The American Heritage

CHILDREN'S DICTIONARY

Houghton Mifflin Company Boston

Cover Photographs

Clockwise, from top left: **apple,** David Spahn; **French horn,** Jordan Miller; **airplane,** R. Hamilton Smith; **chick,** Steve Chambers, The Picture Cube; **hot-air balloon,** Walter Bibikow.

Homograph Riddle on page B9 from *What's a Frank Frank?* by Giulio Maestro. Copyright © 1984 by Giulio Maestro. Reprinted by permission of Clarion Books/Ticknor & Fields, a Houghton Mifflin Company.

Homophone/Homonym Riddle on page B13 from *Eight Ate* by Marvin Terban, illustrated by Giulio Maestro. Text copyright © 1982 by Marvin Terban. Reprinted by permission of Clarion Books/Ticknor & Fields, a Houghton Mifflin Company.

Program (page 579) content from *BASIC Programming for Kids* by Rosalie Sain Ault. Copyright © 1983 by Ault Education Trust. Reprinted by permission of Houghton Mifflin Company.

State Flags (pages 839–843) from *This is America's Story* by Wilder, Ludlum, and Brown, 5th Ed., pages 760–761. Copyright © 1986. Reprinted by permission of Houghton Mifflin Company. State flags courtesy of *The Texaco Star,* Texaco, Inc.

Map of the World (pages 844–845), Donnelley Cartographic Services, from *America: Past and Present* by David C. King and Charlotte C. Anderson. Copyright © 1980 by Houghton Mifflin Company. Reprinted by permission.

Map of the United States of America (page 846), Robinson Projection, from *America: Past and Present* by David C. King and Charlotte C. Anderson. Copyright © 1980 by Houghton Mifflin Company. Reprinted by permission.

Library of Congress Cataloging-in-Publication Data

The American heritage children's dictionary.

Summary: A dictionary for the elementary school student with introductory explanatory material.
1. English language—Dictionaries, Juvenile.
[1. English language—Dictionaries] I. Houghton Mifflin Company.
PF1628.5.A44 1986 423 86–7349
ISBN 0-395-42529-8

Printed in the United States of America

Table of Contents

Staff

Anne H. Soukhanov
Senior Editor

Pamela B. DeVinne
Coordinating Editor, Dictionaries

Howard Webber
Publisher

Margery S. Berube
Director of Editorial Operations

Kaethe Ellis • *Coordinating Editor, Reference*
David A. Jost • *Editor*
David R. Pritchard • *Editor*
Susan Innes • *Assistant Editor*
James P. Marciano • *Assistant Editor*
Dolores R. Harris • *Senior Editor, Dictionary*
Marion Severynse • *Editor*

Contributing Editors

Paul Acker
Charles R. Ault, Jr.
Ruth S. Beebe
Ronald J. Bogus
John K. Bollard
Robert L. Cherry
Karis Crawford
Walter M. Havighurst
Eleanor Jacovina
Ramona Michaelis
Trudy Nelson
Anne D. Steinhardt

Proofreading

Kathryn Blatt
Susan Boulanger
Elizabeth Collins
Judi Drummond
Rhonda Holmes
Susan Kidney

Christopher Leonesio • *Production Manager*
Patricia McTiernan • *Editorial Production Assistant*
Donna L. Muise • *Editorial Production Assistant*
Margaret Anne Miles • *Administrative Assistant*

Composition Keyboarding

Brenda Bregoli Sturtevant
Celester Jackson
Ron Perkins

Design

Kirchoff/Wohlberg, Inc. • *Text Design*
Ligature, Inc. • *Cover Design*

Preface

Your new dictionary is not just a book with a big list of words. It is really a chest full of hidden treasure. In this treasure chest you can find facts about our language that will help you be a better reader, a better writer, a better speaker, and a better speller.

The dictionary shows you how to spell hard words like *Doberman pinscher*. It tells you how to say words like *aunt:* you can say this word in two ways. It gives you the meanings of words like *aerobics* and *computer*. It shows you how to use words in sentences. The dictionary shows you how to divide words into syllables so that you can remember how to spell them. And the dictionary lists all the forms of words; for example, we write one *ox* but we write two *oxen*.

You'll also find some special boxes of information in your dictionary. The blue Vocabulary Builder boxes show you how to make new words out of word parts. The yellow History boxes tell you interesting stories, or histories, about the words in our language, like *hippopotamus*. The blue and white Synonym boxes are another special feature in your dictionary. They give you lists of words called *synonyms* that have the same or almost the same meanings. And the yellow and white Language Detective boxes tell you about different words that people in various parts of our country use for the same thing, like *darning needle* for *dragonfly*.

In the back of your dictionary you'll find the Children's Thesaurus. The Thesaurus gives you even more synonyms and antonyms. Next comes a section that gives you interesting facts about the states in our Union. You can also turn to the colorful map and look up the locations of the states. You can find countries of the world on a second map. Have fun with your dictionary!

A message to parents The *American Heritage Children's Dictionary* is entirely new. This dictionary combines our resources in dictionary-making as publishers of the *American Heritage Dictionary* with our skills in meeting the educational needs of children as publishers of leading textbooks in reading and English. The word list is based on a computerized study of the words that children need and use. The definitions show meanings clearly, with full-sentence illustrative examples. Over 800 color photos and drawings provide additional information about the ideas conveyed by words.

A logical but lively section that shows what a dictionary is and does is located at the front of the book. Learning how to use a dictionary to obtain from it the full treasury of information it contains is one of the significant educational achievements your child can make. That skill is essential for lifelong learning, and developing it was one of our main aims as we prepared the *American Heritage Children's Dictionary*.

Howard Webber, *Publisher*

Preview of the Dictionary

Guide Words → **giggle • gladiolus**

Synonym Box →

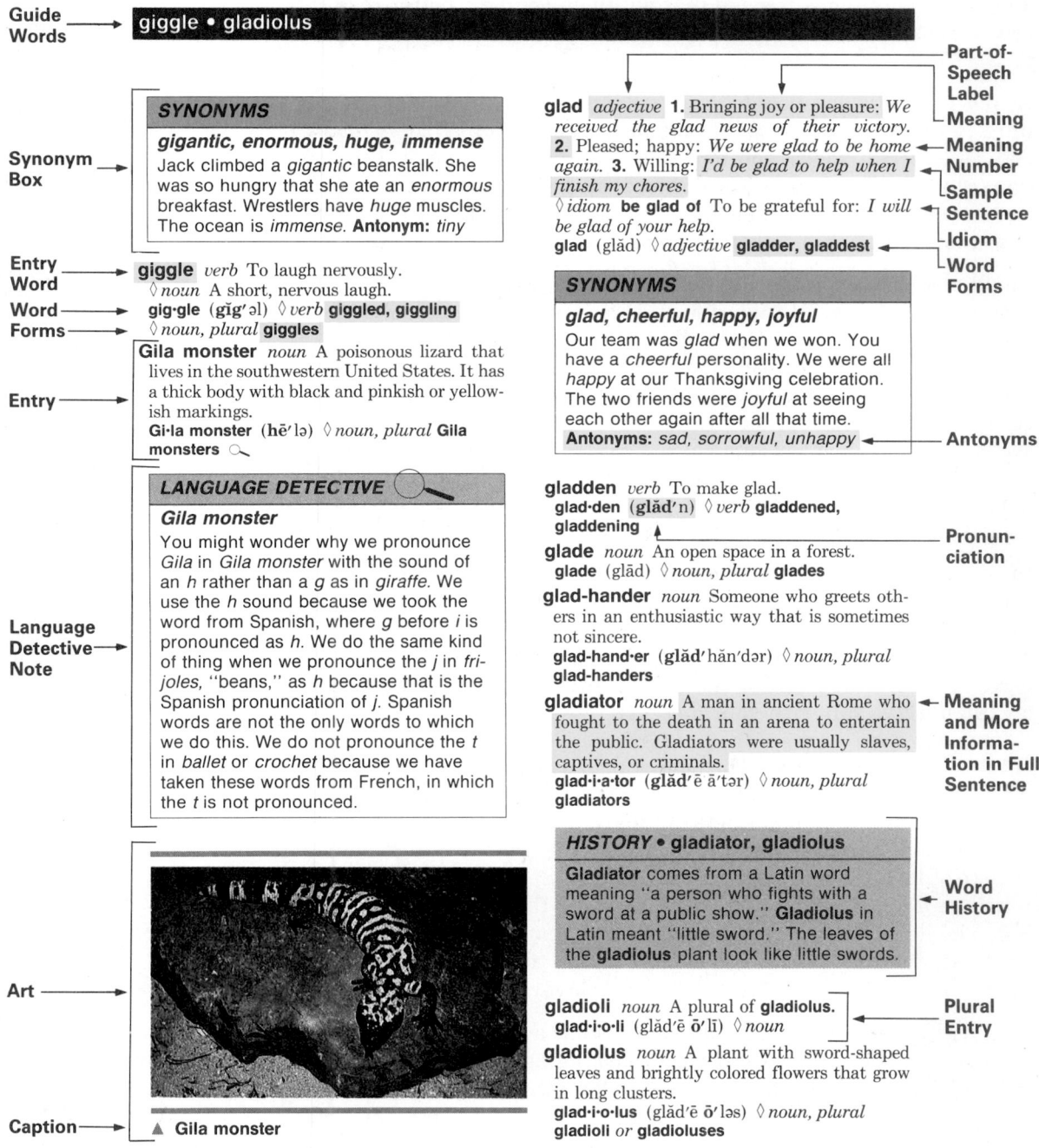

> ***SYNONYMS***
>
> ***gigantic, enormous, huge, immense***
>
> Jack climbed a *gigantic* beanstalk. She was so hungry that she ate an *enormous* breakfast. Wrestlers have *huge* muscles. The ocean is *immense*. **Antonym:** *tiny*

Entry Word →
giggle *verb* To laugh nervously.
◊ *noun* A short, nervous laugh.
Word Forms →
gig·gle (gĭg′əl) ◊ *verb* **giggled, giggling**
◊ *noun, plural* **giggles**

Entry →
Gila monster *noun* A poisonous lizard that lives in the southwestern United States. It has a thick body with black and pinkish or yellowish markings.
Gi·la monster (hē′lə) ◊ *noun, plural* **Gila monsters**

Language Detective Note →

> ***LANGUAGE DETECTIVE***
>
> ***Gila monster***
>
> You might wonder why we pronounce *Gila* in *Gila monster* with the sound of an *h* rather than a *g* as in *giraffe*. We use the *h* sound because we took the word from Spanish, where *g* before *i* is pronounced as *h*. We do the same kind of thing when we pronounce the *j* in *frijoles*, "beans," as *h* because that is the Spanish pronunciation of *j*. Spanish words are not the only words to which we do this. We do not pronounce the *t* in *ballet* or *crochet* because we have taken these words from French, in which the *t* is not pronounced.

Art →

Caption → ▲ **Gila monster**

glad *adjective* **1.** Bringing joy or pleasure: *We received the glad news of their victory.* **2.** Pleased; happy: *We were glad to be home again.* **3.** Willing: *I'd be glad to help when I finish my chores.*
◊ *idiom* **be glad of** To be grateful for: *I will be glad of your help.*
glad (glăd) ◊ *adjective* **gladder, gladdest**

← Part-of-Speech Label
← Meaning
← Meaning Number
← Sample Sentence
← Idiom
← Word Forms

> ***SYNONYMS***
>
> ***glad, cheerful, happy, joyful***
>
> Our team was *glad* when we won. You have a *cheerful* personality. We were all *happy* at our Thanksgiving celebration. The two friends were *joyful* at seeing each other again after all that time.
> **Antonyms:** *sad, sorrowful, unhappy* ← Antonyms

gladden *verb* To make glad.
glad·den (glăd′n) ◊ *verb* **gladdened, gladdening** ← Pronunciation

glade *noun* An open space in a forest.
glade (glād) ◊ *noun, plural* **glades**

glad-hander *noun* Someone who greets others in an enthusiastic way that is sometimes not sincere.
glad-hand·er (glăd′hăn′dər) ◊ *noun, plural* **glad-handers**

gladiator *noun* A man in ancient Rome who fought to the death in an arena to entertain the public. Gladiators were usually slaves, captives, or criminals. ← Meaning and More Information in Full Sentence
glad·i·a·tor (glăd′ē ā′tər) ◊ *noun, plural* **gladiators**

> ***HISTORY* • gladiator, gladiolus**
>
> **Gladiator** comes from a Latin word meaning "a person who fights with a sword at a public show." **Gladiolus** in Latin meant "little sword." The leaves of the **gladiolus** plant look like little swords.

← Word History

gladioli *noun* A plural of **gladiolus.**
glad·i·o·li (glăd′ē ō′lī) ◊ *noun* ← Plural Entry

gladiolus *noun* A plant with sword-shaped leaves and brightly colored flowers that grow in long clusters.
glad·i·o·lus (glăd′ē ō′ləs) ◊ *noun, plural* **gladioli** *or* **gladioluses**

Samples taken from pages 309 and 311.

Introduction What Is a Dictionary?

A **dictionary** is a book of words listed in alphabetical order. A dictionary tells you how to spell words. It gives you the meanings of words in its definitions. It tells you how to say words aloud. It shows you how words are used in sentences. It also shows you how word endings change when a word is used in different ways.

The word you wish to find in the dictionary is called the **entry word**. Entry words are printed in heavy, dark letters. Information about the entry word comes next. An entry word and all the information about it are called the **entry**:

The word **foot** is an entry word. →

Everything the dictionary tells you about it is an entry. →

foot *noun* **1.** The part of the leg of a person or animal on which it stands or walks. **2.** Something that resembles a foot in form, use, or position: *There is a rug at the foot of the stairs. Put the blanket over the foot of the bed.* **3.** A unit of length equal to 12 inches.
◊ *verb* To pay: *I'll foot the bill for dinner.*
◊ *idiom* **on foot** Walking rather than riding.
foot (fo͝ot) ◊ *noun, plural* **feet** ◊ *verb* **footed, footing**

Alphabetical Order The A–Z Word List

Your dictionary lists thousands of entry words. To help you find an entry word quickly, the dictionary lists it in **alphabetical order** from **A** to **Z**. All the words that begin with **A** are listed together. All the words that begin with **B** are listed together, and so on through the alphabet.

Words that begin with the same letter are put into alphabetical order using the second letter, or the third letter, if the second letter is the same, and so on. Notice that **beagle** comes before **beak**, which in turn comes before **beaker**:

Guidewords The First and Last Entry Words on a Page

Guidewords are like bookends. They hold together all the words on one page in the dictionary.

To find the exact page where a word is located, look at the **guidewords.** Guidewords appear at the top of every page in the A–Z list. Here are the guidewords on page 279:

float • florist

The first guideword, *float,* is the first entry on page 279. The second guideword, *florist,* is the last entry on page 279. The words *flock, floe, flood, floodlight, floor, flop, floppy,* and *floppy disk,* which come between *float* and *florist* in the alphabet, are located on page 279.

Word Hunt

Look at page 282. The guidewords on page 282 are **flying fish** and **fold**[1]. Read the entry words on page 282. Then decide which of these words would be on page 282:

foghorn	**flycatcher**
flying saucer	**foam rubber**
folder	**foggy**

Homographs Words with the Same Spelling

Homographs are words that are spelled the same way but have different meanings and may be pronounced differently. They are words that have different histories, or backgrounds. Homographs are followed by little raised numbers: ¹ ². These numbers keep the entries separate.

bat¹ *noun* A strong wooden stick or club used for hitting a ball, as in baseball.
◊ *verb* To hit with or as if with a bat: *The cat batted the ball of yarn back and forth.*
◊ *idiom* **at bat** Having a turn as a hitter in baseball: *Our team is at bat first.*
bat¹ (băt) ◊ *noun, plural* **bats** ◊ *verb* **batted, batting**

bat² *noun* A small, furry animal with a body like a mouse and thin, leathery wings. Bats are active at night and are the only mammals that can fly.
bat² (băt) ◊ *noun, plural* **bats**

Homograph Riddles

These riddles come from What's a Frank Frank? Tasty Homograph Riddles by Giulio Maestro. Clarion Books published it in 1984. If you like these riddles, read the book for even more fun with words!

1. **What's a frank frank?**
   A hot dog who gives his honest opinion.
2. **Why did the duck duck the angry bee?**
   He didn't want to get the point.
3. **When does a trunk carry a trunk?**
   When an elephant goes on vacation.
4. **When are scales on scales?**
   When fish are getting weighed.

Meanings The Ideas Conveyed by Words

Your dictionary tells you what words mean. The meaning of an entry word is called its **definition**. The definition comes after the entry word and the part-of-speech label in the entry.

Words with only one meaning. Some words, like *fetch,* have only one meaning:

The phrase is the definition of **fetch**.

fetch *verb* To go after and return with; get: *Shall I fetch your bags for you?*
fetch (fĕch) ◊ *verb* **fetched, fetching**

The phrase is the definition of **fable**.

The sentence gives you more information about **fable.**

fable *noun* **1.** A story that is meant to teach a useful lesson. A fable often has animal characters that speak and act like human beings. **2.** A story that is not based on fact.
fa·ble (fā′ bəl) ◊ *noun, plural* **fables**

The sample sentence in slanting letters shows you how to use **floppy** when you say or write it yourself.

floppy *adjective* Tending to or able to flop: *The dog had floppy ears.*
flop·py (flŏp′ ē) ◊ *adjective* **floppier, floppiest**

Words with more than one meaning. Some words, like *jump,* have more than one meaning. Heavy, dark numbers introduce new definitions. Look at the many definitions listed for the entry word **jump**:

The verb **jump** has three definitions.

The noun **jump** has two definitions.

jump *verb* **1.** To rise up or move through the air by using the leg muscles; leap: *Grasshoppers can jump very high.* **2.** To move or jerk without wanting to, as in surprise: *I jumped when I heard the noise.* **3.** To leap over: *The horse jumped the fence.*
◊ *noun* **1.** An act of jumping or the distance jumped. **2.** A sudden movement or jerk, as in surprise.
jump (jŭmp) ◊ *verb* **jumped, jumping** ◊ *noun, plural* **jumps**

Different entry words with the same meaning. Sometimes two or more entry words have the same meaning. You will find a full definition at the word that is used most often. The words *mountain lion* and *cougar,* for example, have the same meaning. Because *mountain lion* is the word people use more often, the full definition of the word is found at the entry for *mountain lion*. Look at the two entries. Notice that the definition of the word **cougar** sends you to the full definition at the entry word **mountain lion.**

The definition at **cougar** sends you to **mountain lion.**

cougar *noun* The mountain lion.
cou·gar (ko͞o′gər) ◊ *noun, plural* **cougars**

mountain lion *noun* A large, tawny animal that belongs to the cat family. It lives in western North America and South America.
mountain lion ◊ *noun, plural* **mountain lions**

Idioms Phrases Having Meanings of Their Own

An **idiom** is a group of words that has a special meaning different from the separate meanings the words usually have. An idiom and its definition appear near the end of the entry for the most important word in the idiom. For example, in the idiom **by heart,** the most important word is **heart.**

heart *noun* **1.** The hollow, muscular organ that pumps blood throughout the body.

....

The idiom **by heart** follows the definitions for **heart.** Notice how different the definition of **by heart** is from any definition of **heart** itself.

◊ *idiom* **by heart** Entirely by memory: *We learned the poem by heart.*
heart (härt) ◊ *noun, plural* **hearts**

If there are two or more idioms in an entry, the idioms are in alphabetical order.

Fun With Idioms
1. Look up the idiom **on the fence** in your dictionary. Read the meaning. Can you draw a funny picture that shows what this idiom really means? 2. Look up these idioms: **out of the blue** **up in the air** **out of hand** **walk on air** Now draw a funny picture that shows what each of these idioms really means.

Syllabication The Division of Words into Syllables

A **syllable** is a word part with one vowel sound. The word *ditch* is a one-syllable word. The word *native* is a two-syllable word. If a word has only one syllable, the dictionary does not divide it. If a word has more than one syllable, the dictionary divides the word into syllables. Heavy, dark dots divide entry words with two or more syllables.

caterpillar *noun* The wormlike larva of a moth or butterfly that has just hatched from its egg. A caterpillar has a long body that is often covered with hair or bristles.
cat·er·pil·lar (**kăt'** ər pĭl'ər) ◊ *noun, plural* **caterpillars**

Heavy, dark dots divide **caterpillar** into four syllables at the end of the entry. →

Pronunciation How to Say a Word

The dictionary shows you how to pronounce a word, how to say it aloud. A special spelling, called the **pronunciation,** appears after the divided entry word near the end of the entry. The pronunciation appears in parentheses:

insect *noun* **1.** Any of a large group of animals that have six legs, a body with three main divisions, and usually wings. Flies, bees, grasshoppers, butterflies, and moths are insects. **2.** An animal, as a spider, that is similar to but not a true insect.
in·sect (**ĭn'**sĕkt') ◊ *noun, plural* **insects**

The pronunciation comes after the entry word divided into syllables.

Pronunciation symbols. In order to show how we say words aloud, your dictionary uses a special group of letters and symbols that stand for the sounds in a word. This group of letters and symbols is shown in the **Full Pronunciation Key** on page B16. The Full Pronunciation Key shows the letter or symbol used for each sound in English. For each sound listed in the Key, you'll find one or more sample words. Sample words help explain the sounds by showing how the sound is said in a word you know. A shorter form of the Pronunciation Key is on every left-hand page of the A–Z list where it is easy to find:

This is the **Short Pronunciation Key.** →

ă	pat	ĭ	pit	oi	**oil**	th	**bath**
ā	pay	ī	ride	ŏŏ	**book**	*th*	**bathe**
â	care	î	fierce	ōō	**boot**	ə	**ago, item**
ä	father	ŏ	pot	ou	**out**		**pencil**
ĕ	pet	ō	**go**	ŭ	**cut**		**atom**
ē	be	ô	paw, for	û	**fur**		**circus**

Homophones Words that Sound Alike

Homophones are words that sound alike but have different spellings and meanings. Look at the spellings for **cent, scent,** and **sent.** Pronounce each one, using the pronunciation at each entry. The dictionary gives you a list of words that sound alike at the end of each entry for a homophone.

The words **cent, scent,** and **sent** are homophones.

cent *noun* A coin used in the United States and Canada. One hundred cents equals one dollar.
cent (sĕnt) ◊ *noun, plural* **cents**
‖*These sound alike:* **cent, scent, sent**

scent *noun* **1.** A distinctive smell. —See Synonyms at **smell.** **2.** A perfume. **3.** The trail of a hunted animal or fugitive. **4.** The sense of smell.
◊ *verb* To sense by or as if by smelling.
scent (sĕnt) ◊ *noun, plural* **scents** ◊ *verb* **scented, scenting**
‖*These sound alike:* **scent, cent, sent**

I have **SENT** the letter.

sent *verb* Past tense and past participle of **send.**
sent (sĕnt) ◊ *verb*
‖*These sound alike:* **sent, cent, scent**

Homophone/Homonym Riddle

This riddle comes from Eight Ate: A Feast of Homonym Riddles by Marvin Terban. Giulio Maestro drew the funny pictures in this book. Clarion Books published the book in 1982. If you like this riddle, read the book for even more fun with words!

What are nervous little outdoor cloth houses?

Tense tents.

Word Parts Prefixes and Suffixes, and Vocabulary Builders

When you add a prefix or a suffix to a base word or root word, you make a new word. You can find separate entries for **prefixes** and **suffixes** in your dictionary.

Your dictionary also includes **Vocabulary Builders** at all prefix and suffix entries. Use the Vocabulary Builders to help expand your vocabulary:

The Vocabulary Builder at the entry **re–** gives you words using the prefix that are not in the dictionary and also gives you their definitions. →

***VOCABULARY BUILDER* • re–**

Many words that are formed with **re–** are not entries in this dictionary. But you can figure out what these words mean by looking up the meanings of the root words and the prefix. For example:
rearrange = to arrange again
repay = to pay back

Synonyms and Antonyms Words with the Same and Opposite Meanings

Synonym boxes. Hundreds of boxes with the title "Synonyms" appear in this dictionary. These synonym boxes list **synonyms,** words that have the same or nearly the same meaning. Learning synonyms helps increase your vocabulary. Many of the synonym boxes also include antonyms. Antonyms are words that have opposite or nearly opposite meanings from the synonyms. You will find antonyms at the ends of many synonym boxes.

This is the synonym box at **quick.** →

These are synonyms of the word **quick.** →

Sample sentences illustrate the synonyms of **quick.** →

This is the antonym of **quick** and its synonyms. →

SYNONYMS

quick, fast[1], hasty, rapid
Be as *quick* as you can in putting on your coat. He is so *fast* that nobody can beat him. She was too *hasty* in doing her work and made several mistakes. The train made *rapid* progress down the hill. **Antonym:** *slow*

The entries for **fast[1], hasty,** and **rapid** will tell you to look up **quick** in order to find their synonyms.

Word Histories Family Backgrounds of Words

America is a big country, and its people come from many lands. Our language is similar to America itself because it contains immigrants from many other languages. For example, the word *hacienda* comes to English from Spanish, and the word *dachshund* comes to English from German. Word history paragraphs give you the family backgrounds of many words:

hippopotamus *noun* A large African river animal with dark, almost hairless skin, short legs, a broad snout, and a wide mouth.
hip·po·pot·a·mus (hĭp′ə **pŏt′** ə məs) ◊ *noun, plural* **hippopotamuses**

The word history tells you that the word **hippopotamus** came into English from two other languages.

***HISTORY* • hippopotamus**

Hippopotamus comes into English through Latin from two Greek words meaning "river horse."

The dictionary gives word histories for all *homographs*.

Language Detective Notes Interesting Facts about Words

People throughout our country often pronounce and use words in very different ways, depending on the parts of the country that they live in. The Language Detective Notes explain some of the ways that we Americans use the English language from region to region:

frying pan *noun* A shallow pan with a long handle, used for frying foods.
frying pan ◊ *noun, plural* **frying pans**

The Language Detective Note at **frying pan** tells you that this utensil can be called a *skillet* or a *spider,* depending on the part of the country that you live in.

LANGUAGE DETECTIVE

frying pan

The term *frying pan* is used all over the United States, but many people use a different word for a frying pan that is made out of cast iron. In a large area between the North and South, a cast-iron frying pan is usually called a *skillet.* In New England, in some other parts of the North, and along the coasts of New Jersey, Virginia, North Carolina, and South Carolina some people call it a *spider. Frying pans* got the name *spider* because they had legs on the bottom so that they could be set over a fire.

FULL PRONUNCIATION KEY

Sounds	Sample Words
ă	as in r**a**t, l**au**gh
ā	**a**pe, **ai**d, p**ay**
â	**ai**r, c**a**re, w**ea**r
ä	f**a**ther, ko**a**la, y**a**rd
b	**b**i**b**, ca**bb**age
ch	**ch**ur**ch**, sti**tch**
d	**d**ee**d**, mail**ed**, pu**dd**le
ĕ	p**e**t, pl**ea**sure, **a**ny
ē	b**e**, b**ee**, **ea**sy, pian**o**
f	**f**ast, **f**i**f**e, o**ff**, **ph**rase, rou**gh**
g	**g**a**g**, **g**et, fin**g**er
h	**h**at, **wh**o
hw	**wh**ich, **wh**ere
ĭ	**i**f, p**i**t, b**u**sy
ī	b**y**, p**ie**, h**igh**
î	d**ear**, d**eer**, f**ier**ce, m**ere**
j	**j**u**dg**e, **g**em
k	**c**at, **k**i**ck**, s**ch**ool
kw	**ch**oir, **qu**ick
l	**l**id, need**le**, ta**ll**
m	**am**, **m**an, du**mb**
n	**n**o, sudd**en**
ng	thi**ng**, i**n**k
ŏ	h**o**rrible, p**o**t
ō	g**o**, r**ow**, t**oe**, th**ough**
ô	**a**ll, c**au**ght, f**o**r, p**aw**
oi	b**oy**, n**oi**se, **oi**l

Sounds	Sample Words
ou	as in c**ow**, **ou**t
o͝o	f**u**ll, t**oo**k, w**o**lf
o͞o	b**oo**t, fr**ui**t, fl**ew**
p	**p**o**p**, ha**pp**y
r	**r**oa**r**, **rh**yme
s	mi**ss**, **s**au**c**e, **sc**ene, **s**ee
sh	di**sh**, **sh**ip, **s**ugar, ti**ss**ue
t	**t**igh**t**, stopp**ed**
th	ba**th**, **th**in
th	ba**th**e, **th**is
ŭ	c**u**t, fl**oo**d, r**ou**gh, s**o**me
û	circle, f**ur**, h**ear**d, t**er**m, t**ur**n, **ur**ge, w**or**d
v	ca**v**e, **v**al**v**e, **v**ine
w	**w**ith, **w**olf
y	**y**es, **y**olk, oni**o**n
yo͝o	c**u**re
yo͞o	ab**u**se, **u**se
z	ro**s**e, si**z**e, **x**ylophone, **z**ebra
zh	gara**g**e, plea**s**ure, vi**s**ion
ə	**a**bout, sil**e**nt, penc**i**l, lem**o**n, circ**u**s

Stress

Shown by accent marks ʹ and ′ and by heavy, dark letters.

dic•tion•ar•y (**dĭk**′shə nĕr′ē)

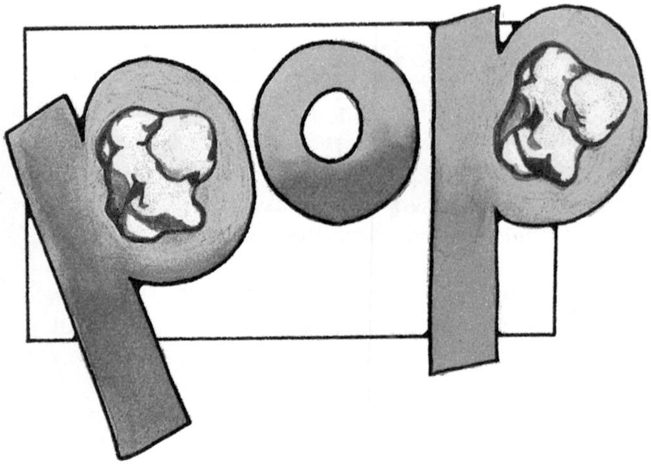

Aardvark

Aa

A is the first letter of the English alphabet. Did you know that it has a long history?

Over 3,500 years ago, people in the Middle East were using symbols that became the letters of our alphabet. This ancient Middle Eastern symbol is a form of the letter that became our letter *A*.

A

The ancient Greeks borrowed their alphabet from people in the Middle East. Here is a form of the Greek letter that became our letter *A*.

A

The ancient Romans borrowed their alphabet from a people who had taken their own letter symbols from the Greeks. Here is a form of the Roman letter *A* that was used for carving letters into stone. These letters became the model for our printed capital letters.

As people wrote quickly, especially with pens, the capital letters began to take the shapes of small letters. Here is a small-letter *a* that was developed about 1 200 years ago.

Aa *Aa*	Aa	Aa	Aa
Handwriting	Sans Serif Type	Serif Type	Computer Printing

a *or* **A** *noun* **1.** The first letter of the English alphabet. **2.** The highest mark, as in school.
a *or* **A** (ā) ◊ *noun, plural* **a's** *or* **A's**

a *indefinite article* **1.** One: *I didn't hear a word you said.* **2.** Any; each: *A beaver builds dams.* **3.** Such a: *This is a person you can trust.* **4.** An example or kind of: *Water is a liquid.*
◊ *preposition* In or to each; per: *We paid five dollars a person for the tickets. An apple a day keeps the doctor away.*
a (ə *or* ā) ◊ *indefinite article* ◊ *preposition*

aardvark *noun* An African animal with large ears, a snout shaped like a tube, and sharp claws. The aardvark uses its claws to dig into the nests of ants and termites and catches these insects with its long, sticky tongue.
aard·vark (**ärd′**värk′) ◊ *noun, plural* **aardvarks**

abacus *noun* A device made of beads strung on parallel wires on a frame. An abacus can be used to do arithmetic by hand.
ab·a·cus (**ăb′** ə kəs) ◊ *noun, plural* **abacuses**

abalone *noun* A shellfish with a large, flat shell that is shaped like an ear and lined with brightly colored mother-of-pearl.
ab·a·lo·ne (ăb′ə **lō′**nē) ◊ *noun, plural* **abalones**

abandon *verb* **1.** To leave, especially because of trouble or danger; desert: *During the terrible storm at sea, the crew had to abandon the sinking ship.* **2.** To have, make, or do no longer: *Although the situation seemed impossible, we never abandoned hope.*
a·ban·don (ə **băn′**dən) ◊ *verb* **abandoned, abandoning**

abandoned *adjective* No longer used or lived in; deserted: *Our parents warned us not to play in the abandoned house.*
a·ban·doned (ə **băn′**dənd) ◊ *adjective*

abate *verb* To become or make less in amount or intensity: *The storm has abated.*
a·bate (ə **bāt′**) ◊ *verb* **abated, abating**

abbess *noun* The nun who is in charge of the other nuns in a convent.
ab·bess (**ăb′**ĭs) ◊ *noun, plural* **abbesses**

abbey *noun* A monastery or convent.
ab·bey (ăb′ē) ◊ *noun, plural* **abbeys**

▲ **abbey**

abbot *noun* The monk who is in charge of the other monks in a monastery.
ab·bot (ăb′ət) ◊ *noun, plural* **abbots**

abbreviate *verb* To make shorter by leaving out letters from a word or group of words: *We abbreviate United States of America as U.S.A. and Junior as Jr.*
ab·bre·vi·ate (ə **brē′** vē āt′) ◊ *verb* **abbreviated, abbreviating**

abbreviation *noun* A letter or group of letters that come from abbreviating a word or group of words.
ab·bre·vi·a·tion (ə brē′vē **ā′**shən) ◊ *noun, plural* **abbreviations**

abdicate *verb* To give up power or authority officially: *The queen abdicated her power. The king abdicated.*
ab·di·cate (**ăb′** dĭ kāt′) ◊ *verb* **abdicated, abdicating**

abdomen *noun* **1.** The part of the body between the chest and about where the legs join. The abdomen contains organs, such as the stomach and intestines, that help digest food. **2.** The last of the three sections of the body of an insect.
ab·do·men (**ăb′** də mən) ◊ *noun, plural* **abdomens**

ă	pat	ĭ	pit	oi	**oi**l	th	ba**th**
ā	pay	ī	ride	ŏŏ	b**oo**k	*th*	ba**th**e
â	care	î	fierce	ōō	b**oo**t	ə	**a**go, it**e**m
ä	father	ŏ	pot	ou	**ou**t		penc**i**l
ĕ	pet	ō	go	ŭ	cut		at**o**m
ē	be	ô	paw, for	û	fur		circ**u**s

abide *verb* **1.** To live in a place; reside: *The monarch will abide in the castle for life.* **2.** To put up with: *I cannot abide that noise.*
◊ *idiom* **abide by 1.** To live up to; fulfill: *We will abide by the rules.* **2.** To agree to; submit to: *I will abide by your decision.*
a·bide (ə **bīd′**) ◊ *verb* **abided, abiding**

ability *noun* **1.** The quality of being able to do something; power: *Most people have the ability to dance.* **2.** Power to do something, especially as a result of practice; skill: *You have real ability as a dancer.*
a·bil·i·ty (ə **bĭl′** ĭ tē) ◊ *noun, plural* **abilities**

SYNONYMS

ability, aptitude, skill, talent

Most people have the *ability* to sing. He has a natural *aptitude* for thinking out difficult problems. This nicely made furniture shows her *skill* as a carpenter. He has a real *talent* as a singer.

ablaze *adjective* On fire: *Smoke was everywhere, and the house was ablaze.*
a·blaze (ə **blāz′**) ◊ *adjective*

able *adjective* **1.** Having what is necessary to do something: *I will be able to see you tomorrow.* **2.** Having special power to do something: *She is an able mechanic.*
a·ble (**ā′** bəl) ◊ *adjective* **abler, ablest**

-able The suffix *-able* forms adjectives and means "capable of" or "able to." A *breakable* vase is a vase that is capable of being broken. The suffix *-able* also means "worthy of" or "deserving." A *lovable* puppy is a puppy that deserves love.

***VOCABULARY BUILDER* • -able**

Many words that are formed with **-able** are not entries in this dictionary. But you can figure out what these words mean by looking up the meanings of the root words and the suffix. For example:
honorable = deserving honor
washable = able to be washed

abnormal *adjective* Not usual or normal: *The cold snap made us wonder about the abnormal June weather.*
ab·nor·mal (ăb **nôr′**məl) ◊ *adjective*

aboard *adverb & preposition* On, onto, or inside a vehicle, such as a ship, train, or bus: *All aboard! The ship is leaving. We went aboard the train.*
a·board (ə **bôrd′**) ◊ *adverb & preposition*

abode *noun* The place where one lives: *The forest is the abode of many wild animals.*
a·bode (ə **bōd′**) ◊ *noun, plural* **abodes**

abolish *verb* To get rid of; put an end to: *Abraham Lincoln abolished slavery.*
a·bol·ish (ə **bŏl′**ĭsh) ◊ *verb* **abolished, abolishing**

abolition *noun* The act of getting rid of.
ab·o·li·tion (ăb′ə **lĭsh′**ən) ◊ *noun*

abominable *adjective* **1.** Causing disgust or hatred: *Kidnaping is an abominable crime.* **2.** Not at all pleasing or agreeable: *The cold, rainy weather has been abominable.*
a·bom·i·na·ble (ə **bŏm′**ə nə bəl) ◊ *adjective*

aborigine *noun* A member of the group of people first known to have lived in a place: *Colonists from Europe came into contact with aborigines in many parts of the world.*
ab·o·rig·i·ne (ăb′ə **rĭj′**ə nē) ◊ *noun, plural* **aborigines**

abound *verb* To be present in large numbers or amounts; be full of: *Fish abound in that river. The forest abounds in wildlife.*
a·bound (ə **bound′**) ◊ *verb* **abounded, abounding**

about *preposition* **1.** Around on all sides: *The explorers looked about them.* —See Synonyms at **around. 2.** Close in time to: *It is about midnight.* **3.** Almost the same as: *That is about the right size.* **4.** Concerned with: *That book is about astronomy.*
◊ *adverb* **1.** Nearly; almost: *That answer is just about right.* **2.** On the point of: *I am about to go.*
a·bout (ə **bout′**) ◊ *preposition* ◊ *adverb*

above *adverb* Over or directly over but not touching: *Look at the clouds above.*
◊ *preposition* **1.** Over or directly over but not touching: *The clouds are above us.* **2.** At or to a higher level than: *Look above the building.* **3.** Taller than: *That tree rises above the other trees.* **4.** Higher in rank, degree, or number: *Ten is above nine.* **5.** Beyond the level or reach of: *That scientific theory is above my understanding.*
a·bove (ə **bŭv′**) ◊ *adverb* ◊ *preposition*

abreast *adverb* Side by side in a line.
a·breast (ə **brĕst′**) ◊ *adverb*

▲ **abreast**
Standing four abreast

abridge *verb* To make shorter by using fewer words to say the same thing: *We read an abridged version of "Winnie the Pooh."*
a·bridge (ə **brĭj′**) ◊ *verb* **abridged, abridging**

abroad *adverb* In or to a place outside one's own country: *We went abroad to India.*
a·broad (ə **brôd′**) ◊ *adverb*

abrupt *adjective* **1.** Taking place without warning: *I made an abrupt change in plans.* **2.** So quick in speech or behavior as to seem rude: *I said good-by in an abrupt way.*
a·brupt (ə **brŭpt′**) ◊ *adjective*

abscess *noun* A mass of pus surrounded by an inflamed area. An abscess forms where there is an infection in the body.
ab·scess (**ăb′**sĕs′) ◊ *noun, plural* **abscesses**

absence *noun* **1.** The condition of being away from someone or from a place: *Absence can make you love someone more.* **2.** The time during which someone or something is away: *After an absence of four days, I returned to work.* **3.** The fact of not existing or not being present: *The absence of color in that drawing makes it dull.*
ab·sence (**ăb′**səns) ◊ *noun, plural* **absences**

absent *adjective* **1.** Not present in a place or with someone: *Two students are absent today.* **2.** Not existing, even though often needed or wanted: *Fish are completely absent from the lake.*
ab·sent (**ăb′** sənt) ◊ *adjective*

absentee *noun* A person who is absent.
ab·sen·tee (ăb′sən **tē′**) ◊ *noun, plural* **absentees**

absent-minded *adjective* Not paying attention; forgetful: *I am so absent-minded that I am always losing my glasses.*
ab·sent-mind·ed (**ăb′** sənt **mīn′** dĭd) ◊ *adjective*

absolute *adjective* **1.** Lacking nothing; complete: *There was absolute silence during study period.* **2.** Without any limit in any way: *You have my absolute trust. A ruler who can do anything he or she wants is called an absolute monarch.* **3.** Without any doubt; certain: *I have absolute proof that this is so.*
ab·so·lute (**ăb′** sə lo͞ot′) ◊ *adjective*

absolve *verb* To free from blame or punishment: *The police absolved the suspect.*
ab·solve (ăb **zŏlv′**) ◊ *verb* **absolved, absolving**

absorb *verb* **1.** To take in; soak up: *A sponge absorbs water.* **2.** To take in and make part of something: *The United States has absorbed people from all over the world.* **3.** To take in and keep from going back or through: *Thick rugs absorb sound.* **4.** To hold the attention; engross: *The movie absorbed the audience from start to finish.*
ab·sorb (ăb **sôrb′**) ◊ *verb* **absorbed, absorbing**

absorbent *adjective* Able to take in or soak up: *These towels are very absorbent.*
ab·sorb·ent (ăb **sôr′** bənt) ◊ *adjective*

absorbing *adjective* Holding all one's attention: *That is an absorbing mystery novel.*
ab·sorb·ing (ăb **sôr′** bĭng) ◊ *adjective*

absorption *noun* The process of absorbing.
ab·sorp·tion (ăb **sôrp′** shən) ◊ *noun*

ă	pat	ĭ	pit	oi	**oi**l	th	ba**th**
ā	pay	ī	ride	o͝o	book	*th*	ba**th**e
â	care	î	fierce	o͞o	boot	ə	ago, item
ä	father	ŏ	pot	ou	**ou**t		pencil
ĕ	pet	ō	go	ŭ	cut		atom
ē	be	ô	paw, for	û	fur		circus

abstain *verb* To keep oneself from by choice: *We abstained from eating too much.*
ab·stain (ăb **stān′**) ◊ *verb* **abstained, abstaining**

abstinence *noun* The act of abstaining from things that appeal to the senses.
ab·sti·nence (**ăb′** stə nəns) ◊ *noun, plural* **abstinences**

abstract *adjective* **1.** Thought of apart from anything in the real world: *I have an abstract idea of what to do, but I haven't worked out my plan. We do not have to think of snow to think of the abstract quality of whiteness.* **2.** Hard to understand: *You explain things in a way that is too abstract for me.*
ab·stract (**ăb′** străkt′) ◊ *adjective*

absurd *adjective* Not making any sense; silly: *It is absurd to say it is sunny during a blizzard.*
ab·surd (əb **sûrd′**) ◊ *adjective*

absurdity *noun* **1.** The condition or quality of being absurd; foolishness. **2.** Something that is absurd.
ab·surd·i·ty (əb **sûr′** dĭ tē) ◊ *noun, plural* **absurdities**

abundance *noun* An amount that is large or more than enough: *In cities there is an abundance of things to do.*
a·bun·dance (ə **bŭn′** dəns) ◊ *noun, plural* **abundances**

abundant *adjective* Large or more than enough in amount; plentiful.
a·bun·dant (ə **bŭn′** dənt) ◊ *adjective*

abuse *verb* **1.** To use in a way that is not right; misuse: *The government abused its power by too much taxation.* **2.** To give bad treatment that causes injury; mistreat: *My feet hurt because I abused them by running too long.* **3.** To speak to or about in words that do injury.
◊ *noun* **1.** Use or treatment that is not right; misuse: *It is an abuse of our vacation to work the whole time.* **2.** An unfair or wrong practice or custom: *In a game it is hard to stop abuses of the rules by people who want to cheat.* **3.** Words that injure someone.
a·buse ◊ *verb* (ə **byo͞oz′**) **abused, abusing** ◊ *noun* (ə **byo͞os′**), *plural* **abuses**

abyss *noun* A hole, gulf, or space that seemingly cannot be measured.
a·byss (ə **bĭs′**) ◊ *noun, plural* **abysses**

a.c. *or* **A.C.** Abbreviations for *alternating current.*

academic *adjective* Of or relating to a school or college.
ac·a·dem·ic (ăk′ə **dĕm′**ĭk) ◊ *adjective*

academy *noun* **1.** A school where a special field of study is taught: *She went to a police academy.* **2.** A secondary school, especially a private one.
a·cad·e·my (ə **kăd′**ə mē) ◊ *noun, plural* **academies**

accelerate *verb* To go or cause to go faster: *The driver stepped on the gas and accelerated the car.* —See Synonyms at **speed.**
ac·cel·er·ate (ăk **sĕl′**ə rāt′) ◊ *verb* **accelerated, accelerating**

acceleration *noun* An increase in speed.
ac·cel·er·a·tion (ăk sĕl′ə **rā′**shən) ◊ *noun*

accelerator *noun* A control for increasing speed, especially the gas pedal of a car.
ac·cel·er·a·tor (ăk **sĕl′**ə rā′tər) ◊ *noun, plural* **accelerators**

accent *noun* **1.** The stress or force with which a speaker says one syllable of a word compared with the other syllables of a word. In the word *butter* the accent is on the first syllable. **2.** A mark showing stress or accent. In this dictionary we show the strongest accent with the mark **′** and the next strongest accent with the mark ′, as in the word (**ăk′**sĕnt′). **3.** A way of speaking or pronouncing that is typical of a certain group. An accent can be typical of a social group, of a part of the country, or of speakers from one country speaking the language of another country. ◊ *verb* **1.** To give more stress to in pronouncing: *We accent the first syllable in the word "butter."* **2.** To mark with a stress mark.
ac·cent (**ăk′**sĕnt′) ◊ *noun, plural* **accents** ◊ *verb* **accented, accenting**

accept *verb* **1.** To receive when offered, often to receive gladly: *I accept your friendship.* **2.** To say yes to; consent to: *I accept your invitation.* **3.** To permit to come into a place or join a group, often with approval: *Our class has begun to accept the new student.* **4.** To think of as usual, correct, true, or satisfactory: *I accept your answer.*
ac·cept (ăk **sĕpt′**) ◊ *verb* **accepted, accepting**

acceptable *adjective* **1.** Worth being accepted: *Your apology is acceptable.* **2.** Up to a level high enough to be accepted: *My test answers were acceptable.* **3.** Not up to a high level but good enough to be accepted: *This work is acceptable, but it's not your best.* **4.** Received gladly; welcome.
ac·cept·a·ble (ăk **sĕp′**tə bəl) ◊ *adjective*

acceptance *noun* The act of accepting or the condition of being accepted: *I will try to get acceptance for your offer. My singing met with acceptance from the audience.*
ac·cept·ance (ăk **sĕp′**təns) ◊ *noun, plural* **acceptances**

access *noun* **1.** The action of going to or into; an approaching or entering: *Access to the palace was not easy.* **2.** Permission or ability to enter or use: *We have access to the pool.* **3.** A way or means of going to or into: *The only access was through a tunnel.*
ac·cess (**ăk′**sĕs′) ◊ *noun, plural* **accesses**

access code *noun* A special code that allows access to information or data that has been stored in a computer.
access code ◊ *noun, plural* **access codes**

▲ **access code**
Access code shown on screen

accessible *adjective* Easy to reach or obtain: *The freeway is accessible from here. These books are accessible in the library.*
ac·ces·si·ble (ăk **sĕs′**ə bəl) ◊ *adjective*

accessory *noun* **1.** Something that is not necessary but adds to the appearance or usefulness of something else: *The red scarf was a cheerful accessory with the black coat.* **2.** Someone who helps commit a crime.
ac·ces·so·ry (ăk **sĕs′**ə rē) ◊ *noun, plural* **accessories**

accident *noun* **1.** Something that happens without being planned ahead of time: *Our meeting was a lucky accident.* **2.** An unexpected and undesirable event: *An accident held up traffic for miles.*
ac·ci·dent (**ăk′**sĭ dənt) ◊ *noun, plural* **accidents**

accidental *adjective* Happening without being expected or intended.
ac·ci·den·tal (ăk′sĭ **dĕn′**tl) ◊ *adjective*

accidentally *adverb* In an unexpected or unintended way.
ac·ci·den·tal·ly (ăk′sə **dĕn′**tl ē) ◊ *adverb*

acclaim *verb* To give enthusiastic approval or praise to: *We acclaim Marie Curie for the discovery of radium.*
◊ *noun* Enthusiastic praise or approval.
ac·claim (ə **klām′**) ◊ *verb* **acclaimed, acclaiming** ◊ *noun*

accommodate *verb* **1.** To do a favor or service for. **2.** To provide with a place to stay. **3.** To have room for; hold: *The auditorium can accommodate 500 people.*
ac·com·mo·date (ə **kŏm′**ə dāt′) ◊ *verb* **accommodated, accommodating**

accommodations *plural noun* Food and shelter: *We found accommodations at a fine hotel in Chicago.*
ac·com·mo·da·tions (ə kŏm′ə **dā′**shənz) ◊ *plural noun*

accompaniment *noun* **1.** Something that goes along with or adds to something else: *Crisp toast is a good accompaniment for cheese.* **2.** A musical part played as a support, especially for a soloist.
ac·com·pa·ni·ment (ə **kŭm′**pə nĭ mənt) ◊ *noun, plural* **accompaniments**

accompany *verb* **1.** To go along with: *I accompanied them to the concert.* **2.** To happen together with: *Thunder ordinarily accompanies lightning.* **3.** To play a musical accompaniment for.
ac·com·pa·ny (ə **kŭm′**pə nē) ◊ *verb* **accompanied, accompanying**

ă	pat	ĭ	pit	oi	**oil**	th	**bath**
ā	pay	ī	ride	ŏŏ	**book**	*th*	**bathe**
â	care	î	fierce	ōō	**boot**	ə	ago, item
ä	father	ŏ	pot	ou	**out**		pencil
ĕ	pet	ō	go	ŭ	**cut**		atom
ē	be	ô	paw, for	û	**fur**		circus

accomplice *noun* Someone who helps another to do something wrong or illegal.
ac·com·plice (ə **kŏm′**plĭs) ◊ *noun, plural* **accomplices**

accomplish *verb* To carry out: *We accomplished the job quickly.* —See Synonyms at **perform.**
ac·com·plish (ə **kŏm′**plĭsh) ◊ *verb* **accomplished, accomplishing**

accomplished *adjective* Skillful because of practice and study: *My parents are accomplished musicians.*
ac·com·plished (ə **kŏm′**plĭsht) ◊ *adjective*

accomplishment *noun* **1.** The act of accomplishing or carrying out. **2.** Something accomplished: *The first walk on the moon was quite an accomplishment.* **3.** A skill gained through training and practice: *That class increased your accomplishments as a musician.*
ac·com·plish·ment (ə **kŏm′**plĭsh mənt) ◊ *noun, plural* **accomplishments**

accord *verb* **1.** To give; grant: *Our Constitution accords every citizen certain rights.* **2.** To be in agreement or harmony: *Your ideas accord with mine.*
◊ *noun* **1.** Agreement; harmony. **2.** A formal act of agreeing; treaty.
◊ *idiom* **of one's own accord** Without outside help or influence: *The fire went out of its own accord.*
ac·cord (ə **kôrd′**) ◊ *verb* **accorded, according** ◊ *noun, plural* **accords**

accordance *noun* A state of agreement: *You should play the game in accordance with the rules.*
ac·cor·dance (ə **kôr′**dns) ◊ *noun*

accordingly *adverb* **1.** In keeping with a particular case: *Learn the rules and act accordingly.* **2.** Consequently; therefore.
ac·cord·ing·ly (ə **kôr′**dĭng lē) ◊ *adverb*

according to *preposition* **1.** As said or shown by: *According to the mayor, we need a new hospital.* **2.** In agreement with: *We built the model according to the instructions.*

accordion *noun* A portable keyboard instrument in which air is forced past reeds to create musical tones.
ac·cor·di·on (ə **kôr′**dē ən) ◊ *noun, plural* **accordions**

account *noun* **1.** A written or spoken description of events: *They gave us an exciting*

account of their trip. **2.** A set of reasons; explanation. **3.** A record of money received or spent. **4.** Importance; worth.
◊ *verb* **1.** To believe to be; consider. **2.** To give the reason for; explain: *We cannot account for these mistakes.* **3.** To be responsible for: *Carelessness accounts for many accidents in the home.*
◊ *idioms* **on account of** Because of: *We were late on account of traffic.* **on no account** Under no circumstances; never: *On no account should you touch a live wire.*
ac·count (ə **kount′**) ◊ *noun, plural* **accounts** ◊ *verb* **accounted, accounting**

accountant *noun* A person who records the money received or spent by a business.
ac·count·ant (ə **koun′**tənt) ◊ *noun, plural* **accountants**

accounting *noun* The business or job of an accountant.
ac·count·ing (ə **koun′**tĭng) ◊ *noun*

accumulate *verb* To gather together; collect: *We accumulated a large collection of books. Snow began to accumulate shortly after midnight.*
ac·cu·mu·late (ə **kyo͞o′**myə lāt′) ◊ *verb* **accumulated, accumulating**

accumulation *noun* **1.** The act of accumulating. **2.** An amount accumulated.
ac·cu·mu·la·tion (ə kyo͞o′myə **lā′**shən) ◊ *noun, plural* **accumulations**

accuracy *noun* **1.** Freedom from error: *Always check the accuracy of your answers.* **2.** Precision; exactness.
ac·cu·ra·cy (**ăk′**yər ə sē) ◊ *noun*

accurate *adjective* Free from mistakes; exactly right: *Do you think the story is accurate?* —See Synonyms at **correct.**
ac·cu·rate (**ăk′**yər ĭt) ◊ *adjective*

accusation *noun* A statement that a person is guilty of wrongdoing.
ac·cu·sa·tion (ăk′yo͞o **zā′**shən) ◊ *noun, plural* **accusations**

accuse *verb* To blame for wrongdoing: *They were accused of stealing.*
ac·cuse (ə **kyo͞oz′**) ◊ *verb* **accused, accusing**

accustom *verb* To make used to: *As a security guard, you must accustom yourself to staying awake at night.*
ac·cus·tom (ə **kŭs′**təm) ◊ *verb* **accustomed, accustoming**

accustomed *adjective* **1.** Usual; habitual: *We sat in our accustomed places at the front of the room.* **2.** Used to; familiar with: *Explorers are accustomed to hardship.*
ac·cus·tomed (ə **kŭs′**təmd) ◊ *adjective*

ace *noun* A person who can do something very well.
ace (ās) ◊ *noun, plural* **aces**

ache *verb* **1.** To feel a dull, steady pain: *I ache all over.* **2.** To want very much; long: *I am aching to get home.*
◊ *noun* A steady pain: *I have an ache in my back.* —See Synonyms at **pain.**
ache (āk) ◊ *verb* **ached, aching** ◊ *noun, plural* **aches**

achieve *verb* **1.** To succeed in doing or accomplishing. —See Synonyms at **reach.** **2.** To get with great work or effort: *They finally achieved success and fame.*
a·chieve (ə **chēv′**) ◊ *verb* **achieved, achieving**

achievement *noun* **1.** The act or process of achieving. **2.** Something that has been achieved: *The invention of the computer is a great achievement.*
a·chieve·ment (ə **chēv′**mənt) ◊ *noun, plural* **achievements**

acid *noun* A chemical compound that has a sour taste. When dissolved in water, acids turn blue litmus paper to red.
◊ *adjective* **1.** Composed of or containing an acid. **2.** Having a sour taste.
ac·id (**ăs′**ĭd) ◊ *noun, plural* **acids** ◊ *adjective*

acidity *noun* The condition or quality of being acid.
a·cid·i·ty (ə **sĭd′**ĭ tē) ◊ *noun*

acknowledge *verb* **1.** To admit the existence or truth of: *It is hard to acknowledge one's mistakes* **2.** To recognize the authority of: *They were acknowledged as experts in science.* **3.** To notice and make an answer to: *Our parents acknowledged the neighbors' invitation to the wedding.*
ac·knowl·edge (ăk **nŏl′**ĭj) ◊ *verb* **acknowledged, acknowledging**

acknowledgment *noun* **1.** Something done to respond to or recognize another's action. **2.** The act of acknowledging; recognition: *I bowed my head in acknowledgment of guilt.*
ac·knowl·edg·ment (ăk **nŏl′**ĭj mənt) ◊ *noun, plural* **acknowledgments**

acne *noun* A condition in which the oil glands of the skin become infected and form pimples.
ac·ne (ăk′nē) ◊ *noun*

acorn *noun* The nut of an oak tree.
a·corn (ā′kôrn′) ◊ *noun, plural* **acorns**

▲ **acorn**

acquaint *verb* To make or become familiar or informed: *We acquainted ourselves with the subject by reading a few books about it.*
ac·quaint (ə **kwānt′**) ◊ *verb* **acquainted, acquainting**

acquaintance *noun* **1.** Knowledge of something. **2.** A person whom one knows.
ac·quaint·ance (ə **kwān′**təns) ◊ *noun, plural* **acquaintances**

acquire *verb* To get; gain: *They worked hard to acquire new skills.*
ac·quire (ə **kwīr′**) ◊ *verb* **acquired, acquiring**

acquisition *noun* **1.** The act or process of acquiring. **2.** Something acquired.
ac·qui·si·tion (ăk′wĭ **zĭsh′**ən) ◊ *noun, plural* **acquisitions**

acquit *verb* **1.** To state that a person is innocent of a crime or wrongdoing. **2.** To conduct oneself in a certain way: *The new graduates acquitted themselves with dignity.*
ac·quit (ə **kwĭt′**) ◊ *verb* **acquitted, acquitting**

acre *noun* A unit of area equal to 4,840 square yards.
a·cre (ā′kər) ◊ *noun, plural* **acres**

***HISTORY* • acre**

Acre goes back to a word that first meant "a field, a pasture for cattle." Then people began to use **acre** for a measure of land, based on the size of a field that could be plowed in one day.

acreage *noun* Land area measured in acres.
a·cre·age (ā′kər ĭj) ◊ *noun*

acrid *adjective* **1.** Tasting or smelling harsh or bitter. **2.** Sharp and unpleasant: *There is an acrid tone to your remarks.*
ac·rid (ăk′rĭd) ◊ *adjective*

acrobat *noun* A person who is skilled in actions or stunts such as swinging from a trapeze or walking on a tightrope.
ac·ro·bat (**ăk′**rə băt′) ◊ *noun, plural* **acrobats**

▲ **acrobat**

across *preposition* **1.** To the other side of: *They rode bicycles across the continent.* **2.** On the other side of: *The bus station is across the street.* **3.** At an angle to: *A frog leaped across our path.*
◊ *adverb* From one side to the other: *A big ocean wave can be 100 feet across.*
a·cross (ə **krôs′**) ◊ *preposition* ◊ *adverb*

act *verb* **1.** To perform an action: *By acting quickly, we prevented the fire from spreading.* **2.** To conduct oneself; behave: *You act as if*

ă	pat	ĭ	pit	oi	**oil**	th	bath
ā	pay	ī	ride	ŏŏ	book	*th*	bathe
â	care	î	fierce	ōō	boot	ə	ago, item
ä	father	ŏ	pot	ou	**out**		pencil
ĕ	pet	ō	go	ŭ	cut		atom
ē	be	ô	paw, for	û	fur		circus

you are tired. **3.** To perform a part, especially in a play or movie: *Only a few of my friends have ever acted.* **4.** To have an effect: *The medicine acts quickly.*
◊ *noun* **1.** A thing done: *It was a brave act to rescue the drowning child.* **2.** The process of doing something: *The police caught the burglar in the act of breaking into the house.* **3.** One of the main divisions, especially of a play: *The first act takes place in a factory.* **4.** A law that has been passed.
act (ăkt) ◊ *verb* **acted, acting** ◊ *noun, plural* **acts**

action *noun* **1.** A thing done; act: *Take responsibility for your actions.* **2.** The activity or fact of doing something: *Verbs show action.* **3.** The way in which something works: *Let's study the action of the lock.* **4.** Battle: *The soldier was wounded in action.*
ac·tion (ăk′shən) ◊ *noun, plural* **actions**

active *adjective* **1.** Moving about; performing actions: *Athletes are more active than office workers.* **2.** Functioning; working: *Have you seen an active coal mine?* **3.** Taking part in activities: *The club has 20 active members.* **4.** Full of energy; busy.
ac·tive (ăk′tĭv) ◊ *adjective*

SYNONYMS

active, energetic, lively

He was very *active* during the game, not stopping for a moment's rest. My *energetic* sister keeps busy all day. We danced in a very *lively* way.

activity *noun* **1.** Something done for fun: *Stamp collecting is my favorite activity.* **2.** Energetic movement or action: *The store was a scene of great activity.*
ac·tiv·i·ty (ăk tĭv′ĭ tē) ◊ *noun, plural* **activities**

actor *noun* A person who acts a part, especially in a play or motion picture.
ac·tor (ăk′tər) ◊ *noun, plural* **actors**

actress *noun* A girl or woman who acts a part, especially in a play or motion picture.
ac·tress (ăk′trĭs) ◊ *noun, plural* **actresses**

actual *adjective* Really existing or happening. —See Synonyms at **real.**
ac·tu·al (ăk′cho͞o əl) ◊ *adjective*

actually *adverb* In fact; really.
ac·tu·al·ly (ăk′cho͞o ə lē) ◊ *adverb*

acute *adjective* **1.** Very sharp; keen: *The bat has an acute sense of hearing.* **2.** Sharp and very strong: *A toothache can cause acute pain.* **3.** Happening suddenly and lasting only for a short time: *I had an acute attack of asthma.* **4.** Very serious; critical: *We have an acute fuel shortage.*
a·cute (ə kyo͞ot′) ◊ *adjective*

acute accent *noun* A mark used over a vowel to show its quality or length. The accent over the *é* in *café* is an acute accent.
acute accent ◊ *noun, plural* **acute accents**

acute angle *noun* An angle that is smaller than a right angle. It measures between zero and 90 degrees.
acute angle ◊ *noun, plural* **acute angles**

▲ **acute angle**

ad *noun* An advertisement.
ad (ăd) ◊ *noun, plural* **ads**
‖*These sound alike:* **ad, add**

A.D. The abbreviation for the Latin words *anno Domini,* which mean "in the year of the Lord." *A.D.* is used for dates after the birth of Christ: *This antique jar was used in Rome about A.D. 300.*

adage *noun* A short saying. "Haste makes waste" is an adage.
ad·age (ăd′ĭj) ◊ *noun, plural* **adages**

adapt *verb* To change so as to be suitable for a different condition or purpose: *We put legs on a large tray to adapt it for use as a table.*
a·dapt (ə dăpt′) ◊ *verb* **adapted, adapting**

adaptable *adjective* Able to adapt or be adapted easily.
a·dapt·a·ble (ə dăp′tə bəl) ◊ *adjective*

adaptation *noun* The act or process of adapting to new conditions.
ad·ap·ta·tion (ăd′əp tā′shən) ◊ *noun*

add *verb* **1.** To find the sum of two or more numbers: *If you add 6 to 8, you get a total of 14.* **2.** To put on as a new part: *We want to add a new deck to the house.* **3.** To put in as

something extra: *I add honey to my tea.* **4.** To say as something extra: *My parents said good night and added, "Brush your teeth."*
◊ *idiom* **add up to** To mean: *Those warning signs add up to trouble.*
add (ăd) ◊ *verb* **added, adding**
‖*These sound alike:* **add, ad**

addend *noun* A number to be added to another number: *In 9 + 2 = 11, the numbers 9 and 2 are addends.*
ad·dend (**ăd′**ĕnd′ *or* ə **dĕnd′**) ◊ *noun, plural* **addends**

adder *noun* **1.** A poisonous snake of northern Europe and Asia. **2.** A nonpoisonous snake of North America.
ad·der (**ăd′**ər) ◊ *noun, plural* **adders**

▲ **adder**
Poisonous puff adder

addict *noun* **1.** A person who has a very strong desire for something habit-forming and harmful, especially a drug. **2.** A devoted fan: *They are rock music addicts.*
◊ *verb* To cause to have a very strong desire for something: *You are addicted to television.*
ad·dict ◊ *noun* (**ăd′**ĭkt), *plural* **addicts** ◊ *verb* (ə **dĭkt′**) **addicted, addicting**

addiction *noun* The condition of being addicted, especially to harmful, habit-forming drugs.
ad·dic·tion (ə **dĭk′**shən) ◊ *noun*

ă	pat	ĭ	pit	oi	oil	th	bath
ā	pay	ī	ride	o͝o	book	*th*	bathe
â	care	î	fierce	o͞o	boot	ə	ago, item
ä	father	ŏ	pot	ou	out		pencil
ĕ	pet	ō	go	ŭ	cut		atom
ē	be	ô	paw, for	û	fur		circus

addition *noun* **1.** The act or process of finding the sum of two or more numbers. **2.** The act of adding something extra: *The addition of fruit makes the cereal taste good.* **3.** A person or thing added: *The baby is a new addition to our family.*
◊ *idioms* **in addition** Also; besides: *We went shopping and in addition saw a movie.* **in addition to** Along with; besides: *In addition to cars, there were many bicycles on the ferry.*
ad·di·tion (ə **dĭsh′**ən) ◊ *noun, plural* **additions**

additional *adjective* Being extra; more: *We needed additional money for our trip.*
ad·di·tion·al (ə **dĭsh′**ə nəl) ◊ *adjective*

additive *noun* A small amount of something added to something else: *Additives are often used in packaged foods.*
ad·di·tive (**ăd′**ĭ tĭv) ◊ *noun, plural* **additives**

address *noun* **1.** The place where someone lives, works, or receives mail: *What is your home address?* **2.** A direction for delivery on a piece of mail: *Write the address clearly.* **3.** A formal speech.
◊ *verb* **1.** To speak to: *We addressed the principal politely.* **2.** To give a speech to: *The mayor will address our club.* **3.** To put directions for delivery on a piece of mail. —See Synonyms at **send.** **4.** To direct one's efforts or attention toward: *We addressed ourselves to our homework.*
ad·dress ◊ *noun* (ə **drĕs′** *or* **ăd′**rĕs′ *for senses 1, 2*), *plural* **addresses** ◊ *verb* (ə **drĕs′**) **addressed, addressing**

adenoids *plural noun* Small growths in the nose above the throat. Adenoids can swell and make it hard to breathe and speak.
ad·e·noids (**ăd′**n oidz′) ◊ *plural noun*

adept *adjective* Very skillful: *He is adept at cooking. She is an adept mechanic.*
a·dept (ə **dĕpt′**) ◊ *adjective*

adequate *adjective* **1.** Enough to meet a need; sufficient: *Do they have adequate food and clothing?* **2.** Passable, but not really good: *The book report was barely adequate.*
ad·e·quate (**ăd′**ĭ kwĭt) ◊ *adjective*

adhere *verb* **1.** To stick or hold fast: *The wallpaper adheres to the wall.* **2.** To remain loyal: *We adhered to our promises.*
ad·here (ăd **hîr′**) ◊ *verb* **adhered, adhering**

adhesive *adjective* Tending to stick fast to

something; sticky: *We put new adhesive tiles on the kitchen floor.*
◊ *noun* An adhesive substance, such as glue.
ad·he·sive (ăd **hē′**sĭv) ◊ *adjective* ◊ *noun, plural* **adhesives**

▲ **adhesive**

adhesive tape *noun* A tape coated with a sticky substance on one side and often used to hold bandages in place.

adjacent *adjective* Next or close to: *Your room is adjacent to mine.*
ad·ja·cent (ə **jā′**sənt) ◊ *adjective*

adjective *noun* A word used to describe a noun or a pronoun. For example, in the sentence *It was frightening to see three very big dogs racing toward us,* the words *frightening, three,* and *big* are adjectives.
ad·jec·tive (**ăj′**ĭk tĭv) ◊ *noun, plural* **adjectives**

adjoin *verb* To be next to or connected with: *The dining room adjoins the kitchen.*
ad·join (ə **join′**) ◊ *verb* **adjoined, adjoining**

adjourn *verb* To bring or come to a close until later: *We voted to adjourn the meeting.*
ad·journ (ə **jûrn′**) ◊ *verb* **adjourned, adjourning**

adjust *verb* **1.** To change, set, or regulate so as to improve or make right: *Can you adjust the color controls on the TV?* **2.** To become used to: *We have to adjust to city life.*
ad·just (ə **jŭst′**) ◊ *verb* **adjusted, adjusting**

adjustment *noun* **1.** The act or process of adjusting. **2.** The state of being adjusted. **3.** Something used to adjust a device.
ad·just·ment (ə **jŭst′**mənt) ◊ *noun, plural* **adjustments**

ad-lib *verb* To make up something, such as speech or music, while performing.
ad-lib (ăd **lĭb′**) ◊ *verb* **ad-libbed, ad-libbing**

administer *verb* **1.** To be the director or manager of; manage: *My friend administers the summer program.* **2.** To give or deal out; dispense: *A judge administers justice.*
ad·min·is·ter (ăd **mĭn′**ĭ stər) ◊ *verb* **administered, administering**

administration *noun* **1.** The act or process of administering. **2.** The work of managing something; management. **3.** The persons who manage the operation of something, such as a school, business, or government.
ad·min·is·tra·tion (ăd mĭn′ĭ **strā′**shən) ◊ *noun, plural* **administrations**

administrator *noun* A person in charge of directing or managing something.
ad·min·is·tra·tor (ăd **mĭn′**ĭ strā′tər) ◊ *noun, plural* **administrators**

admirable *adjective* Worthy of admiration: *Honesty is admirable.*
ad·mi·ra·ble (**ăd′**mər ə bəl) ◊ *adjective*

admiral *noun* A Navy or Coast Guard officer ranking above a vice admiral.
ad·mi·ral (**ăd′**mər əl) ◊ *noun, plural* **admirals**

admiration *noun* **1.** Great pleasure and delight: *We gazed at the sunset in admiration.* **2.** Very high respect: *The team felt great admiration for the coach.* **3.** Praise and approval: *We want attention and admiration.*
ad·mi·ra·tion (ăd′mə **rā′**shən) ◊ *noun*

admire *verb* **1.** To regard with great pleasure and delight. **2.** To feel great respect for: *We admire your courage.*
ad·mire (ăd **mīr′**) ◊ *verb* **admired, admiring**

HISTORY • **admire, admiral**

The spelling of the word **admire** influenced that of **admiral,** which sometimes used to be spelled *amiral.* Originally the two words were unrelated. **Admire** came from a Latin word that meant "to wonder at," but **admiral** came from an Arabic phrase that meant "commander of the sea."

admission *noun* **1.** The act of admitting. **2.** The right to enter: *You should apply early*

for admission to college. **3.** A price charged or paid to enter a place. **4.** An admitting of something, such as a confession of guilt.
ad·mis·sion (ăd **mĭsh'** ən) ◊ *noun, plural* **admissions**

admit *verb* **1.** To make known that something is true or a fact: *I must admit that you are right.* **2.** To allow or permit to enter: *This pass will admit one person free.* **3.** To make possible; allow: *That problem seems to admit no solution.*
ad·mit (ăd **mĭt'**) ◊ *verb* **admitted, admitting**

admittance *noun* Permission or the right to enter.
ad·mit·tance (ăd **mĭt'** ns) ◊ *noun*

admonish *verb* To criticize for a fault in a kind but serious way: *I admonished them for their lateness.*
ad·mon·ish (ăd **mŏn'** ĭsh) ◊ *verb* **admonished, admonishing**

admonition *noun* A criticism or kind but serious warning.
ad·mo·ni·tion (ăd'mə **nĭsh'** ən) ◊ *noun, plural* **admonitions**

ado *noun* Needless fuss and bother.
a·do (ə **do͞o'**) ◊ *noun*

adobe *noun* **1.** Brick made of clay and straw that is dried in the sun. **2.** A structure, such as a house, built with adobe.
a·do·be (ə **dō'** bē) ◊ *noun, plural* **adobes**

adolescence *noun* The time of life during which a young person is growing up.
ad·o·les·cence (ăd'l **ĕs'** əns) ◊ *noun*

adolescent *noun* A person who is between 13 and 19 years old; teen-ager.
ad·o·les·cent (ăd'l **ĕs'** ənt) ◊ *noun, plural* **adolescents**

adopt *verb* **1.** To take another person's child and raise it as one's own. **2.** To take and make one's own: *Samuel Clemens adopted the name Mark Twain.* **3.** To accept and use or follow: *Our school has adopted the new way of doing arithmetic.*
a·dopt (ə **dŏpt'**) ◊ *verb* **adopted, adopting**

ă	pat	ĭ	pit	oi	**oil**	th	**bath**
ā	pay	ī	ride	o͝o	**book**	*th*	**bathe**
â	care	î	fierce	o͞o	**boot**	ə	ago, item
ä	father	ŏ	pot	ou	**out**		pencil
ĕ	pet	ō	go	ŭ	cut		atom
ē	be	ô	paw, for	û	fur		circus

adoption *noun* The act of adopting or the condition of being adopted.
a·dop·tion (ə **dŏp'** shən) ◊ *noun, plural* **adoptions**

adorable *adjective* Delightful; charming.
a·dor·a·ble (ə **dôr'** ə bəl) ◊ *adjective*

adoration *noun* The act of adoring.
ad·o·ra·tion (ăd'ə **rā'** shən) ◊ *noun*

adore *verb* **1.** To worship as a divine being. **2.** To love with deep devotion: *We adore our sisters and brothers.* **3.** To have a great liking for: *I adore ghost stories.*
a·dore (ə **dôr'**) ◊ *verb* **adored, adoring**

adorn *verb* To decorate with something beautiful; ornament.
a·dorn (ə **dôrn'**) ◊ *verb* **adorned, adorning**

adrift *adverb & adjective* Drifting without direction: *The storm set the boat adrift.*
a·drift (ə **drĭft'**) ◊ *adverb & adjective*

▲ **adrift**

adroit *adjective* Skillful or clever at handling something difficult.
a·droit (ə **droit'**) ◊ *adjective*

adulation *noun* Too much praise.
ad·u·la·tion (ăj'ə **lā'** shən) ◊ *noun*

adult *noun* **1.** A person who is fully developed and mature; grownup. **2.** A fully grown animal or plant.
◊ *adjective* Fully grown. —See Synonyms at **mature.**
a·dult (ə **dŭlt'** *or* **ăd'** ŭlt') ◊ *noun, plural* **adults** ◊ *adjective*

▲ **adult**
Adult dog with puppy

adulthood *noun* The time or state of being an adult.
a•dult•hood (ə dŭlt′ho͝od′) ◊ *noun*

advance *verb* **1.** To move forward, onward, or ahead: *The quarterback advanced the ball ten yards.* **2.** To help the growth or progress of: *Our studies advance our knowledge of the world.* **3.** To raise or rise to a higher rank or position. **4.** To put forward; suggest. **5.** To give ahead of time: *The company advanced me a week's pay.*
◊ *noun* **1.** Forward or onward movement. **2.** Progress or improvement. **3.** Money given ahead of time: *Can you get an advance on your allowance?* **4.** A rise in price, amount, or value.
◊ *idiom* **in advance** Ahead of time: *We made all our plans in advance.*
ad•vance (əd văns′) ◊ *verb* **advanced, advancing** ◊ *noun, plural* **advances**

advanced *adjective* **1.** Being beyond others in progress or development: *Ancient Greece was an advanced civilization.* **2.** Being beyond a beginning level: *She studied advanced math.* **3.** Far along in years or course: *He died at the advanced age of 97.*
ad•vanced (əd vănst′) ◊ *adjective*

advancement *noun* The act of advancing or the condition of being advanced.
ad•vance•ment (ăd văns′mənt) ◊ *noun, plural* **advancements**

advantage *noun* **1.** A benefit that puts a person in a favorable position: *They gave the children the advantages of education.* **2.** Personal benefit: *We turned the handicap to our advantage.* **3.** A favorable position: *My early start gave me an advantage.*
◊ *idiom* **take advantage of 1.** To put to good use; benefit by: *Let's take advantage of this chance to learn to swim.* **2.** To use in an unfair way: *Don't take advantage of your friend's willingness to do all the work.*
ad•van•tage (əd văn′tĭj) ◊ *noun, plural* **advantages**

advantageous *adjective* Giving an advantage; beneficial.
ad•van•ta•geous (ăd′vən tā′jəs) ◊ *adjective*

advent *noun* The coming or arrival of a new person or thing.
ad•vent (ăd′vĕnt′) ◊ *noun, plural* **advents**

adventure *noun* **1.** A bold, dangerous, or risky undertaking: *They set out on a daring space adventure.* **2.** An unusual or exciting experience: *The storm made our hike a real adventure.*
ad•ven•ture (əd vĕn′chər) ◊ *noun, plural* **adventures**

adventurous *adjective* Willing to risk danger in order to have exciting adventures.
ad•ven•tur•ous (əd vĕn′chər əs) ◊ *adjective*

adverb *noun* A word used to modify a verb, an adjective, or another adverb. Adverbs can be used to show time, place, manner, or degree. For example, in the sentence *Early in the morning I felt fine, but later on I became very tired,* the words *early, fine, later,* and *very* are adverbs.
ad•verb (ăd′vûrb′) ◊ *noun, plural* **adverbs**

adversary *noun* A person or group that opposes another; enemy.
ad•ver•sar•y (ăd′vər sĕr′ē) ◊ *noun, plural* **adversaries**

adverse *adjective* **1.** Not favorable or helpful: *The pill had an adverse effect, and I felt worse.* **2.** Acting in an opposite direction: *Adverse currents prevented swimming.*
ad•verse (ăd vûrs′ *or* ăd′vûrs′) ◊ *adjective*

adversity *noun* Bad luck; misfortune.
ad•ver•si•ty (ăd vûr′sĭ tē) ◊ *noun, plural* **adversities**

advertise *verb* **1.** To announce to the public: *The poster advertised the circus.* **2.** To call public attention to a product. **3.** To give out a public notice or request.
ad•ver•tise (ăd′vər tīz′) ◊ *verb* **advertised, advertising**

advertisement *noun* A public notice to call attention to something, such as a product, a service, or a coming event.
ad·ver·tise·ment (ăd′vər **tīz′**mənt *or* ăd-**vûr′**tĭs mənt) ◊ *noun, plural* **advertisements**

advice *noun* An idea or suggestion about how to solve a problem.
ad·vice (əd **vīs′**) ◊ *noun*

advisable *adjective* Wise or sensible to do: *It is advisable to see a dentist regularly.*
ad·vis·a·ble (əd **vī′**zə bəl) ◊ *adjective*

advise *verb* **1.** To give advice to or offer advice. **2.** To give information to; notify.
ad·vise (əd **vīz′**) ◊ *verb* **advised, advising**

advisory *adjective* Advising or having the power to advise.
ad·vi·so·ry (əd **vī′**zə rē) ◊ *adjective*

advocate *verb* To be or speak in favor of: *We advocate equal rights for everyone.*
◊ *noun* A person who supports a cause.
ad·vo·cate ◊ *verb* (**ăd′**və kāt′) **advocated, advocating** ◊ *noun* (**ăd′**və kĭt *or* **ad′**və kāt′), *plural* **advocates**

adz *or* **adze** *noun* An axlike tool with a curved blade that is used for shaping large pieces of wood.
adz *or* **adze** (ădz) ◊ *noun, plural* **adzes**

aerial *adjective* Of or in the air.
◊ *noun* A radio or television antenna.
aer·i·al (**âr′**ē əl) ◊ *adjective* ◊ *noun, plural* **aerials**

aerobics *noun* (*used with a singular or plural verb*) Regular exercises, such as biking, running, or swimming, that help strengthen the heart and lungs: *Aerobics is* (or *are*) *fun.*
aer·o·bics (â **rō′**bĭks) ◊ *noun*

aeronautics *noun* (*used with a singular verb*) The science of the design, building, and operation of aircraft.
aer·o·nau·tics (âr′ə **nô′**tĭks) ◊ *noun*

aerospace *noun* **1.** The earth's atmosphere and outer space. **2.** The science that deals with flight in outer space.
aer·o·space (**âr′**ə spās′) ◊ *noun*

ă	pat	ĭ	pit	oi	**oil**	th	**bath**
ā	pay	ī	ride	ŏŏ	book	*th*	**bathe**
â	care	î	fierce	ōō	boot	ə	ago, item
ä	father	ŏ	pot	ou	**out**		pencil
ĕ	pet	ō	go	ŭ	cut		atom
ē	be	ô	paw, for	û	fur		circus

afar *adverb* Far away; far off: *We heard a shout afar.*
a·far (ə **fär′**) ◊ *adverb*

affable *adjective* Pleasant and friendly in dealing with others.
af·fa·ble (**ăf′**ə bəl) ◊ *adjective*

affair *noun* **1.** A matter that concerns one: *The problem is your affair, not mine.* **2.** An action, event, or happening: *The wedding was a grand affair.* **3. affairs** Business matters: *A lawyer takes care of my affairs.*
af·fair (ə **fâr′**) ◊ *noun, plural* **affairs**

affect[1] *verb* **1.** To cause a change in; have an effect on: *Eating junk food can affect your health.* **2.** To touch the feelings of.
af·fect[1] (ə **fĕkt′**) ◊ *verb* **affected, affecting**

> **SYNONYMS**
>
> ***affect*[1]*, impress, influence, move***
>
> His unkindness to me *affected* my feelings toward him. Her ideas *impressed* me favorably. I *influenced* them to change their minds about the election. Hearing their sad story *moved* me to offer help.

affect[2] *verb* To pretend to feel or have; assume: *They affected deep sorrow, but it was all an act.*
af·fect[2] (ə **fĕkt′**) ◊ *verb* **affected, affecting**

> ***HISTORY* • affect**[1]**, affect**[2]
>
> **Affect**[1] comes from a Latin word that meant "to have an influence on." **Affect**[2] comes from a related Latin word that meant "to strive after."

affection *noun* A feeling of fondness or love for a person, animal, or thing.
af·fec·tion (ə **fĕk′**shən) ◊ *noun, plural* **affections**

affectionate *adjective* Having or showing affection; loving.
af·fec·tion·ate (ə **fĕk′**shə nĭt) ◊ *adjective*

affirm *verb* **1.** To declare to be true; confirm. **2.** To say in a confident way; assert.
af·firm (ə **fûrm′**) ◊ *verb* **affirmed, affirming**

affirmative *adjective* Saying that something is so, as with the word *yes.*
af·firm·a·tive (ə **fûr′**mə tĭv) ◊ *adjective*

affix *verb* To add on; attach: *I affixed the stamp to the envelope.*
◊ *noun* A letter or group of letters added to a word to change its meaning; a prefix or suffix.
af·fix ◊ *verb* (ə **fĭks′**) **affixed, affixing** ◊ *noun* (**ăf′**ĭks′), *plural* **affixes**

afflict *verb* To cause to suffer, as from disease, pain, or trouble.
af·flict (ə **flĭkt′**) ◊ *verb* **afflicted, afflicting**

affliction *noun* **1.** A state of being afflicted. **2.** A cause of pain or suffering.
af·flic·tion (ə **flĭk′**shən) ◊ *noun, plural* **afflictions**

affluence *noun* A great deal of money or property; wealth.
af·flu·ence (**ăf′**lo͞o əns) ◊ *noun*

afford *verb* **1.** To be able to pay for or spare: *We can't afford a new TV set. I can't afford the time.* **2.** To be able to do or bear without causing harm: *You can't afford to go without sleep.* **3.** To give or furnish; provide: *The cabin afforded protection from the rain.*
af·ford (ə **fôrd′**) ◊ *verb* **afforded, affording**

affront *verb* To insult on purpose.
◊ *noun* An open insult.
af·front (ə **frŭnt′**) ◊ *verb* **affronted, affronting** ◊ *noun, plural* **affronts**

afield *adverb* Away from home; to or at a distance: *They went far afield to find water.*
a·field (ə **fēld′**) ◊ *adverb*

afire *adjective & adverb* On or as if on fire.
a·fire (ə **fīr′**) ◊ *adjective & adverb*

afloat *adjective & adverb* **1.** Floating on or as if on water. **2.** Passing around: *Strange rumors soon were afloat.*
a·float (ə **flōt′**) ◊ *adjective & adverb*

afoot *adjective & adverb* **1.** On foot; walking. **2.** Going on; happening: *Big plans were afoot for the surprise party.*
a·foot (ə **fo͝ot′**) ◊ *adjective & adverb*

afraid *adjective* **1.** Filled with fear; scared. **2.** Filled with regret; sorry.
a·fraid (ə **frād′**) ◊ *adjective*

LANGUAGE DETECTIVE

afraid

Usually the last syllable of *afraid* rhymes with *paid.* However, if you live in eastern Virginia, you may pronounce *afraid* so that the last syllable rhymes with *bed.*

afresh *adverb* Again; anew: *Take a clean piece of paper and start afresh.*
a·fresh (ə **frĕsh′**) ◊ *adverb*

African *noun* A person who was born in or lives in Africa.
◊ *adjective* Of or relating to Africa or the Africans.
Af·ri·can (**ăf′**rĭ kən) ◊ *noun, plural* **Africans** ◊ *adjective*

African violet *noun* A house plant with white, pink, or purple flowers.
African violet ◊ *noun, plural* **African violets**

▲ **African violet**

Afro *noun* A full, rounded hair style for thick, very curly hair.
Af·ro (**ăf′**rō) ◊ *noun, plural* **Afros**

Afro-American *noun* An American who has African ancestors.
Af·ro-A·mer·i·can (ăf′rō ə **mĕr′**ĭ kən) ◊ *noun, plural* **Afro-Americans**

aft *adverb* Toward or at the rear of a ship or aircraft.
aft (ăft) ◊ *adverb*

after *preposition* **1.** Behind in place or order: *The clowns came after the elephants in the parade.* **2.** With the aim of following, catching, or getting: *We ran after the fire engine.*
◊ *conjunction* Following the time that: *We can eat after we get home.*
◊ *adverb* Following in time or place: *We left the party shortly after.*
af·ter (**ăf′**tər) ◊ *preposition* ◊ *conjunction* ◊ *adverb*

afternoon *noun* The part of the day from noon until sunset.
af·ter·noon (ăf′tər **no͞on′**) ◊ *noun, plural* **afternoons**

afterward *or* **afterwards** *adverb* At a later time: *We ate and afterward we took a walk.*
af·ter·ward (ăf′ tər wərd) *or* **af·ter·wards** (ăf′ tər wərdz) ◊ *adverb*

again *adverb* Once more: *If you don't win, try again.*
a·gain (ə gĕn′) ◊ *adverb*

against *preposition* **1.** In a direction or course opposite to: *It's hard to swim against the current.* **2.** In or into contact with: *I leaned against a tree to rest.* **3.** Opposed to; resisting: *Are you for or against the plan?* **4.** Contrary to: *I went skiing against my better judgment.* **5.** As protection from: *We wore warm jackets against the cold.*
a·gainst (ə gĕnst′) ◊ *preposition*

agate *noun* **1.** A mineral that is a type of quartz. The colors of agate appear in streaks or cloudy masses. **2.** A playing marble made of a material that looks like agate.
ag·ate (ăg′ ĭt) ◊ *noun, plural* **agates**

▲ **agate**
Above: Agate
Below: A marble made of agate

age *noun* **1.** The period or length of time during which someone or something has existed; lifetime. **2.** A specified time in life: *I learned to read at the age of five.* **3.** The time in life when a person is granted legal rights, such as voting. **4.** The later part of life. **5.** A period of time noted for a special feature: *We live in the space age.* **6.** A long period of time.
◊ *verb* **1.** To become or cause to become old. **2.** To become or allow to become ready for use: *Many kinds of cheese need to age.*
age (āj) ◊ *noun, plural* **ages** ◊ *verb* **aged, aging**

ă	pat	ĭ	pit	oi	**oil**	th	ba**th**
ā	pay	ī	ride	ŏŏ	book	*th*	ba**th**e
â	care	î	fierce	ōō	boot	ə	ago, item
ä	father	ŏ	pot	ou	**out**		pencil
ĕ	pet	ō	go	ŭ	cut		atom
ē	be	ô	paw, for	û	fur		circus

aged *adjective* **1.** Of the age of: *Our family adopted a child aged five.* **2.** Very old.
aged (ājd *for sense 1;* ā′ jĭd *for sense 2*) ◊ *adjective*

agency *noun* **1.** Someone or something through which an act or goal is achieved. **2.** A business or organization with the power to act for others: *My friend found a job through an employment agency.*
a·gen·cy (ā′ jən sē) ◊ *noun, plural* **agencies**

agent *noun* **1.** A person or company that acts for another: *A ticket agent reserved seats for us.* **2.** A means by which something is done or caused: *Wind is an agent of soil erosion.*
a·gent (ā′ jənt) ◊ *noun, plural* **agents**

aggravate *verb* **1.** To make worse: *Ice water aggravated my toothache.* **2.** To make irritated, as by constant bothering.
ag·gra·vate (ăg′ rə vāt′) ◊ *verb* **aggravated, aggravating**

aggregate *noun* The whole or total amount.
◊ *verb* To total up to; amount to.
ag·gre·gate ◊ *noun* (ăg′ rə gĭt′), *plural* **aggregates** ◊ *verb* (ăg′ rə gāt′) **aggregated, aggregating**

aggression *noun* **1.** An attack, as of one country on another, made without cause. **2.** Unfriendly action or behavior.
ag·gres·sion (ə grĕsh′ ən) ◊ *noun, plural* **aggressions**

aggressive *adjective* **1.** Quick to attack or start a fight. **2.** Very active and forceful and sometimes too bold: *The aggressive salesperson wouldn't leave us alone.*
ag·gres·sive (ə grĕs′ ĭv) ◊ *adjective*

aggressor *noun* A person or country that attacks another without cause.
ag·gres·sor (ə grĕs′ ər) ◊ *noun, plural* **aggressors**

aggrieved *adjective* **1.** Feeling unhappy or troubled. **2.** Feeling wrongly treated.
ag·grieved (ə grēvd′) ◊ *adjective*

aghast *adjective* Shocked by something terrible or wrong.
a·ghast (ə găst′) ◊ *adjective*

agile *adjective* **1.** Able to move quickly and easily; nimble. **2.** Quick to understand.
ag·ile (ăj′ əl) ◊ *adjective*

agility *noun* Quickness and ease in moving or thinking.
a·gil·i·ty (ə jĭl′ ĭ tē) ◊ *noun*

agitate *verb* **1.** To shake or stir up with a back-and-forth motion: *The storm agitated the waves.* **2.** To upset the mind or feelings of; disturb. **3.** To try to stir up public interest in a cause: *The workers agitated for equal pay for equal work.*
ag·i·tate (ăj′ĭ tāt′) ◊ *verb* **agitated, agitating**

agitator *noun* A device that stirs or shakes, as in a washing machine.
ag·i·ta·tor (ăj′ĭ tā′tər) ◊ *noun, plural* **agitators**

ago *adjective & adverb* Before the present time: *They moved to Chicago five years ago.*
a·go (ə **gō′**) ◊ *adjective & adverb*

agog *adjective* Full of great excitement: *We were agog when we won the trophy.*
a·gog (ə **gŏg′**) ◊ *adjective*

agonizing *adjective* Causing great pain or suffering.
ag·o·niz·ing (**ăg′** ə nī′zĭng) ◊ *adjective*

agony *noun* Great pain or suffering.
ag·o·ny (**ăg′** ə nē) ◊ *noun*

agree *verb* **1.** To have or share the same opinion; concur: *I agree with you that it's too hot to work.* **2.** To express one's willingness or approval; consent: *My cousin agreed to take me fishing.* **3.** To be in harmony; be alike: *Your stories don't agree.* **4.** To arrive at an understanding: *The buyer and the seller agreed on a price.* **5.** To be suitable or healthful: *The climate here agrees with me.* **6.** To get along well together.
a·gree (ə **grē′**) ◊ *verb* **agreed, agreeing**

agreeable *adjective* **1.** Giving pleasure or delight; pleasing: *The field of wild flowers was an agreeable sight.* —See Synonyms at **pleasant. 2.** Willing to agree: *They were agreeable to our plans for the school play.*
a·gree·a·ble (ə **grē′** ə bəl) ◊ *adjective*

agreement *noun* **1.** The act or fact of agreeing. **2.** An arrangement or understanding between people or groups.
a·gree·ment (ə **grē′**mənt) ◊ *noun, plural* **agreements**

agricultural *adjective* Of or having to do with farms or farming.
ag·ri·cul·tur·al (ăg′rĭ **kŭl′**chər əl) ◊ *adjective*

agriculture *noun* The science, activity, and business of cultivating the soil, growing crops, and raising livestock; farming.
ag·ri·cul·ture (**ăg′** rĭ kŭl′chər) ◊ *noun*

> ***HISTORY* • agriculture**
>
> The word **agriculture** comes from two Latin words, *agri cultura,* that meant "the cultivation of land."

aground *adverb & adjective* On or onto the shore or a reef or shoal: *The ship ran aground during the storm.*
a·ground (ə **ground′**) ◊ *adverb & adjective*

ah *interjection* An expression used to show surprise, delight, relief, or disgust.
ah (ä) ◊ *interjection*

aha *interjection* An expression used to show satisfaction, pleasure, or triumph.
a·ha (ä **hä′**) ◊ *interjection*

ahead *adverb & adjective* **1.** In, at, or toward the front; farther forward: *We moved ahead in line. The road ahead is icy.* **2.** In advance: *To get tickets you have to phone ahead.* **3.** Forward or onward: *Go ahead with your science project.*
a·head (ə **hĕd′**) ◊ *adverb & adjective*

ahead of *preposition* **1.** In front of: *They pushed ahead of us in line.* **2.** Earlier than: *We arrived at the football game ahead of everyone else.*

ahoy *interjection* An expression used to hail a person or a passing ship or to attract attention: *Ship ahoy! Ahoy there!*
a·hoy (ə **hoi′**) ◊ *interjection*

aid *verb* To give help to; assist: *Glasses aid my sight. A map aids us in finding our way.* ◊ *noun* **1.** Help or assistance given. —See Synonyms at **help. 2.** Someone or something that helps or is helpful.
aid (ād) ◊ *verb* **aided, aiding** ◊ *noun, plural* **aids**
‖*These sound alike:* **aid, aide**

aide *noun* A person who acts as a helper.
aide (ād) ◊ *noun, plural* **aides**
‖*These sound alike:* **aide, aid**

ail *verb* **1.** To be ill: *My cousin is ailing.* **2.** To cause distress to: *What ails you?*
ail (āl) ◊ *verb* **ailed, ailing**
‖*These sound alike:* **ail, ale**

ailment *noun* An illness or disease.
ail·ment (**āl′**mənt) ◊ *noun, plural* **ailments**

aim *verb* **1.** To point a weapon or instrument: *Aim the telescope at the star.* **2.** To direct to

or toward someone or something: *I aimed my talk at the younger children.* **3.** To have as a goal or purpose.
◊ *noun* **1.** The pointing of a weapon at a target. **2.** A purpose or goal.
aim (ām) ◊ *verb* **aimed, aiming** ◊ *noun, plural* **aims**

ain't Nonstandard contraction for "am not," "is not," "are not," "have not," "has not."
ain't (ānt) ◊ *contraction*

LANGUAGE DETECTIVE

ain't

The word *ain't* is not considered to be proper English. Because of this, you should not use *ain't* in writing, and you should use it in speaking only if you want to be humorous.

air *noun* **1.** The colorless, odorless, tasteless mixture of gases that surrounds the earth. The two main gases in air are nitrogen and oxygen. **2.** The open space above the earth: *The batter hit the ball high into the air.* **3.** Aircraft: *I like to travel by air. The company ships goods by air.* **4.** A general look or appearance: *The judge had a dignified air.* **5. airs** An affected, unnatural way of acting: *Don't put on airs just because you won the contest.* **6.** A radio or television broadcasting system: *Is that program still on the air?* **7.** A melody or tune.
◊ *verb* **1.** To expose to the air so as to dry or freshen: *Let's air these winter clothes.* **2.** To let fresh air through: *Open the window and air the room.* **3.** To express in public: *I need to air my complaints.*
◊ *idiom* **up in the air** Not settled; undecided.
air (âr) ◊ *noun, plural* **airs** ◊ *verb* **aired, airing**
‖*These sound alike:* **air, heir**

air-condition *verb* To cause fresh air to circulate through an enclosed space by means of an air conditioner.
air-con·di·tion (âr′kən dĭsh′ən) ◊ *verb* **air-conditioned, air-conditioning**

air conditioner *noun* A device that cools the air in an enclosed space and controls the humidity.
air conditioner ◊ *noun, plural* **air conditioners**

aircraft *noun* A vehicle, such as an airplane, helicopter, glider, or dirigible, that can travel through the air.
air·craft (âr′krăft′) ◊ *noun, plural* **aircraft**

air force *noun* Often **Air Force** The branch of a nation's armed forces that is equipped with aircraft.
air force ◊ *noun, plural* **air forces**

airline *noun* A company that carries passengers and freight by aircraft.
air·line (âr′līn′) ◊ *noun, plural* **airlines**

airmail *noun* **1.** Mail carried by aircraft. **2.** The system of carrying mail by aircraft.
air·mail (âr′māl′) ◊ *noun*

airman *noun* An Air Force enlisted person ranking below a sergeant.
air·man (âr′mən) ◊ *noun, plural* **airmen**

airplane *noun* A vehicle with fixed wings that is heavier than air but can fly through it. Airplanes are driven by propellers or jet engines.
air·plane (âr′plān′) ◊ *noun, plural* **airplanes**

airport *noun* A place with marked, open spaces where aircraft can take off and land.
air·port (âr′pôrt′) ◊ *noun, plural* **airports**

▲ **airport**
Runways and gate area of an airport

ă	pat	ĭ	pit	oi	oil	th	bath
ā	pay	ī	ride	o͝o	book	*th*	bathe
â	care	î	fierce	o͞o	boot	ə	ago, item
ä	father	ŏ	pot	ou	out		pencil
ĕ	pet	ō	go	ŭ	cut		atom
ē	be	ô	paw, for	û	fur		circus

airship *noun* A large cigar-shaped aircraft filled with gas; dirigible.
air·ship (âr′shĭp′) ◊ *noun, plural* **airships**

airtight *adjective* **1.** So tight that no air can pass in or out: *An airtight seal protected the food in the package.* **2.** Having no weak points; sound: *My bus was late, so I had an airtight excuse for being tardy.*
air·tight (âr′tīt′) ◊ *adjective*

airy *adjective* **1.** With air moving about freely: *The room was light and airy.* **2.** Light as air; delicate: *The airy curtains fluttered in the breeze.*
air·y (âr′ē) ◊ *adjective* **airier, airiest**

aisle *noun* A narrow space for walking between rows of seats, as in a theater.
aisle (īl) ◊ *noun, plural* **aisles**
‖*These sound alike:* **aisle, I'll, isle**

ajar *adjective & adverb* Partly open: *Please leave the door ajar.*
a·jar (ə jär′) ◊ *adjective & adverb*

AK The abbreviation for *Alaska* that is used with a Zip Code.

akimbo *adjective & adverb* With the hands on the hips and the elbows bent outward.
a·kim·bo (ə kĭm′bō) ◊ *adjective & adverb*

akin *adjective* **1.** Having the same origin or ancestors; related. **2.** Similar in nature or kind: *My friend's feelings are akin to mine.*
a·kin (ə kĭn′) ◊ *adjective*

AL The abbreviation for *Alabama* that is used with a Zip Code.

Ala. An abbreviation for *Alabama.*

alarm *noun* **1.** Sudden fear caused by a feeling that danger is near: *The passengers felt alarm when the airplane began to shake.* **2.** A warning that danger is near: *I smelled smoke and spread the alarm.* **3.** A bell, light, or other signal that warns people of possible danger. —See Synonyms at **warning.**
◊ *verb* To fill with sudden fear; frighten.
a·larm (ə lärm′) ◊ *noun, plural* **alarms** ◊ *verb* **alarmed, alarming**

alarm clock *noun* A clock that can be set to sound a bell or buzzer at a certain time in order to wake a person up.
alarm clock ◊ *noun, plural* **alarm clocks**

alas *interjection* An expression used to show sorrow, regret, or grief.
a·las (ə lăs′) ◊ *interjection*

albatross *noun* A large sea bird with a hooked beak, webbed feet, and long wings.
al·ba·tross (ăl′bə trôs′) ◊ *noun, plural* **albatrosses**

▲ **albatross**

album *noun* **1.** A book with blank pages in which such things as photographs or stamps can be kept. **2.** A phonograph record or set of records in one case.
al·bum (ăl′bəm) ◊ *noun, plural* **albums**

alcohol *noun* **1.** Any of several liquids that are colorless, burn easily, and have many uses. One kind of alcohol is made from fruits, grains, or sugar and is found in drinks like wine and whiskey. Alcohols are also used in medicines, chemicals, and fuels. **2.** A drink that contains alcohol; liquor.
al·co·hol (ăl′kə hôl′) ◊ *noun, plural* **alcohols**

alcoholic *adjective* **1.** Of or containing alcohol. **2.** Of or suffering from alcoholism.
◊ *noun* A person suffering from alcoholism.
al·co·hol·ic (ăl′kə hô′lĭk) ◊ *adjective* ◊ *noun, plural* **alcoholics**

alcoholism *noun* A disease in which people get into the habit of drinking too much alcohol and find it hard to stop.
al·co·ho·ism (ăl′kə hô lĭz′əm) ◊ *noun*

alcove *noun* A small part of a room that is set back from the main part.
al·cove (ăl′kōv′) ◊ *noun, plural* **alcoves**

alder *noun* A tree or shrub with rounded leaves that grows in cool, damp places.
al·der (ôl′dər) ◊ *noun, plural* **alders**

ale *noun* An alcoholic drink made of malt and hops.
ale (āl) ◊ *noun, plural* **ales**
‖*These sound alike:* **ale, ail**

alert *adjective* **1.** Quick to notice or act: *The alert child caught the blue dish as it fell.* **2.** Watching out for danger; attentive: *A good driver must always be alert.*
◊ *verb* To make aware or ready; warn: *The siren alerted us to the danger.*
◊ *noun* A warning signal.
a·lert (ə lûrt′) ◊ *adjective* ◊ *verb* **alerted, alerting** ◊ *noun, plural* **alerts**

alfalfa *noun* A plant with purple flowers that is related to clover. Alfalfa is grown as feed for cattle and other livestock.
al·fal·fa (ăl făl′fə) ◊ *noun*

al·gae *plural noun* Any of a large group of green, red, or brown plants that grow in water but lack true roots, stems, and leaves.
al·gae (ăl′jē) ◊ *plural noun*

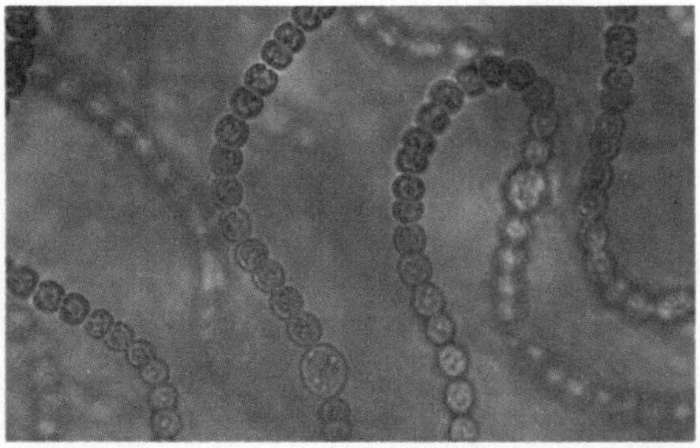

▲ **algae**
Magnified 450 times

algebra *noun* A branch of mathematics dealing with problems that involve known and unknown numbers and their relations. The unknown numbers are often represented by letters or other symbols.
al·ge·bra (ăl′jə brə) ◊ *noun*

alias *noun* A name that a person uses to hide his or her real name.
a·li·as (ā′lē əs) ◊ *noun, plural* **aliases**

alibi *noun* **1.** A claim that a person was somewhere else when a crime was committed: *They were out of town when the money was taken, and this alibi kept them from being accused.* **2.** An excuse: *I won't accept any more of your alibis.*
al·i·bi (ăl′ə bī′) ◊ *noun, plural* **alibis**

ă	pat	ĭ	pit	oi	oil	th	bath
ā	pay	ī	ride	ŏŏ	book	*th*	bathe
â	care	î	fierce	ōō	boot	ə	ago, item
ä	father	ŏ	pot	ou	out		pencil
ĕ	pet	ō	go	ŭ	cut		atom
ē	be	ô	paw, for	û	fur		circus

alien *adjective* **1.** Of or coming from another country; foreign. **2.** Not natural; contrary: *Jealousy is alien to my nature.*
◊ *noun* **1.** A person who lives in one country while still being a citizen of another; foreigner. **2.** In science fiction, an intelligent being from somewhere other than the earth.
a·li·en (ā′lē ən *or* āl′yən) ◊ *adjective* ◊ *noun, plural* **aliens**

alight[1] *adjective* Lit up; glowing: *The house was alight with festive candles.*
a·light[1] (ə līt′) ◊ *adjective*

alight[2] *verb* **1.** To come down and settle gently: *A bird alighted on the branch.* **2.** To get off; get down: *The bus stopped and two passengers alighted.*
a·light[2] (ə līt′) ◊ *verb* **alighted** *or* **alit, alighting**

HISTORY **• alight**[1]**, alight**[2]

Alight[1] comes from an old English phrase, *on light,* in the same way that **afire** comes from *on fire.* **Alight**[2] comes from an old English word that meant "to take the weight off something."

align *verb* **1.** To arrange in a straight line; line up: *The chairs were aligned in two rows.* **2.** To put into the proper relationship; adjust: *Please align the wheels of my car.*
a·lign (ə līn′) ◊ *verb* **aligned, aligning**

alike *adjective* Being like one another; similar: *The twins look very much alike.*
◊ *adverb* In the same way or manner: *We must try to treat everyone alike.*
a·like (ə līk′) ◊ *adjective* ◊ *adverb*

alimentary canal *noun* The connected parts of the body through which food passes as it is being digested. The alimentary canal includes the esophagus, the stomach, and the large and small intestines.
al·i·men·ta·ry canal (ăl′ə mĕn′tə rē) ◊ *noun, plural* **alimentary canals**

alimony *noun* Money that must be paid regularly to support a person's spouse during

a legal separation or a person's former spouse after a divorce.
al·i·mo·ny (ăl′ ə mō′nē) ◊ *noun, plural* **alimonies**

alit *verb* A past tense and a past participle of **alight²**.
a·lit (ə lĭt′) ◊ *verb*

alive *adjective* **1.** Having life; living: *My grandfather is dead, but my grandmother is still alive.* **2.** In existence; active: *The baseball team kept its pennant hopes alive by winning last night.* **3.** Swarming: *The pond was alive with fish.*
a·live (ə līv′) ◊ *adjective*

all *adjective* **1.** The total number of; every one of: *All five children are good students.* **2.** The whole of: *It rained all night.* **3.** Any: *The case was proven beyond all doubt.*
◊*pronoun* Each and every one: *All aboard the capsized ship were saved.*
◊*adverb* **1.** Entirely: *You're all wrong.* **2.** Apiece: *The score is tied at five all.*
all (ôl) ◊ *adjective* ◊ *pronoun* ◊ *adverb*
‖*These sound alike:* **all, awl**

all-around *adjective* **1.** Able to do many things well: *You're an all-around athlete.* **2.** Covering a wide range; broad.
all-a·round (ôl′ ə round′) ◊ *adjective*

allege *verb* To declare to be true without offering proof.
al·lege (ə lĕj′) ◊ *verb* **alleged, alleging**

allegiance *noun* Faithful devotion to one's country, a person, or a cause; loyalty.
al·le·giance (ə lē′jəns) ◊ *noun, plural* **allegiances**

allergic *adjective* **1.** Having an allergy or allergies: *I'm sneezing because I'm allergic to dust.* **2.** Resulting from an allergy.
al·ler·gic (ə lûr′ jĭk) ◊ *adjective*

allergy *noun* A disorder in which a person has an abnormal, often unpleasant physical reaction to a food, an animal's fur, or some other substance. A person with an allergy may develop a rash or experience sneezing or difficulty in breathing.
al·ler·gy (ăl′ ər jē) ◊ *noun, plural* **allergies**

alley *noun* **1.** A narrow street or passageway between or behind buildings. **2.** A long, narrow wooden lane down which bowling balls are rolled.
al·ley (ăl′ē) ◊ *noun, plural* **alleys**

alliance *noun* An agreement between nations, organizations, or individuals to act together for a common purpose.
al·li·ance (ə lī′ əns) ◊ *noun, plural* **alliances**

allied *adjective* Joined in an alliance.
al·lied (ə līd′ *or* ăl′īd′) ◊ *adjective*

alligator *noun* A large reptile with sharp teeth and long, powerful jaws. Alligators look like crocodiles but have a shorter, broader snout.
al·li·ga·tor (ăl′ ĭ gā′tər) ◊ *noun, plural* **alligators**

▲ **alligator**

allot *verb* **1.** To give out in shares; distribute: *The prize money was allotted equally to the three winners.* **2.** To set aside for a particular purpose; assign: *Be sure to allot enough time for study.*
al·lot (ə lŏt′) ◊ *verb* **allotted, allotting**

allow *verb* **1.** To let do or happen; permit: *No ball playing allowed! Please allow me to finish.* —See Synonyms at **let. 2.** To permit to have; let have: *Allow us five minutes to explain our project.* **3.** To permit the presence of; let in: *No dogs are allowed in the store.* **4.** To provide; allot: *The speaker allowed time for discussion.* **5.** To take into account: *One must allow for unexpected delays.*
al·low (ə lou′) ◊ *verb* **allowed, allowing**

allowance *noun* **1.** An amount of something given at regular times or for a specific purpose: *I get an allowance of a dollar a week, and I'm saving the money to buy a new pair of roller skates.* **2.** An amount taken off a price for a special reason; discount.
al·low·ance (ə lou′ əns) ◊ *noun, plural* **allowances**

alloy *noun* A metal made by melting and mixing together another metal and one or more other elements. Brass is an alloy of copper and zinc.
al·loy (ăl′oi) ◊ *noun, plural* **alloys**

all right *adjective & adverb* **1.** Satisfactory but not excellent; good enough: *These peaches are all right, but they could be fresher.* **2.** Without errors; correct: *I checked your figures and they're perfectly all right.* **3.** Not hurt or sick; safe: *We came out of the crash all right.* **4.** Very well; yes: *All right, I'll go.* **5.** Without a doubt: *That's it all right!*

all-round *adjective* All-around.
all-round (ôl′**round**′) ◊ *adjective*

allude *verb* To hint at someone or something unnamed; refer indirectly: *Were you alluding to me when you said that someone had lied?*
al·lude (ə **lo͞od**′) ◊ *verb* **alluded, alluding**

allure *noun* Strong attraction; fascination: *Do you feel the allure of the sea?*
al·lure (ə **lo͝or**′) ◊ *noun*

ally *verb* To join or unite so as to work or fight for the same goal: *The United States allied itself with Great Britain and France during World War II.*
◊ *noun* A person or country that has joined with another for a special purpose.
al·ly ◊ *verb* (ə **lī**′) **allied, allying** ◊ *noun* (**ăl**′ī′ *or* ə **lī**′), *plural* **allies**

almanac *noun* A book published once a year containing calendars, statistics, and information on many different subjects.
al·ma·nac (**ôl**′mə năk′) ◊ *noun, plural* **almanacs**

almighty *adjective* Having complete power over everything.
◊ *noun* **Almighty** God.
al·might·y (ôl **mī**′tē) ◊ *adjective* ◊ *noun*

almond *noun* **1.** An oval, good-tasting nut with a soft, light brown shell. **2.** A tree on which almonds grow.
al·mond (**ä**′mənd *or* **äl**′mənd) ◊ *noun, plural* **almonds**

ă	pat	ĭ	pit	oi	**oil**	th	ba**th**
ā	pay	ī	ride	o͝o	book	*th*	ba**th**e
â	care	î	fierce	o͞o	boot	ə	ago, item
ä	father	ŏ	pot	ou	**out**		pencil
ĕ	pet	ō	go	ŭ	cut		atom
ē	be	ô	paw, for	û	fur		circus

▲ **almond**
The branch of an almond tree

almost *adverb* Just short of; nearly: *The muffins are almost done.*
al·most (**ôl**′mōst′) ◊ *adverb*

alms *noun* Money or goods given to the poor as charity.
alms (ämz) ◊ *noun, plural* **alms**

aloft *adverb* **1.** High above the ground: *The first fliers went aloft in balloons.* **2.** High on the mast or rigging of a ship: *The sailor climbed aloft to look for land.*
a·loft (ə **lôft**′) ◊ *adverb*

aloha *interjection* An expression used in Hawaii as a greeting or farewell. It is the Hawaiian word for "love."
a·lo·ha (ə **lō**′ə *or* ə **lō**′hä′) ◊ *interjection*

alone *adjective* Without anyone or anything else: *The person next door is alone all day.*
◊ *adverb* Without help.
◊ *idiom* **leave** *or* **let alone** To keep from bothering or interrupting: *Leave the dog alone until it finishes eating.*
a·lone (ə **lōn**′) ◊ *adjective* ◊ *adverb*

SYNONYMS

alone, lonely, solitary

I am *alone* in my room reading a book. I'm a bit *lonely* right now because my friends are on vacation. Explorers sometimes lead a *solitary* life.

along *preposition* **1.** Following the length of: *The parade moved along the main street.* **2.** At a place on: *We stopped along the way for a rest.*

◊ *adverb* **1.** Farther on; forward: *It's time to move along.* **2.** As a companion: *Bring your friend along.* **3.** In association; together: *Yogurt along with fruit makes a good dessert.*
a·long (ə **lông'**) ◊ *preposition* ◊ *adverb*

alongside *preposition & adverb* By the side of; side by side with: *The boat pulled up alongside the dock. The police car pulled up alongside.*
a·long·side (ə **lông'**sīd') ◊ *preposition & adverb*

aloof *adjective* Cool and distant in manner; not friendly.
a·loof (ə **lo͞of'**) ◊ *adjective*

aloud *adverb* Not in a whisper or to oneself; out loud: *I read the story aloud to the class.*
a·loud (ə **loud'**) ◊ *adverb*

alpaca *noun* A South American animal related to the llama. Its long, silky fur is shorn and woven into a warm cloth.
al·pac·a (ăl **păk'**ə) ◊ *noun, plural* **alpacas**

▲ **alpaca**

alphabet *noun* The letters used to represent the different sounds of a language, arranged in a set order.
al·pha·bet (**ăl'**fə bĕt') ◊ *noun, plural* **alphabets**

***HISTORY* • alphabet**

Alphabet comes from the names for the first two letters in the ancient Greek alphabet: *alpha* and *beta*.

alphabetical *adjective* Arranged in the order of the letters of the alphabet.
al·pha·bet·i·cal (ăl'fə **bĕt'**ĭ kəl) ◊ *adjective*

alphabetize *verb* To arrange in alphabetical order.
al·pha·bet·ize (**ăl'**fə bĭ tīz') ◊ *verb* **alphabetized, alphabetizing**

already *adverb* By this time: *I ran to the station, but the bus had already left.*
al·read·y (ôl **rĕd'**ē) ◊ *adverb*

also *adverb* In addition; besides: *My watch tells time and also gives the date.*
al·so (**ôl'**sō) ◊ *adverb*

Alta. The abbreviation for *Alberta.*

altar *noun* A table or a raised place used in religious ceremonies.
al·tar (**ôl'**tər) ◊ *noun, plural* **altars**
‖*These sound alike:* **altar, alter**

alter *verb* To change in some way; make or become different: *The tailor altered the jacket to fit me.*
al·ter (**ôl'**tər) ◊ *verb* **altered, altering**
‖*These sound alike:* **alter, altar**

alteration *noun* **1.** The act or process of changing or altering. **2.** A change.
al·ter·a·tion (ôl'tə **rā'**shən) ◊ *noun, plural* **alterations**

alternate *verb* **1.** To appear or happen by turns, first one and then the other: *Blue alternates with red in this striped pattern.* **2.** To take turns in doing something: *My friend and I alternate mowing the grass.* **3.** To pass back and forth: *The clown's face alternated between joy and sorrow.*
◊ *adjective* **1.** Appearing or happening in turns: *We had alternate periods of rain and sunshine all day long.* **2.** Every other; every second: *Our team plays on alternate Saturdays, or once every two weeks.* **3.** In place of another: *We should make an alternate plan, in case the first plan doesn't work.*
◊ *noun* A person or thing acting or ready to act in place of another; substitute: *If our class representative cannot attend a student council meeting, the alternate goes.*
al·ter·nate ◊ *verb* (**ôl'**tər nāt') **alternated, alternating** ◊ *adjective* (**ôl'**tər nĭt) ◊ *noun* (**ôl'**tər nĭt), *plural* **alternates**

alternating current *noun* An electric current that flows first in one direction, then in the other direction, at regular intervals.

alternative *noun* **1.** One of two or more possibilities that can be chosen: *If you don't like the school lunch, you have the alternative of bringing your own.* **2.** A choice between two or more possibilities: *The alternative is between studying late for the test or getting a full night's sleep.* —See Synonyms at **choice.**
al·ter·na·tive (ôl **tûr′** nə tĭv) ◊ *noun, plural* **alternatives**

although *conjunction* Even though.
al·though (ôl ***thō′***) ◊ *conjunction*

altitude *noun* A height measured from sea level or from the earth's surface: *The airplane flew at an altitude of 30,000 feet.*
al·ti·tude (**ăl′** tĭ to͞od′ *or* **ăl′** tĭ tyo͞od′) ◊ *noun, plural* **altitudes**

alto *noun* **1.** A low singing voice of a woman or boy, or a high singing voice of a man. **2.** A person having such a voice.
al·to (**ăl′** tō) ◊ *noun, plural* **altos**

altogether *adverb* **1.** Completely: *Soon the noise faded away altogether.* **2.** With all included or counted: *Altogether there are 36 teachers in the school.* **3.** Considering everything; on the whole: *Altogether you deserved the scolding you got.*
al·to·geth·er (ôl′tə **gĕ*th*′** ər) ◊ *adverb*

aluminum *noun* A lightweight, silver-white metal that is one of the elements. It is used to make pots and pans, tools, airplanes, parts of buildings, and many other things.
a·lu·mi·num (ə **lo͞o′** mə nəm) ◊ *noun*

always *adverb* **1.** At all times; every single time: *I always leave at six o'clock.* **2.** For as long as one can imagine; forever: *They will always be friends.*
al·ways (**ôl′** wāz *or* **ôl′** wĭz) ◊ *adverb*

am *verb* First person singular present tense of **be.**
am (ăm *or* əm) ◊ *verb*

a.m. *or* **A.M.** Abbreviations for the Latin words *ante meridiem,* which mean "before noon." *A.M.* is used for the time between midnight and noon: *Breakfast is at 7:30 a.m.*

ă	pat	ĭ	pit	oi	**oil**	th	ba**th**
ā	pay	ī	ride	o͝o	**book**	*th*	ba**the**
â	care	î	fierce	o͞o	**boot**	ə	ago, item
ä	father	ŏ	pot	ou	**out**		pencil
ĕ	pet	ō	go	ŭ	cut		atom
ē	be	ô	paw, for	û	fur		circus

amateur *noun* **1.** A person who engages in an art, science, or sport for enjoyment rather than for money: *Only amateurs can compete in the Olympics.* **2.** A person who does something without much skill.
am·a·teur (**ăm′** ə chər *or* **ăm′** ə tər) ◊ *noun, plural* **amateurs**

amaze *verb* To fill with surprise or wonder; astonish: *The idea of water carving a deep canyon out of solid rock amazes me.*
a·maze (ə **māz′**) ◊ *verb* **amazed, amazing**

amazement *noun* Great surprise; wonder.
a·maze·ment (ə **māz′** mənt) ◊ *noun*

ambassador *noun* An official of the highest rank who represents his or her government in another country.
am·bas·sa·dor (ăm **băs′** ə dər) ◊ *noun, plural* **ambassadors**

amber *noun* **1.** A clear, brownish-yellow material that is the hardened resin of ancient pine trees. Amber sometimes has fossil insects that were trapped in it and is used for making jewelry and ornaments. **2.** A brownish yellow color.
am·ber (**ăm′** bər) ◊ *noun, plural* **ambers**

ambiguity *noun* **1.** The condition of being ambiguous. **2.** Something that has two or more possible meanings.
am·bi·gu·i·ty (ăm′bĭ **gyo͞o′** ĭ tē) ◊ *noun, plural* **ambiguities**

ambiguous *adjective* Having two or more possible meanings. The sentence *Joe told Bill that he had to leave* is ambiguous, because it is not clear whether Joe or Bill has to leave.
am·big·u·ous (ăm **bĭg′** yo͞o əs) ◊ *adjective*

ambition *noun* **1.** A strong desire to get or become something: *Her ambition was to become a great scientist.* **2.** Something that is strongly desired: *I finally achieved my ambition of sailing across the ocean.*
am·bi·tion (ăm **bĭsh′** ən) ◊ *noun, plural* **ambitions**

ambitious *adjective* **1.** Eager to succeed or to gain fame or power: *The ambitious kid learned very quickly.* **2.** Needing a lot of effort to succeed: *They have an ambitious plan to turn the desert into farm land.*
am·bi·tious (ăm **bĭsh′** əs) ◊ *adjective*

amble *verb* To walk or move along at a slow pace: *The horses ambled out of the corral.*
am·ble (**ăm′** bəl) ◊ *verb* **ambled, ambling**

ambulance *noun* A large automobile especially equipped to rush sick and injured people to a hospital.
am·bu·lance (**ăm′**byə ləns) ◊ *noun, plural* **ambulances**

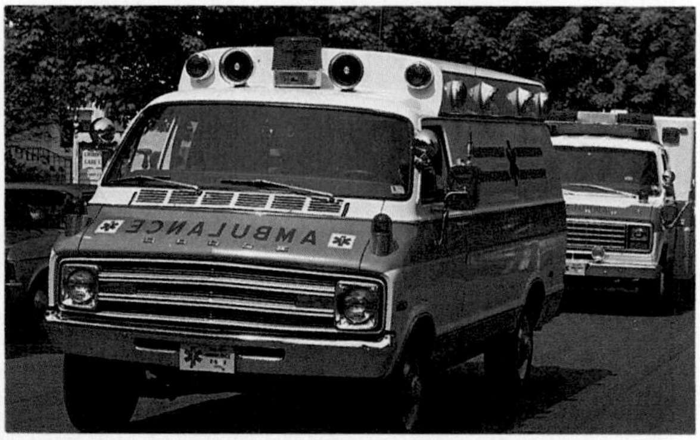

▲ **ambulance**

ambush *noun* **1.** A surprise attack made from a hiding place. **2.** A hidden place from which a surprise attack is made or planned. ◊ *verb* To attack from a concealed position.
am·bush (**ăm′**bŏŏsh′) ◊ *noun, plural* **ambushes** ◊ *verb* **ambushed, ambushing**

ameba *noun* Another spelling for **amoeba.**
a·me·ba (ə **mē′**bə) ◊ *noun, plural* **amebas**

amen *interjection* **1.** Used at the end of a prayer to mean "so be it" or "truly." **2.** Used to express agreement with a statement.
a·men (ä **mĕn′**) ◊ *interjection*

amend *verb* To change so as to improve or correct.
a·mend (ə **mĕnd′**) ◊ *verb* **amended, amending**

amendment *noun* A change made to improve, correct, or add something: *An amendment to the United States Constitution limits the President to two full terms in office.*
a·mend·ment (ə **mĕnd′**mənt) ◊ *noun, plural* **amendments**

amends *plural noun* Something that is paid or given to make up for a wrong or mistake: *I tried to make amends for my rudeness.*
a·mends (ə **mĕndz′**) ◊ *plural noun*

Amer. The abbreviation for *America* and *American.*

American *noun* **1.** A person who was born in, lives in, or is a citizen of the United States. **2.** A person who was born in or lives in North, Central, or South America.
◊ *adjective* **1.** Of or relating to the United States, its people, or its culture. **2.** Of or relating to North, Central, or South America or their peoples.
A·mer·i·can (ə **mĕr′**ĭ kən) ◊ *noun, plural* **Americans** ◊ *adjective*

amethyst *noun* A clear, purple or violet form of quartz used as a gem.
am·e·thyst (**ăm′**ə thĭst) ◊ *noun, plural* **amethysts**

amiable *adjective* Friendly and pleasant; good-natured.
a·mi·a·ble (**ā′**mē ə bəl) ◊ *adjective*

amid *preposition* In the middle of: *The swimmer's head appeared amid the waves.*
a·mid (ə **mĭd′**) ◊ *preposition*

amidships *adverb* In or toward the middle part of a ship.
a·mid·ships (ə **mĭd′**shĭps′) ◊ *adverb*

amidst *preposition* In the middle of: *The scarecrow stood amidst the corn.*
a·midst (ə **mĭdst′**) ◊ *preposition*

amino acid *noun* Any of a group of chemical compounds containing carbon, hydrogen, oxygen, and nitrogen. Living organisms need amino acids to make protein.
a·mi·no acid (ə **mē′**nō) ◊ *noun, plural* **amino acids**

amiss *adjective* Wrong; faulty; improper: *I can find nothing amiss.*
◊ *idiom* **take amiss** To feel offended by: *I hope you won't take my remark amiss.*
a·miss (ə **mĭs′**) ◊ *adjective*

ammonia *noun* **1.** A colorless gas with a strong, irritating smell. It is composed of nitrogen and hydrogen. **2.** A liquid with ammonia dissolved in it, used to clean things.
am·mo·nia (ə **mōn′**yə) ◊ *noun*

ammunition *noun* Bullets, bombs, or anything else that can be fired from a gun or that can explode and cause damage.
am·mu·ni·tion (ăm′yə **nĭsh′**ən) ◊ *noun*

amnesia *noun* A partial or total loss of memory, especially when caused by shock or an injury to the brain.
am·ne·sia (ăm **nē′**zhə) ◊ *noun*

amoeba *or* **ameba** *noun* A tiny water animal that has only one cell and can be seen only through a microscope. It changes shape

as it moves and surrounds its food.
a·moe·ba *or* **a·me·ba** (ə **mē′**bə) ◊ *noun, plural* **amoebas** *or* **amebas**

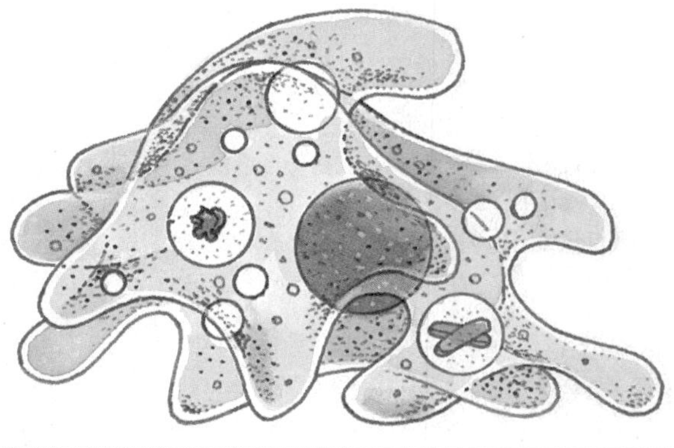

▲ **amoeba**

among *preposition* **1.** In or through the middle of: *A tall church stood out among the low houses.* **2.** In the company of; with: *I was glad to be among friends again.* **3.** With portions to each of: *The pudding was shared among them.* **4.** Through all or most of: *Measles spread among the ship's crew.*
a·mong (ə **mŭng′**) ◊ *preposition*

amount *noun* **1.** The total of two or more quantities; sum: *The amount of your bill is $8.72.* **2.** Quantity: *A very small amount of rain falls on the desert.*
◊ *verb* **1.** To add up in number or quantity: *My potato crop amounted to six bushels this year.* **2.** To be the same as; be equal: *Disobeying orders often amounts to mutiny.*
a·mount (ə **mount′**) ◊ *noun, plural* **amounts** ◊ *verb* **amounted, amounting**

ampersand *noun* The character or sign (&) that stands for *and.*
am·per·sand (**ăm′**pər sănd′) ◊ *noun, plural* **ampersands**

amphibian *noun* **1.** A cold-blooded animal that lives in water and breathes with gills during its early life. It develops lungs and breathes air as an adult. Frogs, toads, and salamanders are amphibians. **2.** A vehicle that can travel both on land and in water. **3.** An aircraft that can take off from and land on either ground or water.
am·phib·i·an (ăm **fĭb′**ē ən) ◊ *noun, plural* **amphibians**

ă	pat	ĭ	pit	oi	oil	th	bath
ā	pay	ī	ride	o͝o	book	*th*	bathe
â	care	î	fierce	o͞o	boot	ə	ago, item
ä	father	ŏ	pot	ou	out		pencil
ĕ	pet	ō	go	ŭ	cut		atom
ē	be	ô	paw, for	û	fur		circus

▲ **amphibian**
The red-legged frog is an amphibian.

amphibious *adjective* Able to live both on land and in water.
am·phib·i·ous (ăm **fĭb′**ē əs) ◊ *adjective*

amphitheater *noun* A round theater that has rows of seats rising gradually outward from a stage or arena at the center.
am·phi·the·a·ter (**ăm′**fə thē′ə tər) ◊ *noun, plural* **amphitheaters**

▲ **amphitheater**

ample *adjective* **1.** More than enough; plenty of: *Our big house has ample room for over-*

night guests. **2.** Large in size, number, extent, or capacity: *I stored my trunk in that ample closet.*
am·ple (ăm′pəl) ◊ *adjective* **ampler, amplest**

amplify *verb* **1.** To make fuller or more complete by adding material; expand: *Let me amplify my earlier remarks.* **2.** To make stronger or louder: *An electronic device amplified the speaker's voice.*
am·pli·fy (ăm′plə fī′) ◊ *verb* **amplified, amplifying**

amputate *verb* To cut off all or some of a body part, as a leg, arm, or finger.
am·pu·tate (ăm′pyə tāt′) ◊ *verb* **amputated, amputating**

amt. The abbreviation for *amount.*

amuse *verb* **1.** To give enjoyment to; entertain pleasantly: *Playing checkers amuses me.* **2.** To cause to laugh or smile: *The clown's tricks amused us all.*
a·muse (ə **myo͞oz′**) ◊ *verb* **amused, amusing**

SYNONYMS

amuse, entertain

I *amused* my friends with the trick I played on them. We *entertained* the audience with our play. **Antonym:** *bore*

amusement *noun* **1.** A feeling of being entertained: *The group sang for their own amusement.* **2.** Something that provides enjoyment or entertainment: *Reading and seeing movies are among my amusements.*
a·muse·ment (ə **myo͞oz′**mənt) ◊ *noun, plural* **amusements**

amusing *adjective* Pleasantly entertaining: *The circus clowns and animals could do some amusing tricks.* —See Synonyms at **funny.**
a·mus·ing (ə **myo͞o′**zĭng) ◊ *adjective*

an *indefinite article* The form of *a* that is used before words beginning with a vowel or with an *h* that is not pronounced: *an elephant; an hour.*
an (ăn *or* ən) ◊ *indefinite article*

anaconda *noun* A very large, nonpoisonous South American snake. The anaconda coils around and crushes animals before eating them.
an·a·con·da (ăn′ə **kŏn′**də) ◊ *noun, plural* **anacondas**

▲ **anaconda**

analysis *noun* **1.** The separation of a physical substance into its parts for study of each part. An analysis of water shows that it is made up of hydrogen and oxygen. **2.** A study of something, of its parts, or of how the parts fit together. A person can do an analysis of a book or an election.
a·nal·y·sis (ə **năl′**ĭ sĭs) ◊ *noun, plural* **analyses**

analyze *verb* **1.** To separate into parts to find out what these parts are: *They analyzed the ore and found iron in it.* **2.** To study carefully in order to determine what something is, what its parts are, or how its parts fit together: *Our class analyzed the way our government works.*
an·a·lyze (ăn′ə līz′) ◊ *verb* **analyzed, analyzing**

anatomy *noun* **1.** The arrangement and relationship of the parts of living things: *We studied the anatomy of the snake.* **2.** The scientific study of the structure of living things: *People who are studying to be doctors take courses in anatomy.*
a·nat·o·my (ə **năt′**ə mē) ◊ *noun*

ancestor *noun* A person from whom one is descended.
an·ces·tor (**ăn′**sĕs′tər) ◊ *noun, plural* **ancestors**

ancestral *adjective* Of, belonging to, or coming from an ancestor.
an·ces·tral (ăn **sĕs′**trəl) ◊ *adjective*

ancestry *noun* People who make up a line of descent; ancestors: *I am of Native American ancestry.*
an·ces·try (**ăn′**sĕs′trē) ◊ *noun*

anchor *noun* A heavy metal device that is attached to a ship by a cable. An anchor is dropped overboard and keeps the ship in place by its weight or by catching on the bottom of a body of water.
◊ *verb* **1.** To hold or be held in one place by an anchor; drop anchor: *The ship anchored in the bay.* **2.** To hold in one place as if by an anchor: *I anchored the tent with pegs.*
an·chor (ăng′kər) ◊ *noun, plural* **anchors**
◊ *verb* **anchored, anchoring**

***HISTORY* • anchor, angle, ankle**

Anchor, angle, and **ankle** all go back to a prehistoric word that meant "something bent."

anchovy *noun* A small fish that is related to the herring. One kind that is found in the Mediterranean Ocean is eaten for its strong, sharp flavor.
an·cho·vy (ăn′chō vē) ◊ *noun, plural* **anchovies**

ancient *adjective* **1.** Having existed for a long time: *They discovered an ancient treasure.* **2.** Having to do with times long past: *The ancient Greeks and Romans gave us many valuable ideas.* —See Synonyms at **old.**
an·cient (ān′shənt) ◊ *adjective*

and *conjunction* **1.** Together with or along with; as well as: *My cousin and I went to the store and to the library.* **2.** Added to; plus: *Two and two makes four.*
and (ănd *or* ənd) ◊ *conjunction*

andiron *noun* One of a pair of metal supports for holding up wood in a fireplace.
and·i·ron (ănd′ī′ərn) ◊ *noun, plural* **andirons**

anecdote *noun* A short story about something interesting or humorous that has happened: *I told the class an anecdote about our fishing trip.*
an·ec·dote (ăn′ĭk dōt′) ◊ *noun, plural* **anecdotes**

ă	pat	ĭ	pit	oi	**oil**	th	ba**th**
ā	pay	ī	ride	ŏŏ	**book**	*th*	ba**the**
â	care	î	fierce	ōō	**boot**	ə	ago, item
ä	father	ŏ	pot	ou	**out**		pencil
ĕ	pet	ō	go	ŭ	cut		atom
ē	be	ô	paw, for	û	fur		circus

anemia *noun* An unhealthy physical condition that occurs when there is a lack of blood, of red blood cells, or of hemoglobin.
a·ne·mi·a (ə nē′mē ə) ◊ *noun, plural* **anemias**

anemometer *noun* An instrument that measures how strongly the wind is blowing.
an·e·mom·e·ter (ăn′ə mŏm′ĭ tər) ◊ *noun, plural* **anemometers**

anesthetic *noun* A drug that causes a loss of feeling or of consciousness. A dentist gives a patient an anesthetic before drilling into a tooth so that there will be no pain.
an·es·thet·ic (ăn′ĭs thĕt′ĭk) ◊ *noun, plural* **anesthetics**

anew *adverb* Once more; again.
a·new (ə nōō′ *or* ə nyōō′) ◊ *adverb*

angel *noun* **1.** A spiritual being that serves God and acts as God's messenger. **2.** A person who is like an angel, for example, by being kind or innocent.
an·gel (ān′jəl) ◊ *noun, plural* **angels**

anger *noun* A strong feeling of not being pleased with someone or something.
◊ *verb* To make or become angry.
an·ger (ăng′gər) ◊ *noun* ◊ *verb* **angered, angering**

angle *noun* **1.** The figure made by two lines that begin at the same point. **2.** A sharp corner. **3.** A way of looking at something; point of view: *From that angle, this looks like a good idea.*
◊ *verb* To turn so as to make an angle: *We angled to the right.*
an·gle (ăng′gəl)
◊ *noun, plural* **angles**
◊ *verb* **angled, angling**

▲ **angle**
A right angle

angry *adjective* **1.** Feeling, showing, or resulting from anger: *You say you aren't angry, but your face looks angry.* **2.** Having a threatening look: *Those angry, dark storm clouds are coming closer.*
an·gry (ăng′grē) ◊ *adjective* **angrier, angriest**

anguish *noun* Strong pain or suffering of body or mind: *They were in great anguish un-*

til their lost puppy was found.
an·guish (**ăng′** gwish) ◊ *noun*

angular *adjective* Having one or more angles or sharp corners.
an·gu·lar (**ăng′** gyə lər) ◊ *adjective*

animal *noun* **1.** A living being that is not a plant. Unlike plants, most animals move from place to place, have sense organs, and eat food rather than make it. Human beings, horses, fish, and ants are all animals. **2.** An animal other than a human being, and especially a mammal.
an·i·mal (**ăn′** ə məl) ◊ *noun, plural* **animals**

animated *adjective* **1.** Full of life or spirit; lively: *I talked in an animated way about my trip to the circus.* **2.** Made so as to seem alive: *We watched an animated cartoon.*
an·i·mat·ed (**ăn′** ə mā′tĭd) ◊ *adjective*

animosity *noun* A strong feeling of dislike that may show in action: *The two enemies felt animosity toward each other.*
an·i·mos·i·ty (ăn′ə **mŏs′** ĭ tē) ◊ *noun*

ankle *noun* **1.** The joint between the foot and leg. **2.** The lower leg from the calf down to and including the ankle joint.
an·kle (**ang′** kəl) ◊ *noun, plural* **ankles**

anklet *noun* A short sock reaching to just above the ankle.
an·klet (**ăng′** klĭt) ◊ *noun, plural* **anklets**

annex *verb* To add to something else, especially something else that is larger or more important: *The city annexed two suburbs.*
◊ *noun* An extra building that is added to or stands near another, bigger building and is used for some related purpose.
an·nex ◊ *verb* (ə **nĕks′**) **annexed, annexing**
◊ *noun* (**ăn′** ĕks′), *plural* **annexes**

annexation *noun* The act of annexing: *The annexation of the Republic of Texas by the United States took place in 1845.*
an·nex·a·tion (ăn′ĭk **sā′** shən) ◊ *noun, plural* **annexations**

annihilate *verb* To destroy completely: *The explosion annihilated the rock.*
an·ni·hi·late (ə **nī′** ə lāt′) ◊ *verb* **annihilated, annihilating**

anniversary *noun* The return every year of the date of a special event: *My parents' wedding anniversary is in April.*
an·ni·ver·sa·ry (ăn′ə **vûr′** sə rē) ◊ *noun, plural* **anniversaries**

***HISTORY* • anniversary, annual**

Anniversary and **annual** are related to the Latin word for "year." **Anniversary** literally means "returning yearly."

announce *verb* **1.** To make known to people officially: *The principal announced a holiday.* **2.** To make known the presence, readiness, or arrival of: *Dad announced supper.* **3.** To serve as an announcer of: *She announced the game on the radio.*
an·nounce (ə **nouns′**) ◊ *verb* **announced, announcing**

announcement *noun* **1.** The act of officially making known to people: *We listened to the radio announcement.* **2.** A public statement that makes something known in writing or in speech: *We were eager to hear the announcement of the winner of the race.*
an·nounce·ment (ə **nouns′** mənt) ◊ *noun, plural* **announcements**

announcer *noun* A person who speaks to the public on radio, television, or a public-address system.
an·nounc·er (ə **noun′** sər) ◊ *noun, plural* **announcers**

annoy *verb* To cause to lose patience or become angry, especially by continuing to bother: *Your loud talking annoyed me.*
an·noy (ə **noi′**) ◊ *verb* **annoyed, annoying**

SYNONYMS

annoy, bother, irritate

Your constant fiddling with that paper clip *annoys* me. It *bothers* me to hear you say mean things about them. I am *irritated* by your lateness.

annoyance *noun* **1.** The act of annoying: *I watched your constant annoyance of our neighbor.* **2.** The feeling of being annoyed: *I felt annoyance at being teased.* **3.** Something that annoys; nuisance: *Mosquitoes are an annoyance.*
an·noy·ance (ə **noi′** əns) ◊ *noun, plural* **annoyances**

annual *adjective* **1.** Happening or appearing every year: *The annual town picnic is next week.* **2.** For a period of a year: *Our annual*

rainfall was higher than usual. **3.** Living for only one growing season: *There are annual plants and perennial plants.*
◊ *noun* A plant that grows from seed, blossoms, produces seed, and dies in a single growing season. Petunias, tomatoes, and wheat are annuals.
an·nu·al (**ăn′** yo͞o əl) ◊ *adjective* ◊ *noun, plural* **annuals**

anoint *verb* To put oil on as part of a religious ceremony such as baptism.
a·noint (ə **noint′**) ◊ *verb* **anointed, anointing**

anonymous *adjective* **1.** Having a name that is not known or not given: *An anonymous author wrote this book.* **2.** By or from someone whose name is not known or not given: *We received an anonymous letter.*
a·non·y·mous (ə **nŏn′** ə məs) ◊ *adjective*

another *adjective* **1.** Being a second or an additional one: *I'd love another helping.* **2.** Some other and later: *Let's go on another day.* **3.** Different: *I have another idea.*
◊ *pronoun* **1.** An additional person or thing: *First one left and then another and another.* **2.** Someone or something else: *One person says this while another says that.*
an·oth·er (ə **nŭ*th*′** ər) ◊ *adjective* ◊ *pronoun*

ans. The abbreviation for *answer.*

answer *noun* **1.** Something said or written in return to a question, statement, request, or letter; reply. **2.** A reply or solution to something such as a problem: *What is your answer to the riddle?* **3.** Something, such as an action, made in return to something else: *I rang the doorbell, but there was no answer.*
◊ *verb* **1.** To say, write, or do something in reply or in reply to. **2.** To be responsible: *I have to answer for my actions.* **3.** To match or correspond: *This person answers to the description that you gave me.*
an·swer (**ăn′** sər) ◊ *noun, plural* **answers**
◊ *verb* **answered, answering**

ant *noun* An insect that lives in social groups called colonies. Ants live in various places, including tunnels in the ground or holes in dead wood.
ant (ănt) ◊ *noun, plural* **ants**

ă	pat	ĭ	pit	oi	**oi**l	th	ba**th**
ā	pay	ī	ride	o͝o	b**oo**k	*th*	ba**th**e
â	care	î	fierce	o͞o	b**oo**t	ə	ago, item
ä	father	ŏ	**po**t	ou	**ou**t		pencil
ĕ	pet	ō	**go**	ŭ	cut		atom
ē	be	ô	paw, for	û	fur		circus

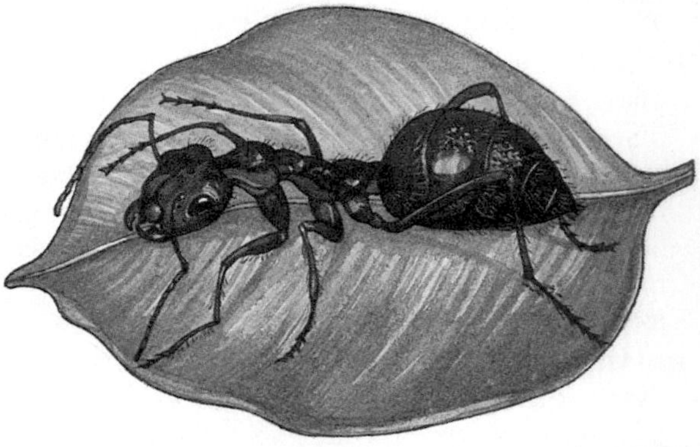

▲ **ant**
A honey ant magnified 6 times

antagonism *noun* A state or feeling of being against somebody or something: *There was antagonism between us.*
an·tag·o·nism (ăn **tăg′** ə nĭz′əm) ◊ *noun*

antagonist *noun* Someone who is against and acts against somebody or something.
an·tag·o·nist (ăn **tăg′** ə nĭst) ◊ *noun, plural* **antagonists**

Antarctic *adjective* Of or relating to the region surrounding the South Pole.
Ant·arc·tic (ănt **ärk′** tĭk *or* ănt **är′** tĭk) ◊ *adjective*

anteater *noun* A Central or South American animal that feeds on ants or other insects. An anteater uses its long snout and long, sticky tongue to catch the ants.
ant·eat·er (**ănt′** ē′tər) ◊ *noun, plural* **anteaters**

▲ **anteater**

antelope *noun* One of several African and Asian animals that have horns without branches. Antelopes are related to cattle but are slenderer and faster.
an·te·lope (an′ təl ōp′) ◊ *noun, plural* **antelope** *or* **antelopes**

antenna *noun* **1.** One of a pair of thin, movable organs on the head of insects or animals. An antenna can be used in touching and smelling. **2.** A device used to send or receive such things as radio waves.
an·ten·na (ăn **tĕn′** ə) ◊ *noun, plural* **antennas**

anthem *noun* **1.** A song that expresses such things as patriotism or praise: *The national anthem of America is "The Star-Spangled Banner."* **2.** A song with words usually from the Bible and usually sung by a choir.
an·them (**ăn′** thəm) ◊ *noun, plural* **anthems**

anther *noun* The part of a flower that produces and contains pollen. The anther is at the tip of the stamen.
an·ther (**ăn′** thər) ◊ *noun, plural* **anthers**

anthill *noun* A mound of earth made by ants in digging a nest.
ant·hill (**ănt′** hĭl′) ◊ *noun, plural* **anthills**

▲ **anthill**

anthology *noun* A collection of writings, such as stories, by various authors: *We are reading an anthology of poetry.*
an·thol·o·gy (ăn **thŏl′** ə jē) ◊ *noun, plural* **anthologies**

anthracite *noun* A very hard form of coal that gives off little smoke when it burns.
an·thra·cite (**ăn′** thrə sīt′) ◊ *noun*

anthropology *noun* The scientific study of human beings.
an·thro·pol·o·gy (ăn′thrə **pŏl′** ə jē) ◊ *noun*

anti– The prefix *anti–* means "opposing" or "against." *Antifreeze* is a substance that works against freezing.

> ***VOCABULARY BUILDER* • anti–**
>
> Many words that are formed with **anti–** are not entries in this dictionary. But you can figure out what these words mean by looking up the meanings of the root words and the prefix. For example:
> **antipollution** = acting or working against pollution
> **antiwar** = opposing war

antibiotic *noun* A substance, such as penicillin, that kills or slows the growth of such things as bacteria. Antibiotics help to treat and prevent disease.
an·ti·bi·ot·ic (ăn′tē bī **ŏt′** ĭk) ◊ *noun, plural* **antibiotics**

antibody *noun* A substance made in the body that can act against a foreign substance, such as a virus.
an·ti·bod·y (**ăn′** tĭ bŏd′ē) ◊ *noun, plural* **antibodies**

antic *noun* An action that is odd or funny and makes no sense; prank.
an·tic (**ăn′** tĭk) ◊ *noun, plural* **antics**

anticipate *verb* **1.** To think of ahead of time: *I anticipated that I couldn't go.* **2.** To deal with ahead of time: *I anticipated trouble by what I did.* **3.** To look forward to; expect.
an·tic·i·pate (ăn **tĭs′** ə pāt′) ◊ *verb* **anticipated, anticipating**

anticipation *noun* **1.** The act of thinking of something in advance. **2.** The act of looking forward to something.
an·tic·i·pa·tion (ăn tĭs′ə **pā′** shən) ◊ *noun*

antidote *noun* A substance that works against a poison: *If we swallow poison we must call a doctor to find out the antidote.*
an·ti·dote (**ăn′** tĭ dōt′) ◊ *noun, plural* **antidotes**

antifreeze *noun* A substance, such as alcohol, that is added to a liquid to lower the point at which it freezes.
an·ti·freeze (**ăn′** tĭ frēz′) ◊ *noun*

antique *noun* Something, such as a piece of furniture, that was made in the past.
◊ *adjective* Made in the past: *In the museum*

we saw antique pewter plates. —See Synonyms at **old.**
an·tique (ăn **tēk′**) ◊ *noun, plural* **antiques** ◊ *adjective*

▲ **antique**
An antique shop displaying its wares

antiquity *noun* Times that are long past.
an·tiq·ui·ty (ăn **tĭk′**wĭ tē) ◊ *noun*

antiseptic *noun* A substance, such as iodine, that kills some germs or stops their growth.
an·ti·sep·tic (ăn′tĭ **sĕp′**tĭk) ◊ *noun, plural* **antiseptics**

antitoxin *noun* An antibody made in the body to act against a poison made by a living organism, such as a bacteria or a bee.
an·ti·tox·in (ăn′tē **tŏk′**sĭn) ◊ *noun, plural* **antitoxins**

antler *noun* A bony growth on the head of such animals as deer or antelopes. Antlers grow in pairs and are often branched.
ant·ler (**ănt′**lər) ◊ *noun, plural* **antlers**

antonym *noun* A word that is opposite or nearly opposite in meaning to another word. *Fast* is the antonym of *slow.*
an·to·nym (**ăn′**tə nĭm′) ◊ *noun, plural* **antonyms**

anvil *noun* A heavy block, usually of iron and steel. Metals can be hammered and shaped on an anvil.
an·vil (**ăn′**vĭl) ◊ *noun, plural* **anvils**

ă	pat	ĭ	pit	oi	**oi**l	th	ba**th**
ā	pay	ī	ride	ŏŏ	book	*th*	ba**th**e
â	care	î	fierce	ōō	boot	ə	ago, item
ä	father	ŏ	pot	ou	**ou**t		pencil
ĕ	pet	ō	go	ŭ	cut		atom
ē	be	ô	paw, for	û	fur		circus

▲ **anvil**

anxiety *noun* **1.** A feeling of being afraid or nervous about something uncertain or in the future: *He felt anxiety about being on time.* **2.** Strong interest or desire mixed with nervousness: *Her anxiety to win was strong.*
anx·i·e·ty (ăng **zī′**ĭ tē) ◊ *noun, plural* **anxieties**

anxious *adjective* **1.** Feeling nervous or afraid about something uncertain: *I am anxious about whether I will get there.* **2.** Having a strong desire; eager: *I was anxious to get home before it rained.*
anx·ious (**ăngk′**shəs) ◊ *adjective*

any *adjective* **1.** One or some, no matter which, out of three or more: *Take any books you want.* **2.** Every: *Any kid in my club can come to the party.* **3.** One or some of which the number or amount is not known: *Do we have any milk?* **4.** As much as is wanted or needed: *Have any amount you want.*
◊ *pronoun* Any person or persons; any thing or things: *Did any of you go?*
◊ *adverb* At all: *I don't feel any better.*
an·y (**ĕn′**ē) ◊ *adjective* ◊ *pronoun* ◊ *adverb*

anybody *pronoun* Any person at all; anyone: *Anybody would have done that.*
an·y·bod·y (**ĕn′**ē bŏd′ē) ◊ *pronoun*

anyhow *adverb* In any case; just the same: *I know the answer, but I'm asking anyhow.*
an·y·how (**ĕn′**ē hou′) ◊ *adverb*

anyone *pronoun* Any person; anybody: *I don't want to see anyone right now.*
an·y·one (**ĕn′**ē wŭn′) ◊ *pronoun*

anyplace *adverb* Anywhere: *Move the chair anyplace you like.*
an·y·place (**ĕn′**ē plās′) ◊ *adverb*

anything *pronoun* Any thing whatever: *Is there anything left in the box?*
◊ *adverb* At all: *I'm not anything like you.*
an·y·thing (ĕn′ē thĭng′) ◊ *pronoun* ◊ *adverb*

anytime *adverb* At any time: *Come over anytime you feel like it.*
an·y·time (ĕn′ē tīm′) ◊ *adverb*

anyway *adverb* In any case; just the same: *The ball curved, but I caught it anyway.*
an·y·way (ĕn′ē wā′) ◊ *adverb*

anywhere *adverb* To, in, or at any place: *They travel anywhere they want to.*
an·y·where (ĕn′ē hwâr′) ◊ *adverb*

aorta *noun* The main artery that carries blood from the left side of the heart to all the organs except the lungs.
a·or·ta (ā ôr′tə) ◊ *noun, plural* **aortas**

apart *adverb* **1.** Away from each other in time or position: *We saw two trees about ten feet apart.* **2.** In or into separate pieces; to pieces: *I took the camera apart.* **3.** One from another: *It was almost impossible for us to tell the twins apart.*
a·part (ə pärt′) ◊ *adverb*

apartment *noun* One or more rooms usually used as a place to live.
a·part·ment (ə pärt′mənt) ◊ *noun, plural* **apartments**

apathy *noun* Lack of feeling or interest; indifference: *My parents do not feel apathy about the election.*
ap·a·thy (ăp′ə thē) ◊ *noun*

ape *noun* One of a class of related mammals, such as the gibbon, orangutan, gorilla, or chimpanzee. Most apes can walk upright for a short way.
◊ *verb* To follow as a pattern; mimic: *Some people try to ape rock stars.*
ape (āp) ◊ *noun, plural* **apes** ◊ *verb* **aped, aping**

aperture *noun* **1.** A hole or opening: *We saw light through a small aperture in the wall.* **2.** The opening in the lens of a camera through which light can pass.
ap·er·ture (ăp′ər chər) ◊ *noun, plural* **apertures**

aphid *noun* A tiny insect with a soft body that is shaped like a pear. Aphids feed on the juices of plants and are harmful to plants.
a·phid (ā′fĭd *or* ăf′ĭd) ◊ *noun, plural* **aphids**

▲ aphid

apiece *adverb* To or for each one; each: *Give them an apple apiece.*
a·piece (ə pēs′) ◊ *adverb*

apologetic *adjective* Expressing, making, or feeling like making an apology: *I was apologetic for not keeping my promise.*
a·pol·o·get·ic (ə pŏl′ə jĕt′ĭk) ◊ *adjective*

apologize *verb* To make an apology; say one is sorry.
a·pol·o·gize (ə pŏl′ə jīz′) ◊ *verb* **apologized, apologizing**

apology *noun* A statement that one is sorry for something, such as a mistake or a wrong action: *I owe you an apology.*
a·pol·o·gy (ə pŏl′ə jē) ◊ *noun, plural* **apologies**

Apostle *noun* One of the early missionaries of Christ including the twelve disciples and Saint Paul.
A·pos·tle (ə pŏs′əl) ◊ *noun, plural* **Apostles**

apostrophe *noun* A punctuation mark (') that is used: **1.** To show that one or more letters or numbers have been left out, as in the contraction *aren't* for *are not* or *'86* for *1986.* **2.** With the letter *s* to form a possessive noun such as *Lee's* in the phrase *Lee's book.* **3.** To indicate the plural of letters or numbers, as in four *x's* or five *7's.*
a·pos·tro·phe (ə pŏs′trə fē′) ◊ *noun, plural* **apostrophes**

apothecary *noun* A druggist.
a·poth·e·car·y (ə pŏth′ĭ kĕr′ē) ◊ *noun, plural* **apothecaries**

appall *verb* To cause to feel fear, horror, amazement, or confusion.
ap·pall (ə pôl′) ◊ *verb* **appalled, appalling**

apparatus *noun* All the things used for a particular job or purpose. Equipment in a laboratory is an example of apparatus.
ap·pa·ra·tus (ăp′ə **răt′**əs *or* ăp′ə **rā′**təs) ◊ *noun, plural* **apparatus** *or* **apparatuses**

apparel *noun* The things that are worn by a person; clothing.
ap·par·el (ə **păr′**əl) ◊ *noun*

apparent *adjective* **1.** Easily seen; visible: *The tear in my shirt was apparent.* **2.** Easily understood; obvious: *It was apparent that we needed to do more work.* **3.** Seeming to be true or real but not necessarily so: *Their apparent excitement was actually real.*
ap·par·ent (ə **pâr′**ənt) ◊ *adjective*

appeal *noun* **1.** A request for something that is really needed: *During the blizzard the governor made an appeal for everyone to stay home.* **2.** The power to attract or interest: *That story has a strong appeal for me.* **3.** The bringing of a legal case from a lower court to a higher court to be heard again.
◊ *verb* **1.** To make a request for something really needed: *I appeal to you to help me.* **2.** To be attractive or interesting: *That game appeals to us.* **3.** To bring or ask to bring a legal case from a lower court to a higher court to be heard again.
ap·peal (ə **pēl′**) ◊ *noun, plural* **appeals** ◊ *verb* **appealed, appealing**

appear *verb* **1.** To come into view: *A ship appeared on the horizon.* **2.** To come before the public: *I have appeared in two plays.* **3.** To seem or look: *The coat appears to be navy blue.* **4.** To present oneself formally before a court of law.
ap·pear (ə **pîr′**) ◊ *verb* **appeared, appearing**

appearance *noun* **1.** The act or an example of appearing: *The sudden appearance of the clown made the children laugh.* **2.** The way something or someone looks: *Your smile gave you a happy appearance.*
ap·pear·ance (ə **pîr′**əns) ◊ *noun, plural* **appearances**

ă	pat	ĭ	pit	oi	**oil**	th	ba**th**
ā	pay	ī	ride	o͝o	book	*th*	ba*th*e
â	care	î	fierce	o͞o	boot	ə	ago, item
ä	father	ŏ	pot	ou	**out**		pencil
ĕ	pet	ō	go	ŭ	cut		atom
ē	be	ô	paw, for	û	fur		circus

appease *verb* **1.** To make calm, quiet, or peaceful: *I appeased the angry child with kind words.* **2.** To satisfy: *A glass of water appeased my thirst.*
ap·pease (ə **pēz′**) ◊ *verb* **appeased, appeasing**

appendices *noun* A plural of **appendix.**
ap·pen·di·ces (ə **pĕn′**dĭ sēz′) ◊ *noun*

appendicitis *noun* Inflammation of the appendix of the large intestine.
ap·pen·di·ci·tis (ə pĕn′dĭ **sī′**tĭs) ◊ *noun*

appendix *noun* **1.** A section of a book containing additional information such as tables and charts. **2.** A slender, closed tube that is attached to the large intestine.
ap·pen·dix (ə **pĕn′**dĭks) ◊ *noun, plural* **appendixes** *or* **appendices**

appetite *noun* **1.** The desire for food. **2.** A desire or liking: *I have an appetite for work.*
ap·pe·tite (**ăp′**ĭ tīt′) ◊ *noun, plural* **appetites**

appetizer *noun* A food or drink taken before a meal to increase the appetite.
ap·pe·tiz·er (**ăp′**ĭ tī′zər) ◊ *noun, plural* **appetizers**

appetizing *adjective* Appealing to the appetite: *A peach makes an appetizing snack.*
ap·pe·tiz·ing (**ăp′**ĭ tī′zĭng) ◊ *adjective*

applaud *verb* **1.** To express enjoyment or approval especially by clapping the hands. **2.** To express praise for: *We applauded the president's decision.*
ap·plaud (ə **plôd′**) ◊ *verb* **applauded, applauding**

applause *noun* **1.** Enjoyment or approval expressed especially by the clapping of hands. **2.** Publicly expressed approval; praise.
ap·plause (ə **plôz′**) ◊ *noun*

apple *noun* A firm, rounded, often red-skinned fruit that can be eaten.
ap·ple (**ăp′**əl) ◊ *noun, plural* **apples**

appliance *noun* A device, such as a toaster or an electric stove, designed for a task.
ap·pli·ance (ə **plī′**əns) ◊ *noun, plural* **appliances**

applicable *adjective* Capable of being applied; appropriate.
ap·pli·ca·ble (**ăp′**lĭ kə bəl) ◊ *adjective*

applicant *noun* A person who applies for something, as a loan or a job.
ap·pli·cant (**ăp′**lĭ kənt) ◊ *noun, plural* **applicants**

application *noun* **1.** The act or an example of applying: *The application of varnish made the desk shine.* **2.** Something, such as a medicine, that is applied. **3.** The capacity of being put to a specific use: *Biology has practical applications.* **4.** A request, as for a job: *I made an application for a loan.*
ap·pli·ca·tion (ăp′lĭ **kā′**shən) ◊ *noun, plural* **applications**

apply *verb* **1.** To spread or put on: *We applied glue to the edges of the paper.* **2.** To put into action or use: *He applied the brakes to stop the truck.* **3.** To devote one's attention or effort: *She applied herself to her studies.* **4.** To have to do with: *This rule applies to you.* **5.** To make a request, as for employment or admission.
ap·ply (ə **plī′**) ◊ *verb* **applied, applying**

appoint *verb* **1.** To choose or name for an office, position, or duty. **2.** To decide on; fix: *I appointed 3:00 for the meeting.*
ap·point (ə **point′**) ◊ *verb* **appointed, appointing**

appointment *noun* **1.** The act or an example of appointing: *The appointment of a new judge was reported in the newspaper.* **2.** An office or position to which a person has been appointed: *I accepted the appointment as chairperson.* **3.** An arrangement to meet at a particular time or place.
ap·point·ment (ə **point′**mənt) ◊ *noun, plural* **appointments**

appraise *verb* **1.** To fix the value of: *The expert appraised the house.* **2.** To judge the quality, importance, or value of: *The teacher appraised the pupil's drawing.*
ap·praise (ə **prāz′**) ◊ *verb* **appraised, appraising**

appreciate *verb* **1.** To enjoy and understand: *I appreciate books.* **2.** To be thankful for: *The child appreciated your help.* **3.** To be aware of; realize: *I appreciate your problems.* **4.** To rise in price or value.
ap·pre·ci·ate (ə **prē′**shē āt′) ◊ *verb* **appreciated, appreciating**

appreciation *noun* **1.** Enjoyment and understanding: *You show a great appreciation of art.* **2.** A feeling or expression of gratitude: *We showed our appreciation by sending flowers.* **3.** A rise in price or value.
ap·pre·ci·a·tion (ə prē′shē **ā′**shən) ◊ *noun*

appreciative *adjective* Showing or feeling appreciation: *The appreciative audience applauded.*
ap·pre·cia·tive (ə **prē′**shə tĭv) ◊ *adjective*

apprehend *verb* **1.** To seize and arrest: *The police apprehended them.* **2.** To understand: *I didn't apprehend what you said.*
ap·pre·hend (ăp′rĭ **hĕnd′**) ◊ *verb* **apprehended, apprehending**

apprehension *noun* **1.** The act of seizing and arresting. **2.** The ability to understand or an act of understanding. **3.** Fear of what may happen.
ap·pre·hen·sion (ăp′rĭ **hĕn′**shən) ◊ *noun*

apprehensive *adjective* Fearful of what may happen: *I felt apprehensive about diving into the deep water.*
ap·pre·hen·sive (ăp′rĭ **hĕn′**sĭv) ◊ *adjective*

apprentice *noun* A person who is learning a craft or trade by working for a skilled worker.
ap·pren·tice (ə **prĕn′**tĭs) ◊ *noun, plural* **apprentices**

▲ **apprentice**
A potter and his apprentice

approach *verb* **1.** To come near or nearer: *The car approached the garage.* **2.** To begin to deal with or work on: *I didn't know how to approach my science homework.* **3.** To go to with a request or plan: *We approached our parents to ask permission.*
◊ *noun* **1.** The act of approaching: *Snow announced the approach of winter.* **2.** A way of beginning to deal with or work on something: *I tried a new approach to the problem.* **3.** A way of reaching a place.
ap·proach (ə **prōch′**) ◊ *verb* **approached, approaching** ◊ *noun, plural* **approaches**

approachable *adjective* Easy to approach and deal with.
ap·proach·a·ble (ə **prō′**chə bəl) ◊ *adjective*

appropriate *adjective* Suitable, as for a particular occasion; proper: *White shorts are appropriate for playing tennis.*
◊ *verb* **1.** To set apart for a particular use: *Congress appropriated money for education.* **2.** To take for oneself, often without permission: *You appropriated my bike for the day.*
ap·pro·pri·ate ◊ *adjective* (ə **prō′**prē ĭt) ◊ *verb* (ə **prō′**prē āt′) **appropriated, appropriating**

approval *noun* **1.** Favorable judgment: *The voters expressed their approval by electing the candidate.* **2.** Official consent: *We went to the party with our parents' approval.*
ap·prov·al (ə **prōō′**vəl) ◊ *noun*

approve *verb* **1.** To think favorably of: *Do you approve of my behavior?* **2.** To consent to officially: *The Senate approved the treaty.*
ap·prove (ə **prōōv′**) ◊ *verb* **approved, approving**

approximate *adjective* Almost exact or correct: *My approximate height is five feet.*
◊ *verb* To come close to; approach: *The recording approximates the sound of the tuba.*
ap·prox·i·mate ◊ *adjective* (ə **prŏk′**sə mĭt) ◊ *verb* (ə **prŏk′**sə māt′) **approximated, approximating**

approximately *adverb* Close to; almost exactly; nearly; about: *We drove approximately 100 miles today.*
ap·prox·i·mate·ly (ə **prŏk′**sə mĭt lē) ◊ *adverb*

approximation *noun* Something that is almost but not quite exact or correct: *Is this only an approximation of the true cost?*
ap·prox·i·ma·tion (ə prŏk′sə **mā′**shən) ◊ *noun, plural* **approximations**

Apr. The abbreviation for *April.*

apricot *noun* A juicy, yellow-orange fruit similar to a peach.
ap·ri·cot (**ăp′**rĭ kŏt′ *or* **ā′**prĭ kŏt′) ◊ *noun, plural* **apricots**

ă	pat	ĭ	pit	oi	oil	th	bath
ā	pay	ī	ride	ŏŏ	book	*th*	bathe
â	care	î	fierce	ōō	boot	ə	ago, item
ä	father	ŏ	pot	ou	out		pencil
ĕ	pet	ō	go	ŭ	cut		atom
ē	be	ô	paw, for	û	fur		circus

▲ **apricot**

April *noun* The fourth month of the year. April has 30 days.
A·pril (**ā′**prəl) ◊ *noun*

apron *noun* A garment worn over the front of the body to protect the clothes.
a·pron (**ā′**prən) ◊ *noun, plural* **aprons**

apt *adjective* **1.** Exactly suitable; appropriate: *Your apt answer proves that you have read the poem.* **2.** Inclined; likely: *You are apt to drop things when you hurry.* **3.** Quick to learn: *My cousin is an apt music student.*
apt (ăpt) ◊ *adjective*

aptitude *noun* **1.** A natural ability or talent: *She has an aptitude for learning languages.* —See Synonyms at **ability. 2.** Quickness to learn: *He skipped the fourth grade because of his aptitude.*
ap·ti·tude (**ăp′**tĭ tōōd′ *or* **ăp′**tĭ tyōōd′) ◊ *noun, plural* **aptitudes**

aquarium *noun* **1.** A water-filled container, as a tank, for keeping and displaying water animals and often water plants. **2.** A building where water animals and water plants are displayed to the public.
a·quar·i·um (ə **kwâr′**ē əm) ◊ *noun, plural* **aquariums**

aquatic *adjective* **1.** Of, living in, or growing in water: *The water lily is an aquatic plant.* **2.** Taking place in or on water.
a·quat·ic (ə **kwăt′**ĭk) ◊ *adjective*

aqueduct *noun* **1.** A large pipe or channel that carries water from a distant source. **2.** A structure like a bridge for carrying an aqueduct across low ground or a river.
aq·ue·duct (**ăk′**wĭ dŭkt′) ◊ *noun, plural* **aqueducts**

▲ **aqueduct**

AR The abbreviation for *Arkansas* that is used with a Zip Code.

Arab *noun* **1.** A person who was born in or lives in Arabia. **2.** A member of one of the Arabic-speaking peoples of the Middle East and northern Africa.
◊ *adjective* Of or relating to Arabia or the Arabs.
Ar·ab (ăr′ əb) ◊ *noun, plural* **Arabs**
◊ *adjective*

Arabian *noun* A person who was born in or lives in Arabia.
◊ *adjective* Of or relating to Arabia, the Arabians, or the Arabs.
A·ra·bi·an (ə rā′ bē ən) ◊ *noun, plural* **Arabians** ◊ *adjective*

Arabic *noun* A Semitic language spoken in Arabia, the Middle East, and parts of northern Africa.
◊ *adjective* Of or relating to the Arabs or their language.
Ar·a·bic (ăr′ ə bĭk) ◊ *noun* ◊ *adjective*

Arabic numeral *noun* One of the numerals formed with the symbols 1, 2, 3, 4, 5, 6, 7, 8, 9, and 0.
Arabic numeral ◊ *noun, plural* **Arabic numerals**

arbitrary *adjective* Based on or likely to rely on one's own wishes, opinions, or feelings rather than reason, rule, or law: *When I said "Never mind why, just do as I say," I was being arbitrary.*
ar·bi·trar·y (är′ bĭ trĕr′ē) ◊ *adjective*

arbitrate *verb* **1.** To make a decision that settles a dispute between two sides: *The teacher offered to arbitrate between us.* **2.** To submit to or settle by arbitration: *We agreed to arbitrate our quarrel.*
ar·bi·trate (är′ bĭ trāt′) ◊ *verb* **arbitrated, arbitrating**

arbitration *noun* The settlement of a dispute by a third person or group who hears the arguments and makes a decision.
ar·bi·tra·tion (är′bĭ **trā′**shən) ◊ *noun, plural* **arbitrations**

arbor *noun* A shaded place closed in by shrubs or trees or a frame on which climbing plants such as vines grow.
ar·bor (är′ bər) ◊ *noun, plural* **arbors**

▲ **arbor**

arc *noun* A part of a curved line, especially of a circle.
arc (ärk) ◊ *noun, plural* **arcs**
‖ *These sound alike:* **arc, ark**

arch *noun* **1.** A curved structure that extends across an opening and serves as a support. **2.** Something curved like an arch.
◊ *verb* To form or cause to form an arch.
arch (ärch) ◊ *noun, plural* **arches** ◊ *verb* **arched, arching**

archaeologist *noun* A person who practices archaeology.
ar·chae·ol·o·gist (är′kē **ŏl′** ə jĭst) ◊ *noun, plural* **archaeologists**

archaeology *noun* The scientific study of past human activities, life, and customs as they are shown by the tools, monuments, and pottery remaining from past societies.
ar·chae·ol·o·gy (är′kē **ŏl′** ə jē) ◊ *noun*

archbishop *noun* A bishop of the highest rank.
arch·bish·op (**ärch′ bĭsh′** əp) ◊ *noun, plural* **archbishops**

archer *noun* A person who shoots with a bow and arrows.
arch·er (är′ chər) ◊ *noun, plural* **archers**

archery *noun* The sport or skill of shooting with a bow and arrows.
arch·er·y (är′ chə rē) ◊ *noun*

archipelago *noun* **1.** A sea with a large group of islands. **2.** A large group of islands.
ar·chi·pel·a·go (är′kə **pĕl′** ə gō′) ◊ *noun, plural* **archipelagoes** *or* **archipelagos**

architect *noun* A person who designs buildings and oversees their construction.
ar·chi·tect (**är′** kĭ tĕkt′) ◊ *noun, plural* **architects**

architecture *noun* **1.** The art of designing buildings. **2.** A style of building. **3.** The organization and connection of the various parts of a computer system.
ar·chi·tec·ture (**är′** kĭ tĕk′chər) ◊ *noun*

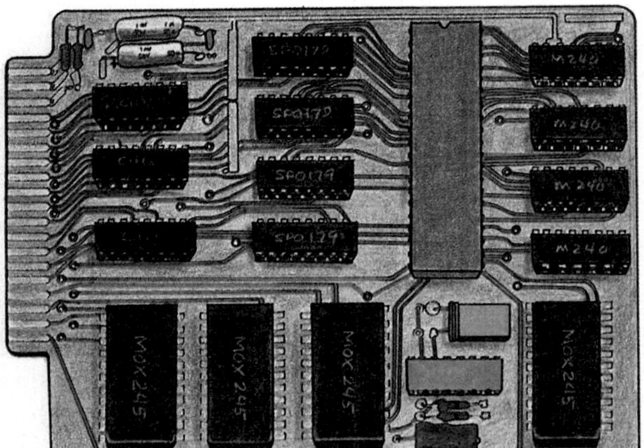

▲ **architecture**
An example of systems architecture

ă	pat	ĭ	pit	oi	**oil**	th	ba**th**
ā	pay	ī	ride	o͝o	**book**	*th*	ba**the**
â	care	î	fierce	o͞o	**boot**	ə	ago, item
ä	father	ŏ	pot	ou	**out**		pencil
ĕ	pet	ō	go	ŭ	**cut**		atom
ē	be	ô	paw, for	û	**fur**		circus

archway *noun* **1.** A passageway under an arch. **2.** An arch that covers a passageway.
arch·way (**ärch′** wā′) ◊ *noun, plural* **archways**

arctic *adjective* **1.** Extremely cold. **2. Arctic** Of or relating to the region surrounding the North Pole.
arc·tic (**ärk′** tĭk *or* **är′** tĭk) ◊ *adjective*

ardent *adjective* Having or showing great enthusiasm: *I am an ardent tennis fan.*
ar·dent (**är′** dnt) ◊ *adjective*

are *verb* **1.** Second person singular present tense of **be. 2.** First, second, and third person plural present tense of **be.**
are (är) ◊ *verb*

area *noun* **1.** A region, as of land: *The family moved from the city to a farming area.* **2.** The amount of surface within particular limits: *The area of the apartment is 2,000 square feet.* **3.** A field of study, interest, or activity: *Mathematics is my special area.*
ar·e·a (**âr′** ē ə) ◊ *noun, plural* **areas**

Area Code *noun* A series of three numbers assigned to each telephone service area within a country. An Area Code is used in dialing directly between such areas.
Area Code ◊ *noun, plural* **Area Codes**

arena *noun* **1.** An enclosed area in which shows or sports events are given. **2.** A building that has an arena. **3.** An area of conflict or activity: *A member of Congress works in the political arena.*
a·re·na (ə **rē′** nə) ◊ *noun, plural* **arenas**

aren't Contraction of "are not."
aren't (ärnt) ◊ *contraction*

argue *verb* **1.** To give reasons for or against something: *The senator argued in favor of the law.* —See Synonyms at **discuss. 2.** To discuss something with someone who has a different opinion; dispute.
ar·gue (**är′** gyo͞o) ◊ *verb* **argued, arguing**

argument *noun* **1.** An angry quarrel; dispute. **2.** A discussion with someone who has a different opinion: *We had an argument about politics.* **3.** A reason for or against something: *My argument was that I should be elected because I had more experience.*
ar·gu·ment (**är′** gyə mənt) ◊ *noun, plural* **arguments**

arid *adjective* Having little or no rainfall; dry: *The settlers irrigated the arid land.*
ar·id (**ăr′** ĭd) ◊ *adjective*

arise *verb* **1.** To get up from sitting or lying down. **2.** To move upward; ascend: *A mist arose from the lake.* **3.** To come into being: *A problem arose that had to be solved.*
a·rise (ə **rīz′**) ◊ *verb* **arose, arisen, arising**

arisen *verb* Past participle of **arise.**
a·ris·en (ə **rĭz′** ən) ◊ *verb*

aristocracy *noun* **1.** A social class usually based on birth whose members often enjoy more wealth and status than the rest of society. **2.** A group of people considered to be superior because of their intelligence or wealth.
ar·is·toc·ra·cy (ăr′ĭ **stŏk′** rə sē) ◊ *noun, plural* **aristocracies**

aristocrat *noun* A person who belongs to an aristocracy.
a·ris·to·crat (ə **rĭs′** tə krăt′) ◊ *noun, plural* **aristocrats**

aristocratic *adjective* Of, relating to, or like the aristocracy; noble.
a·ris·to·crat·ic (ə rĭs′tə **krăt′** ĭk) ◊ *adjective*

arithmetic *noun* **1.** The branch of mathematics that has to do with the addition, subtraction, multiplication, and division of numbers. **2.** The use of addition, subtraction, multiplication, or division.
a·rith·me·tic (ə **rĭth′** mə tĭk′) ◊ *noun*

Ariz. An abbreviation for *Arizona.*

ark *noun* **1.** The ship built by Noah for saving himself and his family from the Flood. **2.** A chest containing the Ten Commandments on stone tablets that was carried by the ancient Hebrews.
ark (ärk) ◊ *noun, plural* **arks**
‖*These sound alike:* **ark, arc**

Ark. An abbreviation for *Arkansas.*

arm¹ *noun* **1.** An upper limb of the human body that connects the hand and wrist to the shoulder. **2.** A part that resembles an arm in shape, use, or position.
arm¹ (ärm) ◊ *noun, plural* **arms**

arm² *noun* **1.** A weapon, especially a firearm. **2. arms** The use of weapons; warfare. **3. arms** The designs or emblems on the coat of arms of a family or nation.
◊ *verb* **1.** To equip with weapons. **2.** To prepare for war by taking up weapons: *The militia armed for the attack.* **3.** To provide with a means of defense.
arm² (ärm) ◊ *noun, plural* **arms** ◊ *verb* **armed, arming**

> ***HISTORY* • arm¹, arm²**
>
> **Arm¹,** like most words for the basic parts of the body, is a native English word. **Arm²** is from a French word that came from a Latin word meaning "weapons."

armada *noun* A big fleet of warships.
ar·ma·da (är **mä′** də) ◊ *noun, plural* **armadas**

armadillo *noun* A burrowing animal of southern North America and South America whose body is covered with bony plates.
ar·ma·dil·lo (är′mə **dĭl′** ō) ◊ *noun, plural* **armadillos**

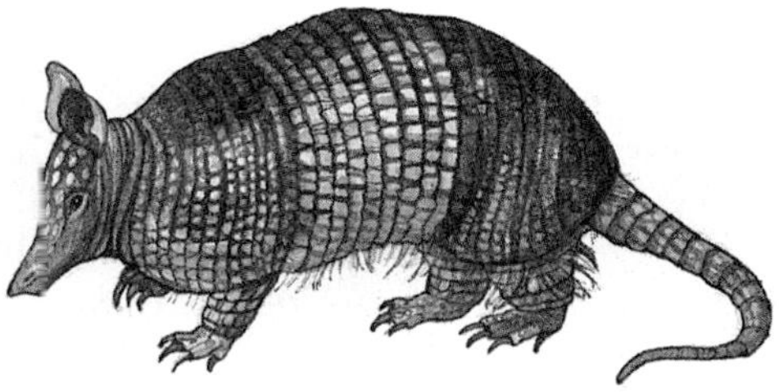

▲ **armadillo**

armament *noun* **1.** The weapons of a ship, airplane, or tank. **2.** The military forces and war equipment of a country.
ar·ma·ment (**är′** mə mənt) ◊ *noun, plural* **armaments**

armchair *noun* A chair with supports at the sides for the arms.
arm·chair (**ärm′** châr′) ◊ *noun, plural* **armchairs**

armistice *noun* A temporary stop in fighting agreed on by the two sides; truce.
ar·mi·stice (**är′** mĭ stĭs) ◊ *noun, plural* **armistices**

armor *noun* **1.** A heavy covering, especially of metal, worn to protect the body in battle. **2.** A protective covering, such as the metal plates on a tank.
ar·mor (**är′** mər) ◊ *noun*

armored *adjective* Protected by or covered with armor.
ar·mored (**är′** mərd) ◊ *adjective*

armory *noun* **1.** A place where military weapons are stored or made. **2.** A headquarters for soldiers where they train.
ar·mor·y (är′mə rē) ◊ *noun, plural* **armories**

armpit *noun* The hollow under the arm at the shoulder.
arm·pit (ärm′pĭt′) ◊ *noun, plural* **armpits**

army *noun* **1.** A large body of men and women organized and trained for land warfare. **2.** Often **Army** All the land forces of a country. **3.** A large group of people organized for a particular purpose. **4.** A large group of persons or things: *An army of people ran the marathon race.*
ar·my (är′mē) ◊ *noun, plural* **armies**

aroma *noun* A pleasant smell; fragrance: *We sniffed the aroma of fresh apple pie.*
a·ro·ma (ə rō′mə) ◊ *noun, plural* **aromas**

arose *verb* Past tense of **arise.**
a·rose (ə rōz′) ◊ *verb*

around *preposition* **1.** Near to; close to: *I go to the beach around July 1.* **2.** In or to various places in: *We drove around the city.* **3.** In a circle surrounding: *I wore a belt around my waist.* **4.** On all sides of: *Vines had grown up around the tower.* **5.** On or to the farther side of: *I ran around the corner.*
◊ *adverb* **1.** In circumference: *The ball measured one foot around.* **2.** In a circle: *The wheel turned around.* **3.** Close at hand; nearby: *I waited around all day.* **4.** Here and there: *I wandered around in the museum.* **5.** To each member of a group: *There is enough food to go around.* **6.** In or to the opposite direction: *I turned the car around and drove back to town.*
a·round (ə round′) ◊ *preposition* ◊ *adverb*

SYNONYMS

around, about, round

The dog chased the cat *around* the tree. We looked *about* us in the field. The wheel went *round* and *round* the axle.

ă	pat	ĭ	pit	oi	oil	th	bath
ā	pay	ī	ride	o͝o	book	*th*	bathe
â	care	î	fierce	o͞o	boot	ə	ago, item
ä	father	ŏ	pot	ou	out		pencil
ĕ	pet	ō	go	ŭ	cut		atom
ē	be	ô	paw, for	û	fur		circus

arouse *verb* **1.** To awaken from sleep. **2.** To stir up; excite: *The story aroused my anger.*
a·rouse (ə rouz′) ◊ *verb* **aroused, arousing**

arrange *verb* **1.** To put in order: *I arranged the food on the plate.* **2.** To plan for; prepare: *Can we arrange buses to pick us up?* **3.** To make a musical arrangement of.
ar·range (ə rānj′) ◊ *verb* **arranged, arranging**

arrangement *noun* **1.** The act or an example of arranging; order in which things are arranged: *I studied the alphabetical arrangement of the books on the shelf.* **2.** A set of things that have been arranged: *I put a flower arrangement on the table.* **3.** Often **arrangements** Planning done beforehand; preparation: *We made arrangements for our vacation.* **4.** A piece of music that has been adapted for instruments or voices for which it was not first written.
ar·range·ment (ə rānj′mənt) ◊ *noun, plural* **arrangements**

array *noun* **1.** An orderly arrangement: *The soldiers lined up in battle array.* **2.** An impressive display or group: *The jeweler showed us a huge array of diamonds.* **3.** Splendid clothing: *The king and queen appeared in rich array.*
◊ *verb* **1.** To arrange in order: *The officer arrayed the troops for inspection.* **2.** To dress, especially in fine clothes.
ar·ray (ə rā′) ◊ *noun* ◊ *verb* **arrayed, arraying**

arrest *verb* **1.** To seize and hold by authority of law: *The detective arrested the thief.* **2.** To stop the motion or progress of; check: *We built a dam to arrest the flow of the stream.* **3.** To capture and hold; attract: *The parade arrested our attention.*
◊ *noun* The act of arresting or the condition of being arrested.
ar·rest (ə rĕst′) ◊ *verb* **arrested, arresting**
◊ *noun, plural* **arrests**

arrival *noun* **1.** The act of arriving: *We waited for the arrival of our guests.* **2.** Someone or something that has arrived: *We welcomed the new arrival in our class.*
ar·ri·val (ə rī′vəl) ◊ *noun, plural* **arrivals**

arrive *verb* **1.** To reach a place: *They arrived early.* **2.** To reach a goal: *The two friends arrived at an understanding.* **3.** To come: *The day to start school arrived.*
ar·rive (ə rīv′) ◊ *verb* **arrived, arriving**

arrogant *adjective* Too proud of oneself; conceited and haughty.
ar·ro·gant (ăr′ ə gənt) ◊ *adjective*

arrow *noun* **1.** A straight, thin shaft that is shot from a bow. An arrow has a pointed head at one end and feathers at the other. **2.** Something, such as a sign or mark used to show direction, that is similar in shape to an arrow.
ar·row (ăr′ ō) ◊ *noun, plural* **arrows**

arrowhead *noun* The tip of an arrow.
ar·row·head (ăr′ ō-hĕd′) ◊ *noun, plural* **arrowheads**

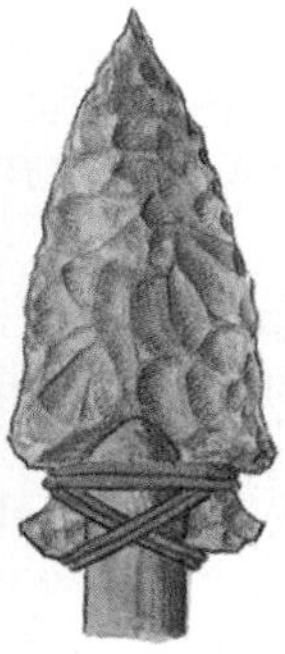

▲ **arrowhead**

arsenal *noun* A place where weapons and ammunition are stored and manufactured.
ar·se·nal (är′ sə nəl) ◊ *noun, plural* **arsenals**

arsenic *noun* A highly poisonous chemical element that is usually brittle and gray.
ar·se·nic (är′ sə nĭk) ◊ *noun*

art *noun* **1.** An activity, such as painting or sculpture, in which something beautiful is created. **2.** Works created by artists. **3.** A skill gained through practice, experience, or study: *You have mastered the art of public speaking.* **4.** An activity that calls for skill: *I learned the art of sewing.*
art (ärt) ◊ *noun, plural* **arts**

artery *noun* **1.** A blood vessel that carries blood from the heart to all parts of the body. **2.** A main channel or route, as a river.
ar·ter·y (är′ tə rē) ◊ *noun, plural* **arteries**

arthritis *noun* A painful inflammation and swelling of the joints of the body.
ar·thri·tis (är **thrī′** tĭs) ◊ *noun*

arthropod *noun* Any of a group of animals, as spiders and lobsters, that have jointed legs and a body made up of segments.
ar·thro·pod (är′ thrə pŏd′) ◊ *noun, plural* **arthropods**

article *noun* **1.** A piece of writing that forms an independent part of a newspaper, magazine, or book: *Write an article about your hobbies.* **2.** A section of a written document. **3.** An individual thing; item: *A bed is an article of furniture.* **4.** A word such as *a, an,* or *the* that is used to introduce a noun and clarify or limit it.
ar·ti·cle (är′ tĭ kəl) ◊ *noun, plural* **articles**

articulate *verb* To speak or express clearly: *Articulate your words so that we can understand what you are saying.*
ar·tic·u·late (är **tĭk′** yə lāt′) ◊ *verb* **articulated, articulating**

artificial *adjective* **1.** Made by human beings rather than occurring in nature: *These are artificial pearls.* **2.** Not genuine or natural; pretended: *That is an artificial smile.*
ar·ti·fi·cial (är′tə **fĭsh′** əl) ◊ *adjective*

artificial respiration *noun* A method of forcing air into and out of the lungs of a person who has stopped breathing.

artillery *noun* Large guns that are mounted on wheels or tracks because they are too heavy to carry.
ar·til·ler·y (är **tĭl′** ə rē) ◊ *noun*

artisan *noun* A person who works at a craft that requires manual skill.
ar·ti·san (är′ tĭ zən) ◊ *noun, plural* **artisans**

artist *noun* **1.** A person who practices an art, such as painting, sculpture, or music. **2.** A person whose work shows skill.
art·ist (är′ tĭst) ◊ *noun, plural* **artists**

artistic *adjective* **1.** Of or relating to art or artists. **2.** Showing skill and good taste: *This is an artistic flower arrangement.*
ar·tis·tic (är **tĭs′** tĭk) ◊ *adjective*

as *adverb* **1.** To the same extent or degree; equally: *You'll never meet anyone as nice.* **2.** For instance: *At the zoo we saw large animals, such as tigers and lions.*
◊ *conjunction* **1.** To the same extent or degree that: *The peach was sweet as sugar.* **2.** In the same way that: *I always do as I am told.* **3.** At the same time that: *I whistled as I worked.* **4.** Since; because: *I stayed home, as I was sick.*
◊ *preposition* **1.** In a manner similar to; like: *He appeared on stage as a clown.* **2.** In the role or function of: *She acted as a friend.*
as (ăz *or* əz) ◊ *adverb* ◊ *conjunction* ◊ *preposition*

asbestos *noun* A mineral that separates into strands that can be woven to make fireproof material.
as·bes·tos (ăs **bĕs′** təs) ◊ *noun*

ascend *verb* To go or move up; rise.
as·cend (ə sĕnd′) ◊ *verb* **ascended, ascending**

ascent *noun* **1.** The act or an example of ascending: *We watched the ascent of the rocket.* **2.** An upward slope.
as·cent (ə sĕnt′) ◊ *noun, plural* **ascents**
‖*These sound alike:* **ascent, assent**

ash¹ *noun* The solid material that is left after something has been burned completely. Ashes are grayish-white to black in color.
ash¹ (ăsh) ◊ *noun, plural* **ashes**

ash² *noun* A tree with leaflets in a featherlike arrangement and strong, tough wood.
ash² (ăsh) ◊ *noun, plural* **ashes**

> ***HISTORY* • ash¹, ash²**
>
> **Ash¹** and **ash²** have always meant what they mean now, though they were not always pronounced alike. They come from two different old English words.

ashamed *adjective* **1.** Feeling shame or guilt. **2.** Held back through fear or shame: *Don't be ashamed to ask for help.*
a·shamed (ə shāmd′) ◊ *adjective*

ashore *adverb* On or to the shore: *The crew of the ship stepped ashore.*
a·shore (ə shôr′) ◊ *adverb*

Asian *noun* A person who was born in or lives in Asia.
◊ *adjective* Of or relating to Asia or the Asians.
A·sian (ā′zhən) ◊ *noun, plural* **Asians** ◊ *adjective*

Asian American *noun* A person who was born in an Asian country and now lives in the United States.
◊ *adjective* Of or relating to Asian Americans.
Asian American ◊ *noun, plural* **Asian Americans** ◊ *adjective*

aside *adverb* **1.** To or on one side: *Stand aside.* **2.** Away from another or others; apart: *Let's put our money aside.* **3.** Out of one's thoughts or mind: *I put my fears aside.*
a·side (ə sīd′) ◊ *adverb*

ask *verb* **1.** To put a question to: *My parents asked me what time it was.* **2.** To seek an answer to: *Why do you ask that question?* **3.** To make a request: *My friend asked for an apple.*
ask (ăsk) ◊ *verb* **asked, asking**

> ***SYNONYMS***
>
> ***ask, examine, question***
>
> We *asked* them how they were feeling. The judge *examined* the witness during the trial. The police *questioned* the suspect. **Antonyms:** *answer, reply*

askew *adverb & adjective* At or to one side.
a·skew (ə skyo͞o′) ◊ *adverb & adjective*

asleep *adjective* **1.** Not awake; sleeping. **2.** Without feeling; numb: *My foot is asleep.*
◊ *adverb* Into a state of sleep.
a·sleep (ə slēp′) ◊ *adjective* ◊ *adverb*

asparagus *noun* A plant with spear-shaped stalks that are eaten as a vegetable.
as·par·a·gus (ə spăr′ə gəs) ◊ *noun*

aspect *noun* A way in which someone or something looks, appears, or may be viewed.
as·pect (ăs′pĕkt′) ◊ *noun, plural* **aspects**

aspen *noun* A poplar tree whose leaves flutter in the lightest breeze.
as·pen (ăs′pən) ◊ *noun, plural* **aspens**

▲ **aspen**

ă	pat	ĭ	pit	oi	oil	th	bath
ā	pay	ī	ride	o͝o	book	*th*	bathe
â	care	î	fierce	o͞o	boot	ə	ago, item
ä	father	ŏ	pot	ou	out		pencil
ĕ	pet	ō	go	ŭ	cut		atom
ē	be	ô	paw, for	û	fur		circus

asphalt *noun* **1.** A thick, sticky, dark mixture of petroleum tars used in paving, roofing, and waterproofing. **2.** A paving material composed of sand, gravel, and asphalt.
as·phalt (ăs′fôlt′) ◊ *noun*

aspiration *noun* A strong desire to achieve something; ambition.
as·pi·ra·tion (ăs′pə **rā′**shən) ◊ *noun, plural* **aspirations**

aspire *verb* To have a great ambition; desire strongly: *They aspire to fame.*
as·pire (ə **spīr′**) ◊ *verb* **aspired, aspiring**

aspirin *noun* A drug that is used to relieve pain and fever.
as·pi·rin (**ăs′**pə rĭn) ◊ *noun*

assail *verb* To attack with blows or words.
as·sail (ə **sāl′**) ◊ *verb* **assailed, assailing**

assassin *noun* A murderer, especially one who kills an important person.
as·sas·sin (ə **săs′**ĭn) ◊ *noun, plural* **assassins**

assassinate *verb* To attack and kill an important person.
as·sas·si·nate (ə **săs′**ə nāt′) ◊ *verb* **assassinated, assassinating**

assault *noun* **1.** A violent attack. **2.** An unlawful effort or threat to harm someone.
◊ *verb* To attack with force or violence.
as·sault (ə **sôlt′**) ◊ *noun, plural* **assaults**
◊ *verb* **assaulted, assaulting**

assemblage *noun* A collection of persons or things.
as·sem·blage (ə **sĕm′**blĭj) ◊ *noun, plural* **assemblages**

assemble *verb* **1.** To bring or come together as a group. **2.** To put together the parts of: *The mechanic assembled the engine.* **3.** To fit together: *The unit assembles easily.*
as·sem·ble (ə **sĕm′**bəl) ◊ *verb* **assembled, assembling**

assembly *noun* **1.** A group of persons who are gathered together for a common purpose. **2. Assembly** A specific group or body of lawmakers. **3.** The act or process of assembling parts. **4.** A number of parts that work together as a unit.
as·sem·bly (ə **sĕm′**blē) ◊ *noun, plural* **assemblies**

assent *noun* Acceptance or approval.
as·sent (ə **sĕnt′**) ◊ *noun*
‖*These sound alike:* **assent, ascent**

assert *verb* **1.** To state positively; affirm: *They assert their innocence.* **2.** To insist on; defend: *In 1776 the American Colonies asserted their independence.*
as·sert (ə **sûrt′**) ◊ *verb* **asserted, asserting**

assess *verb* **1.** To estimate the value of property for taxes. **2.** To set the amount of a tax or fine. **3.** To charge or tax: *Each member will be assessed 50 cents.*
as·sess (ə **sĕs′**) ◊ *verb* **assessed, assessing**

asset *noun* **1.** A valuable quality or possession: *An outgoing personality is an asset in making friends.* **2. assets** All the property owned by a person or an organization.
as·set (**ăs′**ĕt′) ◊ *noun, plural* **assets**

assign *verb* **1.** To set apart for a purpose: *We haven't assigned a date for the picnic.* **2.** To appoint to a post or duty. **3.** To give out; allot: *A counselor assigned bunks to us.*
as·sign (ə **sīn′**) ◊ *verb* **assigned, assigning**

assignment *noun* **1.** The act of assigning: *Assignment of team positions will be done by the coach.* **2.** A task or job assigned: *The English assignment is a book report.* —See Synonyms at **task.**
as·sign·ment (ə **sīn′**mənt) ◊ *noun, plural* **assignments**

assimilate *verb* **1.** To take in and use as nourishment: *The body assimilates protein.* **2.** To take into the mind: *It's not easy to assimilate so many ideas.*
as·sim·i·late (ə **sĭm′**ə lāt′) ◊ *verb* **assimilated, assimilating**

assist *verb* To give help; aid.
◊ *noun* An act of assisting.
as·sist (ə **sĭst′**) ◊ *verb* **assisted, assisting**
◊ *noun, plural* **assists**

assistance *noun* The act or result of helping; aid. —See Synonyms at **help.**
as·sis·tance (ə **sĭs′**təns) ◊ *noun*

assistant *noun* One who assists; helper.
◊ *adjective* Acting as a helper to another: *I am the assistant manager of the shop.*
as·sis·tant (ə **sĭs′**tənt) ◊ *noun, plural* **assistants** ◊ *adjective*

associate *verb* **1.** To connect in one's mind: *I associate elephants with the circus.* **2.** To join as a partner, member, or friend.
◊ *noun* **1.** A person who works with another; partner. **2.** A friend or companion.
◊ *adjective* **1.** Closely joined with another and

sharing in responsibility or authority: *She is an associate judge.* **2.** Not having full rights and privileges: *He is an associate member of the club.*
as·so·ci·ate ◊ *verb* (ə **sō′**shē āt′) **associated, associating** ◊ *noun* (ə **sō′**shē ĭt), *plural* **associates** ◊ *adjective* (ə **sō′**shē ĭt)

association *noun* **1.** The act of associating or the condition of being associated. **2.** A group of people organized for a common purpose. **3.** A mental connection made between thoughts or feelings and a person, place, or thing: *What associations do you have with the word "teen-ager"?*
as·so·ci·a·tion (ə sō′sē **ā′**shən) ◊ *noun, plural* **associations**

associative *adjective* Of or relating to a rule that the combinations by which the same groups of numbers are multiplied or added will not change their product or sum. For example, (4 × 2) × 8 will give the same product as (8 × 4) × 2. In both examples the product is 64.
associative (ə **sō′**shē ā′tĭv) ◊ *adjective*

assort *verb* To sort into groups according to kinds; classify.
as·sort (ə **sôrt′**) ◊ *verb* **assorted, assorting**

assorted *adjective* Of different kinds: *We chose from assorted desserts.*
as·sort·ed (ə **sôr′**tĭd) ◊ *adjective*

assortment *noun* A collection of different kinds.
as·sort·ment (ə **sôrt′**mənt) ◊ *noun, plural* **assortments**

assume *verb* **1.** To take for granted; suppose: *I assume you know where you're going.* **2.** To take upon oneself; undertake: *She will assume the duties of class president.* **3.** To pretend to be or have; feign: *He assumed a bold manner to hide his fear.*
as·sume (ə **so͞om′**) ◊ *verb* **assumed, assuming**

assurance *noun* **1.** The act of assuring; a guarantee. **2.** Freedom from doubt; certainty: *They answered with assurance that it was against the rules.* **3.** Confidence in one's own ability.
as·sur·ance (ə **sho͝or′**əns) ◊ *noun, plural* **assurances**

assure *verb* **1.** To tell with confidence: *I can assure you that it's going to rain.* **2.** To make certain; guarantee: *We assured the success of the party by hiring a rock band.* **3.** To give confidence to; reassure: *The doctor assured me that I would recover.*
as·sure (ə **sho͝or′**) ◊ *verb* **assured, assuring**

aster *noun* A plant that is related to the daisy and that has white, pink, purple, or yellow flowers.
as·ter (**ăs′**tər) ◊ *noun, plural* **asters**

▲ **aster**

asterisk *noun* A symbol (*) used in printing or in writing to direct the reader to another part of the page.
as·ter·isk (**ăs′**tə rĭsk′) ◊ *noun, plural* **asterisks**

astern *adverb* **1.** Behind a ship or airplane. **2.** At or toward the rear of a ship. **3.** With the back of the ship first; backward.
a·stern (ə **stûrn′**) ◊ *adverb*

asteroid *noun* One of the thousands of small planets that orbit the sun, mostly in the region between Mars and Jupiter. Asteroids range in size from about one to several hundred miles in diameter.
as·ter·oid (**ăs′**tə roid′) ◊ *noun, plural* **asteroids**

asthma *noun* A usually chronic ailment whose main symptoms are wheezing, coughing, and difficulty in breathing.
asth·ma (**ăz′**mə) ◊ *noun*

ă	pat	ĭ	pit	oi	**oil**	th	ba**th**
ā	pay	ī	ride	o͝o	book	*th*	ba*th*e
â	care	î	fierce	o͞o	boot	ə	ago, item
ä	father	ŏ	pot	ou	**out**		pencil
ĕ	pet	ō	go	ŭ	cut		atom
ē	be	ô	paw, for	û	fur		circus

astir *adjective* Up and about; active: *Our family was astir early in the morning.*
a·stir (ə **stûr′**) ◊ *adjective*

astonish *verb* To surprise greatly; amaze.
as·ton·ish (ə **stŏn′**ĭsh) ◊ *verb* **astonished, astonishing**

astonishment *noun* Sudden great surprise.
as·ton·ish·ment (ə **stŏn′**ĭsh mənt) ◊ *noun*

astound *verb* To astonish.
a·stound (ə **stound′**) ◊ *verb* **astounded, astounding**

astray *adverb* Away from the right path or direction.
a·stray (ə **strā′**) ◊ *adverb*

astride *preposition* With one leg on each side of: *The child sat astride the pony.*
◊ *adverb* With one leg on each side: *On the elephant was an acrobat riding astride.*
a·stride (ə **strīd′**) ◊ *preposition* ◊ *adverb*

astringent *noun* A substance that tends to tighten living tissue: *I use an astringent on my face.*
as·trin·gent (ə **strĭn′**jənt) ◊ *noun, plural* **astringents**

astronaut *noun* A person trained to travel in a spacecraft.
as·tro·naut (**ăs′**trə nôt′) ◊ *noun, plural* **astronauts**

▲ **astronaut**

astronautics *noun* (*used with a singular verb*) The science of the design, construction, and operation of spacecraft.
as·tro·nau·tics (ăs′trə **nô′**tĭks) ◊ *noun*

astronomer *noun* An expert in astronomy.
as·tron·o·mer (ə **strŏn′**ə mər) ◊ *noun, plural* **astronomers**

astronomic *or* **astronomical** *adjective* **1.** Of or relating to astronomy. **2.** Extremely large; immense: *The budget is astronomic.*
as·tro·nom·ic (ăs′trə **nŏm′**ĭk) *or* **as·tro·nom·i·cal** (ăs′trə **nŏm′**ĭ kəl) ◊ *adjective*

astronomy *noun* The scientific study and observation of the part of the universe beyond the earth, including stars, planets, comets, and galaxies.
as·tron·o·my (ə **strŏn′**ə mē) ◊ *noun*

asylum *noun* **1.** An institution for people who are unable to care for themselves, especially those who are mentally ill. **2.** A place of shelter; refuge. **3.** Protection given to a refugee from another country.
a·sy·lum (ə **sī′**ləm) ◊ *noun, plural* **asylums**

at *preposition* **1.** Used to indicate position, location, or state: *Will you be at home? The two nations were at war.* **2.** Used to indicate a direction or goal: *Look at us! I jumped at the chance to go.* **3.** Used to indicate time: *We had lunch at noon.* **4.** Used to indicate manner, means, or cause: *Work at your own pace. I laughed at the clown.*
at (ăt *or* ət) ◊ *preposition*

ate *verb* Past tense of **eat.**
ate (āt) ◊ *verb*
‖*These sound alike:* **ate, eight**

athlete *noun* A person who is trained in or is good at physical exercises, games, or sports that require strength, speed, and agility.
ath·lete (**ath′**lēt′) ◊ *noun, plural* **athletes**

athletic *adjective* **1.** Of or for athletics or athletes. **2.** Having a strong, muscular body.
ath·let·ic (ăth **lĕt′**ĭk) ◊ *adjective*

athletics *noun* (*used with a plural verb*) Athletic activities; sports.
ath·let·ics (ăth **lĕt′**ĭks) ◊ *noun*

atlas *noun* A book of maps.
at·las (**ăt′**ləs) ◊ *noun, plural* **atlases**

atmosphere *noun* **1.** The gas that surrounds a body in space, especially the air that surrounds the earth. **2.** The air or climate of a place: *The desert has a dry atmosphere.* **3.** The general environment in a place: *We like the busy atmosphere of the classroom.*
at·mos·phere (**ăt′**mə sfîr′) ◊ *noun, plural* **atmospheres**

atmospheric *adjective* Of, in, relating to, or coming from the atmosphere.
at·mos·pher·ic (at′mə **sfîr′**ĭk) ◊ *adjective*

atoll *noun* A coral island or a string of coral islands and reefs surrounding a lagoon.
at·oll (**ăt′**tôl′) ◊ *noun, plural* **atolls**

atom *noun* **1.** The smallest unit of an element that can exist by itself or in combination with other units. An atom is made up of neutrons and protons in a main nucleus surrounded by electrons. **2.** An atom viewed as a source of nuclear energy. **3.** A tiny bit: *I don't think there is an atom of truth in that story you're telling me.*
at·om (**ăt′**əm) ◊ *noun, plural* **atoms**

atomic *adjective* **1.** Of an atom or atoms. **2.** Of or using nuclear energy; nuclear.
a·tom·ic (ə **tŏm′**ĭk) ◊ *adjective*

atomic bomb *noun* A bomb whose very great explosive force is a result of energy being released by the splitting of atomic nuclei.
atomic bomb ◊ *noun, plural* **atomic bombs**

atomic energy *noun* Energy that is released as a result of the splitting or combining of atomic nuclei.

atone *verb* To make up for a wrong.
a·tone (ə **tōn′**) ◊ *verb* **atoned, atoning**

atop *preposition* On top of: *The picture shows us atop a high hill.*
a·top (ə **tŏp′**) ◊ *preposition*

atrocious *adjective* Extremely evil or cruel; wicked: *Murder is an atrocious crime.*
a·tro·cious (ə **trō′**shəs) ◊ *adjective*

attach *verb* **1.** To fasten one thing to another: *I attached a name tag to my dog's collar.* **2.** To bind by ties of affection or loyalty: *We are attached to our cousins.* **3.** To think of as having or belonging to: *I attach no importance to your complaints.* **4.** To add at the end; append: *Please attach your signature to the document.*
at·tach (ə **tăch′**) ◊ *verb* **attached, attaching**

attachment *noun* **1.** The act of attaching or state of being attached. **2.** A device that can be attached, as to a small appliance. **3.** A bond of affection or loyalty.
at·tach·ment (ə **tăch′**mənt) ◊ *noun, plural* **attachments**

attack *verb* **1.** To make a sudden violent move against; assault. **2.** To criticize strongly or in an unfriendly way. **3.** To afflict: *Flu attacked many people.* **4.** To start work with purpose and energy.
◊ *noun* **1.** The act of attacking. **2.** Sudden illness: *I had an attack of indigestion.*
at·tack (ə **tăk′**) ◊ *verb* **attacked, attacking** ◊ *noun, plural* **attacks**

attain *verb* **1.** To achieve a goal: *I hope to attain my ambition of becoming a lawyer.* **2.** To arrive at; reach.
at·tain (ə **tān′**) ◊ *verb* **attained, attaining**

attempt *verb* To make an effort; try: *The baby is attempting to crawl.*
◊ *noun* An effort or try.
at·tempt (ə **tĕmpt′**) ◊ *verb* **attempted, attempting** ◊ *noun, plural* **attempts**

attend *verb* **1.** To be present at: *All our friends attended the party.* **2.** To act as a servant or companion to: *The page attended the king.* **3.** To take care of: *Parents attend their babies.* **4.** To apply oneself: *Attend to your tasks.* **5.** To pay attention.
at·tend (ə **tĕnd′**) ◊ *verb* **attended, attending**

attendance *noun* **1.** The act or practice of attending: *My attendance at school is excellent.* **2.** The number of persons present: *Attendance was large at the play.*
at·ten·dance (ə **tĕn′**dəns) ◊ *noun*

attendant *noun* A person who is present at a specific place, such as a parking lot, in order to wait on those using the facilities.
at·ten·dant (ə **tĕn′**dənt) ◊ *noun, plural* **attendants**

attention *noun* **1.** The ability to concentrate: *The story held our attention for more than an hour.* **2.** The act of noticing or giving careful thought: *Your letter has come to our attention.* **3.** Thoughtful care and kindness: *They gave their aging parents much attention.* **4. attentions** Polite or thoughtful acts done especially to win a person's favor. **5.** A military posture with the body held very straight, arms at the sides, and heels together.
at·ten·tion (ə **tĕn′**shən) ◊ *noun, plural* **attentions**

ă	pat	ĭ	pit	oi	oil	th	bath
ā	pay	ī	ride	ŏŏ	book	*th*	bathe
â	care	î	fierce	ōō	boot	ə	ago, item
ä	father	ŏ	pot	ou	out		pencil
ĕ	pet	ō	go	ŭ	cut		atom
ē	be	ô	paw, for	û	fur		circus

SYNONYMS

attention, concentration

Class, please give me your *attention.* It took real *concentration* to understand that arithmetic problem.

attentive *adjective* **1.** Giving attention to something; alert. **2.** Considerate and polite.
at·ten·tive (ə **tĕn′**tĭv) ◊ *adjective*

attic *noun* The space in a building just under the roof.
at·tic (**ăt′**ĭk) ◊ *noun, plural* **attics**

attitude *noun* **1.** A state of mind; point of view: *Take a positive attitude toward studying.* **2.** A position of the body showing a certain mood or condition.
at·ti·tude (**ăt′**ĭ to͞od′ *or* **ăt′**ĭ tyo͞od′) ◊ *noun, plural* **attitudes**

attorney *noun* A lawyer.
at·tor·ney (ə **tûr′**nē) ◊ *noun, plural* **attorneys**

attract *verb* **1.** To draw to itself: *A magnet attracts nails.* **2.** To draw by exciting interest or emotion: *They like to attract attention by wearing strange outfits.*
at·tract (ə **trăkt′**) ◊ *verb* **attracted, attracting**

attraction *noun* **1.** The act or power of attracting. **2.** Something that attracts.
at·trac·tion (ə **trăk′**shən) ◊ *noun, plural* **attractions**

attractive *adjective* **1.** Having the power of attracting. **2.** Pleasing to the eye or mind.
at·trac·tive (ə **trăk′**tĭv) ◊ *adjective*

attribute *verb* **1.** To view as the cause of: *They attribute their athletic ability to practice.* **2.** To view as a quality of someone or something: *We attribute bravery to heroic men and women.*
◊ *noun* A quality belonging to a person or thing.
at·trib·ute ◊ *verb* (ə **trĭb′**yo͞ot) **attributed, attributing** ◊ *noun* (**ăt′**rə byo͞ot′), *plural* **attributes**

auburn *adjective* Reddish brown in color.
au·burn (**ô′**bərn) ◊ *adjective*

auction *noun* A public sale in which things are sold to those who offer the most money.
◊ *verb* To sell at an auction.
auc·tion (**ôk′**shən) ◊ *noun, plural* **auctions** ◊ *verb* **auctioned, auctioning**

auctioneer *noun* A manager of an auction.
auc·tion·eer (ôk′shə **nîr′**) ◊ *noun, plural* **auctioneers**

audacious *adjective* Daring to take risks; fearless. —See Synonyms at **bold.**
au·da·cious (ô **dā′**shəs) ◊ *adjective*

audacity *noun* **1.** Courage and daring; boldness. **2.** Rude or impudent behavior.
au·dac·i·ty (ô **dăs′**ĭ tē) ◊ *noun*

audible *adjective* Loud enough to be heard.
au·di·ble (**ô′**də bəl) ◊ *adjective*

audience *noun* **1.** The people gathered to see or hear something, such as a play, movie, concert, or game. **2.** The members of the public who pay attention to a book, radio broadcast, or television program.
au·di·ence (**ô′**dē əns) ◊ *noun, plural* **audiences**

audio *adjective* **1.** Of or dealing with sound or hearing. **2.** Of or for reproduction or broadcasting of sound.
◊ *noun* Sound or an electrical signal that corresponds to sound.
au·di·o (**ô′**dē ō′) ◊ *adjective* ◊ *noun, plural* **audios**

audio-visual *adjective* Of or relating to teaching materials, such as films with recordings, that use sight and sound.
au·di·o-vis·u·al (ô′dē ō **vĭzh′**o͞o əl) ◊ *adjective*

audition *noun* A short performance to test the ability of a musician, singer, dancer, or actor.
◊ *verb* To test or perform in an audition.
au·di·tion (ô **dĭsh′**ən) ◊ *noun, plural* **auditions** ◊ *verb* **auditioned, auditioning**

auditorium *noun* A large room or a building used for public gatherings, such as meetings, plays, concerts, or sports events.
au·di·to·ri·um (ô′dĭ **tôr′**ē əm) ◊ *noun, plural* **auditoriums**

Aug. The abbreviation for *August.*

augment *verb* To make larger; increase: *I augment my weekly allowance by working part-time after school.*
aug·ment (ôg **mĕnt′**) ◊ *verb* **augmented, augmenting**

august *adjective* Noble and majestic.
au·gust (ô **gŭst′**) ◊ *adjective*

August *noun* The eighth month of the year. August has 31 days.
Au·gust (**ô′**gəst) ◊ *noun*

auk *noun* A black and white sea bird with a thick body and short wings.
auk (ŏk) ◊ *noun, plural* **auks**

▲ **auk**

aunt *noun* **1.** The sister of one's father or mother. **2.** The wife of one's uncle.
aunt (ănt *or* änt) ◊ *noun, plural* **aunts**

LANGUAGE DETECTIVE

aunt

The way you pronounce *aunt* may depend on what part of the country you come from. If you live in the eastern part of New England or Virginia, then you probably pronounce *aunt* with the same vowel sound as *are.* Some people in large cities like New York and Philadelphia also use this pronunciation. But if you live in any other part of the United States, you probably pronounce *aunt* with the same vowel as *at,* so that it sounds the same as *ant.* Both pronunciations of *aunt* are correct.

auricle *noun* **1.** The outside part of the ear. **2.** A chamber of the heart that receives blood from a vein.
au·ri·cle (ôr′ĭ kəl) ◊ *noun, plural* **auricles**

aurora borealis *noun* Bands of flashing and moving light that can be seen in the night sky mainly in the regions near the North Pole. The aurora borealis is thought to have a magnetic and electrical origin.
au·ro·ra bo·re·al·is (ə rôr′ə bôr′ē **ăl′**ĭs) ◊ *noun*

Australian *noun* A person who was born in or lives in Australia.
◊ *adjective* Of or relating to Australia or the Australians.
Aus·tra·lian (ô **strāl′** yən) ◊ *noun, plural* **Australians** ◊ *adjective*

authentic *adjective* **1.** Worthy of belief; true: *This is an authentic story about forest fires by a forest ranger.* **2.** Being the real thing; genuine: *Those are authentic dinosaur bones.*
au·then·tic (ô **thĕn′** tĭk) ◊ *adjective*

author *noun* A person who writes a book, story, play, or magazine article.
au·thor (**ô′** thər) ◊ *noun, plural* **authors**

authoritative *adjective* **1.** Having or coming from proper authority; official. **2.** Having or showing expert knowledge: *The astronaut wrote an authoritative book on space travel.*
au·thor·i·ta·tive (ə **thôr′** ĭ tā′tĭv) ◊ *adjective*

authority *noun* **1.** The right and power to control persons or things: *The principal has the authority to close the school.* —See Synonyms at **power. 2.** Persons with controlling power: *Report the accident to the authorities.* **3.** A source of expert information: *Lee is an authority on whales.*
au·thor·i·ty (ə **thôr′** ĭ tē) ◊ *noun, plural* **authorities**

authorization *noun* **1.** The act of authorizing. **2.** Permission given by someone who has authority.
au·thor·i·za·tion (ô′thər ĭ **zā′** shən) ◊ *noun, plural* **authorizations**

authorize *verb* To give authority, approval, or power to: *The school board authorized them to teach a class in sign language.*
au·thor·ize (**ô′** thə rīz′) ◊ *verb* **authorized, authorizing**

auto *noun* An automobile.
au·to (**ô′** tō) ◊ *noun, plural* **autos**

autobiography *noun* The story of a person's life written by that person.
au·to·bi·og·ra·phy (ô′tō bī **ŏg′** rə fē) ◊ *noun, plural* **autobiographies**

autograph *noun* A person's signature in his or her own handwriting.

ă	pat	ĭ	pit	oi	**oil**	th	bath
ā	pay	ī	ride	o͝o	book	*th*	bathe
â	care	î	fierce	o͞o	boot	ə	ago, item
ä	father	ŏ	pot	ou	**out**		pencil
ĕ	pet	ō	go	ŭ	cut		atom
ē	be	ô	paw, for	û	fur		circus

◊ *verb* To write one's signature in or on: *I asked the author to autograph my book.*
au·to·graph (ô′tə grăf′) ◊ *noun, plural* **autographs** ◊ *verb* **autographed, autographing**

automate *verb* To make something, such as a process, machine, or factory, automatic.
au·to·mate (ô′tə māt′) ◊ *verb* **automated, automating**

automatic *adjective* **1.** Capable of operating by or regulating itself. **2.** Done without thought or control: *Breathing is automatic.*
◊ *noun* An automatic device or machine.
au·to·mat·ic (ô′tə **măt′**ĭk) ◊ *adjective* ◊ *noun, plural* **automatics**

automation *noun* **1.** The automatic operation or control of a process, machine, or system by devices that replace human workers. **2.** The ways and means of making a process, machine, or system automatic.
au·to·ma·tion (ô′tə **mā′**shən) ◊ *noun*

automobile *noun* A usually four-wheeled vehicle that is powered by a gasoline engine and that can carry passengers.
au·to·mo·bile (ô′tə mə bēl′) ◊ *noun, plural* **automobiles**

autumn *noun* The season of the year between summer and winter, lasting from late September to late December in the Northern Hemisphere.
au·tumn (ô′təm) ◊ *noun, plural* **autumns**

HISTORY • autumn

The season that follows summer used to be called **harvest.** Then two new terms began to be used: **autumn** and "fall of the leaf," later shortened to **fall. Autumn** became the more usual term in England, and **fall** the more usual term in America.

auxiliary *adjective* **1.** Giving help or support. **2.** Added as a supplement; extra.
◊ *noun* **1.** A person, group, or thing that gives help or support. **2.** An auxiliary verb.
aux·il·ia·ry (ôg **zĭl′**yə rē) ◊ *adjective* ◊ *noun, plural* **auxiliaries**

auxiliary verb *noun* A verb that accompanies another verb to show such things as number, person, or tense. *Can, do, may, must, shall,* and *will* are examples of auxiliary verbs.
auxiliary verb ◊ *noun, plural* **auxiliary verbs**

available *adjective* **1.** Possible to obtain: *Tickets are still available.* **2.** Ready to serve or be used: *I'm available to work today.*
a·vail·a·ble (ə **vā′**lə bəl) ◊ *adjective*

avalanche *noun* Much snow, ice, or earth that falls down the side of a mountain.
av·a·lanche (**ăv′**ə lănch′) ◊ *noun, plural* **avalanches**

HISTORY • avalanche

Avalanche is one of the few English words that come from Switzerland. In the Swiss Alps, avalanches are particularly common and severe.

Ave. The abbreviation for *Avenue.*

avenue *noun* A usually wide street.
av·e·nue (**ăv′**ə no͞o′ *or* **ăv′**ə nyo͞o′) ◊ *noun, plural* **avenues**

average *noun* **1.** A number found by adding up two or more quantities and dividing the sum by the number of quantities. The average of 1, 3, 5, and 7 is 4 or $1 + 3 + 5 + 7 = 16 \div 4 = 4$. **2.** Something that is about midway between extremes: *Your reading skill is close to the average for your age.*
◊ *verb* **1.** To find the average of. **2.** To amount to as an average: *The temperature averages 75 degrees.*
◊ *adjective* **1.** Found by averaging: *In our school the average size of a class is 26.* **2.** Typical, usual, or ordinary: *The average two-year-old loves teddy bears.*
av·er·age (**ăv′**ər ĭj) ◊ *noun, plural* **averages** ◊ *verb* **averaged, averaging** ◊ *adjective*

averse *adjective* Being opposed to something: *Are you averse to homework?*
a·verse (ə **vûrs′**) ◊ *adjective*

avert *verb* To turn away or aside: *I averted my eyes from the bright sun.*
a·vert (ə **vûrt′**) ◊ *verb* **averted, averting**

aviation *noun* **1.** The operation of aircraft. **2.** The design and construction of aircraft.
a·vi·a·tion (ā′vē **ā′**shən) ◊ *noun*

aviator *noun* A person who flies aircraft.
a·vi·a·tor (ā′vē ā′tər) ◊ *noun, plural* **aviators**

avid *adjective* **1.** Very eager: *The dictator was avid for power.* **2.** Very enthusiastic: *They are avid sports fans.*
av·id (**ăv′**ĭd) ◊ *adjective*

avocado *noun* A dark green, pear-shaped edible fruit that grows on a tropical American tree. An avocado has smooth, yellow-green flesh and a large seed.
av·o·ca·do (ăv′ə **kä′**dō *or* ä′və **kä′**dō) ◊ *noun, plural* **avocados**

▲ **avocado**

avoid *verb* **1.** To keep away from: *Go early to avoid the crowds.* **2.** To keep from happening: *Study hard to avoid failure.*
a·void (ə **void′**) ◊ *verb* **avoided, avoiding**

await *verb* **1.** To wait for: *We await our test scores.* **2.** To be in store for: *We got up early and found breakfast awaiting us.*
a·wait (ə **wāt′**) ◊ *verb* **awaited, awaiting**

awake *verb* To wake up: *The alarm clock awoke me at seven. I always awake at dawn.*
◊ *adjective* Not asleep.
a·wake (ə **wāk′**) ◊ *verb* **awoke** *or* **awaked, awaked** *or* **awoken, awaking** ◊ *adjective*

awaken *verb* To wake up: *I awakened early because of the noise.*
a·wak·en (ə **wā′**kən) ◊ *verb* **awakened, awakening**

award *verb* To give for outstanding performance or quality: *The faculty committee awarded Lee the prize for the best essay.*
◊ *noun* Something awarded.
a·ward (ə **wôrd′**) ◊ *verb* **awarded, awarding** ◊ *noun, plural* **awards**

aware *adjective* Conscious of something: *We are aware of the time.*
a·ware (ə **wâr′**) ◊ *adjective*

away *adverb* **1.** At or to a distance: *The lake is two miles away.* **2.** In or to a different direction: *Don't look away now.* **3.** From one's presence or possession: *My old bicycle was given away by my parents.* **4.** Out of existence: *The smoke faded away.* **5.** In a steady or continuous way: *We chopped away until the log split.*
◊ *adjective* **1.** Absent: *I am away from my desk.* **2.** At a distance: *I was miles away.*
a·way (ə **wā′**) ◊ *adverb* ◊ *adjective*

ă	pat	ĭ	pit	oi	oil	th	bath
ā	pay	ī	ride	ŏŏ	book	*th*	bathe
â	care	î	fierce	ōō	boot	ə	ago, item
ä	father	ŏ	pot	ou	out		pencil
ĕ	pet	ō	go	ŭ	cut		atom
ē	be	ô	paw, for	û	fur		circus

awe *noun* A feeling of wonder, fear, and respect: *The astronauts gazed in awe at the distant planet earth.*
◊ *verb* To fill with awe: *The sunset awed us.*
awe (ô) ◊ *noun* ◊ *verb* **awed, awing**

awful *adjective* **1.** Causing fear; frightening: *There is an awful stillness before a tornado.* **2.** Very bad; horrible: *That movie was awful.*
aw·ful (**ô′**fəl) ◊ *adjective*

awfully *adverb* **1.** Very: *I'm awfully tired.* **2.** Very badly: *You behaved awfully.*
aw·ful·ly (**ô′**fə lē *or* **ô′**flē) ◊ *adverb*

awhile *adverb* For a short time: *Let's wait awhile.*
a·while (ə **hwīl′**) ◊ *adverb*

awkward *adjective* **1.** Not graceful; clumsy: *Seals are awkward when out of the water.* **2.** Not natural in behavior or speech: *The child was shy and awkward around guests.* **3.** Difficult to handle or manage: *That's an awkward bundle.*
awk·ward (**ôk′**wərd) ◊ *adjective*

awl *noun* A pointed tool for making holes in wood or leather.
awl (ôl) ◊ *noun, plural* **awls**
‖*These sound alike:* **awl, all**

awning *noun* A piece of material put up like a roof just outside a door or window to provide shade.
awn·ing (**ô′**nĭng) ◊ *noun, plural* **awnings**

awoke *verb* A past tense of **awake.**
a·woke (ə **wōk′**) ◊ *verb*

awoken *verb* A past participle of **awake.**
a·wok·en (ə **wō′**kən) ◊ *verb*

ax *or* **axe** *noun* A heavy chopping tool with a long handle and a sharp blade.
ax *or* **axe** (ăks) ◊ *noun, plural* **axes**

axes *noun* Plural of **axis.**
ax·es (**ăk′**sēz′) ◊ *noun*

axiom *noun* **1.** An established rule, principle, or law. **2.** A statement that is assumed to be true without proof.
ax·i·om (**ăk′**sē əm) ◊ *noun, plural* **axioms**

axis *noun* A straight line around which an object turns or is thought to turn: *The earth's axis passes through both of its poles.*
ax·is (ăk′sĭs) ◊ *noun, plural* **axes**

axle *noun* A bar or shaft on which one or more wheels turn.
ax·le (ăk′səl) ◊ *noun, plural* **axles**

aye *interjection* Yes.
◊ *noun* A vote of "yes."
aye (ī) ◊ *interjection* ◊ *noun, plural* **ayes**
‖*These sound alike:* **aye, eye, I**

AZ The abbreviation for *Arizona* that is used with a Zip Code.

azalea *noun* A shrub with clusters of showy pink, red, or white flowers.
a·zal·ea (ə zāl′yə) ◊ *noun, plural* **azaleas**

▲ **azalea**

azure *noun* A light to medium blue color.
az·ure (ăzh′ər) ◊ *noun*

Badger

Bb

B is the second letter of the English alphabet. Did you know that it has a long history?

9 Over 3,500 years ago, people in the Middle East were using symbols that became the letters of our alphabet. This ancient Middle Eastern symbol is a form of the letter that became our letter *B*.

B The ancient Greeks borrowed their alphabet from people in the Middle East. Here is a form of the Greek letter that became our letter *B*.

B The ancient Romans borrowed their alphabet from a people who had taken their own letter symbols from the Greeks. Here is a form of the Roman letter *B* that was used for carving letters into stone. These letters became the model for our printed capital letters.

b As people wrote quickly, especially with pens, the capital letters began to take the shapes of small letters. Here is a small-letter *b* that was developed about 1,200 years ago.

Bb *Bb*	Bb	Bb	Bb
Handwriting	Sans Serif Type	Serif Type	Computer Printing

b *or* **B** *noun* The second letter of the English alphabet.
b *or* **B** (bē) ◊ *noun, plural* **b's** *or* **B's**

baa *noun* The sound that a sheep makes.
◊ *verb* To make this sound.
baa (bă *or* bä) ◊ *noun, plural* **baas** ◊ *verb* **baaed, baaing**

babble *verb* **1.** To make a series of sounds that have no meaning: *The babies babbled as they played.* **2.** To talk on and on about things that are not important; chatter. **3.** To make a low murmuring sound, as a brook.
◊ *noun* **1.** A series or mixture of sounds that have no meaning. **2.** A low murmuring sound.
bab·ble (băb′əl) ◊ *verb* **babbled, babbling** ◊ *noun, plural* **babbles**

ă	pat	ĭ	pit	oi	oil	th	bath
ā	pay	ī	ride	o͝o	book	*th*	bathe
â	care	î	fierce	o͞o	boot	ə	ago, item
ä	father	ŏ	pot	ou	out		pencil
ĕ	pet	ō	go	ŭ	cut		atom
ē	be	ô	paw, for	û	fur		circus

babe *noun* A baby; infant.
babe (bāb) ◊ *noun, plural* **babes**

baboon *noun* A large African monkey with a long, doglike face.
ba·boon (bă **bo͞on′**) ◊ *noun, plural* **baboons**

baby *noun* **1.** A very young child; infant. **2.** The youngest member of a family. **3.** A person who acts like a baby.
◊ *verb* To treat like a baby. —See Synonyms at **pamper.**
ba·by (**bā′**bē) ◊ *noun, plural* **babies** ◊ *verb* **babied, babying**

baby-sat *verb* Past tense of **baby-sit.**
ba·by-sat (**bā′**bē săt′) ◊ *verb*

baby-sit *verb* To take care of a child or children when the parents are not at home.
ba·by-sit (**bā′**bē sĭt′) ◊ *verb* **baby-sat, baby-sitting**

baby sitter *noun* A person who baby-sits.
baby sitter ◊ *noun, plural* **baby sitters**

bachelor *noun* An unmarried man.
bach·e·lor (**băch′**ə lər *or* **băch′**lər) ◊ *noun, plural* **bachelors**

back *noun* **1.** The part of the human body on the other side from the chest, between the neck and the buttocks. **2.** The upper part of an animal's body, where the spine is. **3.** The backbone. **4.** The part of something that is away from the main or front part: *The delivery entrance is at the back of the building.* **5.** The rear or reverse side of something: *The backs of the farmer's hands were sunburned.*
◊ *adverb* **1.** Toward the rear; backward: *Step back, please.* **2.** To a former place, time, or condition: *Think back to last year.* **3.** In return: *If you're hit, don't hit back.*
◊ *adjective* **1.** Located at the back: *Let's sit on the back porch.* **2.** Past; old: *Do you save back issues of that magazine?*
◊ *verb* **1.** To move or cause to move backward: *The principal backed slowly toward the door.* **2.** To give support to: *If you run for team captain, I'll back you.*
◊ *idiom* **back down** To give up and stop insisting on something.
back (băk) ◊ *noun, plural* **backs** ◊ *adverb* ◊ *adjective* ◊ *verb* **backed, backing**

backbone *noun* **1.** The series of connected bones in the middle of the back; spine. **2.** Strength of character; courage: *Standing up to bullies takes plenty of backbone.*
back·bone (**băk'**bōn') ◊ *noun, plural* **backbones**

background *noun* **1.** The part of a picture, scene, or view that appears far away. **2.** The general surface on which designs or figures are shown: *The flag had white stars on a blue background.* **3.** A person's past experience, training, and education.
back·ground (**băk'**ground') ◊ *noun, plural* **backgrounds**

backhand *noun* A stroke, as of a tennis racket, made with the back of the hand facing forward.
back·hand (**băk'**hănd') ◊ *noun, plural* **backhands**

backpack *noun* A bag worn on the back to carry camping supplies. It is sometimes mounted on a light metal frame.
back·pack (**băk'**păk') ◊ *noun, plural* **backpacks**

backward *adverb* **1.** In a direction opposite to forward: *I jumped backward to get out of the way.* **2.** With the back first: *Helicopters can fly backward.* **3.** In reverse order or direction: *Count backward from ten to one.*
◊ *adjective* **1.** Directed or moving toward the back: *I left without a backward glance.* **2.** Behind others in progress or development: *Rich nations lend money to backward countries.*
back·ward (**băk'**wərd) ◊ *adverb* ◊ *adjective*

backwards *adverb* Backward.
back·wards (**băk'**wərdz) ◊ *adverb*

back yard *noun* A yard at the back of a house.
back yard ◊ *noun, plural* **back yards**

bacon *noun* The salted and smoked meat from the back and sides of a pig.
ba·con (**bā'**kən) ◊ *noun*

bacteria *plural noun* Tiny one-celled organisms. Some bacteria help digest food; other bacteria cause diseases.
bac·te·ri·a (băk **tîr'** ē ə) ◊ *plural noun*

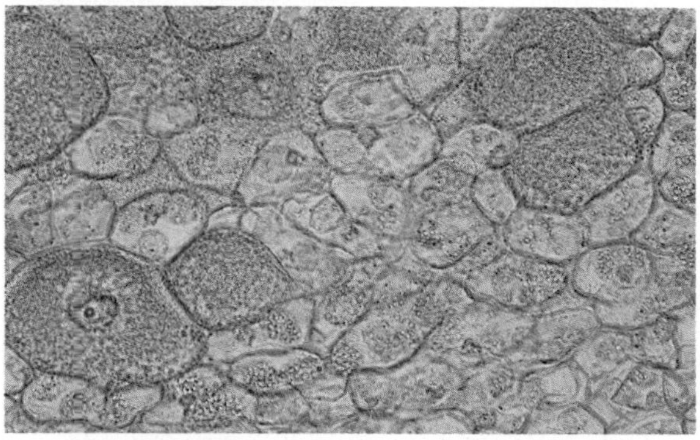

▲ **bacteria**
Magnified 225 times

bad *adjective* **1.** Not good; inferior: *The food was so bad that no one touched it.* **2.** Disagreeable; unpleasant: *Are you in a bad mood today?* **3.** Causing distress: *I'm afraid I have bad news.* **4.** Incorrect; improper: *It is very bad manners to interrupt.* **5.** Disobedient; naughty: *They were bad children today.* **6.** Causing harm: *Sugar is bad for your teeth.* **7.** In poor health; ill: *I feel bad today.* **8.** Severe; intense: *A bad storm knocked down the fence.* **9.** Sorry; regretful: *I feel very bad about what happened.* **10.** Rotten; spoiled: *The milk has turned bad.*
bad (băd) ◊ *adjective* **worse, worst**

bade *verb* A past tense of **bid.**
bade (băd *or* bād) ◊ *verb*

badge *noun* Something worn to show that a person belongs to a certain group, has a certain rank, or has been given an honor.
badge (băj) ◊ *noun, plural* **badges**

badger *noun* A burrowing animal with short legs and thick, grayish fur.
◊ *verb* To trouble with many questions or protests; pester.
badg·er (băj′ər) ◊ *noun, plural* **badgers**
◊ *verb* **badgered, badgering**

badly *adverb* **1.** In a bad way; not well: *The package was badly wrapped.* **2.** Very much; greatly: *I badly want a new bicycle.*
bad·ly (băd′lē) ◊ *adverb*

badminton *noun* A game in which players use light rackets to hit a shuttlecock back and forth over a high net.
bad·min·ton (băd′mĭnt′n) ◊ *noun*

baffle *verb* To be too difficult or confusing to understand or solve: *I figured out most of the problems, but the last one baffled me.*
baf·fle (băf′əl) ◊ *verb* **baffled, baffling**

bag *noun* **1.** A container made of paper, cloth, or other soft material: *We put our garbage in plastic bags.* **2.** Something, as a purse or a suitcase, that can be used like a bag.
bag (băg) ◊ *noun, plural* **bags**

LANGUAGE DETECTIVE

bag

People sometimes use different words for the same thing, depending on where they live. What do you call the paper container that you carry groceries home in? If you live in the northern United States, you probably call it a *paper bag.* If you live in the southern United States you probably call it a *paper sack.* But if you live in a large area between the North and the South and also in some parts of the South, you might even call it a *poke.*

ă	pat	ĭ	pit	oi	oil	th	bath
ā	pay	ī	ride	ŏŏ	book	*th*	bathe
â	care	î	fierce	ōō	boot	ə	ago, item
ä	father	ŏ	pot	ou	out		pencil
ĕ	pet	ō	go	ŭ	cut		atom
ē	be	ô	paw, for	û	fur		circus

baggage *noun* The suitcases and other containers that a person carries when traveling.
bag·gage (băg′ĭj) ◊ *noun*

baggy *adjective* Fitting loosely: *The clown wore baggy pants.*
bag·gy (băg′ē) ◊ *adjective* **baggier, baggiest**

bagpipe *noun* A musical instrument consisting of a leather bag and a number of pipes. The player blows air into the bag through a tube and then squeezes the bag to force the air through the pipes.
bag·pipe (băg′pīp′) ◊ *noun, plural* **bagpipes**

▲ **bagpipe**

bail[1] *noun* Money given for the temporary release of an arrested person from jail. The money is held by a court and returned when the person appears for trial.
◊ *verb* To set free by providing bail: *The lawyer bailed the prisoner out of jail.*
bail[1] (bāl) ◊ *noun* ◊ *verb* **bailed, bailing**
‖*These sound alike:* **bail, bale**

bail[2] *verb* To remove water from a boat by repeatedly filling a container and emptying it: *We bailed the canoe with a juice can.*
◊ *idiom* **bail out** To jump out of an aircraft with a parachute.
bail[2] (bāl) ◊ *verb* **bailed, bailing**
‖*These sound alike:* **bail, bale**

bait *noun* **1.** Food placed on a hook or in a trap to attract and catch fish, birds, or other animals. **2.** Something used to lure or attract a person or animal.
◊ *verb* **1.** To put bait on: *I baited the hook with a worm.* **2.** To tease or insult with repeated remarks.
bait (bāt) ◊ *noun* ◊ *verb* **baited, baiting**

bake *verb* **1.** To cook in an oven with steady, dry heat: *We baked bread today.* **2.** To harden or dry by heating in or as if in an oven: *The ground baked in the hot sun.*
bake (bāk) ◊ *verb* **baked, baking**

baker *noun* A person who bakes and sells foods such as bread, cakes, and pastries.
bak·er (bā′ kər) ◊ *noun, plural* **bakers**

bakery *noun* A place where foods such as bread, cake, and pastries are baked or sold.
bak·e·ry (bā′ kə rē) ◊ *noun, plural* **bakeries**

baking powder *noun* A powder used in cooking to make dough or batter rise.

balance *noun* **1.** A device for weighing things. **2.** A condition in which two numbers, amounts, or forces are equal: *The number of boys and girls in the class is in balance, ten boys and ten girls.* **3.** Something left over; remainder: *After school, we spent the balance of the afternoon swimming.* **4.** A steady or stable position: *I lost my balance and fell.*
◊ *verb* **1.** To make equal in number, amount, or force: *Balance the weights on both sides of the scale.* **2.** To put in a steady or stable condition: *I balanced the ball on my head.* **3.** To weigh or compare in or as if in a balance: *A judge balances justice and mercy.*
bal·ance (băl′ əns) ◊ *noun, plural* **balances**
◊ *verb* **balanced, balancing**

▲ **balance**
Weighing berries on a balance

balcony *noun* **1.** A platform that sticks out from the wall of a building. Balconies often have railings around them. **2.** An upper section of seats that sticks out over the main floor of a theater or auditorium.
bal·co·ny (băl′ kə nē) ◊ *noun, plural* **balconies**

bald *adjective* **1.** Lacking hair on the top of the head. **2.** Lacking natural or usual covering: *The fire left a bald spot in the lawn.*
bald (bôld) ◊ *adjective* **balder, baldest**

bald eagle *noun* A North American eagle with a dark body and a white head and tail.
bald eagle ◊ *noun, plural* **bald eagles**

▲ **bald eagle**

bale *noun* A large bundle of raw or finished material tied up tightly: *The barn was filled with bales of hay.*
bale (bāl) ◊ *noun, plural* **bales**
‖*These sound alike:* **bale, bail**

balk *verb* To stop short and refuse to go on: *My pony jumped across the deep ravine, but all the others balked.*
balk (bôk) ◊ *verb* **balked, balking**

ball¹ *noun* **1.** Something that is round or nearly round: *The sun is a fiery ball. I wound the string into a ball.* **2.** A round object used in a game or sport: *A basketball is larger than a tennis ball.* **3.** A game, especially baseball, that is played with a ball. **4.** A baseball pitch that is not swung at by the batter and not thrown over home plate between the batter's knees and shoulders.
ball¹ (bôl) ◊ *noun, plural* **balls**
‖*These sound alike:* **ball, bawl**

ball² *noun* A formal social dance.
ball² (bôl) ◊ *noun, plural* **balls**
‖*These sound alike:* **ball, bawl**

HISTORY • ball[1], ball[2]

Ball[1] comes from an old Scandinavian word meaning "a ball" or "something round." **Ball[2]** is from an old French word that goes back to a Greek word meaning "to dance."

ballad *noun* A poem or song that tells a story, usually about love.
bal·lad (băl′əd) ◊ *noun, plural* **ballads**

ballast *noun* A heavy material carried in a vessel to give it weight and keep it steady.
bal·last (băl′əst) ◊ *noun*

ball bearing *noun* A bearing in which the moving part slides on a number of loose steel balls in a groove. Ball bearings reduce friction between machine parts.
ball bearing ◊ *noun, plural* **ball bearings**

ballerina *noun* A woman who is a leading dancer in a ballet company.
bal·le·ri·na (băl′ə **rē′**nə) ◊ *noun, plural* **ballerinas**

ballet *noun* A kind of dancing with formal poses, turns, and leaps.
bal·let (bă **lā′** *or* **băl′**ā′) ◊ *noun*

balloon *noun* **1.** A large bag filled with hot air or some other gas that is lighter than normal air; hot-air balloon. **2.** A small, usually brightly colored rubber bag that floats when filled with air or another gas.
◊ *verb* To swell out like a balloon.
bal·loon (bə **lo͞on′**) ◊ *noun, plural* **balloons** ◊ *verb* **ballooned, ballooning**

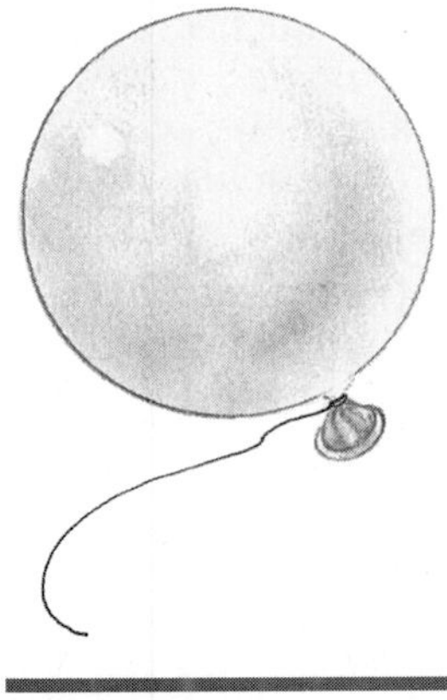

▲ **balloon**

ballot *noun* **1.** A piece of paper on which a voter marks a choice or choices. **2.** The act or a method of voting: *In a democracy, decisions are made by ballot.*
bal·lot (băl′ət) ◊ *noun, plural* **ballots**

ball-point pen *noun* A pen with a small metal ball at its writing tip. The ball turns in its socket and inks itself by touching an inner supply.
ball-point pen (**bôl′**point′) ◊ *noun, plural* **ball-point pens**

ballroom *noun* A large room for dancing.
ball·room (**bôl′**ro͞om′ *or* **bôl′**ro͝om′) ◊ *noun, plural* **ballrooms**

balmy *adjective* Mild and pleasant: *Spring soon came and balmy breezes blew.*
balm·y (**bä′**mē) ◊ *adjective* **balmier, balmiest**

balsa *noun* A tropical American tree with very light wood that is used to make rafts and model airplanes.
bal·sa (**bôl′**sə) ◊ *noun, plural* **balsas**

balsam *noun* A North American fir tree that yields a fragrant substance that is used in medicines and perfumes.
bal·sam (**bôl′**səm) ◊ *noun, plural* **balsams**

bamboo *noun* A tall, tropical grass that has hollow, woody stems. The stems are used for window blinds, fishing poles, and many other objects.
bam·boo (băm **bo͞o′**) ◊ *noun, plural* **bamboos**

ban *verb* To forbid by law; make illegal: *Billboards are banned on this highway.*
◊ *noun* A law or official order that forbids something.
ban (băn) ◊ *verb* **banned, banning** ◊ *noun, plural* **bans**

banana *noun* A curved fruit with sweet, soft flesh and yellow or reddish skin that peels off easily. Bananas grow in bunches on large tropical plants.
ba·nan·a (bə **năn′**ə) ◊ *noun, plural* **bananas**

band[1] *noun* **1.** A strip of metal, cloth, or other flexible material used to tie or hold things together: *The trunk was strapped with leather bands.* **2.** A stripe of color or material: *The blue pitcher has yellow bands around the neck.* **3.** A range of radio frequencies.
◊ *verb* To put a band on: *If you band the*

ă	pat	ĭ	pit	oi	**oi**l	th	ba**th**
ā	pay	ī	ride	o͝o	book	*th*	ba**the**
â	care	î	fierce	o͞o	boot	ə	ago, item
ä	father	ŏ	pot	ou	**ou**t		pencil
ĕ	pet	ō	go	ŭ	cut		atom
ē	be	ô	paw, for	û	fur		circus

bird's leg, you can identify it later.
band¹ (bănd) ◊ *noun, plural* **bands** ◊ *verb* **banded, banding**

band² *noun* **1.** A group of people or animals acting together: *A band of outlaws held up the stagecoach.* **2.** A group of musicians who play together.
◊ *verb* To form or gather in a group: *The settlers banded together for protection.*
band² (bănd) ◊ *noun, plural* **bands** ◊ *verb* **banded, banding**

***HISTORY* • band¹, band²**

Band¹ and **band²** come from two old French words that came from two Germanic words. The first word meant "a bond, tie, or link" and gave us **band¹**. The other word meant "a banner" and thus "a troop of men fighting under one banner." This meaning was then extended to include any group acting as one, such as a **band²** of musicians.

bandage *noun* A strip of cloth or other material used to cover and protect a wound or injury.
◊ *verb* To cover with a bandage.
band·age (**băn′** dĭj) ◊ *noun, plural* **bandages** ◊ *verb* **bandaged, bandaging**

bandanna *noun* A large, brightly colored handkerchief.
ban·dan·na (băn **dăn′** ə) ◊ *noun, plural* **bandannas**

bandit *noun* A robber, often one who is a member of a gang.
ban·dit (**băn′** dĭt) ◊ *noun, plural* **bandits**

bang *noun* **1.** A loud, sharp, sudden noise: *The door slammed shut with a bang.* **2.** A sudden, noisy blow; thump: *A bang on the side of the head shook me up.*
◊ *verb* **1.** To make a loud, sharp, sudden noise: *The guns banged in the distance.* **2.** To strike or move with a loud noise: *The cook banged the pots and pans together.*
bang (băng) ◊ *noun, plural* **bangs** ◊ *verb* **banged, banging**

bangs *plural noun* Hair cut straight across the forehead.
bangs (băngz) ◊ *plural noun*

***HISTORY* • bang, bangs**

Bang probably comes from an old Scandinavian word made up to imitate the noisy sound it describes. The origin of **bangs** is not known for certain, but it may be short for *bangtail,* a slang word for a kind of horse. You could then wear your hair in a *bangtail* in front and a *ponytail* behind.

banish *verb* **1.** To force to leave a country or place; exile: *The ruler banished the outlaws.* **2.** To drive out or away; expel: *Banish such thoughts from your mind.*
ban·ish (**băn′** ĭsh) ◊ *verb* **banished, banishing**

banister *noun* The railing supported by posts along a staircase.
ban·is·ter (**băn′** ĭ stər) ◊ *noun, plural* **banisters**

banjo *noun* A musical instrument with a round body, a long neck, and four or five strings.
ban·jo (**băn′** jo) ◊ *noun, plural* **banjos** *or* **banjoes**

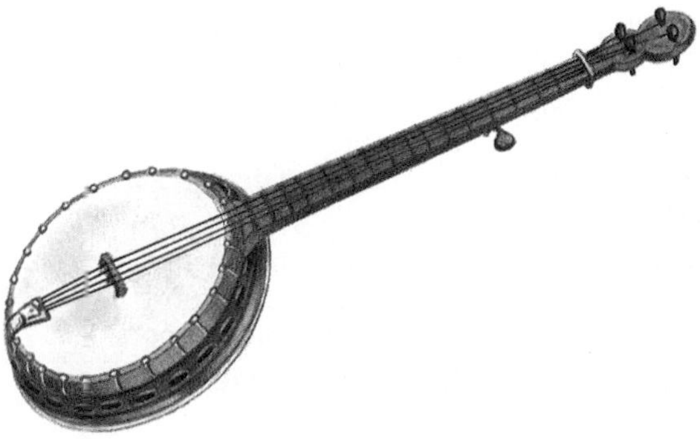

▲ **banjo**

bank¹ *noun* **1.** The sloping ground along the edge of a river or lake: *The stream overflowed its banks.* **2.** A mound, pile, or heap: *Banks of earth surrounded the fort.*
◊ *verb* To form into a bank; pile up: *They banked the snow against the house wall.*
bank¹ (băngk) ◊ *noun, plural* **banks** ◊ *verb* **banked, banking**

bank² *noun* **1.** A container used for saving coins and other money. **2.** A place of business

where money is kept and loans are made. **3.** A place for storing supplies of something: *This hospital has a blood bank.*
◊ *verb* To put or keep in a bank: *I bank most of my earnings.*
◊ *idiom* **bank on** To rely on; count on: *I'm banking on you to get the job done.*
bank² (băngk) ◊ *noun, plural* **banks** ◊ *verb* **banked, banking**

HISTORY • bank¹, bank²

Bank¹ and **bank²** go back to the same Germanic word. This word meant both "a mound of earth," as in **bank¹**, and also "a bench or table." From this second meaning came a special sense of "a table on which money was exchanged." This meaning passed into Italian, then French, and then into English as **bank²**.

banker *noun* A person who owns or works in a bank.
bank·er (**băng′** kər) ◊ *noun, plural* **bankers**

banking *noun* The occupation or business of running a bank.
bank·ing (**băng′** kĭng) ◊ *noun*

bankrupt *adjective* **1.** Legally declared unable to pay personal or company debts. **2.** Completely without money.
◊ *verb* To make bankrupt.
bank·rupt (**băngk′** rŭpt′) ◊ *adjective* ◊ *verb* **bankrupted, bankrupting**

banner *noun* A flag or similar piece of material with words or a special design on it.
ban·ner (**băn′** ər) ◊ *noun, plural* **banners**

banquet *noun* A large, formal meal for many people.
ban·quet (**băng′** kwĭt) ◊ *noun, plural* **banquets**

banter *verb* To tease or joke in a playful, good-humored way: *The rival team members bantered before the game.*
ban·ter (**băn′** tər) ◊ *verb* **bantered, bantering**

ă	pat	ĭ	pit	oi	**oi**l	th	ba**th**
ā	pay	ī	ride	o͝o	book	*th*	ba*th*e
â	care	î	fierce	o͞o	boot	ə	ago, item
ä	father	ŏ	pot	ou	**ou**t		pencil
ĕ	pet	ō	go	ŭ	cut		atom
ē	be	ô	paw, for	û	fur		circus

baptism *noun* A religious ceremony in which a person is sprinkled with or dipped in water as a sign of having sins washed away. Through baptism, a person is admitted to membership in a Christian church.
bap·tism (**băp′** tĭz′əm) ◊ *noun, plural* **baptisms**

baptize *verb* **1.** To sprinkle with or dip into water in the ceremony of baptism. **2.** To give a name to a person at baptism.
bap·tize (băp **tīz′** *or* **băp′** tīz′) ◊ *verb* **baptized, baptizing**

bar *noun* **1.** A narrow, straight piece of metal or other rigid material. Bars are often used to close an opening. **2.** A solid, rectangular piece of a substance: *Soap comes in bars.* **3.** A stripe, band, or similar narrow marking. **4.** Something that stands in the way or blocks progress; obstacle. **5.** A place with a counter at which alcoholic drinks and sometimes food are served. **6.** The occupation of a lawyer. **7.** One of the upright lines drawn across a musical staff to divide it into equal units of time. **8.** A unit of music between two such lines; measure.
◊ *verb* **1.** To close or fasten with a bar: *The guard slammed and barred the gate.* **2.** To block; obstruct: *Fallen branches barred the way.* **3.** To keep out; exclude: *Regulations bar hunters from national parks and wildlife sanctuaries.*
bar (bär) ◊ *noun, plural* **bars** ◊ *verb* **barred, barring**

barb *noun* A sharp point that sticks out backward, as on a fishhook.
barb (bärb) ◊ *noun, plural* **barbs**

barbarian *noun* A person who is uncivilized, savage, or brutal.
bar·bar·i·an (bär **bâr′** ē ən) ◊ *noun, plural* **barbarians**

barbecue *noun* **1.** A grill, pit, or fireplace, often outdoors, for cooking food over an open fire or hot coals. **2.** A social gathering at which food is cooked over a barbecue.
◊ *verb* To cook over a barbecue.
bar·be·cue (**bär′** bĭ kyo͞o′) ◊ *noun, plural* **barbecues** ◊ *verb* **barbecued, barbecuing**

barbed wire *noun* Strands of wire with sharp hooks or barbs at regular intervals, used in fences.
barbed wire (bärbd) ◊ *noun*

barber *noun* A person whose work is cutting hair and shaving or trimming beards.
bar·ber (bär′bər) ◊ *noun, plural* **barbers**

bare *adjective* **1.** Without clothing or covering; naked: *The sand tickled my bare feet.* **2.** Without the usual furnishings or supplies; empty: *The cupboard had bare shelves.* **3.** Without additions or decorations; plain: *Just tell me the bare facts.* **4.** With nothing left over; mere: *The candidate won the close election with a bare majority.*
◊ *verb* To open up to view; uncover.
bare (bâr) ◊ *adjective* **barer, barest** ◊ *verb* **bared, baring**
‖*These sound alike:* **bare, bear**

bareback *adverb & adjective* On the back of a horse without a saddle: *Can you ride the pony bareback?*
bare·back (bâr′băk′) ◊ *adverb & adjective*

▲ **bareback**

barefoot *adjective & adverb* Without shoes or other covering on the feet: *A barefoot kid was playing in the grass. Let's run barefoot.*
bare·foot (bâr′fo͝ot′) ◊ *adjective & adverb*

barely *adverb* Almost not; hardly; just: *We could barely see the shore in the dark.*
bare·ly (bâr′lē) ◊ *adverb*

bargain *noun* **1.** An agreement between two sides, often involving payment or a trade; deal: *We made a bargain that they would cook dinner if we did the dishes.* **2.** Something offered or bought at a low price: *At five dollars this shirt is a bargain.*
◊ *verb* To discuss the terms of an agreement or a price to be paid.
bar·gain (bär′gĭn) ◊ *noun, plural* **bargains** ◊ *verb* **bargained, bargaining**

barge *noun* A large boat with a flat bottom, used to carry freight on rivers and canals.
barge (bärj) ◊ *noun, plural* **barges**

▲ **barge**

baritone *noun* **1.** A man's singing voice that is higher than a bass. **2.** A singer having such a voice.
bar·i·tone (băr′ĭ tōn′) ◊ *noun, plural* **baritones**

bark¹ *noun* The short, gruff sound made by a dog and certain other animals.
◊ *verb* **1.** To make the sound of a bark. **2.** To speak sharply; shout: *The sergeant barked orders to the marching troops.*
bark¹ (bärk) ◊ *noun, plural* **barks** ◊ *verb* **barked, barking**

bark² *noun* The protective outer covering of the trunks, branches, and roots of trees.
bark² (bärk) ◊ *noun, plural* **barks**

***HISTORY* • bark¹, bark²**

Bark¹ comes from an old English word that was made up to imitate the sound a dog makes. **Bark²** was borrowed from an old Scandinavian word that meant "the outer covering of a tree."

barley *noun* A grass whose seeds are a kind of grain. Barley is used as food and for making beer and whiskey.
bar·ley (bär′lē) ◊ *noun*

barn *noun* A large farm building used for storing grain and hay and for sheltering cattle and other livestock.
barn (bärn) ◊ *noun, plural* **barns**

barnacle *noun* A small, hard-shelled sea animal that attaches itself to the bottoms of ships and to underwater rocks.
bar·na·cle (**bär′** nə kəl) ◊ *noun, plural* **barnacles**

▲ **barnacle**

barnyard *noun* The usually fenced area of ground around a barn.
barn·yard (**bärn′** yärd′) ◊ *noun, plural* **barnyards**

barometer *noun* An instrument that measures the pressure of the atmosphere. The data recorded by a barometer is used to forecast the weather.
ba·rom·e·ter (bə **rŏm′** ĭ tər) ◊ *noun, plural* **barometers**

baron *noun* A nobleman of the lowest rank.
bar·on (**băr′** ən) ◊ *noun, plural* **barons**
‖*These sound alike:* **baron, barren**

barracks *noun* (*used with a singular or plural verb*) A building or group of buildings used to house troops or workers.
bar·racks (**băr′** əks) ◊ *noun*

barrel *noun* **1.** A large container with bulging sides and round, flat ends. Barrels are usually made of narrow strips of wood held together by hoops. **2.** The long tube of a gun, through which the bullet travels. **3.** A large quantity: *We had a barrel of fun.*
bar·rel (**băr′** əl) ◊ *noun, plural* **barrels**

barren *adjective* Not able to produce growing plants or crops.
bar·ren (**băr′** ən) ◊ *adjective*
‖*These sound alike:* **barren, baron**

barrette *noun* A small clasp used to hold the hair in place.
bar·rette (bə **rĕt′**) ◊ *noun, plural* **barrettes**

barricade *noun* A quickly built structure set up to block passage or keep back attackers. ◊ *verb* To close off with a barricade.
bar·ri·cade (**băr′** ĭ kād′) ◊ *noun, plural* **barricades** ◊ *verb* **barricaded, barricading**

barrier *noun* Something that blocks movement or passage: *Cows crossing the road are a barrier to traffic.*
bar·ri·er (**băr′** ē ər) ◊ *noun, plural* **barriers**

barter *verb* To trade one thing for another without using money: *The farmer bartered the corn for eggs.*
◊ *noun* The act of bartering.
bar·ter (**bär′** tər) ◊ *verb* **bartered, bartering** ◊ *noun*

base¹ *noun* **1.** The lowest part; bottom: *We camped at the base of the cliff.* **2.** A part on which something rests or is placed for support: *The house was built on a base of solid rock.* **3.** The main part of something: *This paint has an oil base.* **4.** A starting point or central place: *The explorers set up a base at the foot of the mountain.* **5.** One of the four corners of a baseball diamond that a runner must touch to score a run. **6.** A chemical substance that combines with an acid to form a salt. A base turns red litmus paper blue.
◊ *verb* To use as a base for; support: *Base your answers on the facts.*
base¹ (bās) ◊ *noun, plural* **bases** ◊ *verb* **based, basing**
‖*These sound alike:* **base, bass²**

base² *adjective* **1.** Not honorable; mean or shameful: *Lying and cheating are base acts.* **2.** Not of great value: *Iron is a base metal.*
base² (bās) ◊ *adjective* **baser, basest**
‖*These sound alike:* **base, bass²**

ă	pat	ĭ	pit	oi	oil	th	bath
ā	pay	ī	ride	o͝o	book	*th*	bathe
â	care	î	fierce	o͞o	boot	ə	ago, item
ä	father	ŏ	pot	ou	out		pencil
ĕ	pet	ō	go	ŭ	cut		atom
ē	be	ô	paw, for	û	fur		circus

***HISTORY* • base¹, base²**

Base¹ comes from an ancient Greek word meaning "a platform." **Base²** comes from a Latin word meaning "low." The two words are not related.

baseball *noun* **1.** A game played with a bat and ball by two teams of nine players each. Baseball is played on a field with four bases laid out in a diamond pattern. A run is scored when a player is able to touch all the bases while his or her team is at bat. **2.** The ball used in this game.
base·ball (bās′bôl′) ◊ *noun, plural* **baseballs**

▲ **baseball**

basement *noun* The lowest floor of a building, usually below ground level.
base·ment (bās′mənt) ◊ *noun, plural* **basements**

bases *noun* Plural of **basis.**
ba·ses (bā′sēz′) ◊ *noun*

base word *noun* A word to which a prefix, suffix, or ending can be added. The base word of *shortness* is *short.*
base word ◊ *noun, plural* **base words**

bashful *adjective* Timid and uncomfortable with other people. —See Synonyms at **shy.**
bash·ful (băsh′fəl) ◊ *adjective*

basic *adjective* Forming the base or main part of something: *The ability to read is basic to an education.*
ba·sic (bā′sĭk) ◊ *adjective*

BASIC *noun* A simple computer programming language that is widely used, especially with personal computers.
BA·SIC (bā′sĭk) ◊ *noun*

basin *noun* **1.** A round, shallow bowl often used for holding water to wash in. **2.** A shallow area filled with water. **3.** The land that is drained by a river and all the streams that flow into it.
ba·sin (bā′sən) ◊ *noun, plural* **basins**

basis *noun* Something that serves as the base or main support of anything; foundation: *Working hard is the basis for success.*
ba·sis (bā′sĭs) ◊ *noun, plural* **bases**

bask *verb* To rest in a pleasant warmth: *Turtles like to bask on logs in the sun.*
bask (băsk) ◊ *verb* **basked, basking**

basket *noun* **1.** A container made of woven grasses, fibers, or strips of wood. **2.** A metal hoop with a net hanging from it that is used in basketball.
bas·ket (băs′kĭt) ◊ *noun, plural* **baskets**

basketball *noun* **1.** A game played by two teams of five players each on a court with a raised basket at each end. Players score by throwing the ball through the basket defended by the other team. **2.** The large, round ball used in this game.
bas·ket·ball (băs′kĭt bôl′) ◊ *noun, plural* **basketballs**

bass¹ *noun* Any of several freshwater or saltwater fishes caught for food or sport.
bass¹ (băs) ◊ *noun, plural* **bass** *or* **basses**

bass² *noun* **1.** The lowest range of musical tones. **2.** The lowest singing voice of a man. **3.** A singer having such a voice.
bass² (bās) ◊ *noun, plural* **basses**
‖*These sound alike:* **bass², base**

***HISTORY* • bass¹, bass²**

Bass¹ comes from an old English word meaning "a fish with a spiny back." **Bass²**, like **base²**, comes from a Latin word that meant "low." **Bass¹** and **bass²** are spelled the same, but are pronounced differently.

bassoon *noun* A musical instrument having a long wooden body connected to the mouthpiece by a curved metal tube.
bas·soon (bə so͞on′) ◊ *noun, plural* **bassoons**

baste¹ *verb* To sew loosely with large stitches so as to hold together until the final sewing is done.
baste¹ (bāst) ◊ *verb* **basted, basting**

baste² *verb* To moisten food with melted fat or other liquid while cooking.
baste² (bāst) ◊ *verb* **basted, basting**

HISTORY • baste[1], baste[2]

Baste[1] comes from an old French word meaning "fiber," and thus "to sew with fiber." The origin of **baste[2]** is unknown.

bat[1] *noun* A strong wooden stick or club used for hitting a ball, as in baseball.
◊ *verb* To hit with or as if with a bat: *The cat batted the ball of yarn back and forth.*
◊ *idiom* **at bat** Having a turn as a hitter in baseball: *Our team is at bat first.*
bat[1] (băt) ◊ *noun, plural* **bats** ◊ *verb* **batted, batting**

▲ **bat[2]**

bat[2] *noun* A small, furry animal with a body like a mouse and thin, leathery wings. Bats are active at night and are the only mammals that can fly.
bat[2] (băt) ◊ *noun, plural* **bats**

HISTORY • bat[1], bat[2]

Bat[1] comes from an old English word meaning "a wooden club." Now it usually refers to the club used in baseball. **Bat[2]** comes from an old Scandinavian word that meant "to flap or flutter."

batch *noun* An amount prepared at one time: *We baked a batch of rolls.*
batch (băch) ◊ *noun, plural* **batches**

bath *noun* **1.** The act of washing the body in water. **2.** The water used for a bath: *The bath is too hot.* **3.** A bathroom.
bath (băth) ◊ *noun, plural* **baths**

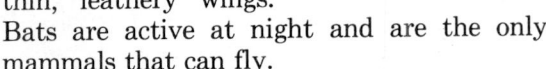

ă	pat	ĭ	pit	oi	oil	th	bath
ā	pay	ī	ride	o͝o	book	*th*	bathe
â	care	î	fierce	o͞o	boot	ə	ago, item
ä	father	ŏ	pot	ou	out		pencil
ĕ	pet	ō	go	ŭ	cut		atom
ē	be	ô	paw, for	û	fur		circus

bathe *verb* **1.** To take a bath: *I bathe every morning.* **2.** To give a bath to: *Will you help me bathe the baby?* **3.** To seem to wash or pour over; flood: *Moonlight bathed the porch.* **4.** To go swimming.
bathe (bā*th*) ◊ *verb* **bathed, bathing**

bathing suit *noun* A piece of clothing worn for swimming.
bathing suit ◊ *noun, plural* **bathing suits**

bathroom *noun* A room containing a toilet and sink and often a bathtub or shower.
bath·room (**băth′**ro͞om′ *or* **băth′**ro͝om′) ◊ *noun, plural* **bathrooms**

bathtub *noun* A tub to bathe in.
bath·tub (**băth′**tŭb′) ◊ *noun, plural* **bathtubs**

baton *noun* **1.** A thin stick used by the leader of an orchestra or band. **2.** A rod twirled by the leader of a marching band.
ba·ton (bə **tŏn′**) ◊ *noun, plural* **batons**

▲ **baton**
An orchestra conductor uses a baton.

battalion *noun* A large body of soldiers organized as a unit. Two or more battalions form a regiment.
bat·tal·ion (bə **tăl′**yən) ◊ *noun, plural* **battalions**

batter[1] *verb* To strike or pound over and over again with heavy blows.
bat·ter[1] (**băt′**ər) ◊ *verb* **battered, battering**

batter[2] *noun* A baseball player who is at bat.
bat·ter[2] (**băt′**ər) ◊ *noun, plural* **batters**

batter[3] *noun* A beaten mixture of flour, eggs, and milk or water that becomes solid when cooked. Batter is used to make pancakes, cakes, and biscuits.
bat·ter[3] (**băt′**ər) ◊ *noun, plural* **batters**

HISTORY • batter[1], batter[2], batter[3]

Batter[1] comes from an old French word meaning "to beat." **Batter[3]** also probably comes from this French word, since a **batter[3]** is something you must beat. **Batter[2]** comes from **bat[1]** plus the ending **-er,** which together mean "someone who bats."

battery *noun* **1.** A set of electric cells that work together to supply electric current. **2.** A small dry cell designed to power a flashlight or other portable electric device. **3.** A group of similar things acting together: *The senator faced a battery of cameras at the hearing.*
bat·ter·y (băt′ə rē) ◊ *noun, plural* **batteries**

battle *noun* **1.** A fight between two armed forces, usually in war. **2.** A hard struggle or contest: *The battle against childhood diseases is endless.*
◊ *verb* To fight in a battle.
bat·tle (băt′l) ◊ *noun, plural* **battles** ◊ *verb* **battled, battling**

battlefield *noun* A place where a battle is fought.
bat·tle·field (băt′l fēld′) ◊ *noun, plural* **battlefields**

battlement *noun* A low, protective wall built along the top edge of a castle or fort. Battlements had openings for soldiers to shoot through.
bat·tle·ment (băt′l mənt) ◊ *noun, plural* **battlements**

battleship *noun* A warship of the largest size and having the heaviest guns and armor.
bat·tle·ship (băt′l shĭp′) ◊ *noun, plural* **battleships**

bawl *verb* To cry or shout loudly: *"Who goes there?" bawled the sentry.*
◊ *idiom* **bawl out** To scold: *I was bawled out for losing the keys to the house.*
bawl (bôl) ◊ *verb* **bawled, bawling**
‖ *These sound alike:* **bawl, ball**

bay[1] *noun* A part of the sea that extends into the land.
bay[1] (bā) ◊ *noun, plural* **bays**

bay[2] *adjective* Reddish brown: *We rode bay horses in the parade.*
bay[2] (bā) ◊ *adjective*

bay[3] *verb* To bark with long, deep cries.
◊ *noun* A long, howling bark.
bay[3] (bā) ◊ *verb* **bayed, baying** ◊ *noun, plural* **bays**

HISTORY • bay[1], bay[2], bay[3]

These three words spelled **bay** all came from French during the Middle Ages. The French words all had different origins. **Bay[1]** goes back to a Spanish word meaning "a gulf." The other two words go back to Latin words. **Bay[2]** is from a word meaning "chestnut brown" and **bay[3]** is from a word meaning "to howl."

bayonet *noun* A knife attached to the muzzle of a rifle for use in close combat.
bay·o·net (bā′ə nĭt) ◊ *noun, plural* **bayonets**

bayou *noun* A creek that moves slowly through a marsh or swamp. Bayous are found in the southern United States.
bay·ou (bī′o͞o) ◊ *noun, plural* **bayous**

bazaar *noun* **1.** A market made up of a street lined with shops and stalls. **2.** A fair or sale, usually to raise money for a charity: *We baked bread for the club's bazaar.*
ba·zaar (bə zär′) ◊ *noun, plural* **bazaars**

▲ **bazaar**

B.C. 1 The abbreviation for *before Christ. B.C.* is used for dates before the birth of Christ: *200 B.C. was 150 years earlier than 50*

B.C. **2.** The abbreviation for *British Columbia,* Canada.

be *verb* **1.** To live; exist: *There once was a poor woodcutter.* **2.** To occupy a certain place or position: *The house is over there.* **3.** To take place: *The concert was last night.* **4.** To equal in identity or meaning: *A grade of A is excellent.* **5.** To belong to a specified class or group: *Lizards are reptiles.* **6.** To have or show a specified quality or characteristic: *We are always glad to see them.*
◊ *auxiliary verb* Used with other verbs: *When were you promoted? I was eating lunch when the phone rang.*
be (bē) ◊ *verb*
‖*These sound alike:* **be, bee**

INFLECTED FORMS OF THE VERB be

	First Person	Second Person	Third Person
Present Tense			
singular	**am**	**are**	**is**
plural	**are**	**are**	**are**
Present Participle			
	being	**being**	**being**
Past Tense			
singular	**was**	**were**	**was**
plural	**were**	**were**	**were**
Past Participle			
	been	**been**	**been**

beach *noun* The sandy or pebbly shore of the sea or a lake.
◊ *verb* To haul or drive onto the shore.
beach (bēch) ◊ *noun, plural* **beaches** ◊ *verb* **beached, beaching**
‖*These sound alike:* **beach, beech**

beacon *noun* **1.** A light or fire used as a warning or guide. **2.** A radio transmitter that sends out signals to warn or guide ships and airplanes.
bea·con (bē′kən) ◊ *noun, plural* **beacons**

ă	pat	ĭ	pit	oi	**oil**	th	**bath**
ā	pay	ī	ride	o͝o	**book**	*th*	**bathe**
â	care	î	fierce	o͞o	**boot**	ə	**ago, item**
ä	father	ŏ	pot	ou	**out**		**pencil**
ĕ	pet	ō	**go**	ŭ	**cut**		**atom**
ē	be	ô	paw, for	û	**fur**		**circus**

▲ **beacon**
A lighthouse beacon

bead *noun* **1.** A small, usually round piece of glass, plastic, wood, or other material, having a hole through which string can be drawn. **2.** Any small, round object, as a drop of moisture: *There were beads of sweat on the runner's forehead.*
◊ *verb* To decorate with beads.
bead (bēd) ◊ *noun, plural* **beads** ◊ *verb* **beaded, beading**

beagle *noun* A small hound with a smooth coat, short legs, and drooping ears.
bea·gle (bē′gəl) ◊ *noun, plural* **beagles**

beak *noun* **1.** The hard, projecting mouth parts of a bird; bill. **2.** Something that looks like a bird's beak.
beak (bēk) ◊ *noun, plural* **beaks**

beaker *noun* A container with straight sides and a lip for pouring, used in laboratories.
beak·er (bē′kər) ◊ *noun, plural* **beakers**

beam *noun* **1.** A long, sturdy piece of wood or metal used in building as a horizontal support for floors or ceilings. **2.** A ray of light, as from a flashlight or the sun.
◊ *verb* **1.** To send out rays of light; shine. **2.** To smile broadly.
beam (bēm) ◊ *noun, plural* **beams** ◊ *verb* **beamed, beaming**

bean *noun* **1.** An oval, often flat seed that is used for food. There are many kinds of beans, such as kidney beans and lima beans. **2.** The long, narrow pod in which these seeds grow. Some kinds of bean pods are eaten as a vegetable. **3.** A seed or pod similar to a bean, such as a coffee bean.
bean (bēn) ◊ *noun, plural* **beans**

B

bear¹ *verb* **1.** To hold up; support: *That broken chair will not bear your weight. The president must bear the burden of leadership.* **2.** To move while supporting: *These ships bear cargo from many lands.* —See Synonyms at **carry.** **3.** To have as a visible characteristic; show: *The twins bear little resemblance to each other.* **4.** To put up with; endure: *They bore their hardships with courage.* **5.** To give birth to: *She has borne three children.* **6.** To come into being: *I was born July 4, 1975.* **7.** To bring forth; yield: *Our apple trees will bear well this year.*
bear¹ (bâr) ◊ *verb* **bore, borne** *or* **born** (for sense 6), **bearing**
‖*These sound alike:* **bear, bare**

bear² *noun* A large animal with a shaggy coat, a very short tail, and a flat-footed walk, feeding mainly on fruit and insects.
bear² (bâr) ◊ *noun, plural* **bears**
‖*These sound alike:* **bear, bare**

***HISTORY* • bear¹, bear²**

Bear¹ comes from an old English word that meant both "to carry" and "to have a child." **Bear²** comes from the old English name for this animal.

beard *noun* **1.** The hair on the chin and cheeks of a man. **2.** A hairlike growth, as on an ear of grain.
beard (bîrd) ◊ *noun, plural* **beards**

▲ **beard**

bearing *noun* **1.** The way a person looks, acts, and moves: *The new judge has a dignified bearing.* **2.** Relationship in thought or meaning: *Your question has no bearing on the subject.* **3.** A part of a machine that supports a moving part and allows it to turn with little friction. **4. bearings** Awareness of one's position or situation: *The hikers lost their bearings in the dark.*
bear·ing (bâr′ĭng) ◊ *noun, plural* **bearings**

beast *noun* **1.** An animal other than a human being, especially a large, four-footed animal. **2.** A cruel or savage person.
beast (bēst) ◊ *noun, plural* **beasts**

beat *verb* **1.** To strike again and again. **2.** To mark or count in strokes: *Let's beat time to the music.* **3.** To throb; pulsate: *My heart beat wildly.* **4.** To move up and down; flap: *Hummingbirds beat their wings fast.* **5.** To stir rapidly so as to mix: *Beat the egg whites.* **6.** To win against: *We beat their team.* —See Synonyms at **defeat.** **7.** To be superior to: *We beat the old record.*
◊ *noun* **1.** A sound, stroke, or blow made again and again. **2.** A pulse, as of the heart. **3.** A basic unit of time that makes up meter in music: *There are four beats in this measure.* **4.** A regular route: *The officers know everyone on their beat.*
beat (bēt) ◊ *verb* **beat, beaten** *or* **beat, beating** ◊ *noun, plural* **beats**
‖*These sound alike:* **beat, beet**

beaten *verb* A past participle of **beat.**
beat·en (bēt′n) ◊ *verb*

beautiful *adjective* Being very pleasing to the senses or the mind: *Beautiful music filled the air. The redwood trees are beautiful.*
beau·ti·ful (byo͞o′tə fəl) ◊ *adjective*

SYNONYMS

beautiful, lovely, pretty

There was a *beautiful* sunset yesterday. Your letter to me contains many *lovely* thoughts. The baby has a *pretty* little face. **Antonyms:** *homely, ugly*

beautify *verb* To make beautiful.
beau·ti·fy (byo͞o′tə fī′) ◊ *verb* **beautified, beautifying**

beauty *noun* **1.** A quality that pleases the senses or the mind: *We were charmed by the beauty of the singer's voice. There is great beauty in the poetry.* **2.** A person or thing that is beautiful: *We appreciate the beauties of the countryside.*
beau·ty (byo͞o′tē) ◊ *noun, plural* **beauties**

beaver *noun* An animal related to the rat and squirrel, having thick brown fur, a broad, flat tail, and webbed hind feet for swimming. Beavers live in and near lakes and streams

and gnaw down trees to build dams and houses in the water.
bea·ver (bē′ vər) ◊ *noun, plural* **beavers**

▲ **beaver**

became *verb* Past tense of **become.**
be·came (bĭ **kām′**) ◊ *verb*

because *conjunction* For the reason that: *I left because I was sick.*
be·cause (bĭ **kôz′**) ◊ *conjunction*

because of *preposition* On account of: *I stayed home because of illness.*

beckon *verb* To signal with a movement of the head or hand: *I beckoned them to enter the shop.*
beck·on (**bĕk′** ən) ◊ *verb* **beckoned, beckoning**

become *verb* **1.** To grow or come to be: *The children became restless.* **2.** To be suitable or appropriate to: *Such bad behavior does not become you. The new suit becomes you.*
◊ *idiom* **become of** To happen to: *What became of your blue shirt?*
be·come (bĭ **kŭm′**) ◊ *verb* **became, become, becoming**

bed *noun* **1.** A piece of furniture for resting and sleeping. **2.** A small piece of ground for growing things: *We planted a bed of roses.* **3.** The ground under a body of water: *The creek bed is muddy.* **4.** A base; foundation: *The brick path sits on a bed of sand.*
◊ *verb* To provide with a place to sleep.
bed (bĕd) ◊ *noun, plural* **beds** ◊ *verb* **bedded, bedding**

ă	pat	ĭ	pit	oi	**oil**	th	ba**th**
ā	pay	ī	ride	o͝o	book	*th*	ba**th**e
â	care	î	fierce	o͞o	boot	ə	ago, item
ä	father	ŏ	pot	ou	**out**		pencil
ĕ	pet	ō	go	ŭ	cut		atom
ē	be	ô	paw, for	û	fur		circus

bedbug *noun* A small, wingless, biting insect that has a flat reddish body and is sometimes found in bedding.
bed·bug (**bĕd′** bŭg′) ◊ *noun, plural* **bedbugs**

bedclothes *plural noun* Coverings on a bed.
bed·clothes (**bĕd′** klōz′) ◊ *plural noun*

bedding *noun* **1.** Bedclothes. **2.** Straw or hay for animals to sleep on.
bed·ding (**bĕd′** ĭng) ◊ *noun*

bedlam *noun* Confusion or uproar: *There was bedlam in the store during the sale.*
bed·lam (**bĕd′** ləm) ◊ *noun*

bedraggled *adjective* Limp and soiled, as if having been dragged through the mud.
be·drag·gled (bĭ **drăg′** əld) ◊ *adjective*

bedrock *noun* The solid rock that is beneath the soil and other material on the surface of the earth.
bed·rock (**bĕd′** rŏk′) ◊ *noun*

bedroom *noun* A room to sleep in.
bed·room (**bĕd′** ro͞om′ *or* **bĕd′** ro͝om′) ◊ *noun, plural* **bedrooms**

bedside *noun* The space beside a bed.
bed·side (**bĕd′** sīd′) ◊ *noun*

bedspread *noun* A top cover for a bed.
bed·spread (**bĕd′** sprĕd′) ◊ *noun, plural* **bedspreads**

bedstead *noun* The frame supporting the springs and mattress of a bed.
bed·stead (**bĕd′** stĕd′) ◊ *noun, plural* **bedsteads**

bee *noun* **1.** An insect that is related to the wasp and ant and has four wings, a hairy body, and usually a stinger. Bees gather nectar from flowers for food. **2.** A gathering for competition or work: *We won the spelling bee at our school.*
bee (bē) ◊ *noun, plural* **bees**
‖*These sound alike:* **bee, be**

beebread *noun* A brownish substance made by bees from pollen and nectar and fed to their young.
bee·bread (**bē′** brĕd′) ◊ *noun*

beech *noun* A tree with smooth, light-gray bark, strong wood, and edible nuts.
beech (bēch) ◊ *noun, plural* **beeches**
‖*These sound alike:* **beech, beach**

▲ beech

beef *noun* The meat of a steer, bull, or cow.
beef (bēf) ◊ *noun*

beehive *noun* **1.** A shelter for a swarm of bees. **2.** A very busy place.
bee·hive (bē′hīv′) ◊ *noun, plural* **beehives**

beeline *noun* The fastest, most direct course.
bee·line (bē′līn′) ◊ *noun, plural* **beelines**

been *verb* Past participle of **be.**
been (bĭn) ◊ *verb*
‖*These sound alike:* **been, bin**

beer *noun* An alcoholic drink made from malt and hops.
beer (bîr) ◊ *noun, plural* **beers**

beeswax *noun* The wax made by honeybees for building their honeycombs. Beeswax is used to make candles and crayons.
bees·wax (bēz′wăks′) ◊ *noun*

beet *noun* A leafy plant with a thick, round, dark-red root eaten as a vegetable.
beet (bēt) ◊ *noun, plural* **beets**
‖*These sound alike:* **beet, beat**

beetle *noun* An insect with hard, glossy front wings that cover the hind wings when at rest. Some beetles are harmful to plants.
bee·tle (bēt′l) ◊ *noun, plural* **beetles**

***HISTORY* • beetle**

Beetle is a native English word and is related to the word **bite.** Beetles have mouth parts designed for biting.

before *adverb* **1.** In the past: *I've heard that before.* **2.** In front: *Go on before; I'll follow.* **3.** Earlier: *Class ends at noon, not before.* ◊*preposition* **1.** Ahead of; earlier than: *The dog got home before me.* **2.** In front of: *Please eat what's set before you.* **3.** In the presence of: *They were brought before the judge.* ◊ *conjunction* **1.** In advance of the time when: *We left before the concert began.* **2.** Sooner than: *I'd fail before I'd cheat.*
be·fore (bĭ fôr′) ◊ *adverb* ◊*preposition* ◊ *conjunction*

beforehand *adverb* Ahead of time.
be·fore·hand (bĭ fôr′hănd′) ◊ *adverb*

befriend *verb* To act as a friend to.
be·friend (bĭ frĕnd′) ◊ *verb* **befriended, befriending**

beg *verb* **1.** To ask earnestly as a favor. **2.** To ask humbly for charity.
beg (bĕg) ◊ *verb* **begged, begging**

began *verb* Past tense of **begin.**
be·gan (bĭ găn′) ◊ *verb*

beggar *noun* A person who begs for a living.
beg·gar (bĕg′ər) ◊ *noun, plural* **beggars**

begin *verb* **1.** To start to do: *I began taking piano lessons last year.* **2.** To come into being. **3.** To have as a starting point: *Proper nouns begin with capital letters.*
be·gin (bĭ gĭn′) ◊ *verb* **began, begun, beginning**

SYNONYMS

begin, commence, embark, start

In a week the seeds should *begin* to sprout. The graduation festivities *commenced* at noon. They *embarked* on careers as firefighters. *Start* at dawn if you want to reach town by noon.
Antonyms: *close, end, finish*

beginner *noun* A person who is just starting to learn or to do something.
be·gin·ner (bĭ gĭn′ər) ◊ *noun, plural* **beginners**

beginning *noun* **1.** The act or process of bringing or being brought into existence; a start. **2.** The time at which something begins. **3.** The first or earliest part.
be·gin·ning (bĭ gĭn′ĭng) ◊ *noun, plural* **beginnings**

begun *verb* Past participle of **begin.**
be·gun (bĭ gŭn′) ◊ *verb*

behalf *noun* Interest or benefit: *The oldest student spoke on behalf of all the others.*
be·half (bĭ hăf′) ◊ *noun*

behave *verb* **1.** To function in a certain way: *The car behaves well on ice.* **2.** To conduct oneself in a given way: *You behaved badly.*
be·have (bĭ hāv′) ◊ *verb* **behaved, behaving**

behavior *noun* **1.** The way in which a person behaves. **2.** The way in which something acts or reacts under given circumstances: *Scientists study the behavior of mice.*
be·hav·ior (bĭ hāv′yər) ◊ *noun, plural* **behaviors**

behead *verb* To cut off the head of.
be·head (bĭ hĕd′) ◊ *verb* **beheaded, beheading**

beheld *verb* Past tense and past participle of **behold.**
be·held (bĭ hĕld′) ◊ *verb*

behind *preposition* **1.** To or at the back of: *The orchard is behind the barn.* **2.** Later than: *The bus is behind schedule.* **3.** At a lower level than: *I am behind the others in math.* **4.** In support of: *The voters are behind the senator.*
◊ *adverb* **1.** In, to, or toward the back: *A gate led into the yard behind.* **2.** In the place or situation being left: *My friends stayed behind.* **3.** In or to a lower level: *You're falling behind in your homework.*
be·hind (bĭ hīnd′) ◊ *preposition* ◊ *adverb*

behold *verb* To look at; see.
be·hold (bĭ hōld′) ◊ *verb* **beheld, beholding**

beige *noun* A light yellowish brown.
beige (bāzh) ◊ *noun*

being *noun* **1.** The state or fact of existing. **2.** Someone or something that exists.
be·ing (bē′ĭng) ◊ *noun, plural* **beings**

belated *adjective* Being, coming, or happening late; delayed.
be·lat·ed (bĭ lā′tĭd) ◊ *adjective*

ă	pat	ĭ	pit	oi	oil	th	bath
ā	pay	ī	ride	ŏŏ	book	*th*	bathe
â	care	î	fierce	ōō	boot	ə	ago, item
ä	father	ŏ	pot	ou	out		pencil
ĕ	pet	ō	go	ŭ	cut		atom
ē	be	ô	paw, for	û	fur		circus

belfry *noun* A tower or a room in a tower in which a bell or bells are hung.
bel·fry (bĕl′frē) ◊ *noun, plural* **belfries**

belief *noun* **1.** Confidence; trust: *We have a strong belief in justice for all.* **2.** Something accepted as true.
be·lief (bĭ lēf′) ◊ *noun, plural* **beliefs**

believe *verb* **1.** To accept as true or real. **2.** To have faith or confidence: *I believe in a proper diet.* **3.** To accept the truthfulness of: *I believe you when you say you're sick.* **4.** To think or expect: *I believe it will snow.* —See Synonyms at **suppose.**
be·lieve (bĭ lēv′) ◊ *verb* **believed, believing**

bell *noun* **1.** A hollow, usually cup-shaped metal device that makes a clear musical tone when struck. **2.** The sound of a bell. **3.** Something shaped like a bell.
bell (bĕl) ◊ *noun, plural* **bells**

bellhop *noun* A person employed by a hotel to carry luggage and run errands.
bell·hop (bĕl′hŏp′) ◊ *noun, plural* **bellhops**

▲ **bellhop**

belligerent *adjective* **1.** Eager to fight; warlike. **2.** Engaged in warfare.
bel·lig·er·ent (bə lĭj′ər ənt) ◊ *adjective*

bellow *verb* To give a loud roar, like that made by a bull.
bel·low (bĕl′ō) ◊ *verb* **bellowed, bellowing**

bellows *noun* (*used with a singular or plural verb*) A device that produces a strong blast of

air when its sides are squeezed.
bel·lows (**bĕl′**ōz) ◊ *noun*

belly *noun* **1.** The front part of the human body below the chest. **2.** The stomach. **3.** The underside of an animal's body.
bel·ly (**bĕl′**ē) ◊ *noun, plural* **bellies**

belong *verb* To have a proper place.
◊ *idiom* **belong to 1.** To be the property of: *This watch once belonged to my grandparents.* **2.** To be a member of.
be·long (bĭ **lông′**) ◊ *verb* **belonged, belonging**

belongings *plural noun* A person's possessions.
be·long·ings (bĭ **lông′**ĭngz) ◊ *plural noun*

beloved *adjective* Very much loved; dear.
be·lov·ed (bĭ **lŭv′**ĭd *or* bĭ **lŭvd′**) ◊ *adjective*

below *adverb* In or to a lower place or position: *Look at the valley below.*
◊ *preposition* At or to a lower place, level, or position than: *Your bunk is below mine. It is two degrees below zero.*
be·low (bĭ **lō′**) ◊ *adverb* ◊ *preposition*

belt *noun* **1.** A band of flexible material worn around the waist for decoration or to support clothing, tools, or weapons. **2.** A band forming a closed loop that passes over wheels or pulleys and transfers motion from one to another or carries objects. **3.** A geographic region marked by a specific feature: *Iowa is in the corn belt.*
◊ *verb* **1.** To encircle with or as if with a belt. **2.** To fasten with a belt. **3.** To hit hard.
belt (bĕlt) ◊ *noun, plural* **belts** ◊ *verb* **belted, belting**

bench *noun* **1.** A long seat. **2.** A sturdy table on which work is done. **3.** A judge's office or position.
◊ *verb* To remove a player from a game.
bench (bĕnch) ◊ *noun, plural* **benches** ◊ *verb* **benched, benching**

bend *verb* **1.** To be, make, or become curved or crooked: *I bent my knee. Bend the tube.* **2.** To move from an upright position; stoop: *I bent over to pick up the ball.* **3.** To take or cause to take a direction; turn: *The road bends to the right.*
◊ *noun* Something that is bent: *A boat came around the bend in the river.*
bend (bĕnd) ◊ *verb* **bent, bending** ◊ *noun, plural* **bends**

beneath *preposition* **1.** Underneath: *Clean beneath the table.* **2.** Not worthy of: *This job is beneath me.*
◊ *adverb* In a lower position.
be·neath (bĭ **nēth′**) ◊ *preposition* ◊ *adverb*

benediction *noun* A blessing recited by a member of the clergy at the end of a religious service.
ben·e·dic·tion (bĕn′ĭ **dĭk′**shən) ◊ *noun, plural* **benedictions**

beneficial *adjective* Helpful; favorable: *Rain is beneficial to our crops.*
ben·e·fi·cial (bĕn′ə **fĭsh′**əl) ◊ *adjective*

benefit *noun* Something that is of help: *Eating properly is to your own benefit.*
◊ *verb* **1.** To be helpful or useful to. **2.** To receive help or useful service: *I benefited from studying hard.*
ben·e·fit (**bĕn′**ə fĭt) ◊ *noun, plural* **benefits** ◊ *verb* **benefited, benefiting**

benevolent *adjective* Inclined to do good.
be·nev·o·lent (bə **nĕv′**ə lənt) ◊ *adjective*

bent *verb* Past tense and past participle of **bend.**
bent (bĕnt) ◊ *verb*

beret *noun* A soft, round, flat cap.
be·ret (bə **rā′**) ◊ *noun, plural* **berets**

berry *noun* **1.** A usually small, juicy fruit that has many seeds. **2.** A seed or dried kernel, as of wheat.
ber·ry (**bĕr′**ē) ◊ *noun, plural* **berries**
‖ *These sound alike:* **berry, bury**

berth *noun* **1.** A bunk, as on a ship. **2.** Docking space at a wharf.
berth (bûrth) ◊ *noun, plural* **berths**
‖ *These sound alike:* **berth, birth**

beset *verb* To surround and attack from all sides: *I am beset with problems.*
be·set (bĭ **sĕt′**) ◊ *verb* **beset, besetting**

beside *preposition* **1.** At the side of: *Sit beside me.* **2.** Compared with: *You are short beside your parents.* **3.** Apart from: *That is beside the point.*
be·side (bĭ **sīd′**) ◊ *preposition*

besides *adverb* In addition: *We have fish, eggs, and milk besides.*
◊ *preposition* **1.** In addition to: *Besides swimming, we enjoy archery.* **2.** Other than: *There's nothing to eat besides bread.*
be·sides (bĭ **sīdz′**) ◊ *adverb* ◊ *preposition*

besiege *verb* **1.** To surround with troops in order to capture. **2.** To crowd around and hem in: *Enthusiastic fans besieged the famous movie star.*
be·siege (bĭ **sēj′**) ◊ *verb* **besieged, besieging**

best *verb* To get the better of: *We bested the other team easily.*
◊ *noun* **1.** Someone or something that is best: *Unhappiness can come to the best of us.* **2.** One's greatest effort: *Give the science examination your best.*
◊ *adjective* Superlative of **good.**
◊ *adverb* Superlative of **well.**
best (bĕst) ◊ *verb* **bested, besting** ◊ *noun* ◊ *adjective* ◊ *adverb*

bet *noun* **1.** An agreement between two persons taking opposite sides, as in a contest, that the person who is right will collect something from the person who is wrong. **2.** Something risked in a bet.
◊ *verb* **1.** To make or risk in a bet. **2.** To say with confidence: *I bet you don't know the answer to that problem.*
bet (bĕt) ◊ *noun, plural* **bets** ◊ *verb* **bet, betting**

betray *verb* **1.** To help an enemy of: *The traitors betrayed their country.* **2.** To be disloyal to: *My friend betrayed me.*
be·tray (bĭ **trā′**) ◊ *verb* **betrayed, betraying**

better *verb* **1.** To do in a more excellent way than; surpass: *That athlete has bettered your record.* **2.** To improve: *You can better your life by studying medicine.*
◊ *noun* Someone or something that is more excellent or higher in quality than another.
◊ *adjective* Comparative of **good.**
◊ *adverb* Comparative of **well.**
bet·ter (**bĕt′** ər) ◊ *verb* **bettered, bettering** ◊ *noun, plural* **betters** ◊ *adjective* ◊ *adverb*

between *preposition* **1.** In the position separating: *A few trees stand between the house and the road.* **2.** By the combined efforts of: *Between us we moved the desk.* **3.** By comparing: *Choose between good and evil.* **4.** Shared by both of: *There was a debate between the two students.*
◊ *adverb* In a space, position, or time between others.
be·tween (bĭ **twēn′**) ◊ *preposition* ◊ *adverb*

ă	pat	ĭ	pit	oi	**oi**l	th	ba**th**
ā	pay	ī	ride	ŏŏ	b**oo**k	*th*	ba*th*e
â	care	î	fierce	ōō	b**oo**t	ə	ago, item
ä	father	ŏ	pot	ou	**ou**t		pencil
ĕ	pet	ō	go	ŭ	cut		atom
ē	be	ô	paw, for	û	fur		circus

beverage *noun* A liquid for drinking.
bev·er·age (**bĕv′** ər ĭj) ◊ *noun, plural* **beverages**

beware *verb* To be careful; look out: *Beware of the dog.*
be·ware (bĭ **wâr′**) ◊ *verb*

bewilder *verb* To puzzle greatly.
be·wil·der (bĭ **wĭl′** dər) ◊ *verb* **bewildered, bewildering**

beyond *preposition* **1.** On or to the far side of: *The forest is beyond the lake.* **2.** Past the understanding, reach, or range of: *The situation is beyond help.*
◊ *adverb* On or to the far side: *I looked at the horizon beyond.*
be·yond (bĭ **yŏnd′**) ◊ *preposition* ◊ *adverb*

bias *noun* **1.** A slanted line that crosses the weave of a fabric. **2.** A strong feeling for or against without enough reason; prejudice.
◊ *verb* To cause to have prejudice.
bi·as (**bī′** əs) ◊ *noun, plural* **biases** ◊ *verb* **biased, biasing**

bib *noun* **1.** A napkin tied under a child's chin to keep the front of the clothes clean during meals. **2.** The part of an apron or pair of overalls worn over the chest.
bib (bĭb) ◊ *noun, plural* **bibs**

Bible *noun* **1.** The book of the sacred writings of the Christian religion that includes the Old and New Testaments. **2.** The sacred book of Judaism, consisting of the Old Testament. **3.** A book containing the sacred writings of any religion.
Bi·ble (**bī′** bəl) ◊ *noun*

biblical *adjective* Of, relating to, or taken from the Bible.
bib·li·cal (**bĭb′** lĭ kəl) ◊ *adjective*

bibliography *noun* A list of the works of an author or of writings on a subject.
bib·li·og·ra·phy (bĭb′lē **ŏg′** rə fē) ◊ *noun, plural* **bibliographies**

bicker *verb* To quarrel about something unimportant: *The children bickered over whose turn it was to wash the dishes.*
bick·er (**bĭk′** ər) ◊ *verb* **bickered, bickering**

bicuspid *noun* A tooth with two points. An adult has eight bicuspids.
bi·cus·pid (bī-kŭs′pĭd) ◊ *noun, plural* **bicuspids**

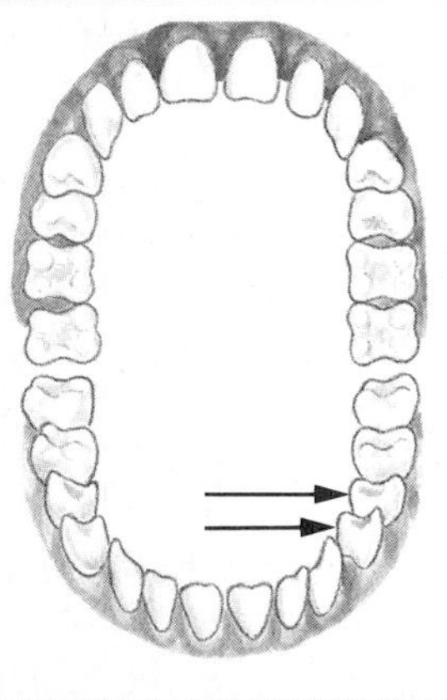

▲ **bicuspid**

bicycle *noun* A vehicle with two wheels mounted one behind the other, a seat for the rider, and pedals.
◊ *verb* To ride a bicycle: *I bicycled home.*
bi·cy·cle (bī′sĭk′əl) ◊ *noun, plural* **bicycles** ◊ *verb* **bicycled, bicycling**

bid *verb* **1.** To order; command: *My parents bade me look in the mirror.* **2.** To say or express to: *We bid them farewell.* **3.** To offer as a price: *I bid a dollar for the old magazine.*
◊ *noun* **1.** An offer to pay or accept a certain amount for something: *We're looking for a higher bid.* **2.** An amount bid.
bid (bĭd) ◊ *verb* **bid** *or* **bade, bidden** *or* **bid, bidding** ◊ *noun, plural* **bids**

bidden *verb* A past participle of **bid.**
bid·den (bĭd′n) ◊ *verb*

bide *verb* To wait: *Bide here for a while.*
bide (bīd) ◊ *verb* **bided, biding**

big *adjective* **1.** Of great size; large. **2.** Of great importance: *Graduation was a big event in my life.*
big (bĭg) ◊ *adjective* **bigger, biggest**

SYNONYMS

big, great, large

A hippopotamus is a really *big* animal. We drove past *great* fields of corn. We own a *large* factory that covers two blocks. **Antonyms:** *little, small*

bike *noun* A bicycle.
◊ *verb* To ride a bicycle.
bike (bīk) ◊ *noun, plural* **bikes** ◊ *verb* **biked, biking**

bile *noun* A bitter, greenish liquid produced by the liver and that helps to digest fats.
bile (bīl) ◊ *noun*

bilingual *adjective* Speaking two languages very well.
bi·lin·gual (bī lĭng′gwəl) ◊ *adjective*

bill¹ *noun* **1.** A statement of the cost of goods sold, work done, or services performed. **2.** A piece of paper money. **3.** A written or printed advertisement. **4.** A draft of a law presented for approval to a legislature.
◊ *verb* **1.** To send a bill to: *The store billed us on the first of the month.* **2.** To advertise: *The play is billed as a comedy.*
bill¹ (bĭl) ◊ *noun, plural* **bills** ◊ *verb* **billed, billing**

bill² *noun* The hard, horny beak of a bird.
bill² (bĭl) ◊ *noun, plural* **bills**

***HISTORY* • bill¹, bill²**

Bill¹ comes from an old French word meaning "a blob of sealing wax," or "a document with a wax seal on it." This word came from a Latin word meaning "bubble." **Bill²** comes from an old English word that, like the modern English word, meant "a bird's beak."

billboard *noun* A large upright board on which advertisements are displayed.
bill·board (bĭl′bôrd′) ◊ *noun, plural* **billboards**

billfold *noun* A wallet.
bill·fold (bĭl′fōld′) ◊ *noun, plural* **billfolds**

billion *noun* The amount of one thousand millions; 1,000,000,000.
◊ *adjective* Being equal to a thousand millions in number.
bil·lion (bĭl′yən) ◊ *noun, plural* **billions** ◊ *adjective*

billow *verb* To rise in a great wave or surge: *Flames and smoke billowed over the prairie.*
bil·low (bĭl′ō) ◊ *verb* **billowed, billowing**

bin *noun* A container for storage: *The coal bin is in the cellar.*
bin (bĭn) ◊ *noun, plural* **bins**
‖*These sound alike:* **bin, been**

binary digit *noun* Either of the numbers 0 or 1, used as the basis for calculations in computers; bit.
bi·na·ry digit (bī′nə rē) ◊ *noun, plural* **binary digits**

bind *verb* **1.** To fasten together by or as if by tying: *A ribbon binds my hair.* **2.** To put a bandage on. **3.** To hold with or as if with bonds; oblige: *We are bound to obey you.*
bind (bīnd) ◊ *verb* **bound, binding**

binoculars *plural noun* A device for making distant objects look closer that consists of two small telescopes joined together.
bin·oc·u·lars (bə **nŏk′**-yə lərz) ◊ *plural noun*

▲ **binoculars**

biodegradable *adjective* Capable of being broken down by natural processes.
bi·o·de·grad·a·ble (bī′ō dĭ **grā′**də bəl) ◊ *adjective*

biographic *or* **biographical** *adjective* Of or relating to biography: *I need a biographic dictionary.*
bi·o·graph·ic (bī′ə **grăf′**ĭk) *or* **bi·o·graph·i·cal** (bī′ə **grăf′**ĭ kəl) ◊ *adjective*

biography *noun* A person's life story.
bi·og·ra·phy (bī **ŏg′**rə fē) ◊ *noun, plural* **biographies**

biology *noun* A science, such as botany or zoology, that deals with living things and life processes.
bi·ol·o·gy (bī **ŏl′**ə jē) ◊ *noun*

biomass *noun* The total amount of living matter found within a certain ecological environment.
bi·o·mass (**bī′**ō măs′) ◊ *noun*

bionic *adjective* Of, having, or made of electronic or mechanical parts that strengthen or replace a part of the body.
bi·on·ic (bī **ŏn′**ĭk) ◊ *adjective*

biplane *noun* An airplane having two sets of wings, one above the other.
bi·plane (**bī′**plān′) ◊ *noun, plural* **biplanes**

ă	pat	ĭ	pit	oi	**oi**l	th	ba**th**
ā	pay	ī	ride	ŏŏ	b**oo**k	*th*	ba**th**e
â	care	î	fierce	ōō	b**oo**t	ə	ago, item
ä	father	ŏ	pot	ou	**ou**t		pencil
ĕ	pet	ō	go	ŭ	c**u**t		atom
ē	be	ô	paw, for	û	f**u**r		circus

birch *noun* A tree that has hard wood and smooth bark that peels off easily.
birch (bûrch) ◊ *noun, plural* **birches**

bird *noun* A warm-blooded animal that lays eggs and that has two wings and a body covered with feathers.
bird (bûrd) ◊ *noun, plural* **birds**

birdseed *noun* Seeds for feeding birds.
bird·seed (**bûrd′**sēd′) ◊ *noun*

birth *noun* **1.** The fact of being born; the act of bearing offspring. **2.** A beginning or origin, as of an idea.
birth (bûrth) ◊ *noun, plural* **births**
‖*These sound alike:* **birth, berth**

birthday *noun* **1.** The day of a person's birth. **2.** A day on which something begins.
birth·day (**bûrth′**dā′) ◊ *noun, plural* **birthdays**

birthmark *noun* A mark on the body that was there at one's birth.
birth·mark (**bûrth′**märk′) ◊ *noun, plural* **birthmarks**

birthplace *noun* A place of birth or origin.
birth·place (**bûrth′**plās′) ◊ *noun, plural* **birthplaces**

birthright *noun* A right to which a person is entitled because of his or her birth.
birth·right (**bûrth′**rīt′) ◊ *noun, plural* **birthrights**

biscuit *noun* A small cake of baked bread dough.
bis·cuit (**bĭs′**kĭt) ◊ *noun, plural* **biscuits**

bisect *verb* To cut into two equal parts.
bi·sect (**bī′**sĕkt′) ◊ *verb* **bisected, bisecting**

bishop *noun* **1.** A high-ranking member of the clergy who is usually in charge of a church district. **2.** A chess piece.
bish·op (**bĭsh′**əp) ◊ *noun, plural* **bishops**

bison *noun* A large animal of western North America that has a shaggy, dark-brown mane and short, curved horns.
bi·son (**bī′**sən) ◊ *noun, plural* **bison**

bit¹ *noun* **1.** A tiny piece: *I ate the last bit of fish.* **2.** A brief amount of time: *Wait a bit.* **3.** A small role, as in a play.
bit¹ (bĭt) ◊ *noun, plural* **bits**

bit² *noun* **1.** A drilling tool. **2.** The metal mouthpiece of a bridle, used to control a horse.
bit² (bĭt) ◊ *noun, plural* **bits**

bit³ *noun* The smallest unit of information that a computer can recognize; binary digit.
bit³ (bĭt) ◊ *noun, plural* **bits**

> ***HISTORY* • bit¹, bit², bit³**
>
> **Bit¹** comes from an old English word meaning "a piece bitten off." **Bit²** comes from a related old English word meaning "a bite." This word then came to mean "a cutting edge" and then "the mouthpiece of a horse's bridle." Both **bit¹** and **bit²** are related to **bite. Bit³** is an abbreviation of **binary digit.**

bit⁴ *verb* Past tense and a past participle of **bite.**
bit⁴ (bĭt) ◊ *verb*

bite *verb* **1.** To grip, cut into, or tear off with or as if with the teeth. **2.** To wound with teeth, fangs, or a stinger. **3.** To cause to sting or smart: *The cold wind bit my face.* **4.** To take or swallow bait: *The trout bit.*
◊ *noun* **1.** A gripping or cutting of something with the teeth. **2.** A wound or injury made by biting or stinging. **3.** An amount of food taken into the mouth at one time. **4.** A light meal or snack: *Let's have a bite of lunch.*
bite (bīt) ◊ *verb* **bit, bitten** *or* **bit, biting**
◊ *noun, plural* **bites**
‖*These sound alike:* **bite, byte**

bitten *verb* A past participle of **bite.**
bit·ten (bĭt′n) ◊ *verb*

bitter *adjective* **1.** Sharp and unpleasant: *The fruit is bitter. We nearly froze in the bitter cold.* **2.** Hard to accept, admit, or bear: *Face the bitter truth.*
bit·ter (bĭt′ər) ◊ *adjective* **bitterer, bitterest**

bituminous coal *noun* A soft coal that burns with a smoky flame.
bi·tu·mi·nous coal (bĭ to͞o′mə nəs) ◊ *noun*

black *noun* **1.** The darkest of all colors; the opposite of white. **2.** A paint or dye of the darkest color. **3.** Often **Black** A member of a dark-skinned people.
◊ *adjective* **1.** Of or nearly of the color black. **2.** Having no light: *It was a black night.* **3.** Often **Black** Of or relating to a dark-skinned race. **4.** Very dirty.
black (blăk) ◊ *noun, plural* **blacks** ◊ *adjective* **blacker, blackest**

blackberry *noun* The blackish juicy berry of a thorny plant related to the raspberry.
black·ber·ry (blăk′bĕr′ē) ◊ *noun, plural* **blackberries**

blackbird *noun* A bird with black or mostly black feathers.
black·bird (blăk′bûrd′) ◊ *noun, plural* **blackbirds**

blackboard *noun* A hard, smooth, dark-colored panel for writing on with chalk.
black·board (blăk′bôrd′) ◊ *noun, plural* **blackboards**

blacken *verb* To make or become black.
black·en (blăk′ən) ◊ *verb* **blackened, blackening**

black hole *noun* A small heavenly body that has a very strong field of gravity and that is thought to be a collapsed star.
black hole ◊ *noun, plural* **black holes**

blackmail *noun* **1.** The demanding of money from a person by threatening to reveal something that might damage his or her reputation. **2.** Money paid as blackmail.
◊ *verb* To threaten with blackmail.
black·mail (blăk′māl′) ◊ *noun* ◊ *verb* **blackmailed, blackmailing**

blackout *noun* The act of putting out all lights at night to protect against enemy aircraft raids during a war.
black·out (blăk′out′) ◊ *noun, plural* **blackouts**

blacksmith *noun* A person who heats iron and hammers it into objects such as horseshoes and tools.
black·smith (blăk′smĭth′) ◊ *noun, plural* **blacksmiths**

▲ **blacksmith**

blacktop *noun* Black road-paving material.
black·top (blăk′tŏp′) ◊ *noun*

bladder *noun* An elastic sac in the body that stores urine from the kidneys.
blad·der (blăd′ər) ◊ *noun, plural* **bladders**

blade *noun* **1.** The flat, sharp-edged part of a cutting instrument, such as a knife, saw, razor, or sword. **2.** A wide, flat part, as of an oar, fan, or propeller. **3.** A thin, narrow leaf of grass. **4.** The broad, flat part of a leaf. **5.** The metal runner of an ice skate.
blade (blād) ◊ *noun, plural* **blades**

blame *verb* **1.** To hold at fault. **2.** To find fault with: *I can't blame the baby for crying.* **3.** To place responsibility for: *Don't blame the mistake on me.*
◊ *noun* Responsibility for a fault.
blame (blām) ◊ *verb* **blamed, blaming** ◊ *noun*

bland *adjective* **1.** Pleasant or smooth in manner. **2.** Not irritating; soothing: *I ate only bland foods in the hospital.*
bland (blănd) ◊ *adjective* **blander, blandest**

blank *adjective* **1.** Free of marks or decoration: *Give me a blank piece of paper.* —See Synonyms at **empty. 2.** Having empty spaces to be filled in: *Fill in this blank form.* **3.** Showing a lack of attention.
◊ *noun* **1.** An empty place or space: *My mind was a complete blank during the test. Fill in the blanks on the paper.* **2.** A paper or form with empty spaces to be filled in. **3.** A cartridge filled with powder but no bullet.
blank (blăngk) ◊ *adjective* **blanker, blankest** ◊ *noun, plural* **blanks**

blanket *noun* **1.** A covering for beds, used to keep a sleeper warm. **2.** A covering or layer: *A blanket of snow is on the ground.*
◊ *verb* To cover with or as if with a blanket.
blan·ket (blăng′kĭt) ◊ *noun, plural* **blankets** ◊ *verb* **blanketed, blanketing**

blare *noun* A loud, harsh noise, as of a horn.
◊ *verb* To make this sound: *Trumpets blared.*
blare (blâr) ◊ *noun, plural* **blares** ◊ *verb* **blared, blaring**

ă	pat	ĭ	pit	oi	oil	th	bath
ā	pay	ī	ride	ŏŏ	book	*th*	bathe
â	care	î	fierce	ōō	boot	ə	ago, item
ä	father	ŏ	pot	ou	out		pencil
ĕ	pet	ō	go	ŭ	cut		atom
ē	be	ô	paw, for	û	fur		circus

blast *noun* **1.** A strong gust of wind. **2.** A strong rush or stream of air or gas from an opening. **3.** An explosion.
◊ *verb* **1.** To blow up with an explosive. **2.** To destroy or ruin.
◊ *idiom* **blast off** To begin flight propelled by rockets.
blast (blăst) ◊ *noun, plural* **blasts** ◊ *verb* **blasted, blasting**

blastoff *noun* The launch of a spacecraft.
blast·off (blăst′ôf′) ◊ *noun, plural* **blastoffs**

▲ **blastoff**

blaze[1] *noun* **1.** A brightly burning flame or fire. **2.** A bright light: *We were dazzled by the sun's blaze.* **3.** A brilliant display: *The flowers were a blaze of color.*
◊ *verb* To burn or shine brightly.
blaze[1] (blāz) ◊ *noun, plural* **blazes** ◊ *verb* **blazed, blazing**

blaze² *noun* **1.** A white spot on an animal's face. **2.** A mark cut on the bark of a tree to indicate a trail.
◊ *verb* **1.** To mark a tree with a blaze. **2.** To indicate with blazes: *Let's blaze a new trail.*
blaze² (blāz) ◊ *noun, plural* **blazes** ◊ *verb* **blazed, blazing**

***HISTORY* • blaze¹, blaze²**

Blaze¹ comes from an old English word meaning "a torch or bright fire." **Blaze²** comes from an old German word meaning "a white mark." Both go back to the same Germanic word meaning "a bright or white object."

bleach *verb* To make lighter or white by means of sunlight or a chemical substance.
◊ *noun* A chemical substance that is used for bleaching.
bleach (blēch) ◊ *verb* **bleached, bleaching** ◊ *noun, plural* **bleaches**

bleachers *plural noun* Seats in rows placed one above another for people watching an event or performance, as in a stadium.
bleach·ers (blē′chərz) ◊ *plural noun*

▲ **bleachers**

bleak *adjective* **1.** Exposed to wind or weather: *Little grows on a bleak mountain.* **2.** Cold and harsh: *The bleak wind chilled us.*
bleak (blēk) ◊ *adjective* **bleaker, bleakest**

bleat *noun* The cry of a goat, sheep, or calf.
◊ *verb* To make this sound.
bleat (blēt) ◊ *noun, plural* **bleats** ◊ *verb* **bleated, bleating**

bled *verb* Past tense and past participle of **bleed**.
bled (blĕd) ◊ *verb*

bleed *verb* **1.** To lose blood. **2.** To feel sorrow or pity: *My heart bleeds for you.*
bleed (blēd) ◊ *verb* **bled, bleeding**

blemish *noun* A mark that makes something less than perfect; flaw.
◊ *verb* To spoil by or as if by a blemish.
blem·ish (blĕm′ĭsh) ◊ *noun, plural* **blemishes** ◊ *verb* **blemished, blemishing**

blend *verb* To combine completely: *Blend the milk and flour.* —See Synonyms at **mix.**
◊ *noun* A mixture made by blending.
blend (blĕnd) ◊ *verb* **blended, blending** ◊ *noun, plural* **blends**

bless *verb* **1.** To make holy by a ceremony; consecrate. **2.** To glorify. **3.** To give good fortune to: *We are blessed with good health.*
bless (blĕs) ◊ *verb* **blessed** *or* **blest, blessing**

blessing *noun* **1.** A prayer asking the favor of God or giving thanks. **2.** Approval: *I went on the trip with my parents' blessing.* **3.** Something that brings happiness or well-being: *Good health is a blessing.*
bless·ing (blĕs′ĭng) ◊ *noun, plural* **blessings**

blest *verb* A past tense and past participle of **bless**.
blest (blĕst) ◊ *verb*

blew *verb* Past tense of **blow¹**.
blew (blo͞o) ◊ *verb*
‖ *These sound alike:* **blew, blue**

blight *noun* **1.** A disease that withers or destroys plants. **2.** Something harmful.
blight (blīt) ◊ *noun, plural* **blights**

blimp *noun* An airship.
blimp (blĭmp) ◊ *noun, plural* **blimps**

blind *adjective* **1.** Unable to see; sightless. **2.** Depending on aircraft instruments rather than on visual landmarks: *The pilot made a blind landing in the fog.* **3.** Unwilling or unable to notice or understand: *I am not blind to your mistakes.* **4.** Without thinking ahead or using good judgment: *The spoiled child was in a blind rage.* **5.** Hidden from sight: *Watch out for blind intersections.*

◊ *noun* Something that shuts out light or limits sight: *Close the window blinds.*
◊ *verb* **1.** To cause to lose the sense of sight. **2.** To cause to lose judgment or good sense: *Greed blinded them to the danger.*
◊ *adverb* With instruments as the only guide: *The pilot had to fly blind.*
blind (blīnd) ◊ *adjective* **blinder, blindest** ◊ *noun, plural* **blinds** ◊ *verb* **blinded, blinding** ◊ *adverb*

blindfold *verb* To cover the eyes of with or as if with a strip of material.
◊ *noun* A covering for the eyes.
blind·fold (**blīnd′**fōld′) ◊ *verb* **blindfolded, blindfolding** ◊ *noun, plural* **blindfolds**

blink *verb* **1.** To close and open the eyes rapidly: *The bright lights made us blink.* **2.** To flash or seem to flash off and on: *We could see lights blinking on the shore.*
◊ *noun* An act of blinking.
◊ *idiom* **on the blink** Out of order.
blink (blĭngk) ◊ *verb* **blinked, blinking** ◊ *noun, plural* **blinks**

bliss *noun* Very great happiness; joy.
bliss (blĭs) ◊ *noun*

blister *noun* **1.** A thin, fluid-filled sac that forms on the skin as a result of a burn or an irritation. **2.** A blisterlike swelling, as on a painted surface.
◊ *verb* To form or cause to form blisters.
blis·ter (**blĭs′**tər) ◊ *noun, plural* **blisters** ◊ *verb* **blistered, blistering**

blizzard *noun* A very long, heavy snowstorm with strong winds.
bliz·zard (**blĭz′**ərd) ◊ *noun, plural* **blizzards**

bloat *verb* To swell or cause to swell with or as if with a liquid or gas.
bloat (blōt) ◊ *verb* **bloated, bloating**

blob *noun* A small mass of something soft or thick, such as paint or wax.
blob (blŏb) ◊ *noun, plural* **blobs**

block *noun* **1.** A solid piece of a material, such as wood or stone, that has one or more flat sides. **2.** A pulley or set of pulleys enclosed in a casing. **3.** Something that obstructs passage or progress; obstacle. **4.** An area in a city or town enclosed by four streets. **5.** The length of one side of a city block.
◊ *verb* To stop or slow down passage through or the progress of; obstruct: *Fallen trees blocked the road. They blocked our attempts to join the club.*
block (blŏk) ◊ *noun, plural* **blocks** ◊ *verb* **blocked, blocking**

blockade *noun* The closing off of an area to prevent movement of people and supplies.
◊ *verb* To close off with a blockade.
block·ade (blŏ **kād′**) ◊ *noun, plural* **blockades** ◊ *verb* **blockaded, blockading**

blockhouse *noun* A small houselike fort with holes from which to fire at an enemy.
block·house (**blŏk′**hous′) ◊ *noun, plural* **blockhouses**

blond *or* **blonde** *adjective* **1.** Having fair hair and skin. **2.** Light-colored: *I like the look of the blond furniture.*
◊ *noun* A blond person.
blond *or* **blonde** (blŏnd) ◊ *adjective* **blonder, blondest** ◊ *noun, plural* **blonds** *or* **blondes**

blood *noun* **1.** The fluid circulated by the heart through the arteries, veins, and capillaries of persons and animals. Blood carries oxygen to all parts of the body and carries away waste materials. **2.** Family relationship; kinship: *We are related by blood.*
blood (blŭd) ◊ *noun*

bloodhound *noun* A hound with drooping ears and a keen sense of smell.
blood·hound (**blŭd′**hound′) ◊ *noun, plural* **bloodhounds**

blood pressure *noun* Pressure of the blood against the walls of the arteries.
blood pressure ◊ *noun*

bloodshot *adjective* Being red and irritated: *My eyes are bloodshot from fatigue.*
blood·shot (**blŭd′**shŏt′) ◊ *adjective*

bloodstream *noun* The blood circulating through a living body.
blood·stream (**blŭd′**strēm′) ◊ *noun, plural* **bloodstreams**

blood vessel *noun* An elastic passage in the body through which blood circulates; an artery, vein, or capillary.
blood vessel ◊ *noun, plural* **blood vessels**

ă	pat	ĭ	pit	oi	**oi**l	th	ba**th**
ā	pay	ī	ride	o͝o	book	*th*	ba**th**e
â	care	î	fierce	o͞o	boot	ə	ago, item
ä	father	ŏ	pot	ou	**ou**t		pencil
ĕ	pet	ō	go	ŭ	cut		atom
ē	be	ô	paw, for	û	fur		circus

bloody *adjective* **1.** Stained or covered with blood. **2.** Marked by the shedding of blood.
blood·y (blŭd′ē) ◊ *adjective* **bloodier, bloodiest**

bloom *noun* **1.** The flower or blossoms of a plant. **2.** The condition or time of flowering: *The roses were all in bloom.* **3.** A state or time of beauty, health, and energy: *The children were in the bloom of youth.*
◊ *verb* **1.** To bear flowers; blossom. **2.** To do well, as in a state of beauty or health.
bloom (blo͞om) ◊ *noun, plural* **blooms** ◊ *verb* **bloomed, blooming**

blossom *noun* **1.** A flower, especially of a fruit-bearing plant. **2.** The condition or time of flowering.
◊ *verb* **1.** To come into flower; bloom. **2.** To develop gradually: *The ugly duckling blossomed into a beautiful swan.*
blos·som (blŏs′əm) ◊ *noun, plural* **blossoms** ◊ *verb* **blossomed, blossoming**

blot *noun* **1.** A stain or spot, as of ink. **2.** Something that spoils or brings disgrace: *The bad grade is a blot on my record.*
◊ *verb* **1.** To spot or stain. **2.** To hide from view: *Storm clouds blotted out the sunlight.* **3.** To soak up with absorbent material.
blot (blŏt) ◊ *noun, plural* **blots** ◊ *verb* **blotted, blotting**

blotch *noun* **1.** A large spot or stain, as of ink or color. **2.** A blemish on the skin.
blotch (blŏch) ◊ *noun, plural* **blotches**

blotter *noun* A piece or pad of thick, absorbent paper used to dry wet ink.
blot·ter (blŏt′ər) ◊ *noun, plural* **blotters**

blouse *noun* **1.** A shirtlike outer garment for women and girls that covers the body from neck to waist. **2.** A loose garment like a smock. **3.** The jacket of a uniform.
blouse (blous) ◊ *noun, plural* **blouses**

blow[1] *verb* **1.** To move, usually with speed and power: *The wind blew all night.* **2.** To be moved or cause to move by means of a current of air: *My hat blew off.* **3.** To send out a stream of air: *Blow on your soup to cool it.* **4.** To sound or cause to sound by the force of air or steam: *The whistle blows at noon.* **5.** To clear by forcing air through: *I blew my nose.* **6.** To shape by forcing air into: *Can you blow a bubble?* **7.** To cause an electrical fuse to melt and open a circuit. **8.** To break or destroy by an explosion: *The dynamite blew the bridge to bits.*
◊ *idiom* **blow up 1.** To come into being: *A storm blew up.* **2.** To explode: *The building blew up.* **3.** To fill with air or a gas: *We blew up balloons.* **4.** To lose one's temper.
blow[1] (blō) ◊ *verb* **blew, blown, blowing**

blow[2] *noun* **1.** A sudden hard hit, as with the fist or a weapon. **2.** A sudden attack. **3.** A sudden shock or great misfortune.
blow[2] (blō) ◊ *noun, plural* **blows**

***HISTORY* • blow[1], blow[2]**

Blow[1] comes from an old English word that meant "to blow" and also "to breathe." **Blow[2]** comes from a word that meant "a sudden hit" and was used in northern England during the Middle Ages. Its history before that is not known for certain.

blown *verb* Past participle of **blow[1]**.
blown (blōn) ◊ *verb*

blowtorch *noun* A small device in which a blast of air makes the flame hot enough to melt soft metals.
blow·torch (blō′tôrch′) ◊ *noun, plural* **blowtorches**

▲ **blowtorch**

blubber *noun* The thick layer of fat under the skin of certain sea animals, such as seals.
blub·ber (blŭb′ər) ◊ *noun*

blue *noun* The color of a clear sky.
◊ *adjective* **1.** Of the color blue. **2.** Having a gray or purplish color, as from cold or a

bruise. **3.** Sad and gloomy.
◊ *idiom* **out of the blue** Suddenly and at an unexpected time or place.
blue (blo͞o) ◊ *noun, plural* **blues** ◊ *adjective* **bluer, bluest**
‖*These sound alike:* **blue, blew**

blueberry *noun* A round, juicy, dark-blue berry that grows on a low bush.
blue·ber·ry (**blo͞o′**bĕr′ē) ◊ *noun, plural* **blueberries**

bluebird *noun* A North American songbird with blue feathers.
blue·bird (**blo͞o′**bûrd′) ◊ *noun, plural* **bluebirds**

bluegrass *noun* A lawn and pasture grass with bluish or grayish leaves and stems.
blue·grass (**blo͞o′**grăs′) ◊ *noun*

blue jay *noun* A North American bird with a crested head and mostly blue feathers.
blue jay ◊ *noun, plural* **blue jays**

▲ **blue jay**

blue jeans *plural noun* Pants made of blue denim.

blueprint *noun* **1.** A photographic copy of an original drawing, as of a building plan, made with white lines on a blue background. **2.** A careful plan.
blue·print (**blo͞o′**prĭnt′) ◊ *noun, plural* **blueprints**

ă	pat	ĭ	pit	oi	**oi**l	th	ba**th**
ā	pay	ī	ride	o͝o	book	*th*	ba**th**e
â	care	î	fierce	o͞o	boot	ə	ago, item
ä	father	ŏ	pot	ou	**ou**t		pencil
ĕ	pet	ō	go	ŭ	cut		atom
ē	be	ô	paw, for	û	fur		circus

blues *noun* (*used with a singular or plural verb*) **1.** A type of slow, sad-sounding jazz. **2.** Low spirits; melancholy: *The blues is* (or *are*) *not much fun.*
blues (blo͞oz) ◊ *noun*

bluff[1] *verb* To mislead by a false display of strength or confidence.
◊ *noun* The act or an example of bluffing.
bluff[1] (blŭf) ◊ *verb* **bluffed, bluffing** ◊ *noun, plural* **bluffs**

bluff[2] *noun* A high, steep headland, cliff, or riverbank.
◊ *adjective* Gruff and blunt in a friendly way.
bluff[2] (blŭf) ◊ *noun, plural* **bluffs** ◊ *adjective* **bluffer, bluffest**

***HISTORY* • bluff[1], bluff[2]**

Bluff[1] comes from a Dutch word that meant "to boast." **Bluff**[2] may come from a Dutch word meaning "broad" or "flat."

blunder *noun* A foolish or stupid mistake. —See Synonyms at **error.**
◊ *verb* **1.** To make a stupid mistake. **2.** To move in a clumsy way; stumble.
blun·der (**blŭn′**dər) ◊ *noun, plural* **blunders** ◊ *verb* **blundered, blundering**

blunderbuss *noun* A gun with a wide muzzle that was formerly used for shooting at close range without exact aim.
blun·der·buss (**blŭn′**dər bŭs′) ◊ *noun, plural* **blunderbusses**

blunt *adjective* **1.** Having a thick, dull edge or end; not sharp or pointed. —See Synonyms at **dull. 2.** Very direct and frank without regard for others' feelings.
◊ *verb* To make less sharp or effective.
blunt (blŭnt) ◊ *adjective* **blunter, bluntest** ◊ *verb* **blunted, blunting**

blur *verb* **1.** To make or become dim or hard to see. **2.** To smudge or smear: *I blurred my report by spilling milk on it.*
◊ *noun* Something that is blurred.
blur (blûr) ◊ *verb* **blurred, blurring** ◊ *noun, plural* **blurs**

blurt *verb* To say suddenly and without thought: *I was embarrassed after I blurted out my secret.*
blurt (blûrt) ◊ *verb* **blurted, blurting**

blush *verb* **1.** To become red in the face, as from shame. **2.** To feel ashamed.
◊ *noun* **1.** A reddening of the face, as from shame. **2.** A rosy color.
blush (blŭsh) ◊ *verb* **blushed, blushing** ◊ *noun, plural* **blushes**

bluster *verb* **1.** To blow loud and hard: *Winds blustered around the house.* **2.** To make noisy boasts or threats.
◊ *noun* **1.** A loud, hard blowing, as of the wind. **2.** Loud, boastful, or threatening talk.
bluster (blŭs′tər) ◊ *verb* **blustered, blustering** ◊ *noun, plural* **blusters**

Blvd. The abbreviation for *Boulevard.*

boa *noun* A large, nonpoisonous snake that coils around and crushes its prey.
bo·a (bō′ə) ◊ *noun, plural* **boas**

boar *noun* **1.** A male pig. **2.** A wild pig.
boar (bôr) ◊ *noun, plural* **boars**
‖*These sound alike:* **boar, bore**

board *noun* **1.** A piece of sawed lumber that has more length and width than thickness; plank. **2.** A flat piece of hard material that has a special use: *Here's a notice for your bulletin board.* **3.** Food served daily to paying guests. **4.** A group of persons who are in charge of something.
◊ *verb* **1.** To close up with boards. **2.** To give or receive daily meals for a charge. **3.** To go aboard: *We boarded the plane.*
board (bôrd) ◊ *noun, plural* **boards** ◊ *verb* **boarded, boarding**

boarding school *noun* A school at which students may live during the school year.
boarding school ◊ *noun, plural* **boarding schools**

boast *verb* **1.** To praise oneself, one's belongings, or one's actions. **2.** To have and take pride in having: *The valley boasts many beautiful gardens.*
◊ *noun* A boastful statement.
boast (bōst) ◊ *verb* **boasted, boasting** ◊ *noun, plural* **boasts**

SYNONYMS

boast, brag, crow²

He *boasted* about his wealth. She *bragged* about her home run. I *crowed* over solving the puzzle first.

boat *noun* **1.** A small craft for traveling on water. **2.** A large seagoing vessel; ship.
◊ *verb* To travel by boat.
boat (bōt) ◊ *noun, plural* **boats** ◊ *verb* **boated, boating**

bob¹ *verb* To move or cause to move with a quick, up-and-down motion.
bob¹ (bŏb) ◊ *verb* **bobbed, bobbing**

bob² *noun* **1.** A short haircut. **2.** A float or cork for a fishing line.
◊ *verb* To cut short.
bob² (bŏb) ◊ *noun, plural* **bobs** ◊ *verb* **bobbed, bobbing**

***HISTORY* • bob¹, bob²**

Bob¹ perhaps comes from an old French word meaning "to mock." The origin of **bob²** is not known.

bobbin *noun* A spool that holds thread or yarn in place, as for sewing.
bob·bin (bŏb′ĭn) ◊ *noun, plural* **bobbins**

bobby pin *noun* A small metal hairpin with ends pressed close together to hold the hair in place.
bob·by pin (bŏb′ē) ◊ *noun, plural* **bobby pins**

bobcat *noun* A North American wild cat. A bobcat has reddish-brown fur with black spots and a short tail.
bob·cat (bŏb′kăt′) ◊ *noun, plural* **bobcats**

▲ **bobcat**

bobolink *noun* A black, white, and tan American songbird.
bob·o·link (bŏb′ə lĭngk′) ◊ *noun, plural* **bobolinks**

bobsled *noun* A long racing sled with two sets of runners, a steering wheel, and brakes. ◊ *verb* To ride or race in a bobsled.
bob·sled (bŏb′slĕd′) ◊ *noun, plural* **bobsleds** ◊ *verb* **bobsledded, bobsledding**

bobwhite *noun* A brown and white North American quail. The call of a bobwhite sounds like its name.
bob·white (bŏb **hwīt′**) ◊ *noun, plural* **bobwhites**

bode *verb* To be a sign of: *A rough sea boded trouble for the passengers on board.*
bode (bōd) ◊ *verb* **boded, boding**

bodice *noun* The fitted part of a dress from the shoulder to the waist.
bod·ice (**bŏd′**ĭs) ◊ *noun, plural* **bodices**

body *noun* **1.** The whole physical structure of a living person or animal. **2.** The main part of a person or animal; trunk. **3.** The main or central part of an object: *The body of the car was full of dents.* **4.** A separate mass of matter: *The Pacific Ocean is a vast body of water.* **5.** A group acting together: *The student body voted to adopt a dress code.*
bod·y (**bŏd′**ē) ◊ *noun, plural* **bodies**

bodyguard *noun* A person or group of persons who protect someone.
bod·y·guard (**bŏd′**ē gärd′) ◊ *noun, plural* **bodyguards**

bog *noun* Soft, water-soaked ground; marsh. ◊ *verb* To cause to sink in or as if in a bog: *Rain had bogged the village in a sea of mud.*
bog (bôg) ◊ *noun, plural* **bogs** ◊ *verb* **bogged, bogging**

boil¹ *verb* **1.** To reach or cause to reach a temperature at which bubbles form and steam is given off: *Water boils at 212°F.* **2.** To cook or become cooked in boiling liquid. **3.** To become very upset.
◊ *noun* The condition of boiling.
boil¹ (boil) ◊ *verb* **boiled, boiling** ◊ *noun*

boil² *noun* A painful pus-filled swelling of the skin. It is caused by an infection.
boil² (boil) ◊ *noun, plural* **boils**

ă	pat	ĭ	pit	oi	**oi**l	th	ba**th**
ā	pay	ī	ride	ŏŏ	book	*th*	ba**th**e
â	care	î	fierce	ōō	boot	ə	ago, item
ä	father	ŏ	pot	ou	**ou**t		pencil
ĕ	pet	ō	go	ŭ	cut		atom
ē	be	ô	paw, for	û	fur		circus

***HISTORY* • boil¹, boil²**

Boil¹ came from French during the Middle Ages. The French word came from a Latin word meaning "to bubble." **Boil²** is a native English word that has not changed in meaning.

boiler *noun* **1.** A vessel that is used in making steam for heating or power. **2.** A container, such as a kettle, used to boil or heat liquids. **3.** A tank for storing hot water.
boil·er (**boi′**lər) ◊ *noun, plural* **boilers**

boisterous *adjective* Not restrained or disciplined; unruly: *Our class was loud and boisterous.*
bois·ter·ous (**boi′**stər əs) ◊ *adjective*

bold *adjective* **1.** Having or showing no fear; brave: *The American pioneers were bold men and women.* **2.** Having or showing a lack of respect or polite behavior; impudent: *My bold remarks angered you.*
bold (bōld) ◊ *adjective* **bolder, boldest**

SYNONYMS

bold, audacious, daring

Knights were *bold.* A few *audacious* explorers discovered the New World. It was a *daring* test pilot who first broke the sound barrier. **Antonym:** *timid*

boll *noun* A rounded seed pod of a plant such as cotton or flax.
boll (bōl) ◊ *noun, plural* **bolls**
‖*These sound alike:* **boll, bowl**

bolster *noun* A long pillow or cushion.
◊ *verb* To give support to; strengthen: *Pillars bolster the roof.*
bol·ster (**bōl′**stər) ◊ *noun, plural* **bolsters** ◊ *verb* **bolstered, bolstering**

bolt *noun* **1.** A rod or pin with spiral grooves cut around it so that a nut can be screwed onto it. Bolts are used to hold things together. **2.** A bar that slides to fasten a door or gate. **3.** The part of a lock that is pushed out or withdrawn at a turn of the key. **4.** A large roll, as of cloth. **5.** A flash of lightning or a thunderbolt. **6.** A sudden dash or dart: *The prisoner made a bolt for freedom.*

◊ *verb* **1.** To lock with a bolt: *Bolt the door.* **2.** To make off suddenly: *The horse bolted from the stable.* **3.** To eat quickly and with little chewing; gulp.
bolt (bōlt) ◊ *noun, plural* **bolts** ◊ *verb* **bolted, bolting**

bomb *noun* A container filled with an explosive that blows up when it strikes something or when a timing device in it sets it off.
◊ *verb* To attack with bombs.
bomb (bŏm) ◊ *noun, plural* **bombs** ◊ *verb* **bombed, bombing**

bombard *verb* **1.** To attack, as with bombs or explosive shells. **2.** To attack or bother, as with questions or insults.
bom·bard (bŏm **bärd′**) ◊ *verb* **bombarded, bombarding**

bomber *noun* A military airplane that carries and drops bombs.
bomb·er (**bŏm′**ər) ◊ *noun, plural* **bombers**

bond *noun* **1.** Something that binds, ties, or fastens together, as a cord or rope. **2.** A force that unites; tie: *Our relatives feel close bonds with one another.* **3.** A certificate issued by a government or corporation for borrowing money. It guarantees that the person who buys the certificate will be repaid with interest on a certain date.
bond (bŏnd) ◊ *noun, plural* **bonds**

bondage *noun* Slavery.
bond·age (**bŏn′**dĭj) ◊ *noun*

bone *noun* **1.** One of the many pieces that make up the skeleton of most animals with backbones. **2.** The hard, dense tissue of which such pieces are composed.
◊ *verb* To remove the bones from: *Our butcher boned a leg of lamb.*
bone (bōn) ◊ *noun, plural* **bones** ◊ *verb* **boned, boning**

bonfire *noun* A large outdoor fire.
bon·fire (**bŏn′**fīr′) ◊ *noun, plural* **bonfires**

bonnet *noun* **1.** A hat tied with ribbons under the chin and worn by women and very young children. **2.** A headdress of feathers worn by some Native Americans.
bon·net (**bŏn′**ĭt) ◊ *noun, plural* **bonnets**

bonus *noun* Something given or paid in addition to what is usual or expected: *I received a $100 bonus for finishing the job early.*
bo·nus (**bō′**nəs) ◊ *noun, plural* **bonuses**

bony *adjective* **1.** Of or like bone. **2.** Full of bones: *The fish we caught were too bony to eat.* **3.** Having bones that stick out or show through; thin: *The old horse was bony.*
bon·y (**bō′**nē) ◊ *adjective* **bonier, boniest**

boo *noun* A sound made to show dislike: *The performer was greeted with boos.*
◊ *interjection* An expression used to show dislike or to frighten or surprise: *I shouted "Boo!" as I jumped out.*
◊ *verb* To make such sounds or show dislike of by such sounds: *They booed the referee.*
boo (bo͞o) ◊ *noun, plural* **boos** ◊ *interjection* ◊ *verb* **booed, booing**

book *noun* **1.** A group of pages bound together along one side and placed between covers. **2.** A long written or printed work: *I wrote a book about birds.* **3.** A main division of a larger written or printed work: *Genesis is a book of the Bible.*
◊ *verb* To arrange for ahead of time; make reservations for: *The tickets are booked.*
book (bo͝ok) ◊ *noun, plural* **books** ◊ *verb* **booked, booking**

bookcase *noun* A piece of furniture with shelves for holding books.
book·case (**bo͝ok′**kās′) ◊ *noun, plural* **bookcases**

bookend *noun* A prop placed at the end of a row of books to keep them upright.
book·end (**bo͝ok′**ĕnd′) ◊ *noun, plural* **bookends**

bookkeeping *noun* The work or skill of keeping records of a business, as money received or owed.
book·keep·ing (**bo͝ok′**kē′pĭng) ◊ *noun*

booklet *noun* A small book or pamphlet.
book·let (**bo͝ok′**lĭt) ◊ *noun, plural* **booklets**

bookmark *noun* Something, such as a ribbon or a piece of paper, placed between the pages of a book to mark one's place.
book·mark (**bo͝ok′**märk′) ◊ *noun, plural* **bookmarks**

bookmobile *noun* A vehicle, such as a van, used as a traveling library.
book·mo·bile (**bo͝ok′**mō bēl′) ◊ *noun, plural* **bookmobiles**

boom¹ *noun* **1.** A loud, deep, hollow sound, like the sound of thunder. **2.** A sudden increase, as in growth of business or of a place.
◊ *verb* **1.** To make a loud, deep, hollow sound.

2. To grow or develop rapidly; flourish.
boom[1] (bo͞om) ◊ *noun, plural* **booms** ◊ *verb* **boomed, booming**

boom[2] *noun* **1.** A long pole used to stretch out the bottom of a sail. **2.** A long pole that holds or guides something lifted by a derrick.
boom[2] (bo͞om) ◊ *noun, plural* **booms**

> ***HISTORY* • boom[1], boom[2]**
>
> **Boom[1]** first appears in English during the later Middle Ages. It was made up in imitation of the sound it describes. **Boom[2]** comes from an old Dutch word meaning "pole."

boomerang *noun* A curved stick made for throwing, especially one that comes back to the thrower.
boo·mer·ang (**bo͞o′** mə-răng′) ◊ *noun, plural* **boomerangs**

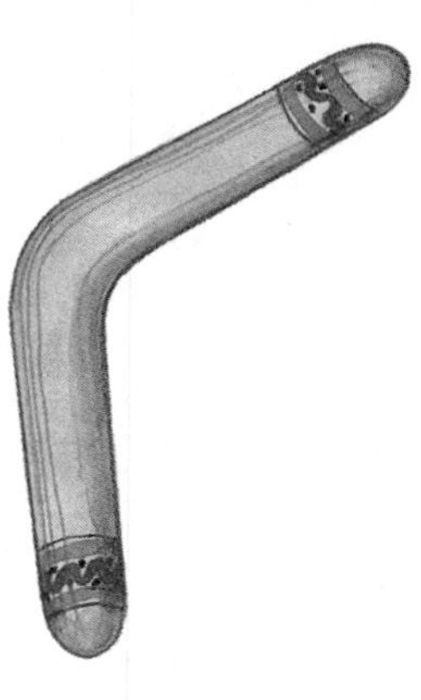

▲ **boomerang**

boon *noun* An often unexpected help or benefit: *It was a boon to find a compass when we were lost.*
boon (bo͞on) ◊ *noun, plural* **boons**

boost *verb* **1.** To lift by pushing from below: *Boost me into the saddle.* —See Synonyms at **lift.** **2.** To make greater in quantity: *The company boosted its sales this year.*
◊ *noun* A push upward.
boost (bo͞ost) ◊ *verb* **boosted, boosting** ◊ *noun, plural* **boosts**

booster *noun* **1.** A device used to help launch a vehicle such as a rocket. **2.** A dose of something, such as a vaccine, given in order to continue immunity.
boost·er (**bo͞o′** stər) ◊ *noun, plural* **boosters**

ă	pat	ĭ	pit	oi	oil	th	bath
ā	pay	ī	ride	o͝o	book	*th*	bathe
â	care	î	fierce	o͞o	boot	ə	ago, item
ä	father	ŏ	pot	ou	out		pencil
ĕ	pet	ō	go	ŭ	cut		atom
ē	be	ô	paw, for	û	fur		circus

boot *noun* A covering for the foot that usually covers the ankle as well and often part of the leg.
◊ *verb* To kick: *I booted the football.*
boot (bo͞ot) ◊ *noun, plural* **boots** ◊ *verb* **booted, booting**

booth *noun* **1.** A small stall or stand where things are shown or sold, as at a fair. **2.** A small structure, such as a telephone booth, that is completely or partly enclosed.
booth (bo͞oth) ◊ *noun, plural* **booths**

▲ **booth**

booty *noun* Something taken by force, as in war.
boo·ty (**bo͞o′** tē) ◊ *noun*

border *noun* **1.** The line or narrow area at the furthest boundary of something: *The plate has a pattern of flowers around its border.* **2.** The line where an area, as a country, ends and another area begins. **3.** Something, as a strip, that makes an edge or a trim to an edge.
◊ *verb* **1.** To share a boundary with; be next to: *Canada borders on the United States.* **2.** To put something on that makes an edge or a trim to an edge.
bor·der (**bôr′** dər) ◊ *noun, plural* **borders** ◊ *verb* **bordered, bordering**

> ***SYNONYMS***
>
> ***border, edge, margin, rim***
>
> I want to put a *border* of small stones around the garden. There is a strong railing at the *edge* of the canyon to prevent accidents. Don't write in the *margin.* The *rim* of my cup has a band of gold around it.

bore[1] *verb* **1.** To make a hole or a hole in, as with a drill: *The carpenter bored the wood.* **2.** To make a hole or tunnel, as by digging or drilling.
bore[1] (bôr) ◊ *verb* **bored, boring**
‖*These sound alike:* **bore, boar**

bore² *verb* To cause to feel that one has had enough, as by seeming dull or uninteresting: *The speaker bored the audience.*
◊ *noun* A person or thing that causes boredom: *The movie was such a bore that we left.*
bore² (bôr) ◊ *verb* **bored, boring** ◊ *noun, plural* **bores**
‖*These sound alike:* **bore, boar**

> ***HISTORY* • bore¹, bore²**
>
> **Bore¹** is a native English word, but the origin of **bore²** is unknown.

bore³ *verb* Past tense of **bear¹**.
bore³ (bôr) ◊ *verb*
‖*These sound alike:* **bore, boar**

boredom *noun* The state of being bored.
bore·dom (**bôr′** dəm) ◊ *noun*

born *adjective* Having something, such as an ability, from birth: *I am a born singer.*
◊ *verb* A past participle of **bear¹**.
born (bôrn) ◊ *adjective* ◊ *verb*
‖*These sound alike:* **born, borne**

borne *verb* A past participle of **bear¹**.
borne (bôrn) ◊ *verb*
‖*These sound alike:* **borne, born**

borough *noun* **1.** A unit of government in some states that is like a town or village. **2.** A political division of New York City.
bor·ough (**bûr′** ō) ◊ *noun, plural* **boroughs**
‖*These sound alike:* **borough, burro, burrow**

borrow *verb* **1.** To get from someone else with the understanding that what is gotten will be returned or replaced: *The book I borrowed from the library is due today.* **2.** To take and use as one's own; adopt: *I borrowed that idea from my friend.*
bor·row (**bŏr′** ō) ◊ *verb* **borrowed, borrowing**

bosom *noun* The front part of the human chest: *I held the baby close to my bosom.*
◊ *adjective* Close to each other; intimate: *We are bosom friends.*
bos·om (**bo͝oz′** əm) ◊ *noun, plural* **bosoms**
◊ *adjective*

boss *noun* A person, such as an employer, who is in charge.
◊ *verb* To give orders to; order around: *Please don't boss me around.*
boss (bôs) ◊ *noun, plural* **bosses** ◊ *verb* **bossed, bossing**

botanical *adjective* Of or relating to plants or botany.
bo·tan·i·cal (bə **tăn′** ĭ kəl) ◊ *adjective*

botany *noun* The scientific study of plants.
bot·a·ny (**bŏt′** n ē) ◊ *noun*

both *pronoun* The one as well as the other; the two alike: *I talked to both of them.*
◊ *adjective* The two; the one as well as the other: *Both sides of the valley are steep.*
◊ *conjunction* Used with the conjunction *and* to show that two things are being mentioned: *Both you and I are going.*
both (bōth) ◊ *pronoun* ◊ *adjective*
◊ *conjunction*

bother *verb* **1.** To disturb or irritate: *That constant little noise bothers me.* —See Synonyms at **annoy. 2.** To concern, worry, or trouble: *High places bother me.* **3.** To take the trouble; concern oneself: *Don't bother to get up.*
◊ *noun* **1.** Someone or something that bothers or annoys. **2.** Unnecessary or annoying effort or excitement; fuss.
both·er (**bŏ*th*′** ər) ◊ *verb* **bothered, bothering**
◊ *noun, plural* **bothers**

bottle *noun* A container, usually made of glass or plastic, with a narrow neck and mouth and no handle.
◊ *verb* **1.** To put in a bottle: *This machine bottles water.* **2.** To hold in, as if in a bottle; restrain: *I bottle up my anger sometimes.*
bot·tle (**bŏt′** l) ◊ *noun, plural* **bottles** ◊ *verb* **bottled, bottling**

bottom *noun* **1.** The lowest part of something. **2.** The lowest outside part of something: *The bottom of the jar left a wet circle on the table.* **3.** The land under a body of water. **4.** Something, such as a truth, that can be thought of as lying below other things; basis: *I want to get to the bottom of that problem immediately.*
bot·tom (**bŏt′** əm) ◊ *noun, plural* **bottoms**

bough *noun* A branch of a tree, especially a main branch.
bough (bou) ◊ *noun, plural* **boughs**
‖*These sound alike:* **bough, bow², bow³**

bought *verb* Past tense and past participle of **buy.**
bought (bôt) ◊ *verb*

boulder *noun* A large rounded rock.
boul·der (**bōl′** dər) ◊ *noun, plural* **boulders**

boulevard *noun* A broad street, often with trees and grass planted in the center or along the sides.
boul·e·vard (bŏŏl′ə värd′) ◊ *noun, plural* **boulevards**

bounce *verb* **1.** To come back or up after hitting a surface. **2.** To cause to bounce: *I bounced the tennis ball into the water.* **3.** To move or jump as if bouncing.
◊ *noun* **1.** An act of coming back or up after hitting a surface. **2.** A movement or jump like a bounce.
bounce (bouns) ◊ *verb* **bounced, bouncing** ◊ *noun, plural* **bounces**

bound[1] *verb* To leap upward or forward: *The deer bounded away.*
◊ *noun* An act of bounding; leap.
bound[1] (bound) ◊ *verb* **bounded, bounding** ◊ *noun, plural* **bounds**

bound[2] *noun* **1.** A line where something comes to an end: *The ball went out of bounds.* **2.** A limit: *Our joy knew no bounds.*
◊ *verb* To be the bound or boundary of.
bound[2] (bound) ◊ *noun, plural* **bounds** ◊ *verb* **bounded, bounding**

bound[3] *adjective* Ready or intending to go; on the way: *I am bound for home.*
bound[3] (bound) ◊ *adjective*

***HISTORY* • bound[1], bound[2], bound[3]**

Bound[1] comes from an old French word that first meant "to resound" and then "to bounce." **Bound[2]** comes from an old French word meaning "boundary." **Bound[3]** comes from an old Scandinavian word meaning "prepared."

bound[4] *adjective* **1.** Having a duty; obliged: *I am bound by my promise.* **2.** Certain or almost certain to happen: *It is bound to rain tomorrow.*
◊ *verb* Past tense and past participle of **bind.**
bound[4] (bound) ◊ *adjective* ◊ *verb*

ă	pat	ĭ	pit	oi	**oil**	th	ba**th**
ā	pay	ī	ride	ŏŏ	book	*th*	ba**th**e
â	care	î	fierce	ōō	boot	ə	ago, item
ä	father	ŏ	pot	ou	**out**		pencil
ĕ	pet	ō	go	ŭ	cut		atom
ē	be	ô	paw, for	û	fur		circus

boundary *noun* **1.** A line or limit where something, such as a country, comes to an end. **2.** Something that indicates or shows a boundary: *The wall is the boundary of our property.*
bound·a·ry (**boun′**də rē) ◊ *noun, plural* **boundaries**

bountiful *adjective* **1.** Willing and free in giving; generous: *The monarch was bountiful.* **2.** Providing more than enough; in a great amount: *Crops are bountiful this year.*
boun·ti·ful (**boun′**tə fəl) ◊ *adjective*

bounty *noun* **1.** The quality of giving or something that is given in a free and willing way. **2.** Something, such as a reward, given by a government for doing something, such as killing a wild animal.
boun·ty (**boun′**tē) ◊ *noun, plural* **bounties**

bouquet *noun* A bunch of flowers, especially when they are tied together: *I gave a bouquet of roses to my teacher.*
bou·quet (bō **kā′** *or* bōō **kā′**) ◊ *noun, plural* **bouquets**

▲ **bouquet**

bout *noun* **1.** A contest, such as a boxing match, between opponents. **2.** A period or occurrence, as of a disease; attack: *I had a bout of flu.*
bout (bout) ◊ *noun, plural* **bouts**

boutique *noun* A shop or store that sells such things as gifts or clothes.
bou·tique (bōō **tēk′**) ◊ *noun, plural* **boutiques**

bow[1] *noun* **1.** A weapon for shooting arrows. A bow is made of a piece of flexible material, such as wood, and a string stretched between its two ends. **2.** A stick with horsehair stretched from end to end. A bow is used to play a string instrument, such as the violin. **3.** A knot tied with loops or something tied in such a knot: *Put a bow on that package.* **4.** Something that is bent or curved; bend: *The river makes a bow around the mountain.*
bow[1] (bō) ◊ *noun, plural* **bows**

bow² *verb* **1.** To bend the body, head, or knee to show such things as agreement, respect, or greeting. **2.** To give in: *They refused to bow to pressure.*
◊ *noun* A bending of the body or head, as when showing respect or thanks.
bow² (bou) ◊ *verb* **bowed, bowing** ◊ *noun, plural* **bows**
‖ *These sound alike:* **bow², bough, bow³**

bow³ *noun* The front part of a ship or boat.
bow³ (bou) ◊ *noun, plural* **bows**
‖ *These sound alike:* **bow³, bough, bow²**

***HISTORY* • bow¹, bow², bow³**

Bow¹ and **bow²** come from related old English words that shared a sense of "to bend." A **bow¹** is made from bent wood or other material. When you **bow²**, you bend your body. **Bow³** comes from an old German word that first meant "shoulder" and then "the front of a boat."

bowels *plural noun* The part of the digestive system below the stomach.
bow·els (bou′əlz) ◊ *plural noun*

bowl¹ *noun* **1.** A round, hollow container or dish. **2.** The amount that a bowl holds: *Eat a bowl of soup.* **3.** Something, such as a football stadium, that is shaped like a bowl.
bowl¹ (bōl) ◊ *noun, plural* **bowls**
‖ *These sound alike:* **bowl, boll**

bowl² *verb* **1.** To roll a ball or take a turn in bowling. **2.** To play the game of bowling.
◊ *idiom* **bowl over** To surprise greatly: *We were bowled over by the news.*
bowl² (bōl) ◊ *verb* **bowled, bowling**
‖ *These sound alike:* **bowl, boll**

***HISTORY* • bowl¹, bowl²**

Bowl¹ is from an old English word that meant "any round container" and also "pot." **Bowl²** comes from an old French word meaning "ball."

bowlegged *adjective* Having legs that curve outward at or below the knee.
bow·leg·ged (bō′lĕg′ĭd) ◊ *adjective*

bowling *noun* A game in which a ball is rolled on a green or down an alley to try to knock down wooden pins.
bowl·ing (bō′lĭng) ◊ *noun*

box¹ *noun* **1.** A stiff container often with four sides, a bottom, and a top. **2.** The amount that a box holds: *I couldn't eat a whole box of raisins.* **3.** Something shaped or closed in like a box: *We sat in a box seat.*
◊ *verb* To put in or as if in a box: *Would you please box this gift?*
box¹ (bŏks) ◊ *noun, plural* **boxes** ◊ *verb* **boxed, boxing**

box² *verb* **1.** To hit or slap with the hand. **2.** To take part in a boxing match.
box² (bŏks) ◊ *verb* **boxed, boxing**

***HISTORY* • box¹, box²**

Box¹ probably goes back to a Greek word for a kind of tree from which boxes were made. The origin of **box²** is not known.

boxcar *noun* A railway car that is closed on all sides and at the top.
box·car (bŏks′kär′) ◊ *noun, plural* **boxcars**

▲ **boxcar**

boxer *noun* A dog of medium size with a short, smooth coat and a short, square face.
box·er (bŏk′sər) ◊ *noun, plural* **boxers**

boxing *noun* The sport of fighting an opponent with the fists, especially with padded gloves and according to special rules.
box·ing (bŏk′sĭng) ◊ *noun*

boy *noun* A young male person.
boy (boi) ◊ *noun, plural* **boys**

boycott *verb* To refuse as part of an organized group to use, buy from, or deal with a store, company, person, or nation. Boycotting may be an act of protest or punishment.
◊ *noun* The action of boycotting.
boy·cott (boi′kŏt′) ◊ *verb* **boycotted, boycotting** ◊ *noun, plural* **boycotts**

boyhood *noun* The period of time or state of being a boy: *I had a happy boyhood.*
boy·hood (boi′hŏŏd′) ◊ *noun, plural* **boyhoods**

boyish *adjective* Of or relating to a boy.
boy·ish (boi′ĭsh) ◊ *adjective*

brace *noun* **1.** Something that provides support or strength: *I wore a brace on my leg after the accident.* **2. braces** An arrangement of wires and bands for straightening teeth. **3.** A handle used to hold and turn a bit.
◊ *verb* **1.** To support or strengthen with or as with a brace. **2.** To prepare for something difficult or unpleasant: *I braced myself for the dive into the icy water.* **3.** To fill with energy, life, or strength: *The clear air braced the skiers.*
brace (brās) ◊ *noun, plural* **braces** ◊ *verb* **braced, bracing**

bracelet *noun* A band or chain that is worn around the wrist or arm as jewelry or for identification.
brace·let (brās′lĭt) ◊ *noun, plural* **bracelets**

bracket *noun* **1.** A support that sticks out from a surface, such as a wall. A bracket may be used to hold up a shelf or a candle. **2.** One of a pair of symbols [ ] used to enclose letters, words, or numerals in written or printed material. **3.** A group or division within a series: *This book is written for the 10-to-11 age bracket.*
◊ *verb* To put the symbols [ ] around.
brack·et (brăk′ĭt) ◊ *noun, plural* **brackets** ◊ *verb* **bracketed, bracketing**

ă	pat	ĭ	pit	oi	oil	th	bath
ā	pay	ī	ride	ŏŏ	book	*th*	bathe
â	care	î	fierce	ōō	boot	ə	ago, item
ä	father	ŏ	pot	ou	out		pencil
ĕ	pet	ō	go	ŭ	cut		atom
ē	be	ô	paw, for	û	fur		circus

brag *verb* To speak with too much pride about oneself in an attempt to show off. —See Synonyms at **boast.**
brag (brăg) ◊ *verb* **bragged, bragging**

braid *verb* To weave or twist together three or more strands into a rope shape: *The baker braided the dough into a fancy loaf.*
◊ *noun* A length of something, such as hair, that has been braided.
braid (brād) ◊ *verb* **braided, braiding** ◊ *noun, plural* **braids**

Braille *noun* A system of writing and printing for blind people. In Braille things such as letters are represented by different patterns of raised dots. These dot patterns are read with the finger tips.
Braille (brāl) ◊ *noun*

▲ **Braille**
Reading a trail marker in Braille

brain *noun* **1.** The main organ of the nervous system in human beings and other animals with backbones. The brain is located at the upper end of the spinal cord and is enclosed by the skull. The brain is made up of a complex mass of nerves. It controls all voluntary actions such as speaking and many involuntary actions such as breathing. In human beings the brain is the center of memory, learning, and emotion. **2. brains** The ability to think and learn; intelligence. —See Synonyms at **mind.**
brain (brān) ◊ *noun, plural* **brains**

brainstorm *noun* A sudden smart idea.
brain·storm (brān′stôrm′) ◊ *noun, plural* **brainstorms**

brake *noun* A device for slowing or stopping motion, as of a vehicle.

◊ *verb* To slow, stop, or cause to slow or stop by using one or more brakes.
brake (brāk) ◊ *noun, plural* **brakes** ◊ *verb* **braked, braking**
‖*These sound alike:* **brake, break**

bramble *noun* A plant, such as the blackberry, that has thorny stems and edible fruits.
bram·ble (brăm′bəl) ◊ *noun, plural* **brambles**

▲ **bramble**

bran *noun* The broken outer coat of the seed of grains such as wheat or rye. When flour or meal is made the bran is sifted out. It is used in cereals and in animal foods.
bran (brăn) ◊ *noun*

branch *noun* **1.** A part that grows out from a trunk, limb, or stem of a plant. **2.** Something similar to a branch, as a stream that flows into a river. **3.** A part of something larger: *The United States government is divided into the executive, legislative, and judicial branches.*
◊ *verb* To divide or spread into or as if into branches of a tree.
branch (brănch) ◊ *noun, plural* **branches** ◊ *verb* **branched, branching**

brand *noun* **1.** Something such as a name or symbol that identifies a product as coming from a certain company or maker; trademark. **2.** A mark burned into something. Brands are used on cattle to show who owns them. **3.** A mark of shame or disgrace.
◊ *verb* **1.** To mark by burning in a brand. **2.** To mark or label with shame or disgrace: *The people branded them liars.*
brand (brănd) ◊ *noun, plural* **brands** ◊ *verb* **branded, branding**

brand-new *adjective* Completely new.
brand-new (**brănd′no͞o′** *or* **brand′nyo͞o′**) ◊ *adjective*

brandy *noun* An alcoholic drink made from substances such as fermented fruit juice.
bran·dy (brăn′dē) ◊ *noun, plural* **brandies**

brass *noun* **1.** A metal made chiefly of copper and zinc. **2.** A musical instrument, such as a trumpet or trombone, that is made of brass or a similar metal.
brass (brăs) ◊ *noun, plural* **brasses**

brat *noun* A child who behaves badly.
brat (brăt) ◊ *noun, plural* **brats**

brave *adjective* Having or showing the ability to face danger or pain without fear: *I tried to be brave when I broke my leg.*
◊ *noun* A Native American warrior.
◊ *verb* To deal with in a brave way: *They braved the fierce storm to rescue the lost hikers.*
brave (brāv) ◊ *adjective* **braver, bravest** ◊ *noun, plural* **braves** ◊ *verb* **braved, braving**

> ***SYNONYMS***
>
> ***brave, courageous, fearless***
>
> The *brave* sailor rescued the drowning person. The *courageous* explorer reached the South Pole. The *fearless* cowboy finally tamed the wild horse.
> **Antonym:** *cowardly*

bravery *noun* The condition or quality of being brave; courage.
brav·er·y (brā′və rē) ◊ *noun*

brawny *adjective* Having strong, large muscles: *Football players are brawny.*
brawn·y (brô′nē) ◊ *adjective* **brawnier, brawniest**

bray *noun* A donkey's loud, harsh cry.
◊ *verb* To make this sound.
bray (brā) ◊ *noun, plural* **brays** ◊ *verb* **brayed, braying**

breach *noun* An opening that is made by breaking through something solid: *Water was pouring through a breach in the dike.*
◊ *verb* To make a hole in; break through: *Soldiers breached the enemy's line.*
breach (brēch) ◊ *noun, plural* **breaches** ◊ *verb* **breached, breaching**

bread *noun* **1.** A food made from flour or meal that is mixed with water or milk, kneaded, and baked. **2.** Food and other necessities: *We must work to earn our daily bread.*
bread (brĕd) ◊ *noun, plural* **breads**
‖*These sound alike:* **bread, bred**

breadth *noun* The distance from side to side; width: *The length of a football field is about twice its breadth.*
breadth (brĕdth) ◊ *noun, plural* **breadths**

break *verb* **1.** To separate into two or more pieces as the result of force or strain; crack or split: *The rock broke the window. We pulled until the rope broke.* **2.** To pull apart; separate: *I broke a branch from the tree.* **3.** To crack a bone of; fracture: *I fell from the ladder and broke my ankle.* **4.** To make or become unusable; ruin: *My watch broke.* **5.** To force one's way; penetrate: *We broke through the dense jungle.* **6.** To appear or happen suddenly: *The sun broke through the clouds.* **7.** To fail to keep or follow: *An honorable person never breaks a promise.* **8.** To lessen in force; check or subside: *Most fevers reach a peak and then break.* **9.** To put an end to; stop: *Your vote broke the tie. I broke the habit of biting my nails.* **10.** To do better than; surpass: *My friend broke the school record for the 100-yard dash.* **11.** To make known; reveal: *Break the news to them gently.* **12.** To train to obey; tame: *It takes skill to break a wild horse.* **13.** To collapse or crash into surf or spray: *Waves broke onto the shore.*
◊ *noun* **1.** A broken place; a crack or opening: *The x-rays showed a break in the left wrist.* **2.** A period of rest or relaxation: *Let's take a break before study hall.* **3.** An attempt to escape: *Local police were alerted after the prison break.* **4.** A sudden change or departure: *There was a break in the heat wave.* **5.** An unexpected event: *What a lucky break that rain put out the fire.*
◊ *idioms* **break down 1.** To stop working properly. **2.** To have a mental or physical collapse. **break in 1.** To enter by force: *The bears broke in and wrecked the cabin.* **2.** To prepare something new for use: *I'm breaking in my new shoes.* **3.** To interrupt or intrude. **break off** To stop suddenly: *The speaker broke off in the middle of a sentence.* **break up** To bring or come to an end: *The meeting broke up at noon.*
break (brāk) ◊ *verb* **broke, broken, breaking** ◊ *noun, plural* **breaks**
‖*These sound alike:* **break, brake**

breakdown *noun* **1.** A failure to work properly. **2.** A sudden loss of health.
break·down (**brāk′**doun′) ◊ *noun, plural* **breakdowns**

breaker *noun* A wave that breaks into foam on a shore.
break·er (**brā′**kər) ◊ *noun, plural* **breakers**

breakfast *noun* The first meal of the day. ◊ *verb* To eat breakfast.
break·fast (**brĕk′**fəst) ◊ *noun, plural* **breakfasts** ◊ *verb* **breakfasted, breakfasting**

breakthrough *noun* A sudden advance that shows the way toward further progress.
break·through (**brāk′**thro͞o′) ◊ *noun, plural* **breakthroughs**

breast *noun* **1.** One of the glands in a female mammal that produces milk to feed her young offspring. **2.** The upper part of the front surface of the body, from the neck to the abdomen; chest.
breast (brĕst) ◊ *noun, plural* **breasts**

breastbone *noun* The bone in the middle of the chest, to which the ribs attach.
breast·bone (**brĕst′**bōn′) ◊ *noun, plural* **breastbones**

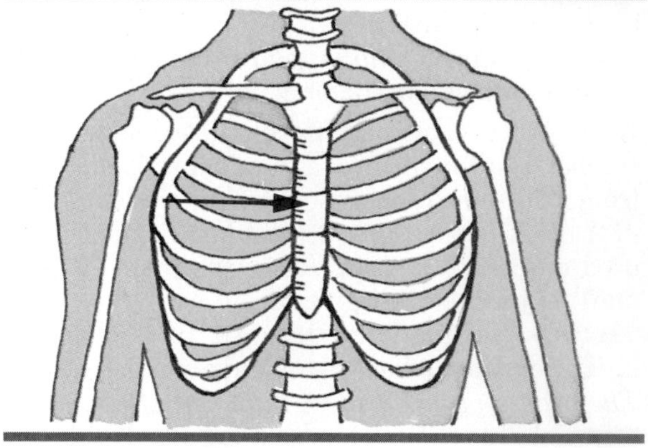

▲ **breastbone**

ă	pat	ĭ	pit	oi	**oil**	th	**bath**
ā	pay	ī	ride	o͝o	**book**	*th*	**bathe**
â	care	î	fierce	o͞o	**boot**	ə	**ago, item**
ä	father	ŏ	pot	ou	**out**		pencil
ĕ	pet	ō	go	ŭ	**cut**		atom
ē	be	ô	paw, for	û	**fur**		circus

breath *noun* **1.** The air taken into the lungs and forced out when a person breathes. **2.** The ability to breathe normally or easily: *I became short of breath as I ran up the hill.* **3.** The act of breathing: *Hold your breath.* **4.** A slight breeze: *There was not a breath of air in that hot auditorium.*
breath (brĕth) ◊ *noun, plural* **breaths**

breathe *verb* **1.** To take air into the lungs and force it out; inhale and exhale: *All mammals breathe air.* **2.** To say in the quietest way; whisper: *Don't breathe a word of this.*
breathe (brēth) ◊ *verb* **breathed, breathing**

breathless *adjective* **1.** Out of breath; panting: *We were breathless after running up the stairs.* **2.** Holding the breath from excitement or suspense.
breath·less (**brĕth′** lĭs) ◊ *adjective*

breathtaking *adjective* Filling a person with wonder or awe; very exciting: *The cliff offered a breathtaking view of the canyon.*
breath·tak·ing (**brĕth′** tā′kĭng) ◊ *adjective*

bred *verb* Past tense and past participle of **breed.**
bred (brĕd) ◊ *verb*
‖*These sound alike:* **bred, bread**

breeches *plural noun* **1.** Short trousers ending at or just below the knees. **2.** Trousers; pants.
breech·es (**brĭch′** ĭz) ◊ *plural noun*

breed *verb* **1.** To produce offspring; reproduce: *Mosquitoes breed rapidly.* **2.** To raise animals or plants; grow: *That farmer breeds cattle. Scientists are breeding improved types of grain.* **3.** To bring about; give rise to: *Lying always breeds trouble.*
◊ *noun* A particular type or variety of animal or plant: *Poodles and collies are breeds of dogs. This is a hardy breed of corn for cold climates.*
breed (brēd) ◊ *verb* **bred, breeding** ◊ *noun, plural* **breeds**

breeding *noun* Training in proper ways of behaving: *Fine manners show breeding.*
breed·ing (**brē′** dĭng) ◊ *noun*

breeze *noun* A light wind.
◊ *verb* To move quickly and without effort: *I breezed through the test and passed easily.*
breeze (brēz) ◊ *noun, plural* **breezes** ◊ *verb* **breezed, breezing**

breve *noun* A mark (˘) placed over a vowel to show that it has a short sound. In the pronunciation of the word *bat* (băt), the breve is placed over the *ă.*
breve (brĕv *or* brēv) ◊ *noun, plural* **breves**

brew *verb* **1.** To make beer or ale from malt and hops. **2.** To make by boiling or steeping: *We brewed tea for lunch.* **3.** To think up; plan: *They're brewing a scheme for getting revenge.* **4.** To be taking form: *A storm is brewing in the east.*
◊ *noun* A drink made by brewing.
brew (broo͞) ◊ *verb* **brewed, brewing** ◊ *noun, plural* **brews**

briar *noun* A brier.
bri·ar (**brī′** ər) ◊ *noun, plural* **briars**
‖*These sound alike:* **briar, brier**

bribe *noun* Money or something else valuable offered or given to try to make a person act dishonestly.
◊ *verb* To give a bribe to: *The outlaws tried to bribe the sheriff into letting them go.*
bribe (brīb) ◊ *noun, plural* **bribes** ◊ *verb* **bribed, bribing**

brick *noun* **1.** An oblong block of clay, baked by the sun or in an oven until hard. Bricks are used for building and paving. **2.** These blocks considered as a building material.
brick (brĭk) ◊ *noun, plural* **bricks**

bricklayer *noun* A person who builds walls or other structures with bricks.
brick·lay·er (**brĭk′** lā′ər) ◊ *noun, plural* **bricklayers**

bride *noun* A woman recently married or about to be married.
bride (brīd) ◊ *noun, plural* **brides**

bridegroom *noun* A man recently married or about to be married.
bride·groom (**brīd′** groo͞m′ *or* **brīd′** gro͝om′) ◊ *noun, plural* **bridegrooms**

bridge *noun* **1.** A structure built over a river, railroad, or other obstacle so that people or vehicles can cross from one side to the other. **2.** The upper bony ridge of the human nose. **3.** A platform above the main deck of a ship. The captain or the officer in charge usually runs the ship from the bridge.
◊ *verb* To build a bridge over: *We chopped down a tree to bridge the stream.*
bridge (brĭj) ◊ *noun, plural* **bridges** ◊ *verb* **bridged, bridging**

bridle *noun* The straps, bit, and reins that are placed over a horse's head and used to control the animal.
◊ *verb* To put a bridle on: *I saddled and bridled my favorite horse.*
bri·dle (**brīd′** l) ◊ *noun, plural* **bridles** ◊ *verb* **bridled, bridling**

▲ **bridle**

brief *adjective* Short in time or length: *The walkers stopped for a brief rest. Write a brief outline of the book.*
◊ *verb* To give instructions, information, or advice to: *The leader briefed the campers about what to expect on the hike.*
brief (brēf) ◊ *adjective* **briefer, briefest** ◊ *verb* **briefed, briefing**

brier *noun* A shrub with thorny stems.
bri·er (**brī′** ər) ◊ *noun, plural* **briers**
‖*These sound alike:* **brier, briar**

brig *noun* **1.** A sailing ship with two masts and square sails. **2.** A prison on a ship.
brig (brĭg) ◊ *noun, plural* **brigs**

brigade *noun* **1.** A large army unit. **2.** A group organized to do a job together: *Our town has a volunteer fire brigade.*
bri·gade (brĭ **gād′**) ◊ *noun, plural* **brigades**

bright *adjective* **1.** Giving off or filled with a lot of light: *The bright sun lit up the meadow.* **2.** Strong or clear in color; vivid: *The fire engine was painted bright red.* **3.** Quick in understanding or thinking; smart: *The class was easy for the brighter children.*
bright (brīt) ◊ *adjective* **brighter, brightest**

brighten *verb* To make or become bright or brighter: *Sunlight brightened the room.*
bright·en (**brīt′** n) ◊ *verb* **brightened, brightening**

brilliance *noun* The quality or condition of being brilliant.
bril·liance (**brĭl′** yəns) ◊ *noun*

brilliant *adjective* **1.** Shining very brightly: *A brilliant sun blazed in the sky.* **2.** Very vivid in color: *The sky was a brilliant blue.* **3.** Very intelligent. **4.** Splendid; magnificent: *The actor gave a brilliant performance.*
bril·liant (**brĭl′** yənt) ◊ *adjective*

brim *noun* **1.** The rim or upper edge of a cup or glass. **2.** The part of a hat that sticks out at the lower front edge.
◊ *verb* To be full almost to the point of overflowing: *The cup is brimming with milk.*
brim (brĭm) ◊ *noun, plural* **brims** ◊ *verb* **brimmed, brimming**

brine *noun* Water with a large amount of salt: *The pickles were packed in brine.*
brine (brīn) ◊ *noun*

bring *verb* **1.** To take with oneself; cause to come along; convey: *Please bring me a peach from the kitchen.* **2.** To cause to occur or arrive: *North winds bring cooler weather.* **3.** To cause to do something: *What brought you to give away your best scarf?* **4.** To result in: *The flood brought death to hundreds.* **5.** To put in a certain condition: *Bring the liquid to a boil. I brought the bicycle to a stop.* **6.** To sell for: *Those diamonds will bring high prices.*
◊ *idiom* **bring up 1.** To take care of; raise or rear. **2.** To introduce into discussion.
bring (brĭng) ◊ *verb* **brought, bringing**

brink *noun* **1.** The upper edge of a steep place: *From the brink of the cliff, you can look straight down.* **2.** The very edge; verge: *I am on the brink of tears.*
brink (brĭngk) ◊ *noun, plural* **brinks**

brisk *adjective* **1.** Moving or acting quickly; lively: *If we walk at a brisk pace, we'll get there on time.* **2.** Very active: *Business is brisk when the store has a sale.* **3.** Fresh and invigorating: *It was a brisk day.*
brisk (brĭsk) ◊ *adjective* **brisker, briskest**

ă	pat	ĭ	pit	oi	oil	th	bath
ā	pay	ī	ride	o͝o	book	*th*	bathe
â	care	î	fierce	o͞o	boot	ə	ago, item
ä	father	ŏ	pot	ou	out		pencil
ĕ	pet	ō	go	ŭ	cut		atom
ē	be	ô	paw, for	û	fur		circus

bristle *noun* A short, coarse, stiff hair or hairlike part of an animal, as a hog.
◊ *verb* **1.** To raise the bristles stiffly: *The dog bristled and showed its teeth.* **2.** To stand out stiffly like bristles: *The child's short hair bristled.* **3.** To show sudden anger: *I bristled when they called me a baby.*
bris·tle (**brĭs′** əl) ◊ *noun, plural* **bristles** ◊ *verb* **bristled, bristling**

Brit. The abbreviation for *Britain* and *British.*

British *noun* (*used with a plural verb*) The people of Great Britain.
◊ *adjective* Of or relating to Great Britain, the British, or the kind of English used by them.
Brit·ish (**brĭt′** ĭsh) ◊ *noun* ◊ *adjective*

brittle *adjective* Hard and easily broken: *The brittle branch snapped in my hand.*
brit·tle (**brĭt′** l) ◊ *adjective*

broach *verb* To begin to discuss; bring up: *How can I broach this subject?*
broach (brōch) ◊ *verb* **broached, broaching**

broad *adjective* **1.** Wide from side to side: *The piano was too broad to fit through the door.* **2.** Large in size, extent, or scope: *The menu offers a broad choice of desserts.* **3.** Full; complete: *The theft occurred in broad daylight.*
broad (brôd) ◊ *adjective* **broader, broadest**

broadcast *verb* **1.** To send out over a wide area by radio or television: *All the networks will broadcast the governor's speech.* **2.** To make known over a wide area: *The rumor was quickly broadcast through the town.*
◊ *noun* **1.** An act of broadcasting. **2.** A radio or television program.
broad·cast (**brôd′** kăst′) ◊ *verb* **broadcast** *or* **broadcasted, broadcasting** ◊ *noun, plural* **broadcasts**

broaden *verb* To make or become broad or broader: *This narrow highway should be broadened.*
broad·en (**brôd′** n) ◊ *verb* **broadened, broadening**

brocade *noun* A heavy cloth with a rich, raised design woven into it.
bro·cade (brō **kād′**) ◊ *noun, plural* **brocades**

broccoli *noun* A plant with dark green stalks and tightly clustered flower buds that are eaten as a vegetable.
broc·co·li (**brŏk′** ə lē) ◊ *noun*

▲ **broccoli**

broil *verb* **1.** To cook directly under or over a source of heat: *Let's broil the fish we caught. The fish broiled for ten minutes.* **2.** To make or be very hot: *The desert sun broiled the travelers in the caravan. The tourists broiled under the tropical sun.*
broil (broil) ◊ *verb* **broiled, broiling**

broiler *noun* A pan, grill, or a part of a stove for broiling foods.
broil·er (**broi′** lər) ◊ *noun, plural* **broilers**

broke *adjective* Having no money at all.
◊ *verb* Past tense of **break.**
broke (brōk) ◊ *adjective* ◊ *verb*

broken *adjective* **1.** In pieces; shattered: *If you walk barefoot, look out for broken glass.* **2.** Not working properly; out of order: *My watch is broken.* **3.** Not kept or followed: *After a broken promise, it is hard to count on a person.*
◊ *verb* Past participle of **break.**
bro·ken (**brō′** kən) ◊ *adjective* ◊ *verb*

broker *noun* A person who buys or sells property for other people.
bro·ker (**brō′** kər) ◊ *noun, plural* **brokers**

bronchial tube *noun* Any of the tubes in the chest formed by branches of the windpipe. There are two large bronchial tubes, each leading into a lung. Inside the lungs are many smaller bronchial tubes.
bron·chi·al tube (**brŏng′** kē əl) ◊ *noun, plural* **bronchial tubes**

bronchitis *noun* An illness caused by the infection and swelling of the lining of the bronchial tubes. Bronchitis may cause a bad cough and a hoarse voice.
bron·chi·tis (brŏng **kī′** tĭs) ◊ *noun*

bronco *noun* A small wild or half-wild horse of western North America.
bron·co (**brŏng′**kō) ◊ *noun, plural* **broncos**

bronze *noun* **1.** A yellowish brown metal that is a mixture of copper and tin and sometimes other elements. Bronze is used for statues, bells, machine parts, and other things. **2.** A yellowish brown color.
◊ *verb* To make or become the color of bronze: *The sun bronzed their faces.*
bronze (brŏnz) ◊ *noun* ◊ *verb* **bronzed, bronzing**

brooch *noun* A large ornamental pin.
brooch (brōch *or* bro͞och) ◊ *noun, plural* **brooches**

brood *noun* **1.** Young birds that are hatched at the same time. **2.** The children in one family.
◊ *verb* **1.** To sit on and hatch eggs. **2.** To think or worry quietly for a long time: *When you make a mistake, don't brood about it.*
brood (bro͞od) ◊ *noun, plural* **broods** ◊ *verb* **brooded, brooding**

▲ **brooch**

brook *noun* A small, natural stream.
brook (bro͝ok) ◊ *noun, plural* **brooks**

broom *noun* A device for sweeping. A broom has straw bristles or a brush attached at the end of a long stick.
broom (bro͞om *or* bro͝om) ◊ *noun, plural* **brooms**

broth *noun* A clear soup made from the water in which meat or fish have been boiled.
broth (brôth) ◊ *noun, plural* **broths**

brother *noun* A boy or man having the same mother and father as another person.
broth·er (**brŭ*th*′**ər) ◊ *noun, plural* **brothers**

ă	pat	ĭ	pit	oi	**oil**	th	**bath**
ā	pay	ī	ride	o͝o	book	*th*	bathe
â	care	î	fierce	o͞o	boot	ə	ago, item
ä	father	ŏ	pot	ou	**out**		pencil
ĕ	pet	ō	go	ŭ	cut		atom
ē	be	ô	paw, for	û	fur		circus

brotherhood *noun* **1.** The relationship of being a brother or brothers. **2.** Close friendship and good will among human beings; fellowship. **3.** All the members of the same profession, labor union, or other group.
broth·er·hood (**brŭ*th*′**ər ho͝od′) ◊ *noun, plural* **brotherhoods**

brother-in-law *noun* **1.** The brother of one's husband or wife. **2.** The husband of one's sister.
broth·er-in-law (**brŭ*th*′**ər ĭn lô′) ◊ *noun, plural* **brothers-in-law**

brought *verb* Past tense and past participle of **bring.**
brought (brôt) ◊ *verb*

brow *noun* **1.** The forehead. **2.** Either of the lines of hair above the eyes; eyebrow.
brow (brou) ◊ *noun, plural* **brows**

brown *noun* The color of chocolate or most kinds of soil.
◊ *adjective* Of the color brown.
◊ *verb* **1.** To make or become brown: *The sun browned my skin.* **2.** To cook until brown on the outside: *Meat browns quickly.*
brown (broun) ◊ *noun, plural* **browns** ◊ *adjective* **browner, brownest** ◊ *verb* **browned, browning**

brownie *noun* **1.** A small imaginary creature that is like an elf and is said to perform household chores while people are asleep. **2.** A square of a rich chocolate cake that often has nuts in it.
brown·ie (**brou′**nē) ◊ *noun, plural* **brownies**

browse *verb* **1.** To look over or read in a casual way: *I browsed through some magazines while I waited.* **2.** To feed on leaves, young shoots, and other plants, as deer do.
browse (brouz) ◊ *verb* **browsed, browsing**

bruise *noun* **1.** An injury that leaves a mark on the skin but does not break it. **2.** An injury to the surface of a fruit or plant.
◊ *verb* To make or become discolored as a result of a bruise: *A fall bruised my knee.*
bruise (bro͞oz) ◊ *noun, plural* **bruises** ◊ *verb* **bruised, bruising**

brunette *adjective* Having brown or black hair.
◊ *noun* A person with brown or black hair.
bru·nette (bro͞o **nĕt′**) ◊ *adjective* ◊ *noun, plural* **brunettes**

brush¹ *noun* **1.** A device for scrubbing, grooming the hair, or applying liquids. A brush is made of bristles, hairs, or wire fastened to a hard back or a short handle. **2.** A cleaning or grooming with a brush. **3.** A bushy tail of an animal, especially a fox. **4.** A light touch of something passing; graze.
◊ *verb* **1.** To clean, polish, sweep, or groom with a brush: *Brush your teeth.* **2.** To apply with a brush: *I brushed the paint on evenly.* **3.** To remove with or as if with a brush: *I brushed the crumbs from the table.* **4.** To touch lightly in passing; graze: *My horse brushed the fence in jumping.*
brush¹ (brŭsh) ◊ *noun, plural* **brushes** ◊ *verb* **brushed, brushing**

brush² *noun* **1.** Land that is covered with a thick growth of shrubs or small trees. **2.** Broken branches and twigs.
brush² (brŭsh) ◊ *noun*

***HISTORY* • brush¹, brush²**

Brush¹ comes from an old French word meaning "a brush" or "a broom." **Brush²** comes from another old French word that meant "twigs." The two French words were probably related, since brushes were often made from twigs.

Brussels sprout *noun* One of the small green heads that grow thickly on the stalk of a type of cabbage plant. Brussels sprouts are eaten as a vegetable.
Brus·sels sprout (brŭs′əlz) ◊ *noun, plural* **Brussels sprouts**

▲ **Brussels sprout**

brutal *adjective* Cruel and harsh; savage.
bru·tal (bro͞ot′l) ◊ *adjective*

brutality *noun* **1.** The quality of being brutal. **2.** A brutal act.
bru·tal·i·ty (bro͞o tăl′ĭ tē) ◊ *noun, plural* **brutalities**

brute *noun* **1.** An animal, especially a four-footed one; beast. **2.** A cruel person.
◊ *adjective* Entirely physical: *We lifted the barrel by brute force.*
brute (bro͞ot) ◊ *noun, plural* **brutes** ◊ *adjective*

bu. The abbreviation for *bushel* or *bushels.*

bubble *noun* A ball of air or other gas, often with a thin film around it. Bubbles form in boiling water and in soaps or shaken liquids.
◊ *verb* To form or rise in bubbles: *A stew bubbled on the stove.*
bub·ble (bŭb′əl) ◊ *noun, plural* **bubbles** ◊ *verb* **bubbled, bubbling**

buck *noun* A full-grown male deer, antelope, or rabbit.
◊ *verb* **1.** To leap upward with the head down: *The bronco bucked and kicked.* **2.** To charge into or against; struggle against: *The little boat bucked a strong wind.*
buck (bŭk) ◊ *noun, plural* **bucks** ◊ *verb* **bucked, bucking**

▲ **buck**
A mule deer buck

bucket *noun* A round, open container with a curved handle, used for carrying things such

as water, coal, and sand; pail.
buck·et (bŭk′ĭt) ◊ *noun, plural* **buckets**

buckle *noun* **1.** A clasp used to fasten one end of a strap or belt to the other. **2.** An ornament that looks like such a clasp.
◊ *verb* **1.** To fasten with a buckle: *Buckle your safety belt.* **2.** To bend, bulge, or crumple under pressure or heat.
buck·le (bŭk′əl) ◊ *noun, plural* **buckles**
◊ *verb* **buckled, buckling**

buckskin *noun* A very soft, strong, yellow leather made from the skins of deer or sheep.
buck·skin (bŭk′skĭn′) ◊ *noun*

buckwheat *noun* A plant with small seeds that are often ground into flour.
buck·wheat (bŭk′hwēt′) ◊ *noun*

bud *noun* **1.** A small swelling on a branch or stem, containing a flower, shoot, or leaves that have not yet developed. **2.** A flower or leaf that has not opened up yet.
◊ *verb* To form or produce a bud or buds: *Spring flowers will soon bud.*
bud (bŭd) ◊ *noun, plural* **buds** ◊ *verb* **budded, budding**

Buddha *noun* 563?–483? B.C. The Indian philosopher who founded the religion of Buddhism.
Bud·dha (bo͞o′də) ◊ *noun*

Buddhism *noun* The religion based on the teachings of Buddha. Buddhism is practiced mainly in eastern and central Asia.
Bud·dhism (bo͞o′dĭz′əm) ◊ *noun*

buddy *noun* A close friend; pal.
bud·dy (bŭd′ē) ◊ *noun, plural* **buddies**

budge *verb* To move or cause to move slightly: *We couldn't budge the heavy rock.*
budge (bŭj) ◊ *verb* **budged, budging**

budget *noun* A plan for how money will be spent: *Our budget includes amounts for food, clothing, and rent.*
◊ *verb* To plan in advance how to spend.
bud·get (bŭj′ĭt) ◊ *noun, plural* **budgets**
◊ *verb* **budgeted, budgeting**

ă	pat	ĭ	pit	oi	**oil**	th	ba**th**
ā	pay	ī	ride	o͝o	**book**	*th*	ba**the**
â	care	î	fierce	o͞o	**boot**	ə	ago, item
ä	father	ŏ	pot	ou	**out**		pencil
ĕ	pet	ō	go	ŭ	cut		atom
ē	be	ô	paw, for	û	fur		circus

buff *noun* **1.** A soft, thick, yellowish leather made from the skin of a buffalo, elk, or ox. **2.** A yellowish tan color. **3.** A stick or wheel covered with soft material and used for polishing objects.
◊ *adjective* Yellowish tan.
◊ *verb* To polish with a buff.
buff (bŭf) ◊ *noun, plural* **buffs** ◊ *adjective*
◊ *verb* **buffed, buffing**

buffalo *noun* **1.** Any of several oxlike African or Asian animals with large, outward-curving horns. **2.** The bison.
buf·fa·lo (bŭf′ə lō′) ◊ *noun, plural* **buffaloes** *or* **buffalos** *or* **buffalo**

buffet *noun* **1.** A long piece of furniture with drawers for storing china, silverware, and table linens. **2.** A meal at which guests serve themselves from dishes arranged on a table or buffet.
buf·fet (bə **fā**′) ◊ *noun, plural* **buffets**

bug *noun* **1.** A kind of insect that has mouth parts used for piercing or sucking. Some bugs have four wings, and some have none. **2.** An insect or similar creature. **3.** A very small organism that causes disease; germ. **4.** Something wrong with a machine, system, or plan: *We must get rid of the bugs in the new computer program.* **5.** A hidden microphone that allows private conversations to be overheard.
◊ *verb* To put a hidden microphone in a place to listen in on conversations.
bug (bŭg) ◊ *noun, plural* **bugs** ◊ *verb* **bugged, bugging**

buggy *noun* A small, light carriage pulled by a horse.
bug·gy (bŭg′ē) ◊ *noun, plural* **buggies**

▲ **buggy**

bugle *noun* A brass musical instrument. A bugle is like a trumpet and usually has no valves.
bu·gle (byo͞o′gəl) ◊ *noun, plural* **bugles**

build *verb* **1.** To make or form by putting together materials or parts; construct: *Engineers build bridges and dams.* **2.** To bring into being by working step by step: *You need to exercise to build strong muscles.* **3.** To progress toward a peak; grow steadily: *The excitement built because the game was tied.*
◊ *noun* The way a person or animal is shaped: *You are tall and slender in build.*
build (bĭld) ◊ *verb* **built, building** ◊ *noun, plural* **builds**

building *noun* **1.** A permanent structure built for people to live or gather in or for some other purpose. **2.** The work or business of making large structures such as buildings, ships, or bridges.
build·ing (bĭl′dĭng) ◊ *noun, plural* **buildings**

built *verb* Past tense and past participle of **build.**
built (bĭlt) ◊ *verb*

built-in *adjective* Built as a permanent part of a larger structure: *Our kitchen has built-in cupboards.*
built-in (bĭlt′ĭn′) ◊ *adjective*

bulb *noun* **1.** A rounded underground plant part, as of a tulip or an onion, from which a new plant can grow. **2.** A rounded part or object: *I put a new bulb in the electric lamp.*
bulb (bŭlb) ◊ *noun, plural* **bulbs**

bulge *noun* An outward curve or swelling: *The apple made a bulge in my coat pocket.*
◊ *verb* To swell or cause to swell outward.
bulge (bŭlj) ◊ *noun, plural* **bulges** ◊ *verb* **bulged, bulging**

bulk *noun* **1.** Great size, mass, or volume: *We couldn't move the couch because of its bulk.* **2.** The major portion; greater part: *The bulk of our money goes for rent.*
bulk (bŭlk) ◊ *noun*

bull *noun* **1.** The fully grown male of cattle. **2.** The male of certain large mammals, as the elephant or the moose.
bull (bo͝ol) ◊ *noun, plural* **bulls**

bulldog *noun* A stocky dog with a large head, short hair, and strong, square jaws.
bull·dog (bo͝ol′dôg′) ◊ *noun, plural* **bulldogs**

▲ **bulldog**

bulldozer *noun* A powerful tractor with a metal blade in front for moving earth, rocks, and small trees.
bull·doz·er (bo͝ol′dō′zər) ◊ *noun, plural* **bulldozers**

bullet *noun* A piece of metal that is shaped to be fired from a small firearm, as a pistol.
bul·let (bo͝ol′ĭt) ◊ *noun, plural* **bullets**

bulletin *noun* **1.** A short announcement on a matter of public interest, as in a newspaper or on television. **2.** A small newspaper, magazine, or pamphlet published regularly by an organization.
bul·le·tin (bo͝ol′ĭ tn) ◊ *noun, plural* **bulletins**

bullfinch *noun* A European bird with a short, thick bill and a red breast.
bull·finch (bo͝ol′fĭnch′) ◊ *noun, plural* **bullfinches**

bullfrog *noun* A large frog with a deep, hollow croak.
bull·frog (bo͝ol′frôg′) ◊ *noun, plural* **bullfrogs**

▲ **bullfrog**

bull's-eye *noun* **1.** The small circle in the center of a target. **2.** A shot that hits the center of a target.
bull's-eye (bo͝olz'ī') ◊ *noun, plural* **bull's-eyes**

bully *noun* A person who teases, picks on, or hurts smaller or weaker people.
◊ *verb* To treat as a bully does.
bul·ly (bo͝ol'ē) ◊ *noun, plural* **bullies** ◊ *verb* **bullied, bullying**

bulrush *noun* Any of several tall, grasslike plants that grow in wet places.
bul·rush (bo͝ol'rŭsh') ◊ *noun, plural* **bulrushes**

bumblebee *noun* A large, hairy bee that flies with a humming sound.
bum·ble·bee (bŭm'bəl bē') ◊ *noun, plural* **bumblebees**

bump *verb* **1.** To hit or knock against someone or something with force: *I bumped my head on the door.* **2.** To move with jerks and jolts: *The old car bumped down the road.*
◊ *noun* **1.** A heavy blow, collision, or jolt. **2.** A swelling, as from a blow or the sting of an insect.
bump (bŭmp) ◊ *verb* **bumped, bumping** ◊ *noun, plural* **bumps**

bumper *noun* A bar attached to the front or rear of a motor vehicle to reduce damage or shock in case of a collision.
◊ *adjective* Fuller, larger, or better than usual: *The farmer harvested a bumper crop.*
bump·er (bŭm'pər) ◊ *noun, plural* **bumpers** ◊ *adjective*

bun *noun* A biscuit or roll, often sweetened.
bun (bŭn) ◊ *noun, plural* **buns**

bunch *noun* **1.** A group of things of the same kind that are growing, fastened, or placed together: *I put the bunch of keys in my pocket.* **2.** A group of people: *You are the nicest one in our bunch.*
◊ *verb* To gather into or form a bunch.
bunch (bŭnch) ◊ *noun, plural* **bunches** ◊ *verb* **bunched, bunching**

ă	pat	ĭ	pit	oi	**oil**	th	ba**th**
ā	pay	ī	ride	o͝o	book	*th*	ba**th**e
â	care	î	fierce	o͞o	boot	ə	ago, item
ä	father	ŏ	pot	ou	**out**		pencil
ĕ	pet	ō	go	ŭ	cut		atom
ē	be	ô	paw, for	û	fur		circus

bundle *noun* A number of things bound or wrapped together; package: *We carried the bundle to the post office.*
◊ *verb* To make into or tie in a bundle: *I bundled the old magazines together.*
bun·dle (bŭn'dl) ◊ *noun, plural* **bundles** ◊ *verb* **bundled, bundling**

bungalow *noun* A small one-story house.
bun·ga·low (bŭng'gə lō') ◊ *noun, plural* **bungalows**

bungle *verb* To manage, do, or handle badly: *The pitcher bungled the game.*
bun·gle (bŭng'gəl) ◊ *verb* **bungled, bungling**

bunk *noun* A narrow bed built like a shelf against a wall.
bunk (bŭngk) ◊ *noun, plural* **bunks**

bunny *noun* A rabbit.
bun·ny (bŭn'ē) ◊ *noun, plural* **bunnies**

bunt *verb* To bat a baseball lightly so that the ball doesn't go very far.
◊ *noun* A baseball that is bunted.
bunt (bŭnt) ◊ *verb* **bunted, bunting** ◊ *noun, plural* **bunts**

bunting *noun* **1.** A light cloth used for making flags. **2.** Flags made of bunting and used especially for holiday decoration.
bun·ting (bŭn'tĭng) ◊ *noun*

buoy *noun* **1.** A floating object that is anchored in water to warn of danger or to mark a channel. **2.** A life preserver.
buoy (bo͞o'ē *or* boi) ◊ *noun, plural* **buoys**

▲ **buoy**

bur *noun* A seed, fruit, nut, or flower head enclosed in a rough, prickly covering.
bur (bûr) ◊ *noun, plural* **burs**
‖*These sound alike:* **bur, burr**

burden *noun* **1.** Something that is carried; load: *The horses pulled a heavy burden of logs.* **2.** Something that is hard to bear: *We worry about the burden of high taxes.*
◊ *verb* To load with a burden: *Don't burden me with your complaints.*
bur·den (bûr′dn) ◊ *noun, plural* **burdens**
◊ *verb* **burdened, burdening**

burdensome *adjective* Very hard to bear; tiring.
bur·den·some (bûr′dn səm) ◊ *adjective*

bureau *noun* **1.** A chest of drawers, especially one with a mirror. **2.** An office for a particular kind of business: *We opened a travel bureau.* **3.** A department of a government: *The Bureau of Motor Vehicles issues automobile licenses.*
bu·reau (byo͝or′ō) ◊ *noun, plural* **bureaus**

burglar *noun* A person who breaks into a building in order to steal.
bur·glar (bûr′glər) ◊ *noun, plural* **burglars**

burial *noun* The act of placing a dead body in a grave, a tomb, or the sea.
bur·i·al (bĕr′ē əl) ◊ *noun, plural* **burials**

burlap *noun* A coarse cloth made of hemp or jute and used especially to make bags, sacks, and wall coverings.
bur·lap (bûr′lăp′) ◊ *noun*

burn *verb* **1.** To be or set on fire: *The logs burned in the fireplace. When I finished reading the letter, I burned it.* **2.** To undergo or cause to undergo damage, destruction, or injury by fire or heat: *The house burned to the ground. I burned my fingers with a match.* **3.** To produce by fire or heat: *The spark burned a hole in the rug.* **4.** To produce light: *The sun burned bright in the sky.* **5.** To feel or cause to feel strong emotion: *We burned with anger.* **6.** To feel or cause to feel a burning sensation: *My cheeks burned.*
◊ *noun* Damage or an injury produced by burning.
burn (bûrn) ◊ *verb* **burned** *or* **burnt, burning**
◊ *noun, plural* **burns**

burner *noun* The part of a stove, furnace, or lamp in which a flame is produced.
burn·er (bûr′nər) ◊ *noun, plural* **burners**

burnoose *noun* A long, loose, flowing cloak with a hood that is worn by Arabs.
bur·noose (bər no͞os′) ◊ *noun, plural* **burnooses**

burnt *verb* A past tense and past participle of **burn.**
burnt (bûrnt) ◊ *verb*

burr *noun* A bur.
burr (bûr) ◊ *noun, plural* **burrs**
‖*These sound alike:* **burr, bur**

burro *noun* A small donkey, usually used for riding or for carrying loads.
bur·ro (bûr′ō) ◊ *noun, plural* **burros**
‖*These sound alike:* **burro, borough, burrow**

▲ **burro**

burrow *noun* A hole dug in the ground by a small animal, such as a rabbit or a mole.
◊ *verb* **1.** To make a burrow. **2.** To move or work one's way by or as if by digging: *I burrowed under the covers.* **3.** To look for; search: *I had to burrow in the library for the books I needed.*
bur·row (bûr′ō) ◊ *noun, plural* **burrows**
◊ *verb* **burrowed, burrowing**
‖*These sound alike:* **burrow, borough, burro**

burst *verb* **1.** To break or cause to break open suddenly and violently: *The balloon burst. Ice burst the water pipe.* **2.** To come, go, or do suddenly and with force: *They burst into the room.* **3.** To be or seem to be full to the point of breaking open: *I am bursting with pride.* **4.** To give sudden expression to one's feelings: *They burst out laughing.*
◊ *noun* A sudden outbreak; spurt: *I heard a burst of laughter. With a burst of speed the car passed the truck.*
burst (bûrst) ◊ *verb* **burst, bursting,** ◊ *noun, plural* **bursts**

bury *verb* **1.** To put a dead body in a grave, a tomb, or the sea. **2.** To hide by placing in the

ground and covering with earth: *The dog buried the bone in the garden.* **3.** To cover from view; hide: *I buried my face in the pillow.* **4.** To be or become absorbed: *We buried ourselves in our books.*
bur·y (bĕr′ē) ◊ *verb* **buried, burying**
‖*These sound alike:* **bury, berry**

bus *noun* A large motor vehicle used for carrying passengers.
◊ *verb* To send, take, or go in a bus.
bus (bŭs) ◊ *noun, plural* **buses** *or* **busses**
◊ *verb* **bused, busing** *or* **bussed, bussing**

bush *noun* An often low woody plant with many branches; shrub.
bush (bo͝osh) ◊ *noun, plural* **bushes**

bushel *noun* A unit of capacity for dry things equal to 4 pecks or 32 quarts.
bush·el (bo͝osh′əl) ◊ *noun, plural* **bushels**

bushy *adjective* Thick and shaggy: *Squirrels have bushy tails.*
bush·y (bo͝osh′ē) ◊ *adjective* **bushier, bushiest**

business *noun* **1.** A person's occupation, activity, or work: *Our neighbor is in the business of selling cars.* **2.** Selling and buying; trade. **3.** A commercial establishment such as a store or factory. **4.** A matter of concern or interest: *That is none of your business.*
busi·ness (bĭz′nĭs) ◊ *noun, plural* **businesses**

> ***SYNONYMS***
>
> ***business, commerce, industry***
>
> They were in the shoe *business* before they became actors. There are many regulations for *commerce* between states. Our city is the center of the steel *industry.*

businessman *noun* A man who is engaged in business.
busi·ness·man (bĭz′nĭs măn′) ◊ *noun, plural* **businessmen**

ă	pat	ĭ	pit	oi	oil	th	bath
ā	pay	ī	ride	o͝o	book	*th*	bathe
â	care	î	fierce	o͞o	boot	ə	ago, item
ä	father	ŏ	pot	ou	out		pencil
ĕ	pet	ō	go	ŭ	cut		atom
ē	be	ô	paw, for	û	fur		circus

businesswoman *noun* A woman who is engaged in business.
busi·ness·wom·an (bĭz′nĭs wo͝om′ən) ◊ *noun, plural* **businesswomen**

busses *noun* A plural of **bus.**
bus·ses (bŭs′ĭz) ◊ *noun*

bust *noun* A sculpture of a person's head, shoulders, and upper chest.
bust (bŭst) ◊ *noun, plural* **busts**

bustle *verb* To move or cause to move around in a busy or excited way.
◊ *noun* Busy or excited activity; commotion: *There was a lot of bustle as we packed our suitcases.*
bus·tle (bŭs′əl) ◊ *verb* **bustled, bustling**
◊ *noun*

busy *adjective* **1.** Engaged in work or activity: *I am busy studying.* **2.** Crowded with activity: *Today I had a busy morning.* **3.** Being in use: *The phone is busy.*
◊ *verb* To make busy: *I busied myself with making the salad.*
bus·y (bĭz′ē) ◊ *adjective* **busier, busiest**
◊ *verb* **busied, busying**

busybody *noun* A person who pries into the affairs of others.
bus·y·bod·y (bĭz′ē bŏd′ē) ◊ *noun, plural* **busybodies**

but *conjunction* **1.** While on the contrary: *Usually nights are cold, but tonight the air is hot and sticky.* **2.** Nevertheless: *The plan may not work out, but we must try it.* **3.** Without the result that: *It never rains but it pours.*
◊ *adverb* No more than; only: *They had skated but a few moments when the bell rang.*
◊ *preposition* With the exception of; except: *I had nothing to wear but an old suit.*
but (bŭt) ◊ *conjunction* ◊ *adverb*
◊ *preposition*
‖*These sound alike:* **but, butt**

butcher *noun* **1.** A person whose work is killing animals and preparing their meat for food. **2.** A person who sells meat.
◊ *verb* **1.** To kill and prepare animals for food. **2.** To ruin by bad work; bungle.
butch·er (bo͝och′ər) ◊ *noun, plural* **butchers**
◊ *verb* **butchered, butchering**

butler *noun* The chief male servant of a household.
but·ler (bŭt′lər) ◊ *noun, plural* **butlers**

butt¹ *noun* A person who is the target of ridicule or scorn: *The child was the butt of the bully's jokes.*
butt¹ (bŭt) ◊ *noun, plural* **butts**
‖*These sound alike:* **butt, but**

butt² *verb* To hit or push with the head or horns: *The goat butted the wall.*
◊ *noun* A blow or push with the head or horns.
butt² (bŭt) ◊ *verb* **butted, butting** ◊ *noun, plural* **butts**
‖*These sound alike:* **butt, but**

butt³ *noun* **1.** The thicker end: *Rest the butt of the rifle on the ground.* **2.** An unused end: *Put the cigarette butts in the garbage.*
butt³ (bŭt) ◊ *noun, plural* **butts**
‖*These sound alike:* **butt, but**

***HISTORY* • butt¹, butt², butt³**

Butt¹ comes from an old French word meaning "target." **Butt²** also comes from an old French word. This French word came from a prehistoric Germanic word meaning "to strike." It is distantly related to **beat. Butt³** probably came from a Scandinavian word that meant "a block of wood."

butte *noun* A hill that rises sharply and has a flat top.
butte (byo͞ot) ◊ *noun, plural* **buttes**

butter *noun* **1.** A soft, yellowish fatty food that is separated from milk or cream by churning. **2.** A substance that is like butter in use and consistency.
◊ *verb* To put butter on or in.
but·ter (bŭt′ər) ◊ *noun, plural* **butters** ◊ *verb* **buttered, buttering**

buttercup *noun* A common plant with glossy yellow cup-shaped flowers.
but·ter·cup (bŭt′ər kŭp′) ◊ *noun, plural* **buttercups**

butterfat *noun* The fat in milk from which butter is made.
but·ter·fat (bŭt′ər făt′) ◊ *noun*

butterfly *noun* An insect with four broad, often colorful wings and a narrow body. It flies mainly in the daytime.
but·ter·fly (bŭt′ər flī′) ◊ *noun, plural* **butterflies**

▲ **butterfly**
Left: The pupa stage of development
Right: An adult butterfly

buttermilk *noun* The thick, sour liquid that remains after butter has been churned from milk or cream.
but·ter·milk (bŭt′ər mĭlk′) ◊ *noun*

butterscotch *noun* A candy or a flavoring made from brown sugar and butter.
but·ter·scotch (bŭt′ər skŏch′) ◊ *noun*

button *noun* **1.** A disk or knob used to fasten together parts of a garment or as decoration. **2.** A part that resembles a button: *I pushed the button to turn on the light.*
◊ *verb* To fasten or close with buttons: *Don't forget to button your coat.*
but·ton (bŭt′n) ◊ *noun, plural* **buttons** ◊ *verb* **buttoned, buttoning**

buttonhole *noun* A slit or hole through which a button passes.
but·ton·hole (bŭt′n hōl′) ◊ *noun, plural* **buttonholes**

buttress *noun* **1.** A structure, often of stone, built against a wall to support or strengthen it. **2.** Something that serves to support or strengthen.
but·tress (bŭt′rĭs) ◊ *noun, plural* **buttresses**

buy *verb* To get by paying the price for: *We bought a new car.*
◊ *noun* Something offered for sale or bought at a lower price than usual; bargain: *The coat was a good buy.*
buy (bī) ◊ *verb* **bought, buying** ◊ *noun, plural* **buys**
‖*These sound alike:* **buy, by**

SYNONYMS

buy, purchase

We need to *buy* a larger car. The manager *purchases* all the machinery for the factory. **Antonym:** *sell*

buyer *noun* **1.** A person who buys; customer. **2.** A person who is employed to buy merchandise for a retail store.
buy·er (bī′ər) ◊ *noun, plural* **buyers**

buzz *verb* **1.** To make a low, humming sound like that of a bee: *The alarm clock buzzed.* **2.** To be full of a low murmur or humming sound: *The courtroom buzzed with excitement.* **3.** To fly a plane low over.
◊ *noun* A buzzing sound: *I heard the buzz of the mosquito.*
buzz (bŭz) ◊ *verb* **buzzed, buzzing** ◊ *noun, plural* **buzzes**

buzzard *noun* A vulture.
buz·zard (bŭz′ərd) ◊ *noun, plural* **buzzards**

buzzer *noun* An electrical device that makes a buzzing noise, used to give a signal.
buzz·er (bŭz′ər) ◊ *noun, plural* **buzzers**

by *preposition* **1.** Through the action of: *The homework was assigned by the teacher.* **2.** With the help or use of: *We crossed the river by ferry.* **3.** According to: *The team always played by the rules.* **4.** In the course of; during: *We slept by day.* **5.** In the amount of: *The actor received letters by the hundreds.* **6.** Up to and beyond; past: *A car drove by us.* **7.** Next to; near: *We went jogging by the river.* **8.** Not later than: *We had to get there by evening.* **9.** In the matter of: *She is a carpenter by trade.* **10.** With the difference of or to the extent of: *My brother is shorter than I by three inches.*
◊ *adverb* **1.** Close at hand; nearby: *We just sat by and watched.* **2.** Aside: *We put money by for later use.* **3.** Past: *A truck went by.*
◊ *idiom* **by and by** Before long; soon.
by (bī) ◊ *preposition* ◊ *adverb*
‖ *These sound alike:* **by, buy**

bygone *adjective* Gone by; past: *The photograph brings back memories of bygone days.*
by·gone (bī′gôn′) ◊ *adjective*

by-pass *noun* A road that goes around a crowded area such as a city or town.
◊ *verb* To go around by using a by-pass.
by-pass (bī′păs′) ◊ *noun, plural* **by-passes** ◊ *verb* **by-passed, by-passing**

by-product *noun* Something that is produced while making another product.
by-prod·uct (bī′prŏd′əkt) ◊ *noun, plural* **by-products**

bystander *noun* A person who is present but does not take part in what is happening.
by·stand·er (bī′stăn′dər) ◊ *noun, plural* **bystanders**

byte *noun* A sequence of adjacent binary digits operated on as a unit by a computer and usually shorter than a word.
byte (bīt) ◊ *noun, plural* **bytes**
‖ *These sound alike:* **byte, bite**

byway *noun* A road that leads off a main road but is used less often.
by·way (bī′wā′) ◊ *noun, plural* **byways**

ă	pat	ĭ	pit	oi	oil	th	bath
ā	pay	ī	ride	o͝o	book	*th*	bathe
â	care	î	fierce	o͞o	boot	ə	ago, item
ä	father	ŏ	pot	ou	out		pencil
ĕ	pet	ō	go	ŭ	cut		atom
ē	be	ô	paw, for	û	fur		circus

Cobra

Cc

C is the third letter of the English alphabet. Did you know that it has a long history?

Over 3 500 years ago, people in the Middle East were using symbols that became the letters of our alphabet. This ancient Middle Eastern symbol is a form of the letter that became our letter *C*.

The ancient Greeks borrowed their alphabet from people in the Middle East. Here is a form of the Greek letter that became our letter *C*.

The ancient Romans borrowed their alphabet from a people who had taken their own letter symbols from the Greeks. Here is a form of the Roman letter *C* that was used for carving letters into stone. These letters became the model for our printed capital letters.

As people wrote quickly, especially with pens, the capital letters began to take the shapes of small letters. Here is a small-letter *c* that was developed about 1,200 years ago.

Cc *Cc*	Cc	Cc	Cc
Handwriting	Sans Serif Type	Serif Type	Computer Printing

c *or* **C** *noun* **1.** The third letter of the English alphabet. **2.** The Roman numeral for the number 100.
c *or* **C** (sē) ◊ *noun, plural* **c's** *or* **C's**

C The abbreviation for *Celsius* and *centigrade.*

CA The abbreviation for *California* used with a Zip Code.

cab *noun* **1.** An automobile that can be hired to carry passengers; taxicab. **2.** A carriage for hire that is pulled by one horse. **3.** The covered compartment for the operator or driver of a machine such as a crane or truck.
cab (kăb) ◊ *noun, plural* **cabs**

cabbage *noun* A plant with a rounded head of tightly overlapping leaves. Cabbage is eaten as a vegetable.
cab·bage (kăb′ĭj) ◊ *noun, plural* **cabbages**

cabin *noun* **1.** A small, simply built house. **2.** A private room for a passenger or crew member on a ship. **3.** A part of an airplane for the crew, passengers, or cargo.
cab·in (kăb′ĭn) ◊ *noun, plural* **cabins**

cabinet *noun* **1.** A case or cupboard with drawers, shelves, or compartments for storing or displaying objects: *Put the letters in the filing cabinet.* **2.** A group of people who act as official advisers, especially to a head of state.
cab·i·net (kăb′ə nĭt) ◊ *noun, plural* **cabinets**

cable *noun* **1.** A strong, thick rope made of fiber, as hemp, or of strands of steel wire. **2.** A bundle of insulated wires that carry electric current. **3.** A telegraph message sent by underwater cable.
◊ *verb* To send a telegraph message to by underwater cable.
ca·ble (kā′bəl) ◊ *noun, plural* **cables** ◊ *verb* **cabled, cabling**

cable car *noun* **1.** A car or bus that runs on tracks and is pulled by a cable. **2.** A car that hangs from a cable and is pulled along by it. Cable cars are used on hills and mountains.
cable car ◊ *noun, plural* **cable cars**

cable television *noun* A system for receiving television programs in which signals from faraway stations are picked up by one large antenna and then sent by cables to the television sets of people who pay for the service.

caboose *noun* A car at the end of a freight train, where the crew can cook and sleep.
ca·boose (kə **bo͞os′**) ◊ *noun, plural* **cabooses**

cacao *noun* A tropical tree that bears pods that are used to make chocolate and cocoa.
ca·ca·o (kə **kä′** ō) ◊ *noun, plural* **cacaos**

cackle *verb* **1.** To make the shrill, broken sound of a hen that has just laid an egg. **2.** To laugh or speak in a shrill, noisy way.
◊ *noun* An act or sound of cackling.
cack·le (**kăk′** əl) ◊ *verb* **cackled, cackling** ◊ *noun, plural* **cackles**

cacti *noun* A plural of **cactus.**
cac·ti (**kăk′** tī′) ◊ *noun*

cactus *noun* One of many kinds of plants that have thick, often spiny stems without leaves and that grow in hot, dry places.
cac·tus (**kăk′** təs) ◊ *noun, plural* **cacti** *or* **cactuses**

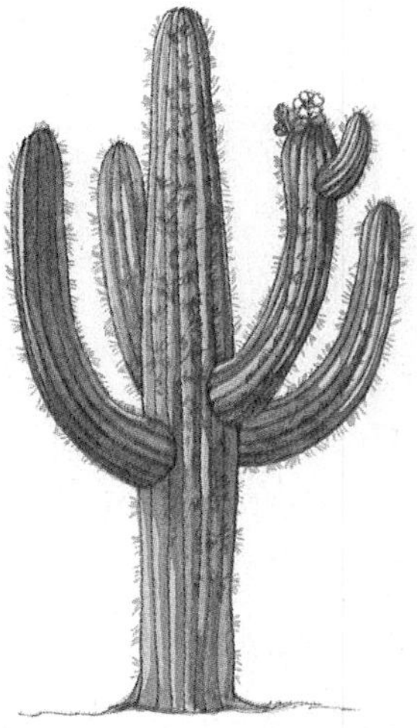

▲ **cactus**

cadet *noun* A student at a military or naval school who is training to be an officer.
ca·det (kə **dĕt′**) ◊ *noun, plural* **cadets**

ă	pat	ĭ	pit	oi	oil	th	bath
ā	pay	ī	ride	o͝o	book	*th*	bathe
â	care	î	fierce	o͞o	boot	ə	ago, item
ä	father	ŏ	pot	ou	out		pencil
ĕ	pet	ō	go	ŭ	cut		atom
ē	be	ô	paw, for	û	fur		circus

café *noun* A small restaurant or bar.
ca·fé (kă **fā′**) ◊ *noun, plural* **cafés**

cafeteria *noun* A restaurant in which the customers buy their food at a counter and carry it to their tables.
caf·e·te·ri·a (kăf′ĭ **tîr′** ē ə) ◊ *noun, plural* **cafeterias**

caffeine *noun* A bitter, stimulating substance that is found in coffee and tea.
caf·feine (kă **fēn′** *or* **kăf′** ēn′) ◊ *noun*

cage *noun* **1.** An enclosure that has openings covered with wire mesh or bars and is used for confining birds or animals. **2.** Something that is like a cage in shape or use: *The cashier at the movie theater sat in a cage.*
◊ *verb* To put in or as if in a cage.
cage (kāj) ◊ *noun, plural* **cages** ◊ *verb* **caged, caging**

cake *noun* **1.** A baked food made from a sweetened batter, as of flour, liquid, and eggs. **2.** A thin mixture of dough or batter that is baked or fried and is usually round and flat. **3.** Something, as soap, that is shaped or molded into a solid mass.
◊ *verb* **1.** To form or cause to form a cake: *Clay cakes as it dries.* **2.** To cover with a compact layer: *Mud caked my boots.*
cake (kāk) ◊ *noun, plural* **cakes** ◊ *verb* **caked, caking**

cal. The abbreviation for *calorie.*

Cal. An abbreviation for *California.*

calcium *noun* A silvery, moderately hard metallic chemical element that is found in substances such as milk, bone, and shells.
cal·ci·um (**kăl′** sē əm) ◊ *noun*

calculate *verb* **1.** To find by using addition, subtraction, multiplication, or division: *I calculated the amount of fabric I would need to make the bedspread.* **2.** To make an estimate of: *Can you calculate the cost of the electricity you use?*
cal·cu·late (**kăl′** kyə lāt′) ◊ *verb* **calculated, calculating**

calculation *noun* The act, process, or result of calculating.
cal·cu·la·tion (kăl′kyə **lā′** shən) ◊ *noun, plural* **calculations**

calculator *noun* A machine that solves mathematical problems.
cal·cu·la·tor (**kăl′** kyə lā′tər) ◊ *noun, plural* **calculators**

C

calendar *noun* **1.** A chart that shows the months, weeks, and days of the year. **2.** A schedule of events or things to be done.
cal·en·dar (kăl′ən dər) ◊ *noun, plural* **calendars**

calf¹ *noun* **1.** The young of cattle; a young cow or bull. **2.** The young of certain large animals, as the elephant or whale.
calf¹ (kăf) ◊ *noun, plural* **calves**

calf² *noun* The muscular back part of the human leg between the knee and the ankle.
calf² (kăf) ◊ *noun, plural* **calves**

***HISTORY* • calf¹, calf²**

Calf¹ comes from an old English word that meant "the young of a cow." **Calf²** comes from an old Scandinavian word for the lower back part of the leg.

calico *noun* Cotton cloth printed with a brightly colored pattern.
◊ *adjective* Marked with spots of color: *The children found a calico cat.*
cal·i·co (kăl′ĭ kō) ◊ *noun, plural* **calicoes** *or* **calicos** ◊ *adjective*

▲ **calico**

Calif. An abbreviation for *California.*

call *verb* **1.** To speak or say in a loud voice: *The teacher called a list of names.* **2.** To send for; summon: *We called the doctor.* **3.** To give a name to; name: *They called the dog "Spot."* **4.** To communicate with by telephone: *Call me on Thursday.* **5.** To rouse, as from sleep; awaken: *Call me just before eight.* **6.** To make a brief stop or visit: *We called at every house.*
◊ *noun* **1.** A loud cry or shout: *I heard a call for help.* **2.** The cry of an animal, especially a bird: *We tried to copy the call of the owl.* **3.** The act of calling on the telephone: *Try to keep your calls short.* **4.** A short visit.
◊ *idiom* **call for 1.** To go and get: *I'll call for you at eight.* **2.** To demand; require: *Making a model airplane calls for patience.*
call (kôl) ◊ *verb* **called, calling** ◊ *noun, plural* **calls**

caller *noun* A person who makes a short visit.
call·er (kô′lər) ◊ *noun, plural* **callers**

calling *noun* An occupation or profession.
call·ing (kô′lĭng) ◊ *noun, plural* **callings**

callus *noun* A small area of skin that has become hard and thick, usually because of pressure or rubbing.
cal·lus (kăl′əs) ◊ *noun, plural* **calluses**

calm *adjective* **1.** Without disturbance or much motion; still: *The sea is calm.* **2.** Not excited or upset; quiet: *I tried to stay calm when I heard the bad news.*
◊ *noun* **1.** Lack of motion or disturbance. **2.** Lack of excitement or upset; quiet: *A loud noise broke the calm of the evening.*
◊ *verb* To become or make calm: *I calmed down after the argument.*
calm (käm) ◊ *adjective* **calmer, calmest** ◊ *noun* ◊ *verb* **calmed, calming**

SYNONYMS

calm, peaceful, tranquil

Now that all the excitement is over I feel *calm.* After leading very active lives, we enjoyed a *peaceful* old age. The little village seemed very *tranquil* all the time.

calorie *noun* **1.** A unit for measuring the amount of heat energy. A calorie is equal to the amount of heat needed to raise one gram of water one degree Celsius. **2.** A unit of heat used for measuring the amount of heat energy in food: *An apple has 80 calories.*
cal·o·rie (kăl′ə rē) ◊ *noun, plural* **calories**

calves *noun* Plural of **calf¹** and **calf²**.
calves (kăvz) ◊ *noun*

came *verb* Past tense of **come.**
came (kām) ◊ *verb*

camel *noun* A large animal with a long neck and one or two humps. Camels are found in northern Africa and western Asia. They are

used in dry, sandy deserts for riding and carrying loads.
cam·el (kăm′əl) ◊ *noun, plural* **camels**

▲ **camel**

camera *noun* **1.** A device for taking photographs or motion pictures. Most cameras consist of a box that has a lens through which an image is recorded on film. **2.** A device that receives an image and changes it into electrical signals for television.
cam·er·a (kăm′ər ə) ◊ *noun, plural* **cameras**

camouflage *noun* The disguising of people, animals, or things, especially in order to make them look like what is around them.
◊ *verb* To hide or disguise by camouflage.
cam·ou·flage (kăm′ə fläzh′) ◊ *noun* ◊ *verb* **camouflaged, camouflaging**

camp *noun* An outdoor area with temporary shelters such as tents or cabins.
◊ *verb* To set up or stay in a camp.
camp (kămp) ◊ *noun, plural* **camps** ◊ *verb* **camped, camping**

campaign *noun* Organized activity to gain a goal, as electing a candidate to office.
◊ *verb* To take part in a campaign.
cam·paign (kăm **pān′**) ◊ *noun, plural* **campaigns** ◊ *verb* **campaigned, campaigning**

camper *noun* **1.** A person who camps, as a child who goes to a summer camp. **2.** A place to live in, as a trailer or van, that can be used during long trips or for camping.
camp·er (kăm′pər) ◊ *noun, plural* **campers**

campfire *noun* An outdoor fire used for warmth or cooking.
camp·fire (kămp′fīr′) ◊ *noun, plural* **campfires**

camphor *noun* A white substance with a strong smell. It is used in medicine and for making plastics.
cam·phor (kăm′fər) ◊ *noun*

campus *noun* The grounds and buildings of a college or school.
cam·pus (kăm′pəs) ◊ *noun, plural* **campuses**

can¹ *auxiliary verb* **1.** Have the knowledge or skill to: *You can skate well.* **2.** Have the physical or mental ability to: *I can lift those weights.* **3.** Be able to by nature or design: *This plane can fly higher than any other.* **4.** Feel free to: *I can let you go now.* **5.** Be able to on the basis of logic, rules, or right: *We can cross the street when the light is green.* **6.** Have permission to: *My parents said we can go.* **7.** May possibly or probably: *That could never happen to a careful person.*
can¹ (kăn) ◊ *auxiliary verb, past tense* **could**

can² *noun* A metal or plastic container, often in the shape of a cylinder, that is airtight or has a tight-fitting cover.
◊ *verb* To preserve in a sealed can or jar: *We can summer vegetables for use in winter.*
can² (kăn) ◊ *noun, plural* **cans** ◊ *verb* **canned, canning**

***HISTORY* • can¹, can²**

Can¹ comes from an old English verb meaning "to know how." **Can²** first meant "cup." It is difficult to tell whether this word was borrowed from Latin or was a native English word.

Can. The abbreviation for *Canada* and *Canadian.*

Canadian *noun* A person who was born in or lives in Canada.
◊ *adjective* Of or relating to Canada or the Canadians.
Ca·na·di·an (kə **nā′**dē ən) ◊ *noun, plural* **Canadians** ◊ *adjective*

ă	pat	ĭ	pit	oi	**oil**	th	**bath**
ā	pay	ī	ride	o͝o	book	*th*	**bathe**
â	care	î	fierce	o͞o	**boot**	ə	ago, item
ä	father	ŏ	pot	ou	**out**		pencil
ĕ	pet	ō	go	ŭ	cut		atom
ē	be	ô	paw, for	û	fur		circus

canal *noun* A waterway that is made by artificial means, as by digging. Canals are used for carrying water to dry areas or draining water from wet areas. Canals also join bodies of water so ships can move between them.
ca·nal (kə năl′) ◊ *noun, plural* **canals**

▲ **canal**

canary *noun* A songbird, often yellow in color, that can be kept as a pet in a cage.
ca·nar·y (kə nâr′ ē) ◊ *noun, plural* **canaries**

***HISTORY* • canary**

A **canary** takes its name from the *Canary Islands* where this bird was found. In Latin and Spanish, the place name meant "Island of Dogs." It seems the first explorers were more impressed by the dogs they saw on these islands than by the birds.

cancel *verb* **1.** To give up; call off: *I canceled my dentist appointment.* **2.** To mark to show that a postage stamp or check cannot be used again.
can·cel (kăn′səl) ◊ *verb* **canceled, canceling**

cancer *noun* A disease involving abnormal cells that do not stop growing. Cancer can spread from where it begins in the body and destroy healthy tissues and organs.
can·cer (kăn′sər) ◊ *noun*

candidate *noun* A person who seeks or is put forward by others for an office or honor.
can·di·date (kăn′dĭ dāt′) ◊ *noun, plural* **candidates**

candle *noun* A solid stick of wax or tallow with a wick inside that is lit and burned to give light.
can·dle (kăn′dl) ◊ *noun, plural* **candles**

candlestick *noun* A holder for a candle.
can·dle·stick (kăn′dl stĭk′) ◊ *noun, plural* **candlesticks**

candy *noun* A sweet food made from sugar or syrup, often mixed with chocolate or nuts.
can·dy (kăn′dē) ◊ *noun, plural* **candies**

cane *noun* **1.** A stick used for help in walking. **2.** A thin, hollow or woody plant stem that usually has joints. **3.** A plant or grass with such a stem, as bamboo or sugar cane.
cane (kān) ◊ *noun, plural* **canes**

cannibal *noun* **1.** A person who eats human flesh. **2.** An animal that feeds on others of its own kind.
can·ni·bal (kăn′ ə bəl) ◊ *noun, plural* **cannibals**

cannon *noun* A heavy gun mounted on wheels or on a fixed base.
can·non (kăn′ən) ◊ *noun, plural* **cannons** *or* **cannon**

cannot *verb* Can not.
can·not (kăn′ŏt′ *or* kă nŏt′) ◊ *verb*

canoe *noun* A light, slender boat with pointed ends that is propelled by paddles.
ca·noe (kə no͞o′) ◊ *noun, plural* **canoes**

▲ **canoe**

canopy *noun* A covering suspended over a bed, throne, or entrance to a building.
can·o·py (kăn′ ə pē) ◊ *noun, plural* **canopies**

can't Contraction of "can not."
can't (kănt) ◊ *contraction*

cantaloupe *noun* A melon with a ribbed, rough rind and sweet orange flesh.
can·ta·loupe (**kăn′**tl ōp′) ◊ *noun, plural* **cantaloupes**

canteen *noun* **1.** A container for carrying liquid, as drinking water. **2.** A store, as in a factory or on a military base, where supplies and refreshments are sold or provided.
can·teen (kăn **tēn′**) ◊ *noun, plural* **canteens**

canter *noun* A slow, easy gallop.
◊ *verb* To run at a canter.
can·ter (**kăn′**tər) ◊ *noun, plural* **canters**
◊ *verb* **cantered, cantering**

canvas *noun* **1.** A heavy coarse cloth of cotton, hemp, or flax that is used for making tents and sails and is the material on which artists make oil paintings. **2.** An oil painting on canvas.
can·vas (**kăn′**vəs) ◊ *noun, plural* **canvases**

canyon *noun* A deep valley with steep walls on both sides that was formed by running water; gorge.
can·yon (**kăn′**yən) ◊ *noun, plural* **canyons**

▲ **canyon**

ă	pat	ĭ	pit	oi	**oil**	th	**bath**
ā	pay	ī	ride	o͝o	**book**	*th*	**bathe**
â	care	î	fierce	o͞o	**boot**	ə	ago, item
ä	father	ŏ	pot	ou	**out**		pencil
ĕ	pet	ō	go	ŭ	**cut**		atom
ē	be	ô	paw, for	û	**fur**		circus

cap *noun* **1.** A covering for the head that has no brim but sometimes has a visor. **2.** Something that resembles a cap: *Put the cap back on the toothpaste.* **3.** A small amount of explosive enclosed in paper for use in a toy gun.
◊ *verb* To cover with or as if with a cap: *Snow capped the mountains.*
cap (kăp) ◊ *noun, plural* **caps** ◊ *verb* **capped, capping**

capable *adjective* Having or showing the ability, power, or strength needed for a particular activity or purpose: *You are capable of being a great athlete.*
ca·pa·ble (**kā′**pə bəl) ◊ *adjective*

capacity *noun* **1.** The ability to hold, receive, or contain: *The bottle has a capacity of three quarts.* **2.** Mental or physical ability: *You have a great capacity for happiness.* **3.** The position in which a person functions; role: *I was acting in my capacity as bus monitor.*
ca·pac·i·ty (kə **păs′**ĭ tē) ◊ *noun, plural* **capacities**

cape¹ *noun* A garment without sleeves that is worn hanging loose over the shoulders.
cape¹ (kāp) ◊ *noun, plural* **capes**

cape² *noun* A point of land that juts out into a body of water, as a sea.
cape² (kāp) ◊ *noun, plural* **capes**

***HISTORY* • cape¹, cape²**

Both **cape¹** and **cape²** go back to a Latin word meaning "head." **Cape¹** first meant a covering for the head, then the upper part of a cloak, then the cloak itself. A **cape²** sticks out like a "head" of land.

caper *noun* A playful trick; prank.
ca·per (**kā′**pər) ◊ *noun, plural* **capers**

capillary *noun* One of the tiny blood vessels that connect the smallest arteries to the smallest veins.
cap·il·lar·y (**kăp′**ə lĕr′ē) ◊ *noun, plural* **capillaries**

capital *noun* **1.** A city where a state or national government is located. **2.** Wealth that is used to produce more wealth. **3.** A letter, as A, B, or C, of the large size used at the beginning of a sentence.
◊ *adjective* **1.** Very important; chief: *Sending astronauts to the moon was a capital advance*

in space flight. **2.** Punishable by death.
cap·i·tal (kăp′ĭ tl) ◊ *noun, plural* **capitals** ◊ *adjective*
‖*These sound alike:* **capital, capitol**

capitalism *noun* An economic system in which factories, farms, and other properties are privately owned.
cap·i·tal·ism (kăp′ĭ tl ĭz′əm) ◊ *noun*

capitalize *verb* **1.** To begin with a capital letter: *Capitalize the first word in every sentence.* **2.** To write or print in capital letters.
cap·i·tal·ize (kăp′ĭ tl īz′) ◊ *verb* **capitalized, capitalizing**

capitol *noun* **1. Capitol** The domed building in Washington, D.C., in which the Congress of the United States meets. **2.** The building in which a state legislature meets.
cap·i·tol (kăp′ĭ tl) ◊ *noun, plural* **capitols**
‖*These sound alike:* **capitol, capital**

capsize *verb* To turn bottom side up; overturn: *The ship capsized in the storm.*
cap·size (kăp′sīz′ *or* kăp **sīz′**) ◊ *verb* **capsized, capsizing**

capsule *noun* **1.** A small container, as of gelatin, that contains medicine to be taken by mouth. **2.** A compartment in a spacecraft, especially one that carries the crew.
cap·sule (kăp′səl) ◊ *noun, plural* **capsules**

▲ **capsule**
A space capsule

captain *noun* **1.** The leader of a group; chief. **2.** The person in command of a ship. **3.** A Navy or Coast Guard officer ranking below an admiral. **4.** An Army, Air Force, or Marine Corps officer ranking below a major.
◊ *verb* To lead as captain.
cap·tain (kăp′tən) ◊ *noun, plural* **captains** ◊ *verb* **captained, captaining**

caption *noun* A title or explanation that goes with an illustration or photograph.
cap·tion (kăp′shən) ◊ *noun, plural* **captions**

captive *adjective* Held prisoner or kept under the control of another.
◊ *noun* A person or animal held captive.
cap·tive (kăp′tĭv) ◊ *adjective* ◊ *noun, plural* **captives**

captivity *noun* The condition or a period of being a captive: *Very few pandas have been born in captivity.*
cap·tiv·i·ty (kăp **tĭv′**ĭ tē) ◊ *noun, plural* **captivities**

capture *verb* To seize and hold, as by force or skill: *The play captured my imagination.* —See Synonyms at **catch.**
◊ *noun* The act of capturing.
cap·ture (kăp′chər) ◊ *verb* **captured, capturing** ◊ *noun, plural* **captures**

car *noun* **1.** An automobile. **2.** A vehicle, as a railroad car, that has wheels and moves on rails or tracks. **3.** The part of an elevator in which passengers ride.
car (kär) ◊ *noun, plural* **cars**

caramel *noun* **1.** A smooth, chewy candy. **2.** Sugar heated to a brown syrup and used for coloring, flavoring, and sweetening foods.
car·a·mel (kăr′ə məl *or* **kär′**məl) ◊ *noun, plural* **caramels**

caravan *noun* A group of people or vehicles who travel together.
car·a·van (kăr′ə văn′) ◊ *noun, plural* **caravans**

carbohydrate *noun* A compound, as sugar or starch, that is composed of carbon, hydrogen, and oxygen.
car·bo·hy·drate (kär′bō **hī′**drāt′) ◊ *noun, plural* **carbohydrates**

carbon *noun* A chemical element that is found in all living things. Its pure crystal form is a diamond.
car·bon (**kär′**bən) ◊ *noun*

carbon dioxide *noun* A colorless and odorless gas that is composed of carbon and oxygen and does not burn. Carbon dioxide is

produced when animals breathe and when fuel containing carbon burns. It is used in fire extinguishers and soft drinks.
carbon di·ox·ide (dī ŏk′sīd′) ◊ *noun*

carburetor *noun* The part of an engine that mixes gasoline with air so that it will burn properly.
car·bu·re·tor (**kär′**bə rā′tər) ◊ *noun, plural* **carburetors**

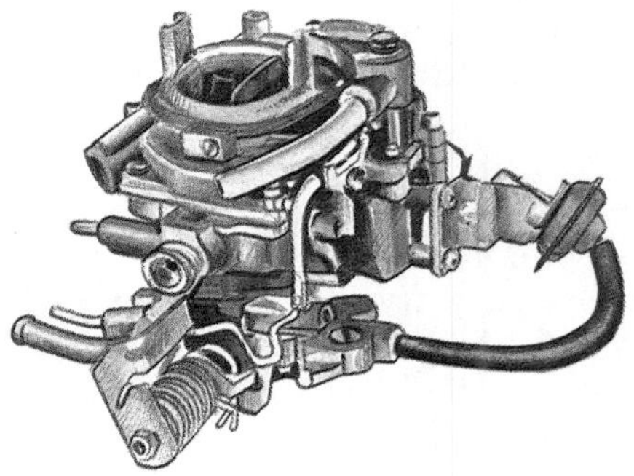

▲ **carburetor**

carcass *noun* The body of a dead animal.
car·cass (**kär′**kəs) ◊ *noun, plural* **carcasses**

card *noun* **1.** An often rectangular piece of stiff paper, thin plastic, or pasteboard on which messages can be written or that bears printed information: *I'm going to send a birthday card to my friend.* **2.** One of a set of cards bearing numbers. They are used in playing various games. **3. cards** A game played with a set of cards.
card (kärd) ◊ *noun, plural* **cards**

cardboard *noun* A stiff, heavy paper used for making cards, boxes, and posters.
card·board (**kärd′**bôrd′) ◊ *noun*

cardinal *adjective* Of the highest importance; chief: *The cardinal reason for attending school is to get an education.*
◊ *noun* **1.** A North American songbird with a crest on its head and bright red feathers. **2.** A bright red color.
car·di·nal (**kär′**dn əl) ◊ *adjective* ◊ *noun, plural* **cardinals**

▲ **cardinal**
A male cardinal

cardinal number *noun* A number used in counting to tell how many. One, ten, and twenty are cardinal numbers.
cardinal number ◊ *noun, plural* **cardinal numbers**

cardinal point *noun* One of the four main directions on a compass. They are north, south, east, and west.
cardinal point ◊ *noun, plural* **cardinal points**

care *noun* **1.** A feeling of fear, concern, or worry: *We are seldom totally free from care.* **2.** Serious attention or effort: *Devote more care to your work.* **3.** Caution, as in avoiding harm or damage: *Handle glass with care.* **4.** The responsibility of supervising or protecting; charge: *Are you in the doctor's care?*
◊ *verb* **1.** To be concerned or interested: *Who cares what happens?* **2.** To have a wish or liking: *I don't care to go out.* **3.** To provide care: *I know how to care for a garden.*
care (kâr) ◊ *noun, plural* **cares** ◊ *verb* **cared, caring**

career *noun* A profession or occupation that a person follows as a life's work: *My cousin chose a career as a scientist.*
ca·reer (kə **rîr′**) ◊ *noun, plural* **careers**

carefree *adjective* Free of care: *We had a carefree vacation at the beach.*
care·free (**kâr′**frē′) ◊ *adjective*

careful *adjective* **1.** Taking the necessary care. **2.** Done or made with care: *The doctor gave the patient a careful examination.*
care·ful (**kâr′**fəl) ◊ *adjective*

ă	pat	ĭ	pit	oi	**oil**	th	**bath**
ā	pay	ī	ride	ŏŏ	**book**	*th*	**bathe**
â	care	î	fierce	ōō	**boot**	ə	**ago, item**
ä	father	ŏ	pot	ou	**out**		pencil
ĕ	pet	ō	go	ŭ	cut		atom
ē	be	ô	paw, for	û	fur		circus

C

SYNONYMS

careful, cautious, prudent

She was a *careful* driver. He was *cautious* on the ice the first time he went skating. We made a *prudent* decision to save money. **Antonym:** *careless*

careless *adjective* **1.** Not taking the necessary care: *Careless writers often make mistakes in spelling.* **2.** Done or made without care: *Careless work merits a low grade.*
care·less (**kâr'** lĭs) ◊ *adjective*

caretaker *noun* A person who is employed to take care of property that belongs to another.
care·tak·er (**kâr'** tā'kər) ◊ *noun, plural* **caretakers**

carfare *noun* The money charged for a ride, as on a streetcar or bus.
car·fare (**kär'** fâr') ◊ *noun*

cargo *noun* The freight carried by a vehicle such as a ship or an airplane.
car·go (**kär'** gō) ◊ *noun, plural* **cargoes** *or* **cargos**

caribou *noun* A large deer of northern North America that is related to the reindeer.
car·i·bou (**kăr'** ə bōō') ◊ *noun, plural* **caribou** *or* **caribous**

carnation *noun* A fragrant flower with many fringed petals that are white, pink, or red.
car·na·tion (kär **nā'** shən) ◊ *noun, plural* **carnations**

carnival *noun* An outdoor show that offers entertainment such as rides and games.
car·ni·val (**kär'** nə vəl) ◊ *noun, plural* **carnivals**

carnivorous *adjective* Feeding on the flesh of animals.
car·niv·o·rous (kär **nĭv'** ər əs) ◊ *adjective*

carol *noun* A song of joy, especially one that is sung at Christmas.
car·ol (**kăr'** əl) ◊ *noun, plural* **carols**

carp *noun* An edible freshwater fish.
carp (kärp) ◊ *noun, plural* **carp** *or* **carps**

carpenter *noun* A person who builds or repairs wooden objects and structures.
car·pen·ter (**kär'** pən tər) ◊ *noun, plural* **carpenters**

carpet *noun* **1.** A heavy woven fabric used as a covering for a floor. **2.** Something that covers a surface like a carpet: *The field was covered with a carpet of flowers.*
◊ *verb* To cover with or as if with a carpet.
car·pet (**kär'** pĭt) ◊ *noun, plural* **carpets**
◊ *verb* **carpeted, carpeting**

car pool *noun* An arrangement among a number of persons who agree to take turns driving to or from a destination.
car pool ◊ *noun, plural* **car pools**

carriage *noun* **1.** A vehicle that has wheels and is used for carrying passengers. **2.** A movable machine part that holds or shifts another part. **3.** The manner in which a person holds his or her body; posture.
car·riage (**kăr'** ĭj) ◊ *noun, plural* **carriages**

▲ **carriage**

carrier *noun* **1.** Someone or something that carries: *I applied for the job as a letter carrier.* **2.** A person or business that deals in transporting goods or passengers.
car·ri·er (**kăr'** ē ər) ◊ *noun, plural* **carriers**

carrot *noun* The long, tapering yellow-orange edible root of a garden plant.
car·rot (**kăr'** ət) ◊ *noun, plural* **carrots**

carry *verb* **1.** To take from one place to another: *Please carry my groceries into the house.* **2.** To hold up the weight of; support: *These columns were designed to carry the roof.* **3.** To keep, wear, or hold on one's person: *I never carry much money with me.* **4.** To hold the body or a part of the body in a particular way: *You carry yourself like a dancer.* **5.** To be transmitted over a distance: *The singer's voice carries very well.* **6.** To offer for sale: *The drugstore carries medicine and cosmetics.* **7.** To sing with accurate pitch: *I can't*

carry a tune. **8.** To put a number into the next column to the left, as in performing addition. **9.** To be the winner in: *The candidate carried the election.* **10.** To print or broadcast: *The newspaper carried the story.*
◊ *idioms* **carry on 1.** To engage in; conduct: *We carried on a conversation during the bus trip.* **2.** To continue in a course of action: *We carried on the game in spite of the rain.* **carry out** To put into practice or effect: *Let's try to carry out our plan.*
car·ry (kăr′ē) ◊ *verb* **carried, carrying**

SYNONYMS

carry, bear[1], transport

We *carried* the basket of food to the picnic. The messenger *bears* the ambassador's gifts to the monarch. Trucks *transport* much of our food.

cart *noun* **1.** A heavy vehicle that has two wheels, is usually pulled by a horse, and is used to transport heavy loads. **2.** A light vehicle that is moved by hand.
◊ *verb* To move in or as if in a cart: *I carted a pile of books back to the library.*
cart (kärt) ◊ *noun, plural* **carts** ◊ *verb* **carted, carting**

cartilage *noun* A tough, white elastic substance that is attached to the surfaces of bones at joints and holds the bones in place.
car·ti·lage (kär′tl ĭj) ◊ *noun*

carton *noun* **1.** A cardboard box made in many sizes and shapes that is used for holding or mailing goods. **2.** A container made of heavy waxed paper or plastic used for holding liquids or small fragile objects.
car·ton (kär′tn) ◊ *noun, plural* **cartons**

cartoon *noun* **1.** A sketch or drawing, often with a caption, showing people or events in a way that is meant to be funny. **2.** A movie made up of such drawings.
car·toon (kär to͞on′) ◊ *noun, plural* **cartoons**

ă	pat	ĭ	pit	oi	oil	th	bath
ā	pay	ī	ride	o͝o	book	*th*	bathe
â	care	î	fierce	o͞o	boot	ə	ago, item
ä	father	ŏ	pot	ou	out		pencil
ĕ	pet	ō	go	ŭ	cut		atom
ē	be	ô	paw, for	û	fur		circus

cartridge *noun* **1.** A tubelike container made of metal, plastic, or cardboard that holds the gunpowder for a bullet. **2.** A container or case that holds something and can easily be inserted into another object. A cartridge may hold ink for a pen, film for a camera, or tape for a tape recorder.
car·tridge (kär′trĭj) ◊ *noun, plural* **cartridges**

cartwheel *noun* **1.** The wheel of a cart. **2.** A handspring in which the body turns over sideways with the arms and legs spread like the spokes of a wheel.
cart·wheel (kärt′hwēl′) ◊ *noun, plural* **cartwheels**

carve *verb* **1.** To make by cutting: *I carved a clown from a bar of soap.* —See Synonyms at **cut. 2.** To cut into pieces for serving: *Will you carve the turkey?*
carve (kärv) ◊ *verb* **carved, carving**

carving *noun* A carved figure or design.
carv·ing (kär′vĭng) ◊ *noun, plural* **carvings**

cascade *noun* A waterfall or group of waterfalls that flows over steep rocks.
◊ *verb* To fall in a cascade or like a cascade: *The cards cascaded to the floor.*
cas·cade (kăs kād′) ◊ *noun, plural* **cascades** ◊ *verb* **cascaded, cascading**

▲ **cascade**

case[1] *noun* **1.** An instance or example of the existence or occurrence of something: *It was a case of mistaken identity. I had a bad case of the flu.* —See Synonyms at **example. 2.** A situation or state of affairs; event: *In that case there is nothing to be done.* **3.** Something that is being investigated: *The police are still trying to solve the murder case.* **4.** A person being treated by a doctor; patient: *The hospi-*

tal has four new cases with pneumonia. **5.** Something to be decided in a court of law. ◊ *idioms* **in any case** No matter what happens: *In any case, you should prepare for the test.* **in case of** If there should be: *In case of rain, close the windows.*
case¹ (kās) ◊ *noun, plural* **cases**

case² *noun* A box or container for shipping, carrying, holding, or protecting something: *Their new TV came in a big packing case.*
case² (kās) ◊ *noun, plural* **cases**

HISTORY • case¹, case²

Case¹ goes back to a Latin word meaning "a falling, an event." **Case²** comes from a different Latin word meaning "a container."

cash *noun* **1.** Money in the form of bills or coins: *How much cash do you have on you?* **2.** Money given at the time something is bought: *I paid cash for my new typewriter.* ◊ *verb* To exchange for or convert into cash: *Maybe the drugstore will cash my check.*
cash (kăsh) ◊ *noun* ◊ *verb* **cashed, cashing**

cashew *noun* The curved, edible nut of a tropical American tree.
cash·ew (**kăsh′** o͞o) ◊ *noun, plural* **cashews**

cashier *noun* **1.** A bank clerk who receives and pays out money to customers. **2.** An employee at a store, hotel, or other business who takes in money for goods and services.
cash·ier (kă **shîr′**) ◊ *noun, plural* **cashiers**

cashmere *noun* The fine, soft wool of an Asian goat.
cash·mere (**kăzh′** mîr′ *or* **kăsh′** mîr′) ◊ *noun, plural* **cashmeres**

cask *noun* A barrel made in various sizes and used for holding liquids.
cask (kăsk) ◊ *noun, plural* **casks**

casket *noun* **1.** A metal or wooden box in which a dead person is buried; coffin. **2.** A small box or case for valuable objects.
cas·ket (**kăs′** kĭt) ◊ *noun, plural* **caskets**

casserole *noun* **1.** A dish, usually made of pottery or glass, in which food is baked and served. **2.** Food baked in such a dish: *We had a shrimp casserole for dinner.*
cas·se·role (**kăs′** ə rōl′) ◊ *noun, plural* **casseroles**

cassette *noun* **1.** A small case that holds plastic tape for recording and playing back sound or images. **2.** A sealed, plastic case containing a roll of film that can be put directly into a camera.
cas·sette (kə **sĕt′**) ◊ *noun, plural* **cassettes**

cast *verb* **1.** To throw or fling: *We cast the fishing net into the water.* **2.** To cause to fall upon something: *The moon cast shadows on the ground.* **3.** To turn or direct: *They cast glances at us from across the street.* **4.** To deposit a ballot: *We cast our votes for a new mayor.* **5.** To give a certain part to in a play or movie: *The director cast an unknown actor in the leading role.* **6.** To form by pouring a liquid or soft material into a mold and letting it harden.
◊ *noun* **1.** The act or an instance of throwing or casting: *I made a good cast and pulled in a 14-inch trout.* **2.** The actors in a play or a movie: *The cast rehearsed for four hours.* **3.** A hard, stiff bandage, made of gauze and plaster or plastic, used to hold the pieces of a broken bone in place or keep a joint from bending. **4.** Something that is cast in a mold. ◊ *idiom* **cast off** To release a ship from a dock or shore: *We cast off the canoe and paddled down the river.*
cast (kăst) ◊ *verb* **cast, casting** ◊ *noun, plural* **casts**

castanet *noun* One of a pair of small pieces of wood, carved like hollow shells, that make a sharp sound when they are struck together with the fingers.
cas·ta·net (kăs′tə-**nĕt′**) ◊ *noun, plural* **castanets**

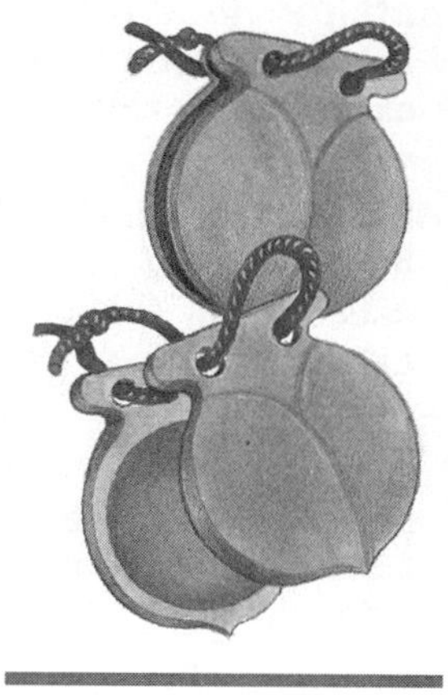

▲ **castanet**

cast iron *noun* A hard and brittle form of iron made by mixing melted iron with other elements and pouring it into a mold.

castle *noun* **1.** A large fort or group of buildings with high, thick walls, towers, and other defenses against attack. **2.** A chess piece.
cas·tle (**kăs′** əl) ◊ *noun, plural* **castles**

casual *adjective* **1.** Not planned or expected; happening by chance: *At the drugstore today I had a casual meeting with an old friend.* **2.** Said or done quickly or without preparation; passing: *The teacher made a casual remark about the rainy weather.* **3.** Suitable for informal wear: *We wore casual clothes.*
cas·u·al (**kăzh′** o͞o əl) ◊ *adjective*

casualty *noun* **1.** A person who is killed or injured in an accident. **2.** A person who is killed, wounded, captured, or missing during a military action. **3.** A serious accident.
cas·u·al·ty (**kăzh′** o͞o əl tē) ◊ *noun, plural* **casualties**

cat *noun* **1.** A soft, furry animal with sharp claws, whiskers, and usually a long tail. Cats are often kept as pets. **2.** A larger animal, as a lion, tiger, or leopard, that is related to and resembles a cat.
cat (kăt) ◊ *noun, plural* **cats**

catalog *or* **catalogue** *noun* **1.** A list of items, usually in alphabetical order, with a description of each item: *I looked up the book in the card catalog in the library.* **2.** A book or pamphlet containing such a list: *I ordered some boots from the store's catalog.*
◊ *verb* To make a catalog of or list in a catalog: *The librarian cataloged the new books.*
cat·a·log *or* **cat·a·logue** (**kăt′**l ôg′) ◊ *noun, plural* **catalogs** *or* **catalogues** ◊ *verb* **cataloged, cataloging** *or* **catalogued, cataloguing**

catalpa *noun* A tree with large heart-shaped leaves and long beanlike pods.
ca·tal·pa (kə **tăl′** pə) ◊ *noun, plural* **catalpas**

catamaran *noun* **1.** A boat with two parallel hulls. **2.** A raft of logs tied together.
cat·a·ma·ran (kăt′ə mə **răn′**) ◊ *noun, plural* **catamarans**

catapult *noun* A large weapon used in ancient times for hurling objects, such as stones and arrows, at the enemy.
cat·a·pult (**kăt′** ə pŭlt′) ◊ *noun, plural* **catapults**

ă	pat	ĭ	pit	oi	oil	th	bath
ā	pay	ī	ride	o͝o	book	*th*	bathe
â	care	î	fierce	o͞o	boot	ə	ago, item
ä	father	ŏ	pot	ou	out		pencil
ĕ	pet	ō	go	ŭ	cut		atom
ē	be	ô	paw, for	û	fur		circus

▲ **catapult**

cataract *noun* **1.** A very large, steep waterfall. **2.** A disease of the eye in which the lens develops a cloudy film, causing a person or animal to become partly or totally blind.
cat·a·ract (**kăt′** ə răkt′) ◊ *noun, plural* **cataracts**

catastrophe *noun* A terrible disaster, as a flood, earthquake, or plane crash, that causes much damage and often loss of life.
ca·tas·tro·phe (kə **tăs′** trə fē) ◊ *noun, plural* **catastrophes**

catbird *noun* A dark-gray North American songbird with a call like the mewing of a cat.
cat·bird (**kăt′** bûrd′) ◊ *noun, plural* **catbirds**

catch *verb* **1.** To get hold of or grasp something that is moving; seize: *I'll throw the ball and you catch it.* **2.** To come upon suddenly; surprise: *We caught our opponents napping.* **3.** To become stuck or lodged: *The bone caught in my throat.* **4.** To arrive in time for: *We caught the last bus home.* **5.** To become or cause to become held or fastened: *This lock will not catch. I caught my finger in the door.* **6.** To attract: *I tried to catch your attention.* **7.** To see, hear, or understand: *I didn't catch what the teacher said.* **8.** To take or get: *Dress warmly or you'll catch a cold. The house caught fire.* **9.** To attend or watch: *We'll catch the football game tomorrow if I can get tickets.* **10.** To act as the catcher in baseball.
◊ *noun* **1.** The act or an instance of grabbing and holding a ball: *The center fielder made a great catch.* **2.** An amount caught: *We brought home a large catch of fish.* **3.** A device, such as a hook or latch, for fastening or

closing something. **4.** A game in which two or more people throw a ball back and forth to one another. **5.** A hidden or tricky condition: *There must be a catch to that last question.* ◊ *idioms* **catch on 1.** To get the idea; understand: *We finally caught on after the teacher explained the problem again.* **2.** To become popular: *The new TV series never caught on.* **catch up** To come up alongside from behind: *They ran so fast I couldn't catch up.*
catch (kăch) ◊ *verb* **caught, catching** ◊ *noun, plural* **catches**

> **SYNONYMS**
>
> ***catch, capture, trap***
>
> I ran to *catch* the ball. The police *captured* the criminal after a long search. The collector *traps* otters for the zoo.

catcher *noun* **1.** Someone or something that catches. **2.** A baseball player who stands behind home plate to catch balls thrown by the pitcher.
catch·er (kăch′ər) ◊ *noun, plural* **catchers**

catching *adjective* **1.** Spread by infection; contagious: *Flu is one of the most catching diseases.* **2.** Likely to spread: *Your sense of humor is catching.*
catch·ing (kăch′ĭng) ◊ *adjective*

category *noun* A division or group within a system; class: *The strings are one category of musical instruments.*
cat·e·go·ry (kăt′ə gôr′ē) ◊ *noun, plural* **categories**

cater *verb* **1.** To provide food, supplies, and sometimes service and entertainment, as for a banquet. **2.** To show preference in business to a particular group of people.
ca·ter (kā′tər) ◊ *verb* **catered, catering**

caterpillar *noun* The wormlike larva of a moth or butterfly that has just hatched from its egg. A caterpillar has a long body that is often covered with hair or bristles.
cat·er·pil·lar (kăt′ər pĭl′ər) ◊ *noun, plural* **caterpillars**

catfish *noun* A usually freshwater fish with long feelers around the mouth that look like big whiskers.
cat·fish (kăt′fĭsh′) ◊ *noun, plural* **catfish** *or* **catfishes**

cathedral *noun* **1.** The main church of the district under the authority of a bishop. **2.** A large or important church.
ca·the·dral (kə thē′drəl) ◊ *noun, plural* **cathedrals**

catkin *noun* A thick cluster of tiny flowers that have down or scales but no petals. Catkins grow on birch, alder, and poplar trees.
cat·kin (kăt′kĭn′) ◊ *noun, plural* **catkins**

catnap *noun* A short nap.
◊ *verb* To take a short nap.
cat·nap (kăt′năp′) ◊ *noun, plural* **catnaps** ◊ *verb* **catnapped, catnapping**

catnip *noun* A plant that has a strong, spicy smell that is very attractive to cats.
cat·nip (kăt′nĭp′) ◊ *noun*

catsup *noun* Ketchup.
cat·sup (kăt′səp *or* kĕch′əp) ◊ *noun*

cattail *noun* A tall plant that has long, narrow leaves and a long, thick cluster of tiny brown flowers. Cattails grow in wet places, such as swamps.
cat·tail (kăt′tāl′) ◊ *noun, plural* **cattails**

cattle *plural noun* Large, heavy animals, as cows, bulls, or oxen, that have hoofs, grow horns, and are raised for milk, meat, or hides.
cat·tle (kăt′l) ◊ *plural noun*

caught *verb* Past tense and past participle of **catch.**
caught (kôt) ◊ *verb*

cauliflower *noun* A vegetable that has a rounded head of small, closely clustered whitish flowers with a few large leaves around the outside.
cau·li·flow·er (kô′lĭ-flou′ər) ◊ *noun*

▲ **cauliflower**

cause *noun* **1.** Someone or something that makes something happen: *What was the cause of the fire?* **2.** An ideal or goal that many people believe in and support: *World peace is a cause we should all work for.*
◊ *verb* To be the cause of; bring about.
cause (kôz) ◊ *noun, plural* **causes** ◊ *verb* **caused, causing**

caution *noun* **1.** Great care so as to avoid possible danger or trouble: *Use caution when you climb that rocky cliff.* **2.** A warning against possible danger or trouble.
◊ *verb* To warn against possible trouble or danger: *I cautioned the children to stay away from the river.*
cau·tion (kô′shən) ◊ *noun, plural* **cautions** ◊ *verb* **cautioned, cautioning**

cautious *adjective* Not taking any chances: *You should be cautious when you are crossing a busy street.* —See Synonyms at **careful.**
cau·tious (kô′shəs) ◊ *adjective*

cavalry *noun* Military troops that were formerly trained to fight on horseback. Cavalry uses armored vehicles today.
cav·al·ry (kăv′əl rē) ◊ *noun, plural* **cavalries**

cave *noun* A hollow area in the earth, usually in the side of a hill or mountain, with an opening to the outside.
◊ *verb* To fall in or cause to fall in because of damage or too much weight; collapse: *The tunnel caved in during the earthquake.*
cave (kāv) ◊ *noun, plural* **caves** ◊ *verb* **caved, caving**

cave man *noun* A human being who lived thousands of years ago in caves.
cave man ◊ *noun, plural* **cave men**

cavern *noun* A very large cave. Many caverns have unusual formations of rock.
cav·ern (kăv′ərn) ◊ *noun, plural* **caverns**

cavity *noun* A hollow place or area; hole: *The dentist filled two cavities in my teeth.*
cav·i·ty (kăv′ĭ tē) ◊ *noun, plural* **cavities**

caw *noun* The hoarse, harsh cry of a crow or raven.
caw (kô) ◊ *noun, plural* **caws**

cease *verb* To come or bring to an end; stop: *The storm ceased at daybreak.*
cease (sēs) ◊ *verb* **ceased, ceasing**

cedar *noun* An evergreen tree with hard, fragrant wood that is used for lining clothes closets and making chests.
ce·dar (sē′dər) ◊ *noun, plural* **cedars**

ă	pat	ĭ	pit	oi	**oi**l	th	ba**th**
ā	pay	ī	ride	o͝o	b**oo**k	*th*	ba**the**
â	care	î	fierce	o͞o	b**oo**t	ə	**a**go, it**e**m
ä	father	ŏ	pot	ou	**ou**t		penc**i**l
ĕ	pet	ō	go	ŭ	c**u**t		at**o**m
ē	be	ô	paw, for	û	f**u**r		circ**u**s

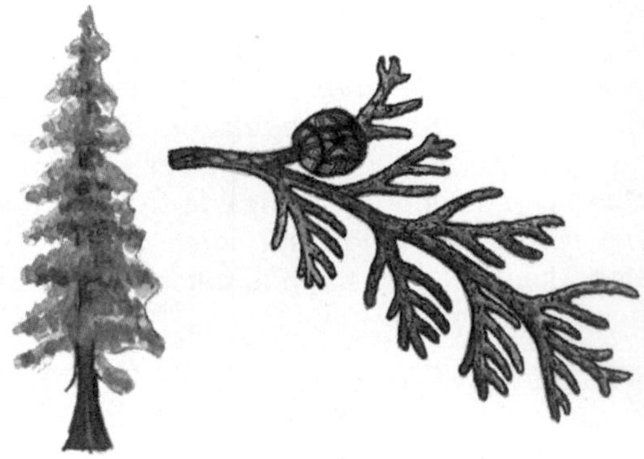

▲ **cedar**

ceiling *noun* **1.** The inside upper surface of a room. **2.** The distance between the earth and the lowest clouds: *The low ceiling delayed our flight by two hours.* **3.** The top limit or amount: *The government put a ceiling on salaries for its employees.*
ceil·ing (sē′lĭng) ◊ *noun, plural* **ceilings**

celebrate *verb* **1.** To have a party or other such activity to honor a special occasion: *We always celebrate my birthday.* **2.** To perform with the proper ceremony or rite: *The minister celebrated the wedding.*
cel·e·brate (sĕl′ə brāt′) ◊ *verb* **celebrated, celebrating**

celebration *noun* The act of celebrating or an instance of celebrating.
cel·e·bra·tion (sĕl′ə **brā′**shən) ◊ *noun, plural* **celebrations**

celebrity *noun* **1.** A famous person. **2.** A well-known reputation; fame: *The gymnasts achieved celebrity in the Olympics.*
ce·leb·ri·ty (sə lĕb′rĭ tē) ◊ *noun, plural* **celebrities**

celery *noun* A plant with crisp, juicy stems that are eaten raw or cooked.
cel·er·y (sĕl′ə rē) ◊ *noun*

cell *noun* **1.** A small room, as in a prison or convent, having little or no furniture. **2.** The smallest and most basic part of a plant or animal. Most cells consist of protoplasm, have a small mass called a nucleus near the center, and are enclosed by a thin membrane. **3.** A

small hole or space in an object or substance: *Bees make honeycombs that have many cells.* **4.** A container holding chemicals that produce electricity.
cell (sĕl) ◊ *noun, plural* **cells**
‖*These sound alike:* **cell, sell**

cellar *noun* A room or rooms under a building where things are stored.
cel·lar (sĕl′ər) ◊ *noun, plural* **cellars**

cello *noun* A stringed musical instrument of the violin family. A cello is larger than a violin and has a lower tone. It is held between the knees while being played.
cel·lo (chĕl′ō) ◊ *noun, plural* **cellos**

▲ **cello**

cellophane *noun* A thin, clear, flexible substance made from cellulose. It is used as a wrapping to keep food fresh.
cel·lo·phane (sĕl′ə-fān′) ◊ *noun*

cellulose *noun* A substance that forms the cell walls of plants and trees. Cellulose is used in making paper, cellophane, cloth, plastics, and explosives.
cel·lu·lose (sĕl′yə lōs′) ◊ *noun*

Celsius *adjective* Of or relating to a temperature scale on which the freezing point of water is 0 degrees and the boiling point of water is 100 degrees.
Cel·si·us (sĕl′sē əs) ◊ *adjective*

Celtic *noun* A group of related languages including Welsh and Irish.
Celt·ic (kĕl′tĭk *or* sĕl′tĭk) ◊ *noun*

cement *noun* **1.** A mixture of powders made from clay and limestone. When water is added, the mixture forms a paste that becomes hard when it dries. Cement is used for sidewalks and as a building material. **2.** A substance, such as glue, that hardens to hold things together.
◊ *verb* **1.** To join or cover with cement. **2.** To bind or strengthen.
ce·ment (sĭ mĕnt′) ◊ *noun, plural* **cements**
◊ *verb* **cemented, cementing**

cemetery *noun* A place where dead people are buried; graveyard.
cem·e·ter·y (sĕm′ĭ tĕr′ē) ◊ *noun, plural* **cemeteries**

census *noun* An official count of the people living in a country or district. A census often includes other information such as the age, sex, or job of each person.
cen·sus (sĕn′səs) ◊ *noun, plural* **censuses**

cent *noun* A coin used in the United States and Canada. One hundred cents equals one dollar.
cent (sĕnt) ◊ *noun, plural* **cents**
‖*These sound alike:* **cent, scent, sent**

centennial *noun* A 100th anniversary.
◊ *adjective* Of or relating to a 100th anniversary: *Our town had its centennial celebration last year.*
cen·ten·ni·al (sĕn tĕn′ē əl) ◊ *noun, plural* **centennials** ◊ *adjective*

center *noun* **1.** A point that is the same distance from every other point of a circle or a sphere. **2.** The middle position, part, or place: *Put the vase of flowers in the center of the table.* **3.** A place where many things are gathered together or many activities take place: *The town built a new civic center.* **4.** A main or principal person, place, or thing. **5.** A player in a middle position in certain sports.
◊ *verb* To place in or at the center.
cen·ter (sĕn′tər) ◊ *noun, plural* **centers**
◊ *verb* **centered, centering**

SYNONYMS

center, core, middle

I shot the arrow into the *center* of the target. We took the seeds out of the *core* of the apple. We swam to the island in the *middle* of the river.

centigrade *adjective* Of or relating to a temperature scale divided into 100 degrees, where 0 degrees is the freezing point of water and 100 degrees is the boiling point of water.
cen·ti·grade (sĕn′tĭ grād′) ◊ *adjective*

centigram *noun* A unit of mass and weight in the metric system. One centigram is equal to $^1/_{100}$ gram.
cen·ti·gram (sĕn′tĭ grăm′) ◊ *noun, plural* **centigrams**

centimeter *noun* A unit of length in the metric system equal to $\frac{1}{100}$ meter.
cen·ti·me·ter (**sĕn'** tə mē'tər) ◊ *noun, plural* **centimeters**

centipede *noun* A wormlike animal that has many pairs of legs. A centipede can give a painful bite.
cen·ti·pede (**sĕn'** tə pēd') ◊ *noun, plural* **centipedes**

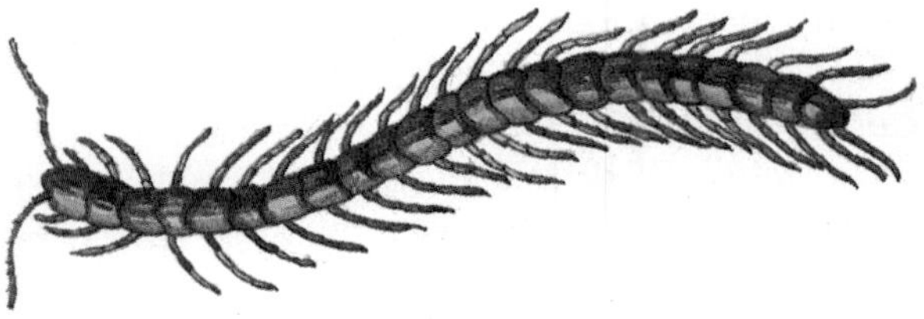

▲ **centipede**
Magnified 2 times

central *adjective* **1.** At or near the center: *The bus station is in the central part of town.* **2.** Most important; chief: *Our central office is in New Jersey.*
cen·tral (**sĕn'** trəl) ◊ *adjective*

century *noun* A period of 100 years: *From 1824 to 1924 is a century. We live in the twentieth century.*
cen·tu·ry (**sĕn'** chə rē) ◊ *noun, plural* **centuries**

ceramic *noun* **1.** A hard, brittle material made by baking clay at a high temperature. Ceramic is used in making pottery, certain kinds of tile, and other articles. **2. ceramics** (*used with a singular verb*) The art or method of making things from ceramic: *Ceramics is my hobby.*
ce·ram·ic (sə **răm'** ĭk) ◊ *noun, plural* **ceramics**

ă	pat	ĭ	pit	oi	**oil**	th	**bath**
ā	pay	ī	ride	o͝o	book	*th*	**bathe**
â	care	î	fierce	o͞o	boot	ə	ago, item
ä	father	ŏ	pot	ou	**out**		pencil
ĕ	pet	ō	go	ŭ	cut		atom
ē	be	ô	paw, for	û	fur		circus

cereal *noun* **1.** The seeds of certain grasses, such as wheat, oats, or corn, used as food. **2.** A food made from the seeds of such plants.
ce·re·al (**sîr'** ē əl) ◊ *noun, plural* **cereals**
‖*These sound alike:* **cereal, serial**

ceremonial *adjective* Of a ceremony: *They performed a ceremonial dance at the festival.*
cer·e·mo·ni·al (sĕr'ə **mō'** nē əl) ◊ *adjective*

ceremony *noun* **1.** A formal act or series of acts performed in honor of an event or special occasion: *Our school had a graduation ceremony today.* **2.** Very polite or formal behavior: *The ruler was welcomed at the airport with great ceremony.*
cer·e·mo·ny (**sĕr'** ə mō'nē) ◊ *noun, plural* **ceremonies**

certain *adjective* **1.** Having no doubt; positive: *Are you certain that you left the book on the bus?* **2.** Beyond doubt; definite: *If you don't study, you face certain failure.* **3.** Known but not named: *Certain laws protect us.* **4.** Agreed on; settled: *I have to work a certain number of hours each week.*
cer·tain (**sûr'** tn) ◊ *adjective*

certainly *adverb* Without a doubt; definitely: *I will certainly be there by noon.*
cer·tain·ly (**sûr'** tn lē) ◊ *adverb*

certainty *noun* The condition or quality of being certain.
cer·tain·ty (**sûr'** tn tē) ◊ *noun*

certificate *noun* An official document that gives information or may be offered as proof of an event or fact: *My birth certificate shows where and when I was born.*
cer·tif·i·cate (sər **tĭf'** ĭ kĭt) ◊ *noun, plural* **certificates**

certify *verb* **1.** To guarantee by an official statement that something is true or correct: *This diploma certifies that you have graduated from high school.* **2.** To guarantee the quality, value, or standard of something.
cer·ti·fy (**sûr'** tə fī') ◊ *verb* **certified, certifying**

chain *noun* **1.** A row of links, usually metal, joined together: *My bicycle chain broke.* **2.** A series of things that are related or connected as if linked together: *They operate a chain of supermarkets in Florida.*
◊ *verb* To hold or fasten with or as if with a chain.
chain (chān) ◊ *noun, plural* **chains** ◊ *verb* **chained, chaining**

chair *noun* A piece of furniture that is built for sitting on. A chair has a seat, a back, and usually four legs. Some chairs have arms.
chair (chậr) ◊ *noun, plural* **chairs**

chairman *noun* A man in charge of a meeting, committee, or other group.
chair·man (**châr′**mən) ◊ *noun, plural* **chairmen**

chairperson *noun* A person in charge of a meeting, committee, or other group.
chair·per·son (**châr′**pûr′sən) ◊ *noun, plural* **chairpersons**

chairwoman *noun* A woman in charge of a meeting, committee, or other group.
chair·wom·an (**châr′**wo͝o′mən) ◊ *noun, plural* **chairwomen**

chalk *noun* **1.** A soft mineral composed mostly of tiny fossil seashells. **2.** A piece of this material used for writing on a blackboard or other surface.
chalk (chôk) ◊ *noun*

challenge *noun* **1.** A call to take part in a contest or fight to see who is better, faster, or stronger: *The Red Team will meet the challenge of the Blue Team.* **2.** Something that requires all of a person's efforts and skills: *That job will be a challenge.*
◊ *verb* **1.** To call to take part in a contest or fight. **2.** To order a person to stop and prove who he or she is: *The guard challenged the intruder at the gate.*
chal·lenge (**chăl′**ənj) ◊ *noun, plural* **challenges** ◊ *verb* **challenged, challenging**

chamber *noun* **1.** A room in a house, especially a bedroom. **2. chambers** A judge's office in a courthouse. **3.** The room or hall where a group of lawmakers or other assembly meets: *The Senate chamber has a gallery for guests.* **4.** A lawmaking group: *The Senate is called the upper chamber of the legislature.* **5.** An enclosed space in a machine or in an animal's body; compartment: *A bird's heart has three chambers.* **6.** The place in a gun where a bullet is put.
cham·ber (**chām′**bər) ◊ *noun, plural* **chambers**

chameleon *noun* A small lizard that can change its color quickly to blend in with its surroundings.
cha·me·leon (kə **mēl′**yən) ◊ *noun, plural* **chameleons**

champion *noun* The winner of a game or contest, accepted as the best of all.
◊ *verb* To fight for or defend a cause or movement: *The senator vowed to champion the rights of poor people everywhere.*
cham·pi·on (**chăm′**pē ən) ◊ *noun, plural* **champions** ◊ *verb* **championed, championing**

championship *noun* **1.** The position or title of champion: *I won the spelling championship.* **2.** A contest to determine a champion.
cham·pi·on·ship (**chăm′**pē ən shĭp′) ◊ *noun, plural* **championships**

chance *noun* **1.** The happening of things without any cause that can be seen or understood; luck: *They found the buried treasure by chance.* **2.** The possibility or probability that something will happen: *We have a good chance of winning the game.* **3.** An opportunity: *They never miss a chance to play basketball.* **4.** A risk or gamble: *I took a chance and left my umbrella at home.*
◊ *verb* **1.** To happen by accident: *They chanced to call when we were out.* **2.** To take a chance with; risk: *Don't chance sailing in a storm.*
chance (chăns) ◊ *noun, plural* **chances** ◊ *verb* **chanced, chancing**

chancellor *noun* A high official in government or education.
chan·cel·lor (**chăn′**sə lər) ◊ *noun, plural* **chancellors**

chandelier *noun* A light fixture with several arms or branches that hold light bulbs or candles. A chandelier hangs from a ceiling.
chan·de·lier (shăn′də **lîr′**) ◊ *noun, plural* **chandeliers**

▲ **chandelier**

change *verb* **1.** To make or become different; alter: *You have changed since last year.* **2.** To take, put, or use something in place of another; exchange: *I'll change this dollar bill for some coins.* **3.** To put fresh clothing or coverings on: *Parents change a baby often. We changed the bed.*
◊ *noun* **1.** The act or result of changing: *We made a change in the schedule.* **2.** Something that is put in place of something else: *You will need seven changes of clothing for camp.* **3.** The money returned when the amount given in paying for something is more than what is owed: *The pad cost 80 cents, so I got back change from my dollar.* **4.** Coins: *Do you need change to operate the machine?*
◊ *idiom* **change hands** To pass from one owner to another.
change (chānj) ◊ *verb* **changed, changing** ◊ *noun, plural* **changes**

SYNONYMS

change, convert, transform

Let's *change* the color of the living room. My parents *converted* the attic into an apartment. Water is *transformed* into steam by heat.

changeover *noun* A change from one activity or way of doing something to another.
change·o·ver (**chānj′** ō′vər) ◊ *noun, plural* **changeovers**

channel *noun* **1.** The part of a river or harbor deep enough for ships to pass through. **2.** A body of water that connects two larger bodies of water: *The English Channel connects the Atlantic Ocean with the North Sea.* **3.** A band of radio waves used for broadcasting, as on television.
◊ *verb* To form a channel or groove in or through something: *The river had channeled a deep gorge through the mountains.*
chan·nel (**chăn′** əl) ◊ *noun, plural* **channels** ◊ *verb* **channeled, channeling**

ă	pat	ĭ	pit	oi	**oil**	th	**bath**
ā	pay	ī	ride	o͝o	**book**	*th*	**bathe**
â	care	î	fierce	o͞o	**boot**	ə	**ago, item**
ä	father	ŏ	pot	ou	**out**		pencil
ĕ	pet	ō	go	ŭ	cut		atom
ē	be	ô	paw, for	û	fur		circus

▲ **channel**

chant *noun* **1.** A melody with many words sung on the same note. **2.** A calling or shouting of words, repeated many times in rhythm: *We heard the chant of the crowd.*
◊ *verb* To sing or shout a chant.
chant (chănt) ◊ *noun, plural* **chants** ◊ *verb* **chanted, chanting**

Chanukah *noun* A Jewish festival, usually in December, that lasts eight days.
Cha·nu·kah (**hä′** nə kə) ◊ *noun*

chaos *noun* Great confusion or disorder.
cha·os (**kā′** ŏs′) ◊ *noun*

chap[1] *verb* To make or become dry, rough, and cracked: *Our lips are chapped from the cold weather.*
chap[1] (chăp) ◊ *verb* **chapped, chapping**

chap[2] *noun* A man or boy; fellow.
chap[2] (chăp) ◊ *noun, plural* **chaps**

HISTORY **• chap**[1]**, chap**[2]

Chap[1] has been around since the end of the Middle Ages. Its history before that is not known for certain. **Chap**[2] has been around almost as long. It was shortened from *chapman,* an old word that meant "merchant."

chapel *noun* **1.** A small church. **2.** A place for religious services in a building such as a hospital or school.
chap·el (**chăp′** əl) ◊ *noun, plural* **chapels**

chaplain *noun* A member of the clergy who leads religious services for a group such as a school or a military unit.
chap·lain (chăp′lən) ◊ *noun, plural* **chaplains**

chaps *plural noun* Heavy leather pants without a seat. Chaps are worn over ordinary pants by cowboys to protect their legs.
chaps (chăps *or* shăps) ◊ *plural noun*

chapter *noun* **1.** A main division of a book. A chapter may have a number or a title or both. **2.** A local branch of a club or other group.
chap·ter (chăp′tər) ◊ *noun, plural* **chapters**

character *noun* **1.** The combination of qualities that makes one person or thing different from another: *The town has a calm and peaceful character.* **2.** A person's moral nature: *Your character determines the way you feel, think, and act.* **3.** Moral strength; honesty: *A person of character would not steal.* **4.** A person in a story, book, play, or movie. **5.** Someone who is unusual and amusing: *That child is really a character.* **6.** A symbol, as a letter or number, used in printing or writing. The 26 capital letters of the alphabet are characters.
char·ac·ter (kăr′ĭk tər) ◊ *noun, plural* **characters**

characteristic *adjective* Showing a special feature or quality; typical: *The zebra has characteristic stripes.*
◊ *noun* A special feature or quality: *Noise is a characteristic of most cities.*
char·ac·ter·is·tic (kăr′ĭk tə **rĭs′**tĭk) ◊ *adjective* ◊ *noun, plural* **characteristics**

characterize *verb* **1.** To describe the character or qualities of; portray: *He characterized her as lively and kind.* **2.** To be a characteristic or quality of; distinguish: *Hardness and strength characterize steel.*
char·ac·ter·ize (kăr′ĭk tə rīz′) ◊ *verb* **characterized, characterizing**

charcoal *noun* A black material made of carbon. It is produced by heating wood or other plant or animal material. Charcoal is used as a fuel, in filters, and for drawing.
char·coal (chär′kōl′) ◊ *noun, plural* **charcoals**

charge *verb* **1.** To ask as payment; set a price: *How much will you charge me for repairing my bike?* **2.** To put off paying for something by recording the amount owed and agreeing to pay later: *Charge the groceries to my account.* **3.** To rush or rush at with force; attack: *The soldiers charged the fort.* **4.** To accuse; blame: *The police charged the suspect with burglary.* **5.** To trust with a duty, task, or responsibility: *The nurse was charged with the care of the children.*
◊ *noun* **1.** An amount asked or made as payment; cost: *There is no charge for this service.* —See Synonyms at **price.** **2.** Care; control; responsibility: *The scientist is in charge of the experiment.* **3.** A statement of blame; accusation. **4.** A rushing, forceful attack.
charge (chärj) ◊ *verb* **charged, charging** ◊ *noun, plural* **charges**

chariot *noun* A two-wheeled cart pulled by horses. Chariots were used in ancient times for battles, races, and parades.
char·i·ot (chăr′ē ət) ◊ *noun, plural* **chariots**

▲ **chariot**

charitable *adjective* **1.** Tolerant or understanding of others: *Be more charitable when you speak of that family; they have their own problems.* **2.** Generous in giving money or other help to needy people. **3.** Of or for helping needy people: *Some hospitals are charitable institutions.*
char·i·ta·ble (chăr′ĭ tə bəl) ◊ *adjective*

charity *noun* **1.** Good will or love toward others. **2.** Tolerance or understanding in judging others. **3.** The giving of money or other help to needy people. **4.** A group or fund organized to help needy people: *Give money to your favorite charity.*
char·i·ty (chăr′ĭ tē) ◊ *noun, plural* **charities**

charm *noun* **1.** The power or ability to please or delight; appeal: *The charm of a good story is that it takes your mind off your troubles.* **2.** A small ornament worn on a bracelet or chain.
◊ *verb* To please greatly; delight.
charm (chärm) ◊ *noun, plural* **charms** ◊ *verb* **charmed, charming**

charming *adjective* Very pleasing; delightful: *Your teacher is a charming person.*
charm·ing (**chär′**mĭng) ◊ *adjective*

chart *noun* **1.** A sheet that gives information in the form of a table, diagram, or graph. **2.** A map for sailors that shows features such as the outlines of coasts, water depths, and positions of rocks.
◊ *verb* **1.** To make a chart of: *Astronomers chart the positions of the stars.* **2.** To plan by or as if by means of a chart.
chart (chärt) ◊ *noun, plural* **charts** ◊ *verb* **charted, charting**

charter *noun* A formal written document from an authority, as a ruler or government, granting rights or privileges or setting forth the function, form, and duties of the body to which it is given.
◊ *verb* **1.** To grant a charter to. **2.** To hire or rent for a limited time.
char·ter (**chär′**tər) ◊ *noun, plural* **charters** ◊ *verb* **chartered, chartering**

chase *verb* **1.** To follow in order to catch or overtake: *We chased the runaway dog.* **2.** To drive away: *A cat chased the bird from its perch.*
◊ *noun* The act of chasing; pursuit.
chase (chās) ◊ *verb* **chased, chasing** ◊ *noun, plural* **chases**

chasm *noun* A deep crack or opening in the surface of the earth.
chasm (**kăz′**əm) ◊ *noun, plural* **chasms**

chat *verb* To talk in a relaxed, friendly way.
◊ *noun* A relaxed, friendly conversation.
chat (chăt) ◊ *verb* **chatted, chatting** ◊ *noun, plural* **chats**

ă	pat	ĭ	pit	oi	**oi**l	th	ba**th**
ā	pay	ī	ride	o͝o	**boo**k	*th*	ba**the**
â	care	î	fierce	o͞o	**boo**t	ə	ago, item
ä	father	ŏ	pot	ou	**ou**t		pencil
ĕ	pet	ō	go	ŭ	cut		atom
ē	be	ô	paw, for	û	fur		circus

chatter *verb* **1.** To make rapid sounds that seem to resemble speech but have no meaning: *Birds and monkeys chattered in the jungle.* **2.** To talk fast and without much purpose; jabber: *All during the meal the guests chattered.* —See Synonyms at **speak.** **3.** To make a rapid series of clicking noises: *Our teeth chattered in the cold.*
◊ *noun* The sound or act of chattering.
chat·ter (**chăt′**ər) ◊ *verb* **chattered, chattering** ◊ *noun*

chatty *adjective* Having the tone or effect of informal conversation: *I wrote them a chatty letter about life at school.*
chat·ty (**chăt′**ē) ◊ *adjective* **chattier, chattiest**

chauffeur *noun* A person who is hired to drive an automobile.
chauf·feur (**shō′**fər *or* shō **fûr′**) ◊ *noun, plural* **chauffeurs**

cheap *adjective* **1.** Low in price; inexpensive: *Tomatoes are cheap in August.* **2.** Charging low prices: *We ate at a cheap restaurant.* **3.** Of little value or poor quality; inferior: *Cheap shoes often wear out quickly.*
cheap (chēp) ◊ *adjective* **cheaper, cheapest**
‖*These sound alike:* **cheap, cheep**

cheat *verb* To act or treat in a dishonest way: *I hope you didn't cheat on your test. They cheated us out of our land.*
◊ *noun* A person who cheats.
cheat (chēt) ◊ *verb* **cheated, cheating** ◊ *noun, plural* **cheats**

check *verb* **1.** To cause to stop suddenly. **2.** To hold back the expression of; curb: *I checked my sudden impulse to giggle.* **3.** To test, examine, or compare to find out if something is correct or in good condition: *Check your answers after doing the arithmetic problems.* **4.** To mark with a sign to show that something has been noted or chosen or is correct: *Read the sentences below, and check the statements that are true.* **5.** To leave something to be kept safe for a time or to be shipped.
◊ *noun* **1.** A stop, especially a sudden stop; halt: *The strike caused a check in production.* **2.** Something that restrains or controls: *Try to keep a check on your enthusiasm.* **3.** Examination or investigation to be sure that something is as it should be: *Make a careful check of your addition.* **4.** A mark made to show

that something has been noted or chosen or is accurate. **5.** A written order to a bank to pay money from a person's account to the one whose name is on the order: *I paid for the coat by check.* **6.** A ticket or slip used for identification or as proof of ownership or claim. **7.** A statement showing the amount due, as at a restaurant; bill. **8.** A pattern of squares.
check (chĕk) ◊ *verb* **checked, checking** ◊ *noun, plural* **checks**

checkerboard *noun* A board divided into 64 squares of alternating colors and used for playing chess or checkers.
check·er·board (**chĕk′** ər bôrd′) ◊ *noun, plural* **checkerboards**

▲ **checkerboard**

checkers *noun* (*used with a singular verb*) A game played on a checkerboard by two players each using 12 round, flat pieces.
check·ers (**chĕk′** ərz) ◊ *noun*

checkup *noun* An examination, as to find out whether someone is in good health or whether something is in good working condition: *We have regular medical checkups.*
check·up (**chĕk′**ŭp′) ◊ *noun, plural* **checkups**

cheek *noun* **1.** The side of the face below the eye and between the nose and ear. **2.** Impudent talk or behavior.
cheek (chēk) ◊ *noun, plural* **cheeks**

cheep *noun* A shrill chirp, like that of a young bird.
◊ *verb* To make this sound; chirp.
cheep (chēp) ◊ *noun, plural* **cheeps** ◊ *verb* **cheeped, cheeping**
‖*These sound alike:* **cheep, cheap**

cheer *verb* **1.** To shout in happiness, approval, encouragement, or enthusiasm: *The audience cheered and clapped.* **2.** To encourage or urge on especially by cheering: *The fans cheered the runner on.* **3.** To make or become happier.
◊ *noun* **1.** A shout of happiness, approval, encouragement, or enthusiasm. **2.** Good spirits; happiness: *On Christmas the children were full of cheer.*
cheer (chîr) ◊ *verb* **cheered, cheering** ◊ *noun, plural* **cheers**

cheerful *adjective* **1.** Showing or full of cheer; happy. —See Synonyms at **glad.** **2.** Producing a feeling of cheer; pleasant: *We painted the room a cheerful yellow.*
cheer·ful (**chîr′** fəl) ◊ *adjective*

cheery *adjective* Bright and cheerful.
cheer·y (**chîr′** ē) ◊ *adjective* **cheerier, cheeriest**

cheese *noun* A food made from the pressed curds of milk.
cheese (chēz) ◊ *noun, plural* **cheeses**

cheetah *noun* A spotted wild cat of Africa and southwestern Asia that has long legs and can run very fast.
chee·tah (**chē′** tə) ◊ *noun, plural* **cheetahs**

▲ **cheetah**

chef *noun* A cook, especially the chief cook of a restaurant.
chef (shĕf) ◊ *noun, plural* **chefs**

chemical *adjective* Of, relating to, or produced by means of chemistry.
◊ *noun* A substance produced by or used in chemistry.
chem·i·cal (**kĕm′** ĭ kəl) ◊ *adjective* ◊ *noun, plural* **chemicals**

chemist *noun* A scientist who specializes in chemistry.
chem·ist (**kĕm′**ĭst) ◊ *noun, plural* **chemists**

chemistry *noun* **1.** The scientific study of the composition, structure, properties, and reactions of matter. **2.** The structure, properties, and reactions of a substance or a system of substances.
chem·is·try (**kĕm′**ĭ strē) ◊ *noun, plural* **chemistries**

cherish *verb* To feel affection for and treat fondly: *The children cherished the kittens.*
cher·ish (**chĕr′**ĭsh) ◊ *verb* **cherished, cherishing**

cherry *noun* **1.** A small, rounded red or yellow fruit with a hard stone. **2.** A deep or bright red color.
cher·ry (**chĕr′**ē) ◊ *noun, plural* **cherries**

chess *noun* A game played on a board by two players, each with 16 pieces.
chess (chĕs) ◊ *noun*

chest *noun* **1.** The part of the body between the neck and the abdomen, enclosed by the ribs and the breastbone. **2.** A box, often with a lid, used for holding, storing, or shipping.
chest (chĕst) ◊ *noun, plural* **chests**

chestnut *noun* **1.** A tree that bears smooth, edible nuts that grow in prickly burs. **2.** A reddish brown color.
chest·nut (**chĕs′**nŭt′) ◊ *noun, plural* **chestnuts**

▲ **chestnut**

chew *verb* To grind or crush with the teeth: *Always chew your food thoroughly.*
chew (cho͞o) ◊ *verb* **chewed, chewing**

chewing gum *noun* Sweet, flavored gum for chewing.
chewing gum ◊ *noun*

ă	pat	ĭ	pit	oi	**oil**	th	bath
ā	pay	ī	ride	o͝o	book	*th*	bathe
â	care	î	fierce	o͞o	boot	ə	ago, item
ä	father	ŏ	pot	ou	**out**		pencil
ĕ	pet	ō	go	ŭ	cut		atom
ē	be	ô	paw, for	û	fur		circus

Chicana *noun* An American woman who was born in Mexico or has Mexican ancestors.
Chi·ca·na (chĭ **kä′**nə *or* shĭ **kä′**nə) ◊ *noun, plural* **Chicanas**

Chicano *noun* An American who was born in Mexico or has Mexican ancestors.
Chi·ca·no (chĭ **kä′**nō *or* shĭ **kä′**nō) ◊ *noun, plural* **Chicanos**

chick *noun* A young chicken or bird.
chick (chĭk) ◊ *noun, plural* **chicks**

chickadee *noun* A small, plump bird that is mostly gray with a darker marking like a cap on the head.
chick·a·dee (**chĭk′**ə dē′) ◊ *noun, plural* **chickadees**

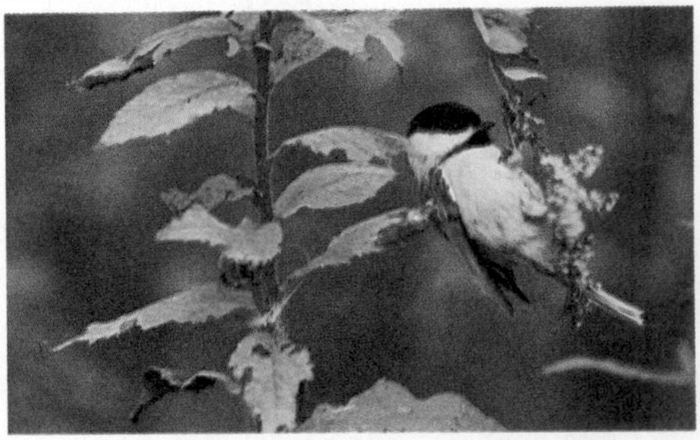
▲ **chickadee**

chicken *noun* **1.** The common domestic fowl; hen or rooster. **2.** The flesh of a chicken used for food.
chick·en (**chĭk′**ən) ◊ *noun, plural* **chickens**

chicken pox *noun* A contagious virus disease, mainly of children, in which the skin breaks out in spots and fever occurs.
chicken pox (pŏks) ◊ *noun*

chief *noun* A person of the highest rank or authority; leader: *The chief of police gave a talk at our school.*
◊ *adjective* **1.** Highest in rank: *My cousin was appointed chief engineer of the project.* **2.** Most important: *The chief problem is to decide what to do first.*
chief (chēf) ◊ *noun, plural* **chiefs** ◊ *adjective*

chiefly *adverb* **1.** Most of all; mainly: *The land was used chiefly for pasture.* **2.** First of all; especially: *Their worries were chiefly about money.*
chief·ly (**chēf′**lē) ◊ *adverb*

chieftain *noun* The leader of a group such as a tribe or clan.
chief·tain (chēf′tən) ◊ *noun, plural* **chieftains**

child *noun* **1.** A baby; infant. **2.** A young boy or girl. **3.** A son or daughter; offspring.
child (chīld) ◊ *noun, plural* **children**

childhood *noun* The time or condition of being a child.
child·hood (chīld′hŏŏd′) ◊ *noun, plural* **childhoods**

childish *adjective* **1.** Of, like, or proper to a child: *The young singers had sweet, childish voices.* **2.** Showing attitudes or qualities not suitable for a mature person: *That was a very childish remark.*
child·ish (chīl′dĭsh) ◊ *adjective*

children *noun* Plural of **child.**
chil·dren (chĭl′drən) ◊ *noun*

chili *noun* **1.** The very sharp-tasting pod of a kind of red pepper. **2.** A spicy dish made of chili, meat, and often beans.
chil·i (chĭl′ē) ◊ *noun, plural* **chilies**
‖*These sound alike:* **chili, chilly**

chill *noun* **1.** Unpleasant coldness: *There was a chill in the dawn air.* **2.** A feeling of coldness, usually with shivering: *Chills and sneezing are signs of a cold.*
◊ *adjective* Unpleasantly cold; chilly: *A chill wind whistled through the branches.*
◊ *verb* To make or become cold or chilly: *The icy wind chilled my face.*
chill (chĭl) ◊ *noun, plural* **chills** ◊ *adjective* ◊ *verb* **chilled, chilling**

chilly *adjective* Cold enough to cause or feel chill. —See Synonyms at **cold.**
chill·y (chĭl′ē) ◊ *adjective* **chillier, chilliest**
‖*These sound alike:* **chilly, chili**

chime *noun* **1.** A set of bells tuned to different pitches and rung to make musical sounds. **2.** A musical sound made by or as if by bells.
◊ *verb* To produce a sound of or like that of a bell or set of chimes.
chime (chīm) ◊ *noun, plural* **chimes** ◊ *verb* **chimed, chiming**

chimney *noun* A hollow, usually vertical structure for the passage of smoke and gases, as from a fireplace, that often rises above the roof of a building.
chim·ney (chĭm′nē) ◊ *noun, plural* **chimneys**

chimpanzee *noun* An African ape with dark hair and a high degree of intelligence.
chim·pan·zee (chĭm′păn **zē′** *or* chĭm **păn′**zē) ◊ *noun, plural* **chimpanzees**

▲ **chimpanzee**

chin *noun* The part of the face below the mouth that is formed by the center of the front of the lower jaw.
◊ *verb* To pull oneself up with the arms while grasping an overhead bar until the chin is level with the bar.
chin (chĭn) ◊ *noun, plural* **chins** ◊ *verb* **chinned, chinning**

china *noun* **1.** Fine, hard porcelain. **2.** Articles, as dishes, made of porcelain or pottery.
chi·na (chī′nə) ◊ *noun*

chinchilla *noun* A South American animal that looks like a squirrel and has soft, pale gray fur.
chin·chil·la (chĭn **chĭl′**ə) ◊ *noun, plural* **chinchillas**

Chinese *noun* **1.** A person who was born or lives in China. **2.** The official language written and spoken by the people of China.
◊ *adjective* Of or relating to China, the Chinese, or their official language.
Chi·nese (chī **nēz′**) ◊ *noun, plural* **Chinese** ◊ *adjective*

chink *noun* A narrow crack or opening.
chink (chĭngk) ◊ *noun, plural* **chinks**

chip *noun* **1.** A small piece that has been chopped, cut, or broken off: *I cleaned up chips of glass after the mirror smashed.* **2.** A mark left when a small piece has broken off: *There is a chip on the rim of my glass.*
◊ *verb* To chop, cut, or break chips from: *I bit into a cherry pit and chipped my tooth.*

◊ *idiom* **chip in** To contribute money: *How many people chipped in for the present?*
chip (chĭp) ◊ *noun, plural* **chips** ◊ *verb* **chipped, chipping**

chipmunk *noun* An animal that resembles a squirrel but is smaller and has a striped back.
chip·munk (**chĭp′**mŭngk′) ◊ *noun, plural* **chipmunks**

▲ **chipmunk**

chirp *noun* The short, high sound made by some small birds and insects.
◊ *verb* To make this sound.
chirp (chûrp) ◊ *noun, plural* **chirps** ◊ *verb* **chirped, chirping**

chisel *noun* A metal tool with a sharp edge for cutting or shaping stone, wood, or metal.
◊ *verb* To cut or shape with a chisel.
chis·el (**chĭz′** əl) ◊ *noun, plural* **chisels** ◊ *verb* **chiseled, chiseling**

chivalry *noun* **1.** The beliefs, customs, and rules followed long ago by knights. **2.** The qualities, such as bravery, courtesy, and honor, that are associated with knights.
chiv·al·ry (**shĭv′** əl rē) ◊ *noun*

chlorine *noun* A chemical element that is a very irritating greenish-yellow gas used especially to purify water and as a bleach.
chlo·rine (**klôr′** ēn′) ◊ *noun*

chlorophyll *noun* A green pigment composed of carbon, hydrogen, magnesium, nitrogen, and oxygen, found in green plants and other living things.
chlo·ro·phyll (**klôr′** ə fĭl) ◊ *noun*

ă pat	ĭ pit	oi	**oil**	th	**bath**		
ā pay	ī ride	o͝o	book	*th*	**bathe**		
â care	î fierce	o͞o	boot	ə	ago, item		
ä father	ŏ pot	ou	**out**		pencil		
ĕ pet	ō go	ŭ	cut		atom		
ē be	ô paw, for	û	fur		circus		

chocolate *noun* **1.** Cacao beans that have been ground and roasted for use in various foods. **2.** A candy made with chocolate.
◊ *adjective* Made with chocolate.
choc·o·late (**chôk′** ə lĭt *or* **chôk′** lĭt) ◊ *noun, plural* **chocolates** ◊ *adjective*

choice *noun* **1.** The act of choosing: *May I help you with your choice of books?* **2.** The freedom or chance to choose. **3.** Someone or something chosen: *Fish, a salad, and fruit were my choices for lunch.* **4.** A variety from which to choose: *We had a wide choice of things to do after school.*
◊ *adjective* Worth being chosen above all others; excellent.
choice (chois) ◊ *noun, plural* **choices** ◊ *adjective* **choicer, choicest**

SYNONYMS

choice, alternative, preference, selection

I had my *choice* of any two outfits in the store. The *alternative* is between going home and staying here. I have a *preference* for oranges. The director made a good *selection* of pieces of music for our chorus to sing.

choir *noun* A group of singers that gives performances, especially in a church.
choir (kwīr) ◊ *noun, plural* **choirs**

choke *verb* **1.** To stop from breathing, as by squeezing the windpipe from outside or blocking the windpipe inside. **2.** To stop breathing, as by having the windpipe blocked: *If we eat slowly, we won't be so likely to choke on food.* **3.** To hold back; control: *I choked back my tears.* **4.** To stop or slow down the growth or action of: *Weeds choked the flowers.*
choke (chōk) ◊ *verb* **choked, choking**

choose *verb* **1.** To pick out, especially on the basis of what one wants and thinks best: *I chose four games to take on my trip.* **2.** To make a decision on the basis of what one prefers: *I chose to go home.*
choose (cho͞oz) ◊ *verb* **chose, chosen, choosing**

chop *verb* **1.** To cut by striking with a heavy, sharp tool, such as an ax: *I chopped each piece of wood in two.* —See Synonyms at **cut.** **2.** To strike once or again and again with or as if with an ax: *I will chop away at this block of ice.* **3.** To cut up into small pieces: *Please chop some onions for supper.*
◊ *noun* **1.** A quick, short blow, as with an ax. **2.** A small slice of meat that contains a rib. **3.** A short, sudden movement of waves.
chop (chŏp) ◊ *verb* **chopped, chopping** ◊ *noun, plural* **chops**

choppy *adjective* **1.** Full of short irregular waves: *The seas were choppy.* **2.** Shifting quickly; not smooth; jerky: *That sentence style is choppy.*
chop·py (**chŏp′**ē) ◊ *adjective* **choppier, choppiest**

chopsticks *plural noun* A pair of thin sticks used as eating utensils, especially in Asian countries.
chop·sticks (**chŏp′**stĭks′) ◊ *plural noun*

▲ **chopsticks**

chord *noun* A combination of two or more musical tones sounded at the same time.
chord (kôrd) ◊ *noun, plural* **chords**
‖*These sound alike:* **chord, cord**

chore *noun* **1.** A small job, usually done on a regular schedule. —See Synonyms at **task.** **2.** An unpleasant or hard job.
chore (chôr) ◊ *noun, plural* **chores**

chorus *noun* **1.** A group of singers who perform together. **2.** A musical piece for such a group. **3.** A section of music that is repeated after each verse of a song; refrain.
cho·rus (**kôr′**əs) ◊ *noun, plural* **choruses**

chose *verb* Past tense of **choose.**
chose (chōz) ◊ *verb*

chosen *verb* Past participle of **choose.**
cho·sen (**chō′**zən) ◊ *verb*

chowder *noun* A thick soup made with clams or fish.
chow·der (**chou′**dər) ◊ *noun, plural* **chowders**

Christ *noun* 4 B.C.?–A.D. 29? The founder of Christianity.
Christ (krīst) ◊ *noun*

christen *verb* **1.** To give a name to at baptism. **2.** To baptize into a Christian church. **3.** To name and dedicate, especially at a ceremony: *They will christen the luxury liner Saturday.*
chris·ten (**krĭs′**ən) ◊ *verb* **christened, christening**

Christian *noun* Someone who believes in and follows the teachings of Christ.
◊ *adjective* **1.** Following the teachings of Christ. **2.** Of Christ, Christianity, or Christians. **3.** Showing qualities such as gentleness, kindness, and humility.
Chris·tian (**krĭs′**chən) ◊ *noun, plural* **Christians** ◊ *adjective*

Christianity *noun* The religion based on the teachings of Christ.
Chris·ti·an·i·ty (krĭs′chē **ăn′**ĭ tē) ◊ *noun*

Christmas *noun* December 25, a holiday celebrated by Christians as the anniversary of the birth of Christ.
Christ·mas (**krĭs′**məs) ◊ *noun*

Christmas tree *noun* An evergreen tree, real or artificial, decorated with ornaments or lights at Christmas time.
Christmas tree ◊ *noun, plural* **Christmas trees**

chrome *noun* Chromium.
chrome (krōm) ◊ *noun*

chromium *noun* A chemical element that is a hard, silvery-gray metal. It does not tarnish in air.
chro·mi·um (**krō′**mē əm) ◊ *noun*

chromosome *noun* A rod-shaped structure in the nucleus of an animal or plant cell. Chromosomes contain genes and have to do with the passing on of hereditary characteristics, such as eye and hair color, from parents to their offspring.
chro·mo·some (**krō′**mə sōm′) ◊ *noun, plural* **chromosomes**

chronicle *noun* A record of events arranged in the order that they happened.
◊ *verb* To record, as in a chronicle: *This almanac chronicles the events of the year.*
chron·i·cle (**krŏn′**ĭ kəl) ◊ *noun, plural* **chronicles** ◊ *verb* **chronicled, chronicling**

chrysanthemum *noun* A plant that has flowers with many little petals.
chry·san·the·mum (krĭ **săn′**thə məm) ◊ *noun, plural* **chrysanthemums**

chub *noun* A freshwater fish that is related to the carp.
chub (chŭb) ◊ *noun, plural* **chub** *or* **chubs**

chubby *adjective* Round and having plenty of flesh; plump: *The baby has a chubby face.*
chub·by (**chŭb′**ē) ◊ *adjective* **chubbier, chubbiest**

chuckle *verb* To laugh quietly.
◊ *noun* A quiet laugh.
chuck·le (**chŭk′**əl) ◊ *verb* **chuckled, chuckling** ◊ *noun, plural* **chuckles**

chug *noun* A sound like a muffled explosion made by or as if by an engine running slowly.
◊ *verb* To make such sounds.
chug (chŭg) ◊ *noun, plural* **chugs** ◊ *verb* **chugged, chugging**

chum *noun* A close friend; pal.
chum (chŭm) ◊ *noun, plural* **chums**

chunk *noun* A short, thick piece, often of irregular shape: *We saw many large chunks of ice floating in the stream.*
chunk (chŭngk) ◊ *noun, plural* **chunks**

chunky *adjective* Short and heavy in build; stocky.
chunk·y (**chŭng′**kē) ◊ *adjective* **chunkier, chunkiest**

church *noun* **1.** A building for Christian services. **2.** Religious services in a church. **3.** An organized group of Christians; congregation.
church (chûrch) ◊ *noun, plural* **churches**

churchyard *noun* A piece of ground near a church, sometimes used as a cemetery.
church·yard (**chûrch′**yärd′) ◊ *noun, plural* **churchyards**

ă	pat	ĭ	pit	oi	oil	th	bath
ā	pay	ī	ride	o͝o	book	*th*	bathe
â	care	î	fierce	o͞o	boot	ə	ago, item
ä	father	ŏ	pot	ou	out		pencil
ĕ	pet	ō	go	ŭ	cut		atom
ē	be	ô	paw, for	û	fur		circus

churn *noun* A device in which cream is beaten vigorously to make butter.
◊ *verb* **1.** To make butter in a churn. **2.** To move or cause to move forcefully: *The water of the lake churned in the storm.*
churn (chûrn) ◊ *noun, plural* **churns** ◊ *verb* **churned, churning**

▲ **churn**

chute *noun* A channel, slope, or passage down which things can fall or slide: *We put our dirty clothes in the laundry chute.*
chute (sho͞ot) ◊ *noun, plural* **chutes**

cicada *noun* An insect with a broad head and transparent wings. The male makes a loud sound with a high pitch.
ci·ca·da (sĭ **kā′**də *or* sĭ **kä′**də) ◊ *noun, plural* **cicadas**

cider *noun* The juice pressed from apples. It is used as a drink and also for making other products, such as vinegar.
ci·der (**sī′**dər) ◊ *noun*

cigar *noun* A small roll of tobacco leaves used for smoking.
ci·gar (sĭ **gär′**) ◊ *noun, plural* **cigars**

cigarette *noun* A small roll of tobacco cut in very small pieces, wrapped in thin paper and used for smoking.
cig·a·rette (sĭg′ə **rĕt′**) ◊ *noun, plural* **cigarettes**

cilia *noun* Plural of **cilium.**
cil·i·a (**sĭl′**ē ə) ◊ *noun*

cilium *noun* A tiny structure shaped like a hair. Cilia stick out from the surface of a cell. Some one-celled creatures use cilia as a means of moving about.
cil·i·um (**sĭl′**ē əm) ◊ *noun, plural* **cilia**

cinch *noun* **1.** A strap that goes around the body of an animal, such as a horse, in order to hold a saddle or a pack on the animal's back. **2.** Something that is easy to do.
cinch (sĭnch) ◊ *noun, plural* **cinches**

cinder *noun* Partly burned material, such as coal or wood, that is no longer flaming.
cin·der (**sĭn′**dər) ◊ *noun, plural* **cinders**

cinema *noun* A motion-picture theater.
cin·e·ma (sĭn′ ə mə) ◊ *noun, plural* **cinemas**

cinnamon *noun* A spice made from the dried or ground bark of a tropical tree.
cin·na·mon (sĭn′ ə mən) ◊ *noun*

circle *noun* **1.** A curved line made up of points that are all at the same distance from an inside point called the center. **2.** The area inside such a curved line. **3.** Something that has the general shape of a circle: *There is a circle of flowers around the statue.* **4.** A group of people who have something in common: *I have a fine circle of friends.*
◊ *verb* **1.** To make a circle around; enclose: *Circle the correct answers.* **2.** To move in a circle: *The bird circled its nest. The plane circled before landing.*
cir·cle (sûr′ kəl) ◊ *noun, plural* **circles** ◊ *verb* **circled, circling**

circuit *noun* **1.** A course or movement that is shaped more or less like a circle: *Each planet makes a circuit around the sun.* **2.** A regular route followed by a judge from place to place in order to hear legal cases. **3.** A closed path through which electricity can flow.
cir·cuit (sûr′ kĭt) ◊ *noun, plural* **circuits**

circuit breaker *noun* An automatic switch that stops the flow of electric current in a circuit if it becomes too strong.
circuit breaker ◊ *noun, plural* **circuit breakers**

circular *adjective* **1.** Shaped like or nearly like a circle: *A Frisbee is circular.* **2.** Forming or moving in a circle: *Wheels move with circular motion.*
◊ *noun* Something, such as an advertisement or notice, that is sent or given to many people: *We gave out circulars to advertise the sale.*
cir·cu·lar (sûr′ kyə lər) ◊ *adjective* ◊ *noun, plural* **circulars**

circulate *verb* **1.** To move in a closed path, such as a circle: *Blood circulates through the body.* **2.** To pass around widely: *Rumors tend to circulate quickly.*
cir·cu·late (sûr′ kyə lāt′) ◊ *verb* **circulated, circulating**

circulation *noun* **1.** Movement in a closed path, such as a circle. **2.** The passage of something, such as money or news, from person to person or from place to place. **3.** The number of copies of something, such as a newspaper, that are sold to the public.
cir·cu·la·tion (sûr′kyə lā′ shən) ◊ *noun, plural* **circulations**

circulatory system *noun* The group of organs, such as the heart, arteries, and veins, that move blood through the body.
cir·cu·la·to·ry system (sûr′ kyə lə tôr′ē) ◊ *noun, plural* **circulatory systems**

circumference *noun* The boundary line around a circle or the length of this line.
cir·cum·fer·ence (sər kŭm′ fər əns) ◊ *noun, plural* **circumferences**

circumstance *noun* A condition, fact, or event that is related to and may affect something or someone else: *Sickness and bad weather were two of the circumstances that caused low attendance at school today.*
cir·cum·stance (sûr′ kəm stăns′) ◊ *noun, plural* **circumstances**

circus *noun* A colorful traveling show that includes performances by acrobats, clowns, and trained animals.
cir·cus (sûr′ kəs) ◊ *noun, plural* **circuses**

▲ **circus**
Elephant act at a circus

cite *verb* To quote the words of as an authority or example: *I cited two sentences from our social studies book to prove my point.*
cite (sīt) ◊ *verb* **cited, citing**
‖ *These sound alike:* **cite, sight, site**

citizen *noun* **1.** A person who is an official member of a political body, such as a country. A person can become a citizen of the United States by being born there or by being given

citizenship by the government. A citizen of the United States gives his or her country certain things, such as payment of taxes, while the United States gives its citizens certain rights, such as freedom of speech. **2.** A person who lives in a city or town.
cit·i·zen (sĭt′ĭ zən) ◊ *noun, plural* **citizens**

citizenship *noun* **1.** The legal position of a citizen of a country, with the duties, rights, and privileges of this position. **2.** The level of a person's behavior in a community: *Their citizenship in school is very good.*
cit·i·zen·ship (sĭt′ĭ zən shĭp′) ◊ *noun*

citrus *noun* One of a group of trees whose fruit is edible and rich in vitamin C. Citrus trees include the orange and lemon.
cit·rus (sĭt′rəs) ◊ *noun, plural* **citruses** *or* **citrus**

▲ **citrus**
Grapefruit, oranges, and lemons are kinds of citrus fruits.

city *noun* **1.** A place where many people live close to one another. Cities are larger than towns and are usually centers of business activity. **2.** The people who live in a city.
cit·y (sĭt′ē) ◊ *noun, plural* **cities**

civic *adjective* **1.** Of or relating to a city or town: *A mayor is a civic officer.* **2.** Of or relating to citizenship: *Voting is a civic duty.*
civ·ic (sĭv′ĭk) ◊ *adjective*

ă	pat	ĭ	pit	oi	**oi**l	th	ba**th**
ā	pay	ī	ride	o͝o	b**oo**k	*th*	ba**th**e
â	care	î	fierce	o͞o	b**oo**t	ə	ago, item
ä	father	ŏ	pot	ou	**ou**t		pencil
ĕ	pet	ō	go	ŭ	c**u**t		atom
ē	be	ô	paw, for	û	f**u**r		circus

civics *noun (used with a singular verb)* The study of how government works and of the rights and duties of citizens.
civ·ics (sĭv′ĭks) ◊ *noun*

civil *adjective* **1.** Of or relating to a citizen of a community or a country: *The laws of the United States protect our civil rights.* **2.** Of or relating to the general public rather than to military or religious matters: *Labor Day is a civil holiday.* **3.** Courteous: *Please give a civil answer to my question.* —See Synonyms at **polite.**
civ·il (sĭv′əl) ◊ *adjective*

civilian *noun* A person who is not in the armed forces.
ci·vil·ian (sĭ vĭl′yən) ◊ *noun, plural* **civilians**

civilization *noun* **1.** A condition of people that shows a high level of development in language, science, agriculture, and art. **2.** The way that a particular people lives in a particular part of the world or at a particular time in history.
civ·i·li·za·tion (sĭv′ə lĭ zā′shən) ◊ *noun, plural* **civilizations**

civilize *verb* To bring from a lower to a higher level of development in such things as language, science, agriculture, and art.
civ·i·lize (sĭv′ə līz′) ◊ *verb* **civilized, civilizing**

civil service *noun* A part of a government that is not concerned with military, legislative, or judicial affairs and that is composed of workers who are appointed, not elected.

clack *noun* A sudden, sharp sound, as that made by two hard objects that are struck together: *We heard the clack of typewriters.*
◊ *verb* To make this sound.
clack (klăk) ◊ *noun, plural* **clacks** ◊ *verb* **clacked, clacking**

clad *verb* A past tense and a past participle of **clothe.**
clad (klăd) ◊ *verb*

claim *noun* **1.** An asking for something that one owns or has a right to: *My parents made a claim for payment of the damages to our car.* **2.** A right to something: *Columbus gave Spain a claim to all the land he discovered.* **3.** Something, such as a piece of land, that somebody demands ownership of: *Miners worked on their claims along the river.*
◊ *verb* **1.** To ask for as something that one owns or has a right to: *I claimed my luggage*

at the airport. **2.** To call for; deserve: *Your homework should claim your full attention.* **3.** To state to be the case; assert: *I claim that I can run faster than you.*
claim (klām) ◊ *noun, plural* **claims** ◊ *verb* **claimed, claiming**

clam *noun* A shellfish that has a shell with two parts hinged together. Clams burrow into sand where they live. The soft body of the clam can be eaten.
◊ *verb* To gather clams, as by digging.
clam (klăm) ◊ *noun, plural* **clams** ◊ *verb* **clammed, clamming**

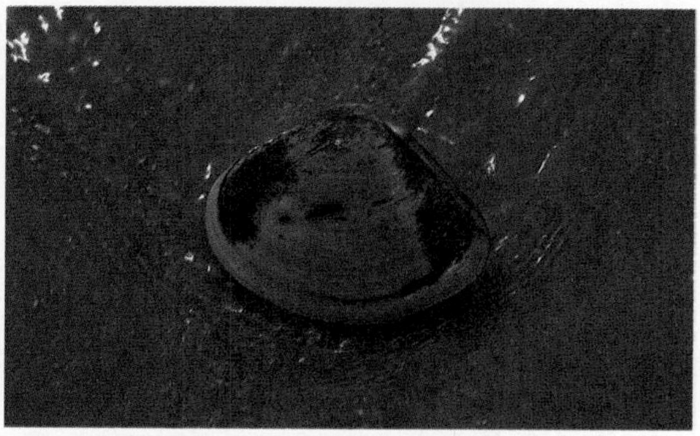

▲ **clam**

clambake *noun* A seashore picnic at which clams and other foods are baked or steamed.
clam·bake (**klăm′**bāk′) ◊ *noun, plural* **clambakes**

clamber *verb* To climb or move with difficulty, as on all fours: *We clambered up the rock.*
clam·ber (**klăm′**bər) ◊ *verb* **clambered, clambering**

clammy *adjective* Damp, sticky, and usually cold.
clam·my (**klăm′**ē) ◊ *adjective* **clammier, clammiest**

clamor *noun* A loud noise, as of a crowd shouting: *There was a clamor in the auditorium when we heard we would have a holiday.*
◊ *verb* To make a loud noise, as of a crowd shouting.
clam·or (**klăm′**ər) ◊ *noun, plural* **clamors** ◊ *verb* **clamored, clamoring**

clamp *noun* A device for gripping or fastening two things together.
◊ *verb* To use a clamp to strengthen something or fasten two things together.
clamp (klămp) ◊ *noun, plural* **clamps** ◊ *verb* **clamped, clamping**

clan *noun* A group of families, as in Scotland, that claim the same ancestor.
clan (klăn) ◊ *noun, plural* **clans**

clang *noun* A loud, ringing, metallic sound.
◊ *verb* To make or cause to make this sound.
clang (klăng) ◊ *noun, plural* **clangs** ◊ *verb* **clanged, clanging**

clank *noun* A loud sound like that of two pieces of heavy metal hitting together: *The iron gate closed with a clank.*
◊ *verb* To make or cause to make this sound.
clank (klăngk) ◊ *noun, plural* **clanks** ◊ *verb* **clanked, clanking**

clap *verb* **1.** To strike the hands together noisily and quickly: *The teacher clapped to get the class's attention.* **2.** To strike the hands together to show approval: *We clapped at the end of the play.* **3.** To slap with the open hand in a friendly way: *I clapped my friend on the shoulder when we met.*
◊ *noun* **1.** The loud sound of thunder. **2.** A friendly slap with the open hand.
clap (klăp) ◊ *verb* **clapped, clapping** ◊ *noun, plural* **claps**

clapper *noun* The part in a bell that hits the side of the bell and makes it ring.
clap·per (**klăp′**ər) ◊ *noun, plural* **clappers**

clarify *verb* To make easier to understand by explaining: *The coach clarified the rules of the game for us.*
clar·i·fy (**klăr′** ə fī′) ◊ *verb* **clarified, clarifying**

clarinet *noun* A musical instrument that has a long tube-shaped body. A clarinet is played by blowing into the mouthpiece while covering holes in the tube with the fingers or keys in order to change pitch.
clar·i·net (klăr′ə **nĕt′**) ◊ *noun, plural* **clarinets**

▲ **clarinet**

clarity *noun* The condition or quality of being clear.
clar·i·ty (**klăr′**ĭ tē) ◊ *noun*

clash *verb* **1.** To make or strike together with a loud, harsh noise, as of two metal objects striking together: *The drums boomed and the cymbals clashed loudly.* **2.** To be against one another; disagree: *The candidates clashed during the debate.*
◊ *noun* **1.** A loud, harsh sound. **2.** A strong disagreement.
clash (klăsh) ◊ *verb* **clashed, clashing**
◊ *noun, plural* **clashes**

clasp *noun* **1.** Something, as a hook or buckle, used to hold two things together. **2.** A strong grasp or hold: *I held the railing with a firm clasp.*
◊ *verb* **1.** To fasten with or as if with a clasp. **2.** To hold or take hold of the hand or the arms: *We clasped hands when we met.*
clasp (klăsp) ◊ *noun, plural* **clasps** ◊ *verb* **clasped, clasping**

class *noun* **1.** A group of things or persons that are alike in some way; kind: *There is a very large class of sports in which a ball is used.* **2.** A group of persons who earn about the same amount and live in a similar way. **3.** A group of students learning together at a regularly scheduled time: *My class is a good group of kids.* **4.** The time during which such a class meets, or the meeting of the class: *No talking is allowed during class.* **5.** A rank or division in terms of such things as quality: *We always travel first class.*
◊ *verb* To place in a group of similar objects or persons; classify.
class (klăs) ◊ *noun, plural* **classes** ◊ *verb* **classed, classing**

classic *adjective* Being the very best.
◊ *noun* **1.** An artist, writer, or work of the best kind: *"Treasure Island" is a classic.* **2. classics** The literature of ancient Greece and Rome.
clas·sic (**klăs′**ĭk) ◊ *adjective* ◊ *noun, plural* **classics**

classical *adjective* **1.** Of or relating to the art, literature, and way of life of ancient Greece and Rome. **2.** Of or relating to music that is composed according to certain forms that have grown up over a long period of time in Europe. Operas and symphonies are examples of classical music.
clas·si·cal (**klăs′**ĭ kəl) ◊ *adjective*

classification *noun* **1.** The act of classifying. **2.** The system that results from classifying.
clas·si·fi·ca·tion (klăs′ə fĭ **kā′**shən) ◊ *noun, plural* **classifications**

classify *verb* To put into groups or classes; sort: *The librarian classified the new books.*
clas·si·fy (**klăs′** ə fī′) ◊ *verb* **classified, classifying**

classmate *noun* A member of the same class in school.
class·mate (**klăs′**māt′) ◊ *noun, plural* **classmates**

classroom *noun* A room in which classes meet in school.
class·room (**klăs′**ro͞om′ *or* **klăs′**ro͝om′) ◊ *noun, plural* **classrooms**

clatter *noun* A loud, rattling sound, as of a horse's hoofs on a street.
◊ *verb* To make or cause to make this sound.
clat·ter (**klăt′** ər) ◊ *noun, plural* **clatters** ◊ *verb* **clattered, clattering**

clause *noun* A group of words containing a subject and a predicate. In the sentence *I ran when he hit the ball,* the words *I ran* and *when he hit the ball* are clauses.
clause (klôz) ◊ *noun, plural* **clauses**

claw *noun* **1.** A sharp, often curved nail on the toe of an animal or bird. **2.** A part that is shaped like a claw and can grab, as on a lobster or crab. **3.** Something that is shaped like a claw, as the part of a hammer used to pull out nails.
◊ *verb* To dig, scratch, or scrape with or as if with claws: *The kitten clawed the couch.*
claw (klô) ◊ *noun, plural* **claws** ◊ *verb* **clawed, clawing**

▲ **claw**

clay *noun* A firm kind of earth made up of small particles. Clay is

ă	pat	ĭ	pit	oi	**oil**	th	**bath**
ā	pay	ī	ride	o͝o	book	*th*	bathe
â	care	î	fierce	o͞o	boot	ə	ago, item
ä	father	ŏ	pot	ou	**out**		pencil
ĕ	pet	ō	**go**	ŭ	cut		atom
ē	be	ô	paw, for	û	**fur**		circus

soft when wet and can be shaped. After heating clay hardens. It is used to make bricks and pottery.
clay (klā) ◊ *noun, plural* **clays**

clean *adjective* **1.** Free from dirt, stains, or clutter: *Put on a clean shirt. My room is clean again.* **2.** Free from guilt; innocent: *A candidate for public office must have a clean record.* **3.** Obeying the rules; fair: *Both teams played a clean game.*
◊ *adverb* So as to leave free from dirt: *I washed the dishes clean.*
◊ *verb* To get rid of dirt or clutter: *We clean the house every Saturday.*
clean (klēn) ◊ *adjective* **cleaner, cleanest** ◊ *adverb* ◊ *verb* **cleaned, cleaning**

> ***SYNONYMS***
>
> ***clean, cleanly, spotless***
>
> I like to keep my room *clean* and beautiful. Cats are *cleanly* animals, always washing themselves with their tongues. After a thorough cleaning, the house looks *spotless.* **Antonyms:** *dirty, filthy, soiled*

cleaner *noun* **1.** A person whose job it is to clean or get rid of dirt. **2.** A machine or substance used in cleaning.
clean·er (klē′nər) ◊ *noun, plural* **cleaners**

cleanly *adjective* Always neat or free from dirt. —See Synonyms at **clean.**
◊ *adverb* In a clean way.
clean·ly ◊ *adjective* (klĕn′lē) **cleanlier, cleanliest** ◊ *adverb* (klēn′lē)

cleanse *verb* To make clean.
cleanse (klĕnz) ◊ *verb* **cleansed, cleansing**

cleanser *noun* A substance, as a powder or liquid, used for cleaning.
cleans·er (klĕn′zər) ◊ *noun, plural* **cleansers**

clear *adjective* **1.** Free from clouds, mist, haze, or dust: *Today the sky was clear.* **2.** Free from anything that makes it hard to see through; transparent: *We could see fish in the clear water.* **3.** Free from anything in the way; open: *We had a clear view of the mountains.* **4.** Easy to see, hear, or understand: *The teacher gave a clear explanation of the science experiment.* **5.** Free from guilt; untroubled: *I have a clear conscience.*
◊ *adverb* In a clear way; distinctly: *Speak loud and clear to your audience.*
◊ *verb* **1.** To become or make free from such things as clouds, rain, or dust: *The sun came out and the weather cleared.* **2.** To become or make easy to see through: *Some time after I threw in the stone, the water cleared up.* **3.** To get rid of; remove: *They will come to clear the dead tree from the road.* **4.** To free from a legal charge. **5.** To pass by, over, or under without touching: *The top of the truck may not clear the top of the tunnel.*
clear (klîr) ◊ *adjective* **clearer, clearest** ◊ *adverb* ◊ *verb* **cleared, clearing**

> ***SYNONYMS***
>
> ***clear, translucent, transparent***
>
> When the sky is *clear,* you can see long distances. I could see only light through the *translucent* glass. I could see the stones on the bottom of the stream through the *transparent* water.

clearance *noun* **1.** The act of clearing: *Clearance of snow from the streets has already begun.* **2.** A space or distance between two objects, as between the top of a truck and the bottom of a bridge.
clear·ance (klîr′əns) ◊ *noun*

clearing *noun* An area of land from which trees and brush have been removed: *We camped in a clearing in the forest.*
clear·ing (klîr′ĭng) ◊ *noun, plural* **clearings**

cleat *noun* A piece of rubber, leather, plastic, or metal attached to a shoe's heel or sole to prevent slipping. Football players wear shoes with cleats.
cleat (klēt) ◊ *noun, plural* **cleats**

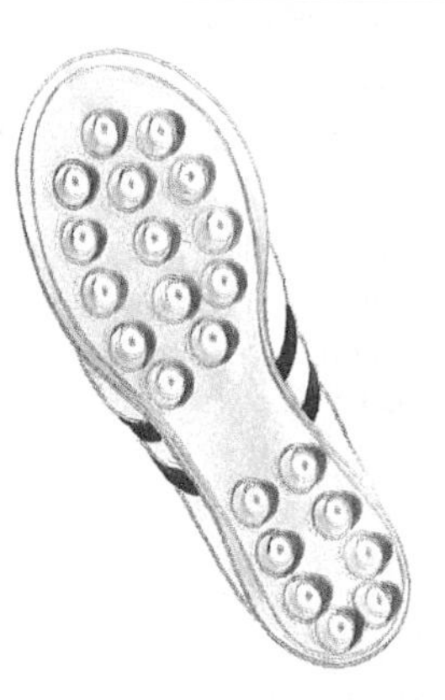

▲ **cleat**

cleaver *noun* A tool with a broad, heavy blade and a short handle used by butchers for cutting meat.
cleav·er (klē′vər) ◊ *noun, plural* **cleavers**

clef *noun* A symbol on

a musical staff that tells which pitch each of the various lines and spaces represents.
clef (klĕf) ◊ *noun, plural* **clefs**

cleft *noun* A crack or split: *I hid the message in a cleft in the rock.*
cleft (klĕft) ◊ *noun, plural* **clefts**

clench *verb* **1.** To take hold of or hold on to tightly: *Clench the football as you run, and you won't drop it.* **2.** To bring together tightly: *I clenched my teeth.*
clench (klĕnch) ◊ *verb* **clenched, clenching**

clergy *noun* All those, as rabbis, priests, and ministers, who are authorized to conduct religious services.
cler·gy (**klûr′**jē) ◊ *noun*

clerical *adjective* **1.** Of or relating to an office worker: *I would like to work as a secretary and do clerical work.* **2.** Of or relating to the clergy: *The minister wore clerical garments for the service.*
cler·i·cal (**klĕr′**ĭ kəl) ◊ *adjective*

clerk *noun* **1.** An office worker who keeps records or files papers. **2.** A person who sells things in a store: *I paid the clerk for what I had bought.*
clerk (klûrk) ◊ *noun, plural* **clerks**

clever *adjective* Having or showing a quick mind; smart: *I tried to be as clever as I could and think what to do before it was too late.*
clev·er (**klĕv′**ər) ◊ *adjective* **cleverer, cleverest**

click *noun* A short, sharp sound, as the sound made by a typewriter key.
◊ *verb* To make or cause to make such a sound: *The door clicked as it shut.*
click (klĭk) ◊ *noun, plural* **clicks** ◊ *verb* **clicked, clicking**

client *noun* Somebody who uses the services of a professional person, as a lawyer.
cli·ent (**klī′**ənt) ◊ *noun, plural* **clients**

cliff *noun* A high, steep face of rock and earth: *We looked down from the cliff to the ocean far below.*
cliff (klĭf) ◊ *noun, plural* **cliffs**

ă	pat	ĭ	pit	oi	oil	th	bath
ā	pay	ī	ride	o͝o	book	*th*	bathe
â	care	î	fierce	o͞o	boot	ə	ago, item
ä	father	ŏ	pot	ou	out		pencil
ĕ	pet	ō	go	ŭ	cut		atom
ē	be	ô	paw, for	û	fur		circus

▲ **cliff**

climate *noun* **1.** The usual weather that occurs in a place, including the average temperature and amounts of rain or wind: *The climate in the polar regions is very harsh.* **2.** A place thought of in terms of its weather conditions.
cli·mate (**klī′**mĭt) ◊ *noun, plural* **climates**

climax *noun* The point in something, as a series of events, that is highest in excitement or interest: *The climax of the Olympics was when our athletes won gold medals.*
cli·max (**klī′**măks′) ◊ *noun, plural* **climaxes**

climb *verb* **1.** To go in various directions, such as up, down, or over, often by use of the hands and feet: *I climbed up the ladder.* **2.** To go upward in a steady motion: *The sun climbed.* —See Synonyms at **rise.** **3.** To grow upward or up on, as a vine does by twining around something.
◊ *noun* **1.** The act of climbing: *We have a*

hard climb up the mountain. **2.** A place to be climbed: *That hill was a good climb.*
climb (klīm) ◊ *verb* **climbed, climbing** ◊ *noun, plural* **climbs**

clinch *verb* **1.** To fasten a nail that sticks through a board, for example, by flattening or bending down the end of the nail. **2.** To make definite or certain: *We clinched the agreement with a handshake.*
clinch (klĭnch) ◊ *verb* **clinched, clinching**

cling *verb* To stick or hold tight to: *Dirt clings to a wet rug. I clung to the hope that I would feel better soon.*
cling (klĭng) ◊ *verb* **clung, clinging**

clinic *noun* A place that gives medical treatment to patients who do not have to stay in a hospital. A clinic is often connected with a hospital or a medical school.
clin·ic (**klĭn′**ĭk) ◊ *noun, plural* **clinics**

clink *noun* A sharp, short sound, as of two glasses hitting together.
◊ *verb* To make or cause to make a clink: *Ice clinked as I carried the glass to the table.*
clink (klĭngk) ◊ *noun, plural* **clinks** ◊ *verb* **clinked, clinking**

clip[1] *verb* **1.** To cut, cut off, or cut out with scissors or shears: *I clipped the ad out of the newspaper.* **2.** To cut the surface growth of: *I had to clip the hedge.*
clip[1] (klĭp) ◊ *verb* **clipped, clipping**

clip[2] *noun* A device that fastens or holds things together: *I use a clip shaped like a bar to hold my hair in place.*
◊ *verb* To fasten with a clip: *We clipped the sheets of music together.*
clip[2] (klĭp) ◊ *noun, plural* **clips** ◊ *verb* **clipped, clipping**

***HISTORY* • clip[1], clip[2]**

Clip[1] comes from an old Scandinavian word meaning "to cut short." **Clip**[2] comes from an old English word that meant both "to fasten" and "to embrace."

clipper *noun* **1. clippers** A device that is used for clipping or cutting: *I have the fingernail clippers.* **2.** A very fast sailing vessel with tall masts.
clip·per (**klĭp′** ər) ◊ *noun, plural* **clippers**

▲ **clipper**

clipping *noun* Something cut out: *I pasted a magazine clipping in my scrapbook.*
clip·ping (**klĭp′**ĭng) ◊ *noun, plural* **clippings**

cloak *noun* **1.** A loose, sleeveless outer garment. **2.** Something that covers or conceals.
◊ *verb* To cover up or hide with or as if with a cloak: *The mountain was cloaked with mist.*
cloak (klōk) ◊ *noun, plural* **cloaks** ◊ *verb* **cloaked, cloaking**

clock *noun* An instrument for measuring and indicating time, often having a numbered dial with moving hands.
◊ *verb* To measure or record the speed of.
clock (klŏk) ◊ *noun, plural* **clocks** ◊ *verb* **clocked, clocking**

clockwise *adverb & adjective* In the direction in which the hands of a clock rotate: *I turned the bulb of the lamp clockwise.*
clock·wise (**klŏk′** wīz′) ◊ *adverb & adjective*

clog *verb* To become or cause to become blocked up: *Traffic clogged the highway.*
clog (klŏg) ◊ *verb* **clogged, clogging**

cloister *noun* A covered walk, usually with open arches, that runs along the sides of a courtyard, as of a church.
clois·ter (**kloi′** stər) ◊ *noun, plural* **cloisters**

close *adjective* **1.** Near in space, time, or relationship: *The airport is close to town.* **2.** Offering little or no space for movement; narrow: *They lived in close quarters.* **3.** Careful and strict: *Pay close attention to what they tell you.* **4.** Lacking fresh air; stuffy: *It's very*

close in this room. **5.** Almost even, as in score: *The presidential election is sure to be close.*
◊ *adverb* In a close manner or position; near: *They stood close by.*
◊ *verb* **1.** To shut: *Please close the doors.* **2.** To stop or cause to stop operating: *The store closes at six o'clock.* **3.** To bring or come to an end; conclude: *I closed the letter with greetings to the family.* —See Synonyms at **end.**
◊ *noun* A conclusion; end: *The meeting came to a close.*
close ◊ *adjective, adverb* (klōs) **closer, closest** ◊ *verb* (klōz) **closed, closing** ◊ *noun* (klōz)

closet *noun* A small room in which clothes or household supplies can be kept.
clos·et (**klŏz′**ĭt) ◊ *noun, plural* **closets**

clot *noun* A lump formed when something, especially a liquid, thickens and sticks together: *When cream is churned, clots form.*
◊ *verb* To form or cause to form clots.
clot (klŏt) ◊ *noun, plural* **clots** ◊ *verb* **clotted, clotting**

cloth *noun* **1.** Material produced by weaving or knitting fibers of cotton, wool, silk, linen, or synthetics. **2.** A piece of cloth used for a particular purpose, as a tablecloth or washcloth.
cloth (klôth) ◊ *noun, plural* **cloths**

clothe *verb* **1.** To put clothes on; dress. **2.** To provide clothes for: *We work hard to feed and clothe our family.* **3.** To cover as if with clothing: *Colorful autumn leaves clothed the trees.*
clothe (klō*th*) ◊ *verb* **clothed** *or* **clad, clothing**

clothes *plural noun* Coverings, as shirts or dresses, worn on the human body; garments.
clothes (klōz) ◊ *plural noun*

clothespin *noun* A clip, as of wood or plastic, for fastening clothes to a line.
clothes·pin (**klōz′**pĭn′) ◊ *noun, plural* **clothespins**

clothing *noun* Clothes.
cloth·ing (**klō′***th*ĭng) ◊ *noun*

cloud *noun* **1.** A visible mass of tiny drops of water or particles of ice floating usually high in the air. **2.** A visible mass, as of dust, steam, or smoke, in the air.
◊ *verb* To cover or become covered with or as if with clouds: *Heavy mist clouded the hills.*
cloud (kloud) ◊ *noun, plural* **clouds** ◊ *verb* **clouded, clouding**

cloudburst *noun* A sudden heavy rainfall.
cloud·burst (**kloud′**bûrst′) ◊ *noun, plural* **cloudbursts**

cloudy *adjective* **1.** Full of or covered with clouds: *The sky was cloudy, so I took my umbrella.* **2.** Not clear: *That water is cloudy.*
cloud·y (**klou′**dē) ◊ *adjective* **cloudier, cloudiest**

clove *noun* The dried flower bud of a tropical Asian plant, used as a spice.
clove (klōv) ◊ *noun, plural* **cloves**

***HISTORY* • clove**

Clove comes from an old French word meaning "nail." If you have ever seen cloves stuck into a baked ham, then you know that they do look like little nails.

clover *noun* Any of several plants with leaves divided into three leaflets and rounded heads of small flowers.
clo·ver (**klō′**vər) ◊ *noun, plural* **clovers**

clown *noun* A performer, especially in a circus, who does tricks or funny stunts.
◊ *verb* To act like a clown.
clown (kloun) ◊ *noun, plural* **clowns** ◊ *verb* **clowned, clowning**

▲ **clown**

ă	pat	ĭ	pit	oi	**oil**	th	bath
ā	pay	ī	ride	ŏŏ	book	*th*	bathe
â	care	î	fierce	ōō	boot	ə	ago, item
ä	father	ŏ	pot	ou	**out**		pencil
ĕ	pet	ō	go	ŭ	cut		atom
ē	be	ô	paw, for	û	fur		circus

club *noun* **1.** A heavy stick used as a weapon. **2.** A stick used to hit a ball in certain games, especially golf. **3.** A group of people who are associated because they share a purpose or interest: *We joined a tennis club.* **4.** The rooms or building used by a club.
◊ *verb* To strike or beat with a club.
club (klŭb) ◊ *noun, plural* **clubs** ◊ *verb* **clubbed, clubbing**

cluck *noun* The low, short sound made by a hen sitting on eggs or calling its chicks.
◊ *verb* To make this sound.
cluck (klŭk) ◊ *noun, plural* **clucks** ◊ *verb* **clucked, clucking**

clue *noun* Something that helps to solve a problem or mystery: *I'll give you one more clue to the riddle.*
clue (klo͞o) ◊ *noun, plural* **clues**

clump *noun* **1.** A thick cluster, as of trees or bushes. **2.** A thick mass, as of dirt. **3.** A heavy, dull sound, as of footsteps.
◊ *verb* **1.** To walk with a heavy, dull sound. **2.** To gather into or form a clump.
clump (klŭmp) ◊ *noun, plural* **clumps** ◊ *verb* **clumped, clumping**

clumsy *adjective* **1.** Lacking grace or skill in motion or action: *I am too clumsy to dance well.* **2.** Done or made without skill: *We put together a clumsy shelter.*
clum·sy (**klŭm′** zē) ◊ *adjective* **clumsier, clumsiest**

clung *verb* Past tense and past participle of **cling.**
clung (klŭng) ◊ *verb*

cluster *noun* A group of similar things growing or grouped close together: *We saw a cluster of stars in the night sky.*
◊ *verb* To grow or gather in a group: *We all clustered around the warm fire.*
clus·ter (**klŭs′** tər) ◊ *noun, plural* **clusters** ◊ *verb* **clustered, clustering**

clutch *verb* **1.** To hold or grasp tightly with or as if with the hands: *I clutched the book in my arms.* **2.** To try to seize or grab: *I clutched at the railing as I lost my balance.*
◊ *noun* **1.** A tight hold or grasp. **2.** A device that connects and disconnects the source of power in machinery. **3.** A lever or pedal that operates a clutch, as in an automobile.
clutch (klŭch) ◊ *verb* **clutched, clutching** ◊ *noun, plural* **clutches**

clutter *noun* A disordered or confused collection; jumble.
◊ *verb* To fill or litter in a disordered or confused way: *Toys cluttered up the room.*
clut·ter (**klŭt′** ər) ◊ *noun, plural* **clutters** ◊ *verb* **cluttered, cluttering**

cm The abbreviation for *centimeter.*

CO The abbreviation for *Colorado* used with a Zip Code.

Co. The abbreviation for *Company* and *County.*

co– The prefix *co–* means "with" or "together." A *copilot* assists and works together with the pilot.

***VOCABULARY BUILDER* • co–**

Many words that are formed with **co–** are not entries in this dictionary. But you can figure out what these words mean by looking up the meanings of the root words and the prefix. For example:
coequal = equal with one another
copartner = a partner with one or more persons

coach *noun* **1.** A large carriage with four wheels that has seats inside and is drawn by horses. **2.** A railroad passenger car. **3.** A class of passenger travel on a train, airplane, or bus at a cheaper fare than first class. **4.** A person who trains or teaches athletes, athletic teams, or performers.
◊ *verb* To teach or train as a coach.
coach (kōch) ◊ *noun, plural* **coaches** ◊ *verb* **coached, coaching**

▲ **coach**

coagulate *verb* To change or cause to change from a liquid to a thickened mass.
co·ag·u·late (kō ăg′ yə lāt′) ◊ *verb* **coagulated, coagulating**

coal *noun* **1.** A black natural solid substance that is formed from partly decayed plant matter, consists mainly of carbon, and is widely used as a fuel. **2.** A piece of coal. **3.** A piece of glowing or burned wood; ember.
coal (kōl) ◊ *noun, plural* **coals**

coarse *adjective* **1.** Not smooth; rough: *I wore a coat of coarse wool.* **2.** Consisting of large particles: *We used coarse gravel on the driveway.*
coarse (kôrs) ◊ *adjective* **coarser, coarsest**
‖*These sound alike:* **coarse, course**

coarsen *verb* To make or become coarse.
coars·en (kôr′ sən) ◊ *verb* **coarsened, coarsening**

coast *noun* The land next to or near the sea; seashore.
◊ *verb* **1.** To move or continue to move without use of power: *The car coasted to a stop.* **2.** To slide down a hill over ice or snow.
coast (kōst) ◊ *noun, plural* **coasts** ◊ *verb* **coasted, coasting**

coastal *adjective* Of, relating to, along, or near a coast: *I fished in coastal waters.*
coast·al (kō′ stəl) ◊ *adjective*

coast guard *noun* Often **Coast Guard** A military force whose job is guarding the coast of a nation.
coast guard ◊ *noun, plural* **coast guards**

coat *noun* **1.** An outer garment with sleeves. **2.** The outer covering, as hair or fur, of an animal. **3.** A layer of a substance, as paint, spread over a surface.
◊ *verb* To cover with a layer.
coat (kōt) ◊ *noun, plural* **coats** ◊ *verb* **coated, coating**

coating *noun* A layer of a substance spread over a surface: *There was a thin coating of frost on the ground.*
coat·ing (kō′ tĭng) ◊ *noun, plural* **coatings**

ă	pat	ĭ	pit	oi	**oil**	th	**bath**
ā	pay	ī	ride	o͝o	**book**	*th*	**bathe**
â	care	î	fierce	o͞o	**boot**	ə	ago, item
ä	father	ŏ	pot	ou	**out**		pencil
ĕ	pet	ō	**go**	ŭ	cut		atom
ē	be	ô	paw, for	û	**fur**		circus

coat of arms *noun* A design, as on a shield, that serves as the emblem of a nation, family, or group.
coat of arms ◊ *noun, plural* **coats of arms**

coax *verb* **1.** To persuade or try to persuade by gentle urging or flattery. **2.** To get by coaxing: *I coaxed a smile from the baby.*
coax (kōks) ◊ *verb* **coaxed, coaxing**

cobalt *noun* A hard, brittle metallic chemical element that looks like nickel and iron.
co·balt (kō′ bôlt′) ◊ *noun*

cobbler *noun* A person who makes or repairs shoes.
cob·bler (kŏb′ lər) ◊ *noun, plural* **cobblers**

cobblestone *noun* A round stone formerly used for paving streets.
cob·ble·stone (kŏb′ əl stōn′) ◊ *noun, plural* **cobblestones**

cobra *noun* A poisonous Asian or African snake that when excited spreads out the skin of its neck to form a hood.
co·bra (kō′ brə) ◊ *noun, plural* **cobras**

cobweb *noun* The web spun by a spider.
cob·web (kŏb′ wĕb′) ◊ *noun, plural* **cobwebs**

cock *noun* **1.** A male chicken; rooster. **2.** A male bird. **3.** A device for controlling the flow of a liquid or gas; faucet or valve.
◊ *verb* **1.** To pull back the hammer of a gun to the firing position. **2.** To tilt or turn up to one side: *The bird cocked its head.*
cock (kŏk) ◊ *noun, plural* **cocks** ◊ *verb* **cocked, cocking**

cockatoo *noun* A crested Australian parrot with usually brightly colored feathers.
cock·a·too (kŏk′ ə to͞o′) ◊ *noun, plural* **cockatoos**

▲ **cockatoo**

cockpit *noun* **1.** An enclosed space in an airplane for the pilot. **2.** An area on the deck of a small boat from which the boat is steered.
cock·pit (**kŏk′**pĭt′) ◊ *noun, plural* **cockpits**

cockroach *noun* A brownish insect with a flat body that is a common household pest.
cock·roach (**kŏk′**rōch′) ◊ *noun, plural* **cockroaches**

cocktail *noun* **1.** A mixed alcoholic drink. **2.** An appetizer, as of seafood or fruit.
cock·tail (**kŏk′**tāl′) ◊ *noun, plural* **cocktails**

cocky *adjective* Too sure of oneself; arrogant.
cock·y (**kŏk′**ē) ◊ *adjective* **cockier, cockiest**

cocoa *noun* **1.** A powder made from ground cacao seeds from which much of the fat has been removed. **2.** A sweet drink made from cocoa and milk or water.
co·coa (**kō′**kō′) ◊ *noun*

coconut *noun* The large nut of a tropical palm tree, the *coconut palm,* with a hard shell, sweet white meat, and a hollow center filled with a liquid called *coconut milk.*
co·co·nut (**kō′**kə nŭt′) ◊ *noun, plural* **coconuts**

cocoon *noun* The silky covering spun by a caterpillar to protect itself until it turns into a fully developed moth or butterfly.
co·coon (kə **kōōn′**) ◊ *noun, plural* **cocoons**

▲ **cocoon**

cod *noun* A large food fish found in cold waters of the northern Atlantic Ocean.
cod (kŏd) ◊ *noun, plural* **cod** *or* **cods**

C.O.D. Abbreviation for *cash on delivery* or *collect on delivery.*

coddle *verb* **1.** To cook in water just below the boiling point: *I coddled eggs for breakfast.* **2.** To treat tenderly; pamper.
cod·dle (**kŏd′**l) ◊ *verb* **coddled, coddling**

code *noun* **1.** A system of signals, symbols, or letters given special meanings and used in sending messages and especially in keeping them. **2.** A system of rules, regulations, or laws: *Our school has a code of behavior.*
◊ *verb* To put into a code.
code (kōd) ◊ *noun, plural* **codes** ◊ *verb* **coded, coding**

coeducation *noun* The education of both sexes at the same school or in the same classes.
co·ed·u·ca·tion (kō′ĕj ə **kā′**shən) ◊ *noun*

coffee *noun* A drink prepared from the ground roasted seeds of a tropical tree.
cof·fee (**kô′**fē) ◊ *noun*

coffin *noun* A box in which a dead person is buried.
cof·fin (**kô′**fĭn) ◊ *noun, plural* **coffins**

cog *noun* One of a series of teeth on the rim of a gear or wheel.
cog (kŏg) ◊ *noun, plural* **cogs**

coil *noun* **1.** A spiral or ring or a series of spirals or rings formed by winding: *Roll that rope into a coil.* **2.** A wire wound in a spiral for carrying electric current.
◊ *verb* To wind into or form a coil: *Vines coiled around the tree.*
coil (koil) ◊ *noun, plural* **coils** ◊ *verb* **coiled, coiling**

coin *noun* A piece of metal issued by a government for use as money.
◊ *verb* **1.** To make coins by stamping metal; mint: *Only the government has the right to coin silver dollars.* **2.** To make coins from metal. **3.** To make up a word or phrase.
coin (koin) ◊ *noun, plural* **coins** ◊ *verb* **coined, coining**

coinage *noun* **1.** The act or process of making coins. **2.** Metal coins. **3.** The act or process of coining words or phrases.
coin·age (**koi′**nĭj) ◊ *noun, plural* **coinages**

coincide *verb* **1.** To occupy the same position in space. **2.** To correspond exactly; be identical: *My opinion coincides with yours.* **3.** To happen at the same time: *Our birthdays coincide.*
co·in·cide (kō′ĭn **sīd′**) ◊ *verb* **coincided, coinciding**

coincidence *noun* **1.** A combination of events or circumstances that is accidental but seems to have been planned or arranged: *It was a coincidence that he was born on his mother's birthday.* **2.** The condition of coinciding in space or time.
co·in·ci·dence (kō **ĭn′**sĭ dəns) ◊ *noun, plural* **coincidences**

coke *noun* The solid material that is left after coal has been heated until the gas has been removed. Coke is used as fuel.
coke (kōk) ◊ *noun*

Col. **1.** An abbreviation for *Colorado.* **2.** The abbreviation for *Colonel.*

cola *noun* A soft drink flavored with an extract from the nuts of a tropical tree.
co·la (kō′lə) ◊ *noun, plural* **colas**

colander *noun* A kitchen utensil that has holes for draining liquids from foods.
col·an·der (kŏl′ən dər) ◊ *noun, plural* **colanders**

cold *adjective* **1.** Having or being at a low temperature or a lower temperature than normal: *The water was cold. I had cold hands and feet.* **2.** Feeling a lack of warmth; chilly: *I was cold without my coat.* **3.** Unfriendly: *That's a cold look you gave me.*
◊ *noun* **1.** Lack of warmth. **2.** The feeling caused by lack of warmth. **3.** A common infection that causes coughing, a running nose, and sneezing.
cold (kōld) ◊ *adjective* **colder, coldest** ◊ *noun, plural* **colds**

> ***SYNONYMS***
>
> ***cold, chilly, cool, icy***
>
> Turn on the *cold* water. The air is *chilly* and damp. Please give me a *cool* drink. In winter *icy* winds blow. **Antonyms:** *hot, torrid*

cold-blooded *adjective* **1.** Having a body temperature that changes according to the temperature of the environment. Fish, frogs, and reptiles are cold-blooded. **2.** Being or done without feeling or emotion.
cold-blood·ed (kōld′blŭd′ĭd) ◊ *adjective*

coliseum *noun* A large stadium or hall for public entertainment or sports events.
col·i·se·um (kŏl′ĭ sē′əm) ◊ *noun, plural* **coliseums**

ă	pat	ĭ	pit	oi	**oil**	th	ba**th**
ā	pay	ī	ride	o͝o	book	*th*	ba**the**
â	care	î	fierce	o͞o	boot	ə	ago, item
ä	father	ŏ	pot	ou	**out**		pencil
ĕ	pet	ō	go	ŭ	cut		atom
ē	be	ô	paw, for	û	fur		circus

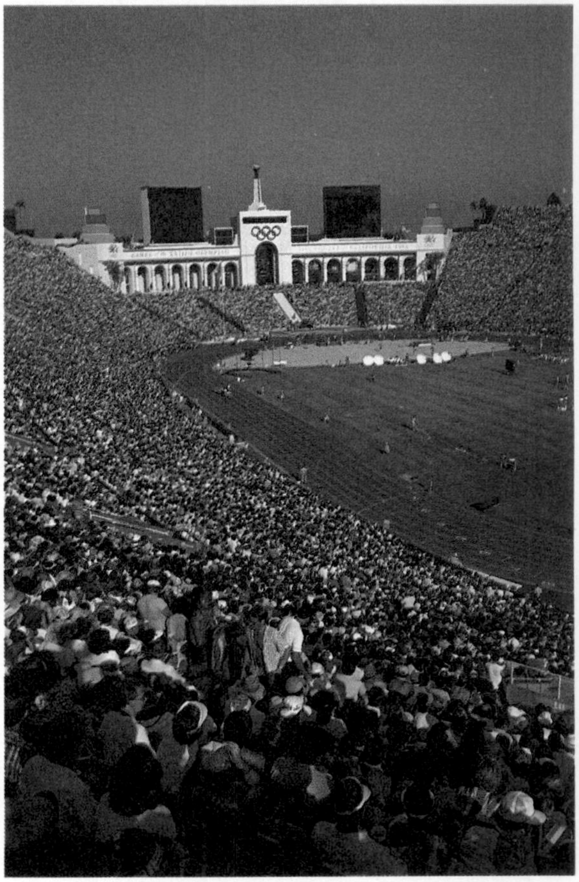

▲ **coliseum**

collaborate *verb* To work with another or others on a project: *The two friends collaborated in writing a play.*
col·lab·o·rate (kə lăb′ə rāt′) ◊ *verb* **collaborated, collaborating**

collage *noun* A picture made by pasting various materials or objects on a surface.
col·lage (kə läzh′) ◊ *noun, plural* **collages**

collapse *verb* **1.** To fall down suddenly; cave in: *Part of the roof collapsed under the weight of the snow.* —See Synonyms at **tumble.** **2.** To break down in strength or health. **3.** To fold together: *I bought a chair that collapses for storage.*
◊ *noun* The act or an example of collapsing: *The collapse of the bridge caused many delays. The country was in a state of collapse at the end of the famine.*
col·lapse (kə lăps′) ◊ *verb* **collapsed, collapsing** ◊ *noun*

collar *noun* **1.** The part of a garment that fits around the neck. **2.** A leather or metal band for the neck of an animal. **3.** The part of a harness that fits over a horse's shoulders. ◊ *verb* To catch and hold by or as if by the collar; capture.
col·lar (kŏl′ər) ◊ *noun, plural* **collars** ◊ *verb* **collared, collaring**

collarbone *noun* A bone that connects the breastbone and the shoulder blade.
col·lar·bone (kŏl′ər bōn′) ◊ *noun, plural* **collarbones**

collards *plural noun* A leafy cabbagelike vegetable that does not form a tight head.
col·lards (kŏl′ərdz) ◊ *plural noun*

colleague *noun* An associate.
col·league (kŏl′ēg′) ◊ *noun, plural* **colleagues**

collect *verb* **1.** To bring or come together in a group: *We collected wood to build a campfire. Crowds collected long before the football game.* **2.** To gather as a hobby or for study: *I collect stamps.* —See Synonyms at **gather. 3.** To get payment of: *I would like to collect the money you owe me.*
col·lect (kə lĕkt′) ◊ *verb* **collected, collecting**

collection *noun* **1.** The act or process of gathering together: *The conductor took care of the collection of fares.* **2.** A group of objects collected for exhibition or study: *That is a fine rock collection.*
col·lec·tion (kə lĕk′shən) ◊ *noun, plural* **collections**

collector *noun* **1.** Someone or something that collects: *I used to be a coin collector.* **2.** A person who is assigned to collect money: *I am the collector of the club's dues.*
col·lec·tor (kə lĕk′tər) ◊ *noun, plural* **collectors**

college *noun* A school attended after high school.
col·lege (kŏl′ĭj) ◊ *noun, plural* **colleges**

collide *verb* **1.** To strike together with force: *The kites collided high in the air.* **2.** To disagree strongly; clash: *The President collided with the Senate over the budget.*
col·lide (kə līd′) ◊ *verb* **collided, colliding**

collie *noun* A large dog with long hair and a narrow snout, often used to herd sheep.
col·lie (kŏl′ē) ◊ *noun, plural* **collies**

▲ **collie**

collision *noun* The act, the process, or an example of colliding; crash.
col·li·sion (kə lĭzh′ən) ◊ *noun, plural* **collisions**

Colo. An abbreviation for *Colorado.*

colon[1] *noun* A punctuation mark (:) used after a word that introduces a quotation, explanation, example, or series.
co·lon[1] (kō′lən) ◊ *noun, plural* **colons**

colon[2] *noun* The main part of the large intestine.
co·lon[2] (kō′lən) ◊ *noun, plural* **colons**

> ***HISTORY* • colon[1], colon[2]**
>
> **Colon[1]** and **colon[2]** come from two different Latin words that in turn came from two ancient Greek words. **Colon[1]** meant "a limb or piece," then "a piece of a sentence." We now use **colon[1]** for a punctuation mark that divides two "pieces" of a sentence. **Colon[2]** had the same meaning it does today.

colonel *noun* An Army, Air Force, or Marine Corps officer ranking below a general.
colo·nel (kûr′nəl) ◊ *noun, plural* **colonels**
‖*These sound alike:* **colonel, kernel**

colonial *adjective* **1.** Of, belonging to, or relating to a colony. **2.** Often **Colonial** Of or relating to the 13 original colonies that became the United States.
co·lo·ni·al (kə lō′nē əl) ◊ *adjective*

colonist *noun* A person who lives in a colony.
col·o·nist (kŏl′ə nĭst) ◊ *noun, plural* **colonists**

colonize *verb* To found a colony or colonies in: *English people colonized Virginia and Massachusetts.*
col·o·nize (**kŏl′** ə nīz′) ◊ *verb* **colonized, colonizing**

colonnade *noun* A series of columns placed the same distance apart.
col·on·nade (kŏl′ə **nād′**) ◊ *noun, plural* **colonnades**

▲ **colonnade**

colony *noun* **1.** A group of people who settle in a distant land but remain citizens of their native country. **2.** A territory ruled by or belonging to another nation. **3.** A group of animals, plants, or organisms of the same kind living or growing together: *A colony of bees built a hive in the tree.* **4. Colonies** The 13 British colonies that became the United States.
col·o·ny (**kŏl′** ə nē) ◊ *noun, plural* **colonies**

color *noun* **1.** The property by which the sense of vision can tell things apart, such as a red rose and a yellow rose, that are alike in size and shape. **2.** A tint other than black or white: *This picture includes all the colors of the rainbow.* **3.** A coloring substance, as a dye or paint. **4.** The natural shade of the skin: *My color was poor because I didn't feel well.*
◊ *verb* To give color to or change the color of: *Color the truck red with a crayon.*
col·or (**kŭl′** ər) ◊ *noun, plural* **colors** ◊ *verb* **colored, coloring**

colorful *adjective* Full of color, especially having several vivid colors: *Many butterflies have colorful wings.*
col·or·ful (**kŭl′** ər fəl) ◊ *adjective*

coloring *noun* **1.** The way something is colored: *Your cheeks have a rosy coloring.* **2.** The act or process of applying color. **3.** A substance used to color something: *They used coloring to hide their gray hair.*
col·or·ing (**kŭl′** ər ĭng) ◊ *noun, plural* **colorings**

colossal *adjective* Very big; enormous.
co·los·sal (kə **lŏs′** əl) ◊ *adjective*

colt *noun* A young horse or related animal such as a zebra, especially a male.
colt (kōlt) ◊ *noun, plural* **colts**

columbine *noun* A garden plant that has colorful flowers with five narrow, projecting spurlike parts.
col·um·bine (**kŏl′** əm bīn′) ◊ *noun, plural* **columbines**

column *noun* **1.** An upright structure used in a building especially as a support; pillar. **2.** Something that looks like a column: *The spinal column is often called the backbone.* **3.** One of two or more vertical sections of printed words on a page: *The weather forecast is in the right column.* **4.** An article that appears regularly in a newspaper or magazine: *I often read the sports column.* **5.** A long straight line, as of soldiers.
col·umn (**kŏl′** əm) ◊ *noun, plural* **columns**

comb *noun* **1.** A strip of hard material, as plastic, that has teeth and is used to smooth and arrange or fasten the hair. **2.** Something resembling a comb in shape or use, as an implement with teeth that is used to separate the fibers of wool. **3.** The brightly colored crest on the top of the head of a rooster or other related birds.
◊ *verb* **1.** To smooth or arrange with a comb. **2.** To search thoroughly: *We combed through the book looking for pictures.*
comb (kōm) ◊ *noun, plural* **combs** ◊ *verb* **combed, combing**

ă	pat	ĭ	pit	oi	oil	th	bath
ā	pay	ī	ride	o͝o	book	*th*	bathe
â	care	î	fierce	o͞o	boot	ə	ago, item
ä	father	ŏ	pot	ou	out		pencil
ĕ	pet	ō	go	ŭ	cut		atom
ē	be	ô	paw, for	û	fur		circus

▲ **comb**
Comb on a rooster

combat *verb* To fight against; battle: *We read about a new drug that combats infection.* ◊ *noun* **1.** Military conflict. **2.** A fight or struggle.
com·bat ◊ *verb* (kəm **băt′** *or* **kŏm′**băt′) **combated, combating** ◊ *noun* (**kŏm′**băt′), *plural* **combats**

combination *noun* **1.** The condition of being combined; union. **2.** Something that results from combining: *An alloy is a combination of metals.* **3.** A series of numbers or letters through which a marked dial is turned to open a lock.
com·bi·na·tion (kŏm′bə **nā′**shən) ◊ *noun, plural* **combinations**

combine *verb* To bring or come together into a single whole or substance; unite: *Music and drama combine in opera. Water and dirt combine to make mud.*
com·bine (kəm **bīn′**) ◊ *verb* **combined, combining**

combustible *adjective* Capable of catching fire and burning.
com·bus·ti·ble (kəm **bŭs′**tə bəl) ◊ *adjective*

combustion *noun* The process of burning.
com·bus·tion (kəm **bŭs′**chən) ◊ *noun, plural* **combustions**

come *verb* **1.** To move toward the speaker or toward a place that is indicated; approach: *The children came quickly when they were called for dinner.* **2.** To reach a particular place, result, or condition: *They came to an agreement.* **3.** To move; progress: *The work was coming along well.* **4.** To extend; reach: *The water only came to my waist.* **5.** To take place; occur or exist: *My birthday comes in May.* **6.** To be a descendant or native; originate: *We come from Chicago.* **7.** To turn out to be; become: *The dream came true.*
◊ *idioms* **come about** To take place; happen; occur. **come across** To find or meet by chance: *I came across an old classmate at the fair.* **come to 1.** To add up to; amount to: *The bill comes to $4.49.* **2.** To wake up after being unconscious; revive.
come (kŭm) ◊ *verb* **came, come, coming**

comedy *noun* A play, movie, or other work that is meant to make people laugh and that ends happily.
com·e·dy (**kŏm′**ĭ dē) ◊ *noun, plural* **comedies**

comet *noun* A mass of material that travels around the sun in a long, slow path. When a comet comes close to the sun, it can be seen in the sky as an object with a glowing head and a long, streaming tail.
com·et (**kŏm′**ĭt) ◊ *noun, plural* **comets**

***HISTORY* • comet**

Comet comes from an old English word that was borrowed from Latin. The Latin word was borrowed from a Greek word meaning "long-haired." To the ancient Greeks, the long "tail" of a comet looked like long, flowing hair.

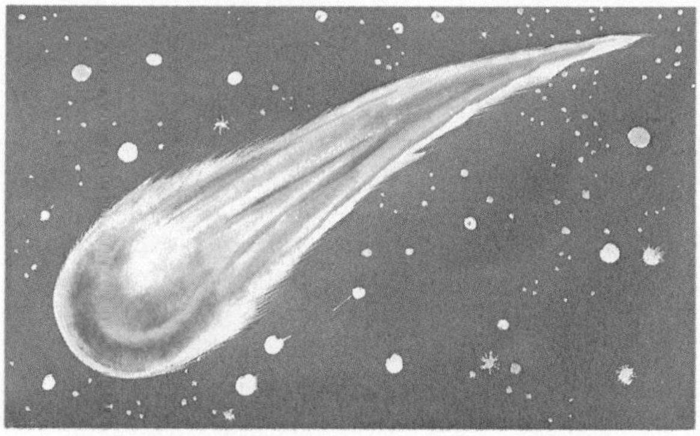

▲ **comet**

comfort *verb* To soothe when sad or frightened: *The police tried to comfort the lost child.* ◊ *noun* **1.** Relief from sadness or fear: *The crying baby held the toy bear for comfort.* **2.** A

feeling of ease and well-being, without pain or other unpleasant sensations. **3.** A thing that gives ease and well-being: *Astronauts miss such comforts as hot baths and wide beds when they are in outer space.*
com·fort (**kŭm′**fərt) ◊ *verb* **comforted, comforting** ◊ *noun, plural* **comforts**

comfortable *adjective* **1.** Giving comfort: *Every living room needs a comfortable couch.* **2.** In a state of comfort; at ease: *We tried to make our guests comfortable.*
com·fort·a·ble (**kŭm′** fər tə bəl) ◊ *adjective*

comic *adjective* **1.** Very funny; amusing: *Kittens and puppies playing together is a comic sight.* **2.** Having to do with comedy.
◊ *noun* **1.** A person who is funny or amusing. **2. comics** Comic strips.
com·ic (**kŏm′**ĭk) ◊ *adjective* ◊ *noun, plural* **comics**

comical *adjective* Causing amusement or laughter. —See Synonyms at **funny.**
com·i·cal (**kŏm′**ĭ kəl) ◊ *adjective*

comic book *noun* A booklet of comic strips.
comic book ◊ *noun, plural* **comic books**

comic strip *noun* A series of cartoons or drawings that tells a story or part of a story.
comic strip ◊ *noun, plural* **comic strips**

comma *noun* A punctuation mark (,) that is used to separate words or groups of words in a sentence.
com·ma (**kŏm′**ə) ◊ *noun, plural* **commas**

command *verb* **1.** To give orders to; direct: *The officer commanded the soldiers to leave.* **2.** To have control or authority over; rule: *The admiral commanded 25 ships.* **3.** To deserve and receive: *Honesty commands respect.*
◊ *noun* **1.** An order or direction. **2.** The authority to give orders: *The major was in command.* **3.** Ability to control or use; mastery: *The student has a good command of two languages.* **4.** A signal that tells a computer to start, stop, or continue a specific operation.
com·mand (kə **mănd′**) ◊ *verb* **commanded, commanding** ◊ *noun, plural* **commands**

ă	pat	ĭ	pit	oi	oil	th	bath
ā	pay	ī	ride	o͝o	book	*th*	bathe
â	care	î	fierce	o͞o	boot	ə	ago, item
ä	father	ŏ	pot	ou	out		pencil
ĕ	pet	ō	go	ŭ	cut		atom
ē	be	ô	paw, for	û	fur		circus

SYNONYMS

command, order

The sergeant *commanded* the troops to march. The doctor *ordered* me not to go to school until I was well.

commander *noun* **1.** A person in charge; leader. **2.** A Navy or Coast Guard officer ranking below a captain.
com·mand·er (kə **măn′**dər) ◊ *noun, plural* **commanders**

commandment *noun* A command; order.
com·mand·ment (kə **mănd′**mənt) ◊ *noun, plural* **commandments**

commemorate *verb* To honor or preserve the memory of.
com·mem·o·rate (kə **mĕm′**ə rāt′) ◊ *verb* **commemorated, commemorating**

commence *verb* To perform the first part of an action; start. —See Synonyms at **begin.**
com·mence (kə **mĕns′**) ◊ *verb* **commenced, commencing**

commencement *noun* **1.** A beginning; start. **2.** A graduation ceremony.
com·mence·ment (kə **mĕns′**mənt) ◊ *noun, plural* **commencements**

▲ **commencement**

commend *verb* To speak highly of; praise: *The coach commended the winning team.*
com·mend (kə **mĕnd′**) ◊ *verb* **commended, commending**

comment *noun* A remark or written note that explains or gives an opinion: *Give me your comments on the book.*
◊ *verb* To make a comment; remark.
com·ment (**kŏm′**ĕnt′) ◊ *noun, plural* **comments** ◊ *verb* **commented, commenting**

commerce *noun* The buying and selling of goods; trade. —See Synonyms at **business.**
com·merce (**kŏm′**ərs) ◊ *noun*

commercial *adjective* **1.** Of or engaged in buying and selling goods: *The stores are located in the commercial part of town.* **2.** Mainly concerned with making money: *Large nets are used in commercial fishing.*
◊ *noun* An advertisement on television or radio.
com·mer·cial (kə **mûr′**shəl) ◊ *adjective* ◊ *noun, plural* **commercials**

commission *noun* **1.** The act of doing something: *They were accused of the commission of a crime.* **2.** Something that a person or group is asked and given power to do; assigned task. **3.** A group of people who are given power to carry out a job or duty: *The city council named a commission to study ways to improve bus service.* **4.** Working condition: *My telephone is out of commission.* **5.** Money paid to someone for each piece of work done or for each thing sold: *The salesperson got a commission on the sale of the house.* **6.** The appointment of a person to a military rank.
◊ *verb* **1.** To give someone the power or right to do something; authorize: *We commissioned an artist to paint our parents' portrait.* **2.** To give someone a military commission. **3.** To put a ship into active service.
com·mis·sion (kə **mĭsh′**ən) ◊ *noun, plural* **commissions** ◊ *verb* **commissioned, commissioning**

commissioner *noun* **1.** A member of a commission. **2.** An official in charge of a government department.
com·mis·sion·er (kə **mĭsh′**ə nər) ◊ *noun, plural* **commissioners**

commit *verb* **1.** To do; perform: *If you sew carelessly, you will commit errors.* **2.** To put in confinement: *The criminal was committed to prison.* **3.** To assign or devote to a certain course or activity; pledge: *We committed ourselves to helping others.*
com·mit (kə **mĭt′**) ◊ *verb* **committed, committing**

commitment *noun* A pledge or obligation.
com·mit·ment (kə **mĭt′**mənt) ◊ *noun, plural* **commitments**

committee *noun* A group of people chosen to do a particular job.
com·mit·tee (kə **mĭt′**ē) ◊ *noun, plural* **committees**

commodity *noun* Something that is bought and sold.
com·mod·i·ty (kə **mŏd′**ĭ tē) ◊ *noun, plural* **commodities**

common *adjective* **1.** Belonging to or shared equally by everybody: *The swamp was drained for common use.* **2.** Found or occurring often; widespread: *Cats and dogs are common pets.* **3.** Often seen; ordinary: *Windy weather is common in March.*
◊ *noun* An area of land belonging to or used by a community as a whole.
com·mon (**kŏm′** ən) ◊ *adjective* **commoner, commonest** ◊ *noun, plural* **commons**

SYNONYMS
common, familiar, ordinary
Computer stores are *common* now. My friend tells the same *familiar* jokes over and over. Today was an *ordinary* day; nothing unusual happened.

common sense *noun* Ordinary good judgment that people have without being taught.

commonwealth *noun* **1.** The people of a nation or state. **2.** A nation or state governed by the people; republic. **3.** Any of certain states of the United States. Kentucky, Massachusetts, Pennsylvania, and Virginia are commonwealths.
com·mon·wealth (**kŏm′**ən wĕlth′) ◊ *noun, plural* **commonwealths**

commotion *noun* Noisy activity; confusion.
com·mo·tion (kə **mō′**shən) ◊ *noun, plural* **commotions**

communicate *verb* **1.** To make known; impart: *A good speaker communicates thoughts clearly.* —See Synonyms at **say. 2.** To have an exchange of thoughts, ideas, or information: *The telephone permits us to communicate over long distances.*
com·mu·ni·cate (kə **myōō′**nĭ kāt′) ◊ *verb* **communicated, communicating**

communication *noun* **1.** The act of making information known. **2.** Exchange of thoughts, information, or messages: *Speech, writing, and gestures are ways of communication.* **3.** A message communicated. **4. communications** A system for sending and receiving messages, as by mail, telephone, radio, or computers.
com·mu·ni·ca·tion (kə myo͞o′nĭ **kā′** shən) ◊ *noun, plural* **communications**

communism *noun* A social system in which factories, farms, and other property are owned by everyone in common.
com·mu·nism (**kŏm′** yə nĭz′əm) ◊ *noun*

communist *noun* A person who believes in or favors communism.
com·mu·nist (**kŏm′** yə nĭst) ◊ *noun, plural* **communists**

community *noun* **1.** A group of people living in one area. **2.** The area in which a group of people live. **3.** A group of people who have close ties and common interests.
com·mu·ni·ty (kə **myo͞o′** nĭ tē) ◊ *noun, plural* **communities**

commute *verb* To travel regularly between home and work or school.
com·mute (kə **myo͞ot′**) ◊ *verb* **commuted, commuting**

commuter *noun* A person who travels regularly between home and work or school: *My parents are commuters.*
com·mut·er (kə **myo͞o′** tər) ◊ *noun, plural* **commuters**

compact¹ *adjective* **1.** Closely packed together; dense: *The flowers grew in compact clusters.* **2.** Arranged or built so as to save space: *We bought a compact car.*
◊ *verb* To pack or press together.
◊ *noun* **1.** A small case containing face powder and a powder puff. **2.** A small car.
com·pact¹ ◊ *adjective* (kəm **păkt′** *or* kŏm-**păkt′**) ◊ *verb* (kəm **păkt′**) **compacted, compacting** ◊ *noun* (**kŏm′** păkt′), *plural* **compacts**

ă	pat	ĭ	pit	oi	oil	th	bath
ā	pay	ī	ride	o͝o	book	*th*	bathe
â	care	î	fierce	o͞o	boot	ə	ago, item
ä	father	ŏ	pot	ou	out		pencil
ĕ	pet	ō	go	ŭ	cut		atom
ē	be	ô	paw, for	û	fur		circus

▲ **compact¹**
A compact car

compact² *noun* A formal agreement.
com·pact² (**kŏm′** păkt′) ◊ *noun, plural* **compacts**

***HISTORY* • compact¹, compact²**

Compact¹ goes back to a Latin word meaning "to put together closely." **Compact²** goes back to a Latin word meaning "to make an agreement."

companion *noun* **1.** A person who often accompanies or associates with another person. **2.** A person hired to live or travel with another person.
com·pan·ion (kəm **păn′** yən) ◊ *noun, plural* **companions**

companionship *noun* The relationship of companions; fellowship.
com·pan·ion·ship (kəm **păn′** yən shĭp′) ◊ *noun*

company *noun* **1.** A group of people; gathering. **2.** A guest or guests: *We're expecting company for dinner.* **3.** A companion or companions: *I was with good company.* **4.** Companionship: *I was grateful for my cousin's company on the train.* **5.** A business: *That insurance company has an office on Main Street.* **6.** A group of performers. **7.** A group of soldiers led by a captain.
com·pa·ny (**kŭm′** pə nē) ◊ *noun, plural* **companies**

comparable *adjective* Alike enough to be compared; similar.
com·pa·ra·ble (**kŏm′** pər ə bəl) ◊ *adjective*

comparative *adjective* **1.** Based on a comparison: *We made a comparative study of customs in four countries.* **2.** Measured in relation to something else; relative: *The comparative size of the sun, as a star, is not large.* ◊ *noun* The form of an adjective or adverb that is used to show a greater degree of what is expressed by the adjective or adverb. For example, *larger, more comfortable,* and *worse* are the comparatives of *large, comfortable,* and *bad.*
com·par·a·tive (kəm **păr'** ə tĭv) ◊ *adjective* ◊ *noun, plural* **comparatives**

compare *verb* **1.** To represent as similar; liken: *We can compare the wings of a bird to those of an airplane.* **2.** To study in order to note similarities and differences: *We compared the habits of bees and spiders.* **3.** To be worthy of comparison: *Cafeteria food can't compare with home cooking.*
com·pare (kəm **pâr'**) ◊ *verb* **compared, comparing**

comparison *noun* **1.** The act of comparing. **2.** Close similarity.
com·par·i·son (kəm **păr'** ĭ sən) ◊ *noun, plural* **comparisons**

compartment *noun* A separate section or space, often set off by walls.
com·part·ment (kəm **pärt'** mənt) ◊ *noun, plural* **compartments**

compass *noun* **1.** An instrument with a magnetic needle that is used to show directions. **2.** A device that is shaped like a V and used for drawing circles and measuring lengths. It is made up of a pair of rigid arms hinged together. One of the arms ends in a sharp point and the other holds a pencil.
com·pass (**kŭm'** pəs) ◊ *noun, plural* **compasses**

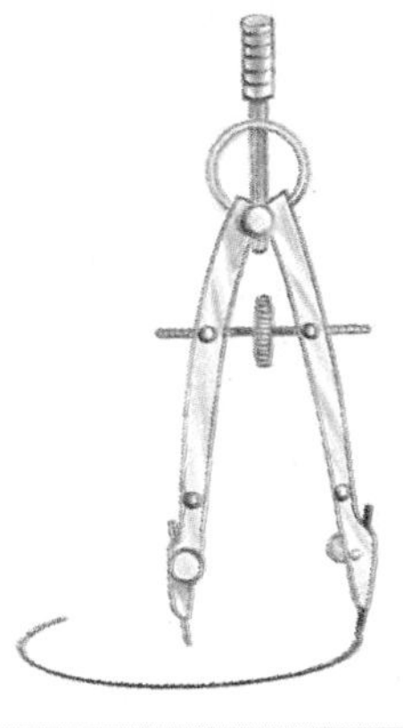

▲ **compass**

compassion *noun* A feeling of sharing the suffering of someone else, together with a desire to help; deep sympathy.
com·pas·sion (kəm **păsh'** ən) ◊ *noun*

compassionate *adjective* Feeling or showing compassion.
com·pas·sion·ate (kəm **păsh'** ə nĭt) ◊ *adjective*

compatible *adjective* Capable of living or existing together in harmony.
com·pat·i·ble (kəm **păt'** ə bəl) ◊ *adjective*

compel *verb* To force to do something: *The sudden storm compelled us to go indoors.*
com·pel (kəm **pĕl'**) ◊ *verb* **compelled, compelling**

compensate *verb* **1.** To make up for something: *A baseball player who is not a speedy runner can compensate by powerful hitting.* **2.** To pay in return for work or injury: *The workers were injured on the job, and their employer compensated them.*
com·pen·sate (**kŏm'** pən sāt') ◊ *verb* **compensated, compensating**

compensation *noun* **1.** Something that balances or makes up for something else: *The crew was one person short, so we all had to work harder in compensation.* **2.** Payment for work or injury.
com·pen·sa·tion (kŏm'pən **sā'** shən) ◊ *noun, plural* **compensations**

compete *verb* To strive against another or others to win something: *The best runners in the class competed in a race.*
com·pete (kəm **pēt'**) ◊ *verb* **competed, competing**

competence *noun* Ability to do something with adequate skill.
com·pe·tence (**kŏm'** pĭ təns) ◊ *noun*

competent *adjective* Able to do something with adequate skill; capable: *A competent mechanic can easily change a tire.*
com·pe·tent (**kŏm'** pĭ tənt) ◊ *adjective*

competition *noun* **1.** The act of struggling to win. **2.** A struggle to win or come out first; contest: *I entered a chess competition and finished third.*
com·pe·ti·tion (kŏm'pĭ **tĭsh'** ən) ◊ *noun, plural* **competitions**

competitive *adjective* **1.** Of, in, or decided by competition: *Our team is competitive in its league.* **2.** Liking to compete: *A competitive person loves to win and hates to lose.*
com·pet·i·tive (kəm **pĕt'** ĭ tĭv) ◊ *adjective*

competitor *noun* A person or group that competes with another or others; opponent:

The two friends were competitors for the class presidency.
com·pet·i·tor (kəm **pĕt′**ĭ tər) ◊ *noun, plural* **competitors**

compile *verb* To put together into a single list or collection.
com·pile (kəm **pīl′**) ◊ *verb* **compiled, compiling**

complacent *adjective* Pleased with oneself.
com·pla·cent (kəm **plā′**sənt) ◊ *adjective*

complain *verb* **1.** To express unhappiness or discontent: *Don't complain about the food.* **2.** To make a report about something one considers wrong or troublesome: *The patient complained of chest pains.*
com·plain (kəm **plān′**) ◊ *verb* **complained, complaining**

complaint *noun* **1.** An expression of unhappiness or discontent. **2.** A cause or reason for complaining. **3.** A formal statement or accusation about something causing discontent: *The storekeeper signed a complaint accusing them of shoplifting.*
com·plaint (kəm **plānt′**) ◊ *noun, plural* **complaints**

complement *noun* Something that completes or makes perfect: *Homework is a necessary complement to classroom study.*
com·ple·ment (**kŏm′**plə mənt) ◊ *noun, plural* **complements**

complementary *adjective* Supplying what is lacking or needed.
com·ple·men·ta·ry (kŏm′plə **mĕn′**tə rē) ◊ *adjective*
‖*These sound alike:* **complementary, complimentary**

complete *adjective* **1.** Having all necessary parts: *A complete chess set has 32 pieces and a board.* **2.** Thorough; full: *A good gymnast has complete control over his or her body.* **3.** Brought to a finish: *We can't go out until our homework is complete.*
◊ *verb* **1.** To add to what is missing; make whole: *Complete the sentences in the exercise by filling in the blanks.* **2.** To bring to an end; finish; conclude: *I have completed five years of school.* —See Synonyms at **end.**
com·plete (kəm **plēt′**) ◊ *adjective* ◊ *verb* **completed, completing**

ă	pat	ĭ	pit	oi	oil	th	bath
ā	pay	ī	ride	o͝o	book	*th*	bathe
â	care	î	fierce	o͞o	boot	ə	ago, item
ä	father	ŏ	pot	ou	out		pencil
ĕ	pet	ō	go	ŭ	cut		atom
ē	be	ô	paw, for	û	fur		circus

completion *noun* The act or process of completing something or the condition of being completed.
com·ple·tion (kəm **plē′**shən) ◊ *noun*

complex *adjective* **1.** Consisting of many connected parts or factors: *The relationship between living things and their environment is complex.* **2.** Difficult to understand: *Computers are used to help solve complex mathematical problems.*
com·plex (kəm **plĕks′** *or* **kŏm′**plĕks′) ◊ *adjective*

complexion *noun* The natural color of a person's skin, especially that of the face.
com·plex·ion (kəm **plĕk′**shən) ◊ *noun, plural* **complexions**

complexity *noun* **1.** The condition of being complex. **2.** Something complex.
com·plex·i·ty (kəm **plĕk′**sĭ tē) ◊ *noun, plural* **complexities**

compliant *adjective* Giving in to the wishes or requests of others: *The child has a very compliant nature.*
com·pli·ant (kəm **plī′**ənt) ◊ *adjective*

complicate *verb* To make hard to understand, solve, or deal with: *The extra information only complicates the problem.*
com·pli·cate (**kŏm′**plĭ kāt′) ◊ *verb* **complicated, complicating**

complicated *adjective* Not easy to understand, deal with, or solve; complex: *Did you do the complicated problem on page 5?*
com·pli·ca·ted (**kŏm′**plĭ kā′tĭd) ◊ *adjective*

complication *noun* Something that complicates: *Both parents work, which adds complications to their family life.*
com·pli·ca·tion (kŏm′plĭ **kā′**shən) ◊ *noun, plural* **complications**

compliment *noun* **1.** An expression of praise. **2. compliments** Good wishes; regards: *Extend my compliments to your parents.*
◊ *verb* To express praise to: *We complimented them on their singing.*
com·pli·ment ◊ *noun* (**kŏm′**plə mənt), *plural* **compliments** ◊ *verb* (**kŏm′**plə mĕnt′) **complimented, complimenting**

complimentary *adjective* **1.** Giving or expressing praise. **2.** Given free: *We received the complimentary tickets to the play.*
com·pli·men·ta·ry (kŏm′plə **mĕn′**tə rē) ◊ *adjective*
‖*These sound alike:* **complimentary, complementary**

comply *verb* To follow a request or rule: *We comply with all fire safety rules.*
com·ply (kəm **plī′**) ◊ *verb* **complied, complying**

component *noun* One of the parts that make up a whole: *A computer consists of thousands of components.*
com·po·nent (kəm **pō′**nənt) ◊ *noun, plural* **components**

▲ **component**
Assembling electronic components

compose *verb* **1.** To make up; form: *Our lungs are composed of air tubes with many branches.* **2.** To make or create by putting parts or elements together: *An artist composes a picture by arranging forms and colors.* **3.** To make calm, controlled, or orderly: *Stop giggling and compose yourself.*
com·pose (kəm **pōz′**) ◊ *verb* **composed, composing**

composer *noun* A writer of music.
com·pos·er (kəm **pō′**zər) ◊ *noun, plural* **composers**

composite *adjective* Made up of parts from different sources.
com·pos·ite (kəm **pŏz′**ĭt) ◊ *adjective*

composition *noun* **1.** The putting together of parts to form a whole. **2.** A work that has been composed, especially a musical work. **3.** A short essay written as a school exercise. **4.** The parts of something and the way in which they are combined: *We examined the rock to find out its composition.*
com·po·si·tion (kŏm′pə **zĭsh′**ən) ◊ *noun, plural* **compositions**

compound *noun* **1.** Something made by combining separate things or ingredients. **2.** A word made by combining two or more other words. *Basketball, up-to-date,* and *test tube* are compounds. **3.** A substance that consists of atoms of two or more different elements combined in molecules: *Water is a compound made up of two parts of hydrogen to one part of oxygen.*
◊ *verb* To make up or put together by combining parts or ingredients: *The pharmacist compounded the medicine that the doctor had ordered for me.*
com·pound ◊ *noun* (**kŏm′**pound′), *plural* **compounds** ◊ *verb* (kəm **pound′**) **compounded, compounding**

comprehend *verb* To understand.
com·pre·hend (kŏm′prĭ **hĕnd′**) ◊ *verb* **comprehended, comprehending**

comprehension *noun* The act or fact of understanding or the ability to understand.
com·pre·hen·sion (kŏm′prĭ **hĕn′**shən) ◊ *noun*

comprehensive *adjective* Including much: *The course ended with a comprehensive review of all that we studied.*
com·pre·hen·sive (kŏm′prĭ **hĕn′**sĭv) ◊ *adjective*

compress *verb* To squeeze or press together.
◊ *noun* A soft pad of cloth, cotton, or other material that is pressed against a wound.
com·press ◊ *verb* (kəm **prĕs′**) **compressed, compressing** ◊ *noun* (**kŏm′**prĕs′), *plural* **compresses**

comprise *verb* To consist of; be composed of; include: *The Union comprises 50 states.*
com·prise (kəm **prīz′**) ◊ *verb* **comprised, comprising**

compromise *noun* A settlement of an argument or dispute reached by each side giving up some of its claims or demands.
◊ *verb* To give up certain demands to settle an argument: *The two sides in the dispute*

compromised and reached an agreement.
com·pro·mise (**kŏm′** prə mīz′) ◊ *noun, plural* **compromises** ◊ *verb* **compromised, compromising**

compulsion *noun* **1.** Pressure that makes it necessary for someone to do something. **2.** An urge that is very hard to control: *I suffered from a compulsion to eat too much.*
com·pul·sion (kəm **pŭl′** shən) ◊ *noun, plural* **compulsions**

compulsory *adjective* Required by law or a rule: *Education is compulsory for children in most countries.*
com·pul·so·ry (kəm **pŭl′** sə rē) ◊ *adjective*

compute *verb* To work out by mathematics; calculate: *We computed our savings.*
com·pute (kəm **pyo͞ot′**) ◊ *verb* **computed, computing**

computer *noun* A complex electronic machine that can accept information, work on the information to solve a problem, and produce an answer or result. Some computers can store whole libraries in a small space and find desired items instantly. Other computers control machinery and print books.
com·put·er (kəm **pyo͞o′** tər) ◊ *noun, plural* **computers**

▲ **computer**
A computer terminal, with keyboard and video display screen; the central processing unit is in the background.

ă	pat	ĭ	pit	oi	**oil**	th	**bath**
ā	pay	ī	ride	o͝o	**book**	*th*	**bathe**
â	care	î	fierce	o͞o	**boot**	ə	**ago, item**
ä	father	ŏ	pot	ou	**out**		pencil
ĕ	pet	ō	**go**	ŭ	**cut**		atom
ē	**be**	ô	paw, for	û	**fur**		circus

computer art *noun* Art produced by computer printers or on video terminals.

computerize *verb* **1.** To process or store information in a computer. **2.** To convert a process, operation, or device so that it can make use of or be controlled by a computer.
com·put·er·ize (kəm **pyo͞o′** tə rīz′) ◊ *verb* **computerized, computerizing**

computer language *noun* A language used to tell a computer what to do and how to do it. BASIC and LOGO are computer languages.
computer language ◊ *noun, plural* **computer languages**

computer literacy *noun* Knowledge and understanding of computers and how to use them.

computer science *noun* The study of the design and use of computers.

computer store *noun* A retail store that sells personal computers, software, computer books, and other items.
computer store ◊ *noun, plural* **computer stores**

comrade *noun* A companion, especially one who shares one's activities.
com·rade (**kŏm′** răd′) ◊ *noun, plural* **comrades**

concave *adjective* Curved inward like the inside surface of a circle or spoon.
con·cave (kŏn **kāv′**) ◊ *adjective*

conceal *verb* To keep someone or something from being noticed or known; hide: *I concealed my money.*
con·ceal (kən **sēl′**) ◊ *verb* **concealed, concealing**

concede *verb* **1.** To admit that something is true, often without wanting to: *We conceded that the other team won the award fair and square.* **2.** To give up on, as in a game or race.
con·cede (kən **sēd′**) ◊ *verb* **conceded, conceding**

conceit *noun* Too high an opinion of oneself.
con·ceit (kən **sēt′**) ◊ *noun*

conceited *adjective* Too proud of oneself.
con·ceit·ed (kən **sē′** tĭd) ◊ *adjective*

conceive *verb* To form in the mind; think up: *Inventors conceived the idea of the airplane by watching birds in flight.*
con·ceive (kən **sēv′**) ◊ *verb* **conceived, conceiving**

concentrate *verb* **1.** To keep or direct one's thoughts, attention, or efforts on something: *I couldn't concentrate on my homework because the TV was on.* **2.** To draw or bring together in one place: *Our population is concentrated in the big cities.*
con·cen·trate (**kŏn′**sən trāt′) ◊ *verb* **concentrated, concentrating**

concentration *noun* **1.** The act of fixing one's mind on something: *Concentration is important when doing your homework.* —See Synonyms at **attention. 2.** A close gathering in one place: *There is a concentration of people in large cities.*
con·cen·tra·tion (kŏn′sən **trā′**shən) ◊ *noun, plural* **concentrations**

concept *noun* A general idea: *The concept of traveling in space fascinates me.*
con·cept (**kŏn′**sĕpt′) ◊ *noun, plural* **concepts**

conception *noun* **1.** An idea: *The study of astronomy gives you some conception of what the universe is like.* **2.** A beginning of an idea: *We studied the automobile from its earliest conception.*
con·cep·tion (kən **sĕp′**shən) ◊ *noun, plural* **conceptions**

concern *verb* **1.** To have to do with; be about: *This fairy tale concerns a prince who turns into a frog.* **2.** To be of importance or interest to: *Their problems don't concern me.* **3.** To worry or trouble: *Your poor grade concerns your parents.*
◊ *noun* **1.** Something of interest or importance: *My chief concern was to get home on time.* **2.** Serious care or interest: *The teacher's concern helped me to improve my grades.* **3.** Worry or anxiety: *I took the test without any concern.* **4.** A business; firm.
con·cern (kən **sûrn′**) ◊ *verb* **concerned, concerning** ◊ *noun, plural* **concerns**

concerning *preposition* With regard to; about: *We read stories concerning visitors from outer space.*
con·cern·ing (kən **sûr′**nĭng) ◊ *preposition*

concert *noun* A musical performance given by a musician or a number of musicians.
con·cert (**kŏn′**sûrt′) ◊ *noun, plural* **concerts**

concerto *noun* A musical composition for a solo instrument and an orchestra.
con·cer·to (kən **chĕr′**tō) ◊ *noun, plural* **concertos**

concession *noun* **1.** An act of yielding: *We settled our argument by mutual concession.* **2.** Something yielded: *My parents made a concession and let me go to a special movie on a school night.* **3.** Permission to operate a business for a special purpose at a certain place: *The town gave our club the concession to sell T-shirts at the ball game.*
con·ces·sion (kən **sĕsh′**ən) ◊ *noun, plural* **concessions**

conch *noun* A tropical sea animal related to the snails. Conch shells are often large and are spiral in shape.
conch (kŏngk *or* kŏnch) ◊ *noun, plural* **conchs** *or* **conches**

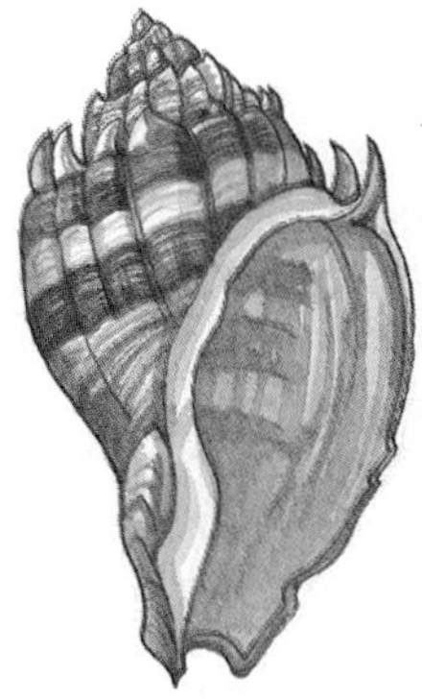
▲ **conch**

concise *adjective* Saying much in a few words; brief: *Write a concise book report.*
con·cise (kən **sīs′**) ◊ *adjective*

conclude *verb* **1.** To bring or come to an end; finish: *The speaker concluded the speech and sat down. The movie concluded with a wild chase.* —See Synonyms at **end. 2.** To think about something and then reach a decision or form an opinion: *I have concluded that the best way to make a friend is to be one.*
con·clude (kən **klo͞od′**) ◊ *verb* **concluded, concluding**

conclusion *noun* **1.** The close or end, as of a play or concert. **2.** A judgment or decision made after careful thought.
con·clu·sion (kən **klo͞o′**zhən) ◊ *noun, plural* **conclusions**

concoct *verb* **1.** To prepare something by putting several different things together. **2.** To make up: *They concocted an excuse for being late.*
con·coct (kən **kŏkt′**) ◊ *verb* **concocted, concocting**

concord *noun* Peaceful agreement.
con·cord (**kŏn′**kôrd′) ◊ *noun*

concrete *noun* A building material made of cement, sand, pebbles, and water. Concrete becomes very hard when it dries.

◊ *adjective* **1.** Made of concrete. **2.** Able to be seen, heard, touched, or otherwise sensed; real: *Shoes and trees are concrete objects.*
con·crete (**kŏn′**krēt′ *or* kŏn **krēt′**) ◊ *noun* ◊ *adjective*

concur *verb* To have the same opinion; agree: *I concur with many people on the need to stop pollution.*
con·cur (kən **kûr′**) ◊ *verb* **concurred, concurring**

concussion *noun* **1.** A violent shaking: *The concussion caused by the earthquake made the buildings sway.* **2.** An injury to the brain caused by a fall or a hard blow.
con·cus·sion (kən **kŭsh′**ən) ◊ *noun, plural* **concussions**

condemn *verb* **1.** To express strong feeling or opinion against: *We condemn violence on television.* **2.** To declare someone guilty and say what the punishment is: *The judge condemned the prisoner to 30 days in jail.* **3.** To declare unsafe: *The city has condemned that old building.*
con·demn (kən **dĕm′**) ◊ *verb* **condemned, condemning**

condensation *noun* The act or process of condensing: *Condensation caused moisture to collect as frost on our car. I read a condensation of the long novel in a magazine.*
con·den·sa·tion (kŏn′dĕn **sā′**shən) ◊ *noun, plural* **condensations**

condense *verb* **1.** To change from a gas to either a liquid or a solid form. If warm water vapor in the air touches a cool surface, the vapor condenses into dew. **2.** To make thicker or more dense, usually by boiling away a liquid or allowing it to evaporate. **3.** To put into a shortened form: *The writer condensed the novel for use in a magazine.*
con·dense (kən **dĕns′**) ◊ *verb* **condensed, condensing**

condescend *verb* To agree to do something that one thinks of as being beneath one's dignity: *I condescended to take out the garbage even though it wasn't my turn.*
con·de·scend (kŏn′dĭ **sĕnd′**) ◊ *verb* **condescended, condescending**

condition *noun* **1.** The way someone or something is: *The house was in poor condition after the flood.* **2.** General health and physical ability. **3.** A satisfactory state for use; working order: *Our car is in good condition.* **4.** A disease or ailment: *The patient has a heart condition.* **5.** Something required or agreed upon if some other thing is to take place: *You may go to the movie on the condition that you do your homework first.* **6. conditions** Circumstances that affect a situation or activity: *We need to improve working conditions at the factory.*
◊ *verb* To put into good operating order or health.
con·di·tion (kən **dĭsh′**ən) ◊ *noun, plural* **conditions** ◊ *verb* **conditioned, conditioning**

conditioner *noun* A device or substance used to improve something in some way.
con·di·tion·er (kən **dĭsh′**ə nər) ◊ *noun, plural* **conditioners**

condominium *noun* An apartment building in which the individual apartments are owned by the people living in them.
con·do·min·i·um (kŏn′də **mĭn′**ē əm) ◊ *noun, plural* **condominiums**

condor *noun* A large bird that lives in the mountains of California and South America.
con·dor (**kŏn′**dər) ◊ *noun, plural* **condors**

▲ **condor**

conduct *verb* **1.** To lead, guide, or direct: *The guide conducts tours through the capitol. A famous composer conducted the orchestra.* **2.** To act as a path for electricity, heat, or

ă	pat	ĭ	pit	oi	**oil**	th	**bath**
ā	pay	ī	ride	o͝o	**book**	*th*	**bathe**
â	care	î	fierce	o͞o	**boot**	ə	ago, item
ä	father	ŏ	**pot**	ou	**out**		pencil
ĕ	pet	ō	go	ŭ	**cut**		atom
ē	be	ô	paw, for	û	**fur**		circus

other forms of energy: *Most metals conduct heat well.* **3.** To behave in a certain way.
◊ *noun* The way a person acts; behavior.
con·duct ◊ *verb* (kən **dŭkt′**) **conducted, conducting** ◊ *noun* (**kŏn′**dŭkt′)

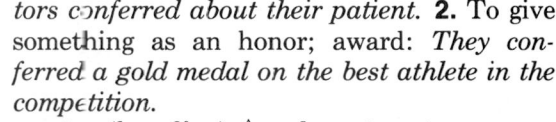

conductor *noun* **1.** A person who guides or leads: *I am the conductor of our school band.* **2.** The person in charge of a railroad train, subway, or cable car. **3.** A substance that provides an easy path for the flow of electricity, heat, or other forms of energy.
con·duc·tor (kən **dŭk′**tər) ◊ *noun, plural* **conductors**

cone *noun* **1.** A solid object that has a flat, round base at one end and tapers to a point at the opposite end. **2.** Something shaped like a cone. **3.** A cluster of overlapping, woody scales that grows on evergreen trees. Inside the cone are the seeds of the tree.
cone (kōn) ◊ *noun, plural* **cones**

▲ **cone**

confederacy *noun* **1.** A group of people or countries joined together for a common purpose. **2. Confederacy** The group of eleven southern states that separated from the United States in 1860 and 1861.
con·fed·er·a·cy (kən **fĕd′**ər ə sē) ◊ *noun, plural* **confederacies**

confederate *adjective* **1.** Belonging to a confederacy. **2. Confederate** Being a part of or having to do with the Confederacy.
◊ *noun* **1.** A person or country that joins with another for a common purpose; ally. **2. Confederate** A person who supported or fought for the Confederacy.
con·fed·er·ate (kən **fĕd′**ər ĭt) ◊ *adjective* ◊ *noun, plural* **confederates**

confederation *noun* A confederacy: *A confederation of Native American tribes met to discuss their problems.*
con·fed·er·a·tion (kən fĕd′ə **rā′**shən) ◊ *noun, plural* **confederations**

confer *verb* **1.** To discuss together: *The doctors conferred about their patient.* **2.** To give something as an honor; award: *They conferred a gold medal on the best athlete in the competition.*
con·fer (kən **fûr′**) ◊ *verb* **conferred, conferring**

conference *noun* A meeting to discuss one or more subjects.
con·fer·ence (**kŏn′**fər əns) ◊ *noun, plural* **conferences**

confess *verb* To admit that one has done something bad or illegal: *I confess that I broke the window.*
con·fess (kən **fĕs′**) ◊ *verb* **confessed, confessing**

confession *noun* The act of confessing or admitting guilt.
con·fes·sion (kən **fĕsh′**ən) ◊ *noun, plural* **confessions**

confetti *noun* (*used with a singular verb*) Small bits of paper that are thrown around at parades, weddings, and parties.
con·fet·ti (kən **fĕt′**ē) ◊ *noun*

▲ **confetti**

confide *verb* To tell someone something, intending that it will be kept a secret: *We confided our plans to our teacher.*
◊ *idiom* **confide in** To share one's secrets with: *I always confide in my best friend.*
con·fide (kən **fīd′**) ◊ *verb* **confided, confiding**

confidence *noun* **1.** A strong feeling of faith in oneself and one's ability: *I have confidence that I will win the race.* **2.** Trust or faith in someone else or in something: *The coach has confidence in the team.*
con·fi·dence (**kŏn′**fĭ dəns) ◊ *noun*

confident *adjective* Feeling sure of oneself: *I am confident that I will win.*
con·fi·dent (**kŏn′**fĭ dənt) ◊ *adjective*

confidential *adjective* **1.** Regarded as secret: *The confidential report was given directly to the president.* **2.** Trusted with secret matters.
con·fi·den·tial (kŏn′fĭ **dĕn′**shəl) ◊ *adjective*

confine *verb* **1.** To keep a person or animal from moving about freely: *I was confined to bed with the flu.* **2.** To put into prison.
◊ *noun* Often **confines** The limits of a space or area; borders: *Have you traveled beyond the confines of your own state?*
con·fine ◊ *verb* (kən **fīn′**) **confined, confining** ◊ *noun* (**kŏn′**fīn′), *plural* **confines**

confirm *verb* **1.** To prove or agree that something is true, correct, or possible: *The newscast confirmed reports of a flu epidemic.* **2.** To make sure of an appointment or arrangement: *Let's confirm our reservations.* **3.** To admit as a full member of a church or synagogue.
con·firm (kən **fûrm′**) ◊ *verb* **confirmed, confirming**

confirmation *noun* **1.** The act of confirming. **2.** Something that confirms; proof. **3.** A ceremony in which a young person is made a full member of a church or synagogue.
con·fir·ma·tion (kŏn′fər **mā′**shən) ◊ *noun, plural* **confirmations**

confirmed *adjective* Firmly settled in a habit or condition: *We are confirmed joggers.*
con·firmed (kən **fûrmd′**) ◊ *adjective*

confiscate *verb* To take something away from someone, in some cases because one has the legal right to do so: *The police confiscated the stolen television sets.*
con·fis·cate (**kŏn′**fĭ skāt′) ◊ *verb* **confiscated, confiscating**

conflict *noun* **1.** Fighting that continues for a long time. **2.** A clash or struggle, as of ideas, feelings, or interests.
◊ *verb* To be in opposition; differ: *What people do often conflicts with what they say.*
con·flict ◊ *noun* (**kŏn′**flĭkt′), *plural* **conflicts** ◊ *verb* (kən **flĭkt′**) **conflicted, conflicting**

conform *verb* To follow or be in agreement with a set standard or rule: *If you don't conform to the traffic laws, you might get hurt.*
con·form (kən **fôrm′**) ◊ *verb* **conformed, conforming**

confront *verb* **1.** To come face to face with; stand before: *Many problems confront us.* **2.** To meet or face with anger or hatred. **3.** To present someone with a challenge or accusation that one is forced to agree with or deny.
con·front (kən **frŭnt′**) ◊ *verb* **confronted, confronting**

confuse *verb* **1.** To be or make unclear in someone's mind; mix up: *The directions confused me and I didn't know what to do.* **2.** To mistake one person or thing for another: *It is easy to confuse one twin with the other.*
con·fuse (kən **fyo͞oz′**) ◊ *verb* **confused, confusing**

confusion *noun* The act of confusing or the condition of being confused: *You can avoid confusion by speaking clearly.*
con·fu·sion (kən **fyo͞o′**zhən) ◊ *noun*

congeal *verb* To become thick or stiff: *The blood on my scratched arm congealed quickly.*
con·geal (kən **jēl′**) ◊ *verb* **congealed, congealing**

congratulate *verb* To give praise or good wishes to someone at a happy event or for something done well.
con·grat·u·late (kən **grăch′**ə lāt′) ◊ *verb* **congratulated, congratulating**

congratulation *noun* **1.** The act of congratulating: *We spoke a few words of congratulation to the winners.* **2. congratulations** Praise or good wishes to someone at a happy event or for something well done.
con·grat·u·la·tion (kən grăch′ə **lā′**shən) ◊ *noun, plural* **congratulations**

congregate *verb* To come together into a crowd; assemble: *Lots of people congregated at the scene of the accident.*
con·gre·gate (**kŏng′**grə gāt′) ◊ *verb* **congregated, congregating**

congregation *noun* **1.** A gathering of people or things. **2.** A group of people gathered for religious worship.
con·gre·ga·tion (kŏng′grə **gā′**shən) ◊ *noun, plural* **congregations**

ă	pat	ĭ	pit	oi	oil	th	bath
ā	pay	ī	ride	o͝o	book	*th*	bathe
â	care	î	fierce	o͞o	boot	ə	ago, item
ä	father	ŏ	pot	ou	out		pencil
ĕ	pet	ō	go	ŭ	cut		atom
ē	be	ô	paw, for	û	fur		circus

congress *noun* **1.** A formal meeting of people who make laws in a republic. **2. Congress** The United States Senate and House of Representatives.
con·gress (**kŏng′** grĭs) ◊ *noun, plural* **congresses**

▲ **congress**
A joint session of the United States Congress

congressman *noun* A member of the United States Congress, especially of the House of Representatives.
con·gress·man (**kŏng′** grĭs mən) ◊ *noun, plural* **congressmen**

congresswoman *noun* A woman who is a member of the United States Congress, especially of the House of Representatives.
con·gress·wom·an (**kŏng′** grĭs wo͝om′ən) ◊ *noun, plural* **congresswomen**

conjunction *noun* A word that joins other words or groups of words in a sentence. *And, or, but,* and *nor* are conjunctions.
con·junc·tion (kən **jŭngk′** shən) ◊ *noun, plural* **conjunctions**

Conn. An abbreviation for *Connecticut.*

connect *verb* **1.** To link or come together; join: *A new road connects the two towns.* —See Synonyms at **join. 2.** To think of as related; associate: *We connect the word "blue" with the color of the sky.* **3.** To plug into an electrical circuit.
con·nect (kə **nĕkt′**) ◊ *verb* **connected, connecting**

connection *noun* **1.** The act of connecting or the condition of being connected. **2.** Something that connects or joins; link: *There is a connection between the moon and the tides of the oceans.* **3.** A transfer from one plane, train, or bus to another.
con·nec·tion (kə **nĕk′** shən) ◊ *noun, plural* **connections**

conquer *verb* **1.** To overcome by force in war: *Has a small country ever conquered a large one?* —See Synonyms at **defeat. 2.** To get control over: *Scientists have still not conquered all diseases.*
con·quer (**kŏng′** kər) ◊ *verb* **conquered, conquering**

conqueror *noun* Someone who conquers.
con·quer·or (**kŏng′** kər ər) ◊ *noun, plural* **conquerors**

conquest *noun* **1.** An act of conquering. **2.** Something conquered: *Spain made conquests in South America.*
con·quest (**kŏn′** kwĕst′) ◊ *noun, plural* **conquests**

conscience *noun* Inner feelings and ideas that tell a person what is right and what is wrong: *My conscience tells me that it is wrong to cheat.*
con·science (**kŏn′** shəns) ◊ *noun, plural* **consciences**

conscious *adjective* **1.** Able to see, feel, and hear and to understand what is happening: *The patient is very ill but is still conscious.* **2.** Able to know; aware: *Are you conscious of your own faults?* **3.** Done with awareness: *Make a conscious effort to speak clearly.*
con·scious (**kŏn′** shəs) ◊ *adjective*

consciousness *noun* **1.** The condition of being conscious: *The ill patient lost consciousness.* **2.** All the thoughts, opinions, and feelings that a person or group has.
con·scious·ness (**kŏn′** shəs nĭs) ◊ *noun*

consecutive *adjective* Following one right after the other: *It rained for five consecutive days.*
con·sec·u·tive (kən **sĕk′** yə tĭv) ◊ *adjective*

consent *verb* To give permission: *My parents consented to my plans.*
◊ *noun* Permission: *I have my teacher's consent to go to the library.*
con·sent (kən **sĕnt′**) ◊ *verb* **consented, consenting** ◊ *noun, plural* **consents**

consequence *noun* Something that happens as a result of another action or condition: *A consequence of cheating is suspension from school.* —See Synonyms at **effect.**
con·se·quence (**kŏn′**sĭ kwĕns′) ◊ *noun, plural* **consequences**

conservation *noun* **1.** The act of conserving: *Conservation of your weekly allowance will make it possible for you to buy a new game.* **2.** Careful use and protection of natural resources, such as forests, water, and oil: *Conservation is one way to make sure we have enough energy in the future.*
con·ser·va·tion (kŏn′sər **vā′**shən) ◊ *noun*

conservative *adjective* **1.** Wanting things to stay as they are or as they used to be. **2.** Careful to avoid risks or trouble: *Conservative drivers are safe drivers.*
◊ *noun* Someone who is conservative.
con·serv·a·tive (kən **sûr′**və tĭv) ◊ *adjective* ◊ *noun, plural* **conservatives**

conserve *verb* To use carefully, so as not to waste, use up, or harm: *Science and common sense teach us to conserve our forests.*
con·serve (kən **sûrv′**) ◊ *verb* **conserved, conserving**

consider *verb* **1.** To think about before deciding: *My parents are considering new jobs in Ohio.* **2.** To think of as; believe to be: *I consider you the best player on the team.* **3.** To keep in mind: *They sing well if you consider that they have never had any lessons.* **4.** To be thoughtful of: *Try to consider the feelings of others.*
con·sid·er (kən **sĭd′**ər) ◊ *verb* **considered, considering**

considerable *adjective* Being fairly large or great in amount, extent, or degree: *It's a considerable distance from the east coast of the United States to the west coast.*
con·sid·er·a·ble (kən **sĭd′**ər ə bəl) ◊ *adjective*

considerate *adjective* Thoughtful of others and their feelings.
con·sid·er·ate (kən **sĭd′**ər ĭt) ◊ *adjective*

ă	pat	ĭ	pit	oi	**oil**	th	ba**th**
ā	pay	ī	ride	ŏŏ	book	*th*	ba**th**e
â	care	î	fierce	ōō	boot	ə	ago, item
ä	father	ŏ	pot	ou	**out**		pencil
ĕ	pet	ō	go	ŭ	cut		atom
ē	be	ô	paw, for	û	fur		circus

consideration *noun* **1.** Careful thought: *Give the idea consideration before you decide what to do.* **2.** Something kept in mind when making a decision: *The health of the community should be an important consideration.* **3.** Thoughtful concern for others.
con·sid·er·a·tion (kən sĭd′ə **rā′**shən) ◊ *noun, plural* **considerations**

consist *verb* To be made up: *A week consists of seven days.*
con·sist (kən **sĭst′**) ◊ *verb* **consisted, consisting**

consistency *noun* **1.** The degree of how thick, firm, or stiff something is: *This glue has the consistency of mud.* **2.** The ability or quality of staying with one way of thinking or acting: *Your behavior lacks consistency; first you're polite and then you're rude.*
con·sis·ten·cy (kən **sĭs′**tən sē) ◊ *noun, plural* **consistencies**

consistent *adjective* Staying with the same ideas, actions, or set of principles: *It helps to have consistent study habits.*
con·sis·tent (kən **sĭs′**tənt) ◊ *adjective*

console *noun* A cabinet for a radio, record player, or television set.
con·sole (**kŏn′**sōl′) ◊ *noun, plural* **consoles**

consolidate *verb* To join together into one: *Several small stores consolidated into one large business.*
con·sol·i·date (kən **sŏl′**ĭ dāt′) ◊ *verb* **consolidated, consolidating**

consonant *noun* A letter of the alphabet that is not a vowel. *B, c, d, f,* and *g* are consonants.
con·so·nant (**kŏn′**sə nənt) ◊ *noun, plural* **consonants**

conspicuous *adjective* Attracting notice: *I see a conspicuous mistake in your work.*
con·spic·u·ous (kən **spĭk′**yōō əs) ◊ *adjective*

conspiracy *noun* A secret plan to do something wrong or illegal; plot.
con·spir·a·cy (kən **spîr′**ə sē) ◊ *noun, plural* **conspiracies**

conspire *verb* To plan together secretly to do something wrong.
con·spire (kən **spīr′**) ◊ *verb* **conspired, conspiring**

constant *adjective* **1.** Always remaining the same: *We kept a constant speed of 55 mph.* **2.** Happening all the time; persistent.

3. Without interruption: *The car is in constant use.* —See Synonyms at **continuous.**
con·stant (**kŏn′**stənt) ◊ *adjective*

constellation *noun* Any of 88 star groups that are shaped somewhat like animals, people, or objects and were named after them.
con·stel·la·tion (kŏn′stə **lā′**shən) ◊ *noun, plural* **constellations**

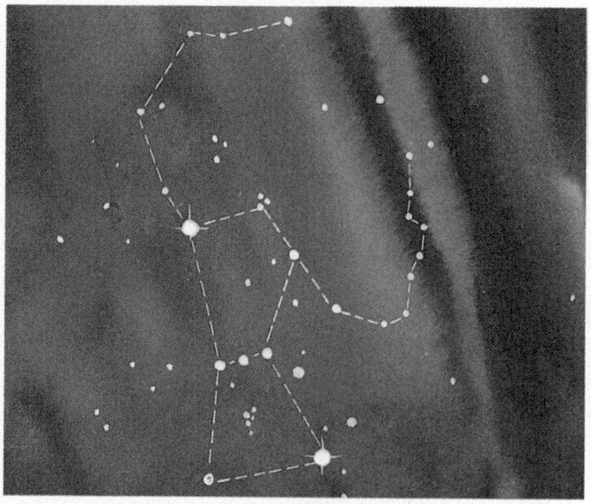

▲ **constellation**
The constellation Orion

constituent *adjective* Being or forming a necessary part: *Hydrogen and oxygen are the constituent parts of water.*
◊ *noun* **1.** A necessary part of which something is composed: *Oxygen is a constituent of water.* **2.** A voter: *Members of legislatures always try to please their constituents.*
con·stit·u·ent (kən **stĭch′**o͞o ənt) ◊ *adjective* ◊ *noun, plural* **constituents**

constitute *verb* To make up; form: *Twelve units constitute a dozen.*
con·sti·tute (**kŏn′**stĭ to͞ot′ *or* **kŏn′**stĭ tyo͞ot′) ◊ *verb* **constituted, constituting**

constitution *noun* **1.** The basic laws and principles under which a country, state, or organization is governed. **2. Constitution** The written constitution of the United States, adopted in 1787 and put into effect in 1789. **3.** The way in which someone or something is made up: *You must eat well in order to build a strong constitution.*
con·sti·tu·tion (kŏn′stĭ **to͞o′**shən *or* kŏn′stĭ-**tyo͞o′**shən) ◊ *noun, plural* **constitutions**

constitutional *adjective* **1.** Of, concerned with, or permitted by a constitution, as of a nation. **2.** Of or in the physical or mental make-up of a person.
con·sti·tu·tion·al (kŏn′stĭ **to͞o′**shə nəl *or* kŏn′stĭ **tyo͞o′**shə nəl) ◊ *adjective*

construct *verb* To make by fitting parts together; build: *We constructed a bookcase.*
con·struct (kən **strŭkt′**) ◊ *verb* **constructed, constructing**

construction *noun* **1.** The act or process of constructing. **2.** The business or work of building. **3.** Something that is put together; structure.
con·struc·tion (kən **strŭk′**shən) ◊ *noun, plural* **constructions**

constructive *adjective* Serving to help or improve; useful: *My teacher gave me some constructive criticism on writing better reports.*
con·struc·tive (kən **strŭk′**tĭv) ◊ *adjective*

consul *noun* An official appointed by a government to live in a foreign city in order to look after commercial interests there and to aid the citizens who live or travel there.
con·sul (**kŏn′**səl) ◊ *noun, plural* **consuls**

consult *verb* **1.** To go to for advice: *If you feel sick, you should consult a doctor.* **2.** To speak together about something: *The team members consulted with the coach.* **3.** To refer to for information.
con·sult (kən **sŭlt′**) ◊ *verb* **consulted, consulting**

consultation *noun* **1.** An act of consulting. **2.** A meeting to discuss or decide on something.
con·sul·ta·tion (kŏn′səl **tā′**shən) ◊ *noun, plural* **consultations**

consume *verb* **1.** To eat or drink up. **2.** To use up: *Cars consume gasoline. School consumes most of our time.* **3.** To buy and use goods and services.
con·sume (kən **so͞om′**) ◊ *verb* **consumed, consuming**

consumer *noun* **1.** Someone who buys and uses goods and services. **2.** A person or thing that consumes.
con·sum·er (kən **so͞o′**mər) ◊ *noun, plural* **consumers**

consumption *noun* The act or process of consuming or an amount consumed.
con·sump·tion (kən **sŭmp′**shən) ◊ *noun*

contact *noun* **1.** A touching or coming together of persons or objects. **2.** The condition of being in communication: *We lost contact with our former neighbors.* **3.** A contact lens.
◊ *verb* To come into contact with; touch.
con·tact (**kŏn′**tăkt′) ◊ *noun, plural* **contacts**
◊ *verb* **contacted, contacting**

contact lens *noun* A very small, thin lens worn directly over the cornea of the eye.
contact lens ◊ *noun, plural* **contact lenses**

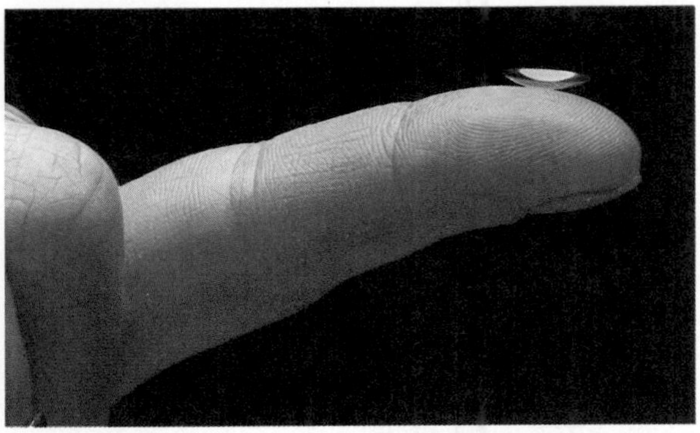

▲ **contact lens**

contagious *adjective* **1.** Spreading by direct or indirect contact: *Measles is a contagious disease.* **2.** Carrying disease.
con·ta·gious (kən **tā′**jəs) ◊ *adjective*

contain *verb* **1.** To have within itself; hold: *Orange juice contains vitamins.* **2.** To consist of or include: *A gallon contains four quarts.* **3.** To hold back; restrain: *I could not contain my laughter.*
con·tain (kən **tān′**) ◊ *verb* **contained, containing**

container *noun* Something, such as a box, can, jar, or barrel, used to hold something.
con·tain·er (kən **tā′**nər) ◊ *noun, plural* **containers**

contaminate *verb* To make impure or unfit for use by mixture or contact; pollute.
con·tam·i·nate (kən **tăm′**ə nāt′) ◊ *verb* **contaminated, contaminating**

ă	pat	ĭ	pit	oi	**oil**	th	**bath**
ā	pay	ī	ride	o͝o	book	*th*	**bathe**
â	care	î	fierce	o͞o	boot	ə	ago, item
ä	father	ŏ	pot	ou	**out**		pencil
ĕ	pet	ō	**go**	ŭ	cut		atom
ē	be	ô	paw, for	û	fur		circus

contemplate *verb* To look at or think about carefully.
con·tem·plate (**kŏn′**təm plāt′) ◊ *verb* **contemplated, contemplating**

contemporary *adjective* Living or occurring during the same period of time.
◊ *noun* A person living at the same time as another.
con·tem·po·rar·y (kən **tĕm′**pə rĕr′ē) ◊ *adjective* ◊ *noun, plural* **contemporaries**

contempt *noun* **1.** A feeling of scorn: *They have only contempt for cowards.* **2.** The state of being scorned: *The whole neighborhood held the bully in contempt.*
con·tempt (kən **tĕmpt′**) ◊ *noun*

contemptible *adjective* Deserving contempt.
con·tempt·i·ble (kən **tĕmp′**tə bəl) ◊ *adjective*

contend *verb* **1.** To fight or struggle: *There were too many problems to contend with.* **2.** To take part in a contest; compete. **3.** To declare to be true; claim: *The workers contend that they are not paid enough.*
con·tend (kən **tĕnd′**) ◊ *verb* **contended, contending**

content¹ *noun* **1.** Often **contents** Something that is contained: *What were the contents of the old trunk?* **2.** Often **contents** The subject matter written or spoken about: *The contents of the letter are secret.* **3.** The amount of one substance contained in another substance: *Some paints have a high oil content.*
con·tent¹ (**kŏn′**tĕnt′) ◊ *noun, plural* **contents**

content² *adjective* Happy with what one is or has; satisfied.
◊ *noun* A feeling of satisfied ease.
◊ *verb* To make pleased or content; satisfy.
con·tent² (kən **tĕnt′**) ◊ *adjective* ◊ *noun*
◊ *verb* **contented, contenting**

HISTORY • **content¹, content²**

Content¹, content², and **contain** all come from a Latin word meaning "to hold together." **Content¹** means "something contained," and relates to the first sense of **contain,** "to hold." **Content²** relates to the third sense of **contain,** "to hold back." You are **content²** when all your desires are "held back" or satisfied.

contented *adjective* Content; satisfied.
con·tent·ed (kən **tĕn′** tĭd) ◊ *adjective*

contention *noun* **1.** An act or example of quarreling or arguing. **2.** A claim or point for which one argues.
con·ten·tion (kən **tĕn′** shən) ◊ *noun, plural* **contentions**

contentment *noun* Happiness and satisfaction; peace of mind.
con·tent·ment (kən **tĕnt′** mənt) ◊ *noun*

contest *noun* **1.** A struggle or fight between two or more people or groups. **2.** A competition, usually for a prize.
◊ *verb* **1.** To compete for, as a prize. **2.** To oppose or argue against; dispute.
con·test ◊ *noun* (**kŏn′** tĕst′), *plural* **contests** ◊ *verb* (kən **tĕst′**) **contested, contesting**

contestant *noun* Someone who takes part in a contest.
con·test·ant (kən **tĕs′** tənt) ◊ *noun, plural* **contestants**

context *noun* The setting of words and ideas in which a particular word or statement appears: *In some contexts "mad" means "insane"; in other contexts it means "angry."*
con·text (**kŏn′** tĕkst′) ◊ *noun, plural* **contexts**

continent *noun* One of the main land masses of the earth, including Africa, Antarctica, Asia, Australia, Europe, North America, and South America.
con·ti·nent (**kŏn′** tə nənt) ◊ *noun, plural* **continents**

▲ **continent**
The continent of North America

continental *adjective* Of, relating to, or like a continent.
con·ti·nen·tal (kŏn′tə **nĕn′** tl) ◊ *adjective*

continual *adjective* **1.** Happening again and again with short pauses in between: *The continual banging of the shutters kept me awake.* **2.** Going on without a break or pause: *There was a continual bubbling of water in the fish tank.* —See Synonyms at **continuous.**
con·tin·u·al (kən **tĭn′** yo͞o əl) ◊ *adjective*

continue *verb* **1.** To keep on or persist in: *The rain continued for days.* **2.** To begin again after stopping; resume: *Our program will continue after a word from our sponsor.* **3.** To stay in the same place, condition, or situation; remain.
con·tin·ue (kən **tĭn′** yo͞o) ◊ *verb* **continued, continuing**

continuous *adjective* Keeping on without stopping: *We heard continuous rain.*
con·tin·u·ous (kən **tĭn′** yo͞o əs) ◊ *adjective*

SYNONYMS

continuous, constant, continual
The water fell in a *continuous* stream. Near the highway there is the *constant* sound of cars. We could hear *continual* coughing during class.

contortion *noun* A twisted position, shape, or facial expression.
con·tor·tion (kən **tôr′** shən) ◊ *noun, plural* **contortions**

contour *noun* The outline of a figure, body, or mass.
con·tour (**kŏn′** to͝or′) ◊ *noun, plural* **contours**

contraband *noun* Goods illegally brought into or taken out of a country.
con·tra·band (**kŏn′** trə bănd′) ◊ *noun*

contract *noun* **1.** A written agreement that the law can enforce. **2.** An official paper showing the conditions of an agreement.
◊ *verb* **1.** To draw together and make shorter: *My stomach muscles contract when I'm afraid.* **2.** To make or become smaller: *The pupils of our eyes contract in bright light.* **3.** To make a written agreement. **4.** To come down with: *I contracted a cold.* **5.** To make two words into one by dropping certain letters: *We contract "is not" to "isn't."*
con·tract ◊ *noun* (**kŏn′** trăkt′), *plural* **contracts** ◊ *verb* (kən **trăkt′**) **contracted, contracting**

contraction *noun* **1.** The act or process of contracting or the condition of being contracted. **2.** A shortened form of a pair of words, such as *isn't* for *is not.*
con·trac·tion (kən **trăk′**shən) ◊ *noun, plural* **contractions**

contradict *verb* **1.** To say the opposite of: *We contradicted their story.* **2.** To disagree with: *Don't contradict your parents.*
con·tra·dict (kŏn′trə **dĭkt′**) ◊ *verb* **contradicted, contradicting**

contradiction *noun* The act of contradicting or the condition of being contradicted.
con·tra·dic·tion (kŏn′trə **dĭk′**shən) ◊ *noun, plural* **contradictions**

contradictory *adjective* Opposing or disagreeing. —See Synonyms at **opposite.**
con·tra·dic·to·ry (kŏn′trə **dĭk′**tə rē) ◊ *adjective*

contralto *noun* **1.** The lowest singing voice of a woman. **2.** A singer with a contralto voice.
con·tral·to (kən **trăl′**tō) ◊ *noun, plural* **contraltos**

contrary *adjective* **1.** Completely different: *My friend and I have contrary points of view.* —See Synonyms at **opposite. 2.** Going against; acting in opposition to: *Don't act contrary to your parents' wishes.* **3.** Tending to be stubborn: *The contrary child wouldn't behave.*
◊ *noun* The opposite: *They say they're happy, but I believe the contrary to be true.*
◊ *idiom* **on the contrary** In the opposite way.
con·tra·ry (**kŏn′**trĕr′ē *or* kən **trâr′**ē *for sense 3*) ◊ *adjective* ◊ *noun, plural* **contraries**

contrast *verb* **1.** To examine and compare in order to show differences: *The story contrasts good and evil.* **2.** To show differences when compared: *Light contrasts with dark.*
◊ *noun* **1.** Comparison, especially in order to show differences: *In contrast to the dry climate of Arizona, it rains a lot in Oregon.* **2.** A noticeable difference between persons or things compared. **3.** A person or thing that is noticeably different from another.
con·trast ◊ *verb* (kən **trăst′** *or* **kŏn′**trăst′) **contrasted, contrasting** ◊ *noun* (**kŏn′**trăst′), *plural* **contrasts**

ă	pat	ĭ	pit	oi	oil	th	bath
ā	pay	ī	ride	o͝o	book	*th*	bathe
â	care	î	fierce	o͞o	boot	ə	ago, item
ä	father	ŏ	pot	ou	out		pencil
ĕ	pet	ō	go	ŭ	cut		atom
ē	be	ô	paw, for	û	fur		circus

contribute *verb* **1.** To give along with others: *Our family contributes time to conservation projects.* **2.** To aid in bringing about: *Exercise contributes to better health.* **3.** To submit for publication especially in a magazine.
con·trib·ute (kən **trĭb′**yo͞ot) ◊ *verb* **contributed, contributing**

contrite *adjective* Sorry for doing wrong.
con·trite (kən **trīt′** *or* **kŏn′**trīt′) ◊ *adjective*

contrive *verb* To plan in a clever way: *They contrived a way to escape. We contrived a little boat out of a large nutshell.*
con·trive (kən **trīv′**) ◊ *verb* **contrived, contriving**

control *verb* **1.** To have authority or influence over; direct: *The school board controls the budget.* **2.** To regulate the operation of: *The pilot controls the helicopter.* **3.** To hold in check; restrain: *You must learn to control your temper.*
◊ *noun* **1.** Authority to direct or regulate: *The team is under the coach's control.* —See Synonyms at **power. 2.** A way of holding in check: *You have little control over your temper.* **3.** Often **controls** The instruments used in setting and regulating a machine.
con·trol (kən **trōl′**) ◊ *verb* **controlled, controlling** ◊ *noun, plural* **controls**

control tower *noun* A tower at an airport from which the takeoffs and landings are controlled by radio and radar.
control tower ◊ *noun, plural* **control towers**

▲ **control tower**

controversy *noun* A dispute or argument between sides holding opposing views.
con·tro·ver·sy (**kŏn′** trə vûr′sē) ◊ *noun, plural* **controversies**

convalesce *verb* To regain health and strength after an illness or injury.
con·va·lesce (kŏn′və **lĕs′**) ◊ *verb* **convalesced, convalescing**

convalescent *adjective* Regaining strength and health after an illness or injury.
◊ *noun* A person who is convalescing.
con·va·les·cent (kŏn′və **lĕs′** ənt) ◊ *adjective* ◊ *noun, plural* **convalescents**

convene *verb* To assemble or cause to assemble: *Congress will convene next month.*
con·vene (kən **vēn′**) ◊ *verb* **convened, convening**

convenience *noun* **1.** The quality or state of being suitable or handy. **2.** Personal comfort or advantage: *The hotel has a restaurant for the guests' convenience.* **3.** Something, as a device or service, that saves time and effort: *This kitchen has all the modern conveniences.*
con·ven·ience (kən **vēn′** yəns) ◊ *noun, plural* **conveniences**

convenient *adjective* **1.** Easy to get to; handy: *They bought a home convenient to the shopping center.* **2.** Suited to one's comfort, needs, or purpose: *What time would be convenient for you?*
con·ven·ient (kən **vēn′** yənt) ◊ *adjective*

convent *noun* **1.** A community of nuns. **2.** A house or building for a community of nuns.
con·vent (**kŏn′** vĕnt′) ◊ *noun, plural* **convents**

convention *noun* **1.** A formal assembly or meeting: *There was a display of new children's books at the teachers' convention.* **2.** A widely accepted practice; custom: *The use of commas is a convention of written English.*
con·ven·tion (kən **vĕn′** shən) ◊ *noun, plural* **conventions**

conventional *adjective* Following accepted practice, customs, or taste.
con·ven·tion·al (kən **vĕn′** shə nəl) ◊ *adjective*

conversation *noun* Informal talk between two or more people.
con·ver·sa·tion (kŏn′vər **sā′** shən) ◊ *noun, plural* **conversations**

converse *verb* To talk with another.
con·verse (kən **vûrs′**) ◊ *verb* **conversed, conversing**

conversion *noun* The act or process of converting or the state of being converted.
con·ver·sion (kən **vûr′** zhən) ◊ *noun, plural* **conversions**

convert *verb* **1.** To change from one form to another. **2.** To change from one use to another —See Synonyms at **change. 3.** To change from one religion or belief to another.
◊ *noun* A person who has adopted a new religion or belief.
con·vert ◊ *verb* (kən **vûrt′**) **converted, converting** ◊ *noun* (**kŏn′** vûrt′), *plural* **converts**

convertible *adjective* Able to be changed into something else.
◊ *noun* A car with a top that can be folded back or taken off.
con·vert·i·ble (kən **vûr′** tə bəl) ◊ *adjective* ◊ *noun, plural* **convertibles**

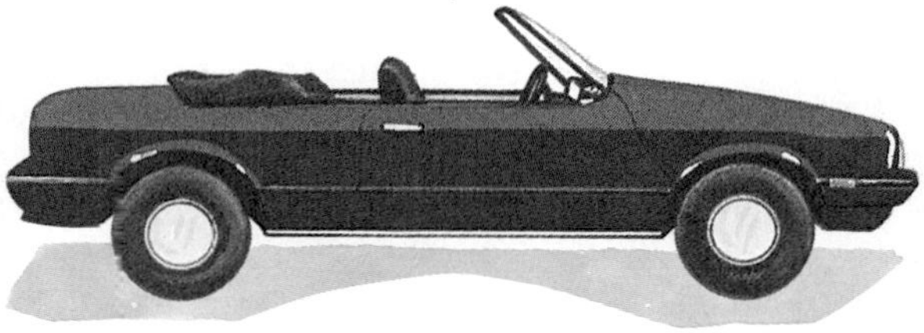

▲ **convertible**

convex *adjective* Curving outward like the outside of a circle.
con·vex (kŏn **vĕks′** *or* **kŏn′** vĕks′) ◊ *adjective*

convey *verb* **1.** To take or carry from one place to another; transport: *A taxi conveyed us to the airport.* **2.** To serve as a way of carrying: *Cables convey electrical power.* **3.** To communicate: *The writer conveys a feeling of excitement in the adventure story.*
con·vey (kən **vā′**) ◊ *verb* **conveyed, conveying**

conveyance *noun* **1.** The act of conveying. **2.** Something that is used to carry passengers or goods.
con·vey·ance (kən **vā′** əns) ◊ *noun, plural* **conveyances**

convict *verb* To find or prove guilty.
◊ *noun* A person serving a prison sentence.
con·vict ◊ *verb* (kən **vĭkt'**) **convicted, convicting** ◊ *noun* (**kŏn'**vĭkt'), *plural* **convicts**

conviction *noun* **1.** The act or process of finding or proving guilty. **2.** The state of being found or proven guilty. **3.** A strong belief.
con·vic·tion (kən **vĭk'**shən) ◊ *noun, plural* **convictions**

convince *verb* To persuade to do or believe: *Can you convince your parents to let you go on the trip?*
con·vince (kən **vĭns'**) ◊ *verb* **convinced, convincing**

convoy *noun* **1.** A group of ships or vehicles protected by an armed escort. **2.** An armed escort. **3.** A group of vehicles traveling together especially for convenience.
con·voy (**kŏn'**voi') ◊ *noun, plural* **convoys**

▲ **convoy**

convulse *verb* To shake or disturb violently: *The earthquake convulsed the village. I was convulsed with laughter.*
con·vulse (kən **vŭls'**) ◊ *verb* **convulsed, convulsing**

ă	pat	ĭ	pit	oi	oil	th	bath
ā	pay	ī	ride	o͝o	book	*th*	bathe
â	care	î	fierce	o͞o	boot	ə	ago, item
ä	father	ŏ	pot	ou	out		pencil
ĕ	pet	ō	go	ŭ	cut		atom
ē	be	ô	paw, for	û	fur		circus

convulsion *noun* A sudden, violent drawing together of the muscles.
con·vul·sion (kən **vŭl'**shən) ◊ *noun, plural* **convulsions**

cook *verb* **1.** To prepare food for eating by using heat. **2.** To undergo cooking.
◊ *noun* A person who cooks.
cook (ko͝ok) ◊ *verb* **cooked, cooking** ◊ *noun, plural* **cooks**

cookie *noun* A usually small, sweet cake.
cook·ie (**ko͝ok'**ē) ◊ *noun, plural* **cookies**

cookout *noun* A picnic at which the food is cooked outdoors.
cook·out (**ko͝ok'**out') ◊ *noun, plural* **cookouts**

cool *adjective* **1.** Somewhat cold. —See Synonyms at **cold. 2.** Giving relief from heat. **3.** Not easily excited or upset; calm. **4.** Not friendly: *They gave me cool looks.*
◊ *verb* To make or become less warm.
◊ *noun* **1.** Something cool. **2.** Calmness of mind: *During the test you lost your cool.*
cool (ko͞ol) ◊ *adjective* **cooler, coolest** ◊ *verb* **cooled, cooling** ◊ *noun*

coop *noun* A cage or pen, especially one for poultry.
◊ *verb* To confine in a small space: *I've been cooped up in my room all day.*
coop (ko͞op) ◊ *noun, plural* **coops** ◊ *verb* **cooped, cooping**

cooperate *verb* To work or act together for a common purpose: *Everyone cooperated in decorating the classroom.*
co·op·er·ate (kō **ŏp'**ə rāt') ◊ *verb* **cooperated, cooperating**

cooperation *noun* The act or process of working or acting together.
co·op·er·a·tion (kō ŏp'ə **rā'**shən) ◊ *noun*

coordinate *adjective* Of equal importance, rank, or degree.
◊ *verb* To work or cause to work together easily or well: *Babies must coordinate their arm and leg muscles when learning to crawl.*
co·or·di·nate ◊ *adjective* (kō **ôr'**dn ĭt) ◊ *verb* (kō **ôr'**dn āt') **coordinated, coordinating**

coordination *noun* **1.** An act of coordinating or the condition of being coordinated. **2.** The organized action of muscles in doing complex movements or tasks.
co·or·di·na·tion (kō ôr'dn **ā'**shən) ◊ *noun*

cope *verb* To deal with successfully.
cope (kōp) ◊ *verb* **coped, coping**

copilot *noun* An assistant pilot in an aircraft.
co·pi·lot (kō′pī′lət) ◊ *noun, plural* **copilots**

copper *noun* A reddish-brown metal that is an excellent conductor of heat and electricity. Copper is a chemical element.
◊ *adjective* Made of or containing copper.
copper (kŏp′ər) ◊ *noun* ◊ *adjective*

copperhead *noun* A poisonous reddish-brown snake of the eastern United States.
cop·per·head (kŏp′ər-hĕd′) ◊ *noun, plural* **copperheads**

▲ **copperhead**

copy *noun* **1.** Something that is made to look exactly like an original. **2.** One of the entire number of books, magazines, or newspapers that are printed at one time.
◊ *verb* **1.** To make something that is exactly like an original. **2.** To follow as a model or pattern: *I copied my friend's clothes.*
cop·y (kŏp′ē) ◊ *noun, plural* **copies** ◊ *verb* **copied, copying**

coral *noun* **1.** A hard, stony substance formed by the skeletons of tiny sea animals massed together in great numbers. It is often white, pink, or reddish. **2.** A yellowish pink or red color.
◊ *adjective* **1.** Made of coral. **2.** Yellowish pink or red.
cor·al (kôr′əl) ◊ *noun, plural* **corals** ◊ *adjective*

coral snake *noun* A poisonous snake marked with red, black, and yellow bands.
coral snake ◊ *noun, plural* **coral snakes**

cord *noun* **1.** A small rope of twisted strands. **2.** An insulated wire fitted with a plug that is used to connect an electrical appliance with an outlet. **3.** Something like a cord: *The spinal cord is in the backbone.*
cord (kôrd) ◊ *noun, plural* **cords**
‖*These sound alike:* **cord, chord**

cordial *adjective* Warm and friendly.
cor·dial (kôr′jəl) ◊ *adjective*

corduroy *noun* **1.** A thick, heavy cotton cloth with a ribbed surface. **2. corduroys** Trousers made of corduroy.
cor·du·roy (kôr′də roi′) ◊ *noun, plural* **corduroys**

core *noun* **1.** The central part of a fruit, such as an apple or pear. —See Synonyms at **center. 2.** The central or most important part; heart: *The core of my problems in school is trouble with reading.*
◊ *verb* To remove the core from: *Please core these apples.*
core (kôr) ◊ *noun, plural* **cores** ◊ *verb* **cored, coring**
‖*These sound alike:* **core, corps**

cork *noun* **1.** The light, spongy, outer bark of a kind of oak tree that is used especially for bottle stoppers and insulation. **2.** A cork, rubber, or plastic stopper for a bottle or jug.
cork (kôrk) ◊ *noun, plural* **corks**

corkscrew *noun* A device that is made of a pointed metal spiral attached to a handle. It is used for pulling corks from bottles.
◊ *adjective* Spiral or twisted in shape.
cork·screw (kôrk′skrōō′) ◊ *noun, plural* **corkscrews** ◊ *adjective*

cormorant *noun* A large blackish water bird with a long neck and a hooked bill.
cor·mo·rant (kôr′mər ənt) ◊ *noun, plural* **cormorants**

corn *noun* **1.** A tall plant grown for its large ears that bear kernels used as food. **2.** The ears or kernels of the corn plant.
corn (kôrn) ◊ *noun*

corncob *noun* The long, hard central part of an ear of corn on which the kernels grow.
corn·cob (kôrn′kŏb′) ◊ *noun, plural* **corncobs**

cornea *noun* The transparent outer coating of the eyeball that covers the pupil and iris.
cor·ne·a (kôr′nē ə) ◊ *noun, plural* **corneas**

corner *noun* **1.** The point or place at which two lines or surfaces meet: *A cabinet sits in a corner of the room.* **2.** The place where two roads or streets meet. **3.** A place or region, especially one that is far away from another: *People arrived from all corners of the world.*
◊ *verb* To drive into a corner: *We cornered the hamster and returned it to its cage.*
cor·ner (kôr′nər) ◊ *noun, plural* **corners** ◊ *verb* **cornered, cornering**

cornet *noun* A brass wind instrument that is like a trumpet but a little shorter.
cor·net (kôr **nĕt′**) ◊ *noun, plural* **cornets**

cornmeal *noun* A coarse meal that is made from ground corn kernels.
corn·meal (**kôrn′**mēl′) ◊ *noun*

cornstalk *noun* The stalk or stem of the corn plant.
corn·stalk (**kôrn′**stôk′) ◊ *noun, plural* **cornstalks**

▲ **cornet**

coronation *noun* The act or ceremony of crowning a monarch.
cor·o·na·tion (kôr′ə **nā′**shən) ◊ *noun, plural* **coronations**

coronet *noun* A small crown worn by members of the nobility.
cor·o·net (kôr′ə **nĕt′**) ◊ *noun, plural* **coronets**

corporal *noun* An Army or Marine Corps officer ranking above private.
cor·po·ral (**kôr′**pər əl) ◊ *noun, plural* **corporals**

***HISTORY* • corporal**

Most of the words beginning with **corp–** go back to Latin *corpus,* meaning "body." A **corps** and a **corporation** are both bodies of people. A **corpuscle** is a "little body" or cell. But **corporal** is an exception. It goes back to an old Italian word, *caporale,* meaning "head of troops." It passed into French and then English, but along the way got confused with the **corp–** words. Its spelling changed under their influence.

ă pat		ĭ pit		oi **oil**		th bath	
ā pay		ī ride		o͝o book		*th* bathe	
â care		î fierce		o͞o boot		ə ago, item	
ä father		ŏ pot		ou **out**		pencil	
ĕ pet		ō go		ŭ cut		atom	
ē be		ô paw, for		û fur		circus	

corporation *noun* An organized group of persons allowed by law to run an enterprise or business as one person.
cor·po·ra·tion (kôr′pə **rā′**shən) ◊ *noun, plural* **corporations**

corps *noun* **1.** Often **Corps** A section or branch of the armed forces having a special function: *The Marine Corps is trained to make landings from the sea.* **2.** A group of people acting or working together: *We belong to a drum and bugle corps.*
corps (kôr) ◊ *noun, plural* **corps**
‖*These sound alike:* **corps, core**

corpse *noun* A dead human body.
corpse (kôrps) ◊ *noun, plural* **corpses**

corpuscle *noun* Any of the cells, such as red or white blood cells, that make up a large part of the blood. Red corpuscles carry oxygen from the lungs to other parts of the body. Some white corpuscles kill disease germs.
cor·pus·cle (**kôr′**pŭs′əl) ◊ *noun, plural* **corpuscles**

corral *noun* A fenced-in area for cattle or horses.
◊ *verb* **1.** To drive into and keep in a corral. **2.** To get hold of: *We corralled all the adventure books in the library.*
cor·ral (kə **răl′**) ◊ *noun, plural* **corrals** ◊ *verb* **corralled, corralling**

correct *verb* **1.** To remove the mistakes from: *Correct your paper before you hand it in.* **2.** To mark the errors in: *The teacher corrected the tests.* **3.** To make right, as by changing or adjusting: *Contact lenses can correct poor eyesight.* **4.** To scold or punish in order to improve: *You should correct the children when they are rude.*
◊ *adjective* **1.** Free from error; accurate: *Your addition is correct.* **2.** Following proper standards: *What is the correct way to eat fried chicken?*
cor·rect (kə **rĕkt′**) ◊ *verb* **corrected, correcting** ◊ *adjective*

SYNONYMS

correct, accurate, right

I think I know the *correct* answer. The witnesses tried to give an *accurate* statement of what they saw. That is the *right* way to spell my name.

C

correction *noun* **1.** The act or process of correcting. **2.** Something that replaces a mistake. **3.** An act of punishing.
cor·rec·tion (kə **rĕk′**shən) ◊ *noun, plural* **corrections**

corrective *adjective* Made, used, or meant to correct.
cor·rec·tive (kə **rĕk′**tĭv) ◊ *adjective*

correspond *verb* **1.** To be in agreement: *Your answers on the test correspond with mine.* **2.** To be very similar: *The eyelids correspond to the shutter of a camera.* **3.** To exchange letters with another person.
cor·re·spond (kôr′ĭ **spŏnd′**) ◊ *verb* **corresponded, corresponding**

correspondence *noun* **1.** The fact of corresponding; agreement: *There is not always an exact correspondence between spelling and pronunciation.* **2.** Communication by writing letters. **3.** The letters exchanged: *We answer all correspondence from our customers.*
cor·re·spon·dence (kôr′ĭ **spŏn′**dəns) ◊ *noun*

correspondent *noun* **1.** A person who communicates with another by writing letters. **2.** A person who reports news, especially from faraway places.
cor·re·spon·dent (kôr′ĭ **spŏn′**dənt) ◊ *noun, plural* **correspondents**

corridor *noun* A hall or passage.
cor·ri·dor (**kôr′**ĭ dər) ◊ *noun, plural* **corridors**

corrode *verb* To wear or be worn away gradually, especially by chemical action: *Sea water corroded the iron pilings.*
cor·rode (kə **rōd′**) ◊ *verb* **corroded, corroding**

corrosion *noun* **1.** The act or process of corroding or the condition of being corroded. **2.** A substance, such as rust, produced by corroding.
cor·ro·sion (kə **rō′**zhən) ◊ *noun*

corrugate *verb* To shape or bend into alternating curved folds and grooves.
cor·ru·gate (**kôr′**ə gāt′) ◊ *verb* **corrugated, corrugating**

corrupt *adjective* **1.** Evil; wicked. **2.** Influenced by others to be dishonest.
◊ *verb* To cause to act wickedly or dishonestly: *Greed corrupts some people.*
cor·rupt (kə **rŭpt′**) ◊ *adjective* ◊ *verb* **corrupted, corrupting**

corsage *noun* A flower or bouquet worn by a woman especially on the shoulder.
cor·sage (kôr **säzh′**) ◊ *noun, plural* **corsages**

▲ **corsage**

cosmetic *noun* A preparation, as powder, rouge, or skin cream, used to make the hair, skin, or complexion beautiful.
cos·met·ic (kŏz **mĕt′**ĭk) ◊ *noun, plural* **cosmetics**

cosmic *adjective* Of or relating to the entire universe.
cos·mic (**kŏz′**mĭk) ◊ *adjective*

cost *noun* **1.** The amount paid or charged for something; price: *The cost of the tickets was $15.* —See Synonyms at **price.** **2.** A loss or penalty; sacrifice.
◊ *verb* To have as a price: *The tickets cost $15 each.*
cost (kôst) ◊ *noun, plural* **costs** ◊ *verb* **cost, costing**

costly *adjective* **1.** Of high cost: *The tickets are costly.* —See Synonyms at **expensive.** **2.** Involving sacrifice or loss.
cost·ly (**kôst′**lē) ◊ *adjective* **costlier, costliest**

costume *noun* **1.** A style of dress typical of a certain time, place, or people: *The fife and drum corps were in Revolutionary costume.* **2.** Clothes worn by a person playing a part or dressing up in disguise: *We changed our costumes between scenes of the school play.*
cos·tume (**kôs′**to͞om′ *or* **kôs′**tyo͞om′) ◊ *noun, plural* **costumes**

cot *noun* A small, narrow bed stretched over a frame that can be folded up.
cot (kŏt) ◊ *noun, plural* **cots**

cottage *noun* A small house in the country.
cot·tage (**kŏt′**ĭj) ◊ *noun, plural* **cottages**

cottage cheese *noun* A soft white cheese made from the curds of skim milk.

cotton *noun* **1.** A plant grown for the fluffy white fibers that surround its seeds. **2.** Thread or cloth made from cotton fibers.
◊ *adjective* Made of cotton.
cot·ton (**kŏt′**n) ◊ *noun* ◊ *adjective*

cottontail *noun* An American rabbit with a short, fluffy white tail.
cot·ton·tail (kŏt′n tāl′) ◊ *noun, plural* **cottontails**

cottonwood *noun* An American tree that has seeds with tufts that look like cotton.
cot·ton·wood (kŏt′n-wo͝od′) ◊ *noun, plural* **cottonwoods**

couch *noun* A sofa.
couch (kouch) ◊ *noun, plural* **couches**

▲ **cottontail**

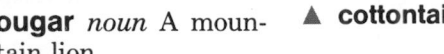

cougar *noun* A mountain lion.
cou·gar (ko͞o′gər) ◊ *noun, plural* **cougars**

cough *verb* **1.** To force air from the lungs with a sudden sharp noise. **2.** To expel by coughing. **3.** To make a sound like that of coughing: *The engine coughed and sputtered.*
◊ *noun* **1.** The act, process, or sound of coughing. **2.** A condition marked by frequent or severe coughing.
cough (kôf) ◊ *verb* **coughed, coughing**
◊ *noun, plural* **coughs**

could *verb* Past tense of **can[1]**.
could (ko͝od *or* kəd) ◊ *verb*

couldn't Contraction of "could not."
could·n't (ko͝od′nt) ◊ *contraction*

council *noun* **1.** A group of persons called together to discuss or settle a problem or question. **2.** A group of persons elected or appointed to make laws or rules.
coun·cil (koun′səl) ◊ *noun, plural* **councils**
‖*These sound alike:* **council, counsel**

councilor *noun* A member of a council.
coun·cil·or (koun′sə lər) ◊ *noun, plural* **councilors**
‖*These sound alike:* **councilor, counselor**

counsel *noun* **1.** Opinion about what should be done; advice: *I won't join the team without your counsel.* **2.** A lawyer or group of lawyers.
◊ *verb* To offer or give advice to.
coun·sel (koun′səl) ◊ *noun* ◊ *verb* **counseled, counseling**
‖*These sound alike:* **counsel, council**

counselor *noun* **1.** A person who gives counsel; adviser. **2.** A lawyer. **3.** A person who supervises children at a summer camp.
coun·sel·or (koun′sə lər) ◊ *noun, plural* **counselors**
‖*These sound alike:* **counselor, councilor**

count[1] *verb* **1.** To find the total of; add up: *Count your change.* **2.** To name the numbers in order up to and including a particular number: *Count three and jump.* **3.** To name numbers in order: *We counted from 1 to 10.* **4.** To include in counting or considering: *There are seven in my family, counting me.* **5.** To have importance, force, or value: *It is not how often you read but what you read that counts.* **6.** To believe to be; consider: *Count yourself lucky to have a bicycle.* **7.** To rely; depend: *You can count on my help.*
◊ *noun* **1.** The act of counting. **2.** A total reached by counting.
count[1] (kount) ◊ *verb* **counted, counting**
◊ *noun, plural* **counts**

count[2] *noun* A European nobleman whose rank corresponds to that of an English earl.
count[2] (kount) ◊ *noun, plural* **counts**

***HISTORY* • count[1], count[2]**

Count[1] comes from an old French word meaning "to add up." **Count[2]** comes from a different old French word that came from a Latin word meaning "companion."

countdown *noun* The act or process of counting aloud the time remaining before an event, such as the launch of a rocket.
count·down (kount′doun′) ◊ *noun, plural* **countdowns**

countenance *noun* **1.** The expression of the human face: *Your grave countenance shows that you are concerned.* **2.** The human face.
coun·te·nance (koun′tə nəns) ◊ *noun, plural* **countenances**

counter[1] *noun* **1.** A flat surface on which goods are sold, food is served, objects are dis-

ă	pat	ĭ	pit	oi	oil	th	bath
ā	pay	ī	ride	o͝o	book	*th*	bathe
â	care	î	fierce	o͞o	boot	ə	ago, item
ä	father	ŏ	pot	ou	out		pencil
ĕ	pet	ō	go	ŭ	cut		atom
ē	be	ô	paw, for	û	fur		circus

played, or work is done. **2.** An object, as of ivory or wood, that is used in counting or in certain games.
count·er¹ (**koun**′tər) ◊ *noun, plural* **counters**

counter² *adjective* Being, acting, or moving in an opposite way or direction; contrary: *Our neighbor's opinion was counter to that of my parents.*
◊ *verb* To move or act in opposition to; oppose: *They tried to counter our impression that they were unfriendly.*
coun·ter² (**koun**′tər) ◊ *adjective* ◊ *verb* **countered, countering**

***HISTORY* • counter¹, counter²**

Counter¹ is related to **count¹**. A **counter¹** (sense 1) first referred to a table on which money was counted, and then to any narrow table. A **counter¹** (sense 2) is something you count or keep score with. **Counter²** comes from an old French word that came from a Latin word meaning "against."

counter– The prefix *counter–* means "opposing" or "against." To *counteract* means "to stop by acting against." The prefix *counter–* also means "corresponding" or "complementary." A *counterpart* is a person or thing that is exactly or very much like another.

***VOCABULARY BUILDER* • counter–**

Many words that are formed with **counter–** are not entries in this dictionary. But you can figure out what these words mean by looking up the meanings of the root words and the prefix. For example:
countercharge = a charge in opposition to another
counterweight = a weight used to balance another

counteract *verb* To check or stop by acting against: *We drank water to counteract our thirst.*
coun·ter·act (koun′tər **ăkt**′) ◊ *verb* **counteracted, counteracting**

counterclockwise *adverb & adjective* In a direction opposite to that of the movement of the hands of a clock.
coun·ter·clock·wise (koun′tər **klŏk**′wīz′) ◊ *adverb & adjective*

counterfeit *verb* To copy or imitate in order to deceive: *They were found guilty of counterfeiting money.*
◊ *adjective* Made in imitation of what is genuine in order to deceive: *The bank destroyed the counterfeit dollar bills.*
◊ *noun* Something counterfeited.
coun·ter·feit (**koun**′tər fĭt) ◊ *verb* **counterfeited, counterfeiting** ◊ *adjective* ◊ *noun, plural* **counterfeits**

counterpart *noun* A person or thing that is exactly or very much like another: *The president of a college is the counterpart of a school principal.*
coun·ter·part (**koun**′tər pärt′) ◊ *noun, plural* **counterparts**

countersign *noun* A secret signal; password.
coun·ter·sign (**koun**′tər sīn′) ◊ *noun, plural* **countersigns**

countless *adjective* Too many to count.
count·less (**kount**′lĭs) ◊ *adjective*

country *noun* **1.** A land in which people live under a single government; nation: *We studied several foreign countries.* **2.** The land of one's birth or citizenship: *They returned to their country at the end of the war.* **3.** The people of a nation: *The country wants peace.* **4.** An area of land; region: *The country near our house is full of forests.* **5.** Land outside of cities or towns; rural area: *They went to the country for their vacation.*
coun·try (**kŭn**′trē) ◊ *noun, plural* **countries**

countryman *noun* **1.** A man from one's own country. **2.** A man who lives in the country.
coun·try·man (**kŭn**′trē mən) ◊ *noun, plural* **countrymen**

countrywoman *noun* **1.** A woman from one's own country. **2.** A woman who lives in the country.
coun·try·wom·an (**kŭn**′trē wo͝om′ən) ◊ *noun, plural* **countrywomen**

county *noun* A unit into which a state or country is divided for local government.
coun·ty (**koun**′tē) ◊ *noun, plural* **counties**

couple *noun* **1.** Two things of the same kind that are connected or considered together;

pair: *I wrote a couple of letters.* **2.** Two persons who are closely associated, especially a man and woman who are married.
◊ *verb* To link, fasten, or join together: *The railroad worker coupled the freight cars.*
cou·ple (kŭp′əl) ◊ *noun, plural* **couples** ◊ *verb* **coupled, coupling**

coupling *noun* **1.** The act of linking or joining. **2.** A device that connects or unites things or parts.
cou·pling (kŭp′lĭng) ◊ *noun, plural* **couplings**

coupon *noun* A printed ticket or form that gives the person holding it the right to a benefit, such as money or a gift.
cou·pon (**ko͞o′**pŏn *or* **kyo͞o′**pŏn) ◊ *noun, plural* **coupons**

courage *noun* The quality that makes a person able to face danger or difficulty bravely.
cour·age (**kûr′**ĭj) ◊ *noun*

courageous *adjective* Having or showing courage. —See Synonyms at **brave.**
cou·ra·geous (kə **rā′**jəs) ◊ *adjective*

courier *noun* A messenger, especially one on urgent, important business.
cour·i·er (**kûr′**ē ər) ◊ *noun, plural* **couriers**

course *noun* **1.** Onward movement from one point to the next: *Everything changed in the course of a single week.* **2.** The direction in which something or someone moves: *Our course took us south.* **3.** A channel in which water flows: *The course of the stream runs beside the road.* **4.** A place where a race is held or a sport is played: *They met at the golf course.* **5.** A series of studies that leads to a degree: *The student finished the four-year course in high school.* **6.** A part of a meal served at one time: *The first course was soup.*
◊ *verb* To flow or move swiftly: *Water coursed over the rocks with a roar.*
course (kôrs) ◊ *noun, plural* **courses** ◊ *verb* **coursed, coursing**
‖*These sound alike:* **course, coarse**

ă	pat	ĭ	pit	oi	oil	th	bath
ā	pay	ī	ride	o͝o	book	*th*	bathe
â	care	î	fierce	o͞o	boot	ə	ago, item
ä	father	ŏ	pot	ou	out		pencil
ĕ	pet	ō	go	ŭ	cut		atom
ē	be	ô	paw, for	û	fur		circus

court *noun* **1.** A courtyard. **2.** A short street. **3.** A level area marked for playing a game, as tennis or basketball. **4.** The place where a ruler lives. **5.** The people who follow a ruler. **6.** An official session led by a judge to hear and make decisions on legal cases. **7.** A room or building in which legal cases are heard.
◊ *verb* **1.** To try to win the love of in order to marry. **2.** To seek the support or favor of; try to please.
court (kôrt) ◊ *noun, plural* **courts** ◊ *verb* **courted, courting**

▲ **court**
A tennis court

courteous *adjective* Considerate toward others. —See Synonyms at **polite.**
cour·te·ous (**kûr′**tē əs) ◊ *adjective*

courtesy *noun* **1.** The quality or condition of being courteous. **2.** A courteous act.
cour·te·sy (**kûr′**tĭ sē) ◊ *noun, plural* **courtesies**

***HISTORY* • courtesy**

Courtesy is related to **court.** Originally **courtesy** meant the kind of manners expected of someone at a king's court.

courthouse *noun* A building in which courts of law are held.
court·house (**kôrt′**hous′) ◊ *noun, plural* **courthouses**

courtier *noun* A member of a ruler's court.
cour·ti·er (**kôr′**tē ər) ◊ *noun, plural* **courtiers**

courtly *adjective* Dignified and polite.
court·ly (**kôrt′**lē) ◊ *adjective* **courtlier, courtliest**

C

courtyard *noun* An open space surrounded by buildings or enclosed by walls.
court·yard (kôrt′ yärd′) ◊ *noun, plural* **courtyards**

▲ **courtyard**

cousin *noun* A child of one's aunt or uncle.
cous·in (kŭz′ ən) ◊ *noun, plural* **cousins**

cove *noun* A small sheltered bay or inlet.
cove (kōv) ◊ *noun, plural* **coves**

cover *verb* **1.** To put something over or on: *I covered my ears with my hands.* **2.** To form a surface layer over: *Dust covered the table.* **3.** To extend over; include: *My diary covered the whole year.* **4.** To go through or over: *We covered 200 miles a day.*
◊ *noun* **1.** A shelter or protection. **2.** Something that covers something else.
cov·er (kŭv′ ər) ◊ *verb* **covered, covering**
◊ *noun, plural* **covers**

covered wagon *noun* A large wagon covered with an arched canvas top.
covered wagon ◊ *noun, plural* **covered wagons**

covering *noun* Something that covers.
cov·er·ing (kŭv′ ər ĭng) ◊ *noun, plural* **coverings**

covet *verb* To wish for eagerly or with envy.
cov·et (kŭv′ ĭt) ◊ *verb* **coveted, coveting**

cow *noun* **1.** The fully grown female of cattle. **2.** The female of certain large mammals, as the elephant or moose.
cow (kou) ◊ *noun, plural* **cows**

coward *noun* A person who has no courage.
cow·ard (kou′ ərd) ◊ *noun, plural* **cowards**

cowardice *noun* Complete lack of courage.
cow·ard·ice (kou′ ər dĭs) ◊ *noun*

cowboy *noun* A man or boy who tends cattle on a ranch.
cow·boy (kou′ boi′) ◊ *noun, plural* **cowboys**

cowcatcher *noun* A frame on the front of a locomotive to clear away things from the track.
cow·catch·er (kou′ kăch′ ər) ◊ *noun, plural* **cowcatchers**

cower *verb* To crouch down or draw back, as from fear.
cow·er (kou′ ər) ◊ *verb* **cowered, cowering**

cowgirl *noun* A woman or girl who tends cattle on a ranch.
cow·girl (kou′ gûrl′) ◊ *noun, plural* **cowgirls**

cowhand *noun* A cowboy or cowgirl.
cow·hand (kou′ hănd′) ◊ *noun, plural* **cowhands**

cowhide *noun* **1.** The hide of a cow. **2.** Leather made from cowhide.
cow·hide (kou′ hīd′) ◊ *noun, plural* **cowhides**

cowl *noun* **1.** A monk's hood. **2.** A robe or cloak with a cowl.
cowl (koul) ◊ *noun, plural* **cowls**

cowlick *noun* A small tuft of hair that stands up from the head and will not lie flat.
cow·lick (kou′ lĭk′) ◊ *noun, plural* **cowlicks**

coy *adjective* Pretending to be shy.
coy (koi) ◊ *adjective* **coyer, coyest**

coyote *noun* An animal similar to a wolf that lives in western North America.
coy·o·te (kī ō′ tē *or* kī′ ōt′) ◊ *noun, plural* **coyotes**

cozy *adjective* Warm and snug.
co·zy (kō′ zē) ◊ *adjective* **cozier, coziest**

crab *noun* An animal that is related to the lobster and shrimp. Crabs have broad, flat bodies and five pairs of legs. The front pair of legs are large and have claws. Crabs often move sideways.
crab (krăb) ◊ *noun, plural* **crabs**

crab apple *noun* A small, sour apple used to make jelly.
crab apple ◊ *noun, plural* **crab apples**

crack *verb* **1.** To break with a sudden sharp sound: *The branch of the tree cracked. We cracked the ice.* **2.** To make or cause to make

a sharp snapping sound: *The rifle cracked.* **3.** To break or cause to break without separating into parts; split: *The mirror cracked.* **4.** To hit suddenly and sharply: *I tripped and cracked my elbow hard on the concrete.*
◊ *noun* **1.** A sharp snapping sound: *We heard the crack of thunder.* **2.** A partial split or break: *There is a crack in the mirror.* **3.** A narrow opening: *The door opened a crack.* **4.** A sharp blow: *The open door of the cabinet gave me a crack on the head.*
crack (krăk) ◊ *verb* **cracked, cracking** ◊ *noun, plural* **cracks**

cracker *noun* A thin, crisp wafer or biscuit.
crack·er (**krăk′**ər) ◊ *noun, plural* **crackers**

crackle *verb* To make slight, sharp, snapping sounds: *The logs crackled in the fireplace.*
◊ *noun* The act or sound of crackling.
crack·le (**krăk′**əl) ◊ *verb* **crackled, crackling** ◊ *noun, plural* **crackles**

cradle *noun* **1.** A small bed for a baby, usually mounted on rockers. **2.** A place of origin; birthplace: *Ancient Greece is often thought of as the cradle of democracy.*
◊ *verb* To place, support, or hold in or as if in a cradle: *The winners cradled the trophies in their arms.*
cra·dle (**krād′**l) ◊ *noun, plural* **cradles** ◊ *verb* **cradled, cradling**

▲ **cradle**

ă	pat	ĭ	pit	oi	**oil**	th	**bath**
ā	pay	ī	ride	o͝o	book	*th*	bathe
â	care	î	fierce	o͞o	boot	ə	ago, item
ä	father	ŏ	pot	ou	**out**		pencil
ĕ	pet	ō	go	ŭ	cut		atom
ē	be	ô	paw, for	û	fur		circus

craft *noun* **1.** Skill in making something, especially with the hands: *The cabinets were built with great craft.* **2.** An occupation or trade that requires special skill, especially with the hands: *We studied the craft of carpenters.* **3.** Skill used to deceive others; cunning. **4.** A boat, ship, or aircraft.
craft (krăft) ◊ *noun, plural* **crafts**

crafty *adjective* Skilled at deceiving others.
craft·y (**krăf′**tē) ◊ *adjective* **craftier, craftiest**

crag *noun* A steep, rugged rock.
crag (krăg) ◊ *noun, plural* **crags**

cram *verb* **1.** To force or squeeze tightly: *I crammed my clothes into the suitcase.* **2.** To fill tightly or too tightly: *The streets are crammed with cars.* **3.** To study very hard just before a test.
cram (krăm) ◊ *verb* **crammed, cramming**

cramp *noun* **1.** A sudden painful contraction of a muscle. **2. cramps** Sharp pains in the abdomen.
◊ *verb* To have or cause to have a cramp.
cramp (krămp) ◊ *noun, plural* **cramps** ◊ *verb* **cramped, cramping**

cranberry *noun* The sour, shiny red berry of a slender vine that grows in damp places. Cranberries are used in making sauces and jellies.
cran·ber·ry (**krăn′**bĕr′ē) ◊ *noun, plural* **cranberries**

HISTORY • cranberry

The first syllable of the word **cranberry** comes from a German word related to the English word **crane.** A part of the cranberry flower reminded people of the long neck of a crane.

crane *noun* **1.** A large wading bird with a long neck, long legs, and a long bill. **2.** A machine for lifting and carrying heavy objects on a swinging arm.
◊ *verb* To stretch the neck in order to get a better view: *We craned forward to see.*
crane (krān) ◊ *noun, plural* **cranes** ◊ *verb* **craned, craning**

cranium *noun* **1.** The skull. **2.** The part of the skull that encloses the brain.
cra·ni·um (**krā′**nē əm) ◊ *noun, plural* **craniums**

crank *noun* A rod or handle that is attached at right angles to a shaft and turned to start or run a machine.
◊ *verb* To start or run by means of a crank.
crank (krăngk) ◊ *noun, plural* **cranks** ◊ *verb* **cranked, cranking**

cranky *adjective* Easily annoyed; irritable.
crank·y (**krăng′** kē) ◊ *adjective* **crankier, crankiest**

crash *verb* **1.** To fall or strike something with sudden noise and damage: *The dishes slid from the shelf and crashed to the floor. The motorcycle crashed into the fence.* **2.** To move forward with force and noise: *Elephants crashed through the jungle.* **3.** To make a very loud noise: *Listen to the thunder crash.*
◊ *noun* **1.** A sudden loud noise. **2.** A smash; collision: *I was hurt in a car crash.*
crash (krăsh) ◊ *verb* **crashed, crashing** ◊ *noun, plural* **crashes**

crate *noun* A case that is used for packing and shipping something.
crate (krāt) ◊ *noun, plural* **crates**

crater *noun* **1.** A hollow area shaped like a bowl at the mouth of a volcano or geyser. **2.** A big hole, as one made by an explosion.
cra·ter (**krā′** tər) ◊ *noun, plural* **craters**

crave *verb* To want very much; desire: *The thirsty runners craved water.*
crave (krāv) ◊ *verb* **craved, craving**

craving *noun* A very strong desire; longing.
crav·ing (**krā′** vĭng) ◊ *noun, plural* **cravings**

crawfish *noun* A crayfish.
craw·fish (**krô′** fĭsh′) ◊ *noun, plural* **crawfish** *or* **crawfishes**

crawl *verb* **1.** To move slowly on the hands and knees; creep: *The baby crawled across the room.* **2.** To move slowly or with great effort: *The car could only crawl in the heavy traffic.*
◊ *noun* **1.** A very slow pace. **2.** A swimming stroke performed by alternately moving the arms down into the water and then pulling them up over the shoulder and kicking the feet rapidly.
crawl (krôl) ◊ *verb* **crawled, crawling** ◊ *noun, plural* **crawls**

crayfish *noun* A freshwater animal that looks like a lobster but is much smaller.
cray·fish (**krā′** fĭsh′) ◊ *noun, plural* **crayfish** *or* **crayfishes**

▲ **crayfish**

crayon *noun* A stick of colored wax, charcoal, or chalk used for drawing or writing.
◊ *verb* To draw or color with a crayon.
cray·on (**krā′** ŏn′ *or* **krā′** ən) ◊ *noun, plural* **crayons** ◊ *verb* **crayoned, crayoning**

craze *noun* Something that is very popular for a short time; fad.
craze (krāz) ◊ *noun, plural* **crazes**

crazy *adjective* **1.** Mentally ill; insane. **2.** Not sensible: *It's crazy to drive too fast.* —See Synonyms at **foolish. 3.** Full of enthusiasm; excited: *I'm crazy about oranges.*
cra·zy (**krā′** zē) ◊ *adjective* **crazier, craziest**

creak *verb* To make or move with a squeaking sound: *The rusty gate creaked.*
◊ *noun* A creaking sound.
creak (krēk) ◊ *verb* **creaked, creaking** ◊ *noun, plural* **creaks**

cream *noun* **1.** The yellowish fatty part of milk. Cream can be separated from milk and is used in cooking and to make butter. **2.** A cosmetic that looks like cream: *I used face cream for my chapped cheeks.* **3.** The best part: *The cream of society attended the opera.*
cream (krēm) ◊ *noun, plural* **creams**

creamy *adjective* **1.** Containing much cream. **2.** Like cream in richness, taste, or color.
cream·y (**krē′** mē) ◊ *adjective* **creamier, creamiest**

crease *noun* A mark or line, usually formed by wrinkling or folding: *When I unpacked the suitcase, the dress was full of creases.*
◊ *verb* To make a crease in or on: *I creased the dress when I put it in the suitcase.*
crease (krēs) ◊ *noun, plural* **creases** ◊ *verb* **creased, creasing**

create *verb* **1.** To bring into being: *Engineers created a new lake by building a dam over the stream.* **2.** To be the cause of; give rise to: *The story created happy feelings.*
cre·ate (krē āt′) ◊ *verb* **created, creating**

creation *noun* **1.** The act or process of creating: *The creation of a poem requires imagination.* **2.** Something that has been created.
cre·a·tion (krē ā′shən) ◊ *noun, plural* **creations**

creative *adjective* Having the ability to create things; having original ideas.
cre·a·tive (krē ā′tĭv) ◊ *adjective*

creature *noun* **1.** A living being, especially an animal. **2.** A human being; person.
crea·ture (krē′chər) ◊ *noun, plural* **creatures**

credit *noun* **1.** Belief or confidence in the truth of something; trust: *I gave full credit to what you told me.* **2.** Good name; reputation: *It is to their credit that they worked without complaining.* **3.** Approval or honor given in recognition of an action or quality: *They shared credit for the book's success.* **4.** A system of buying things and paying for them later.
◊ *verb* To accept the truth of; believe: *Will you credit my explanation for the delay?*
cred·it (krĕd′ĭt) ◊ *noun, plural* **credits** ◊ *verb* **credited, crediting**

creditable *adjective* Good enough to be praised; respectable: *I made a creditable effort to solve the problem.*
cred·it·a·ble (krĕd′ĭ tə bəl) ◊ *adjective*

credit card *noun* A card that entitles the holder to buy on credit.
credit card ◊ *noun, plural* **credit cards**

creditor *noun* A person to whom a debt is owed.
cred·i·tor (krĕd′ĭ tər) ◊ *noun, plural* **creditors**

creed *noun* **1.** A formal statement of the beliefs of a religious faith. **2.** A system of guiding beliefs or principles.
creed (krēd) ◊ *noun, plural* **creeds**

ă	pat	ĭ	pit	oi	oil	th	bath
ā	pay	ī	ride	ŏŏ	book	*th*	bathe
â	care	î	fierce	ōō	boot	ə	ago, item
ä	father	ŏ	pot	ou	out		pencil
ĕ	pet	ō	go	ŭ	cut		atom
ē	be	ô	paw, for	û	fur		circus

creek *noun* A small stream of water, often one that flows into a river.
creek (krēk *or* krĭk) ◊ *noun, plural* **creeks**

LANGUAGE DETECTIVE

creek

Imagine a line drawn across northern Virginia, West Virginia, and Kentucky. If you live south of this line, you probably pronounce *creek* so that it rhymes with *peek*. But what if you live north of the line? If you do, you might rhyme *creek* with *pick*. Or you might even use both pronunciations at different times, without thinking about it at all. Both pronunciations of *creek* are perfectly correct.

▲ **creek**

creep *verb* **1.** To move slowly with the body close to the ground: *The cat crept cautiously along.* **2.** To advance, move, or spread slowly, quietly, or timidly: *A reddish glow crept into my cheeks.* **3.** To grow along the ground or a surface: *Ivy crept up the walls.*
◊ *noun* **1.** A creeping motion. **2. the creeps** A feeling that things are crawling over the skin.
creep (krēp) ◊ *verb* **crept, creeping** ◊ *noun, plural* **creeps**

crepe *noun* A very thin pancake.
crepe (krāp) ◊ *noun, plural* **crepes**

crepe paper *noun* A thin crinkled or puckered paper used for decorations.

crept *verb* Past tense and past participle of **creep.**
crept (krĕpt) ◊ *verb*

crescent *noun* The shape of the moon as it appears in its first or last quarter, with curved edges ending in points.
◊ *adjective* Shaped like a crescent.
cres·cent (**krĕs′** ənt) ◊ *noun, plural* **crescents** ◊ *adjective*

crest *noun* **1.** A natural growth, as a tuft of feathers, on an animal's head. **2.** A plume of feathers or an ornament on top of a helmet. **3.** The top part of something, as of a mountain or wave. **4.** A design at the top of a coat of arms.
crest (krĕst) ◊ *noun, plural* **crests**

▲ **crest**

crevice *noun* A narrow opening; crack.
crev·ice (**krĕv′** ĭs) ◊ *noun, plural* **crevices**

crew *noun* **1.** The people who work together to operate a ship or aircraft. **2.** A group of people who work together.
crew (kro͞o) ◊ *noun, plural* **crews**

crib *noun* **1.** A small bed for a baby, with high sides. **2.** A small building for storing grain. **3.** A rack or manger from which cattle or horses eat.
crib (krĭb) ◊ *noun, plural* **cribs**

cricket[1] *noun* A small, grasshopperlike insect. The male makes a chirping sound by rubbing its front wings together.
crick·et[1] (**krĭk′** ĭt) ◊ *noun, plural* **crickets**

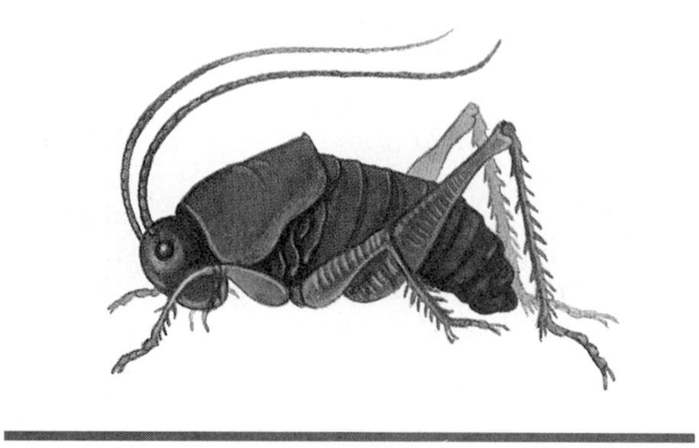

▲ **cricket[1]**

cricket[2] *noun* A game played by two teams of 11 players each, with bats, a ball, and wickets.
crick·et[2] (**krĭk′** ĭt) ◊ *noun*

***HISTORY* • cricket[1], cricket[2]**

Cricket[1] is from an old French word that imitated the sound this insect makes. **Cricket[2]** may come from this same French word, referring to the sound made when the bat hits the ball.

crime *noun* **1.** An action or a failure to act that is against the law. **2.** Unlawful activity in general: *The police fight crime.* **3.** A foolish or disgraceful act: *It's a crime to waste food.*
crime (krīm) ◊ *noun, plural* **crimes**

criminal *noun* A person who has committed a crime or been convicted of one.
◊ *adjective* **1.** Guilty of crime. **2.** Having to do with crime or its punishment: *Law students learn criminal law.*
crim·i·nal (**krĭm′** ə nəl) ◊ *noun, plural* **criminals** ◊ *adjective*

crimson *noun* A purplish red color.
crim·son (**krĭm′** zən) ◊ *noun*

cringe *verb* To shrink back, as in fear: *We cringed whenever the bully came near us.*
cringe (krĭnj) ◊ *verb* **cringed, cringing**

crinkle *verb* **1.** To make or become wrinkled or creased: *Your eyes crinkled merrily at the corners.* **2.** To make a soft, crackling sound; rustle.
crin·kle (**krĭng′** kəl) ◊ *verb* **crinkled, crinkling**

cripple *noun* A person who cannot move normally, as because of injury to a leg.
◊ *verb* **1.** To make into a cripple. **2.** To make useless or helpless; disable: *The storm crippled the ship.*
crip·ple (**krĭp′** əl) ◊ *noun, plural* **cripples** ◊ *verb* **crippled, crippling**

crises *noun* Plural of **crisis.**
cri·ses (**krī′** sēz′) ◊ *noun*

crisis *noun* **1.** A time in the course of something, especially an illness, when there is an important change for the better or for the worse; turning point. **2.** A time of great difficulty or danger when great changes can take place.
cri·sis (**krī′** sĭs) ◊ *noun, plural* **crises**

crisp *adjective* **1.** Firm but easily broken, as fried bacon. **2.** Fresh and firm; not wilted: *Lettuce stays crisp if it's kept cool.* **3.** Cool and refreshing; brisk: *A crisp fall breeze rustled the dry leaves.* **4.** Brief and clear: *"Turn left here" was my crisp order to the driver.*
crisp (krĭsp) ◊ *adjective* **crisper, crispest**

crisscross *verb* **1.** To mark with or form a pattern of crossing lines: *Animal trails crisscross the woods.* **2.** To move back and forth across: *Ships crisscrossed the sea.*
◊ *noun* A pattern of crossing lines.
criss·cross (**krĭs′**krôs′) ◊ *verb* **crisscrossed, crisscrossing** ◊ *noun, plural* **crisscrosses**

critic *noun* **1.** A person whose work is judging the value of books, plays, or other artistic efforts. **2.** A person who finds fault.
crit·ic (**krĭt′**ĭk) ◊ *noun, plural* **critics**

critical *adjective* **1.** Of or relating to a critic or criticism: *Edgar Allan Poe, a famous author, wrote many critical essays.* **2.** Tending to criticize; finding fault: *You're always critical of what I wear.* **3.** Of, being, or relating to a crisis: *The patient is in critical condition.*
crit·i·cal (**krĭt′**ĭ kəl) ◊ *adjective*

criticism *noun* **1.** The act of criticizing. **2.** An expression of an unfavorable opinion: *I accepted your criticism of my behavior.*
crit·i·cism (**krĭt′**ĭ sĭz′əm) ◊ *noun, plural* **criticisms**

criticize *verb* To judge the good and bad qualities of; evaluate.
crit·i·cize (**krĭt′**ĭ sīz′) ◊ *verb* **criticized, criticizing**

croak *noun* A low, hoarse sound, such as that made by a frog or a crow.
◊ *verb* To make this sound or a sound like it.
croak (krōk) ◊ *noun, plural* **croaks** ◊ *verb* **croaked, croaking**

crochet *verb* To make a piece of needlework by looping thread or yarn into connected links with a hooked needle.
cro·chet (krō **shā′**) ◊ *verb* **crocheted, crocheting**

ă	pat	ĭ	pit	oi	**oil**	th	**bath**
ā	pay	ī	ride	o͝o	book	*th*	**bathe**
â	care	î	fierce	o͞o	boot	ə	ago, item
ä	father	ŏ	pot	ou	**out**		pencil
ĕ	pet	ō	**go**	ŭ	cut		atom
ē	be	ô	paw, for	û	fur		circus

crocodile *noun* A large reptile with thick skin, sharp teeth, and long, narrow jaws.
croc·o·dile (**krŏk′**ə dīl′) ◊ *noun, plural* **crocodiles**

▲ **crocodile**

crocus *noun* A low-growing garden plant with flowers that bloom early in spring.
cro·cus (**krō′**kəs) ◊ *noun, plural* **crocuses**

crony *noun* A close friend or companion.
cro·ny (**krō′**nē) ◊ *noun, plural* **cronies**

crook *noun* **1.** A bent or curved part of something: *I held a bag of groceries in the crook of my arm.* **2.** A long staff with a curved end. **3.** A dishonest person.
◊ *verb* To bend or curve.
crook (kro͝ok) ◊ *noun, plural* **crooks** ◊ *verb* **crooked, crooking**

crooked *adjective* **1.** Not straight. **2.** Dishonest: *Don't deal with crooked people.*
crook·ed (**kro͝ok′**ĭd) ◊ *adjective*

croon *verb* To sing or hum softly.
croon (kro͞on) ◊ *verb* **crooned, crooning**

crop *noun* **1.** A plant or plant product that is grown and harvested: *Corn and soybeans are important farm crops.* **2.** The amount of such a product grown or gathered; harvest: *There was a record wheat crop last year.* **3.** A short whip used in horseback riding. **4.** A pouch in the neck of a bird, where food is stored and partially digested.
◊ *verb* To remove the tops or outer parts of: *Goats had cropped the grass.*
◊ *idiom* **crop up** To appear unexpectedly; turn up: *Several problems cropped up at once.*
crop (krŏp) ◊ *noun, plural* **crops** ◊ *verb* **cropped, cropping**

croquet *noun* A lawn game in which each player uses a mallet to hit a wooden ball through a series of hoops.
cro·quet (krō **kā′**) ◊ *noun*

cross *noun* **1.** An upright post with a horizontal piece near the top. **2. Cross** The cross on which Christ died, or a picture or imitation of it. **3.** An emblem or medal in the shape of a cross. **4.** A mark like this (X), formed by two lines that meet and pass beyond each other. **5.** Trouble that tests a person's strength or goodness. **6.** Something produced by mixing breeds or kinds: *A mule is a cross between a horse and a donkey.*
◊ *verb* **1.** To go to the other side of: *Let's cross the street. The bridge crosses the river.* **2.** To lie or go across; intersect: *Elm Street and Main Street cross in the middle of town.* **3.** To place one over the other: *Cross your legs.* **4.** To draw a line across: *Don't forget to cross your t's.* **5.** To mark out or cancel by drawing lines through: *Cross my name off the list.* **6.** To pass while going in opposite directions: *Our letters crossed in the mail.* **7.** To breed an animal or plant with one of another kind.
◊ *adjective* **1.** Placed so as to cross something else: *We turned into a cross street.* **2.** In a bad mood; grumpy. —See Synonyms at **irritable.**
cross (krôs) ◊ *noun, plural* **crosses** ◊ *verb* **crossed, crossing** ◊ *adjective* **crosser, crossest**

crossbar *noun* A horizontal bar or stripe.
cross·bar (**krôs′**bär′) ◊ *noun, plural* **crossbars**

crossbones *plural noun* Two bones placed crosswise, usually under a skull, used as a symbol of death or a warning of danger.
cross·bones (**krôs′**bōnz′) ◊ *plural noun*

crossbow *noun* A weapon for shooting arrows made of a bow fixed on a wooden stock. There are grooves on the stock to direct the arrow.
cross·bow (**krôs′**bō′) ◊ *noun, plural* **crossbows**

▲ **crossbones**

cross-eyed *adjective* Having one or both eyes turn in toward the nose.
cross-eyed (**krôs′**īd′) ◊ *adjective*

crossing *noun* **1.** A place where a street or railroad may be crossed. **2.** An intersection.
cross·ing (**krô′**sĭng) ◊ *noun, plural* **crossings**

crosspiece *noun* A piece, as of wood, that is placed across something else.
cross·piece (**krôs′**pēs′) ◊ *noun, plural* **crosspieces**

cross-reference *noun* A note directing the reader from one part of a book, index, or list to another part that has further information.
cross-ref·er·ence (**krôs′ rĕf′** ər əns) ◊ *noun, plural* **cross-references**

crossroad *noun* **1.** A road that crosses another road. **2. crossroads** (*used with a singular or plural verb*) A place, usually in the countryside, where two or more roads meet.
cross·road (**krŏs′**rōd′) ◊ *noun, plural* **crossroads**

cross section *noun* **1.** A straight cut or slice through a solid object, often made to find out the structure or contents of the object: *A cross section of the tree trunk showed its rings of growth.* **2.** A picture or drawing of such a cut. **3.** A representative sample of something meant to be typical of the whole: *The show appeals to a large cross section of the people.*
cross section ◊ *noun, plural* **cross sections**

crosswalk *noun* A specially marked path for people walking across a street.
cross·walk (**krôs′**wôk′) ◊ *noun, plural* **crosswalks**

crosswise *adverb* So as to cross something: *The wind blew crosswise as we paddled.*
cross·wise (**krôs′**wīz′) ◊ *adverb*

crossword puzzle *noun* A puzzle in which words are fitted into a pattern of numbered squares, one letter to a square.
cross·word puzzle (**krôs′**wûrd′) ◊ *noun, plural* **crossword puzzles**

crotch *noun* A point where a branch grows out from a tree.
crotch (krŏch) ◊ *noun, plural* **crotches**

crouch *verb* To lower the body and keep the arms and legs close; squat.
◊ *noun* The act or posture of crouching.
crouch (krouch) ◊ *verb* **crouched, crouching** ◊ *noun, plural* **crouches**

crow[1] *noun* A large black bird with a harsh, hoarse call.
crow[1] (krō) ◊ *noun, plural* **crows**

crow[2] *noun* **1.** The loud, high-pitched cry of a rooster. **2.** A loud cry of delight or victory.
◊ *verb* **1.** To utter the loud cry of a rooster. **2.** To utter a cry of delight or victory. —See Synonyms at **boast.**
crow[2] (krō) ◊ *noun, plural* **crows** ◊ *verb* **crowed, crowing**

***HISTORY* • crow[1], crow[2]**

Crow[1] and **crow[2]** come from two related old English words. **Crow[2]** was probably a word made to imitate the sound it describes. The **crow[1]** would then be a bird that makes this sound.

crowbar *noun* A straight metal bar that is slightly bent at one end. Crowbars are used to lift or pry up objects.
crow·bar (**krō′** bär′) ◊ *noun, plural* **crowbars**

crowd *noun* **1.** A large number of people gathered together: *A crowd waited for the train.* **2.** People in general: *I do what I want to do; I don't follow the crowd.*
◊ *verb* **1.** To fill with many people or things: *Shoppers crowded the store.* **2.** To press tightly; cram: *We crowded more books onto the shelf.*
crowd (kroud) ◊ *noun, plural* **crowds** ◊ *verb* **crowded, crowding**

crown *noun* **1.** A head covering, often made of gold set with jewels. A crown is worn by a king or queen as a symbol of ruling power. **2.** The authority or government of a king or queen: *The colonists owed taxes to the crown.* **3.** A wreath worn on the head as a mark of victory, honor, or position: *The marathon winner was given a crown of laurel.* **4.** A top part. **5.** The part of a tooth that sticks out above the gums or an artificial substitute for it. **6.** A championship title.
◊ *verb* **1.** To place a crown on the head of, thus officially making a person king or queen: *British monarchs are crowned in Westminster Abbey.* **2.** To declare to be the winner or victor in a ceremony: *The winning driver was crowned champion after the race.* **3.** To cover the top of: *Snow crowned the mountains.*
crown (kroun) ◊ *noun, plural* **crowns** ◊ *verb* **crowned, crowning**

crow's-nest *noun* A small lookout platform near the top of a ship's mast.
crow's-nest (**krōz′** nĕst′) ◊ *noun, plural* **crow's-nests**

▲ **crow's-nest**

crude *adjective* **1.** In a natural state; raw: *Crude oil is piped from wells to refineries.* **2.** Not made with skill or care; rough: *The plastic flower was a crude imitation of the real thing.* **3.** Lacking good manners.
crude (kro͞od) ◊ *adjective* **cruder, crudest**

cruel *adjective* **1.** Liking to cause pain or suffering; unkind. **2.** Causing suffering; painful: *A cruel wind blew into our faces.*
cru·el (**kro͞o′** əl) ◊ *adjective* **crueler, cruelest**

cruelty *noun* **1.** The quality or condition of being cruel. **2.** A cruel act or remark.
cru·el·ty (**kro͞o′** əl tē) ◊ *noun, plural* **cruelties**

cruise *verb* **1.** To sail or travel about in an unhurried way: *A boat was cruising near the coast.* **2.** To drive about in an area without having a definite destination: *The police car cruised the neighborhood.* **3.** To run a vehicle at a high, efficient speed.
◊ *noun* A sea voyage for pleasure.
cruise (kro͞oz) ◊ *verb* **cruised, cruising** ◊ *noun, plural* **cruises**

ă	pat	ĭ	pit	oi	**oi**l	th	ba**th**
ā	pay	ī	ride	o͝o	b**oo**k	*th*	ba**th**e
â	care	î	fierce	o͞o	b**oo**t	ə	**a**go, it**e**m
ä	father	ŏ	pot	ou	**ou**t		penc**i**l
ĕ	pet	ō	**g**o	ŭ	c**u**t		at**o**m
ē	be	ô	paw, for	û	f**u**r		circ**u**s

cruiser *noun* **1.** A medium-sized, fast warship that has less armor and less powerful guns than a battleship. **2.** A large motorboat with a cabin equipped with living facilities. **3.** A police car.
cruis·er (**kroo͞′** zər) ◊ *noun, plural* **cruisers**

crumb *noun* A tiny piece of food, especially of bread or cake.
crumb (krŭm) ◊ *noun, plural* **crumbs**

crumble *verb* To break or fall into small pieces or crumbs.
crum·ble (**krŭm′** bəl) ◊ *verb* **crumbled, crumbling**

crumple *verb* **1.** To crush so as to form creases or wrinkles: *Take care not to crumple your shirt.* **2.** To fall down.
crum·ple (**krŭm′** pəl) ◊ *verb* **crumpled, crumpling**

crunch *verb* **1.** To grind or crush with a noisy or cracking sound; chew noisily. **2.** To make a crushing or cracking sound: *The snow crunched under my boots.*
◊ *noun* The act or sound of crunching.
crunch (krŭnch) ◊ *verb* **crunched, crunching** ◊ *noun, plural* **crunches**

crusade *noun* **1.** Often **Crusade** Any of a series of military expeditions that European Christians made in the eleventh, twelfth, and thirteenth centuries to take the Holy Land from the Moslems. **2.** A strong campaign for a reform or cause: *The citizens launched a crusade against crime.*
◊ *verb* To take part in a crusade: *We crusaded for equal rights.*
cru·sade (kroo͞ **sād′**) ◊ *noun, plural* **crusades** ◊ *verb* **crusaded, crusading**

crusader *noun* A person who takes part in a crusade.
cru·sad·er (kroo͞ **sā′** dər) ◊ *noun, plural* **crusaders**

crush *verb* **1.** To press, squeeze, or bear down on with enough force to break or injure: *The tree fell on the car and crushed it.* **2.** To grind or pound into very fine particles: *This machine crushes rocks into powder.* **3.** To crumple; wrinkle: *Don't crush your suit.* **4.** To put down; subdue.
◊ *noun* **1.** A crowd of people. **2.** A strong, sudden liking for someone.
crush (krŭsh) ◊ *verb* **crushed, crushing** ◊ *noun, plural* **crushes**

crust *noun* **1.** The hard outer layer of bread. **2.** The shell of a pastry. **3.** A hard outer layer or covering: *The earth's crust is between 5 and 25 miles thick.*
◊ *verb* To cover or be covered with a crust.
crust (krŭst) ◊ *noun, plural* **crusts** ◊ *verb* **crusted, crusting**

crustacean *noun* Any of a group of animals that live mostly in water and have a hard outer covering. Lobsters, crabs, and shrimps are crustaceans.
crus·ta·cean (krŭ **stā′** shən) ◊ *noun, plural* **crustaceans**

▲ **crustacean**
Lobsters, crabs, and shrimps are kinds of crustaceans.

crutch *noun* A support used by injured or disabled persons as an aid in walking. A crutch usually is a stick with a padded crosspiece at the top that fits under the arm.
crutch (krŭch) ◊ *noun, plural* **crutches**

cry *verb* **1.** To shed tears; weep. **2.** To call loudly; shout. **3.** To utter a special sound or call, as an animal does.
◊ *noun* **1.** A fit of weeping. **2.** A loud call; shout. **3.** A loud sound that expresses a strong emotion: *With a cry of delight, I found the puppy.* **4.** The special sound or call of an animal: *Do you hear the cries of the gulls?*
cry (krī) ◊ *verb* **cried, crying** ◊ *noun, plural* **cries**

crystal *noun* **1.** A solid piece of matter that has a regular arrangement of flat surfaces and angles between the surfaces. Water vapor forms ice crystals, or snow. **2.** A piece of a transparent mineral, as quartz, with a regular arrangement of flat surfaces and angles.

3. Glass that is clear, colorless, and of high quality. **4.** A clear cover that protects the face of a watch or clock.
crys·tal (krĭs′ təl) ◊ *noun, plural* **crystals**

crystalline *adjective* Of or like crystal.
crys·tal·line (krĭs′ tə lĭn) ◊ *adjective*

crystallize *verb* To form or cause to form crystals.
crys·tal·lize (krĭs′ tə līz′) ◊ *verb* **crystallized, crystallizing**

CT The abbreviation for *Connecticut* used with a Zip Code.

cu. The abbreviation for *cubic.*

cub *noun* A young bear, wolf, or lion.
cub (kŭb) ◊ *noun, plural* **cubs**

Cuban *noun* A person who was born in or lives in Cuba.
◊ *adjective* Of or relating to Cuba or the Cubans.
Cu·ban (kyo͞o′ bən) ◊ *noun, plural* **Cubans** ◊ *adjective*

cube *noun* **1.** A solid figure having six square faces of equal size that meet at right angles. **2.** Something having this shape. **3.** The result of multiplying a number by itself twice. The cube of 3 is $3 \times 3 \times 3 = 27$.
◊ *verb* **1.** To form the cube of a number. **2.** To cut or form into cubes.
cube (kyo͞ob) ◊ *noun, plural* **cubes** ◊ *verb* **cubed, cubing**

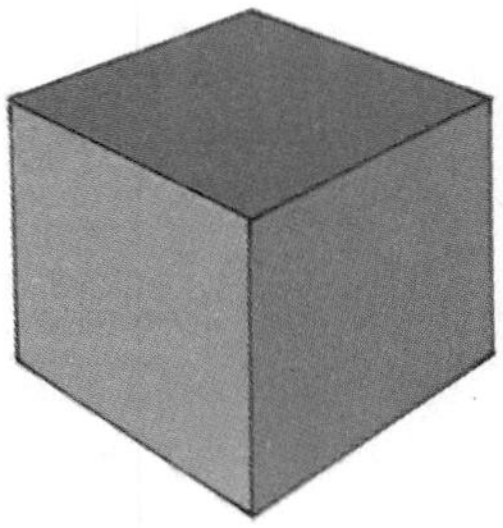
▲ **cube**

cubic *adjective* **1.** Of or relating to a cube; having width, length, and thickness. **2.** Shaped like a cube. **3.** Being a unit that measures the volume of something. A cubic foot is a foot long, a foot wide, and a foot deep.
cu·bic (kyo͞o′ bĭk) ◊ *adjective*

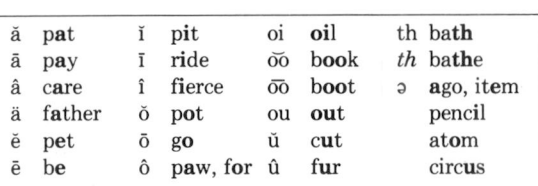

ă	pat	ĭ	pit	oi	**oil**	th	ba**th**
ā	pay	ī	ride	o͝o	**book**	*th*	ba**the**
â	care	î	fierce	o͞o	**boot**	ə	ago, item
ä	father	ŏ	pot	ou	**out**		pencil
ĕ	pet	ō	go	ŭ	cut		atom
ē	be	ô	paw, for	û	fur		circus

cuckoo *noun* **1.** A European bird with grayish feathers and a call that sounds like its name. This bird lays its eggs in the nests of other birds. **2.** An American bird that is related to the European one. The American cuckoo builds its own nests and its call is less like the sound of its name.
cuck·oo (ko͞o′ ko͞o) ◊ *noun, plural* **cuckoos**

cucumber *noun* A long vegetable with green skin and white, watery flesh.
cu·cum·ber (kyo͞o′ kŭm′bər) ◊ *noun, plural* **cucumbers**

cud *noun* Food that has been swallowed by a cow, sheep, or other animal, and then brought up to the mouth for chewing.
cud (kŭd) ◊ *noun, plural* **cuds**

cuddle *verb* **1.** To hold tenderly and close. **2.** To nestle; snuggle: *The kittens cuddled in the big chair.*
cud·dle (kŭd′ l) ◊ *verb* **cuddled, cuddling**

cue[1] *noun* **1.** A word or signal given to remind a performer to begin a speech or movement. **2.** A reminder or suggestion; hint.
◊ *verb* To give a cue: *The band director cued the drums to begin.*
cue[1] (kyo͞o) ◊ *noun, plural* **cues** ◊ *verb* **cued, cuing**
‖*These sound alike:* **cue, queue**

cue[2] *noun* A long, tapering stick used to strike a ball in the game of pool.
cue[2] (kyo͞o) ◊ *noun, plural* **cues**
‖*These sound alike:* **cue, queue**

***HISTORY* • cue**[1]**, cue**[2]

The origin of **cue**[1] is unknown. **Cue**[2] comes from an old French word that came from a Latin word meaning "tail." The long, tapering shape of a pool cue must have reminded people of a tail.

cuff *noun* A band or fold of cloth at the bottom of a sleeve or a trouser leg.
cuff (kŭf) ◊ *noun, plural* **cuffs**

culprit *noun* A person who is guilty of a crime or wrongdoing.
cul·prit (kŭl′ prĭt) ◊ *noun, plural* **culprits**

cultivate *verb* **1.** To prepare and care for land for the raising of crops: *The farmer cultivated the field by plowing it and adding fertilizer.* **2.** To grow and tend: *I cultivate geraniums in*

my garden. **3.** To develop by study or teaching: *The teacher tries to cultivate a love of music in the children.*
cul·ti·vate (kŭl′tə vāt′) ◊ *verb* **cultivated, cultivating**

cultivation *noun* The process of cultivating the soil or a crop.
cul·ti·va·tion (kŭl′tə vā′shən) ◊ *noun*

cultivator *noun* A tool or machine for loosening the earth and destroying weeds around growing plants.
cul·ti·va·tor (kŭl′tə vā′tər) ◊ *noun, plural* **cultivators**

cultural *adjective* Having to do with culture: *The college presents concerts, art exhibits, film festivals, and other cultural events.*
cul·tur·al (kŭl′chər əl) ◊ *adjective*

culture *noun* **1.** The customs, beliefs, laws, ways of living, and all other results of human work and thought that belong to a people: *In most Native American cultures, all land is thought of as common property.* **2.** The qualities of mind and the manners and tastes that result from learning about the arts, sciences, and history; education and refinement: *Our teacher is a person of great culture who speaks three languages, plays the violin, and paints well.* **3.** Development of the mind or body through special training. **4.** The raising of animals or crops. **5.** The growing of living cells or microscopic organisms in a laboratory for medical study.
cul·ture (kŭl′chər) ◊ *noun, plural* **cultures**

culvert *noun* A drain crossing under a road.
cul·vert (kŭl′vərt) ◊ *noun, plural* **culverts**

cumbersome *adjective* Awkward to carry, wear, or manage: *We left our cumbersome baggage at the hotel.*
cum·ber·some (kŭm′bər səm) ◊ *adjective*

cunning *adjective* Clever in deceiving or gaining an advantage; sly.
◊ *noun* The quality or condition of being sly.
cun·ning (kŭn′ĭng) ◊ *adjective* ◊ *noun*

cup *noun* **1.** A small, open container, usually with a handle. Cups are used for drinking liquids. **2.** The contents of a cup: *Would you like a cup of orange juice?* **3.** A unit of capacity used in cooking equal to 16 tablespoons or ½ pint. **4.** Something shaped like a cup: *The robin's nest is a cup of twigs and grass.*
◊ *verb* To shape like a cup: *I cupped my hand behind my ear to hear better.*
cup (kŭp) ◊ *noun, plural* **cups** ◊ *verb* **cupped, cupping**

cupboard *noun* A cabinet, usually with shelves, for storing food or dishes.
cup·board (kŭb′ərd) ◊ *noun, plural* **cupboards**

cupcake *noun* A small cake baked in a cup-shaped container.
cup·cake (kŭp′kāk′) ◊ *noun, plural* **cupcakes**

cupful *noun* The amount a cup will hold.
cup·ful (kŭp′fo͝ol′) ◊ *noun, plural* **cupfuls**

cupola *noun* **1.** A rounded roof; dome. **2.** A small structure built on top of a roof.
cu·po·la (kyo͞o′pə lə) ◊ *noun, plural* **cupolas**

▲ **cupola**

cur *noun* A dog of mixed breed; mongrel.
cur (kûr) ◊ *noun, plural* **curs**

curate *noun* A member of the clergy who assists in a church.
cu·rate (kyo͝or′ĭt) ◊ *noun, plural* **curates**

curb *noun* **1.** A concrete or stone rim along the edge of a sidewalk or road. **2.** Something that stops or holds back.
◊ *verb* To hold back; control: *Can you curb your appetite until dinner?*
curb (kûrb) ◊ *noun, plural* **curbs** ◊ *verb* **curbed, curbing**

curd *noun* The thick part of milk that separates from the watery part when it turns sour. Curds are used to make cheese.
curd (kûrd) ◊ *noun, plural* **curds**

curdle *verb* To form or cause to form into curds: *Add vinegar until the milk curdles.*
cur·dle (kûr′dl) ◊ *verb* **curdled, curdling**

cure *noun* **1.** A medical treatment or a medicine that makes a sick person get better: *Rest and good food may be a cure for your cold.* **2.** A return to good health.
◊ *verb* **1.** To bring back to good health. **2.** To prepare or preserve by using a special process: *They cured the meat by smoking it.*
cure (kyo͝or) ◊ *noun, plural* **cures** ◊ *verb* **cured, curing**

curfew *noun* **1.** A rule requiring people to be off the streets and indoors by a certain time at night. **2.** The time by which people have to be off the streets and indoors.
cur·few (**kûr′**fyo͞o) ◊ *noun, plural* **curfews**

HISTORY **• curfew**

Curfew comes from an old French phrase meaning "cover fire." At curfew time, people were supposed to put out their cooking and heating fires. This was to prevent houses from catching fire while people were asleep.

curiosity *noun* **1.** A desire to know or learn: *We burned with curiosity over what was in the box.* **2.** Something unusual, strange, or rare: *The old wooden skis are a curiosity.*
cu·ri·os·i·ty (kyo͝or′ē **ŏs′**ĭ tē) ◊ *noun, plural* **curiosities**

curious *adjective* **1.** Eager to find out about something: *I was curious, so I opened the mysterious door and peeked in.* **2.** Interesting because of being unusual or remarkable; odd: *Australia is the home of such curious animals as the kangaroo and the platypus.*
cu·ri·ous (**kyo͝or′**ē əs) ◊ *adjective*

curl *verb* **1.** To twist into or form ringlets. **2.** To move in a spiral: *Smoke curled from the chimney.*
◊ *noun* **1.** A ring or coil of hair. **2.** Something with a spiral shape.
curl (kûrl) ◊ *verb* **curled, curling** ◊ *noun, plural* **curls**

ă	pat	ĭ	pit	oi	oil	th	bath
ā	pay	ī	ride	o͝o	book	*th*	bathe
â	care	î	fierce	o͞o	boot	ə	ago, item
ä	father	ŏ	pot	ou	out		pencil
ĕ	pet	ō	go	ŭ	cut		atom
ē	be	ô	paw, for	û	fur		circus

curly *adjective* Having curls or tending to curl.
curl·y (**kûr′**lē) ◊ *adjective* **curlier, curliest**

currant *noun* **1.** The small, sour, red or blackish berry that grows on a prickly shrub. Currants are used for making jelly. **2.** A seedless raisin, used mainly in baking.
cur·rant (**kûr′**ənt) ◊ *noun, plural* **currants**
‖*These sound alike:* **currant, current**

▲ **currant**

currency *noun* The form of money in actual use in a country: *My parents' wallets hold both credit cards and currency.*
cur·ren·cy (**kûr′**ən sē) ◊ *noun, plural* **currencies**

current *adjective* Belonging to the present time: *Newspapers and weekly magazines report on current events.*
◊ *noun* **1.** A mass of liquid or gas that is in motion: *We paddled the canoe into the current of the river.* **2.** A flow of electricity.
cur·rent (**kûr′**ənt) ◊ *adjective* ◊ *noun, plural* **currents**
‖*These sound alike:* **current, currant**

currently *adverb* At the present time; now: *That movie is currently showing.*
cur·rent·ly (**kûr′**ənt lē) ◊ *adverb*

curse *noun* **1.** An appeal for evil or harm to come to someone. **2.** A word or group of words expressing great hatred or anger; oath. **3.** Something that causes great evil or harm: *One of the greatest human curses is poverty.*
◊ *verb* **1.** To wish harm to; place a curse on. **2.** To trouble greatly: *Bad weather cursed the explorers from the start.* **3.** To use angry or violent words; swear.
curse (kûrs) ◊ *noun, plural* **curses** ◊ *verb* **cursed, cursing**

cursor *noun* An indicator often shaped like a square or triangle that appears on a computer screen to show the position where information is to be entered. A cursor may or may not flash.
cur·sor (**kûr′**sər) ◊ *noun, plural* **cursors**

curt *adjective* Rudely impatient and short.
curt (kûrt) ◊ *adjective* **curter, curtest**

curtail *verb* To cut short; reduce: *We must curtail our spending.*
cur·tail (kər tāl′) ◊ *verb* **curtailed, curtailing**

curtain *noun* **1.** A piece of material hanging in a window or other opening. **2.** Something that acts as a screen or cover: *A thick curtain of fog hid the mountain from view.*
cur·tain (kûr′tn) ◊ *noun, plural* **curtains**

curtsy *noun* A bow made by women and girls as a sign of respect. To make a curtsy, you keep one foot forward and lower the body by bending the knees.
◊ *verb* To make a curtsy.
curt·sy (kûrt′sē) ◊ *noun, plural* **curtsies** ◊ *verb* **curtsied, curtsying**

▲ **curtsy**

curvature *noun* The act of curving or the condition of being curved.
cur·va·ture (kûr′və chər) ◊ *noun, plural* **curvatures**

curve *noun* **1.** A line or surface that keeps bending smoothly without sharp angles. **2.** Something shaped like a curve: *The astronauts saw the curve of the earth.*
◊ *verb* To move in or take the shape of a curve: *The road curves sharply just ahead.*
curve (kûrv) ◊ *noun, plural* **curves** ◊ *verb* **curved, curving**

cushion *noun* **1.** A pad or pillow with a soft filling, that is used to sit, lie, or rest on. **2.** Something that softens an impact or blow: *Use a towel as a cushion for your knees when waxing the floor.*
◊ *verb* **1.** To furnish with a cushion. **2.** To lessen the force of: *Snow cushioned my fall.*
cush·ion (ko͝osh′ən) ◊ *noun, plural* **cushions** ◊ *verb* **cushioned, cushioning**

custard *noun* A dessert of milk, sugar, eggs, and flavoring that is similar to pudding.
cus·tard (kŭs′tərd) ◊ *noun, plural* **custards**

custodian *noun* **1.** A person who looks after and protects something; caretaker. **2.** A person who takes care of a building; janitor.
cus·to·di·an (kŭ stō′dē ən) ◊ *noun, plural* **custodians**

custody *noun* **1.** The right or duty to take care of and have control over: *Parents have custody of their children.* **2.** The condition of being arrested or held under guard: *The suspect is still in custody.*
cus·to·dy (kŭs′tə dē) ◊ *noun*

custom *noun* **1.** Something that the members of a group usually do: *Shaking hands when meeting someone is an ancient custom.* **2.** Something that a person regularly does; habit: *Our custom is to vacation in July.*
◊ *adjective* Made especially according to a buyer's needs or instructions.
cus·tom (kŭs′təm) ◊ *noun, plural* **customs** ◊ *adjective*

customary *adjective* According to custom or habit; usual: *This is my customary seat.*
cus·tom·ar·y (kŭs′tə mĕr′ē) ◊ *adjective*

customer *noun* A person who regularly buys goods or services.
cus·tom·er (kŭs′tə mər) ◊ *noun, plural* **customers**

customs *noun* (*used with a singular verb*) A tax that must be paid on goods brought in from another country.
cus·toms (kŭs′təmz) ◊ *noun*

cut *verb* **1.** To go through or into with a sharp edge; pierce or wound: *I cut my hand on the broken glass. The cold wind cut through me like a knife.* **2.** To form, separate, or divide by using a sharp instrument: *We cut cloth for new shirts.* **3.** To allow penetration or separation, as with a sharp instrument: *Butter cuts easily.* **4.** To be able to penetrate or separate easily: *This knife does not cut well.* **5.** To shorten or trim: *I cut the grass every week.* **6.** To grow teeth through the gums: *The baby*

cut two new teeth. **7.** To stop or interrupt: *Electric power was cut for two hours.* **8.** To reduce the size or amount of: *Please don't cut my allowance.* **9.** To get rid of; remove: *We cut the last scene from the play.* **10.** To be absent from on purpose: *If you cut your classes, you may fail.*
◊ *noun* **1.** The result of cutting; a slit, gash, or wound: *The cut on my hand is healing well.* **2.** A piece that has been cut off: *This is a fine cut of meat.* **3.** A reduction: *The workers had to take a cut in pay.* **4.** The style in which something is cut, as clothes or gems.
cut (kŭt) ◊ *verb* **cut, cutting** ◊ *noun, plural* **cuts**

SYNONYMS
cut, carve, chop
We *cut* the paper in two pieces. I *carved* a ship out of a piece of wood. We *chopped* down the tree with an ax.

cute *adjective* Very pretty or charming.
cute (kyo͞ot) ◊ *adjective* **cuter, cutest**

cuticle *noun* **1.** The outer layer of skin. **2.** The strip of hardened skin at the base of a fingernail or toenail.
cu·ti·cle (**kyo͞o′** tĭ kəl) ◊ *noun, plural* **cuticles**

cutlass *noun* A sword with a curved blade.
cut·lass (**kŭt′** ləs) ◊ *noun, plural* **cutlasses**

cutter *noun* **1.** A person who cuts material, such as cloth, glass, or diamonds. **2.** A device for cutting: *Cookie cutters come in many shapes.* **3.** A small, lightly armed boat used by the Coast Guard.
cut·ter (**kŭt′** ər) ◊ *noun, plural* **cutters**

cutting *noun* A part of a plant, such as a leaf or stem, used to grow a new plant.
◊ *adjective* Used for cutting: *Scissors are cutting tools.*
cut·ting (**kŭt′** ĭng) ◊ *noun, plural* **cuttings** ◊ *adjective*

ă	pat	ĭ	pit	oi	oil	th	bath
ā	pay	ī	ride	o͝o	book	*th*	bathe
â	care	î	fierce	o͞o	boot	ə	ago, item
ä	father	ŏ	pot	ou	out		pencil
ĕ	pet	ō	go	ŭ	cut		atom
ē	be	ô	paw, for	û	fur		circus

cycle *noun* **1.** A series of events that is regularly repeated in the same order. **2.** The period of time during which a regularly repeated series of events is completed: *Summer turns to fall in the yearly cycle of the seasons.*
◊ *verb* **1.** To occur in or pass through a cycle. **2.** To ride a bicycle or motorcycle.
cy·cle (**sī′** kəl) ◊ *noun, plural* **cycles** ◊ *verb* **cycled, cycling**

cyclist *noun* A person who rides a bicycle or motorcycle.
cy·clist (**sī′** klĭst) ◊ *noun, plural* **cyclists**

cyclone *noun* **1.** A mass of air that turns rapidly around a center of low pressure, usually bringing rain and strong winds. **2.** A violent windstorm, such as a tornado.
cy·clone (**sī′** klōn′) ◊ *noun, plural* **cyclones**

cylinder *noun* A hollow or solid object shaped like a tube or pipe. The ends of a cylinder are parallel circles of equal size.
cyl·in·der (**sĭl′** ən dər) ◊ *noun, plural* **cylinders**

cylindrical *adjective* Having the shape of a cylinder.
cy·lin·dri·cal (sə **lĭn′** drĭ kəl) ◊ *adjective*

cymbal *noun* One of a pair of brass plates that are hit together as musical percussion instruments.
cym·bal (**sĭm′** bəl) ◊ *noun, plural* **cymbals**
‖ *These sound alike:* **cymbal, symbol**

▲ **cymbal**

cypress *noun* **1.** An evergreen tree that grows in warm regions and has small, scalelike needles, hard wood, and cones. **2.** A similar, related tree that grows in swamps and sheds its needles each year.
cy·press (**sī′** prəs) ◊ *noun, plural* **cypresses**

czar *noun* One of the emperors who ruled Russia before the revolution in 1917.
czar (zär) ◊ *noun, plural* **czars**

czarina *noun* The wife of a Russian czar.
cza·ri·na (zä **rē′** nə) ◊ *noun, plural* **czarinas**

Dalmatian

Dd

D is the fourth letter of the English alphabet. Did you know that it has a long history?

Over 3,500 years ago, people in the Middle East were using symbols that became the letters of our alphabet. This ancient Middle Eastern symbol is a form of the letter that became our letter *D*.

Δ

The ancient Greeks borrowed their alphabet from people in the Middle East. Here is a form of the Greek letter that became our letter *D*.

D

The ancient Romans borrowed their alphabet from a people who had taken their own letter symbols from the Greeks. Here is a form of the Roman letter *D* that was used for carving letters into stone. These letters became the model for our printed capital letters.

d

As people wrote quickly, especially with pens, the capital letters began to take the shapes of small letters. Here is a small-letter *d* that was developed about 1,200 years ago.

Dd *Dd*	Dd	Dd	Dd
Handwriting	Sans Serif Type	Serif Type	Computer Printing

d *or* **D** *noun* **1.** The fourth letter of the English alphabet. **2.** The Roman numeral for the number 500.
d *or* **D** (dē) ◊ *noun, plural* **d's** *or* **D's**

dab *verb* **1.** To apply with short, light strokes: *Dab some ointment on your burn.* **2.** To pat quickly and lightly.
◊ *noun* **1.** A small amount: *Put a dab of jelly on the toast.* **2.** A light stroke or pat.
dab (dăb) ◊ *verb* **dabbed, dabbing** ◊ *noun, plural* **dabs**

dabble *verb* **1.** To splash in and out of water playfully: *She dabbled her feet in the pond.* **2.** To work in a small way and without much effort: *He dabbles at building models.*
dab·ble (**dăb′** əl) ◊ *verb* **dabbled, dabbling**

dace *noun* A small freshwater fish that is related to the minnows.
dace (dās) ◊ *noun, plural* **dace** *or* **daces**

dachshund *noun* A small dog with a long body, drooping ears, and very short legs.
dachs·hund (**däks′** ho͝ont′) ◊ *noun, plural* **dachshunds**

dad *noun* Father.
dad (dăd) ◊ *noun, plural* **dads**

daddy *noun* Father.
dad·dy (**dăd′** ē) ◊ *noun, plural* **daddies**

daddy longlegs *noun* An insect that looks like a spider but has a small, rounded body and long, slender legs.
daddy long·legs (**lông′** lĕgz′) ◊ *noun, plural* **daddy longlegs**

daffodil *noun* A plant that grows from a bulb and has long, narrow leaves and yellow flowers with a trumpet-shaped center.
daf·fo·dil (**dăf′** ə dĭl′) ◊ *noun, plural* **daffodils**

dagger *noun* A short, pointed weapon with sharp edges that is used like a knife.
dag·ger (**dăg′** ər) ◊ *noun, plural* **daggers**

dahlia *noun* Any of several garden plants that are grown for their showy flowers of various colors.
dahl·ia (**dăl′** yə) ◊ *noun, plural* **dahlias**

daily *adjective* Done, happening, or appearing every day or every weekday: *My parents enjoy their daily walk.*

◊ *adverb* Every day: *I exercise daily.*
◊ *noun* A newspaper published every day or every weekday.
dai·ly (**dā′**lē) ◊ *adjective* ◊ *adverb* ◊ *noun, plural* **dailies**

daintily *adverb* In a dainty way.
dain·ti·ly (**dān′**tə lē) ◊ *adverb*

dainty *adjective* **1.** Lovely in a fine, delicate way: *The baby's bonnet had dainty embroidery.* **2.** Having delicate tastes; fussy: *Our kitten is a dainty eater.*
dain·ty (**dān′**tē) ◊ *adjective* **daintier, daintiest**

dairy *noun* **1.** A place where milk is stored or made into butter and cheese. **2.** A company or store that sells milk, cream, butter, and cheese. **3.** A farm that produces milk.
dair·y (**dâr′**ē) ◊ *noun, plural* **dairies**

dais *noun* A raised platform, as for a throne.
da·is (**dā′**ĭs) ◊ *noun, plural* **daises**

daisy *noun* Any of several plants that have flowers with narrow white, yellow, or pink petals around a yellow center.
dai·sy (**dā′**zē) ◊ *noun, plural* **daisies**

dale *noun* A valley.
dale (dāl) ◊ *noun, plural* **dales**

Dalmatian *noun* A large dog that has a short, smooth white coat with black or brown spots.
Dal·ma·tian (dăl **mā′**shən) ◊ *noun, plural* **Dalmatians**

▲ **Dalmatian**

ă	pat	ĭ	pit	oi	**oi**l	th	ba**th**
ā	pay	ī	ride	ŏŏ	b**oo**k	*th*	ba**the**
â	care	î	fierce	ōō	b**oo**t	ə	ago, item
ä	father	ŏ	pot	ou	**ou**t		pencil
ĕ	pet	ō	go	ŭ	cut		atom
ē	be	ô	paw, for	û	fur		circus

dam *noun* A barrier across a waterway to control the flow of water.
◊ *verb* To block or hold back with or as if with a dam.
dam (dăm) ◊ *noun, plural* **dams** ◊ *verb* **dammed, damming**

damage *noun* Harm or injury that causes loss or makes something less valuable.
◊ *verb* To harm or injure: *Some insects damage plants.* —See Synonyms at **harm.**
dam·age (**dăm′**ĭj) ◊ *noun, plural* **damages** ◊ *verb* **damaged, damaging**

damp *adjective* Slightly wet; moist.
◊ *noun* **1.** Slight wetness; moisture: *Don't go out in the damp.* **2.** A poisonous gas that collects in mines.
◊ *verb* To make damp; dampen.
damp (dămp) ◊ *adjective* **damper, dampest** ◊ *noun* ◊ *verb* **damped, damping**

dampen *verb* **1.** To make or become moist: *Dampen the clothes before you iron.* **2.** To lessen or depress: *The long wait dampened their excitement.*
damp·en (**dăm′**pən) ◊ *verb* **dampened, dampening**

dance *verb* **1.** To move with rhythmic steps and motions, usually in time to music. **2.** To skip about or bob up and down: *Moonlight danced on the water.*
◊ *noun* **1.** A set of rhythmic steps and motions, usually performed to music: *I learned a Spanish folk dance.* **2.** A gathering at which people dance: *Our class held a dance at school.* **3.** One round or turn of dancing: *May I have this dance?* **4.** The art of dancing.
dance (dăns) ◊ *verb* **danced, dancing** ◊ *noun, plural* **dances**

dancer *noun* A person who dances.
danc·er (**dăn′**sər) ◊ *noun, plural* **dancers**

dandelion *noun* A common weedy plant with bright yellow flowers and long notched leaves that are sometimes eaten in salads.
dan·de·li·on (**dăn′**dl ī′ən) ◊ *noun, plural* **dandelions**

***HISTORY* • dandelion**

Dandelion comes from an old French phrase meaning "tooth of a lion." The leaves of a dandelion have jagged edges that look a little like lions' teeth.

▲ dandelion

dandruff *noun* Small white flakes of dead skin that are shed from the scalp.
dan·druff (dăn′drəf) ◊ *noun*

dandy *noun* **1.** A man who takes too much pride in his appearance and clothes. **2.** Something very good of its kind.
◊ *adjective* Very good: *That's a dandy idea!*
dan·dy (dăn′dē) ◊ *noun, plural* **dandies**
◊ *adjective* **dandier, dandiest**

Dane *noun* A person who was born in or lives in Denmark.
Dane (dān) ◊ *noun, plural* **Danes**

danger *noun* **1.** The chance of harm or destruction; peril: *The settlers faced danger with courage.* **2.** The condition of being exposed to harm or loss: *We were in danger of falling.* **3.** Something that may cause harm: *Fog is always a danger to pilots.*
dan·ger (dān′jər) ◊ *noun, plural* **dangers**

> ***SYNONYMS***
>
> ***danger, hazard, risk***
>
> The explorer faced many *dangers* in the jungle. People who live near active volcanoes face certain *hazards.* It is a *risk* to swim so far, but if you succeed, you will win a prize.

dangerous *adjective* **1.** Full of danger; risky. **2.** Able or likely to cause harm.
dan·ger·ous (dān′jər əs) ◊ *adjective*

dangle *verb* To swing or cause to swing loosely: *A key dangled from the chain.*
dan·gle (dăng′gəl) ◊ *verb* **dangled, dangling**

Danish *noun* The language of the Danes.
◊ *adjective* Of or relating to Denmark, the Danes, or their language.
Dan·ish (dā′nĭsh) ◊ *noun* ◊ *adjective*

dare *verb* **1.** To be brave or bold enough: *The explorer dared to sail alone across the ocean.* **2.** To challenge: *My friend dared me to climb over the fence.*
◊ *noun* A challenge: *I accept your dare.*
dare (dâr) ◊ *verb* **dared, daring** ◊ *noun, plural* **dares**

daredevil *noun* A person who takes risks.
dare·dev·il (dâr′dĕv′əl) ◊ *noun, plural* **daredevils**

▲ daredevil

daring *adjective* Boldly courageous; fearless. —See Synonyms at **bold.**
◊ *noun* Bold courage.
dar·ing (dâr′ĭng) ◊ *adjective* ◊ *noun*

dark *adjective* **1.** Without light or with very little light: *The night was dark, and we lost our way.* **2.** Of a deep shade closer to black or brown than to lighter shades: *Your eyes are dark.* **3.** Gloomy; dismal: *What a dark view.*
◊ *noun* **1.** Absence of light: *Cats' eyes adjust quickly to the dark.* **2.** Night or nightfall.
dark (därk) ◊ *adjective* **darker, darkest**
◊ *noun*

darken *verb* To make or become dark or darker: *The sky darkened from the storm.*
dark·en (där′kən) ◊ *verb* **darkened, darkening**

darling *noun* A dearly loved person.
◊ *adjective* **1.** Dearest; beloved. **2.** Charming; adorable: *The kittens are darling.*
dar·ling (där′lĭng) ◊ *noun, plural* **darlings**
◊ *adjective*

darn *verb* To mend by weaving thread or yarn across a hole.
darn (därn) ◊ *verb* **darned, darning**

darning needle *noun* A dragonfly.
darning needle ◊ *noun, plural* **darning needles**

dart *verb* **1.** To move suddenly and swiftly: *A squirrel darted across the path.* **2.** To shoot out or send forth swiftly and suddenly: *They darted angry glances at us.*
◊ *noun* **1.** A small, thin object with a sharp point. Darts are usually thrown by hand. **2. darts** (*used with a singular verb*) A game in which darts are thrown at a target.
dart (därt) ◊ *verb* **darted, darting** ◊ *noun, plural* **darts**

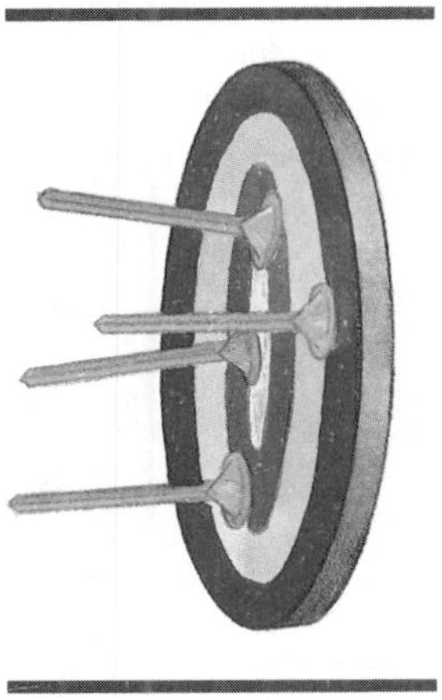

▲ **dart**

dash *verb* **1.** To move with sudden speed; rush: *I dashed out the door.* **2.** To strike, knock, throw, or smash with violent force: *The storm dashed the ship against the rocks.* **3.** To do in a hurry: *I dashed off a note of apology.* **4.** To destroy or ruin: *The rain dashed our hopes for a picnic.*
◊ *noun* **1.** A quick run or rush: *We made a dash for shelter.* **2.** A short, fast race: *I won the 100-yard dash.* **3.** A small amount; bit: *Add just a dash of salt.* **4.** A punctuation mark (—) used to show a pause or omission or to set off part of a sentence from the rest.
dash (dăsh) ◊ *verb* **dashed, dashing** ◊ *noun, plural* **dashes**

dashboard *noun* A panel beneath the windshield of a motor vehicle that contains instruments, dials, and controls.
dash·board (**dăsh′** bôrd′) ◊ *noun, plural* **dashboards**

ă	pat	ĭ	pit	oi	**oil**	th	**bath**
ā	pay	ī	ride	o͝o	**book**	*th*	**bathe**
â	care	î	fierce	o͞o	**boot**	ə	ago, item
ä	father	ŏ	pot	ou	**out**		pencil
ĕ	pet	ō	go	ŭ	cut		atom
ē	be	ô	paw, for	û	fur		circus

data *plural noun* **1.** Facts and figures, especially for use in making decisions. **2.** The basic information that can be produced or processed by a computer.
da·ta (dā′ tə *or* **dăt′** ə) ◊ *plural noun*

date¹ *noun* **1.** The month, day, and year of a happening: *The date of Lincoln's birth was February 12, 1809.* **2.** A statement of calendar time on something: *There is no date on this coin.* **3.** An agreement to meet someone or be somewhere at a particular time: *We made a date to have lunch on Thursday.* **4.** A person with whom one has a social engagement.
◊ *verb* **1.** To mark with a date: *Be sure to date your letter.* **2.** To find out the date of: *They dated the rock by studying the fossils in it.* **3.** To come from a particular period of time: *The building dates from the Civil War.* **4.** To go out with socially.
date¹ (dāt) ◊ *noun, plural* **dates** ◊ *verb* **dated, dating**

date² *noun* The sweet, brown fruit of a kind of palm tree.
date² (dāt) ◊ *noun, plural* **dates**

***HISTORY* • date¹, date²**

Date¹ comes from an old French word that came from a Latin word meaning "given." Originally a **date¹** was the day on which a letter was given to a messenger. **Date²** also comes from Latin through French. The Latin word in turn came from a Greek word meaning "finger." A **date²** is shaped something like a finger, or so the ancient Greeks thought.

datum *noun* A single item of information.
da·tum (dā′ təm *or* **dăt′** əm) ◊ *noun, plural* **data**

daughter *noun* A female offspring or child.
daugh·ter (**dô′** tər) ◊ *noun, plural* **daughters**

daughter-in-law *noun* The wife of one's son.
daugh·ter-in-law (**dô′** tər ĭn lô′) ◊ *noun, plural* **daughters-in-law**

daunt *verb* To cause to lose courage: *The dangers of the trip did not daunt us.*
daunt (dônt) ◊ *verb* **daunted, daunting**

dauntless *adjective* Brave and determined.
daunt·less (**dônt′** lĭs) ◊ *adjective*

D

dawdle *verb* To take more time than necessary: *I dawdled on the way to school and was ten minutes late.*
daw·dle (dôd′l) ◊ *verb* **dawdled, dawdling**

dawn *noun* **1.** The time each morning when the sun comes up. **2.** The first appearance; beginning: *These cave paintings were made before the dawn of history.*
◊ *verb* **1.** To begin to grow light in the morning. **2.** To begin to understand: *It finally dawned on me that I was lost.*
dawn (dôn) ◊ *noun, plural* **dawns** ◊ *verb* **dawned, dawning**

day *noun* **1.** The time of light between sunrise and sunset. **2.** A period of 24 hours from midnight to midnight. **3.** The part of the day devoted to work or study. **4.** A particular period of time; age: *He was the greatest painter of his day.*
day (dā) ◊ *noun, plural* **days**

daybreak *noun* The time each morning when light first appears; dawn.
day·break (dā′brāk′) ◊ *noun*

▲ **daybreak**

daydream *noun* A dreamy imagining in which hopes and wishes come true.
◊ *verb* To have daydreams.
day·dream (dā′drēm′) ◊ *noun, plural* **daydreams** ◊ *verb* **daydreamed, daydreaming**

daylight *noun* **1.** The light of day: *She prefers to read by daylight.* **2.** Dawn: *We were awake before daylight.*
day·light (dā′līt′) ◊ *noun*

daytime *noun* The time between dawn and dark.
day·time (dā′tīm′) ◊ *noun*

daze *verb* To stun with or as if with a blow.
◊ *noun* A dazed condition.
daze (dāz) ◊ *verb* **dazed, dazing** ◊ *noun*

dazzle *verb* **1.** To blind with too much light. **2.** To amaze or impress with a great display: *The fireworks on July 4th dazzled us.*
daz·zle (dăz′əl) ◊ *verb* **dazzled, dazzling**

DC The abbreviation for *District of Columbia* used with a Zip Code.

D.C. An abbreviation for *District of Columbia.*

DE The abbreviation for *Delaware* used with a Zip Code.

de– The prefix *de–* means "to do the opposite of" or "undo." When a person *decodes* a message, he or she changes the message in code back to the original language. The prefix *de–* also means "to remove" or "remove from." When you *defrost* a refrigerator, you remove the frost from the refrigerator.

***VOCABULARY BUILDER* • de–**

Many words that are formed with **de–** are not entries in this dictionary. But you can figure out what these words mean by looking up the meanings of the root words and the prefix. For example:
decompress = to take pressure off
desalt = to remove salt from

deacon *noun* **1.** A church officer who helps the minister. **2.** A member of the clergy who ranks just below a priest.
dea·con (dē′kən) ◊ *noun, plural* **deacons**

dead *adjective* **1.** No longer living: *A dead deer lay in the snow.* **2.** Not working, as because of a loss of power: *The telephone is dead.* **3.** Without activity, interest, or excitement: *College towns are often dead in the summer.* **4.** Complete; total: *There was dead silence in the room. The car came to a dead stop.* **5.** Accurate; exact: *You are a dead shot.*
◊ *noun* **1.** Those who have died. **2.** The darkest, coldest, or most silent time: *The boat slipped away in the dead of night.*
◊ *adverb* **1.** Completely; absolutely: *We were dead tired after our trip.* **2.** Straight; directly: *The town lies dead ahead.*
dead (dĕd) ◊ *adjective* **deader, deadest** ◊ *noun* ◊ *adverb*

deaden *verb* To make less strong or sharp; diminish: *Mufflers help deaden the noise made by motor vehicles.*
dead·en (dĕd′n) ◊ *verb* **deadened, deadening**

deadline *noun* A set time by which something must be done.
dead·line (dĕd′ līn′) ◊ *noun, plural* **deadlines**

deadly *adjective* **1.** Causing or capable of causing death: *A gun is a deadly weapon.* **2.** Intending to harm or destroy: *The friends became deadly enemies.*
dead·ly (dĕd′ lē) ◊ *adjective* **deadlier, deadliest**

deaf *adjective* **1.** Unable to hear or to hear well. **2.** Unwilling to listen or hear: *My parents seem to be deaf to my request for a new bike.*
deaf (dĕf) ◊ *adjective* **deafer, deafest**

deafen *verb* To make deaf, especially for a short time: *The explosion deafened us.*
deaf·en (dĕf′ən) ◊ *verb* **deafened, deafening**

deal *verb* **1.** To have to do with: *Astronomy deals with the stars.* **2.** To do business: *This store deals in used furniture.* **3.** To give; deliver: *The principal had to deal out punishment.* **4.** To act toward; treat: *Deal fairly with your friends.*
◊ *noun* **1.** An agreement, as in business: *I made a deal to sell my bike.* **2.** A bargain: *I got a deal on some used books.*
deal (dēl) ◊ *verb* **dealt, dealing** ◊ *noun, plural* **deals**

dealt *verb* Past tense and past participle of **deal.**
dealt (dĕlt) ◊ *verb*

dear *adjective* **1.** Much loved; precious: *You are my dear friend.* **2.** Used as a term of address in writing letters: *Dear Mr. and Ms. Smith.* **3.** High in price: *Steak is too dear to buy today.*
◊ *noun* A dearly loved person.
dear (dîr) ◊ *adjective* **dearer, dearest** ◊ *noun, plural* **dears**
‖*These sound alike:* **dear, deer**

ă	pat	ĭ	pit	oi	**oi**l	th	**th**bath
ā	pay	ī	ride	ŏŏ	b**oo**k	*th*	ba**th**e
â	care	î	fierce	ōō	b**oo**t	ə	ago, item
ä	father	ŏ	pot	ou	**ou**t		pencil
ĕ	pet	ō	go	ŭ	cut		atom
ē	be	ô	paw, for	û	fur		circus

dearly *adverb* Very much: *I paid dearly for my mistake.*
dear·ly (dîr′ lē) ◊ *adverb*

death *noun* **1.** The end of life. **2.** The state of being dead. **3.** The end or destruction of something: *Loss of the tournament was the death of our hopes for the pennant.*
death (dĕth) ◊ *noun, plural* **deaths**

debate *noun* A discussion of the reasons for and against something: *The town held a debate on building a new school.*
◊ *verb* **1.** To present or discuss reasons for and against: *We debated the proposal before voting.* —See Synonyms at **discuss. 2.** To consider and try to decide: *I debated whether to call home.*
de·bate (dĭ **bāt′**) ◊ *noun, plural* **debates** ◊ *verb* **debated, debating**

debris *noun* The scattered remains of something broken or destroyed.
de·bris (də **brē′**) ◊ *noun*

debt *noun* **1.** Something that is owed to another: *I plan to pay my debts soon.* **2.** The condition of owing: *They are in debt to the bank.*
debt (dĕt) ◊ *noun, plural* **debts**

debtor *noun* A person who owes a debt.
debt·or (dĕt′ ər) ◊ *noun, plural* **debtors**

Dec. The abbreviation for *December.*

decade *noun* A period of ten years.
dec·ade (dĕk′ ād′) ◊ *noun, plural* **decades**

decay *noun* **1.** The breaking down of plant or animal matter by the action of bacteria or fungi. **2.** A gradual decline in health, strength, or soundness.
◊ *verb* **1.** To undergo or cause to undergo decay; rot: *Your teeth will decay if you eat too much sugar.* **2.** To decline in health, strength, or soundness.
de·cay (dĭ **kā′**) ◊ *noun* ◊ *verb* **decayed, decaying**

deceit *noun* The act or practice of deceiving.
de·ceit (dĭ **sēt′**) ◊ *noun, plural* **deceits**

deceitful *adjective* **1.** Practicing deceit. **2.** Intended to deceive; deceptive. —See Synonyms at **dishonest.**
de·ceit·ful (dĭ **sēt′** fəl) ◊ *adjective*

deceive *verb* To cause to believe something that is not true; mislead.
de·ceive (dĭ **sēv′**) ◊ *verb* **deceived, deceiving**

December *noun* The twelfth month of the year. December has 31 days.
De·cem·ber (dĭ **sĕm′** bər) ◊ *noun*

decent *adjective* **1.** According to accepted standards; proper: *It is not decent behavior to cheat on a test.* **2.** Kind or thoughtful: *It is decent of you to help me.* **3.** Fairly good; adequate: *I receive a decent allowance.*
de·cent (**dē′** sənt) ◊ *adjective*

deception *noun* **1.** The act of deceiving. **2.** The fact of being deceived. **3.** Something, as a trick, that deceives.
de·cep·tion (dĭ **sĕp′** shən) ◊ *noun, plural* **deceptions**

deceptive *adjective* Meant to or likely to deceive or mislead.
de·cep·tive (dĭ **sĕp′** tĭv) ◊ *adjective*

decide *verb* **1.** To make up one's mind: *I decided to be a doctor.* **2.** To make a judgment or settle a question or outcome: *Just a few votes decided the election.*
de·cide (dĭ **sīd′**) ◊ *verb* **decided, deciding**

> ***SYNONYMS***
>
> ***decide, determine, resolve***
>
> I *decided* to read a few books. I *determined* which books I would read. I *resolved* that I would read more books this year.

decided *adjective* Definite; sure: *You have a decided advantage in ability.*
de·cid·ed (dĭ **sī′** dĭd) ◊ *adjective*

decimal *noun* A fraction in which the denominator is 10 or a multiple of 10: *The decimal .1 = 1/10, and the decimal .12 = 12/100.* ◊ *adjective* Of or based on 10.
dec·i·mal (**dĕs′** ə məl) ◊ *noun, plural* **decimals** ◊ *adjective*

decimal point *noun* A period at the left of the numerator of a decimal. The periods in .1 and .12 are decimal points.
decimal point ◊ *noun, plural* **decimal points**

decipher *verb* **1.** To change from code; decode. **2.** To make out the meaning of something that is hard to understand or is not clear: *Can you decipher this handwriting?*
de·ci·pher (dĭ **sī′** fər) ◊ *verb* **deciphered, deciphering**

decision *noun* **1.** The act or result of deciding. **2.** Firmness of character or action.
de·ci·sion (dĭ **sĭzh′** ən) ◊ *noun, plural* **decisions**

decisive *adjective* **1.** Deciding or having the power to decide an issue beyond doubt: *The team won a decisive victory.* **2.** Marked by decision; determined: *My reply was decisive.*
de·ci·sive (dĭ **sī′** sĭv) ◊ *adjective*

deck *noun* **1.** One of the floors dividing a ship into different levels. **2.** A platform that is like the deck of a ship. **3.** A pack of playing cards. ◊ *verb* To decorate or dress: *The floats in the parade were decked out with flags.*
deck (dĕk) ◊ *noun, plural* **decks** ◊ *verb* **decked, decking**

▲ **deck**

declaration *noun* **1.** The act of declaring. **2.** Something that is declared; proclamation.
dec·la·ra·tion (dĕk′lə **rā′** shən) ◊ *noun, plural* **declarations**

declarative sentence *noun* A sentence that makes a statement and ends with a period.
de·clar·a·tive sentence (dĭ **klâr′** ə tĭv) ◊ *noun, plural* **declarative sentences**

declare *verb* **1.** To say with emphasis or certainty. **2.** To make known officially or formally: *Congress declared war.*
de·clare (dĭ **klâr′**) ◊ *verb* **declared, declaring**

decline *verb* **1.** To refuse to accept or do: *My friend declined my offer of a ride.* **2.** To sink to a weaker, lower, or inferior state, as of strength. **3.** To slope or bend downward. ◊ *noun* The process or result of declining.
de·cline (dĭ **klīn′**) ◊ *verb* **declined, declining** ◊ *noun, plural* **declines**

decode *verb* To change from code into the original language.
de·code (dē **kōd′**) ◊ *verb* **decoded, decoding**

decompose *verb* To decay; rot.
de·com·pose (dē′kəm **pōz′**) ◊ *verb* **decomposed, decomposing**

decorate *verb* **1.** To furnish with something attractive or beautiful; adorn: *We decorated the room with flowers.* **2.** To award a decoration to: *The sailor was decorated for bravery.*
dec·o·rate (**dĕk′** ə rāt′) ◊ *verb* **decorated, decorating**

decoration *noun* **1.** The act or process of decorating. **2.** Something that decorates; ornament. **3.** Something, as a medal, awarded as a sign of honor.
dec·o·ra·tion (dĕk′ə **rā′**shən) ◊ *noun, plural* **decorations**

decorator *noun* A person who decorates the interiors of houses.
dec·o·ra·tor (**dĕk′** ə rā′tər) ◊ *noun, plural* **decorators**

decoy *noun* **1.** A model of a bird, as a duck, used to lure wild birds into a trap or within gunshot. **2.** Someone or something that lures another into danger or a trap.
◊ *verb* To lure by or as if by using a decoy.
de·coy ◊ *noun* (**dē′**koi′ *or* dĭ **koi′**), *plural* **decoys** ◊ *verb* (dĭ **koi′**) **decoyed, decoying**

decrease *verb* To make or become less or smaller; diminish.
◊ *noun* **1.** The process of decreasing. **2.** The amount by which something decreases.
de·crease ◊ *verb* (dĭ **krēs′**) **decreased, decreasing** ◊ *noun* (**dē′**krēs′ *or* dĭ **krēs′**), *plural* **decreases**

> ***SYNONYMS***
>
> ***decrease, lessen, reduce***
>
> The pilot *decreased* the speed of the plane little by little. The dentist was able to *lessen* my pain. I *reduced* my weight by going on a diet. **Antonym:** *increase*

ă	pat	ĭ	pit	oi	oil	th	bath
ā	pay	ī	ride	o͝o	book	*th*	bathe
â	care	î	fierce	o͞o	boot	ə	ago, item
ä	father	ŏ	pot	ou	out		pencil
ĕ	pet	ō	go	ŭ	cut		atom
ē	be	ô	paw, for	û	fur		circus

decree *noun* An official order or decision.
◊ *verb* To order or decide by decree.
de·cree (dĭ **krē′**) ◊ *noun, plural* **decrees** ◊ *verb* **decreed, decreeing**

dedicate *verb* To set apart for a special purpose; devote: *The scientists dedicated themselves to research.*
ded·i·cate (**dĕd′** ĭ kāt′) ◊ *verb* **dedicated, dedicating**

dedication *noun* **1.** The act of dedicating. **2.** The fact of being dedicated; devotion.
ded·i·ca·tion (dĕd′ĭ **kā′**shən) ◊ *noun*

deduct *verb* To take away one amount from another; subtract: *I bought the paint and deducted the cost from the painter's fee.*
de·duct (dĭ **dŭkt′**) ◊ *verb* **deducted, deducting**

deduction *noun* **1.** The act of deducting; subtraction. **2.** An amount that is or can be deducted.
de·duc·tion (dĭ **dŭk′**shən) ◊ *noun, plural* **deductions**

deed *noun* **1.** Something done; act or action: *Deeds count more than words.* **2.** A legal document that shows the terms of an agreement, especially one transferring real estate from one owner to another.
deed (dēd) ◊ *noun, plural* **deeds**

deep *adjective* **1.** Extending down far below a surface: *I saw a deep crack in the ice.* **2.** Extending far back from front to rear or inward from the outside: *I made curtains with a deep ruffle.* **3.** Located far down or in: *The pipe is deep in the ground.* **4.** Great in degree; profound: *We sat in deep silence.* **5.** Very much occupied; absorbed: *I was deep in thought.* **6.** Hard to understand: *What you said seems like a deep mystery.* **7.** Rich and vivid in color: *The rug was a deep blue.* **8.** Low in pitch: *The singer had a deep voice.*
◊ *adverb* To, in, or at a great depth: *I stuck my hands deep in my pockets.*
◊ *noun* **1.** A part or place located far below a surface: *Fish swam in the deeps of the lake.* **2.** The ocean: *The liner sailed over the deep.*
deep (dēp) ◊ *adjective, adverb* **deeper, deepest** ◊ *noun, plural* **deeps**

deepen *verb* To make or become deeper.
deep·en (**dē′**pən) ◊ *verb* **deepened, deepening**

deer *noun* Any of several animals that have hoofs and chew the cud. The males usually have antlers.
deer (dîr) ◊ *noun, plural* **deer**
‖*These sound alike:* **deer, dear**

***HISTORY* • deer**

Deer is a native English word that first meant "animal," but it now refers to only one particular kind of animal.

▲ **deer**

deface *verb* To mar or ruin the surface or appearance of.
de·face (dĭ fās′) ◊ *verb* **defaced, defacing**

defeat *verb* **1.** To win victory over: *Our baseball team defeated theirs.* **2.** To prevent the success of; frustrate: *Your unfriendly attitude defeats your own purpose of winning friends.* ◊ *noun* **1.** The condition or fact of being defeated. **2.** The act of defeating.
de·feat (dĭ fēt′) ◊ *verb* **defeated, defeating** ◊ *noun, plural* **defeats**

SYNONYMS

defeat, beat, conquer

Which party will *defeat* the other in the election for the Presidency? Our soccer team *beat* their team by a score of 4–3. The Romans *conquered* many parts of the world.

defect *noun* A lack of something necessary for perfection or completeness; flaw.
de·fect (dē′fĕkt′ *or* dĭ **fĕkt′**) ◊ *noun, plural* **defects**

defective *adjective* Lacking a necessary part or quality; imperfect: *I bought some slightly defective china at a very low price.*
de·fec·tive (dĭ **fĕk′**tĭv) ◊ *adjective*

defend *verb* **1.** To protect from attack, harm, danger, or challenge. **2.** To speak, act, or write in support of: *They defended their actions in a letter to the newspaper.*
de·fend (dĭ **fĕnd′**) ◊ *verb* **defended, defending**

defense *noun* **1.** The act of defending. **2.** Something that defends: *Storm windows are a good defense against winter winds.*
de·fense (dĭ **fĕns′**) ◊ *noun, plural* **defenses**

defensive *adjective* Intended or serving to defend: *Defensive walls surrounded the castle.*
de·fen·sive (dĭ **fĕn′**sĭv) ◊ *adjective*

defer[1] *verb* To put off until a future time; postpone: *They were short of money and deferred paying the bills.*
de·fer[1] (dĭ **fûr′**) ◊ *verb* **deferred, deferring**

defer[2] *verb* To yield to another person's wishes, opinion, or decision: *I defer to my parents because they are older and wiser.*
de·fer[2] (dĭ **fûr′**) ◊ *verb* **deferred, deferring**

***HISTORY* • defer[1], defer[2]**

Defer[1] comes from an old French word, which came from a Latin verb meaning "to carry in different directions" and also "to delay." **Defer**[2] also comes from Latin through French. The Latin word meant "to carry or bring," as well as "to submit for judgment."

defiance *noun* Open resistance to authority.
de·fi·ance (dĭ **fī′**əns) ◊ *noun*

defiant *adjective* Showing or marked by defiance: *A raised fist is a defiant gesture.*
de·fi·ant (dĭ **fī′**ənt) ◊ *adjective*

deficiency *noun* A lack of something needed; shortage: *I made up for my educational deficiencies by reading.*
de·fi·cien·cy (dĭ **fĭsh′**ən sē) ◊ *noun, plural* **deficiencies**

deficient *adjective* Lacking something that is needed: *The diet was deficient in vitamins.*
de·fi·cient (dĭ **fĭsh′** ənt) ◊ *adjective*

define *verb* **1.** To explain the meaning of: *Dictionaries define words.* **2.** To fix the limits or extent of: *That list defines your duties.*
de·fine (dĭ **fīn′**) ◊ *verb* **defined, defining**

definite *adjective* **1.** Having exact or fixed limits: *We set a definite time and place to meet.* **2.** Beyond doubt; sure: *It's not definite that I'll go.*
def·i·nite (**dĕf′** ə nĭt) ◊ *adjective*

definition *noun* A statement of the meaning of a word or phrase.
def·i·ni·tion (dĕf′ə **nĭsh′** ən) ◊ *noun, plural* **definitions**

deform *verb* To spoil the shape or appearance of.
de·form (dĭ **fôrm′**) ◊ *verb* **deformed, deforming**

defrost *verb* **1.** To free or become free of ice: *The car's heater defrosts the windshield.* **2.** To thaw or cause to thaw: *I defrosted the frozen vegetables.*
de·frost (dē **frôst′**) ◊ *verb* **defrosted, defrosting**

deft *adjective* Quick and skillful; nimble: *You are certainly deft with that jigsaw.*
deft (dĕft) ◊ *adjective* **defter, deftest**

defy *verb* **1.** To challenge to do something thought of as impossible; dare: *I defy you to jump that high hurdle.* **2.** To resist boldly: *Don't defy the law.* **3.** To be beyond the power of: *What you did defies explanation.*
de·fy (dĭ **fī′**) ◊ *verb* **defied, defying**

degrade *verb* **1.** To lower in rank or degree. **2.** To bring shame or disgrace upon.
de·grade (dĭ **grād′**) ◊ *verb* **degraded, degrading**

degree *noun* **1.** A step or stage in a series or process: *My shyness decreased by degrees.* **2.** Relative amount or extent: *The mechanic has a high degree of skill.* **3.** A title given by a college or university to a student who completes a course of study. **4.** One of the units into which a measuring instrument, as a thermometer, is divided. **5.** A unit of measure equal to 1/360 of the circumference of a circle.
de·gree (dĭ **grē′**) ◊ *noun, plural* **degrees**

deity *noun* **1.** A divine being; god or goddess. **2. Deity** God.
de·i·ty (**dē′** ĭ tē) ◊ *noun, plural* **deities**

dejected *adjective* Feeling depressed and gloomy: *I am dejected because I lost my watch.*
de·ject·ed (dĭ **jĕk′** tĭd) ◊ *adjective*

Del. An abbreviation for *Delaware.*

delay *verb* **1.** To put off; postpone: *We delayed dinner an hour.* **2.** To slow, stop, or prevent for a time: *Rain delayed the game.*
◊ *noun* **1.** The act of delaying or condition of being delayed: *Do your homework without delay.* **2.** The period of time during which someone or something is delayed: *There was a delay of 15 minutes before the train left.*
de·lay (dĭ **lā′**) ◊ *verb* **delayed, delaying**
◊ *noun, plural* **delays**

delegate *noun* A person or group of persons chosen to speak and act for another or others; representative: *Our town sent two delegates to the convention.*
◊ *verb* **1.** To appoint to do a task: *We delegated you to take notices to the classes.* **2.** To entrust to someone else: *The people delegate power to their elected representatives.*
del·e·gate ◊ *noun* (**dĕl′** ə găt′ *or* **dĕl′** ə gĭt), *plural* **delegates** ◊ *verb* (**dĕl′** ə găt′) **delegated, delegating**

delegation *noun* **1.** The act of delegating. **2.** A person or group of persons chosen to represent others.
del·e·ga·tion (dĕl′ə **gā′** shən) ◊ *noun, plural* **delegations**

deliberate *adjective* **1.** Done or said on purpose; intentional: *That was a deliberate lie.* **2.** Not hurried; slow: *You are deliberate in your speech.* **3.** Thinking carefully before doing: *Sending them away was a deliberate choice.*
◊ *verb* To think over or discuss carefully in trying to decide: *I am deliberating whether or not to buy a new typewriter.*
de·lib·er·ate ◊ *adjective* (dĭ **lĭb′** ər ĭt) ◊ *verb* (dĭ **lĭb′** ə rāt′) **deliberated, deliberating**

ă	pat	ĭ	pit	oi	**oil**	th	bath
ā	pay	ī	ride	ŏŏ	book	*th*	bathe
â	care	î	fierce	ōō	boot	ə	ago, item
ä	father	ŏ	pot	ou	**out**		pencil
ĕ	pet	ō	go	ŭ	cut		atom
ē	be	ô	paw, for	û	fur		circus

deliberation *noun* **1.** Careful thought: *The student council decided without enough deliberation.* **2.** Slowness of action: *We walked with deliberation on the icy sidewalk.* **3.** Formal discussion, as in a legislature.
de·lib·er·a·tion (dĭ lĭb′ə **rā′**shən) ◊ *noun, plural* **deliberations**

delicate *adjective* **1.** Very fine in quality, texture, or structure: *I have fair hair and delicate skin.* **2.** Requiring care and skill: *The doctor performed a delicate brain operation.* **3.** Easily broken or damaged; fragile: *I bought some delicate crystal goblets.* **4.** Not physically strong; frail: *Delicate children need rest.* **5.** Requiring tact: *Asking to leave early was a delicate matter.*
del·i·cate (**dĕl′**ĭ kĭt) ◊ *adjective*

delicatessen *noun* A store where cooked or prepared foods, such as smoked meats and salads, are sold.
del·i·ca·tes·sen (dĕl′ĭ kə **tĕs′**ən) ◊ *noun, plural* **delicatessens**

delicious *adjective* Tasting or smelling very good.
de·li·cious (dĭ **lĭsh′**əs) ◊ *adjective*

delight *noun* **1.** Great pleasure: *The baby's face beamed with delight.* —See Synonyms at **joy. 2.** Something that gives delight: *The birthday party was a delight.*
◊ *verb* **1.** To please greatly: *I am delighted to see you.* **2.** To take pleasure: *I delight in your success.*
de·light (dĭ **līt′**) ◊ *noun, plural* **delights**
◊ *verb* **delighted, delighting**

delightful *adjective* Very pleasing: *I had a delightful visit with you.*
de·light·ful (dĭ **līt′**fəl) ◊ *adjective*

delirious *adjective* **1.** Out of one's senses: *The child was delirious from the high fever.* **2.** Wildly excited: *I am delirious with joy that I won the race.*
de·lir·i·ous (dĭ **lîr′**ē əs) ◊ *adjective*

deliver *verb* **1.** To take and turn over to the proper person or at the proper destination: *The mail carrier delivers packages.* **2.** To send to a target aimed at: *The archer delivered an arrow on target.* **3.** To give in words; utter: *The professor delivered a lecture.* **4.** To set free; liberate: *Deliver us from our enemies.*
de·liv·er (dĭ **lĭv′**ər) ◊ *verb* **delivered, delivering**

delivery *noun* **1.** The act of taking and turning something over to another. **2.** A manner of speaking or singing in public.
de·liv·er·y (dĭ **lĭv′**ə rē) ◊ *noun, plural* **deliveries**

dell *noun* A small, secluded valley, often with trees along its slopes.
dell (dĕl) ◊ *noun, plural* **dells**

delphinium *noun* A tall garden plant with long clusters of showy flowers that are usually blue.
del·phin·i·um (dĕl **fĭn′**ē əm) ◊ *noun*

delta *noun* An area of land shaped like a triangle and formed by deposits of sand and mud at the mouth of a river.
del·ta (**dĕl′**tə) ◊ *noun, plural* **deltas**

▲ **delta**

deluge *noun* **1.** A great flood of water. **2.** A heavy downpour of rain. **3.** An overwhelming rush: *The singer received a deluge of letters.*
◊ *verb* **1.** To flood with water. **2.** To overwhelm as if with a flood.
del·uge (**dĕl′**yōōj) ◊ *noun, plural* **deluges**
◊ *verb* **deluged, deluging**

delve *verb* To search hard for facts or information: *The police delved into the crime.*
delve (dĕlv) ◊ *verb* **delved, delving**

demand *verb* **1.** To ask as one's right: *I demanded the money that was owed me.* **2.** To ask urgently and with authority: *The investigators demanded the suspect's name.* **3.** To call for as necessary; require: *The work of a*

lawyer demands skill and concentration. ◊ *noun* **1.** The act of demanding. **2.** An urgent requirement or need: *We earn enough to meet the normal demands of a family.* **3.** The condition of being wanted: *Silver is now in great demand.* **4.** A desire to buy or use something: *The demand for diamonds is great.*
de·mand (dĭ **mănd′**) ◊ *verb* **demanded, demanding** ◊ *noun, plural* **demands**

demerit *noun* A mark entered against a person's record for bad behavior or poor work.
de·mer·it (dĭ **mĕr′**ĭt) ◊ *noun, plural* **demerits**

democracy *noun* **1.** A form of government in which power is held by the people but is usually exercised by their elected representatives. **2.** A political unit, as a nation, in which the government is a democracy. **3.** Belief in or practice of the principle that all individuals in a society are equal.
de·moc·ra·cy (dĭ **mŏk′**rə sē) ◊ *noun, plural* **democracies**

Democrat *noun* A member of the Democratic Party.
Dem·o·crat (**dĕm′**ə krăt′) ◊ *noun, plural* **Democrats**

democratic *adjective* **1.** Of, relating to, or supporting political democracy. **2.** Believing in or practicing the principle of equal rights for all. **3. Democratic** Of or relating to the Democratic Party.
dem·o·crat·ic (dĕm′ə **krăt′**ĭk) ◊ *adjective*

Democratic Party *noun* One of the two major political parties of the United States.

demolish *verb* **1.** To destroy by reducing to ruins: *The explosion demolished the old building.* **2.** To put an end to: *The new discovery demolished old scientific theories.*
de·mol·ish (dĭ **mŏl′**ĭsh) ◊ *verb* **demolished, demolishing**

demon *noun* **1.** An evil spirit. **2.** A very enthusiastic or energetic person.
de·mon (**dē′**mən) ◊ *noun, plural* **demons**

demonstrate *verb* **1.** To show clearly; reveal: *The concert demonstrated your ability to play the flute.* **2.** To describe and explain with the help of experiments or examples: *The doctor demonstrated the harmful effects of tobacco.* —See Synonyms at **prove.** **3.** To make evident by reasoning: *The teacher asked me to demonstrate that a square is a kind of rectangle.* **4.** To show the advantages and method of operation of: *The salesperson demonstrated a new washing machine.* **5.** To take part in a public display, as of support.
dem·on·strate (**dĕm′**ən strāt′) ◊ *verb* **demonstrated, demonstrating**

demonstration *noun* **1.** A clear or logical proof: *The teacher gave a demonstration of the law of gravity.* **2.** A show and explanation of the operation of something for sale. **3.** An outward show, as of feeling: *We were greeted with a demonstration of affection.* **4.** A display of public feeling, as in a rally or parade.
dem·on·stra·tion (dĕm′ən **strā′**shən) ◊ *noun, plural* **demonstrations**

▲ **demonstration**

demonstrator *noun* **1.** A person who demonstrates. **2.** A product used in a demonstration.
dem·on·stra·tor (**dĕm′**ən strā′tər) ◊ *noun, plural* **demonstrators**

demote *verb* To reduce to a lower rank, grade, or position.
de·mote (dĭ **mōt′**) ◊ *verb* **demoted, demoting**

den *noun* **1.** The shelter or retreat of a wild animal. **2.** A cozy private room for personal use, as for study. **3.** A secret place.
den (dĕn) ◊ *noun, plural* **dens**

ă	pat	ĭ	pit	oi	oil	th	bath
ā	pay	ī	ride	o͝o	book	*th*	bathe
â	care	î	fierce	o͞o	boot	ə	ago, item
ä	father	ŏ	pot	ou	out		pencil
ĕ	pet	ō	go	ŭ	cut		atom
ē	be	ô	paw, for	û	fur		circus

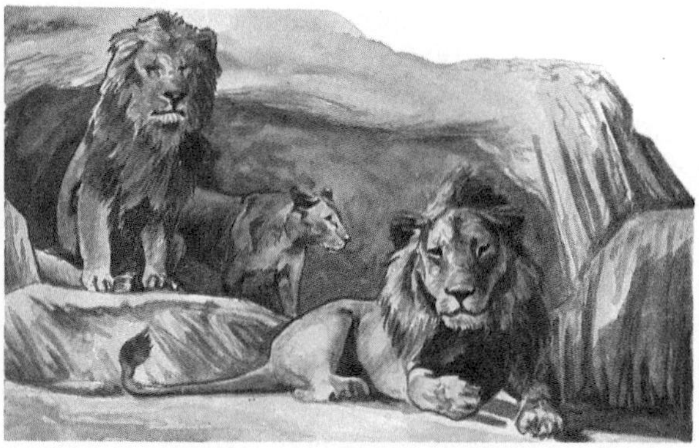

▲ den

denim *noun* **1.** A coarse, heavy cotton cloth. **2. denims** Overalls or pants made of denim.
den·im (dĕn′əm) ◊ *noun, plural* **denims**

denomination *noun* **1.** A name, especially one for a group or class of things. **2.** A religious body consisting of a group of congregations having the same faith. **3.** One of a class of units, as of money: *I asked the cashier for bills of small denomination.*
de·nom·i·na·tion (dĭ nŏm′ə **nā′**shən) ◊ *noun, plural* **denominations**

denominator *noun* The number written below the line in a fraction. In the fraction $^2/_7$, 7 is the denominator.
de·nom·i·na·tor (dĭ **nŏm′** ə nā′tər) ◊ *noun, plural* **denominators**

denote *verb* **1.** To have as the meaning; mean: *The prefix "non–" denotes "not."* **2.** To be a sign of; indicate: *The blue areas on the map denote water.*
de·note (dĭ **nōt′**) ◊ *verb* **denoted, denoting**

denounce *verb* **1.** To declare to be wicked or wrong; condemn. **2.** To give or report information against; accuse.
de·nounce (dĭ **nouns′**) ◊ *verb* **denounced, denouncing**

dense *adjective* Having the parts packed together closely: *The crowd was so dense that I could hardly move.*
dense (dĕns) ◊ *adjective* **denser, densest**

density *noun* **1.** The amount of something per unit of area or volume: *The village had a population density of five people per square mile.* **2.** The condition of being dense.
den·si·ty (**dĕn′**sĭ tē) ◊ *noun, plural* **densities**

dent *noun* A hollow in a surface, as a fender, caused by pressure or a blow.
◊ *verb* To have or make a dent in.
dent (dĕnt) ◊ *noun, plural* **dents** ◊ *verb* **dented, denting**

dental *adjective* **1.** Of or relating to the teeth: *Brushing the teeth helps prevent dental disease.* **2.** Of or relating to the work of a dentist: *I go to a dental clinic.*
den·tal (**dĕn′**tl) ◊ *adjective*

dentine *noun* The hard part of a tooth that lies under the enamel.
den·tine (**dĕn′**tēn′) ◊ *noun*

dentist *noun* A person whose profession is the treatment, care, repair, and prevention of diseases of the teeth.
den·tist (**dĕn′**tĭst) ◊ *noun, plural* **dentists**

▲ dentist

deny *verb* **1.** To declare to be not true: *They couldn't deny the accusation.* **2.** To refuse to give; withhold: *Don't deny your help to friends who need it.*
de·ny (dĭ **nī′**) ◊ *verb* **denied, denying**

depart *verb* **1.** To go away or away from; leave: *We departed for our vacation.* —See Synonyms at **go.** **2.** To turn away, as from a regular course of action: *I departed from my usual practice and took a taxi to school.*
de·part (dĭ **pärt′**) ◊ *verb* **departed, departing**

department *noun* A separate division of an organization, as a government or business.
de·part·ment (dĭ **pärt′**mənt) ◊ *noun, plural* **departments**

department store *noun* A store with separate departments for different kinds of goods.
department store ◊ *noun, plural* **department stores**

departure *noun* **1.** The act of going away. **2.** A turning away, as from a usual way of doing things.
de·par·ture (dĭ **pär′**chər) ◊ *noun, plural* **departures**

depend *verb* **1.** To be determined by something else: *Success depends on hard work.* **2.** To have trust: *You can depend on me to be there.* —See Synonyms at **rely. 3.** To fall back on for help or support: *I will have to depend on my parents for my college education.*
de·pend (dĭ **pĕnd′**) ◊ *verb* **depended, depending**

dependable *adjective* Capable of being depended on; reliable.
de·pend·a·ble (dĭ **pĕn′**də bəl) ◊ *adjective*

dependence *noun* **1.** The condition of being dependent on someone or something else. **2.** The condition or fact of placing trust.
de·pend·ence (dĭ **pĕn′**dəns) ◊ *noun*

dependent *adjective* **1.** Determined by something else. **2.** Relying on someone else for help or support.
◊ *noun* A person who depends on another for help or support.
de·pend·ent (dĭ **pĕn′**dənt) ◊ *adjective* ◊ *noun, plural* **dependents**

depict *verb* **1.** To represent in or as if in a painting. **2.** To represent in words.
de·pict (dĭ **pĭkt′**) ◊ *verb* **depicted, depicting**

deposit *verb* **1.** To lay or put down: *I deposited my books on the table. The wind deposited snow on the sidewalk.* **2.** To put money into a bank account. **3.** To give as partial payment for a purchase or service.
◊ *noun* **1.** An amount of money deposited in a bank account. **2.** The condition of being deposited: *I have $1,000 on deposit.* **3.** An amount of money given as partial payment for a purchase or service. **4.** A mass of material, as a mineral, that builds up by a natural process: *Prospectors looked for gold deposits.*
de·pos·it (dĭ **pŏz′**ĭt) ◊ *verb* **deposited, depositing** ◊ *noun, plural* **deposits**

ă	pat	ĭ	pit	oi	**oil**	th	ba**th**
ā	pay	ī	ride	ŏŏ	book	*th*	ba**the**
â	care	î	fierce	ōō	boot	ə	ago, item
ä	father	ŏ	pot	ou	**out**		pencil
ĕ	pet	ō	go	ŭ	cut		atom
ē	be	ô	paw, for	û	fur		circus

depositor *noun* A person who deposits something, especially money in a bank.
de·pos·i·tor (dĭ **pŏz′**ĭ tər) ◊ *noun, plural* **depositors**

depot *noun* **1.** A railroad or bus station. **2.** A warehouse or storehouse. **3.** A place where military equipment and supplies are stored.
de·pot (**dē′**pō *or* **dĕp′**ō) ◊ *noun, plural* **depots**

▲ **depot**

depress *verb* **1.** To make sad or gloomy: *News of the accident depressed everyone.* **2.** To press down: *The driver depresses the accelerator to increase the speed of the car.* **3.** To cause to lessen in strength or activity: *The decline in business depressed the stock market.*
de·press (dĭ **prĕs′**) ◊ *verb* **depressed, depressing**

depression *noun* **1.** Low spirits; sadness. **2.** A hollow part or area: *My head made a depression in the pillow.* **3.** A period of business decline with much unemployment. **4.** The act of pressing down.
de·pres·sion (dĭ **prĕsh′**ən) ◊ *noun, plural* **depressions**

deprive *verb* To take away from or prevent from having: *Worry deprived me of sleep.*
de·prive (dĭ **prīv′**) ◊ *verb* **deprived, depriving**

depth *noun* **1.** Distance from top to bottom or front to back: *We planted the tulip bulbs at the proper depth.* **2.** A deep part or place, as in a body of water: *The divers worked in the*

depths of the ocean. **3.** The greatest degree of intensity: *I was in the depth of despair.*
depth (dĕpth) ◊ *noun, plural* **depths**

deputy *noun* A person appointed to act for or instead of another.
dep·u·ty (dĕp′ yə tē) ◊ *noun, plural* **deputies**

derby *noun* **1.** A stiff felt hat with a round crown and a narrow, curved brim. **2.** A race for three-year-old horses.
der·by (dûr′ bē) ◊ *noun, plural* **derbies**

derive *verb* To get or receive from a source: *I derive pleasure from music. The word "algebra" derives from Arabic.*
de·rive (dĭ rīv′) ◊ *verb* **derived, deriving**

derrick *noun* **1.** A machine for lifting and moving heavy objects. It consists of a movable beam equipped with pulleys and cables. **2.** A tall framework used to support the equipment used in drilling an oil well.
der·rick (dĕr′ ĭk) ◊ *noun, plural* **derricks**

▲ **derrick**

descend *verb* **1.** To move from a higher to a lower place or position: *The airplane descended for landing.* **2.** To come from a source or origin: *Their ruler descends from a long line of monarchs.*
de·scend (dĭ sĕnd′) ◊ *verb* **descended, descending**

descendant *noun* A person descended from a particular ancestor or ancestors.
de·scen·dant (dĭ sĕn′ dənt) ◊ *noun, plural* **descendants**

descent *noun* **1.** The act of moving downward. **2.** A downward slope. **3.** The fact of descending from a particular ancestor or ancestors: *I am of English descent.*
de·scent (dĭ sĕnt′) ◊ *noun, plural* **descents**
‖*These sound alike:* **descent, dissent**

describe *verb* To use words to tell about: *We described our trip around the world.*
de·scribe (dĭ skrīb′) ◊ *verb* **described, describing**

description *noun* **1.** A statement that describes: *That description of the park makes me feel as if I am there.* **2.** A kind or variety: *At the Thanksgiving Day parade we saw people of every description.*
de·scrip·tion (dĭ skrĭp′ shən) ◊ *noun, plural* **descriptions**

descriptive *adjective* Giving a description.
de·scrip·tive (dĭ skrĭp′ tĭv) ◊ *adjective*

desegregate *verb* To do away with the separation of members of one race from members of another.
de·seg·re·gate (dē sĕg′ rĭ gāt′) ◊ *verb* **desegregated, desegregating**

desert¹ *noun* A dry area, usually covered with sand, in which few plants or animals live. ◊ *adjective* Of or like a desert; not lived in.
des·ert¹ (dĕz′ ərt) ◊ *noun, plural* **deserts** ◊ *adjective*

desert² *verb* To go away from someone or something one has a duty to stay with or support: *The guards deserted their posts.*
de·sert² (dĭ zûrt′) ◊ *verb* **deserted, deserting**

***HISTORY* • desert¹, desert²**

Both **desert¹** and **desert²** go back to a Latin word meaning "to abandon." **Desert¹** originally meant any abandoned area or wasteland, but now it usually refers to a dry, barren, sandy region.

deserve *verb* To be worthy of or have a right to; merit: *You deserved the reward.*
de·serve (dĭ zûrv′) ◊ *verb* **deserved, deserving**

design *noun* **1.** Something, as a drawing, that serves as a pattern: *We saw the architect's design for the new library.* **2.** An arrangement of elements, as lines or shapes, that forms a pattern.
◊ *verb* To make a plan for, as with a drawing: *Architects design buildings.*
de·sign (dĭ zīn′) ◊ *noun, plural* **designs** ◊ *verb* **designed, designing**

designate *verb* **1.** To point out or show; indicate: *A sign designates the boundary.* **2.** To call, as by name or title: *The present time is often designated the Space Age.* **3.** To select for a particular purpose; appoint: *We designate you to represent us.*
des·ig·nate (**dĕs′**ĭg nāt′) ◊ *verb* **designated, designating**

desirable *adjective* Worthy of being desired; pleasing: *That looks like a desirable spot for the picnic.*
de·sir·a·ble (dĭ **zīr′**ə bəl) ◊ *adjective*

desire *noun* **1.** A strong wish; longing: *I have a desire to see the world.* **2.** A wish that is expressed. **3.** Something that is wanted.
◊ *verb* **1.** To have a desire for: *You can have whatever you desire for your birthday.* **2.** To ask for; request.
de·sire (dĭ **zīr′**) ◊ *noun, plural* **desires** ◊ *verb* **desired, desiring**

desk *noun* A piece of furniture with a top for use in reading or writing.
desk (dĕsk) ◊ *noun, plural* **desks**

desolate *adjective* **1.** Without people; deserted: *The beach is desolate in winter.* **2.** In bad condition; ruined. **3.** Extremely unhappy: *We were desolate when the kitten ran away.*
◊ *verb* To cause to be desolate.
des·o·late ◊ *adjective* (**dĕs′**ə lĭt) ◊ *verb* (**dĕs′**ə lāt′) **desolated, desolating**

desolation *noun* **1.** The state of being in bad or ruined condition. **2.** Great sadness.
des·o·la·tion (dĕs′ə **lā′**shən) ◊ *noun*

despair *noun* **1.** Total lack of hope: *They gave up in despair.* **2.** A cause of despair.
◊ *verb* To be without or lose all hope.
de·spair (dĭ **spâr′**) ◊ *noun, plural* **despairs** ◊ *verb* **despaired, despairing**

desperate *adjective* **1.** Without or nearly without hope: *I feel desperate but I will try again.* **2.** Ready to run any risk because of desperation.
des·per·ate (**dĕs′**pər ĭt) ◊ *adjective*

ă	pat	ĭ	pit	oi	**oil**	th	ba**th**
ā	pay	ī	ride	o͝o	book	*th*	ba**the**
â	care	î	fierce	o͞o	boot	ə	ago, item
ä	father	ŏ	pot	ou	**out**		pencil
ĕ	pet	ō	go	ŭ	cut		atom
ē	be	ô	paw, for	û	fur		circus

desperation *noun* A lack of hope that makes a person desperate and very unhappy.
des·per·a·tion (dĕs′pə **rā′**shən) ◊ *noun*

despise *verb* To regard with great dislike: *I despise big black spiders.*
de·spise (dĭ **spīz′**) ◊ *verb* **despised, despising**

despite *preposition* In spite of: *We went downtown despite the stormy skies.*
de·spite (dĭ **spīt′**) ◊ *preposition*

dessert *noun* Food, as fruit, served last at lunch or dinner.
des·sert (dĭ **zûrt′**) ◊ *noun, plural* **desserts**

destination *noun* A place to which someone is going or to which something is sent.
des·ti·na·tion (dĕs′tə **nā′**shən) ◊ *noun, plural* **destinations**

destine *verb* **1.** To determine or decide in advance: *You are destined to be a leader.* **2.** To set apart for a particular use or purpose: *This money is destined for a new TV.*
des·tine (**dĕs′**tĭn) ◊ *verb* **destined, destining**

destitute *adjective* Lacking the resources, as money, needed for life; very poor.
des·ti·tute (**dĕs′**tĭ to͞ot′ *or* **dĕs′**tĭ tyo͞ot′) ◊ *adjective*

destroy *verb* **1.** To completely ruin, as by burning: *The explosion destroyed several homes.* —See Synonyms at **ruin.** **2.** To put to death. **3.** To put an end to.
de·stroy (dĭ **stroi′**) ◊ *verb* **destroyed, destroying**

destroyer *noun* A fast warship that carries torpedoes, missiles, and other weapons.
de·stroy·er (dĭ **stroi′**ər) ◊ *noun, plural* **destroyers**

▲ **destroyer**

destruction *noun* **1.** The act or process of destroying. **2.** The condition of being destroyed.
de·struc·tion (dĭ **strŭk′**shən) ◊ *noun*

destructive *adjective* **1.** Causing destruction: *Destructive storms are unusual in New England.* **2.** Not constructive or helpful: *Destructive criticism of my work made me feel bad.*
de·struc·tive (dĭ **strŭk′**tĭv) ◊ *adjective*

detach *verb* To cause to be separate from something else: *I detached the page from the workbook.*
de·tach (dĭ **tăch′**) ◊ *verb* **detached, detaching**

detail *noun* **1.** A small part of a whole; item: *Give me all the details of your plan.* **2.** The treatment of something item by item: *Tell us the main points; don't go into detail.* **3.** A small group, as of soldiers, given a special duty.
◊ *verb* **1.** To give the details of. **2.** To assign to a special duty.
de·tail (dĭ **tāl′** *or* **dē′**tāl′) ◊ *noun, plural* **details** ◊ *verb* **detailed, detailing**

detain *verb* **1.** To keep from going on; delay. **2.** To keep in custody; confine.
de·tain (dĭ **tān′**) ◊ *verb* **detained, detaining**

detect *verb* To discover or notice the presence or fact of: *I detect anger in your voice.*
de·tect (dĭ **tĕkt′**) ◊ *verb* **detected, detecting**

detective *noun* A person, often a police officer, whose work is to get information about crimes and try to solve them.
de·tec·tive (dĭ **tĕk′**tĭv) ◊ *noun, plural* **detectives**

detector *noun* A device that detects the presence of a substance or agent such as smoke, metal, or radioactivity.
de·tec·tor (dĭ **tĕk′**tər) ◊ *noun, plural* **detectors**

deter *verb* To keep from doing something; discourage: *Rain deterred me from going out.*
de·ter (dĭ **tûr′**) ◊ *verb* **deterred, deterring**

detergent *noun* A cleaning substance that is used instead of soap.
de·ter·gent (dĭ **tûr′**jənt) ◊ *noun, plural* **detergents**

determination *noun* **1.** The act of making a decision or the decision that is made. **2.** The quality of being determined.
de·ter·mi·na·tion (dĭ tûr′mə **nā′**shən) ◊ *noun, plural* **determinations**

determine *verb* **1.** To fix definitely; settle: *Let's determine when you should come.* **2.** To make a decision: *I determined that the story was true.* —See Synonyms at **decide. 3.** To influence or affect: *The weather determines our skiing plans.* **4.** To find out definitely: *I tried to determine what had happened.*
de·ter·mine (dĭ **tûr′**mĭn) ◊ *verb* **determined, determining**

determined *adjective* Having or displaying firmness in sticking to a purpose.
de·ter·mined (dĭ **tûr′**mĭnd) ◊ *adjective*

detest *verb* To dislike very much; hate.
de·test (dĭ **tĕst′**) ◊ *verb* **detested, detesting**

dethrone *verb* To remove from a position of power, especially one held by a king or queen.
de·throne (dē **thrōn′**) ◊ *verb* **dethroned, dethroning**

detour *noun* A way that is used when another way cannot be used.
◊ *verb* To use or cause to use a detour.
de·tour (**dē′**tŏŏr′) ◊ *noun, plural* **detours** ◊ *verb* **detoured, detouring**

▲ **detour**

detract *verb* To take away, as from value or quality: *Dirty hands detract from an otherwise good appearance.*
de·tract (dĭ **trăkt′**) ◊ *verb* **detracted, detracting**

devastate *verb* To destroy or ruin: *Storms devastated much of the small country.*
dev·as·tate (**dĕv′**ə stāt′) ◊ *verb* **devastated, devastating**

develop *verb* **1.** To make more effective or advanced: *Lessons will develop your musical ability.* **2.** To grow or cause to grow: *Swimming develops the muscles.* **3.** To bring or come into being: *Try to develop good reading habits.* **4.** To treat a film with chemicals so that a picture can be seen.
de·vel·op (dĭ **vĕl′** əp) ◊ *verb* **developed, developing**

development *noun* The act of developing or the condition of being developed.
de·vel·op·ment (dĭ **vĕl′** əp mənt) ◊ *noun, plural* **developments**

device *noun* **1.** A piece of equipment that is made for a particular purpose: *A broom is a device for sweeping.* **2.** A plan or trick: *I used the device of disguising my voice.*
de·vice (dĭ **vīs′**) ◊ *noun, plural* **devices**

devil *noun* **1.** Often **Devil** The chief spirit of evil; Satan. **2.** An evil spirit. **3.** An energetic or mischievous person.
dev·il (**dĕv′** əl) ◊ *noun, plural* **devils**

devise *verb* To think of; plan or invent: *I devised a new way of playing the game.*
de·vise (dĭ **vīz′**) ◊ *verb* **devised, devising**

devote *verb* To give time or attention entirely to a particular person, purpose, or activity: *I devoted my life to music.*
de·vote (dĭ **vōt′**) ◊ *verb* **devoted, devoting**

devoted *adjective* Having or showing loyalty and affection; faithful.
de·vot·ed (dĭ **vō′** tĭd) ◊ *adjective*

devotion *noun* Loyalty and affection.
de·vo·tion (dĭ **vō′** shən) ◊ *noun*

devour *verb* **1.** To eat up in a greedy way: *The dog devoured its dinner.* **2.** To take in eagerly: *I devoured every book I could find on the exploration of space.*
de·vour (dĭ **vour′**) ◊ *verb* **devoured, devouring**

devout *adjective* **1.** Having or showing devotion to religion. **2.** Truly meant; sincere: *You have my devout thanks for your help.*
de·vout (dĭ **vout′**) ◊ *adjective*

ă	pat	ĭ	pit	oi	oil	th	bath
ā	pay	ī	ride	o͝o	book	*th*	bathe
â	care	î	fierce	o͞o	boot	ə	ago, item
ä	father	ŏ	pot	ou	out		pencil
ĕ	pet	ō	go	ŭ	cut		atom
ē	be	ô	paw, for	û	fur		circus

dew *noun* Moisture that condenses and collects on cool surfaces, usually at night.
dew (do͞o *or* dyo͞o) ◊ *noun*
‖*These sound alike:* **dew, due**

dewlap *noun* A loose fold of skin hanging under the neck of certain animals, such as a cow or bull.
dew·lap (**do͞o′** lăp′ *or* **dyo͞o′** lăp′) ◊ *noun, plural* **dewlaps**

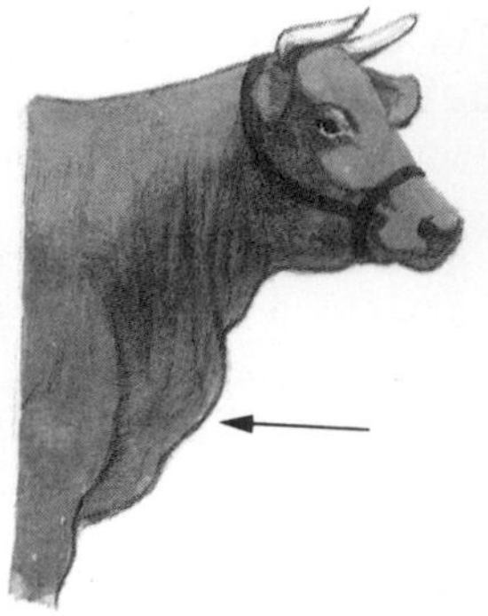
▲ **dewlap**

dexterity *noun* Skill in the use of the hands, body, or mind: *The carpenter had great manual dexterity.*
dex·ter·i·ty (dĕk **stĕr′** ĭ tē) ◊ *noun*

diabetes *noun* A disease in which there is too high a level of sugar in the blood.
di·a·be·tes (dī′ə **bē′** tĭs *or* dī′ə **bē′** tēz′) ◊ *noun*

diadem *noun* A crown or ornamental band worn on the head as a sign of royalty.
di·a·dem (**dī′** ə dĕm′) ◊ *noun, plural* **diadems**

diagnoses *noun* Plural of **diagnosis.**
di·ag·no·ses (dī′əg **nō′** sēz′) ◊ *noun*

diagnosis *noun* The act of identifying a disease and studying the symptoms.
di·ag·no·sis (dī′əg **nō′** sĭs) ◊ *noun, plural* **diagnoses**

diagnostic *adjective* Of, involving, or used in diagnosis.
di·ag·nos·tic (dī′əg **nŏs′** tĭk) ◊ *adjective*

diagonal *adjective* **1.** Slanting from one corner of a figure with four sides, as a square, to another corner. **2.** Having or taking a slanting direction.
◊ *noun* A diagonal line, line segment, or direction.
di·ag·o·nal (dī **ăg′** ə nəl) ◊ *adjective* ◊ *noun, plural* **diagonals**

diagram *noun* Something, as a drawing, that shows how something else works or shows the relationships between its parts.
◊ *verb* To draw or show by a diagram.
di·a·gram (**dī′** ə grăm′) ◊ *noun, plural* **diagrams** ◊ *verb* **diagrammed, diagramming**

dial *noun* **1.** A plate or disk with letters, figures, or marks on which a number or measure-

ment is shown by means of a pointer. **2.** A disk with numbers and letters that is rotated to make telephone calls. **3.** A control that chooses the setting on a radio or television set. **4.** The face of a clock.
◊ *verb* To control, choose, or telephone by means of a dial: *Dial to another TV channel.*
di·al (dī′əl) ◊ *noun, plural* **dials** ◊ *verb* **dialed, dialing**

dialect *noun* A variety of a language that is typical of a particular group or part of a country. A dialect is different from other dialects in such features as the way words are pronounced or used.
di·a·lect (dī′ə lĕkt′) ◊ *noun, plural* **dialects**

dialogue *noun* **1.** A conversation between two or more persons. **2.** The words spoken in conversation by the characters of a written work, as a play.
di·a·logue (dī′ə lôg′) ◊ *noun, plural* **dialogues**

diameter *noun* **1.** A straight line that passes through the center of a circle or sphere from a point on one side to a point on the other side. **2.** The length of a diameter; thickness of something round: *I measured the diameter of the pipe.*
di·am·e·ter (dī ăm′ĭ tər) ◊ *noun, plural* **diameters**

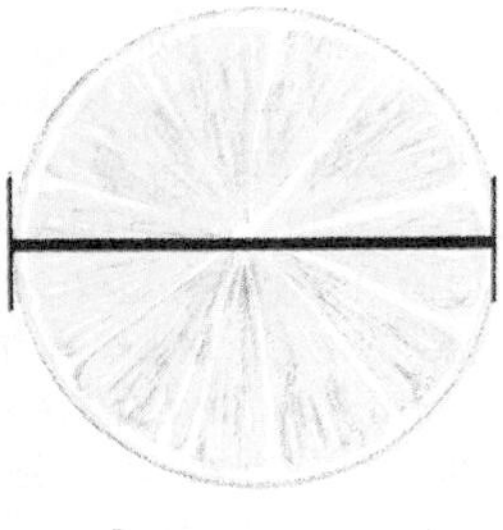

▲ **diameter**

diamond *noun* **1.** An extremely hard mineral that is a crystal form of carbon, is used for cutting and grinding, and is used as jewelry. **2.** A figure (♦) with four equal sides. **3.** A baseball infield.
di·a·mond (dī′ə mənd) ◊ *noun, plural* **diamonds**

diaper *noun* A piece of absorbent material, as cloth, that is placed between a baby's legs and fastened at the waist.
di·a·per (dī′ə pər) ◊ *noun, plural* **diapers**

diaphragm *noun* A wall of muscle that separates the chest from the abdomen.
di·a·phragm (dī′ə frăm′) ◊ *noun, plural* **diaphragms**

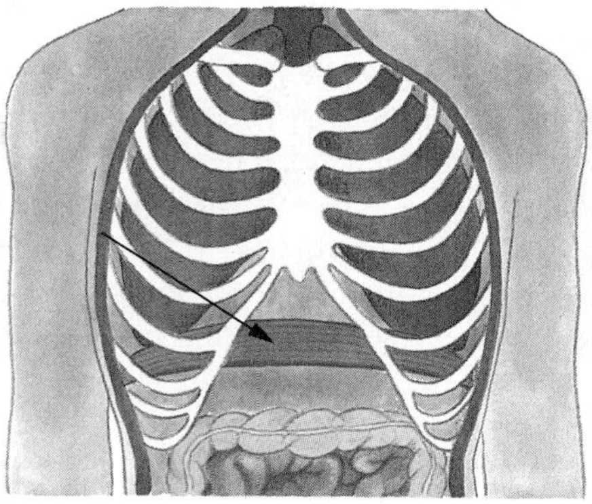

▲ **diaphragm**

diary *noun* **1.** A daily written record of a person's thoughts, activities, opinions, and experiences. **2.** A book for keeping a daily record.
di·a·ry (dī′ə rē) ◊ *noun, plural* **diaries**

dice *verb* To cut into small cubes: *I diced the potatoes for the chowder.*
◊ *noun* Plural of **die²** (sense 2).
dice (dīs) ◊ *verb* **diced, dicing** ◊ *noun*

dictate *verb* **1.** To say or read aloud for another person to write down or a machine to record: *The principal dictated the letter.* **2.** To say with authority; order: *The police dictated where the large, noisy crowd should stand during the parade.*
dic·tate (dĭk′tāt′) ◊ *verb* **dictated, dictating**

dictation *noun* **1.** The act of dictating. **2.** Material to be written down or recorded.
dic·ta·tion (dĭk tā′shən) ◊ *noun*

dictator *noun* A ruler who has complete power and often governs a country in a cruel or unfair way.
dic·ta·tor (dĭk′tā′tər) ◊ *noun, plural* **dictators**

dictionary *noun* A book that contains a list of words in a language in alphabetical order together with the meaning or meanings of each and their pronunciations.
dic·tion·ar·y (dĭk′shə nĕr′ē) ◊ *noun, plural* **dictionaries**

did *verb* Past tense of **do¹**.
did (dĭd) ◊ *verb*

didn't Contraction of "did not."
did·n't (dĭd′nt) ◊ *contraction*

die¹ *verb* **1.** To stop living; become dead: *The flowers died in the spring blizzard.* **2.** To disappear gradually; come to an end: *The winds died away. The fire died down.* **3.** To want very much: *I'm dying to go.*
die¹ (dī) ◊ *verb* **died, dying**
‖*These sound alike:* **die, dye**

die² *noun* **1.** A device or machine part that shapes material by or as if by stamping. **2.** One of a pair of small cubes that are marked on each side with from one to six dots and are used in games.
die² (dī) ◊ *noun, plural* **dies** (for sense 1) *or* **dice** (for sense 2)
‖*These sound alike:* **die, dye**

***HISTORY* • die¹, die²**

Die¹ comes from an old Scandinavian word that meant "to stop living." **Die²** comes from an old French word that came from a Latin word meaning "playing piece."

diesel engine *noun* An engine that burns oil. The oil is burned by the heat of the air compressed in the cylinders instead of by an electric spark, as in a gasoline engine.
die·sel engine (dē′zəl) ◊ *noun, plural* **diesel engines**

diet *noun* **1.** The usual food and drink taken in by a person or animal. **2.** Special foods eaten especially to cause one to lose weight or to improve the health.
◊ *verb* To eat or cause to eat a smaller amount or a particular diet.
di·et (dī′ĭt) ◊ *noun, plural* **diets** ◊ *verb* **dieted, dieting**

differ *verb* **1.** To be unlike: *The two houses differ in size.* **2.** To have a different opinion; disagree: *I differ with you about who really won the debate.*
dif·fer (dĭf′ər) ◊ *verb* **differed, differing**

ă	pat	ĭ	pit	oi	**oil**	th	**bath**
ā	pay	ī	ride	o͝o	book	*th*	bathe
â	care	î	fierce	o͞o	boot	ə	ago, item
ä	father	ŏ	pot	ou	**out**		pencil
ĕ	pet	ō	go	ŭ	cut		atom
ē	be	ô	paw, for	û	fur		circus

difference *noun* **1.** The condition or quality of being different. **2.** The amount left after subtracting one number from another; remainder. **3.** A disagreement or quarrel: *We're friends, but we've had our differences.*
dif·fer·ence (dĭf′ər əns) ◊ *noun, plural* **differences**

different *adjective* **1.** Partly or completely unlike another: *The sea horse is different from any other fish.* **2.** Not identical; separate: *I visited you on two different days.*
dif·fer·ent (dĭf′ər ənt) ◊ *adjective*

difficult *adjective* **1.** Hard to make, do, or understand: *That was a difficult problem.* **2.** Hard to get along with or deal with: *My cousin is a difficult child.*
dif·fi·cult (dĭf′ĭ kŭlt′) ◊ *adjective*

difficulty *noun* **1.** The condition or quality of being difficult: *We were surprised at the difficulty of the book. I walked with difficulty.* **2.** Something that gets in the way; obstacle: *The difficulty was to get there on time.*
dif·fi·cul·ty (dĭf′ĭ kŭl′tē) ◊ *noun, plural* **difficulties**

dig *verb* **1.** To break up, turn over, or remove earth with or as if with a shovel. **2.** To form by or as if by digging: *They dug a tunnel.* **3.** To obtain by digging: *Miners dug coal from the ground.* **4.** To find or make known by searching, studying, or working hard: *I'll dig up the facts somehow.* **5.** To push or cause to push hard; poke: *Thorns dug into my hands when I picked the roses.*
dig (dĭg) ◊ *verb* **dug, digging**

digest *verb* To break food down into a form that is easily taken in and used by the body.
◊ *noun* A shortened version of a written work.
di·gest ◊ *verb* (dĭ jĕst′) **digested, digesting** ◊ *noun* (dī′jĕst′), *plural* **digests**

digestion The process of digesting food.
di·ges·tion (dĭ jĕs′chən) ◊ *noun*

digestive *adjective* Of, relating to, or active in digestion.
di·ges·tive (dĭ jĕs′tĭv) ◊ *adjective*

digit *noun* **1.** A finger or toe. **2.** One of the Arabic numerals, 1, 2, 3, 4, 5, 6, 7, 8, 9, and sometimes 0.
dig·it (dĭj′ĭt) ◊ *noun, plural* **digits**

digital *adjective* **1.** Of or relating to a digit. **2.** Of, relating to, using, or showing information in the form of numerical digits: *We are*

learning how to use a digital computer.
dig·i·tal (dĭj′ ĭ tl) ◊ *adjective*

dignified *adjective* Having or showing dignity: *Behave in a dignified manner.*
dig·ni·fied (dĭg′ nə fīd′) ◊ *adjective*

dignity *noun* **1.** The condition or quality of having worth or of being honorable. **2.** Stately and serious behavior: *The candidates spoke with dignity before the election.*
dig·ni·ty (dĭg′ nĭ tē) ◊ *noun*

dike *noun* A mound or embankment that is built to hold back water and prevent flooding.
dike (dīk) ◊ *noun, plural* **dikes**

▲ **dike**

dilapidated *adjective* Shabby from great neglect: *The windows were broken on the dilapidated old house.*
di·lap·i·dat·ed (dĭ lăp′ ĭ dā′tĭd) ◊ *adjective*

diligent *adjective* Working hard and earnestly: *My friend is a diligent student.*
dil·i·gent (dĭl′ ə jənt) ◊ *adjective*

dilute *verb* To make weaker or more liquid, as by adding water.
di·lute (dĭ lo͞ot′) ◊ *verb* **diluted, diluting**

dim *adjective* **1.** Somewhat dark: *The cat lay in a dim corner of the hall.* **2.** Giving off little light: *Don't try to read by a dim lamp.* **3.** Not easily and clearly seen: *We saw the dim shape of a steeple through the mist.*
◊ *verb* To make or become dim.
dim (dĭm) ◊ *adjective* **dimmer, dimmest**
◊ *verb* **dimmed, dimming**

dime *noun* A coin used in the United States and Canada that is worth ten cents. Ten dimes equal one dollar.
dime (dīm) ◊ *noun, plural* **dimes**

dimension *noun* The measure of length, width, or height: *The dimensions of the room are 20 feet long, 15 feet wide, and 8 feet high.*
di·men·sion (dĭ mĕn′ shən) ◊ *noun, plural* **dimensions**

diminish *verb* To make or become smaller or less: *The drought this spring has greatly diminished our water supply.*
di·min·ish (dĭ mĭn′ ĭsh) ◊ *verb* **diminished, diminishing**

diminutive *adjective* Very small; tiny.
di·min·u·tive (dĭ mĭn′ yə tĭv) ◊ *adjective*

dimple *noun* A small hollow in the flesh, as on the cheek.
dim·ple (dĭm′ pəl) ◊ *noun, plural* **dimples**

▲ **dimple**

din *noun* Loud or confused noise: *We heard the din of the crowd.*
◊ *verb* To make a loud or confused noise.
din (dĭn) ◊ *noun*
◊ *verb* **dinned, dinning**

dine *verb* To eat a meal, especially dinner: *They dined at 7:00.*
dine (dīn) ◊ *verb* **dined, dining**

diner *noun* **1.** A person who dines. **2.** A railroad car in which meals are served or a restaurant that looks like one.
din·er (dī′ nər) ◊ *noun, plural* **diners**

dinghy *noun* A small rowboat.
din·ghy (dĭng′ ē) ◊ *noun, plural* **dinghies**

dingy *adjective* Dirty or dark in appearance: *The dingy room needed a coat of paint.*
din·gy (dĭn′ jē) ◊ *adjective* **dingier, dingiest**

dining room *noun* A room in which meals are served.
dining room ◊ *noun, plural* **dining rooms**

dinner *noun* **1.** The main meal of the day. **2.** A formal meal in honor of a person or an occasion.
din·ner (dĭn′ ər) ◊ *noun, plural* **dinners**

dinosaur *noun* One of a group of reptiles that lived millions of years ago. Some dinosaurs were bigger than elephants and others were the size of cats.
di·no·saur (**dī′** nə sôr′) ◊ *noun, plural* **dinosaurs**

▲ **dinosaur**

diocese *noun* The area or district under the authority of a bishop.
di·o·cese (**dī′** ə sĭs) ◊ *noun, plural* **dioceses**

dip *verb* **1.** To plunge briefly into a liquid: *I dipped the cracker into the soup.* **2.** To take out by or as if by using a ladle: *I dipped some soup from the pot.* **3.** To lower or sink and raise or rise again: *They dipped the flag in salute.* **4.** To sink or slope downward.
◊ *noun* **1.** A brief swim. **2.** An amount taken up by dipping; scoop. **3.** A downward slope or sharp drop.
dip (dĭp) ◊ *verb* **dipped, dipping** ◊ *noun, plural* **dips**

diploma *noun* A document or certificate that shows a student has finished a course of study or earned a degree.
di·plo·ma (dĭ **plō′** mə) ◊ *noun, plural* **diplomas**

ă	pat	ĭ	pit	oi	**oil**	th	ba**th**
ā	pay	ī	ride	o͝o	book	*th*	ba*th*e
â	care	î	fierce	o͞o	boot	ə	ago, item
ä	father	ŏ	pot	ou	**out**		pencil
ĕ	pet	ō	**go**	ŭ	cut		atom
ē	be	ô	paw, for	û	fur		circus

***HISTORY* • diploma, diplomat**

Diploma goes back to a Greek word that meant "something folded," referring especially to an official document. **Diplomats** take their name from the official documents they are often concerned with.

diplomat *noun* **1.** A person whose job it is to represent a government in its relations with other countries. **2.** A person who has skill in dealing with others.
dip·lo·mat (**dĭp′** lə măt′) ◊ *noun, plural* **diplomats**

diplomatic *adjective* **1.** Of or relating to diplomats. **2.** Skillful in dealing with others.
dip·lo·mat·ic (dĭp′lə **măt′** ĭk) ◊ *adjective*

dipper *noun* **1.** A cup with a long handle for scooping up liquids. **2. Dipper** Either of two groups of stars in the northern sky that are shaped somewhat like a dipper. They are called the *Big Dipper* and the *Little Dipper.*
dip·per (**dĭp′** ər) ◊ *noun, plural* **dippers**

direct *verb* **1.** To aim, point, or guide to or toward: *I directed the arrow toward the target. Please direct me to the post office.* **2.** To be in charge of: *My neighbor directs a large company.* **3.** To command; order: *The governor directed them to free the prisoner.*
◊ *adjective* Moving or lying in a straight line: *This street is a direct route into town.*
◊ *adverb* Directly.
di·rect (dĭ **rĕkt′**) ◊ *verb* **directed, directing** ◊ *adjective* ◊ *adverb*

direct current *noun* An electric current that does not change its direction of flow.

direction *noun* **1.** The act of directing. **2.** An instruction or order: *Follow the directions on the package.* **3.** The line or course along which someone or something goes, lies, or points: *Walk in the direction of the town.*
di·rec·tion (dĭ **rĕk′** shən) ◊ *noun, plural* **directions**

directly *adverb* **1.** In a direct line or way: *Go directly to your room.* **2.** Without delay; at once: *I will see you directly after school.*
di·rect·ly (dĭ **rĕkt′** lē) ◊ *adverb*

direct object *noun* A word or words that name the receiver, goal, or result of the action

of a verb. For example, in the sentence *I saw you,* the word *you* is the direct object.
direct object ◊ *noun, plural* **direct objects**

director *noun* A person who directs.
di·rec·tor (dĭ **rĕk′** tər) ◊ *noun, plural* **directors**

▲ **director**
A motion picture director

directory *noun* A book with a list of names and addresses.
di·rec·to·ry (dĭ **rĕk′** tə rē) ◊ *noun, plural* **directories**

dirigible *noun* A large cigar-shaped aircraft filled with gas that is lighter than air. It has a motor and a steering mechanism.
dir·i·gi·ble (**dîr′** ə jə bəl) ◊ *noun, plural* **dirigibles**

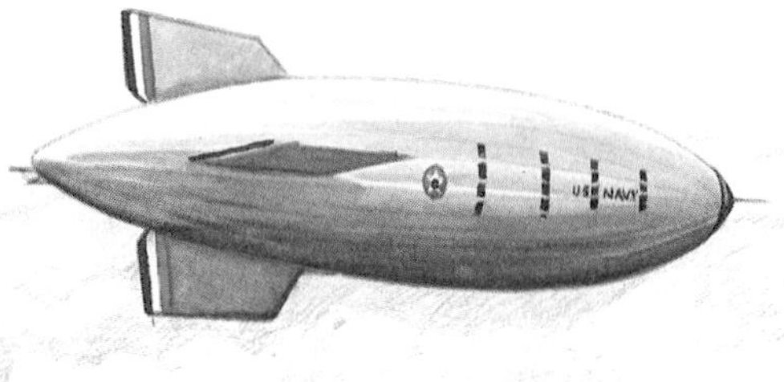

▲ **dirigible**

dirt *noun* **1.** Earth or soil. **2.** A filthy substance, such as mud.
dirt (dûrt) ◊ *noun*

dirty *adjective* **1.** Full of or covered with dirt; not clean. **2.** Not honest or fair; low or mean: *Stealing books is a dirty trick.* **3.** Showing ill will or anger.
◊ *verb* To make or become dirty.
dirt·y (**dûr′** tē) ◊ *adjective* **dirtier, dirtiest** ◊ *verb* **dirtied, dirtying**

dis– The prefix *dis–* means "not" or "opposite." A *dishonest* person is a person who is not honest. The prefix *dis–* also means "not having" or "lack of." When I feel *discomfort,* I feel a lack of comfort.

***VOCABULARY BUILDER* • dis–**

Many words that are formed with **dis–** are not entries in this dictionary. But you can figure out what these words mean by looking up the meanings of the root words and the suffix. For example:
dissimilar = not similar
disunion = a lack of union

disability *noun* **1.** The condition of being disabled. **2.** Something that disables.
dis·a·bil·i·ty (dĭs′ə **bĭl′** ĭ tē) ◊ *noun, plural* **disabilities**

disable *verb* To take away the normal abilities of; cripple: *The injured arm disabled the pitcher for the whole season.*
dis·a·ble (dĭs **ā′** bəl) ◊ *verb* **disabled, disabling**

disadvantage *noun* **1.** A circumstance or condition that makes it harder to do something or to be successful: *A disadvantage of river transportation is its slowness.* **2.** Damage or harm: *The new ruling worked to our disadvantage.*
dis·ad·van·tage (dĭs′əd **văn′** tĭj) ◊ *noun, plural* **disadvantages**

disagree *verb* **1.** To fail to agree; be different: *Your answer to the first problem disagrees with mine.* **2.** To have a different opinion: *Scientists disagree on why the dinosaurs became extinct.* **3.** To have an argument; quarrel.
dis·a·gree (dĭs′ə **grē′**) ◊ *verb* **disagreed, disagreeing**

disagreeable *adjective* **1.** Unpleasant; distasteful. **2.** Tending to cause trouble or get into arguments; quarrelsome.
dis·a·gree·a·ble (dĭs′ə **grē′** ə bəl) ◊ *adjective*

disagreement *noun* **1.** A failure to agree; difference of opinion. **2.** A dispute or quarrel.
dis·a·gree·ment (dĭs′ə **grē′** mənt) ◊ *noun, plural* **disagreements**

disappear *verb* **1.** To pass out of sight; vanish: *The ship disappeared over the horizon.* **2.** To cease to exist.
dis·ap·pear (dĭs′ə **pîr′**) ◊ *verb* **disappeared, disappearing**

disappearance *noun* The act or an example of disappearing.
dis·ap·pear·ance (dĭs′ə **pîr′** əns) ◊ *noun, plural* **disappearances**

disappoint *verb* To fail to satisfy the hopes or wishes of.
dis·ap·point (dĭs′ə **point′**) ◊ *verb* **disappointed, disappointing**

disappointment *noun* **1.** The act of disappointing. **2.** The feeling of being disappointed: *To my disappointment, the game was canceled.* **3.** A person or thing that disappoints: *The picnic was a disappointment.*
dis·ap·point·ment (dĭs′ə **point′** mənt) ◊ *noun, plural* **disappointments**

disapproval *noun* The feeling of considering something or someone wrong or bad.
dis·ap·prov·al (dĭs′ə **prōō′** vəl) ◊ *noun*

disapprove *verb* To have an unfavorable opinion: *We disapprove of smoking.*
dis·ap·prove (dĭs′ə **prōōv′**) ◊ *verb* **disapproved, disapproving**

disarm *verb* **1.** To take weapons from. **2.** To reduce the size of a nation's armed forces or supply of weapons.
dis·arm (dĭs **ärm′**) ◊ *verb* **disarmed, disarming**

disarrange *verb* To upset the order or arrangement of: *The wind disarranged my hair.*
dis·ar·range (dĭs′ə **rānj′**) ◊ *verb* **disarranged, disarranging**

ă	pat	ĭ	pit	oi	oil	th	bath
ā	pay	ī	ride	ŏŏ	book	*th*	bathe
â	care	î	fierce	ōō	boot	ə	ago, item
ä	father	ŏ	pot	ou	out		pencil
ĕ	pet	ō	go	ŭ	cut		atom
ē	be	ô	paw, for	û	fur		circus

disaster *noun* Something, such as a flood, that causes great destruction.
dis·as·ter (dĭ **zăs′** tər) ◊ *noun, plural* **disasters**

▲ **disaster**
Damage caused by an earthquake

disband *verb* To stop being a group; break up: *The club disbanded.*
dis·band (dĭs **bănd′**) ◊ *verb* **disbanded, disbanding**

disbelief *noun* The refusal or unwillingness to believe.
dis·be·lief (dĭs′bĭ **lēf′**) ◊ *noun*

disc *noun* A phonograph record.
disc (dĭsk) ◊ *noun, plural* **discs**
‖*These sound alike:* **disc, disk**

discard *verb* To throw away or get rid of.
dis·card (dĭs **kärd′**) ◊ *verb* **discarded, discarding**

discharge *verb* **1.** To get rid of a load; un-

load: *The ship discharged its cargo.* **2.** To release, as from duty or work; let go: *They were discharged from school.* **3.** To send or pour forth: *The geyser discharged steam.* **4.** To shoot or fire from a weapon.
◊ *noun* **1.** An act of unloading. **2.** Dismissal or release, as from work. **3.** A pouring or flowing out. **4.** An act of firing a weapon or projectile.
dis·charge ◊ *verb* (dĭs **chärj′**) **discharged, discharging** ◊ *noun* (**dĭs′**chärj′), *plural* **discharges**

disciple *noun* A person who believes in and often helps to spread the teachings of another.
dis·ci·ple (dĭ **sī′**pəl) ◊ *noun, plural* **disciples**

discipline *noun* **1.** Training of the mind, body, or character that demands strict obedience and self-control: *It takes years of discipline to become a pianist.* **2.** Punishment intended to correct or train.
◊ *verb* **1.** To train by instruction and control: *You must discipline yourself to speak in public without fear.* **2.** To punish in order to correct or train. —See Synonyms at **punish.**
dis·ci·pline (**dĭs′**ə plĭn) ◊ *noun, plural* **disciplines** ◊ *verb* **disciplined, disciplining**

disc jockey *noun* A radio announcer who plays phonograph records on the air.
disc jockey ◊ *noun, plural* **disc jockeys**

▲ **disc jockey**

disclose *verb* To make known; reveal.
dis·close (dĭs **klōz′**) ◊ *verb* **disclosed, disclosing**

discolor *verb* To spoil the color of; stain.
dis·col·or (dĭs **kŭl′**ər) ◊ *verb* **discolored, discoloring**

discomfort *noun* A lack of comfort.
dis·com·fort (dĭs **kŭm′**fərt) ◊ *noun*

disconcert *verb* To confuse and upset: *With everyone watching me, I became disconcerted and forgot my lines.*
dis·con·cert (dĭs′kən **sûrt′**) ◊ *verb* **disconcerted, disconcerting**

disconnect *verb* To break the connection of or between: *The phone is disconnected.*
dis·con·nect (dĭs′kə **nĕkt′**) ◊ *verb* **disconnected, disconnecting**

discontent *noun* The condition or feeling of being discontented; dissatisfaction.
dis·con·tent (dĭs′kən **tĕnt′**) ◊ *noun*

discontented *adjective* Not satisfied.
dis·con·tent·ed (dĭs′kən **tĕn′**tĭd) ◊ *adjective*

discontinue *verb* To bring or come to an end; stop.
dis·con·tin·ue (dĭs′kən **tĭn′**yo͞o) ◊ *verb* **discontinued, discontinuing**

discord *noun* Lack of agreement or harmony, as among members of a group.
dis·cord (**dĭs′**kôrd′) ◊ *noun*

discount *noun* An amount that is taken off a full or regular price.
◊ *verb* **1.** To subtract from a price. **2.** To have doubts about: *You can discount those rumors.*
dis·count ◊ *noun* (**dĭs′**kount′), *plural* **discounts** ◊ *verb* (**dĭs′**kount′ *or* dĭs **kount′**) **discounted, discounting**

discourage *verb* **1.** To make less hopeful or enthusiastic. **2.** To try to dissuade: *My best friend discouraged me from going.* **3.** To try to prevent or hinder; deter: *They lit a fire to discourage mosquitoes.*
dis·cour·age (dĭ **skûr′**ĭj) ◊ *verb* **discouraged, discouraging**

discourteous *adjective* Not polite; rude.
dis·cour·te·ous (dĭs **kûr′**tē əs) ◊ *adjective*

discourtesy *noun* Lack of courtesy.
dis·cour·te·sy (dĭs **kûr′**tĭ sē) ◊ *noun, plural* **discourtesies**

discover *verb* **1.** To find out; learn: *I looked down and discovered that my knee was bleeding.* **2.** To be the first to find, learn of, or observe: *Columbus discovered America.*
dis·cov·er (dĭ **skŭv′**ər) ◊ *verb* **discovered, discovering**

discovery *noun* **1.** The act of discovering. **2.** Something discovered: *Penicillin was a great scientific discovery.*
dis·cov·er·y (dĭ **skŭv′** ə rē) ◊ *noun, plural* **discoveries**

discredit *verb* **1.** To cast doubt on: *The new scientific study discredits some old theories.* **2.** To refuse to believe in: *I discredited the story as mere rumor.*
dis·cred·it (dĭs **krĕd′**ĭt) ◊ *verb* **discredited, discrediting**

discriminate *verb* **1.** To tell the difference between; distinguish: *Can you discriminate good apples from bad apples by their appearance?* **2.** To treat some people better than others for an unfair reason.
dis·crim·i·nate (dĭ **skrĭm′** ə nāt′) ◊ *verb* **discriminated, discriminating**

discrimination *noun* **1.** The ability to see small differences or make careful and good choices: *The furnishings in their house showed taste and discrimination.* **2.** The treating of some people better than others for an unfair reason; prejudice.
dis·crim·i·na·tion (dĭ skrĭm′ə **nā′**shən) ◊ *noun*

discus *noun* A disk of wood and metal that is hurled for distance in athletic contests.
dis·cus (**dĭs′** kəs) ◊ *noun, plural* **discuses**

▲ **discus**

ă	pat	ĭ	pit	oi	**oil**	th	**bath**
ā	pay	ī	ride	ŏŏ	book	*th*	**bathe**
â	care	î	fierce	ōō	boot	ə	ago, item
ä	father	ŏ	pot	ou	**out**		pencil
ĕ	pet	ō	go	ŭ	cut		atom
ē	be	ô	paw, for	û	fur		circus

discuss *verb* **1.** To talk over. **2.** To consider fully or from different points of view: *Does your history book discuss the Civil War?*
dis·cuss (dĭ **skŭs′**) ◊ *verb* **discussed, discussing**

SYNONYMS

discuss, argue, debate

We *discussed* where we should go for our vacation. I *argued* that the best place to go was the beach. The two candidates for the governorship *debated* the issues with each other.

discussion *noun* **1.** A serious conversation. **2.** An examination or presentation of a subject, as in a book.
dis·cus·sion (dĭ **skŭsh′** ən) ◊ *noun, plural* **discussions**

disease *noun* A condition that keeps the body from functioning normally; illness.
dis·ease (dĭ **zēz′**) ◊ *noun, plural* **diseases**

diseased *adjective* Having a disease.
dis·eased (dĭ **zēzd′**) ◊ *adjective*

disembark *verb* To go or put ashore from a ship: *After the boat docked we disembarked.*
dis·em·bark (dĭs′ĕm **bärk′**) ◊ *verb* **disembarked, disembarking**

disfavor *noun* **1.** Lack of approval; dislike. **2.** The condition of being disapproved of or disliked.
dis·fa·vor (dĭs **fā′**vər) ◊ *noun*

disfigure *verb* To spoil the appearance of.
dis·fig·ure (dĭs **fĭg′** yər) ◊ *verb* **disfigured, disfiguring**

disgrace *noun* **1.** Loss of honor or respect; shame. **2.** Something that brings shame or dishonor: *The dirty halls are a disgrace to the school.*
◊ *verb* To be a cause of shame or dishonor to: *Bad behavior will ruin your reputation and disgrace your family.*
dis·grace (dĭs **grās′**) ◊ *noun, plural* **disgraces** ◊ *verb* **disgraced, disgracing**

disgraceful *adjective* Causing disgrace.
dis·grace·ful (dĭs **grās′** fəl) ◊ *adjective*

disgruntle *verb* To make discontented or dissatisfied.
dis·grun·tle (dĭs **grŭn′** təl) ◊ *verb* **disgruntled, disgruntling**

disguise *noun* Clothes and often make-up worn to hide a person's identity or to look like someone else.
◊ *verb* To change the appearance of with a disguise: *I disguised myself as a clown for the party.*
dis·guise (dĭs **gīz′**) ◊ *noun, plural* **disguises** ◊ *verb* **disguised, disguising**

disgust *noun* A feeling of strong dislike for something sickening or offensive.
◊ *verb* To cause to feel disgust; sicken.
dis·gust (dĭs **gŭst′**) ◊ *noun* ◊ *verb* **disgusted, disgusting**

dish *noun* **1.** A flat or shallow container for holding or serving food. **2.** Something held or served in a dish: *I ate a dish of prunes.* **3.** Food prepared in a particular way: *Soup is my favorite dish in winter.*
dish (dĭsh) ◊ *noun, plural* **dishes**

dishearten *verb* To take away the courage or spirit of; discourage.
dis·heart·en (dĭs **här′**tn) ◊ *verb* **disheartened, disheartening**

dishonest *adjective* Not honest; tending to lie, cheat, or deceive: *It's dishonest to copy someone else's answers.*
dis·hon·est (dĭs **ŏn′**ĭst) ◊ *adjective*

> ***SYNONYMS***
>
> ***dishonest, deceitful, untruthful***
>
> Cheating on tests is *dishonest.* It is *deceitful* to say something when you know it is not true. I know that what they said was *untruthful.*

dishonesty *noun* Lack of honesty.
dis·hon·es·ty (dĭs **ŏn′**ĭ stē) ◊ *noun*

dishonor *noun* Loss of honor, respect, or reputation; disgrace.
◊ *verb* To bring dishonor on; disgrace.
dis·hon·or (dĭs **ŏn′**ər) ◊ *noun* ◊ *verb* **dishonored, dishonoring**

dishonorable *adjective* Causing or deserving loss of honor; disgraceful.
dis·hon·or·a·ble (dĭs **ŏn′**ər ə bəl) ◊ *adjective*

disinfect *verb* To get rid of germs that can cause disease.
dis·in·fect (dĭs′ĭn **fĕkt′**) ◊ *verb* **disinfected, disinfecting**

disinfectant *noun* A substance, as iodine, that kills germs that can cause disease.
dis·in·fec·tant (dĭs′ĭn **fĕk′**tənt) ◊ *noun, plural* **disinfectants**

disintegrate *verb* To break into small, separate pieces or fragments.
dis·in·te·grate (dĭs **ĭn′**tĭ grāt′) ◊ *verb* **disintegrated, disintegrating**

disinterested *adjective* Not having a selfish interest in; impartial: *The counselor gave us some disinterested advice.*
dis·in·ter·est·ed (dĭs **ĭn′**tə rĕs′tĭd) ◊ *adjective*

disk *noun* **1.** A thin, flat, circular object, as a coin. **2.** A flexible circular plate coated with magnetic material on which computer programs and data can be stored.
disk (dĭsk) ◊ *noun, plural* **disks**
‖*These sound alike:* **disk, disc**

▲ **disk**
A computer disk

dislike *verb* To have a feeling of not liking: *I dislike having to get up early.*
◊ *noun* A feeling of not liking: *You'll soon get over your dislike of vegetables.*
dis·like (dĭs **līk′**) ◊ *verb* **disliked, disliking** ◊ *noun, plural* **dislikes**

dislocate *verb* To put or force out of a normal position: *The football player dislocated a shoulder when falling to the ground.*
dis·lo·cate (**dĭs′**lō kāt′) ◊ *verb* **dislocated, dislocating**

dislodge *verb* To force out of position: *We couldn't dislodge the rock from the path.*
dis·lodge (dĭs **lŏj′**) ◊ *verb* **dislodged, dislodging**

disloyal *adjective* Not loyal.
dis·loy·al (dĭs **loi′**əl) ◊ *adjective*

disloyalty *noun* **1.** Lack of loyalty. **2.** A disloyal act.
dis·loy·al·ty (dĭs **loi′**əl tē) ◊ *noun, plural* **disloyalties**

dismal *adjective* Causing, feeling, or showing gloom or depression: *The bad weather put me into a dismal mood.*
dis·mal (**dĭz′**məl) ◊ *adjective*

dismay *verb* To fill with sudden concern or discouragement: *The length of the math assignment dismayed us.*
◊ *noun* A sudden loss of courage or confidence in the face of danger or difficulty.
dis·may (dĭs **mā′**) ◊ *verb* **dismayed, dismaying** ◊ *noun*

dismiss *verb* **1.** To allow or ask to leave; send away: *At two o'clock our teacher dismissed the class.* **2.** To take away the job or office of: *The factory dismissed 200 workers.*
dis·miss (dĭs **mĭs′**) ◊ *verb* **dismissed, dismissing**

dismissal *noun* **1.** The act of dismissing. **2.** The condition of being dismissed.
dis·miss·al (dĭs **mĭs′** əl) ◊ *noun, plural* **dismissals**

dismount *verb* To get off or down: *The rider dismounted from the horse.*
dis·mount (dĭs **mount′**) ◊ *verb* **dismounted, dismounting**

disobedient *adjective* Not obedient.
dis·o·be·di·ent (dĭs′ə **bē′** dē ənt) ◊ *adjective*

disobey *verb* To refuse or fail to obey.
dis·o·bey (dĭs′ə **bā′**) ◊ *verb* **disobeyed, disobeying**

disorder *noun* **1.** Lack of order; confusion: *The kitchen is in disorder.* **2.** A public disturbance; riot. **3.** An illness; sickness.
◊ *verb* To disturb the arrangement of.
dis·or·der (dĭs **ôr′** dər) ◊ *noun, plural* **disorders** ◊ *verb* **disordered, disordering**

disorderly *adjective* **1.** Not neat or tidy. **2.** Not behaving according to rules or customs; unruly.
dis·or·der·ly (dĭs **ôr′** dər lē) ◊ *adjective*

disorganize *verb* To put into confusion: *The interruptions disorganized the class.*
dis·or·gan·ize (dĭs **ôr′** gə nīz′) ◊ *verb* **disorganized, disorganizing**

dispatch *verb* To send off quickly to a certain place or person: *The teacher dispatched a message to the principal's office.* —See Synonyms at **send.**
◊ *noun* **1.** Quick action. —See Synonyms at **hurry. 2.** A written message. **3.** A news report sent to a newspaper.
dis·patch (dĭ **spăch′**) ◊ *verb* **dispatched, dispatching** ◊ *noun, plural* **dispatches**

dispel *verb* To drive away: *Your good spirits dispelled our gloom.*
dis·pel (dĭ **spĕl′**) ◊ *verb* **dispelled, dispelling**

dispense *verb* **1.** To give out in parts or portions; distribute: *The government dispensed emergency food to the flood victims.*
dis·pense (dĭ **spĕns′**) ◊ *verb* **dispensed, dispensing**

dispenser *noun* A container that gives out something one at a time or piece by piece.
dis·pens·er (dĭ **spĕn′**-sər) ◊ *noun, plural* **dispensers**

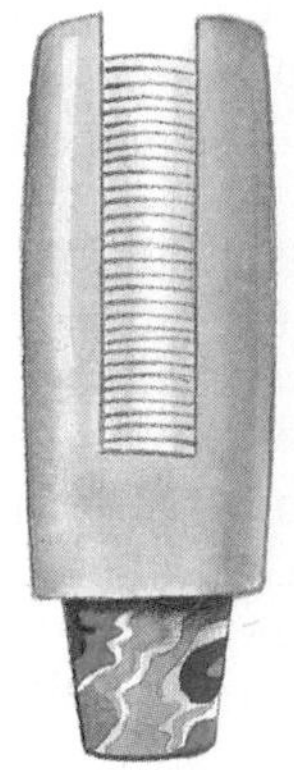

▲ **dispenser**
A paper-cup dispenser

disperse *verb* To move or send in different directions; scatter: *The pods open, and the seeds disperse.*
dis·perse (dĭ **spûrs′**) ◊ *verb* **dispersed, dispersing**

displace *verb* **1.** To put out of the usual place: *The floods displaced many people.* **2.** To take the place of; replace: *Robots have displaced workers in some factories.*
dis·place (dĭs **plās′**) ◊ *verb* **displaced, displacing**

display *verb* **1.** To put on view; exhibit: *The store displayed suits in the window.* —See Synonyms at **show. 2.** To make noticeable; show signs of: *I hate to display my ignorance.*
◊ *noun* **1.** A public showing; exhibition: *A display of moon rocks is in the museum.* **2.** A visual representation of data on a screen.
dis·play (dĭ **splā′**) ◊ *verb* **displayed, displaying** ◊ *noun, plural* **displays**

displease *verb* To make dissatisfied.
dis·please (dĭs **plēz′**) ◊ *verb* **displeased, displeasing**

displeasure *noun* The condition of being displeased; dissatisfaction.
dis·pleas·ure (dĭs **plĕzh′** ər) ◊ *noun*

ă	pat	ĭ	pit	oi	**oil**	th	**bath**
ā	pay	ī	ride	o͝o	book	*th*	**bathe**
â	care	î	fierce	o͞o	boot	ə	ago, item
ä	father	ŏ	pot	ou	**out**		pencil
ĕ	pet	ō	go	ŭ	cut		atom
ē	be	ô	paw, for	û	fur		circus

disposable *adjective* Made to be thrown away after use.
dis·pos·a·ble (dĭ **spō′** zə bəl) ◊ *adjective*

disposal *noun* **1.** The act of throwing out or away: *The sanitation department is in charge of garbage disposal.* **2.** The freedom to use something: *A huge supply of knowledge is at your disposal in the library.*
dis·pos·al (dĭ **spō′** zəl) ◊ *noun*

dispose *verb* **1.** To put in a particular place; arrange: *We disposed our suitcase under our seat.* **2.** To make willing; incline: *They were not disposed to help us.*
◊ *idiom* **dispose of 1.** To finish attending to; settle: *Let's dispose of the matter and turn to something else.* **2.** To get rid of.
dis·pose (dĭ **spōz′**) ◊ *verb* **disposed, disposing**

disposition *noun* **1.** A person's usual mood or attitude: *You have an affectionate disposition.* **2.** A tendency to behave in a certain way: *You show a disposition to help other people.*
dis·po·si·tion (dĭs′pə **zĭsh′** ən) ◊ *noun, plural* **dispositions**

disprove *verb* To prove to be untrue.
dis·prove (dĭs **pro͞ov′**) ◊ *verb* **disproved, disproving**

dispute *verb* **1.** To argue about; debate: *In the debate the students disputed the question of a dress code.* **2.** To question the truth of; doubt: *I dispute the belief that money makes people happy.* **3.** To quarrel.
◊ *noun* An argument or quarrel. —See Synonyms at **fight.**
dis·pute (dĭ **spyo͞ot′**) ◊ *verb* **disputed, disputing** ◊ *noun, plural* **disputes**

disqualify *verb* To make or say to be unfit or not suitable: *Bad eyesight disqualified them for training as pilots.*
dis·qual·i·fy (dĭs **kwŏl′** ə fī′) ◊ *verb* **disqualified, disqualifying**

disregard *verb* To pay little or no attention to: *Don't disregard the rules.*
dis·re·gard (dĭs′rĭ **gärd′**) ◊ *verb* **disregarded, disregarding**

disreputable *adjective* Not respectable, as in appearance: *Your clothes are so sloppy that you look disreputable.*
dis·rep·u·ta·ble (dĭs **rĕp′** yə tə bəl) ◊ *adjective*

disrespect *noun* Lack of respect; rudeness.
dis·re·spect (dĭs′rĭ **spĕkt′**) ◊ *noun*

disrespectful *adjective* Having or showing a lack of respect; rude.
dis·re·spect·ful (dĭs′rĭ **spĕkt′** fəl) ◊ *adjective*

disrupt *verb* To throw into confusion; break up: *The flood disrupted their lives.*
dis·rupt (dĭs **rŭpt′**) ◊ *verb* **disrupted, disrupting**

dissatisfaction *noun* The condition or feeling of not being satisfied.
dis·sat·is·fac·tion (dĭs săt′ĭs **făk′** shən) ◊ *noun*

dissatisfy *verb* To fail to satisfy.
dis·sat·is·fy (dĭs **săt′** ĭs fī′) ◊ *verb* **dissatisfied, dissatisfying**

dissension *noun* Disagreement among the members of a group.
dis·sen·sion (dĭ **sĕn′** shən) ◊ *noun*

dissent *verb* To disagree: *The right to dissent is part of our political system.*
◊ *noun* Difference of opinion; disagreement.
dis·sent (dĭ **sĕnt′**) ◊ *verb* **dissented, dissenting** ◊ *noun*
‖ *These sound alike:* **dissent, descent**

dissipate *verb* **1.** To drive away; scatter: *A strong wind dissipated the clouds.* **2.** To use up in a foolish way; waste: *Don't dissipate your money and time on the project.*
dis·si·pate (**dĭs′** ə pāt′) ◊ *verb* **dissipated, dissipating**

dissolve *verb* **1.** To mix thoroughly with a liquid: *Salt dissolves in water.* —See Synonyms at **melt. 2.** To change from a solid to a liquid.
dis·solve (dĭ **zŏlv′**) ◊ *verb* **dissolved, dissolving**

dissuade *verb* To persuade not to do something: *The lifeguard dissuaded me from swimming across the lake.*
dis·suade (dĭ **swād′**) ◊ *verb* **dissuaded, dissuading**

distance *noun* **1.** The amount of space between two places, things, or points. **2.** A distant place or point: *I can see a train in the distance.*
dis·tance (**dĭs′** təns) ◊ *noun, plural* **distances**

distant *adjective* **1.** Far away in space or time: *Do you see that distant peak on the horizon?* **2.** Far apart in relationship: *You're my distant cousin.*
dis·tant (**dĭs′** tənt) ◊ *adjective*

distaste *noun* Dislike: *I have a great distaste for licorice.*
dis·taste (dĭs **tāst′**) ◊ *noun*

distasteful *adjective* Disagreeable: *The view was spoiled by some distasteful signs.*
dis·taste·ful (dĭs **tāst′**fəl) ◊ *adjective*

distemper *noun* An often fatal disease of animals, as dogs or cats.
dis·tem·per (dĭs **tĕm′**pər) ◊ *noun*

distinct *adjective* **1.** Easy to smell, see, hear, or understand; unmistakable: *A distinct smell of smoke came from the house.* **2.** Not alike; different and separate.
dis·tinct (dĭ **stĭngkt′**) ◊ *adjective*

distinction *noun* **1.** The act of seeing or noting a difference or of treating differently: *Employers should hire men and women without distinction.* **2.** A difference: *What is the distinction between butterflies and moths?* **3.** Something that makes a person or thing different or remarkable: *Jupiter has the distinction of being the largest planet.*
dis·tinc·tion (dĭ **stĭngk′**shən) ◊ *noun, plural* **distinctions**

distinctive *adjective* Setting a person or thing off from others: *Police officers wear distinctive uniforms.*
dis·tinc·tive (dĭ **stĭngk′**tĭv) ◊ *adjective*

distinguish *verb* **1.** To recognize as being different; tell apart: *Counting their legs is one way to distinguish spiders from ants.* **2.** To make different; set apart: *A very long neck distinguishes the giraffe from other animals.* **3.** To hear or see clearly; make out: *Dogs can distinguish sounds that are too high for human ears.* **4.** To make oneself well known or highly regarded.
dis·tin·guish (dĭ **stĭng′**gwĭsh) ◊ *verb* **distinguished, distinguishing**

distort *verb* **1.** To twist out of shape: *The mirror distorted my reflection.* **2.** To tell in a way that is partly false: *Don't distort the facts.*
dis·tort (dĭ **stôrt′**) ◊ *verb* **distorted, distorting**

ă	pat	ĭ	pit	oi	**oil**	th	**bath**
ā	pay	ī	ride	o͝o	book	*th*	**bathe**
â	care	î	fierce	o͞o	boot	ə	ago, item
ä	father	ŏ	pot	ou	**out**		pencil
ĕ	pet	ō	go	ŭ	cut		atom
ē	be	ô	paw, for	û	fur		circus

distract *verb* To draw away the attention of; divert: *The noises from the back yard distracted me from my homework.*
dis·tract (dĭ **străkt′**) ◊ *verb* **distracted, distracting**

distress *noun* Pain or suffering of mind or body.
◊ *verb* To cause distress to.
dis·tress (dĭ **strĕs′**) ◊ *noun* ◊ *verb* **distressed, distressing**

distribute *verb* **1.** To divide and give out in portions. **2.** To give or pass out to several or many: *It's time to distribute the presents.* **3.** To scatter over an area; spread: *Cotton plantations were widely distributed in the South.*
dis·trib·ute (dĭ **strĭb′**yo͞ot) ◊ *verb* **distributed, distributing**

distribution *noun* The act of distributing or the way in which things are distributed.
dis·tri·bu·tion (dĭs′trə **byo͞o′**shən) ◊ *noun, plural* **distributions**

district *noun* **1.** A part, as of a city, that is set aside for a particular purpose: *Our town is divided into three school districts.* **2.** An area or region that has a certain use or character: *The city has several shopping districts.*
dis·trict (**dĭs′**trĭkt) ◊ *noun, plural* **districts**

distrust *noun* Lack of trust; suspicion.
◊ *verb* To have no trust in.
dis·trust (dĭs **trŭst′**) ◊ *noun* ◊ *verb* **distrusted, distrusting**

disturb *verb* **1.** To change the order or arrangement of; move out of place: *Please don't disturb the papers on my desk.* **2.** To trouble or worry: *Your noisy play disturbs me.* **3.** To break in on; interrupt: *The fire sirens disturbed our sleep.*
dis·turb (dĭ **stûrb′**) ◊ *verb* **disturbed, disturbing**

disturbance *noun* **1.** The act of disturbing or the condition of being disturbed. **2.** Something that disturbs; interruption. **3.** An outbreak of disorder; commotion.
dis·tur·bance (dĭ **stûr′**bəns) ◊ *noun, plural* **disturbances**

ditch *noun* A long, narrow trench.
ditch (dĭch) ◊ *noun, plural* **ditches**

dive *verb* **1.** To plunge headfirst into water. **2.** To go or cause to go underwater; submerge: *The submarine dived.* **3.** To make an airplane

plunge downward at a steep angle.
◊ *noun* An act of diving.
dive (dīv) ◊ *verb* **dived** *or* **dove, diving**
◊ *noun, plural* **dives**

diver *noun* **1.** A person who dives. **2.** A person who works underwater.
div·er (dī′ vər) ◊ *noun, plural* **divers**

▲ **diver**

diverse *adjective* Unlike one another; different: *Ours is a nation of diverse peoples.*
di·verse (dĭ vûrs′) ◊ *adjective*

diversion *noun* **1.** An act or example of diverting. **2.** Something amusing.
di·ver·sion (dĭ vûr′ zhən) ◊ *noun, plural* **diversions**

diversity *noun* Difference; variety.
di·ver·si·ty (dĭ vûr′ sĭ tē) ◊ *noun*

divert *verb* **1.** To turn aside from a course or direction: *The police diverted traffic until the road could be repaired.* **2.** To draw the attention away. **3.** To amuse or entertain.
di·vert (dĭ vûrt′) ◊ *verb* **diverted, diverting**

divide *verb* **1.** To separate into two or more parts or groups. —See Synonyms at **separate. 2.** To separate into branches: *The river divides here.* **3.** To split into opposing groups or sides: *Bad feelings have divided the team.* **4.** To give out in equal amounts; share: *The workers divided the money.* **5.** To determine how many times one number contains another: *The teacher told me to divide 20 by 2.*
di·vide (dĭ vīd′) ◊ *verb* **divided, dividing**

dividend *noun* A number to be divided by another: *In 20 ÷ 2, 20 is the dividend.*
div·i·dend (dĭv′ ĭ dĕnd′) ◊ *noun, plural* **dividends**

divine *adjective* **1.** Of, from, or like God or a god. **2.** Holy; sacred.
di·vine (dĭ vīn′) ◊ *adjective*

divinity *noun* **1.** The condition or quality of being divine. **2.** A divine being; deity. **3.** The study of religion; theology.
di·vin·i·ty (dĭ vĭn′ ĭ tē) ◊ *noun, plural* **divinities**

divisible *adjective* Capable of being divided.
di·vis·i·ble (dĭ vĭz′ ə bəl) ◊ *adjective*

division *noun* **1.** The mathematical process of dividing. **2.** The act of dividing or the condition of being divided. **3.** One of the parts or groups into which something is divided. **4.** Something that divides. **5.** An army unit composed of a number of battalions.
di·vi·sion (dĭ vĭzh′ ən) ◊ *noun, plural* **divisions**

divisor *noun* The number by which another number is to be divided: *In 20 ÷ 2, 2 is the divisor.*
di·vi·sor (dĭ vī′ zər) ◊ *noun, plural* **divisors**

divorce *noun* **1.** The legal ending of a marriage. **2.** The complete separation of two things: *In America there is total divorce between church and state.*
◊ *verb* To end a marriage legally.
di·vorce (dĭ vôrs′) ◊ *noun, plural* **divorces**
◊ *verb* **divorced, divorcing**

dizzy *adjective* **1.** Having a feeling of whirling or of being about to fall. **2.** Bewildered or confused.
diz·zy (dĭz′ ē) ◊ *adjective* **dizzier, dizziest**

do[1] *verb* **1.** To carry out an act or action; perform or accomplish: *I don't know what to do.*

2. To act or behave: *Do as I tell you.* **3.** To create or compose: *Do a drawing for me.* **4.** To bring about; effect: *Crying won't do any good.* **5.** To put into action; exert: *I'll do my best to help you.* **6.** To deal with or take care of: *I have a lot of things to do.* **7.** To work at for a living: *What do you do?* **8.** To work out the details of; solve: *Please do these arithmetic problems.* **9.** To be suitable for: *These shoes won't do for running.* **10.** To get along; fare: *How are you doing in school?* **11.** Used as a substitute for a preceding verb: *I try as hard as you do.*
◊ *auxiliary verb* Used: **1.** In questions and negative statements: *Do you see it? I do not want to go.* **2.** For emphasis: *I do want to go.*
do[1] (do͞o) ◊ *verb* **did, done, doing, does**

do[2] *noun* The first tone of the musical scale.
do[2] (dō) ◊ *noun, plural* **dos**
‖*These sound alike:* **do[2], doe, dough**

Doberman pinscher *noun* A large dog with a long head and a smooth black or brown coat.
Do·ber·man pin·scher (dō′bər mən pĭn′shər) ◊ *noun, plural* **Doberman pinschers**

***HISTORY* • Doberman pinscher**

The **Doberman pinscher** gets it name from Ludwig *Dobermann,* who bred the dogs in Germany during the nineteenth century. **Pinscher** is the German word for "terrier."

docile *adjective* Easy to train or handle.
doc·ile (dŏs′əl) ◊ *adjective*

dock *noun* **1.** A platform for loading or unloading. **2.** A group of piers that serves as a landing area for ships and boats. **3.** A waterway between or alongside piers.
◊ *verb* **1.** To guide or come into a dock. **2.** To join two or more spacecraft in space.
dock (dŏk) ◊ *noun, plural* **docks** ◊ *verb* **docked, docking**

ă	pat	ĭ	pit	oi	oil	th	bath
ā	pay	ī	ride	o͝o	book	*th*	bathe
â	care	î	fierce	o͞o	boot	ə	ago, item
ä	father	ŏ	pot	ou	out		pencil
ĕ	pet	ō	go	ŭ	cut		atom
ē	be	ô	paw, for	û	fur		circus

▲ **dock**

doctor *noun* **1.** A physician, dentist, or veterinarian who is trained in and licensed to practice a healing art. **2.** A person who holds the highest degree given by a university.
doc·tor (dŏk′tər) ◊ *noun, plural* **doctors**

doctrine *noun* A principle, belief, or teaching, as of a church, that is held to be true.
doc·trine (dŏk′trĭn) ◊ *noun, plural* **doctrines**

document *noun* An official paper that can be used to give proof or information.
doc·u·ment (dŏk′yə mənt) ◊ *noun, plural* **documents**

dodge *verb* **1.** To move quickly aside: *The quarterback dodged and ran for a touchdown.* **2.** To avoid by moving quickly: *I dodged the snowballs thrown at me.*
dodge (dŏj) ◊ *verb* **dodged, dodging**

dodo *noun* A large, heavy bird that formerly lived on an island in the Indian Ocean and was unable to fly.
do·do (dō′dō) ◊ *noun, plural* **dodoes** *or* **dodos**

doe *noun* **1.** A female deer. **2.** The female of an animal such as the hare or kangaroo.
doe (dō) ◊ *noun, plural* **does**
‖*These sound alike:* **doe, do[2], dough**

does *verb* Third person singular present tense of **do[1]**.
does (dŭz) ◊ *verb*

doesn't Contraction of "does not."
does·n't (dŭz′ənt) ◊ *contraction*

doff *verb* To take off, as a hat.
doff (dôf) ◊ *verb* **doffed, doffing**

dog *noun* An animal with four legs that eats meat and is related to the wolves and foxes.
◊ *verb* To follow after closely or persistently:

My little brothers and sisters have been dogging me all afternoon.
dog (dôg) ◊ *noun, plural* **dogs** ◊ *verb* **dogged, dogging**

dogfish *noun* Any of several small sharks.
dog·fish (dôg′fĭsh′) ◊ *noun, plural* **dogfish** *or* **dogfishes**

dogwood *noun* A tree with small greenish flowers surrounded by showy white or pink leaves that look like petals.
dog·wood (dôg′wo͝od′) ◊ *noun, plural* **dogwoods**

▲ **dogwood**

doily *noun* A small mat used to protect or decorate a table.
doi·ly (doi′lē) ◊ *noun, plural* **doilies**

doings *plural noun* Activities, especially social activities.
do·ings (do͞o′ĭngz) ◊ *plural noun*

dole *noun* **1.** The giving out of goods, especially of money, food, or clothing, as charity. **2.** Something given out as charity.
◊ *verb* **1.** To give out as charity. **2.** To give out in small portions.
dole (dōl) ◊ *noun, plural* **doles** ◊ *verb* **doled, doling**

doll *noun* A small image of a human being used as a child's toy.
doll (dŏl) ◊ *noun, plural* **dolls**

dollar *noun* A unit of money equal to 100 cents that is used in the United States and Canada.
dol·lar (dŏl′ər) ◊ *noun, plural* **dollars**

dolphin *noun* A sea animal that is related to the whales but is smaller and has a snout that looks like a beak. It is an intelligent animal that can be trained by human beings.
dol·phin (dŏl′fĭn) ◊ *noun, plural* **dolphins**

▲ **dolphin**

domain *noun* **1.** All the territory under the control of one ruler or government. **2.** A field of interest or activity.
do·main (dō **mān′**) ◊ *noun, plural* **domains**

dome *noun* A rounded top or roof that looks like half a sphere.
dome (dōm) ◊ *noun, plural* **domes**

▲ **dome**

domestic *adjective* **1.** Of or relating to a home, a household, or family life. **2.** Living with or in the care of human beings; tame. **3.** Of or relating to one's own country; not foreign or imported.
◊ *noun* A person employed in a household, as a maid.
do·mes·tic (də **mĕs′**tĭk) ◊ *adjective* ◊ *noun, plural* **domestics**

domesticate *verb* To train to live with and be of use to human beings; tame.
do·mes·ti·cate (də **mĕs′** tĭ kāt′) ◊ *verb* **domesticated, domesticating**

dominant *adjective* Having the most influence or control: *Our parents are the dominant members of the family.*
dom·i·nant (**dŏm′** ə nənt) ◊ *adjective*

dominate *verb* To have controlling power or occupy a commanding position over.
dom·i·nate (**dŏm′** ə nāt′) ◊ *verb* **dominated, dominating**

domineer *verb* To order others around.
dom·i·neer (dŏm′ə **nîr′**) ◊ *verb* **domineered, domineering**

dominion *noun* **1.** Controlling power; rule. **2.** A territory under the control of one ruler or government; domain.
do·min·ion (də **mĭn′** yən) ◊ *noun, plural* **dominions**

domino *noun* **1.** One of a set of small, dark rectangular blocks marked with light dots. **2. dominoes** (*used with a singular verb*) A game played with a set of these blocks.
dom·i·no (**dŏm′** ə nō′) ◊ *noun, plural* **dominoes**

donate *verb* To give to a fund or cause; contribute: *We donate money to our public television station every year.*
do·nate (**dō′** nāt′) ◊ *verb* **donated, donating**

donation *noun* **1.** The act of donating. **2.** Something donated; contribution.
do·na·tion (dō **nā′** shən) ◊ *noun, plural* **donations**

done *verb* Past participle of **do**[1].
done (dŭn) ◊ *verb*

donkey *noun* An animal related to the horse but smaller and with longer ears.
don·key (**dŏng′** kē) ◊ *noun, plural* **donkeys**

donor *noun* A person who gives, donates, or contributes.
do·nor (**dō′** nər) ◊ *noun, plural* **donors**

don't Contraction of "do not."
don't (dōnt) ◊ *contraction*

ă	pat	ĭ	pit	oi	oil	th	bath
ā	pay	ī	ride	o͝o	book	*th*	bathe
â	care	î	fierce	o͞o	boot	ə	ago, item
ä	father	ŏ	pot	ou	out		pencil
ĕ	pet	ō	go	ŭ	cut		atom
ē	be	ô	paw, for	û	fur		circus

doom *noun* A terrible fate.
◊ *verb* To destine to a terrible fate.
doom (do͞om) ◊ *noun, plural* **dooms** ◊ *verb* **doomed, dooming**

door *noun* **1.** A movable panel that is used to open or close an entrance to a room, building, or vehicle. **2.** A doorway.
door (dôr) ◊ *noun, plural* **doors**

doorbell *noun* A bell at a door that is rung by someone who wishes the door to be opened.
door·bell (**dôr′** bĕl′) ◊ *noun, plural* **doorbells**

doorstep *noun* A step or series of steps leading from an outside door to the ground.
door·step (**dôr′** stĕp′) ◊ *noun, plural* **doorsteps**

doorway *noun* The entrance to a room or building.
door·way (**dôr′** wā′) ◊ *noun, plural* **doorways**

dope *noun* A thick, sticky substance, as that once used to coat and strengthen the cloth covering of airplane wings.
dope (dōp) ◊ *noun, plural* **dopes**

dormant *adjective* Not active for a time.
dor·mant (**dôr′** mənt) ◊ *adjective*

dormitory *noun* A building where a number of people live, as at a school.
dor·mi·to·ry (**dôr′** mĭ tôr′ē) ◊ *noun, plural* **dormitories**

dormouse *noun* A small European animal that is like a squirrel and that sleeps during the day and is active at night.
dor·mouse (**dôr′** mous′) ◊ *noun, plural* **dormice**

dory *noun* A flat-bottomed boat with high sides that is often used in fishing.
do·ry (**dôr′** ē) ◊ *noun, plural* **dories**

▲ **dory**

dose *noun* An amount, as of medicine, given or taken at one time.
◊ *verb* To treat with medicine.
dose (dōs) ◊ *noun, plural* **doses** ◊ *verb* **dosed, dosing**

dot *noun* A small round mark, spot, or point.
◊ *verb* To mark with or as if with dots.
dot (dŏt) ◊ *noun, plural* **dots** ◊ *verb* **dotted, dotting**

dote *verb* To be too fond: *They dote on their only grandchild.*
dote (dōt) ◊ *verb* **doted, doting**

double *adjective* **1.** Twice as much in size, strength, number, or amount. **2.** Made up of two parts: *Double doors opened into the dining room.* **3.** Designed for two. **4.** Acting two parts: *The spy worked as a double agent for two governments.*
◊ *adverb* **1.** Two together: *My friend and I ride double on our horse.* **2.** In two: *I was bent double with laughter.*
◊ *noun* **1.** Someone or something that looks like another. **2.** Something that is twice as much or as many as another.
◊ *verb* **1.** To make or become twice as great or as many. **2.** To fold in two. **3.** To serve an additional purpose: *My bed doubles as a couch.* **4.** To replace or be a substitute for: *That actor can double for the star if need be.* **5.** To turn sharply backward; reverse: *We doubled back and headed for home.*
dou·ble (dŭb′əl) ◊ *adjective* ◊ *adverb* ◊ *noun, plural* **doubles** ◊ *verb* **doubled, doubling**

double bass *noun* The largest and lowest-pitched member of the violin family.
double bass ◊ *noun, plural* **double basses**

▲ **double bass**

double-cross *verb* To betray by doing the opposite of what was agreed on.
dou·ble-cross (dŭb′əl-krôs′) ◊ *verb* **double-crossed, double-crossing**

double-header *noun* Two games played on the same day.
dou·ble-head·er (dŭb′əl hĕd′ər) ◊ *noun, plural* **double-headers**

doublet *noun* A close-fitting jacket worn by men between the fifteenth and seventeenth centuries.
dou·blet (dŭb′lĭt) ◊ *noun, plural* **doublets**

▲ **doublet**

doubly *adverb* In a doubled amount or degree; twice: *I studied doubly hard.*
dou·bly (dŭb′lē) ◊ *adverb*

doubt (dout) ◊ *verb* **1.** To be uncertain or unsure about: *I doubt my ability to win the contest.* **2.** To be distrustful of: *We don't doubt your story.* **3.** To view as unlikely.
◊ *noun* **1.** A lack of belief or certainty. **2.** The condition of being uncertain: *When you're in doubt, look up the word in your dictionary.* **3.** A lack of trust.
doubt (dout) ◊ *verb* **doubted, doubting** ◊ *noun, plural* **doubts**

doubtful *adjective* **1.** Causing uncertainty: *It was a doubtful scheme to get rich quick.* **2.** Of uncertain outcome. **3.** Being undecided about something.
doubt·ful (dout′fəl) ◊ *adjective*

doubtless *adverb* **1.** Without doubt; certainly. **2.** Most likely; probably.
doubt·less (dout′lĭs) ◊ *adverb*

dough *noun* A soft, thick mixture of flour or meal and liquids that is used to make bread and baked goods.
dough (dō) ◊ *noun, plural* **doughs**
‖*These sound alike:* **dough, do², doe**

doughnut *noun* A small, ring-shaped cake of sweetened dough fried in deep fat.
dough·nut (dō′nŭt′) ◊ *noun, plural* **doughnuts**

douse *verb* **1.** To plunge into liquid; immerse. **2.** To wet completely; drench.
douse (dous) ◊ *verb* **doused, dousing**

dove[1] *noun* A pigeon or related bird.
dove[1] (dŭv) ◊ *noun, plural* **doves**

dove[2] *verb* A past tense of **dive.**
dove[2] (dōv) ◊ *verb*

dowel *noun* A round wooden pin that is used to fasten two pieces of wood together.
dow·el (dou′əl) ◊ *noun, plural* **dowels**

down[1] *adverb* **1.** From a higher to a lower place: *The cat climbed down from the roof.* **2.** In or to a lower position, point, condition, or quantity: *The guests sat down.* **3.** From an earlier to a later time: *The necklace was handed down through our family.* **4.** In partial payment at the time of purchase: *I paid $5.00 down.* **5.** In writing: *The police took my statement down.* **6.** To or in a less active state: *The teacher asked the children to quiet down.* **7.** In a serious way: *Let's get down to work.*
◊ *adjective* **1.** Moving or directed downward: *Where is the down escalator?* **2.** Being in a low position: *The blinds are down.* **3.** Being at a lower level: *Car sales are down.*
◊ *preposition* In a downward direction along, through, or into: *I ran down the stairs.*
◊ *noun* **1.** A downward movement; descent. **2.** Any of a series of four plays in football during which a team must advance at least ten yards to keep the ball.
◊ *verb* **1.** To bring, strike, or throw down: *The boxer downed the opponent.* **2.** To swallow hastily: *We downed the milk and ran out.*
down[1] (doun) ◊ *adverb* ◊ *adjective* ◊ *preposition* ◊ *noun, plural* **downs** ◊ *verb* **downed, downing**

down[2] *noun* Fine, soft, fluffy feathers.
down[2] (doun) ◊ *noun*

ă	pat	ĭ	pit	oi	oil	th	bath
ā	pay	ī	ride	o͝o	book	*th*	bathe
â	care	î	fierce	o͞o	boot	ə	ago, item
ä	father	ŏ	pot	ou	out		pencil
ĕ	pet	ō	go	ŭ	cut		atom
ē	be	ô	paw, for	û	fur		circus

***HISTORY* • down[1], down[2]**

Down[1] comes from an old English word meaning "from a hill," and so "downward." It is distantly related to **dune. Down**[2] comes from an old Scandinavian word. Its meaning has not changed.

downcast *adjective* **1.** Directed downward: *The child sat quietly with downcast eyes.* **2.** In low spirits; depressed or sad.
down·cast (doun′kăst′) ◊ *adjective*

downfall *noun* **1.** A sudden loss, as of wealth, reputation, or high position; ruin. **2.** Something that causes a downfall.
down·fall (doun′fôl′) ◊ *noun, plural* **downfalls**

downhearted *adjective* In low spirits.
down·heart·ed (doun′här′tĭd) ◊ *adjective*

downhill *adverb* **1.** Down the slope of a hill: *We raced downhill.* **2.** Toward or into a worsened state: *My health went downhill.*
◊ *adjective* Sloping or going downhill.
down·hill (doun′hĭl′) ◊ *adverb* ◊ *adjective*

downpour *noun* A heavy fall of rain.
down·pour (doun′pôr′) ◊ *noun, plural* **downpours**

downright *adjective* Complete; utter: *That is a downright lie.*
◊ *adverb* Very; completely: *It was a downright foolish thing to do.*
down·right (doun′rīt′) ◊ *adjective* ◊ *adverb*

downstairs *adverb* **1.** Down the stairs. **2.** To or on a lower or main floor.
◊ *adjective* Located on a lower or main floor.
◊ *noun* (*used with a singular verb*) The lower or main floor of a building.
down·stairs (doun′stârz′) ◊ *adverb* ◊ *adjective* ◊ *noun*

downstream *adjective & adverb* In the direction of the current of a stream.
down·stream (doun′strēm′) ◊ *adjective & adverb*

downtown *adjective & adverb* To or in the lower part or business center of a town or city.
down·town (doun′toun′) ◊ *adjective & adverb*

downward *adverb* **1.** From a higher to a lower place, level, or condition: *Cool air moves downward.* **2.** From an earlier to a

more recent time: *People have studied nature downward through history.*
◊ *adjective* Moving from a higher to a lower place, level, or condition: *Follow the downward path.*
down·ward (doun′wərd) ◊ *adverb* ◊ *adjective*

downwards *adverb* Downward.
down·wards (doun′wərdz) ◊ *adverb*

downy *adjective* **1.** Of or like down. **2.** Covered or filled with down.
down·y (dou′nē) ◊ *adjective* **downier, downiest**

dowry *noun* Money or property brought by a bride to her husband.
dow·ry (dou′rē) ◊ *noun, plural* **dowries**

doz. An abbreviation for *dozen* or *dozens.*

doze *verb* To sleep lightly; nap.
◊ *noun* A light sleep; nap.
doze (dōz) ◊ *verb* **dozed, dozing** ◊ *noun, plural* **dozes**

dozen *noun* A set of 12.
doz·en (dŭz′ən) ◊ *noun, plural* **dozens** *or* **dozen**

Dr. The abbreviation for *Doctor.*

drab *adjective* Lacking interest; dull.
drab (drăb) ◊ *adjective* **drabber, drabbest**

draft *noun* **1.** A current of air. **2.** A device that controls a flow of air, as in a fireplace. **3.** The pulling or hauling of a load, as by horses. **4.** A rough outline or sketch before a final form. **5.** The selection of persons for a specific duty and especially for required military service. **6.** A document ordering a bank to pay money to a certain person. **7.** The depth of water needed for a ship to float.
◊ *verb* **1.** To select, especially for required military service. **2.** To make a rough draft of: *The class drafted a letter to the senator.* **3.** To put together; draw up.
◊ *adjective* Used for pulling loads: *Oxen are draft animals.*
draft (drăft) ◊ *noun, plural* **drafts** ◊ *verb* **drafted, drafting** ◊ *adjective*

drag *verb* **1.** To draw along or haul by force. —See Synonyms at **pull.** **2.** To trail or cause to trail along the ground. **3.** To search a body of water with a hook or net. **4.** To move too slowly or with difficulty.
◊ *noun* **1.** The act of dragging. **2.** Something that delays progress.
drag (drăg) ◊ *verb* **dragged, dragging** ◊ *noun, plural* **drags**

dragon *noun* An imaginary fire-breathing monster that is usually pictured as a giant lizard or reptile with wings and claws.
drag·on (drăg′ən) ◊ *noun, plural* **dragons**

dragonfly *noun* A large insect with a long body and four narrow, clear wings.
drag·on·fly (drăg′ən flī′) ◊ *noun, plural* **dragonflies**

> ***LANGUAGE DETECTIVE***
>
> ***dragonfly***
>
> *Dragonfly* is the proper name for this long, four-winged insect, but it has many nicknames in different parts of the country. If you live in the North, you might call it a *darning needle* or a *devil's darning needle.* In a large area between the North and South you might say it is a *snake feeder.* East of the mountains in Virginia you might hear people say *snake doctor.* Farther south it is sometimes called a *mosquito hawk.*

▲ **dragonfly**

drain *verb* **1.** To draw or flow off gradually: *We drained the water from the pool.* **2.** To make or become dry or empty by draining: *Drain the sink.* **3.** To remove water from by natural channels: *The river drains a huge area of land.* **4.** To use up totally; exhaust: *The busy day drained my energy.*
◊ *noun* **1.** A pipe or channel by which liquid is drained off. **2.** A gradual using up.
drain (drān) ◊ *verb* **drained, draining** ◊ *noun, plural* **drains**

drainage *noun* **1.** The act, process, or a way of draining. **2.** A system of drains. **3.** Matter that is drained off.
drain·age (**drā′** nĭj) ◊ *noun*

drake *noun* A male duck.
drake (drāk) ◊ *noun, plural* **drakes**

drama *noun* **1.** A written story meant to be acted out on a stage. **2.** The art and practice of writing and producing works for the stage.
dra·ma (**drä′** mə *or* **drăm′** ə) ◊ *noun, plural* **dramas**

dramatic *adjective* **1.** Of or relating to drama. **2.** Like a drama; exciting.
dra·mat·ic (drə **măt′** ĭk) ◊ *adjective*

dramatist *noun* A writer of plays.
dram·a·tist (**drăm′** ə tĭst) ◊ *noun, plural* **dramatists**

dramatize *verb* **1.** To make a drama of. **2.** To present or portray in a dramatic way.
dram·a·tize (**drăm′** ə tīz′) ◊ *verb* **dramatized, dramatizing**

drank *verb* Past tense of **drink.**
drank (drăngk) ◊ *verb*

drape *verb* **1.** To cover or hang with cloth in loose folds. **2.** To arrange or hang in loose folds.
◊ *noun* Often **drapes** Draperies.
drape (drāp) ◊ *verb* **draped, draping** ◊ *noun, plural* **drapes**

drapery *noun* **1.** Cloth arranged in loose folds. **2. draperies** Long, often heavy curtains that hang straight in loose folds.
drap·er·y (**drā′** pə rē) ◊ *noun, plural* **draperies**

drastic *adjective* Extreme or severe in effect: *We took drastic measures to conserve energy.*
dras·tic (**drăs′** tĭk) ◊ *adjective*

draw *verb* **1.** To cause to move by pulling or hauling. **2.** To pull or take out: *I drew a splinter from my finger.* **3.** To inhale: *I drew a deep breath.* **4.** To move or cause to move in a given direction: *The boat drew near the shore.* **5.** To produce a picture of by marking a surface with lines; sketch. **6.** To get as a response; call forth: *The jokes drew laughter from the audience.* **7.** To attract: *The beautiful weather drew summer visitors.*
◊ *noun* **1.** The act or the outcome of drawing. **2.** A contest that ends in a tie.
◊ *idioms* **draw out** To make longer; stretch. **draw up 1.** To arrange in order: *The troops are drawn up for inspection.* **2.** To write up in a set form: *The lawyer drew up a contract.*
draw (drô) ◊ *verb* **drew, drawn, drawing** ◊ *noun, plural* **draws**

drawback *noun* A disadvantage.
draw·back (**drô′** băk′) ◊ *noun, plural* **drawbacks**

drawbridge *noun* A bridge that can be raised or turned to allow ships to pass through.
draw·bridge (**drô′** brĭj′) ◊ *noun, plural* **drawbridges**

▲ **drawbridge**

drawer *noun* A boxlike compartment in a bureau or table that slides in and out.
drawer (drôr) ◊ *noun, plural* **drawers**

drawing *noun* **1.** The act or art of representing forms and figures on a surface by means of lines. **2.** A picture made by drawing.
draw·ing (**drô′** ĭng) ◊ *noun, plural* **drawings**

drawing room *noun* A formal living room or parlor in a private house.
drawing room ◊ *noun, plural* **drawing rooms**

drawl *verb* To speak slowly with vowels drawn out.

ă	pat	ĭ	pit	oi	**oil**	th	**bath**
ā	pay	ī	ride	o͝o	book	*th*	**bathe**
â	care	î	fierce	o͞o	boot	ə	ago, item
ä	father	ŏ	pot	ou	**out**		pencil
ĕ	pet	ō	go	ŭ	cut		atom
ē	be	ô	paw, for	û	fur		circus

◊*noun* The speech of a person who drawls.
drawl (drôl) ◊*verb* **drawled, drawling** ◊*noun, plural* **drawls**

drawn *verb* Past participle of **draw.**
drawn (drôn) ◊*verb*

drawstring *noun* A cord or ribbon run through a hem and pulled to close an opening.
draw·string (**drô′**strĭng′) ◊*noun, plural* **drawstrings**

dread *noun* Great fear.
◊*verb* To fear greatly.
◊*adjective* Causing great fear; dreadful: *Smallpox is a dread disease.*
dread (drĕd) ◊*noun* ◊*verb* **dreaded, dreading** ◊*adjective*

dreadful *adjective* **1.** Causing dread; terrible. **2.** Very unpleasant, bad, or shocking.
dread·ful (**drĕd′**fəl) ◊*adjective*

dreadnought *noun* A battleship that is heavily armed.
dread·nought (**drĕd′**nôt′) ◊*noun, plural* **dreadnoughts**

dream *noun* **1.** A series of pictures, thoughts, or emotions occurring during sleep. **2.** A daydream. **3.** Something hoped for; aspiration: *We have dreams of world peace.*
◊*verb* **1.** To have a dream or dreams. **2.** To think or believe possible: *I never dreamed my story would be published.*
dream (drēm) ◊*noun, plural* **dreams** ◊*verb* **dreamed** *or* **dreamt, dreaming**

dreamt *verb* A past tense and a past participle of **dream.**
dreamt (drĕmt) ◊*verb*

dreamy *adjective* **1.** Like a dream; vague: *I have only a dreamy memory of my early childhood.* **2.** Likely to daydream: *The dreamy child didn't pay attention in class.*
dream·y (**drē′**mē) ◊*adjective* **dreamier, dreamiest**

dreary *adjective* Gloomy; dismal: *Winter can be a dreary time.*
drear·y (**drîr′**ē) ◊*adjective* **drearier, dreariest**

dredge *noun* A machine that removes earth, mud, or silt, as from the bottom of a body of water, by means of a scoop, a series of buckets, or a suction tube.
◊*verb* To clean out, deepen, or gather with or as if with a dredge.
dredge (drĕj) ◊*noun, plural* **dredges** ◊*verb* **dredged, dredging**

dregs *plural noun* Material that settles to the bottom of a liquid.
dregs (drĕgz) ◊*plural noun*

drench *verb* To wet through and through.
drench (drĕnch) ◊*verb* **drenched, drenching**

dress *noun* **1.** An outer garment consisting of a top and skirt that is worn by women and girls. **2.** Clothing; apparel: *We wore formal dress to the party.*
◊*verb* **1.** To put clothes on: *We dressed the baby in a warm outfit.* **2.** To choose and wear clothes: *They dress with elegance.* **3.** To style the hair by brushing, combing, or curling. **4.** To treat a wound by applying medicine or bandages.
dress (drĕs) ◊*noun, plural* **dresses** ◊*verb* **dressed, dressing**

dresser *noun* A chest of drawers, usually with a mirror.
dress·er (**drĕs′**ər) ◊*noun, plural* **dressers**

dressing *noun* **1.** Material, as a bandage, used to cover a wound. **2.** A sauce for food, as a salad. **3.** A stuffing, as for poultry.
dress·ing (**drĕs′**ĭng) ◊*noun, plural* **dressings**

drew *verb* Past tense of **draw.**
drew (dro͞o) ◊*verb*

dribble *verb* **1.** To drip or cause to drip; trickle: *Water dribbled out of the faucet.* **2.** To drool; slobber: *The baby dribbled juice on the bib.* **3.** To move a ball along by bouncing or kicking, as in basketball.
◊*noun* **1.** A small trickling stream. **2.** The act of dribbling a ball.
drib·ble (**drĭb′**əl) ◊*verb* **dribbled, dribbling** ◊*noun, plural* **dribbles**

drier *adjective* Comparative of **dry.**
dri·er (**drī′**ər) ◊*adjective*

driest *adjective* Superlative of **dry.**
dri·est (**drī′**ĭst) ◊*adjective*

drift *verb* **1.** To be or cause to be carried along by or as if by a current of water or air. **2.** To heap or cause to heap in piles.
◊*noun* **1.** The movement or direction of something drifting. **2.** A mass of material, as sand or snow, heaped in a pile by the wind. **3.** The general meaning of something said or written: *It is hard to see the drift of your conversation.*
drift (drĭft) ◊*verb* **drifted, drifting** ◊*noun, plural* **drifts**

driftwood *noun* Wood that is floating on or has been washed ashore by water.
drift·wood (**drĭft′** wo͝od′) ◊ *noun*

▲ **driftwood**

drill *noun* **1.** A tool used to make holes in solid materials. **2.** Teaching or training in a subject by means of having students repeat something again and again.
◊ *verb* **1.** To bore a hole with a drill. **2.** To teach or train by using drill.
drill (drĭl) ◊ *noun, plural* **drills** ◊ *verb* **drilled, drilling**

drink *verb* **1.** To swallow liquid: *I drink a quart of milk a day.* **2.** To absorb liquid or moisture: *The dry ground drank up the rain.*
◊ *noun* **1.** A kind of liquid for drinking; beverage. **2.** An amount of liquid swallowed.
drink (drĭngk) ◊ *verb* **drank, drunk, drinking** ◊ *noun, plural* **drinks**

drip *verb* **1.** To fall or let fall in drops: *Water dripped from the faucet.* **2.** To be so moist that drops fall: *The grass dripped with dew.*
◊ *noun* **1.** Liquid or moisture that drips. **2.** The sound made by dripping liquid. **3.** The process of dripping.
drip (drĭp) ◊ *verb* **dripped, dripping** ◊ *noun, plural* **drips**

drive *verb* **1.** To steer or operate a motor vehicle, such as a car. **2.** To carry in a vehicle: *Our parents drive us to school.* **3.** To put into and keep in motion: *The motor is driven by electricity.* **4.** To force someone into feeling or acting in a certain way: *Your giggling drives me crazy.* **5.** To force or cause to penetrate: *Drive the nails into the wood.*
◊ *noun* **1.** A ride or short trip in a motor vehicle, such as a car. **2.** A road or driveway. **3.** A special organized effort to achieve a goal: *We began a drive to raise money for the poor.*
drive (drīv) ◊ *verb* **drove, driven, driving** ◊ *noun, plural* **drives**

drive-in *noun* A business establishment, as a bank, designed so that customers can stay in their cars while being served.
drive-in (**drīv′** ĭn′) ◊ *noun, plural* **drive-ins**

driven *verb* Past participle of **drive.**
driv·en (**drĭv′** ən) ◊ *verb*

driveway *noun* A private road connecting a house or garage with the street.
drive·way (**drīv′** wā′) ◊ *noun, plural* **driveways**

drizzle *verb* To rain in very fine drops.
◊ *noun* A fine, misty rain.
driz·zle (**drĭz′** əl) ◊ *verb* **drizzled, drizzling** ◊ *noun, plural* **drizzles**

dromedary *noun* A camel with one hump that is widely used for carrying loads in northern Africa and southwestern Asia.
drom·e·dar·y (**drŏm′** ĭ dĕr′ē) ◊ *noun, plural* **dromedaries**

drone¹ *noun* A male bee, especially a honeybee.
drone¹ (drōn) ◊ *noun, plural* **drones**

drone² *verb* To make or talk with a low, dull humming sound: *An airplane droned far overhead.*
◊ *noun* A low, dull humming sound.
drone² (drōn) ◊ *verb* **droned, droning** ◊ *noun, plural* **drones**

***HISTORY* • drone¹, drone²**

Drone¹ and **drone²** probably both go back to a prehistoric word meaning "to buzz."

droop *verb* **1.** To bend or hang downward; sag: *The flowers began to droop.* **2.** To become weak or depressed: *Our spirits drooped.*
droop (dro͞op) ◊ *verb* **drooped, drooping**

ă pat	ĭ pit	oi **oil**	th ba**th**
ā pay	ī ride	o͝o b**oo**k	*th* ba**th**e
â care	î fierce	o͞o b**oo**t	ə ago, item
ä father	ŏ pot	ou **out**	pencil
ĕ pet	ō go	ŭ cut	atom
ē be	ô paw, for	û fur	circus

drop *noun* **1.** A small quantity of liquid in a rounded mass: *A drop of sweat ran down my forehead.* **2.** Something resembling a drop in shape: *I bought a box of cough drops.* **3. drops** Liquid medicine given in drops. **4.** The act or an instance of falling. **5.** The length, depth, or distance of a fall: *From the cliffs to the ocean it is a drop of 200 feet.*
◊ *verb* **1.** To fall or let fall in drops. **2.** To fall or let fall: *I dropped a dish.* **3.** To go or cause to go lower: *The price of milk dropped.* **4.** To leave out; omit: *You always drop the second "r" in "embarrass."* **5.** To set down; deliver: *The mail carrier dropped off a package.* **6.** To cause to fall, as by striking. **7.** To fall or sink into a less active state: *I dropped off to sleep.* **8.** To stop having to do with: *Let's just drop the subject.* **9.** To say, send, or offer in a casual way: *They dropped hints that they were expecting gifts.*
drop (drŏp) ◊ *noun, plural* **drops** ◊ *verb* **dropped, dropping**

droplet *noun* A tiny drop.
drop·let (**drŏp′**lĭt) ◊ *noun, plural* **droplets**

dropper *noun* A rubber tube with a bulb at one end for drawing in a liquid and releasing it in drops.
drop·per (**drŏp′**ər) ◊ *noun, plural* **droppers**

drought *noun* A period of little or no rain.
drought (drout) ◊ *noun, plural* **droughts**

drove[1] *noun* **1.** A number of animals, as cattle, being driven in a group. **2.** A crowd of people; throng: *Visitors came in droves.*
drove[1] (drōv) ◊ *noun, plural* **droves**

drove[2] *verb* Past tense of **drive.**
drove[2] (drōv) ◊ *verb*

drown *verb* **1.** To die by being submerged in liquid, especially water. **2.** To be loud enough to overpower: *Laughter drowned out my voice.*
drown (droun) ◊ *verb* **drowned, drowning**

drowse *verb* To be half asleep; doze.
drowse (drouz) ◊ *verb* **drowsed, drowsing**

drowsy *adjective* Inclined to sleep; sleepy.
drows·y (**drou′**zē) ◊ *adjective* **drowsier, drowsiest**

drudgery *noun* Hard, boring, or unpleasant work.
drudg·er·y (**drŭj′**ə rē) ◊ *noun*

drug *noun* **1.** A substance used by itself as a medicine or used in making medicine. **2.** An extremely harmful substance that affects the nervous system. Drugs can become habit-forming and cause death.
drug (drŭg) ◊ *noun, plural* **drugs**

druggist *noun* A person who prepares and sells drugs and medicines; pharmacist.
drug·gist (**drŭg′**ĭst) ◊ *noun, plural* **druggists**

drugstore *noun* A store where drugs and medicines are sold.
drug·store (**drŭg′**stôr′) ◊ *noun, plural* **drugstores**

drum *noun* **1.** A percussion instrument consisting of a hollow cylinder with a membrane stretched across one or both ends. **2.** A sound of or like that of a drum. **3.** Something, as a container for oil, shaped like a drum.
◊ *verb* **1.** To play on or beat a drum. **2.** To thump or tap in a rhythmic way: *I drummed on the desk with my fingers.*
drum (drŭm) ◊ *noun, plural* **drums** ◊ *verb* **drummed, drumming**

drum major *noun* A man who leads a marching band.
drum major ◊ *noun, plural* **drum majors**

drum majorette *noun* A girl who leads a marching band.
drum majorette ◊ *noun, plural* **drum majorettes**

drummer *noun* A person who plays a drum.
drum·mer (**drŭm′**ər) ◊ *noun, plural* **drummers**

drumstick *noun* **1.** A stick for beating a drum. **2.** The lower part of the leg of a fowl.
drum·stick (**drŭm′**stĭk′) ◊ *noun, plural* **drumsticks**

drunk *adjective* Affected by drinking alcoholic liquor to the point of losing control over thought and action.
◊ *verb* Past participle of **drink.**
drunk (drŭngk) ◊ *adjective* **drunker, drunkest** ◊ *verb*

dry *adjective* **1.** Free from liquid or moisture; not wet or damp: *We changed into dry clothes.* **2.** Having little or no rainfall; arid: *It was a dry summer.* **3.** Not in or under water: *We swam for dry land.* **4.** Needing or wanting to drink; thirsty. **5.** Lacking water: *A shallow stream is often dry in hot weather.*
◊ *verb* To make or become dry.
dry (drī) ◊ *adjective* **drier, driest** ◊ *verb* **dried, drying**

dry cell *noun* A small cell that produces electricity by means of chemicals in the form of a moist paste. A dry cell is sealed to prevent spilling.
dry cell ◊ *noun, plural* **dry cells**

dry-clean *verb* To clean by using chemicals rather than water.
dry-clean (**drī′**klēn′) ◊ *verb* **dry-cleaned, dry-cleaning**

dry dock *noun* A floating or stationary basin into which a ship can be moved and the water pumped out, used for ship repairs.
dry dock ◊ *noun, plural* **dry docks**

dryer *noun* A device that removes moisture.
dry·er (**drī′**ər) ◊ *noun, plural* **dryers**

dual *adjective* Consisting of two parts.
du·al (**do͞o′**əl *or* **dyo͞o′**əl) ◊ *adjective*
‖*These sound alike:* **dual, duel**

dubious *adjective* **1.** Feeling or showing doubt: *I am dubious about accepting the offer.* **2.** Open to question; doubtful.
du·bi·ous (**do͞o′**bē əs *or* **dyo͞o′**bē əs) ◊ *adjective*

duchess *noun* **1.** The wife or widow of a duke. **2.** A woman holding a rank equal to that of a duke in her own right.
duch·ess (**dŭch′**ĭs) ◊ *noun, plural* **duchesses**

duck¹ *verb* **1.** To lower the head or body quickly: *I ducked to avoid being hit by the ball.* **2.** To avoid meeting or dealing with; evade: *You ducked your responsibility.* **3.** To plunge under water for a moment.
duck¹ (dŭk) ◊ *verb* **ducked, ducking**

duck² *noun* A water bird with a broad, flat bill, short legs, and webbed feet.
duck² (dŭk) ◊ *noun, plural* **ducks**

***HISTORY* • duck¹, duck²**

Duck¹ and **duck²** are native English words that are probably related. **Duck¹** originally meant "to dive," and **duck²** may have originally meant "a bird that dives."

ă	pat	ĭ	pit	oi	**oi**l	th	ba**th**
ā	pay	ī	ride	o͝o	b**oo**k	*th*	ba**the**
â	care	î	fierce	o͞o	b**oo**t	ə	ago, item
ä	father	ŏ	pot	ou	**ou**t		pencil
ĕ	pet	ō	go	ŭ	cut		atom
ē	be	ô	paw, for	û	fur		circus

▲ **duck²**

duckling *noun* A young duck.
duck·ling (**dŭk′**lĭng) ◊ *noun, plural* **ducklings**

duct *noun* A tube through which a liquid or gas flows.
duct (dŭkt) ◊ *noun, plural* **ducts**

due *adjective* **1.** Owed or owing as a right or debt: *Please pay the amount that is still due.* **2.** Appropriate; suitable: *We took due care to be on time.* **3.** Expected, required, or scheduled to come or happen.
◊ *noun* **1.** Something that is due: *Justice was no more than our due.* **2. dues** A charge or fee, as for membership in a club.
◊ *adverb* In a direct line: *We drove due west.*
due (do͞o *or* dyo͞o) ◊ *adjective* ◊ *noun, plural* **dues** ◊ *adverb*
‖*These sound alike:* **due, dew**

duel *noun* A combat between two persons that is arranged in advance and fought with deadly weapons before witnesses.
◊ *verb* To fight in a duel.
du·el (**do͞o′**əl *or* **dyo͞o′**əl) ◊ *noun, plural* **duels** ◊ *verb* **dueled, dueling**
‖*These sound alike:* **duel, dual**

duet *noun* **1.** A musical composition for two voices or two instruments. **2.** Two performers who sing or play a duet.
du·et (do͞o **ĕt′** *or* dyo͞o **ĕt′**) ◊ *noun, plural* **duets**

due to *preposition* **1.** Caused by: *My hesitation was due to fear.* **2.** Because of: *The game was called off due to rain.*

dug *verb* Past tense and past participle of **dig.**
dug (dŭg) ◊ *verb*

D

dugout *noun* **1.** A boat, as a canoe, made by hollowing out a log. **2.** A rough shelter dug in the ground or in a hillside, as one used by soldiers for protection. **3.** A long, low shelter at the side of a baseball field in which team members sit when they are not playing.
dug·out (**dŭg′**out′) ◊ *noun, plural* **dugouts**

▲ **dugout**

duke *noun* A member of the highest level of the British nobility.
duke (do͞ok *or* dyo͞ok) ◊ *noun, plural* **dukes**

dull *adjective* **1.** Not sharp or keen; blunt: *The blade of the ax is dull.* **2.** Not keenly or intensely felt: *First I had a dull ache, then a sharp pain.* **3.** Not interesting; boring: *This story is dull.* **4.** Slow to learn; stupid.
◊ *verb* To make or become dull.
dull (dŭl) ◊ *adjective* **duller, dullest** ◊ *verb* **dulled, dulling**

> ***SYNONYMS***
>
> ***dull, blunt***
>
> The point of my pencil is *dull.* An ax has a sharp end and a *blunt* end.
> **Antonym:** *sharp*

dully *adverb* In a dull manner.
dul·ly (**dŭl′**ē) ◊ *adverb*

duly *adverb* In a due manner; properly: *I am a duly elected member of the club.*
du·ly (**do͞o′**lē *or* **dyo͞o′**lē) ◊ *adverb*

dumb *adjective* Foolish or stupid. —See Synonyms at **foolish.**
dumb (dŭm) ◊ *adjective* **dumber, dumbest**

dumbbell *noun* A short bar with a heavy metal weight at each end that is lifted to develop the muscles of the arms.
dumb·bell (**dŭm′**bĕl′) ◊ *noun, plural* **dumbbells**

▲ **dumbbell**

dummy *noun* An imitation or copy of something that is used as a substitute: *The tailor fitted the tweed coat on a dummy.*
dum·my (**dŭm′**ē) ◊ *noun, plural* **dummies**

dump *verb* **1.** To cast down or discard in a mass: *I dumped my books on the table.* **2.** To empty out a container or vehicle: *The truck dumped a load of sand.*
◊ *noun* **1.** A place where something, as garbage, is dumped. **2.** A place where military supplies, as ammunition, are stored.
dump (dŭmp) ◊ *verb* **dumped, dumping** ◊ *noun, plural* **dumps**

dunce *noun* A stupid person.
dunce (dŭns) ◊ *noun, plural* **dunces**

dune *noun* A ridge or hill of sand heaped up by the wind.
dune (do͞on *or* dyo͞on) ◊ *noun, plural* **dunes**

▲ **dune**

dungaree *noun* **1.** A sturdy cotton fabric. **2. dungarees** Trousers made of this fabric.
dun·ga·ree (dŭng′gə **rē′**) ◊ *noun, plural* **dungarees**

dungeon *noun* A dark underground prison.
dun·geon (**dŭn′**jən) ◊ *noun, plural* **dungeons**

duplicate *adjective* Being exactly like another: *I had a duplicate key made.*
◊ *noun* One of two things that are alike.
◊ *verb* To make an exact copy of.
du·pli·cate (**do͞o′**plĭ kĭt *or* **dyo͞o′**plĭ kĭt) ◊ *adjective* ◊ *noun, plural* **duplicates** ◊ *verb* (**do͞o′**plĭ kāt′ *or* **dyo͞o′**plĭ kāt′) **duplicated, duplicating**

duplication *noun* The act or process of duplicating or the condition of being duplicated.
du·pli·ca·tion (do͞o′plĭ **kā′**shən *or* dyo͞o′plĭ**kā′**shən) ◊ *noun*

durable *adjective* Capable of withstanding hard wear or long use.
du·ra·ble (**do͝or′**ə bəl *or* **dyo͝or′**ə bəl) ◊ *adjective*

duration *noun* The period of time during which something exists or continues.
du·ra·tion (do͞o **rā′**shən *or* dyo͞o **rā′**shən) ◊ *noun*

during *preposition* **1.** Throughout the duration of: *I go skating every afternoon during the winter.* **2.** At some time within the course of: *It rained during the night.*
dur·ing (**do͝or′**ĭng *or* **dyo͝or′**ĭng) ◊ *preposition*

dusk *noun* **1.** The time of evening just before dark. **2.** Partial darkness.
dusk (dŭsk) ◊ *noun, plural* **dusks**

dust *noun* **1.** Fine, dry particles of matter; powder. **2.** A cloud of dust in the air.
◊ *verb* **1.** To remove dust from by wiping or brushing. **2.** To sprinkle with or as if with dust: *Snow dusted the trees.*
dust (dŭst) ◊ *noun* ◊ *verb* **dusted, dusting**

dusty *adjective* **1.** Covered or filled with dust. **2.** Like dust: *Dusty snow was falling.*
dust·y (**dŭs′**tē) ◊ *adjective* **dustier, dustiest**

ă	pat	ĭ	pit	oi	oil	th	bath
ā	pay	ī	ride	o͝o	book	*th*	bathe
â	care	î	fierce	o͞o	boot	ə	ago, item
ä	father	ŏ	pot	ou	out		pencil
ĕ	pet	ō	go	ŭ	cut		atom
ē	be	ô	paw, for	û	fur		circus

Dutch *noun* **1.** (*used with a plural verb*) The people of the Netherlands. **2.** The language of the Netherlands.
◊ *adjective* Of or relating to the Netherlands, its people, or their language.
Dutch (dŭch) ◊ *noun* ◊ *adjective*

Dutch door *noun* A door divided in half horizontally so that either part may be left opened or closed.
Dutch door ◊ *noun, plural* **Dutch doors**

Dutch oven *noun* A large, heavy pot or kettle with a tight lid. A Dutch oven is used for slow cooking.
Dutch oven ◊ *noun, plural* **Dutch ovens**

dutiful *adjective* Showing or having a sense of duty: *Dutiful citizens vote.*
du·ti·ful (**do͞o** tĭ fəl *or* **dyo͞o′**tĭ fəl) ◊ *adjective*

duty *noun* **1.** Something that a person ought to do: *We feel it is our duty to help the poor.* **2.** The obligation to do what is right: *You have a strong sense of duty.* **3.** Action that a person's occupation or position requires: *The candidate can perform the duties of a senator.* **4.** A tax especially on goods imported into a country.
du·ty (**do͞o′**tē *or* **dyo͞o′**tē) ◊ *noun, plural* **duties**

dwarf *noun* **1.** A person, animal, or plant much smaller in size than normal. **2.** A tiny, legendary creature that is sometimes pictured as an ugly person.
◊ *verb* **1.** To keep from growing to natural size; stunt. **2.** To cause to look or seem smaller: *The liner dwarfed the tugboat.*
◊ *adjective* Of unusually small size: *These are dwarf tomatoes.*
dwarf (dwôrf) ◊ *noun, plural* **dwarfs** *or* **dwarves** ◊ *verb* **dwarfed, dwarfing** ◊ *adjective*

▲ **dwarf**

dwarves *noun* A plural of **dwarf.**
dwarves (dwôrvz) ◊ *noun*

dwell *verb* To live as a resident; reside: *A monarch often dwells in a palace.*

dwell (dwĕl) ◊ *verb* **dwelt** *or* **dwelled, dwelling**

dwelling *noun* A place to live in; residence or home.
dwell·ing (**dwĕl**′ĭng) ◊ *noun, plural* **dwellings**

dwelt *verb* A past tense and a past participle of **dwell.**
dwelt (dwĕlt) ◊ *verb*

dwindle *verb* To make or become gradually less; shrink: *Our savings dwindled to nothing.*
dwin·dle (**dwĭn**′dəl) ◊ *verb* **dwindled, dwindling**

dye *noun* **1.** A substance used to change the color of something, as hair or fabric. **2.** A color produced by a dye.
◊ *verb* To color with or as if with a dye.
dye (dī) ◊ *noun, plural* **dyes** ◊ *verb* **dyed, dyeing**
‖*These sound alike:* **dye, die**

dyed-in-the-wool *adjective* Outright: *Our governor is a dyed-in-the-wool conservative politician.*
dyed-in-the-wool (**dīd**′ĭn thə **wo͝ol**′) ◊ *adjective*

dyestuff *noun* A material that is used as or yields a dye.
dye·stuff (**dī**′stŭf′) ◊ *noun, plural* **dyestuffs**

dying *adjective* **1.** About to die. **2.** Drawing to an end: *The coals glowed in the dying fire.*
◊ *verb* Present participle of **die**[1].
dy·ing (**dī**′ĭng) ◊ *adjective* ◊ *verb*

dynamic *adjective* Full of energy; vigorous.
dy·nam·ic (dī **năm**′ĭk) ◊ *adjective*

dynamite *noun* A powerful explosive.
◊ *verb* To blow up with dynamite.
dy·na·mite (**dī**′nə mīt′) ◊ *noun* ◊ *verb* **dynamited, dynamiting**

dynamo *noun* A machine that produces electric current.
dy·na·mo (**dī**′nə mō′) ◊ *noun, plural* **dynamos**

dynast *noun* A ruler, especially one belonging to a dynasty.
dy·nast (**dī**′năst′) ◊ *noun, plural* **dynasts**

dynastic *adjective* Of or having to do with a dynasty.
dy·nas·tic (dī **năs**′tĭk) ◊ *adjective*

dynasty *noun* A succession of rulers of the same family.
dy·nas·ty (**dī**′nə stē) ◊ *noun, plural* **dynasties**

dz. An abbreviation for *dozen* or *dozens.*

Eagle

Ee

E is the fifth letter of the English alphabet. Did you know that it has a long history?

Over 3,500 years ago, people in the Middle East were using symbols that became the letters of our alphabet. This ancient Middle Eastern symbol is a form of the letter that became our letter *E*.

The ancient Greeks borrowed their alphabet from people in the Middle East. Here is a form of the Greek letter that became our letter *E*.

The ancient Romans borrowed their alphabet from a people who had taken their own letter symbols from the Greeks. Here is a form of the Roman letter *E* that was used for carving letters into stone. These letters became the model for our printed capital letters.

As people wrote quickly, especially with pens, the capital letters began to take the shapes of small letters. Here is a small-letter *e* that was developed about 1,200 years ago.

Ee *Ee*	Ee	Ee	Ee
Handwriting	Sans Serif Type	Serif Type	Computer Printing

e *or* **E** *noun* The fifth letter of the English alphabet.
e *or* **E** (ē) ◊ *noun, plural* **e's** *or* **E's**

E. *or* **E** Abbreviations for *east* or *eastern.*

each *adjective* Being one of two or more persons or things thought of separately; every: *Did you speak to each child?*
◊ *pronoun* Every one: *Each of us took a turn riding the pony.*
◊ *adverb* For or to each one; apiece: *We gave the children a dollar each.*
each (ēch) ◊ *adjective* ◊ *pronoun* ◊ *adverb*

each other *pronoun* One another.

eager *adjective* Full of strong desire; impatient: *We're ready and eager to get started.*
ea·ger (ē′ gər) ◊ *adjective* **eagerer, eagerest**

ă	pat	ĭ	pit	oi	**oi**l	th	ba**th**
ā	pay	ī	ride	o͝o	b**oo**k	*th*	ba**th**e
â	care	î	fierce	o͞o	b**oo**t	ə	**a**go, it**e**m
ä	father	ŏ	pot	ou	**ou**t		penc**i**l
ĕ	pet	ō	go	ŭ	c**u**t		at**o**m
ē	be	ô	paw, for	û	f**u**r		circ**u**s

eagle *noun* A large bird with a hooked bill, broad strong wings, and sharp eyesight. Eagles soar high in the air.
ea·gle (ē′ gəl) ◊ *noun, plural* **eagles**

ear¹ *noun* **1.** The part of the body with which people and animals hear, especially the outer part on each side of the head. **2.** The sense of hearing: *The sound of music is pleasant to the ear.* **3.** Favorable attention: *We tried to gain the senator's ear.*
ear¹ (îr) ◊ *noun, plural* **ears**

ear² *noun* The part of a grain plant, as corn or wheat, that bears seeds.
ear² (îr) ◊ *noun, plural* **ears**

HISTORY • ear¹, ear²

Ear¹, like most words for basic parts of the body, is a native English word. **Ear²** comes from a different old English word. It was first applied to grains like wheat and then later to the corn that grew in America.

eardrum *noun* The membrane that separates the middle and outer parts of the ear and vibrates when sound waves strike it.
ear·drum (îr′drŭm′) ◊ *noun, plural* **eardrums**

earl *noun* A member of the British nobility.
earl (ûrl) ◊ *noun, plural* **earls**

early *adjective* **1.** Of or happening near the beginning: *We ate breakfast in the early morning.* **2.** Coming or happening before the usual or expected time: *We ate an early dinner before the baseball game.*
◊ *adverb* **1.** At or near the beginning: *We always get up early in the morning.* **2.** Before the usual or expected time: *I arrived early for my appointment with the dentist.*
ear·ly (ûr′lē) ◊ *adjective, adverb* **earlier, earliest**

earmuffs *plural noun* A pair of ear coverings attached to a flexible band and worn to protect the ears from the cold.
ear·muffs (îr′mŭfs′) ◊ *plural noun*

▲ **earmuffs**

earn *verb* **1.** To gain by working or by supplying service: *Computer programmers earn good salaries.* —See Synonyms at **get.** **2.** To deserve as a result of effort or behavior: *They earned their good grades by working hard.*
earn (ûrn) ◊ *verb* **earned, earning**
‖*These sound alike:* **earn, urn**

earnest *adjective* Not playful or trifling; sincere: *Make an earnest apology for your mistake.* —See Synonyms at **serious.**
ear·nest (ûr′nĭst) ◊ *adjective*

earnings *plural noun* Money that is received as payment for work or as profit from an investment.
earn·ings (ûr′nĭngz) ◊ *plural noun*

earphone *noun* A device that changes electrical signals into sound. Earphones are worn over or in the ear.
ear·phone (îr′fōn′) ◊ *noun, plural* **earphones**

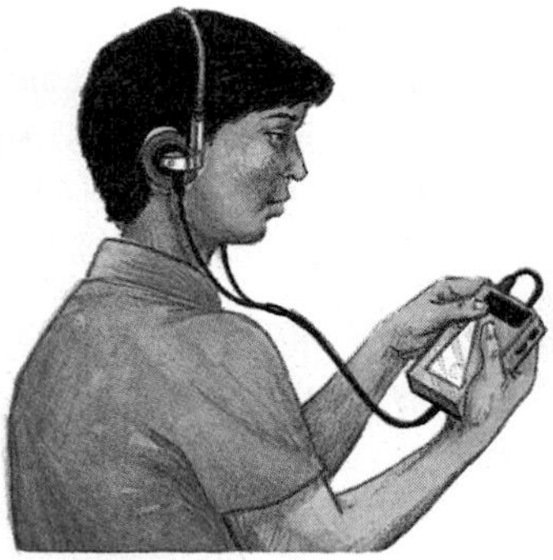

▲ **earphone**

earring *noun* An ornament that is worn clipped to or hanging from the ear.
ear·ring (îr′rĭng′) ◊ *noun, plural* **earrings**

earth *noun* **1.** Often **Earth** The planet on which human beings live. **2.** Dry land as distinguished from the oceans and the air. **3.** The surface of the land; ground. **4.** The substance that forms much of this surface; soil: *Seeds sprouted in the moist earth.*
earth (ûrth) ◊ *noun, plural* **earths**

earthen *adjective* Made of or consisting of earth: *The cabin has an earthen floor.*
earth·en (ûr′thən) ◊ *adjective*

earthly *adjective* **1.** Of or relating to the earth rather than heaven. **2.** Possible to imagine: *What earthly meaning can such nonsense have?*
earth·ly (ûrth′lē) ◊ *adjective*

earthquake *noun* A trembling or shaking of the ground. Earthquakes are caused by sudden movements in masses of rock far below the earth's surface.
earth·quake (ûrth′kwāk′) ◊ *noun, plural* **earthquakes**

earthworm *noun* A worm that lives in soil and has a long body divided into many ringlike segments.
earth·worm (ûrth′wûrm′) ◊ *noun, plural* **earthworms**

ease *noun* **1.** Freedom from worry, pain, or trouble; comfort: *The income we received*

gave us a life of greater ease. **2.** Freedom from hard work or painful effort: *They rode the horses with grace and ease.*
◊ *verb* **1.** To free from worry, pain, or trouble. **2.** To make less; relieve: *A hot bath will ease the pain of sore muscles.* **3.** To move slowly or carefully: *Use a shoehorn to ease your foot into a tight shoe.*
ease (ēz) ◊ *noun* ◊ *verb* **eased, easing**

easel *noun* An upright frame used to support a flat surface, such as an artist's canvas.
ea·sel (ē′zəl) ◊ *noun, plural* **easels**

easily *adverb* **1.** In an easy manner; with ease: *Libraries are arranged so that you can find books easily.* **2.** Without doubt: *That is easily the best meal I have ever eaten.*
eas·i·ly (ē′zə lē) ◊ *adverb*

east *noun* **1.** The direction in which the sun is seen rising in the morning. **2.** Often **East** A region in this direction. **3. East** The part of the United States along or near the coast of the Atlantic Ocean. **4. East** Asia and the islands near it.
◊ *adjective* **1.** Of, in, or toward the east: *We camped on the east side of the lake.* **2.** Coming from the east: *An east wind blew all day.*
◊ *adverb* Toward the east: *We drove east to the camping site.*
east (ēst) ◊ *noun* ◊ *adjective* ◊ *adverb*

Easter *noun* A Christian festival celebrating Christ's return to life. Easter falls each year on the first Sunday following the first full moon on or after March 21.
Eas·ter (ē′stər) ◊ *noun*

easterly *adjective & adverb* **1.** In or toward the east. **2.** From the east: *We were blown off course by easterly winds.*
east·er·ly (ē′stər lē) ◊ *adjective & adverb*

eastern *adjective* **1.** Often **Eastern** Of, in, or toward the east. **2.** Coming from the east.
east·ern (ē′stərn) ◊ *adjective*

eastward *adverb* To or toward the east.
◊ *adjective* Moving to or toward the east: *We began our eastward journey at dawn.*
east·ward (ēst′wərd) ◊ *adverb* ◊ *adjective*

eastwards *adverb* Eastward.
east·wards (ēst′wərdz) ◊ *adverb*

easy *adjective* **1.** Needing very little effort; not hard: *The homework was easy.* **2.** Free from worry or pain: *The extra income made our life easier.* **3.** Not hurried or forced: *We walked along at an easy pace.* **4.** Not strict or hard to please: *We have an easy teacher.*
eas·y (ē′zē) ◊ *adjective* **easier, easiest**

SYNONYMS

easy, light², simple

This book is *easy* for me to read. I am tired today so I will just do some *light* work this morning. This game is so *simple* that you don't have to think too much while playing it. **Antonym:** *hard*

eat *verb* **1.** To take food into the body by swallowing. **2.** To have a meal: *We eat dinner at six o'clock.* **3.** To wear away or destroy as if by eating: *Rust ate away the iron pipes.*
eat (ēt) ◊ *verb* **ate, eaten, eating**

eaten *verb* Past participle of **eat.**
eat·en (ēt′n) ◊ *verb*

eaves *plural noun* The part of a roof that forms the lower edge and juts out beyond the walls of a building.
eaves (ēvz) ◊ *plural noun*

▲ **eaves**

eavesdrop *verb* To listen secretly to the private conversation of others.
eaves·drop (ēvz′drŏp′) ◊ *verb* **eavesdropped, eavesdropping**

ă	pat	ĭ	pit	oi	oil	th	bath
ā	pay	ī	ride	ŏŏ	book	*th*	bathe
â	care	î	fierce	ōō	boot	ə	ago, item
ä	father	ŏ	pot	ou	out		pencil
ĕ	pet	ō	go	ŭ	cut		atom
ē	be	ô	paw, for	û	fur		circus

ebb *verb* **1.** To flow or fall back, as the tide does after reaching its highest point; recede. **2.** To fade or fall away; weaken: *In the third quarter our hope of winning began to ebb.*
◊ *noun* A flowing out of the tide.
ebb (ĕb) ◊ *verb* **ebbed, ebbing** ◊ *noun, plural* **ebbs**

ebony *noun* The hard, blackish wood of a tree that grows in the tropics. Ebony is used especially for piano keys.
eb·on·y (ĕb′ ə nē) ◊ *noun, plural* **ebonies**

eccentric *adjective* Odd or unusual in appearance or behavior.
ec·cen·tric (ĭk sĕn′ trĭk) ◊ *adjective*

echo *noun* A repeated sound that is caused by the reflection of sound waves.
◊ *verb* To repeat a sound by or as if by an echo: *My shout echoed in the cave.*
ech·o (ĕk′ ō) ◊ *noun, plural* **echoes** ◊ *verb* **echoed, echoing**

eclipse *noun* The partial or complete blocking of light from one heavenly body by another. In a solar eclipse the moon passes between the sun and the earth. In a lunar eclipse the earth passes between the sun and the moon.
◊ *verb* **1.** To block the light of; darken. **2.** To make unimportant by comparison; overshadow: *This news eclipses everything else.*
e·clipse (ĭ klĭps′) ◊ *noun, plural* **eclipses** ◊ *verb* **eclipsed, eclipsing**

▲ **eclipse**
A solar eclipse

ecology *noun* The science of the relationships between plants and animals and their environment.
e·col·o·gy (ĭ kŏl′ ə jē) ◊ *noun*

economic *adjective* Of or relating to the making and managing of goods and services.
ec·o·nom·ic (ĕk′ə nŏm′ĭk *or* ē′kə nŏm′ĭk) ◊ *adjective*

economical *adjective* **1.** Being careful about spending money; thrifty. **2.** Running with little waste or expense, as an automobile.
ec·o·nom·i·cal (ĕk′ə nŏm′ĭ kəl *or* ē′kə nŏm′ĭ-kəl) ◊ *adjective*

economics *noun* (*used with a singular verb*) The science that deals with the production, distribution, development, and use of money, goods, and services.
ec·o·nom·ics (ĕk′ə nŏm′ĭks *or* ē′kə nŏm′ĭks) ◊ *noun*

economize *verb* To save money; spend less: *We economize by using coupons at the grocery store.*
e·con·o·mize (ĭ kŏn′ ə mīz′) ◊ *verb* **economized, economizing**

economy *noun* **1.** The careful and thrifty use of money and goods. **2.** The way in which the resources of a country, community, or business are managed.
e·con·o·my (ĭ kŏn′ ə mē) ◊ *noun, plural* **economies**

ecosystem *noun* The plants, animals, and nonliving things that make up an environment and have an effect on each other.
e·co·sys·tem (ĕk′ ō sĭs′təm *or* ē′ kō sĭs′təm) ◊ *noun, plural* **ecosystems**

-ed[1] The suffix *-ed* is added to nouns to form adjectives and means "having," "like," or "having the qualities of." *Horned* means "having horns." *Hooked* means "shaped like a hook." *Wretched* means "having the qualities of a wretch" or "miserable."

***VOCABULARY BUILDER* • -ed[1]**

Many words that are formed with **-ed** are not entries in this dictionary. But you can figure out what these words mean by looking up the meanings of the root words and the suffix. For example:
honeyed = having the qualities of honey
kindhearted = having a kind heart

-ed² The suffix *-ed* is added to verbs to show that something happened in the past. When you talk about a shirt fading at some past time, you say that the shirt *faded* or that it has *faded.* When you talk about trying a new food at some past time, you say that you *tried* the food or that you have *tried* it. When you talk about dropping a package at some past time, you say that you *dropped* the package or that you have *dropped* it.

VOCABULARY BUILDER • -ed²

In this dictionary you will find **-ed** forms given at most verb entries. Words with the suffix **-ed** can be used as adjectives. For example, a shirt that has lost its color is a *faded* shirt. Sometimes these adjectives have their own entries. For example, *accomplished* means "skilled because of practice or study" and has its own entry.

edge *noun* **1.** The line or point where an object or area ends. —See Synonyms at **border.** **2.** The usually thin, sharp side of a blade. **3.** An advantage: *We had a slight edge over the other team.*
◊ *verb* **1.** To move gradually: *We edged our way through the crowd.* **2.** To sharpen. **3.** To put an edge or border on.
edge (ĕj) ◊ *noun, plural* **edges** ◊ *verb* **edged, edging**

edible *adjective* Capable of being eaten; safe to eat.
ed·i·ble (**ĕd′** ə bəl) ◊ *adjective*

edit *verb* **1.** To make written material ready for publication by correcting, revising, or marking directions for a printer. **2.** To supervise the publication of something, as a newspaper or magazine.
ed·it (**ĕd′**ĭt) ◊ *verb* **edited, editing**

edition *noun* **1.** The entire number of copies of a book, magazine, or newspaper printed at one time. **2.** The form in which a publication is issued: *There is a paperback edition of that novel.*
e·di·tion (ĭ **dĭsh′**ən) ◊ *noun, plural* **editions**

editor *noun* **1.** A person who edits. **2.** A person who writes editorials.
ed·i·tor (**ĕd′**ĭ tər) ◊ *noun, plural* **editors**

editorial *noun* An article in a newspaper or magazine or a statement broadcast on radio or television that gives the opinions of the editors or management.
◊ *adjective* **1.** Of or relating to an editor. **2.** Giving opinions rather than reporting the news.
ed·i·to·ri·al (ĕd′ĭ **tôr′** ē əl) ◊ *noun, plural* **editorials** ◊ *adjective*

educate *verb* **1.** To provide with formal schooling. **2.** To provide with formal instruction; teach.
ed·u·cate (**ĕj′** ə kāt′) ◊ *verb* **educated, educating**

education *noun* **1.** The act or process of giving or receiving formal instruction. **2.** The knowledge or skill gained from instruction or training.
ed·u·ca·tion (ĕj′ə **kā′**shən) ◊ *noun*

educational *adjective* **1.** Of or relating to education. **2.** Giving information or providing a learning experience: *The sixth graders saw an educational film on fire safety.*
ed·u·ca·tion·al (ĕj′ə **kā′**shə nəl) ◊ *adjective*

eel *noun* A long, slippery, snakelike fish.
eel (ēl) ◊ *noun, plural* **eels**

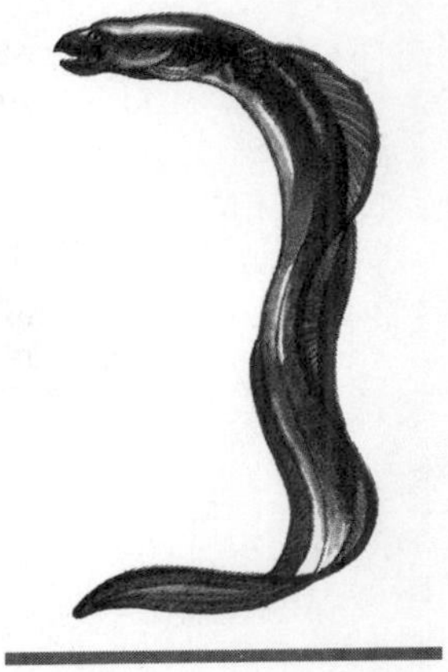
▲ **eel**

eerie *or* **eery** *adjective* Causing an uneasy feeling; weird: *An eerie blue light appeared in the distance.*
ee·rie *or* **ee·ry** (**îr′** ē) ◊ *adjective* **eerier, eeriest**

effect *noun* **1.** Something brought about by a cause: *The effect of too much sun can be a bad sunburn.* **2.** The ability to bring about a desired result; influence: *Our talk had a good effect on the children.* **3. effects** Personal belongings.

ă	pat	ĭ	pit	oi	**oil**	th	bath
ā	pay	ī	ride	ŏŏ	book	*th*	bathe
â	care	î	fierce	ōō	boot	ə	ago, item
ä	father	ŏ	pot	ou	**out**		pencil
ĕ	pet	ō	go	ŭ	cut		atom
ē	be	ô	paw, for	û	fur		circus

◊ *verb* To cause to occur: *Science has effected many changes in our society.*
ef·fect (ĭ **fĕkt′**) ◊ *noun, plural* **effects** ◊ *verb* **effected, effecting**

> ***SYNONYMS***
>
> ***effect, consequence, result***
> The *effect* of opening the window was to give me a chill. The *consequence* of this action would not be seen for years. As a *result* of all that has happened today we will have to miss the play tonight.
> **Antonym:** *cause*

effective *adjective* **1.** Having or producing a desired effect: *There are two vaccines that are effective against polio.* **2.** In operation; in force: *The new rule will become effective immediately.*
ef·fec·tive (ĭ **fĕk′**tĭv) ◊ *adjective*

efficiency *noun* **1.** The condition or quality of being efficient. **2.** The measure of how well something operates.
ef·fi·cien·cy (ĭ **fĭsh′**ən sē) ◊ *noun, plural* **efficiencies**

efficient *adjective* Bringing about a desired result without waste of time, materials, or energy: *They are efficient office workers.*
ef·fi·cient (ĭ **fĭsh′**ənt) ◊ *adjective*

effort *noun* **1.** The use of physical or mental energy to do something; exertion: *Doing it this way will save time and effort.* **2.** An earnest attempt; try: *Please make an effort to arrive on time.*
ef·fort (**ĕf′**ərt) ◊ *noun, plural* **efforts**

effortless *adjective* Easily done.
ef·fort·less (**ĕf′**ərt lĭs) ◊ *adjective*

egg[1] *noun* **1.** A female cell of an animal that unites with a male cell to produce a new animal. **2.** The round or oval body laid by a female bird, fish, insect, or reptile that is surrounded by a shell or membrane and contains a developing young animal. The young animal hatches from the egg. **3.** The contents of an egg, especially an egg produced by a hen and used as food.
egg[1] (ĕg) ◊ *noun, plural* **eggs**

egg[2] *verb* To urge into action; encourage: *They quarreled after we egged them on.*
egg[2] (ĕg) ◊ *verb* **egged, egging**

> ***HISTORY* • egg[1], egg[2]**
>
> **Egg[1]** was borrowed from the Scandinavian word for a bird's egg. **Egg[2]** was borrowed from a different Scandinavian word that is distantly related to **edge.**

eggplant *noun* A plant that has egg-shaped fruit with a shiny purple skin. The eggplant is eaten as a vegetable.
egg·plant (**ĕg′**plănt′) ◊ *noun, plural* **eggplants**

▲ **eggplant**

Egyptian *noun* **1.** A person who was born in or lives in Egypt. **2.** The language of the ancient Egyptians.
◊ *adjective* Of or relating to Egypt, the Egyptians, or the language of ancient Egypt.
E·gyp·tian (ĭ **jĭp′**shən) ◊ *noun, plural* **Egyptians** ◊ *adjective*

eight *noun* A number, written 8, that is equal to the sum of 7 + 1.
◊ *adjective* Being one more than seven.
eight (āt) ◊ *noun, plural* **eights** ◊ *adjective*
‖ *These sound alike:* **eight, ate**

eighteen *noun* A number, written 18, that is equal to the sum of 17 + 1.
◊ *adjective* Being one more than seventeen.
eight·een (ā′**tēn′**) ◊ *noun, plural* **eighteens** ◊ *adjective*

eighteenth *noun* **1.** The number in a series that matches the number eighteen. **2.** One of eighteen equal parts, written $1/18$.
◊ *adjective* Coming after the seventeenth.
eight·eenth (ā′**tēnth′**) ◊ *noun, plural* **eighteenths** ◊ *adjective*

eighth *noun* **1.** The number in a series that matches the number eight. **2.** One of eight equal parts, written 1/8.
◊ *adjective* Coming after the seventh.
eighth (ātth) ◊ *noun, plural* **eighths**
◊ *adjective*

eightieth *noun* **1.** The number in a series that matches the number eighty. **2.** One of eighty equal parts, written 1/80.
◊ *adjective* Coming after the seventy-ninth.
eight·i·eth (ā′tē ĭth) ◊ *noun, plural* **eightieths**
◊ *adjective*

eighty *noun* A number, written 80, that is equal to the product of 10 × 8.
◊ *adjective* Being equal to ten times eight.
eight·y (ā′tē) ◊ *noun, plural* **eighties**
◊ *adjective*

either *pronoun* One or the other of two: *They went a mile before either spoke.*
◊ *adjective* **1.** Being one or the other; any one of two: *Read either book if you want a great adventure story.* **2.** Each of the two: *Candles stood on either side of the vase.*
◊ *conjunction* Used with *or* to present choices or possibilities: *We can either walk or ride. This answer is either right or wrong.*
◊ *adverb* Likewise; also: *I didn't go to the party, and my friends didn't either.*
ei·ther (ē′*th*ər *or* ī′*th*ər) ◊ *pronoun*
◊ *adjective* ◊ *conjunction* ◊ *adverb*

eject *verb* To throw out forcefully: *The rifle ejects empty shells after firing.*
e·ject (ĭ **jĕkt′**) ◊ *verb* **ejected, ejecting**

elaborate *adjective* Planned or made with careful attention or much detail: *They made elaborate costumes for the play.*
◊ *verb* To say more on a subject; give details: *The press secretary elaborated on the mayor's earlier statement about new housing.*
e·lab·o·rate ◊ *adjective* (ĭ **lăb′**ər ĭt) ◊ *verb* (ĭ **lăb′**ə rāt′) **elaborated, elaborating**

elapse *verb* To go by; pass: *Months elapsed before I heard from my friend again.*
e·lapse (ĭ **lăps′**) ◊ *verb* **elapsed, elapsing**

ă	pat	ĭ	pit	oi	oil	th	bath
ā	pay	ī	ride	o͝o	book	*th*	bathe
â	care	î	fierce	o͞o	boot	ə	ago, item
ä	father	ŏ	pot	ou	out		pencil
ĕ	pet	ō	go	ŭ	cut		atom
ē	be	ô	paw, for	û	fur		circus

elastic *adjective* Capable of returning to a normal shape after being stretched or pressed together. Rubber bands are elastic.
◊ *noun* A fabric or tape woven with strands of rubber to make it stretch.
e·las·tic (ĭ **lăs′**tĭk) ◊ *adjective* ◊ *noun, plural* **elastics**

elate *verb* To make happy or joyful.
e·late (ĭ **lāt′**) ◊ *verb* **elated, elating**

elbow *noun* **1.** The joint or bend between the lower and the upper arm. **2.** Something, as a length of pipe, that has a sharp bend in it.
◊ *verb* To push, jostle, or shove with or as if with the elbows.
el·bow (**ĕl′**bō′)
◊ *noun, plural* **elbows**
◊ *verb* **elbowed, elbowing**

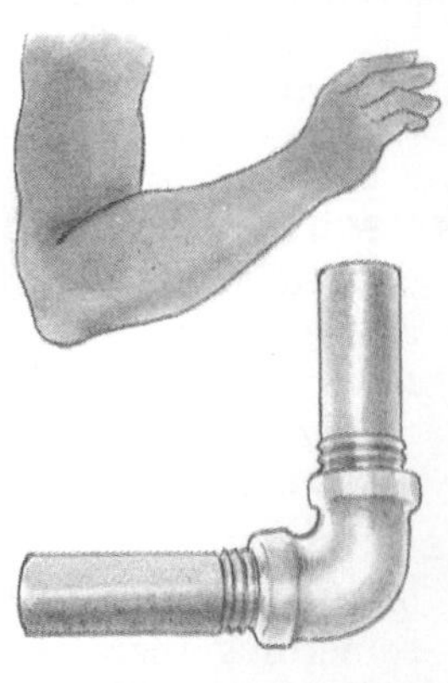
▲ **elbow**

elder *adjective* (*used only of persons*) Older: *Her elder brother just got married.*
◊ *noun* A person who is older.
eld·er (**ĕl′**dər) ◊ *adjective* ◊ *noun, plural* **elders**

elderly *adjective* Approaching old age.
eld·er·ly (**ĕl′**dər lē) ◊ *adjective*

eldest *adjective* (*used only of persons*) Oldest: *His eldest daughter is a judge.*
eld·est (**ĕl′**dĭst) ◊ *adjective*

elect *verb* **1.** To choose by vote: *We elected a class president.* **2.** To make a choice; decide: *I elected to go in my cousin's place.*
e·lect (ĭ **lĕkt′**) ◊ *verb* **elected, electing**

election *noun* The act or process of electing or the condition of being elected.
e·lec·tion (ĭ **lĕk′**shən) ◊ *noun, plural* **elections**

electric *adjective* **1.** Of, relating to, or produced by electricity: *An electric current runs through the wiring of a house.* **2.** Having an exciting or thrilling effect: *Seeing the spacecraft launch gave me an electric feeling.*
e·lec·tric (ĭ **lĕk′**trĭk) ◊ *adjective*

electrical *adjective* Of, relating to, or powered by electricity.
e·lec·tri·cal (ĭ **lĕk′**trĭ kəl) ◊ *adjective*

electric guitar *noun* A guitar whose sound is turned into electrical signals that are amplified and sent to a loudspeaker.
electric guitar ◊ *noun, plural* **electric guitars**

▲ **electric guitar**

electrician *noun* A person whose work is installing, repairing, or operating electric equipment.
e·lec·tri·cian (ĭ lĕk **trĭsh′** ən) ◊ *noun, plural* **electricians**

electricity *noun* **1.** A natural form of energy that can also be produced by artificial means to generate light, heat, and motion. **2.** Power transmitted by electrical means.
e·lec·tric·i·ty (ĭ lĕk **trĭs′** ĭ tē) ◊ *noun*

electromagnet *noun* A piece of iron that becomes a magnet when an electric current is passed through a wire coiled around it.
e·lec·tro·mag·net (ĭ lĕk′trō **măg′** nĭt) ◊ *noun, plural* **electromagnets**

electron *noun* A tiny particle that has a negative electric charge and is found outside the nucleus of an atom.
e·lec·tron (ĭ **lĕk′** trŏn′) ◊ *noun, plural* **electrons**

electronic *adjective* Of or relating to electrons or electronics.
e·lec·tron·ic (ĭ lĕk **trŏn′** ĭk) ◊ *adjective*

electronics *noun* (*used with a singular verb*) **1.** The science that is concerned with electrons and with devices and systems that make use of electrons. **2.** The commercial industry of electronic devices and systems. Electronics has led to the development of radio, television, computers, and space flight.
e·lec·tron·ics (ĭ lĕk **trŏn′** ĭks) ◊ *noun*

elegance *noun* Refinement and grace in the way a person appears or behaves.
el·e·gance (**ĕl′** ĭ gəns) ◊ *noun*

elegant *adjective* Marked by good taste and refinement: *We had dinner last night in an elegant restaurant.*
el·e·gant (**ĕl′** ĭ gənt) ◊ *adjective*

element *noun* **1.** A basic or essential part of a whole: *A noun and a verb are elements of a sentence.* **2.** The most basic part of a subject: *To be good readers we must learn the elements of reading.* **3.** One of over 100 basic substances that cannot be broken down by ordinary chemical means: *Water is made up of the elements hydrogen and oxygen.* **4. elements** The forces of weather, such as cold, wind, or rain.
el·e·ment (**ĕl′** ə mənt) ◊ *noun, plural* **elements**

elementary *adjective* Of or relating to the most basic parts of a subject; introductory.
el·e·men·ta·ry (ĕl′ə **mĕn′** tə rē) ◊ *adjective*

elementary school *noun* A school for the first six to eight years of a child's formal classroom instruction.
elementary school ◊ *noun, plural* **elementary schools**

elephant *noun* A very large Asian or African mammal with a long, flexible trunk and long, curved tusks.
el·e·phant (**ĕl′** ə fənt) ◊ *noun, plural* **elephants**

▲ **elephant**

elevate *verb* To raise to a higher place, position, or level; lift up.
el·e·vate (ĕl′ ə vāt′) ◊ *verb* **elevated, elevating**

elevation *noun* **1.** A raised place or position. **2.** Height above the surface of the earth or above sea level.
el·e·va·tion (ĕl′ə **vā′**shən) ◊ *noun, plural* **elevations**

elevator *noun* **1.** A platform or small room that can be raised or lowered in a vertical shaft to carry people or freight from one level to another. **2.** A building for storing grain.
el·e·va·tor (**ĕl′** ə vā′tər) ◊ *noun, plural* **elevators**

▲ **elevator**

eleven *noun* A number, written 11, that is equal to the sum of 10 + 1.
◊ *adjective* Being one more than ten.
e·lev·en (ĭ **lĕv′** ən) ◊ *noun, plural* **elevens** ◊ *adjective*

eleventh *noun* **1.** The number in a series that matches the number eleven. **2.** One of eleven equal parts, written 1/11.
◊ *adjective* Coming after the tenth.
e·lev·enth (ĭ **lĕv′** ənth) ◊ *noun, plural* **elevenths** ◊ *adjective*

ă	pat	ĭ	pit	oi	**oil**	th	ba**th**
ā	pay	ī	ride	o͝o	**book**	*th*	ba**the**
â	care	î	fierce	o͞o	**boot**	ə	**a**go, it**e**m
ä	father	ŏ	pot	ou	**out**		penc**i**l
ĕ	pet	ō	go	ŭ	cut		at**o**m
ē	be	ô	paw, for	û	fur		circ**u**s

elf *noun* A tiny, often mischievous, imaginary creature with magical powers.
elf (ĕlf) ◊ *noun, plural* **elves**

eligible *adjective* Fit, qualified, or worthy to be chosen.
el·i·gi·ble (**ĕl′**ĭ jə bəl) ◊ *adjective*

eliminate *verb* To get rid of; do away with: *We must work to eliminate world hunger.*
e·lim·i·nate (ĭ **lĭm′** ə nāt′) ◊ *verb* **eliminated, eliminating**

elk *noun* A North American deer with very large antlers.
elk (ĕlk) ◊ *noun, plural* **elk** *or* **elks**

▲ **elk**

ellipse *noun* A closed curve shaped like an egg or oval with both ends alike.
el·lipse (ĭ **lĭps′**) ◊ *noun, plural* **ellipses**

elm *noun* A tall shade tree with arching or curving branches.
elm (ĕlm) ◊ *noun, plural* **elms**

elope *verb* To run away to get married without the consent of one's parents.
e·lope (ĭ **lōp′**) ◊ *verb* **eloped, eloping**

eloquent *adjective* Showing clear, forceful, and effective use of language: *The speaker made an eloquent appeal for human rights.*
el·o·quent (**ĕl′** ə kwənt) ◊ *adjective*

else *adjective* **1.** Other; different: *Ask somebody else.* **2.** In addition; more: *Would you like anything else?*
◊ *adverb* **1.** In a different time, place, or manner: *How else could it have been done?* **2.** If

not; otherwise: *Be careful or else you will make a mistake.*
else (ĕls) ◊ *adjective* ◊ *adverb*

elsewhere *adverb* To or in a different or other place: *We decided to go elsewhere for our vacation.*
else·where (**ĕls′**hwâr′) ◊ *adverb*

elude *verb* To avoid or escape by being skillful, cunning, or quick; evade: *The fox eluded the hunters.*
e·lude (ĭ **lo͞od′**) ◊ *verb* **eluded, eluding**

elves *noun* Plural of **elf.**
elves (ĕlvz) ◊ *noun*

emancipate *verb* To set free from slavery or control; liberate.
e·man·ci·pate (ĭ **măn′**sə pāt′) ◊ *verb* **emancipated, emancipating**

embalm *verb* To treat a dead body with substances that prevent or slow decay.
em·balm (ĕm **bäm′**) ◊ *verb* **embalmed, embalming**

embankment *noun* A mound, as of earth or stone, to hold back water, support a roadway, or prevent floods.
em·bank·ment (ĕm **băngk′**mənt) ◊ *noun, plural* **embankments**

embargo *noun* An order by a government that forbids ships engaged in trade or commerce to enter or leave its ports.
em·bar·go (ĕm **bär′**gō) ◊ *noun, plural* **embargoes**

embark *verb* **1.** To go on board a ship or an airplane: *We embarked on a cruise.* **2.** To set out on a venture or task: *They embarked on a campaign to get people to vote.* —See Synonyms at **begin.**
em·bark (ĕm **bärk′**) ◊ *verb* **embarked, embarking**

embarrass *verb* To cause to feel nervous or ill at ease; fluster: *It embarrassed me when I dropped my lunch tray.*
em·bar·rass (ĕm **băr′**əs) ◊ *verb* **embarrassed, embarrassing**

embarrassment *noun* **1.** The condition of being embarrassed: *My face turned red with embarrassment.* **2.** Something that embarrasses: *Coughing at a concert can be a real embarrassment.*
em·bar·rass·ment (ĕm **băr′**əs mənt) ◊ *noun, plural* **embarrassments**

embassy *noun* **1.** An ambassador and his or her staff. **2.** The official headquarters of an ambassador.
em·bas·sy (**ĕm′**bə sē) ◊ *noun, plural* **embassies**

embed *verb* To fix or become fixed firmly in a surrounding substance: *The workers embedded the big posts in concrete.*
em·bed (ĕm **bĕd′**) ◊ *verb* **embedded, embedding**

ember *noun* A piece of glowing coal or wood in the ashes of a fire.
em·ber (**ĕm′**bər) ◊ *noun, plural* **embers**

embezzle *verb* To take money or property that was left in one's care for one's own use: *The president of the firm embezzled a large sum of the company's money.*
em·bez·zle (ĕm **bĕz′**əl) ◊ *verb* **embezzled, embezzling**

emblem *noun* An object or picture of an object that represents something else; symbol: *The eagle is the national emblem of the United States.*
em·blem (**ĕm′**bləm) ◊ *noun, plural* **emblems**

▲ **emblem**

embody *verb* To represent in a visible form: *The Statue of Liberty embodies the spirit of freedom.*
em·bod·y (ĕm **bŏd′**ē) ◊ *verb* **embodied, embodying**

emboss *verb* To decorate with a raised design: *The leather wallet was embossed with my initials.*
em·boss (ĕm **bôs′**) ◊ *verb* **embossed, embossing**

embrace *verb* **1.** To clasp or hold in the arms, especially as a sign of affection; hug: *They embraced and then said good-by.* **2.** To take up willingly or eagerly: *We left the farm and embraced life in the city.* **3.** To take in as a part or member; include: *My education embraced all the language arts.*
◊ *noun* An act of clasping in the arms; hug.
em·brace (ĕm **brās′**) ◊ *verb* **embraced, embracing** ◊ *noun, plural* **embraces**

embroider *verb* **1.** To decorate by sewing designs with a needle and thread: *Did you embroider this pillow?* **2.** To add made-up details to in order to add interest; exaggerate: *I embroidered the story about my trip.*
em·broi·der (ĕm **broi′**dər) ◊ *verb* **embroidered, embroidering**

embroidery *noun* An embroidered fabric or design.
em·broi·der·y (ĕm **broi′**də rē) ◊ *noun, plural* **embroideries**

▲ **embroidery**

embryo *noun* **1.** An animal in its earliest stages of growth, just after its development from an egg cell. **2.** A tiny young plant contained within a seed.
em·bry·o (**ĕm′**brē ō′) ◊ *noun, plural* **embryos**

emerald *noun* **1.** A bright-green stone that is used as a gem. **2.** A bright green color.
em·er·ald (**ĕm′**ər əld) ◊ *noun, plural* **emeralds**

emerge *verb* **1.** To come into view; appear: *The butterfly emerged from the cocoon.* **2.** To come into existence; arise: *A new spirit of freedom emerged.*
e·merge (ĭ **mûrj′**) ◊ *verb* **emerged, emerging**

emergency *noun* A situation that develops suddenly and unexpectedly and calls for immediate action.
e·mer·gen·cy (ĭ **mûr′**jən sē) ◊ *noun, plural* **emergencies**

emery *noun* A mineral used in a crushed or powdered form for grinding and polishing.
em·er·y (**ĕm′**ə rē) ◊ *noun*

emigrant *noun* A person who leaves a country or region to settle in another.
em·i·grant (**ĕm′**ĭ grənt) ◊ *noun, plural* **emigrants**

ă	pat	ĭ	pit	oi	**oi**l	th	ba**th**
ā	pay	ī	ride	o͝o	b**oo**k	*th*	ba**th**e
â	care	î	fierce	o͞o	b**oo**t	ə	ago, item
ä	father	ŏ	pot	ou	**ou**t		pencil
ĕ	pet	ō	go	ŭ	c**u**t		atom
ē	be	ô	paw, for	û	f**u**r		circus

emigrate *verb* To leave a country or region to settle in another: *In 1908 my grandparents emigrated from Italy to America.*
em·i·grate (**ĕm′**ĭ grāt′) ◊ *verb* **emigrated, emigrating**

eminent *adjective* Standing out above all others; distinguished: *An eminent surgeon operated on the patient.*
em·i·nent (**ĕm′**ə nənt) ◊ *adjective*

emissary *noun* A person sent on a mission or errand as the representative of another.
em·is·sar·y (**ĕm′**ĭ sĕr′ē) ◊ *noun, plural* **emissaries**

emit *verb* To give off or send forth: *The sun emits light and heat.*
e·mit (ĭ **mĭt′**) ◊ *verb* **emitted, emitting**

emotion *noun* A strong feeling, as love, sorrow, hate, or joy.
e·mo·tion (ĭ **mō′**shən) ◊ *noun, plural* **emotions**

emotional *adjective* **1.** Of or relating to emotion or the emotions: *Winning gave us emotional satisfaction.* **2.** Easily affected by emotion: *Emotional people often cry at sad movies.* **3.** Appealing to or arousing the emotions: *The politician used emotional language in the speech.*
e·mo·tion·al (ĭ **mō′**shə nəl) ◊ *adjective*

emperor *noun* The male ruler of an empire.
em·per·or (**ĕm′**pər ər) ◊ *noun, plural* **emperors**

emphases *noun* Plural of **emphasis.**
em·pha·ses (**ĕm′**fə sēz′) ◊ *noun*

emphasis *noun* **1.** Special importance given to something: *Our school puts a strong emphasis on learning foreign languages.* **2.** Stress given to a particular syllable or word in reading or speaking.
em·pha·sis (**ĕm′**fə sĭs) ◊ *noun, plural* **emphases**

emphasize *verb* To give emphasis to; stress: *My parents emphasized the need to learn a second language in school.*
em·pha·size (**ĕm′**fə sīz′) ◊ *verb* **emphasized, emphasizing**

empire *noun* **1.** A group of territories or nations headed by a single ruler. **2.** A country under the rule of an emperor or empress.
em·pire (**ĕm′**pīr′) ◊ *noun, plural* **empires**

employ *verb* **1.** To engage the services of; hire: *The construction company employed*

many workers to build the skyscraper. **2.** To make use of: *The carpenter employed lumber to make the chest.*
◊ *noun* The condition of being employed: *We were in the employ of the government.*
em·ploy (ĕm **ploi′**) ◊ *verb* **employed, employing** ◊ *noun*

employee *noun* A person who works for an employer in return for wages or a salary.
em·ploy·ee (ĕm **ploi′**ē) ◊ *noun, plural* **employees**

employer *noun* A person or business that employs people for wages or a salary.
em·ploy·er (ĕm **ploi′**ər) ◊ *noun, plural* **employers**

employment *noun* **1.** The work in which one is engaged or activity to which one devotes time: *I got regular employment on a fishing boat.* **2.** The act of employing or the condition of being employed: *The level of employment in that country was rising.*
em·ploy·ment (ĕm **ploi′**mənt) ◊ *noun, plural* **employments**

empress *noun* **1.** The female ruler of an empire. **2.** The wife or widow of an emperor.
em·press (**ĕm′**prĭs) ◊ *noun, plural* **empresses**

empty *adjective* **1.** Containing nothing: *You can fill the empty bottle with orange juice.* **2.** Lacking purpose, value, or meaning: *Everything you said was empty talk.*
◊ *verb* **1.** To make or become empty: *I emptied my glass and asked for more.* **2.** To transfer or pour off: *Empty the ashes into a bucket.* **3.** To flow or discharge: *The river empties into the ocean.*
emp·ty (**ĕmp′**tē) ◊ *adjective* ◊ *verb* **emptied, emptying**

> ***SYNONYMS***
>
> ***empty, blank, vacant***
>
> When the movers left, all the rooms were *empty.* I am about to write something on this *blank* piece of paper. The house at the corner has been *vacant* for a long time. **Antonym:** *full*

emu *noun* A large Australian bird that is related to and looks like the ostrich.
e·mu (ē′myo͞o′) ◊ *noun, plural* **emus**

▲ **emu**

enable *verb* To give the means, ability, strength, or opportunity to do something: *Space flight enables us to explore the moon.*
en·a·ble (ĕn **ā′**bəl) ◊ *verb* **enabled, enabling**

enact *verb* **1.** To make into law: *Congress enacted a bill to curb the use of drugs.* **2.** To act out, as on a stage: *They enacted the roles of hero and heroine in the play.*
en·act (ĕn **ăkt′**) ◊ *verb* **enacted, enacting**

enamel *noun* **1.** A substance baked onto the surface of metal, porcelain, pottery, or glass for decoration or protection. **2.** A paint that dries to make a hard, glossy surface. **3.** The hard substance that covers the exposed part of a tooth.
◊ *verb* To coat or decorate with enamel.
e·nam·el (ĭ **năm′**əl) ◊ *noun, plural* **enamels** ◊ *verb* **enameled, enameling**

enchant *verb* **1.** To put under a magic spell; bewitch. **2.** To delight completely; charm.
en·chant (ĕn **chănt′**) ◊ *verb* **enchanted, enchanting**

enchantment *noun* **1.** An act of enchanting. **2.** The condition or quality of being enchanted.
en·chant·ment (ĕn **chănt′**mənt) ◊ *noun, plural* **enchantments**

encircle *verb* **1.** To form a circle around; surround: *The sea encircled the island.* **2.** To pass in a circle around: *It takes the earth one year to encircle the sun.*
en·cir·cle (ĕn **sûr′**kəl) ◊ *verb* **encircled, encircling**

enclose *verb* **1.** To close in on all sides; surround: *A high fence encloses the garden.* **2.** To put in the same envelope or package

with something else: *I enclosed my class picture with the letter.*
en·close (ĕn **klōz′**) ◊ *verb* **enclosed, enclosing**

enclosure *noun* **1.** The act or process of enclosing. **2.** Something, as a wall, that encloses. **3.** An enclosed area. **4.** Something put into an envelope or package with something else.
en·clo·sure (ĕn **klō′**zhər) ◊ *noun, plural* **enclosures**

encompass *verb* **1.** To take in; include. **2.** To form a circle around; encircle.
en·com·pass (ĕn **kŭm′**pəs) ◊ *verb* **encompassed, encompassing**

encore *noun* **1.** A request by an audience for an additional performance, usually expressed by clapping. **2.** An additional performance given in response to applause.
en·core (**ŏn′**kôr′) ◊ *noun, plural* **encores**

encounter *noun* An often unexpected meeting with a person or thing: *The campers had an encounter with a skunk.*
◊ *verb* **1.** To meet, especially unexpectedly: *We had to learn the meanings of the new words we encountered.* **2.** To be faced with; experience: *I never expected to encounter so much opposition to my plan.*
en·coun·ter (ĕn **koun′**tər) ◊ *noun, plural* **encounters** ◊ *verb* **encountered, encountering**

encourage *verb* **1.** To give courage, hope, or confidence to: *The doctor's report encouraged me somewhat.* **2.** To urge or inspire: *The teacher encouraged the students to make use of the library.* **3.** To help bring about; foster: *Many people feel that violence on television encourages real violence.*
en·cour·age (ĕn **kûr′**ĭj) ◊ *verb* **encouraged, encouraging**

encouragement *noun* **1.** The act of encouraging. **2.** Something that encourages: *The promise of a surprise gift if I succeeded was an encouragement to keep trying.*
en·cour·age·ment (ĕn **kûr′**ĭj mənt) ◊ *noun, plural* **encouragements**

ă	pat	ĭ	pit	oi	oil	th	bath
ā	pay	ī	ride	ŏŏ	book	*th*	bathe
â	care	î	fierce	ōō	boot	ə	ago, item
ä	father	ŏ	pot	ou	out		pencil
ĕ	pet	ō	go	ŭ	cut		atom
ē	be	ô	paw, for	û	fur		circus

encyclopedia *noun* A book or set of books containing articles usually arranged in alphabetical order and covering a wide variety of subjects or one particular field.
en·cy·clo·pe·di·a (ĕn sī′klə **pē′**dē ə) ◊ *noun, plural* **encyclopedias**

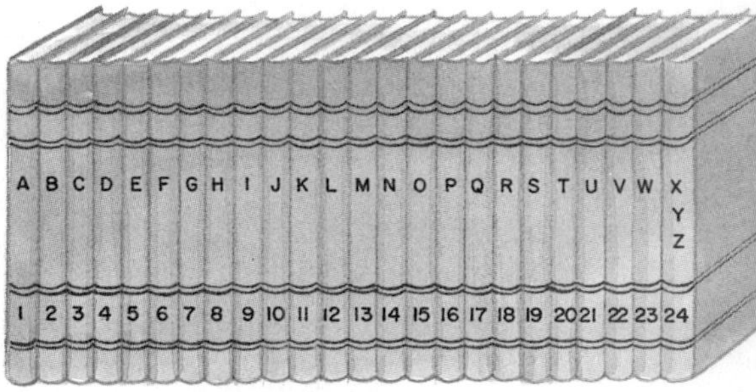

▲ **encyclopedia**

end *noun* **1.** The first or last part of something that has length: *They sat at opposite ends of the table.* **2.** The extreme edge or limit of something, as a space or area: *The city lies at the eastern end of the lake.* **3.** The point at which something stops or finishes; conclusion: *Summer is coming to an end.* **4.** The purpose of an action; goal.
◊ *verb* To bring or come to a finish.
end (ĕnd) ◊ *noun, plural* **ends** ◊ *verb* **ended, ending**

SYNONYMS

end, close, complete, conclude, finish

Tomorrow our long trip across the country will *end.* The assembly has to *close* now because we've run out of time. The construction of our new house will not be *completed* until next fall. The ambassador hopes to *conclude* negotiations tomorrow. I have just about *finished* reading that book. **Antonyms:** *begin, start*

endanger *verb* To expose to danger: *The oil spill endangered thousands of birds.*
en·dan·ger (ĕn **dān′**jər) ◊ *verb* **endangered, endangering**

endeavor *verb* To make a serious effort: *We endeavor to achieve world peace.*
◊ *noun* A serious effort; attempt.
en·deav·or (ĕn **dĕv′**ər) ◊ *verb* **endeavored, endeavoring** ◊ *noun, plural* **endeavors**

ending *noun* **1.** The last part, as of a book; end: *The play has a happy ending.* **2.** A letter or letters added to the end of a word, especially to make an inflected form. The ending *-ed* is added to the verb *pick* to make the past tense *picked.*
end·ing (**ĕn′**dĭng) ◊ *noun, plural* **endings**

endorse *verb* **1.** To write one's signature on the back of a check in order to receive payment. **2.** To give approval of or support to: *Many senators have already endorsed the new bill.*
en·dorse (ĕn **dôrs′**) ◊ *verb* **endorsed, endorsing**

endow *verb* **1.** To provide with property, income, or a source of income: *The wealthy graduate endowed the college.* **2.** To provide with a talent, ability, or quality: *Nature endowed the child with intelligence and charm.*
en·dow (ĕn **dou′**) ◊ *verb* **endowed, endowing**

endurance *noun* The ability to withstand strain, pain, hardship, or use: *Running the marathon tests a person's endurance.*
en·dur·ance (ĕn **dŏŏr′**əns *or* ĕn **dyŏŏr′**əns) ◊ *noun*

endure *verb* **1.** To put up with; bear: *I can no longer endure your rudeness.* **2.** To continue to exist; last: *Their friendship endured for years.*
en·dure (ĕn **dŏŏr′** *or* ĕn **dyŏŏr′**) ◊ *verb* **endured, enduring**

enemy *noun* **1.** A person, animal, or group that hates or wishes harm to another; foe: *All citizens should be enemies of prejudice.* **2.** A country that is at war with one's own country. **3.** Something harmful in its effects: *Weather is sometimes the farmer's worst enemy.*
en·e·my (**ĕn′**ə mē) ◊ *noun, plural* **enemies**

energetic *adjective* Full of energy; vigorous. —See Synonyms at **active.**
en·er·get·ic (ĕn′ər **jĕt′**ĭk) ◊ *adjective*

energy *noun* **1.** Usable heat or electric power for doing physical work such as moving or lifting objects. Water, oil, and the sun are sources of energy. **2.** The ability to act, work, or put forth mental or physical effort. **3.** Strength and vigor in action: *Good food helps give us energy.*
en·er·gy (**ĕn′**ər jē) ◊ *noun, plural* **energies**

enforce *verb* To force others to obey: *The police department enforces the law.*
en·force (ĕn **fôrs′**) ◊ *verb* **enforced, enforcing**

Eng. The abbreviation for *England* or *English.*

engage *verb* **1.** To make arrangements to get the services or use of; hire: *We engaged a hotel room for our vacation.* **2.** To attract and hold: *The book engaged my full attention.* **3.** To take part; involve oneself: *They engaged in the study of music.* **4.** To require the use of; occupy: *Sewing engages much of my free time.* **5.** To promise to do something, especially to pledge oneself to marry.
en·gage (ĕn **gāj′**) ◊ *verb* **engaged, engaging**

engagement *noun* **1.** The act of engaging or the condition of being engaged. **2.** A promise to marry. **3.** A promise to appear at a certain time; appointment.
en·gage·ment (ĕn **gāj′**mənt) ◊ *noun, plural* **engagements**

engine *noun* **1.** A machine that uses energy, as that produced by oil or steam, to make something run or move; motor. **2.** A railroad locomotive.
en·gine (**ĕn′**jən) ◊ *noun, plural* **engines**

▲ **engine**

engineer *noun* **1.** A person who works in a branch of engineering. **2.** A person who runs a railroad locomotive.
◊ *verb* To achieve by skill or cleverness.
en·gi·neer (ĕn′jə **nîr′**) ◊ *noun, plural* **engineers** ◊ *verb* **engineered, engineering**

engineering *noun* The use of scientific knowledge and rules for practical purposes, as designing and building bridges, roads, and tunnels.
en·gi·neer·ing (ĕn′jə **nîr′**ĭng) ◊ *noun*

English *noun* **1.** (*used with a plural verb*) The people of England. **2.** The language of

Great Britain, the United States, and many other countries.
◊ *adjective* Of or relating to England, the English, or the English language.
Eng·lish (ĭng′glĭsh) ◊ *noun* ◊ *adjective*

English horn *noun* A musical instrument that is similar to an oboe but is larger and has a lower pitch.
English horn ◊ *noun, plural* **English horns**

engrave *verb* **1.** To carve or cut a design or letters into a surface, as of stone, metal, or wood: *I had my initials engraved on the picture frame.* **2.** To print from an engraved surface.
en·grave (ĕn **grāv′**) ◊ *verb* **engraved, engraving**

▲ **English horn**

engraving *noun* **1.** The art or technique of carving or cutting something into a surface, as of stone, metal, or wood. **2.** An engraved surface used for printing. **3.** A print made from an engraved plate.
en·grav·ing (ĕn **grā′** vĭng) ◊ *noun, plural* **engravings**

▲ **engraving**

ă	pat	ĭ	pit	oi	**oil**	th	ba**th**
ā	pay	ī	ride	ŏŏ	book	*th*	ba**the**
â	care	î	fierce	ōō	boot	ə	ago, item
ä	father	ŏ	pot	ou	**out**		pencil
ĕ	pet	ō	go	ŭ	cut		atom
ē	be	ô	paw, for	û	fur		circus

engulf *verb* To swallow up or cover completely by or as if by overflowing: *The flood engulfed the farms and destroyed the crops.*
en·gulf (ĕn **gŭlf′**) ◊ *verb* **engulfed, engulfing**

enhance *verb* To make greater, as in value or beauty; heighten: *Beautiful colored illustrations enhanced the book.*
en·hance (ĕn **hăns′**) ◊ *verb* **enhanced, enhancing**

enjoy *verb* **1.** To receive pleasure from: *We enjoy living in the country.* **2.** To have as a benefit or advantage: *I'm glad you enjoy good health.*
◊ *idiom* **enjoy oneself** To have a good time: *Did you enjoy yourself during your vacation?*
en·joy (ĕn **joi′**) ◊ *verb* **enjoyed, enjoying**

enjoyable *adjective* Giving joy or happiness: *We had an enjoyable trip to the zoo.*
en·joy·a·ble (ĕn **joi′** ə bəl) ◊ *adjective*

enjoyment *noun* **1.** The act or condition of enjoying something: *One of the best things in life is the enjoyment of good food.* **2.** A form or source of pleasure: *We work in the garden for enjoyment.* —See Synonyms at **joy.**
en·joy·ment (ĕn **joi′**mənt) ◊ *noun, plural* **enjoyments**

enlarge *verb* To make or become larger: *I asked the photographer to enlarge the picture.*
en·large (ĕn **lärj′**) ◊ *verb* **enlarged, enlarging**

enlargement *noun* **1.** The act of enlarging or the condition of being enlarged. **2.** A photographic print larger than the original.
en·large·ment (ĕn **lärj′**mənt) ◊ *noun, plural* **enlargements**

enlighten *verb* To give knowledge or understanding to; instruct: *We were enlightened by the teacher's discussion.*
en·light·en (ĕn **līt′**n) ◊ *verb* **enlightened, enlightening**

enlist *verb* **1.** To join or persuade to join the armed forces as a volunteer: *They enlisted in the navy after they finished high school.* **2.** To get the help or support of: *I enlisted my best friend in planning the party.*
en·list (ĕn **lĭst′**) ◊ *verb* **enlisted, enlisting**

enormous *adjective* Extremely large; huge. —See Synonyms at **gigantic.**
e·nor·mous (ĭ **nôr′**məs) ◊ *adjective*

enough *adjective* Being as much or as many as needed to meet a requirement; adequate: *There is enough food for everybody.*

◊*pronoun* An adequate quantity or number: *The child ate enough for two.*
◊*adverb* To or in an adequate amount or degree: *You know them well enough not to believe what they say.*
e·nough (ĭ **nŭf′**) ◊*adjective* ◊*pronoun* ◊*adverb*

enrage *verb* To make extremely angry.
en·rage (ĕn **rāj′**) ◊*verb* **enraged, enraging**

enrich *verb* **1.** To make rich or richer: *The success of the new business has enriched the owners.* **2.** To improve the quality of by adding certain elements or ingredients: *Fertilizer enriches the soil.*
en·rich (ĕn **rĭch′**) ◊*verb* **enriched, enriching**

enroll *verb* To place or be placed on a list or roll: *In September we enroll in school.*
en·roll (ĕn **rōl′**) ◊*verb* **enrolled, enrolling**

enrollment *noun* **1.** The act of enrolling or the process of being enrolled: *Elementary school enrollment begins tomorrow.* **2.** The number of people enrolled: *The school has an enrollment of 600 students.*
en·roll·ment (ĕn **rōl′**mənt) ◊*noun, plural* **enrollments**

en route *adverb* On or along the way: *We'll pick you up en route to the ball game.*
en route (ŏn **ro͞ot′**) ◊*adverb*

ensign *noun* **1.** A national flag or banner that is displayed on ships and airplanes. **2.** A Navy or Coast Guard officer having the lowest rank.
en·sign (**ĕn′**sən) ◊*noun, plural* **ensigns**

▲ **ensign**

ensure *verb* To make sure or certain; guarantee: *Proper diet helps ensure good health.*
en·sure (ĕn **sho͝or′**) ◊*verb* **ensured, ensuring**

entangle *verb* To make tangled; snarl: *Don't entangle the fishing lines.*
en·tan·gle (ĕn **tăng′**gəl) ◊*verb* **entangled, entangling**

enter *verb* **1.** To come or go in or into: *The ship entered the harbor.* **2.** To become a member of; join: *At 16 you're too young to enter the army.* **3.** To make a beginning in: *They decided to enter the medical profession.* **4.** To cause to be admitted; register: *We have decided to enter you in a private school.* **5.** To record in writing: *Enter the total amount in the box below.*
en·ter (**ĕn′**tər) ◊*verb* **entered, entering**

enterprise *noun* **1.** An important undertaking or project, especially one that is complicated and sometimes risky: *Traveling around the world in a sailboat is a dangerous enterprise.* **2.** A business activity or organization.
en·ter·prise (**ĕn′**tər prīz′) ◊*noun, plural* **enterprises**

entertain *verb* **1.** To hold the attention of in an agreeable way: *We entertained them with stories about our trip to Hawaii.* —See Synonyms at **amuse. 2.** To have as a guest: *We entertained friends for dinner.*
en·ter·tain (ĕn′tər **tān′**) ◊*verb* **entertained, entertaining**

entertainer *noun* A person, such as a singer or dancer, who performs for the entertainment of the public.
en·ter·tain·er (ĕn′tər **tā′**nər) ◊*noun, plural* **entertainers**

entertainment *noun* **1.** The act of entertaining. **2.** Something, as a show, that is intended to entertain. **3.** The pleasure that comes from being entertained; amusement: *I read the novel for entertainment.*
en·ter·tain·ment (ĕn′tər **tān′**mənt) ◊*noun, plural* **entertainments**

enthrall *verb* To hold as if under a magic spell; fascinate: *The beauty of the singer's voice enthralled the audience.*
en·thrall (ĕn **thrôl′**) ◊*verb* **enthralled, enthralling**

enthusiasm *noun* A very strong, positive feeling for something; strong interest or admiration: *The children dive and swim with enthusiasm.*
en·thu·si·asm (ĕn **tho͞o′**zē ăz′əm) ◊*noun*

enthusiastic *adjective* Full of or showing enthusiasm: *My parents are enthusiastic skiers.*
en·thu·si·as·tic (ĕn thōō′zē **ăs′** tĭk) ◊ *adjective*

entire *adjective* Having no part missing or left out; whole or complete.
en·tire (ĕn **tīr′**) ◊ *adjective*

entirety *noun* **1.** The condition of being entire and complete. **2.** An entire amount or extent; whole.
en·tire·ty (ĕn **tīr′** tē) ◊ *noun, plural* **entireties**

entitle *verb* **1.** To give a title to; name: *The article is entitled "Our American Heritage."* **2.** To give a right or privilege to: *This coupon entitles you to a discount.*
en·ti·tle (ĕn **tīt′**l) ◊ *verb* **entitled, entitling**

entrance[1] *noun* **1.** The act or an example of entering: *The audience applauded the singer's entrance.* **2.** A door or passageway: *We used the back entrance to the building.* **3.** Permission or right to enter; admission: *They were refused entrance to the theater.*
en·trance[1] (**ĕn′** trəns) ◊ *noun, plural* **entrances**

entrance[2] *verb* To fill with great pleasure and wonder: *The beauty of the mountains entranced the hikers.*
en·trance[2] (ĕn **trăns′**) ◊ *verb* **entranced, entrancing**

> ***HISTORY* • entrance[1], entrance[2]**
>
> **Entrance[1]** is related to **enter**, and **entrance[2]** to **trance**. Their different pronunciations reflect their different origins.

entreat *verb* To ask earnestly; beg: *I entreated them to help me.*
en·treat (ĕn **trēt′**) ◊ *verb* **entreated, entreating**

entrust *verb* To give over to another for protection, care, or action: *I entrusted my cat to a friend while I was away.*
en·trust (ĕn **trŭst′**) ◊ *verb* **entrusted, entrusting**

ă	pat	ĭ	pit	oi	**oil**	th	**bath**
ā	pay	ī	ride	ŏŏ	**book**	*th*	**bathe**
â	care	î	fierce	ōō	**boot**	ə	ago, item
ä	father	ŏ	pot	ou	**out**		pencil
ĕ	pet	ō	go	ŭ	cut		atom
ē	be	ô	paw, for	û	fur		circus

entry *noun* **1.** The act or right of entering: *You need a passport for entry into the country.* **2.** A place, as a passage or door, through which to enter. **3.** The act of including an item in a record, as a diary or list. **4.** Something entered in a record or list: *A word or phrase that is entered and defined in a dictionary is an entry.* **5.** Someone or something entered in a race or contest.
en·try (**ĕn′** trē) ◊ *noun, plural* **entries**

enunciate *verb* To pronounce words: *Try to enunciate more clearly.*
e·nun·ci·ate (ĭ **nŭn′** sē āt′) ◊ *verb* **enunciated, enunciating**

envelop *verb* To enclose completely with or as if with a covering; wrap up: *The baby is enveloped in a blanket.*
en·vel·op (ĕn **vĕl′** əp) ◊ *verb* **enveloped, enveloping**

envelope *noun* A flat, paper wrapper used mainly for mailing letters.
en·ve·lope (**ĕn′** və lōp′) ◊ *noun, plural* **envelopes**

envious *adjective* Feeling or showing envy.
en·vi·ous (**ĕn′** vē əs) ◊ *adjective*

environment *noun* Surroundings and conditions that affect natural processes and the growth and development of living things: *We grew up in a warm and loving environment.*
en·vi·ron·ment (ĕn **vī′** rən mənt) ◊ *noun, plural* **environments**

envy *noun* **1.** A feeling of discontent at the advantages or success enjoyed by another together with a strong desire to have them for oneself: *I was filled with envy when I saw their new car.* **2.** An object of envy: *The new car was the envy of all their friends.*
◊ *verb* To feel envy toward or because of.
en·vy (**ĕn′** vē) ◊ *noun, plural* **envies** ◊ *verb* **envied, envying**

epic *noun* A long poem about the achievements and adventures of heroes.
◊ *adjective* **1.** Of an epic: *I'm reading an epic novel about frontier life.* **2.** Like something in an epic; tremendous: *The landing on the moon in 1969 was an epic achievement.*
ep·ic (**ĕp′** ĭk) ◊ *noun, plural* **epics** ◊ *adjective*

epidemic *noun* An outbreak of a disease that spreads rapidly and widely.
ep·i·dem·ic (ĕp′ĭ **dĕm′** ĭk) ◊ *noun, plural* **epidemics**

episode *noun* **1.** An event or series of events in a person's life: *Owning my own horse was an important episode of my childhood.* **2.** A distinct part of a story or a separate part of a continuing story.
ep·i·sode (ĕp′ĭ sōd′) ◊ *noun, plural* **episodes**

epoch *noun* A period in history marked by certain important events or developments; era: *The years of the American Revolution were an epoch in United States history.*
ep·och (ĕp′ək) ◊ *noun, plural* **epochs**

equal *adjective* **1.** Being exactly the same in amount, extent, or other measured quality: *Three feet are equal to one yard.* —See Synonyms at **same. 2.** Having the same rights and privileges: *All persons are equal under the law.* **3.** Having the necessary strength, ability, or determination: *I tried to run one more lap, but I wasn't equal to it.*
◊ *noun* Someone or something that is equal to another: *I'm much younger, but they treat me as an equal.*
◊ *verb* **1.** To be the same as: *Two pints equal one quart.* **2.** To do something equal to: *They equaled the world's record in the mile run.*
e·qual (ē′kwəl) ◊ *adjective* ◊ *noun, plural* **equals** ◊ *verb* **equaled, equaling**

equality *noun* The condition of being equal.
e·qual·i·ty (ĭ **kwŏl′**ĭ tē) ◊ *noun*

equation *noun* A mathematical statement that two quantities are equal. For example, $3 \times 2 = 6$ is an equation.
e·qua·tion (ĭ **kwā′**zhən) ◊ *noun, plural* **equations**

equator *noun* An imaginary line around the middle of the earth at an equal distance from the North and South Poles. The equator divides the earth into the Northern Hemisphere and the Southern Hemisphere.
e·qua·tor (ĭ **kwā′**tər) ◊ *noun, plural* **equators**

equatorial *adjective* **1.** Of or near the equator. **2.** Typical of the equator or the regions near it.
e·qua·to·ri·al (ē′kwə **tôr′**ē əl *or* ĕk′wə **tôr′**ē-əl) ◊ *adjective*

equilibrium *noun* Balance between opposite forces: *When the weights on each side of a scale are equal, the scale is in equilibrium.*
e·qui·lib·ri·um (ē′kwə **lĭb′**rē əm) ◊ *noun*

equinox *noun* Either of the two times of the year at which the sun is exactly above the equator and day and night are equal in length everywhere on earth. The equinoxes take place at about March 21 and September 23.
e·qui·nox (ē′kwə nŏks′ *or* **ĕk′**wə nŏks′) ◊ *noun, plural* **equinoxes**

equip *verb* To supply with things that are needed or wanted; provide: *We equipped ourselves with packs for the hike.*
e·quip (ĭ **kwĭp′**) ◊ *verb* **equipped, equipping**

equipment *noun* The things that are needed for a purpose: *The store sells tents and other camping equipment.*
e·quip·ment (ĭ **kwĭp′**mənt) ◊ *noun*

▲ **equipment**
Camping equipment

equivalent *adjective* Equal: *A meter is equivalent to 39.37 inches.*
◊ *noun* Something that is equal: *A dime is the equivalent of two nickels.*
e·quiv·a·lent (ĭ **kwĭv′**ə lənt) ◊ *adjective* ◊ *noun, plural* **equivalents**

-er¹ The suffix *-er* forms the comparative of adjectives and adverbs and means "more." *Drier* weather is more dry than other weather. *Hotter* water is more hot than other water. A *rarer* coin is more rare than other coins. A car that drives *slower* drives more slowly than other cars.

-er² The suffix *-er* forms nouns meaning "one that does a certain action." A *baker* is a person who bakes. A *flier* is someone or something that flies. A *runner* is someone or something that runs. The suffix *-er* also forms nouns meaning "a person who was born in or lives in a place." An *islander* is a person who lives on an island. The suffix *-er* also forms nouns meaning "one who is." A *foreigner* is one who is *foreign.*

VOCABULARY BUILDER • -er²

Many words that are formed with **-er** are not entries in this dictionary. But you can figure out what these words mean by looking up the meanings of the root words and the suffix. For example:
bidder = a person who makes a bid
designer = a person who thinks up designs
Easterner = a person who was born in or lives in the eastern part of the United States
planner = a person who makes plans
six-footer = a person who is six feet tall

era *noun* A period of history, often starting or ending with an important event: *The Declaration of Independence was the end of the Colonial era in America.*
e·ra (îr′ə) ◊ *noun, plural* **eras**

erase *verb* **1.** To remove by rubbing or wiping: *I erased the misspelled word and wrote it correctly.* **2.** To remove writing or a recording from: *Don't erase the tape yet.*
e·rase (ĭ rās′) ◊ *verb* **erased, erasing**

HISTORY • erase

Erase comes from a Latin word that meant "to scratch out." The ancient Romans sometimes wrote on wax tablets. They erased something by scratching it out of the wax.

eraser *noun* A piece of rubber, a felt pad, or some other object used to rub out marks.
e·ras·er (ĭ rā′sər) ◊ *noun, plural* **erasers**

ă	pat	ĭ	pit	oi	**oil**	th	**bath**
ā	pay	ī	ride	ŏŏ	book	*th*	**bathe**
â	care	î	fierce	ōō	boot	ə	ago, item
ä	father	ŏ	pot	ou	**out**		pencil
ĕ	pet	ō	go	ŭ	cut		atom
ē	be	ô	paw, for	û	fur		circus

erect *adjective* Standing upright; vertical: *The dancer had a proud, erect posture.*
◊ *verb* **1.** To build; construct: *Workers are erecting a new skyscraper downtown.* **2.** To raise upright; set on end: *It took six campers to erect the heavy tent.*
e·rect (ĭ rĕkt′) ◊ *adjective* ◊ *verb* **erected, erecting**

ermine *noun* A kind of weasel that has brownish fur for most of the year and valuable white fur in the winter.
er·mine (ûr′mĭn) ◊ *noun, plural* **ermine** *or* **ermines**

erode *verb* To wear away or become worn away bit by bit: *Flowing water eroded the bare hillside.*
e·rode (ĭ rōd′) ◊ *verb* **eroded, eroding**

erosion *noun* The process of being worn away bit by bit, as by water or wind.
e·ro·sion (ĭ rō′zhən) ◊ *noun*

▲ **erosion**

errand *noun* **1.** A short trip taken to perform a task. **2.** The purpose of such a trip: *My errand was to mail a letter.*
er·rand (ĕr′ənd) ◊ *noun, plural* **errands**

erratic *adjective* Not following a steady or usual course; irregular: *Our rowboat's course was erratic after we lost the oars.*
er·rat·ic (ĭ răt′ĭk) ◊ *adjective*

error *noun* Something that is incorrect or wrong: *There's an error in your addition.*
er·ror (ĕr′ər) ◊ *noun, plural* **errors**

> **SYNONYMS**
>
> ***error, blunder, mistake***
>
> It was an *error* in judgment when you spent your entire allowance on video games. I made that *blunder* because I just didn't know what I was doing. You made only two *mistakes* on your spelling test.

erupt *verb* To burst out violently: *Lava and ash erupted from the volcano.*
e·rupt (ĭ rŭpt′) ◊ *verb* **erupted, erupting**

escalator *noun* A moving staircase that carries people between floors of a building.
es·ca·la·tor (ĕs′kə lā′tər) ◊ *noun, plural* **escalators**

escape *verb* **1.** To get free: *The prisoners escaped by climbing the wall.* **2.** To succeed in avoiding: *I fell off the ladder but managed to escape injury.*
◊ *noun* **1.** The act of getting free or avoiding something bad. **2.** A way of getting one's mind off worries or cares.
es·cape (ĭ skāp′) ◊ *verb* **escaped, escaping** ◊ *noun, plural* **escapes**

escort *noun* **1.** One or more persons going along with another to give protection or show respect: *The visiting foreign leader was given a police escort.* **2.** One or more ships or planes traveling with another to give protection. **3.** A man who goes with a woman to a party or other social event.
◊ *verb* To go with as an escort: *Police escorted the senator during the parade.*
es·cort ◊ *noun* (ĕs′kôrt′), *plural* **escorts** ◊ *verb* (ĭ skôrt′) **escorted, escorting**

Eskimo *noun* **1.** A member of a people who were born in or live in the Arctic regions of North America and Asia. **2.** The language of the Eskimos.
◊ *adjective* Of or relating to the Eskimos or their language.
Es·ki·mo (ĕs′kə mō′) ◊ *noun, plural* **Eskimos** *or* **Eskimo** ◊ *adjective*

esophagus *noun* The tube that connects the throat with the stomach.
e·soph·a·gus (ĭ sŏf′ə gəs) ◊ *noun*

especially *adverb* **1.** In a special way; specifically: *These coats are designed especially for tall people.* **2.** More than usually; very.
es·pe·cial·ly (ĭ spĕsh′ə lē) ◊ *adverb*

espionage *noun* The use of spies by a government to get secret information about another country.
es·pi·o·nage (ĕs′pē ə näzh′) ◊ *noun*

essay *noun* A short piece of writing that gives the author's opinions on a certain subject; composition.
es·say (ĕs′ā′) ◊ *noun, plural* **essays**

essence *noun* The basic quality of a thing that makes it what it is: *The essence of democracy is faith in the people.*
es·sence (ĕs′əns) ◊ *noun, plural* **essences**

essential *adjective* **1.** Very important; vital: *It is essential that you pay attention.* **2.** Being an absolutely necessary part of something; basic: *Eating regularly is essential to good health.*
◊ *noun* A basic thing that cannot be done without: *Bring a small bag with your toothbrush and other essentials.*
es·sen·tial (ĭ sĕn′shəl) ◊ *adjective* ◊ *noun, plural* **essentials**

-est The suffix *-est* forms the superlative of adjectives and adverbs and means "most." The *happiest* person in a group is the person who is the most happy. The *hoarsest* person with a cold is the person who is most hoarse. The *thinnest* person in a room is the person who is the most thin. The runner who runs *fastest* is the runner who runs faster than anyone else.

establish *verb* **1.** To begin or set up; found; create: *My grandparents established the lumber company in 1920.* **2.** To show to be true: *I established my identity by showing my passport.* —See Synonyms at **prove.**
es·tab·lish (ĭ stăb′lĭsh) ◊ *verb* **established, establishing**

establishment *noun* **1.** The act of establishing or condition of being established: *They used their savings for the establishment of the business.* **2.** A business, club, or home, including its members or residents.
es·tab·lish·ment (ĭ **stăb′**lĭsh mənt) ◊ *noun, plural* **establishments**

estate *noun* **1.** A large piece of land in the country, usually with a large house. **2.** Everything that a person owns, especially the property left by someone who has died.
es·tate (ĭ **stāt′**) ◊ *noun, plural* **estates**

esteem *verb* To think highly of; respect: *I esteem them for their honesty.*
◊ *noun* Great respect; honor.
es·teem (ĭ **stēm′**) ◊ *verb* **esteemed, esteeming** ◊ *noun*

estimate *verb* To guess about; calculate roughly: *Can you estimate my weight?*
◊ *noun* A rough calculation; guess.
es·ti·mate ◊ *verb* (**ĕs′**tə māt′) **estimated, estimating** ◊ *noun* (**ĕs′**tə mĭt), *plural* **estimates**

estimation *noun* **1.** A general opinion; judgment: *They are fine people in my estimation.* **2.** High regard; esteem.
es·ti·ma·tion (ĕs′tə **mā′**shən) ◊ *noun, plural* **estimations**

estuary *noun* The wide lower part of a river where its current is met by the tides of the ocean.
es·tu·ar·y (**ĕs′**cho͞o ĕr′ē) ◊ *noun, plural* **estuaries**

etc. The abbreviation for the Latin words *et cetera,* which mean "and the other things of the same type."

etch *verb* To make a drawing or design by cutting lines with acid on a metal or glass plate. The lines are then filled with ink and paper is pressed against the plate.
etch (ĕch) ◊ *verb* **etched, etching**

etching *noun* A design or picture printed from an etched plate.
etch·ing (**ĕch′**ĭng) ◊ *noun, plural* **etchings**

▲ **etching**

eternal *adjective* **1.** Having no beginning and no end; lasting forever: *The movement of the tides is eternal.* **2.** Going on and on; seeming never to stop: *Stop that eternal giggling.*
e·ter·nal (ĭ **tûr′**nəl) ◊ *adjective*

eternity *noun* **1.** All of time without beginning or end. **2.** A very long time: *The pyramids were built to last for an eternity.*
e·ter·ni·ty (ĭ **tûr′**nĭ tē) ◊ *noun, plural* **eternities**

ether *noun* A liquid that evaporates easily and is used in medicine to make people unconscious for surgical operations.
e·ther (**ē′**thər) ◊ *noun, plural* **ethers**

ethnic *adjective* Of or being a group of people within a larger society who continue to have their own national origin, language, or way of life: *Italians, Chinese, and Puerto Ricans are among the ethnic groups living in New York.*
eth·nic (**ĕth′**nĭk) ◊ *adjective*

etiquette *noun* Rules that tell people how to behave in various social situations: *According to etiquette, you should stand up when a guest comes into the room.*
et·i·quette (**ĕt′**ĭ kĭt) ◊ *noun*

etymology *noun* The history of a word, including where it or its parts came from and how it got its present form and meaning.
et·y·mol·o·gy (ĕt′ə **mŏl′**ə jē) ◊ *noun, plural* **etymologies**

eucalyptus *noun* A tall tree that grows in warm regions. Its leaves yield a strong-smelling oil used in medicine, and its wood is used for building.
eu·ca·lyp·tus (yo͞o′kə **lĭp′**təs) ◊ *noun, plural* **eucalyptuses**

ă	pat	ĭ	pit	oi	**oi**l	th	ba**th**
ā	pay	ī	ride	o͝o	b**oo**k	*th*	ba**the**
â	care	î	fierce	o͞o	b**oo**t	ə	ago, item
ä	father	ŏ	pot	ou	**ou**t		pencil
ĕ	pet	ō	go	ŭ	cut		atom
ē	be	ô	paw, for	û	fur		circus

▲ eucalyptus

European *noun* A person who was born in or lives in Europe. Germans, Italians, and Spaniards are Europeans.
◊ *adjective* Of or relating to Europe or the Europeans.
Eu·ro·pe·an (yo͝or′ə **pē′**ən) ◊ *noun, plural* **Europeans** ◊ *adjective*

evacuate *verb* **1.** To leave or send away from a dangerous place: *The residents quickly evacuated the burning building.* **2.** To remove the contents of.
e·vac·u·ate (ĭ **văk′**yo͞o āt′) ◊ *verb* **evacuated, evacuating**

evade *verb* To escape or avoid, especially by clever planning: *The politician evaded the question by giving a vague answer.*
e·vade (ĭ **vād′**) ◊ *verb* **evaded, evading**

evaluate *verb* To find out, judge, or estimate the value of: *The teacher evaluates your work at the end of each term.*
e·val·u·ate (ĭ **văl′**yo͞o āt′) ◊ *verb* **evaluated, evaluating**

evaporate *verb* **1.** To change into a vapor or gas: *Alcohol evaporates quickly.* **2.** To disappear; vanish: *My confidence evaporated as my turn came to sing.*
e·vap·o·rate (ĭ **văp′**ə rāt′) ◊ *verb* **evaporated, evaporating**

eve *noun* The evening or day before a special day: *We were excited on the eve of the big game.*
eve (ēv) ◊ *noun, plural* **eves**

even *adjective* **1.** Equal in size or amount: *Cut the cake in even pieces.* **2.** Having the same score; tied: *The teams were even after the first half.* **3.** Equally matched; fair: *The wrestlers are about the same size, so it should be an even contest.* **4.** At the same height; level: *The ledge is even with the bottom of the first-floor windows.* **5.** Without bumps, gaps, or rough parts; smooth: *We sanded the floor to make it even.* **6.** Not changing suddenly; steady: *On the highway we drove at an even rate of speed.* **7.** Capable of being divided by 2 without having anything left over: *We know that 6, 18, and 100 are even numbers.*
◊ *adverb* **1.** To a greater degree: *Texas is a large state, and Alaska is even larger.* **2.** At the same time as: *Even as we watched, the building collapsed.* **3.** In spite of: *Even with a head start, I knew I could not win the race.* **4.** Though it seems unlikely: *Even I could see through that trick.*
◊ *verb* To make or become even: *Even the ground with a rake.*
e·ven (**ē′**vən) ◊ *adjective* ◊ *adverb* ◊ *verb* **evened, evening**

evening *noun* The time between sunset and the time to go to bed; early night.
eve·ning (**ēv′**nĭng) ◊ *noun, plural* **evenings**

event *noun* **1.** Something that happens; occurrence: *The town newspaper reports events such as accidents, marriages, and births.* **2.** A single contest in a program of sports: *The runners got ready for the next event, the 100-yard dash.*
◊ *idiom* **in the event of** If something should happen: *In the event of the President's death, the Vice President becomes President.*
e·vent (ĭ **vĕnt′**) ◊ *noun, plural* **events**

eventide *noun* Evening.
e·ven·tide (**ē′**vən tīd′) ◊ *noun*

eventual *adjective* Happening in the end: *We never lost hope of eventual victory.*
e·ven·tu·al (ĭ **vĕn′**cho͞o əl) ◊ *adjective*

ever *adverb* **1.** At all times; always: *I am ever ready to help you.* **2.** At any time: *Have you ever caught a fish?* **3.** In any way: *How could I ever forget that day?*
ev·er (**ĕv′** ər) ◊ *adverb*

evergreen *adjective* Having leaves or needles that stay green all year: *Pines, firs, and hollies are evergreen trees.*

◊ *noun* An evergreen tree, shrub, or plant.
ev·er·green (ĕv′ər grēn′) ◊ *adjective* ◊ *noun, plural* **evergreens**

▲ **evergreen**

everlasting *adjective* Lasting forever; eternal: *We are thankful for the everlasting beauty of nature.*
ev·er·last·ing (ĕv′ər **lăs′** tĭng) ◊ *adjective*

every *adjective* Each one of a group with no exceptions: *There is a desk for every student in the class.*
eve·ry (**ĕv′** rē) ◊ *adjective*

everybody *pronoun* Every person; everyone: *Everybody makes a mistake sometimes.*
eve·ry·bod·y (**ĕv′** rē bŏd′ē) ◊ *pronoun*

everyday *adjective* Ordinary; usual: *Everyday problems, like getting up on time, were hard for them.*
eve·ry·day (**ĕv′** rē dā′) ◊ *adjective*

everyone *pronoun* Every person; everybody: *When everyone sits down, the class will begin.*
eve·ry·one (**ĕv′** rē wŭn′) ◊ *pronoun*

everything *pronoun* **1.** All things: *Everything in the store is for sale.* **2.** The most important fact or thing: *Their children are everything to them.*
eve·ry·thing (**ĕv′** rē thĭng′) ◊ *pronoun*

everywhere *adverb* In every place; in all places: *I looked everywhere for my lost keys.*
eve·ry·where (**ĕv′** rē hwâr′) ◊ *adverb*

ă	pat	ĭ	pit	oi	**oi**l	th	ba**th**
ā	pay	ī	ride	o͝o	book	*th*	ba**th**e
â	care	î	fierce	o͞o	boot	ə	ago, item
ä	father	ŏ	pot	ou	**ou**t		pencil
ĕ	pet	ō	go	ŭ	cut		atom
ē	be	ô	paw, for	û	fur		circus

evidence *noun* Facts or signs that help one find out the truth or come to a conclusion; indication: *The broken window was evidence that a burglary had taken place.*
◊ *idiom* **in evidence** Easily seen or noticed; obvious.
ev·i·dence (**ĕv′** ĭ dəns) ◊ *noun*

evident *adjective* Easy to see or notice; obvious: *From the dark clouds it was evident that it would soon rain.*
ev·i·dent (**ĕv′** ĭ dənt) ◊ *adjective*

evil *adjective* **1.** Bad, wrong, or wicked. **2.** Causing harm; harmful.
◊ *noun* **1.** The condition or fact of being bad or wicked; sin. **2.** Something that causes harm: *Poverty is a great evil in our society.*
e·vil (**ē′** vəl) ◊ *adjective* **eviler, evilest** ◊ *noun, plural* **evils**

evolution *noun* Slow, gradual change or development: *We studied the evolution of flowers from seeds and buds.*
ev·o·lu·tion (ĕv′ə **lo͞o′** shən) ◊ *noun, plural* **evolutions**

evolve *verb* **1.** To arrive at gradually; develop: *We evolved a plan for doing household chores that satisfied the whole family.* **2.** To develop gradually from something else: *Scientists think that birds probably evolved from reptiles.*
e·volve (ĭ **vŏlv′**) ◊ *verb* **evolved, evolving**

ewe *noun* A female sheep.
ewe (yo͞o) ◊ *noun, plural* **ewes**
‖*These sound alike:* **ewe, yew, you**

ex– The prefix *ex–* means "former." A person who was formerly a president is an *ex-president.*

***VOCABULARY BUILDER* • ex–**

Many words that are formed with **ex–** are not entries in this dictionary. But you can figure out what these words mean by looking up the meanings of the root words and the prefix. A hyphen is always used between *ex–* and the root word. For example:
ex-actor = a person who was formerly an actor
ex-student = a person who was formerly a student

E

exact *adjective* Accurate in every detail: *It cost me about five dollars—the exact amount was $5.03.*
ex·act (ĭg **zăkt′**) ◊ *adjective*

exactly *adverb* **1.** Without any change or mistake; accurately: *Be sure that you follow the recipe exactly.* **2.** In every respect; quite: *You may do exactly as you please.*
ex·act·ly (ĭg **zăkt′** lē) ◊ *adverb*

exaggerate *verb* To describe something as being larger than it really is: *When I said the fish was two feet long, I was exaggerating.*
ex·ag·ger·ate (ĭg **zăj′** ə rāt′) ◊ *verb* **exaggerated, exaggerating**

examination *noun* **1.** The act of looking at carefully; inspection: *A close examination of the jewel showed that it was a fake.* **2.** A set of questions designed to test knowledge or skills.
ex·am·i·na·tion (ĭg zăm′ə **nā′**shən) ◊ *noun, plural* **examinations**

examine *verb* **1.** To look at carefully: *Examine the plant cells under a microscope.* **2.** To question in order to get information or test knowledge: *The lawyer examined the witness.* —See Synonyms at **ask.**
ex·am·ine (ĭg **zăm′**ĭn) ◊ *verb* **examined, examining**

example *noun* **1.** Something that is picked out or studied because it is like other things of the same kind: *Water is one example of liquid substances.* **2.** Someone or something that should be copied; model: *Their courage was an example to all of us.* **3.** A problem or question with its answer, given to show how to do similar problems or answer similar questions.
ex·am·ple (ĭg **zăm′**pəl) ◊ *noun, plural* **examples**

SYNONYMS

example, case[1], instance

That is an *example* of bad handwriting. There has not been a single *case* of tardiness in school this year. What I say is true even if I can't think of an *instance* to back it up.

exasperate *verb* To irritate or make angry.
ex·as·per·ate (ĭg **zăs′**pə rāt′) ◊ *verb* **exasperated, exasperating**

excavate *verb* **1.** To dig or dig out: *The workers excavated a hole for the swimming pool.* **2.** To uncover by digging and expose to view: *They excavated the ruins of an ancient Roman city.*
ex·ca·vate (**ĕks′**kə vāt′) ◊ *verb* **excavated, excavating**

▲ **excavate**

excavation *noun* **1.** The act or process of excavating. **2.** A hole formed by excavating.
ex·ca·va·tion (ĕks′kə **vā′**shən) ◊ *noun, plural* **excavations**

exceed *verb* **1.** To be greater than: *A mountain exceeds a hill in size.* **2.** To go beyond: *Be careful not to exceed the speed limit.*
ex·ceed (ĭk **sēd′**) ◊ *verb* **exceeded, exceeding**

exceedingly *adverb* To an unusual degree: *The center of the sun is exceedingly hot.*
ex·ceed·ing·ly (ĭk **sē′**dĭng lē) ◊ *adverb*

excel *verb* To be better than others: *You excel in English and arithmetic.*
ex·cel (ĭk **sĕl′**) ◊ *verb* **excelled, excelling**

excellence *noun* The condition or quality of being excellent; superiority.
ex·cel·lence (**ĕk′**sə ləns) ◊ *noun*

excellent *adjective* Of the highest quality.
ex·cel·lent (**ĕk′**sə lənt) ◊ *adjective*

except *preposition* Not including; but: *They invited everyone except me.*
◊ *conjunction* If it were not for the fact that: *I could leave early, except I don't want to.*
ex·cept (ĭk **sĕpt′**) ◊ *preposition* ◊ *conjunction*

exception *noun* **1.** The condition of being left out; omission: *Everyone is here without exception.* **2.** Something or someone that is different from most others: *We always went to the mountains on vacation, but that summer was an exception.*
ex·cep·tion (ĭk **sĕp′**shən) ◊ *noun, plural* **exceptions**

exceptional *adjective* **1.** Not ordinary or average; unusual: *There has been an exceptional amount of snow this winter.* **2.** Well above average in quality or ability; superior: *They are exceptional students.*
ex·cep·tion·al (ĭk **sĕp′**shə nəl) ◊ *adjective*

excess *noun* **1.** An amount greater than is needed or usual: *There was an excess of food at the picnic.* **2.** An amount by which something is greater than another; surplus: *We were left with an excess of two gallons over what the container would hold.*
◊ *adjective* More than is needed or usual.
ex·cess (ĭk **sĕs′** *or* **ĕk′**sĕs) ◊ *noun, plural* **excesses** ◊ *adjective*

excessive *adjective* Greater than is normal, proper, or necessary: *You have taken an excessive amount of time for this job.*
ex·ces·sive (ĭk **sĕs′**ĭv) ◊ *adjective*

exchange *verb* **1.** To give one thing for another; trade: *The traders exchanged cheap trinkets for valuable furs.* **2.** To replace something returned with something else: *The store will exchange the gift for you.*
◊ *noun* **1.** A giving of one thing for another: *Your skates for my bike is not a fair exchange.* **2.** Replacement of something returned: *This store will allow exchanges but not refunds.* **3.** A place where things, as stocks or bonds, are bought or sold.
ex·change (ĭks **chānj′**) ◊ *verb* **exchanged, exchanging** ◊ *noun, plural* **exchanges**

excite *verb* **1.** To stir up; arouse: *News of the party excited the children.* **2.** To make more active; stimulate: *Do not excite the bees.*
ex·cite (ĭk **sīt′**) ◊ *verb* **excited, exciting**

ă	pat	ĭ	pit	oi	oil	th	bath
ā	pay	ī	ride	o͝o	book	*th*	bathe
â	care	î	fierce	o͞o	boot	ə	ago, item
ä	father	ŏ	pot	ou	out		pencil
ĕ	pet	ō	go	ŭ	cut		atom
ē	be	ô	paw, for	û	fur		circus

excitement *noun* **1.** The condition of being excited: *As the game continued, the excitement increased.* **2.** Something that excites: *I looked forward to the excitement of my first airplane ride.*
ex·cite·ment (ĭk **sīt′**mənt) ◊ *noun, plural* **excitements**

exciting *adjective* Causing great excitement; rousing: *We took an exciting trip down the river on a raft.*
ex·cit·ing (ĭk **sī′**tĭng) ◊ *adjective*

exclaim *verb* To cry out or speak suddenly, as from surprise or strong feeling: *"Look who's here!" I exclaimed.*
ex·claim (ĭk **sklām′**) ◊ *verb* **exclaimed, exclaiming**

exclamation *noun* **1.** A sudden, strong outcry: *There were many exclamations of pleasure at the gifts.* **2.** Something said suddenly and strongly, as in surprise.
ex·cla·ma·tion (ĕk′sklə **mā′**shən) ◊ *noun, plural* **exclamations**

exclamation mark *noun* An exclamation point.
exclamation mark ◊ *noun, plural* **exclamation marks**

exclamation point *noun* A punctuation mark (!) used after an exclamation.
exclamation point ◊ *noun, plural* **exclamation points**

exclamatory sentence *noun* A sentence that shows excitement or strong feeling and ends with an exclamation point.
ex·clam·a·to·ry sentence (ĭk **sklăm′**ə tôr′ē) ◊ *noun, plural* **exclamatory sentences**

exclude *verb* **1.** To keep out or shut out; bar: *Dogs are excluded from this store.* **2.** To leave out; omit.
ex·clude (ĭk **sklo͞od′**) ◊ *verb* **excluded, excluding**

exclusive *adjective* **1.** Not shared with others; sole: *The company has exclusive rights to publish this book.* **2.** Total; complete: *Give the speaker your exclusive attention.* **3.** Admitting only certain people or groups and keeping out others: *They belong to an exclusive private club.*
ex·clu·sive (ĭk **sklo͞o′**sĭv) ◊ *adjective*

excursion *noun* A short pleasure trip.
ex·cur·sion (ĭk **skûr′**zhən) ◊ *noun, plural* **excursions**

excuse *verb* **1.** To forgive: *Please excuse me for what I said yesterday.* —See Synonyms at **pardon. 2.** To serve as a reason or apology for; justify: *Nothing excuses such rudeness.* **3.** To release from a duty or promise: *All students in the sixth grade will be excused from study hall this afternoon.*
◊ *noun* **1.** Something given as a reason for excusing: *You must bring a written excuse for your absence from school.* **2.** Something that excuses or justifies: *There is no excuse for such rude behavior.*
ex·cuse ◊ *verb* (ĭk **skyo͞oz′**) **excused, excusing** ◊ *noun* (ĭk **skyo͞os′**), *plural* **excuses**

execute *verb* **1.** To perform; do: *We executed a difficult dance step.* **2.** To put into effect; carry out: *Town governments execute local laws.* **3.** To put to death as a legal penalty.
ex·e·cute (**ĕk′** sĭ kyo͞ot′) ◊ *verb* **executed, executing**

execution *noun* **1.** The act of performing or doing: *The execution of our plan requires teamwork.* **2.** A putting to death according to law.
ex·e·cu·tion (ĕk′sĭ **kyo͞o′**shən) ◊ *noun, plural* **executions**

executive *noun* **1.** A person who helps manage and make decisions for a company or organization. **2.** The branch of government concerned with putting the country's laws into effect.
◊ *adjective* **1.** Having to do with management and the making of decisions: *The company is run by an executive board.* **2.** Of or pertaining to the branch of government concerned with putting laws into effect.
ex·ec·u·tive (ĭg **zĕk′** yə tĭv) ◊ *noun, plural* **executives** ◊ *adjective*

exempt *verb* To free from a duty or rule that applies to others; excuse: *Good students are exempted from attending study hall.*
◊ *adjective* Freed from a duty or rule that applies to others; excused.
ex·empt (ĭg **zĕmpt′**) ◊ *verb* **exempted, exempting** ◊ *adjective*

exercise *noun* **1.** The act of using or putting into practice: *The government must be careful in its exercise of power.* **2.** Physical activity for the good of the body: *We try to get some exercise every day.* **3.** A lesson or problem designed to improve understanding or skill: *Do the vocabulary exercise at the end of the chapter.* **4. exercises** A ceremony: *Graduation exercises are usually held in June.*
◊ *verb* **1.** To put into use or practice: *Exercise your right to vote.* **2.** To do physical activity for the good of the body: *You should exercise every day.*
ex·er·cise (**ĕk′** sər sīz′) ◊ *noun, plural* **exercises** ◊ *verb* **exercised, exercising**

▲ **exercise**

exert *verb* To put into use; apply: *I exerted all my strength to move the stone.*
ex·ert (ĭg **zûrt′**) ◊ *verb* **exerted, exerting**

exhale *verb* **1.** To breathe out. **2.** To give off as if by breathing out: *Cars exhale fumes.*
ex·hale (ĕks **hāl′**) ◊ *verb* **exhaled, exhaling**

exhaust *verb* **1.** To use up: *The diver exhausted the air supply.* **2.** To wear out completely; tire: *The long swim exhausted me.*
◊ *noun* **1.** The waste gases that escape from an engine. **2.** A device or system that pumps such gases out or allows them to escape.
ex·haust (ĭg **zôst′**) ◊ *verb* **exhausted, exhausting** ◊ *noun, plural* **exhausts**

exhaustion *noun* **1.** The act of using up a supply. **2.** Very great fatigue: *My exhaustion lasted for hours after the race.*
ex·haus·tion (ĭg **zôs′**chən) ◊ *noun*

exhibit *verb* **1.** To show or demonstrate: *She exhibits a talent for teaching.* **2.** To present for the public to view; display: *He exhibits his paintings at a gallery.* —See Synonyms at **show.**

◊ *noun* Something put on display, as at a museum or gallery.
ex·hib·it (ĭg **zĭb′**ĭt) ◊ *verb* **exhibited, exhibiting** ◊ *noun, plural* **exhibits**

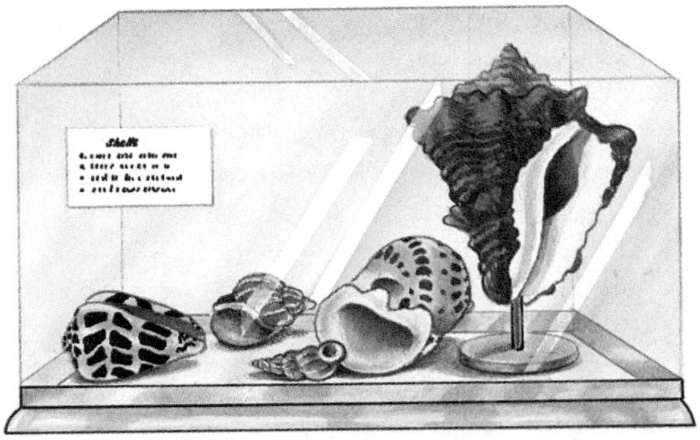

▲ **exhibit**

exhibition *noun* **1.** The act of displaying: *The athlete's exhibition of strength was amazing.* **2.** A display for the public.
ex·hi·bi·tion (ĕk′sə **bĭsh′**ən) ◊ *noun, plural* **exhibitions**

exhilarate *verb* To make cheerful, lively, or full of energy: *We were exhilarated by our brisk walk in the snow.*
ex·hil·a·rate (ĭg **zĭl′**ə rāt′) ◊ *verb* **exhilarated, exhilarating**

exile *noun* **1.** A forced removal from one's own country. **2.** A person who has been forced to leave his or her country.
◊ *verb* To send into exile.
ex·ile (**ĕg′**zīl′ *or* **ĕk′**sīl′) ◊ *noun, plural* **exiles** ◊ *verb* **exiled, exiling**

exist *verb* **1.** To be real: *Ghosts do not exist.* **2.** To have life; live: *Most living beings cannot exist for long without food and water.* **3.** To be found; occur: *Some form of life may exist on other planets.*
ex·ist (ĭg **zĭst′**) ◊ *verb* **existed, existing**

existence *noun* **1.** The fact or condition of being: *Very few horse-drawn carriages are still in existence.* **2.** A way of living: *The explorers led a dangerous existence.* **3.** Occurrence; presence: *Do you believe in the existence of life on other planets?*
ex·is·tence (ĭg **zĭs′**təns) ◊ *noun, plural* **existences**

ă	pat	ĭ	pit	oi	**oi**l	th	ba**th**
ā	pay	ī	ride	ŏŏ	b**oo**k	*th*	ba**th**e
â	care	î	fierce	ōō	b**oo**t	ə	ago, item
ä	father	ŏ	pot	ou	**ou**t		pencil
ĕ	pet	ō	go	ŭ	c**u**t		atom
ē	be	ô	paw, for	û	f**u**r		circus

exit *noun* **1.** A way out. **2.** The act of going away or out: *We made a hasty exit from the room when the bell rang.*
◊ *verb* To go out; leave.
ex·it (**ĕg′**zĭt *or* **ĕk′**sĭt) ◊ *noun, plural* **exits** ◊ *verb* **exited, exiting**

exotic *adjective* From another part of the world; foreign: *We saw pictures of exotic birds from the jungles of Brazil.*
ex·ot·ic (ĭg **zŏt′**ĭk) ◊ *adjective*

▲ **exotic**
An exotic bird

expand *verb* To make or become larger in size, volume, or amount: *Gases expand when heated.* —See Synonyms at **spread.**
ex·pand (ĭk **spănd′**) ◊ *verb* **expanded, expanding**

expanse *noun* A wide and open area, as of land, sea, or sky: *The Sahara is a vast expanse of desert.*
ex·panse (ĭk **spăns′**) ◊ *noun, plural* **expanses**

expansion *noun* **1.** The act of expanding or condition of being expanded; growth: *There are plans for expansion of the school to make room for more students.* **2.** An expanded or expanding part: *The suburbs are an expansion of cities.*
ex·pan·sion (ĭk **spăn′**shən) ◊ *noun, plural* **expansions**

expect *verb* **1.** To look for as likely to happen or appear: *The farmers expect an early frost*

this year. **2.** To look for as proper or appropriate: *I expect an apology.* **3.** To suppose or think: *I expect you're right.*
ex·pect (ĭk **spĕkt′**) ◊ *verb* **expected, expecting**

expectation *noun* **1.** The act of expecting; anticipation: *The dog wagged its tail in expectation of a bone.* **2. expectations** Hopes or prospects: *The reward fell short of our expectations.*
ex·pec·ta·tion (ĕk′spĕk **tā′**shən) ◊ *noun, plural* **expectations**

expedition *noun* **1.** A journey made for a definite purpose: *The explorer was sent on an expedition to discover new lands.* —See Synonyms at **trip. 2.** The group making such a journey: *The expedition returned a year later.*
ex·pe·di·tion (ĕk′spĭ **dĭsh′**ən) ◊ *noun, plural* **expeditions**

expel *verb* **1.** To force out: *When exhaling, we expel air from the lungs.* **2.** To put out; dismiss.
ex·pel (ĭk **spĕl′**) ◊ *verb* **expelled, expelling**

expenditure *noun* **1.** The act of spending: *Training a dog requires the expenditure of time and effort.* **2.** Something that is spent: *My expenditures this week amount to $3.52.*
ex·pen·di·ture (ĭk **spĕn′**dĭ chər) ◊ *noun, plural* **expenditures**

expense *noun* **1.** Something paid out; cost: *We cannot afford the expense of a long vacation.* —See Synonyms at **price. 2.** Something requiring the spending of money: *Sending children to college can be a heavy expense.*
ex·pense (ĭk **spĕns′**) ◊ *noun, plural* **expenses**

expensive *adjective* Having a high price: *I can't afford that expensive toy.*
ex·pen·sive (ĭk **spĕn′**sĭv) ◊ *adjective*

SYNONYMS

expensive, costly

I can't buy *expensive* Christmas presents this year. Those are very *costly* jewels. **Antonym:** *cheap*

experience *noun* **1.** Something that one has taken part in or lived through: *The experience of being in an earthquake is never forgotten.* **2.** Knowledge or skill gotten through practice: *You will need education and experience to get a good job.*
◊ *verb* To have something happen to oneself: *We experienced a great adventure when we rode rafts down the long river.*
ex·pe·ri·ence (ĭk **spîr′**ē əns) ◊ *noun, plural* **experiences** ◊ *verb* **experienced, experiencing**

experienced *adjective* Having gotten skill or knowledge through experience.
ex·pe·ri·enced (ĭk **spîr′**ē ənst) ◊ *adjective*

experiment *noun* A test used to find out or prove something.
◊ *verb* To conduct an experiment: *They were the first scientists to experiment with rockets.*
ex·per·i·ment (ĭk **spĕr′**ə mĕnt′) ◊ *noun, plural* **experiments** ◊ *verb* **experimented, experimenting**

experimental *adjective* Based on or tested by experiments: *There is no experimental evidence for that theory.*
ex·per·i·men·tal (ĭk spĕr′ə **mĕn′**tl) ◊ *adjective*

expert *noun* A person who has great knowledge or skill in a special area: *My teacher is an expert on American history.*
◊ *adjective* Having or displaying special knowledge or skill in a field.
ex·pert ◊ *noun* (**ĕk′**spûrt′), *plural* **experts** ◊ *adjective* (**ĕk′**spûrt′ *or* ĭk **spûrt′**)

expiration *noun* **1.** The act of coming to an end: *You must renew your library card before its date of expiration.* **2.** The act or process of breathing out.
ex·pi·ra·tion (ĕk′spə **rā′**shən) ◊ *noun, plural* **expirations**

expire *verb* **1.** To come to an end: *My club membership expires next month.* **2.** To die. **3.** To breathe out; exhale: *We expire used air from our lungs.*
ex·pire (ĭk **spīr′**) ◊ *verb* **expired, expiring**

explain *verb* **1.** To make clear or understandable; clarify: *The science teacher explained atoms to us.* **2.** To give reasons for; account for: *We were asked to explain our noisy behavior during class.*
ex·plain (ĭk **splān′**) ◊ *verb* **explained, explaining**

explanation *noun* **1.** The act or process of explaining: *The explanation of fractions was very helpful.* **2.** Something that explains.
ex·pla·na·tion (ĕk′splə **nā′**shən) ◊ *noun, plural* **explanations**

E

explicit *adjective* Clearly stated so that nothing is misunderstood: *The doctor gave me explicit instructions on when to take the medicine.*
ex·plic·it (ĭk **splĭs′**ĭt) ◊ *adjective*

explode *verb* **1.** To burst or cause to burst with a loud noise; blow up: *Suddenly the tank exploded.* **2.** To burst forth noisily: *We exploded with laughter during the show.*
ex·plode (ĭk **splōd′**) ◊ *verb* **exploded, exploding**

exploit *noun* A very brave or daring act: *This book tells about the exploits of King Arthur's knights.*
◊ *verb* **1.** To make full, practical use of: *The company plans to exploit its oil wells.* **2.** To make unfair use of for selfish reasons: *The ancient Egyptians exploited their slave laborers.*
ex·ploit ◊ *noun* (**ĕk′**sploit′), *plural* **exploits** ◊ *verb* (ĭk **sploit′**) **exploited, exploiting**

exploration *noun* The act of exploring: *Spain began the exploration of the New World.*
ex·plo·ra·tion (ĕk′splə **rā′**shən) ◊ *noun, plural* **explorations**

explore *verb* **1.** To go into or travel through an unknown or unfamiliar place for the purpose of discovery: *The Spanish explored the New World.* **2.** To look into or through closely; examine: *We must explore every possibility for peace.*
ex·plore (ĭk **splôr′**) ◊ *verb* **explored, exploring**

explorer *noun* A person who explores unknown or little-known places.
ex·plor·er (ĭk **splôr′**ər) ◊ *noun, plural* **explorers**

explosion *noun* **1.** The act of bursting apart suddenly with great force and noise. **2.** A sudden outburst: *We heard an explosion of loud laughter.*
ex·plo·sion (ĭk **splō′**zhən) ◊ *noun, plural* **explosions**

ă	pat	ĭ	pit	oi	oil	th	bath
ā	pay	ī	ride	ŏŏ	book	*th*	bathe
â	care	î	fierce	ōō	boot	ə	ago, item
ä	father	ŏ	pot	ou	out		pencil
ĕ	pet	ō	go	ŭ	cut		atom
ē	be	ô	paw, for	û	fur		circus

explosive *adjective* Capable of exploding or causing an explosion: *Gasoline fumes are highly explosive.*
◊ *noun* A substance that can explode: *Dynamite is a powerful explosive.*
ex·plo·sive (ĭk **splō′**sĭv) ◊ *adjective* ◊ *noun, plural* **explosives**

export *verb* To send to another country for trade or sale: *The United States exports wheat to many countries.*
◊ *noun* **1.** The act of exporting: *The Arab countries depend on the export of oil.* **2.** Something that is exported: *Automobiles are a major export of Japan.*
ex·port ◊ *verb* (ĭk **spôrt′**) **exported, exporting** ◊ *noun* (**ĕk′**spôrt′), *plural* **exports**

expose *verb* **1.** To leave or be without cover or protection: *We were all exposed to chicken pox when my cousin caught it.* **2.** To leave open to some action or influence: *We were exposed to good books at an early age.* **3.** To make known: *They exposed the plot to rob the bank.* **4.** To permit light to reach and act on a photographic film or plate.
ex·pose (ĭk **spōz′**) ◊ *verb* **exposed, exposing**

exposition *noun* A large public display; exhibition.
ex·po·si·tion (ĕk′spə **zĭsh′**ən) ◊ *noun, plural* **expositions**

exposure *noun* **1.** The act of exposing or the condition of being exposed: *The newspaper's exposure of their crimes led to their arrest.* **2.** Position in relation to the sun, wind, or points of the compass: *A room with a western exposure will get the afternoon sun.* **3.** The act of permitting light to reach and act on a photographic film or the length of time that the film is exposed to light.
ex·po·sure (ĭk **spō′**zhər) ◊ *noun, plural* **exposures**

express *verb* **1.** To make known; reveal: *This story expresses the writer's love of animals.* **2.** To put into words; state: *I must express my opinion to the teacher.*
◊ *adjective* **1.** Special; particular: *They painted the house for the express purpose of selling it.* **2.** Sent by or traveling on fast direct transportation: *The express package arrived in one day. We took an express bus home.*
◊ *noun* **1.** A train, bus, or elevator that travels

quickly to its destination with few or no stops. **2.** A system for the rapid delivery of goods and mail.
ex·press (ĭk sprĕs′) ◊ *verb* **expressed, expressing** ◊ *adjective* ◊ *noun, plural* **expresses**

expression *noun* **1.** The act of expressing: *We believe in the free expression of ideas.* **2.** A way of showing thoughts or feelings: *I sent them flowers as an expression of thanks.* **3.** A look that shows mood or feeling. **4.** A particular way of saying something: *"Sleep like a log" is a familiar expression.*
ex·pres·sion (ĭk sprĕsh′ən) ◊ *noun, plural* **expressions**

expressive *adjective* Expressing something or full of expression: *"Wonderful!" is expressive of great pleasure.*
ex·pres·sive (ĭk sprĕs′ĭv) ◊ *adjective*

expressly *adverb* **1.** Especially; particularly: *This ship was designed expressly for exploring the Arctic waters.* **2.** In a definite way; plainly: *The rules expressly forbid it.*
ex·press·ly (ĭk sprĕs′lē) ◊ *adverb*

expressway *noun* A wide highway built for high-speed travel.
ex·press·way (ĭk sprĕs′wā′) ◊ *noun, plural* **expressways**

▲ **expressway**

expulsion *noun* The act of forcing out or the condition of being forced out.
ex·pul·sion (ĭk spŭl′shən) ◊ *noun, plural* **expulsions**

exquisite *adjective* Highly pleasing because of its beauty or excellence: *The sunset was exquisite.*
ex·qui·site (ĕk′skwĭz ĭt) ◊ *adjective*

extend *verb* **1.** To make longer; lengthen: *We extended the table to seat more people.* —See Synonyms at **spread. 2.** To stretch out; reach: *Their land extends from the river to the mountains.* **3.** To make greater or larger; expand: *The empire sought to extend its boundaries.* **4.** To offer or grant: *We extended our congratulations to the winner.*
ex·tend (ĭk stĕnd′) ◊ *verb* **extended, extending**

extension *noun* **1.** The act of extending or condition of being extended: *We had hoped for the extension of the deadline to the end of the week.* **2.** Something that forms an addition or enlargement: *We built an extension to our house.* **3.** An additional telephone connected to the main line.
ex·ten·sion (ĭk stĕn′shən) ◊ *noun, plural* **extensions**

extensive *adjective* Large in quantity or area; broad: *We own extensive land by the ocean.*
ex·ten·sive (ĭk stĕn′sĭv) ◊ *adjective*

extent *noun* **1.** The area or distance over which something extends: *The Sahara is a desert of vast extent.* **2.** The scope or range of something: *The extent of our scientific knowledge has increased greatly since Benjamin Franklin's time.*
ex·tent (ĭk stĕnt′) ◊ *noun, plural* **extents**

exterior *adjective* Outer or outside; external: *We painted the exterior walls of the house.* ◊ *noun* A part or surface that is outside.
ex·te·ri·or (ĭk stîr′ē ər) ◊ *adjective* ◊ *noun, plural* **exteriors**

exterminate *verb* To get rid of by destroying completely; wipe out: *This spray will exterminate the termites.*
ex·ter·mi·nate (ĭk stûr′mə nāt′) ◊ *verb* **exterminated, exterminating**

external *adjective* On or for the outside or outer surface: *This medicine is for external use only.*
ex·ter·nal (ĭk stûr′nəl) ◊ *adjective*

extinct *adjective* **1.** No longer existing in living form: *The dodo bird has been extinct for 300 years.* **2.** No longer active; extinguished:

A lake can form in the crater of an extinct volcano.
ex·tinct (ĭk **stĭngkt′**) ◊ *adjective*

extinction *noun* **1.** The act or process of destroying completely: *The flow of lava from the volcano caused the extinction of all plant life in the area.* **2.** The condition of being extinct: *The buffalo was hunted almost to extinction.*
ex·tinc·tion (ĭk **stĭngk′**shən) ◊ *noun, plural* **extinctions**

extinguish *verb* **1.** To put out a fire or flame. **2.** To put an end to; destroy: *The storm extinguished their last hope for rescue.*
ex·tin·guish (ĭk **stĭng′**gwĭsh) ◊ *verb* **extinguished, extinguishing**

extinguisher *noun* A device used to put out fires, especially a sealed container from which chemicals are sprayed.
ex·tin·guish·er (ĭk **stĭng′**gwĭ shər) ◊ *noun, plural* **extinguishers**

▲ **extinguisher**

extra *adjective* More than what is usual, expected, or needed: *We baby-sit to earn extra spending money.*
◊ *adverb* Especially; unusually: *The children were extra quiet today.*
◊ *noun* **1.** Often **extras** Something additional for which one pays an added charge. **2.** A special edition of a newspaper.
ex·tra (**ĕk′**strə) ◊ *adjective* ◊ *adverb* ◊ *noun, plural* **extras**

extract *verb* To take or pull out: *The dentist extracted one of my teeth.*
◊ *noun* Something drawn out of a natural substance for use as flavoring.
ex·tract ◊ *verb* (ĭk **străkt′**) **extracted, extracting** ◊ *noun* (**ĕk′**străkt′), *plural* **extracts**

ă	pat	ĭ	pit	oi	oil	th	bath
ā	pay	ī	ride	ŏŏ	book	*th*	bathe
â	care	î	fierce	ōō	boot	ə	ago, item
ä	father	ŏ	pot	ou	out		pencil
ĕ	pet	ō	go	ŭ	cut		atom
ē	be	ô	paw, for	û	fur		circus

extraordinary *adjective* Very unusual; remarkable: *Landing on the moon was an extraordinary accomplishment.*
ex·traor·di·nar·y (ĭk **strôr′**dn ĕr′ē *or* ĕk′strə-**ôr′**dn ĕr′ē) ◊ *adjective*

extravagance *noun* **1.** Wasteful or unwise spending of money: *Your extravagance will lead you into debt.* **2.** A going beyond the limits of reason: *The extravagance of your claims makes us doubt your story.*
ex·trav·a·gance (ĭk **străv′**ə gəns) ◊ *noun, plural* **extravagances**

extravagant *adjective* **1.** Costing or spending too much; wasteful. **2.** Going beyond the limits of reason; excessive.
ex·trav·a·gant (ĭk **străv′**ə gənt) ◊ *adjective*

extreme *adjective* **1.** Very great or intense: *The Arctic explorers suffered from the extreme cold.* **2.** The farthest possible: *The piano was placed at the extreme end of the room.* **3.** Very unusual: *They hold extreme political opinions.*
◊ *noun* Either of two ends of a scale or range: *In this region we experience extremes in hot and cold weather.*
ex·treme (ĭk **strēm′**) ◊ *adjective* ◊ *noun, plural* **extremes**

extremity *noun* **1.** The farthest point; end: *Alaska is at the western extremity of North America.* **2. extremities** The hands or feet.
ex·trem·i·ty (ĭk **strĕm′**ĭ tē) ◊ *noun, plural* **extremities**

exult *verb* To rejoice greatly: *We exulted in our team's victory.*
ex·ult (ĭg **zŭlt′**) ◊ *verb* **exulted, exulting**

eye *noun* **1.** The organ of sight in people and animals. **2.** The colored part of the eye; iris: *I have green eyes.* **3.** The area around the eye: *My hair keeps falling in my eyes.* **4.** The ability to see: *You need sharp eyes to see the boat on the horizon.* **5.** The ability to estimate or judge: *The coach had an eye for new talent.* **6.** A marking that resembles an eye, as a bud on a potato or a spot on a peacock's tail feather. **7.** The hole in a needle that the thread goes through. **8.** The loop to which a hook links for fastening.
◊ *verb* To look at; regard: *We eyed the strange new food with caution.*
eye (ī) ◊ *noun, plural* **eyes** ◊ *verb* **eyed, eying**
‖*These sound alike:* **eye, aye, I**

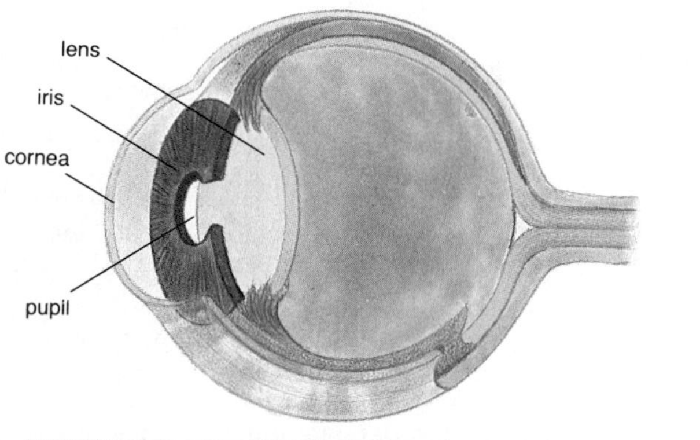

▲ **eye**

eyeball *noun* The ball-shaped part of the eye, enclosed by the socket and eyelids.
eye·ball (ī′bôl′) ◊ *noun, plural* **eyeballs**

eyebrow *noun* **1.** The bony ridge of the skull just above the eye. **2.** The arch of short hairs covering this ridge.
eye·brow (ī′brou′) ◊ *noun, plural* **eyebrows**

eyeglasses *plural noun* A pair of lenses in a frame worn in front of the eyes to improve poor vision; spectacles.
eye·glass·es (ī′glăs′ĭz) ◊ *plural noun*

▲ **eyeglasses**

eyelash *noun* **1.** A row of hairs that forms a fringe along the edge of each eyelid. **2.** Any one of the hairs in this row.
eye·lash (ī′lăsh′) ◊ *noun, plural* **eyelashes**

eyelet *noun* **1.** A small hole for a lace, cord, or hook to fit through: *Laces are threaded through eyelets in a shoe.* **2.** A metal ring used as a rim to strengthen such a hole.
eye·let (ī′lĭt) ◊ *noun, plural* **eyelets**
‖*These sound alike:* **eyelet, islet**

eyelid *noun* Either of a pair of folds of skin with which the eye can be opened and closed.
eye·lid (ī′lĭd′) ◊ *noun, plural* **eyelids**

eyepiece *noun* The lens or the set of lenses closest to the eye in a telescope or microscope.
eye·piece (ī′pēs′) ◊ *noun, plural* **eyepieces**

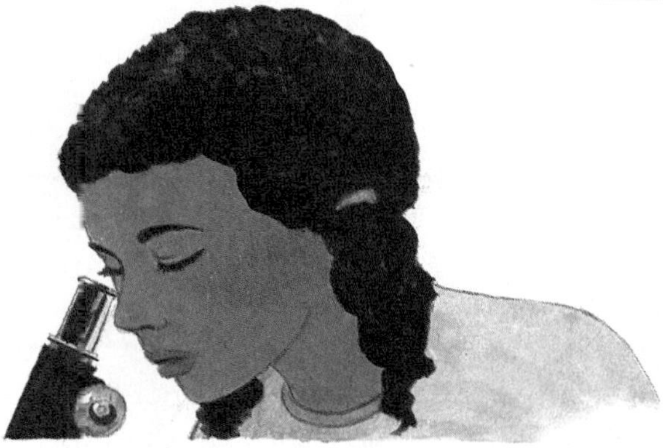

▲ **eyepiece**

eyesight *noun* The ability to see; vision.
eye·sight (ī′sīt′) ◊ *noun*

eyesore *noun* Something that is extremely unpleasant or ugly: *The garbage dump is an eyesore.*
eye·sore (ī′sôr′) ◊ *noun, plural* **eyesores**

eyetooth *noun* Either of the two pointed teeth of the upper jaw.
eye·tooth (ī′to͝oth′) ◊ *noun, plural* **eyeteeth**

Fox

Ff

F is the sixth letter of the English alphabet. Did you know that it has a long history?

Over 3,500 years ago, people in the Middle East were using symbols that became the letters of our alphabet. This ancient Middle Eastern symbol is a form of the letter that became our letter *F*.

The ancient Greeks borrowed their alphabet from people in the Middle East. Here is a form of the Greek letter that became our letter *F*.

The ancient Romans borrowed their alphabet from a people who had taken their own letter symbols from the Greeks. Here is a form of the Roman letter *F* that was used for carving letters into stone. These letters became the model for our printed capital letters.

As people wrote quickly, especially with pens, the capital letters began to take the shapes of small letters. Here is a small-letter *f* that was developed about 1,200 years ago.

Ff *Ff*	Ff	Ff	Ff
Handwriting	Sans Serif Type	Serif Type	Computer Printing

f *or* **F** *noun* **1.** The sixth letter of the English alphabet. **2. F** A failing grade in school.
f *or* **F** (ĕf) ◊ *noun, plural* **f's** *or* **F's**

F The abbreviation for *Fahrenheit.*

fa *noun* The fourth tone of the musical scale.
fa (fä) ◊ *noun*

fable *noun* **1.** A story that is meant to teach a useful lesson. A fable often has animal characters that speak and act like human beings. **2.** A story that is not based on fact.
fa·ble (fā′bəl) ◊ *noun, plural* **fables**

fabric *noun* A material that is produced by joining fibers together, as by weaving; cloth.
fab·ric (**făb′**rĭk) ◊ *noun, plural* **fabrics**

fabulous *adjective* Like a fable, as in being amazing or hard to believe: *The museum has a fabulous collection of jewels.*
fab·u·lous (**făb′**yə ləs) ◊ *adjective*

ă	pat	ĭ	pit	oi	**oil**	th	ba**th**
ā	pay	ī	ride	ŏŏ	**book**	*th*	ba**th**e
â	care	î	fierce	ōō	**boot**	ə	ago, item
ä	father	ŏ	pot	ou	**out**		pencil
ĕ	pet	ō	go	ŭ	cut		atom
ē	be	ô	paw, for	û	fur		circus

face *noun* **1.** The front part of the head from the forehead to the chin. **2.** An expression on the face: *You have a happy face.* **3.** A twisting of the muscles of the face; grimace: *Don't make faces.* **4.** The front, outer, or upper surface: *The face of my watch is broken.*
◊ *verb* **1.** To have the face or front toward: *Turn around and face the class.* **2.** To deal with boldly, firmly, or bravely: *I just can't face the problem today.*
face (fās) ◊ *noun, plural* **faces** ◊ *verb* **faced, facing**

facet *noun* A flat, polished surface of a cut gem.
fac·et (**făs′**ĭt) ◊ *noun, plural* **facets**

facial *adjective* Of or relating to the face.
fa·cial (fā′shəl) ◊ *adjective*

facilitate *verb* To make easier; ease: *Airplanes facilitate travel over long distances.*
fa·cil·i·tate (fə **sĭl′**ĭ tāt′) ◊ *verb* **facilitated, facilitating**

facility *noun* **1.** Ease in moving, acting, or doing something; skill or aptitude: *The pianist reads music with facility.* **2.** Something that provides a service or convenience: *The house is pretty, but it lacks storage facilities.*
fa·cil·i·ty (fə sĭl′ĭ tē) ◊ *noun, plural* **facilities**

fact *noun* **1.** Something that has really happened or that really exists: *It is a fact that the sun is a star.* **2.** What has actually happened or is the case: *The fact is that they're telling the truth.*
fact (făkt) ◊ *noun, plural* **facts**

factor *noun* **1.** Something that brings about a result: *A willingness to work hard is an important factor in achieving success.* **2.** One of two or more numbers that when multiplied together form a product: *2 and 3 are factors of 6.*
fac·tor (făk′tər) ◊ *noun, plural* **factors**

factory *noun* A building or group of buildings in which goods are manufactured; plant.
fac·to·ry (făk′tə rē) ◊ *noun, plural* **factories**

▲ **factory**

factual *adjective* Of or based on facts: *Just give a factual account of what happened.*
fac·tu·al (făk′cho͞o əl) ◊ *adjective*

faculty *noun* **1.** One of the powers of the body or mind: *Hearing and sight are human faculties.* **2.** An ability for doing something; aptitude. **3.** The teaching staff of a school, college, or university.
fac·ul·ty (făk′əl tē) ◊ *noun, plural* **faculties**

fad *noun* Something that is very popular for a short time; craze.
fad (făd) ◊ *noun, plural* **fads**

***HISTORY* • fad**

Fad was originally short for *fiddle-faddle,* an old word meaning "nonsense."

F

fade *verb* **1.** To lose or cause to lose brightness: *The material faded in the laundry.* **2.** To lose freshness; wither: *The flowers are beginning to fade.* **3.** To become faint or dim: *The sound of the music faded away.*
fade (fād) ◊ *verb* **faded, fading**

Fahrenheit *adjective* Of or relating to a temperature scale that indicates the freezing point of water as 32 degrees and the boiling point of water as 212 degrees.
Fahr·en·heit (făr′ən hīt′) ◊ *adjective*

fail *verb* **1.** To be unsuccessful: *Many students failed the test.* **2.** To neglect or omit: *You failed to keep your promise.* **3.** To stop functioning; break down: *The brakes on the car failed.* **4.** To be of little or no use to; disappoint: *I won't fail you this time.* **5.** To lose power or strength: *I hope your health isn't failing.* **6.** To become bankrupt: *A number of downtown stores have failed.*
fail (fāl) ◊ *verb* **failed, failing**

failure *noun* **1.** Lack of success: *The experiment ended in failure.* **2.** An example of failing: *Failure to brush your teeth can result in tooth decay.* **3.** Someone or something that has failed.
fail·ure (fāl′yər) ◊ *noun, plural* **failures**

faint *adjective* **1.** Not distinct or clear; dim: *We heard a faint sound.* **2.** Dizzy and weak and about to become unconscious.
◊ *noun* A sudden loss of consciousness.
◊ *verb* To lose consciousness for a short time.
faint (fānt) ◊ *adjective* **fainter, faintest** ◊ *noun, plural* **faints** ◊ *verb* **fainted, fainting**
‖*These sound alike:* **faint, feint**

fair[1] *adjective* **1.** Pleasing in appearance; lovely: *The king married a fair maiden.* **2.** Light in color: *I have fair hair and fair skin.* **3.** Not wet, cloudy, or stormy; clear: *The morning was fair and sunny.* **4.** Free of bias; just: *The prisoner was given a fair trial.* **5.** According to the rules: *The team had a*

sense of fair play. **6.** Neither good nor bad: *My cousin is just a fair student.*
◊ *adverb* In a fair manner: *Let's play fair.*
fair¹ (fâr) ◊ *adjective* **fairer, fairest** ◊ *adverb*
‖*These sound alike:* **fair, fare**

fair² *noun* **1.** A gathering of persons at a particular place and time to buy and sell goods. **2.** A display, as of farm and home products, often together with entertainment. **3.** An exhibition and sale of articles to benefit a charity: *We made pies for the church fair.*
fair² (fâr) ◊ *noun, plural* **fairs**
‖*These sound alike:* **fair, fare**

HISTORY • fair¹, fair²

Fair¹ comes from an old English word meaning "pleasing, beautiful." **Fair²** comes through French from a Latin word meaning "holidays."

fairground *noun* An open area where fairs or exhibitions are held.
fair·ground (fâr′ground′) ◊ *noun, plural* **fairgrounds**

▲ **fairground**

ă	pat	ĭ	pit	oi	**oil**	th	ba**th**
ā	pay	ī	ride	o͝o	book	*th*	ba**th**e
â	care	î	fierce	o͞o	boot	ə	ago, item
ä	father	ŏ	pot	ou	**out**		pencil
ĕ	pet	ō	go	ŭ	cut		atom
ē	be	ô	paw, for	û	fur		circus

fairly *adverb* **1.** In a fair manner: *Our teacher treats all students fairly.* **2.** To a moderate degree: *I am feeling fairly well today.*
fair·ly (fâr′lē) ◊ *adverb*

fairy *noun* A tiny imaginary being in human form who has magical powers.
fair·y (fâr′ē) ◊ *noun, plural* **fairies**

faith *noun* **1.** Confidence or trust even without proof: *Have faith in yourself; you will succeed.* **2.** A religion: *People of every faith attended the mayor's funeral.* **3.** Loyalty to a person or to one's obligations.
faith (fāth) ◊ *noun, plural* **faiths**

faithful *adjective* Firm in allegiance; loyal: *A faithful friend helps in times of trouble.*
faith·ful (fāth′fəl) ◊ *adjective*

fake *verb* **1.** To make believe: *We faked a happiness we didn't really feel.* **2.** To make or imitate in order to deceive; counterfeit.
◊ *noun* Someone or something that is not what it pretends to be: *The experts discovered several fakes in the art collection.*
◊ *adjective* Not genuine; counterfeit: *I bought a pretty ring with a fake emerald.*
fake (fāk) ◊ *verb* **faked, faking** ◊ *noun, plural* **fakes** ◊ *adjective*

falcon *noun* A hawk with long wings and hooked claws, especially one that is trained to hunt small animals and birds.
fal·con (făl′kən *or* fôl′kən) ◊ *noun, plural* **falcons**

▲ **falcon**

fall *verb* **1.** To drop or come down freely under the influence of weight or gravity: *The book fell off the table.* —See Synonyms at **tumble.** **2.** To come down from an erect position suddenly, as through lack or loss of sup-

port: *I slipped on the ice and fell.* **3.** To be wounded, killed, or defeated: *Many soldiers fell in the battle.* **4.** To happen as if by dropping: *A hush fell over the crowd.* **5.** To become lower, as in value or intensity: *The temperature fell below freezing.* **6.** To take place at a particular time: *Thanksgiving always falls on a Thursday.* **7.** To pass from one condition into another: *The tired child fell asleep right after dinner.*
◊ *noun* **1.** The act or an example of falling. **2.** An amount that has fallen: *There was a heavy fall of rain.* **3.** The season that follows summer; autumn. **4.** Often **falls** A stream of water that falls from a height; waterfall. **5.** A decline in amount, value, or degree: *We expect a fall in the price of clothing.* **6.** A loss of power, as through defeat: *Constant wars led to the fall of the empire.*
◊ *idioms* **fall back on** To turn to for help when others fail. **fall out** To have an argument; quarrel.
fall (fôl) ◊ *verb* **fell, fallen, falling** ◊ *noun, plural* **falls**

fallen *verb* Past participle of **fall.**
fall·en (fô′lən) ◊ *verb*

fallout *noun* Tiny radioactive particles in the atmosphere after a nuclear explosion.
fall·out (fôl′out′) ◊ *noun, plural* **fallouts**

false *adjective* **1.** Not true, real, honest, or correct: *Is that conclusion false?* **2.** Lacking loyalty: *They turned out to be false friends.* **3.** Based on mistaken ideas or information.
false (fôls) ◊ *adjective* **falser, falsest**

SYNONYMS

false, incorrect, wrong

Please decide whether the statements on the test are true or *false*. You have an *incorrect* total for that addition problem. I was *wrong* when I predicted that it was going to snow last night.
Antonyms: *correct, right, true*

falsehood *noun* A statement that is not true; lie.
false·hood (fôls′hŏŏd′) ◊ *noun, plural* **falsehoods**

falter *verb* **1.** To act or speak in an unsteady way: *I faltered as I walked up the steep staircase.* **2.** To hesitate in deciding or doing: *Their courage faltered.*
fal·ter (fôl′tər) ◊ *verb* **faltered, faltering**

fame *noun* The condition or quality of being well known and usually respected.
fame (fām) ◊ *noun*

familiar *adjective* **1.** Well known, as from frequent experience: *I heard the familiar voice of the announcer.* —See Synonyms at **common.** **2.** Having a good knowledge of: *I am familiar with the roads here.* **3.** Of, resulting from, or marked by a close personal tie; friendly: *We are on familiar terms with our neighbors.*
fa·mil·iar (fə mĭl′yər) ◊ *adjective*

family *noun* **1.** A group consisting of parents and their children. **2.** The children of a father and mother; offspring: *We are a large family.* **3.** A group of persons related by blood; relatives. **4.** All the members of a household who live under one roof. **5.** A group of things that share certain features or properties: *English is a member of a larger family of languages.* **6.** A group of related plants or animals. Dogs, wolves, coyotes, and foxes belong to the same family of animals.
fam·i·ly (făm′ə lē) ◊ *noun, plural* **families**

famine *noun* An extreme and widespread lack of food.
fam·ine (făm′ĭn) ◊ *noun, plural* **famines**

famous *adjective* Very well known.
fa·mous (fā′məs) ◊ *adjective*

fan¹ *noun* An instrument, as a device shaped like a semicircle and waved by hand or one with rotating blades and powered by electricity, for stirring the air.
◊ *verb* To cause air to blow on with or as if with a fan: *The wind fanned the flames.*
fan¹ (făn) ◊ *noun, plural* **fans** ◊ *verb* **fanned, fanning**

fan² *noun* A person with an enthusiastic interest in or admiration for someone or something: *My friend is a basketball fan.*
fan² (făn) ◊ *noun, plural* **fans**

***HISTORY* • fan¹, fan²**

Fan¹ comes from a Latin word for a device that was used to blow the husks away from grains of wheat. **Fan²** is a fairly recent American word. Originally it was short for **fanatic**.

fanatic *noun* A person with unreasonable enthusiasm for or devotion to his or her beliefs, ideas, or feelings.
◊ *adjective* Enthusiastic or devoted beyond all reason.
fa·nat·ic (fə **năt′**ĭk) ◊ *noun, plural* **fanatics** ◊ *adjective*

fancy *noun* **1.** The ability to picture in one's mind; imagination: *The story is partly fact and partly fancy.* **2.** An idea or thought; notion: *I had a sudden fancy to buy a hat.* **3.** A liking or fondness: *The singer caught the public's fancy.*
◊ *adjective* **1.** Not plain or simple; elaborate. **2.** Of higher quality than the usual: *The store carries fancy fruits.*
◊ *verb* **1.** To picture in the mind; imagine: *Do you fancy yourself an actor?* **2.** To have a liking for; enjoy: *I fancy big hats.*
fan·cy (**făn′**sē) ◊ *noun, plural* **fancies** ◊ *adjective* **fancier, fanciest** ◊ *verb* **fancied, fancying**

fang *noun* A long, pointed tooth, such as one with which a poisonous snake injects its venom or an animal seizes and holds its prey.
fang (făng) ◊ *noun, plural* **fangs**

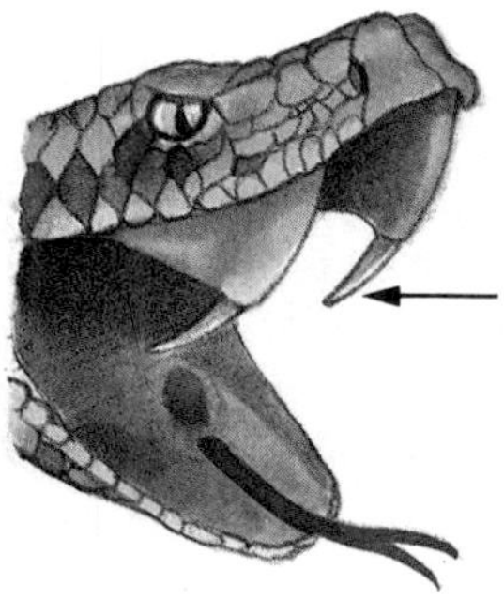

▲ **fang**

fantastic *adjective* **1.** Very strange or odd: *The tapestry had all sorts of fantastic designs.* **2.** Very remarkable: *You did a fantastic job.*
fan·tas·tic (făn **tăs′**tĭk) ◊ *adjective*

fantasy *noun* **1.** Imagination; fancy: *Your claim that you are a singer is pure fantasy.* **2.** Something that is a creation of the imagination.
fan·ta·sy (**făn′**tə sē) ◊ *noun, plural* **fantasies**

far *adverb* **1.** To or at a great distance: *I worked far into the afternoon.* **2.** To or at a definite distance, degree, or point: *So far we haven't received a letter from our friends.* **3.** To a great degree; much: *I feel far happier now.*
◊ *adjective* **1.** Being at a great distance; remote: *We traveled to a far country.* **2.** Being the more distant of two: *A chair stood in the far corner of the room.* **3.** Long; lengthy: *You're a very far way from home.*
far (fär) ◊ *adverb, adjective* **farther** *or* **further, farthest** *or* **furthest**

faraway *adjective* **1.** Very distant; remote: *I saw a flash of lightning over the faraway hills.* **2.** Lost in thought: *There was a faraway look in the child's eyes.*
far·a·way (**fär′** ə **wā′**) ◊ *adjective*

fare *noun* **1.** The money a person must pay to travel, as on a plane, train, or bus. **2.** A passenger who pays a fare.
◊ *verb* To get along; progress: *How are you faring with your project?*
fare (fâr) ◊ *noun, plural* **fares** ◊ *verb* **fared, faring**
‖*These sound alike:* **fare, fair**

farewell *interjection* An expression used to show good wishes at parting.
◊ *noun* Good wishes at parting.
fare·well (fâr **wĕl′**) ◊ *interjection* ◊ *noun, plural* **farewells**

farm *noun* A piece of land on which crops or animals are raised.
◊ *verb* **1.** To engage in farming. **2.** To cultivate or produce a crop on.
farm (färm) ◊ *noun, plural* **farms** ◊ *verb* **farmed, farming**

▲ **farm**

ă	pat	ĭ	pit	oi	**oil**	th	ba**th**
ā	pay	ī	ride	o͝o	**book**	*th*	ba**the**
â	care	î	fierce	o͞o	**boot**	ə	ago, item
ä	father	ŏ	pot	ou	**out**		pencil
ĕ	pet	ō	go	ŭ	cut		atom
ē	be	ô	paw, for	û	fur		circus

farmer *noun* A person who owns or operates a farm.
farm·er (fär′mər) ◊ *noun, plural* **farmers**

farming *noun* The business of growing crops or raising livestock; agriculture.
farm·ing (fär′mĭng) ◊ *noun*

far-sighted *adjective* Able to see distant objects more easily than those nearby.
far-sight·ed (fär′sī′tĭd) ◊ *adjective*

farther *adverb* **1.** To or at a greater distance: *Could anything be farther from the truth?* **2.** In addition; besides. **3.** A comparative of **far.**
◊ *adjective* **1.** More distant: *We docked the boat on the farther shore of the lake.* **2.** A comparative of **far.**
far·ther (fär′*th*ər) ◊ *adverb* ◊ *adjective*

farthest *adverb* **1.** To or at the greatest distance: *Of all the students, I ran farthest.* **2.** To the most advanced point or stage: *We honored the graduates who had gone farthest in their careers.* **3.** A superlative of **far.**
◊ *adjective* **1.** Most distant: *We rode to the farthest limits of our property in the country.* **2.** A superlative of **far.**
far·thest (fär′*th*ĭst) ◊ *adverb* ◊ *adjective*

fascinate *verb* To attract and hold the interest and attention of.
fas·ci·nate (făs′ə nāt′) ◊ *verb* **fascinated, fascinating**

fashion *noun* **1.** A way of doing something: *Try to do your work in an orderly fashion.* **2.** A style, as of dressing or behaving, that is popular at a certain time: *I bought a coat in the latest fashion.*
◊ *verb* To give a form or shape to: *We fashioned figures from clay.*
fash·ion (făsh′ən) ◊ *noun, plural* **fashions** ◊ *verb* **fashioned, fashioning**

fashionable *adjective* Following the current style or latest fashion; stylish.
fash·ion·a·ble (făsh′ə nə bəl) ◊ *adjective*

fast[1] *adjective* **1.** Moving, acting, or done quickly: *Fast drivers often get speeding tickets.* —See Synonyms at **quick. 2.** Indicating a time ahead of the actual time: *My watch is fast.* **3.** Firmly fixed, attached, or fastened: *Keep a fast grip on the rope.* **4.** Loyal; firm: *They became fast friends.*
◊ *adverb* **1.** With speed; rapidly: *You are driving too fast.* **2.** In a firm way; securely: *Hold fast to the railing.* **3.** To the greatest extent possible: *I was fast asleep.*
fast[1] (făst) ◊ *adjective, adverb* **faster, fastest**

fast[2] *verb* To go without all or certain foods, as for religious reasons or in protest.
◊ *noun* The act or a period of fasting.
fast[2] (făst) ◊ *verb* **fasted, fasting** ◊ *noun, plural* **fasts**

> ***HISTORY* • fast[1], fast[2]**
>
> **Fast[1]** and **fast[2]** come from related old English words. **Fast[1]** originally meant "firm" or "firmly" and then came to mean "swift" or "swiftly." **Fast[2]** meant "to hold firm" and came to refer especially to abstaining firmly from food.

fasten *verb* **1.** To attach firmly; secure: *We fastened our skis to a rack on the roof of the car.* **2.** To make or become fast or closed: *Fasten your seat belts.*
fas·ten (făs′ən) ◊ *verb* **fastened, fastening**

fastener *noun* Something, as a lock, bolt, or clasp, used to fasten things together.
fas·ten·er (făs′ə nər) ◊ *noun, plural* **fasteners**

fat *noun* **1.** An oily substance found in plant and animal tissues. **2.** Tissue, especially of an animal, that contains a high amount of fat.
◊ *adjective* **1.** Having much or too much body fat; heavy or plump. **2.** Full of fat: *I prefer fish to fat meat.*
fat (făt) ◊ *noun, plural* **fats** ◊ *adjective* **fatter, fattest**

fatal *adjective* Causing or capable of causing death.
fa·tal (fāt′l) ◊ *adjective*

fate *noun* **1.** The invisible force or power that is believed to determine future events; destiny: *They were sure that fate was responsible for their meeting.* **2.** Something that happens as though it were decided by fate: *We still don't know the fate of the plane's passengers.*
fate (fāt) ◊ *noun, plural* **fates**

father *noun* **1.** A male parent. **2.** A priest.
fa·ther (fä′*th*ər) ◊ *noun, plural* **fathers**

father-in-law *noun* The father of one's husband or wife.
fa·ther-in-law (fä′*th*ər ĭn lô′) ◊ *noun, plural* **fathers-in-law**

fathom *noun* A unit of length equal to six feet that is used mainly in measuring the depth of water.
◊ *verb* **1.** To measure the depth of water, especially with a line that has a weight at one end. **2.** To get to the bottom of and understand: *Your behavior is difficult to fathom.*
fath·om (făth′əm) ◊ *noun, plural* **fathoms** *or* **fathom** ◊ *verb* **fathomed, fathoming**

fatigue *noun* The condition of being tired, as from hard work or strain; exhaustion.
◊ *verb* To tire, as with hard work or strain.
fa·tigue (fə tēg′) ◊ *noun* ◊ *verb* **fatigued, fatiguing**

fatten *verb* To make or become fat.
fat·ten (făt′n) ◊ *verb* **fattened, fattening**

faucet *noun* A device for controlling the flow of liquid, as from a pipe; tap.
fau·cet (fô′sĭt) ◊ *noun, plural* **faucets**

LANGUAGE DETECTIVE

faucet

What do you call the thing that turns the water on and off in your sink? The word you use may depend on where you live. In the North the most common word for this device is *faucet.* In much of the rest of the country the most common word for it is *spigot,* although *faucet* is used too. Another widely used word for the device is *tap.*

fault *noun* **1.** Responsibility for a mistake or offense: *Failing the test was my own fault.* **2.** Something that keeps something else from being perfect; defect. **3.** A mistake; error: *The teacher found many faults in spelling and grammar in my report.*
fault (fôlt) ◊ *noun, plural* **faults**

favor *noun* **1.** A kind or helpful act. **2.** Approval or support: *Our parents viewed our idea of working after school with favor.* **3.** A gift or decorative item, as for party guests.
◊ *verb* **1.** To do a favor for; oblige: *Please favor us with another song.* **2.** To approve or support: *I favor increasing aid for schools.* **3.** To show preference for, especially in an unfair way: *Teachers try to avoid favoring one student over another.*
fa·vor (fā′vər) ◊ *noun, plural* **favors** ◊ *verb* **favored, favoring**

favorable *adjective* **1.** Offering aid or advantage; helpful: *The ship set sail when the wind was favorable.* **2.** Expressing favor: *The reviews of the movie were very favorable.*
fa·vor·a·ble (fā′vər ə bəl) ◊ *adjective*

favorite *noun* Someone or something that is preferred above all others.
◊ *adjective* Preferred above all others.
fa·vor·ite (fā′vər ĭt) ◊ *noun, plural* **favorites** ◊ *adjective*

fawn *noun* A young deer, especially one that is less than a year old.
fawn (fôn) ◊ *noun, plural* **fawns**

▲ **fawn**

FBI The abbreviation for *Federal Bureau of Investigation.*

fear *noun* A feeling caused by a sense of danger or the expectation that something harmful or evil may happen.
◊ *verb* **1.** To be afraid of: *You have nothing to fear.* **2.** To have a very uneasy feeling: *I feared that you were lost.*
fear (fîr) ◊ *noun, plural* **fears** ◊ *verb* **feared, fearing**

fearful *adjective* **1.** Feeling fear: *I was fearful of losing my way in the forest.* **2.** Causing fear: *I heard a fearful explosion.*
fear·ful (fîr′fəl) ◊ *adjective*

ă	pat	ĭ	pit	oi	**oi**l	th	ba**th**
ā	pay	ī	ride	o͝o	b**oo**k	*th*	ba**the**
â	care	î	fierce	o͞o	b**oo**t	ə	ago, item
ä	father	ŏ	pot	ou	**ou**t		pencil
ĕ	pet	ō	go	ŭ	c**u**t		atom
ē	be	ô	paw, for	û	f**u**r		circus

fearless *adjective* Having no fear; afraid of nothing. —See Synonyms at **brave.**
fear·less (fîr′lĭs) ◊ *adjective*

feast *noun* A fancy meal; banquet: *We prepared a feast for the wedding.*
◊ *verb* **1.** To eat well and with pleasure. **2.** To take great delight in: *We feasted our eyes on the toys in the window.*
feast (fēst) ◊ *noun, plural* **feasts** ◊ *verb* **feasted, feasting**

feat *noun* An act or accomplishment that shows skill, strength, or bravery: *The gymnasts performed remarkable feats.*
feat (fēt) ◊ *noun, plural* **feats**
‖*These sound alike:* **feat, feet**

feather *noun* One of the light horny structures forming the outer covering of a bird.
feath·er (fĕ*th*′ər) ◊ *noun, plural* **feathers**

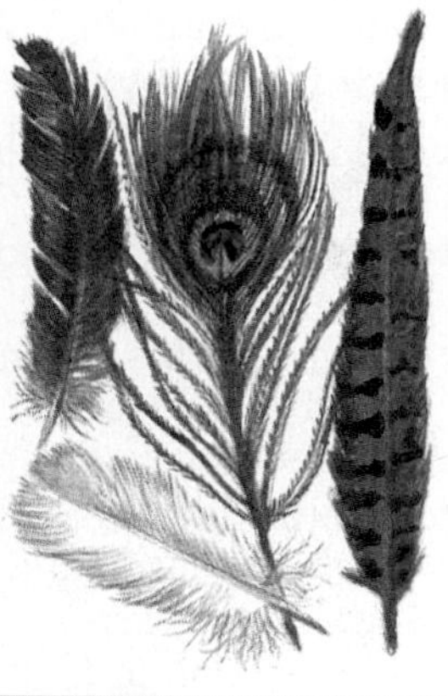

▲ **feather**

feature *noun* **1.** The part, characteristic, or quality that is most noticeable. **2.** One of the distinct parts, as the chin or nose, of the face. **3.** A full-length movie.
◊ *verb* To make or be a noticeable part: *The museum's exhibit features paintings of Colonial times.*
fea·ture (fē′chər) ◊ *noun, plural* **features** ◊ *verb* **featured, featuring**

Feb. The abbreviation for *February.*

February *noun* The second month of the year. February has 28 days except in leap year when it has 29.
Feb·ru·ar·y (fĕb′ro͞o ĕr′ē *or* fĕb′yo͞o ĕr′ē) ◊ *noun*

fed *verb* Past tense and past participle of **feed.**
fed (fĕd) ◊ *verb*

federal *adjective* **1.** Of or relating to a form of government in which separate states are united under one central authority. **2.** Of, relating to, or being a nation that is united under a federal government.
fed·er·al (fĕd′ər əl) ◊ *adjective*

federation *noun* A union by agreement of states, nations, or other groups.
fed·er·a·tion (fĕd′ə rā′shən) ◊ *noun, plural* **federations**

fee *noun* **1.** A fixed charge: *We had to pay an admission fee to attend the football game.* **2.** A charge for a service, especially for professional services.
fee (fē) ◊ *noun, plural* **fees**

feeble *adjective* **1.** Lacking or showing a lack of strength; weak. **2.** Lacking in power or effect: *I made a feeble attempt to answer.*
fee·ble (fē′bəl) ◊ *adjective* **feebler, feeblest**

feed *verb* **1.** To give food to: *We fed the elephants.* **2.** To provide as food: *They fed peanuts to the elephant.* **3.** To use as food; eat: *Young turtles feed on insects.*
◊ *noun* Food, especially for animals.
feed (fēd) ◊ *verb* **fed, feeding** ◊ *noun*

feel *verb* **1.** To be or become aware of through the sense of touch: *I felt leaves brush against my cheek.* **2.** To touch in order to test or examine: *The nurse felt my forehead to see if I had a fever.* **3.** To be aware of by means of a physical sensation: *They felt the warmth of the sun.* **4.** To be aware of being in a certain condition: *I felt sleepy.* **5.** To have an opinion or feeling: *They feel strongly about equal rights for women.* **6.** To seem to be, especially to the sense of touch: *This cloth feels like satin.*
◊ *noun* A mental or physical feeling or sensation: *I liked the soft feel of the rose petal.*
feel (fēl) ◊ *verb* **felt, feeling** ◊ *noun*

feeler *noun* A slender part, as an insect's antenna, used for touching or feeling.
feel·er (fē′lər) ◊ *noun, plural* **feelers**

▲ **feeler**

feeling *noun* **1.** The sense of touch: *I lost all feeling in my injured hand.* **2.** A physical sensation: *A feeling of hunger led me to the refrigerator.* **3.** An emotion, as pity or joy. **4. feelings** The state of someone's emotions: *We tried to*

hide our feelings. **5.** What a person feels about something: *You know my feeling about people who cheat.*
feel·ing (fē′lĭng) ◊ *noun, plural* **feelings**

feet *noun* Plural of **foot.**
feet (fēt) ◊ *noun*
‖*These sound alike:* **feet, feat**

feign *verb* To pretend: *I feigned sickness so I wouldn't have to mow the lawn.*
feign (fān) ◊ *verb* **feigned, feigning**

feint *noun* A movement, attack, or blow that is aimed at one point or part to divert attention away from the real objective.
◊ *verb* To make a feint.
feint (fānt) ◊ *noun, plural* **feints** ◊ *verb* **feinted, feinting**
‖*These sound alike:* **feint, faint**

feline *adjective* Of or typical of a cat or related animal.
◊ *noun* A cat or related animal, such as a lion, tiger, or leopard.
fe·line (fē′līn′) ◊ *adjective* ◊ *noun, plural* **felines**

fell[1] *verb* To cut or knock down: *They felled trees to build a cabin.*
fell[1] (fĕl) ◊ *verb* **felled, felling**

fell[2] *verb* Past tense of **fall.**
fell[2] (fĕl) ◊ *verb*

fellow *noun* **1.** A man or boy. **2.** A comrade; companion.
◊ *adjective* Being another of the same kind: *We voted with our fellow citizens.*
fel·low (fĕl′ō) ◊ *noun, plural* **fellows** ◊ *adjective*

fellowship *noun* **1.** Friendly association of people; companionship. **2.** A union of friends or groups sharing a common interest.
fel·low·ship (fĕl′ō shĭp′) ◊ *noun, plural* **fellowships**

felt[1] *noun* A smooth cloth made by pressing wool, fur, or other fibers together instead of weaving them.
felt[1] (fĕlt) ◊ *noun, plural* **felts**

ă	pat	ĭ	pit	oi	**oi**l	th	ba**th**
ā	pay	ī	ride	ŏŏ	b**oo**k	*th*	ba**the**
â	care	î	fierce	ōō	b**oo**t	ə	**a**go, it**e**m
ä	father	ŏ	pot	ou	**ou**t		penc**i**l
ĕ	pet	ō	go	ŭ	cut		at**o**m
ē	be	ô	paw, for	û	fur		circ**u**s

felt[2] *verb* Past tense and past participle of **feel.**
felt[2] (fĕlt) ◊ *verb*

female *adjective* Of or belonging to the sex that can give birth to young or produce eggs.
◊ *noun* A female person or animal.
fe·male (fē′māl′) ◊ *adjective* ◊ *noun, plural* **females**

feminine *adjective* Of, relating to, or belonging to women or girls.
fem·i·nine (fĕm′ə nĭn) ◊ *adjective*

fence *noun* A structure set up to prevent entry into an area or to mark it off.
◊ *idiom* **on the fence** Undecided.
fence (fĕns) ◊ *noun, plural* **fences**

fencing *noun* The sport of fighting with long, slender swords.
fenc·ing (fĕn′sĭng) ◊ *noun*

fender *noun* A cover or guard mounted above and around a wheel, as of a car or bicycle.
fen·der (fĕn′dər) ◊ *noun, plural* **fenders**

ferment *verb* To undergo or cause to undergo fermentation.
◊ *noun* Great excitement; tumult.
fer·ment (fûr′mĕnt′) ◊ *verb* **fermented, fermenting** ◊ *noun*

fermentation *noun* A chemical process by which the sugar in a liquid turns into alcohol and a gas. Yeast or certain bacteria can cause fermentation in fruit juices.
fer·men·ta·tion (fûr′mĕn tā′shən) ◊ *noun, plural* **fermentations**

fern *noun* Any of a group of plants that usually have feathery leaves with many leaflets and that reproduce by sending out spores.
fern (fûrn) ◊ *noun, plural* **ferns**

ferocious *adjective* Very cruel and savage.
fe·ro·cious (fə rō′shəs) ◊ *adjective*

ferret *noun* An animal with yellowish or white fur that is related to the weasel. It is often trained to hunt for rats and rabbits.
◊ *verb* To search hard and find: *I finally ferreted out the lost socks.*
fer·ret (fĕr′ĭt) ◊ *noun, plural* **ferrets** ◊ *verb* **ferreted, ferreting**

Ferris wheel *noun* A large, upright, rotating wheel with seats attached to its rim. People ride on Ferris wheels at carnivals and amusement parks.
Fer·ris wheel (fĕr′ĭs′) ◊ *noun, plural* **Ferris wheels**

▲ Ferris wheel

ferry *noun* A boat or boat service used to carry people, cars, or goods across water.
◊ *verb* **1.** To carry in a boat across a body of water. **2.** To take a ferry.
fer·ry (fĕr′ ē) ◊ *noun, plural* **ferries** ◊ *verb* **ferried, ferrying**

fertile *adjective* **1.** Good for plants to grow in: *The fertile soil near the river is good for growing corn.* **2.** Capable of producing offspring. **3.** Capable of developing into a complete plant or animal: *Most chicken eggs are not fertile.* **4.** Producing many ideas; creative: *You have a fertile imagination.*
fer·tile (fûr′ tl) ◊ *adjective*

fertilize *verb* **1.** To make fertile. **2.** To put fertilizer in or on.
fer·til·ize (fûr′ tl īz′) ◊ *verb* **fertilized, fertilizing**

fertilizer *noun* A substance, such as manure or chemicals, that is added to soil so that plants or grass will grow better.
fer·til·iz·er (fûr′ tl ī′zər) ◊ *noun, plural* **fertilizers**

festival *noun* **1.** A day or period of celebrating; holiday. **2.** A series of special cultural events, such as films, concerts, or exhibitions.
fes·ti·val (fĕs′ tə vəl) ◊ *noun, plural* **festivals**

festive *adjective* Merry; joyous: *We were in a festive mood after our birthday party.*
fes·tive (fĕs′ tĭv) ◊ *adjective*

festivity *noun* An activity that is part of a celebration: *The festivities included parades, banquets, and balls.*
fes·tiv·i·ty (fĕ stĭv′ ĭ tē) ◊ *noun, plural* **festivities**

fetch *verb* To go after and return with; get: *Shall I fetch your bags for you?*
fetch (fĕch) ◊ *verb* **fetched, fetching**

feud *noun* A long, bitter quarrel between two people, families, or groups. —See Synonyms at **fight**.
◊ *verb* To carry on a feud.
feud (fyōōd) ◊ *noun, plural* **feuds** ◊ *verb* **feuded, feuding**

feudalism *noun* A political and economic system in Europe during the Middle Ages. Under feudalism, a lord granted land and protection to people who gave the lord services and part of their crops in return.
feu·dal·ism (fyōōd′l ĭz′əm) ◊ *noun*

fever *noun* A body temperature that is higher than normal.
fe·ver (fē′ vər) ◊ *noun, plural* **fevers**

feverish *adjective* **1.** Having a fever. **2.** Very excited or restless.
fe·ver·ish (fē′ vər ĭsh) ◊ *adjective*

few *adjective* Amounting to a small number: *The bag held a few apples.*
◊ *noun* (*used with a plural verb*) A small number: *Most of the kids went home, but a few stayed to help clean up.*
◊ *pronoun* (*used with a plural verb*) A small number of persons or things: *Few in the back of the room were able to hear the speaker.*
few (fyōō) ◊ *adjective* **fewer, fewest** ◊ *noun* ◊ *pronoun*

fez *noun* A high felt cap that is shaped like an upside-down flower pot. Fezzes are worn in eastern Mediterranean countries.
fez (fĕz) ◊ *noun, plural* **fezzes**

F

fib *noun* A lie: *I told a fib about my age.*
◊ *verb* To tell a lie.
fib (fĭb) ◊ *noun, plural* **fibs** ◊ *verb* **fibbed, fibbing**

fiber *noun* **1.** A long, thin strand of natural or artificial material: *Cotton, wool, and nylon fibers can be spun into yarn.* **2.** Any part of food that cannot be broken down by the body and that helps in the process of digestion.
fi·ber (fī′bər) ◊ *noun, plural* **fibers**

fiction *noun* **1.** Something that is imaginary rather than real: *Legends are often mixtures of fact and fiction.* **2.** Written works that tell about made-up events and characters.
fic·tion (fĭk′shən) ◊ *noun, plural* **fictions**

fiddle *noun* A violin.
◊ *verb* To play a violin.
fid·dle (fĭd′l) ◊ *noun, plural* **fiddles** ◊ *verb* **fiddled, fiddling**

▲ **fiddle**

fidget *verb* To move in a nervous or restless way.
fidg·et (fĭj′ĭt) ◊ *verb* **fidgeted, fidgeting**

field *noun* **1.** A broad area of open or cleared land. **2.** An area of land where a crop is grown, a natural product is obtained, or a special activity is done: *There are oil fields in Oklahoma.* **3.** An area of interest or activity: *They hope to enter the field of medicine.*
field (fēld) ◊ *noun, plural* **fields**

fielder *noun* A baseball player who has a position in the outfield.
field·er (fēl′dər) ◊ *noun, plural* **fielders**

field glasses *plural noun* Binoculars for outdoor use.

field trip *noun* A trip made by a group to observe and learn.
field trip ◊ *noun, plural* **field trips**

ă	pat	ĭ	pit	oi	**oi**l	th	ba**th**
ā	pay	ī	ride	ŏŏ	b**oo**k	*th*	ba**th**e
â	care	î	fierce	ōō	b**oo**t	ə	ago, item
ä	father	ŏ	pot	ou	**ou**t		pencil
ĕ	pet	ō	go	ŭ	cut		atom
ē	be	ô	paw, for	û	fur		circus

fiend *noun* **1.** An evil spirit; demon. **2.** An evil or wicked person.
fiend (fēnd) ◊ *noun, plural* **fiends**

fierce *adjective* **1.** Wild and savage; dangerous: *Tigers can be fierce animals.* **2.** Very strong or extreme: *A fierce winter wind was blowing.* —See Synonyms at **intense.**
fierce (fîrs) ◊ *adjective* **fiercer, fiercest**

fiery *adjective* **1.** Of or glowing like fire: *The fiery sunset lit up the western sky.* —See Synonyms at **hot. 2.** Full of feeling or emotion: *The politician gave a fiery speech.*
fier·y (fīr′ē) ◊ *adjective* **fierier, fieriest**

fiesta *noun* A festival or celebration, especially in a Spanish-speaking country.
fi·es·ta (fē ĕs′tə) ◊ *noun, plural* **fiestas**

fife *noun* A small high-pitched musical instrument similar to a flute. Fifes are played mainly in marching bands.
fife (fīf) ◊ *noun, plural* **fifes**

fifteen *noun* The number, written 15, that is equal to the sum of 14 + 1.
◊ *adjective* Being one more than fourteen.
fif·teen (fĭf′tēn′) ◊ *noun, plural* **fifteens** ◊ *adjective*

fifteenth *noun* **1.** The number in a series that matches the number fifteen. **2.** One of fifteen equal parts, written 1/15.
◊ *adjective* Coming after the fourteenth.
fif·teenth (fĭf′tēnth′) ◊ *noun, plural* **fifteenths** ◊ *adjective*

fifth *noun* **1.** The number in a series that matches the number five. **2.** One of five equal parts, written 1/5.
◊ *adjective* Coming after the fourth.
fifth (fĭfth) ◊ *noun, plural* **fifths** ◊ *adjective*

fiftieth *noun* **1.** The number in a series that matches the number fifty. **2.** One of fifty equal parts, written 1/50.
◊ *adjective* Coming after the forty-ninth.
fif·ti·eth (fĭf′tē ĭth) ◊ *noun, plural* **fiftieths** ◊ *adjective*

fifty *noun* The number, written 50, that is equal to the product of 10 × 5.
◊ *adjective* Being equal to ten times five.
fif·ty (fĭf′tē) ◊ *noun, plural* **fifties** ◊ *adjective*

fig *noun* A sweet-tasting fruit that is shaped like a pear and has many small seeds. Figs grow on trees in warm regions.
fig (fĭg) ◊ *noun, plural* **figs**

▲ **fig**

fight *noun* **1.** A meeting between animals, persons, or groups in which each side, using bodies or weapons, tries to hurt the other or gain power over the other. **2.** An angry disagreement; quarrel. **3.** A hard struggle or effort: *In my fight to reach the top of the cliff, I injured my knee.*
◊ *verb* **1.** To use the body or weapons to try to hurt or gain power over: *The army fought the invaders and turned them back.* **2.** To take part in a fight. **3.** To struggle against: *It's up to everyone to fight injustice.* **4.** To quarrel or argue: *They often fight over money.* **5.** To try hard: *They fought to keep the leaking boat afloat.*
fight (fīt) ◊ *noun, plural* **fights** ◊ *verb* **fought, fighting**

> ***SYNONYMS***
>
> ***fight, dispute, feud, quarrel***
>
> My cousin and I get on each other's nerves and sometimes we have a *fight.* The two drivers had a *dispute* about who caused the accident. The *feud* between those two families went on for years. I would like to end our *quarrel* so that we can be friends again.

figure *noun* **1.** A written symbol that stands for a number. **2.** **figures** Calculations that involve numbers; arithmetic: *I'm good at figures.* **3.** An amount represented in numbers: *Next to the name of each town was a population figure.* **4.** A design or pattern, as on cloth. **5.** A distinct shape or outline, as a square, circle, or rectangle. **6.** A shape or form: *A tall figure stood in the doorway.* **7.** A person, especially a well-known one: *The President is a public figure.*
◊ *verb* **1.** To work out by using numbers; calculate: *Can you figure the sales tax on our bill?* **2.** To work out by thinking: *The guide figured a way to cross the mountains.*
fig·ure (fĭg′yər) ◊ *noun, plural* **figures** ◊ *verb* **figured, figuring**

figured *adjective* Decorated with designs or a pattern: *I picked out a figured wallpaper for my bedroom.*
fig·ured (fĭg′yərd) ◊ *adjective*

figurehead *noun* **1.** A carved figure placed on the prow of a ship as a decoration. **2.** A person who is called a leader but has no real power.
fig·ure·head (fĭg′yər hĕd′) ◊ *noun, plural* **figureheads**

figure of speech *noun* An expression in which words are used in an imaginative or colorful way. "It's raining cats and dogs" is a figure of speech.
figure of speech ◊ *noun, plural* **figures of speech**

filament *noun* A fine wire or thread.
fil·a·ment (fĭl′ə mənt) ◊ *noun, plural* **filaments**

filbert *noun* A hazelnut of a kind that is grown for eating.
fil·bert (fĭl′bərt) ◊ *noun, plural* **filberts**

file¹ *noun* **1.** A collection of papers, cards, records, or other information arranged in order: *The cook has a large file of recipes.* **2.** A collection of related data for a computer, stored on a tape or disk. **3.** A container in which papers or records are kept and arranged in order: *The office has a large metal file where students' records are stored.* **4.** A line of persons, animals, or things placed one behind the other.
◊ *verb* **1.** To put away in a file: *I filed copies of the letters in my desk drawer.* **2.** To send in; submit: *The reporter filed the story by phoning it in to the newspaper office.* **3.** To walk in a line or lines: *The nine judges, wearing black robes, filed in.*
file¹ (fīl) ◊ *noun, plural* **files** ◊ *verb* **filed, filing**

file² *noun* A steel tool with a rough surface used in smoothing, shaping, and cutting.

◊ *verb* To smooth, shape, or cut with a file.
file² (fīl) ◊ *noun, plural* **files** ◊ *verb* **filed, filing**

> ***HISTORY* • file¹, file²**
>
> **File¹** comes through French from a Latin word meaning "thread." People standing "single file" are lined up straight as a thread. Originally, an office **file¹** was a group of papers threaded together with string or wire. **File²** comes from the old English name for the steel tool.

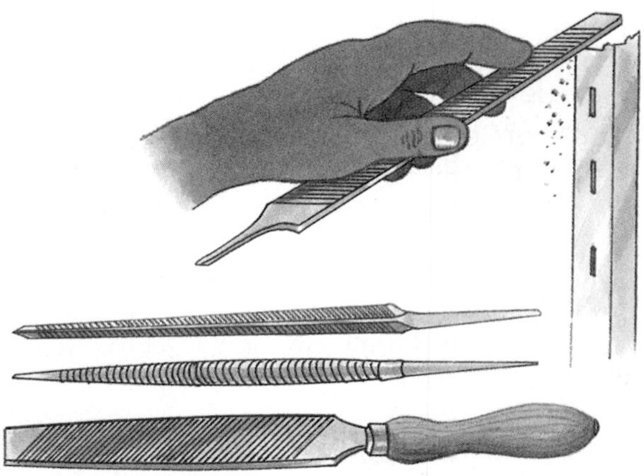

▲ **file²**

filing *noun* A particle scraped off by a file.
fil·ing (fī′lĭng) ◊ *noun, plural* **filings**

fill *verb* **1.** To make or become full: *Fill the glass with milk.* **2.** To take up all the space of; occupy: *People soon filled all the seats in the hall.* **3.** To do the job or tasks of: *The student filled the office of class president well.* **4.** To put writing or information in; complete: *Fill in the blanks.* **5.** To stop or plug up: *We filled the hole in the roof with tar.* **6.** To put together or give what is asked for; supply: *The pharmacist filled my prescription.*
fill (fĭl) ◊ *verb* **filled, filling**

ă	pat	ĭ	pit	oi	**oi**l	th	ba**th**
ā	pay	ī	ride	ŏŏ	b**oo**k	*th*	ba**th**e
â	care	î	fierce	ōō	b**oo**t	ə	**a**go, it**e**m
ä	father	ŏ	pot	ou	**ou**t		penc**i**l
ĕ	pet	ō	go	ŭ	c**u**t		at**o**m
ē	be	ô	paw, for	û	f**u**r		circ**u**s

fillet *noun* A lean piece of meat or fish with the bones cut out.
fil·let (fĭ lā′ *or* fĭl′ā′) ◊ *noun, plural* **fillets**

filling *noun* Something used to fill a space, cavity, or container.
fill·ing (fĭl′ĭng) ◊ *noun, plural* **fillings**

filly *noun* A young female horse.
fil·ly (fĭl′ē) ◊ *noun, plural* **fillies**

film *noun* **1.** A thin strip of material coated with a chemical that changes when light strikes it. Film is used in taking photographs. **2.** A motion picture; movie. **3.** A thin layer; coating: *A film of dust covered the boxes in the attic.*
◊ *verb* To make a movie of: *I filmed the porpoises while swimming alongside them.*
film (fĭlm) ◊ *noun, plural* **films** ◊ *verb* **filmed, filming**

filter *noun* **1.** A device with tiny holes or narrow passageways in it. A liquid or gas is passed through a filter in order to get rid of dirt or other unwanted matter. **2.** A sheet of material that changes the colors of light passing through it by blocking certain light waves and letting others pass through.
◊ *verb* **1.** To pass through a filter: *Filter this water before drinking it.* **2.** To remove or separate with a filter: *The screen filters leaves from the water.* **3.** To pass slowly; seep: *Sunlight filtered through the clouds.*
fil·ter (fĭl′tər) ◊ *noun, plural* **filters** ◊ *verb* **filtered, filtering**

filth *noun* Dirty or disgusting matter.
filth (fĭlth) ◊ *noun*

filthy *adjective* Extremely dirty.
filth·y (fĭl′thē) ◊ *adjective* **filthier, filthiest**

fin *noun* **1.** One of the thin, flat parts that stick out from the body of a water animal. Fish use their fins for moving through water and for balancing themselves. **2.** Something shaped or used like a fin.
fin (fĭn) ◊ *noun, plural* **fins**
‖ *These sound alike:* **fin, Finn**

final *adjective* **1.** Coming at the end: *We took a final spelling test at the end of the school year.* —See Synonyms at **last. 2.** Not to be reconsidered; conclusive: *You're not going out tonight, and that's final.*
◊ *noun* **1.** The last game in a series of games

or a tournament. **2.** The last examination in a school course.
fi·nal (fī′nəl) ◊ *adjective* ◊ *noun, plural* **finals**

finale *noun* The last part of a show or a piece of music.
fi·na·le (fĭ nä′lē) ◊ *noun, plural* **finales**

finalist *noun* A contestant in the finals of a competition.
fi·nal·ist (fī′nə lĭst) ◊ *noun, plural* **finalists**

finally *adverb* After a long while; at last.
fi·nal·ly (fī′nə lē) ◊ *adverb*

finance *noun* **1.** The management and use of money, especially by government, banks, and businesses. **2. finances** Money resources or funds of a person, business, or government.
◊ *verb* To provide money for: *We financed our education with extra jobs.*
fi·nance (fĭ **năns′** *or* **fī′**năns′) ◊ *noun, plural* **finances** ◊ *verb* **financed, financing**

financial *adjective* Of or having to do with finance: *The store was a financial failure and soon closed.*
fi·nan·cial (fĭ **năn′**shəl *or* fī **năn′**shəl) ◊ *adjective*

finch *noun* A bird with a short, thick bill used for cracking seeds. The cardinal and canary are finches.
finch (fĭnch) ◊ *noun, plural* **finches**

▲ **finch**

find *verb* **1.** To come upon by accident: *I found a mitten on the stairs.* **2.** To look for and discover: *Please help me find my pen.* **3.** To learn: *Are you surprised to find that sound is a form of energy?* **4.** To get by investigating or calculating; determine: *Find the answers to these problems.* **5.** To meet with; encounter: *Ants are found almost everywhere.*
◊ *noun* Something found; discovery: *New gold finds brought many miners to California.*
◊ *idiom* **find out** To get information about; discover: *Scientists try to find out as much as they can about the world.*
find (fīnd) ◊ *verb* **found, finding** ◊ *noun, plural* **finds**

finding *noun* One of the results of a study or investigation: *When you have finished the experiment, include your findings in a report.*
find·ing (**fīn′**dĭng) ◊ *noun, plural* **findings**

fine[1] *adjective* **1.** Consisting of small particles: *The gravel was almost as fine as sand.* **2.** Very thin, light, or small: *You can see through this fine silk.* **3.** Of high quality; excellent: *This shop sells only the finest foods.* **4.** In good health: *I'm feeling fine now.*
◊ *adverb* Very well: *The two of us are getting along just fine.*
fine[1] (fīn) ◊ *adjective* **finer, finest** ◊ *adverb*

fine[2] *noun* A sum of money that has to be paid as a penalty for breaking a law or rule.
◊ *verb* To order to pay a fine: *The judge fined them $50 each for speeding.*
fine[2] (fīn) ◊ *noun, plural* **fines** ◊ *verb* **fined, fining**

***HISTORY* • fine[1], fine[2]**

Fine[1] and **fine[2]** both go back to a Latin word meaning "end." This word was sometimes used to mean "the ultimate" and thus "excellent" or **fine[1]**. A **fine[2]** was at one time a fee paid when completing a legal transfer of property.

finery *noun* Fine or fancy clothes and ornaments: *I am decked out in my spring finery.*
fin·er·y (**fī′**nə rē) ◊ *noun, plural* **fineries**

finger *noun* **1.** One of the five extensions of the hand. **2.** The part of a glove that fits over a finger.
◊ *verb* To feel, touch, or handle with the fingers: *I fingered a tune on the piano.*
fin·ger (**fĭng′**gər) ◊ *noun, plural* **fingers** ◊ *verb* **fingered, fingering**

fingernail *noun* The thin layer of horny, transparent material at the tip of each finger.
fin·ger·nail (**fĭng′**gər nāl′) ◊ *noun, plural* **fingernails**

fingerprint *noun* A mark with a pattern of fine, curved lines, made by pressing the fleshy end of a finger against a surface. Fingerprints are used as identification because no two people have exactly the same fingerprints.
◊ *verb* To record the fingerprints of.
fin·ger·print (fĭng′ gər-prĭnt′) ◊ *noun, plural* **fingerprints** ◊ *verb* **fingerprinted, fingerprinting**

▲ **fingerprint**

finish *verb* **1.** To bring or come to an end; get done: *I have finished my lunch.* —See Synonyms at **end. 2.** To use all of; use up.
◊ *noun* The conclusion; end: *The finish of the race was exciting.*
fin·ish (fĭn′ĭsh) ◊ *verb* **finished, finishing** ◊ *noun, plural* **finishes**
‖*These sound alike:* **finish, Finnish**

Finn *noun* A person who was born in or lives in Finland.
Finn (fĭn) ◊ *noun, plural* **Finns**
‖*These sound alike:* **Finn, fin**

Finnish *noun* The language of the Finns.
◊ *adjective* Of or relating to Finland, the Finns, or their language.
Fin·nish (fĭn′ĭsh) ◊ *noun* ◊ *adjective*
‖*These sound alike:* **Finnish, finish**

fiord *noun* Another spelling for **fjord.**
fiord (fyôrd) ◊ *noun, plural* **fiords**

fir *noun* A tall evergreen tree that bears cones and has rather flat, short needles.
fir (fûr) ◊ *noun, plural* **firs**
‖*These sound alike:* **fir, fur**

fire *noun* **1.** The flame, light, and heat given off when something is burning. **2.** Something that is burning, especially a pile of burning fuel. **3.** Great enthusiasm; strong emotion: *The poet read with a voice full of fire.* **4.** The shooting of a gun or guns.
◊ *verb* **1.** To set on fire; burn. **2.** To treat with great heat, as by baking: *I fired a clay pot in the kiln.* **3.** To set off; launch: *They fired the rocket.* **4.** To shoot a gun. **5.** To stir up; excite: *Adventure stories fire my imagination.* **6.** To dismiss from a job.
fire (fīr) ◊ *noun, plural* **fires** ◊ *verb* **fired, firing**

firearm *noun* A small weapon that shoots bullets or other missiles by exploding gunpowder. Pistols and rifles are firearms.
fire·arm (fīr′ärm′) ◊ *noun, plural* **firearms**

firecracker *noun* A small explosive charge in a paper tube. Firecrackers are set off to make noise during celebrations.
fire·crack·er (fīr′krăk′ər) ◊ *noun, plural* **firecrackers**

firedog *noun* An andiron.
fire·dog (fīr′dôg′) ◊ *noun, plural* **firedogs**

fire engine *noun* A truck that carries firefighters and equipment to fight a fire.
fire engine ◊ *noun, plural* **fire engines**

fire escape *noun* An outside stairway attached to a building, used as an emergency exit in case of a fire.
fire escape ◊ *noun, plural* **fire escapes**

fire extinguisher *noun* A portable device containing chemicals that can be sprayed on a fire to put it out.
fire extinguisher ◊ *noun, plural* **fire extinguishers**

firefighter *noun* A person whose job is putting out fires.
fire·fight·er (fīr′fī′tər) ◊ *noun, plural* **firefighters**

firefly *noun* A beetle that flies at night and gives off a flashing light from the rear part of its body.
fire·fly (fīr′flī′) ◊ *noun, plural* **fireflies**

firehouse *noun* A fire station.
fire·house (fīr′hous′) ◊ *noun, plural* **firehouses**

fireman *noun* **1.** A firefighter. **2.** A man who takes care of the fires in a furnace or steam engine.
fire·man (fīr′mən) ◊ *noun, plural* **firemen**

fireplace *noun* A structure for holding a fire for heating or cooking. An indoor fireplace is

ă	pat	ĭ	pit	oi	oil	th	bath
ā	pay	ī	ride	o͝o	book	*th*	bathe
â	care	î	fierce	o͞o	boot	ə	ago, item
ä	father	ŏ	pot	ou	out		pencil
ĕ	pet	ō	go	ŭ	cut		atom
ē	be	ô	paw, for	û	fur		circus

an opening in the wall of a room with a chimney leading up from it.
fire·place (fīr′plās′) ◊ *noun, plural* **fireplaces**

fireproof *adjective* Made of material or materials that do not burn, crack, or break when exposed to heat.
fire·proof (fīr′pro͞of′) ◊ *adjective*

fireside *noun* **1.** The area around a fireplace. **2.** A home: *The tired hikers longed for the comfort of their own fireside.*
fire·side (fīr′sīd′) ◊ *noun, plural* **firesides**

fire station *noun* A building for firefighters and their trucks and equipment.
fire station ◊ *noun, plural* **fire stations**

firewood *noun* Wood used to make fires.
fire·wood (fīr′wo͝od′) ◊ *noun*

fireworks *plural noun* Explosives used to produce colored lights, smoke, and noise for entertainment at celebrations.
fire·works (fīr′wûrks′) ◊ *plural noun*

▲ **fireworks**

firm¹ *adjective* **1.** Not giving way when pressed or pushed; solid: *The firm ground of the track was ideal for running.* **2.** Fixed in place: *The pole was firm in the ground.* **3.** Not changing or varying; steady: *Our friendship is firm.* **4.** Strong and sure: *Keep a firm grip on the handlebars.* **5.** Not giving in: *My parents are firm about not letting me stay out too late.*
firm¹ (fûrm) ◊ *adjective* **firmer, firmest**

firm² *noun* A company formed by two or more persons who go into business together.
firm² (fûrm) ◊ *noun, plural* **firms**

***HISTORY* • firm¹, firm²**

Firm¹ comes from a Latin word that meant "fixed, certain." **Firm²** goes back to a related Latin word meaning "to confirm." This developed into an Italian word meaning "to confirm by signature" and then "a signature or business trademark." The Italian word was borrowed into English as **firm²**.

first *noun* **1.** The number in a series that matches the number one. **2.** A person or thing that is first: *Would the first in line come here?*
◊ *adjective* Coming before all others: *The first house on the block is mine.*
◊ *adverb* **1.** Before all others: *I'll go first.* **2.** For the first time: *I first ate fish at camp.*
first (fûrst) ◊ *noun, plural* **firsts** ◊ *adjective* ◊ *adverb*

first aid *noun* Emergency care given to an injured or sick person before a doctor comes.

first-class *adjective* **1.** Of or for the best kind of seats or rooms: *We bought first-class airline tickets.* **2.** Of the highest quality; excellent: *That is a first-class band.*
◊ *adverb* In first-class seats or rooms.
first-class (fûrst′klăs′) ◊ *adjective* ◊ *adverb*

firsthand *adjective* Coming from the original source: *I heard a firsthand account of the concert from someone who was there.*
◊ *adverb* From direct experience or observation: *The astronauts have a chance to learn firsthand about life in space.*
first·hand (fûrst′hănd′) ◊ *adjective* ◊ *adverb*

first-rate *adjective* Of the best quality.
first-rate (fûrst′rāt′) ◊ *adjective*

F

firth *noun* A long, narrow inlet of the sea in Scotland.
firth (fûrth) ◊ *noun, plural* **firths**

fish *noun* Any of a large group of cold-blooded water animals having a backbone, fins, and gills for breathing.
◊ *verb* **1.** To catch or try to catch fish. **2.** To try to find something by groping: *I fished around for the light switch.*
fish (fĭsh) ◊ *noun, plural* **fish** *or* **fishes** ◊ *verb* **fished, fishing**

fisher *noun* A North American animal that is related to the mink and weasel. Fishers have thick, dark-brown fur.
fish·er (**fĭsh′** ər) ◊ *noun, plural* **fishers**

▲ **fisher**

fisherman *noun* Someone who fishes.
fish·er·man (**fĭsh′** ər mən) ◊ *noun, plural* **fishermen**

fishery *noun* **1.** A place where fish are caught. **2.** A place where fish are bred.
fish·er·y (**fĭsh′** ə rē) ◊ *noun, plural* **fisheries**

fishhook *noun* A hook used to catch fish.
fish·hook (**fĭsh′**ho͝ok′) ◊ *noun, plural* **fishhooks**

fishy *adjective* **1.** Tasting or smelling of fish. **2.** Causing suspicion; questionable: *That is a fishy excuse for being late to class.*
fish·y (**fĭsh′** ē) ◊ *adjective* **fishier, fishiest**

ă	pat	ĭ	pit	oi	oil	th	bath
ā	pay	ī	ride	o͝o	book	*th*	bathe
â	care	î	fierce	o͞o	boot	ə	ago, item
ä	father	ŏ	pot	ou	out		pencil
ĕ	pet	ō	go	ŭ	cut		atom
ē	be	ô	paw, for	û	fur		circus

fission *noun* The breaking up of the nucleus of an atom, with the release of large amounts of energy.
fis·sion (**fĭsh′** ən) ◊ *noun*

fist *noun* The hand closed tightly, with the fingers bent against the palm.
fist (fĭst) ◊ *noun, plural* **fists**

fit¹ *verb* **1.** To be the proper size and shape for: *Does the shoe fit you?* **2.** To be appropriate for: *That song fits the celebration.* **3.** To change to a required size and shape; adjust: *The tailor fitted the pants perfectly.* **4.** To place or pack snugly: *Can you fit all your things in one bag?* **5.** To equip or provide: *We fitted the car with snow tires.*
◊ *noun* The way something fits: *I can adjust the cap for a perfect fit.*
◊ *adjective* **1.** Appropriate: *Do what you think fit.* **2.** Good enough: *The food was not fit to eat.* **3.** Physically sound: *I keep fit with exercise.* —See Synonyms at **healthy.**
fit¹ (fĭt) ◊ *verb* **fitted** *or* **fit, fitting** ◊ *noun* ◊ *adjective* **fitter, fittest**

fit² *noun* **1.** A sudden, violent physical reaction or a strong emotion; outburst: *I had a fit of coughing. Fits of laughter broke out.* **2.** A sudden attack of a disease.
fit² (fĭt) ◊ *noun, plural* **fits**

***HISTORY* • fit¹, fit²**

Fit¹ may be related to an old Scandinavian word meaning "to knit." **Fit²** comes from an old English word that probably meant "fight." Later, **fit²** meant "a bad experience."

fitful *adjective* Starting and stopping: *I worried half the night and had a fitful sleep.*
fit·ful (**fĭt′** fəl) ◊ *adjective*

fitting *adjective* Suitable to the occasion or circumstances; appropriate: *They received a fitting reward for their brave deeds.*
fit·ting (**fĭt′** ĭng) ◊ *adjective*

five *noun* The number, written 5, that is equal to the sum of 4 + 1.
◊ *adjective* Being one more than four.
five (fīv) ◊ *noun, plural* **fives** ◊ *adjective*

fix *verb* **1.** To place or fasten firmly: *We fixed the lightning rod to the chimney.* **2.** To direct steadily: *We fixed our eyes on the*

screen. **3.** To set or decide definitely: *We tried to fix a time for the party.* **4.** To set right; mend: *I fixed the broken radio.* **5.** To put together; make ready: *There is no time to fix dinner.*
◊ *noun* A difficult situation: *We were in a fix when we lost the oars for our boat.*
fix (fĭks) ◊ *verb* **fixed, fixing** ◊ *noun, plural* **fixes**

fixture *noun* Something fixed or attached permanently in a place: *There are two light fixtures on the ceiling.*
fix·ture (**fĭks′**chər) ◊ *noun, plural* **fixtures**

▲ **fixture**
A light fixture

fizz *verb* To make a hissing or sputtering sound.
◊ *noun* A hissing or sputtering sound.
fizz (fĭz) ◊ *verb* **fizzed, fizzing** ◊ *noun, plural* **fizzes**

fjord *noun* A long, narrow inlet of the sea between steep cliffs or slopes.
fjord (fyôrd) ◊ *noun, plural* **fjords**

▲ **fjord**

FL The abbreviation for *Florida* used with a Zip Code.

Fla. An abbreviation for *Florida.*

flag *noun* A piece of cloth with a design that is used as a symbol, emblem, or signal.
◊ *verb* To signal with or as if with a flag.
flag (flăg) ◊ *noun, plural* **flags** ◊ *verb* **flagged, flagging**

flagpole *noun* A pole for flying a flag.
flag·pole (**flăg′**pōl′) ◊ *noun, plural* **flagpoles**

flair *noun* A natural talent or aptitude.
flair (flâr) ◊ *noun, plural* **flairs**
‖*These sound alike:* **flair, flare**

flake *noun* A small, thin piece of something.
◊ *verb* To come off in flakes.
flake (flāk) ◊ *noun, plural* **flakes** ◊ *verb* **flaked, flaking**

flame *noun* **1.** The hot, visible, and often bright gases given off by a fire. **2.** A condition of active burning: *The paper suddenly burst into flame.*
◊ *verb* To burn brightly; blaze: *The logs flamed up.*
flame (flām) ◊ *noun, plural* **flames** ◊ *verb* **flamed, flaming**

flamingo *noun* A tropical wading bird that has long legs, a long neck, and reddish or pinkish feathers.
fla·min·go (flə **mĭng′** gō) ◊ *noun, plural* **flamingos** *or* **flamingoes**

▲ **flamingo**

flammable *adjective* Easy to set fire to and able to burn very rapidly: *Gasoline is a flammable substance.*
flam·ma·ble (**flăm′**ə bəl) ◊ *adjective*

flank *noun* **1.** The fleshy part of the body between the ribs and the hip. **2.** The far left or

right side of a body of soldiers, a fort, or a naval fleet.
◊ *verb* To be placed or located at the side of: *Two chairs flanked the fireplace.*
flank (flăngk) ◊ *noun, plural* **flanks** ◊ *verb* **flanked, flanking**

flannel *noun* A soft woven cloth with a nap, usually made of wool or cotton.
flan·nel (**flăn′** əl) ◊ *noun*

flap *verb* **1.** To move or cause to move wings or arms up and down. **2.** To move or swing while fixed at one edge or corner; flutter.
◊ *noun* A flat piece attached along one side and hanging loose on the other, often forming a cover for an opening: *I licked the flap of the envelope and sealed it.*
flap (flăp) ◊ *verb* **flapped, flapping** ◊ *noun, plural* **flaps**

flapjack *noun* A pancake.
flap·jack (**flăp′**jăk′) ◊ *noun, plural* **flapjacks**

flare *verb* **1.** To burn with a sudden or unsteady flame: *The candles flared briefly just before going out.* **2.** To burst out like a flame: *Tempers flared during the discussion.* **3.** To spread outward in a shape like that of a cone: *The full skirt flared out.*
◊ *noun* **1.** A sudden or unsteady blaze of light. **2.** Something that produces a bright flame for signaling or lighting.
flare (flâr) ◊ *verb* **flared, flaring** ◊ *noun, plural* **flares**
‖*These sound alike:* **flare, flair**

flash *verb* **1.** To give out a sudden, bright light: *The fireworks flashed in the sky.* **2.** To appear or occur for an instant only: *A thought flashed through my mind.* **3.** To cause to appear suddenly and for an instant: *I flashed a warning glance at them.* **4.** To move rapidly: *A car flashed by.*
◊ *noun* **1.** A short, sudden burst of light: *We were startled by the flash of lightning.* **2.** A very short time: *We finished lunch in a flash.*
flash (flăsh) ◊ *verb* **flashed, flashing** ◊ *noun, plural* **flashes**

ă	pat	ĭ	pit	oi	**oil**	th	bath
ā	pay	ī	ride	ŏŏ	book	*th*	bathe
â	care	î	fierce	ōō	boot	ə	ago, item
ä	father	ŏ	pot	ou	**out**		pencil
ĕ	pet	ō	go	ŭ	cut		atom
ē	be	ô	paw, for	û	fur		circus

flash bulb *noun* A light bulb that produces a bright flash for taking photographs.
flash bulb ◊ *noun, plural* **flash bulbs**

flashlight *noun* A lamp powered by batteries that is small enough to be carried around.
flash·light (**flăsh′**līt′) ◊ *noun, plural* **flashlights**

flask *noun* A bottle or other container with a narrow neck.
flask (flăsk) ◊ *noun, plural* **flasks**

flat *adjective* **1.** Having a smooth, even surface: *The flat land stretched for miles in every direction.* **2.** Lying horizontally on a surface: *My book is flat on the table.* **3.** Having a wide or long surface and not much depth or thickness: *Arrange the vegetables on a flat plate.* **4.** Having lost contained air; deflated: *Our car had a flat tire.* **5.** Not changing; fixed: *We pay a flat rate for every telephone call.* **6.** Not glossy: *Flat paint is more difficult to clean.* **7.** Lower in musical pitch than is correct. **8.** Without flavor: *The sauce tastes flat.*
◊ *noun* **1.** A flat surface or part: *I hit the table with the flat of my hand.* **2.** Often **flats** An area of level, low ground: *We dug clams in the mud flats at low tide.* **3.** A deflated tire. **4.** A musical note that is one half step lower than the natural tone. **5.** A sign (♭) showing that a musical note is one half step lower in pitch than usual.
flat (flăt) ◊ *adjective* **flatter, flattest** ◊ *noun, plural* **flats**

flatcar *noun* A railroad car that has no sides or roof and is used for carrying freight.
flat·car (**flăt′**kär′) ◊ *noun, plural* **flatcars**

flatfish *noun* A fish, such as a flounder or sole, that has a flattened body and both eyes on its upper side.
flat·fish (**flăt′**fĭsh′) ◊ *noun, plural* **flatfish** *or* **flatfishes**

flatten *verb* To make or become flat.
flat·ten (**flăt′**n) ◊ *verb* **flattened, flattening**

flatter *verb* **1.** To praise in a way that is not sincere, especially in order to get something in return. **2.** To please or gratify: *I was flattered by their interest in my drawings.* **3.** To make more attractive than is really the case: *The photograph flatters you.*
flat·ter (**flăt′** ər) ◊ *verb* **flattered, flattering**

flattery *noun* Insincere praise.
flat·ter·y (**flăt′** ə rē) ◊ *noun, plural* **flatteries**

flavor *noun* **1.** The quality that causes something to have a certain taste: *The sauce had a burnt flavor.* **2.** A flavoring.
◊ *verb* To give flavor to.
fla·vor (flā′vər) ◊ *noun, plural* **flavors** ◊ *verb* **flavored, flavoring**

flavoring *noun* An ingredient that is used to flavor food.
fla·vor·ing (flā′vər ĭng) ◊ *noun, plural* **flavorings**

flaw *noun* A defect; blemish: *There is a flaw in the crystal vase.*
◊ *verb* To make or become defective.
flaw (flô) ◊ *noun, plural* **flaws** ◊ *verb* **flawed, flawing**

flawless *adjective* Without a flaw; perfect: *The singer gave a flawless recital.*
flaw·less (flô′lĭs) ◊ *adjective*

flax *noun* A plant with blue flowers. It is grown for its stems that contain a light-colored fiber from which linen is made.
flax (flăks) ◊ *noun*

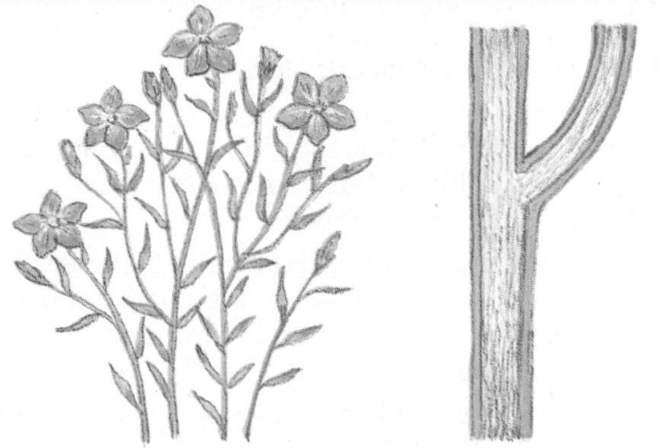

▲ **flax**

flaxen *adjective* **1.** Made of flax. **2.** Having the pale-yellow color of flax fiber.
flax·en (flăk′sən) ◊ *adjective*

flea *noun* A small, wingless insect that sucks blood from animals and human beings.
flea (flē) ◊ *noun, plural* **fleas**
‖*These sound alike:* **flea, flee**

fleck *noun* A small, irregular mark.
◊ *verb* To mark with flecks; spot.
fleck (flĕk) ◊ *noun, plural* **flecks** ◊ *verb* **flecked, flecking**

fled *verb* Past tense and past participle of **flee.**
fled (flĕd) ◊ *verb*

fledgling *noun* A young bird that is learning to fly.
fledg·ling (flĕj′lĭng) ◊ *noun, plural* **fledglings**

flee *verb* To run away.
flee (flē) ◊ *verb* **fled, fleeing**
‖*These sound alike:* **flee, flea**

fleece *noun* The wool forming the coat of an animal, especially a sheep.
fleece (flēs) ◊ *noun, plural* **fleeces**

fleet[1] *noun* **1.** A group of warships under the command of one person. **2.** The navy of a country. **3.** A number of boats, ships, or vehicles that form a group: *The company owns a fleet of cars for its sales force to use.*
fleet[1] (flēt) ◊ *noun, plural* **fleets**

fleet[2] *adjective* Able to move very quickly: *Few animals can outrun the fleet antelope.*
fleet[2] (flēt) ◊ *adjective* **fleeter, fleetest**

> ***HISTORY* • fleet[1], fleet[2]**
>
> **Fleet[1]** comes from an old English word meaning "a ship" or "a place, such as a river, where ships float." **Fleet[2]** comes from a different but related old English word meaning "to flow, go swiftly."

fleeting *adjective* Very brief: *I caught a fleeting glimpse of an eagle.*
fleet·ing (flē′tĭng) ◊ *adjective*

flesh *noun* **1.** The soft parts of the body, especially the muscles. **2.** The meat of animals eaten as food. **3.** The pulpy, usually edible part of a fruit or vegetable.
flesh (flĕsh) ◊ *noun*

flew *verb* Past tense of **fly[1].**
flew (flo͞o) ◊ *verb*
‖*These sound alike:* **flew, flu, flue**

flex *verb* To bend or cause to bend.
flex (flĕks) ◊ *verb* **flexed, flexing**

flexible *adjective* **1.** Able to bend or be bent: *Baskets are woven out of flexible twigs.* **2.** Able to change or adapt to suit new conditions: *My schedule is flexible, so come whenever you can.*
flex·i·ble (flĕk′sə bəl) ◊ *adjective*

flick *noun* A light, quick blow or stroke.
◊ *verb* To hit or move with a flick: *I flicked the dust off my coat.*
flick (flĭk) ◊ *noun, plural* **flicks** ◊ *verb* **flicked, flicking**

flicker¹ *verb* **1.** To burn or shine with an unsteady light: *The candles flickered before going out.* **2.** To move in a quick, wavering way: *Shadows flickered on the wall.*
◊ *noun* **1.** An uneven or unsteady light. **2.** A short, quick movement or expression.
flick·er¹ (flĭk′ər) ◊ *verb* **flickered, flickering** ◊ *noun, plural* **flickers**

flicker² *noun* A woodpecker with a brown back and a spotted breast.
flick·er² (flĭk′ər) ◊ *noun, plural* **flickers**

***HISTORY* • flicker¹, flicker²**

Flicker¹ comes from an old English word meaning "to flutter." **Flicker²** may come from **flick,** referring to the quick flight of this bird.

flied *verb* Past tense and past participle of **fly¹** (sense 6).
flied (flīd) ◊ *verb*

flier *or* **flyer** *noun* Someone or something that flies, especially the pilot of an aircraft.
fli·er *or* **fly·er** (flī′ər) ◊ *noun, plural* **fliers** *or* **flyers**

flight¹ *noun* **1.** The act or process of flying: *The bird's flight was almost too swift to see.* **2.** A scheduled airplane trip: *We took a flight to Dallas.* **3.** A group flying together: *I saw a flight of geese headed south for the winter.* **4.** A series of stairs.
flight¹ (flīt) ◊ *noun, plural* **flights**

flight² *noun* The act of fleeing; escape.
flight² (flīt) ◊ *noun, plural* **flights**

***HISTORY* • flight¹, flight²**

Flight¹ comes from an old English word meaning "flying, flight." **Flight²** appeared first in English about 800 years ago and meant, then as now, "the act of fleeing, running away."

ă	pat	ĭ	pit	oi	oil	th	bath
ā	pay	ī	ride	o͝o	book	*th*	bathe
â	care	î	fierce	o͞o	boot	ə	ago, item
ä	father	ŏ	pot	ou	out		pencil
ĕ	pet	ō	go	ŭ	cut		atom
ē	be	ô	paw, for	û	fur		circus

flightless *adjective* Unable to fly: *Ostriches and penguins are flightless birds.*
flight·less (flīt′lĭs) ◊ *adjective*

flimsy *adjective* Easily damaged or destroyed; not strong: *The flimsy jacket tore the first time I wore it.*
flim·sy (flĭm′zē) ◊ *adjective* **flimsier, flimsiest**

flinch *verb* To shrink as from pain or fear.
flinch (flĭnch) ◊ *verb* **flinched, flinching**

fling *verb* To throw hard; hurl: *I flung my coat on the chair.*
◊ *noun* **1.** An act of flinging; throw. **2.** A lively Scottish dance.
fling (flĭng) ◊ *verb* **flung, flinging** ◊ *noun, plural* **flings**

flint *noun* A very hard type of stone that makes sparks when struck with steel.
flint (flĭnt) ◊ *noun, plural* **flints**

flip *verb* **1.** To move or turn by tossing in the air: *Let's flip a coin to decide who goes first.* **2.** To move with a light, quick blow: *I flipped the switch but the light did not come on.*
◊ *noun* **1.** An act of flipping: *Give the hamburger a flip.* **2.** A somersault.
flip (flĭp) ◊ *verb* **flipped, flipping** ◊ *noun, plural* **flips**

flippant *adjective* Disrespectful, especially in a way that is humorous or not serious.
flip·pant (flĭp′ənt) ◊ *adjective*

flipper *noun* **1.** A wide, flat limb, as of a seal, adapted for swimming. **2.** A wide, flat rubber shoe worn for swimming and skin diving.
flip·per (flĭp′ər) ◊ *noun, plural* **flippers**

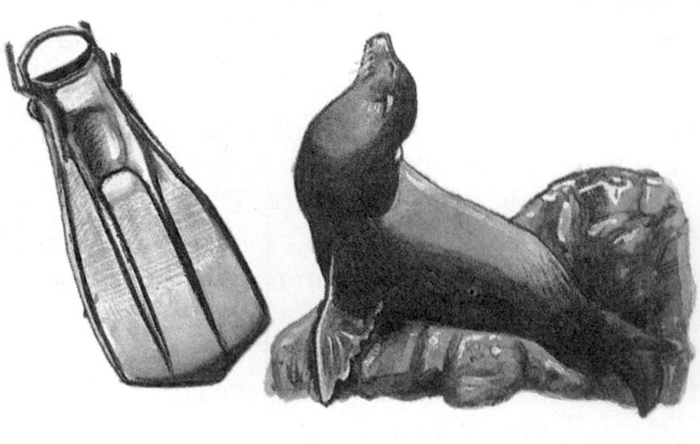

▲ **flipper**

flirt *verb* To act romantically, especially in a playful or teasing way.

◊ *noun* Someone who flirts.
flirt (flûrt) ◊ *verb* **flirted, flirting** ◊ *noun, plural* **flirts**

float *verb* **1.** To be held up in or at the top of a liquid or air: *Balloons floated in the air. Divers tried to float the sunken ship.* **2.** To move or cause to move in or through liquid or air: *Lumberjacks floated logs down the river.*
◊ *noun* **1.** A cork or other floating object on a fishing line. **2.** An anchored raft used by swimmers. **3.** A large, flat vehicle carrying an exhibit in a parade.
float (flōt) ◊ *verb* **floated, floating** ◊ *noun, plural* **floats**

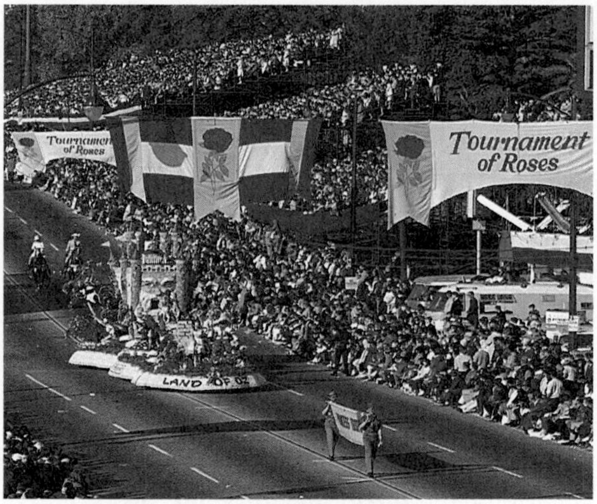

▲ **float**

flock *noun* **1.** A group of animals, such as birds or sheep, that live, travel, or feed together. **2.** A large group of people; crowd.
◊ *verb* To gather or travel in a flock.
flock (flŏk) ◊ *noun, plural* **flocks** ◊ *verb* **flocked, flocking**

floe *noun* A large, flat mass of floating ice.
floe (flō) ◊ *noun, plural* **floes**
‖*These sound alike:* **floe, flow**

flood *noun* **1.** A large flow of water over dry land. **2.** A large amount or flow: *A flood of settlers from Europe came to America.*
◊ *verb* **1.** To fill or cover with water: *The rains flooded the cellar. The river floods in the spring.* **2.** To fill or overwhelm with or as if with a flood: *Letters of complaint flooded in.*
flood (flŭd) ◊ *noun, plural* **floods** ◊ *verb* **flooded, flooding**

▲ **flood**

floodlight *noun* A lamp that produces a broad and very bright beam of light.
flood·light (flŭd′līt′) ◊ *noun, plural* **floodlights**

floor *noun* **1.** The surface of a room on which one stands. **2.** The ground or lowest surface, as of a forest or ocean. **3.** A story or level of a building.
◊ *verb* **1.** To provide with a floor. **2.** To knock down: *The swinging door floored me.* **3.** To confuse or surprise greatly: *The results of the election simply floored us.*
floor (flôr) ◊ *noun, plural* **floors** ◊ *verb* **floored, flooring**

flop *verb* **1.** To fall heavily and noisily: *I flopped down on the couch.* **2.** To move about in a clumsy way, often with a thumping or flapping noise. **3.** To fail completely.
◊ *noun* **1.** The action or sound of flopping. **2.** A complete failure: *The play was a flop.*
flop (flŏp) ◊ *verb* **flopped, flopping** ◊ *noun, plural* **flops**

floppy *adjective* Tending to or able to flop: *The dog had floppy ears.*
flop·py (flŏp′ē) ◊ *adjective* **floppier, floppiest**

floppy disk *noun* A flexible plastic disk coated with magnetic material and used to store computer data.
floppy disk ◊ *noun, plural* **floppy disks**

florist *noun* Someone whose business is the selling of flowers and plants.
flo·rist (flôr′ĭst) ◊ *noun, plural* **florists**

floss *noun* **1.** A soft, shiny silk or cotton thread used in embroidery. **2.** A strong thread used to clean between the teeth.
floss (flôs) ◊ *noun, plural* **flosses**

flounder[1] *verb* To move or act clumsily or with difficulty: *We floundered through deep snow to get to the store.*
floun·der[1] (**floun′** dər) ◊ *verb* **floundered, floundering**

flounder[2] *noun* Any of several flatfishes often used for food.
floun·der[2] (**floun′** dər) ◊ *noun, plural* **flounder** *or* **flounders**

> ***HISTORY* • flounder[1], flounder[2]**
>
> **Flounder**[1] may have been made up by combining **blunder** and *founder*, a word that once meant "to stumble violently." **Flounder**[2] comes through French from the old Scandinavian name for this fish.

flour *noun* A fine powder or meal made by grinding wheat or another grain. Flour is also made from potatoes and beans.
◊ *verb* To cover or coat with flour.
flour (flour) ◊ *noun, plural* **flours** ◊ *verb* **floured, flouring**

flourish *verb* **1.** To grow very well; thrive: *Most flowers flourish in full sunlight.* **2.** To do well; prosper: *Their business flourished and they became rich.* **3.** To wave in a vigorous or dramatic way: *The conductor of the orchestra flourished the baton.*
◊ *noun* **1.** A vigorous or dramatic waving motion. **2.** A bit of added decoration: *I signed my name with flourishes.*
flour·ish (**flûr′** ĭsh) ◊ *verb* **flourished, flourishing** ◊ *noun, plural* **flourishes**

flow *verb* **1.** To move or run freely in or as if in a stream: *Air flowed in through the window. Traffic flowed along the new highway.* **2.** To move in a steady and smooth way: *I was nervous about giving the book report, but once I began talking the words flowed.* **3.** To hang loosely and gracefully: *Long hair flowed out from under the magician's hat.*
◊ *noun* **1.** The act or process of flowing: *A dam controls the flow of water.* **2.** A flowing mass; stream: *The lava flow almost reached the town.* **3.** A continuous output or outpouring: *The telephone rang and interrupted the flow of my thoughts.*
flow (flō) ◊ *verb* **flowed, flowing** ◊ *noun, plural* **flows**
‖*These sound alike:* **flow, floe**

flower *noun* **1.** The part of a plant that produces seeds, usually with colorful petals. **2.** A plant that is grown chiefly for its flowers. **3.** The best example of something: *Ancient Athens is often considered the flower of democracy.*
◊ *verb* To produce flowers; bloom.
flow·er (**flou′** ər) ◊ *noun, plural* **flowers** ◊ *verb* **flowered, flowering**

flown *verb* Past participle of **fly**[1].
flown (flōn) ◊ *verb*

flu *noun* Influenza.
flu (flo͞o) ◊ *noun*
‖*These sound alike:* **flu, flew, flue**

flue *noun* An enclosed passage, as a pipe in a chimney, through which smoke, steam, or air may pass.
flue (flo͞o) ◊ *noun, plural* **flues**
‖*These sound alike:* **flue, flew, flu**

fluff *noun* A light, soft substance, such as that made of bits of fur or feathers: *The chicks looked like little round balls of fluff.*
◊ *verb* To make light and puffy by patting, poking, or shaking into a soft, light mass: *The nurse fluffed the patient's pillow.*
fluff (flŭf) ◊ *noun, plural* **fluffs** ◊ *verb* **fluffed, fluffing**

fluffy *adjective* **1.** Having hair, feathers, or fibers that stand out in a soft, full mass. **2.** Light, soft, and airy: *Beat the egg whites until they are fluffy.*
fluff·y (**flŭf′** ē) ◊ *adjective* **fluffier, fluffiest**

fluid *noun* A substance, such as air or water, that flows easily and takes the shape of its container. All liquids and gases are fluids.
◊ *adjective* Capable of flowing: *Mercury remains fluid at ordinary temperatures.*
flu·id (**flo͞o′** ĭd) ◊ *noun, plural* **fluids** ◊ *adjective*

ă	pat	ĭ	pit	oi	oil	th	bath
ā	pay	ī	ride	o͝o	book	*th*	bathe
â	care	î	fierce	o͞o	boot	ə	ago, item
ä	father	ŏ	pot	ou	out		pencil
ĕ	pet	ō	go	ŭ	cut		atom
ē	be	ô	paw, for	û	fur		circus

fluid ounce *noun* A unit of capacity for liquids that is equal to 1/16 pint.
fluid ounce ◊ *noun, plural* **fluid ounces**

flume *noun* **1.** A narrow gorge with a stream flowing or rushing through it. **2.** An artificial channel for flowing water.
flume (flo͞om) ◊ *noun, plural* **flumes**

flung *verb* Past tense and past participle of **fling.**
flung (flŭng) ◊ *verb*

flunk *verb* **1.** To fail a test or examination. **2.** To give a failing grade to.
flunk (flŭngk) ◊ *verb* **flunked, flunking**

flurry *noun* **1.** A sudden gust of wind. **2.** A brief, light fall of snow. **3.** A sudden burst or stir, as of interest.
flur·ry (flûr′ē) ◊ *noun, plural* **flurries**

flush *verb* **1.** To turn red in the face; blush: *I flushed at the compliment.* **2.** To wash out with a sudden, rapid flow of water: *The plumber flushed out the water pipes.*
◊ *noun* **1.** A blush or glow. **2.** A sudden flow or gush of liquid. **3.** A rush of excitement: *The first flush of enthusiasm soon faded.*
◊ *adjective* In line or on a level; even: *The door is flush with the wall.*
flush (flŭsh) ◊ *verb* **flushed, flushing** ◊ *noun, plural* **flushes** ◊ *adjective*

fluster *verb* To make nervous, upset, or confused: *The hard question flustered me.*
flus·ter (flŭs′tər) ◊ *verb* **flustered, flustering**

flute *noun* A musical instrument played by blowing across or into a hole near one end. Different notes are sounded by covering holes along its length with the fingers.
flute (flo͞ot) ◊ *noun, plural* **flutes**

▲ **flute**

flutter *verb* **1.** To flap the wings rapidly in flying or trying to fly: *A moth fluttered around the porch light.* **2.** To wave, flap, or beat rapidly: *My heart is fluttering with excitement. The curtains fluttered in the breeze.*
◊ *noun* **1.** A quick flapping or beating motion. **2.** A condition of nervous excitement: *The cast of the play was in a flutter on opening night.*
flut·ter (flŭt′ər) ◊ *verb* **fluttered, fluttering** ◊ *noun, plural* **flutters**

fly¹ *verb* **1.** To move through the air with the aid of wings or parts like wings: *Some birds cannot fly. A plane flew over our house.* **2.** To travel through air or space in an aircraft or spacecraft: *Have you ever flown in a jet?* **3.** To operate or pilot an aircraft or spacecraft: *I have always wanted to learn to fly a plane.* **4.** To carry or transport by air: *Plans were quickly made to fly supplies to the people stranded by the flood.* **5.** To move or cause to move through the air or before the wind: *Let's fly our kites today.* **6.** To hit a baseball high in the air so that it travels in an arc: *The first three batters flied out to the center fielder.* **7.** To move or go by swiftly: *I flew to the door. Time flies when you're having fun.*
◊ *noun* **1.** A baseball hit high in the air. **2.** A cloth flap covering a zipper or set of buttons.
◊ *idiom* **on the fly** In a hurry.
fly¹ (flī) ◊ *verb* **flew** *or* **flied** (for sense 6), **flown** *or* **flied** (for sense 6), **flying** ◊ *noun, plural* **flies**

fly² *noun* A winged insect, especially one of a group that includes the common housefly and many others that have a single pair of thin, clear wings.
fly² (flī) ◊ *noun, plural* **flies**

> ***HISTORY* • fly¹, fly²**
>
> **Fly¹** and **fly²** are related native English words. **Fly²** originally meant "an insect that flies."

flycatcher *noun* Any of several birds that catch flying insects.
fly·catch·er (flī′kăch′ər) ◊ *noun, plural* **flycatchers**

flyer *noun* Another spelling for **flier.**
fly·er (flī′ər) ◊ *noun, plural* **flyers**

flying fish *noun* A fish with large side fins that are spread out like wings as it leaps above the water.
flying fish ◊ *noun, plural* **flying fishes**

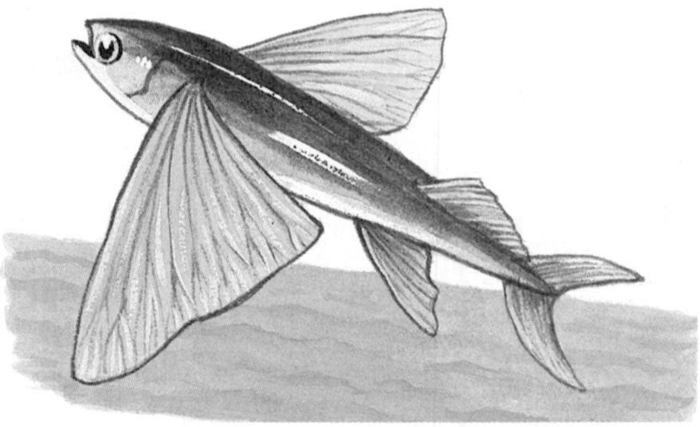

▲ **flying fish**

flying saucer *noun* An unidentified object with a disklike shape that is reported as having been seen flying in the sky.
flying saucer ◊ *noun, plural* **flying saucers**

foal *noun* A young horse, donkey, or zebra.
foal (fōl) ◊ *noun, plural* **foals**

foam *noun* A mass of very small bubbles.
◊ *verb* To form foam or come forth in foam.
foam (fōm) ◊ *noun* ◊ *verb* **foamed, foaming**

foam rubber *noun* A light, spongy form of rubber made by forcing air bubbles into liquid rubber and letting it harden. Foam rubber is used for mattresses and pillows.

focal *adjective* Of, at, or relating to a focus.
fo·cal (fō′kəl) ◊ *adjective*

focus *noun* **1.** A point at which rays of light meet after having been bent or reflected by a lens. **2.** The distance from the surface of a lens or mirror to the point where the rays of light meet. **3.** The adjustment of a lens, an eye, or a camera that gives the best image: *The camera is out of focus.* **4.** A center of interest or activity: *The focus of this chapter is the American Revolution.*
◊ *verb* **1.** To adjust in order to produce a clear image. **2.** To bring or come to a focus: *A camera lens focuses light on the film.* **3.** To concentrate or center; fix: *We focused our attention on the lesson.*
fo·cus (fō′kəs) ◊ *noun, plural* **focuses** ◊ *verb* **focused, focusing**

fodder *noun* Dry food for farm animals.
fod·der (fŏd′ər) ◊ *noun*

foe *noun* An enemy.
foe (fō) ◊ *noun, plural* **foes**

fog *noun* A mass of water droplets floating near the surface of the ground or water.
◊ *verb* To cover or become covered with fog: *Steam fogged the bathroom mirror.*
fog (fôg) ◊ *noun, plural* **fogs** ◊ *verb* **fogged, fogging**

foggy *adjective* **1.** Full of, having, or covered by fog. **2.** Confused or vague: *I haven't the foggiest idea of how to solve this problem.*
fog·gy (fô′gē) ◊ *adjective* **foggier, foggiest**

foghorn *noun* A horn that is blown to warn ships of danger in foggy weather.
fog·horn (fôg′hôrn′) ◊ *noun, plural* **foghorns**

foil[1] *verb* To keep from being successful; thwart: *The alarm foiled the thief.*
foil[1] (foil) ◊ *verb* **foiled, foiling**

foil[2] *noun* A very thin, flexible sheet of metal: *Wrap the meat in aluminum foil.*
foil[2] (foil) ◊ *noun, plural* **foils**

foil[3] *noun* A long, light, slender sword with a blunt point that is used in fencing.
foil[3] (foil) ◊ *noun, plural* **foils**

HISTORY • foil[1], foil[2], foil[3]

Foil[1] comes from an old English word that first meant "to trample." **Foil[2]** comes from a French word that came from a Latin word meaning "leaf." The origin of **foil[3]** is unknown.

fold[1] *verb* **1.** To bend or double over so that one part lies over another: *I have to fold the clean clothes and put them away.* **2.** To bend close to the body: *They folded their arms over their chests.*
◊ *noun* A line or crease formed by folding: *The paper tore easily along the fold.*
fold[1] (fōld) ◊ *verb* **folded, folding** ◊ *noun, plural* **folds**

ă	pat	ĭ	pit	oi	**oi**l	th	ba**th**
ā	pay	ī	ride	o͝o	book	*th*	ba**th**e
â	care	î	fierce	o͞o	boot	ə	ago, item
ä	father	ŏ	pot	ou	**ou**t		pencil
ĕ	pet	ō	go	ŭ	cut		atom
ē	be	ô	paw, for	û	fur		circus

fold² *noun* A pen for sheep or other domestic animals.
fold² (fōld) ◊ *noun, plural* **folds**

***HISTORY* • fold¹, fold²**

Fold¹ comes from an old English word that meant "to wrap up, fold." **Fold²** comes from a different old English word that meant "a pen for animals."

folder *noun* **1.** A folded sheet of cardboard or heavy paper used to hold loose papers. **2.** A booklet or pamphlet made of one or more folded sheets of paper.
fold·er (fōl′dər) ◊ *noun, plural* **folders**

foliage *noun* The leaves of plants or trees.
fo·li·age (fō′lē ĭj) ◊ *noun*

▲ **foliage**

folk *noun* **1.** The people who make up a nation or tribe. **2.** People of a certain kind: *City folk are used to noise and bustle.* **3. folks** People in general: *Folks in this town don't like strangers.* **4. folks** One's family or relatives: *My folks spend summers in Maine.*
folk (fōk) ◊ *noun, plural* **folk** *or* **folks**

folk dance *noun* A traditional dance of the people of a country or region.
folk dance ◊ *noun, plural* **folk dances**

folklore *noun* The beliefs, legends, customs, and other traditions handed down by a people from generation to generation.
folk·lore (fōk′lôr′) ◊ *noun*

folk music *noun* Music that is traditional among the people of a country or region. It is usually passed from person to person, and its composers are often unknown.

folk singer *noun* Someone who sings and often composes folk songs.
folk singer ◊ *noun, plural* **folk singers**

folk song *noun* A song that is part of the folk music of a people.
folk song ◊ *noun, plural* **folk songs**

folktale *noun* A traditional story handed down by the people of a country or region from one generation to the next.
folk·tale (fōk′tāl′) ◊ *noun, plural* **folktales**

follow *verb* **1.** To go or come after: *The ducklings followed their mother to the pond.* **2.** To move or go along or take the same course as: *I followed the trail for a mile until it joined the road.* **3.** To come after in order or time: *Night follows day.* **4.** To be or come as a result: *If you break the rules, trouble will follow.* **5.** To take as a guide; act in agreement with: *Follow the directions when you build the airplane model.* —See Synonyms at **obey. 6.** To work at for a livelihood: *I want to follow the trade of a printer.* **7.** To pay attention to or keep up with, especially so as to understand: *It was hard to follow their conversation.*
fol·low (fŏl′ō) ◊ *verb* **followed, following**

follower *noun* An admirer or disciple.
fol·low·er (fŏl′ō ər) ◊ *noun, plural* **followers**

following *adjective* Coming immediately after; next: *School ended on Friday, and we left on our vacation the following day.*
◊ *noun* A group of admirers or disciples.
fol·low·ing (fŏl′ō ĭng) ◊ *adjective* ◊ *noun*

follow-up *noun* Something, such as a letter or visit, that makes a previous action more effective.
fol·low-up (fŏl′ō ŭp′) ◊ *noun, plural* **follow-ups**

fond *adjective* **1.** Loving or affectionate: *They wished me a fond good night.* **2.** Having a liking for: *My cousin is very fond of skiing.*
fond (fŏnd) ◊ *adjective* **fonder, fondest**

font *noun* A basin that holds water used for baptism.
font (fŏnt) ◊ *noun, plural* **fonts**

food *noun* **1.** Anything that a plant, animal, or person can take in and use for energy and for life and growth; nourishment. **2.** Something that encourages an activity or growth: *The speech gave us food for thought.*
food (fo͞od) ◊ *noun, plural* **foods**

food chain *noun* A series of plants and animals in which each kind is a source of nourishment for the next in the series.
food chain ◊ *noun, plural* **food chains**

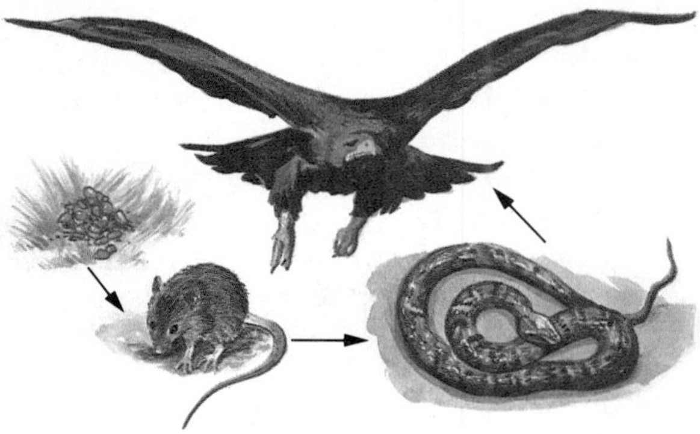

▲ **food chain**

fool *noun* **1.** A person who lacks judgment or good sense. **2.** A person who was formerly kept by a monarch or nobleman to entertain people.
◊ *verb* **1.** To trick or deceive: *You can't fool me by wearing a costume; I recognize you.* **2.** To act or speak in a playful or teasing manner; joke: *I'm not fooling; I mean it.*
fool (fo͞ol) ◊ *noun, plural* **fools** ◊ *verb* **fooled, fooling**

foolish *adjective* Lacking in judgment or good sense.
fool·ish (fo͞o′lĭsh) ◊ *adjective*

SYNONYMS

foolish, crazy, dumb, silly

It was *foolish* to go out in that cold weather without a coat. It is a *crazy* idea to think that someone can work all day and all night. It would be *dumb* to make square wheels. We've played this game so long that we're getting *silly*.
Antonym: *wise*

ă	pat	ĭ	pit	oi	oil	th	bath
ā	pay	ī	ride	o͝o	book	*th*	bathe
â	care	î	fierce	o͞o	boot	ə	ago, item
ä	father	ŏ	pot	ou	out		pencil
ĕ	pet	ō	go	ŭ	cut		atom
ē	be	ô	paw, for	û	fur		circus

foot *noun* **1.** The part of the leg of a person or animal on which it stands or walks. **2.** Something that resembles a foot in form, use, or position: *There is a rug at the foot of the stairs. Put the blanket over the foot of the bed.* **3.** A unit of length equal to 12 inches.
◊ *verb* To pay: *I'll foot the bill for dinner.*
◊ *idiom* **on foot** Walking rather than riding.
foot (fo͝ot) ◊ *noun, plural* **feet** ◊ *verb* **footed, footing**

football *noun* **1.** A game played with an inflated oval ball on a long field with goals at either end. Two teams of 11 players each try to carry the ball across the opponent's goal line or to kick it between the opponent's goal posts in order to score. **2.** The ball used in this game.
foot·ball (fo͝ot′bôl′) ◊ *noun, plural* **footballs**

foothill *noun* A low hill at or near the foot of a mountain or mountain range.
foot·hill (fo͝ot′hĭl′) ◊ *noun, plural* **foothills**

▲ **foothill**

foothold *noun* A place to put the foot so that it will not slip, as when climbing.
foot·hold (fo͝ot′hōld′) ◊ *noun, plural* **footholds**

footing *noun* **1.** A firm placing or position of the feet: *It's easy to lose your footing when the sidewalk is icy.* **2.** A foothold. **3.** Rank, position, or relationship with respect to others: *All students in this class will begin on an equal footing.*
foot·ing (fo͝ot′ĭng) ◊ *noun, plural* **footings**

footman *noun* A male servant who opens doors and waits on tables.
foot•man (fo͝ot′mən) ◊ *noun, plural* **footmen**

footnote *noun* A note at the bottom of a page that explains something in the text.
foot•note (fo͝ot′nōt′) ◊ *noun, plural* **footnotes**

footprint *noun* A mark left by a foot.
foot•print (fo͝ot′prĭnt′) ◊ *noun, plural* **footprints**

footstep *noun* **1.** A step of the foot. **2.** The sound of a step. **3.** A footprint.
foot•step (fo͝ot′stĕp′) ◊ *noun, plural* **footsteps**

footstool *noun* A low stool on which to rest the feet while sitting.
foot•stool (fo͝ot′sto͞ol′) ◊ *noun, plural* **footstools**

for *preposition* **1.** Directed or sent to: *There's a package for you on the table.* **2.** As a result of: *She cheered for joy.* **3.** Through the duration of: *He worked for an hour.* **4.** In order to go to or reach: *We started for home early in the morning.* **5.** With the purpose of finding, getting, having, keeping, or saving: *I was looking for a bargain.* **6.** In favor, support, or defense of: *The senator stands for lower taxes.* **7.** In the amount or at the price of: *I bought a book for $15.* **8.** With respect to; concerning: *Regular exercise is good for health.* **9.** In view of the normal character of: *This book is pretty short for a novel.* **10.** In spite of: *For all their experience they do a poor job.* **11.** On behalf or in honor of: *We gave a dinner party for the mayor.* **12.** In place of: *We used our hands for paddles.* **13.** Intended to belong to or be used by: *This is a recording for children.*
◊ *conjunction* Because; since: *We should leave soon, for it is getting late.*
for (fôr) ◊ *preposition* ◊ *conjunction*
‖ *These sound alike:* **for, fore, four**

forage *noun* Food, as plants or grass, for grazing animals.
◊ *verb* To hunt around, especially for food; search: *Raccoons foraged in the garbage.*
for•age (fôr′ĭj) ◊ *noun* ◊ *verb* **foraged, foraging**

forbad *verb* A past tense of **forbid.**
for•bad (fər băd′) ◊ *verb*

forbade *verb* A past tense of **forbid.**
for•bade (fər băd′ *or* fər bād′) ◊ *verb*

forbid *verb* **1.** To order against with authority; prohibit: *The rules forbid running in the hallways.* **2.** To order not to do something: *I forbid you to go.*
for•bid (fər bĭd′) ◊ *verb* **forbade** *or* **forbad, forbidden, forbidding**

forbidden *verb* Past participle of **forbid.**
for•bid•den (fər bĭd′n) ◊ *verb*

force *noun* **1.** Strength; power: *The force of the explosion shattered windows in nearby buildings.* **2.** Power, pressure, or violence used on something or someone: *The window was stuck, and we had to open it by force.* **3.** Something, as a push or pull, that changes the speed or direction in which something moves: *The force of gravity keeps us on earth.* **4.** A group of people organized and trained for a particular purpose: *Our city has a large police force.* **5.** The state of being in effect: *The old rules are no longer in force.*
◊ *verb* **1.** To make do something; compel: *The storm forced me to stay on the island until the next day.* **2.** To move, push, or drive by pressure: *The pump forces water up into the pipe.* **3.** To make, get, or produce by the use of force: *We forced our way through the crowd.* **4.** To break or pry open by using force: *I lost the key and had to force the lock.*
force (fôrs) ◊ *noun, plural* **forces** ◊ *verb* **forced, forcing**

forceful *adjective* Full of force; powerful.
force•ful (fôrs′fəl) ◊ *adjective*

forceps *noun* An instrument that looks like a pair of tongs. It is used for delicate grasping, holding, or pulling, as by surgeons or jewelers.
for•ceps (fôr′səps) ◊ *noun, plural* **forceps**

▲ **forceps**

ford *noun* A shallow place in a body of water, as a river, where one can wade across.
◊ *verb* To cross a body of water at a ford.
ford (fôrd) ◊ *noun, plural* **fords** ◊ *verb* **forded, fording**

fore *adjective & adverb* In, at, or toward the front.
◊ *noun* The front part.
fore (fôr) ◊ *adjective & adverb* ◊ *noun*
‖*These sound alike:* **fore, for, four**

fore– The prefix *fore–* means "earlier" or "in advance." To *forecast* is to tell in advance what is to happen. The prefix *fore–* also means "front" or "in front of." The *forehead* is the front part of the face above the eyes. The *foreground* is the part of a picture that is in front.

***VOCABULARY BUILDER* • fore–**

Many words that are formed with **fore–** are not entries in this dictionary. But you can figure out what these words mean by looking up the meanings of the root words and the prefix. For example:
forecourt = the part of a tennis court in front of the net
forejudge = to judge in advance

forearm *noun* The part of the arm between the wrist and the elbow.
fore·arm (fôr′ärm′) ◊ *noun, plural* **forearms**

forecast *verb* To tell in advance what is going to happen, especially after studying available information and evidence; predict: *Who can forecast the future?*
◊ *noun* A prediction of coming events or conditions: *I listened to the weather forecast.*
fore·cast (fôr′kăst′) ◊ *verb* **forecast** *or* **forecasted, forecasting** ◊ *noun, plural* **forecasts**

forefather *noun* An ancestor.
fore·fa·ther (fôr′fä′*th*ər) ◊ *noun, plural* **forefathers**

ă	pat	ĭ	pit	oi	**oil**	th	ba**th**
ā	pay	ī	ride	o͝o	b**oo**k	*th*	ba**the**
â	care	î	fierce	o͞o	b**oo**t	ə	ago, item
ä	father	ŏ	pot	ou	**ou**t		pencil
ĕ	pet	ō	go	ŭ	cut		atom
ē	be	ô	paw, for	û	fur		circus

forefinger *noun* The index finger.
fore·fin·ger (fôr′fĭng′gər) ◊ *noun, plural* **forefingers**

forefoot *noun* One of the front feet of an animal, such as a dog, that has four feet.
fore·foot (fôr′fo͝ot′) ◊ *noun, plural* **forefeet**

▲ **forefoot**

foreground *noun* A part of a scene or picture that is or seems to be closest to the person who is looking at it.
fore·ground (fôr′-ground′) ◊ *noun, plural* **foregrounds**

forehead *noun* The front part of the face above the eyes.
fore·head (fôr′ĭd *or* fôr′hĕd′) ◊ *noun, plural* **foreheads**

foreign *adjective* **1.** Being outside of one's own country: *We went to a foreign school.* **2.** Of or from another country: *I tried to learn a foreign language.* **3.** Related to or dealing with other nations or governments.
for·eign (fôr′ĭn) ◊ *adjective*

foreigner *noun* A person from a foreign country.
for·eign·er (fôr′ə nər) ◊ *noun, plural* **foreigners**

foreleg *noun* One of the front legs of an animal with four legs.
fore·leg (fôr′lĕg′) ◊ *noun, plural* **forelegs**

foreman *noun* **1.** A person who is in charge of a group of workers, as at a factory. **2.** The member of a jury who acts as chairman and announces the verdict to the court.
fore·man (fôr′mən) ◊ *noun, plural* **foremen**

foremost *adjective* First in rank, position, or importance; chief.
fore·most (fôr′mōst′) ◊ *adjective*

forerunner *noun* Something that comes before and signals the approach of another: *The harpsichord was the forerunner of the piano.*
fore·run·ner (fôr′rŭn′ər) ◊ *noun, plural* **forerunners**

foresaw *verb* Past tense of **foresee.**
fore·saw (fôr sô′) ◊ *verb*

foresee *verb* To see or know in advance: *I foresee trouble.*
fore·see (fôr sē′) ◊ *verb* **foresaw, foreseen, foreseeing**

foreseen *verb* Past participle of **foresee.**
fore·seen (fôr sēn′) ◊ *verb*

foresight *noun* **1.** The ability to foresee. **2.** Care or steps taken to get ready for the future: *During the blizzard I was glad I'd had the foresight to buy enough groceries.*
fore·sight (fôr′sīt′) ◊ *noun*

forest *noun* A dense growth of trees covering a large area.
for·est (fôr′ĭst) ◊ *noun, plural* **forests**

forestall *verb* To prevent, put off, or interfere with by taking action in advance: *I left the room to forestall questions.*
fore·stall (fôr stôl′) ◊ *verb* **forestalled, forestalling**

forester *noun* A person trained in forestry.
for·est·er (fôr′ĭ stər) ◊ *noun, plural* **foresters**

forestry *noun* The science and work of developing and caring for forests.
for·est·ry (fôr′ĭ strē) ◊ *noun*

foretell *verb* To tell of in advance; predict: *The prophet foretold a glorious future for the young ruler.*
fore·tell (fôr tĕl′) ◊ *verb* **foretold, foretelling**

foretold *verb* Past tense and past participle of **foretell.**
fore·told (fôr tōld′) ◊ *verb*

forever *adverb* **1.** For all time; always: *I'll be your friend forever.* **2.** At all times; constantly: *Why are you forever complaining and finding fault?*
for·ev·er (fər ĕv′ər) ◊ *adverb*

forewoman *noun* **1.** A woman in charge of a group of workers, as at a factory. **2.** The chairwoman and spokesperson of a jury.
fore·wom·an (fôr′wo͝om′ən) ◊ *noun, plural* **forewomen**

forfeit *verb* To lose or give up because of a fault, error, or offense: *By failing to appear, the team forfeited the game.*
◊ *noun* Something lost or given up because of a fault, error, or offense.
for·feit (fôr′fĭt) ◊ *verb* **forfeited, forfeiting** ◊ *noun, plural* **forfeits**

forgave *verb* Past tense of **forgive.**
for·gave (fər gāv′) ◊ *verb*

forge[1] *noun* A furnace or hearth where metal is heated so that it can be shaped by hammering or bending.
◊ *verb* **1.** To shape metal by heating in a forge and hammering. **2.** To make, shape, or form by or as if by forging: *The coach forged the basketball team into champions.* **3.** To copy or imitate in order to deceive; counterfeit: *Do you know who forged the signature?*
forge[1] (fôrj) ◊ *noun, plural* **forges** ◊ *verb* **forged, forging**

▲ **forge**[1]

forge[2] *verb* To move forward in a slow and steady way: *The ship forged ahead through the stormy sea.*
forge[2] (fôrj) ◊ *verb* **forged, forging**

***HISTORY* • forge[1], forge[2]**

Forge[1] comes through French from a Latin word meaning "a blacksmith's workshop." The origin of **forge**[2] is unknown.

forget *verb* **1.** To be unable to bring to mind; fail to remember: *I forgot my friend's new address.* **2.** To fail by accident to do, take, or use: *Don't forget to take your keys.*
for·get (fər gĕt′) ◊ *verb* **forgot, forgotten** *or* **forgot, forgetting**

forgetful *adjective* Apt to forget: *I am so forgetful I often leave my keys at home.*
for·get·ful (fər gĕt′fəl) ◊ *adjective*

F

forget-me-not *noun* A small low plant with clusters of blue flowers.
for·get-me-not (fər gĕt′ mē nŏt′) ◊ *noun, plural* **forget-me-nots**

▲ **forget-me-not**

forgive *verb* To stop being angry at or blaming; excuse: *Forgive me for behaving so badly.* —See Synonyms at **pardon.**
for·give (fər gĭv′) ◊ *verb* **forgave, forgiven, forgiving**

forgiven *verb* Past participle of **forgive.**
for·giv·en (fər gĭv′ ən) ◊ *verb*

forgiveness *noun* The act of forgiving or condition of being forgiven.
for·give·ness (fər gĭv′ nĭs) ◊ *noun*

forgot *verb* Past tense and a past participle of **forget.**
for·got (fər gŏt′) ◊ *verb*

forgotten *verb* A past participle of **forget.**
for·got·ten (fər gŏt′ n) ◊ *verb*

fork *noun* **1.** A utensil with a handle and several prongs for use in lifting and eating food. **2.** A pitchfork. **3.** The place where something divides into two or more parts: *Swallows built a nest in a fork of the tree.*
◊ *verb* **1.** To pick up, carry, or pitch with a fork. **2.** To divide into branches: *If you look at the map, you'll see that the interstate highway forks here.*
fork (fôrk) ◊ *noun, plural* **forks** ◊ *verb* **forked, forking**

forlorn *adjective* Left alone and miserable.
for·lorn (fôr lôrn′) ◊ *adjective*

form *noun* **1.** The shape, structure, or outline of something: *The biscuits were made in the form of a circle.* **2.** The state, character, or way in which a thing exists; kind or sort: *Light is a form of energy.* **3.** A customary way of doing something: *They sent my parents a copy of the report as a matter of form.* **4.** A printed sheet with blanks for information: *I filled out a medical form before going to camp.* **5.** Any of the different ways a word may be spelled or pronounced: *Feet is the plural form of foot.*
◊ *verb* **1.** To give form to; shape: *We mixed flour and water to form paste.* —See Synonyms at **make. 2.** To come or cause to come into being: *Buds form in the spring.* **3.** To make up; constitute: *Three small streams joined to form a great river.*
form (fôrm) ◊ *noun, plural* **forms** ◊ *verb* **formed, forming**

formal *adjective* Following the usual forms, customs, or rules: *I received a formal wedding invitation.*
◊ *noun* Something, as a dance, that requires a person to dress up.
for·mal (fôr′ məl) ◊ *adjective* ◊ *noun, plural* **formals**

formation *noun* **1.** The act or process of forming: *Cold caused the formation of frost on the window.* **2.** Something that is formed. **3.** A particular arrangement: *They marched in parade formation.*
for·ma·tion (fôr mā′ shən) ◊ *noun, plural* **formations**

former *adjective* **1.** Coming or happening earlier in time: *I met my former teacher.* **2.** Being the first or first mentioned of two: *I play golf and tennis but enjoy the former sport more.*
for·mer (fôr′ mər) ◊ *adjective*

formula *noun* **1.** A set of symbols showing the composition of a chemical compound: *H_2O is the formula for water.* **2.** A set of symbols in mathematics that expresses a rule or principle: *The teacher gave us the formula for finding the area of a triangle.*
for·mu·la (fôr′ myə lə) ◊ *noun, plural* **formulas**

ă	pat	ĭ	pit	oi	**oi**l	th	ba**th**
ā	pay	ī	ride	o͝o	b**oo**k	*th*	ba**th**e
â	care	î	fierce	o͞o	b**oo**t	ə	**a**go, it**e**m
ä	father	ŏ	pot	ou	**ou**t		penc**i**l
ĕ	pet	ō	go	ŭ	cut		at**o**m
ē	be	ô	paw, for	û	fur		circ**u**s

forsake *verb* To give up or leave; abandon: *Do not forsake a friend who needs help.*
for·sake (fôr sāk′) ◊ *verb* **forsook, forsaken, forsaking**

forsaken *verb* Past participle of **forsake.**
for·sak·en (fôr sā′kən) ◊ *verb*

forsook *verb* Past tense of **forsake.**
for·sook (fôr so͝ok′) ◊ *verb*

forsythia *noun* A garden shrub with yellow flowers that bloom early in spring.
for·syth·i·a (fôr sĭth′ē ə) ◊ *noun, plural* **forsythias**

fort *noun* A fortified area or building.
fort (fôrt) ◊ *noun, plural* **forts**

▲ **fort**

forth *adverb* **1.** Out into view: *The bushes put forth leaves and flowers.* **2.** Forward in time, order, or place; onward: *From this day forth I will work harder.*
forth (fôrth) ◊ *adverb*
‖*These sound alike:* **forth, fourth**

fortieth *noun* **1.** The number in a series that matches the number forty. **2.** One of forty equal parts, written 1/40.
◊ *adjective* Coming after the thirty-ninth.
for·ti·eth (fôr′tē ĭth) ◊ *noun, plural* **fortieths** ◊ *adjective*

fortification *noun* **1.** The act or process of fortifying. **2.** Something, as a wall or moat, that fortifies, strengthens, or defends.
for·ti·fi·ca·tion (fôr′tə fĭ kā′shən) ◊ *noun, plural* **fortifications**

fortify *verb* **1.** To make strong, as against attack: *They fortified the castle by digging deep trenches around it.* **2.** To improve the quality of, as by adding; enrich: *The flour was fortified with vitamins.*
for·ti·fy (fôr′tə fī′) ◊ *verb* **fortified, fortifying**

fortress *noun* A fort or fortification.
for·tress (fôr′trĭs) ◊ *noun, plural* **fortresses**

fortunate *adjective* Having good fortune; lucky: *I feel fortunate to have met them.*
for·tu·nate (fôr′chə nĭt) ◊ *adjective*

fortune *noun* **1.** The luck that comes to a person; chance: *I had the good fortune to meet many nice people during my visit.* **2.** What will happen to a person in the future; fate. **3.** A large amount of money or property; wealth: *Our neighbor has a fortune in twentieth-century paintings.*
for·tune (fôr′chən) ◊ *noun, plural* **fortunes**

fortuneteller *noun* A person who claims to be able to predict future events.
for·tune·tell·er (fôr′chən tĕl′ər) ◊ *noun, plural* **fortunetellers**

forty *noun* A number, written 40, that is equal to the product of 10×4.
◊ *adjective* Being equal to ten times four.
for·ty (fôr′tē) ◊ *noun, plural* **forties** ◊ *adjective*

forum *noun* **1.** The public square of an ancient Roman city where people gathered for meetings and business. **2.** A meeting for discussing openly matters of public interest.
fo·rum (fôr′əm) ◊ *noun, plural* **forums**

forward *adjective* **1.** At, near, or belonging to the front of something: *I like to sit in the forward part of a train.* **2.** Going or moving toward a position in front: *The runner made a move forward.*
◊ *adverb* **1.** To or toward the front: *Please step forward.* **2.** In the future: *I look forward to seeing you.*
◊ *noun* A player in certain games, as basketball, who is part of the front line.
◊ *verb* To send on, especially to a new destination or address: *We have moved, but the post office forwards all our mail.*
for·ward (fôr′wərd) ◊ *adjective* ◊ *adverb* ◊ *noun, plural* **forwards** ◊ *verb* **forwarded, forwarding**

forwards *adverb* Forward.
for·wards (fôr′wərdz) ◊ *adverb*

fossil *noun* The remains or traces of a plant or animal of an earlier age. Fossils are embedded in rock or in the earth's crust.
fos·sil (fŏs′əl) ◊ *noun, plural* **fossils**

▲ **fossil**

foster *verb* To aid the growth and development of: *Concerts foster interest in music.*
◊ *adjective* Receiving, sharing, or giving care like that of a parent although not related by blood or adoption: *There are three foster children in our home.*
fos·ter (fô′stər) ◊ *verb* **fostered, fostering** ◊ *adjective*

fought *verb* Past tense and past participle of **fight.**
fought (fôt) ◊ *verb*

foul *adjective* **1.** Sickening in taste, smell, or appearance: *We opened the windows to get rid of the foul air in the attic.* **2.** Stormy and unpleasant: *Foul weather kept us indoors.* **3.** Not according to the rules; unfair. **4.** Being outside a foul line: *The batter hit a foul ball.*
◊ *noun* A violation of a rule of play in a game or sport.
◊ *verb* **1.** To make or become foul: *Black smoke fouled the air.* **2.** To commit a foul in a game or sport.
foul (foul) ◊ *adjective* **fouler, foulest** ◊ *noun, plural* **fouls** ◊ *verb* **fouled, fouling**
‖*These sound alike:* **foul, fowl**

foul line *noun* Either of the two straight lines that run from home plate through first or third base to the end of a baseball field.
foul line ◊ *noun, plural* **foul lines**

found¹ *verb* To bring into being; establish: *They are trying to found a new company.*
found¹ (found) ◊ *verb* **founded, founding**

ă	pat	ĭ	pit	oi	**oil**	th	**bath**
ā	pay	ī	ride	o͝o	**book**	*th*	**bathe**
â	care	î	fierce	o͞o	**boot**	ə	ago, item
ä	father	ŏ	pot	ou	**out**		pencil
ĕ	pet	ō	**go**	ŭ	cut		atom
ē	be	ô	paw, for	û	**fur**		circus

found² *verb* Past tense and past participle of **find.**
found² (found) ◊ *verb*

foundation *noun* **1.** The act of founding; creation. **2.** The basis on which something rests or is developed: *That rumor has no foundation in fact.* **3.** The base that supports a structure: *The foundation of the school was made of huge blocks of granite.*
foun·da·tion (foun **dā**′shən) ◊ *noun, plural* **foundations**

foundry *noun* A place where metals are melted and then molded.
foun·dry (**foun**′drē) ◊ *noun, plural* **foundries**

fountain *noun* **1.** A stream or jet of water, as for drinking or for decoration. **2.** A point of origin; source: *Our geography book is a fountain of information about the world.*
foun·tain (**foun**′tən) ◊ *noun, plural* **fountains**

fountain pen *noun* A pen using ink that goes through a tube to the writing point.
fountain pen ◊ *noun, plural* **fountain pens**

four *noun* A number, written 4, that is equal to the sum of 3 + 1.
◊ *adjective* Being one more than three.
four (fôr) ◊ *noun, plural* **fours** ◊ *adjective*
‖*These sound alike:* **four, for, fore**

fourteen *noun* A number, written 14, that is equal to the sum of 13 + 1.
◊ *adjective* Being one more than thirteen.
four·teen (**fôr′ tēn′**) ◊ *noun, plural* **fourteens** ◊ *adjective*

fourteenth *noun* **1.** The number in a series that matches the number fourteen. **2.** One of fourteen equal parts, written 1/14.
◊ *adjective* Coming after the thirteenth.
four·teenth (**fôr′ tēnth′**) ◊ *noun, plural* **fourteenths** ◊ *adjective*

fourth *noun* **1.** The number in a series that matches the number four. **2.** One of four equal parts, written 1/4.
◊ *adjective* Coming after the third.
fourth (fôrth) ◊ *noun, plural* **fourths** ◊ *adjective*
‖*These sound alike:* **fourth, forth**

fowl *noun* A bird, as a chicken, duck, turkey, or pheasant, that is raised or hunted for food.
fowl (foul) ◊ *noun, plural* **fowl** *or* **fowls**
‖*These sound alike:* **fowl, foul**

fox *noun* An animal that has a pointed snout, upright ears, a long, bushy tail, and thick fur.

Foxes are related to the dog and wolf.
fox (fŏks) ◊ *noun, plural* **foxes**

▲ **fox**

foxfire *noun* A phosphorescent glow on rotting wood in swamps.
fox·fire (**fŏks'**fīr') ◊ *noun*

foxhound *noun* A hound with a smooth coat that is trained to hunt foxes.
fox·hound (**fŏks'**hound') ◊ *noun, plural* **foxhounds**

fraction *noun* **1.** Two numbers with a line between them that express a part of a whole. The fraction $^7/_{10}$ means that the whole is divided into 10 equal amounts, and 7 of them make up the part expressed by the fraction. The 10 is called the denominator and the 7 is called the numerator of the fraction. **2.** A part of a whole; portion: *Only a small fraction of the people voted.*
frac·tion (**frăk'**shən) ◊ *noun, plural* **fractions**

fracture *noun* **1.** The act of breaking or condition of being broken. **2.** A break or crack, as in a bone.
◊ *verb* To break or cause to break: *I fell and fractured a rib.*
frac·ture (**frăk'**chər) ◊ *noun, plural* **fractures** ◊ *verb* **fractured, fracturing**

fragile *adjective* Easily damaged or broken; delicate: *The crystal vase is fragile.*
frag·ile (**frăj'**əl) ◊ *adjective*

fragment *noun* **1.** A piece or part broken off from a whole: *I dropped the plate, and it shattered into fragments.* **2.** Something that is incomplete: *We only heard a fragment of their conversation.*
frag·ment (**frăg'**mənt) ◊ *noun, plural* **fragments**

fragrance *noun* A sweet or pleasant odor: *I breathed in the fragrance of pine.* —See Synonyms at **smell.**
fra·grance (**frā'**grəns) ◊ *noun, plural* **fragrances**

fragrant *adjective* Having a pleasant odor.
fra·grant (**frā'**grənt) ◊ *adjective*

frail *adjective* **1.** Lacking physical strength; weak: *I feel frail after my bout of flu.* **2.** Easily broken or damaged; fragile: *That antique chair is frail.*
frail (frāl) ◊ *adjective* **frailer, frailest**

frame *noun* **1.** A structure that shapes or supports something: *The frame of the umbrella is made of metal.* **2.** An open structure or rim used to enclose, hold, or border something: *We put the photograph in a silver frame.* **3.** The structure of the human body: *That athlete has a large frame.*
◊ *verb* **1.** To put together; construct: *The lawyer framed the questions in a careful way.* **2.** To enclose in or as if in a frame: *Your hair frames your face perfectly.*
frame (frām) ◊ *noun, plural* **frames** ◊ *verb* **framed, framing**

framework *noun* A structure that consists of fitted and connected parts and encloses or supports something: *The skyscraper has a framework of steel.*
frame·work (**frām'**wûrk') ◊ *noun, plural* **frameworks**

franc *noun* A unit of money used in France, Switzerland, and various other countries.
franc (frăngk) ◊ *noun, plural* **francs**
‖*These sound alike:* **franc, frank**

frank *adjective* Free and open in expressing one's thoughts and feelings: *You might as well be frank; I really want to know the truth.*
frank (frăngk) ◊ *adjective* **franker, frankest**
‖*These sound alike:* **frank, franc**

frankfurter *noun* A smoked sausage of beef, beef and pork, or chicken.
frank·furt·er (**frăngk'**fər tər) ◊ *noun, plural* **frankfurters**

frantic *adjective* Very much excited, as from fear or worry: *The frantic parents looked everywhere for their lost child.*
fran·tic (**frăn'**tĭk) ◊ *adjective*

fraud *noun* **1.** The use of deceit to cheat or get an unfair advantage; trickery: *The mayor won the election by fraud.* **2.** A person who is

not what he or she pretends to be. —See Synonyms at **impostor.**
fraud (frôd) ◊ *noun, plural* **frauds**

fray *verb* To wear or become worn away, especially along an edge, so that loose threads show: *The rope frayed and broke.*
fray (frā) ◊ *verb* **frayed, fraying**

freckle *noun* A small brown spot on the skin.
freck·le (**frĕk′** əl) ◊ *noun, plural* **freckles**

▲ **freckle**

free *adjective* **1.** Not controlled by another or others: *The United States is a free country.* **2.** Able to do, act, or think as one wishes: *Feel perfectly free to refuse the invitation.* **3.** Not affected by or subject to something: *The tests showed that I was free of infection.* **4.** Given or provided without a charge: *We won a free meal at a fancy restaurant.*
◊ *adverb* Without charge.
◊ *verb* To set or make free: *We opened the cage and freed the bird.*
free (frē) ◊ *adjective* **freer, freest** ◊ *adverb* ◊ *verb* **freed, freeing**

freedom *noun* **1.** The condition of being free. **2.** The right to use or enjoy something freely.
free·dom (**frē′** dəm) ◊ *noun, plural* **freedoms**

freeway *noun* A wide highway on which vehicles may travel without paying tolls.
free·way (**frē′** wā′) ◊ *noun, plural* **freeways**

freeze *verb* **1.** To change from a liquid to a solid by loss of heat: *The pond froze over during the cold night.* **2.** To be uncomfortably cold: *I forgot my gloves, and my hands are freezing.* **3.** To make or become motionless or unable to move: *I heard a noise and froze in my tracks.*
◊ *noun* A period of very cold weather.
freeze (frēz) ◊ *verb* **froze, frozen, freezing** ◊ *noun, plural* **freezes**

freezer *noun* A refrigerator or a very cold compartment in a refrigerator for freezing foods and storing them.
freez·er (**frē′** zər) ◊ *noun, plural* **freezers**

freight *noun* **1.** Goods carried by a train, ship, truck, or other vehicle. **2.** The act or business of moving goods from one place to another.
freight (frāt) ◊ *noun*

freighter *noun* A ship that is used to move goods from one port to another.
freight·er (**frā′** tər) ◊ *noun, plural* **freighters**

French *noun* **1.** (*used with a plural verb*) The people of France. **2.** The language of France.
◊ *adjective* Of or relating to France, the French, or the French language.
French (frĕnch) ◊ *noun* ◊ *adjective*

French-Canadian *noun* A Canadian who has French ancestors.
◊ *adjective* Of or relating to the French-Canadians.
French-Ca·na·di·an (frĕnch′kə **nā′** dē ən) ◊ *noun, plural* **French-Canadians** ◊ *adjective*

French fries *plural noun* Long, narrow pieces of potatoes fried in deep fat until crisp.

French horn *noun* A brass musical instrument with a coiled tube and a wide bell at the end. It is played by pressing valves while blowing into the mouthpiece.
French horn ◊ *noun, plural* **French horns**

▲ **French horn**

frenzy *noun* Wild excitement: *The crowd went into a frenzy when the home team won.*
fren·zy (**frĕn′** zē) ◊ *noun, plural* **frenzies**

ă	pat	ĭ	pit	oi	**oil**	th	bath
ā	pay	ī	ride	ŏŏ	book	*th*	bathe
â	care	î	fierce	ōō	boot	ə	ago, item
ä	father	ŏ	pot	ou	**out**		pencil
ĕ	pet	ō	go	ŭ	cut		atom
ē	be	ô	paw, for	û	fur		circus

frequency *noun* **1.** The number of times that something happens within a certain amount of time: *Snowstorms in our area are increasing in frequency during the winter months.* **2.** The condition of happening often: *The frequency of your complaints annoys us.*
fre·quen·cy (frē′kwən sē) ◊ *noun, plural* **frequencies**

frequent *adjective* Occurring or appearing often: *I am a frequent visitor at the museum.*
fre·quent (frē′kwənt) ◊ *adjective*

fresh *adjective* **1.** Just made, grown, or gathered: *We ate warm, fresh bread with our salad.* —See Synonyms at **new.** **2.** Containing little or no salt: *Ships carry fresh water for drinking.* **3.** New; additional: *The detective looked for fresh clues.* **4.** New and unusual; different: *Let's take a fresh approach to the math problems.* **5.** Not yet used or soiled; clean: *Here are some fresh paper towels.* **6.** Rested; revived: *I feel fresh as a daisy.* **7.** Clean and refreshing: *They went out for some fresh air.* **8.** Having no respect or modesty; rude: *Don't make fresh remarks to your elders.* —See Synonyms at **impertinent.**
fresh (frĕsh) ◊ *adjective* **fresher, freshest**

freshen *verb* To make or become clean and tidy: *I took a shower to freshen up.*
fresh·en (frĕsh′ən) ◊ *verb* **freshened, freshening**

freshman *noun* A student in the first year of high school or college.
fresh·man (frĕsh′mən) ◊ *noun, plural* **freshmen**

freshwater *adjective* Of or living in water that is not salty: *Trout are freshwater fish.*
fresh·wa·ter (frĕsh′wô′tər) ◊ *adjective*

fret *verb* To be or cause to be uneasy or troubled; worry: *Later I fretted over whether I had done the right thing.*
fret (frĕt) ◊ *verb* **fretted, fretting**

Fri. The abbreviation for *Friday.*

friction *noun* **1.** The rubbing of one object or surface against another: *Constant friction wore out the heels of my shoes.* **2.** A force that slows down the motion of an object that is touching something else as it moves: *Friction causes a rolling ball to stop finally.* **3.** Disagreement; conflict: *We try to avoid friction in our household.*
fric·tion (frĭk′shən) ◊ *noun, plural* **frictions**

Friday *noun* The sixth day of the week.
Fri·day (frī′dē) ◊ *noun, plural* **Fridays**

> ***HISTORY* • Friday**
>
> Four of the seven days of the week were named after the gods that the English believed in before they became Christians. **Friday** was named after the queen of these gods.

friend *noun* **1.** A person one knows, likes, and enjoys being with. **2.** Someone who supports a group, cause, or movement.
friend (frĕnd) ◊ *noun, plural* **friends**

friendly *adjective* **1.** Showing or encouraging friendship: *My new neighbor gave me a friendly smile.* **2.** Liking to meet and talk with others; amiable: *A friendly guide asked us if we needed directions.*
friend·ly (frĕnd′lē) ◊ *adjective* **friendlier, friendliest**

friendship *noun* **1.** The condition of being friends. **2.** A feeling of warmth toward another person.
friend·ship (frĕnd′shĭp′) ◊ *noun, plural* **friendships**

fright *noun* Sudden, strong fear; terror.
fright (frīt) ◊ *noun, plural* **frights**

frighten *verb* **1.** To make or become afraid; alarm: *The flash of lightning frightened us.* **2.** To drive or force by causing fear: *The loud noise frightened the birds away.*
fright·en (frīt′n) ◊ *verb* **frightened, frightening**

> ***SYNONYMS***
>
> ***frighten, scare, terrify***
>
> I was so *frightened* by the noise that I could hardly move. The police officer *scared* the robbers. If I were ever chased by a lion, I would be *terrified.*

frightful *adjective* Causing fear; alarming: *I was awakened by a frightful clap of thunder.*
fright·ful (frīt′fəl) ◊ *adjective*

frigid *adjective* Extremely cold: *Frigid winds blew from the north.*
frig·id (frĭj′ĭd) ◊ *adjective*

fringe *noun* **1.** A border or edge of hanging threads or strips. Fringes are used on curtains and bedspreads for decoration. **2.** Something that is similar to a fringe: *The lawn ended with a fringe of bushes.*
fringe (frĭnj) ◊ *noun, plural* **fringes**

▲ **fringe**

Frisbee *noun* Trademark for a saucer-shaped toy. It glides through the air when it is thrown back and forth between several players.
Fris·bee (**frĭz′**bē) ◊ *noun, plural* **Frisbees**

frisky *adjective* Energetic, lively, and playful.
frisk·y (**frĭs′**kē) ◊ *adjective* **friskier, friskiest**

fritter *verb* To waste money or time bit by bit: *Don't fritter away your money on junk food.*
frit·ter (**frĭt′**ər) ◊ *verb* **frittered, frittering**

fro *adverb* Away; back.
◊ *idiom* **to and fro** Back and forth: *I pushed the swing to and fro.*
fro (frō) ◊ *adverb*

frock *noun* A girl's or woman's dress.
frock (frŏk) ◊ *noun, plural* **frocks**

frog *noun* A small animal with smooth skin, webbed feet, and long hind legs. Frogs are amphibians and live in or near water. They swim well and can make long jumps.
frog (frôg) ◊ *noun, plural* **frogs**

frogman *noun* A swimmer who uses an oxygen tank and other equipment to work underwater.
frog·man (**frôg′**măn′) ◊ *noun, plural* **frogmen**

frolic *verb* To behave playfully; romp: *The dogs frolicked in the fresh snow.*
frol·ic (**frŏl′**ĭk) ◊ *verb* **frolicked, frolicking**

ă	pat	ĭ	pit	oi	**oil**	th	**bath**
ā	pay	ī	ride	o͝o	book	*th*	bathe
â	care	î	fierce	o͞o	boot	ə	ago, item
ä	father	ŏ	pot	ou	**out**		pencil
ĕ	pet	ō	go	ŭ	cut		atom
ē	be	ô	paw, for	û	fur		circus

from *preposition* **1.** Beginning at; starting with: *We walked home from the station.* **2.** Originating with or in: *Bring a note from your parents.* **3.** Because of: *I was weak from hunger.* **4.** Out of: *I took a book from the shelf.* **5.** So as not to be engaged in: *The noise kept me from concentrating.* **6.** At a distance measured in relation to: *The sea is four miles from here.* **7.** As opposed to: *You're old enough to know right from wrong.*
from (frŭm *or* frŏm *or* frəm) ◊ *preposition*

frond *noun* The leaf of a fern or a palm tree.
frond (frŏnd) ◊ *noun, plural* **fronds**

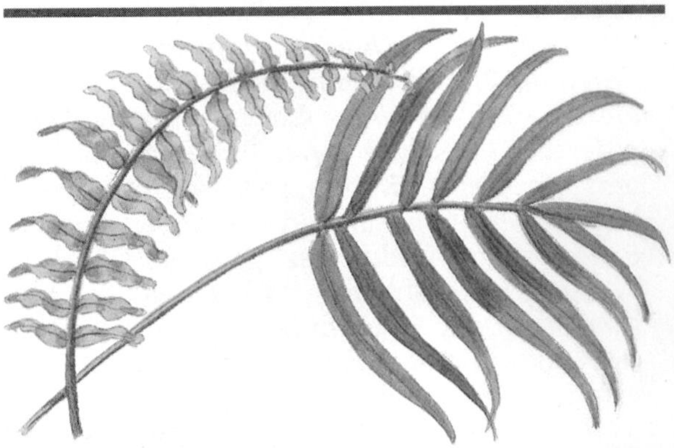

▲ **frond**

front *noun* **1.** The forward part or surface of a thing or place: *The front of a shirt has buttons.* **2.** The area directly ahead of the forward part: *There was a line in front of the theater.* **3.** A leading position: *Our team is still in front.* **4.** Land next to a body of water or a street: *There are wharves on the river front.* **5.** The boundary between two masses of air at different temperatures.
◊ *adjective* In or facing the front: *The front door is locked.*
◊ *verb* To look out; face: *Our building fronts on the park.*
front (frŭnt) ◊ *noun, plural* **fronts** ◊ *adjective* ◊ *verb* **fronted, fronting**

frontier *noun* **1.** A boundary between countries or the land along such a boundary. **2.** A remote area beyond which people do not live: *The American frontier gradually moved westward.* **3.** A subject, field, or area of activity that is just beginning to be studied or understood.
fron·tier (frŭn **tîr′**) ◊ *noun, plural* **frontiers**

frost *noun* **1.** A covering of small ice particles formed from frozen water vapor: *Our windows were covered with frost.* **2.** Air temperatures below freezing.
◊ *verb* **1.** To cover with or as if with frost. **2.** To cover with frosting.
frost (frôst) ◊ *noun, plural* **frosts** ◊ *verb* **frosted, frosting**

frostbite *noun* Injury to a part of the body as a result of exposure to very cold temperatures.
frost·bite (**frôst′** bīt′) ◊ *noun*

frosting *noun* A coating of sugar and other ingredients, used to decorate cakes or cookies.
frost·ing (**frô′** stĭng) ◊ *noun, plural* **frostings**

froth *noun* A mass of bubbles in or on a liquid; foam: *Look at the froth on the milk.*
◊ *verb* To pour forth bubbles; foam.
froth (frôth) ◊ *noun, plural* **froths** ◊ *verb* **frothed, frothing**

frown *verb* **1.** To wrinkle the forehead as a sign that one is puzzled, unhappy, or thinking. **2.** To look with disapproval; be against: *The teacher frowns on lateness.*
◊ *noun* The act of wrinkling the forehead when puzzled, unhappy, or thinking.
frown (froun) ◊ *verb* **frowned, frowning** ◊ *noun, plural* **frowns**

froze *verb* Past tense of **freeze.**
froze (frōz) ◊ *verb*

frozen *verb* Past participle of **freeze.**
fro·zen (**frō′** zən) ◊ *verb*

frugal *adjective* **1.** Careful in spending and managing money; thrifty: *Frugal people save leftover food.* **2.** Costing little: *We had a frugal lunch of leftovers.*
fru·gal (**fro͞o′** gəl) ◊ *adjective*

fruit *noun* **1.** The part of a flowering plant that contains seeds, as a pod, berry, or nut. **2.** A seed-bearing plant part that is fleshy or juicy, eaten as food. Apples, oranges, grapes, strawberries, and bananas are fruits.
fruit (fro͞ot) ◊ *noun, plural* **fruit** *or* **fruits**

frustrate *verb* **1.** To keep from reaching a goal or carrying out a plan: *I wanted to study that afternoon, but constant interruptions frustrated me.* **2.** To cause to feel puzzled or helpless; discourage: *The hard questions on the test frustrated us.*
frus·trate (**frŭs′** trāt′) ◊ *verb* **frustrated, frustrating**

fry *verb* To cook over direct heat in hot oil or fat: *Fry the chicken lightly in butter.*
fry (frī) ◊ *verb* **fried, frying**

frying pan *noun* A shallow pan with a long handle, used for frying foods.
frying pan ◊ *noun, plural* **frying pans**

LANGUAGE DETECTIVE

frying pan

The term *frying pan* is used all over the United States, but many people use a different word for a frying pan that is made out of cast iron. In a large area between the North and South, a cast-iron frying pan is usually called a *skillet.* In New England, in some other parts of the North, and along the coasts of New Jersey, Virginia, North Carolina, and South Carolina some people call it a *spider.* *Frying pans* got the name *spider* because they had legs on the bottom so that they could be set over a fire.

▲ **frying pan**

ft. The abbreviation for *foot* or *feet.*

fudge *noun* A soft candy, often flavored with chocolate.
fudge (fŭj) ◊ *noun*

fuel *noun* A substance that is burned to give off heat or produce energy. Coal, wood, oil, gas, and gasoline are fuels.
fu·el (**fyo͞o′** əl) ◊ *noun, plural* **fuels**

fugitive *noun* A person who is running away, especially from the police.
fu·gi·tive (**fyo͞o′** jĭ tĭv) ◊ *noun, plural* **fugitives**

-ful The suffix *-ful* forms adjectives and means "full of," "having," or "having the qualities of." A *beautiful* view is a view that is full of beauty. The suffix *-ful* also means "able to" or "apt to." A *forgetful* person is a person who is apt to forget. The suffix *-ful* also means "an amount that fills." A *cupful* is the amount that fills a cup.

***VOCABULARY BUILDER* • -ful**

Many words that are formed with **-ful** are not entries in this dictionary. But you can figure out what these words mean by looking up the meanings of the root words and the suffix. For example:
bucketful = the amount that fills a bucket
resentful = apt to resent
tasteful = having good taste

fulcrum *noun* The point on which a lever turns or is supported when it is moving or lifting something.
ful·crum (**fo͝ol′**krəm) ◊ *noun, plural* **fulcrums**

fulfill *verb* **1.** To do what is called for; carry out: *You may leave after you have fulfilled all your duties.* —See Synonyms at **perform. 2.** To measure up to; satisfy.
ful·fill (fo͝ol **fĭl′**) ◊ *verb* **fulfilled, fulfilling**

full *adjective* **1.** Holding as much as possible; filled: *Water trickled down the side of the full bucket.* **2.** Not missing a part; complete: *I waited a full hour.* **3.** Having a lot; having many: *The sidewalk was full of cracks.* **4.** Rounded in shape or outline; plump: *The child has a full round face.* **5.** Not tight or narrow: *Those are very full curtains.*
◊ *adverb* To a complete extent; entirely: *I knew full well what you meant.*
full (fo͝ol) ◊ *adjective* **fuller, fullest** ◊ *adverb*

fully *adverb* **1.** Totally or completely: *I am fully aware of what I am doing.* **2.** At least; no less than: *Fully half the class is here.*
ful·ly (**fo͝ol′**ē) ◊ *adverb*

ă	pat	ĭ	pit	oi	**oil**	th	**bath**
ā	pay	ī	ride	o͝o	book	*th*	bathe
â	care	î	fierce	o͞o	boot	ə	ago, item
ä	father	ŏ	pot	ou	**out**		pencil
ĕ	pet	ō	go	ŭ	cut		atom
ē	be	ô	paw, for	û	fur		circus

fumble *verb* **1.** To feel, touch, or handle in a clumsy way: *I fumbled nervously with my keys.* **2.** To deal with badly; bungle. —See Synonyms at **botch. 3.** To lose one's grip on; drop: *The quarterback fumbled the ball.*
◊ *noun* An act of fumbling.
fum·ble (**fŭm′**bəl) ◊ *verb* **fumbled, fumbling** ◊ *noun, plural* **fumbles**

fume *noun* An irritating or strong-smelling smoke, vapor, or gas: *The fumes from the cigar were making me sick.*
◊ *verb* **1.** To produce or give off fumes. **2.** To feel angry; seethe: *I fumed over the insult.*
fume (fyo͞om) ◊ *noun, plural* **fumes** ◊ *verb* **fumed, fuming**

fun *noun* A good time; pleasure: *Have fun at the circus.*
fun (fŭn) ◊ *noun*

function *noun* **1.** The proper activity; purpose or use: *The function of a knife is to cut.* **2.** A formal social gathering or official ceremony, as a wedding.
◊ *verb* To have or perform a function; serve: *This post functions as a support.*
func·tion (**fŭngk′**shən) ◊ *noun, plural* **functions** ◊ *verb* **functioned, functioning**

fund *noun* **1.** A source of supply; stock: *Their experience gave them a large fund of knowledge.* **2.** A sum of money raised or kept for a certain purpose: *The family has a vacation fund.* **3. funds** Available money; ready cash: *I'm temporarily out of funds.*
fund (fŭnd) ◊ *noun, plural* **funds**

fundamental *adjective* Forming a foundation; basic: *Food is a fundamental human need.*
◊ *noun* A basic part, principle, fact, or skill: *Reading is a fundamental of education.*
fun·da·men·tal (fŭn′də **mĕn′**tl) ◊ *adjective* ◊ *noun, plural* **fundamentals**

funeral *noun* The ceremonies held when a dead person is buried or cremated.
fu·ner·al (**fyo͞o′**nər əl) ◊ *noun, plural* **funerals**

fungi *noun* A plural of **fungus.**
fun·gi (**fŭn′**jī) ◊ *noun*

fungus *noun* Any of a group of plants that have no flowers and leaves and no green coloring. Mushrooms, molds, and mildew are fungi.
fun·gus (**fŭng′** gəs) ◊ *noun, plural* **fungi** *or* **funguses**

F

funnel *noun* **1.** A utensil that looks like a cone with an open tube at the bottom. A funnel is used to help pour a liquid or other substance into a container with a small mouth. **2.** The smokestack of a ship or locomotive.
fun·nel (fŭn′əl) ◊ *noun, plural* **funnels**

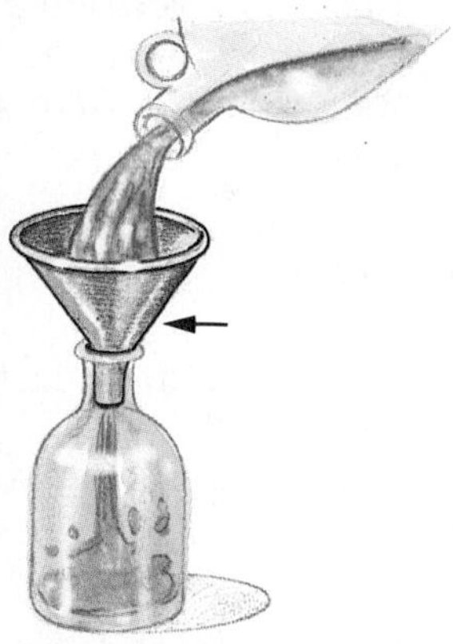

▲ **funnel**

funnies *plural noun* Comic strips.
fun·nies (fŭn′ēz) ◊ *plural noun*

funny *adjective* **1.** Causing amusement or laughter; humorous. **2.** Strange; odd; curious: *I heard a funny noise.*
fun·ny (fŭn′ē) ◊ *adjective* **funnier, funniest**

SYNONYMS

funny, amusing, comical, humorous, laughable

My friend's jokes are very *funny.* The otters are *amusing* when they play together. We found it *comical* to watch the clowns at the circus. I wrote a *humorous* letter to a friend about the first day in my new school. The sack race was a *laughable* event. **Antonym:** *serious*

fur *noun* **1.** The thick, soft hair covering the body of certain animals. Cats, rabbits, hamsters, and foxes have fur. **2.** The hair-covered skin or skins of such animals.
fur (fûr) ◊ *noun, plural* **furs**
‖*These sound alike:* **fur, fir**

furious *adjective* **1.** Full of or marked by very great anger; raging. **2.** Fierce; violent: *The furious storm lasted for three days.* —See Synonyms at **intense.**
fu·ri·ous (fyo͝or′ē əs) ◊ *adjective*

furl *verb* To roll up and fasten: *The crew furled all the sails.*
furl (fûrl) ◊ *verb* **furled, furling**

furlong *noun* A unit of distance equal to ⅛ mile or 220 yards.
fur·long (fûr′lông′) ◊ *noun, plural* **furlongs**

furlough *noun* A vacation or leave of absence from duty: *The workers were on furlough.*
fur·lough (fûr′lō) ◊ *noun, plural* **furloughs**

furnace *noun* An enclosed chamber in which fuel is burned to produce heat.
fur·nace (fûr′nĭs) ◊ *noun, plural* **furnaces**

furnish *verb* **1.** To equip with furniture: *We are furnishing a new home.* **2.** To supply; give: *The company furnishes the bats and balls for our baseball league.*
fur·nish (fûr′nĭsh) ◊ *verb* **furnished, furnishing**

furnishings *plural noun* Furniture and other equipment for a house or office.
fur·nish·ings (fûr′nĭ shĭngz) ◊ *plural noun*

furniture *noun* The movable objects that are needed to make a room or office fit for living or working. Chairs, tables, and beds are pieces of furniture.
fur·ni·ture (fûr′nə chər) ◊ *noun*

furrow *noun* A long, narrow groove cut in the ground by a plow or other tool. Farmers plow furrows and plant seeds in them.
◊ *verb* To make furrows in.
fur·row (fûr′ō) ◊ *noun, plural* **furrows** ◊ *verb* **furrowed, furrowing**

▲ **furrow**

furry *adjective* Made of, covered with, or like fur: *Velvet is a thick, furry cloth.*
fur·ry (fûr′ē) ◊ *adjective* **furrier, furriest**

further *adverb* **1.** To a greater extent; more: *We will explore the matter further.* **2.** In addition; also: *We hope to return, and further we expect to.* **3.** At or to a more distant point: *I sat beneath the lamp, and they sat a little further away.* **4.** A comparative of **far.**
◊ *adjective* **1.** More distant: *You couldn't be*

further from the right answer. **2.** Additional: *Keep tuned in for further bulletins.* **3.** A comparative of **far.**
◊ *verb* To help the progress of; advance: *The teacher furthered many careers.*
fur·ther (fûr′ *th*ər) ◊ *adverb* ◊ *adjective* ◊ *verb* **furthered, furthering**

furthermore *adverb* In addition; moreover: *Fresh vegetables are nutritious; furthermore, they are cheaper than frozen ones.*
fur·ther·more (fûr′ *th*ər môr′) ◊ *adverb*

furthest *adverb* **1.** To the greatest extent or degree: *I went furthest into the cold lake water.* **2.** At or to the most distant point: *Of all the known planets, Pluto orbits furthest from the sun.* **3.** A superlative of **far.**
◊ *adjective* **1.** Most distant: *My guess was furthest from the correct answer.* **2.** A superlative of **far.**
fur·thest (fûr′ *th*ĭst) ◊ *adverb* ◊ *adjective*

furtive *adjective* Done in a quiet or sly way, so as not to be noticed; sneaky: *"I have plenty of time," said the guest with a furtive glance at the clock.*
fur·tive (fûr′ tĭv) ◊ *adjective*

fury *noun* **1.** Violent anger; rage. **2.** Violent, uncontrolled motion or force.
fu·ry (fyo͝or′ ē) ◊ *noun, plural* **furies**

fuse[1] *noun* A long wick or cord that is lighted at one end to carry a flame to and set off an explosive charge at the other end.
fuse[1] (fyo͞oz) ◊ *noun, plural* **fuses**

fuse[2] *verb* **1.** To make or become soft or liquid by heating; melt: *The metal was heated until it fused.* **2.** To mix together or unite by or as if by melting; blend: *We fused the pipes with solder.*
◊ *noun* A device in an electric circuit that prevents fires and accidents. It contains a wire that melts and breaks the circuit when the current becomes dangerously strong.
fuse[2] (fyo͞oz) ◊ *verb* **fused, fusing** ◊ *noun, plural* **fuses**

ă	pat	ĭ	pit	oi	oil	th	bath
ā	pay	ī	ride	o͝o	book	*th*	bathe
â	care	î	fierce	o͞o	boot	ə	ago, item
ä	father	ŏ	pot	ou	out		pencil
ĕ	pet	ō	go	ŭ	cut		atom
ē	be	ô	paw, for	û	fur		circus

HISTORY • fuse[1], fuse[2]

Fuse[1] comes through French from a Latin word meaning "spindle." **Fuse[2]** comes from a Latin word meaning "to melt."

fuselage *noun* The body of an airplane, to which the wings and tail are attached.
fu·se·lage (fyo͞o′ sə läzh′) ◊ *noun, plural* **fuselages**

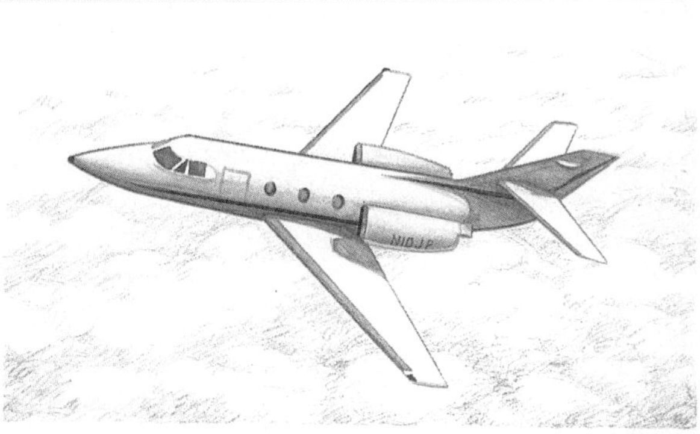

▲ **fuselage**

fusillade *noun* **1.** The firing of many guns at the same time or rapidly, one after another. **2.** A rapid outburst: *The crowd of reporters fired a fusillade of questions at the mayor.*
fu·sil·lade (fyo͞o′ sə läd′) ◊ *noun, plural* **fusillades**

fusion *noun* **1.** The act or process of melting or mixing different things into one thing by heating. **2.** A mixture or blend that is formed by fusing two or more things: *The fusion of copper and zinc makes the metal brass.*
fu·sion (fyo͞o′ zhən) ◊ *noun, plural* **fusions**

fuss *noun* **1.** A lot of needless or unhelpful activity; commotion: *The fire department asked us to leave the building without noise or fuss.* **2.** A display of concern or worry: *Why make a fuss about a small mistake?*
◊ *verb* To get excited or concerned over something: *We fussed over every detail of the party.*
fuss (fŭs) ◊ *noun, plural* **fusses** ◊ *verb* **fussed, fussing**

fussy *adjective* Hard to please; often dissatisfied: *Some people are fussy eaters.*

fuss·y (fŭs′ē) ◊ *adjective* **fussier, fussiest**

fusty *adjective* **1.** Smelling of mildew or decay; musty. **2.** Old-fashioned.
fus·ty (fŭs′tē) ◊ *adjective* **fustier, fustiest**

futile *adjective* Having no useful results; useless: *I made a futile effort to catch my hat when the wind blew it off.*
fu·tile (fyo͞ot′l *or* fyo͞o′tīl) ◊ *adjective*

futility *noun* The quality or condition of being futile.
fu·til·i·ty (fyo͞o tĭl′ĭ tē) ◊ *noun, plural* **futilities**

future *noun* **1.** The time that is to come: *We must plan now for the future.* **2.** Chance of success; outlook: *The future of the wilderness looks bleak if we do not take care of our natural resources.*
◊ *adjective* Occurring in time that is to come; coming after the present: *We will talk about our plans at some future date.*
fu·ture (fyo͞o′chər) ◊ *noun, plural* **futures**
◊ *adjective*

future tense *noun* A verb tense used to express action in the future. It is formed in English with the auxiliary verbs *shall* and *will*: *I shall be back tonight. They will leave in half an hour.*
future tense ◊ *noun, plural* **future tenses**

fuze *noun* A mechanical or electrical device that is used to make an explosive charge, such as dynamite, go off.
fuze (fyo͞oz) ◊ *noun, plural* **fuzes**

fuzz *noun* Soft, short fibers or hairs; down.
fuzz (fŭz) ◊ *noun*

fuzzy *adjective* **1.** Covered with fuzz: *Some peaches have fuzzy skin.* **2.** Not clear; blurred: *The photograph was so fuzzy that we couldn't make out the faces.*
fuzz·y (fŭz′ē) ◊ *adjective* **fuzzier, fuzziest**

Gnu

Gg

G is the seventh letter of the English alphabet. Did you know that it has a long history?

Over 3,500 years ago, people in the Middle East were using symbols that became the letters of our alphabet. This ancient Middle Eastern symbol is a form of the letter that became our letter *G*.

The ancient Greeks borrowed their alphabet from people in the Middle East. Here is a form of the Greek letter that became our letter *G*.

The ancient Romans borrowed their alphabet from a people who had taken their own letter symbols from the Greeks. Here is a form of the Roman letter *G* that was used for carving letters into stone. These letters became the model for our printed capital letters.

As people wrote quickly, especially with pens, the capital letters began to take the shapes of small letters. Here is a small-letter *g* that was developed about 1,200 years ago.

Gg *Gg*	Gg	Gg	Gg
Handwriting	Sans Serif Type	Serif Type	Computer Printing

g *or* **G** *noun* The seventh letter of the English alphabet.
g *or* **G** (jē) ◊ *noun, plural* **g's** *or* **G's**

g *or* **gm** Abbreviations for *gram* or *grams.*

GA The abbreviation for *Georgia* used with a Zip Code.

Ga. An abbreviation for *Georgia.*

gable *noun* The three-cornered section at the end of a building with a sloping roof.
ga·ble (gā′bəl) ◊ *noun, plural* **gables**

gadget *noun* A small mechanical device: *A bottle opener is a kitchen gadget.*
gadg·et (găj′ĭt) ◊ *noun, plural* **gadgets**

gag *noun* **1.** Something put into or over the mouth to prevent a person from speaking or crying out. **2.** A playful joke or trick.
◊ *verb* **1.** To prevent from speaking or crying out by using a gag. **2.** To feel a tightening in the throat, as a person does before vomiting.
gag (găg) ◊ *noun, plural* **gags** ◊ *verb* **gagged, gagging**

gaiety *noun* The condition of being cheerful or merry.
gai·e·ty (gā′ĭ tē) ◊ *noun*

gaily *adverb* **1.** In a cheerful or merry way: *I whistled gaily as I skipped off.* **2.** In a bright or colorful way: *The gym was gaily decorated for the big party.*
gai·ly (gā′lē) ◊ *adverb*

gain *verb* **1.** To get or obtain by effort: *We gained experience by working in a number of jobs.* —See Synonyms at **reach. 2.** To develop gradually; pick up: *The movement gained strength.* **3.** To get an advantage; profit: *We all gained from the experience.* **4.** To arrive at; reach: *We hoped to gain the top of the mountain by noon.*
◊ *noun* **1.** Something gotten or won. **2.** Bene-

ă	pat	ĭ	pit	oi	**oil**	th	ba**th**
ā	pay	ī	ride	o͝o	book	*th*	ba*th*e
â	care	î	fierce	o͞o	boot	ə	ago, item
ä	father	ŏ	pot	ou	**out**		pencil
ĕ	pet	ō	go	ŭ	cut		atom
ē	be	ô	paw, for	û	fur		circus

fit; advantage: *If you study hard, the gains you achieve will be great.* **3.** An increase: *Did you have a weight gain or loss?*
gain (gān) ◊ *verb* **gained, gaining** ◊ *noun, plural* **gains**

gait *noun* A way of walking or running.
gait (gāt) ◊ *noun, plural* **gaits**
‖*These sound alike:* **gait, gate**

gal. The abbreviation for *gallon* or *gallons.*

gala *adjective* Of or suited to a holiday; festive: *Christmas is a gala day.*
ga·la (gā′lə *or* găl′ə) ◊ *adjective*

galaxy *noun* A very large group of stars. Our sun and its planets are in a single galaxy.
gal·ax·y (găl′ək sē) ◊ *noun, plural* **galaxies**

gale *noun* **1.** A very strong wind. **2.** A noisy outburst: *I heard gales of laughter coming from the kitchen.*
gale (gāl) ◊ *noun, plural* **gales**

gall *noun* **1.** A liquid produced by the liver; bile. **2.** Impudence; nerve: *They had the gall to attend our party without invitations.*
gall (gôl) ◊ *noun*

gallant *adjective* Heroic and courageous: *A gallant knight killed the dragon.*
gal·lant (găl′ənt) ◊ *adjective*

gallantry *noun* Heroic courage.
gal·lant·ry (găl′ən trē) ◊ *noun*

galleon *noun* A large sailing ship of former times with three masts and several decks.
gal·le·on (găl′ē ən) ◊ *noun, plural* **galleons**

▲ **galleon**

gallery *noun* **1.** A long, narrow room or passageway; hall. **2.** A balcony in a theater or assembly hall. **3.** A building or group of rooms for showing artistic works. —See Synonyms at **museum**.
gal·le·ry (găl′ə rē) ◊ *noun, plural* **galleries**

galley *noun* **1.** A long, low ship of former times driven by sails and oars. **2.** The kitchen on a ship or airplane.
gal·ley (găl′ē) ◊ *noun, plural* **galleys**

gallon *noun* A unit of capacity for liquids equal to four quarts.
gal·lon (găl′ən) ◊ *noun, plural* **gallons**

gallop *noun* A fast way of running by a horse or other animal with four feet.
◊ *verb* **1.** To ride at a gallop. **2.** To run fast.
gal·lop (găl′əp) ◊ *noun, plural* **gallops** ◊ *verb* **galloped, galloping**

galore *adjective* In great numbers or abundance: *I found bargains galore.*
ga·lore (gə **lôr′**) ◊ *adjective*

galoshes *plural noun* Waterproof overshoes, often of rubber, that are worn in rainy or snowy weather.
ga·losh·es (gə **lŏsh′**əz) ◊ *plural noun*

gam *noun* A school or herd of whales.
gam (găm) ◊ *noun, plural* **gams**

gamble *verb* **1.** To bet money on the outcome of a game or contest. **2.** To take a chance: *They gambled on having no rain for the picnic.*
◊ *noun* A risky action or undertaking.
gam·ble (găm′bəl) ◊ *verb* **gambled, gambling** ◊ *noun, plural* **gambles**
‖*These sound alike:* **gamble, gambol**

gambol *verb* To skip about playfully; frolic.
gam·bol (găm′bəl) ◊ *verb* **gamboled, gamboling**
‖*These sound alike:* **gambol, gamble**

game *noun* **1.** Something done for amusement. **2.** A sport or other form of play carried on according to a special set of rules. **3.** The equipment needed for a game: *This store sells toys and games.* **4.** Wild animals, birds, or fish hunted for food or sport. **5.** The flesh of such animals, used as food.
◊ *adjective* **1.** Full of courage and spirit; plucky: *That child is a game runner.* **2.** Ready and willing: *I'm game for anything.*
game (gām) ◊ *noun, plural* **games** ◊ *adjective* **gamer, gamest**

gander *noun* A fully grown male goose.
gan·der (**găn′** dər) ◊ *noun, plural* **ganders**

▲ **gander**

gang *noun* **1.** A group of people who gather together regularly on a social basis. **2.** An organized group of criminals. **3.** A group of people who work together: *A railroad gang repaired the tracks.*
gang (găng) ◊ *noun, plural* **gangs**

gangplank *noun* A movable ramp used as a bridge for getting on and off a ship.
gang·plank (**găng′** plăngk′) ◊ *noun, plural* **gangplanks**

▲ **gangplank**

gangway *noun* **1.** A passageway along either side of a ship's deck. **2.** A gangplank.
gang·way (**găng′** wā′) ◊ *noun, plural* **gangways**

ă	pat	ĭ	pit	oi	**oil**	th	ba**th**
ā	pay	ī	ride	o͝o	**book**	*th*	ba**the**
â	care	î	fierce	o͞o	**boot**	ə	ago, item
ä	father	ŏ	pot	ou	**out**		pencil
ĕ	pet	ō	go	ŭ	**cut**		atom
ē	be	ô	paw, for	û	**fur**		circus

gap *noun* **1.** An opening or break, as in a wall. **2.** A blank space: *There are some gaps in my knowledge.* **3.** A pass through mountains.
gap (găp) ◊ *noun, plural* **gaps**

gape *verb* **1.** To open the mouth wide, as in yawning. **2.** To stare with the mouth open: *We gaped in amazement at the show.* **3.** To open wide: *Cracks gaped in the ground after the earthquake.*
◊ *noun* **1.** An act or example of gaping. **2.** A wide gap or opening.
gape (gāp) ◊ *verb* **gaped, gaping** ◊ *noun, plural* **gapes**

garage *noun* **1.** A building or part of a building in which cars are kept. **2.** A shop where cars are repaired and serviced.
ga·rage (gə **räzh′**) ◊ *noun, plural* **garages**

garb *noun* Clothing or a way of dressing.
◊ *verb* To clothe: *The judge was garbed in black robes.*
garb (gärb) ◊ *noun, plural* **garbs** ◊ *verb* **garbed, garbing**

garbage *noun* Food and trash to be thrown away, as from a kitchen.
gar·bage (**gär′** bĭj) ◊ *noun*

garden *noun* A piece of land where flowers, vegetables, or fruit are grown.
◊ *verb* To raise plants in a garden.
gar·den (**gär′** dn) ◊ *noun, plural* **gardens** ◊ *verb* **gardened, gardening**

▲ **garden**

gardener *noun* A person who works in or takes care of a garden.

gar·den·er (gär′dn ər) ◊ *noun, plural* **gardeners**

gardenia *noun* A white flower with a sweet smell and shiny evergreen leaves.
gar·de·nia (gär **dē′** nyə) ◊ *noun, plural* **gardenias**

gargle *verb* To rinse the throat or mouth with a liquid that is moved around in the back of the mouth by breathing out.
◊ *noun* A liquid that is used for gargling.
gar·gle (**gär′** gəl) ◊ *verb* **gargled, gargling** ◊ *noun, plural* **gargles**

gargoyle *noun* A spout in the shape of a very ugly or strange human or animal. This spout sticks out from the gutter of a roof to carry off water after a rainfall.
gar·goyle (**gär′** goil′) ◊ *noun, plural* **gargoyles**

garland *noun* A wreath of flowers or leaves.
gar·land (**gär′** lənd) ◊ *noun, plural* **garlands**

garlic *noun* A plant that is related to the onion. The strong-tasting bulb of garlic is used to flavor food.
gar·lic (**gär′** lĭk) ◊ *noun*

garment *noun* An article of clothing.
gar·ment (**gär′** mənt) ◊ *noun, plural* **garments**

garner *verb* To gather and store: *Squirrels garner nuts for the winter.*
gar·ner (**gär′** nər) ◊ *verb* **garnered, garnering**

garnet *noun* A deep-red stone that is used as a gem.
gar·net (**gär′** nĭt) ◊ *noun, plural* **garnets**

garnish *verb* To decorate food with something that adds color or flavor: *We garnished the melon with strawberries.*
◊ *noun* Something that is put on or around food to give it color or flavor.
gar·nish (**gär′** nĭsh) ◊ *verb* **garnished, garnishing** ◊ *noun, plural* **garnishes**

garret *noun* A room or space in a house directly under a sloping roof.
gar·ret (**găr′** ĭt) ◊ *noun, plural* **garrets**

garrison *noun* **1.** A military base. **2.** The troops stationed at a military base.
◊ *verb* To station troops at a base.
gar·ri·son (**găr′** ĭ sən) ◊ *noun, plural* **garrisons** ◊ *verb* **garrisoned, garrisoning**

garter *noun* An elastic band worn on the leg to hold up a stocking or sock.
gar·ter (**gär′** tər) ◊ *noun, plural* **garters**

garter snake *noun* A nonpoisonous North American snake with long yellow stripes on a green or brown background.
garter snake ◊ *noun, plural* **garter snakes**

gas *noun* **1.** A substance that is neither solid nor liquid and that can expand to fill any container completely. The air we breathe is made up of gases such as nitrogen and oxygen. **2.** A gaseous substance that is burned as fuel. **3.** A poisonous, irritating, or choking gaseous substance used as a weapon. **4.** Gasoline.
gas (găs) ◊ *noun, plural* **gases**

gaseous *adjective* Of or like gas: *The sun is in a gaseous state.*
gas·e·ous (**găs′** ē əs) ◊ *adjective*

gash *verb* To make a long, deep cut in.
◊ *noun* A long, deep cut.
gash (găsh) ◊ *verb* **gashed, gashing** ◊ *noun, plural* **gashes**

gas mask *noun* A face covering that protects against breathing in poisonous gases.
gas mask ◊ *noun, plural* **gas masks**

gasoline *noun* A liquid made from petroleum. Gasoline burns easily and is used as a fuel to make engines run.
gas·o·line (**găs′** ə lēn′ *or* găs′ə **lēn′**) ◊ *noun*

gasp *verb* **1.** To catch the breath sharply, as from shock. **2.** To draw in breath with great effort: *We gasped for air.* **3.** To say breathlessly: *I gasped out a few words.*
◊ *noun* An act of gasping.
gasp (găsp) ◊ *verb* **gasped, gasping** ◊ *noun, plural* **gasps**

gate *noun* **1.** A movable part that serves as a door in a wall or fence. **2.** An opening in a wall or fence.
gate (gāt) ◊ *noun, plural* **gates**
‖*These sound alike:* **gate, gait**

gateway *noun* **1.** An opening, as in a wall or fence, that may be closed with a gate. **2.** A way to enter or approach something: *Denver is the gateway to the Rockies.*
gate·way (**gāt′** wā′) ◊ *noun, plural* **gateways**

gather *verb* **1.** To bring or come together into one place; collect: *I gathered the papers together.* **2.** To pick up from many sources: *Squirrels gather nuts.* **3.** To bring into being or action: *It took us a while to gather our courage.* **4.** To gain or increase by degrees: *The sled gathered speed as it moved down the hill.* **5.** To draw together into small folds: *The*

skirt was gathered at the waist.
gath·er (găth′ ər) ◊ *verb* **gathered, gathering**

SYNONYMS

gather, assemble, collect
We *gathered* food together for our picnic. I have now *assembled* all the parts of my model. I have *collected* stamps for several years.

gathering *noun* A coming together of people; assembly.
gath·er·ing (găth′ ər ĭng) ◊ *noun, plural* **gatherings**

gaudy *adjective* Too fancy and bright to be in good taste: *I wore a gaudy costume with sequins all over it to my cousin's Halloween party.*
gaud·y (gô′ dē) ◊ *adjective* **gaudier, gaudiest**

gauge *noun* **1.** A standard of measurement, as for the distance between two rails on a railroad. **2.** An instrument for measuring, as one that measures the amount of rain that has fallen.
◊ *verb* To measure precisely, especially by using a gauge.
gauge (gāj) ◊ *noun, plural* **gauges** ◊ *verb* **gauged, gauging**

▲ **gauge**

ă	pat	ĭ	pit	oi	**oil**	th	**bath**
ā	pay	ī	ride	o͝o	**book**	*th*	**bathe**
â	care	î	fierce	o͞o	**boot**	ə	ago, item
ä	father	ŏ	**pot**	ou	**out**		pencil
ĕ	pet	ō	**go**	ŭ	cut		atom
ē	be	ô	paw, for	û	fur		circus

gaunt *adjective* Very thin and bony.
gaunt (gônt) ◊ *adjective* **gaunter, gauntest**

gauntlet *noun* A metal glove worn with a suit of armor to protect the hand.
gaunt·let (gônt′ lĭt) ◊ *noun, plural* **gauntlets**

gauze *noun* A very thin, loosely woven cloth used especially for bandages.
gauze (gôz) ◊ *noun*

gave *verb* Past tense of **give.**
gave (gāv) ◊ *verb*

gavel *noun* A small wooden mallet used by the person in charge of a meeting or trial to signal for attention or order.
gav·el (găv′ əl) ◊ *noun, plural* **gavels**

gawk *verb* To stare at in a stupid way; gape.
gawk (gôk) ◊ *verb* **gawked, gawking**

gay *adjective* **1.** Merry; cheerful: *The music was lively and gay.* **2.** Brightly colored: *The package was tied with gay ribbons.*
gay (gā) ◊ *adjective* **gayer, gayest**

gaze *verb* To look steadily and long: *They gazed in wonder at the high mountains.* —See Synonyms at **watch.**
◊ *noun* A long, steady look.
gaze (gāz) ◊ *verb* **gazed, gazing** ◊ *noun, plural* **gazes**

gazelle *noun* A swift, slender antelope of Africa and Asia.
ga·zelle (gə zĕl′) ◊ *noun, plural* **gazelles**

▲ **gazelle**

gazette *noun* A newspaper.
ga·zette (gə zĕt′) ◊ *noun, plural* **gazettes**

G

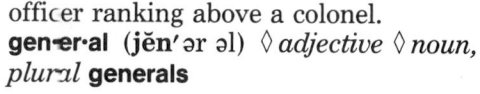

gear *noun* **1.** A wheel with teeth that fit into the teeth of another wheel. **2.** Equipment, such as tools or clothing, used for a particular activity: *I packed our fishing gear.*
◊ *verb* To make fit; adjust or adapt: *The workbook is geared to your grade level.*
gear (gîr) ◊ *noun, plural* **gears** ◊ *verb* **geared, gearing**

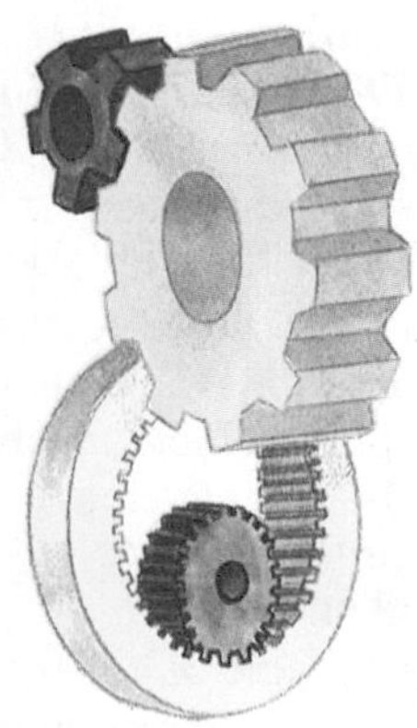

▲ **gear**

gearshift *noun* A device for changing from one gear to another, as in an automobile.
gear·shift (gîr′shĭft′) ◊ *noun, plural* **gearshifts**

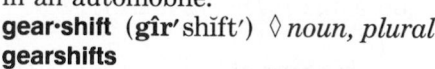

geese *noun* Plural of **goose.**
geese (gēs) ◊ *noun*

Geiger counter *noun* An instrument used to detect and measure radiation.
Gei·ger counter (gī′gər) ◊ *noun, plural* **Geiger counters**

gelatin *noun* A thick substance like jelly or glue that is obtained by boiling the skin, bones, and waste tissue of animals. Gelatin is used in making glue, film, and desserts.
gel·a·tin (jĕl′ə tən) ◊ *noun*

gem *noun* **1.** A precious stone, especially one cut and polished as a jewel. **2.** A person or thing that is very valuable: *Our baby sitter is a real gem.*
gem (jĕm) ◊ *noun, plural* **gems**

gene *noun* A tiny part of an animal or plant cell that determines a characteristic that will be passed on to the animal's or plant's offspring.
gene (jēn) ◊ *noun, plural* **genes**

genera *noun* Plural of **genus.**
gen·er·a (jĕn′ər ə) ◊ *noun*

general *adjective* **1.** Of or involving all: *All the states take part in a general election.* **2.** Widespread: *The general opinion is that taxes are too high.* **3.** Not limited or specialized: *A general store sells food, clothing, and tools.* **4.** Highest in rank: *My cousin is the general manager of our local bank.*
◊ *noun* An Army, Air Force, or Marine Corps officer ranking above a colonel.
gen·er·al (jĕn′ər əl) ◊ *adjective* ◊ *noun, plural* **generals**

***HISTORY* • general**

General comes from an old French word that meant "belonging to the same group." In the past, an army chief was called a *captain general,* meaning "captain of the whole group." This title was then shortened to **general,** meaning "officer of the highest rank."

generalize *verb* To make a general rule from observing individual examples.
gen·er·al·ize (jĕn′ər ə līz′) ◊ *verb* **generalized, generalizing**

generally *adverb* **1.** As a rule; usually: *I generally ride my bike to school.* **2.** Widely; commonly: *That fact is not generally known.* **3.** In general terms; without going into detail: *Generally speaking, we enjoyed the trip.*
gen·er·al·ly (jĕn′ər ə lē) ◊ *adverb*

generate *verb* To bring about or produce: *Water and steam generate electricity.*
gen·er·ate (jĕn′ə rāt′) ◊ *verb* **generated, generating**

generation *noun* **1.** All of the offspring that are at the same stage of descent from a common ancestor: *My grandparents, parents, and I represent three generations of our family.* **2.** A group of people who grow up at about the same time and have similar ideas and customs: *We are a generation of achievers.* **3.** The average length of time between the birth of parents and the birth of their children. **4.** The act or process of generating.
gen·er·a·tion (jĕn′ə **rā′**shən) ◊ *noun, plural* **generations**

generator *noun* A machine that converts mechanical energy into electric energy.
gen·er·a·tor (jĕn′ə rā′tər) ◊ *noun, plural* **generators**

generic *adjective* Not having a trademark or brand name; belonging to an entire group or class of products.
ge·ner·ic (jə **nĕr′**ĭk) ◊ *adjective*

generosity *noun* The quality of being generous; willingness to give or share.
gen·er·os·i·ty (jĕn′ə **rŏs′**ĭ tē) ◊ *noun*

generous *adjective* Willing to give or share; unselfish: *They are generous contributors to charity.*
gen·er·ous (jĕn′ər əs) ◊ *adjective*

genetics *noun* (*used with a singular verb*) A branch of biology that studies how characteristics are passed from parents to offspring.
ge·net·ics (jə **nĕt′**ĭks) ◊ *noun*

genial *adjective* Cheerful and friendly: *Our neighbor has a genial personality.*
gen·ial (**jēn′**yəl) ◊ *adjective*

genie *noun* A magic spirit who is believed to grant people's wishes.
ge·nie (**jē′**nē) ◊ *noun, plural* **genies**

genius *noun* **1.** Outstanding mental or creative ability: *He is a man of genius.* **2.** A person having such ability. **3.** A strong natural talent: *She has a genius for leadership.*
gen·ius (**jēn′**yəs) ◊ *noun, plural* **geniuses**

gentile *or* **Gentile** *noun* A person who is not Jewish.
◊ *adjective* Not Jewish.
gen·tile *or* **Gen·tile** (**jĕn′**tīl′) ◊ *noun, plural* **gentiles** *or* **Gentiles** ◊ *adjective*

gentle *adjective* **1.** Mild and soft: *A gentle breeze rustled the leaves.* **2.** Kindly and thoughtful: *You have a gentle nature.* **3.** Easily managed; tame: *That is a gentle pony.*
gen·tle (**jĕn′**tl) ◊ *adjective* **gentler, gentlest**

gentleman *noun* **1.** A man of high birth or social standing. **2.** A man who is polite, considerate, and refined.
gen·tle·man (**jĕn′**tl mən) ◊ *noun, plural* **gentlemen**

gentlewoman *noun* **1.** A woman of high birth or social standing. **2.** A woman who is polite, considerate, and gracious.
gen·tle·wom·an (**jĕn′**tl wŏŏm′ən) ◊ *noun, plural* **gentlewomen**

gently *adverb* In a gentle manner.
gen·tly (**jĕnt′**lē) ◊ *adverb*

genuflect *verb* To bend one knee to or toward the ground as an act of respect.
gen·u·flect (**jĕn′**yə flĕkt′) ◊ *verb* **genuflected, genuflecting**

genuine *adjective* **1.** Not false; real or pure: *The necklace is genuine gold.* —See Synonyms at **real. 2.** Sincere; honest: *They showed genuine interest in my work.*
gen·u·ine (**jĕn′**yōō ĭn) ◊ *adjective*

genus *noun* A group of closely related plants or animals. A genus usually includes several species. Dogs, wolves, and coyotes belong to the same genus.
ge·nus (**jē′**nəs) ◊ *noun, plural* **genera** *or* **genuses**

geoduck *noun* A very large, edible clam of the Pacific coast of North America that has a hard, thin shell. Geoducks sometimes weigh as much as 12 pounds.
geo·duck (**gōō′**ē dŭk′) ◊ *noun, plural* **geoducks**

geographic *or* **geographical** *adjective* Of or relating to geography.
ge·o·graph·ic (jē′ə **grăf′**ĭk) *or* **ge·o·graph·i·cal** (jē′ə **grăf′**ĭ kəl) ◊ *adjective*

geography *noun* **1.** The study of the earth and its plant and animal life. Geography includes the study of continents, mountains, oceans, and rivers, and of countries, populations, products, and climates around the world. **2.** The natural features of a region or place.
ge·og·ra·phy (jē **ŏg′**rə fē) ◊ *noun*

geologic *or* **geological** *adjective* Of or relating to geology.
ge·o·log·ic (jē′ə **lŏj′**ĭk) *or* **ge·o·log·i·cal** (jē′ə-**lŏj′**ĭ kəl) ◊ *adjective*

geologist *noun* A scientist who specializes in geology.
ge·ol·o·gist (jē **ŏl′**ə jĭst) ◊ *noun, plural* **geologists**

geology *noun* **1.** The scientific study of the origin, history, and structure of the earth. Geology includes the study of the layers of soil, rock, and minerals that make up the earth's crust. **2.** The geologic features of a region.
ge·ol·o·gy (jē **ŏl′**ə jē) ◊ *noun*

geometric *or* **geometrical** *adjective* **1.** Of or relating to geometry. **2.** Made up of simple shapes formed from straight lines or curves: *The rug has a geometric design.*
ge·o·met·ric (jē′ə **mĕt′**rĭk) *or* **ge·o·met·ri·cal** (jē′ə **mĕt′**rĭk əl) ◊ *adjective*

ă	pat	ĭ	pit	oi	**oil**	th	**bath**
ā	pay	ī	ride	ŏŏ	**book**	*th*	**bathe**
â	care	î	fierce	ōō	**boot**	ə	**ago, item**
ä	father	ŏ	pot	ou	**out**		pencil
ĕ	pet	ō	go	ŭ	cut		atom
ē	be	ô	paw, for	û	fur		circus

▲ geometric

geometry *noun* The branch of mathematics that deals with the measurement and relationship of points, lines, surfaces, angles, and solids.
ge·om·e·try (jē ŏm′ĭ trē) ◊ *noun*

geranium *noun* A plant with clusters of red, pink, or white flowers.
ge·ra·ni·um (jĭ rā′nē əm) ◊ *noun, plural* **geraniums**

gerbil *noun* A mouselike animal with long hind legs and a long tail.
ger·bil (jûr′bĭl) ◊ *noun, plural* **gerbils**

▲ gerbil

germ *noun* **1.** A very tiny organism that can cause disease. **2.** A tiny living cell or structure from which a new organism may develop; a seed or bud.
germ (jûrm) ◊ *noun, plural* **germs**

German *noun* **1.** A person who was born in or lives in East Germany or West Germany. **2.** The language of Germany, Austria, and part of Switzerland.
◊ *adjective* Of or relating to Germany, the Germans, or their language.
Ger·man (jûr′mən) ◊ *noun, plural* **Germans** ◊ *adjective*

Germanic *noun* A prehistoric language that is the ancestor of various languages, such as English, German, and Dutch.
◊ *adjective* Of or relating to Germanic.
Ger·man·ic (jûr măn′ĭk) ◊ *noun* ◊ *adjective*

German shepherd *noun* A large dog with a thick brownish or black coat. German shepherds are often trained to assist the police and to guide the blind.
German shepherd ◊ *noun, plural* **German shepherds**

germinate *verb* To begin or cause to begin to grow; sprout: *Seeds need water and warmth to germinate.*
ger·mi·nate (jûr′mə nāt′) ◊ *verb* **germinated, germinating**

gesture *noun* **1.** A motion of the hands, arms, head, or body used while speaking or in place of speech to help express a feeling or idea. **2.** An outward show, as of courtesy or friendship: *Sending flowers was a thoughtful gesture.*
◊ *verb* To make or use gestures; signal: *We gestured to our friends to follow us.*
ges·ture (jĕs′chər) ◊ *noun, plural* **gestures** ◊ *verb* **gestured, gesturing**

get *verb* **1.** To become: *The sick patient is getting better every day.* **2.** To arrive; reach: *When will we get to Atlanta?* **3.** To move or go: *I can't get around too well with a broken leg.* **4.** To have to: *I've got to go now.* **5.** To obtain or receive: *I get five dollars a week.* **6.** To be able or allowed: *I get to stay up late on Saturday nights.* **7.** To go after; fetch: *Please get my books.* **8.** To reach or make contact with: *Try to get me at my house.* **9.** To come down with a sickness: *I'm getting a cold.* **10.** To capture or catch: *We chased our dog and got it.* **11.** To persuade: *Get them to change their minds.* **12.** To understand: *I don't get what you're saying.* **13.** To make ready; prepare: *I'll get dinner.* **14.** To cause to be or become: *I got my hair cut.*
◊ *idioms* **get along 1.** To be or remain on friendly terms: *Try to get along with your brothers and sisters.* **2.** To manage: *I can get along without your help.* **get off 1.** To start

out: *We get off to school early every morning.* **2.** To escape punishment: *They got off with just a scolding.* **get out of** To avoid: *You're always trying to get out of your chores.* **get over** To recover from: *I'm just getting over a cold.* **get together** To meet: *Let's get together after school.* **get up 1.** To arise from bed: *What time did you get up this morning?* **2.** To stand up: *The dog sat down and refused to get up.*
get (gĕt) ◊ *verb* **got, got** *or* **gotten, getting**

SYNONYMS
get, earn, obtain, win
I have to go *get* some bread at the store. I *earn* my allowance by doing chores around the house. She *obtained* a rare stamp for her collection. He thinks he will *win* the race.

geyser *noun* A natural hot spring that throws out a spray of steam and water from time to time.
gey·ser (gī′zər) ◊ *noun, plural* **geysers**

▲ **geyser**

ă	pat	ĭ	pit	oi	**oil**	th	ba**th**
ā	pay	ī	ride	o͝o	book	*th*	ba**the**
â	care	î	fierce	o͞o	boot	ə	ago, item
ä	father	ŏ	pot	ou	**out**		pencil
ĕ	pet	ō	go	ŭ	cut		atom
ē	be	ô	paw, for	û	fur		circus

ghastly *adjective* **1.** Horrible; dreadful: *A ghastly tornado wrecked the town.* **2.** Deathly pale: *You looked ghastly when you were sick.*
ghast·ly (găst′lē) ◊ *adjective* **ghastlier, ghastliest**

ghetto *noun* A section of a city lived in by members of a minority group.
ghet·to (gĕt′ō) ◊ *noun, plural* **ghettos** *or* **ghettoes**

ghost *noun* The spirit of a dead person.
ghost (gōst) ◊ *noun, plural* **ghosts**

ghostly *adjective* Of or resembling a ghost: *A ghostly figure appeared on the stage.*
ghost·ly (gōst′lē) ◊ *adjective* **ghostlier, ghostliest**

giant *noun* **1.** A huge, very strong, imaginary creature resembling a human being. **2.** Someone or something that is very large, powerful, or important: *That company is a giant in the electronics industry.*
◊ *adjective* Extremely large; huge.
gi·ant (jī′ənt) ◊ *noun, plural* **giants** ◊ *adjective*

gibbon *noun* A small ape of southeastern Asia. Gibbons live in trees and swing from branch to branch with their long arms.
gib·bon (gĭb′ən) ◊ *noun, plural* **gibbons**

gibe *noun* A scornful remark; jeer.
◊ *verb* To make scornful or jeering remarks.
gibe (jīb) ◊ *noun, plural* **gibes** ◊ *verb* **gibed, gibing**

giblet *noun* Often **giblets** The heart, liver, or gizzard of a fowl eaten as food.
gib·let (jĭb′lĭt) ◊ *noun, plural* **giblets**

giddy *adjective* **1.** Having a whirling feeling; dizzy: *We were giddy from the summer heat.* **2.** Causing dizziness: *We spun around at a giddy speed.* **3.** Silly or playful: *I was in a giddy mood at the party.*
gid·dy (gĭd′ē) ◊ *adjective* **giddier, giddiest**

gift *noun* **1.** Something given; present. **2.** A special talent or ability: *My friend has a gift for science and arithmetic.*
gift (gĭft) ◊ *noun, plural* **gifts**

gifted *adjective* Having special ability: *You are a gifted athlete.*
gift·ed (gĭf′tĭd) ◊ *adjective*

gigantic *adjective* Being like a giant in size, strength, or power: *Some of the dinosaurs were gigantic creatures.*
gi·gan·tic (jī găn′tĭk) ◊ *adjective*

SYNONYMS

gigantic, enormous, huge, immense

Jack climbed a *gigantic* beanstalk. She was so hungry that she ate an *enormous* breakfast. Wrestlers have *huge* muscles. The ocean is *immense.* **Antonym:** *tiny*

giggle *verb* To laugh nervously.
◊ *noun* A short, nervous laugh.
gig·gle (gĭg′əl) ◊ *verb* **giggled, giggling** ◊ *noun, plural* **giggles**

Gila monster *noun* A poisonous lizard that lives in the southwestern United States. It has a thick body with black and pinkish or yellowish markings.
Gi·la monster (hē′lə) ◊ *noun, plural* **Gila monsters**

LANGUAGE DETECTIVE

Gila monster

You might wonder why we pronounce *Gila* in *Gila monster* with the sound of an *h* rather than a *g* as in *giraffe.* We use the *h* sound because we took the word from Spanish, where *g* before *i* is pronounced as *h.* We do the same kind of thing when we pronounce the *j* in *frijoles,* "beans," as *h* because that is the Spanish pronunciation of *j.* Spanish words are not the only words to which we do this. We do not pronounce the *t* in *ballet* or *crochet* because we have taken these words from French, in which the *t* is not pronounced.

▲ **Gila monster**

gild *verb* To cover with a thin layer of gold.
gild (gĭld) ◊ *verb* **gilded** *or* **gilt, gilding**
‖*These sound alike:* **gild, guild**

gill *noun* A body part of certain water animals, such as fish, used for taking oxygen from the water.
gill (gĭl) ◊ *noun, plural* **gills**

gilt *noun* A thin layer of gold that is applied to another surface.
◊ *verb* A past tense and a past participle of **gild.**
gilt (gĭlt) ◊ *noun* ◊ *verb*
‖*These sound alike:* **gilt, guilt**

gin¹ *noun* A strong, clear alcoholic liquor made from grain and flavored with juniper berries.
gin¹ (jĭn) ◊ *noun*

gin² *noun* A machine that separates the seeds from the fibers of cotton.
gin² (jĭn) ◊ *noun, plural* **gins**

HISTORY • gin¹, gin²

Gin¹ was first made in Holland. The word **gin¹** comes from the Dutch word for "juniper," whose berry is used to flavor this drink. **Gin²** is a shorter form of the word **engine.**

ginger *noun* The root of a tropical plant, having a sharp, spicy flavor. Powdered ginger is used as a spice.
gin·ger (jĭn′jər) ◊ *noun*

ginger ale *noun* A soft drink flavored with ginger.

gingerbread *noun* A cake flavored with ginger and molasses.
gin·ger·bread (jĭn′jər brĕd′) ◊ *noun, plural* **gingerbreads**

gingerly *adverb* In a very cautious or careful way: *He gingerly patted the large dog.*
◊ *adjective* Very cautious or careful: *She took gingerly steps into the cold lake.*
gin·ger·ly (jĭn′jər lē) ◊ *adverb* ◊ *adjective*

gingham *noun* A cotton cloth that is usually woven in checks, stripes, or plaids.
ging·ham (gĭng′əm) ◊ *noun*

giraffe *noun* A tall African animal with short horns, a very long neck and legs, and a tan coat with brown blotches.
gi·raffe (jĭ răf′) ◊ *noun, plural* **giraffes**

girder *noun* A heavy, horizontal beam that is used to support floors and the frameworks of structures, such as buildings or bridges.
gird·er (gûr′dər) ◊ *noun, plural* **girders**

girdle *noun* **1.** A belt, sash, or band worn around the waist. **2.** Something that surrounds: *Just beyond the planet Mars is a girdle of asteroids.*
gir·dle (gûr′dl) ◊ *noun, plural* **girdles**

girl *noun* **1.** A young female person. **2.** A sweetheart.
girl (gûrl) ◊ *noun, plural* **girls**

HISTORY **• girl**

In the Middle Ages, the word **girl** meant "a young person" and was used for both boys and girls. It was only later that **girl** came to mean "a young female person."

girlhood *noun* The period of time or state of being a girl: *I had a happy girlhood.*
girl·hood (gûrl′ho͝od′) ◊ *noun, plural* **girlhoods**

girlish *adjective* Of or relating to a girl.
girl·ish (gûr′lĭsh) ◊ *adjective*

girth *noun* **1.** The distance or measurement around something. **2.** A strap put around the body of a horse or pack animal to hold a saddle or load on its back.
girth (gûrth) ◊ *noun, plural* **girths**

give *verb* **1.** To make a gift of: *My sister gave me a new watch.* **2.** To pay: *He gave me five dollars for the book.* **3.** To hand over; pass: *Please give me the newspaper.* **4.** To let have; cause to have: *The teacher gave me permission to leave.* **5.** To provide; supply: *Milk gives us calcium.* **6.** To offer: *We gave them our thanks.* **7.** To cause to take place: *My neighbor gives good parties.* **8.** To produce: *Cows give milk.* **9.** To cause by some action: *The bump gave me a bruise.* **10.** To yield, as to pressure: *We pushed and the door gave.* ◊ *noun* The quality of being able to yield to pressure: *A mattress should have some give.* ◊ *idioms* **give in** To admit defeat; surrender: *We were losing but we didn't give in.* **give out** **1.** To make known; announce: *I gave out the good news.* **2.** To break down; fail: *My watch gave out.* **3.** To become used up; run out: *The supply of books just gave out.* **give up** **1.** To admit defeat: *The losing team refused to give up.* **2.** To stop; abandon: *I won't give up trying.* **3.** To let go of; part with: *They had to give up their place in line.*
give (gĭv) ◊ *verb* **gave, given, giving** ◊ *noun*

given *adjective* **1.** Stated or agreed on in advance: *Each student will write a report on a given country.* **2.** Having a tendency; inclined: *You are given to arguing.* ◊ *verb* Past participle of **give.**
giv·en (gĭv′ən) ◊ *adjective* ◊ *verb*

gizzard *noun* A large, muscular part of a bird's digestive system in which food is ground up.
giz·zard (gĭz′ərd) ◊ *noun, plural* **gizzards**

glacial *adjective* **1.** Of or having to do with glaciers. **2.** Very cold; icy.
gla·cial (glā′shəl) ◊ *adjective*

glacier *noun* A large mass of ice that moves very slowly down a mountain or through a valley. Glaciers are formed from snow on the tops of huge mountains.
gla·cier (glā′shər) ◊ *noun, plural* **glaciers**

▲ **glacier**

ă	pat	ĭ	pit	oi	**oil**	th	**bath**
ā	pay	ī	ride	o͝o	**book**	*th*	**bathe**
â	care	î	fierce	o͞o	**boot**	ə	ago, item
ä	father	ŏ	pot	ou	**out**		pencil
ĕ	pet	ō	go	ŭ	cut		atom
ē	be	ô	paw, for	û	fur		circus

glad *adjective* **1.** Bringing joy or pleasure: *We received the glad news of their victory.* **2.** Pleased; happy: *We were glad to be home again.* **3.** Willing: *I'd be glad to help when I finish my chores.*
◊ *idiom* **be glad of** To be grateful for: *I will be glad of your help.*
glad (glăd) ◊ *adjective* **gladder, gladdest**

SYNONYMS

glad, cheerful, happy, joyful
Our team was *glad* when we won. You have a *cheerful* personality. We were all *happy* at our Thanksgiving celebration. The two friends were *joyful* at seeing each other again after all that time.
Antonyms: *sad, sorrowful, unhappy*

gladden *verb* To make glad.
glad·den (**glăd′**n) ◊ *verb* **gladdened, gladdening**

glade *noun* An open space in a forest.
glade (glād) ◊ *noun, plural* **glades**

glad-hander *noun* Someone who greets others in an enthusiastic way that is sometimes not sincere.
glad-hand·er (**glăd′**hăn′dər) ◊ *noun, plural* **glad-handers**

gladiator *noun* A man in ancient Rome who fought to the death in an arena to entertain the public. Gladiators were usually slaves, captives, or criminals.
glad·i·a·tor (**glăd′**ē ā′tər) ◊ *noun, plural* **gladiators**

***HISTORY* • gladiator, gladiolus**

Gladiator comes from a Latin word meaning "a person who fights with a sword at a public show." **Gladiolus** in Latin meant "little sword." The leaves of the **gladiolus** plant look like little swords.

gladioli *noun* A plural of **gladiolus.**
glad·i·o·li (glăd′ē **ō′**lī) ◊ *noun*

gladiolus *noun* A plant with sword-shaped leaves and brightly colored flowers that grow in long clusters.
glad·i·o·lus (glăd′ē **ō′**ləs) ◊ *noun, plural* **gladioli** *or* **gladioluses**

▲ **gladiolus**

glamorous *adjective* Charming and fascinating: *A glamorous movie star arrived at the theater.*
glam·or·ous (**glăm′**ər əs) ◊ *adjective*

glamour *noun* The quality of being charming, fascinating, and exciting: *The glamour of Hollywood has always attracted people.*
glam·our (**glăm′**ər) ◊ *noun*

glance *verb* **1.** To look quickly: *I glanced at my watch.* **2.** To strike a surface so as to fly off to one side: *The stone glanced off our windshield.*
◊ *noun* A quick look.
glance (glăns) ◊ *verb* **glanced, glancing** ◊ *noun, plural* **glances**

gland *noun* An organ in the body that makes some special substance that the body uses or gives off. Glands can make tears for the eyes or saliva for the mouth.
gland (glănd) ◊ *noun, plural* **glands**

glare *verb* **1.** To stare at in an angry way. **2.** To shine with a blinding light: *The hot sun glared down on us.*
◊ *noun* **1.** An angry stare. **2.** A blinding light: *The glare from the lamp hurts my eyes.*
glare (glâr) ◊ *verb* **glared, glaring** ◊ *noun, plural* **glares**

glaring *adjective* **1.** Staring angrily. **2.** Shining with a blinding light. **3.** Too bright and showy: *The curtains were a glaring red.* **4.** Very easily seen; obvious: *I made a glaring error in this arithmetic problem.*
glar·ing (**glâr′**ĭng) ◊ *adjective*

glass *noun* **1.** A hard, usually clear substance that breaks easily. Glass is used for making windowpanes, containers, and lenses. **2.** A

container made of glass and used for drinking. **3.** The amount that a glass holds: *I drank a glass of milk.* **4.** A mirror: *I looked at myself in the glass.* **5. glasses** A pair of corrective lenses set in a frame and worn over the eyes to aid vision.
glass (glăs) ◊ *noun, plural* **glasses**

glassy *adjective* Like glass: *We skated on the glassy surface of the frozen pond.*
glass·y (**glăs'** ē) ◊ *adjective* **glassier, glassiest**

glaze *noun* **1.** A thin, smooth, shiny coating, as on paper or fabric. **2.** A thin, glassy coating of ice. **3.** A coating applied to ceramics before they are baked in a kiln.
◊ *verb* **1.** To put glass into: *The carpenter glazed all the windows.* **2.** To apply a glaze to: *We glazed the pottery and put it in the kiln.*
glaze (glāz) ◊ *noun, plural* **glazes** ◊ *verb* **glazed, glazing**

gleam *noun* **1.** A beam or flash of bright light: *We saw a gleam of light through the crack under the door.* **2.** A soft, steady glow: *The pale gleam of moonlight streamed into the room.* **3.** A brief or faint appearance: *A gleam of hope shows in your eyes.*
◊ *verb* To shine brightly or softly.
gleam (glēm) ◊ *noun, plural* **gleams** ◊ *verb* **gleamed, gleaming**

glean *verb* **1.** To gather what has been left in a field by reapers. **2.** To gather something, such as information, little by little.
glean (glēn) ◊ *verb* **gleaned, gleaning**

glee *noun* A feeling of delight; joy.
glee (glē) ◊ *noun*

glee club *noun* A group of singers who usually perform short pieces.
glee club ◊ *noun, plural* **glee clubs**

gleeful *adjective* Full of glee; joyous.
glee·ful (**glē'** fəl) ◊ *adjective*

glen *noun* A narrow valley.
glen (glĕn) ◊ *noun, plural* **glens**

ă	pat	ĭ	pit	oi	oil	th	bath
ā	pay	ī	ride	ŏŏ	book	*th*	bathe
â	care	î	fierce	ōō	boot	ə	ago, item
ä	father	ŏ	pot	ou	out		pencil
ĕ	pet	ō	go	ŭ	cut		atom
ē	be	ô	paw, for	û	fur		circus

glide *verb* To move smoothly, quietly, and with ease: *The submarine glided through the deep, cold water.*
◊ *noun* The act or process of gliding.
glide (glīd) ◊ *verb* **glided, gliding** ◊ *noun, plural* **glides**

glider *noun* An aircraft without an engine that glides on currents of air.
glid·er (**glī'** dər) ◊ *noun, plural* **gliders**

glimmer *noun* A dim, unsteady light.
◊ *verb* To shine with a dim, unsteady light.
glim·mer (**glĭm'** ər) ◊ *noun, plural* **glimmers** ◊ *verb* **glimmered, glimmering**

glimpse *noun* A very quick look: *We caught a glimpse of the house as we drove by.*
◊ *verb* To get a quick look at.
glimpse (glĭmps) ◊ *noun, plural* **glimpses** ◊ *verb* **glimpsed, glimpsing**

glint *noun* A brief flash, as of light.
◊ *verb* To flash; gleam: *The water glinted like silver in the moonlight.*
glint (glĭnt) ◊ *noun, plural* **glints** ◊ *verb* **glinted, glinting**

glisten *verb* To shine with reflected light: *Sunshine made the snow glisten.*
glis·ten (**glĭs'** ən) ◊ *verb* **glistened, glistening**

glitch *noun* A sudden, small problem or breakdown, especially in one of the parts of a computer.
glitch (glĭch) ◊ *noun, plural* **glitches**

glitter *noun* Sparkling light or brightness: *I love the winter with its frosty glitter.*
◊ *verb* To sparkle brilliantly.
glit·ter (**glĭt'** ər) ◊ *noun* ◊ *verb* **glittered, glittering**

gloaming *noun* Twilight.
gloam·ing (**glō'** mĭng) ◊ *noun*

gloat *verb* To look at or think about something with great pleasure and with selfish or spiteful satisfaction: *Good sports don't gloat when they win.*
gloat (glōt) ◊ *verb* **gloated, gloating**

glob *noun* **1.** A drop: *There are globs of paint all over the floor.* **2.** A large, rounded mass: *That big glob of dough will make three loaves of bread.*
glob (glŏb) ◊ *noun, plural* **globs**

global *adjective* **1.** Shaped like a globe. **2.** Of or relating to the entire earth: *The problem of hunger is of global importance.*
glob·al (**glō'** bəl) ◊ *adjective*

globe *noun* **1.** Something shaped like a ball; sphere. **2.** A map of the earth or heavens that is shaped like a globe. **3.** The earth.
globe (glōb) ◊ *noun, plural* **globes**

▲ **globe**

gloom *noun* **1.** Partial or complete darkness: *I peered into the gloom of the cave.* **2.** Low spirits: *The big defeat brought gloom to the team.*
gloom (gloom) ◊ *noun*

gloomy *adjective* **1.** Partly or completely dark: *We use our headlights when we drive on a gloomy winter day.* **2.** Showing or filled with gloom; sad: *I can tell by your gloomy face that the news is bad.* **3.** Causing low spirits.
gloom·y (gloo′mē) ◊ *adjective* **gloomier, gloomiest**

glorify *verb* **1.** To praise highly: *The nation glorified the hero by building a monument.* **2.** To give glory to through worship.
glo·ri·fy (glôr′ə fī′) ◊ *verb* **glorified, glorifying**

glorious *adjective* **1.** Having or deserving great honor, praise, and fame: *The team won a glorious victory.* **2.** Having great beauty; magnificent: *We saw a glorious sunset.*
glo·ri·ous (glôr′ē əs) ◊ *adjective*

glory *noun* **1.** Great honor, praise, and fame given by others: *The captain of the winning team got all the glory for the victory.* **2.** Something that brings honor, praise, and fame. **3.** Great beauty; magnificence.
◊ *verb* To rejoice proudly: *The Olympic swimming team gloried in its victory.*
glo·ry (glôr′ē) ◊ *noun, plural* **glories** ◊ *verb* **gloried, glorying**

gloss *noun* A bright shine on a smooth surface: *I polished my shoes to give them a gloss.*
gloss (glôs) ◊ *noun, plural* **glosses**

glossary *noun* A list of difficult words with their meanings, usually found at the end of a book: *I looked the word up in the glossary of my science book.*
glos·sa·ry (glô′sə rē) ◊ *noun, plural* **glossaries**

glossy *adjective* Having a smooth and shiny surface: *Satin is a glossy fabric.*
gloss·y (glô′sē) ◊ *adjective* **glossier, glossiest**

glove *noun* A covering for the hand that has a separate section for each finger.
glove (glŭv) ◊ *noun, plural* **gloves**

glow *verb* **1.** To shine brightly with heat but without flame: *The coals in the fireplace glowed.* **2.** To shine without giving off heat: *Some insects glow in the dark.* **3.** To show a bright, warm color: *The autumn leaves glowed in the sunlight.* **4.** To have a healthy, ruddy color: *Your cheeks are glowing.*
◊ *noun* **1.** A steady light like that produced by something hot but not flaming: *I can see the glow of the lamp in the window.* **2.** Bright, warm color: *The glow of the gold ring caught my eye.* **3.** Warmth of emotion.
glow (glō) ◊ *verb* **glowed, glowing** ◊ *noun, plural* **glows**

glowworm *noun* An insect larva or insect that gives off a glowing light in the dark.
glow·worm (glō′wûrm′) ◊ *noun, plural* **glowworms**

glue *noun* A thick, sticky substance that is used to stick things together.
◊ *verb* To stick with or as if with glue.
glue (gloo) ◊ *noun, plural* **glues** ◊ *verb* **glued, gluing**

glum *adjective* Frowning or sullen; gloomy.
glum (glŭm) ◊ *adjective* **glummer, glummest**

gm An abbreviation for *gram* or *grams.*

gnarled *adjective* Thick, twisted, and full of knots: *The orchard was full of gnarled old apple and peach trees.*
gnarled (närld) ◊ *adjective*

LANGUAGE DETECTIVE

gnarled

In the few English words that begin with *gn–*, the letter *g* is never pronounced. *Gnarled* comes from a word meaning "a swelling," and was originally spelled with a *k* instead of a *g*. *Gnash, gnat,* and *gnaw* all developed from the basic meaning "to bite." *Gnome* comes from a Latin word that may have been borrowed from Greek. *Gnu* was borrowed from the African name for the animal.

gnash *verb* To strike or grind the teeth together, as in pain or anger.
gnash (năsh) ◊ *verb* **gnashed, gnashing**

gnat *noun* A very small biting insect with two wings.
gnat (năt) ◊ *noun, plural* **gnats**

gnaw *verb* **1.** To chew or bite on: *The mouse gnawed the cheese.* **2.** To wear away bit by bit: *Waves gnawed the sandy beach.*
gnaw (nô) ◊ *verb* **gnawed, gnawing**

gnome *noun* A legendary dwarflike creature that was supposed to live underground and guard treasure hoards.
gnome (nōm) ◊ *noun, plural* **gnomes**

▲ **gnome**

gnu *noun* A large African antelope with a short mane, a long tail, and curved horns.
gnu (no͞o *or* nyo͞o) ◊ *noun, plural* **gnus**
‖ *These sound alike:* **gnu, new, knew**

go *verb* **1.** To pass from one place to another; move along: *We're going for a walk.* **2.** To move away from a place; leave: *We must go now.* **3.** To begin or continue to act, operate, or move; function: *The car wouldn't go.* **4.** To have as a usual place or position; belong: *This book goes on the bottom shelf.* **5.** To reach from one place or point to another; extend: *The curtains go from the ceiling to the floor.* **6.** To be given: *Most of our money goes for food and rent.* **7.** To be consumed, lost, or used up: *Our food went, and we had to turn back from the hike.* **8.** To turn out: *How did your day go?* **9.** To pass by; elapse: *I was so busy that the day went quickly.* **10.** To be suitable or appropriate: *Those shoes go well with that outfit.*
go (gō) ◊ *verb* **went, gone, going, goes**

ă	pat	ĭ	pit	oi	**oil**	th	**bath**
ā	pay	ī	ride	o͝o	book	*th*	**bathe**
â	care	î	fierce	o͞o	boot	ə	ago, item
ä	father	ŏ	pot	ou	**out**		pencil
ĕ	pet	ō	go	ŭ	cut		atom
ē	be	ô	paw, for	û	fur		circus

SYNONYMS

go, depart, leave[1]

I will have to *go* home soon. The knight *departed* on a long journey. I hate to *leave* before finishing the job.
Antonyms: *arrive, come*

goad *noun* **1.** A stick with a pointed end used for moving animals along. **2.** Something that makes a person do something.
◊ *verb* To urge on with or as if with a goad.
goad (gōd) ◊ *noun, plural* **goads** ◊ *verb* **goaded, goading**

goal *noun* **1.** Something wanted or worked for; purpose: *My goal in life is to help other people.* **2.** The finish line of a race. **3.** A structure or area into which players must drive a ball or puck in order to score in certain games. **4.** A score awarded for driving a ball or puck into a goal.
goal (gōl) ◊ *noun, plural* **goals**

goalie *noun* A player assigned to protect a goal, as in hockey.
goal·ie (gō′lē) ◊ *noun, plural* **goalies**

▲ **goalie**

goat *noun* An animal that has hoofs, horns, and a beard and is raised for its meat, milk, and hide.
goat (gōt) ◊ *noun, plural* **goats**

gobble *verb* To eat quickly or in a greedy manner.
gob·ble (gŏb′əl) ◊ *verb* **gobbled, gobbling**

goblet *noun* A drinking glass with a stem and base.
gob·let (gŏb′lĭt) ◊ *noun, plural* **goblets**

goblin *noun* A mischievous, ugly creature or elf in folklore.
gob·lin (gōb′lĭn) ◊ *noun, plural* **goblins**

god *noun* **1. God** A being that is thought to have powers above those of human beings and is felt to be worthy of worship. **2.** An image that is worshiped; idol.
god (gŏd) ◊ *noun, plural* **gods**

godchild *noun* A person for whom another serves as sponsor at baptism.
god·child (gŏd′chīld′) ◊ *noun, plural* **godchildren**

goddess *noun* A female god.
god·dess (gŏd′ĭs) ◊ *noun, plural* **goddesses**

godfather *noun* A man or boy who acts as a sponsor at baptism.
god·fa·ther (gŏd′fä′*th*ər) ◊ *noun, plural* **godfathers**

godmother *noun* A woman or girl who acts as a sponsor at baptism.
god·moth·er (gŏd′mŭ*th*′ər) ◊ *noun, plural* **godmothers**

goes *verb* Third person singular present tense of **go.**
goes (gōz) ◊ *verb*

goggles *plural noun* A pair of glasses worn for protection against wind, dust, sparks, or glare.
gog·gles (gŏg′əlz) ◊ *plural noun*

▲ **goggles**

gold *noun* **1.** A soft, yellow metallic chemical element used in making coins and jewelry. **2.** A deep yellow color.
◊ *adjective* Being the color of gold.
gold (gōld) ◊ *noun* ◊ *adjective*

golden *adjective* **1.** Made of or containing gold. **2.** Having the color of gold. **3.** Very favorable; excellent: *You have a golden opportunity to travel and learn.*
gold·en (gōl′dən) ◊ *adjective*

goldenrod *noun* A plant with branching clusters of small yellow flowers that bloom in late summer or fall.
gold·en·rod (gōl′dən rŏd′) ◊ *noun*

goldfinch *noun* A North American bird with yellow feathers and a black forehead, wings, and tail.
gold·finch (gōld′fĭnch′) ◊ *noun, plural* **goldfinches**

goldfish *noun* A small golden-orange or reddish freshwater fish that is often kept in home aquariums.
gold·fish (gōld′fĭsh′) ◊ *noun, plural* **goldfish** *or* **goldfishes**

golf *noun* A game played by hitting a small, hard ball with one of a set of clubs. Players try to hit the ball around a large outdoor course into one hole after another using as few strokes as possible.
◊ *verb* To play golf.
golf (gŏlf) ◊ *noun* ◊ *verb* **golfed, golfing**

gondola *noun* **1.** A long, narrow boat used to carry passengers on the canals of Venice, Italy. **2.** The cabin of a dirigible. **3.** A basket that is suspended from a balloon. **4.** A closed car that hangs from a cable and is used to carry passengers up high mountains.
gon·do·la (gŏn′dl ə) ◊ *noun, plural* **gondolas**

▲ **gondola**

gone *verb* Past participle of **go.**
gone (gôn) ◊ *verb*

gong *noun* A metal disk that makes a loud, ringing tone when hit.
gong (gông) ◊ *noun, plural* **gongs**

good *adjective* **1.** Having positive or desirable qualities: *Last week I read a good book.*

2. Suitable for a particular use: *Aluminum is a good material for pots and pans.* **3.** Providing a benefit; helpful: *Exercise is good for your health.* **4.** Giving enjoyment; pleasant: *We had a good time at the party.* **5.** Better than the average: *Are you a good student?* **6.** Not weakened or damaged; sound: *The old dog's teeth are still good.* **7.** Behaving properly: *Good children don't tell lies.* **8.** Helpful and considerate; kind: *Be good to your parents and your friends.*
◊ *noun* **1.** Something that is good: *You have to accept the bad with the good.* **2.** Something that is a benefit: *I'm doing this for your own good.* **3. goods** Things that can be bought and sold: *Businesses sell goods and services.* **4. goods** Personal belongings: *Our neighbors sold their household goods before they moved to Florida.*
good (go͝od) ◊ *adjective* **better, best** ◊ *noun, plural* **goods**

good-by *or* **good-bye** *interjection* An expression used to say farewell.
◊ *noun* An expression of farewell.
good-by *or* **good-bye** (go͝od **bī′**) ◊ *interjection* ◊ *noun, plural* **good-bys** *or* **good-byes**

goodhearted *adjective* Kind and generous.
good·heart·ed (**go͝od′ här′** tĭd) ◊ *adjective*

goodly *adjective* **1.** Rather large: *A goodly number of people came to the play.* **2.** Nice looking; handsome.
good·ly (**go͝od′** lē) ◊ *adjective* **goodlier, goodliest**

good-natured *adjective* Having or showing a nice disposition; cheerful.
good-na·tured (**go͝od′ nā′** chərd) ◊ *adjective*

goodness *noun* The quality or condition of being good.
good·ness (**go͝od′** nĭs) ◊ *noun*

good will *noun* **1.** A kindly or friendly attitude. **2.** The value of the good relationship a business has with its customers.

ă	pat	ĭ	pit	oi	**oil**	th	**bath**
ā	pay	ī	ride	o͝o	book	*th*	**bathe**
â	care	î	fierce	o͞o	boot	ə	ago, item
ä	father	ŏ	pot	ou	**out**		pencil
ĕ	pet	ō	go	ŭ	cut		atom
ē	be	ô	paw, for	û	fur		circus

goose *noun* A water bird that has a long neck and a short, pointed bill.
goose (go͞os) ◊ *noun, plural* **geese**

gopher *noun* A burrowing North American animal with pouches like pockets in its cheeks.
go·pher (**gō′** fər) ◊ *noun, plural* **gophers**

▲ **gopher**

gorge *noun* A deep, narrow passage, as between mountains.
◊ *verb* To eat in a greedy way.
gorge (gôrj) ◊ *noun, plural* **gorges** ◊ *verb* **gorged, gorging**

gorgeous *adjective* Extremely beautiful.
gor·geous (**gôr′** jəs) ◊ *adjective*

gorilla *noun* A large African ape with a heavy, thick body and dark hair.
go·ril·la (gə **rĭl′** ə) ◊ *noun, plural* **gorillas**
‖ *These sound alike:* **gorilla, guerrilla**

▲ **gorilla**

goshawk *noun* A large hawk with broad, rounded wings and gray or brownish plumage.
gos·hawk (gŏs′hôk′) ◊ *noun, plural* **goshawks**

gosling *noun* A young goose.
gos·ling (gŏz′lĭng) ◊ *noun, plural* **goslings**

gospel *noun* **1.** Often **Gospel** The teachings of Christ and the Apostles. **2.** Something that is never doubted or questioned: *We took the teacher's words as gospel.*
gos·pel (gŏs′pəl) ◊ *noun, plural* **gospels**

gossip *noun* **1.** Rumor and talk, often not true, that people repeat. **2.** A person who repeats rumors about other people.
◊ *verb* To engage in or spread rumors.
gos·sip (gŏs′əp) ◊ *noun, plural* **gossips** ◊ *verb* **gossiped, gossiping**

got *verb* Past tense and a past participle of **get.**
got (gŏt) ◊ *verb*

gotten *verb* A past participle of **get.**
got·ten (gŏt′n) ◊ *verb*

gouge *noun* **1.** A chisel with a rounded blade for cutting grooves, especially in wood. **2.** A groove or hole made with or as if with a gouge.
◊ *verb* To cut or dig out with a gouge.
gouge (gouj) ◊ *noun, plural* **gouges** ◊ *verb* **gouged, gouging**

gourd *noun* **1.** The fruit of a vine that is related to the pumpkin, squash, and cucumber. **2.** A bowl, ladle, or cup that is made from the dried, hard, hollowed-out shell of a gourd.
gourd (gôrd) ◊ *noun, plural* **gourds**

▲ **gourd**
Several kinds of gourds

Gov. The abbreviation for *Governor.*

govern *verb* **1.** To direct the public affairs of a country or state; rule: *Congress and the President govern the United States.* **2.** To control the actions and behavior of. **3.** To determine: *The size of crops governs the price of food.*
gov·ern (gŭv′ərn) ◊ *verb* **governed, governing**

SYNONYMS

govern, rule

We elect a President to help *govern* the United States. The monarch *ruled* the people for many years.

government *noun* **1.** The act or process of governing, especially the direction of the public affairs of a country, state, or city. **2.** A form or system by which a political unit, as a country, is governed: *In a democratic government elected representatives make the laws.* **3.** A group of people who govern a political unit, as a country: *My parents joined the government as lawyers.*
gov·ern·ment (gŭv′ərn mənt) ◊ *noun, plural* **governments**

governor *noun* **1.** The person elected as the head of a state in the United States. **2.** A person who is appointed to govern a colony or territory.
gov·er·nor (gŭv′ər nər) ◊ *noun, plural* **governors**

govt. The abbreviation for *government.*

gown *noun* **1.** A loose, flowing robe, as that worn by graduates, judges, and members of the clergy. **2.** A woman's dress, especially a formal one.
gown (goun) ◊ *noun, plural* **gowns**

grab *verb* To seize suddenly; snatch: *The monkey grabbed the peanut out of my hand.*
◊ *noun* The act or an example of grabbing: *I made a grab for the falling glass of water.*
grab (grăb) ◊ *verb* **grabbed, grabbing** ◊ *noun, plural* **grabs**

grace *noun* **1.** Ease, elegance, and beauty of movement or form: *We admired the grace of the dancer.* **2.** A charming or pleasing quality or type of behavior: *We should all learn the social graces at an early age.* **3.** A short prayer of thanks before or after a meal.
◊ *verb* **1.** To give honor to; favor: *The royal family graced the ball with their presence.* **2.** To add beauty to: *A vase full of lilies graced the table.*
grace (grās) ◊ *noun, plural* **graces** ◊ *verb* **graced, gracing**

graceful *adjective* Showing grace, as in movement: *The deer is a graceful animal.*
grace·ful (grās′fəl) ◊ *adjective*

gracious *adjective* Courteous and kind: *Gracious hosts always try to make their guests comfortable.*
gra·cious (**grā′**shəs) ◊ *adjective*

grackle *noun* A blackbird with glossy blackish feathers and a harsh, husky voice.
grack·le (**grăk′**əl) ◊ *noun, plural* **grackles**

grade *noun* **1.** A position in a scale of quality, rank, order, or value: *The rank of commander is one grade lower than that of captain.* **2.** A group of things of the same quality, rank, or value; class: *Eggs are sorted into grades according to size.* **3.** The degree to which something, as a road or railroad track, slopes. **4.** A class or year in a school: *The twins will enter the fourth grade next fall.* **5.** A mark showing the quality of a student's work: *I got a good grade in science.*
◊ *verb* **1.** To put into grades, as of quality; sort: *The farmer graded the peaches.* **2.** To give a mark or grade to: *The teacher will grade all the tests.* **3.** To adjust to a desirable slope: *Bulldozers graded the highway.*
grade (grād) ◊ *noun, plural* **grades** ◊ *verb* **graded, grading**

grade school *noun* An elementary school.
grade school ◊ *noun, plural* **grade schools**

gradual *adjective* Happening or moving little by little: *There was a gradual improvement in the weather.*
grad·u·al (**grăj′** o͞o əl) ◊ *adjective*

graduate *verb* **1.** To finish a course of study and receive a diploma: *My cousin graduated from high school last year.* **2.** To divide into or mark with evenly spaced lines: *The ruler is graduated in inches.*
◊ *noun* A person who has graduated from a school or college.
grad·u·ate ◊ *verb* (**grăj′** o͞o āt′) **graduated, graduating** ◊ *noun* (**grăj′** o͞o ĭt), *plural* **graduates**

graduation *noun* **1.** The act or process of graduating from a school or college. **2.** A ceremony at which graduating students receive their diplomas.
grad·u·a·tion (grăj′ o͞o **ā′**shən) ◊ *noun, plural* **graduations**

graft *verb* **1.** To join a plant, shoot, or bud to another plant so that the two grow together as a single plant. **2.** To transplant or implant tissue, bone, or an organ from one part of the body to another part of the body by surgery.
◊ *noun* **1.** A grafted plant shoot or bud. **2.** Tissue, bone, or an organ of the body that has been grafted.
graft (grăft) ◊ *verb* **grafted, grafting** ◊ *noun, plural* **grafts**

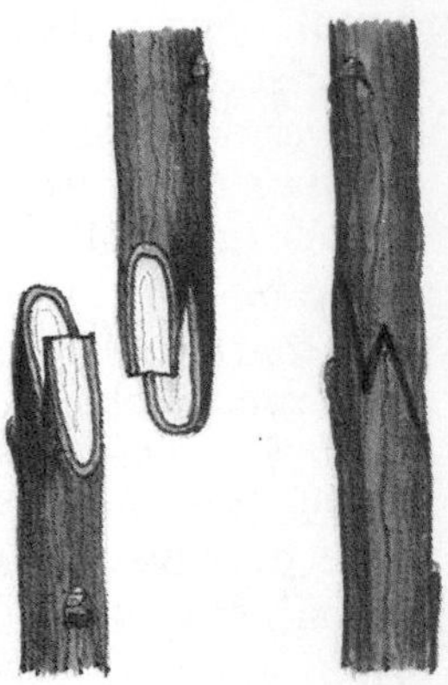

▲ **graft**
A plant graft

grain *noun* **1.** The small, hard, edible seed of cereal plants, especially of wheat, corn, or rice. **2.** A small, hard particle, as of salt or sand. **3.** Cereal plants, as wheat or rye: *I saw a painting of a field of golden grain.* **4.** The markings, pattern, or texture of a substance such as wood, stone, or marble.
grain (grān) ◊ *noun, plural* **grains**

gram *noun* A unit of mass and weight in the metric system. One gram is equal to 1/1000 kilogram.
gram (grăm) ◊ *noun, plural* **grams**

grammar *noun* **1.** The study of the forms of words and how they are used in sentences. **2.** The rules for combining words into the phrases and sentences of a language. **3.** The use of language according to the rules of grammar.
gram·mar (**grăm′**ər) ◊ *noun*

grammar school *noun* A school for the first six to eight years of a child's formal education.
grammar school ◊ *noun, plural* **grammar schools**

grammatical *adjective* **1.** Of or relating to grammar. **2.** Following the rules of grammar: *Although the sentence was grammatical, it didn't make much sense.*
gram·mat·i·cal (grə **măt′**ĭ kəl) ◊ *adjective*

ă	pat	ĭ	pit	oi	**oil**	th	**bath**
ā	pay	ī	ride	o͝o	book	*th*	**bathe**
â	care	î	fierce	o͞o	boot	ə	ago, item
ä	father	ŏ	pot	ou	**out**		pencil
ĕ	pet	ō	go	ŭ	cut		atom
ē	be	ô	paw, for	û	fur		circus

granary *noun* A building for storing grain.
gran·a·ry (**grăn′**ə rē *or* **grā′**nə rē) ◊ *noun, plural* **granaries**

▲ **granary**

grand *adjective* **1.** Very pleasing; wonderful: *I had a grand time on my vacation.* **2.** Large and very fine in appearance: *The inside of the capitol is truly grand.* **3.** Ranking higher or being more important than others: *We won the grand prize.* **4.** Including everything; complete: *I spent a grand total of $15.00.*
grand (grănd) ◊ *adjective* **grander, grandest**

> ***SYNONYMS***
>
> ***grand, magnificent, majestic***
>
> The mansion was built in the *grand* style. The food at the royal feast was *magnificent*. The Rockies are *majestic* mountains.

grandchild *noun* A child of one's son or daughter.
grand·child (**grănd′**chīld′) ◊ *noun, plural* **grandchildren**

grandchildren *noun* Plural of **grandchild.**
grand·chil·dren (**grănd′**chĭl′drən) ◊ *noun*

granddaughter *noun* A daughter of one's son or daughter.
grand·daugh·ter (**grănd′**dô′tər) ◊ *noun, plural* **granddaughters**

grandeur *noun* The quality or condition of being grand; greatness or splendor: *We admired the grandeur of the mountains.*
gran·deur (**grăn′**jər) ◊ *noun*

grandfather *noun* The father of one's father or mother.
grand·fa·ther (**grănd′**fä′*th*ər) ◊ *noun, plural* **grandfathers**

grandmother *noun* The mother of one's father or mother.
grand·moth·er (**grănd′**mŭ*th*′ər) ◊ *noun, plural* **grandmothers**

grandparent *noun* A parent of one's father or mother.
grand·par·ent (**grănd′**păr′ənt) ◊ *noun, plural* **grandparents**

grandson *noun* A son of one's son or daughter.
grand·son (**grănd′**sŭn′) ◊ *noun, plural* **grandsons**

grandstand *noun* The main seating area for spectators, as at a stadium.
grand·stand (**grănd′**stănd′) ◊ *noun, plural* **grandstands**

granite *noun* A hard rock that is used in buildings and monuments.
gran·ite (**grăn′**ĭt) ◊ *noun*

granny *or* **grannie** *noun* A grandmother.
gran·ny *or* **gran·nie** (**grăn′**ē) ◊ *noun, plural* **grannies**

granola *noun* Rolled oats mixed with various ingredients, such as dried fruit, brown sugar, and nuts. Granola is eaten especially as a breakfast cereal.
gra·no·la (grə **nō′**lə) ◊ *noun*

grant *verb* **1.** To give or allow: *Please grant their request.* **2.** To admit that something is true: *I'll grant that you look a lot better now.* ◊ *noun* **1.** The act of granting. **2.** Something, as a sum of money or a piece of land, that is granted.
grant (grănt) ◊ *verb* **granted, granting** ◊ *noun, plural* **grants**

grape *noun* A juicy fruit with smooth skin that grows in clusters on a climbing vine. Grapes are eaten raw, dried for raisins, and used for making jelly or jam.
grape (grāp) ◊ *noun, plural* **grapes**

grapefruit *noun* A large, round fruit that has yellow skin, is related to the orange, and has a somewhat sour taste.
grape·fruit (**grāp′**fro͞ot′) ◊ *noun, plural* **grapefruit** *or* **grapefruits**

G

grapevine *noun* A vine on which grapes grow.
grape·vine (grāp′vīn′) ◊ *noun, plural* **grapevines**

▲ **grapevine**

graph *noun* A drawing or diagram that shows the relationships between things.
graph (grăf) ◊ *noun, plural* **graphs**

graphics *noun* (*used with a singular or plural verb*) **1.** The making of drawings according to mathematical rules, as in engineering work. **2.** Pictures or charts drawn by a computer and displayed on its screen.
graph·ics (grăf′ĭks) ◊ *noun*

graphite *noun* A rather soft black carbon that is used in making lead pencils.
graph·ite (grăf′īt′) ◊ *noun*

grasp *verb* **1.** To seize and hold firmly with or as if with the hand: *I grasped the railing so I wouldn't fall.* **2.** To take into the mind; understand: *Do you grasp the problem?*
◊ *noun* **1.** The act of grasping. **2.** The ability to achieve; reach: *Victory seemed within the team's grasp.* **3.** Understanding: *The student has a good grasp of social studies.*
grasp (grăsp) ◊ *verb* **grasped, grasping**
◊ *noun, plural* **grasps**

grass *noun* **1.** One of a large group of plants with narrow leaves, jointed stems, and clusters of small flowers. **2.** Green plants on which grazing animals feed. **3.** Ground, such as a lawn or pasture, covered with grass.
grass (grăs) ◊ *noun, plural* **grasses**

grasshopper *noun* An insect with two pairs of wings and long hind legs used for jumping.
grass·hop·per (grăs′hŏp′ər) ◊ *noun, plural* **grasshoppers**

▲ **grasshopper**

grassland *noun* An area of land, such as a prairie, covered with grass.
grass·land (grăs′lănd′) ◊ *noun, plural* **grasslands**

grate¹ *verb* **1.** To break into fragments or shreds by rubbing against a rough surface: *I grated a little nutmeg on the top of the custard.* **2.** To rub or rub against with a harsh grinding or scraping sound. **3.** To have an unpleasant or annoying effect: *That loud music grates on my nerves.*
grate¹ (grāt) ◊ *verb* **grated, grating**
‖*These sound alike:* **grate, great**

grate² *noun* **1.** A framework of parallel or crossed bars or wires over an opening, as a window. **2.** A framework of metal bars used to hold burning fuel in a furnace or fireplace.
grate² (grāt) ◊ *noun, plural* **grates**
‖*These sound alike:* **grate, great**

HISTORY • grate¹, grate²

Grate¹ is from an old French word meaning "to scratch" and is distantly related to the word **scratch. Grate²** goes back to a Latin word meaning "frame, basket," and is distantly related to the word **crate.**

ă	pat	ĭ	pit	oi	oil	th	bath
ā	pay	ī	ride	ŏŏ	book	*th*	bathe
â	care	î	fierce	ōō	boot	ə	ago, item
ä	father	ŏ	pot	ou	out		pencil
ĕ	pet	ō	go	ŭ	cut		atom
ē	be	ô	paw, for	û	fur		circus

grateful *adjective* Feeling or showing gratitude; thankful: *I have a lot to be grateful for.*
grate·ful (**grāt′** fəl) ◊ *adjective*

grater *noun* A kitchen tool that has slits and holes with sharp edges, on which to grate or shred food.
grat·er (**grā′** tər) ◊ *noun, plural* **graters**

gratify *verb* To give pleasure or satisfaction to: *Your success gratified your parents.*
grat·i·fy (**grăt′** ə fī′) ◊ *verb* **gratified, gratifying**

grating *noun* A frame of parallel bars set across an opening, as in a bank or post office, in order to block it.
grat·ing (**grā′** tĭng) ◊ *noun, plural* **gratings**

gratitude *noun* A feeling of being thankful; appreciation.
grat·i·tude (**grăt′** ĭ to͞od′ *or* **grăt′** ĭ tyo͞od′) ◊ *noun*

grave[1] *noun* **1.** A hole in the ground in which a corpse is buried. **2.** A place of burial; tomb: *The sea was the sailor's grave.*
grave[1] (grāv) ◊ *noun, plural* **graves**

grave[2] *adjective* **1.** Very important: *World hunger is a grave problem.* **2.** Having a serious appearance or way of acting: *Why do you have a grave expression on your face?* —See Synonyms at **serious.**
grave[2] (grāv) ◊ *adjective* **graver, gravest**

> ***HISTORY* • grave[1], grave[2]**
>
> **Grave**[1] goes back to an old English word that meant "a place dug out for a burial." **Grave**[2] is from a Latin word that meant "heavy" and also "weighty, serious, solemn." **Gravity** is related to this Latin word.

gravel *noun* A loose mixture of small pieces of rock, used for covering roads and paths.
grav·el (**grăv′** əl) ◊ *noun*

gravelly *adjective* **1.** Containing gravel. **2.** Harsh or irritating in sound, as a voice.
grav·el·ly (**grăv′** ə lē) ◊ *adjective*

graveyard *noun* A place for burying the dead; cemetery.
grave·yard (**grāv′** yärd′) ◊ *noun, plural* **graveyards**

gravitation *noun* The force that makes all the objects in the universe tend to move toward one another. Gravitation keeps the planets in our solar system from flying out of their orbits around the sun.
grav·i·ta·tion (grăv′ĭ **tā′** shən) ◊ *noun*

gravity *noun* **1.** The natural force that causes smaller objects to move toward the center of the earth. A ball that is tossed in the air falls back to the ground because of the pull of gravity. **2.** Great importance: *They haven't realized the gravity of the threat of famine yet.*
grav·i·ty (**grăv′** ĭ tē) ◊ *noun, plural* **gravities**

gravy *noun* A sauce made from the juice that comes out of meat during cooking.
gra·vy (**grā′** vē) ◊ *noun, plural* **gravies**

gray *noun* A color made by mixing black and white.
◊ *adjective* Of the color gray.
gray (grā) ◊ *noun, plural* **grays** ◊ *adjective* **grayer, grayest**

graze[1] *verb* To feed on growing grass: *Cattle grazed in the pasture.*
graze[1] (grāz) ◊ *verb* **grazed, grazing**

graze[2] *verb* To touch or scrape lightly in passing.
◊ *noun* A light touch of something passing.
graze[2] (grāz) ◊ *verb* **grazed, grazing** ◊ *noun, plural* **grazes**

> ***HISTORY* • graze[1], graze[2]**
>
> **Graze**[1] comes from an old English word that meant "to feed on growing grass." **Graze**[2] was first used to refer to things such as bullets glancing off a surface, as a wall or the ground. Perhaps **graze**[2] came from **graze**[1] with the idea that the bullets were taking the grass off close to the ground.

grease *noun* **1.** Animal fat when melted or soft. This kind of grease is used in cooking. **2.** Very thick, sticky oil or a similar material, used on the moving parts of machines to make them operate properly.
◊ *verb* To smear grease on or pack grease in: *Always grease a cake pan before using it.*
grease (grēs) ◊ *noun, plural* **greases** ◊ *verb* **greased, greasing**

greasy *adjective* **1.** Covered or soiled with grease: *I usually have to wash the greasy pots and pans.* **2.** Containing grease; oily: *Too*

much greasy food isn't good for you.
greas·y (**grē′**sē *or* **grē′**zē) ◊ *adjective*
greasier, greasiest

LANGUAGE DETECTIVE

greasy
The way you pronounce *greasy* depends on where you live. If you live in the northern United States, you probably pronounce *greasy* as (**grē′**sē). If you live in the southern United States, you probably pronounce *greasy* as (**grē′**zē). You might also use this pronunciation if you live in New York City, New Jersey, or Philadelphia. Both pronunciations of *greasy* are correct.

great *adjective* **1.** Very large in size, number, or amount: *A great number of people welcomed the senator.* —See Synonyms at **big.** **2.** More than usual. **3.** Important; remarkable: *Our art museum has great paintings and sculptures.*
great (grāt) ◊ *adjective* **greater, greatest**
‖*These sound alike:* **great, grate**

Great Dane *noun* A large, powerful dog with a smooth, short coat.
Great Dane ◊ *noun, plural* **Great Danes**

▲ **Great Dane**

ă	pat	ĭ	pit	oi	**oil**	th	ba**th**
ā	pay	ī	ride	ŏŏ	**book**	*th*	ba**th**e
â	care	î	fierce	ōō	**boot**	ə	**a**go, it**e**m
ä	father	ŏ	pot	ou	**out**		penc**i**l
ĕ	pet	ō	go	ŭ	**cut**		at**o**m
ē	be	ô	paw, for	û	**fur**		circ**u**s

great-grandchild *noun* A child of one's grandchild.
great-grand·child (**grāt′ grănd′**chīld′) ◊ *noun, plural* **great-grandchildren**

great-grandfather *noun* The father of any of one's grandparents.
great-grand·fa·ther (**grāt′ grănd′** fä′*th*ər) ◊ *noun, plural* **great-grandfathers**

great-grandmother *noun* The mother of any of one's grandparents.
great-grand·moth·er (**grāt′ grănd′** mŭ*th*′ər) ◊ *noun, plural* **great-grandmothers**

great-grandparent *noun* The mother or father of one's grandparent.
great-grand·par·ent (**grāt′ grănd′** păr′ənt) ◊ *noun, plural* **great-grandparents**

greatly *adverb* To a great degree; very much: *Families vary greatly in size.*
great·ly (**grāt′**lē) ◊ *adverb*

greed *noun* A selfish desire for more than what one needs or deserves.
greed (grēd) ◊ *noun*

Greek *noun* **1.** A person who was born in or lives in Greece. **2.** The language of the Greeks.
◊ *adjective* Of or relating to Greece, the Greeks, or their language.
Greek (grēk) ◊ *noun, plural* **Greeks**
◊ *adjective*

green *noun* **1.** The color of most plant leaves and growing grass. **2. greens** Leaves and stems of plants used as food: *We had turnip greens for dinner.* **3.** A grassy area or park in the center of town: *We often play soccer on the village green.* **4.** The area of smooth, short grass around a hole on a golf course.
◊ *adjective* **1.** Of the color green. **2.** Covered with grass, trees, or other plant growth: *Green meadows spread for miles into the distance.* **3.** Not ripe: *Green oranges are not good to eat.* **4.** Not having training or experience: *A truck full of green recruits drove into the naval base.*
green (grēn) ◊ *noun, plural* **greens**
◊ *adjective* **greener, greenest**

greenhouse *noun* A room or building made of glass in which plants that need a warm, even temperature are grown.
green·house (**grēn′**hous′) ◊ *noun, plural* **greenhouses**

▲ **greenhouse**

green thumb *noun* An unusual ability to make plants grow well.

greet *verb* **1.** To welcome or speak to in a friendly or polite way: *We greeted our guests at the door.* **2.** To respond to; meet: *The announcement of the team's victory was greeted with cheers from everyone.*
greet (grēt) ◊ *verb* **greeted, greeting**

greeting *noun* **1.** An act or expression of welcome: *Our hosts gave us a warm greeting.* **2. greetings** Friendly wishes.
greet·ing (**grē′** tĭng) ◊ *noun, plural* **greetings**

grenade *noun* A small bomb usually thrown by hand.
gre·nade (grə **nād′**) ◊ *noun, plural* **grenades**

grew *verb* Past tense of **grow.**
grew (gro͞o) ◊ *verb*

greyhound *noun* A slender dog with long legs, a smooth coat, and a narrow head. Greyhounds can run very fast.
grey·hound (**grā′**hound′) ◊ *noun, plural* **greyhounds**

grid *noun* A pattern of vertical and horizontal lines that form squares. Grids are used on maps and charts to locate places.
grid (grĭd) ◊ *noun, plural* **grids**

griddle *noun* A heavy, flat metal plate with a handle or a large, flat metal surface on big stoves, used for cooking foods such as pancakes or bacon.
grid·dle (**grĭd′**l) ◊ *noun, plural* **griddles**

gridiron *noun* **1.** A grill that is used for broiling food. **2.** A football field.
grid·i·ron (**grĭd′**ī′ərn) ◊ *noun, plural* **gridirons**

grief *noun* Great sadness; deep sorrow: *We all felt grief over the death of our cat.*
grief (grēf) ◊ *noun, plural* **griefs**

grieve *verb* **1.** To feel very sad; mourn. **2.** To cause to feel very sad.
grieve (grēv) ◊ *verb* **grieved, grieving**

grievous *adjective* Causing grief or pain.
griev·ous (**grē′** vəs) ◊ *adjective*

grill *noun* A cooking device with parallel thin metal bars on which food, as meat or fish, may be broiled.
◊ *verb* **1.** To cook on a grill. **2.** To question closely, severely, and for a long time.
grill (grĭl) ◊ *noun, plural* **grills** ◊ *verb* **grilled, grilling**

grim *adjective* **1.** Harsh; stern: *Why do you have such a grim expression on your face?* **2.** Refusing to give up: *We climbed the mountain with grim determination.*
grim (grĭm) ◊ *adjective* **grimmer, grimmest**

grimace *noun* A tightening and twisting of the face muscles, as in pain or disgust.
◊ *verb* To make a grimace: *The acrobat grimaced during the circus performance.*
grim·ace (**grĭm′**ĭs *or* grĭ **mās′**) ◊ *noun, plural* **grimaces** ◊ *verb* **grimaced, grimacing**

grime *noun* Heavy dirt: *The mechanic's hands were covered with grime.*
grime (grīm) ◊ *noun*

grimy *adjective* Covered with grime; very dirty: *Please ask the mechanic to clean that grimy windshield.*
grim·y (**grī′**mē) ◊ *adjective* **grimier, grimiest**

grin *verb* To smile broadly: *The child grinned with delight at the birthday present.*
◊ *noun* A very broad smile.
grin (grĭn) ◊ *verb* **grinned, grinning** ◊ *noun, plural* **grins**

grind *verb* **1.** To rub, pound, or crush something into powder or very small pieces: *Our grocery store has a machine that grinds coffee beans.* **2.** To shape, sharpen, or make smooth by rubbing: *I had new lenses ground for my eyeglasses.* **3.** To rub together noisily; grate: *Some people grind their teeth at night in their sleep.*
grind (grīnd) ◊ *verb* **ground, grinding**

grindstone *noun* A round, flat stone wheel that spins on a rod set in a frame. It is used for grinding and sharpening knives and tools or for smoothing and polishing objects.
grind·stone (**grīnd′**stōn′) ◊ *noun, plural* **grindstones**

▲ **grindstone**

grip *noun* **1.** A tight hold; firm grasp: *I got a good grip on the handlebars as I went down the hill.* **2.** A part designed to be grasped and held; handle. **3.** Power or control: *Try to keep a grip on your emotions.*
◊ *verb* To grasp firmly and hold on to: *The little child gripped my hand as we walked.*
grip (grĭp) ◊ *noun, plural* **grips** ◊ *verb* **gripped, gripping**

gristle *noun* Tough, white tissue in meat.
gris·tle (**grĭs′** əl) ◊ *noun*

grit *noun* **1.** Tiny rough bits of sand or stone. **2.** The quality of staying with something and not giving up; endurance: *It takes grit to keep studying a subject that is very difficult for you.*
◊ *verb* To clamp or grind the teeth together, as in determination: *I gritted my teeth as I waded into the cold ocean water.*
grit (grĭt) ◊ *noun, plural* **grits** ◊ *verb* **gritted, gritting**

grits *plural noun* Very coarsely ground grain, especially corn.
grits (grĭts) ◊ *plural noun*

grizzled *adjective* Streaked or marked with gray: *The old dog had a grizzled muzzle.*
griz·zled (**grĭz′** əld) ◊ *adjective*

grizzly bear *noun* A large, grayish or brownish bear of western North America.
griz·zly bear (**grĭz′** lē) ◊ *noun, plural* **grizzly bears**

ă	pat	ĭ	pit	oi	**oil**	th	ba**th**
ā	pay	ī	ride	o͝o	book	*th*	ba**th**e
â	care	î	fierce	o͞o	boot	ə	ago, item
ä	father	ŏ	pot	ou	**out**		pencil
ĕ	pet	ō	go	ŭ	cut		atom
ē	be	ô	paw, for	û	fur		circus

▲ **grizzly bear**

groan *verb* To make a deep sound low in the throat that expresses pain, grief, annoyance, or good-natured disapproval.
◊ *noun* The deep sound made in groaning; moan.
groan (grōn) ◊ *verb* **groaned, groaning** ◊ *noun, plural* **groans**
‖*These sound alike:* **groan, grown**

grocer *noun* A storekeeper who sells food and various household supplies.
gro·cer (**grō′** sər) ◊ *noun, plural* **grocers**

grocery *noun* **1.** A store selling food and various household supplies. **2.** **groceries** The goods sold by a grocer.
gro·cer·y (**grō′** sə rē) ◊ *noun, plural* **groceries**

groggy *adjective* Unsteady and dazed, as from an illness, a blow, or lack of sleep.
grog·gy (**grŏg′** ē) ◊ *adjective* **groggier, groggiest**

groom *noun* **1.** A person who takes care of horses. **2.** A bridegroom.
◊ *verb* **1.** To clean, brush, feed, and take care of horses. **2.** To make neat and attractive in appearance: *We groomed ourselves carefully for the party.*
groom (gro͞om *or* gro͝om) ◊ *noun, plural* **grooms** ◊ *verb* **groomed, grooming**

groove *noun* **1.** A long, narrow cut or channel: *The heavy wheels of the wagon left deep grooves in the earth.* **2.** The track on a phonograph record that the needle follows.
groove (gro͞ov) ◊ *noun, plural* **grooves**

grope *verb* **1.** To reach about or search blindly or uncertainly: *I groped for the light switch in the dark.* **2.** To feel one's way slowly without seeing clearly: *We groped our way down the long, dark hallway.*
grope (grōp) ◊ *verb* **groped, groping**

gross *adjective* **1.** Without anything taken out; total: *My cousin's gross income is $20,000 a year.* **2.** Extreme; obvious: *The people thought the new law was a gross injustice.*
◊ *noun* **1.** Twelve dozen; 144: *We ordered three gross of pencils.* **2.** A total amount received: *The theater's gross for the evening was high.*
gross (grōs) ◊ *adjective* **grosser, grossest** ◊ *noun, plural* **gross** (for sense 1) *or* **grosses** (for sense 2)

grotesque *adjective* Very ugly or unnatural in appearance: *Grotesque faces are carved over the doorway of the old building.*
gro·tesque (grō **tĕsk′**) ◊ *adjective*

grouch *noun* A person who is often cross, grumbling, or complaining.
grouch (grouch) ◊ *noun, plural* **grouches**

grouchy *adjective* Cross, grumbling, or complaining: *Some people are grouchy when they first wake up.* —See Synonyms at **irritable.**
grouch·y (**grou′**chē) ◊ *adjective* **grouchier, grouchiest**

ground¹ *noun* **1.** The solid surface of the earth; land. **2.** Often **grounds** An area or plot of land set aside and used for a special purpose: *We stayed overnight in the camp grounds.* **3. grounds** The land that surrounds a house or other building: *According to the rules, we can't go off the school grounds during lunch.* **4.** Often **grounds** The reasons for a belief, action, or thought: *What grounds do you have for doubting me?* **5. grounds** The bits of solid coffee left over in a coffee pot after boiling water has strained through; dregs.
◊ *verb* **1.** To cause to touch the bottom of a body of water: *The boat was grounded in shallow water.* **2.** To base or establish: *We grounded our argument on the facts.* **3.** To stop an aircraft or pilot from flying. **4.** To connect an electric wire to the ground so that dangerous electricity passes off into it.
ground¹ (ground) ◊ *noun, plural* **grounds** ◊ *verb* **grounded, grounding**

ground² *verb* Past tense and past participle of **grind.**
ground² (ground) ◊ *verb*

ground hog *noun* A woodchuck.
ground hog ◊ *noun, plural* **ground hogs**

group *noun* **1.** A number of persons or things gathered or located together: *A group of people are waiting for the bus.* **2.** A number of persons or things thought of as a class because they are similar: *The choir on TV tonight is a children's group.*
◊ *verb* To arrange or gather in a group: *The coach grouped us according to ability.*
group (gro͞op) ◊ *noun, plural* **groups** ◊ *verb* **grouped, grouping**

grouse *noun* A bird that has a plump body and brownish or grayish feathers. Grouse are often hunted for food.
grouse (grous) ◊ *noun, plural* **grouse** *or* **grouses**

▲ **grouse**

grove *noun* A group of trees with open ground between them.
grove (grōv) ◊ *noun, plural* **groves**

grow *verb* **1.** To become larger in size as a result of a natural process: *Our class studied how crystals grow.* **2.** To be capable of living and flourishing, especially in a particular climate or environment: *Many house plants won't grow outdoors.* **3.** To cause to grow; raise: *We grow zucchini and carrots in our garden.* **4.** To increase or spread: *The singer's fame grew rapidly.* **5.** To become: *It grows dark early during winter.*
◊ *idiom* **grow up** To become an adult: *I want to be a surgeon when I grow up.*
grow (grō) ◊ *verb* **grew, grown, growing**

G

growl *noun* A low, deep, angry sound, as the one made by a dog.
◊ *verb* **1.** To make a low, deep, angry sound. **2.** To speak in a gruff, angry way: *The coach growled at the players who were late.*
growl (groul) ◊ *noun, plural* **growls** ◊ *verb* **growled, growling**

grown *adjective* Having reached an adult age; mature.
◊ *verb* Past participle of **grow.**
grown (grōn) ◊ *adjective* ◊ *verb*
‖*These sound alike:* **grown, groan**

grownup *noun* A fully grown person; adult.
grown·up (**grōn′**up′) ◊ *noun, plural* **grownups**

grown-up *adjective* For or characteristic of adults: *Behave in a grown-up manner when you answer the telephone.* —See Synonyms at **mature.**
grown-up (**grōn′**ŭp′) ◊ *adjective*

growth *noun* **1.** The process of growing: *Exercise and good food are important to the proper growth of a child.* **2.** Complete physical development; mature age: *Most cats reach full growth by the age of one year.* **3.** Something that grows or has grown: *A thick growth of weeds covered the yard.*
growth (grōth) ◊ *noun, plural* **growths**

grub *verb* To dig in the ground: *We helped the farmer grub for potatoes.*
◊ *noun* A beetle after it has hatched from an egg and before it is a fully grown insect. A grub looks like a small, thick worm.
grub (grŭb) ◊ *verb* **grubbed, grubbing** ◊ *noun, plural* **grubs**

grudge *noun* A continuing feeling of resentment, dislike, or anger, caused by an insult or injury: *Don't bear a grudge against me because I accidentally broke your record.*
◊ *verb* To be unwilling or reluctant to give or allow, often because of envy: *Don't grudge your cousin's pleasure at winning the race.*
grudge (grŭj) ◊ *noun, plural* **grudges** ◊ *verb* **grudged, grudging**

ă	pat	ĭ	pit	oi	**oil**	th	ba**th**
ā	pay	ī	ride	o͝o	book	*th*	ba*th*e
â	care	î	fierce	o͞o	boot	ə	ago, item
ä	father	ŏ	pot	ou	**out**		pencil
ĕ	pet	ō	go	ŭ	cut		atom
ē	be	ô	paw, for	û	fur		circus

grueling *adjective* Extremely tiring.
gru·el·ing (**gro͞o′**ə lĭng) ◊ *adjective*

gruesome *adjective* Causing shock or horror; terrible.
grue·some (**gro͞o′**səm) ◊ *adjective*

gruff *adjective* **1.** Having a harsh, deep sound. **2.** Not very friendly; stern.
gruff (grŭf) ◊ *adjective* **gruffer, gruffest**

grumble *verb* To complain in a sullen or discontented way; mutter: *The students grumbled about their homework assignments.*
◊ *noun* A mutter of complaint.
grum·ble (**grŭm′**bəl) ◊ *verb* **grumbled, grumbling** ◊ *noun, plural* **grumbles**

grumpy *adjective* Easily angered or upset; irritable: *I'm grumpy this morning.*
grump·y (**grŭm′**pē) ◊ *adjective* **grumpier, grumpiest**

grunt *noun* **1.** A short, deep, harsh sound made by a pig. **2.** A similar sound made deep in the throat: *I lifted the heavy suitcases with a grunt.*
◊ *verb* **1.** To make a short deep, harsh sound. **2.** To say or speak with such a sound: *I grunted a good morning to the others.*
grunt (grŭnt) ◊ *noun, plural* **grunts** ◊ *verb* **grunted, grunting**

guarantee *noun* **1.** A way of making sure of a certain outcome or result: *Buying a ticket ahead of time is a guarantee of a good seat at the show.* **2.** A personal promise: *You have my guarantee that I'll finish the job on time.* **3.** A promise that a product made by someone will be repaired or replaced if anything goes wrong with it during a certain amount of time.
◊ *verb* **1.** To make certain: *Hard work and musical talent guaranteed us places in the band.* **2.** To promise: *The carpenter guaranteed the work would be finished by Tuesday.* **3.** To give a guarantee for: *The company guarantees this watch for a year.*
guar·an·tee (găr′ən **tē′**) ◊ *noun, plural* **guarantees** ◊ *verb* **guaranteed, guaranteeing**

guard *verb* **1.** To protect from harm or danger; defend. **2.** To supervise, so as to prevent escape: *The prisoner in the courtroom was guarded carefully.* **3.** To take precautions: *Guard against a head cold by dressing properly in cold weather.*
◊ *noun* **1.** A person or group that keeps watch

or protects: *The palace guard stood in line at attention.* **2.** Protection; control: *The house is under guard by the police.* **3.** A device or substance that protects or shields the user: *The bicycle has mud guards.* **4.** Either of two players on a football team's offensive line on each side of the center. **5.** Either of two players stationed farthest from the opponents' basket in basketball.
guard (gärd) ◊ *verb* **guarded, guarding** ◊ *noun, plural* **guards**

▲ **guard**

guardian *noun* **1.** Someone or something that guards, protects, or defends. **2.** A person who is appointed by a court of law to take care of someone who is unable to take care of himself or herself.
guard·i·an (**gär′** dē ən) ◊ *noun, plural* **guardians**

guerrilla *or* **guerilla** *noun* A member of a small, loosely organized group of soldiers fighting to overthrow a government. Guerrillas move and attack quickly in sudden raids and ambushes.
guer·ril·la *or* **gue·ril·la** (gə **rĭl′** ə) ◊ *noun, plural* **guerrillas** *or* **guerillas**
‖*These sound alike:* **guerrilla, gorilla**

guess *verb* **1.** To form an opinion without enough information to be sure of it; estimate: *I'd guess there were 6,000 people at the concert.* **2.** To form such an opinion and be right: *Can you guess the answer to this riddle?* **3.** To believe, without proof, that something is true, real, or accurate; suppose: *The car isn't here, so I guess my parents have gone out for the day.*
◊ *noun* An opinion or estimate arrived at by guessing: *If you're not sure of the answer, at least make a guess.*
guess (gĕs) ◊ *verb* **guessed, guessing** ◊ *noun, plural* **guesses**

guest *noun* **1.** A person who is at another person's home for a visit or a meal; visitor: *Our parents cooked a special meal for their dinner guests.* **2.** A person who visits a hotel, motel, or restaurant: *The motel manager showed the guests to their room.*
guest (gĕst) ◊ *noun, plural* **guests**

guidance *noun* **1.** Help or advice; counsel: *It is useful to have some guidance in choosing a career.* **2.** Leadership; supervision: *I learned how to roller-skate under the guidance of an instructor.*
guid·ance (**gīd′** ns) ◊ *noun*

guide *noun* Someone or something that shows the way, directs, leads, or teaches: *Our guide led us safely out of the woods.*
◊ *verb* To show the way to; direct: *The ranger agreed to guide us through the steep mountains.*
guide (gīd) ◊ *noun, plural* **guides** ◊ *verb* **guided, guiding**

> ***SYNONYMS***
>
> ***guide, lead[1], steer***
>
> Our counselor *guided* us on our hike through the woods. Our captain will *lead* our team onto the field. It is hard work to *steer* a truck on these winding mountain roads.

guided missile *noun* A missile whose course can be controlled while it is in flight.
guided missile ◊ *noun, plural* **guided missiles**

guideword *noun* A word that appears at the top of a page in dictionaries and certain other reference books. It tells you the first and last words on that page.
guide·word (**gīd′** wûrd′) ◊ *noun, plural* **guidewords**

guild *noun* **1.** An association of people who share an occupation, interest, or cause: *The sculptor was a member of an artists' guild.*

2. A union of merchants or craftsmen in the Middle Ages who set standards of work and looked after their own interests.
guild (gĭld) ◊ *noun, plural* **guilds**
‖*These sound alike:* **guild, gild**

guillotine *noun* A device for executing people by cutting off their heads. A guillotine is made of a heavy blade that slides up and down between two large, tall posts.
guil·lo·tine (**gĭl′** ə tēn′) ◊ *noun, plural* **guillotines**

guilt *noun* **1.** The fact of having done wrong; blame for a crime or bad deed: *The police couldn't prove the suspect's guilt.* **2.** A feeling of responsibility or deep shame for having done something bad or illegal: *I felt guilt for having quarreled with my friend.*
guilt (gĭlt) ◊ *noun*
‖*These sound alike:* **guilt, gilt**

guilty *adjective* **1.** Having committed a crime or bad deed: *The jury found them guilty of stealing.* **2.** Feeling deep shame: *I felt guilty about lying to my parents.*
guilt·y (**gĭl′** tē) ◊ *adjective* **guiltier, guiltiest**

guinea pig *noun* A small, furry animal with short ears, short legs, and a tail so short that it cannot be seen. Guinea pigs are often kept as pets.
guin·ea pig (**gĭn′** ē) ◊ *noun, plural* **guinea pigs**

guitar *noun* A musical instrument with a long neck attached to a sound box that is usually shaped like a pear with a flat back and front. Standard guitars have either 6 or 12 strings that are plucked or strummed with the fingers or a pick.
gui·tar (gĭ **tär′**) ◊ *noun, plural* **guitars**

gulch *noun* A shallow canyon or ravine.
gulch (gŭlch) ◊ *noun, plural* **gulches**

gulf *noun* **1.** A large area of a sea or ocean that is partly enclosed by land. **2.** A deep break in the earth, as one caused by an earthquake. **3.** A big difference, as of opinions.
gulf (gŭlf) ◊ *noun, plural* **gulfs**

ă	pat	ĭ	pit	oi	**oil**	th	**bath**
ā	pay	ī	ride	o͝o	book	*th*	**bathe**
â	care	î	fierce	o͞o	boot	ə	ago, item
ä	father	ŏ	pot	ou	**out**		pencil
ĕ	pet	ō	go	ŭ	cut		atom
ē	be	ô	paw, for	û	fur		circus

gull *noun* A bird with long wings, usually gray and white feathers, and webbed feet. Gulls live on coasts, rivers, and lakes.
gull (gŭl) ◊ *noun, plural* **gulls**

▲ **gull**

gullible *adjective* Easily tricked or fooled: *Gullible people will believe almost anything.*
gul·li·ble (**gŭl′** ə bəl) ◊ *adjective*

gully *noun* A ditch or channel cut in the earth by flowing water, especially after a heavy rain.
gul·ly (**gŭl′** ē) ◊ *noun, plural* **gullies**

gulp *verb* **1.** To swallow quickly or greedily in large amounts: *We gulped down our lunch because we were late.* **2.** To breathe air in deeply and quickly: *I gulped when I saw lightning strike a tree across the street.*
◊ *noun* A large, quick swallow: *Take a big gulp of air before swimming the length of the pool and back.*
gulp (gŭlp) ◊ *verb* **gulped, gulping** ◊ *noun, plural* **gulps**

gum¹ *noun* **1.** A thick, sticky juice produced by some plants and trees. Gum is used in making glue, candies, and rubber. **2.** Chewing gum.
◊ *verb* **1.** To seal or fasten in place with gum. **2.** To become sticky or clogged with or as if with gum.
gum¹ (gŭm) ◊ *noun, plural* **gums** ◊ *verb* **gummed, gumming**

gum² *noun* The firm flesh that is around the teeth.
gum² (gŭm) ◊ *noun, plural* **gums**

HISTORY **• gum¹, gum²**

Your **gum²** may seem soft like **gum¹**, but these two words are not related. **Gum¹** goes back to an Egyptian word for the sticky stuff that comes from certain trees. **Gum²** comes from an old English word that first meant "the inside of the mouth."

gumdrop *noun* A small piece of stiff, jellied candy.
gum·drop (gŭm′drŏp′) ◊ *noun, plural* **gumdrops**

gun *noun* **1.** A weapon that shoots bullets through a heavy metal tube. Pistols, rifles, and cannons are guns. **2.** A device that shoots out something under pressure: *I painted the wall with a spray gun.*
◊ *verb* To shoot with a gun.
gun (gŭn) ◊ *noun, plural* **guns** ◊ *verb* **gunned, gunning**

gunboat *noun* A light, maneuverable warship equipped with guns.
gun·boat (gŭn′bōt′) ◊ *noun, plural* **gunboats**

gunner *noun* A person in the military whose job is to fire large guns.
gun·ner (gŭn′ər) ◊ *noun, plural* **gunners**

gunpowder *noun* A powder that explodes when set on fire. Gunpowder is used for shooting bullets out of guns and in making explosives and fireworks.
gun·pow·der (gŭn′pou′dər) ◊ *noun, plural* **gunpowders**

gunwale *noun* The upper edge of the side of a ship, boat, or canoe.
gun·wale (gŭn′əl) ◊ *noun, plural* **gunwales**

guppy *noun* A small, brightly colored tropical freshwater fish. Guppies are often kept in home aquariums.
gup·py (gŭp′ē) ◊ *noun, plural* **guppies**

gurgle *verb* **1.** To flow with a bubbling sound: *The milk gurgled out of the bottle.* **2.** To make low, bubbling sounds: *The baby gurgled when I came into the room.*
◊ *noun* A bubbling sound.
gur·gle (gûr′gəl) ◊ *verb* **gurgled, gurgling** ◊ *noun, plural* **gurgles**

gush *verb* **1.** To flow or pour out of suddenly and in a great amount: *Oil gushed out of the ground.* **2.** To show or talk with so much feeling and enthusiasm that it seems silly or embarrassing to others: *Family and friends gushed over the new baby.*
◊ *noun* A sudden or large flow: *The pipe burst open with a gush of hot water.*
gush (gŭsh) ◊ *verb* **gushed, gushing** ◊ *noun, plural* **gushes**

gust *noun* A sudden, strong rush of wind.
gust (gŭst) ◊ *noun, plural* **gusts**

gut *noun* **1.** The stomach or intestines. **2.** String made from the intestines of certain animals. Gut is used for the strings of some musical instruments, such as violins.
gut (gŭt) ◊ *noun, plural* **guts**

gutter *noun* **1.** A ditch along the side of a street for draining off water. **2.** A pipe or trough along the edge of a roof for carrying off water.
gut·ter (gŭt′ər) ◊ *noun, plural* **gutters**

guy[1] *noun* A rope, chain, or cable used for steadying, guiding, or fastening something.
guy[1] (gī) ◊ *noun, plural* **guys**

guy[2] *noun* **1.** A man; fellow. **2.** A person.
guy[2] (gī) ◊ *noun, plural* **guys**

HISTORY • guy[1], guy[2]

Guy[1] is probably from a Dutch word that meant "a rope used in sailing." **Guy**[2] has a more interesting history. On November 5, 1605, a man named Guy Fawkes tried to blow up the British rulers in Parliament. Since then English children have celebrated November 5 as Guy Fawkes Day, which is something like our Halloween. Children carrying scarecrows called *Guys* go around to neighbors' houses and ask for "a penny for the Guy." From these figures, **guy**[2] also came to mean "a raggedy-looking person." About a hundred years ago, Americans started using **guy**[2] as a slang word for "man."

guzzle *verb* To drink greedily.
guz·zle (gŭz′əl) ◊ *verb* **guzzled, guzzling**

gym *noun* **1.** A gymnasium. **2.** A class in physical exercises or sports.
gym (jĭm) ◊ *noun, plural* **gyms**

gymnasium *noun* A room or building with equipment for physical exercises and training and for indoor sports.
gym·na·si·um (jĭm nā′zē əm) ◊ *noun, plural* **gymnasiums**

gymnast *noun* A person who is skilled in gymnastics.
gym·nast (jĭm′năst′) ◊ *noun, plural* **gymnasts**

G

gymnastic *adjective* Of or having to do with gymnastics or gymnasts.
gym·nas·tic (jĭm **năs′** tĭk) ◊ *adjective*

gymnastics *noun* (*used with a singular or plural verb*) Physical exercises done with the use of floor mats, stationary bars, and other equipment in a gymnasium.
gym·nas·tics (jĭm **năs′** tĭks) ◊ *noun*

Gypsy *noun* A member of a wandering group of people who came from India in the fourteenth and fifteenth centuries and now live in many different parts of the world.
Gyp·sy (**jĭp′** sē) ◊ *noun, plural* **Gypsies**

gypsy moth *noun* A small moth. The caterpillars of the gypsy moth feed on leaves and do great damage to trees.
gypsy moth ◊ *noun, plural* **gypsy moths**

gyrate *verb* To move in a circle or a spiral; whirl: *The figure skater gyrated in an incredibly fast spin.*
gy·rate (**jī′** rāt′) ◊ *verb* **gyrated, gyrating**

ă	pat	ĭ	pit	oi	**oil**	th	ba**th**
ā	pay	ī	ride	o͝o	book	*th*	ba**th**e
â	care	î	fierce	o͞o	boot	ə	ago, item
ä	father	ŏ	pot	ou	**out**		pencil
ĕ	pet	ō	go	ŭ	cut		atom
ē	be	ô	paw, for	û	fur		circus

gyrfalcon *noun* A large falcon of northern regions, with white or grayish feathers.
gyr·fal·con (**jûr′** făl′kən *or* **jûr′** fôl′kən) ◊ *noun, plural* **gyrfalcons**

gyroscope *noun* An instrument consisting of a mounted wheel that can spin rapidly and freely on an axis. A spinning gyroscope resists any change in its direction, even when the base is tilted. Gyroscopes are used to keep ships and aircraft steady.
gy·ro·scope (**jī′** rə skōp′) ◊ *noun, plural* **gyroscopes**

▲ **gyroscope**

gyroscopic *adjective* **1.** Of or relating to a gyroscope. **2.** Operated by a gyroscope.
gy·ro·scop·ic (jī′rə **skŏp′** ĭk) ◊ *adjective*

Hyena

Hh

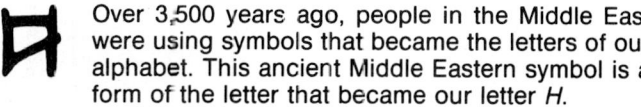

H is the eighth letter of the English alphabet. Did you know that it has a long history?

Over 3,500 years ago, people in the Middle East were using symbols that became the letters of our alphabet. This ancient Middle Eastern symbol is a form of the letter that became our letter *H*.

H

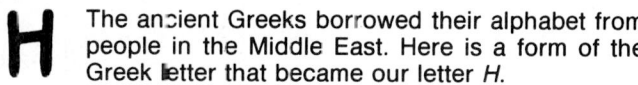

The ancient Greeks borrowed their alphabet from people in the Middle East. Here is a form of the Greek letter that became our letter *H*.

H

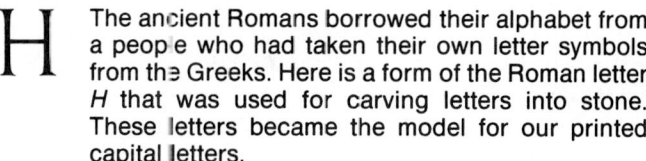

The ancient Romans borrowed their alphabet from a people who had taken their own letter symbols from the Greeks. Here is a form of the Roman letter *H* that was used for carving letters into stone. These letters became the model for our printed capital letters.

h

As people wrote quickly, especially with pens, the capital letters began to take the shapes of small letters. Here is a small-letter *h* that was developed about 1,200 years ago.

Hh *Hh*	Hh	Hh	Hh
Handwriting	Sans Serif Type	Serif Type	Computer Printing

h *or* **H** *noun* The eighth letter of the English alphabet.
h *or* **H** (āch) ◊ *noun, plural* **h's** *or* **H's**

ha *interjection* An expression that is used to show surprise or triumph: *Ha! I win!*
ha (hä) ◊ *interjection*

habit *noun* **1.** An activity or action done so often that one does it without thinking: *I have a habit of getting up early every morning.* **2.** Clothing that is worn for a particular activity, such as horseback riding, or by members of certain religious groups.
hab·it (**hăb′**ĭt) ◊ *noun, plural* **habits**

habitat *noun* The place where an animal or plant naturally lives and grows.
hab·i·tat (**hăb′**ĭ tăt′) ◊ *noun, plural* **habitats**

habitation *noun* A place, such as a room or building, to live in; residence.
hab·i·ta·tion (hăb′ĭ **tā′**shən) ◊ *noun, plural* **habitations**

habitual *adjective* **1.** Done again and again: *Habitual tardiness is irritating to the teachers.* **2.** Behaving according to habit; regular: *Farmers are habitual early risers.*
ha·bit·u·al (hə **bĭch′**o͞o əl) ◊ *adjective*

hacienda *noun* In Spanish-speaking countries and the southwestern United States, a large estate, especially one used for farming or for raising animals.
ha·ci·en·da (hä′sē **ĕn′**də) ◊ *noun, plural* **haciendas**

hack *verb* To cut with heavy blows; chop roughly: *We hacked our way through the thick jungle.*
◊ *noun* A rough, irregular cut.
hack (hăk) ◊ *verb* **hacked, hacking** ◊ *noun, plural* **hacks**

had *verb* Past tense and past participle of **have.**
had (hăd) ◊ *verb*

haddock *noun* An ocean fish that is related to the cod. It is often eaten as food.
had·dock (**hăd′**ək) ◊ *noun, plural* **haddock** *or* **haddocks**

hadn't Contraction of "had not."
had·n't (**hăd′**nt) ◊ *contraction*

haggard *adjective* Looking very worn from worry, suffering, hunger, or fatigue.
hag·gard (hăg′ərd) ◊ *adjective*

hail[1] *noun* **1.** Small round pieces of frozen rain that fall to the earth, often during thunderstorms. **2.** A large quantity that falls hard like a shower of hail: *The strong wind shook a hail of nuts from the tree.*
◊ *verb* **1.** To fall as hail: *It hailed all night.* **2.** To pour down like a shower of hail: *The fans hailed cheers on our team.*
hail[1] (hāl) ◊ *noun* ◊ *verb* **hailed, hailing**
‖*These sound alike:* **hail, hale**

hail[2] *verb* **1.** To greet or welcome by calling out: *We hailed our friends who were across the street.* **2.** To congratulate by cheering with enthusiasm: *The crowd hailed the winner of the race.* **3.** To call or signal to: *We hailed a taxi to take us home.*
hail[2] (hāl) ◊ *verb* **hailed, hailing**
‖*These sound alike:* **hail, hale**

***HISTORY* • hail[1], hail[2]**

Hail[1] comes from an old English word that may have come from a Germanic word meaning "pellet." **Hail[2]** comes from an old Scandinavian word that meant "healthy." It was short for a phrase that meant "be healthy."

hailstone *noun* A piece or lump of hail.
hail·stone (hāl′stōn′) ◊ *noun, plural* **hailstones**

hair *noun* **1.** A fine, thin strand that grows from the skin of animals and human beings. **2.** A mass or covering of these strands: *My friend has red hair.* **3.** A fine, thin strand, as on a plant or an insect.
hair (hâr) ◊ *noun, plural* **hairs**
‖*These sound alike:* **hair, hare**

haircut *noun* The act of cutting hair or the way in which it is cut.
hair·cut (hâr′kŭt′) ◊ *noun, plural* **haircuts**

ă	pat	ĭ	pit	oi	**oi**l	th	ba**th**
ā	pay	ī	ride	o͝o	book	*th*	bathe
â	care	î	fierce	o͞o	boot	ə	ago, item
ä	father	ŏ	pot	ou	**ou**t		pencil
ĕ	pet	ō	go	ŭ	cut		atom
ē	be	ô	paw, for	û	fur		circus

hairdo *noun* The way in which hair is arranged.
hair·do (hâr′do͞o′) ◊ *noun, plural* **hairdos**

hairdresser *noun* A person who cuts or arranges hair.
hair·dress·er (hâr′drĕs′ər) ◊ *noun, plural* **hairdressers**

hairy *adjective* Having much hair or covered with hair: *Gorillas are hairy animals.*
hair·y (hâr′ē) ◊ *adjective* **hairier, hairiest**

hale *adjective* Strong and healthy.
hale (hāl) ◊ *adjective* **haler, halest**
‖*These sound alike:* **hale, hail**

half *noun* **1.** Either of two equal parts into which a thing can be divided: *Do you want half of my sandwich?* **2.** Either of two time periods that make up a sports event, such as a football or basketball game.
◊ *adjective* Being one of two equal parts: *I need a half dozen eggs.*
◊ *adverb* **1.** To the extent of one half: *The gas tank was half empty.* **2.** Not completely; partly: *I was half asleep.*
half (hăf) ◊ *noun, plural* **halves** ◊ *adjective* ◊ *adverb*

half brother *noun* A brother related through only one parent.
half brother ◊ *noun, plural* **half brothers**

halfhearted *adjective* Showing little enthusiasm or interest.
half·heart·ed (hăf′här′tĭd) ◊ *adjective*

half-mast *noun* The position that is halfway up a mast or pole. A flag is lowered to half-mast out of respect for someone who has just died or as a signal of distress.
half-mast (hăf′măst′) ◊ *noun*

half sister *noun* A sister related through only one parent.
half sister ◊ *noun, plural* **half sisters**

halfway *adjective* **1.** Midway between two points; in the middle. **2.** Incomplete; partial: *Halfway measures won't solve the problem.*
◊ *adverb* **1.** To or at half the distance: *I'll meet you halfway between your house and mine.* **2.** One half: *The fire alarm rang halfway through the third period.*
half·way (hăf′wā′) ◊ *adjective* ◊ *adverb*

halibut *noun* A large flatfish of northern ocean waters, used as food.
hal·i·but (hăl′ə bət) ◊ *noun, plural* **halibut** *or* **halibuts**

hall *noun* **1.** A passageway in a house or building; corridor. **2.** An entrance room in a building. **3.** A large building or room for public gatherings; auditorium. **4.** A college or university building.
hall (hôl) ◊ *noun, plural* **halls**
‖*These sound alike:* **hall, haul**

hallelujah *interjection* An expression that is used to show praise or joy.
hal·le·lu·jah (hăl′ə **lo͞o′** yə) ◊ *interjection*

Halloween *noun* October 31, a holiday that children celebrate by wearing masks and costumes and by asking for treats.
Hal·low·een (hăl′ə **wēn′**) ◊ *noun*

▲ **Halloween**

hallway *noun* **1.** A passageway in a building; corridor. **2.** An entrance hall.
hall·way (**hôl′** wā′) ◊ *noun, plural* **hallways**

halo *noun* **1.** A ring of light or bright haze around a shining object. **2.** A ring of light around the head of a saint or other holy person, as in a religious painting.
ha·lo (**hā′** lō) ◊ *noun, plural* **halos** *or* **haloes**

halt *noun* A temporary stop; pause.
◊ *verb* To come or bring to a stop: *The government has hopes to halt inflation this year.* —See Synonyms at **stop.**
halt (hôlt) ◊ *noun, plural* **halts** ◊ *verb* **halted, halting**

halter *noun* **1.** A rope or strap that fits around the head of an animal, as a horse. A halter is used to lead or tie the animal. **2.** A blouse with a band that ties around the neck, leaving the back and shoulders bare.
hal·ter (**hôl′** tər) ◊ *noun, plural* **halters**

halve *verb* **1.** To divide into two equal parts. **2.** To reduce by half: *The store halved its prices during the big sale.*
halve (hăv) ◊ *verb* **halved, halving**
‖*These sound alike:* **halve, have**

halves *noun* Plural of **half.**
halves (hăvz) ◊ *noun*

halyard *noun* A rope used to lower or raise a sail or flag.
hal·yard (**hăl′** yərd) ◊ *noun, plural* **halyards**

ham *noun* **1.** The thigh of the hind leg of certain animals, especially a hog. **2.** The meat from the thigh of a hog, eaten as food. **3.** An amateur radio operator.
ham (hăm) ◊ *noun, plural* **hams**

hamburger *noun* **1.** Ground beef. **2.** A patty of ground beef, fried or broiled and usually served in a roll or bun.
ham·burg·er (**hăm′** bûr′gər) ◊ *noun, plural* **hamburgers**

***HISTORY* • hamburger**

Hamburger is named after *Hamburg,* a large city in West Germany.

hamlet *noun* A small village.
ham·let (**hăm′** lĭt) ◊ *noun, plural* **hamlets**

hammer *noun* **1.** A hand tool with a metal head and a long handle. Hammers are used especially for driving nails. **2.** The part of a gun that strikes the firing pin, causing the gun to go off. **3.** One of the padded wooden pieces that strike the strings of a piano.
◊ *verb* **1.** To pound or drive in with a hammer. **2.** To beat, shape, or flatten with a hammer: *The mechanic hammered out the dent in the fender.* **3.** To strike or pound with heavy, loud blows. **4.** To communicate by repeating over and over; drill.
ham·mer (**hăm′** ər) ◊ *noun, plural* **hammers** ◊ *verb* **hammered, hammering**

hammerhead shark *noun* A large shark that has at each side of the head a long, sideways fleshy projection with an eye at the end.
ham·mer·head shark (**hăm′** ər hĕd′) ◊ *noun, plural* **hammerhead sharks**

hammock *noun* A swinging bed or couch made of a strong net or cloth that is hung by

H

ropes between two vertical supports.
ham·mock (hăm′ək) ◊ *noun, plural* **hammocks**

▲ **hammock**

hamper¹ *verb* To get in the way of; impede: *Snow hampered the rescue efforts.*
ham·per¹ (hăm′pər) ◊ *verb* **hampered, hampering**

hamper² *noun* A large covered basket used for holding laundry or carrying food.
ham·per² (hăm′pər) ◊ *noun, plural* **hampers**

***HISTORY* • hamper¹, hamper²**

Hamper¹ first appeared in writing about 650 years ago. Its history before that is not known for certain. **Hamper²** comes from an old French word for a kind of wicker basket.

hamster *noun* A small animal with soft fur, large cheek pouches, and a short tail. Hamsters are often kept as pets.
ham·ster (hăm′stər) ◊ *noun, plural* **hamsters**

hand *noun* **1.** The part of the arm that is below the wrist. The hand includes the palm, four fingers, and the thumb. **2.** A pointer that moves around a circular dial, as on a clock. **3.** A style of handwriting: *You wrote the note in a clear hand.* **4.** Physical assistance; help: *Give me a hand with these boxes.* **5. hands** Possession or control: *The town is in enemy hands.* **6.** A round of applause: *The audience gave us a big hand.* **7.** A person who works with the hands; laborer. **8.** An active part: *We all had a hand in planning the class trip.* **9.** A side or direction: *Please sit on my right hand.* **10.** An agreement to marry someone: *He asked for her hand in marriage.* **11.** A unit of length equal to four inches, used to measure the height of a horse.
◊ *verb* To give or pass with the hand: *Will you please hand me the flashlight? Hand over the money.*
◊ *idioms* **hand down** To pass on to those who are younger: *The story was handed down from one generation to the next.* **on hand** Available for use: *I keep extra food on hand for emergencies.* **out of hand** Out of control: *The fire soon got out of hand.*
hand (hănd) ◊ *noun, plural* **hands** ◊ *verb* **handed, handing**

handbag *noun* A bag carried in the hand or on the arm, used to hold personal items such as money, papers, and keys; pocketbook.
hand·bag (hănd′băg′) ◊ *noun, plural* **handbags**

handbook *noun* A small book of instructions or facts.
hand·book (hănd′bo͝ok′) ◊ *noun, plural* **handbooks**

handcuff *noun* One of a pair of metal rings that are chained together and that can be locked around a prisoner's wrists.
◊ *verb* To put handcuffs on.
hand·cuff (hănd′kŭf′) ◊ *noun, plural* **handcuffs** ◊ *verb* **handcuffed, handcuffing**

handful *noun* **1.** An amount that can be held in the hand: *I drew a handful of coins from my pocket.* **2.** A small number: *Only a handful of people attended the movie.*
hand·ful (hănd′fo͝ol′) ◊ *noun, plural* **handfuls**

handicap *noun* **1.** Something that makes progress or success difficult: *Losing our best player was a handicap to the team.* **2.** A limitation caused by a physical or mental disability. **3.** An advantage given to a weaker side, or a disadvantage given to a stronger side, at the start of a contest.
◊ *verb* **1.** To put at a disadvantage; hinder:

ă	pat	ĭ	pit	oi	**oil**	th	ba**th**
ā	pay	ī	ride	o͝o	**book**	*th*	ba**the**
â	care	î	fierce	o͞o	**boot**	ə	ago, item
ä	father	ŏ	pot	ou	**out**		pencil
ĕ	pet	ō	go	ŭ	cut		atom
ē	be	ô	paw, for	û	fur		circus

The heavy snowstorm on the mountain handicapped the rescue team. **2.** To affect with a physical or mental handicap.
hand·i·cap (hăn′dē kăp′) ◊ *noun, plural* **handicaps** ◊ *verb* **handicapped, handicapping**

handicraft *noun* **1.** A craft or trade requiring skilled use of the hands. **2.** An object made by the skilled use of the hands.
hand·i·craft (hăn′dē krăft′) ◊ *noun, plural* **handicrafts**

handkerchief *noun* A small square of cloth used to wipe the nose or face.
hand·ker·chief (hăng′kər chĭf) ◊ *noun, plural* **handkerchiefs**

handle *noun* The part of a tool, door, or container that is made to be held or pulled with the hand.
◊ *verb* **1.** To touch, hold, or use with the hands: *Please do not handle the toys on sale.* **2.** To manage properly; control: *Can you handle a 10-speed bike?* **3.** To deal in; buy and sell: *Drugstores handle a wide variety of goods.* **4.** To deal with; treat: *Handle the horse with firmness and kindness.*
han·dle (hăn′dl) ◊ *noun, plural* **handles** ◊ *verb* **handled, handling**

handlebar *noun* A curved metal bar for steering a bicycle or motorcycle.
han·dle·bar (hăn′dl bär′) ◊ *noun, plural* **handlebars**

▲ **handlebar**

handmade *adjective* Made by hand.
hand·made (hănd′mād′) ◊ *adjective*

handout *noun* Something given to a needy person.
hand·out (hănd′out′) ◊ *noun, plural* **handouts**

handrail *noun* A narrow rail to be held with the hand for support.
hand·rail (hănd′rāl′) ◊ *noun, plural* **handrails**

handshake *noun* The act of grasping a person's hand, as when saying hello.
hand·shake (hănd′shāk′) ◊ *noun, plural* **handshakes**

handsome *adjective* **1.** Pleasing in appearance; good-looking. **2.** Generous; large: *I got a handsome reward for finding the lost pet.*
hand·some (hăn′səm) ◊ *adjective* **handsomer, handsomest**

handspring *noun* The act of flipping the body completely forward or backward from an upright position, landing first on the hands and then on the feet.
hand·spring (hănd′sprĭng′) ◊ *noun, plural* **handsprings**

handstand *noun* The act of balancing the body on the hands with the feet in the air.
hand·stand (hănd′stănd′) ◊ *noun, plural* **handstands**

handwriting *noun* **1.** Writing done by hand. **2.** A person's style of writing.
hand·writ·ing (hănd′rī′tĭng) ◊ *noun*

handy *adjective* **1.** Skillful in using the hands. **2.** Within easy reach: *Leave the dictionary on the table where it will be handy.* **3.** Useful; convenient: *An alarm clock is a handy thing to have when traveling.* —See Synonyms at **useful.**
hand·y (hăn′dē) ◊ *adjective* **handier, handiest**

hang *verb* **1.** To fasten or be attached at the upper end only: *Hang the clothes on the line.* **2.** To fasten or be attached so as to swing freely, as on hinges. **3.** To execute or be executed by suspending or being suspended from a rope tied around the neck. **4.** To remain over a place without moving; hover.
hang (hăng) ◊ *verb* **hung** *or* **hanged** (for sense 3), **hanging**

hangar *noun* A building in which aircraft are kept and repaired.
han·gar (hăng′ər) ◊ *noun, plural* **hangars**
‖ *These sound alike:* **hangar, hanger**

hanger *noun* A frame of wire, wood, or plastic used for hanging clothes.
hang·er (hăng′ər) ◊ *noun, plural* **hangers**
‖ *These sound alike:* **hanger, hangar**

H

hang glider *noun* A large frame that looks like a kite, from which a rider hangs while gliding down from a height.
hang glider ◊ *noun, plural* **hang gliders**

▲ **hang glider**

hangnail *noun* A small flap of skin that hangs from the side or base of a fingernail.
hang·nail (**hăng′** nāl′) ◊ *noun, plural* **hangnails**

Hanukkah *noun* Chanukah.
Ha·nuk·kah (**hä′** nə kə) ◊ *noun*

haphazard *adjective* Having no plan or order; mixed up: *Why did you put the volumes of the encyclopedia back in haphazard order?*
hap·haz·ard (hăp **hăz′** ərd) ◊ *adjective*

ă	pat	ĭ	pit	oi	**oil**	th	bath
ā	pay	ī	ride	o͝o	book	*th*	bathe
â	care	î	fierce	o͞o	boot	ə	ago, item
ä	father	ŏ	pot	ou	**out**		pencil
ĕ	pet	ō	go	ŭ	cut		atom
ē	be	ô	paw, for	û	fur		circus

happen *verb* **1.** To take place; occur: *Tell me everything that happened today.* **2.** To take place by accident or chance: *I just happened to be passing their house.*
hap·pen (**hăp′** ən) ◊ *verb* **happened, happening**

happening *noun* An event or occurrence.
hap·pen·ing (**hăp′** ə nĭng) ◊ *noun, plural* **happenings**

happy *adjective* **1.** Showing or feeling pleasure or joy: *I'm happy that we're all home safe.* —See Synonyms at **glad.** **2.** Marked by success or good fortune: *The story has a happy ending.*
hap·py (**hăp′** ē) ◊ *adjective* **happier, happiest**

happy-go-lucky *adjective* Having no troubles or worries.
hap·py-go-luck·y (**hăp′** ē gō **lŭk′** ē) ◊ *adjective*

harass *verb* **1.** To bother again and again; pester. **2.** To attack or raid again and again.
har·ass (hə **răs′** *or* **hăr′** əs) ◊ *verb* **harassed, harassing**

harbor *noun* **1.** A sheltered place along a coast where ships can safely anchor or dock; port. **2.** A shelter; refuge.
◊ *verb* **1.** To give shelter to. **2.** To keep in the mind; hold: *Don't harbor grudges.*
har·bor (**här′** bər) ◊ *noun, plural* **harbors**
◊ *verb* **harbored, harboring**

hard *adjective* **1.** Not bending or yielding when pushed; firm: *The steel blade is hard.* **2.** Difficult to solve, understand, or express: *There were some hard questions on the test.* **3.** Done or working with much steady effort: *It took years of hard work to build the canal.* **4.** Strict and demanding; stern: *Our teacher is hard but fair.* **5.** Having much force or momentum; forceful: *I felt a hard wind at my back.* **6.** Difficult to get through; trying: *It's been a hard winter.*
◊ *adverb* **1.** With much effort: *This year I began to study hard.* **2.** With much force, pressure, or intensity; heavily: *Press hard on the doorbell.* **3.** With much pain, distress, or resentment: *The family took the bad news hard.*
hard (härd) ◊ *adjective, adverb* **harder, hardest**

hard copy *noun* Data from a computer printed on paper.

harden *verb* **1.** To make or become hard or harder: *Allow the clay to harden.* **2.** To make rugged; toughen: *All-day hikes hardened the campers.*
hard·en (**här'** dn) ◊ *verb* **hardened, hardening**

hardheaded *adjective* Very stubborn.
hard·head·ed (**härd'hĕd'** ĭd) ◊ *adjective*

hardhearted *adjective* Lacking sympathy or pity.
hard·heart·ed (**härd' här'** tĭd) ◊ *adjective*

hardly *adverb* **1.** Only just; barely: *They hardly noticed me.* **2.** Not at all: *I hardly expected to win the grand prize.*
hard·ly (**härd'** lē) ◊ *adverb*

hardship *noun* Something that causes suffering or difficulty: *The early pioneers suffered great hardships on the frontier.*
hard·ship (**härd'** shĭp') ◊ *noun, plural* **hardships**

hardware *noun* **1.** Articles made of metal and used for making and repairing other things. Tools, nails, bolts, and hinges are hardware. **2.** The physical parts of a computer system, including the keyboard, video display screen, memory storage devices, and printer.
hard·ware (**härd'** wâr') ◊ *noun*

hardwood *noun* The wood of a tree that has leaves and flowers rather than needles and cones. Oak, maple, and ash are hardwoods.
hard·wood (**härd'** wo͝od') ◊ *noun, plural* **hardwoods**

hardy *adjective* Strong and healthy.
har·dy (**här'** dē) ◊ *adjective* **hardier, hardiest**

hare *noun* An animal that is related to and looks like a rabbit. A hare has longer ears and larger hind feet than a rabbit.
hare (hâr) ◊ *noun, plural* **hares**
‖*These sound alike:* **hare, hair**

▲ **hare**

harm *noun* Injury or damage: *Locusts cause great harm to crops.*
◊ *verb* To cause harm to; hurt.
harm (härm) ◊ *noun* ◊ *verb* **harmed, harming**

SYNONYMS

harm, damage, mar

Looking directly at the sun can *harm* your eyes. Freezing weather *damaged* the orange trees. That deep scratch *mars* the appearance of the table top.

harmful *adjective* Causing harm.
harm·ful (**härm'** fəl) ◊ *adjective*

harmless *adjective* Causing little or no harm: *Some snakes are harmless.*
harm·less (**härm'** lĭs) ◊ *adjective*

harmonica *noun* A small, bar-shaped musical instrument with a row of metal reeds inside. A player blows through holes along the front to make the reeds vibrate.
har·mon·i·ca (här **mŏn'** ĭ kə) ◊ *noun, plural* **harmonicas**

harmonious *adjective* **1.** Sounding pleasant; melodious. **2.** Going well together: *The room was painted in harmonious colors.* **3.** Getting along well together; friendly.
har·mo·ni·ous (här **mō'** nē əs) ◊ *adjective*

harmonize *verb* **1.** To sing or play in musical harmony. **2.** To be in or bring into harmony: *The colors of your coat, hat, and muffler should harmonize.*
har·mo·nize (**här'** mə nīz') ◊ *verb* **harmonized, harmonizing**

harmony *noun* **1.** The sounding together of musical notes in a chord. **2.** A pleasing combination of the parts that make up a whole: *The harmony of the garden will be spoiled if you mix red and orange flowers in one plot.* **3.** Friendly relations: *Cats and dogs can live in harmony in the same household.*
har·mo·ny (**här'** mə nē) ◊ *noun, plural* **harmonies**

harness *noun* A set of leather straps and metal pieces used to attach an animal to a vehicle or plow.
◊ *verb* **1.** To put a harness on. **2.** To attach by means of a harness. **3.** To bring under control for use; put to work: *Solar heating devices harness the energy of the sun.*
har·ness (**här'** nĭs) ◊ *noun, plural* **harnesses** ◊ *verb* **harnessed, harnessing**

harp *noun* A musical instrument made up of a large triangular frame on which a series of

H

strings are stretched. A player plucks the strings to make sounds.
harp (härp) ◊ *noun, plural* **harps**

▲ **harp**

harpoon *noun* A barbed spear with a rope, used in hunting whales and large fish.
◊ *verb* To strike or kill with a harpoon.
har·poon (här po͞on′) ◊ *noun, plural* **harpoons** ◊ *verb* **harpooned, harpooning**

harpsichord *noun* A keyboard instrument that looks like a small piano. A harpsichord's strings are plucked by leather picks or quills rather than being struck by hammers.
harp·si·chord (härp′sĭ kôrd′) ◊ *noun, plural* **harpsichords**

harrow *noun* A farm tool made up of a heavy frame with rows of metal teeth or upright disks. A harrow is used to break up and level off plowed ground.
◊ *verb* To drag a harrow over.
har·row (hăr′ō) ◊ *noun, plural* **harrows** ◊ *verb* **harrowed, harrowing**

harsh *adjective* **1.** Unpleasant to hear or taste. **2.** Very severe or demanding; cruel.
harsh (härsh) ◊ *adjective* **harsher, harshest**

ă	pat	ĭ	pit	oi	**oil**	th	ba**th**
ā	pay	ī	ride	o͝o	**book**	*th*	ba**the**
â	care	î	fierce	o͞o	**boot**	ə	ago, item
ä	father	ŏ	pot	ou	**out**		pencil
ĕ	pet	ō	go	ŭ	cut		atom
ē	be	ô	paw, for	û	fur		circus

harvest *noun* **1.** The act or process of gathering a crop: *The farmer hired extra workers for the harvest.* **2.** The crop that is gathered or is ready for gathering: *Everyone helped to bring in the corn harvest.*
◊ *verb* To gather: *We harvested the corn.*
har·vest (här′vĭst) ◊ *noun, plural* **harvests** ◊ *verb* **harvested, harvesting**

harvester *noun* A machine for harvesting crops; reaper.
har·vest·er (här′vĭ stər) ◊ *noun, plural* **harvesters**

has *verb* Third person singular present tense of **have.**
has (hăz) ◊ *verb*

hash *noun* A mixture of chopped meat and potatoes browned and cooked together.
hash (hăsh) ◊ *noun, plural* **hashes**

hasn't Contraction of "has not."
has·n't (hăz′ənt) ◊ *contraction*

haste *noun* **1.** Speed in moving or acting: *We ate with great haste to get to school on time.* **2.** Careless speed; rush: *In my haste, I forgot my umbrella.* —See Synonyms at **hurry.**
haste (hāst) ◊ *noun*

hasten *verb* **1.** To move or act swiftly; hurry: *I hastened home to tell my family the good news.* **2.** To cause to happen faster or sooner: *Warm weather and showers hastened the growth of the plants.*
has·ten (hā′sən) ◊ *verb* **hastened, hastening**

hasty *adjective* **1.** Acting or done fast: *We had a hasty meal and then left.* —See Synonyms at **quick.** **2.** Done too quickly to be accurate or wise; rash: *Don't make a hasty decision about summer camp.*
hast·y (hā′stē) ◊ *adjective* **hastier, hastiest**

hat *noun* A covering for the head, especially one with a crown and a brim.
hat (hăt) ◊ *noun, plural* **hats**

hatch¹ *verb* **1.** To come or cause to come out of an egg or eggs: *Ten chicks hatched today. The hen hatched a brood of ten chicks.* **2.** To think up, especially in secret; plot: *We hatched a scheme to surprise the twins on their birthday.*
hatch¹ (hăch) ◊ *verb* **hatched, hatching**

hatch² *noun* **1.** A small door: *The bus has an escape hatch in the roof.* **2.** An opening in the deck of a ship leading to another deck.
hatch² (hăch) ◊ *noun, plural* **hatches**

HISTORY • hatch[1], hatch[2]

Hatch[1] first appeared in written records about 750 years ago. Its history before that is not known for certain. **Hatch[2]** comes from an old English word for a small door or gate.

hatchery *noun* A place where eggs, especially of fish or chickens, are hatched.
hatch·er·y (hăch′ə rē) ◊ *noun, plural* **hatcheries**

▲ **hatchery**

hatchet *noun* A small ax with a short handle.
hatch·et (hăch′ĭt) ◊ *noun, plural* **hatchets**

hate *verb* To feel strong dislike for; detest: *We hate injustice. Our team hates to lose.*
◊ *noun* Strong dislike; hatred.
hate (hāt) ◊ *verb* **hated, hating** ◊ *noun, plural* **hates**

hateful *adjective* **1.** Deserving or causing hatred. **2.** Full of hatred.
hate·ful (hāt′fəl) ◊ *adjective*

hatred *noun* Very strong dislike.
ha·tred (hā′trĭd) ◊ *noun, plural* **hatreds**

haughty *adjective* Proud about oneself and looking down on others; arrogant.
haugh·ty (hô′tē) ◊ *adjective* **haughtier, haughtiest**

haul *verb* **1.** To pull or carry with effort; drag: *We hauled the sled up the hill.* —See Synonyms at **pull. 2.** To move from one place to another, as with a truck.
◊ *noun* **1.** The act of hauling. **2.** The distance over which something is carried or someone travels: *It's a long haul across country.* **3.** An amount gathered, caught, or taken in: *We brought home a big haul of fish.*
haul (hôl) ◊ *verb* **hauled, hauling** ◊ *noun, plural* **hauls**
‖*These sound alike:* **haul, hall**

haunch *noun* The hip, buttock, and upper thigh of a person or animal.
haunch (hônch) ◊ *noun, plural* **haunches**

haunt *verb* **1.** To come to the mind of again and again: *The thought of that test has haunted me ever since I took it.* **2.** To visit, live in, or appear to in the form of a ghost.
◊ *noun* A place that is visited often: *That playground is a favorite haunt of ours.*
haunt (hônt) ◊ *verb* **haunted, haunting** ◊ *noun, plural* **haunts**

have *verb* **1.** To be in possession of; own: *I have a bicycle.* **2.** To possess as a feature or characteristic: *Everyone in our family has blue eyes.* **3.** To consist of or contain: *A year has 365 days.* **4.** To hold in one's mind: *I have my doubts.* **5.** To be in a certain relationship to: *You have many friends.* **6.** To give birth to: *Our cat is having kittens soon.* **7.** To accept; take: *Will you have another orange?* **8.** To go through; experience: *I have a cold.* **9.** To allow; permit: *I won't have you talk like that.* **10.** To cause to do or to be done: *We had a fence put around the yard.* **11.** To be forced or obliged: *I have to go now.*
◊ *auxiliary verb* Used with a past participle to show that an action has already been completed: *They have eaten. The class had ended by the time I arrived.*
◊ *idiom* **have to do with** To be about: *Biology has to do with plants and animals.*
have (hăv) ◊ *verb* **had, having, has**
‖*These sound alike:* **have, halve**

haven *noun* A safe place; shelter: *Their home was a haven for stray animals.*
ha·ven (hā′vən) ◊ *noun, plural* **havens**

haven't Contraction of "have not."
have·n't (hăv′ənt) ◊ *contraction*

havoc *noun* Very great destruction.
hav·oc (hăv′ək) ◊ *noun*

hawk[1] *noun* A large bird with a short, hooked bill, strong claws, and keen eyesight. Hawks

H

catch small birds and animals for food.
hawk¹ (hôk) ◊ *noun, plural* **hawks**

▲ **hawk¹**

hawk² *verb* To offer for sale by shouting in the street; peddle.
hawk² (hôk) ◊ *verb* **hawked, hawking**

***HISTORY* • hawk¹, hawk²**

Hawk¹ comes from the old English name for this bird. **Hawk²** is a verb made from *hawker,* an old word for a person who peddles items on the street.

hay *noun* Grass, clover, and other plants, cut and dried and used as fodder.
◊ *verb* To cut grass or other plants so as to make them into hay.
hay (hā) ◊ *noun* ◊ *verb* **hayed, haying**
‖ *These sound alike:* **hay, hey**

hay fever *noun* An allergy caused by pollen from plants that floats in the air. Hay fever causes itching eyes and running noses.

hayloft *noun* An upper floor in a barn or stable for storing hay.
hay·loft (hā′lôft′) ◊ *noun, plural* **haylofts**

haystack *noun* A large pile of hay.
hay·stack (hā′stăk′) ◊ *noun, plural* **haystacks**

ă	pat	ĭ	pit	oi	oil	th	bath
ā	pay	ī	ride	o͝o	book	*th*	bathe
â	care	î	fierce	o͞o	boot	ə	ago, item
ä	father	ŏ	pot	ou	out		pencil
ĕ	pet	ō	go	ŭ	cut		atom
ē	be	ô	paw, for	û	fur		circus

hazard *noun* Something that may cause injury or harm: *Piles of oily rags are a fire hazard.* —See Synonyms at **danger.**
◊ *verb* To take a chance; risk: *I wouldn't hazard a guess about the weather.*
haz·ard (hăz′ərd) ◊ *noun, plural* **hazards**
◊ *verb* **hazarded, hazarding**

***HISTORY* • hazard**

Hazard goes back to an Arabic word meaning "dice." The word passed through Spanish and French into English, where it came to mean also "chance" or "risk" and then "a source of danger."

hazardous *adjective* Full of danger; risky: *Smoking is hazardous to your health.*
haz·ard·ous (hăz′ər dəs) ◊ *adjective*

haze *noun* Fine dust, smoke, or water vapor floating in the air.
haze (hāz) ◊ *noun, plural* **hazes**

hazel *noun* **1.** A shrub or small tree that has edible nuts with smooth brown shells. **2.** A yellowish-brown color.
◊ *adjective* Yellowish brown.
ha·zel (hā′zəl) ◊ *noun, plural* **hazels**
◊ *adjective*

hazy *adjective* **1.** Marked by or covered with haze: *It was a humid day with a hazy sun.* **2.** Not clear: *I have a hazy memory of those early years.* —See Synonyms at **vague.**
haz·y (hā′zē) ◊ *adjective* **hazier, haziest**

he *pronoun* The male one mentioned earlier: *I wrote to my cousin, but he hasn't replied.*
he (hē) ◊ *pronoun*

head *noun* **1.** The top part of the body, containing the brain, eyes, ears, nose, mouth, and jaws. **2.** The brain; mind: *I can do arithmetic in my head.* **3.** A mental ability: *I have a good head for arithmetic.* **4.** A rounded or enlarged end of something: *A pin has a point and a head.* **5.** A person who leads or rules; leader: *The principal is the head of the school.* **6.** The leading position; front: *The bugler marched at the head of the column.* **7.** The uppermost part of something; top: *Place the label at the head of each column.* **8.** A single animal or person: *We sold seven head of cattle. The tickets cost $4.50 a head.* **9. heads**

(*used with a singular verb*) The side of a coin having the principal design and the date. **10.** A point when something decisive happens; climax: *The quarrel finally came to a head.* **11.** Self-control; composure: *I managed to keep my head during the hurricane.*
◊ *adjective* Most important; ranking first: *Our neighbor is the head librarian at school.*
◊ *verb* **1.** To set out in a certain direction: *Let's head for home.* **2.** To cause to go in a certain direction; aim: *We headed our horses up the hill.* **3.** To be in charge of; lead. **4.** To be at the top of: *Who heads the class?*
◊ *idiom* **over one's head** Beyond one's ability to understand.
head (hĕd) ◊ *noun, plural* **heads** *or* **head** (for sense 8) ◊ *adjective* ◊ *verb* **headed, heading**

headache *noun* **1.** A pain in the head. **2.** Something that causes trouble; problem.
head·ache (**hĕd'**āk') ◊ *noun, plural* **headaches**

headband *noun* A band that is worn on or around the head.
head·band (**hĕd'**bănd') ◊ *noun, plural* **headbands**

headdress *noun* A fancy covering or decoration worn on the head.
head·dress (**hĕd'**drĕs') ◊ *noun, plural* **headdresses**

▲ **headdress**

headfirst *adverb* With the head leading; headlong: *I dove headfirst into the pool.*
head·first (**hĕd'fûrst'**) ◊ *adverb*

heading *noun* Something, such as a title, that is put at the head of a page or chapter.
head·ing (**hĕd'**ĭng) ◊ *noun, plural* **headings**

headland *noun* A point of high land that sticks out into a body of water.
head·land (**hĕd'**lănd') ◊ *noun, plural* **headlands**

headlight *noun* A light mounted on the front of a motor vehicle or a bicycle.
head·light (**hĕd'**līt') ◊ *noun, plural* **headlights**

headline *noun* A group of words that is printed in large type over a newspaper article. Headlines tell what the articles are about.
head·line (**hĕd'**līn') ◊ *noun, plural* **headlines**

headlong *adverb* **1.** With the head leading; headfirst: *I fell headlong into the mud.* **2.** Much too fast and without thinking: *They ran headlong into the street.*
head·long (**hĕd'**lông') ◊ *adverb*

headmaster *noun* A man who is a school principal, usually of a private school.
head·mas·ter (**hĕd'**măs'tər) ◊ *noun, plural* **headmasters**

headmistress *noun* A woman who is a school principal, usually of a private school.
head·mis·tress (**hĕd'**mĭs'trĭs) ◊ *noun, plural* **headmistresses**

head-on *adjective & adverb* With the front end hitting or directed toward something: *The cars met in a head-on collision. The sled struck the tree head-on.*
head-on (**hĕd'**ŏn') ◊ *adjective & adverb*

headphone *noun* An earphone that is held over the head by a headband.
head·phone (**hĕd'**fōn') ◊ *noun, plural* **headphones**

headquarters *plural noun* (*sometimes used with a singular verb*) **1.** The offices of a commander or leader, from which orders are given out: *Headquarters has* (or *have*) *ordered us to retreat.* **2.** A center of operations: *The headquarters of the company are* (or *is*) *currently in Arizona.*
head·quar·ters (**hĕd'**kwôr'tərz) ◊ *plural noun*

headrest *noun* A cushion attached to the top of the back of a seat, as in a motor vehicle. A headrest helps to prevent neck injuries in case of an accident.
head·rest (**hĕd'**rĕst') ◊ *noun, plural* **headrests**

head start *noun* An advantage given at the beginning, as to a runner in a race.
head start ◊ *noun, plural* **head starts**

H

headstone *noun* A memorial stone put at the top of a grave.
head·stone (hĕd′stōn′) ◊ *noun, plural* **headstones**

headstrong *adjective* Insisting on having one's own way; stubborn. —See Synonyms at **obstinate.**
head·strong (hĕd′strông′) ◊ *adjective*

headwaters *plural noun* Lakes and streams located at the source of a river. They join to form the main channel of the river.
head·wa·ters (hĕd′wô′tərz) ◊ *plural noun*

headway *noun* Movement forward; progress.
head·way (hĕd′wā′) ◊ *noun*

heal *verb* To make or become healthy again: *The wound healed quickly.*
heal (hēl) ◊ *verb* **healed, healing**
‖*These sound alike:* **heal, heel, he'll**

health *noun* **1.** The condition of the body or mind: *Bad eating habits can put you in poor health.* **2.** Freedom from disease or injury: *We wish you a speedy return to health.*
health (hĕlth) ◊ *noun*

health food *noun* Food that is grown without chemical fertilizers and that is prepared without using preservatives.

healthful *adjective* Being good for people's health.
health·ful (hĕlth′fəl) ◊ *adjective*

healthy *adjective* **1.** In good health. **2.** Good for the health; healthful. **3.** Showing good health: *Your cheeks have a healthy glow.*
health·y (hĕl′thē) ◊ *adjective* **healthier, healthiest**

SYNONYMS

healthy, fit[1], sound[2], well[2]

I had the flu, but now I'm *healthy* again. You should follow a regular program of exercise to keep yourself *fit.* Good dental care helps maintain *sound* teeth. We were lucky to stay *well* last winter.

ă	pat	ĭ	pit	oi	**oil**	th	**bath**
ā	pay	ī	ride	ŏŏ	**book**	*th*	**bathe**
â	care	î	fierce	ōō	**boot**	ə	ago, item
ä	father	ŏ	pot	ou	**out**		pencil
ĕ	pet	ō	go	ŭ	cut		atom
ē	be	ô	paw, for	û	fur		circus

heap *noun* **1.** A pile of things thrown together: *My toys lay in a heap on the floor.* **2. heaps** A great amount: *The game was heaps of fun.*
◊ *verb* **1.** To put in a heap; pile up. **2.** To fill to overflowing.
heap (hēp) ◊ *noun, plural* **heaps** ◊ *verb* **heaped, heaping**

hear *verb* **1.** To take in sounds through the ear: *We heard a dog barking. The child doesn't hear well.* **2.** To listen to: *I love to hear stories about the sea.* **3.** To receive information: *I've heard about that book.* **4.** To receive communication, as by letter: *We have not heard from them lately.*
hear (hîr) ◊ *verb* **heard, hearing**
‖*These sound alike:* **hear, here**

heard *verb* Past tense and past participle of **hear.**
heard (hûrd) ◊ *verb*
‖*These sound alike:* **heard, herd**

hearing *noun* **1.** The sense by which sound is picked up; ability to hear. **2.** The distance within which sounds can be picked up: *Stay within hearing of the baby.* **3.** A chance to be heard: *The teacher gave both sides of the argument a fair hearing.*
hear·ing (hîr′ĭng) ◊ *noun, plural* **hearings**

hearing aid *noun* A small electronic device that makes sounds louder and that is worn by a person with a hearing loss.
hearing aid ◊ *noun, plural* **hearing aids**

hearken *verb* To listen closely.
hear·ken (här′kən) ◊ *verb* **hearkened, hearkening**

hearsay *noun* Something heard from another person; gossip.
hear·say (hîr′sā′) ◊ *noun*

heart *noun* **1.** The hollow, muscular organ that pumps blood throughout the body. **2.** The part of a person's mind that feels emotions, such as love: *These words come from the heart.* **3.** Love; affection: *The children won my heart.* **4.** Inner strength; courage: *I didn't have the heart to tell you that you lost the contest.* **5.** The central or main part: *We live in the heart of the city.* **6.** Something that is shaped like a heart.
◊ *idiom* **by heart** Entirely by memory: *We learned the poem by heart.*
heart (härt) ◊ *noun, plural* **hearts**

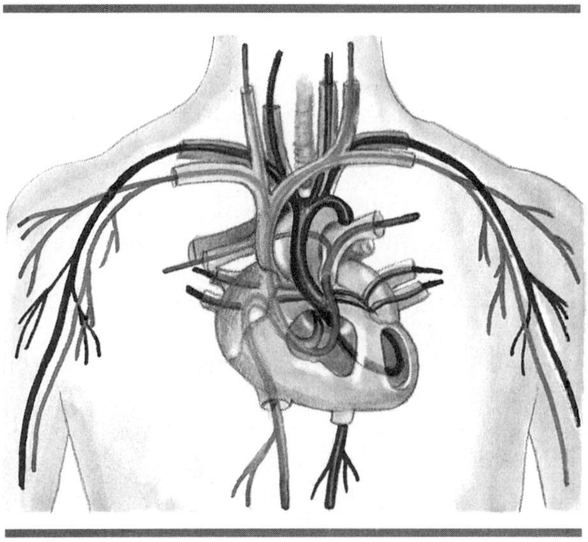

▲ heart

heartache *noun* Deep sorrow.
heart·ache (härt′āk′) ◊ *noun, plural* **heartaches**

heartbeat *noun* A single pumping movement of the heart.
heart·beat (härt′bēt′) ◊ *noun, plural* **heartbeats**

heartbroken *adjective* Feeling great sorrow.
heart·bro·ken (härt′brō′kən) ◊ *adjective*

hearten *verb* To cheer up.
heart·en (här′tn) ◊ *verb* **heartened, heartening**

heartfelt *adjective* Deeply felt; sincere.
heart·felt (härt′fĕlt′) ◊ *adjective*

hearth *noun* **1.** The floor of a fireplace and the area in front of it, usually made of stone or brick. **2.** Family life; home: *I longed to be at my own hearth once again.*
hearth (härth) ◊ *noun, plural* **hearths**

heartily *adverb* **1.** In a warm, friendly, enthusiastic way: *They welcomed me heartily.* **2.** With appetite or enjoyment.
heart·i·ly (här′tl ē) ◊ *adverb*

heartless *adjective* Very cruel.
heart·less (härt′lĭs) ◊ *adjective*

hearty *adjective* **1.** Very warm, friendly, and enthusiastic: *They gave us a hearty welcome.* **2.** Strong and healthy: *The explorers were young and hearty.* **3.** Giving much nourishment: *We cooked a hearty soup.* **4.** Requiring much food: *I have a hearty appetite.*
heart·y (här′tē) ◊ *adjective* **heartier, heartiest**

heat *noun* **1.** The condition of being hot; warmth: *I could feel the heat of the sun.* **2.** High temperature: *We left town to escape the summer heat.* **3.** Warmth provided for a house or room, as by a furnace: *Turn up the heat.* **4.** A round in a race: *The runners lined up for the first heat.*
◊ *verb* To make or become warm or hot: *The sun heats the earth. The soup heated slowly.*
heat (hēt) ◊ *noun, plural* **heats** ◊ *verb* **heated, heating**

heater *noun* A device that supplies heat.
heat·er (hē′tər) ◊ *noun, plural* **heaters**

heath *noun* **1.** An open, uncultivated stretch of land covered with low-growing shrubs or plants. **2.** A plant that grows on such land.
heath (hēth) ◊ *noun, plural* **heaths**

heathen *noun* A person who does not believe in a religion.
hea·then (hē′*th*ən) ◊ *noun, plural* **heathens** *or* **heathen**

heather *noun* A low shrub with tiny evergreen leaves and small, bell-shaped purplish flowers.
heath·er (hĕ*th*′ər) ◊ *noun*

▲ heather

heave *verb* **1.** To lift with effort or force: *We heaved the box onto the shelf.* **2.** To throw with effort or force: *The pitcher heaved the ball.* **3.** To utter with effort: *I heaved a sigh.* **4.** To pull with effort: *They heaved on the anchor line.*
◊ *noun* **1.** An act of lifting or pulling: *With a final heave, we got the box onto the shelf.* **2.** A forceful throw: *Give the ball a heave.*
heave (hēv) ◊ *verb* **heaved, heaving** ◊ *noun, plural* **heaves**

H

heaven *noun* **1.** Often **heavens** The sky over the earth; upper regions of the air: *Stars twinkled in the heavens.* **2.** Often **Heaven** In Christianity and some other religions, the dwelling place of God and the angels. **3.** A place of great happiness: *The cool forest was heaven on a hot day.*
heav·en (hĕv′ən) ◊ *noun, plural* **heavens**

heavenly *adjective* **1.** Of or in the heavens: *The sun and the planets are heavenly bodies.* **2.** Very pleasing: *This has been a heavenly day.*
heav·en·ly (hĕv′ən lē) ◊ *adjective*

heavily *adverb* In a heavy way: *The rain came down heavily all night.*
heav·i·ly (hĕv′ə lē) ◊ *adverb*

heavy *adjective* **1.** Weighing a lot. **2.** Greater than usual in amount, size, or effect: *We got caught in heavy traffic.* **3.** Sturdy or thick: *We bought some heavy winter clothing.* **4.** Hard to do or bear: *Shoveling snow is heavy work.* **5.** Feeling sad or worried: *I watched you leave with a heavy heart.* **6.** Weighed down: *The branches are heavy with apples.* **7.** Very important or serious: *A judge has heavy responsibilities.*
heav·y (hĕv′ē) ◊ *adjective* **heavier, heaviest**

SYNONYMS

heavy, massive

That 50-pound crate is much too *heavy* to carry home. A *massive* boulder blocked the entrance to the cave.
Antonym: *light*

Hebrew *noun* **1.** A member of one of the Jewish peoples of ancient times. **2.** The language of the ancient Hebrews. **3.** The language of the Israelis.
◊ *adjective* Of or relating to the Hebrews or to ancient or modern Hebrew.
He·brew (hē′brōō) ◊ *noun, plural* **Hebrews** ◊ *adjective*

ă	pat	ĭ	pit	oi	oil	th	bath
ā	pay	ī	ride	ŏŏ	book	*th*	bathe
â	care	î	fierce	ōō	boot	ə	ago, item
ä	father	ŏ	pot	ou	out		pencil
ĕ	pet	ō	go	ŭ	cut		atom
ē	be	ô	paw, for	û	fur		circus

hectic *adjective* Full of activity, confusion, or excitement.
hec·tic (hĕk′tĭk) ◊ *adjective*

he'd Contraction of "he had" or "he would."
he'd (hēd) ◊ *contraction*
‖*These sound alike:* **he'd, heed**

hedge *noun* A row of shrubs or small trees that are planted close together and form a fence or boundary.
◊ *verb* To enclose with or as if with a hedge: *We hedged our yard with yews.*
hedge (hĕj) ◊ *noun, plural* **hedges** ◊ *verb* **hedged, hedging**

hedgehog *noun* **1.** A small animal whose back is covered with short, stiff spines. Hedgehogs are found in Europe, Asia, and Africa. **2.** The porcupine.
hedge·hog (hĕj′hôg′) ◊ *noun, plural* **hedgehogs**

▲ **hedgehog**

heed *verb* To pay close attention to: *You should heed your teacher's advice.*
◊ *noun* Close attention or notice.
heed (hēd) ◊ *verb* **heeded, heeding** ◊ *noun*
‖*These sound alike:* **heed, he'd**

heedless *adjective* Not paying attention: *They were heedless of the risks when they skated on the thin ice.*
heed·less (hēd′lĭs) ◊ *adjective*

heel *noun* **1.** The rounded back part of the human foot. **2.** The part of a sock, shoe, or stocking that covers the rounded back part of the foot. **3.** The built-up part of a shoe or boot that is under the rounded back part of the foot.
heel (hēl) ◊ *noun, plural* **heels**
‖*These sound alike:* **heel, heal, he'll**

heifer *noun* A young cow that has not borne a calf.
heif·er (hĕf′ər) ◊ *noun, plural* **heifers**

height *noun* **1.** The distance from bottom to top: *The height of Mount Everest is about 29,000 feet above sea level.* **2.** The distance from foot to head: *My height increased two inches this year.* **3.** Often **heights** A high place: *I am afraid of heights.* **4.** The highest point; peak: *At the height of the storm, the lights went out.*
height (hīt) ◊ *noun, plural* **heights**

heighten *verb* **1.** To make or become greater in degree or quantity; increase. **2.** To make or become high or higher.
height·en (hīt′n) ◊ *verb* **heightened, heightening**

heir *noun* A person who receives or has the right to receive the property or title of another when the other person dies.
heir (âr) ◊ *noun, plural* **heirs**
‖*These sound alike:* **heir, air**

heiress *noun* A female heir.
heir·ess (âr′ĭs) ◊ *noun, plural* **heiresses**

heirloom *noun* A family possession passed down from one generation to the next.
heir·loom (âr′lo͞om′) ◊ *noun, plural* **heirlooms**

held *verb* Past tense and past participle of **hold**[1].
held (hĕld) ◊ *verb*

helicopter *noun* An aircraft without wings that is kept in the air by horizontal propellers that rotate above the craft.
hel·i·cop·ter (hĕl′ĭ kŏp′tər) ◊ *noun, plural* **helicopters**

▲ **helicopter**

heliport *noun* A place where helicopters land and take off.
hel·i·port (hĕl′ə pôrt′) ◊ *noun, plural* **heliports**

helium *noun* A very light gas that will not burn and is used in dirigibles and balloons. Helium is a chemical element.
he·li·um (hē′lē əm) ◊ *noun*

hell *noun* Often **Hell** In Christianity and certain other religions, the place where wicked people are punished after they die.
hell (hĕl) ◊ *noun*

he'll Contraction of "he will" or "he shall."
he'll (hēl) ◊ *contraction*
‖*These sound alike:* **he'll, heal, heel**

hello *interjection* An expression that is used as a greeting or to attract attention.
hel·lo (hĕ **lō′** *or* hə **lō′**) ◊ *interjection*

helm *noun* The steering device of a ship.
helm (hĕlm) ◊ *noun, plural* **helms**

helmet *noun* A head covering made of a hard material such as metal. A helmet is worn to protect the head, as in some sports.
hel·met (hĕl′mĭt) ◊ *noun, plural* **helmets**

▲ **helmet**
Several kinds of helmets

help *verb* **1.** To give or do what is needed or useful; assist: *I helped my parents with the dishes.* **2.** To give relief from: *This medicine will help your cold.* **3.** To prevent or change: *I cannot help what happened.* **4.** To keep from: *We couldn't help laughing.* **5.** To wait on, as in a store: *I asked the clerk to help me.*
◊*noun* **1.** An act or example of helping. **2.** Someone or something that helps: *Summer help is hard to find these days.*

H

◊ *idiom* **help oneself to 1.** To serve oneself: *Help yourself to the food.* **2.** To take without permission: *They helped themselves to my lunch.*
help (hĕlp) ◊ *verb* **helped, helping** ◊ *noun*

SYNONYMS
help, aid, assistance Our club provides a great deal of *help* to the needy in our town. Many people offered *aid* to the victims of the hurricane. I need your *assistance* in moving the picnic table to a shady spot.

helpful *adjective* Providing help. —See Synonyms at **useful.**
help·ful (**hĕlp′** fəl) ◊ *adjective*

helping *noun* Food for one person.
help·ing (**hĕl′** pĭng) ◊ *noun, plural* **helpings**

helping verb *noun* An auxiliary verb.
helping verb ◊ *noun, plural* **helping verbs**

helpless *adjective* Not able to take care of or defend oneself.
help·less (**hĕlp′** lĭs) ◊ *adjective*

hem *noun* The finished edge or border of a garment or piece of cloth. A hem is made by folding an edge under and sewing it down.
◊ *verb* To fold back and sew down the edge of: *I hemmed the trousers.*
hem (hĕm) ◊ *noun, plural* **hems** ◊ *verb* **hemmed, hemming**

hemisphere *noun* **1.** One half of a sphere. **2. Hemisphere** Either of the halves into which the earth is divided by the equator (the *Northern Hemisphere* and the *Southern Hemisphere*) or by a meridian (the *Eastern Hemisphere* and the *Western Hemisphere*). The Eastern Hemisphere includes Europe, Asia, and Africa. The Western Hemisphere includes North and South America.
hem·i·sphere (**hĕm′** ĭ sfîr′) ◊ *noun, plural* **hemispheres**

ă	pat	ĭ	pit	oi	**oil**	th	**bath**
ā	pay	ī	ride	ŏŏ	book	*th*	bathe
â	care	î	fierce	ōō	boot	ə	ago, item
ä	father	ŏ	pot	ou	**out**		pencil
ĕ	pet	ō	go	ŭ	cut		atom
ē	be	ô	paw, for	û	fur		circus

hemlock *noun* **1.** An evergreen tree with short, flat needles and small cones. **2.** A poisonous plant with leaves like feathers and clusters of small, whitish flowers.
hem·lock (**hĕm′** lŏk′) ◊ *noun, plural* **hemlocks**

▲ **hemlock**

hemoglobin *noun* The material in red blood cells that carries oxygen from the lungs to the rest of the body.
he·mo·glo·bin (hē′mə **glō′** bĭn) ◊ *noun*

hemp *noun* A tall plant with stems that yield a tough fiber used in making rope.
hemp (hĕmp) ◊ *noun*

hen *noun* **1.** A fully grown female chicken. **2.** The female of some other birds, such as the peacock and turkey.
hen (hĕn) ◊ *noun, plural* **hens**

hence *adverb* For this reason; therefore: *This necklace is gold; hence, it is expensive.*
hence (hĕns) ◊ *adverb*

her *pronoun* The objective case of **she:** *Do you see her? They sent her flowers. I have a message for her.*
◊ *adjective* Relating or belonging to her: *Where did she put her hat?*
her (hûr) ◊ *pronoun* ◊ *adjective*

herald *noun* A person who carried messages or made announcements, as for a king.
her·ald (**hĕr′** əld) ◊ *noun, plural* **heralds**

herb *noun* A plant whose leaves, roots, or other parts are used to flavor food or are used

as medicine. Parsley and thyme are herbs.
herb (ûrb *or* hûrb) ◊ *noun, plural* **herbs**

▲ **herb**

herd *noun* A group of animals of one kind, such as cattle, that stay together or are kept together.
◊ *verb* **1.** To gather, keep, or lead together. **2.** To tend or watch over sheep or cattle.
herd (hûrd) ◊ *noun, plural* **herds** ◊ *verb* **herded, herding**
‖ *These sound alike:* **herd, heard**

here *adverb* **1.** At or in this place: *Put it here. Stay here.* **2.** At this time; now: *I think I'll stop reading here.* **3.** To this place: *Come here and sit beside me.*
◊ *noun* This place: *I went there from here.*
◊ *interjection* An expression used to answer to one's name in a roll call, to call an animal, or to get someone's attention.
here (hîr) ◊ *adverb* ◊ *noun* ◊ *interjection*
‖ *These sound alike:* **here, hear**

hereafter *adverb* From now on; after this: *Hereafter I will be your friend.*
here·af·ter (hîr **ăf′** tər) ◊ *adverb*

hereby *adverb* By this means: *The letter said, "You are hereby ordered to report for duty."*
here·by (hîr **bī′**) ◊ *adverb*

heredity *noun* The passing of characteristics from parents to offspring: *My height comes from my heredity.*
he·red·i·ty (hə **rĕd′** ĭ tē) ◊ *noun*

here's Contraction of "here is."
here's (hîrz) ◊ *contraction*

heritage *noun* Something handed down to later generations from earlier generations: *Freedom of speech is part of our national heritage.*
her·i·tage (**hĕr′** ĭ tĭj) ◊ *noun, plural* **heritages**

hermit *noun* A person who lives alone and far away from other people.
her·mit (**hûr′** mĭt) ◊ *noun, plural* **hermits**

hermit crab *noun* A crab that has a soft abdomen not covered by a protective shell. A hermit crab lives in and carries around the empty shell of a mollusk, such as a snail.
hermit crab ◊ *noun, plural* **hermit crabs**

hero *noun* **1.** A person who is admired for great courage, special achievements, or noble character. **2.** The main male character in a story, poem, or play.
he·ro (**hîr′** ō) ◊ *noun, plural* **heroes**

heroic *adjective* **1.** Very brave or daring: *Many heroic men and women have died in defense of liberty.* **2.** Of or relating to heroes.
he·ro·ic (hĭ **rō′** ĭk) ◊ *adjective*

heroine *noun* **1.** A woman or girl admired for her great courage, special achievements, or noble character. **2.** The main female character in a story, poem, or play.
her·o·ine (**hĕr′** ō ĭn) ◊ *noun, plural* **heroines**

heron *noun* A wading bird with a long neck, long legs, and a long, pointed bill.
her·on (**hĕr′** ən) ◊ *noun, plural* **herons**

herring *noun* A fish of the northern Atlantic Ocean, caught in large numbers for food.
her·ring (**hĕr′** ĭng) ◊ *noun, plural* **herring** *or* **herrings**

hers *pronoun* The one or ones that belong to her: *That hat is hers. If his desk is occupied, use hers.*
hers (hûrz) ◊ *pronoun*

herself *pronoun* Her own self: *She blamed herself. She herself saw it.*
her·self (hər **sĕlf′**) ◊ *pronoun*

he's Contraction of "he is" or "he has."
he's (hēz) ◊ *contraction*

hesitant *adjective* Doubtful or uncertain: *I am hesitant about going to the party.*
hes·i·tant (**hĕz′** ĭ tənt) ◊ *adjective*

hesitate *verb* **1.** To pause or hold back because of feeling unsure: *I hesitated before diving off the high board.* **2.** To speak with many pauses; stammer.
hes·i·tate (**hĕz′** ĭ tāt′) ◊ *verb* **hesitated, hesitating**

H

hesitation *noun* The act or an example of hesitating.
hes·i·ta·tion (hĕz′ĭ **tā′**shən) ◊ *noun, plural* **hesitations**

hew *verb* **1.** To chop or shape with an ax; cut: *The hunters hewed a path through the jungle.* **2.** To cut down with an ax.
hew (hyo͞o) ◊ *verb* **hewed, hewn** *or* **hewed, hewing**
‖*These sound alike:* **hew, hue**

hewn *verb* A past participle of **hew.**
hewn (hyo͞on) ◊ *verb*

hey *interjection* An expression that shows surprise or pleasure or that is used to attract attention: *Hey, that's nice! Hey, watch out!*
hey (hā) ◊ *interjection*
‖*These sound alike:* **hey, hay**

hi *interjection* An expression that is used as a greeting.
hi (hī) ◊ *interjection*
‖*These sound alike:* **hi, high**

HI The abbreviation for *Hawaii* used with a Zip Code.

hibernate *verb* To spend the winter sleeping, as some animals do: *Woodchucks and some bears hibernate.*
hi·ber·nate (**hī′**bər nāt′) ◊ *verb* **hibernated, hibernating**

HISTORY • hibernate

Hibernate comes from the Latin word for winter. Winter is, of course, the time when some animals hibernate.

hiccup *noun* **1.** A sudden, quick catching of the breath in the throat that causes a clicking sound. **2. hiccups** An attack in which a person has one hiccup after another.
◊ *verb* To have the hiccups.
hic·cup (**hĭk′**ŭp) ◊ *noun, plural* **hiccups**
◊ *verb* **hiccupped, hiccupping**

hickory *noun* A tall North American tree that has hard, tough wood. The hickory bears edible nuts that have a smooth, hard shell.
hick·o·ry (**hĭk′**ə rē) ◊ *noun, plural* **hickories**

▲ **hickory**

hid *verb* Past tense and a past participle of **hide[1].**
hid (hĭd) ◊ *verb*

hidden *verb* A past participle of **hide[1].**
hid·den (**hĭd′**n) ◊ *verb*

hide[1] *verb* **1.** To keep or put out of sight: *We hid behind a tree.* **2.** To keep from being known; conceal: *I could barely hide my disappointment.* **3.** To cut off from sight; cover up: *Clouds hid the moon.*
hide[1] (hīd) ◊ *verb* **hid, hidden** *or* **hid, hiding**

hide[2] *noun* The skin of an animal.
hide[2] (hīd) ◊ *noun, plural* **hides**

HISTORY • hide[1], hide[2]

Hide[1] comes from an old English word that meant "to put or keep out of sight." **Hide[2]** goes back to a related old English word that meant "the skin of an animal."

hide-and-seek *noun* A children's game in which one player tries to find the others who are hiding.
hide-and-seek (**hīd′**n **sēk′**) ◊ *noun*

hideaway *noun* A hiding place.
hide·a·way (**hīd′**ə wā′) ◊ *noun, plural* **hideaways**

ă	pat	ĭ	pit	oi	**oil**	th	**bath**
ā	pay	ī	ride	o͝o	**book**	*th*	**bathe**
â	care	î	fierce	o͞o	**boot**	ə	**ago, item**
ä	father	ŏ	pot	ou	**out**		pencil
ĕ	pet	ō	go	ŭ	**cut**		atom
ē	be	ô	paw, for	û	**fur**		circus

hideous *adjective* Very ugly or disgusting.
hid·e·ous (hĭd′ē əs) ◊ *adjective*

hieroglyphic *noun* A picture or symbol that represented words or sounds in the writing system used in ancient Egypt.
hi·er·o·glyph·ic (hī′ər-ə glĭf′ĭk) ◊ *noun, plural* **hieroglyphics**

▲ **hieroglyphic**

high *adjective* **1.** Having great height: *The mountains are high.* **2.** Having a specified height: *The cabinet is four feet high.* **3.** At a great distance above the ground: *The balloon was high in the sky.* **4.** Greater than average in degree, amount, or size: *I ran a high temperature when I was sick. That store charges high prices.* **5.** Greater than others in rank or importance: *Our neighbor is a high official in the government.* **6.** Sharp; shrill: *A soprano's voice is high.*
◊ *adverb* At or to a high place or level: *Eagles fly high in the sky.*
◊ *noun* **1.** A high point or level: *Prices reached a new high.* **2.** An arrangement of gears that gives the fastest speed.
high (hī) ◊ *adjective, adverb* **higher, highest** ◊ *noun, plural* **highs**
‖*These sound alike:* **high, hi**

highland *noun* A high or hilly area.
high·land (hī′lənd) ◊ *noun, plural* **highlands**

highlight *noun* An outstanding event.
high·light (hī′līt′) ◊ *noun, plural* **highlights**

highly *adverb* **1.** To a great degree: *Dogs have a highly developed sense of smell.* **2.** In a very favorable way: *I think highly of you.*
high·ly (hī′lē) ◊ *adverb*

Highness *noun* A title of honor for a member of a royal family.
High·ness (hī′nĭs) ◊ *noun, plural* **Highnesses**

high-rise *noun* **1.** A very tall building; skyscraper. **2.** A bicycle that has very long handlebars.
high-rise (hī′rīz′) ◊ *noun, plural* **high-rises**

▲ **high-rise**

high school *noun* A school attended by students who have completed elementary school or junior high school. It usually includes the ninth or tenth grades through the twelfth grade.
high school ◊ *noun, plural* **high schools**

high seas *plural noun* The open waters of an ocean or sea beyond the limits of any country's control.
high seas ◊ *plural noun*

high-strung *adjective* Very nervous or sensitive: *The horse is high-strung and well-bred.*
high-strung (hī′strŭng′) ◊ *adjective*

high technology *noun* Technology that has to do with very advanced, complex devices such as computers.

high tide *noun* The time when the ocean reaches its highest level on the shore.
high tide ◊ *noun, plural* **high tides**

H

highway *noun* A main public road.
high·way (hī′wā′) ◊ *noun, plural* **highways**

highwayman *noun* A man who robs travelers on a public road.
high·way·man (hī′wā′mən) ◊ *noun, plural* **highwaymen**

hijack *verb* To take control of by force, as an airplane.
hi·jack (hī′jăk′) ◊ *verb* **hijacked, hijacking**

hike *verb* To go on a long walk for pleasure or exercise.
◊ *noun* A long walk.
hike (hīk) ◊ *verb* **hiked, hiking** ◊ *noun, plural* **hikes**

hill *noun* **1.** A raised, usually rounded part of the earth's surface. **2.** A small mound of earth, such as one made by ants.
hill (hĭl) ◊ *noun, plural* **hills**

hillside *noun* The side of a hill.
hill·side (hĭl′sīd′) ◊ *noun, plural* **hillsides**

hilltop *noun* The top of a hill.
hill·top (hĭl′tŏp′) ◊ *noun, plural* **hilltops**

hilly *adjective* Having many hills: *San Francisco is a hilly city.*
hill·y (hĭl′ē) ◊ *adjective* **hillier, hilliest**

hilt *noun* The handle of a sword or dagger.
hilt (hĭlt) ◊ *noun, plural* **hilts**

him *pronoun* The objective case of **he:** *I can see him. They sent him a book. Don't laugh at him.*
him (hĭm) ◊ *pronoun*
‖ *These sound alike:* **him, hymn**

himself *pronoun* His own self: *He found himself in a strange place. He himself made the mistake.*
him·self (hĭm sĕlf′) ◊ *pronoun*

hind *adjective* Being at the rear or back: *The dog stood on its hind legs.*
hind (hīnd) ◊ *adjective*

hinder *verb* To get in the way of, slow up, or make difficult: *The heavy rain hindered highway construction.*
hin·der (hĭn′dər) ◊ *verb* **hindered, hindering**

ă	pat	ĭ	pit	oi	oil	th	bath
ā	pay	ī	ride	o͝o	book	*th*	bathe
â	care	î	fierce	o͞o	boot	ə	ago, item
ä	father	ŏ	pot	ou	out		pencil
ĕ	pet	ō	go	ŭ	cut		atom
ē	be	ô	paw, for	û	fur		circus

hindrance *noun* A person or thing that hinders; obstacle: *Strong winds are a hindrance to mountain climbers.*
hin·drance (hĭn′drəns) ◊ *noun, plural* **hindrances**

hinge *noun* A device with joints on which something, such as a door, turns.
hinge (hĭnj) ◊ *noun, plural* **hinges**

hint *noun* **1.** A slight sign or suggestion: *Your smile gave no hint of how angry you felt.* **2.** A piece of useful information; clue: *Here are some hints to help you solve the riddle.*
◊ *verb* To make known or suggest by a hint.
hint (hĭnt) ◊ *noun, plural* **hints** ◊ *verb* **hinted, hinting**

hip *noun* The part of the body that projects outward on each side between the waist and thigh.
hip (hĭp) ◊ *noun, plural* **hips**

hippo *noun* A hippopotamus.
hip·po (hĭp′ō) ◊ *noun, plural* **hippos**

hippopotamus *noun* A large African river animal with dark, almost hairless skin, short legs, a broad snout, and a wide mouth.
hip·po·pot·a·mus (hĭp′ə pŏt′ə məs) ◊ *noun, plural* **hippopotamuses**

***HISTORY* • hippopotamus**

Hippopotamus comes into English through Latin from two Greek words meaning "river horse."

▲ **hippopotamus**

hire *verb* **1.** To use the work or services of; employ. **2.** To pay for using temporarily;

rent: *We can hire a car at the airport.*
◊ *noun* **1.** Money that is given as payment for doing work or for the use of something. **2.** The act or fact of hiring; employment.
hire (hīr) ◊ *verb* **hired, hiring** ◊ *noun*

his *adjective* Relating or belonging to him: *Where did he put his glasses?*
◊ *pronoun* The one or ones that belong to him: *The red scarf on the chair is his. They needed extra records for the party so he lent them his.*
his (hĭz) ◊ *adjective* ◊ *pronoun*

Hispanic *noun* An American who has Spanish or Latin-American ancestors.
◊ *adjective* Of or relating to Hispanics or to the people, language, and culture of Spain, Portugal, or Latin America.
His·pan·ic (hĭ **spăn′**ĭk) ◊ *noun, plural* **Hispanics** ◊ *adjective*

hiss *noun* A sound like a long *s: We could hear the hiss of air escaping from a tire.*
◊ *verb* To make a hiss.
hiss (hĭs) ◊ *noun, plural* **hisses** ◊ *verb* **hissed, hissing**

historian *noun* A person who writes about or specializes in the study of history.
his·to·ri·an (hĭ **stôr′** ē ən) ◊ *noun, plural* **historians**

historic *adjective* Important or famous in history: *The historic battle changed the fate of two nations.*
his·tor·ic (hĭ **stôr′**ĭk) ◊ *adjective*

historical *adjective* **1.** Of or relating to history. **2.** Based on or concerned with events in history.
his·tor·i·cal (hĭ **stôr′**ĭ kəl) ◊ *adjective*

history *noun* **1.** The continuing events of the past leading up to the present: *The invention of the printing press was one of the most important in history.* **2.** A written record of past events. **3.** The study of past events as a special field of knowledge. **4.** An account of things that have happened; story.
his·to·ry (**hĭs′** tə rē) ◊ *noun, plural* **histories**

hit *verb* **1.** To give a punch, slap, or blow to: *The ball hit me on the arm.* **2.** To strike or strike against: *The two boats hit in midstream.* **3.** To get to: *The ride was smooth until we hit a bumpy road.* **4.** To propel by striking with a bat or racket: *I hit the ball into the field.* **5.** To affect or impress strongly, as if by a blow: *The bad news hit me hard.*
◊ *noun* **1.** A blow, stroke, or shot that hits something aimed at. **2.** A great success: *The show is the hit of the season.* **3.** A baseball struck so that the batter can reach a base safely.
◊ *idiom* **hit it off** To get along well together.
hit (hĭt) ◊ *verb* **hit, hitting** ◊ *noun, plural* **hits**

hitch *verb* **1.** To tie or fasten by a knot, ring, or hook: *We hitched a dog team to the sled.* **2.** To raise or pull with a tug or jerk: *I hitched up my socks.*
◊ *noun* **1.** A short pull or tug. **2.** An unexpected difficulty or delay: *Heavy traffic put a hitch in our plans.*
hitch (hĭch) ◊ *verb* **hitched, hitching** ◊ *noun, plural* **hitches**

hive *noun* **1.** A natural or artificial home for honeybees. **2.** A colony of bees.
hive (hīv) ◊ *noun, plural* **hives**

▲ **hive**

hives *plural noun* An allergic reaction that is marked by red itchy patches on the skin.
hives (hīvz) ◊ *plural noun*

ho *interjection* An expression that is used to show surprise or to attract attention.
ho (hō) ◊ *interjection*
‖*These sound alike:* **ho, hoe**

hoard *noun* A supply that is stored away.
◊ *verb* To save and store away, often secretly or greedily.
hoard (hôrd) ◊ *noun, plural* **hoards** ◊ *verb* **hoarded, hoarding**
‖*These sound alike:* **hoard, horde**

hoarse *adjective* **1.** Low, rough, or harsh in sound: *The cry of the crow is hoarse.* **2.** Having a low, rough, or harsh voice: *We shouted until we were hoarse.*
hoarse (hôrs) ◊ *adjective* **hoarser, hoarsest**
‖*These sound alike:* **hoarse, horse**

hoax *noun* **1.** An act meant to deceive or fool others **2.** Something false that is put before the public as real.
hoax (hōks) ◊ *noun, plural* **hoaxes**

H

hobble *verb* To walk with a slow, awkward motion; limp.
◊ *noun* An awkward or limping walk.
hob·ble (hŏb′əl) ◊ *verb* **hobbled, hobbling** ◊ *noun, plural* **hobbles**

hobby *noun* An activity done for pleasure in one's spare time: *Building models is my favorite hobby.*
hob·by (hŏb′ē) ◊ *noun, plural* **hobbies**

hobo *noun* A person without a steady income who wanders about from place to place.
ho·bo (hō′bō) ◊ *noun, plural* **hoboes** *or* **hobos**

hockey *noun* A game played by two teams who try to drive a puck or ball through a goal with curved sticks. Hockey is played on ice with a puck or on a field with a ball.
hock·ey (hŏk′ē) ◊ *noun*

hoe *noun* A tool with a flat blade on a long handle. A hoe is used for breaking up soil and for weeding.
◊ *verb* To loosen, dig, or weed with a hoe.
hoe (hō) ◊ *noun, plural* **hoes** ◊ *verb* **hoed, hoeing**
‖*These sound alike:* **hoe, ho**

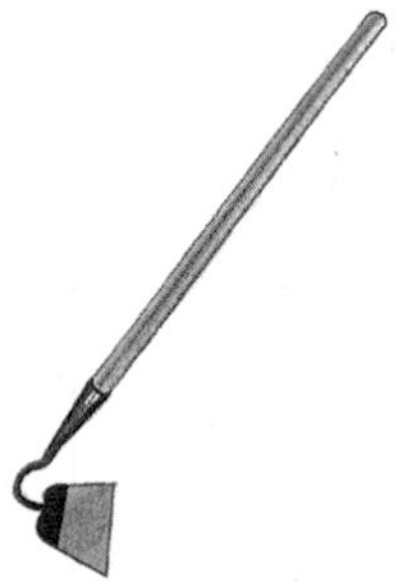

▲ **hoe**

hog *noun* A pig that is fully grown, especially one raised for meat.
◊ *verb* To take or use more than one's fair share of something.
hog (hôg) ◊ *noun, plural* **hogs** ◊ *verb* **hogged, hogging**

hoist *verb* To lift or haul up, often with a mechanical device.
◊ *noun* **1.** A device, such as a pulley or crane, for lifting or hauling up. **2.** A pull or lift: *Give me a hoist over the fence.*
hoist (hoist) ◊ *verb* **hoisted, hoisting** ◊ *noun, plural* **hoists**

ă	pat	ĭ	pit	oi	**oil**	th	**bath**
ā	pay	ī	ride	o͝o	**book**	*th*	**bathe**
â	care	î	fierce	o͞o	**boot**	ə	**ago, item**
ä	father	ŏ	pot	ou	**out**		**pencil**
ĕ	pet	ō	go	ŭ	**cut**		**atom**
ē	be	ô	paw, for	û	**fur**		**circus**

hold¹ *verb* **1.** To have or keep in the arms or hands: *The baby is learning to hold a cup.* **2.** To keep from moving or from doing: *Hold your dog on the leash!* **3.** To keep in a certain place or position: *Hold your head high.* **4.** To have or take as contents; contain: *This box holds a dozen apples.* **5.** To support: *Will that rope hold a heavy load?* **6.** To remain firm or fast: *The knot will not hold.* **7.** To keep on without changing: *Do you think our good luck will hold?* **8.** To have or occupy: *The senator held office for two terms.* **9.** To cause to take place; conduct: *We can hold the meeting at my house.* **10.** To keep the interest of: *The magician held our attention with amazing tricks.* **11.** To be or cause to be loyal or faithful, as to a duty: *I'm going to hold you to your promises.* **12.** To be true: *This basic rule holds in all cases.* **13.** To stop or delay: *Please hold dinner until I get home.*
◊ *noun* **1.** An act or means of holding something: *Keep a firm hold on the railing.* **2.** Something that is held or used for support, as in climbing.
◊ *idiom* **hold up 1.** To stop or interfere with; delay: *The accident held up traffic.* **2.** To remain in good condition; last: *This car should hold up for many years.* **3.** To rob, especially by threatening with a weapon: *The robber held up the bank.*
hold¹ (hōld) ◊ *verb* **held, holding** ◊ *noun, plural* **holds**

hold² *noun* A compartment in a ship or airplane for storing cargo.
hold² (hōld) ◊ *noun, plural* **holds**

***HISTORY* • hold¹, hold²**

Hold¹ goes back to an old English word that meant "to contain, grasp." **Hold²** comes from the word **hull**, "the outer covering of a seed or fruit." The original spelling of **hold²** probably changed under the influence of **hold¹**.

holder *noun* A thing or device for holding or handling something.
hold·er (hōl′dər) ◊ *noun, plural* **holders**

holdup *noun* **1.** An armed robbery. **2.** A delay.
hold·up (hōld′ŭp′) ◊ *noun, plural* **holdups**

hole *noun* **1.** An opening into or through something: *I tore a hole in my shirt.* **2.** A hollow place or space: *The batter hit the ball through the hole between second and third base.* **3.** An animal's shelter or burrow.
hole (hōl) ◊ *noun, plural* **holes**
‖ *These sound alike:* **hole, whole**

holiday *noun* **1.** A day or period of time set aside to honor someone or to celebrate a special event. **2.** A vacation.
hol·i·day (hŏl′ĭ dā′) ◊ *noun, plural* **holidays**

holiness *noun* The quality or condition of being holy.
ho·li·ness (hō′lē nĭs) ◊ *noun*

hollow *adjective* **1.** Having a space or opening inside: *The squirrel hid in a hollow log.* **2.** Echoing as if coming from an empty place: *We heard a hollow boom of thunder.*
◊ *noun* **1.** An opening, space, or dent in or within something. **2.** A small valley.
◊ *verb* To make or become hollow.
hol·low (hŏl′ō) ◊ *adjective* **hollower, hollowest** ◊ *noun, plural* **hollows** ◊ *verb* **hollowed, hollowing**

holly *noun* An evergreen tree or shrub that has shiny, prickly leaves and bright-red berries often used for Christmas decorations.
hol·ly (hŏl′ē) ◊ *noun, plural* **hollies**

▲ **holly**

hollyhock *noun* A tall garden plant with a long cluster of large, colorful flowers.
hol·ly·hock (hŏl′ē hŏk′) ◊ *noun, plural* **hollyhocks**

holocaust *noun* Total destruction and great loss of life.
ho·lo·caust (hŏl′ə kôst′) ◊ *noun, plural* **holocausts**

holster *noun* A case shaped to hold a pistol and usually worn on a belt.
hol·ster (hōl′stər) ◊ *noun, plural* **holsters**

holy *adjective* **1.** Of or having to do with the worship of God or a divine being; sacred: *The Bible and the Koran are holy books.* **2.** Very religious; saintly. **3.** Deserving very special respect.
ho·ly (hō′lē) ◊ *adjective* **holier, holiest**
‖ *These sound alike:* **holy, wholly**

homage *noun* **1.** Special public honor or respect: *The crowd cheered in homage to the astronauts.* **2.** A ceremony of the Middle Ages in which a vassal pledged loyalty to a lord.
hom·age (hŏm′ĭj) ◊ *noun*

home *noun* **1.** The place in which one lives. **2.** A family in its dwelling place; household. **3.** The place in which one was born, grew up, or has lived for a long time. **4.** A natural dwelling place; habitat: *The forest is the home of many animals and plants.* **5.** A place or institution for the care and shelter of those who cannot care for themselves. **6.** A goal or place of safety in some games, such as baseball.
◊ *adverb* To or at home: *We raced home from school.*
home (hōm) ◊ *noun, plural* **homes** ◊ *adverb*

▲ **home**
Sliding into home in a baseball game

homeland *noun* The country in which one was born or has lived for a long time.
home·land (hōm′lănd′) ◊ *noun, plural* **homelands**

homely *adjective* Not good-looking.
home·ly (hōm′lē) ◊ *adjective* **homelier, homeliest**

H

homemade *adjective* Made at home.
home·made (**hōm′mād′**) ◊ *adjective*

homemaker *noun* A person who manages a household.
home·mak·er (**hōm′**mā′kər) ◊ *noun, plural* **homemakers**

homer *noun* A home run.
hom·er (**hō′**mər) ◊ *noun, plural* **homers**

homeroom *noun* A classroom in which a group of pupils of the same grade gather each day, as before the start of classes.
home·room (**hōm′**ro͞om′ *or* **hōm′**ro͝om′) ◊ *noun, plural* **homerooms**

home run *noun* A hit in baseball that allows the batter to touch all bases and score a run.
home run ◊ *noun, plural* **home runs**

homesick *adjective* Unhappy and longing for home and family.
home·sick (**hōm′**sĭk′) ◊ *adjective*

homespun *noun* A plain, loosely woven cloth originally made of yarn spun at home. ◊ *adjective* **1.** Spun or woven at home. **2.** Made of homespun. **3.** Plain and simple.
home·spun (**hōm′**spŭn′) ◊ *noun* ◊ *adjective*

homestead *noun* **1.** A house with the land and buildings belonging to it. **2.** A piece of land that is given by the government to a settler who claims it and builds a home on it.
home·stead (**hōm′**stĕd′) ◊ *noun, plural* **homesteads**

homeward *adverb & adjective* Toward or moving toward home.
home·ward (**hōm′**wərd) ◊ *adverb & adjective*

homework *noun* School assignments to be done at home.
home·work (**hōm′**wûrk′) ◊ *noun*

homey *adjective* Like a home; comfortable and pleasant.
home·y (**hō′**mē) ◊ *adjective* **homier, homiest**

homing pigeon *noun* A pigeon that is trained to fly back home carrying messages.
hom·ing pigeon (**hō′**mĭng) ◊ *noun, plural* **homing pigeons**

ă	pat	ĭ	pit	oi	**oi**l	th	ba**th**
ā	pay	ī	ride	o͝o	b**oo**k	*th*	ba**the**
â	care	î	fierce	o͞o	b**oo**t	ə	**a**go, it**e**m
ä	father	ŏ	pot	ou	**ou**t		penc**i**l
ĕ	pet	ō	go	ŭ	c**u**t		at**o**m
ē	be	ô	paw, for	û	f**u**r		circ**u**s

hominy *noun* Hulled and dried kernels of corn, often ground into a coarse white meal, and cooked by boiling.
hom·i·ny (**hŏm′**ə nē) ◊ *noun*

homogenize *verb* To mix the cream in milk so that it does not rise to the top.
ho·mog·e·nize (hə **mŏj′**ə nīz′) ◊ *verb* **homogenized, homogenizing**

homograph *noun* One of two or more words that are spelled the same way but have different meanings and may be pronounced differently. Examples are *wound*[1] (wo͞ond) and *wound*[2] (wound).
hom·o·graph (**hŏm′**ə grăf′) ◊ *noun, plural* **homographs**

homonym *noun* One of two or more words that are pronounced alike and have the same spelling but have different meanings and origins. Examples are *die*[1] (to stop living) and *die*[2] (stamping or shaping device).
hom·o·nym (**hŏm′**ə nĭm) ◊ *noun, plural* **homonyms**

homophone *noun* One of two or more words that sound alike but have different meanings and spellings. Examples are *mail* and *male.*
hom·o·phone (**hŏm′**ə fōn′) ◊ *noun, plural* **homophones**

honest *adjective* **1.** Not lying, stealing, or cheating. **2.** Being just what it appears to be; genuine. **3.** Not hiding anything; straightforward: *Give me your honest opinion.*
hon·est (**ŏn′**ĭst) ◊ *adjective*

honesty *noun* The quality of being honest.
hon·es·ty (**ŏn′**ĭ stē) ◊ *noun*

honey *noun* A sweet, thick, syrupy substance made by bees from the nectar of flowers and used as food.
hon·ey (**hŭn′**ē) ◊ *noun, plural* **honeys**

honeybee *noun* A bee that makes honey.
hon·ey·bee (**hŭn′**ē bē′) ◊ *noun, plural* **honeybees**

honeycomb *noun* **1.** A wax structure with many small, six-sided cells that is made by honeybees to hold honey. **2.** An object full of many small openings or spaces.
◊ *verb* To fill or become filled with many small openings or spaces: *Small animals had honeycombed the cliff with caves.*
hon·ey·comb (**hŭn′**ē kōm′) ◊ *noun, plural* **honeycombs** ◊ *verb* **honeycombed, honeycombing**

▲ **honeycomb**

honeydew melon *noun* A melon with a smooth whitish rind and sweet green flesh.
hon·ey·dew melon (**hŭn′**ē do͞o) ◊ *noun, plural* **honeydew melons**

honeymoon *noun* A trip or vacation taken by a newly married couple.
hon·ey·moon (**hŭn′**ē mo͞on′) ◊ *noun, plural* **honeymoons**

honeysuckle *noun* A vine with fragrant yellow, white, or pink flowers shaped like tubes.
hon·ey·suck·le (**hŭn′**ē sŭk′əl) ◊ *noun*

honk *noun* A loud, harsh sound such as that made by a goose or an automobile horn.
◊ *verb* To make this sound.
honk (hôngk) ◊ *noun, plural* **honks** ◊ *verb* **honked, honking**

honor *noun* **1.** Special respect or high regard: *We display the flag to show honor to the United States.* **2.** A special privilege or mark of excellence: *Election as class president is an honor.* **3.** A person who is highly respected: *That young doctor is an honor to the profession.* **4.** High moral standards. **5.** High standing among others; reputation. **6. Honor** A title of respect for a high-ranking official, such as a judge or mayor: *Your Honor, the jury has finally reached a verdict.* **7. honors** Special recognition for excellent schoolwork.
◊ *verb* To show special respect for.
hon·or (**ŏn′**ər) ◊ *noun, plural* **honors** ◊ *verb* **honored, honoring**

honorary *adjective* Given as an honor without fulfilling the usual requirements: *The college gave the ambassador an honorary degree.*
hon·or·ar·y (**ŏn′**ə rĕr′ē) ◊ *adjective*

hood *noun* **1.** A covering for the head and neck and sometimes the face, often attached to a coat, cape, or robe. **2.** Something shaped or used like a hood. **3.** The hinged metal cover over the engine of a motor vehicle.
◊ *verb* To cover with or as if with a hood: *Clouds hooded the mountain tops.*
hood (ho͝od) ◊ *noun, plural* **hoods** ◊ *verb* **hooded, hooding**

hoodlum *noun* **1.** A gangster or criminal. **2.** A young person who is tough or mean.
hood·lum (**ho͞od′**ləm) ◊ *noun, plural* **hoodlums**

hoof *noun* **1.** A tough, protective covering of horn on the feet of certain animals, such as horses, cattle, deer, and pigs. **2.** The hoofed foot of an animal.
hoof (ho͝of *or* ho͞of) ◊ *noun, plural* **hoofs** *or* **hooves**

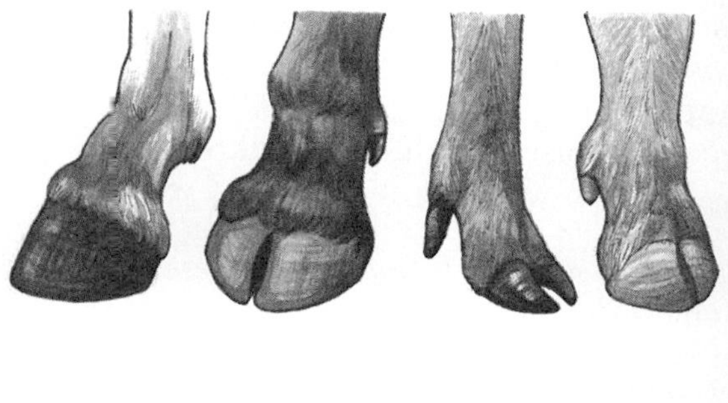

▲ **hoof**
Several kinds of hoofs

hoofed *adjective* Having hoofs.
hoofed (ho͝oft *or* ho͞oft) ◊ *adjective*

hook *noun* **1.** A curved or bent object, often of metal, that is used to catch, hold, fasten, or pull something. **2.** Something that is curved or bent like a hook.
◊ *verb* **1.** To fasten with or as if with a hook. **2.** To catch with a hook: *I hooked a 10-pound bass.* **3.** To move, throw, or extend in a curve or bend: *The road hooked around the lake.*
◊ *idiom* **hook up** To connect to a system or a source of power: *I hooked up the TV antenna.*
hook (ho͝ok) ◊ *noun, plural* **hooks** ◊ *verb* **hooked, hooking**

hooked *adjective* Shaped like a hook.
hooked (ho͝okt) ◊ *adjective*

H

hoop *noun* **1.** A circular band that holds the sides of a barrel together. **2.** A circular object: *A toy hoop can be spun around the body.* **3.** A circular frame once used to make a woman's skirt stand out.
hoop (ho͞op *or* ho͝op) ◊ *noun, plural* **hoops**

hooray *interjection* Another spelling for **hurrah.**
hoo·ray (ho͝o **rā′**) ◊ *interjection*

hoot *noun* **1.** The deep, hollow cry of an owl. **2.** A shout of scorn or disapproval.
◊ *verb* **1.** To make a deep, hollow cry. **2.** To shout with scorn or disapproval.
hoot (ho͞ot) ◊ *noun, plural* **hoots** ◊ *verb* **hooted, hooting**

hooves *noun* A plural of **hoof.**
hooves (ho͝ovz *or* ho͞ovz) ◊ *noun*

hop *verb* **1.** To move with light, quick leaps or springs: *The rabbit hopped away.* **2.** To jump on one foot. **3.** To jump over: *I hopped the fence in a single bound.*
◊ *noun* A light, springy leap or jump.
hop (hŏp) ◊ *verb* **hopped, hopping** ◊ *noun, plural* **hops**

hope *verb* To wish and at the same time expect or trust that the wish will come true.
◊ *noun* **1.** A feeling of confident expectation or trust. **2.** A reason or cause for hope: *You are the team's only hope for success.* **3.** What one wishes or hopes for.
hope (hōp) ◊ *verb* **hoped, hoping** ◊ *noun, plural* **hopes**

hopeful *adjective* **1.** Feeling or showing hope. **2.** Giving hope; encouraging.
hope·ful (**hōp′**fəl) ◊ *adjective*

hopeless *adjective* **1.** Having no hope: *The lost hikers felt hopeless.* **2.** Offering no hope: *The search for my wallet proved hopeless.* **3.** Beyond improvement.
hope·less (**hōp′**lĭs) ◊ *adjective*

hopper *noun* **1.** A hopping insect. **2.** A container for holding something such as coal or grain. A hopper often has a wide, open top and a narrow bottom opening through which its contents can be removed.
hop·per (**hŏp′**ər) ◊ *noun, plural* **hoppers**

hopscotch *noun* A game in which players toss a small object into the numbered spaces of a pattern of rectangles marked on the ground. The players hop or jump through the spaces and back to pick up the object.
hop·scotch (**hŏp′**skŏch′) ◊ *noun*

horde *noun* A large crowd or swarm.
horde (hôrd) ◊ *noun, plural* **hordes**
‖*These sound alike:* **horde, hoard**

horizon *noun* **1.** The line along which the earth and sky appear to meet. **2.** The limits of a person's experience or knowledge.
ho·ri·zon (hə **rī′**zən) ◊ *noun, plural* **horizons**

▲ **horizon**

horizontal *adjective* Parallel to the horizon; level or straight across: *Floors are horizontal and walls are vertical.*
◊ *noun* A horizontal line, line segment, or object.
hor·i·zon·tal (hôr′ĭ **zŏn′**tl) ◊ *adjective* ◊ *noun, plural* **horizontals**

hormone *noun* A substance produced by certain glands and carried by the blood to bodily organs and tissue. Hormones regulate some bodily functions and control growth.
hor·mone (**hôr′**mōn′) ◊ *noun, plural* **hormones**

horn *noun* **1.** One of a pair of hard, bony, usually curved and pointed growths on the heads of hoofed animals such as cattle, sheep, and goats. **2.** A growth that looks like a horn, as on the head of a snail or an owl. **3.** The hard, smooth substance forming the outer covering of animal horns, or a similar substance: *The*

ă	pat	ĭ	pit	oi	**oil**	th	ba**th**
ā	pay	ī	ride	o͝o	book	*th*	ba**the**
â	care	î	fierce	o͞o	boot	ə	ago, item
ä	father	ŏ	pot	ou	**out**		pencil
ĕ	pet	ō	go	ŭ	cut		atom
ē	be	ô	paw, for	û	fur		circus

handle of this knife is made of horn. **4.** A container made from an animal's horn: *Horns were once used to carry gunpowder.* **5.** A brass wind instrument, such as a French horn or trumpet. **6.** Something shaped like a horn. **7.** A device used to project sound, as from a loudspeaker. **8.** A usually electrical signaling device that produces a loud tone.
horn (hôrn) ◊ *noun, plural* **horns**

horned *adjective* Having horns.
horned (hôrnd) ◊ *adjective*

horned toad *noun* A lizard of southwestern North America with hornlike growths on the head, a broad, spiny body, and a short tail.
horned toad ◊ *noun, plural* **horned toads**

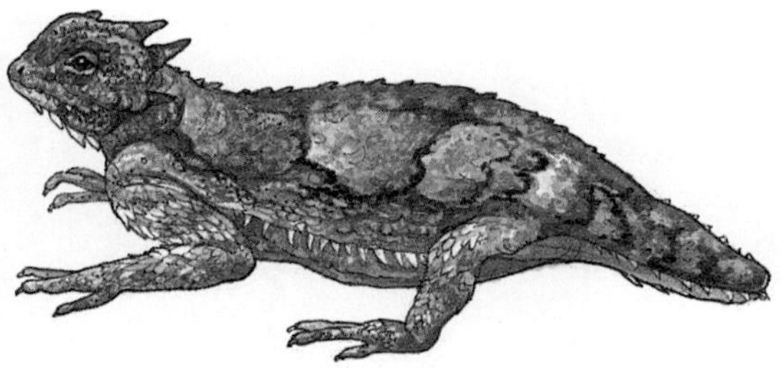

▲ **horned toad**

hornet *noun* Any of several large stinging wasps that often build large, papery nests.
hor•net (**hôr′**nĭt) ◊ *noun, plural* **hornets**

horrible *adjective* **1.** Causing horror; dreadful. **2.** Very unpleasant: *What is that horrible taste?*
hor•ri•ble (**hôr′**ə bəl) ◊ *adjective*

horrid *adjective* **1.** Causing horror. **2.** Very unpleasant.
hor•rid (**hôr′**ĭd) ◊ *adjective*

horror *noun* **1.** Great fear, terror, or shock. **2.** A cause of horror.
hor•ror (**hôr′**ər) ◊ *noun, plural* **horrors**

horse *noun* **1.** A large hoofed animal that has a long mane and tail. Horses are used for riding, pulling vehicles, and carrying loads. **2.** A supporting frame with legs. **3.** A piece of equipment used for gymnastic exercises.
horse (hôrs) ◊ *noun, plural* **horses**
‖ *These sound alike:* **horse, hoarse**

horseback *noun* The back of a horse. ◊ *adverb* On the back of a horse.
horse•back (**hôrs′**băk′) ◊ *noun* ◊ *adverb*

horsehair *noun* The hair from the mane or tail of a horse.
horse•hair (**hôrs′**hâr′) ◊ *noun*

horseman *noun* A man who is skilled at riding and handling horses.
horse•man (**hôrs′**mən) ◊ *noun, plural* **horsemen**

horseplay *noun* Rough, noisy play.
horse•play (**hôrs′**plā′) ◊ *noun*

horsepower *noun* A unit for measuring the power of an engine, equal to the energy used in raising 550 pounds one foot in one second.
horse•pow•er (**hôrs′**pou′ər) ◊ *noun*

horseshoe *noun* **1.** A U-shaped iron plate fitted and nailed to the rim of a horse's hoof. **2. horseshoes** (*used with a singular verb*) A game in which players try to toss horseshoes around a stake. **3.** A thing shaped like a horseshoe.
horse•shoe (**hôrs′**sho͞o′) ◊ *noun, plural* **horseshoes**

horseshoe crab *noun* A sea animal with a large oval shell and a stiff, pointed tail.
horseshoe crab ◊ *noun, plural* **horseshoe crabs**

horsewoman *noun* A woman who is skilled at riding and handling horses.
horse•wom•an (**hôrs′**wo͝om′ən) ◊ *noun, plural* **horsewomen**

hose *noun* **1.** Stockings or socks. **2.** A long flexible tube used for carrying fluid or air. ◊ *verb* To wash or spray with a hose.
hose (hōz) ◊ *noun, plural* **hose** (for sense 1) *or* **hoses** (for sense 2) ◊ *verb* **hosed, hosing**

hosiery *noun* Stockings and socks.
ho•sier•y (**hō′**zhə rē) ◊ *noun*

hospitable *adjective* Friendly and generous to guests; cordial.
hos•pi•ta•ble (**hŏs′**pĭ tə bəl *or* hŏ **spĭt′**ə bəl) ◊ *adjective*

hospital *noun* A medical institution that treats sick and injured people.
hos•pi•tal (**hŏs′**pĭ təl) ◊ *noun, plural* **hospitals**

hospitality *noun* Friendly, cordial treatment of guests.
hos•pi•tal•i•ty (hŏs′pĭ **tăl′**ĭ tē) ◊ *noun*

H

hospitalize *verb* To put in a hospital.
hos·pi·tal·ize (**hŏs′** pĭ tə līz′) ◊ *verb* **hospitalized, hospitalizing**

host[1] *noun* A person, group, or institution that receives or entertains guests.
host[1] (hōst) ◊ *noun, plural* **hosts**

host[2] *noun* **1.** An army. **2.** A great number; multitude.
host[2] (hōst) ◊ *noun, plural* **hosts**

***HISTORY* • host[1], host[2]**

Host[1] came into English through French from a Latin word that meant both "guest" and "one who receives guests." **Host**[2] came into English through French from a Latin word that meant "enemy" and then "army."

hostage *noun* A person given to or held by an enemy as security for the fulfillment of certain demands.
hos·tage (**hŏs′** tĭj) ◊ *noun, plural* **hostages**

hostel *noun* An inexpensive lodging house for travelers and tourists especially of high-school or college age.
hos·tel (**hŏs′** təl) ◊ *noun, plural* **hostels**
‖*These sound alike:* **hostel, hostile**

hostess *noun* **1.** A woman who receives or entertains guests. **2.** A woman who greets and serves patrons, as at a restaurant.
host·ess (**hō′** stĭs) ◊ *noun, plural* **hostesses**

hostile *adjective* **1.** Of or relating to an enemy. **2.** Not friendly: *Don't give me such a hostile look.*
hos·tile (**hŏs′** təl) ◊ *adjective*
‖*These sound alike:* **hostile, hostel**

hostility *noun* **1.** A hostile condition or action. **2. hostilities** Open warfare.
hos·til·i·ty (hŏ **stĭl′** ĭ tē) ◊ *noun, plural* **hostilities**

hot *adjective* **1.** Having or giving off great heat: *The iron is hot.* **2.** Having or causing a higher body heat than is normal or comfortable. **3.** Tasting sharp or spicy. **4.** Full of emotion; fiery: *It was a hot debate.*
hot (hŏt) ◊ *adjective* **hotter, hottest**

SYNONYMS

hot, fiery

Last summer there were many *hot* days over 95 degrees. I couldn't walk on the *fiery* pavement in my bare feet.
Antonyms: *cold, freezing*

hot-air balloon *noun* A large bag filled with hot air or a gas that is lighter than air. It often has a basket attached beneath it for carrying passengers and equipment.
hot-air balloon (**hŏt′ âr′**) ◊ *noun, plural* **hot-air balloons**

▲ **hot-air balloon**

hot dog *noun* A frankfurter, especially one that is cooked and served in a long roll.
hot dog ◊ *noun, plural* **hot dogs**

hotel *noun* A house or building that provides lodging and often meals to travelers for pay.
ho·tel (hō **tĕl′**) ◊ *noun, plural* **hotels**

hothouse *noun* A heated building, usually with a glass roof and sides, for growing plants; greenhouse.
hot·house (**hŏt′** hous′) ◊ *noun, plural* **hothouses**

hound *noun* **1.** Any of several kinds of dogs that were originally bred and trained for

ă	pat	ĭ	pit	oi	**oil**	th	ba**th**
ā	pay	ī	ride	ŏŏ	book	*th*	ba**the**
â	care	î	fierce	ōō	boot	ə	ago, item
ä	father	ŏ	pot	ou	**out**		pencil
ĕ	pet	ō	go	ŭ	cut		atom
ē	be	ô	paw, for	û	fur		circus

hunting. Hounds have a good sense of smell, short hair, and usually drooping ears. **2.** A dog.
◊ *verb* To urge or ask over and over; pester.
hound (hound) ◊ *noun, plural* **hounds** ◊ *verb* **hounded, hounding**

hour *noun* **1.** A unit of time that is equal to 60 minutes: *There are 24 hours in a day.* **2.** A particular time of day: *At what hour does the store open?* **3.** A customary time for doing something: *Our dinner hour is usually around six.* **4. hours** The time for study or work: *Our school hours are from eight to three.*
hour (our) ◊ *noun, plural* **hours**
‖*These sound alike:* **hour, our**

hourglass *noun* An instrument for measuring time. It is made of two glass chambers with a narrow neck connecting them. A quantity of sand in the top takes one hour to pass down to the bottom chamber.
hour·glass (our′ glăs′) ◊ *noun, plural* **hourglasses**

▲ **hourglass**

hourly *adjective* **1.** Happening or done every hour. **2.** By the hour: *I get an hourly wage for yard work.*
◊ *adverb* Every hour: *News broadcasts are run hourly.*
hour·ly (our′ lē) ◊ *adjective* ◊ *adverb*

house *noun* **1.** A building people live in; residence: *We moved into our new house.* **2.** A building, such as a schoolhouse or firehouse, that is used for a certain purpose. **3.** A business firm. **4.** The people who live in a private residence: *The sound of thunder woke up the whole house.* **5.** An audience, as at a movie or a concert: *There was a full house at the opening night of the play.* **6.** A group of people who make laws: *The House of Representatives and the Senate are the two houses of the United States Congress.*
◊ *verb* To provide living quarters or accommodations for: *The motel can house 120 overnight guests.*
house ◊ *noun* (hous), *plural* **houses** ◊ *verb* (houz) **housed, housing**

houseboat *noun* A large boat with a flat bottom that is designed for people to live on.
house·boat (hous′ bōt′) ◊ *noun, plural* **houseboats**

housefly *noun* A common fly that is found in or around homes. It carries and spreads the germs of many diseases.
house·fly (hous′ flī′) ◊ *noun, plural* **houseflies**

household *noun* **1.** The people who live in a residence. **2.** A home and its activities.
house·hold (hous′ hōld′) ◊ *noun, plural* **households**

housekeeper *noun* Someone who is hired to take care of a home.
house·keep·er (hous′ kē′pər) ◊ *noun, plural* **housekeepers**

housekeeping *noun* The care and management of a household.
house·keep·ing (hous′ kē′pĭng) ◊ *noun*

House of Commons *noun* In the British or Canadian government, the lower house of Parliament. Its members are elected by the people and have the power to make laws.

House of Lords *noun* In the British government, the upper house of Parliament. Its members are nobles and important clergymen.

House of Representatives *noun* **1.** The lower house of the United States Congress. Its members are elected every two years. **2.** The lower branch of the legislature in most states of the United States.

housewarming *noun* A party to celebrate moving into a new home.
house·warm·ing (hous′ wôr′mĭng) ◊ *noun, plural* **housewarmings**

housewife *noun* A woman who takes care of or shares in taking care of a household.
house·wife (hous′ wīf′) ◊ *noun, plural* **housewives**

housework *noun* Housekeeping tasks, such as cleaning and cooking.
house·work (hous′ wûrk′) ◊ *noun*

housing *noun* **1.** Buildings where people live. **2.** Something that covers, holds, or protects a machine or any of its parts.
hous·ing (hou′ zĭng) ◊ *noun, plural* **housings**

hovel *noun* A small, dirty house.
hov·el (hŭv′ əl) ◊ *noun, plural* **hovels**

hover *verb* **1.** To stay in one place in the air:

H

The hummingbird hovered over the flower. **2.** To stay or wait nearby: *The dogs hovered around me while I was fixing their dinner.*
hov·er (hŭv′ər) ◊ *verb* **hovered, hovering**

how *adverb* **1.** In what way; by what means: *How can you prove you're right?* **2.** In what condition: *How do you feel now?* **3.** To what extent, amount, or degree: *How do you like your new bike?* **4.** By what reason; why: *How is it you're always late to class?*
how (hou) ◊ *adverb*

howdah *noun* A seat, usually with a canopy and railing, for riding on the back of an elephant or camel.
how·dah (hou′də) ◊ *noun, plural* **howdahs**

however *adverb* **1.** By whatever way or means: *However you get there, be there on time.* **2.** To whatever degree or amount: *However I tried, I couldn't make friends with their new dog.*
◊ *conjunction* In spite of that; nevertheless: *It was growing very dark; however, we were not worried because we had a flashlight.*
how·ev·er (hou ĕv′ər) ◊ *adverb* ◊ *conjunction*

howl *noun* **1.** A long, wailing cry, such as the one made by a dog, wolf, or coyote. **2.** A loud cry or scream.
◊ *verb* **1.** To make a long, wailing cry. **2.** To produce a sound similar to this: *The wind howled through the trees.* **3.** To cry or scream, as in pain. **4.** To yell or shout with laughter: *We all howled during the funny movie.*
howl (houl) ◊ *noun, plural* **howls** ◊ *verb* **howled, howling**

hr. The abbreviation for *hour* or *hours.*

ht. The abbreviation for *height.*

hub *noun* **1.** The middle or center part of a wheel. **2.** A center of activity or importance: *Our town is the business hub of the region.*
hub (hŭb) ◊ *noun, plural* **hubs**

huckleberry *noun* A blackish, edible berry related to the blueberry.
huck·le·ber·ry (hŭk′əl bĕr′ē) ◊ *noun, plural* **huckleberries**

ă	pat	ĭ	pit	oi	oil	th	bath
ā	pay	ī	ride	ŏŏ	book	*th*	bathe
â	care	î	fierce	ōō	boot	ə	ago, item
ä	father	ŏ	pot	ou	out		pencil
ĕ	pet	ō	go	ŭ	cut		atom
ē	be	ô	paw, for	û	fur		circus

▲ **huckleberry**

huddle *noun* A closely packed group or crowd: *There was a huddle around the warmth of the campfire.*
◊ *verb* To crowd close or put close together.
hud·dle (hŭd′l) ◊ *noun, plural* **huddles** ◊ *verb* **huddled, huddling**

hue *noun* Color: *We enjoyed the orange and reddish hues of the sunset.*
hue (hyōō) ◊ *noun, plural* **hues**
‖*These sound alike:* **hue, hew**

huff *noun* A fit of anger or annoyance.
◊ *verb* To blow, as from exhaustion: *We huffed and puffed up the hill.*
huff (hŭf) ◊ *noun, plural* **huffs** ◊ *verb* **huffed, huffing**

hug *verb* To put one's arms around and hold closely, especially to show love; embrace: *The old friends hugged when they met.*
◊ *noun* A tight clasp with the arms, especially to show love; embrace.
hug (hŭg) ◊ *verb* **hugged, hugging** ◊ *noun, plural* **hugs**

huge *adjective* Very big; enormous. —See Synonyms at **gigantic.**
huge (hyōōj) ◊ *adjective* **huger, hugest**

hulk *noun* **1.** A worn-out old ship that is no longer able to move under its own power. **2.** A heavy, clumsy ship. **3.** A large, clumsy person or thing.
hulk (hŭlk) ◊ *noun, plural* **hulks**

hull *noun* **1.** The body or frame of a ship or boat, including only its sides and bottom. **2.** The cluster of small leaves near the stem of a strawberry and some other fruits. **3.** The outer covering of certain seeds, fruits, or nuts.
◊ *verb* To remove the hull or hulls from:

Would you help me hull these berries?
hull (hŭl) ◊ *noun, plural* **hulls** ◊ *verb* **hulled, hulling**

hum *verb* **1.** To make musical tones or produce a tune as in singing but with the lips kept closed: *Sometimes I hum popular songs.* **2.** To produce a soft, low, continuous sound: *The wind is humming through the trees.* **3.** To be full of busy activity: *Our classroom really hums in the mornings.*
◊ *noun* **1.** The act or sound of humming. **2.** The sound of activity.
hum (hŭm) ◊ *verb* **hummed, humming** ◊ *noun, plural* **hums**

human *adjective* Of or characteristic of people: *Many people can't afford basic human comforts, like food, shelter, and clothing.*
◊ *noun* A person.
hu·man (**hyōō′**mən) ◊ *adjective* ◊ *noun, plural* **humans**

humane *adjective* Showing or having kindness and thoughtful concern for others: *We believe in humane treatment of all creatures.*
hu·mane (hyōō **mān′**) ◊ *adjective*

humanity *noun* **1.** The human race; people: *Humanity has made great progress in space exploration and medicine.* **2.** The condition or quality of being human. **3.** Kindness and thoughtful concern: *The veterinarian treated the animals with great humanity.*
hu·man·i·ty (hyōō **măn′**ĭ tē) ◊ *noun*

humble *adjective* **1.** Not thinking or speaking too highly about oneself or about one's own talents, abilities, or accomplishments. **2.** Having a low rank or being unimportant; lowly: *The family lived in a humble cottage.*
hum·ble (**hŭm′**bəl) ◊ *adjective* **humbler, humblest**

humid *adjective* Having a large amount of water or water vapor in the air; damp.
hu·mid (**hyōō′**mĭd) ◊ *adjective*

humidity *noun* Moisture in the air.
hu·mid·i·ty (hyōō **mĭd′**ĭ tē) ◊ *noun*

humiliate *verb* To hurt the self-respect or pride of: *Losing the game humiliated me.*
hu·mil·i·ate (hyōō **mĭl′**ē āt′) ◊ *verb* **humiliated, humiliating**

hummingbird *noun* A very small, brightly colored bird with a long, slender bill. Its wings flutter so fast that they make a humming sound.
hum·ming·bird (**hŭm′**ĭng bûrd′) ◊ *noun, plural* **hummingbirds**

▲ **hummingbird**

humor *noun* **1.** The quality of being comical or funny: *I could find no humor in the dull jokes.* **2.** The ability to see and enjoy what is comical or funny: *Since you have such a good sense of humor, you might enjoy this cartoon.* **3.** State of mind; mood: *Are you in a good or bad humor today?*
◊ *verb* To go along with the wishes of: *Let's humor them and go to the party.*
hu·mor (**hyōō′**mər) ◊ *noun, plural* **humors** ◊ *verb* **humored, humoring**

humorous *adjective* Funny, amusing, or comical. —See Synonyms at **funny.**
hu·mor·ous (**hyōō′**mər əs) ◊ *adjective*

hump *noun* A natural, rounded lump, as on the back of a camel.
hump (hŭmp) ◊ *noun, plural* **humps**

humus *noun* Dark soil formed from dead leaves and other decayed plant parts. Humus contains substances that help plants grow.
hu·mus (**hyōō′**məs) ◊ *noun*

hunch *noun* A feeling or a belief without any reason for it: *I have a hunch that it will snow soon.*
◊ *verb* To bend and draw up, as the shoulders or back, so as to form a hump.
hunch (hŭnch) ◊ *noun, plural* **hunches** ◊ *verb* **hunched, hunching**

hunchback *noun* A person with a back that is badly curved.
hunch·back (**hŭnch′**băk′) ◊ *noun, plural* **hunchbacks**

hundred *noun* The number, written 100, that is equal to the product of 10 × 10.

H

◊ *adjective* Being equal to ten times ten.
hun·dred (hŭn′drĭd) ◊ *noun, plural* **hundreds** ◊ *adjective*

hundredth *noun* **1.** The number in a series that matches the number 100. **2.** One of a hundred equal parts, written 1/100.
◊ *adjective* Coming after the ninety-ninth.
hun·dredth (hŭn′drĭdth) ◊ *noun, plural* **hundredths** ◊ *adjective*

hung *verb* A past tense and a past participle of **hang.**
hung (hŭng) ◊ *verb*

hunger *noun* **1.** A strong desire for food. **2.** Lack of food: *People still die from hunger in some parts of the world.*
◊ *verb* To have a strong desire for something: *The little orphan hungered for affection.*
hun·ger (hŭng′gər) ◊ *noun, plural* **hungers** ◊ *verb* **hungered, hungering**

hungrily *adverb* In a hungry way.
hun·gri·ly (hŭng′grə lē) ◊ *adverb*

hungry *adjective* **1.** Wanting food. **2.** Having a strong desire for something: *The puppy is hungry for attention.*
hun·gry (hŭng′grē) ◊ *adjective* **hungrier, hungriest**

hunk *noun* A large piece, as of bread or meat.
hunk (hŭngk) ◊ *noun, plural* **hunks**

hunt *verb* **1.** To look for wild animals, so as to capture or kill them. **2.** To make a careful search: *Help me hunt for my glasses.*
◊ *noun* **1.** The act or activity of hunting for wild animals, birds, or fish. **2.** A careful search: *We had an Easter egg hunt.*
hunt (hŭnt) ◊ *verb* **hunted, hunting** ◊ *noun, plural* **hunts**

hunter *noun* A person or animal that hunts.
hunt·er (hŭn′tər) ◊ *noun, plural* **hunters**

hurdle *noun* **1.** A barrier, usually consisting of a horizontal bar held in place by two upright supports. Hurdles are used in certain track and field events. **2. hurdles** (*used with a singular verb*) A race in which the runners jump over hurdles. **3.** A problem or difficulty.
◊ *verb* To jump over: *The horse hurdled the fence with ease.*
hur·dle (hûr′dl) ◊ *noun, plural* **hurdles** ◊ *verb* **hurdled, hurdling**

▲ **hurdle**

hurl *verb* To throw with a great force; fling. —See Synonyms at **throw.**
hurl (hûrl) ◊ *verb* **hurled, hurling**

hurrah *interjection* An expression that is used as a shout of joy or praise.
hur·rah (ho͝o **rä′**) ◊ *interjection*

hurray *interjection* Another spelling for **hurrah.**
hur·ray (ho͝o **rā′**) ◊ *interjection*

hurricane *noun* A very powerful storm with extremely strong winds over 75 miles per hour and heavy rains.
hur·ri·cane (hûr′ĭ kān′) ◊ *noun, plural* **hurricanes**

hurried *adjective* Done in a hurry; rushed.
hur·ried (hûr′ēd) ◊ *adjective*

hurry *verb* **1.** To act or move quickly: *Don't hurry through your work.* —See Synonyms at **speed. 2.** To take, send, or move quickly: *The ambulance hurried the patient to the hospital.*
◊ *noun* **1.** The act of hurrying: *In my hurry this morning I must have forgotten my keys.* **2.** The need or wish to go or do quickly: *We were in a hurry to finish our chores before dinner.*
hur·ry (hûr′ē) ◊ *verb* **hurried, hurrying** ◊ *noun*

ă pat	ĭ pit	oi	**oil**	th	ba**th**		
ā pay	ī ride	o͝o	**book**	*th*	ba**the**		
â care	î fierce	o͞o	**boot**	ə	ago, item		
ä father	ŏ pot	ou	**out**		pencil		
ĕ pet	ō go	ŭ	cut		atom		
ē be	ô paw, for	û	fur		circus		

SYNONYMS

hurry, haste, dispatch

I am in a *hurry* and can't talk to you now. That sloppy job shows the sock was mended in *haste.* We ate our Thanksgiving dinner with *dispatch* and sat back very full and very happy.

hurt *verb* **1.** To cause pain or injury to: *I fell and hurt my wrist.* **2.** To have a feeling of pain: *Does your ankle still hurt?* **3.** To cause painful or bad feelings in: *It hurt me that I wasn't invited to the party.* **4.** To have a bad effect on: *The dogs can't hurt that old couch.*
◊ *noun* A pain or injury.
◊ *adjective* **1.** Physically injured: *I have a hurt finger.* **2.** Upset or offended: *When you are mean to someone, it causes hurt feelings.*
hurt (hûrt) ◊ *verb* **hurt, hurting** ◊ *noun, plural* **hurts** ◊ *adjective*

husband *noun* A man who is married.
hus·band (hŭz′bənd) ◊ *noun, plural* **husbands**

hush *noun* A stopping of noise; silence: *A hush fell on the classroom.*
hush (hŭsh) ◊ *noun, plural* **hushes**

husk *noun* The dry or leaflike outer covering, as of an ear of corn or a nut.
◊ *verb* To remove the husk or husks from.
husk (hŭsk) ◊ *noun, plural* **husks** ◊ *verb* **husked, husking**

LANGUAGE DETECTIVE

husk

Part of the fun of eating corn on the cob is peeling off the outer covering before cooking the corn. The word you use for this covering depends on where you live. If you live in Virginia, West Virginia, Kentucky, or farther south, you probably say *shuck* or *corn shuck,* and you might even call the corn a "roasting ear." But if you live north of these states, you probably say *husk* or *corn husk* and call the part you cook an "ear of corn." *Husk* and *shuck* are also used as verbs. In the northern United States you *husk* the corn before cooking it, but in the southern United States you *shuck* it.

husky[1] *adjective* **1.** Hoarse or deep: *You have a husky voice.* **2.** Big and strong: *It took four husky workers to move our piano.*
husk·y[1] (hŭs′kē) ◊ *adjective* **huskier, huskiest**

husky[2] *noun* A dog with a thick, furry coat. Huskies are used for pulling sleds in the far north.
husk·y[2] (hŭs′kē) ◊ *noun, plural* **huskies**

HISTORY • husky[1], husky[2]

Husky[1] first meant "tough or dry like a husk." **Husky**[2], which refers to a sled dog, is not related to **husky**[1].

▲ **husky**[2]

hustle *verb* **1.** To push or shove roughly. **2.** To hurry; rush: *We can get there in time if we hustle.*
hus·tle (hŭs′əl) ◊ *verb* **hustled, hustling**

hut *noun* A small, simple, roughly built house or shelter; shack.
hut (hŭt) ◊ *noun, plural* **huts**

hyacinth *noun* A plant that grows from a bulb and has a cluster of fragrant, variously colored flowers.
hy·a·cinth (hī′ə sĭnth) ◊ *noun, plural* **hyacinths**

hybrid *noun* A plant or animal that has parents of different species or varieties. A mule is a hybrid that has a horse for its mother and a donkey for its father.
hy·brid (hī′brĭd) ◊ *noun, plural* **hybrids**

hydrant *noun* An outlet from a water pipe that sticks up out of the ground, usually near

a curb. Fire hoses are connected to hydrants to get water for putting out fires.
hy·drant (**hī′** drənt) ◊ *noun, plural* **hydrants**

hydroelectric *adjective* Generating electricity from water power: *Hoover Dam and Niagara Falls have large hydroelectric power stations.*
hy·dro·e·lec·tric (hī′drō ĭ **lĕk′** trĭk) ◊ *adjective*

hydrogen *noun* A gas that is very light and burns easily. It is a chemical element and mixes with oxygen to make water.
hy·dro·gen (**hī′** drə jən) ◊ *noun*

hydrogen bomb *noun* An extremely destructive bomb that can completely destroy a large city. When the bomb is set off, hydrogen atoms combine to form helium atoms, and energy is released in a tremendous explosion.
hydrogen bomb ◊ *noun, plural* **hydrogen bombs**

hydroplane *noun* A motorboat designed so that only a small part of its hull touches the water when it goes at high speeds.
hy·dro·plane (**hī′** drə plān′) ◊ *noun, plural* **hydroplanes**

▲ **hydroplane**

ă	pat	ĭ	pit	oi	**oil**	th	ba**th**
ā	pay	ī	ride	ŏŏ	book	*th*	ba*th*e
â	care	î	fierce	ōō	boot	ə	ago, item
ä	father	ŏ	pot	ou	**out**		pencil
ĕ	pet	ō	go	ŭ	cut		atom
ē	be	ô	paw, for	û	fur		circus

hyena *noun* An animal of Asia and Africa that looks rather like a large dog. It has thick, coarse hair and strong jaws and often eats dead animals. The call of the hyena sounds like wild, hysterical laughter.
hy·e·na (hī **ē′** nə) ◊ *noun, plural* **hyenas**

hygiene *noun* The rules of cleanliness and good health.
hy·giene (**hī′** jēn′) ◊ *noun*

hymn *noun* A song of joy, praise, or thanksgiving, especially when sung to God.
hymn (hĭm) ◊ *noun, plural* **hymns**
‖*These sound alike:* **hymn, him**

hymnal *noun* A book or collection of hymns.
hym·nal (**hĭm′** nəl) ◊ *noun, plural* **hymnals**

hyphen *noun* A punctuation mark (-) used to connect words (like *high-school class*), parts of a compound word (like *baby-sit*), or parts of a word divided between two lines.
hy·phen (**hī′** fən) ◊ *noun, plural* **hyphens**

hyphenate *verb* To put a hyphen in.
hy·phen·ate (**hī′** fə nāt′) ◊ *verb* **hyphenated, hyphenating**

hypnotism *noun* The method or process of hypnotizing a person.
hyp·no·tism (**hĭp′** nə tĭz′əm) ◊ *noun*

hypnotize *verb* To put someone into a relaxed, sleeplike, but alert state. People who have been hypnotized are very likely to do what they are told to do.
hyp·no·tize (**hĭp′** nə tīz′) ◊ *verb* **hypnotized, hypnotizing**

hypocrisy *noun* The act or fact of pretending to be good, kind, or honest.
hy·poc·ri·sy (hĭ **pŏk′** rĭ sē) ◊ *noun*

hypocrite *noun* A person who tries to deceive other people by pretending to be good, kind, or honest.
hyp·o·crite (**hĭp′** ə krĭt′) ◊ *noun, plural* **hypocrites**

hypotenuse *noun* The longest side of a triangle that contains an angle of 90 degrees.
hy·pot·e·nuse (hī **pŏt′** n ōōs′) ◊ *noun, plural* **hypotenuses**

hysterical *adjective* So excited or upset that one laughs and cries uncontrollably.
hys·ter·i·cal (hĭ **stĕr′** ĭ kəl) ◊ *adjective*

hysterics *noun* (*used with a singular verb*) Uncontrolled laughing or crying or both.
hys·ter·ics (hĭ **stĕr′** ĭks) ◊ *noun*

Iguana

Ii

I is the ninth letter of the English alphabet. Did you know that it has a long history?

Over 3,500 years ago, people in the Middle East were using symbols that became the letters of our alphabet. This ancient Middle Eastern symbol is a form of the letter that became our letter *I*.

I
The ancient Greeks borrowed their alphabet from people in the Middle East. Here is a form of the Greek letter that became our letter *I*.

I
The ancient Romans borrowed their alphabet from a people who had taken their own letter symbols from the Greeks. Here is a form of the Roman letter *I* that was used for carving letters into stone. These letters became the model for our printed capital letters.

ı
As people wrote quickly, especially with pens, the capital letters began to take the shapes of small letters. Here is a small-letter *i* that was developed about 1,200 years ago.

Ii *Ii*	Ii	Ii	Ii
Handwriting	Sans Serif Type	Serif Type	Computer Printing

i *or* **I** *noun* **1.** The ninth letter of the English alphabet. **2.** The Roman numeral for the number 1.
i *or* **I** (ī) ◊ *noun, plural* **i's** *or* **I's**

I *pronoun* The person who is the speaker or writer: *"I am tired today." I like cats a lot, but cats don't seem to like me.*
I (ī) ◊ *pronoun*
‖ *These sound alike:* **I, aye, eye**

IA The abbreviation for *Iowa* used with a Zip Code.

Ia. An abbreviation for *Iowa.*

ice *noun* **1.** Water that has been frozen solid. **2.** A frozen dessert made of crushed ice flavored with sweet fruit juice or syrup.
◊ *verb* **1.** To make cold or keep cold with ice: *We iced the bottles of juice for the picnic.* **2.** To become covered with ice: *The streets iced over during the freezing rain.* **3.** To put icing on.
ice (īs) ◊ *noun, plural* **ices** ◊ *verb* **iced, icing**

iceberg *noun* A very large mass of ice floating in the ocean. Icebergs are pieces of a glacier that have broken off. They can be very dangerous to ships.
ice·berg (īs′bûrg′) ◊ *noun, plural* **icebergs**

***HISTORY* • iceberg**

Iceberg comes from a Scandinavian word meaning "ice mountain."

icebox *noun* **1.** A box into which ice is put to store and cool food. **2.** A refrigerator.
ice·box (īs′bŏks′) ◊ *noun, plural* **iceboxes**

icebreaker *noun* A ship built for breaking a passage through ice-covered water.
ice·break·er (īs′brā′kər) ◊ *noun, plural* **icebreakers**

ice cap *noun* A sheet of ice and snow that covers an area of land year round.
ice cap ◊ *noun, plural* **ice caps**

ice cream *noun* A smooth, sweet, frozen food made of milk or cream and sweeteners. It comes in many flavors.
ice cream ◊ *noun, plural* **ice creams**

ice hockey *noun* Hockey played on ice.

icehouse *noun* A place where ice is stored.
ice·house (īs′hous′) ◊ *noun, plural* **icehouses**

ice pack *noun* **1.** A floating mass of solid ice. **2.** A folded cloth or bag that is filled with ice and put on sore parts of the body.
ice pack ◊ *noun, plural* **ice packs**

ice pick *noun* A pointed tool for chipping or breaking ice.
ice pick ◊ *noun, plural* **ice picks**

ice skate *noun* A boot or shoe with a metal blade or runner attached to the sole, worn for skating on ice.
ice skate ◊ *noun, plural* **ice skates**

▲ **ice skate**

ice-skate *verb* To skate on ice.
ice-skate (īs′skāt′) ◊ *verb* **ice-skated, ice-skating**

icicle *noun* A slender, pointed, hanging piece or stick of ice. An icicle is formed by water that freezes as it is dripping.
i·ci·cle (ī′sĭ kəl) ◊ *noun, plural* **icicles**

icing *noun* A smooth, sweet mixture of sugar, butter, and eggs; frosting. It is used to cover cakes and cookies.
ic·ing (ī′sĭng) ◊ *noun, plural* **icings**

icy *adjective* **1.** Covered with ice; frozen: *I slid on the icy sidewalk.* **2.** Feeling as cold as ice: *I wore a ski mask as a protection against icy winter winds.* —See Synonyms at **cold.** **3.** Without warmth of feeling; unfriendly: *Why did you give me such an icy stare?*
ic·y (ī′sē) ◊ *adjective* **icier, iciest**

ID The abbreviation for *Idaho* used with a Zip Code.

ă	pat	ĭ	pit	oi	oil	th	bath
ā	pay	ī	ride	ŏŏ	book	*th*	bathe
â	care	î	fierce	ōō	boot	ə	ago, item
ä	father	ŏ	pot	ou	out		pencil
ĕ	pet	ō	go	ŭ	cut		atom
ē	be	ô	paw, for	û	fur		circus

I'd Contraction of "I had," "I would," or "I should."
I'd (īd) ◊ *contraction*

idea *noun* **1.** A thought or plan carefully formed in the mind: *I have some ideas as to how I want to change my bedroom around.* **2.** An opinion or belief: *I have my ideas about what is right and wrong.*
i·de·a (ī **dē**′ə) ◊ *noun, plural* **ideas**

ideal *noun* A person or thing that is thought of as being perfect.
◊ *adjective* Thought of as being the best possible: *It's an ideal day for swimming.*
i·de·al (ī **dē**′əl) ◊ *noun, plural* **ideals** ◊ *adjective*

identical *adjective* **1.** Being exactly alike: *The twins bought identical shirts.* —See Synonyms at **same. 2.** Being the very same: *Those are the identical words I used.*
i·den·ti·cal (ī **dĕn**′tĭ kəl) ◊ *adjective*

identification *noun* Something that is used to prove who a person is or what something is: *I used my library card as identification.*
i·den·ti·fi·ca·tion (ī dĕn′tə fĭ **kā**′shən) ◊ *noun, plural* **identifications**

identify *verb* To recognize and acknowledge as being a certain person or thing: *I identified my pocketbook by telling what was in it.*
i·den·ti·fy (ī **dĕn**′tə fī′) ◊ *verb* **identified, identifying**

identity *noun* **1.** Who a person is or what a thing is: *Some people try to hide their identities by wearing dark glasses.* **2.** The condition of being exactly the same: *The identity of the two signatures was never in doubt.*
i·den·ti·ty (ī **dĕn**′tĭ tē) ◊ *noun, plural* **identities**

idiom *noun* An expression with a special meaning that cannot be understood from the meaning of the individual words in the phrase. For example, *to fly off the handle* is an idiom that means "to lose one's temper."
id·i·om (**ĭd**′ē əm) ◊ *noun, plural* **idioms**

idiot *noun* **1.** A stupid person. **2.** A person who does a thoughtless or foolish act: *I was an idiot to lose my ticket.*
id·i·ot (**ĭd**′ē ət) ◊ *noun, plural* **idiots**

idle *adjective* **1.** Not working or being used: *The machines in the factory were idle during the strike.* **2.** Avoiding work; lazy: *That idle loafer just sits around doing nothing.* **3.** Not

proven to be true: *It is wrong to spread idle gossip about other people.*
◊ *verb* **1.** To run at a low speed and out of gear: *The engine idled smoothly.* **2.** To spend time doing nothing: *I idled away the day.*
i·dle (īd′l) ◊ *adjective* **idler, idlest** ◊ *verb* **idled, idling**
‖*These sound alike:* **idle, idol**

idol *noun* **1.** An object that is worshiped as a god. **2.** A person who is admired or loved very much: *That famous singer is an idol to people all over the world.*
i·dol (īd′l) ◊ *noun, plural* **idols**
‖*These sound alike:* **idol, idle**

i.e. The abbreviation for the Latin words *id est,* which mean "that is."

if *conjunction* **1.** On the condition that: *I will go only if you go.* **2.** Supposing that; in case that: *Even if the rumor is true, what can we do about it?* **3.** Whether: *I wonder if they are working.*
if (ĭf) ◊ *conjunction*

igloo *noun* An Eskimo house or hut shaped like a dome. An igloo is often made from blocks of ice or hard snow.
ig·loo (ĭg′lo͞o) ◊ *noun, plural* **igloos**

***HISTORY* • igloo**

Igloo comes from the Eskimo word for house.

▲ **igloo**

igneous *adjective* Formed or made from molten rock that has hardened. Lava and granite are igneous rocks.
ig·ne·ous (ĭg′nē əs) ◊ *adjective*

ignite *verb* To set fire to or catch fire: *We ignited the bonfire.*
ig·nite (ĭg nīt′) ◊ *verb* **ignited, igniting**

ignition *noun* **1.** The act or process of igniting. **2.** An electrical system in a gasoline engine that controls the sparks that fire the gasoline vapors.
ig·ni·tion (ĭg nĭsh′ən) ◊ *noun, plural* **ignitions**

ignorance *noun* The condition of being ignorant; lack of knowledge.
ig·no·rance (ĭg′nər əns) ◊ *noun*

ignorant *adjective* **1.** Without education or knowledge: *They are ignorant but not stupid and will learn quickly.* **2.** Having the wrong information or not enough information.
ig·no·rant (ĭg′nər ənt) ◊ *adjective*

ignore *verb* To pay no attention to: *Whenever I try to talk to you, you ignore me.* —See Synonyms at **refuse.**
ig·nore (ĭg nôr′) ◊ *verb* **ignored, ignoring**

iguana *noun* A large tropical American lizard with a ridge of spines along the back.
i·gua·na (ĭ gwä′nə) ◊ *noun, plural* **iguanas**

▲ **iguana**

IL The abbreviation for *Illinois* used with a Zip Code.

ill *adjective* **1.** Not healthy; sick: *They have been ill with colds.* **2.** Not favorable; bad: *If you don't tell the truth, you'll do yourself an ill service.*
◊ *adverb* Unkindly, badly, or cruelly: *You*

I

shouldn't speak ill of someone you don't know. ◊ *noun* Something that causes harm or suffering: *Crime and poverty are social ills.*
ill (ĭl) ◊ *adjective, adverb* **worse, worst** ◊ *noun, plural* **ills**

Ill. An abbreviation for *Illinois.*

I'll Contraction of "I will" or "I shall."
I'll (īl) ◊ *contraction*
‖*These sound alike:* **I'll, aisle, isle**

illegal *adjective* Against the law or the rules: *It is illegal to drive an automobile without a license.*
il·le·gal (ĭ **lē′** gəl) ◊ *adjective*

illiterate *adjective* Not knowing how to read and write.
il·lit·er·ate (ĭ **lĭt′** ər ĭt) ◊ *adjective*

illness *noun* A sickness or disease: *Pneumonia is a serious illness.*
ill·ness (**ĭl′** nĭs) ◊ *noun, plural* **illnesses**

illuminate *verb* To light up; shine light on: *Moonlight illuminated the valley.*
il·lu·mi·nate (ĭ **lo͞o′** mə nāt′) ◊ *verb* **illuminated, illuminating**

illusion *noun* **1.** Something that fools one of the senses: *Extreme heat can create an illusion of water on a highway in the summer.* **2.** An idea or belief that is mixed up or mistaken: *Some people have the illusion that they will make good grades even if they don't study.*
il·lu·sion (ĭ **lo͞o′** zhən) ◊ *noun, plural* **illusions**

illustrate *verb* **1.** To explain or clarify by using examples, pictures, stories, or comparisons. **2.** To add photographs, drawings, diagrams, or maps that explain or decorate printed material, such as books, magazines, or newspapers.
il·lus·trate (**ĭl′** ə strāt′ *or* ĭ **lŭs′** trāt′) ◊ *verb* **illustrated, illustrating**

illustration *noun* **1.** Something, such as a picture, diagram, or map, that clarifies, explains, or decorates something such as a book or magazine. **2.** An example, explanation, or proof: *A rock falling to the ground is an illustration of gravity.*
il·lus·tra·tion (ĭl′ə **strā′** shən) ◊ *noun, plural* **illustrations**

illustrator *noun* An artist who illustrates books or magazines.
il·lus·tra·tor (**ĭl′** ə strā′tər) ◊ *noun, plural* **illustrators**

illustrious *adjective* Very much admired; famous: *Mark Twain was an illustrious writer.*
il·lus·tri·ous (ĭ **lŭs′** trē əs) ◊ *adjective*

ill will *noun* Unfriendly feeling; hatred.

I'm Contraction of "I am."
I'm (īm) ◊ *contraction*

image *noun* **1.** A picture of a real object formed by a lens, mirror, or other device: *When I looked through the telescope, the image was blurred.* **2.** A picture in the mind: *Images of food came into the hungry child's head.* **3.** A representation of a person or thing, such as a statue or a figure in a painting. **4.** A person or thing that looks just like another: *I am the image of my cousin.*
im·age (**ĭm′** ĭj) ◊ *noun, plural* **images**

imaginary *adjective* Existing only in the imagination; not real: *Ghosts and goblins are imaginary creatures.*
i·mag·i·nar·y (ĭ **măj′** ə nĕr′ē) ◊ *adjective*

imagination *noun* **1.** The ability of the mind to form pictures of things that are not present or real. **2.** Creative power; originality: *The author's imagination is evident in this exciting story.*
i·mag·i·na·tion (ĭ măj′ə **nā′** shən) ◊ *noun*

imaginative *adjective* **1.** Having a strong imagination: *An imaginative person can make up stories about strangers waiting at an airport.* **2.** Showing or having to do with imagination: *Fiction is imaginative writing.*
i·mag·i·na·tive (ĭ **măj′** ə nə tĭv) ◊ *adjective*

imagine *verb* **1.** To form a mental picture or idea of: *Can you imagine a blue horse with a yellow mane?* **2.** To make a guess; think: *How do you imagine the story will turn out?*
i·mag·ine (ĭ **măj′** ĭn) ◊ *verb* **imagined, imagining**

imitate *verb* **1.** To copy the actions, looks, or sounds of: *Little children imitate their parents.* **2.** To look like; resemble: *This wallpaper imitates wood paneling.*
im·i·tate (**ĭm′** ĭ tāt′) ◊ *verb* **imitated, imitating**

ă	pat	ĭ	pit	oi	**oi**l	th	ba**th**
ā	pay	ī	ride	o͝o	b**oo**k	*th*	ba**th**e
â	care	î	fierce	o͞o	b**oo**t	ə	ago, item
ä	father	ŏ	pot	ou	**ou**t		pencil
ĕ	pet	ō	go	ŭ	cut		atom
ē	be	ô	paw, for	û	fur		circus

imitation *noun* **1.** The act or process of imitating or copying: *I learned the song through imitation.* **2.** Something made to look or seem just like something else; copy: *This vase is an imitation of one in the museum.*
im·i·ta·tion (ĭm′ĭ **tā′**shən) ◊ *noun, plural* **imitations**

immaculate *adjective* Perfectly clean.
im·mac·u·late (ĭ **măk′**yə lĭt) ◊ *adjective*

immature *adjective* Not fully grown or developed. —See Synonyms at **young.**
im·ma·ture (ĭm′ə **tŏŏr′** *or* ĭm′ə **tyŏŏr′** *or* ĭm′ə **chŏŏr′**) ◊ *adjective*

immeasurable *adjective* Too great, far, or deep to be measured.
im·meas·ur·a·ble (ĭ **mĕzh′**ər ə bəl) ◊ *adjective*

immediate *adjective* **1.** Taking place at once or very soon; happening with no delay: *A broken bone needs immediate medical care.* **2.** Nearby; close: *Is there a gas station in the immediate area?* **3.** Coming next or very soon: *Let's plan to meet in the immediate future.* **4.** Next in line or relation: *George Washington's immediate successor was John Adams.*
im·me·di·ate (ĭ **mē′**dē ĭt) ◊ *adjective*

immediately *adverb* **1.** At once; right away: *If you hear an alarm, leave the building immediately.* **2.** Without anything else between; next: *June comes immediately after May.*
im·me·di·ate·ly (ĭ **mē′**dē ĭt lē) ◊ *adverb*

immense *adjective* Of great size, extent, or degree: *An elephant is truly an immense animal.* —See Synonyms at **gigantic.**
im·mense (ĭ **mĕns′**) ◊ *adjective*

immerse *verb* **1.** To cover completely with a liquid; submerge: *I immersed the dish in the soapy water.* **2.** To involve deeply; absorb: *I immersed myself in the new book.*
im·merse (ĭ **mûrs′**) ◊ *verb* **immersed, immersing**

immigrant *noun* A person who comes into a foreign country to live after he or she has left an earlier homeland.
im·mi·grant (**ĭm′**ĭ grənt) ◊ *noun, plural* **immigrants**

immigrate *verb* To come into a foreign country to live.
im·mi·grate (**ĭm′**ĭ grāt′) ◊ *verb* **immigrated, immigrating**

> ***HISTORY* • immigrate, emigrate**
>
> **Immigrate** comes from a Latin word meaning "to move in." **Emigrate** comes from a related Latin word meaning "to move out."

imminent *adjective* About to happen: *A thunderstorm looks imminent.*
im·mi·nent (**ĭm′**ə nənt) ◊ *adjective*

immoral *adjective* Going against what is fair, right, or good.
im·mor·al (ĭ **môr′**əl) ◊ *adjective*

immortal *adjective* Living or lasting forever: *This composer wrote a few immortal songs.*
im·mor·tal (ĭ **môr′**tl) ◊ *adjective*

immortality *noun* **1.** The condition of being immortal. **2.** Fame that will last forever.
im·mor·tal·i·ty (ĭm′ôr **tăl′**ĭ tē) ◊ *noun*

immovable *adjective* Not capable of moving or of being moved; fixed.
im·mov·a·ble (ĭ **mōō′**və bəl) ◊ *adjective*

immune *adjective* **1.** Protected from a disease: *Once you get chicken pox, you are usually immune to getting it again.* **2.** Not likely to have to undergo something; safe: *The island was immune to attack by land.*
im·mune (ĭ **myōōn′**) ◊ *adjective*

immunity *noun* **1.** The ability to resist disease. **2.** Freedom from having to undergo something unpleasant.
im·mu·ni·ty (ĭ **myōō′**nĭ tē) ◊ *noun, plural* **immunities**

immunize *verb* To give immunity to, especially by inoculating: *We were all immunized against polio.*
im·mu·nize (**ĭm′**yə nīz′) ◊ *verb* **immunized, immunizing**

imp *noun* A mischievous child.
imp (ĭmp) ◊ *noun, plural* **imps**

impact *noun* **1.** The action of one object striking against another; collision: *The impact of the ball broke the windowpane.* **2.** The effect of something on an observer, reader, or listener: *The movie had an emotional impact on me.*
im·pact (**ĭm′**păkt′) ◊ *noun, plural* **impacts**

impair *verb* To weaken in strength, quantity, or quality: *Fatigue impaired their judgment.*
im·pair (ĭm **pâr′**) ◊ *verb* **impaired, impairing**

I

impala *noun* A small African antelope that has curved, spreading horns.
im·pa·la (ĭm **păl**′ ə) ◊ *noun, plural* **impalas**

▲ **impala**

impartial *adjective* Not favoring either side: *An impartial judge can settle our argument.*
im·par·tial (ĭm **pär**′ shəl) ◊ *adjective*

impassable *adjective* Impossible to travel on or over: *Mud made the road impassable.*
im·pass·a·ble (ĭm **păs**′ ə bəl) ◊ *adjective*

impatient *adjective* Not able or willing to wait or put up with something calmly: *The impatient caller knocked louder and louder on the door.*
im·pa·tient (ĭm **pā**′ shənt) ◊ *adjective*

impeach *verb* To charge a public official with wrongdoing in office.
im·peach (ĭm **pēch**′) ◊ *verb* **impeached, impeaching**

impede *verb* To obstruct or slow down; block: *The stalled car impeded traffic.*
im·pede (ĭm **pēd**′) ◊ *verb* **impeded, impeding**

imperative *adjective* **1.** Expressing a command, order, or request: *An imperative sentence gives a command or makes a request and ends with a period.* **2.** Very important to do; urgent: *Speed was imperative, so I ran all the way with the message.*
im·per·a·tive (ĭm **pĕr**′ ə tĭv) ◊ *adjective*

ă	pat	ĭ	pit	oi	oil	th	bath
ā	pay	ī	ride	ŏŏ	book	*th*	bathe
â	care	î	fierce	ōō	boot	ə	ago, item
ä	father	ŏ	pot	ou	out		pencil
ĕ	pet	ō	go	ŭ	cut		atom
ē	be	ô	paw, for	û	fur		circus

imperfect *adjective* Having faults or mistakes; not perfect.
im·per·fect (ĭm **pûr**′ fĭkt) ◊ *adjective*

imperial *adjective* Relating to an empire, emperor, or empress: *India was an imperial possession of Great Britain until 1947.*
im·pe·ri·al (ĭm **pîr**′ ē əl) ◊ *adjective*

impersonate *verb* To act the character or part of; pretend to be: *It's against the law to impersonate a doctor.*
im·per·son·ate (ĭm **pûr**′ sə nāt′) ◊ *verb* **impersonated, impersonating**

impertinence *noun* **1.** Discourteous, rude behavior. **2.** An impertinent act or remark.
im·per·ti·nence (ĭm **pûr**′ tn əns) ◊ *noun, plural* **impertinences**

impertinent *adjective* Showing disrespect or bad manners; discourteous: *It is impertinent to talk back to your grandparents.*
im·per·ti·nent (ĭm **pûr**′ tn ənt) ◊ *adjective*

SYNONYMS

impertinent, fresh, impudent, insolent

You disgraced yourself with that *impertinent* behavior. Don't be so *fresh* when you answer my questions. It's very *impudent* of them to insult everybody. Bullies often act in an *insolent* way to others.

impetuous *adjective* Acting suddenly.
im·pet·u·ous (ĭm **pĕch**′ ōō əs) ◊ *adjective*

implant *verb* **1.** To set or fix firmly; establish securely: *Parents try to implant their own basic values in their children.* **2.** To put into the body by surgery: *The team of doctors implanted an artificial heart in the patient's chest.*
im·plant (ĭm **plănt**′) ◊ *verb* **implanted, implanting**

implement *noun* A specially made object used in doing a task or a kind of work; tool: *Plows, pitchforks, and rakes are farm implements.*
im·ple·ment (**ĭm**′ plə mənt) ◊ *noun, plural* **implements**

implore *verb* To ask earnestly or anxiously; beg: *We implore you to help us.*
im·plore (ĭm **plôr′**) ◊ *verb* **implored, imploring**

imply *verb* To say or mean something without expressing it directly; suggest: *My note said "See you soon," which implies that I plan to visit you.*
im·ply (ĭm **plī′**) ◊ *verb* **implied, implying**

impolite *adjective* Not polite; discourteous: *It is impolite to interrupt people.*
im·po·lite (ĭm′pə **līt′**) ◊ *adjective* **impoliter, impolitest**

import *verb* To bring in from another country for trade, sale, or use: *The United States imports oil and exports grain.*
◊ *noun* Something that is imported from another country.
im·port ◊ *verb* (ĭm **pôrt′**) **imported, importing** ◊ *noun* (**ĭm′** pôrt′), *plural* **imports**

importance *noun* The condition or quality of being important; significance.
im·por·tance (ĭm **pôr′** tns) ◊ *noun*

important *adjective* **1.** Strongly affecting the course of events or the nature of things; significant: *This is an important message. Eating, sleeping, and exercising are all important to your health.* **2.** Having rank, fame, or authority: *Some important people approved of the plan.*
im·por·tant (ĭm **pôr′** tnt) ◊ *adjective*

impose *verb* **1.** To place a burden on someone; inflict: *The heavy work imposed a great strain on us.* **2.** To force to accept: *The judge imposed a fine on the factory owners and the striking workers.* **3.** To take advantage of; cause inconvenience: *I don't want to impose on you by staying too long.*
im·pose (ĭm **pōz′**) ◊ *verb* **imposed, imposing**

imposing *adjective* Tending to cause awe or admiration; impressive: *The White House is an imposing mansion.*
im·pos·ing (ĭm **pō′** zĭng) ◊ *adjective*

impossible *adjective* **1.** Not capable of happening or existing: *Human travel to another solar system is still impossible.* **2.** Not likely to happen or be done: *It will be impossible to get there without driving.* **3.** Difficult to deal with or tolerate.
im·pos·si·ble (ĭm **pŏs′** ə bəl) ◊ *adjective*

impostor *noun* A person who tries to fool people by pretending to be someone else.
im·pos·tor (ĭm **pŏs′** tər) ◊ *noun, plural* **imposters**

> **SYNONYMS**
>
> ***impostor, fraud, phony***
>
> That man was not the king but only an *impostor.* We bought that jewelry from a *fraud.* Even though she acts friendly, we know she's a *phony.*

impoverish *verb* **1.** To make poor: *Two bad harvests impoverished the farmer.* **2.** To take away the natural strength or richness of: *Floods impoverished the soil.*
im·pov·er·ish (ĭm **pŏv′** ər ĭsh) ◊ *verb* **impoverished, impoverishing**

impracticable *adjective* Not capable of being done, carried out, or put into practice.
im·prac·ti·ca·ble (ĭm **prăk′** tĭ kə bəl) ◊ *adjective*

impractical *adjective* Not practical: *It is impractical to build a house on sand.*
im·prac·ti·cal (ĭm **prăk′** tĭ kəl) ◊ *adjective*

impress *verb* **1.** To have a strong, often favorable effect on the mind or feelings of: *The size of the tall building impressed me.* —See Synonyms at **affect. 2.** To put firmly in someone's mind: *The coach impressed us with the importance of fair play.*
im·press (ĭm **prĕs′**) ◊ *verb* **impressed, impressing**

impression *noun* **1.** An effect, image, or feeling that stays in the mind: *My new friend made a good impression on my parents.* **2.** A vague notion, memory, or feeling: *I have the impression that we've met before.* **3.** A mark made on a surface by pressure: *There was an impression in the cushion where I had sat.*
im·pres·sion (ĭm **prĕsh′** ən) ◊ *noun, plural* **impressions**

impressive *adjective* Making a strong, lasting impression: *A cathedral is an impressive building.*
im·pres·sive (ĭm **prĕs′** ĭv) ◊ *adjective*

imprint *noun* **1.** A mark or pattern made by something pressed on a surface: *I saw the imprints of feet in the sand.* **2.** A strong influence: *Settlers from many countries made a strong imprint on American life.*

I

◊ *verb* **1.** To make a mark or pattern on a surface by pressing or stamping: *I imprinted my name on the card.* **2.** To fix firmly in the mind or memory.
im·print ◊ *noun* (**ĭm′** prĭnt′), *plural* **imprints** ◊ *verb* (ĭm **prĭnt′**) **imprinted, imprinting**

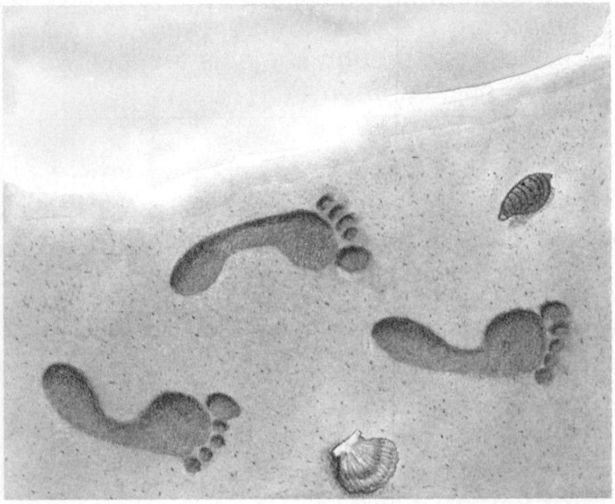

▲ **imprint**

imprison *verb* To put in prison.
im·pris·on (ĭm **prĭz′** ən) ◊ *verb* **imprisoned, imprisoning**

improper *adjective* **1.** Not proper; incorrect. **2.** Showing or having bad manners.
im·prop·er (ĭm **prŏp′** ər) ◊ *adjective*

improper fraction *noun* A fraction in which the numerator is greater than or equal to the denominator. For example, $\frac{4}{3}$ and $\frac{3}{3}$ are improper fractions.
improper fraction ◊ *noun, plural* **improper fractions**

improve *verb* To make or become better: *I improved my tennis serve by practicing.*
im·prove (ĭm **pro͞ov′**) ◊ *verb* **improved, improving**

improvement *noun* **1.** A change or addition that makes something better: *Painting the room yellow is a great improvement.* **2.** The act or process of improving.
im·prove·ment (ĭm **pro͞ov′** mənt) ◊ *noun, plural* **improvements**

improvise *verb* **1.** To make up and perform without planning or rehearsing beforehand: *The governor had not prepared a speech, so she improvised one.* **2.** To make from whatever materials happen to be around: *He improvised a meal for his unexpected guests.*
im·pro·vise (**ĭm′** prə vīz′) ◊ *verb* **improvised, improvising**

impudent *adjective* Rude and disrespectful: *It is impudent to talk back to your parents.* —See Synonyms at **impertinent.**
im·pu·dent (**ĭm′** pyə dənt) ◊ *adjective*

impulse *noun* **1.** A short, sudden burst or flow, as of energy: *An electrical impulse makes the light blink.* **2.** A sudden wish or urge to do something; whim: *I acted on impulse when I bought the puppy.*
im·pulse (**ĭm′** pŭls′) ◊ *noun, plural* **impulses**

impulsive *adjective* Acting on impulse rather than by thinking things through or planning carefully.
im·pul·sive (ĭm **pŭl′** sĭv) ◊ *adjective*

impure *adjective* Not pure or clean; dirty: *The water in that polluted river is impure, so don't drink it.*
im·pure (ĭm **pyo͝or′**) ◊ *adjective*

impurity *noun* **1.** The state or quality of being impure. **2.** A substance that, when present, makes another substance impure: *The impurities in the water made the spring unfit for drinking.*
im·pu·ri·ty (ĭm **pyo͝or′** ĭ tē) ◊ *noun, plural* **impurities**

in *preposition* **1.** Surrounded by; inside: *Put your things in this drawer.* **2.** Into a certain space: *Get in the car, please.* **3.** At the time of; during: *Call me in the morning.* **4.** By means of; with the use of: *We paid in cash.* **5.** Used to show condition, manner, or purpose: *I am in trouble. Are you in a hurry? They went in search of their friends.*
◊ *adverb* **1.** To or toward the inside: *Come in and sit down.* **2.** Within a certain place, as an office: *Is the doctor in?* **3.** To or toward a certain place: *They drove in from the country.*
in (ĭn) ◊ *preposition* ◊ *adverb*
‖*These sound alike:* **in, inn**

ă	pat	ĭ	pit	oi	**oi**l	th	ba**th**
ā	pay	ī	ride	o͝o	b**oo**k	*th*	ba**the**
â	care	î	fierce	o͞o	b**oo**t	ə	ago, item
ä	father	ŏ	pot	ou	**ou**t		pencil
ĕ	pet	ō	go	ŭ	cut		atom
ē	be	ô	paw, for	û	fur		circus

IN The abbreviation for *Indiana* used with a Zip Code.

in. The abbreviation for *inch* or *inches.*

inability *noun* The condition or fact of being unable to do something; lack of ability.
in·a·bil·i·ty (ĭn′ə **bĭl′**ĭ tē) ◊ *noun, plural* **inabilities**

inaccurate *adjective* Not correct or exact; not accurate: *It is inaccurate to say that a whale is a fish.*
in·ac·cu·rate (ĭn **ăk′**yər ĭt) ◊ *adjective*

inactive *adjective* Not active or not tending to be active: *Many animals are inactive at night.*
in·ac·tive (ĭn **ăk′**tĭv) ◊ *adjective*

inadvisable *adjective* Not sensible or recommended; unwise.
in·ad·vis·a·ble (ĭn′əd **vī′**zə bəl) ◊ *adjective*

inalienable *adjective* Not capable of being given up or taken away: *Freedom of speech is one of our inalienable rights.*
in·al·ien·a·ble (ĭn **āl′**yə nə bəl) ◊ *adjective*

inanimate *adjective* Not living: *A rock is an inanimate object.*
in·an·i·mate (ĭn **ăn′**ə mĭt) ◊ *adjective*

inappropriate *adjective* Not suitable or appropriate.
in·ap·pro·pri·ate (ĭn′ə **prō′**prē ĭt) ◊ *adjective*

inattention *noun* Lack of attention: *Inattention to the instructions can cause you to make errors on the test.*
in·at·ten·tion (ĭn′ə **tĕn′**shən) ◊ *noun*

inattentive *adjective* Not paying attention.
in·at·ten·tive (ĭn′ə **tĕn′**tĭv) ◊ *adjective*

inaudible *adjective* Too soft or quiet to be heard: *A cat's footsteps are inaudible.*
in·au·di·ble (ĭn **ô′**də bəl) ◊ *adjective*

inaugurate *verb* **1.** To place in office with a ceremony: *Every four years a President of the United States is inaugurated.* **2.** To open or begin using with a ceremony: *The city inaugurated a new subway system this year.*
in·au·gu·rate (ĭ **nô′**gyə rāt′) ◊ *verb* **inaugurated, inaugurating**

***HISTORY* • inaugurate**

Inaugurate goes back to a Latin word meaning "omen." To **inaugurate** was to begin with good omens.

inauguration *noun* The formal ceremony of inaugurating.
in·au·gu·ra·tion (ĭ nô′gyə **rā′**shən) ◊ *noun, plural* **inaugurations**

▲ **inauguration**

inborn *adjective* Present in a person or animal from birth: *Most birds have an inborn instinct to build nests at the right time.*
in·born (**ĭn′**bôrn′) ◊ *adjective*

Inc. The abbreviation for *Incorporated.*

incapable *adjective* Lacking the ability to do something.
in·ca·pa·ble (ĭn **kā′**pə bəl) ◊ *adjective*

incense *noun* A substance that gives off a pleasant smell when it is burned.
in·cense (**ĭn′**sĕns′) ◊ *noun, plural* **incenses**

incentive *noun* Something that urges a person to do something or make a special effort; stimulus: *A prize for the winner is the incentive for those who will run in the race.*
in·cen·tive (ĭn **sĕn′**tĭv) ◊ *noun, plural* **incentives**

incessant *adjective* Never stopping; going on and on.
in·ces·sant (ĭn **sĕs′**ənt) ◊ *adjective*

inch *noun* A unit of length equal to $1/12$ of a foot.
◊ *verb* To move very slowly or a little bit at a time: *We inched toward the door and hoped no one would notice us.*
inch (ĭnch) ◊ *noun, plural* **inches** ◊ *verb* **inched, inching**

I

inchworm *noun* A caterpillar that moves by first looping and then stretching out its body.
inch·worm (**inch'**-wûrm') ◊ *noun, plural* **inchworms**

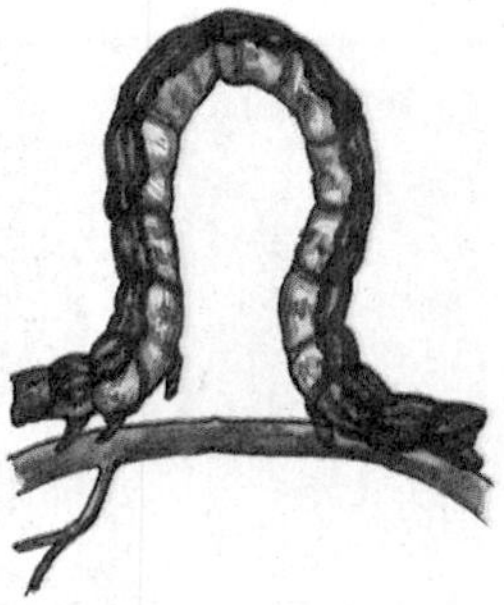
▲ **inchworm**

incident *noun* **1.** A thing that happens, especially something brief and unimportant: *A funny incident happened on the playground today.* **2.** An event that causes some trouble: *The newspaper reported the fire and similar incidents.*
in·ci·dent (**ĭn'** sĭ dənt) ◊ *noun, plural* **incidents**

incidentally *adverb* By the way: *Incidentally, what time is it?*
in·ci·den·tal·ly (ĭn'sĭ **dĕn'** tl ē) ◊ *adverb*

incinerator *noun* A furnace for burning garbage and other waste materials.
in·cin·er·a·tor (ĭn **sĭn'** ə rā'tər) ◊ *noun, plural* **incinerators**

incite *verb* To move to action; urge on: *The speaker incited us to acts of patriotism.*
in·cite (ĭn **sīt'**) ◊ *verb* **incited, inciting**

inclination *noun* **1.** The act of leaning or slanting. **2.** A tendency to act in a certain way: *I have an inclination to keep quietly to myself.* **3.** A natural or usual preference.
in·cli·na·tion (ĭn'klə **nā'** shən) ◊ *noun, plural* **inclinations**

incline *verb* To lean, slant, or slope: *The road inclines steeply.*
◊ *noun* A surface that inclines; slope.
in·cline ◊ *verb* (ĭn **klīn'**) **inclined, inclining** ◊ *noun* (**ĭn'** klīn'), *plural* **inclines**

inclined *adjective* **1.** Having a slope; slanting. **2.** Having a preference or tendency.
in·clined (ĭn **klīnd'**) ◊ *adjective*

ă	pat	ĭ	pit	oi	**oil**	th	ba**th**
ā	pay	ī	ride	o͝o	book	*th*	ba**th**e
â	care	î	fierce	o͞o	boot	ə	ago, item
ä	father	ŏ	pot	ou	**out**		pencil
ĕ	pet	ō	go	ŭ	cut		atom
ē	be	ô	paw, for	û	fur		circus

include *verb* **1.** To be made up of, at least in part: *The class includes several foreign students.* **2.** To put into a group, set, or total: *Include an apple in my lunch box, please.*
in·clude (ĭn **klo͞od'**) ◊ *verb* **included, including**

inclusion *noun* **1.** The act of including or the condition of being included. **2.** Something that is included.
in·clu·sion (ĭn **klo͞o'** zhən) ◊ *noun, plural* **inclusions**

income *noun* The amount of money that a person or business receives during a certain period of time.
in·come (**ĭn'** kŭm') ◊ *noun, plural* **incomes**

income tax *noun* A tax on a person's income.
income tax ◊ *noun, plural* **income taxes**

incompetent *adjective* Not capable of doing a good job.
in·com·pe·tent (ĭn **kŏm'** pĭ tənt) ◊ *adjective*

incomplete *adjective* Not complete: *This incomplete chess set is missing a pawn.*
in·com·plete (ĭn'kəm **plēt'**) ◊ *adjective*

inconsiderate *adjective* Not considerate of others; thoughtless: *Loud laughter in the library is inconsiderate.*
in·con·sid·er·ate (ĭn'kən **sĭd'** ər ĭt) ◊ *adjective*

inconspicuous *adjective* Not easily seen or noticed; not obvious.
in·con·spic·u·ous (ĭn'kən **spĭk'** yo͞o əs) ◊ *adjective*

inconvenience *noun* **1.** Lack of comfort; difficulty. **2.** Something that causes difficulty or discomfort: *Having to go downstairs to answer the phone is an inconvenience.*
◊ *verb* To cause inconvenience for; trouble: *Don't inconvenience yourself on my account.*
in·con·ven·ience (ĭn'kən **vēn'** yəns) ◊ *noun, plural* **inconveniences** ◊ *verb* **inconvenienced, inconveniencing**

inconvenient *adjective* Causing bother or difficulty; troublesome.
in·con·ven·ient (ĭn'kən **vēn'** yənt) ◊ *adjective*

incorporate *verb* **1.** To put or join into a single larger thing; include: *We peeled the stamps from the envelope and incorporated them into our collections.* **2.** To form into a legal corporation: *The two partners decided to incorporate their business.*
in·cor·po·rate (ĭn **kôr'** pə rāt') ◊ *verb* **incorporated, incorporating**

incorrect *adjective* Not correct or proper; wrong. —See Synonyms at **false.**
in·cor·rect (ĭn′kə **rĕkt′**) ◊ *adjective*

increase *verb* To make or become greater or larger: *I increased my spending money by taking a job after school.*
◊ *noun* **1.** The act of increasing; growth: *When you get to high school, you will find an increase in homework.* **2.** The amount or rate by which something is increased: *There has been an increase in the price of the tickets.*
in·crease ◊ *verb* (ĭn **krēs′**) **increased, increasing** ◊ *noun* (**ĭn′**krēs′), *plural* **increases**

incredible *adjective* **1.** Too unlikely to be believed: *Your silly excuse is incredible.* **2.** Astonishing; amazing: *Some birds fly incredible distances when they migrate.*
in·cred·i·ble (ĭn **krĕd′**ə bəl) ◊ *adjective*

incubator *noun* A device in which an unusually small newborn baby or some other delicate living thing is kept warm and safe while it develops.
in·cu·ba·tor (**ĭng′**kyə bā′tər) ◊ *noun, plural* **incubators**

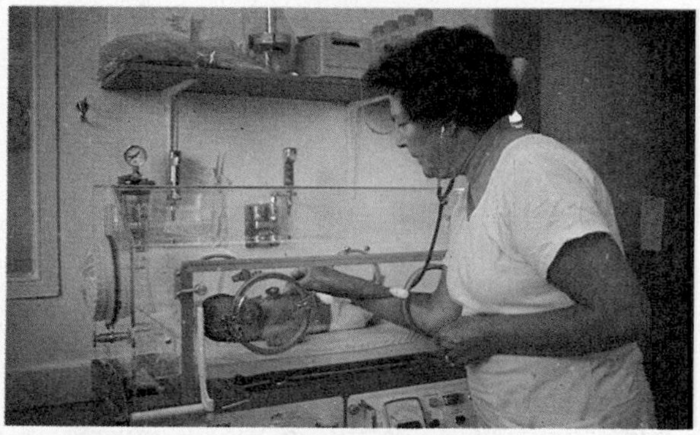

▲ **incubator**

incur *verb* To bring upon oneself: *The dog incurred my anger by pulling down the curtains.*
in·cur (ĭn **kûr′**) ◊ *verb* **incurred, incurring**

incurable *adjective* Not capable of being cured: *Some diseases are still incurable.*
in·cur·a·ble (ĭn **kyo͝or′**ə bəl) ◊ *adjective*

Ind. An abbreviation for *Indiana.*

indebted *adjective* Owing something to another: *I am indebted to you for your help.*
in·debt·ed (ĭn **dĕt′**ĭd) ◊ *adjective*

indecision *noun* The condition of not being able to make up one's mind.
in·de·ci·sion (ĭn′dĭ **sĭzh′**ən) ◊ *noun*

indeed *adverb* In fact; really: *My parents were indeed pleased with my grades.*
in·deed (ĭn **dēd′**) ◊ *adverb*

indefinite *adjective* **1.** Not fixed or limited: *We're staying for an indefinite period of time.* **2.** Not clear; vague: *We saw the indefinite outline of a tree through the mist.* **3.** Not decided; uncertain: *Our plans are indefinite.*
in·def·i·nite (ĭn **dĕf′**ə nĭt) ◊ *adjective*

indent *verb* To begin the first line of a paragraph farther in from the margin than the other lines.
in·dent (ĭn **dĕnt′**) ◊ *verb* **indented, indenting**

independence *noun* The quality or condition of being independent.
in·de·pend·ence (ĭn′dĭ **pĕn′**dəns) ◊ *noun*

Independence Day *noun* July 4, a national holiday in honor of the adoption of the Declaration of Independence in 1776.

independent *adjective* **1.** Not governed by a foreign country; ruling itself: *Many colonies in Africa became independent nations in the 1950's.* **2.** Not controlled by other people. **3.** Earning one's own living: *My older sisters and brothers have moved away from home and are now independent.*
in·de·pend·ent (ĭn′dĭ **pĕn′**dənt) ◊ *adjective*

index *noun* **1.** An alphabetized list of things or persons, used to keep track of them and to find out where they are located: *We keep a card index of all the books in our library.* **2.** An alphabetized list of the names and subjects in a printed work, giving the page or pages where each can be found: *Consult the index to find information on domestic cats.*
◊ *verb* **1.** To make or write an index for: *The editor indexed the book.* **2.** To put or arrange in an index: *Every subject in the textbook is indexed.*
in·dex (**ĭn′**dĕks′) ◊ *noun, plural* **indexes** ◊ *verb* **indexed, indexing**

index finger *noun* The finger next to the thumb.
index finger ◊ *noun, plural* **index fingers**

Indian *noun* **1.** A person who was born in or lives in India. **2.** A member of one of the peoples who lived in North, Central, or South America long before explorers and colonists arrived.

I

◊ *adjective* **1.** Of or relating to India or its people. **2.** Of or relating to any of the peoples who lived in North, Central, or South America long before European explorers and colonists arrived.
In·di·an (**ĭn′**dē ən) ◊ *noun, plural* **Indians**
◊ *adjective*

Indian paintbrush *noun* A plant with clusters of bright-red, petallike leaves encircling small, greenish flowers.
Indian paintbrush
◊ *noun, plural* **Indian paintbrushes**

▲ **Indian paintbrush**

indicate *verb* **1.** To show or point out: *A compass indicates direction.* **2.** To serve as a sign of: *Dark clouds indicated rain.*
in·di·cate (**ĭn′**dĭ kāt′)
◊ *verb* **indicated, indicating**

indication *noun* Something that indicates; symbol. —See Synonyms at **sign**.
in·di·ca·tion (ĭn′dĭ **kā′**shən) ◊ *noun, plural* **indications**

indifferent *adjective* Having or showing no interest; not caring: *I was concentrating so hard that I was indifferent to the noise and excitement outside.*
in·dif·fer·ent (ĭn **dĭf′**ər ənt) ◊ *adjective*

indigestible *adjective* Hard to digest.
in·di·gest·i·ble (ĭn′dĭ **jĕs′**tə bəl) ◊ *adjective*

indigestion *noun* A stomach ache that is caused by improper digestion of food.
in·di·ges·tion (ĭn′dĭ **jĕs′**chən) ◊ *noun*

indignant *adjective* Feeling or showing indignation; angry.
in·dig·nant (ĭn **dĭg′**nənt) ◊ *adjective*

indignation *noun* Anger caused by something unjust, unworthy, or mean.
in·dig·na·tion (ĭn′dĭg **nā′**shən) ◊ *noun*

ă	pat	ĭ	pit	oi	**oil**	th	bath
ā	pay	ī	ride	ŏŏ	book	*th*	bathe
â	care	î	fierce	ōō	boot	ə	ago, item
ä	father	ŏ	pot	ou	**out**		pencil
ĕ	pet	ō	go	ŭ	cut		atom
ē	be	ô	paw, for	û	fur		circus

indigo *noun* **1.** A plant that yields a blue dye. **2.** A dark-blue dye that is obtained from the indigo plant or made artificially.
in·di·go (**ĭn′**dĭ gō′)
◊ *noun, plural* **indigos** *or* **indigoes**

▲ **indigo**

indirect *adjective* **1.** Not going in a direct way; roundabout: *We took an indirect route to the town.* **2.** Not straightforward or to the point: *Pouting is an indirect way of showing displeasure.* **3.** Not directly connected; secondary: *An indirect benefit of a night light is a feeling of safety.*
in·di·rect (ĭn′də **rĕkt′**) ◊ *adjective*

individual *adjective* **1.** Of, relating to, or meant for a single or separate person or thing. **2.** Having a special quality; distinctive: *You have a very individual style of dressing.*
◊ *noun* A single person, plant, or animal considered separately from a group.
in·di·vid·u·al (ĭn′də **vĭj′**ōō əl) ◊ *adjective*
◊ *noun, plural* **individuals**

individuality *noun* The qualities that make a person or thing different from others.
in·di·vid·u·al·i·ty (ĭn′də vĭj′ōō **ăl′**ĭ tē) ◊ *noun, plural* **individualities**

individually *adverb* As individuals; separately: *The principal knew all the students individually.*
in·di·vid·u·al·ly (ĭn′də **vĭj′**ōō ə lē) ◊ *adverb*

indivisible *adjective* Not capable of being divided or separated.
in·di·vis·i·ble (ĭn′də **vĭz′**ə bəl) ◊ *adjective*

indoor *adjective* **1.** Of or relating to the inside of a building. **2.** Located, done, or used indoors.
in·door (**ĭn′**dôr′) ◊ *adjective*

indoors *adverb* In or into a building.
in·doors (ĭn **dôrz′**) ◊ *adverb*

induct *verb* **1.** To place formally in office. **2.** To call into military service; draft.
in·duct (ĭn **dŭkt′**) ◊ *verb* **inducted, inducting**

indulge *verb* **1.** To yield to the desires of one-

self or another. —See Synonyms at **pamper.** **2.** To allow oneself some special pleasure: *I indulged in a trip to the movies.*
in·dulge (ĭn **dŭlj'**) ◊ *verb* **indulged, indulging**

industrial *adjective* **1.** Of or having to do with industry: *Steel and gasoline are industrial products.* **2.** Having much industry: *The United States is an industrial nation.*
in·dus·tri·al (ĭn **dŭs'**trē əl) ◊ *adjective*

industrialize *verb* To make or become industrial; develop industries in.
in·dus·tri·al·ize (ĭn **dŭs'**trē ə līz') ◊ *verb* **industrialized, industrializing**

industrious *adjective* Working hard as a steady habit.
in·dus·tri·ous (ĭn **dŭs'**trē əs) ◊ *adjective*

industry *noun* **1.** A making or producing of goods on a large scale by businesses and factories. **2.** A large-scale enterprise that provides a product or service: *Hollywood is the capital of the motion-picture industry.* —See Synonyms at **business.** **3.** Hard work; effort.
in·dus·try (**ĭn'**də strē) ◊ *noun, plural* **industries**

inedible *adjective* Not suitable or fit to eat.
in·ed·i·ble (ĭn **ĕd'**ə bəl) ◊ *adjective*

inequality *noun* **1.** The quality or condition of being unequal or uneven. **2.** A condition in which some people are favored over others.
in·e·qual·i·ty (ĭn'ĭ **kwŏl'**ĭ tē) ◊ *noun, plural* **inequalities**

inert *adjective* Unable to move or act: *Rocks are inert objects.*
in·ert (ĭ **nûrt'**) ◊ *adjective*

inevitable *adjective* Certain to happen.
in·ev·i·ta·ble (ĭn **ĕv'**ĭ tə bəl) ◊ *adjective*

inexcusable *adjective* Impossible to excuse.
in·ex·cus·a·ble (ĭn'ĭk **skyōō'**zə bəl) ◊ *adjective*

inexpensive *adjective* Not expensive.
in·ex·pen·sive (ĭn'ĭk **spĕn'**sĭv) ◊ *adjective*

inexperienced *adjective* Lacking experience or practice.
in·ex·pe·ri·enced (ĭn'ĭk **spîr'**ē ənst) ◊ *adjective*

infallible *adjective* **1.** Not capable of making a mistake: *No person is infallible.* **2.** Not capable of failing: *I know an infallible cure for hiccups.*
in·fal·li·ble (ĭn **făl'**ə bəl) ◊ *adjective*

infancy *noun* **1.** The condition or time of being an infant. **2.** The earliest years or stage of something.
in·fan·cy (**ĭn'**fən sē) ◊ *noun, plural* **infancies**

infant *noun* A child from the earliest period of life up to about two years of age; baby.
in·fant (**ĭn'**fənt) ◊ *noun, plural* **infants**

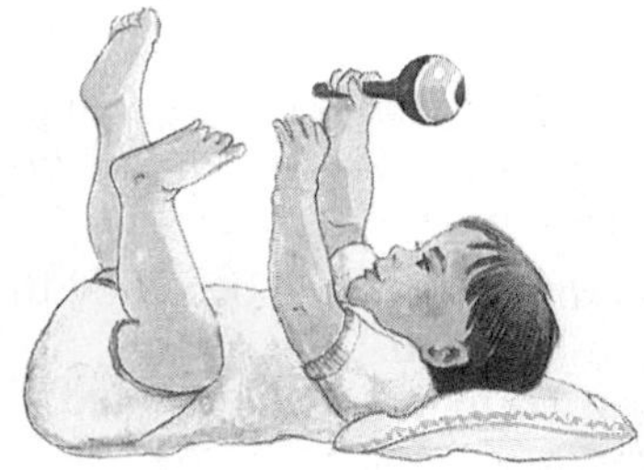

▲ **infant**

infantry *noun* The branch of an army made up of units trained to fight on foot.
in·fan·try (**ĭn'**fən trē) ◊ *noun, plural* **infantries**

infect *verb* **1.** To cause to come in contact with germs or bacteria that cause disease. **2.** To transmit a disease or virus to.
in·fect (ĭn **fĕkt'**) ◊ *verb* **infected, infecting**

infection *noun* **1.** The act or process of infecting. **2.** A disease that can be passed from one person or animal to another.
in·fec·tion (ĭn **fĕk'**shən) ◊ *noun, plural* **infections**

infectious *adjective* Caused or spread by germs: *Influenza is an infectious disease.*
in·fec·tious (ĭn **fĕk'**shəs) ◊ *adjective*

infer *verb* To conclude from evidence: *We inferred from the black clouds that a storm was coming up.*
in·fer (ĭn **fûr'**) ◊ *verb* **inferred, inferring**

inferior *adjective* **1.** Low or lower in order, degree, or rank: *I had to take an inferior position on the second team.* **2.** Low or lower, as in quality or ability: *Your grades are inferior this semester.*
◊ *noun* A person or thing that is inferior.
in·fe·ri·or (ĭn **fîr'**ē ər) ◊ *adjective* ◊ *noun, plural* **inferiors**

I

infest *verb* To live in or overrun in large numbers so as to be harmful or unpleasant: *Gnats and mosquitoes infested the field by the river.*
in·fest (ĭn **fĕst′**) ◊ *verb* **infested, infesting**

infield *noun* The playing area of a baseball field inside the bases.
in·field (**ĭn′**fēld′) ◊ *noun, plural* **infields**

infielder *noun* A baseball player whose position is in the infield.
in·field·er (**ĭn′**fēl′dər) ◊ *noun, plural* **infielders**

infinite *adjective* Having or seeming to have no limits; endless: *The universe is infinite.*
in·fi·nite (**ĭn′**fə nĭt) ◊ *adjective*

inflame *verb* To make or become affected by bodily inflammation.
in·flame (ĭn **flām′**) ◊ *verb* **inflamed, inflaming**

inflammable *adjective* Tending to catch fire easily; flammable.
in·flam·ma·ble (ĭn **flăm′**ə bəl) ◊ *adjective*

inflammation *noun* Redness, heat, swelling, and pain that is caused by an injury, infection, or irritation.
in·flam·ma·tion (ĭn′flə **mā′**shən) ◊ *noun, plural* **inflammations**

inflatable *adjective* Made ready for use by inflating: *I bought an inflatable raft.*
in·flat·a·ble (ĭn **flā′**tə bəl) ◊ *adjective*

inflate *verb* To fill with gas and expand: *Did you inflate the tires on the bicycle?*
in·flate (ĭn **flāt′**) ◊ *verb* **inflated, inflating**

inflation *noun* **1.** The act or process of filling with gas and expanding. **2.** A continuing rise in the prices of goods and services.
in·fla·tion (ĭn **flā′**shən) ◊ *noun, plural* **inflations**

inflect *verb* To add an inflection to a word.
in·flect (ĭn **flĕkt′**) ◊ *verb* **inflected, inflecting**

inflected form *noun* A form of a word with an inflection.
inflected form ◊ *noun, plural* **inflected forms**

ă	pat	ĭ	pit	oi	**oil**	th	bath
ā	pay	ī	ride	o͝o	book	*th*	bathe
â	care	î	fierce	o͞o	boot	ə	ago, item
ä	father	ŏ	pot	ou	**out**		pencil
ĕ	pet	ō	go	ŭ	cut		atom
ē	be	ô	paw, for	û	fur		circus

inflection *noun* An ending added to a word to show whether a noun is singular or plural, whether a verb shows present or past action, or whether an adjective is a comparative or superlative. For example, the ending *-s* is added to the noun *book* to make it plural.
in·flec·tion (ĭn **flĕk′**shən) ◊ *noun, plural* **inflections**

inflexible *adjective* Not easily bent; stiff and rigid.
in·flex·i·ble (ĭn **flĕk′**sə bəl) ◊ *adjective*

inflict *verb* **1.** To give by or as if by an attack: *Extreme cold can inflict frostbite.* **2.** To cause to be suffered or endured: *Our parents inflict punishment only for serious wrongdoing.*
in·flict (ĭn **flĭkt′**) ◊ *verb* **inflicted, inflicting**

influence *noun* **1.** The power to cause changes or have an effect without using direct force: *Use your influence to get them to study more.* **2.** Someone or something that has the power to produce change without use of direct force.
◊ *verb* To have an influence on. —See Synonyms at **affect.**
in·flu·ence (**ĭn′**flo͞o əns) ◊ *noun, plural* **influences** ◊ *verb* **influenced, influencing**

influential *adjective* Having an influence: *Television news is very influential.*
in·flu·en·tial (ĭn′flo͞o **ĕn′**shəl) ◊ *adjective*

influenza *noun* A disease caused by viruses that is easily passed from one person to another. It is usually like a bad cold, with fever and often pain in the muscles.
in·flu·en·za (ĭn′flo͞o **ĕn′**zə) ◊ *noun*

inform *verb* **1.** To tell about something; notify: *Please inform me as to the time of your arrival.* **2.** To give information that accuses someone of a wrongful act.
in·form (ĭn **fôrm′**) ◊ *verb* **informed, informing**

informal *adjective* **1.** Made or done without following set rules or custom: *We have an informal agreement to ride to school together.* **2.** Casual; relaxed: *The atmosphere in the classroom was informal.*
in·for·mal (ĭn **fôr′**məl) ◊ *adjective*

information *noun* **1.** Facts and understanding of a subject gotten by studying or being taught. **2.** Knowledge about a certain event; news.
in·for·ma·tion (ĭn′fər **mā′**shən) ◊ *noun*

infrequent *adjective* Not seen or happening often: *The bus made infrequent stops along the route.*
in·fre·quent (ĭn **frē′**kwənt) ◊ *adjective*

infuriate *verb* To make very angry; enrage.
in·fu·ri·ate (ĭn **fyo͝or′**ē āt′) ◊ *verb* **infuriated, infuriating**

-ing The suffix *-ing* is added to verbs to show that something is happening in the present. When a dog digs for a bone and is in the middle of this action, we say that the dog is *digging* for the bone. The suffix *-ing* also forms nouns and has three different meanings. It can mean "action" or "process." *Reading* means "the action of reading" in the sentence "Reading is fun." The suffix *-ing* also means "the result of an action or process." A *drawing* is a picture that results from the action of drawing. The suffix *-ing* also means "something connected with or used for a certain thing." *Clothing* is used to clothe or dress someone.

VOCABULARY BUILDER • -ing

In this dictionary you will find **-ing** forms given at all verb entries. Words with the suffix **-ing** can be used as adjectives. For example, in baseball when a run ties the score, it is the *tying* run. Sometimes these adjectives have their own entries because they have come to have special meanings. For example, *interesting* means "causing interest or attention" and has its own entry.

ingenious *adjective* Very smart, clever, and creative: *That is an ingenious solution to the problem.*
in·gen·ious (ĭn **jēn′**yəs) ◊ *adjective*

ingenuity *noun* Inventive or imaginative skill; cleverness: *You needed a lot of ingenuity to solve that puzzle.*
in·ge·nu·i·ty (ĭn′jə **no͞o′**ĭ tē) ◊ *noun*

ingenuous *adjective* Frank and open; honest: *The child gave a completely ingenuous answer to the question.*
in·gen·u·ous (ĭn **jĕn′**yo͞o əs) ◊ *adjective*

ingot *noun* A mass of metal shaped like a bar or block.
in·got (**ĭng′**gət) ◊ *noun, plural* **ingots**

▲ **ingot**

ingratitude *noun* Lack of gratitude.
in·grat·i·tude (ĭn **grăt′**ĭ to͞od′ *or* ĭn **grăt′**ĭ tyo͞od′) ◊ *noun*

ingredient *noun* One of the parts that make up a mixture or combination: *Flour is an ingredient of bread.*
in·gre·di·ent (ĭn **grē′**dē ənt) ◊ *noun, plural* **ingredients**

inhabit *verb* To live in or on: *Dinosaurs inhabited the earth millions of years ago.*
in·hab·it (ĭn **hăb′**ĭt) ◊ *verb* **inhabited, inhabiting**

inhabitant *noun* A resident of a place.
in·hab·i·tant (ĭn **hăb′**ĭ tənt) ◊ *noun, plural* **inhabitants**

inhale *verb* **1.** To draw in by breathing: *We inhaled the fresh air.* **2.** To breathe in: *They inhaled deeply.*
in·hale (ĭn **hāl′**) ◊ *verb* **inhaled, inhaling**

inherit *verb* **1.** To receive money or property after someone's death. **2.** To receive by heredity: *I inherited my parents' dark eyes.*
in·her·it (ĭn **hĕr′**ĭt) ◊ *verb* **inherited, inheriting**

inheritance *noun* **1.** The act or process of inheriting. **2.** Something inherited.
in·her·i·tance (ĭn **hĕr′**ĭ təns) ◊ *noun, plural* **inheritances**

inhospitable *adjective* Not being friendly to visitors.
in·hos·pi·ta·ble (ĭn **hŏs′**pĭ tə bəl *or* ĭn′hŏ **spĭt′**ə bəl) ◊ *adjective*

initial *adjective* Of or happening at the beginning; first: *My initial skiing lesson was a total failure.*
◊ *noun* The first letter of a word or name.

◊ *verb* To mark or sign with the first letter or letters of one's name.
in·i·tial (ĭ **nĭsh'** əl) ◊ *adjective* ◊ *noun, plural* **initials** ◊ *verb* **initialed, initialing**

initiate *verb* **1.** To set going; start: *Who initiated this rumor?* **2.** To admit to membership in a club, often with a special ceremony.
in·i·ti·ate (ĭ **nĭsh'** ē āt') ◊ *verb* **initiated, initiating**

initiation *noun* **1.** The act or process of initiating. **2.** Admission into a club or society.
in·i·ti·a·tion (ĭ nĭsh'ē **ā'** shən) ◊ *noun, plural* **initiations**

initiative *noun* The ability to begin or carry out a task or a plan: *To succeed in life you must have initiative and determination.*
in·i·tia·tive (ĭ **nĭsh'** ə tĭv) ◊ *noun, plural* **initiatives**

inject *verb* **1.** To force or drive a medicine into the body. **2.** To bring or put in: *I tried to inject some humor into my book report.*
in·ject (ĭn **jĕkt'**) ◊ *verb* **injected, injecting**

injection *noun* **1.** The act or process of injecting. **2.** Something injected, especially a liquid medicine.
in·jec·tion (ĭn **jĕk'** shən) ◊ *noun, plural* **injections**

injure *verb* To cause harm or damage to; hurt: *I fell and injured my foot.*
in·jure (**ĭn'** jər) ◊ *verb* **injured, injuring**

injury *noun* **1.** An act that damages or harms. **2.** Damage or harm, especially to the body.
in·ju·ry (**ĭn'** jə rē) ◊ *noun, plural* **injuries**

injustice *noun* **1.** Unfair treatment of a person or thing. **2.** An unfair act.
in·jus·tice (ĭn **jŭs'** tĭs) ◊ *noun, plural* **injustices**

ink *noun* A colored liquid used for writing or printing.
ink (ĭngk) ◊ *noun, plural* **inks**

inkling *noun* A slight sign; hint: *A headache was the first inkling that I was sick.*
ink·ling (**ĭngk'** lĭng) ◊ *noun, plural* **inklings**

ă pat	ĭ pit	oi	**oil**	th	bath		
ā pay	ī ride	o͝o	book	*th*	bathe		
â care	î fierce	o͞o	boot	ə	ago, item		
ä father	ŏ pot	ou	**out**		pencil		
ĕ pet	ō go	ŭ	cut		atom		
ē be	ô paw, for	û	fur		circus		

inkwell *noun* A small container for ink.
ink·well (**ĭngk'** wĕl') ◊ *noun, plural* **inkwells**

▲ **inkwell**

inky *adjective* **1.** Covered, stained, discolored, or smeared with ink. **2.** Dark or black like ink: *Look at the inky clouds.*
ink·y (**ĭng'** kē) ◊ *adjective* **inkier, inkiest**

inland *adjective* Of or located in the interior of a country or region. ◊ *adverb* In, toward, or into the interior of a country or region.
in·land (**ĭn'** lənd) ◊ *adjective* ◊ *adverb*

in-law *noun* A relative by marriage.
in-law (**ĭn'** lô') ◊ *noun, plural* **in-laws**

inlet *noun* A small or narrow body of water, as a bay or cove, along a coast.
in·let (**ĭn'** lĕt') ◊ *noun, plural* **inlets**

inn *noun* A place that offers meals and lodging for travelers.
inn (ĭn) ◊ *noun, plural* **inns**
‖ *These sound alike:* **inn, in**

inner *adjective* Located farther inside: *We heard singing in an inner room of the house.*
in·ner (**ĭn'** ər) ◊ *adjective*

inning *noun* One of the divisions of a baseball game when each team comes to bat.
in·ning (**ĭn'** ĭng) ◊ *noun, plural* **innings**

innkeeper *noun* A person who owns or manages an inn.
inn·keep·er (**ĭn'** kē'pər) ◊ *noun, plural* **innkeepers**

innocence *noun* The quality, condition, or fact of being innocent.
in·no·cence (**ĭn'** ə səns) ◊ *noun*

innocent *adjective* Not guilty of a crime or fault: *The jury found them innocent.*
in·no·cent (**ĭn'** ə sənt) ◊ *adjective*

inoculate *verb* To inject with a vaccine in order to cure or protect against a disease.
in·oc·u·late (ĭ **nŏk'** yə lāt') ◊ *verb* **inoculated, inoculating**

input *noun* The information and instructions that are entered in a computer system.
in·put (**ĭn'** po͝ot') ◊ *noun*

inquire *verb* To ask in order to find out: *We inquired the way to the airport.*
in·quire (ĭn **kwīr′**) ◊ *verb* **inquired, inquiring**

inquiry *noun* **1.** The act or process of asking in order to find out. **2.** A request for information; question.
in·quir·y (ĭn **kwīr′**ē *or* **ĭn′**kwə rē) ◊ *noun, plural* **inquiries**

inquisitive *adjective* Curious and eager to learn: *The child has an inquisitive mind.*
in·quis·i·tive (ĭn **kwĭz′**ĭ tĭv) ◊ *adjective*

inroad *noun* A hostile invasion; raid.
in·road (**ĭn′**rōd′) ◊ *noun, plural* **inroads**

insane *adjective* **1.** Mentally ill. **2.** Very foolish: *What an insane idea!*
in·sane (ĭn **sān′**) ◊ *adjective*

insanity *noun* **1.** Mental illness. **2.** Extreme foolishness.
in·san·i·ty (ĭn **săn′**ĭ tē) ◊ *noun, plural* **insanities**

inscribe *verb* To write, print, carve, or engrave something on or in.
in·scribe (ĭn **skrīb′**) ◊ *verb* **inscribed, inscribing**

inscription *noun* **1.** The act or an example of inscribing. **2.** Something that is inscribed: *An interesting inscription is on the gate.*
in·scrip·tion (ĭn **skrĭp′**shən) ◊ *noun, plural* **inscriptions**

▲ **inscription**

insect *noun* **1.** Any of a large group of animals that have six legs, a body with three main divisions, and usually wings. Flies, bees, grasshoppers, butterflies, and moths are insects. **2.** An animal, as a spider, that is similar to but not a true insect.
in·sect (**ĭn′**sĕkt′) ◊ *noun, plural* **insects**

insecticide *noun* A poisonous chemical used to kill insects.
in·sec·ti·cide (ĭn **sĕk′**tĭ sīd′) ◊ *noun, plural* **insecticides**

insecure *adjective* **1.** Not firm or steady; shaky: *I had only an insecure hold on the rope.* **2.** Not secure; unsafe.
in·se·cure (ĭn′sĭ **kyŏŏr′**) ◊ *adjective*

insert *verb* To put, set, or fit into: *Insert the key in the lock.*
◊ *noun* Something that is inserted or meant to be inserted.
in·sert ◊ *verb* (ĭn **sûrt′**) **inserted, inserting**
◊ *noun* (**ĭn′**sûrt′), *plural* **inserts**

inside *noun* The inner part, side, or surface; interior: *The inside of the house looked better than the outside.*
◊ *adjective* Inner or interior: *This jacket has an inside pocket.*
◊ *adverb* **1.** Into or in the interior; within: *I'm staying inside because of my cold.* **2.** On the inner side: *I scrubbed the tub inside and out until it was thoroughly clean.*
◊ *preposition* In, on, or into the inner side or part of: *A bear lives inside the cave.*
◊ *idiom* **inside out** With the inner surface turned out: *The socks are turned inside out.*
in·side (**ĭn′**sīd′ *or* ĭn **sīd′**) ◊ *noun, plural* **insides** ◊ *adjective* ◊ *adverb* ◊ *preposition*

insignia *noun* An official emblem of rank or membership.
in·sig·ni·a (ĭn **sĭg′**nē ə) ◊ *noun, plural* **insignias**

▲ **insignia**

insignificant *adjective* Not meaningful or important.
in·sig·nif·i·cant (ĭn′sĭg **nĭf′**ĭ kənt) ◊ *adjective*

insincere *adjective* Not sincere: *Don't give me such an insincere apology.*
in·sin·cere (ĭn′sĭn **sîr′**) ◊ *adjective*

insinuate *verb* To introduce in a gradual or sly way: *They tried to insinuate themselves into our club.*
in·sin·u·ate (ĭn **sĭn′**yōō āt′) ◊ *verb* **insinuated, insinuating**

insist *verb* **1.** To demand: *I insist on watching the ball game.* **2.** To state strongly and repeatedly: *They insisted that we were wrong.*
in·sist (ĭn **sĭst′**) ◊ *verb* **insisted, insisting**

insistent *adjective* **1.** Demanding firmly: *They were insistent that we go on without them.* **2.** Repeating persistently: *We heard the insistent cry of a bluejay.*
in·sis·tent (ĭn **sĭs′**tənt) ◊ *adjective*

insolence *noun* Disrespect for authority.
in·so·lence (**ĭn′**sə ləns) ◊ *noun*

insolent *adjective* Showing insolence; rude: *You should never give your teacher an insolent reply.* —See Synonyms at **impertinent.**
in·so·lent (**ĭn′**sə lənt) ◊ *adjective*

inspect *verb* **1.** To look over carefully. **2.** To examine in an official or formal way.
in·spect (ĭn **spĕkt′**) ◊ *verb* **inspected, inspecting**

inspection *noun* **1.** The act or an example of inspecting. **2.** An official examination or review: *Elevators must undergo an annual safety inspection.*
in·spec·tion (ĭn **spĕk′**shən) ◊ *noun, plural* **inspections**

inspector *noun* **1.** A person who makes inspections. **2.** A high-ranking police officer.
in·spec·tor (ĭn **spĕk′**tər) ◊ *noun, plural* **inspectors**

inspiration *noun* **1.** The power of exciting the mind or emotions. **2.** Someone or something that inspires. **3.** A sudden, original idea.
in·spi·ra·tion (ĭn′spə **rā′**shən) ◊ *noun, plural* **inspirations**

inspire *verb* **1.** To fill with great emotion: *The songs inspired us.* **2.** To move to action: *The promise of money inspired me to work hard.* **3.** To be the cause or source of: *The book inspired a movie.*
in·spire (ĭn **spīr′**) ◊ *verb* **inspired, inspiring**

install *verb* To set in position for use or service: *They installed the telephone today.*
in·stall (ĭn **stôl′**) ◊ *verb* **installed, installing**

ă	pat	ĭ	pit	oi	**oil**	th	bath
ā	pay	ī	ride	o͝o	**book**	*th*	bathe
â	care	î	fierce	o͞o	**boot**	ə	ago, item
ä	father	ŏ	pot	ou	**out**		pencil
ĕ	pet	ō	go	ŭ	cut		atom
ē	be	ô	paw, for	û	fur		circus

installment *noun* One of a series of payments: *The TV cost $400; we paid for it in four installments of $100 each.*
in·stall·ment (ĭn **stôl′**mənt) ◊ *noun, plural* **installments**

instance *noun* A case or example: *There were a few failures but many instances of success.* —See Synonyms at **example.**
in·stance (**ĭn′**stəns) ◊ *noun, plural* **instances**

instant *noun* A very brief period of time; second. —See Synonyms at **moment.**
◊ *adjective* **1.** Immediate: *The song was an instant success.* **2.** Designed for quick preparation: *I made a cup of instant cocoa.*
in·stant (**ĭn′**stənt) ◊ *noun, plural* **instants** ◊ *adjective*

instantly *adverb* At once; immediately.
in·stant·ly (**ĭn′**stənt lē) ◊ *adverb*

instead *adverb* In place of another: *Since you're sick, I'll go instead.*
in·stead (ĭn **stĕd′**) ◊ *adverb*

instep *noun* **1.** The arched middle part of the human foot. **2.** The part of a shoe, stocking, or sock that covers the instep.
in·step (**ĭn′**stĕp′) ◊ *noun, plural* **insteps**

instill *verb* To put into a person's mind over a period of time: *The coach instilled in us a sense of fair play.*
in·still (ĭn **stĭl′**) ◊ *verb* **instilled, instilling**

instinct *noun* **1.** An inner feeling or way of behaving that is automatic rather than learned. **2.** A natural talent or ability.
in·stinct (**ĭn′**stĭngkt′) ◊ *noun, plural* **instincts**

instinctive *adjective* Of, relating to, or coming from instinct: *Nest building is instinctive behavior in most birds.*
in·stinc·tive (ĭn **stĭngk′**tĭv) ◊ *adjective*

institute *verb* **1.** To organize and get established: *They instituted a new basketball program.* **2.** To start: *Congress instituted an investigation.*
◊ *noun* A place for specialized study.
in·sti·tute (**ĭn′**stĭ to͞ot′ *or* **ĭn′**stĭ tyo͞ot′) ◊ *verb* **instituted, instituting** ◊ *noun, plural* **institutes**

institution *noun* **1.** An established custom, practice, or pattern of behavior: *The family is an institution in American life.* **2.** An established organization. A school, hospital, or museum is an institution.
in·sti·tu·tion (ĭn′stĭ **to͞o′**shən *or* ĭn′stĭ**tyo͞o′**shən) ◊ *noun, plural* **institutions**

instruct *verb* **1.** To pass on knowledge or skill to. **2.** To give orders to; direct: *We instructed them to be on time.*
in·struct (ĭn **strŭkt′**) ◊ *verb* **instructed, instructing**

instruction *noun* **1.** Something that is taught; a lesson or series of lessons. **2.** The act or profession of teaching. **3.** Often **instructions** A direction or an order.
in·struc·tion (ĭn **strŭk′**shən) ◊ *noun, plural* **instructions**

instructor *noun* A person who instructs.
in·struc·tor (ĭn **strŭk′** tər) ◊ *noun, plural* **instructors**

instrument *noun* **1.** A tool or implement for doing a certain kind of work: *The dentist picked up several instruments.* **2.** A device used in making music.
in·stru·ment (**ĭn′**strə mənt) ◊ *noun, plural* **instruments**

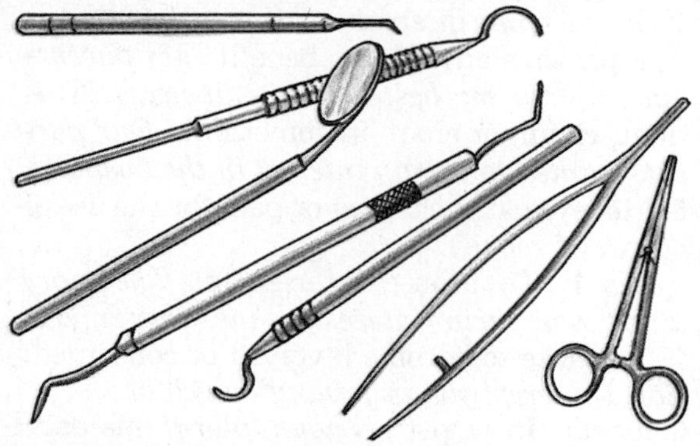

▲ **instrument**
Dental instruments

insulate *verb* To cover, surround, or line with a material that slows or prevents heat, electricity, or sound from passing through: *We insulated the house so it would stay warmer in the winter.*
in·su·late (**ĭn′**sə lāt′) ◊ *verb* **insulated, insulating**

insulation *noun* **1.** The act or process of insulating. **2.** The condition of being insulated. **3.** Material used for insulating buildings.
in·su·la·tion (ĭn′sə **lā′**shən) ◊ *noun*

insult *verb* To speak to or treat impolitely and disrespectfully: *Don't insult me by calling me dishonest.*
◊ *noun* An insulting action or remark.
in·sult ◊ *verb* (ĭn **sŭlt′**) **insulted, insulting** ◊ *noun* (**ĭn′**sŭlt′), *plural* **insults**

insurance *noun* **1.** A promise by a company that it will pay a certain amount for a loss in return for regular payments. Insurance can be bought to protect against losses caused by such things as accident, fire, or theft. **2.** The business of selling insurance.
in·sur·ance (ĭn **shoor′**əns) ◊ *noun*

insure *verb* **1.** To issue or get insurance on or for. **2.** To make sure of; ensure: *Use your seat belt to insure your safety.*
in·sure (ĭn **shoor′**) ◊ *verb* **insured, insuring**

intact *adjective* Not harmed or damaged.
in·tact (ĭn **tăkt′**) ◊ *adjective*

intake *noun* **1.** An opening through which a liquid or gas enters something, such as a container or pipe. **2.** The act or process of taking in. **3.** The amount of a thing taken in.
in·take (**ĭn′**tāk′) ◊ *noun, plural* **intakes**

integrate *verb* **1.** To combine into a whole; unite: *We tried to integrate all our ideas into one plan.* **2.** To open to people of all races without restriction.
in·te·grate (**ĭn′**tĭ grāt′) ◊ *verb* **integrated, integrating**

integration *noun* The act, process, or result of integrating.
in·te·gra·tion (ĭn′tĭ **grā′**shən) ◊ *noun*

integrity *noun* Complete honesty.
in·teg·ri·ty (ĭn **tĕg′**rĭ tē) ◊ *noun*

intellect *noun* The ability to think and learn.
in·tel·lect (**ĭn′**tl ĕkt′) ◊ *noun, plural* **intellects**

intellectual *adjective* Of, relating to, or requiring use of the brain: *Reading is an intellectual activity.*
◊ *noun* A smart person.
in·tel·lec·tu·al (ĭn′tl **ĕk′**chōō əl) ◊ *adjective* ◊ *noun, plural* **intellectuals**

intelligence *noun* **1.** The ability to learn, think, understand, and know. —See Synonyms at **mind.** **2.** Information, especially secret information, as about an enemy.
in·tel·li·gence (ĭn **tĕl′**ə jəns) ◊ *noun*

intelligent *adjective* Having or showing the ability to learn, think, understand, and know.
in·tel·li·gent (ĭn **tĕl′**ə jənt) ◊ *adjective*

intend *verb* To have in mind as an aim or goal; plan: *I intend to go to college.*
in·tend (ĭn **tĕnd′**) ◊ *verb* **intended, intending**

I

intense *adjective* **1.** Very strong: *The sun emits intense light.* **2.** Having or showing deep feelings.
in·tense (ĭn tĕns′) ◊ *adjective*

SYNONYMS
intense, fierce, furious, violent The *intense* heat from the fireplace soon warmed us. It was impossible to make any headway against the *fierce* blizzard. The *furious* storm raged all night, and in the morning we found many trees knocked down. The *violent* tornado leveled all the buildings on Main Street.

intensity *noun* **1.** The quality or condition of being intense. **2.** The degree or extent to which something is intense: *The two colors differ in intensity.*
in·ten·si·ty (ĭn tĕn′sĭ tē) ◊ *noun, plural* **intensities**

intensive *adjective* Of, relating to, or marked by intensity; thorough: *We made an intensive study of the pyramids.*
in·ten·sive (ĭn tĕn′sĭv) ◊ *adjective*

intent *adjective* **1.** Showing concentration: *The judge listened with an intent expression on her face.* **2.** Having the mind or thoughts set on a goal; determined: *He is intent on winning the marathon.*
◊ *noun* **1.** Aim; purpose: *Was it your intent to laugh at me?* **2.** Meaning: *I don't understand the intent of your first sentence.*
in·tent (ĭn tĕnt′) ◊ *adjective* ◊ *noun, plural* **intents**

intention *noun* An aim, purpose, or plan: *It isn't my intention to fool you.*
in·ten·tion (ĭn tĕn′shən) ◊ *noun, plural* **intentions**

intentional *adjective* Done on purpose: *I trust that bump wasn't intentional.*
in·ten·tion·al (ĭn tĕn′shə nəl) ◊ *adjective*

intercept *verb* To stop, seize, or take on the way from one place to another: *The opposing team intercepted the ball.*
in·ter·cept (ĭn′tər sĕpt′) ◊ *verb* **intercepted, intercepting**

interchangeable *adjective* Capable of being switched: *The parts of the two machines are interchangeable.*
in·ter·change·a·ble (ĭn′tər chān′jə bəl) ◊ *adjective*

intercom *noun* A system that usually has loudspeakers and microphones and is used for communicating between one part of a building and another.
in·ter·com (ĭn′tər kŏm′) ◊ *noun, plural* **intercoms**

interest *noun* **1.** A feeling of wanting to give special attention to something: *The adventure book held my interest from the very first page.* **2.** The quality of causing this feeling: *A boring movie lacks interest.* **3.** Something that a person wants to give special attention to: *Music is one of my interests.* **4.** Something that is to a person's advantage; benefit: *My parents always have my best interests at heart.* **5.** A right, claim, or share in something: *Our parents wanted to buy an interest in the business.* **6.** Money that is charged or paid for the use of borrowed money.
◊ *verb* **1.** To arouse interest in: *The story about your trip interested me very much.* **2.** To cause to become involved or concerned: *Can I interest you in joining our club?*
in·ter·est (ĭn′tə rĭst′) ◊ *noun, plural* **interests** ◊ *verb* **interested, interesting**

interesting *adjective* Causing interest or attention: *We had a long and interesting talk.*
in·ter·est·ing (ĭn′tər ĭ stĭng) ◊ *adjective*

interfere *verb* **1.** To get or be in the way so as to hinder: *Noise interferes with my sleep.* **2.** To meddle in the affairs of others.
in·ter·fere (ĭn′tər fîr′) ◊ *verb* **interfered, interfering**

interference *noun* The act, the process, or an example of interfering.
in·ter·fer·ence (ĭn′tər fîr′əns) ◊ *noun*

interior *noun* An inner part; inside.
◊ *adjective* Of or located on the inside; inner: *Ancient paintings are on the interior walls of the cave.*
in·te·ri·or (ĭn tîr′ē ər) ◊ *noun, plural* **interiors** ◊ *adjective*

ă	pat	ĭ	pit	oi	**oil**	th	ba**th**
ā	pay	ī	ride	ŏŏ	book	*th*	ba*th*e
â	care	î	fierce	ōō	boot	ə	ago, item
ä	father	ŏ	pot	ou	**out**		pencil
ĕ	pet	ō	go	ŭ	cut		atom
ē	be	ô	paw, for	û	fur		circus

interjection *noun* A word, such as *ouch,* that expresses emotion.
in·ter·jec·tion (ĭn′tər **jĕk′**shən) ◊ *noun, plural* **interjections**

interlude *noun* An event, episode, or period of time that comes between others.
in·ter·lude (**ĭn′**tər lo͞od′) ◊ *noun, plural* **interludes**

intermediate *adjective* Being or occurring between or in the middle: *We teach beginning, intermediate, and advanced swimming.* ◊ *noun* Someone or something in between.
in·ter·me·di·ate (ĭn′tər **mē′**dē ĭt) ◊ *adjective* ◊ *noun, plural* **intermediates**

intermission *noun* An interruption in activity, as one between the acts of a play.
in·ter·mis·sion (ĭn′tər **mĭsh′**ən) ◊ *noun, plural* **intermissions**

internal *adjective* Of or located within something; inner: *The driver received internal injuries in the accident.*
in·ter·nal (ĭn **tûr′**nəl) ◊ *adjective*

international *adjective* Of, relating to, or carried on between two or more countries or peoples.
in·ter·na·tion·al (ĭn′tər **năsh′**ə nəl) ◊ *adjective*

interpret *verb* **1.** To explain the meaning or importance of: *Scientists interpret data.* **2.** To see or understand in a certain way: *We interpret a frown as a sign of disapproval.*
in·ter·pret (ĭn **tûr′**prĭt) ◊ *verb* **interpreted, interpreting**

interpretation *noun* The act, process, or result of interpreting.
in·ter·pre·ta·tion (ĭn tûr′prĭ **tā′**shən) ◊ *noun, plural* **interpretations**

interrogate *verb* To question closely.
in·ter·ro·gate (ĭn **tĕr′**ə gāt′) ◊ *verb* **interrogated, interrogating**

interrogative *adjective* Of, relating to, or having the nature of a question: *An interrogative sentence asks a question and ends with a question mark.*
in·ter·rog·a·tive (ĭn′tə **rŏg′**ə tĭv) ◊ *adjective*

interrupt *verb* **1.** To hinder or stop by breaking in: *I didn't want to interrupt the conversation.* **2.** To break off for a time: *The storm interrupted our electrical power.*
in·ter·rupt (ĭn′tə **rŭpt′**) ◊ *verb* **interrupted, interrupting**

interruption *noun* The act of interrupting or the condition of being interrupted.
in·ter·rup·tion (ĭn′tə **rŭp′**shən) ◊ *noun, plural* **interruptions**

intersect *verb* To divide or cut by lying across or passing through; cross: *Two main highways intersect north of town.*
in·ter·sect (ĭn′tər **sĕkt′**) ◊ *verb* **intersected, intersecting**

intersection *noun* **1.** The act or process of intersecting. **2.** The point where two or more things intersect: *There is a traffic light at the intersection.*
in·ter·sec·tion (ĭn′tər **sĕk′**shən) ◊ *noun, plural* **intersections**

▲ **intersection**

interstate *adjective* Of, existing between, or connecting two or more states.
in·ter·state (**ĭn′**tər stāt′) ◊ *adjective*

interval *noun* A period of time between two events or actions: *An interval of two weeks passed before I answered the letter.*
in·ter·val (**ĭn′**tər vəl) ◊ *noun, plural* **intervals**

intervene *verb* **1.** To be or come between things, points, or events: *A day of calm intervened between the busy weeks.* **2.** To come in or between in order to adjust, stop, or change: *The referee intervened to stop play.*
in·ter·vene (ĭn′tər **vēn′**) ◊ *verb* **intervened, intervening**

interview *noun* **1.** A meeting of people face to face: *The principal asked the new student to report for an interview.* **2.** A conversation

I

between a reporter and a person during which the reporter asks for facts, information, or statements.
◊ *verb* To have an interview with.
in·ter·view (ĭn′tər vyōō′) ◊ *noun, plural* **interviews** ◊ *verb* **interviewed, interviewing**

intestine *noun* The lower part of the digestive canal that extends below the stomach. Food is digested completely and water is absorbed in the intestines.
in·tes·tine (ĭn **tĕs′** tĭn) ◊ *noun, plural* **intestines**

intimate *adjective* Very closely acquainted; familiar.
in·ti·mate (**ĭn′** tə mĭt) ◊ *adjective*

intimidate *verb* To frighten by threats.
in·tim·i·date (ĭn **tĭm′** ĭ dāt′) ◊ *verb* **intimidated, intimidating**

into *preposition* **1.** To the inside of: *I went into the house.* **2.** To the activity or occupation of: *My friend is going into banking.* **3.** To the condition or form of: *We got into trouble.* **4.** In such a way as to be in contact with; against: *The bike bumped into a tree.*
in·to (**ĭn′** tōō) ◊ *preposition*

intolerant *adjective* Not willing or able to tolerate: *Don't be intolerant of people whose opinions differ from yours.*
in·tol·er·ant (ĭn **tŏl′** ər ənt) ◊ *adjective*

intricate *adjective* Complicated; complex.
in·tri·cate (**ĭn′** trĭ kĭt) ◊ *adjective*

intrigue *verb* **1.** To catch the interest or arouse the curiosity of. **2.** To plot secretly.
◊ *noun* A secret plot or scheme.
in·trigue (ĭn **trēg′**) ◊ *verb* **intrigued, intriguing** ◊ *noun, plural* **intrigues**

introduce *verb* **1.** To make known by name: *Let me introduce my newest friend to you.* **2.** To provide with a beginning knowledge of something: *This class will introduce you to science.* **3.** To bring or put in something new or different: *Try to introduce excitement into your story.*
in·tro·duce (ĭn′trə **dōōs′** *or* ĭn′trə **dyōōs′**) ◊ *verb* **introduced, introducing**

introduction *noun* **1.** A part, as of a book, that leads into or explains what will follow. **2.** The act or process of introducing: *The brother and sister made the introductions at their party.* **3.** Something that introduces: *Collecting rocks is an excellent introduction to geology.*
in·tro·duc·tion (ĭn′trə **dŭk′** shən) ◊ *noun, plural* **introductions**

introductory *adjective* Serving to introduce.
in·tro·duc·to·ry (ĭn′trə **dŭk′** tə rē) ◊ *adjective*

invade *verb* **1.** To enter by force as an enemy: *The rebels invaded the capital.* **2.** To enter in great numbers: *In the summer tourists invade the mountain village.*
in·vade (ĭn **vād′**) ◊ *verb* **invaded, invading**

invalid *noun* A sick person.
in·va·lid (**ĭn′** və lĭd) ◊ *noun, plural* **invalids**

invaluable *adjective* Having a value that is greater than one can measure; priceless: *The museum has many invaluable jewels.*
in·val·u·a·ble (ĭn **văl′** yōō ə bəl) ◊ *adjective*

invasion *noun* The act of invading.
in·va·sion (ĭn **vā′** zhən) ◊ *noun, plural* **invasions**

invent *verb* To make or produce something that did not exist before: *Who invented the elevator?*
in·vent (ĭn **vĕnt′**) ◊ *verb* **invented, inventing**

invention *noun* **1.** An original device, system, or process: *The cotton gin was an important invention.* **2.** The act or process of inventing: *No one person can take credit for the invention of the printing press.*
in·ven·tion (ĭn **vĕn′** shən) ◊ *noun, plural* **inventions**

inventive *adjective* Having or showing the ability to invent.
in·ven·tive (ĭn **vĕn′** tĭv) ◊ *adjective*

inventor *noun* A person who invents things.
in·ven·tor (ĭn **vĕn′** tər) ◊ *noun, plural* **inventors**

inventory *noun* **1.** A detailed list, as of goods or items that one owns. **2.** The process of making an inventory. **3.** The supply of goods on hand, as in a store; stock.
◊ *verb* To make an inventory of.
in·ven·to·ry (**ĭn′** vən tôr′ē) ◊ *noun, plural* **inventories** ◊ *verb* **inventoried, inventorying**

ă	pat	ĭ	pit	oi	**oil**	th	ba**th**
ā	pay	ī	ride	ŏŏ	book	*th*	ba**th**e
â	care	î	fierce	ōō	boot	ə	ago, item
ä	father	ŏ	pot	ou	**out**		pencil
ĕ	pet	ō	go	ŭ	cut		atom
ē	be	ô	paw, for	û	fur		circus

invert *verb* **1.** To turn upside down: *If you invert the glass, the water will spill.* **2.** To reverse the order of: *If you invert "I will" you have "will I?"*
in·vert (ĭn vûrt′) ◊ *verb* **inverted, inverting**

invertebrate *noun* An animal that has no backbone. Worms, clams, insects, and lobsters are invertebrates.
◊ *adjective* Having no backbone.
in·ver·te·brate (ĭn vûr′tə brĭt *or* ĭn vûr′tə-brāt′) ◊ *noun, plural* **invertebrates** ◊ *adjective*

invest *verb* To put money to use in order to earn interest or make a profit: *They invested money in stocks.*
in·vest (ĭn vĕst′) ◊ *verb* **invested, investing**

investigate *verb* To look into carefully.
in·ves·ti·gate (ĭn vĕs′tĭ gāt′) ◊ *verb* **investigated, investigating**

investigation *noun* The act or process of investigating.
in·ves·ti·ga·tion (ĭn vĕs′tĭ gā′shən) ◊ *noun, plural* **investigations**

investigator *noun* A person who investigates.
in·ves·ti·ga·tor (ĭn vĕs′tĭ gā′tər) ◊ *noun, plural* **investigators**

investment *noun* **1.** The act or process of investing. **2.** Money that is invested. **3.** Something in which money is invested.
in·vest·ment (ĭn vĕst′mənt) ◊ *noun, plural* **investments**

investor *noun* A person or group that invests money.
in·ves·tor (ĭn vĕs′tər) ◊ *noun, plural* **investors**

invigorate *verb* To give energy or strength to: *Regular exercise in the cool autumn air invigorated us.*
in·vig·or·ate (ĭn vĭg′ə rāt′) ◊ *verb* **invigorated, invigorating**

invincible *adjective* Too strong and powerful to be defeated: *The army seemed invincible.*
in·vin·ci·ble (ĭn vĭn′sə bəl) ◊ *adjective*

invisible *adjective* Not capable of being seen; not visible: *Air is invisible.*
in·vis·i·ble (ĭn vĭz′ə bəl) ◊ *adjective*

invitation *noun* **1.** A spoken or written request for someone to come somewhere or do something. **2.** The act of inviting.
in·vi·ta·tion (ĭn′vĭ tā′shən) ◊ *noun, plural* **invitations**

invite *verb* To ask to come somewhere or do something: *How many guests did you invite to the party?*
in·vite (ĭn vīt′) ◊ *verb* **invited, inviting**

involuntary *adjective* **1.** Not controlled by the will: *Sneezing is an involuntary act.* **2.** Not done willingly or on purpose: *My errors on the test were involuntary.*
in·vol·un·tar·y (ĭn vŏl′ən tĕr′ē) ◊ *adjective*

involve *verb* **1.** To have as a feature or result: *Producing a good school play involves hard work.* **2.** To take in as a part; include: *Opera involves music and drama.* **3.** To get mixed up in: *They became involved in an argument.* **4.** To hold the interest of: *I was so involved in my work that I didn't hear my friend come into the room.*
in·volve (ĭn vŏlv′) ◊ *verb* **involved, involving**

inward *adverb* Toward the inside or center: *Look inward beyond the mouth of the cave.*
◊ *adjective* Directed toward or located on the inside or interior: *Open the door with an inward pull on the handle.*
in·ward (ĭn′wərd) ◊ *adverb* ◊ *adjective*

inwardly *adverb* **1.** On or toward the inside. **2.** To oneself; privately: *I laughed inwardly but said nothing.*
in·ward·ly (ĭn′wərd lē) ◊ *adverb*

iodine *noun* **1.** A chemical element that is found in seaweed and sea water. It is used in medicine and photography. **2.** A brown liquid medication that is used to kill germs on wounds.
i·o·dine (ī′ə dīn′) ◊ *noun*

iris *noun* **1.** The colored part of the eye around the pupil. **2.** A plant with long, narrow, pointed leaves and purplish flowers.
i·ris (ī′rĭs) ◊ *noun, plural* **irises**

Irish *noun* **1.** (*used with a plural verb*) The people of Ireland. **2.** The Celtic language of Ireland.
◊ *adjective* Of or relating to Ireland or the language of Ireland.
I·rish (ī′rĭsh) ◊ *noun* ◊ *adjective*

▲ **iris**

I

irksome *adjective* Causing annoyance.
irk·some (ûrk′səm) ◊ *adjective*

iron *noun* **1.** A hard, gray metal that can be magnetized. Iron is used in making many tools and machines. **2.** A metal appliance with a handle and flat bottom that is used when heated to smooth wrinkles in cloth and clothing. **3. irons** Chains that are used to keep a prisoner under control. **4.** A golf club with a metal head.
◊ *adjective* **1.** Of, relating to, or made of iron. **2.** Strong like iron: *You have an iron will.*
◊ *verb* To press with a heated iron.
i·ron (ī′ərn) ◊ *noun, plural* **irons** ◊ *adjective* ◊ *verb* **ironed, ironing**

ironstone *noun* A heavy, hard white pottery.
i·ron·stone (ī′ərn stōn′) ◊ *noun*

ironware *noun* Things made of iron.
i·ron·ware (ī′ərn wâr′) ◊ *noun*

irregular *adjective* **1.** Not being standard, even, or uniform in shape, size, length, or arrangement: *There is an irregular row of elm trees along the road.* **2.** Not done or happening at regular intervals: *The ill patient's breathing was irregular.*
ir·reg·u·lar (ĭ **rĕg′**yə lər) ◊ *adjective*

irregularity *noun* **1.** The condition of being irregular. **2.** Something that is irregular.
ir·reg·u·lar·i·ty (ĭ rĕg′yə **lăr′**ĭ tē) ◊ *noun, plural* **irregularities**

irresistible *adjective* Too strong or great to be resisted: *The puppy is irresistible.*
ir·re·sist·i·ble (ĭr′ĭ **zĭs′**tə bəl) ◊ *adjective*

irresponsible *adjective* Not having or showing a sense of responsibility; unreliable.
ir·re·spon·si·ble (ĭr′ĭ **spŏn′**sə bəl) ◊ *adjective*

irrigate *verb* To supply with water by means of a system of ditches, pipes, and canals.
ir·ri·gate (**ĭr′**ĭ gāt′) ◊ *verb* **irrigated, irrigating**

irrigation *noun* **1.** The process of irrigating. **2.** A system of ditches, pipes, and canals used to irrigate land.
ir·ri·ga·tion (ĭr′ĭ **gā′**shən) ◊ *noun*

ă	pat	ĭ	pit	oi	**oi**l	th	ba**th**
ā	pay	ī	ride	o͝o	b**oo**k	*th*	ba**th**e
â	care	î	fierce	o͞o	b**oo**t	ə	**a**go, it**e**m
ä	father	ŏ	pot	ou	**ou**t		penc**i**l
ĕ	pet	ō	go	ŭ	c**u**t		at**o**m
ē	be	ô	paw, for	û	f**u**r		circ**u**s

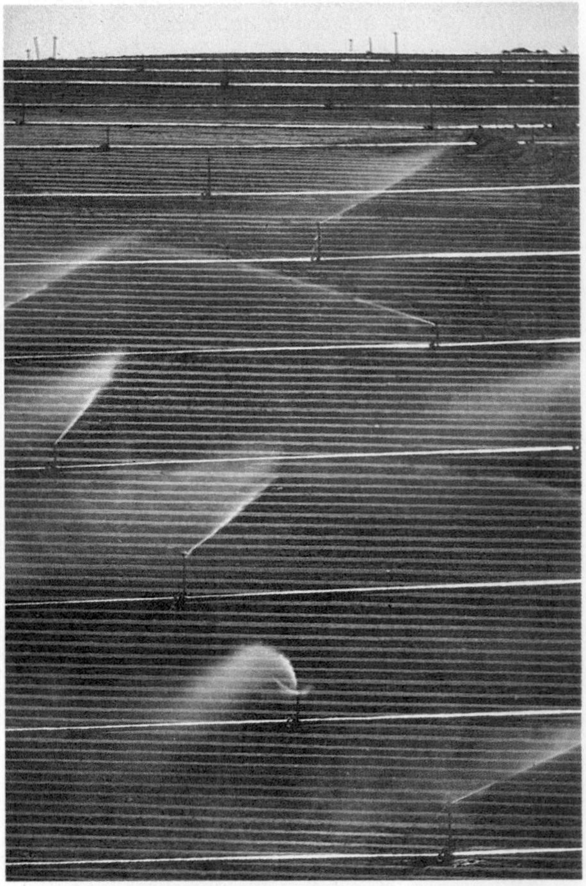

▲ **irrigation**

irritable *adjective* Easily annoyed.
ir·ri·ta·ble (**ĭr′**ĭ tə bəl) ◊ *adjective*

> ***SYNONYMS***
>
> ***irritable, cross, grouchy***
>
> The baby is teething and has been *irritable* for several days. Your *cross* answer to my question hurt my feelings. I am feeling very *grouchy* because I didn't sleep well.

irritably *adverb* In a cross or annoyed way or manner.
ir·ri·ta·bly (**ĭr′**ĭ tə blē) ◊ *adverb*

irritate *verb* **1.** To make angry or impatient: *Your endless questions irritate me.* —See Synonyms at **annoy. 2.** To cause to become sore or sensitive: *The smoke irritated my eyes.*
ir·ri·tate (**ĭr′**ĭ tāt′) ◊ *verb* **irritated, irritating**

irritation *noun* **1.** The act or process of irritating. **2.** The condition of being irritated. **3.** Something that irritates.
ir·ri·ta·tion (ĭr′ĭ **tā′**shən) ◊ *noun, plural* **irritations**

is *verb* Third person singular present tense of **be.**
is (ĭz) ◊ *verb*

-ish The suffix *-ish* forms adjectives and means "like," "resembling," or "having the qualities of." A *childish* voice is a voice that sounds like a child's. The suffix *-ish* also means "somewhat" or "approximately." A *yellowish* suit is somewhat yellow in color.

VOCABULARY BUILDER • -ish

Many words that are formed with **-ish** are not entries in this dictionary. But you can figure out what these words mean by looking up the meanings of the root words and the suffix. For example:
clownish = having the qualities of a clown
darkish = somewhat dark
sweetish = somewhat sweet

Islam *noun* A religion based on the teachings of the prophet Mohammed.
Is·lam (**ĭs′**ləm) ◊ *noun*

island *noun* **1.** A piece of land that is encircled by water. **2.** Something that looks like an island in shape or position.
is·land (**ī′**lənd) ◊ *noun, plural* **islands**

HISTORY • island, isle

These two words are actually not related. **Island** used to be spelled *iland,* from an old English word meaning "land by the water." **Isle** came through French from a Latin word meaning "island." Later, people wrongly assumed the two words were related. So they put the *s* in **island** to make it look more like **isle.**

islander *noun* A person living on an island.
is·land·er (**ī′**lən dər) ◊ *noun, plural* **islanders**

isle *noun* An island, especially a small one.
isle (īl) ◊ *noun, plural* **isles**
‖*These sound alike:* **isle, aisle, I'll**

islet *noun* A little island.
is·let (**ī′**lĭt) ◊ *noun, plural* **islets**
‖*These sound alike:* **islet, eyelet**

isn't Contraction of "is not."
is·n't (**ĭz′**ənt) ◊ *contraction*

isolate *verb* To set or keep apart from others.
i·so·late (**ī′**sə lāt′) ◊ *verb* **isolated, isolating**

isolation *noun* **1.** The condition of being isolated. **2.** The act or process of isolating.
i·so·la·tion (ī′sə **lā′**shən) ◊ *noun*

Israeli *noun* A person who was born in or lives in Israel.
◊ *adjective* Of or relating to Israel or the Israelis.
Is·rae·li (ĭz **rā′**lē) ◊ *noun, plural* **Israelis**
◊ *adjective*

issue *noun* **1.** The act of giving out or publishing: *The government's issue of the new stamp will be tomorrow.* **2.** Something that is issued at one time: *Did you see the July issue of that magazine?* **3.** Something that is being discussed or argued about: *Let's talk about the issue of free school lunches.*
◊ *verb* To give out or publish officially.
is·sue (**ĭsh′**o͞o) ◊ *noun, plural* **issues** ◊ *verb* **issued, issuing**

-ist The suffix *-ist* forms nouns and means "a person who does, makes, or has to do with a certain thing." A *cyclist* does cycling. A *novelist* writes novels. The suffix *-ist* also means "a person who plays a certain musical instrument or works with a certain device." A *violinist* plays the violin. A *machinist* works with machine-operated tools. The suffix *-ist* also means "someone who specializes in a certain art or branch of learning." A *geologist* specializes in geology.

VOCABULARY BUILDER • -ist

Many words that are formed with *-ist* are not entries in this dictionary. But you can figure out what these words mean by looking up the meanings of the root words and the suffix. For example:
biologist = a person who specializes in biology
cartoonist = a person who makes cartoons
organist = a person who plays the organ

I

isthmus *noun* A narrow strip of land that runs between two bodies of water and joins two bodies of land.
isth·mus (**ĭs′**məs) ◊ *noun, plural* **isthmuses**

▲ **isthmus**

it *pronoun* **1.** The thing or matter mentioned earlier: *They inspected the house carefully before they bought it.* **2.** The whole situation: *How can you stand it?* **3.** Used as the subject of certain verbs: *It has been snowing since early this morning.*
it (ĭt) ◊ *pronoun*

Italian *noun* **1.** A person who was born in or lives in Italy. **2.** The language of Italy.
◊ *adjective* Of or relating to Italy, the Italians, or their language.
I·tal·ian (ĭ **tăl′**yən) ◊ *noun, plural* **Italians** ◊ *adjective*

italic *adjective* Of, in, or relating to a style of printing with the letters slanting to the right: *This is italic print.*
◊ *noun* Often **italics** Italic printing.
i·tal·ic (ĭ **tăl′**ĭk) ◊ *adjective* ◊ *noun, plural* **italics**

ă	pat	ĭ	pit	oi	**oil**	th	ba**th**
ā	pay	ī	ride	o͝o	book	*th*	ba**the**
â	care	î	fierce	o͞o	boot	ə	ago, item
ä	father	ŏ	pot	ou	**out**		pencil
ĕ	pet	ō	go	ŭ	cut		atom
ē	be	ô	paw, for	û	fur		circus

italicize *verb* **1.** To print in italics: *Please italicize the titles of books.* **2.** To underline to show that in printing what is underlined is to be printed in italics.
i·tal·i·cize (ĭ **tăl′**ĭ sīz′) ◊ *verb* **italicized, italicizing**

itch *noun* A tickling feeling in the skin that makes one want to scratch.
◊ *verb* To have, cause, or cause to have a tickling feeling in the skin.
itch (ĭch) ◊ *noun, plural* **itches** ◊ *verb* **itched, itching**

itchy *adjective* Having or causing a tickling feeling in the skin.
itch·y (**ĭch′**ē) ◊ *adjective* **itchier, itchiest**

item *noun* **1.** A single thing, as in a list or group: *That item of clothing is no longer made.* **2.** A piece of news or information: *We clipped items from the newspaper for social studies class.*
i·tem (**ī′**təm) ◊ *noun, plural* **items**

itemize *verb* To list item by item.
i·tem·ize (**ī′**tə mīz′) ◊ *verb* **itemized, itemizing**

it'll Contraction of "it will" or "it shall."
it'll (**ĭt′**l) ◊ *contraction*

its *adjective* Relating or belonging to it: *Everything was in its place.*
its (ĭts) ◊ *adjective*
‖*These sound alike:* **its, it's**

it's Contraction of "it is" or "it has."
it's (ĭts) ◊ *contraction*
‖*These sound alike:* **it's, its**

itself *pronoun* Its own self: *The team surprised itself by winning.*
it·self (ĭt **sĕlf′**) ◊ *pronoun*

I've Contraction of "I have."
I've (īv) ◊ *contraction*

ivied *adjective* Covered with ivy: *The ivied wall is really made of brick.*
i·vied (**ī′**vēd) ◊ *adjective*

ivory *noun* **1.** The yellowish white substance that forms the tusks of animals such as elephants or walruses. Ivory was once used for making piano keys. **2.** A pale yellow to yellowish white color.
i·vo·ry (**ī′**və rē) ◊ *noun*

ivy *noun* **1.** A climbing vine with evergreen leaves and black berries that grows on houses and walls. **2.** A plant that is like ivy.
i·vy (**ī′**vē) ◊ *noun, plural* **ivies**

Jaguar

Jj

J is the tenth letter of the English alphabet. Did you know that it has a long history?

Over 3,500 years ago, people in the Middle East were using symbols that became the letters of our alphabet. This ancient Middle Eastern symbol is a form of the letter that became our letter *J*.

The ancient Greeks borrowed their alphabet from people in the Middle East. Here is a form of the Greek letter that became our letter *J*.

The ancient Romans borrowed their alphabet from a people who had taken their own letter symbols from the Greeks. The letter *J* is a later development of the Roman letter *I*. Here is a form of the Roman letter *I* that was used for carving letters into stone. These letters became the model for our printed capital letters.

As people wrote quickly, especially with pens, the capital letters began to take the shapes of small letters. Here is a small-letter *j* that was used in the Middle Ages.

Jj *Jj*	Jj	Jj	Jj
Handwriting	Sans Serif Type	Serif Type	Computer Printing

j *or* **J** *noun* The tenth letter of the English alphabet.
j *or* **J** (jā) ◊ *noun, plural* **j's** *or* **J's**

jab *verb* To poke or pierce with something pointed: *You accidentally jabbed me with your elbow.*
◊ *noun* An act of jabbing; poke.
jab (jăb) ◊ *verb* **jabbed, jabbing** ◊ *noun, plural* **jabs**

jabber *verb* To talk in a fast, confused, or foolish way: *We jabbered for hours.*
◊ *noun* Jabbering talk.
jab·ber (jăb′ər) ◊ *verb* **jabbered, jabbering** ◊ *noun*

jacaranda *noun* A tropical American tree with pale-purple flower clusters.
jac·a·ran·da (jăk′ə **răn′** də) ◊ *noun, plural* **jacarandas**

jack *noun* **1.** A mechanical device used to raise or move a heavy object, such as an automobile, in order to change a tire. **2. jacks** (*used with a singular verb*) A children's game played with a set of small six-pointed metal pieces and a small ball. The object of the game is to pick up the pieces as the ball bounces. **3.** One of the pieces used in the game of jacks.
◊ *verb* To raise or move by or as if by a jack.
jack (jăk) ◊ *noun, plural* **jacks** ◊ *verb* **jacked, jacking**

jackal *noun* A wild animal of Africa and Asia that is similar to a coyote or a large dog. Jackals often eat what is left of the prey killed by other animals, such as lions.
jack·al (jăk′əl) ◊ *noun, plural* **jackals**

jacket *noun* **1.** A short coat. **2.** An outer covering, as for a book or record.
jack·et (jăk′ĭt) ◊ *noun, plural* **jackets**

jack-in-the-box *noun* A toy that is made of a box with a figure inside that pops up when the lid is opened.
jack-in-the-box (jăk′ĭn *th*ə bŏks′) ◊ *noun, plural* **jack-in-the-boxes**

jackknife *noun* A large pocketknife.
jack·knife (jăk′nīf′) ◊ *noun, plural* **jackknives**

jack-o'-lantern *noun* A lantern made from a hollowed-out pumpkin. A jack-o'-lantern has a carved face and a candle inside for light.
jack-o'-lan·tern (jăk′ə-lăn′tərn) ◊ *noun, plural* **jack-o'-lanterns**

▲ **jack-o'-lantern**

jackpot *noun* The top prize that is given in a game or contest.
jack·pot (jăk′pŏt′) ◊ *noun, plural* **jackpots**

jack rabbit *noun* A hare with long ears and strong legs. Jack rabbits are found in western North America and Central America.
jack rabbit ◊ *noun, plural* **jack rabbits**

▲ **jack rabbit**

jade *noun* A hard green or white stone. Jade is used for jewelry and ornamental objects.
jade (jād) ◊ *noun, plural* **jades**

jagged *adjective* Having an edge or a surface that is ragged or full of parts that stick out.
jag·ged (jăg′ĭd) ◊ *adjective*

jaguar *noun* A large wild cat with a coat that is marked with rings and spots. Jaguars are found in the southwestern United States and in parts of South America.
jag·uar (jăg′wär′) ◊ *noun, plural* **jaguars**

jail *noun* A place for keeping persons who are waiting for trial or are serving sentences for crimes.
◊ *verb* To put or keep in jail; imprison.
jail (jāl) ◊ *noun, plural* **jails** ◊ *verb* **jailed, jailing**

jam¹ *verb* **1.** To squeeze or wedge into or become stuck in a tight position: *I jammed the cork into the bottle.* **2.** To crowd or pack tightly: *Thousands of people jammed the stadium.* **3.** To bruise or crush by squeezing: *I jammed my finger in the door.* **4.** To push suddenly or hard: *The driver jammed on the brakes.*
◊ *noun* **1.** A large group of things or people crowded so close together that moving around is hard or impossible: *We got into a traffic jam.* **2.** A difficult situation: *I'm in a jam because I didn't study for the test.*
jam¹ (jăm) ◊ *verb* **jammed, jamming** ◊ *noun, plural* **jams**

jam² *noun* A sweet food made by boiling fruit and sugar together until the mixture is thick.
jam² (jăm) ◊ *noun, plural* **jams**

***HISTORY* • jam¹, jam²**

Jam¹ and **jam²** both first appeared in written English about 200 years ago. **Jam¹** may have been a word made up to sound like what it means. **Jam²** may then have come from **jam¹**, since fruit is usually mashed or "jammed together" to make **jam²**.

Jan. The abbreviation for *January.*

jangle *noun* A harsh, confused, or unpleasant sound.
◊ *verb* To make or cause to make a jangle.
jan·gle (jăng′gəl) ◊ *noun, plural* **jangles** ◊ *verb* **jangled, jangling**

janitor *noun* A person who cleans and takes care of a building.
jan·i·tor (jăn′ĭ tər) ◊ *noun, plural* **janitors**

January *noun* The first month of the year. January has 31 days.
Jan·u·ar·y (jăn′yo͞o ĕr′ē) ◊ *noun*

ă	pat	ĭ	pit	oi	**oil**	th	**bath**
ā	pay	ī	ride	o͝o	book	*th*	**bathe**
â	care	î	fierce	o͞o	boot	ə	ago, item
ä	father	ŏ	pot	ou	**out**		pencil
ĕ	pet	ō	**go**	ŭ	cut		atom
ē	be	ô	paw, for	û	fur		circus

Japanese *noun* **1.** A person who was born in or lives in Japan. **2.** The language of Japan. ◊ *adjective* Of or relating to Japan, the Japanese, or their language.
Jap·a·nese (jăp′ə nēz′) ◊ *noun, plural* **Japanese** ◊ *adjective*

jar[1] *noun* A container with a wide mouth. Jars are usually made of glass, pottery, or plastic.
jar[1] (jär) ◊ *noun, plural* **jars**

jar[2] *verb* **1.** To shake or cause to shake strongly; rock: *The explosion jarred buildings for miles.* **2.** To be upsetting or painful to: *The news that my dog was lost jarred me.* ◊ *noun* A strong shaking movement, as from being hit; jolt.
jar[2] (jär) ◊ *verb* **jarred, jarring** ◊ *noun, plural* **jars**

***HISTORY* • jar**[1]**, jar**[2]

Jar[1] goes back to an Arabic word meaning "earthen pot." The word passed through French before arriving in English. **Jar**[2] was probably a word made up to sound like what it means.

jasmine *noun* A vine or shrub with flowers that are usually very sweet smelling.
jas·mine (jăz′mĭn) ◊ *noun, plural* **jasmines**

▲ **jasmine**

jaunt *noun* A short trip taken for fun.
jaunt (jônt) ◊ *noun, plural* **jaunts**

javelin *noun* A light spear that is thrown for distance in an athletic contest.
jave·lin (jăv′lĭn) ◊ *noun, plural* **javelins**

jaw *noun* **1.** One of a pair of structures that hold the teeth and form the framework and shape of the mouth. The jaws are made of bone and cartilage. **2.** One of two parts of a device, such as a pair of pliers, that can be opened or closed like jaws.
jaw (jô) ◊ *noun, plural* **jaws**

▲ **jaw**
Skeleton of a dinosaur's jaw

jay *noun* Any of several birds related to the crow but smaller. Jays often have blue, green, or yellow feathers. They have a loud, harsh call.
jay (jā) ◊ *noun, plural* **jays**

jaywalk *verb* To cross a street in the middle of a block or when the traffic light is red.
jay·walk (jā′wôk′) ◊ *verb* **jaywalked, jaywalking**

jazz *noun* A type of music with a strong rhythm. Jazz developed in the United States from work songs, hymns, and spirituals.
jazz (jăz) ◊ *noun*

jealous *adjective* **1.** Concerned about losing someone's affection to another person: *Don't be jealous just because your best friend has other friends besides you.* **2.** Having a bad feeling toward another person who is a competitor; envious.
jeal·ous (jĕl′əs) ◊ *adjective*

jealousy *noun* A jealous feeling or attitude.
jeal·ous·y (jĕl′ə sē) ◊ *noun, plural* **jealousies**

jeans *plural noun* Trousers made of a strong, usually cotton cloth.
jeans (jēnz) ◊ *plural noun*

jeer *verb* To speak or speak to in a way that shows scorn or makes fun: *Good sports do not jeer at the members of the other teams.* ◊ *noun* A jeering sound or statement.
jeer (jîr) ◊ *verb* **jeered, jeering** ◊ *noun, plural* **jeers**

jelly *noun* A soft, semisolid food. One kind of jelly is made by boiling sugar and fruit juice along with a substance that sets or hardens the liquid.

J

◊ *verb* To make into or become jelly.
jel·ly (jĕl′ē) ◊ *noun, plural* **jellies** ◊ *verb* **jellied, jellying**

jellyfish *noun* A sea animal with a dome-shaped body that is filled with a jellylike material. Many jellyfish have long tentacles that can give an unpleasant or dangerous sting.
jel·ly·fish (jĕl′ē fĭsh′) ◊ *noun, plural* **jellyfish** *or* **jellyfishes**

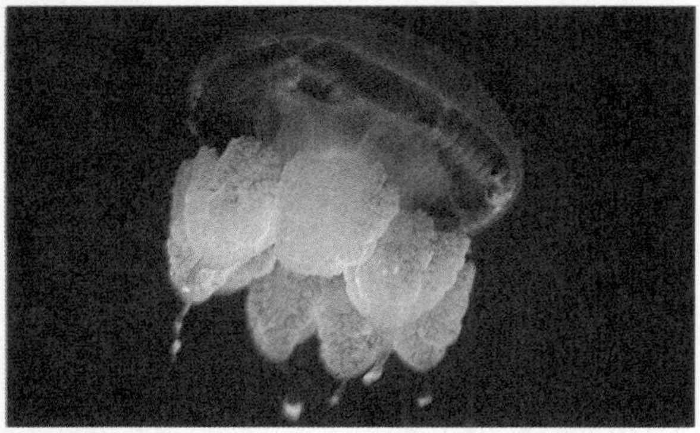

▲ **jellyfish**

jeopardize *verb* To put in jeopardy; endanger: *Don't jeopardize your health by eating junk food.*
jeop·ard·ize (jĕp′ər dīz′) ◊ *verb* **jeopardized, jeopardizing**

jeopardy *noun* Danger of dying, being injured, or being lost; peril: *The villagers' lives were in jeopardy during the blizzard.*
jeop·ard·y (jĕp′ər dē) ◊ *noun*

jerk *verb* **1.** To give a quick, sudden movement to: *I had to jerk the window open.* **2.** To make or move with sudden, sharp movements: *I felt the fishing line jerk.*
◊ *noun* A sudden, sharp motion.
jerk (jûrk) ◊ *verb* **jerked, jerking** ◊ *noun, plural* **jerks**

jerkin *noun* A short, tight jacket, usually with no sleeves. People wore jerkins until around 1700.
jer·kin (jûr′kĭn) ◊ *noun, plural* **jerkins**

ă	pat	ĭ	pit	oi	**oil**	th	**bath**
ā	pay	ī	ride	ŏŏ	book	*th*	bathe
â	care	î	fierce	ōō	boot	ə	ago, item
ä	father	ŏ	pot	ou	**out**		pencil
ĕ	pet	ō	go	ŭ	cut		atom
ē	be	ô	paw, for	û	fur		circus

jerky *adjective* Marked by or moving with jerks: *We had a jerky ride over the rough road.*
jerk·y (jûr′kē) ◊ *adjective* **jerkier, jerkiest**

jersey *noun* **1.** A soft cloth made of material such as wool or cotton. **2.** A sweater or shirt that can be pulled over the head.
jer·sey (jûr′zē) ◊ *noun, plural* **jerseys**

jest *noun* **1.** Something said or done for fun or amusement: *Nobody thought my jest about the food was funny.* **2.** A mood or manner that is not serious; playfulness.
◊ *verb* To make a jest or joke.
jest (jĕst) ◊ *noun, plural* **jests** ◊ *verb* **jested, jesting**

jester *noun* A person who was employed in former times to entertain a monarch.
jest·er (jĕs′tər) ◊ *noun, plural* **jesters**

Jesus Christ *noun* Christ.
Je·sus Christ (jē′zŭs) ◊ *noun*

jet *noun* **1.** A stream of liquid, vapor, or gas that is forced out of a small opening or nozzle by great pressure. **2.** An airplane that is propelled by a jet engine.
jet (jĕt) ◊ *noun, plural* **jets**

jet engine *noun* An engine that is driven by a jet of gases from fuel burned inside the engine itself.
jet engine ◊ *noun, plural* **jet engines**

jet-propelled *adjective* Powered or driven forward by one or more jet engines.
jet-pro·pelled (jĕt′prə **pĕld′**) ◊ *adjective*

jet stream *noun* A very strong current of winds that blows from a westerly direction seven to eight miles above the earth.

jetty *noun* **1.** A landing place, such as a pier, where ships are tied up and are loaded or unloaded. **2.** A structure, such as a wall, that is built out into a body of water. A jetty is used to protect the coast from strong waves.
jet·ty (jĕt′ē) ◊ *noun, plural* **jetties**

Jew *noun* **1.** A person whose religion is Judaism. **2.** A descendant of the Hebrew people mentioned in the Bible.
Jew (jōō) ◊ *noun, plural* **Jews**

jewel *noun* **1.** A precious stone; gem. **2.** A valuable ornament, as a ring or necklace, especially one made of precious metal and set with gems. **3.** Something or someone that is greatly admired or valued: *The island is con-*

sidered the jewel of the Caribbean Sea.
jew·el (jo͞o′əl) ◊ *noun, plural* **jewels**

jeweler *noun* A person who makes, repairs, or sells jewelry.
jew·el·er (jo͞o′ə lər) ◊ *noun, plural* **jewelers**

jewelry *noun* Ornaments, such as bracelets or necklaces, that are worn as decorations. Jewelry is made of precious metals and gems or of substitutes for them.
jew·el·ry (jo͞o′əl rē) ◊ *noun*

Jewish *adjective* Of or relating to the Jews, their religion, or their culture.
Jew·ish (jo͞o′ĭsh) ◊ *adjective*

jib *noun* A triangular sail that is set in front of the mast and stretched to the bow.
jib (jĭb) ◊ *noun, plural* **jibs**

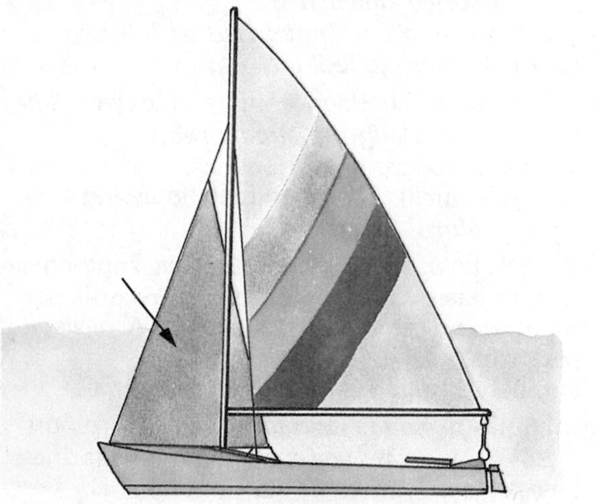

▲ **jib**

jiffy *noun* A small amount of time: *I'll be done in a jiffy.* —See Synonyms at **moment.**
jif·fy (jĭf′ē) ◊ *noun, plural* **jiffies**

jig *noun* A fast, lively dance.
jig (jĭg) ◊ *noun, plural* **jigs**

jiggle *verb* To move or cause to move up and down or back and forth with short, quick jerks: *We jiggled the latch to open the gate.*
◊ *noun* A jiggling motion.
jig·gle (jĭg′əl) ◊ *verb* **jiggled, jiggling** ◊ *noun, plural* **jiggles**

jigsaw *noun* A saw with a narrow blade that is set upright in a frame. A jigsaw is used for cutting curved or wavy lines.
jig·saw (jĭg′sô′) ◊ *noun, plural* **jigsaws**

▲ **jigsaw**

jigsaw puzzle *noun* A puzzle that is made of differently shaped pieces that are fitted together to form a picture.
jigsaw puzzle ◊ *noun, plural* **jigsaw puzzles**

jingle *verb* To make or cause to make a tinkling or ringing sound.
◊ *noun* **1.** A jingling sound. **2.** A simple, catchy verse or song, often used in radio or television commercials.
jin·gle (jĭng′gəl) ◊ *verb* **jingled, jingling** ◊ *noun, plural* **jingles**

jinx *noun* Someone or something that is felt to bring bad luck.
jinx (jĭngks) ◊ *noun, plural* **jinxes**

job *noun* **1.** A piece of work: *Who gets the job of sweeping the floor?* —See Synonyms at **task. 2.** A position of employment: *My cousin has a job in a bookstore.* **3.** Something that must be done; responsibility: *Your job is not to fall asleep while you are baby-sitting.*
job (jŏb) ◊ *noun, plural* **jobs**

jockey *noun* A person who rides horses in races.
jock·ey (jŏk′ē) ◊ *noun, plural* **jockeys**

jog *verb* **1.** To give a slight push to; nudge: *I felt someone jogging my elbow.* **2.** To run or ride at a slow, steady speed: *I jog every morning before breakfast.*
◊ *noun* **1.** A slight push; nudge. **2.** A slow, steady pace.
jog (jŏg) ◊ *verb* **jogged, jogging** ◊ *noun, plural* **jogs**

joggle *verb* To shake or cause to shake a little bit: *I joggled the catch and the door opened.*
jog·gle (jŏg′əl) ◊ *verb* **joggled, joggling**

J

join *verb* **1.** To bring or come together, as by fastening: *We joined the two pieces of the puzzle.* **2.** To become or be connected with: *Two rivers join each other near my home.* **3.** To enter into the company of: *Please join us for lunch.* **4.** To become a member of: *I would like to join the club.* **5.** To take part; participate: *Let's all join in the singing.*
join (join) ◊ *verb* **joined, joining**

> ***SYNONYMS***
>
> ***join, connect, unite***
>
> Let's *join* hands in a circle. The Panama Canal *connects* the Atlantic and Pacific Oceans. Let us *unite* into a strong group behind the cause of conservation.
> **Antonyms:** *part, separate*

joint *noun* **1.** A place where two or more bones come together. There are joints at the elbows and knees. **2.** A place where two or more things, such as pipes, come together.
◊ *adjective* Done or shared by two or more: *We made a joint effort to help them.*
joint (joint) ◊ *noun, plural* **joints** ◊ *adjective*

joke *noun* Something, such as a trick or short story, that is meant to be funny.
◊ *verb* To say or do something as a joke: *I was only joking when I said that.*
joke (jōk) ◊ *noun, plural* **jokes** ◊ *verb* **joked, joking**

jokingly *adverb* In a joking way or manner.
jok·ing·ly (jō′kĭng lē) ◊ *adverb*

jolly *adjective* Full of good spirits and fun; merry: *Santa Claus has a jolly laugh.*
jol·ly (jŏl′ē) ◊ *adjective* **jollier, jolliest**

jolt *verb* To move, ride, or cause to move in a jerky way: *The bus jolted to a stop.*
◊ *noun* **1.** A sudden jerk or bump. **2.** A feeling or something that causes a feeling of sudden shock or surprise.
jolt (jōlt) ◊ *verb* **jolted, jolting** ◊ *noun, plural* **jolts**

ă	pat	ĭ	pit	oi	**oil**	th	ba**th**
ā	pay	ī	ride	o͝o	book	*th*	ba*th*e
â	care	î	fierce	o͞o	boot	ə	ago, item
ä	father	ŏ	pot	ou	**out**		pencil
ĕ	pet	ō	go	ŭ	cut		atom
ē	be	ô	paw, for	û	fur		circus

jonquil *noun* A garden plant with sweet-smelling yellow or white flowers. Jonquils are similar to daffodils.
jon·quil (jŏng′kwĭl) ◊ *noun, plural* **jonquils**

▲ **jonquil**

jostle *verb* To shove and push against: *The crowd jostled one another as each person tried to get a good look at the movie star.*
jos·tle (jŏs′əl) ◊ *verb* **jostled, jostling**

jot *verb* To write down quickly or in a short form: *I jotted down a few notes on a pad that I had with me.*
jot (jŏt) ◊ *verb* **jotted, jotting**

jounce *verb* To bounce up and down: *The bus jounced along the bumpy road.*
◊ *noun* A rough, jolting bounce.
jounce (jouns) ◊ *verb* **jounced, jouncing** ◊ *noun, plural* **jounces**

journal *noun* **1.** A record that is kept on a regular basis. One kind of journal records personal experiences and feelings. **2.** A newspaper or magazine.
jour·nal (jûr′nəl) ◊ *noun, plural* **journals**

journalism *noun* The gathering and reporting of news, as by newspapers and magazines.
jour·nal·ism (jûr′nə lĭz′əm) ◊ *noun*

journalist *noun* A person who works in journalism, especially a reporter or editor.
jour·nal·ist (jûr′nə lĭst) ◊ *noun, plural* **journalists**

journey *noun* Travel from one place to another: *We made the long journey home.* —See Synonyms at **trip.**
◊ *verb* To make a journey.
jour·ney (jûr′nē) ◊ *noun, plural* **journeys** ◊ *verb* **journeyed, journeying**

joust *noun* A combat with lances between two knights on horses.
◊ *verb* To take part in a joust.
joust (joust) ◊ *noun, plural* **jousts** ◊ *verb* **jousted, jousting**

jovial *adjective* Full of fun and good cheer; jolly: *We had a jovial family dinner.*
jo·vi·al (jō′vē əl) ◊ *adjective*

jowl *noun* The flesh under the lower jaw, especially when plump or hanging loosely.
jowl (joul) ◊ *noun, plural* **jowls**

joy *noun* **1.** A feeling of great happiness or delight: *We felt joy at being with our family again.* **2.** A source or cause of joy: *The child was a joy to be with.*
joy (joi) ◊ *noun, plural* **joys**

> ***SYNONYMS***
>
> ***joy, delight, enjoyment, pleasure***
> We felt great *joy* at being together after so long. We took *delight* in the good news. Walking in the country is a source of constant *enjoyment* to me. I took *pleasure* in hearing my name pronounced correctly. **Antonym:** *sorrow*

joyful *adjective* Feeling, showing, or causing joy. —See Synonyms at **glad.**
joy·ful (**joi′**fəl) ◊ *adjective*

joyous *adjective* Joyful.
joy·ous (**joi′**əs) ◊ *adjective*

Jr. The abbreviation for *Junior.*

jubilant *adjective* Showing great joy and triumph: *The crowd was jubilant after the team won the game.*
ju·bi·lant (**jo͞o′**bə lənt) ◊ *adjective*

jubilee *noun* **1.** A special anniversary, such as the twenty-fifth or fiftieth, or the celebration of a special anniversary. **2.** A time of celebration.
ju·bi·lee (**jo͞o′**bə lē′) ◊ *noun, plural* **jubilees**

Judaism *noun* The religion of the Jewish people.
Ju·da·ism (**jo͞o′**də ĭz′əm) ◊ *noun*

judge *noun* **1.** A public official who listens to and makes decisions about cases in a court of law. **2.** A person who decides the winner of a contest or race. **3.** A person who knows enough to make decisions or give opinions about something: *My parents are good judges of character.*
◊ *verb* **1.** To listen to and make a decision about in a court of law: *Different kinds of courts have the power to judge different kinds of cases.* **2.** To form an opinion about: *Try not to judge others unfairly.*
judge (jŭj) ◊ *noun, plural* **judges**
◊ *verb* **judged, judging**

judgment *noun* **1.** A decision that is made in a court of law. **2.** An opinion that is formed by thinking carefully about something: *My judgment is that it is too dangerous to swim during a storm.* **3.** The ability to form opinions: *They showed good judgment in deciding not to enter the deep cave.*
judg·ment (**jŭj′**mənt) ◊ *noun, plural* **judgments**

judicial *adjective* Of or relating to judges, courts of law, or justice.
ju·di·cial (jo͞o **dĭsh′**əl) ◊ *adjective*

judicious *adjective* Having or showing good sense or judgment: *It was a judicious decision to stay home during the storm.*
ju·di·cious (jo͞o **dĭsh′**əs) ◊ *adjective*

jug *noun* A large glass, pottery, or plastic container for liquids. A jug has a narrow mouth and a small handle.
jug (jŭg) ◊ *noun, plural* **jugs**

juggle *verb* To keep two or more objects, such as balls, in the air at one time by tossing and catching them.
jug·gle (**jŭg′**əl) ◊ *verb* **juggled, juggling**

juggler *noun* A person who juggles objects in order to entertain people.
jug·gler (**jŭg′**lər) ◊ *noun, plural* **jugglers**

▲ **juggler**

juice *noun* **1.** A liquid contained in meats or in the fruit, stem, or roots of plants: *Orange juice is rich in vitamins.* **2.** Fluid, such as digestive juices, made in an animal's body.
juice (jo͞os) ◊ *noun, plural* **juices**

July *noun* The seventh month of the year. July has 31 days.
Ju·ly (jo͞o **lī′**) ◊ *noun*

jumble *verb* To mix or throw together without any neatness or order: *We jumbled all the clothes together before doing the laundry.*
◊ *noun* A group of things that is mixed or thrown together without any order.
jum·ble (**jŭm′**bəl) ◊ *verb* **jumbled, jumbling** ◊ *noun, plural* **jumbles**

jumbo *adjective* Very large: *We saw a jumbo elephant at the circus.*
jum·bo (**jŭm′**bō) ◊ *adjective*

jump *verb* **1.** To rise up or move through the air by using the leg muscles; leap: *Grasshoppers can jump very high.* **2.** To move or jerk without wanting to, as in surprise: *I jumped when I heard the noise.* **3.** To leap over: *The horse jumped the fence.*
◊ *noun* **1.** An act of jumping or the distance jumped. **2.** A sudden movement or jerk, as in surprise.
jump (jŭmp) ◊ *verb* **jumped, jumping** ◊ *noun, plural* **jumps**

jumper *noun* A dress without sleeves that is worn over a blouse or sweater.
jum·per (**jŭm′**pər) ◊ *noun, plural* **jumpers**

junction *noun* **1.** The act of joining or condition of being joined. **2.** The place where things join or meet: *There was an accident at the junction of the two highways.*
junc·tion (**jŭngk′**-shən) ◊ *noun, plural* **junctions**

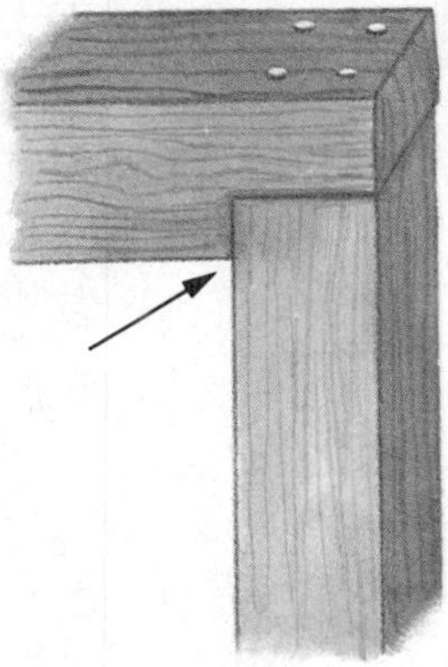

▲ **junction**

June *noun* The sixth month of the year. June has 30 days.
June (jo͞on) ◊ *noun*

jungle *noun* A heavy growth of tropical trees and plants or land that is covered with such growth.
jun·gle (**jŭng′** gəl) ◊ *noun, plural* **jungles**

▲ **jungle**

ă	pat	ĭ	pit	oi	**oil**	th	**bath**
ā	pay	ī	ride	o͝o	**book**	*th*	**bathe**
â	care	î	fierce	o͞o	**boot**	ə	**ago, item**
ä	father	ŏ	pot	ou	**out**		pencil
ĕ	pet	ō	go	ŭ	**cut**		atom
ē	be	ô	paw, for	û	**fur**		circus

junior *adjective* **1.** Of or for younger or smaller persons. **2. Junior** Younger. Used with the name of a son named after his father: *William Smith, Junior, was the eldest son of the family.* **3.** Of lower rank or shorter length of service: *My aunt is a junior partner in a law firm.* **4.** Of or relating to the third year of a four-year high school or college.
◊ *noun* **1.** A person who is younger or of lesser rank than another: *She was sixteen years his junior.* **2.** A student in the third year of a four-year high school or college.
jun·ior (**jo͞on′** yər) ◊ *adjective* ◊ *noun, plural* **juniors**

juniper *noun* An evergreen tree or shrub with small berrylike cones.
ju·ni·per (**jo͞o′** nə pər) ◊ *noun, plural* **junipers**

junk¹ *noun* Materials, such as rags or machine parts, that are thrown away but can be used again in some way.
junk¹ (jŭngk) ◊ *noun*

junk² *noun* A ship with a flat bottom that sails in the waters around Southeast Asia.
junk² (jŭngk) ◊ *noun, plural* **junks**

HISTORY **• junk¹, junk²**

Junk¹ comes from a word once used by sailors to mean "old, worn-out rope." Junk² goes back to a Southeast Asian word for "a seagoing ship." This word was taken into Portuguese and from there into English.

▲ junk²

junk food *noun* Food that is usually high in calories but is not very nutritious.
junk food ◊ *noun, plural* **junk foods**

Jupiter *noun* The planet that is fifth in distance from the sun. Jupiter is the largest planet in our solar system.
Ju·pi·ter (jōō′pĭ tər) ◊ *noun*

juror *noun* A member of a jury.
ju·ror (jŏŏr′ər) ◊ *noun, plural* **jurors**

jury *noun* **1.** A group of citizens who are chosen to listen to the facts and evidence on cases presented in a court of law. **2.** A group of judges who are given the power to pick a winner or award prizes in a contest.
ju·ry (jŏŏr′ē) ◊ *noun, plural* **juries**

just *adjective* Following what is right or fair: *A just government makes laws that are fair to the poor as well as to the rich.*
◊ *adverb* **1.** Exactly; precisely: *Do just what I told you.* **2.** At the very instant: *Just then a flash of lightning turned the whole sky white.* **3.** Only a moment ago: *The store just ran out of bread.* **4.** By a small extra amount; barely: *I just made it to the bus on time.* **5.** Nothing more than; merely: *I am just a fan of football, not a player.*
just (jŭst) ◊ *adjective* ◊ *adverb*

justice *noun* **1.** The quality of being just or fair: *Good teachers treat their students with justice.* **2.** The carrying out of the law or the way in which the law is carried out: *The courts ensure that justice is achieved.* **3.** A judge, such as one who is a member of the United States Supreme Court.
jus·tice (jŭs′tĭs) ◊ *noun, plural* **justices**

justify *verb* **1.** To show or prove to be right or just. **2.** To show to be sound or sensible.
jus·ti·fy (jŭs′tə fī′) ◊ *verb* **justified, justifying**

jut *verb* To stick sharply upward or outward: *In the desert the big cactus plants seem to jut up as high as the sky.*
jut (jŭt) ◊ *verb* **jutted, jutting**

jute *noun* A plant that grows in tropical Asia and yields a fiber that is used to make rope, twine, and rough cloth such as burlap.
jute (jōōt) ◊ *noun, plural* **jutes**

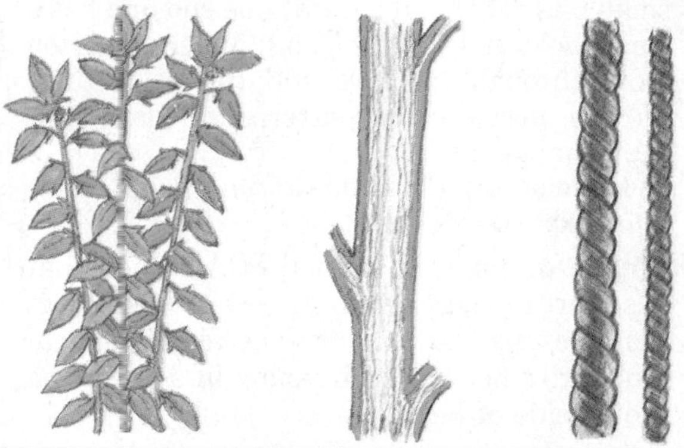

▲ jute

juvenile *adjective* **1.** Youthful; young. **2.** Immature or childish. **3.** Of or for young people.
◊ *noun* A young person.
ju·ve·nile (jōō′və nəl *or* jōō′və nīl′) ◊ *adjective* ◊ *noun, plural* **juveniles**

J

Kiwi

Kk

K is the eleventh letter of the English alphabet. Did you know that it has a long history?

Over 3,500 years ago, people in the Middle East were using symbols that became the letters of our alphabet. This ancient Middle Eastern symbol is a form of the letter that became our letter *K*.

K

The ancient Greeks borrowed their alphabet from people in the Middle East. Here is a form of the Greek letter that became our letter *K*.

K

The ancient Romans borrowed their alphabet from a people who had taken their own letter symbols from the Greeks. Here is a form of the Roman letter *K* that was used for carving letters into stone. These letters became the model for our printed capital letters.

As people wrote quickly, especially with pens, the capital letters began to take the shapes of small letters. Here is a small-letter *k* that was used in the Middle Ages.

Kk *Kk*	Kk	Kk	Kk
Handwriting	Sans Serif Type	Serif Type	Computer Printing

k, K *noun* The eleventh letter of the English alphabet.
k, K (kā) ◊ *noun, plural* **k's** *or* **K's**

kaleidoscope *noun* A tube that contains small bits of colored glass at one end and has a small hole at the other end. When a person looks through the hole and turns the tube, mirrors inside show patterns of glass that keep changing.
ka·lei·do·scope (kə lī′də skōp′) ◊ *noun, plural* **kaleidoscopes**

kangaroo *noun* An animal of Australia that has short forelegs and long, powerful hind legs that are used for leaping. The female kangaroo carries her newborn young in a pouch on the outside of her body.
kan·ga·roo (kăng′gə **ro͞o′**) ◊ *noun, plural* **kangaroos**

Kans. An abbreviation for *Kansas.*

katydid *noun* A green insect related to the grasshoppers. The males rub their front wings together to make a shrill sound.
ka·ty·did (**kā′**tē dĭd′) ◊ *noun, plural* **katydids**

kayak *noun* **1.** An Eskimo canoe made of skins stretched over a light wooden frame. The top of a kayak is closed except for an opening in the middle in which the paddler sits. **2.** A light canoe of the same design covered with canvas.
kay·ak (**kī′**ăk′) ◊ *noun, plural* **kayaks**

keel *noun* A strong piece of wood or metal that runs along the bottom of a ship or boat. ◊ *idiom* **keel over 1.** To turn upside down; capsize: *The boat pitched suddenly and keeled over.* **2.** To fall down; collapse.
keel (kēl) ◊ *noun, plural* **keels**

keen *adjective* **1.** Very quick or sensitive, especially in seeing, hearing, tasting, or smelling: *Dogs have a keen sense of smell.* **2.** Full

ă	pat	ĭ	pit	oi	**oil**	th	ba**th**
ā	pay	ī	ride	o͝o	**book**	*th*	ba**the**
â	care	î	fierce	o͞o	**boot**	ə	ago, item
ä	father	ŏ	pot	ou	**out**		pencil
ĕ	pet	ō	go	ŭ	cut		atom
ē	be	ô	paw, for	û	fur		circus

of enthusiasm and interest; eager: *My friend is a keen sports fan.*
keen (kēn) ◊ *adjective* **keener, keenest**

keep *verb* **1.** To hold in one's possession; have and not give up: *You may keep my book for a week.* **2.** To continue or cause to continue in a certain condition, position, or place: *The light kept me awake.* **3.** To continue to do: *Keep guessing until you get the right answer.* **4.** To stay fresh or unspoiled: *Most fruits don't keep long.* **5.** To move in the same way or on the same course: *Traffic keeps to the left in England.* **6.** To put in a safe, handy place: *Do you keep your money in a bank?* **7.** To take care of; manage: *We take turns keeping house.* **8.** To carry out; fulfill: *You didn't keep your word.* **9.** To prevent or stop: *The storm kept us from going to the movie.* **10.** To detain or delay: *I wonder what is keeping them.*
◊ *noun* **1.** Food, clothing, and a place to live: *They earn their keep by doing chores.* **2.** The main tower or strongest part of a castle.
◊ *idiom* **keep up 1.** To maintain the pace set by others: *I found it difficult to keep up with the rest of the class.* **2.** To maintain in good condition: *We all helped in keeping up the yard.*
keep (kēp) ◊ *verb* **kept, keeping** ◊ *noun, plural* **keeps**

SYNONYMS

keep, reserve, retain, withhold

He *kept* almost all the money that he earned. Let's *reserve* some of the food just in case we need it later. She was not sure how long she would *retain* her job. I will *withhold* money from you until you finish the job.

keeper *noun* A person who watches over, guards, or takes care of something: *My friend found a job as a zoo keeper.*
keep·er (kē′pər) ◊ *noun, plural* **keepers**

keeping *noun* **1.** Care; custody; charge: *I put my wallet in the keeping of our teacher during recess.* **2.** Agreement; harmony: *Be sure the clothes you wear to the party are in keeping with the occasion.*
keep·ing (kē′pĭng) ◊ *noun*

keepsake *noun* Something that is kept as a remembrance of a person or occasion.
keep·sake (kēp′sāk′) ◊ *noun, plural* **keepsakes**

keg *noun* A small barrel.
keg (kĕg) ◊ *noun, plural* **kegs**

kelp *noun* A large brown seaweed.
kelp (kĕlp) ◊ *noun*

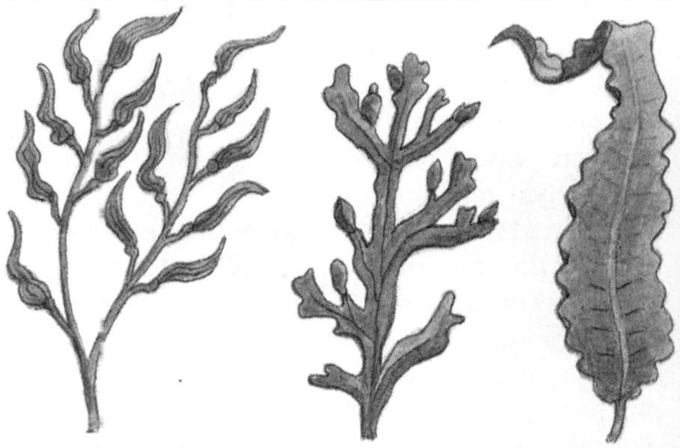

▲ **kelp**
Several kinds of kelp

kennel *noun* **1.** A small shelter for one or more dogs. **2.** Often **kennels** A place where dogs are bred, trained, or left by their owners to be cared for.
ken·nel (kĕn′əl) ◊ *noun, plural* **kennels**

kept *verb* Past tense and past participle of **keep.**
kept (kĕpt) ◊ *verb*

kerchief *noun* A square scarf worn over the head or around the neck.
ker·chief (kûr′chĭf) ◊ *noun, plural* **kerchiefs**

kernel *noun* **1.** A grain or seed, especially of corn, wheat, or a similar cereal plant. **2.** The part found inside the shell of a nut.
ker·nel (kûr′nəl) ◊ *noun, plural* **kernels**
‖*These sound alike:* **kernel, colonel**

kerosene *noun* A thin, light-colored oil that is obtained mainly from petroleum. Kerosene is used as a fuel.
ker·o·sene (kĕr′ə sēn′) ◊ *noun*

ketchup *noun* A thick spicy sauce, usually made with tomatoes, used as a seasoning.
ketch·up (kĕch′əp) ◊ *noun*

kettle *noun* A metal pot, usually with a lid, that is used for boiling liquids or for cooking.
ket·tle (kĕt′l) ◊ *noun, plural* **kettles**

K

kettledrum *noun* A large drum with a bowl-shaped brass or copper body and a top made of parchment.
ket·tle·drum (kĕt′l-drŭm′) ◊ *noun, plural* **kettledrums**

▲ **kettledrum**

key¹ *noun* **1.** A small piece of notched metal that is inserted into a lock to open or close it. **2.** A small piece of notched metal that is used to wind springs, as in toys and clocks. **3.** Something that solves a problem or explains a puzzle; solution: *The detective believes the missing gun is the key to the mystery.* **4.** The single most important element: *The key to winning the game was the last touchdown.* **5.** A list or chart that explains the symbols, colors, or abbreviations used in things such as maps. **6.** One of a set of buttons or levers pressed by the fingers to operate a machine or play a musical instrument. **7.** A group of musical tones in which all the tones are related. There is one basic tone or note in every key, and all the other tones are related to it: *The song is written in the key of D.*
◊ *adjective* Very important; chief: *Voters in three key states determined the outcome of the election.*
◊ *verb* To regulate the musical pitch of: *The musicians keyed their instruments just before the concert began.*
key¹ (kē) ◊ *noun, plural* **keys** ◊ *adjective* ◊ *verb* **keyed, keying**
‖*These sound alike:* **key, quay**

key² *noun* A low-lying island or reef along a coast.
key² (kē) ◊ *noun, plural* **keys**
‖*These sound alike:* **key, quay**

ă	pat	ĭ	pit	oi	oil	th	bath
ā	pay	ī	ride	ŏŏ	book	*th*	bathe
â	care	î	fierce	ōō	boot	ə	ago, item
ä	father	ŏ	pot	ou	out		pencil
ĕ	pet	ō	go	ŭ	cut		atom
ē	be	ô	paw, for	û	fur		circus

HISTORY • key¹, key²

Key¹ is from an old English word meaning "a device to open or close a lock." **Key²** was borrowed from a Spanish word meaning "sandbar, small island."

keyboard *noun* A set of keys, as on a piano, organ, typewriter, or computer.
key·board (kē′bôrd′) ◊ *noun, plural* **keyboards**

▲ **keyboard**

keyhole *noun* The hole in a lock where a key fits.
key·hole (kē′hōl′) ◊ *noun, plural* **keyholes**

keystone *noun* The middle stone at the top of an arch. The keystone holds or locks the other stones together.
key·stone (kē′stōn′) ◊ *noun, plural* **keystones**

khaki *noun* **1.** A yellowish brown color. **2.** A strong, heavy cloth of this color. Khaki is used for military uniforms.
khak·i (kăk′ē *or* kä′kē) ◊ *noun, plural* **khakis**

kick *verb* **1.** To strike with the foot. **2.** To lash out with the feet or hoofs. **3.** To make repeated motions with the feet or legs, as in swimming. **4.** To move something by kicking: *I kicked the football.* **5.** To spring back, as a gun does when being fired.
◊ *noun* **1.** A blow with the foot. **2.** Any of several leg movements used in swimming. **3.** The backward spring of a firearm.
kick (kĭk) ◊ *verb* **kicked, kicking** ◊ *noun, plural* **kicks**

kickoff *noun* A kick in football or soccer that begins the play.
kick·off (kĭk′ôf′) ◊ *noun, plural* **kickoffs**

kid *noun* **1.** A young goat. **2.** A child or young person.
◊ *verb* **1.** To make fun of; tease: *My friends are kidding me about being in the play.* **2.** To

be playful, amusing, or silly: *Stop kidding around.*
kid (kĭd) ◊ *noun, plural* **kids** ◊ *verb* **kidded, kidding**

kidnap *verb* To carry off and hold by force, usually for ransom.
kid·nap (**kĭd′**năp′) ◊ *verb* **kidnapped, kidnapping** *or* **kidnaped, kidnaping**

kidney *noun* Either of a pair of bodily organs that separate waste matter from the blood and pass it through the bladder in the form of urine.
kid·ney (**kĭd′**nē) ◊ *noun, plural* **kidneys**

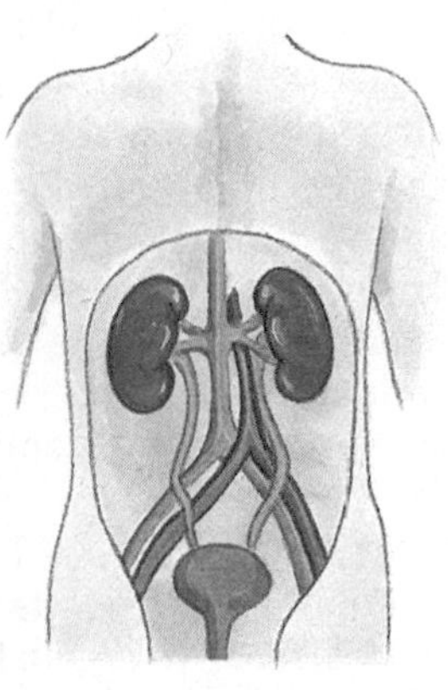
▲ kidney

kidney bean *noun* A reddish seed from the ripened pod of the common bean plant.
kidney bean ◊ *noun, plural* **kidney beans**

kill *verb* **1.** To cause the death of: *Most wild animals kill other animals only for food.* **2.** To put an end to; eliminate: *The snowstorm killed our hopes for a trip to New York.* **3.** To cause great pain to; hurt intensely: *These new boots are killing my feet.* **4.** To make time pass: *I killed two hours watching the soccer team practice.*
◊ *noun* **1.** An act of killing. **2.** Something that has been killed.
kill (kĭl) ◊ *verb* **killed, killing** ◊ *noun, plural* **kills**

killdeer *noun* A North American bird that has two dark bands across the breast. A killdeer has a call that sounds like its name.
kill·deer (**kĭl′**dîr′) ◊ *noun, plural* **killdeer** *or* **killdeers**

kiln *noun* An oven or furnace used to harden, dry, or burn pottery, bricks, grain, or lumber.
kiln (kĭln *or* kĭl) ◊ *noun, plural* **kilns**

kilo *noun* **1.** A kilogram. **2.** A kilometer.
ki·lo (**kē′**lō *or* **kĭl′**ō) ◊ *noun, plural* **kilos**

kilogram *noun* The basic unit of mass and weight in the metric system. One kilogram is equal to 1,000 grams or 2.205 pounds.
kil·o·gram (**kĭl′**ə grăm′) ◊ *noun, plural* **kilograms**

kilometer *noun* A unit of length in the metric system equal to 1,000 meters.
kil·o·me·ter (kĭ **lŏm′**ĭ tər *or* **kĭl′**ə mē′tər) ◊ *noun, plural* **kilometers**

LANGUAGE DETECTIVE

kilometer

A majority of speakers in the United States put the strongest stress on the second syllable of *kilometer,* but many others put the stress on the first syllable. Some people prefer this second pronunciation because it matches the stress in other metric words, such as *centimeter* and *millimeter.* Both pronunciations of *kilometer* have been used for more than a hundred years, and both are correct.

kilowatt *noun* A unit of electric power. A kilowatt is equal to 1,000 watts.
kil·o·watt (**kĭl′**ə wŏt′) ◊ *noun, plural* **kilowatts**

kilt *noun* A pleated skirt, usually of a tartan wool, that reaches down to the knees. Kilts are worn by men in Scotland.
kilt (kĭlt) ◊ *noun, plural* **kilts**

▲ kilt

kimono *noun* A long, loose robe that has wide sleeves and is tied with a wide sash. Kimonos are worn by men and women in Japan.
ki·mo·no (kĭ **mō′**nə) ◊ *noun, plural* **kimonos**

K

kin *noun* A person's relatives; family: *Most of my kin were at our Thanksgiving dinner.*
kin (kĭn) ◊ *noun*

kind¹ *adjective* Helpful, considerate, and gentle: *We are always kind to our neighbors. Be kind to animals.*
kind¹ (kīnd) ◊ *adjective* **kinder, kindest**

kind² *noun* **1.** A group of the same or similar things; category: *Violins compose the largest single kind of instrument in the orchestra.* **2.** Sort; type: *We're always looking for the kind of life that will make us happy.*
kind² (kīnd) ◊ *noun, plural* **kinds**

HISTORY • kind¹, kind²

Kind¹ and **kind²** are related, native English words. **Kind¹** meant "natural." During its history it came to mean "of good family" and "well brought up, generous." **Kind²** meant "family" and "group, type."

kindergarten *noun* A class for children from four to six years of age. Kindergarten prepares children for elementary school.
kin·der·gar·ten (**kĭn′** dər gär′tn) ◊ *noun, plural* **kindergartens**

kindle *verb* **1.** To start a fire: *Kindle a fire with these matches, please.* **2.** To begin to burn; catch fire: *The paper kindled on the third match.* **3.** To stir up; arouse; excite: *The speaker kindled our interest in dinosaurs.*
kin·dle (**kĭn′** dl) ◊ *verb* **kindled, kindling**

kindly *adjective* Considerate and helpful.
◊ *adverb* **1.** Out of kindness: *They kindly offered to give us a lift.* **2.** In a kind way: *They greeted us kindly.* **3.** Please: *Kindly read the report to the class.*
kind·ly (**kīnd′** lē) ◊ *adjective* **kindlier, kindliest** ◊ *adverb*

kindness *noun* **1.** The quality or condition of being kind; generosity: *The teacher's kindness made her popular with us.* **2.** A kind act; favor: *Johnny Appleseed did many kindnesses for the pioneers in addition to planting trees.*
kind·ness (**kīnd′** nĭs) ◊ *noun, plural* **kindnesses**

ă	pat	ĭ	pit	oi	**oil**	th	**bath**
ā	pay	ī	ride	ŏŏ	**book**	*th*	**bathe**
â	care	î	fierce	ōō	**boot**	ə	**ago, item**
ä	father	ŏ	pot	ou	**out**		pencil
ĕ	pet	ō	go	ŭ	**cut**		atom
ē	be	ô	paw, for	û	**fur**		circus

king *noun* **1.** A man who rules a nation. **2.** A person or thing that is regarded as the most powerful or outstanding: *The lion is the king of the jungle.* **3.** An important piece in the games of chess and checkers.
king (kĭng) ◊ *noun, plural* **kings**

kingdom *noun* **1.** A country that is ruled by a king or queen. **2.** One of the large groups into which all living things and natural substances are divided. These groups are the animal kingdom, the plant kingdom, and the mineral kingdom.
king·dom (**kĭng′** dəm) ◊ *noun, plural* **kingdoms**

kingfisher *noun* A bird with a large bill and usually a crest on its head.
king·fish·er (**kĭng′** fĭsh′ər) ◊ *noun, plural* **kingfishers**

▲ **kingfisher**

king-size *adjective* Extra large: *The milk came in a king-size container.*
king-size (**kĭng′** sīz′) ◊ *adjective*

king-sized *adjective* King-size.
king-sized (**kĭng′** sīzd′) ◊ *adjective*

kink *noun* **1.** A tight curl or sharp twist, as in a hair, wire, or rope. **2.** A pain or stiff feeling in a muscle, as in the neck or back.
◊ *verb* To form or cause to form a kink: *The animal's tail kinks at the end.*
kink (kĭngk) ◊ *noun, plural* **kinks** ◊ *verb* **kinked, kinking**

kinship *noun* A being related by blood or a shared origin: *The kinship between England and America is strong.*
kin·ship (**kĭn′**shĭp′) ◊ *noun*

kiss *verb* To touch and press with the lips as a sign of love, affection, greeting, or respect. ◊ *noun* **1.** A touch with the lips. **2.** A small piece of candy, especially of chocolate.
kiss (kĭs) ◊ *verb* **kissed, kissing** ◊ *noun, plural* **kisses**

kit *noun* **1.** A set of parts or materials to be assembled: *You can buy a stereo kit.* **2.** A compact set of tools and materials for a certain purpose: *I bought a new sewing kit.*
kit (kĭt) ◊ *noun, plural* **kits**

kitchen *noun* A room where food is cooked or prepared.
kitch·en (**kĭch′** ən) ◊ *noun, plural* **kitchens**

kitchenette *noun* A small kitchen.
kitch·en·ette (kĭch′ə **nĕt′**) ◊ *noun, plural* **kitchenettes**

kite *noun* A light frame, as of wood, covered with paper or plastic. A kite is flown in the wind at the end of a long string.
kite (kīt) ◊ *noun, plural* **kites**

▲ **kite**

kitten *noun* A young cat.
kit·ten (**kĭt′**n) ◊ *noun, plural* **kittens**

km The abbreviation for *kilometer.*

knack *noun* A special talent or skill: *The new mayor has the knack of getting along with many different people.*
knack (năk) ◊ *noun, plural* **knacks**

knapsack *noun* A canvas or leather bag that is designed to be carried on the back. A knapsack is used to hold supplies, as on a hike or march.
knap·sack (**năp′**săk′) ◊ *noun, plural* **knapsacks**

▲ **knapsack**

knead *verb* **1.** To mix and work a substance, as by folding, stretching, or pressing it: *We helped to knead the bread dough.* **2.** To squeeze, press, or roll with the hands, as in massaging: *After the hike I had to knead my leg muscles to get the soreness out of them.*
knead (nēd) ◊ *verb* **kneaded, kneading**
‖*These sound alike:* **knead, need**

knee *noun* **1.** The joint where the human thigh and lower leg come together. **2.** Something that looks like a knee.
knee (nē) ◊ *noun, plural* **knees**

kneecap *noun* A small, movable bone at the front of the knee.
knee·cap (**nē′**kăp′) ◊ *noun, plural* **kneecaps**

kneel *verb* To rest or get down on a bent knee or knees: *We knelt around the campfire.*
kneel (nēl) ◊ *verb* **knelt** *or* **kneeled, kneeling**

knelt *verb* A past tense and a past participle of **kneel.**
knelt (nĕlt) ◊ *verb*

knew *verb* Past tense of **know.**
knew (no͞o *or* nyo͞o) ◊ *verb*
‖*These sound alike:* **knew, gnu, new**

K

knickers *plural noun* Loose, short trousers with legs gathered in just below the knee.
knick·ers (**nĭk′** ərz) ◊ *plural noun*

knickknack *noun* A small ornament.
knick·knack (**nĭk′** năk′) ◊ *noun, plural* **knickknacks**

knife *noun* **1.** A device made of a sharp blade attached to a handle. A knife is used for cutting or carving. **2.** The cutting edge of a machine; blade.
◊ *verb* To cut with a knife.
knife (nīf) ◊ *noun, plural* **knives** ◊ *verb* **knifed, knifing**

knight *noun* **1.** A soldier in the Middle Ages who served and pledged loyalty to a king or lord. In return, the knight was given the right to hold land. **2.** A man in Great Britain who is given the title "knight" by a sovereign for great achievements or service to the country. **3.** A piece in the game of chess.
◊ *verb* To make a person a knight.
knight (nīt) ◊ *noun, plural* **knights** ◊ *verb* **knighted, knighting**
‖*These sound alike:* **knight, night**

knighthood *noun* **1.** The rank of a knight. **2.** Knights as a group.
knight·hood (**nīt′** ho͝od′) ◊ *noun*

knit *verb* **1.** To make a fabric or garment by interlocking yarn or thread in connected loops with special needles, either by hand or by machine: *I am knitting a sweater. Can you knit?* **2.** To draw together in wrinkles: *Try not to knit your brows when you're nervous.* **3.** To grow or bind together: *The broken leg is knitting quickly.*
◊ *noun* A knitted fabric or garment.
knit (nĭt) ◊ *verb* **knit** *or* **knitted, knitting** ◊ *noun, plural* **knits**

knives *noun* Plural of **knife.**
knives (nīvz) ◊ *noun*

knob *noun* **1.** A rounded lump or mass, as on the trunk of a tree. **2.** A rounded dial or handle, as for operating a television or stereo or for opening a drawer or door.
knob (nŏb) ◊ *noun, plural* **knobs**

knock *verb* **1.** To hit with a hard blow or blows: *The batter knocked the ball out of the park.* **2.** To make a loud noise by hitting a hard surface; rap: *I knocked and knocked, but nobody came to the door.* **3.** To hit and cause to fall: *I accidentally knocked over a vase.*
◊ *noun* **1.** A sharp blow: *When I fell I got a terrible knock on the head.* **2.** A rap, as on a door: *We waited for our guest's knock before lighting the candles on the birthday cake.*
knock (nŏk) ◊ *verb* **knocked, knocking** ◊ *noun, plural* **knocks**

knocker *noun* A metal ring or knob attached to a door by a hinge for use in knocking.
knock·er (**nŏk′** ər) ◊ *noun, plural* **knockers**

knoll *noun* A small, rounded hill.
knoll (nōl) ◊ *noun, plural* **knolls**

knot *noun* **1.** A fastening made by tying together one or more pieces of string, rope, or twine. **2.** A tightly twisted roll or clump; tangle: *The dog's fur is full of knots.* **3.** A tight cluster of persons or things: *A knot of spectators stood outside the courtroom.* **4.** A hard spot in wood, darker in color than the surrounding wood. **5.** A unit of speed used by ships and aircraft. A knot is equal to about 6,076 feet per hour.
◊ *verb* To tie or fasten in or with a knot: *I knotted my shoelaces tighter.*
knot (nŏt) ◊ *noun, plural* **knots** ◊ *verb* **knotted, knotting**
‖*These sound alike:* **knot, not**

knothole *noun* A hole in a piece of lumber where a knot has dropped out.
knot·hole (**nŏt′** hōl′) ◊ *noun, plural* **knotholes**

knotty *adjective* **1.** Having many knots: *The floor was made of knotty pine.* **2.** Difficult to solve: *The teacher gave the class a knotty arithmetic problem.*
knot·ty (**nŏt′** ē) ◊ *adjective* **knottier, knottiest**

▲ **knothole**

ă	pat	ĭ	pit	oi	**oil**	th	**bath**
ā	pay	ī	ride	o͝o	**book**	*th*	**bathe**
â	care	î	fierce	o͞o	**boot**	ə	**ago, item**
ä	father	ŏ	pot	ou	**out**		pencil
ĕ	pet	ō	go	ŭ	cut		atom
ē	be	ô	paw, for	û	fur		circus

know *verb* **1.** To understand or have the facts about: *Do you know what causes thunder?* **2.** To be sure: *I know that I'm right.* **3.** To be acquainted or familiar with: *We knew the roads around the lake very well.* **4.** To have skill in or a practical understanding of: *Many people in France know two or more languages.* **5.** To be able to tell apart from others: *I know the house by its red shutters.*
know (nō) ◊ *verb* **knew, known, knowing**
‖ *These sound alike:* **know, no**

know-how *noun* The knowledge and skill required to do something correctly.
know-how (**nō′**hou′) ◊ *noun*

know-it-all *noun* A person who claims to know everything.
know-it-all (**nō′**ĭt ôl′) ◊ *noun, plural* **know-it-alls**

knowledge *noun* **1.** Facts and ideas; information: *Listening in class is a good way to increase your general knowledge.* **2.** Understanding; awareness: *The knowledge that the knife was sharp made me handle it carefully.*
knowl·edge (**nŏl′**ĭj) ◊ *noun*

known *verb* Past participle of **know.**
known (nōn) ◊ *verb*

knuckle *noun* A joint of a finger, especially one of the joints connecting a finger to the rest of the hand.
knuck·le (**nŭk′**əl) ◊ *noun, plural* **knuckles**

koala *noun* A small, furry animal of Australia. Koalas live in eucalyptus trees and feed almost entirely on their leaves and bark. A koala looks like a small bear and the female carries its newborn young in a pouch.
ko·a·la (kō **ä′**lē) ◊ *noun, plural* **koalas**

▲ **koala**

Koran *noun* The sacred book of Islam.
Ko·ran (kô **răn′** *or* kô **rän′**) ◊ *noun*

Korean *noun* **1.** A person who was born in or lives in Korea. **2.** The language of Korea. ◊ *adjective* Of or relating to Korea, the Koreans, or their language.
Ko·re·an (kô **rē′**ən) ◊ *noun, plural* **Koreans** ◊ *adjective*

kosher *adjective* **1.** Following or prepared according to Jewish laws. **2.** Preparing or selling kosher food.
ko·sher (**kō′**shər) ◊ *adjective*

KS The abbreviation for *Kansas* used with a Zip Code.

KY The abbreviation for *Kentucky* used with a Zip Code.

Ky. An abbreviation for *Kentucky.*

K

Leopard

Ll

L is the twelfth letter of the English alphabet. Did you know that it has a long history?

Over 3,500 years ago, people in the Middle East were using symbols that became the letters of our alphabet. This ancient Middle Eastern symbol is a form of the letter that became our letter *L*.

The ancient Greeks borrowed their alphabet from people in the Middle East. Here is a form of the Greek letter that became our letter *L*.

The ancient Romans borrowed their alphabet from a people who had taken their own letter symbols from the Greeks. Here is a form of the Roman letter *L* that was used for carving letters into stone. These letters became the model for our printed capital letters.

As people wrote quickly, especially with pens, the capital letters began to take the shapes of small letters. Here is a small-letter *l* that was developed about 1,200 years ago.

Ll *Ll*	Ll	Ll	Ll
Handwriting	Sans Serif Type	Serif Type	Computer Printing

l *or* **L** *noun* **1.** The twelfth letter of the English alphabet. **2.** The Roman numeral for the number 50.
l *or* **L** (ĕl) ◊ *noun, plural* **l's** *or* **L's**

L The abbreviation for *liter.*

la *noun* The sixth note of the musical scale.
la (lä) ◊ *noun*

LA The abbreviation for *Louisiana* used with a Zip Code.

La. An abbreviation for *Louisiana.*

lab *noun* A laboratory.
lab (lăb) ◊ *noun, plural* **labs**

label *noun* A tag or sticker that is attached to something to tell what it is or what it contains: *The label lists the contents of the can.*
◊ *verb* **1.** To attach a label to: *We labeled each of the jars in our experiment.* **2.** To name or describe with a word or phrase.
la·bel (lā′ bəl) ◊ *noun, plural* **labels** ◊ *verb* **labeled, labeling**

labor *noun* **1.** Hard work: *It took months of labor to dig the tunnel.* **2.** Working people or their union representatives: *Labor supported the bill in Congress.*
◊ *verb* **1.** To work hard: *We labored to learn our lines in the school play.* **2.** To move or act with great effort; struggle: *The train labored up the steep slope.*
la·bor (lā′ bər) ◊ *noun, plural* **labors** ◊ *verb* **labored, laboring**

laboratory *noun* A room or building with special equipment for doing scientific tests and experiments.
lab·o·ra·to·ry (**lăb′** rə tôr′ē) ◊ *noun, plural* **laboratories**

Labor Day *noun* A legal holiday in honor of workers that comes on the first Monday in September.

ă	pat	ĭ	pit	oi	**oi**l	th	ba**th**
ā	pay	ī	ride	o͝o	b**oo**k	*th*	ba**the**
â	care	î	fierce	o͞o	b**oo**t	ə	ago, item
ä	father	ŏ	pot	ou	**ou**t		pencil
ĕ	pet	ō	go	ŭ	c**u**t		atom
ē	be	ô	paw, for	û	f**u**r		circus

labor union *noun* A workers' organization that is formed to protect their interests, such as better wages and working conditions.
labor union ◊ *noun, plural* **labor unions**

lace *noun* **1.** A cord or string that is threaded through holes or around hooks to hold two sides of something together. **2.** A delicate fabric woven in an open, weblike pattern.
◊ *verb* To fasten or tie with a lace.
lace (lās) ◊ *noun, plural* **laces** ◊ *verb* **laced, lacing**

lack *verb* **1.** To be without; not have: *They lacked the curiosity to try the experiment themselves.* **2.** To be in need of: *The town lacked an adequate water supply.*
◊ *noun* An absence or shortage: *The lack of rain caused the crops to die.*
lack (lăk) ◊ *verb* **lacked, lacking** ◊ *noun, plural* **lacks**

lacquer *noun* A liquid coating that is put on wood or metal to give it a glossy finish.
lac·quer (lăk′ər) ◊ *noun, plural* **lacquers**

lacrosse *noun* A game played with long sticks that have mesh pockets for catching, carrying, and throwing a ball. Points are scored in lacrosse by throwing the ball into the opposing team's goal.
la·crosse (lə krôs′) ◊ *noun*

▲ **lacrosse**

lad *noun* A boy or young man.
lad (lăd) ◊ *noun, plural* **lads**

ladder *noun* A device for climbing, made of two long side pieces joined by short rods or bars that serve as steps.
lad·der (lăd′ər) ◊ *noun, plural* **ladders**

laden *adjective* Weighed down with a load.
lad·en (lād′n) ◊ *adjective*

ladle *noun* A spoon with a long handle and a bowl shaped like a cup.
la·dle (lād′l) ◊ *noun, plural* **ladles**

lady *noun* **1.** A woman: *A lady on the bus gave us directions.* **2.** A rich woman or one of high social position. **3.** A girl or woman who has polite manners. **4.** A British noblewoman. **5. Lady** A title for a woman of noble rank.
la·dy (lā′dē) ◊ *noun, plural* **ladies**

ladybug *noun* A small, usually red or yellow beetle that has black spots. The ladybug feeds on insects that are harmful to plants.
la·dy·bug (lā′dē bŭg′) ◊ *noun, plural* **ladybugs**

▲ **ladybug**

lag *verb* To fall behind; move slowly: *The youngest children lagged behind.*
◊ *noun* The act of falling behind; delay.
lag (lăg) ◊ *verb* **lagged, lagging** ◊ *noun, plural* **lags**

lagoon *noun* A shallow body of water along a coast or shore.
la·goon (lə go͞on′) ◊ *noun, plural* **lagoons**

laid *verb* Past tense and past participle of **lay**[1].
laid (lād) ◊ *verb*

lain *verb* Past participle of **lie**[1].
lain (lān) ◊ *verb*
‖*These sound alike:* **lain, lane**

lair *noun* The den or home of a wild animal.
lair (lâr) ◊ *noun, plural* **lairs**

lake *noun* A body of fresh or salt water surrounded by land.
lake (lāk) ◊ *noun, plural* **lakes**

lamb *noun* **1.** A young sheep. **2.** The meat of a lamb.
lamb (lăm) ◊ *noun, plural* **lambs**

lame *adjective* **1.** Not able to walk well; limping: *I was lame after I twisted my ankle.* **2.** Stiff and sore: *Chopping wood gave me a*

L

lame elbow. **3.** Not satisfactory; poor: *That's a lame excuse for being late.*
◊ *verb* To make lame; cripple.
lame (lām) ◊ *adjective* **lamer, lamest** ◊ *verb* **lamed, laming**

lamp *noun* A device that gives off light. Many lamps use electricity to light a bulb or tube. Others burn a fuel, such as oil or gas.
lamp (lămp) ◊ *noun, plural* **lamps**

lance *noun* A long spear used for fighting on horseback.
◊ *verb* To pierce or cut open with a sharp blade: *The nurse lanced the boil.*
lance (lăns) ◊ *noun, plural* **lances** ◊ *verb* **lanced, lancing**

land *noun* **1.** The part of the earth's surface not covered by water. **2.** A particular area of the earth: *Antarctica is a land of ice and snow.* **3.** A country; nation. **4.** Earth; ground: *The farm stood on fertile land.*
◊ *verb* **1.** To come or bring to shore: *The boat landed at the dock.* **2.** To come down or bring to rest on a surface: *The pilot landed the plane safely.* **3.** To succeed in catching or getting: *I hooked a fish but I couldn't land it.*
land (lănd) ◊ *noun, plural* **lands** ◊ *verb* **landed, landing**

landing *noun* **1.** The act of coming to land or of coming to rest after a voyage or flight: *The jet made a landing on the aircraft carrier.* **2.** A place, as a wharf or pier, where boats load and unload. **3.** A level area at the top or bottom of a flight of stairs.
land·ing (lăn′dĭng) ◊ *noun, plural* **landings**

landing field *noun* An area of level land used by aircraft for landing and taking off.
landing field ◊ *noun, plural* **landing fields**

landlady *noun* A woman who owns property, as a house or apartment, that she rents out.
land·la·dy (lănd′lā′dē) ◊ *noun, plural* **landladies**

landlocked *adjective* Entirely or almost entirely surrounded by land: *Bolivia is a landlocked country. We fished for landlocked salmon.*
land·locked (lănd′lŏkt′) ◊ *adjective*

landlord *noun* A man who owns property, as a house or apartment, that he rents out.
land·lord (lănd′lôrd′) ◊ *noun, plural* **landlords**

landmark *noun* **1.** A familiar or easily seen object or building that marks or identifies a place: *The Golden Gate Bridge is a landmark of San Francisco.* **2.** An important event: *The first moon walk was a landmark in the exploration of space.*
land·mark (lănd′märk′) ◊ *noun, plural* **landmarks**

landscape *noun* **1.** A stretch of land that is viewed as scenery: *We watched the desert landscape from the car window.* **2.** A picture of natural scenery.
◊ *verb* To make a piece of land more beautiful or useful, as by planting trees.
land·scape (lănd′skāp′) ◊ *noun, plural* **landscapes** ◊ *verb* **landscaped, landscaping**

landslide *noun* **1.** The sliding of loose earth and rock down a steep slope. **2.** A majority of votes for the winning side in an election.
land·slide (lănd′slīd′) ◊ *noun, plural* **landslides**

lane *noun* **1.** A narrow path or road between fences, hedges, or walls. **2.** A set route, as for ships or aircraft. **3.** A division of a road used by traffic going in one direction. **4.** The part of a bowling alley down which the ball is rolled.
lane (lān) ◊ *noun, plural* **lanes**
‖*These sound alike:* **lane, lain**

language *noun* **1.** Spoken or written human speech. People use language to communicate thoughts and feelings. **2.** A system of words and expressions shared by a people: *People in many countries speak the English language.* **3.** A system of signs or symbols other than words that is used in special kinds of communication: *Many deaf people speak in sign language.* **4.** A computer language.
lan·guage (lăng′gwĭj) ◊ *noun, plural* **languages**

language arts *plural noun* School subjects, such as reading, spelling, and writing, that are designed to improve a student's use of the language.

ă	pat	ĭ	pit	oi	**oi**l	th	ba**th**
ā	pay	ī	ride	ŏŏ	b**oo**k	*th*	ba**the**
â	care	î	fierce	ōō	b**oo**t	ə	**a**go, it**e**m
ä	father	ŏ	pot	ou	**ou**t		penc**i**l
ĕ	pet	ō	go	ŭ	c**u**t		at**o**m
ē	be	ô	paw, for	û	f**u**r		circ**u**s

lantern *noun* A portable container for holding a light, with sides that let the light shine through.
lan·tern (**lăn′** tərn) ◊ *noun, plural* **lanterns**

▲ **lantern**

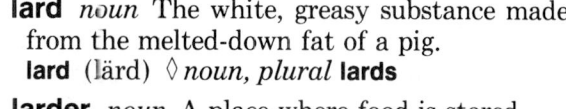

lap¹ *noun* The front part of a sitting person's body from the waist to the knees.
lap¹ (lăp) ◊ *noun, plural* **laps**

lap² *verb* To place or be placed partly over something else; overlap. ◊ *noun* **1.** A part that overlaps another part. **2.** One time over or around something: *I dived into the pool and swam three laps.*
lap² (lăp) ◊ *verb* **lapped, lapping** ◊ *noun, plural* **laps**

lap³ *verb* **1.** To take up with the tip of the tongue: *The kitten lapped up the milk.* **2.** To wash or splash with a light, slapping sound. ◊ *noun* The sound or action of lapping.
lap³ (lăp) ◊ *verb* **lapped, lapping** ◊ *noun, plural* **laps**

***HISTORY* • lap¹, lap², lap³**

Lap¹ comes from an old English word that meant "a flap or fold in clothes." **Lap²** probably comes from **lap¹**. **Lap³** comes from a different old English word that meant "to drink."

lapel *noun* One of the two turned-back flaps of a collar front.
la·pel (lə **pĕl′**) ◊ *noun, plural* **lapels**

lapse *noun* **1.** A slight slip, error, or failure: *I had a lapse of memory.* **2.** Passage of time. ◊ *verb* To pass or fall little by little: *We talked nonstop at first, but soon we lapsed into silence.*
lapse (lăps) ◊ *noun, plural* **lapses** ◊ *verb* **lapsed, lapsing**

larch *noun* A tall tree with cones that sheds its needles every year.
larch (lärch) ◊ *noun, plural* **larches**

lard *noun* The white, greasy substance made from the melted-down fat of a pig.
lard (lärd) ◊ *noun, plural* **lards**

larder *noun* A place where food is stored.
lar·der (**lär′** dər) ◊ *noun, plural* **larders**

large *adjective* Bigger than average in size or amount: *The zoo has large animals such as hippos and elephants.* —See Synonyms at **big.**
large (lärj) ◊ *adjective* **larger, largest**

large intestine *noun* The lower part of the intestine that absorbs water from undigested food.

lariat *noun* A lasso.
lar·i·at (**lăr′** ē ət) ◊ *noun, plural* **lariats**

lark¹ *noun* A European songbird that often sings as it flies high in the air.
lark¹ (lärk) ◊ *noun, plural* **larks**

lark² *noun* A merry adventure or a prank done for fun.
lark² (lärk) ◊ *noun, plural* **larks**

***HISTORY* • lark¹, lark²**

Lark¹ comes from an old English name for this bird. **Lark²** may come from an old Scandinavian word meaning "to play."

larkspur *noun* A tall plant that has a long cluster of usually blue or purplish flowers.
lark·spur (**lärk′** spûr′) ◊ *noun, plural* **larkspurs**

▲ **larkspur**

larva *noun* The wingless, often wormlike form of a newly hatched insect. Caterpillars and grubs are insect larvae.
lar·va (**lär′** və) ◊ *noun, plural* **larvae** *or* **larvas**

larvae *noun* A plural of **larva.**
lar·vae (**lär′** vē) ◊ *noun*

laryngitis *noun* An inflammation of the larynx. Laryngitis causes hoarseness and sometimes a temporary loss of the voice.
lar·yn·gi·tis (lăr′ən **jī′** tĭs) ◊ *noun*

larynx *noun* The upper part of the windpipe, in which the vocal cords are located.
lar•ynx (lăr′ĭngks) ◊ *noun, plural* **larynxes**

laser *noun* A device that sends out a very narrow and extremely powerful beam of light. Laser beams are used to cut through steel and perform delicate surgery.
la•ser (lā′zər) ◊ *noun, plural* **lasers**

lash[1] *noun* **1.** A stroke or blow with a whip. **2.** A whiplike movement. **3.** An eyelash.
◊ *verb* To wave, move, or strike in a sudden or violent way.
lash[1] (lăsh) ◊ *noun, plural* **lashes** ◊ *verb* **lashed, lashing**

lash[2] *verb* To fasten firmly with ropes.
lash[2] (lăsh) ◊ *verb* **lashed, lashing**

***HISTORY* • lash[1], lash[2]**

Lash[1] may originally have been a verb made up to imitate a sound. **Lash**[2] comes from a French word that came from a Latin word meaning "to snare." It is related to **lace.**

lass *noun* A girl or young woman.
lass (lăs) ◊ *noun, plural* **lasses**

lasso *noun* A long rope with a noose at one end that is used to catch horses and cattle.
◊ *verb* To catch with a lasso.
las•so (**lăs′**ō *or* lă **sōō′**) ◊ *noun, plural* **lassos** *or* **lassoes** ◊ *verb* **lassoed, lassoing**

last[1] *adjective* **1.** Coming, being, or placed after all others; final: *We won the last game of the season.* **2.** Being the only one left: *You ate the last apple in the bowl.* **3.** Just past: *I went skating last night.*
◊ *adverb* **1.** At the end: *Beat the eggs, stir in the sugar, and last add the flour.* **2.** Most recently: *You were sick when I last saw you.*
◊ *noun* Someone or something that is last.
◊ *idiom* **at last** After a long time or wait.
last[1] (lăst) ◊ *adjective* ◊ *adverb* ◊ *noun*

ă	pat	ĭ	pit	oi	**oi**l	th	ba**th**
ā	pay	ī	ride	ŏŏ	b**oo**k	*th*	ba**the**
â	care	î	fierce	ōō	b**oo**t	ə	ago, item
ä	father	ŏ	pot	ou	**ou**t		pencil
ĕ	pet	ō	go	ŭ	cut		atom
ē	be	ô	paw, for	û	fur		circus

SYNONYMS

last*[1]*, final
That is the *last* pencil in the box. My *final* word is that I do not want to hear about this again. **Antonym:** *first*

last[2] *verb* **1.** To continue for a time: *The first airplane flight lasted 12 seconds.* **2.** To continue to be in good or usable condition: *A few of the ancient Roman roads have lasted until today.*
last[2] (lăst) ◊ *verb* **lasted, lasting**

***HISTORY* • last[1], last[2]**

Last[1] comes from an old English word that was the earlier form of **latest. Last**[2] comes from an old English word that meant "to follow, endure."

latch *noun* A movable bar that is used to hold a door, gate, or window closed.
◊ *verb* To close or fasten with a latch.
latch (lăch) ◊ *noun, plural* **latches** ◊ *verb* **latched, latching**

late *adjective* **1.** Coming after the expected, usual, or proper time: *We were late for school.* **2.** Being near or toward the end of a time period: *We left in the late afternoon.* **3.** Of a time just past: *This truck is a late model.*
◊ *adverb* **1.** After the usual, expected, or proper time: *The train arrived late.* **2.** Near or toward the end: *Our team scored the winning run late in the game.*
late (lāt) ◊ *adjective, adverb* **later, latest**

lately *adverb* In the near past; recently.
late•ly (lāt′lē) ◊ *adverb*

lateral *adjective* On, of, toward, or from the side: *The quarterback threw a lateral pass.*
lat•er•al (lăt′ər əl) ◊ *adjective*

lathe *noun* A machine for holding a piece of wood or metal while turning it against a cutting tool that shapes it.
lathe (lā*th*) ◊ *noun, plural* **lathes**

lather *noun* **1.** A thick, creamy foam made by mixing soap and water. **2.** Foam from heavy sweating, especially on a horse.
◊ *verb* **1.** To cover with lather. **2.** To form lather.

lath·er (lă*th*′ər) ◊ *noun, plural* **lathers** ◊ *verb* **lathered, lathering**

Latin *noun* **1.** The language of ancient Rome. Latin developed into several important modern languages, including French, Italian, and Spanish. **2.** A member of a people whose language developed from Latin.
◊ *adjective* **1.** Of or relating to the language of the ancient Romans. **2.** Of or relating to the Latins.
Lat·in (lăt′n) ◊ *noun, plural* **Latins** ◊ *adjective*

Latin American *noun* A person who was born in or lives in Latin America.
Latin American ◊ *noun, plural* **Latin Americans**

Latin-American *adjective* Of or relating to Latin America or the Latin Americans.
Lat·in-A·mer·i·can (lăt′n ə **mĕr′**ĭ kən) ◊ *adjective*

latitude *noun* **1.** Distance north or south of the equator measured in degrees. **2.** Freedom of action, speech, or choice.
lat·i·tude (**lăt′**ĭ to͞od′ *or* **lăt′**ĭ tyo͞od′) ◊ *noun, plural* **latitudes**

latter *adjective* **1.** Being the second of two things mentioned: *Of swimming and tennis, I prefer the latter.* **2.** Being closer to the end: *The latter part of the book is the best.*
lat·ter (**lăt′**ər) ◊ *adjective*

lattice *noun* An open framework made of thin strips of wood or metal that cross each other in a regular pattern.
lat·tice (**lăt′**ĭs) ◊ *noun, plural* **lattices**

laugh *verb* To smile and make sounds in the throat to express amusement or scorn.
◊ *noun* The act or sound of laughing.
laugh (lăf) ◊ *verb* **laughed, laughing** ◊ *noun, plural* **laughs**

laughable *adjective* Causing or likely to cause laughter or amusement. —See Synonyms at **funny.**
laugh·a·ble (**lăf′**ə bəl) ◊ *adjective*

laughter *noun* The act or sound of laughing.
laugh·ter (**lăf′**tər) ◊ *noun*

launch¹ *verb* **1.** To throw: *The coach taught us how to launch a javelin.* **2.** To send forcefully upward, as a rocket. **3.** To set afloat: *The new ship was launched today.* **4.** To begin or start: *We launched a new project.*
◊ *noun* The act of launching something.
launch¹ (lônch) ◊ *verb* **launched, launching** ◊ *noun, plural* **launches**

launch² *noun* A motorboat.
launch² (lônch) ◊ *noun, plural* **launches**

> ***HISTORY* • launch¹, launch²**
>
> **Launch¹** comes from an old French word that meant "to throw." It is related to **lance. Launch²** comes from a Portuguese word for a small boat.

launching pad *noun* The platform from which a rocket or space vehicle is launched.
launching pad ◊ *noun, plural* **launching pads**

launder *verb* To wash and iron clothes.
laun·der (**lôn′**dər) ◊ *verb* **laundered, laundering**

laundry *noun* **1.** A place or business where laundering is done. **2.** Clothes that must be washed or that have just been washed.
laun·dry (**lôn′**drē) ◊ *noun, plural* **laundries**

laurel *noun* **1.** A European shrub or tree with glossy, spicy-smelling evergreen leaves that were once used to make victory wreaths. **2. laurels** Honors; glory.
lau·rel (**lôr′**əl) ◊ *noun, plural* **laurels**

▲ **laurel**

lava *noun* **1.** Molten rock that flows from a volcano. **2.** The rock formed when this substance cools and hardens.
la·va (**lä′**və) ◊ *noun, plural* **lavas**

lavatory *noun* A room where one may wash and use the toilet.
lav·a·to·ry (**lăv′** ə tôr′ē) ◊ *noun, plural* **lavatories**

lavender *noun* **1.** A plant with small, sweet-smelling, purplish flowers that yield an oil used in perfume. **2.** A pale purple color.
◊ *adjective* Pale purple in color.
lav·en·der (lăv′ən dər) ◊ *noun, plural* **lavenders** ◊ *adjective*

lavish *adjective* Being much more than is needed: *Don't give me such a lavish helping.*
◊ *verb* To give much more than is needed.
lav·ish (lăv′ĭsh) ◊ *adjective* ◊ *verb* **lavished, lavishing**

law *noun* **1.** A rule that regulates the behavior or activities of a group of people. **2.** A set or system of such rules. **3.** The study, knowledge, or profession of law.
law (lô) ◊ *noun, plural* **laws**

lawful *adjective* Allowed or recognized by law.
law·ful (lô′fəl) ◊ *adjective*

lawn *noun* A piece of ground, as near a house or in a park, planted with grass.
lawn (lôn) ◊ *noun, plural* **lawns**

lawnmower *noun* A machine that cuts grass.
lawn·mow·er (lôn′mō′ər) ◊ *noun, plural* **lawnmowers**

lawsuit *noun* A question, claim, or complaint brought before a court of law.
law·suit (lô′so͞ot′) ◊ *noun, plural* **lawsuits**

lawyer *noun* A person who is trained and qualified to give legal advice to people and to represent them in court.
law·yer (lô′yər) ◊ *noun, plural* **lawyers**

lay¹ *verb* **1.** To put or set down: *You can lay your books on my desk.* **2.** To bring or knock down: *The storm laid the corn flat.* **3.** To put in place: *We helped lay new tiles in the bathroom.* **4.** To produce an egg.
◊ *idioms* **lay away 1.** To save for future use. **2.** To put aside merchandise until it is paid for. **lay off** To dismiss from a job, usually temporarily.
lay¹ (lā) ◊ *verb* **laid, laying**
‖*These sound alike:* **lay, lei**

ă	pat	ĭ	pit	oi	**oil**	th	**bath**
ā	pay	ī	ride	o͝o	**book**	*th*	**bathe**
â	care	î	fierce	o͞o	**boot**	ə	**ago, item**
ä	father	ŏ	pot	ou	**out**		pencil
ĕ	pet	ō	**go**	ŭ	**cut**		atom
ē	be	ô	paw, for	û	**fur**		circus

lay² *verb* Past tense of **lie¹**.
lay² (lā) ◊ *verb*
‖*These sound alike:* **lay, lei**

layer *noun* A single thickness, coating, or sheet of material covering a surface.
◊ *verb* To form, arrange, or split into layers.
lay·er (lā′ər) ◊ *noun, plural* **layers** ◊ *verb* **layered, layering**

lazy *adjective* Not willing to work or be active: *Lazy students usually receive poor grades.*
la·zy (lā′zē) ◊ *adjective* **lazier, laziest**

lb. The abbreviation for *pound.*

lead¹ *verb* **1.** To show or direct along the way, as by going with or ahead of: *The ranger will lead us to the top of the mountain.* **2.** To be or form a way, route, or passage: *The trail leads to a little stream.* **3.** To be or go at the head of: *The color guard will lead the parade.* —See Synonyms at **guide. 4.** To be ahead of or ahead: *Our team is leading by a score of 20 to 15.*
◊ *noun* **1.** The front, first, or winning position: *Our team took the lead in the game.* **2.** The amount by which one is ahead. **3.** The main acting part in a play, movie, or musical performance.
lead¹ (lēd) ◊ *verb* **led, leading** ◊ *noun, plural* **leads**

lead² *noun* **1.** A soft, heavy, gray metal that is easy to bend, melt, and shape. Lead is a chemical element. **2.** Bullets; ammunition. **3.** A thin piece of graphite used as the writing substance in pencils.
lead² (lĕd) ◊ *noun, plural* **leads**
‖*These sound alike:* **lead², led**

***HISTORY* • lead¹, lead²**

Lead¹ and **lead²** have both been in English since the earliest times. But **lead²** may have been borrowed from an ancient language that was the ancestor of modern Irish.

leaden *adjective* **1.** Made of lead. **2.** Dull, dark gray: *The leaden skies meant rain.*
lead·en (lĕd′n) ◊ *adjective*

leader *noun* A person who leads or is able to lead.
lead·er (lē′dər) ◊ *noun, plural* **leaders**

leaf *noun* **1.** A usually thin, flat, green plant part attached to a stem or stalk. **2.** One of the sheets of paper forming the pages of a book. **3.** The movable part of a table top.
◊ *verb* **1.** To produce leaves. **2.** To turn or glance at pages of a book or magazine.
leaf (lēf) ◊ *noun, plural* **leaves** ◊ *verb* **leafed, leafing**

leaflet *noun* **1.** A small or young leaf. **2.** A booklet or pamphlet.
leaf·let (lēf′lĭt) ◊ *noun, plural* **leaflets**

league[1] *noun* **1.** A group of nations, people, or organizations working together for a common goal. **2.** An association of sports teams that compete mainly among themselves.
league[1] (lēg) ◊ *noun, plural* **leagues**

league[2] *noun* A unit of length equal to about three miles.
league[2] (lēg) ◊ *noun, plural* **leagues**

> ***HISTORY* • league[1], league[2]**
>
> **League[1]** comes from a Latin word meaning "to bind." The Latin word passed through Italian and French before coming into English. **League[2]** comes from a different and later Latin word that refers to a measure of distance.

leak *noun* An opening through which gas, air, or fluid can accidentally come in or go out.
◊ *verb* **1.** To escape or pass or allow to escape or pass, especially by accident: *Water leaked from the rusty pail.* **2.** To become or allow to be known by accident or on purpose: *The news leaked out.*
leak (lēk) ◊ *noun, plural* **leaks** ◊ *verb* **leaked, leaking**
‖ *These sound alike:* **leak, leek**

lean[1] *verb* **1.** To bend or slant from an upright position: *Lean your skis against the wall.* **2.** To rest one's weight on for support: *You can lean on my shoulder.* **3.** To rely on for help; depend: *We lean on our friends when we are in trouble.*
lean[1] (lēn) ◊ *verb* **leaned, leaning**

lean[2] *adjective* **1.** Not fat; thin: *A lean and hungry cat came to our door.* **2.** Containing little or no fat: *Please give me a lean piece of meat.*
lean[2] (lēn) ◊ *adjective* **leaner, leanest**

> ***HISTORY* • lean[1], lean[2]**
>
> **Lean[1]** comes from an old English word that meant both "to bend" and "to lie down." **Lean[2]** comes from a different old English word that meant "thin."

leap *verb* To jump or cause to jump quickly or suddenly: *The horse leaped over the fence.* —See Synonyms at **rise.**
◊ *noun* **1.** The act of leaping; jump. **2.** The distance covered by a leap.
leap (lēp) ◊ *verb* **leaped** *or* **leapt, leaping** ◊ *noun, plural* **leaps**

▲ **leap**

leapfrog *noun* A game in which a player bends over and is leaped over by another player.
leap·frog (lēp′frôg′) ◊ *noun*

leapt *verb* A past tense and a past participle of **leap.**
leapt (lĕpt *or* lĕpt) ◊ *verb*

leap year *noun* A year in which there are 366 days, with February 29 being the extra day.
leap year ◊ *noun, plural* **leap years**

learn *verb* **1.** To get knowledge of or skill in through study or instruction: *The third-graders are learning Spanish.* **2.** To get knowledge: *We go to school to learn.* **3.** To find out: *I just learned about your accident.* **4.** To memorize: *I learned the poem.*
learn (lûrn) ◊ *verb* **learned** *or* **learnt, learning**

L

learned *adjective* Having or showing much knowledge or learning.
learn·ed (**lûr′** nĭd) ◊ *adjective*

learning *noun* Knowledge gotten from study or instruction.
learn·ing (**lûr′** nĭng) ◊ *noun*

learnt *verb* A past tense and a past participle of **learn.**
learnt (lûrnt) ◊ *verb*

lease *noun* **1.** A written agreement by which an owner of property allows someone else to use it for a certain period of time in exchange for rent money. **2.** The period of time during which property is leased.
◊ *verb* To grant or get the use of property by lease: *They leased a car for a month.*
lease (lēs) ◊ *noun, plural* **leases** ◊ *verb* **leased, leasing**

leash *noun* A cord, chain, or strap attached to a collar or harness and used to hold or lead an animal.
◊ *verb* To hold, lead, or restrain with a leash: *Leash your dog.*
leash (lēsh) ◊ *noun, plural* **leashes** ◊ *verb* **leashed, leashing**

least *adjective* Smallest in degree or size: *Don't let the least criticism upset you.*
◊ *adverb* In the smallest or lowest degree: *I like tennis best and baseball least.*
◊ *noun* The smallest amount or degree: *The least you can do is offer to help.*
least (lēst) ◊ *adjective* ◊ *adverb* ◊ *noun*

leather *noun* A material made by cleaning and tanning an animal's skin or hide.
leath·er (**lĕ*th*′** ər) ◊ *noun, plural* **leathers**

leave[1] *verb* **1.** To go away from; depart: *Are you leaving before dawn?* —See Synonyms at **go. 2.** To let stay behind: *I left my book in my desk.* **3.** To allow to remain in a certain condition: *The twins left their beds unmade again.* **4.** To have remaining: *Subtracting four from seven leaves three.* **5.** To give to another to do; entrust: *Leave the hard work to me.* **6.** To give in a will: *Our grandparents left us some money.*
leave[1] (lēv) ◊ *verb* **left, leaving**

leave[2] *noun* **1.** Permission: *We asked leave to stay up until midnight.* **2.** Absence from one's work or duty that is officially permitted.
leave[2] (lēv) ◊ *noun, plural* **leaves**

> ***HISTORY* • leave**[1]**, leave**[2]
>
> **Leave**[1] comes from an old English word that meant "to remain." **Leave**[2] comes from a different old English word that meant "permission."

leaves *noun* Plural of **leaf.**
leaves (lēvz) ◊ *noun*

lecture *noun* **1.** A speech that gives information about something. **2.** A serious scolding.
◊ *verb* **1.** To give a lecture. **2.** To scold.
lec·ture (**lĕk′** chər) ◊ *noun, plural* **lectures** ◊ *verb* **lectured, lecturing**

led *verb* Past tense and past participle of **lead**[1]**.**
led (lĕd) ◊ *verb*
‖ *These sound alike:* **led, lead**[2]

ledge *noun* **1.** A narrow shelf that sticks out from a wall. **2.** A flat space like a shelf on the side of a cliff or rock wall.
ledge (lĕj) ◊ *noun, plural* **ledges**

▲ **ledge**

lee *noun* The part or side that is sheltered from the wind.
lee (lē) ◊ *noun, plural* **lees**

leech *noun* A worm that is related to the earthworm and that lives in water. It sucks

ă	pat	ĭ	pit	oi	**oil**	th	**bath**
ā	pay	ī	ride	ŏŏ	book	*th*	**bathe**
â	care	î	fierce	ōō	boot	ə	ago, item
ä	father	ŏ	pot	ou	**out**		pencil
ĕ	pet	ō	go	ŭ	cut		atom
ē	be	ô	paw, for	û	fur		circus

blood from other animals and human beings.
leech (lēch) ◊ *noun, plural* **leeches**

leek *noun* An edible plant that is related to the onion. It is grown for its thick, white stem.
leek (lēk) ◊ *noun, plural* **leeks**
‖*These sound alike:* **leek, leak**

left[1] *noun* The side from which a person begins to read a line of English: *The number 9 is on the left of a clock's face.*
◊ *adjective* Located on or directed toward the left: *I cannot write with my left hand.*
◊ *adverb* To or toward the left: *Turn left.*
left[1] (lĕft) ◊ *noun* ◊ *adjective* ◊ *adverb*

left[2] *verb* Past tense and past participle of **leave[1]**.
left[2] (lĕft) ◊ *verb*

left-hand *adjective* **1.** Located on the left: *Write your name in the upper left-hand corner of the paper.* **2.** On or to the left: *The driver signaled for a left-hand turn.*
left-hand (**lĕft'hănd'**) ◊ *adjective*

left-handed *adjective* **1.** Using the left hand more easily and naturally than the right hand. **2.** Done with or made for the left hand.
left-hand·ed (**lĕft'hăn'**dĭd) ◊ *adjective*

leftover *noun* Something unused or uneaten: *We had leftovers for dinner.*
◊ *adjective* Unused or uneaten.
left·o·ver (**lĕft'**ō'vər) ◊ *noun, plural* **leftovers**
◊ *adjective*

leg *noun* **1.** A limb of an animal or human being that is used to support the body and for moving about. **2.** One of the parts of a pair of trousers or hose that covers the leg. **3.** Something used or shaped like a leg: *The table legs wobbled.* **4.** A stage of a journey or course: *We fell behind in the first leg of the relay.*
leg (lĕg) ◊ *noun, plural* **legs**

legacy *noun* **1.** Something that is left to someone in a will. **2.** Something passed down from an ancestor or predecessor.
leg·a·cy (**lĕg'**ə sē) ◊ *noun, plural* **legacies**

legal *adjective* **1.** Of or having to do with lawyers or the law. **2.** Based on or authorized by law: *Our parents are the legal owners of the house.*
le·gal (**lē'**gəl) ◊ *adjective*

legend *noun* **1.** A story handed down from earlier times. A legend is believed by many people but its truth or accuracy may be questionable. **2.** Words explaining the symbols used in a map or other diagram.
leg·end (**lĕj'**ənd) ◊ *noun, plural* **legends**

legendary *adjective* Based on, like, or told of in legends: *King Arthur was a legendary hero.*
leg·en·dar·y (**lĕj'**ən dĕr'ē) ◊ *adjective*

leggings *plural noun* Leg coverings that are usually made of cloth or leather.
leg·gings (**lĕg'**ĭngz) ◊ *plural noun*

▲ **leggings**

legible *adjective* Plain enough to be read: *The ancient manuscript is still legible.*
leg·i·ble (**lĕj'**ə bəl) ◊ *adjective*

legion *noun* A unit of the ancient Roman army consisting of at least 3,000 foot soldiers and 100 soldiers on horseback.
le·gion (**lē'**jən) ◊ *noun, plural* **legions**

legislation *noun* **1.** The process of making laws. **2.** A law or group of laws that have been proposed or made.
leg·is·la·tion (lĕj'ĭs **lā'**shən) ◊ *noun*

legislative *adjective* **1.** Of or having to do with making laws. **2.** Of or having to do with a legislature.
leg·is·la·tive (**lĕj'**ĭs lā'tĭv) ◊ *adjective*

legislator *noun* **1.** A person who makes laws. **2.** A member of a legislature.
leg·is·la·tor (**lĕj'**ĭs lā'tər) ◊ *noun, plural* **legislators**

legislature *noun* A body of people with the power to make and change laws.
leg·is·la·ture (**lĕj'**ĭs lā'chər) ◊ *noun, plural* **legislatures**

legitimate *adjective* Having rights or being legal under the law.
le·git·i·mate (lə **jĭt'**ə mĭt) ◊ *adjective*

L

lei *noun* A wreath of flowers that is worn around the neck.
lei (lā) ◊ *noun, plural* **leis**
||*These sound alike:* **lei, lay**

leisure *noun* Free time in which to do as one pleases.
lei·sure (lē′zhər *or* **lĕzh′**ər) ◊ *noun*

lemon *noun* A yellow citrus fruit that has sour pulp and juice.
lem·on (**lĕm′**ən) ◊ *noun, plural* **lemons**

lemonade *noun* A drink made of lemon juice, water, and sugar.
lem·on·ade (lĕm′ə **nād′**) ◊ *noun*

lend *verb* **1.** To give or allow the use of with the understanding that it is to be returned: *Please lend me your extra pencil.* **2.** To give money for a time with the understanding that what is borrowed will be returned.
lend (lĕnd) ◊ *verb* **lent, lending**

length *noun* **1.** The distance of a thing measured from one end to the other along its greatest dimension: *The length of the board is four feet and the width is two inches.* **2.** The amount from beginning to end: *My report is too short in length.* **3.** Distance or extent of something: *We are shortening the length of our trip.*
length (lĕngkth) ◊ *noun, plural* **lengths**

lengthen *verb* To make or become longer: *Shadows lengthen as sunset nears.*
length·en (**lĕngk′**thən) ◊ *verb* **lengthened, lengthening**

lengthwise *adverb & adjective* In the direction of the length: *Fold the long piece of paper lengthwise.*
length·wise (**lĕngkth′**wīz′) ◊ *adverb & adjective*

lenient *adjective* Gentle and mild; merciful: *Our teacher is lenient when we're only a minute late.*
le·ni·ent (lē′nē ənt) ◊ *adjective*

lens *noun* **1.** A clear piece of material, as glass, that is curved to bend the rays of light passing through it. **2.** A combination of two or more lenses used to form or magnify an image, as in a camera or telescope. **3.** The clear part of the eye behind the iris that focuses light onto the retina to form images.
lens (lĕnz) ◊ *noun, plural* **lenses**

ă	pat	ĭ	pit	oi	**oil**	th	**bath**
ā	pay	ī	ride	o͝o	book	*th*	**bathe**
â	care	î	fierce	o͞o	boot	ə	ago, item
ä	father	ŏ	pot	ou	**out**		pencil
ĕ	pet	ō	go	ŭ	cut		atom
ē	be	ô	paw, for	û	fur		circus

lent *verb* Past tense and past participle of **lend.**
lent (lĕnt) ◊ *verb*

lentil *noun* The round, flat, edible seed of a pod-bearing plant that is related to the beans and peas.
len·til (**lĕn′**təl *or* **lĕn′**tl) ◊ *noun, plural* **lentils**

leopard *noun* A large wild cat of Africa and Asia that has a light-brown coat with black spots.
leop·ard (**lĕp′**ərd) ◊ *noun, plural* **leopards**

▲ **leopard**

leotard *noun* Often **leotards** A tight-fitting one-piece garment worn especially by dancers.
le·o·tard (lē′ə tärd′) ◊ *noun, plural* **leotards**

less *adjective* **1.** Not as great in amount or quantity: *We have more homework and less time to spare.* **2.** Fewer: *I have less than $5.00 left.*
◊ *adverb* To a smaller extent or degree: *We see you less and less.*
◊ *preposition* Minus; subtracting: *Six less one is five.*
◊ *noun* A smaller amount or share: *We got less than we asked for.*
less (lĕs) ◊ *adjective* ◊ *adverb* ◊ *preposition* ◊ *noun*

-less The suffix *-less* forms adjectives and means "not having" or "without." A *harmless* trick is a trick that does no harm to anyone.

VOCABULARY BUILDER • -less

Many words that are formed with **-less** are not entries in this dictionary. But you can figure out what these words mean by looking up the meanings of the root words and the suffix. For example:
homeless = not having a home
odorless = without any odor

lessen *verb* To make or become less. —See Synonyms at **decrease.**
less·en (lĕs′ən) ◊ *verb* **lessened, lessening**
‖*These sound alike:* **lessen, lesson**

lesser *adjective* Smaller than another.
less·er (lĕs′ər) ◊ *adjective*

lesson *noun* **1.** Something to be learned or taught. **2.** An assignment to be studied.
les·son (lĕs′ən) ◊ *noun, plural* **lessons**
‖*These sound alike:* **lesson, lessen**

let *verb* **1.** To give permission to; allow: *They let us go the movies.* **2.** To cause to; make: *Let me know what happened.* **3.** To permit to move in a certain way: *Let the cat out.* **4.** To permit to escape; release: *I let the air out of the balloon.*
◊ *idioms* **let down** To disappoint: *They let me down by not coming.* **let off 1.** To excuse from work or duty: *The teacher let the students off early.* **2.** To release with little or no punishment: *The principal let us off with a warning.* **let up** To slow down: *By evening the rain had let up a little.*
let (lĕt) ◊ *verb* **let, letting**

SYNONYMS

let, allow, permit

I *let* them do that simply because I wasn't thinking. My parents will *allow* me to go and will even drive me. The principal *permitted* me to go home early.

let's Contraction of "let us."
let's (lĕts) ◊ *contraction*

letter *noun* **1.** A written or printed mark that stands for a speech sound and is used to spell words. There are 26 letters in the English alphabet. **2.** An emblem bearing the initials of a school that is usually awarded to student athletes. **3.** A written message to someone that is usually sent by mail in an envelope.
◊ *verb* To mark or write with letters.
let·ter (lĕt′ər) ◊ *noun, plural* **letters** ◊ *verb* **lettered, lettering**

letter carrier *noun* A person who picks up and delivers mail.
letter carrier ◊ *noun, plural* **letter carriers**

lettering *noun* **1.** The action or art of forming letters. **2.** The letters written or printed on something, as a sign, poster, or greeting card.
let·ter·ing (lĕt′ər ĭng) ◊ *noun, plural* **letterings**

lettuce *noun* A plant grown for its crisp green leaves that are eaten mainly in salad.
let·tuce (lĕt′ĭs) ◊ *noun, plural* **lettuces**

levee *noun* **1.** A bank built along a river to keep it from flooding. **2.** A landing place on a river.
lev·ee (lĕv′ē) ◊ *noun, plural* **levees**
‖*These sound alike:* **levee, levy**

▲ **levee**

level *noun* **1.** A particular height: *I waded in until the water was at chest level.* **2.** A stage in a process or series: *The students are reading at the fourth-grade level.* **3.** A tool that shows whether or not a surface is flat.
◊ *adjective* **1.** Having a flat, even surface: *We found a level piece of ground for our picnic.* **2.** Being at the same height, rank, or position: *My head was level with the teacher's desk.*
◊ *verb* **1.** To make or become even, flat, or horizontal. **2.** To knock down to the ground:

L

The tornado leveled many buildings.
lev·el (lĕv′əl) ◊ *noun, plural* **levels** ◊ *adjective* ◊ *verb* **leveled, leveling**

lever *noun* **1.** A simple machine for lifting a weight. A lever consists of a strong, stiff bar that rests on a fixed point on which it turns. **2.** A bar or handle used to control, adjust, or operate a device or machine.
lev·er (lĕv′ər *or* lē′vər) ◊ *noun, plural* **levers**

levy *verb* To order to be paid: *The town levied a tax on new cars.*
◊ *noun* A tax that is ordered to be paid.
lev·y (lĕv′ē) ◊ *verb* **levied, levying** ◊ *noun, plural* **levies**
‖*These sound alike:* **levy, levee**

liable *adjective* **1.** Responsible under the law: *We are liable for the damage we do to others' property.* **2.** Likely: *Everyone is liable to make mistakes. If you play with matches you're liable to get hurt.*
li·a·ble (lī′ə bəl) ◊ *adjective*

liar *noun* A person who says things that are not true.
li·ar (lī′ər) ◊ *noun, plural* **liars**

liberal *adjective* **1.** Tending to give generously: *My grandparents are liberal givers of birthday presents.* **2.** Generous: *There is a liberal supply of food in the refrigerator.* **3.** Not limited: *A liberal education includes study of math, science, literature, and language.* **4.** Respectful of different people and ideas; tolerant.
lib·er·al (lĭb′ər əl) ◊ *adjective*

liberate *verb* To set free.
lib·er·ate (lĭb′ə rāt′) ◊ *verb* **iiberated, liberating**

liberty *noun* **1.** Freedom from the control of others; independence: *In 1776 the United States won its liberty from Britain.* **2.** Freedom to choose or to do as one pleases. **3.** The state of having free time: *The children were at liberty to go swimming.*
lib·er·ty (lĭb′ər tē) ◊ *noun, plural* **liberties**

ă	pat	ĭ	pit	oi	oil	th	bath
ā	pay	ī	ride	ŏŏ	book	*th*	bathe
â	care	î	fierce	ōō	boot	ə	ago, item
ä	father	ŏ	pot	ou	out		pencil
ĕ	pet	ō	go	ŭ	cut		atom
ē	be	ô	paw, for	û	fur		circus

librarian *noun* A person who works in or is in charge of a library.
li·brar·i·an (lī brâr′ē ən) ◊ *noun, plural* **librarians**

library *noun* **1.** A place where books, magazines, records, and reference materials are kept for reading or borrowing. —See Synonyms at **museum. 2.** A collection of books or records, as in a home.
li·brar·y (lī′brĕr′ ē) ◊ *noun, plural* **libraries**

lice *noun* Plural of **louse.**
lice (līs) ◊ *noun*

license *noun* **1.** Legal permission to do or own something. **2.** A paper that shows that legal permission to do something has been given: *I just got my driver's license.*
◊ *verb* To grant a license to or for.
li·cense (lī′səns) ◊ *noun, plural* **licenses** ◊ *verb* **licensed, licensing**

lichen *noun* A plant that consists of a fungus and an alga growing together. Lichens form a scaly or branching growth on rocks and tree trunks.
li·chen (lī′kən) ◊ *noun, plural* **lichens**
‖*These sound alike:* **lichen, liken**

▲ **lichen**

lick *verb* **1.** To pass the tongue over: *I licked my lips.* **2.** To move or flicker like a tongue: *The flames licked the logs in the fireplace.*
◊ *noun* **1.** A movement of the tongue over something. **2.** A place where animals find and lick natural salt.
lick (lĭk) ◊ *verb* **licked, licking** ◊ *noun, plural* **licks**

licorice *noun* **1.** A plant with a sweet, strong-tasting root used to flavor medicine and candy. **2.** A candy flavored with licorice.
lic·o·rice (lĭk′ə rĭs *or* lĭk′ə rĭsh) ◊ *noun*

lid *noun* **1.** A removable cover, as of a jar or box. **2.** An eyelid.
lid (lĭd) ◊ *noun, plural* **lids**

lie[1] *verb* **1.** To take or be in a flat or resting position: *I lay down under an elm tree.* **2.** To be or rest on a horizontal surface: *Books lay*

on the desk. **3.** To be located or placed: *East of the Philippines lie many tiny islands.* **4.** To remain in a condition or position: *The treasure lay hidden for years.*
lie¹ (lī) ◊ *verb* **lay, lain, lying**
‖*These sound alike:* **lie, lye**

lie² *noun* An untrue statement made on purpose; falsehood.
◊ *verb* To make an untrue statement.
lie² (lī) ◊ *noun, plural* **lies** ◊ *verb* **lied, lying**
‖*These sound alike:* **lie, lye**

HISTORY • lie¹, lie²

Lie¹ comes from an old English word that meant "to be at rest." **Lie²** comes from a different old English word that meant "to say something untrue."

lieutenant *noun* **1.** A low-ranking military officer. **2.** An officer in a police or fire department ranking below a captain.
lieu·ten·ant (lo͞o tĕn′ənt) ◊ *noun, plural* **lieutenants**

life *noun* **1.** The property or quality that separates people, animals, and plants from nonliving things such as rock and metal. The ability to grow is one characteristic of life. **2.** The fact of being alive or staying alive: *I risked my life to save the drowning child.* **3.** The time between birth and death; lifetime: *They lived there for the rest of their lives.* **4.** The time that something exists or works: *Careful driving can prolong the life of a car.* **5.** A human being: *The earthquake claimed hundreds of lives.* **6.** A way of living: *I prefer the outdoor life.* **7.** Liveliness; spirit: *The kitten is full of life.*
life (līf) ◊ *noun, plural* **lives**

lifeboat *noun* A strong boat used for saving lives at sea or from a shore.
life·boat (līf′bōt′) ◊ *noun, plural* **lifeboats**

life buoy *noun* A ring, vest, or belt made of plastic or cork that is used to keep a person afloat in water.
life buoy ◊ *noun, plural* **life buoys**

lifeguard *noun* A person who is hired to look out for the safety of the swimmers at a beach or pool.
life·guard (līf′gärd′) ◊ *noun, plural* **lifeguards**

lifeless *adjective* Having no life.
life·less (līf′lĭs) ◊ *adjective*

lifelike *adjective* Looking alive or seeming very real.
life·like (līf′līk′) ◊ *adjective*

lifelong *adjective* Lasting over a lifetime: *My lifelong ambition was to be a pilot.*
life·long (līf′lông′) ◊ *adjective*

life preserver *noun* A vest, belt, or ring that is filled with air or a very light material for use in keeping a person afloat in water.
life preserver ◊ *noun, plural* **life preservers**

lifesaver *noun* A person who is trained in lifesaving.
life·sav·er (līf′sā′vər) ◊ *noun, plural* **lifesavers**

lifesaving *noun* The skill or practice of saving lives, especially of drowning persons.
life·sav·ing (līf′sā′vĭng) ◊ *noun*

life-size *adjective* Being of the same size as the original person or object: *The artist painted a life-size portrait of the senator.*
life-size (līf′sīz′) ◊ *adjective*

life-sized *adjective* Life-size.
life-sized (līf′sīzd′) ◊ *adjective*

lifetime *noun* The period of time during which a person or thing exists.
life·time (līf′tīm′) ◊ *noun, plural* **lifetimes**

lift *verb* **1.** To raise from a lower to a higher position or condition: *The suitcase is too heavy to lift. The news lifted our spirits.* **2.** To direct upward: *I lifted my eyes from the book.* **3.** To rise from the ground, as an aircraft. **4.** To rise and disappear, as fog.
◊ *noun* **1.** An example of lifting or being lifted: *Give me a lift into the saddle.* **2.** A ride in a vehicle asked or given as a favor. **3.** The extent or height to which something is raised. **4.** A rise in spirits. **5.** A cable with seats attached that is used for carrying people up a ski slope.
lift (lĭft) ◊ *verb* **lifted, lifting** ◊ *noun, plural* **lifts**

SYNONYMS

lift, boost, raise

I tried hard to *lift* the heavy box. *Boost* me into the tree, please. The drawbridge was *raised* for the ship to go through.
Antonym: *lower*

L

liftoff *noun* The vertical takeoff of a rocket or spacecraft.
lift·off (lĭft′ ôf′) ◊ *noun, plural* **liftoffs**

▲ **liftoff**

ligament *noun* A tough band of tissue that connects bones or holds a muscle or body organ in place.
lig·a·ment (lĭg′ ə mənt) ◊ *noun, plural* **ligaments**

light¹ *noun* **1.** A natural or artificial bright form of energy that enables one to see. **2.** A source of light, especially an electric lamp. **3.** The light of day: *We got up before light.* **4.** A source of fire, as a match. **5.** A way of looking at something: *This puts the whole matter in a different light.* **6.** Public attention or knowledge: *New evidence came to light.*
◊ *adjective* **1.** Not dark; bright: *The kitchen is a light, airy room.* **2.** Pale in color.
◊ *verb* **1.** To burn or set burning; ignite. **2.** To make or become bright with light: *We lit the room with candles.* **3.** To guide or show with a light: *Here is an usher to light your way.* **4.** To make lively: *A smile lit the baby's face.*
◊ *idiom* **see the light** To understand something for the first time.
light¹ (līt) ◊ *noun, plural* **lights** ◊ *adjective* **lighter, lightest** ◊ *verb* **lighted** *or* **lit, lighting**

light² *adjective* **1.** Having little weight; not heavy. **2.** Having little force: *A light breeze barely stirred the leaves.* **3.** Small in amount: *We had a light lunch of cheese and fruit.* **4.** Free from care or worry: *I went to school with a light heart.* **5.** Moving easily and quickly: *The gymnasts were light on their feet.* **6.** Not hard to do or deal with. —See Synonyms at **easy.** **7.** Not serious or severe: *I had a light case of the flu.*
◊ *verb* To come to rest; perch.
light² (līt) ◊ *adjective* **lighter, lightest** ◊ *verb* **lighted** *or* **lit, lighting**

***HISTORY* • light¹, light²**

Light¹ comes from an old English word that meant "illumination." **Light²** comes from a different old English word that meant "not heavy."

lighten¹ *verb* To make or become brighter.
light·en¹ (līt′n) ◊ *verb* **lightened, lightening**

lighten² *verb* To make or become less heavy.
light·en² (līt′n) ◊ *verb* **lightened, lightening**

light-footed *adjective* Graceful and nimble.
light-foot·ed (līt′ fo͝ot′ ĭd) ◊ *adjective*

lightheaded *adjective* Dizzy or faint.
light·head·ed (līt′ hĕd′ ĭd) ◊ *adjective*

lighthearted *adjective* Carefree and happy.
light·heart·ed (līt′ här′ tĭd) ◊ *adjective*

lighthouse *noun* A tower with a powerful light at the top that is used to guide ships away from dangerous shores.
light·house (līt′ hous′) ◊ *noun, plural* **lighthouses**

ă	pat	ĭ	pit	oi	**oil**	th	bath
ā	pay	ī	ride	o͝o	book	*th*	bathe
â	care	î	fierce	o͞o	boot	ə	ago, item
ä	father	ŏ	pot	ou	**out**		pencil
ĕ	pet	ō	go	ŭ	cut		atom
ē	be	ô	paw, for	û	fur		circus

▲ **lighthouse**

lighting *noun* Light or lights supplied: *Good lighting is important in the classroom.*
light·ing (lī′tĭng) ◊ *noun*

lightning *noun* The flash of light in the sky when electricity passes between clouds.
light·ning (līt′nĭng) ◊ *noun*

light pen *noun* A device that is used to add, change, or draw information on a computer screen.
light pen ◊ *noun, plural* **light pens**

light-year *noun* A measure of distance equal to the distance that light travels through empty space in a year. One light-year equals about 5.878 trillion miles.
light-year (līt′yîr′) ◊ *noun, plural* **light-years**

likable *adjective* Easy to like.
lik·a·ble (lī′kə bəl) ◊ *adjective*

like[1] *verb* To be fond of; enjoy: *I like playing the drums.*
◊ *noun* The things a person enjoys or prefers: *We have the same likes and dislikes.*
like[1] (līk) ◊ *verb* **liked, liking** ◊ *noun, plural* **likes**

like[2] *preposition* **1.** The same as or similar to: *There was a crash like thunder.* **2.** In the same or a similar manner as: *Please try to act like ladies and gentlemen.* **3.** In character with; typical of: *It's not like you to give up so easily.* **4.** Such as: *Eat green leafy vegetables like lettuce and spinach.* **5.** Likely to: *It looks like rain.* **6.** In the mood for: *Do you feel like taking a walk?*
◊ *adjective* Same or similar: *My parents gave me $5 and a like amount to my cousin.*
◊ *noun* One that is similar to another: *I have never met your like in my entire life.*
like[2] (līk) ◊ *preposition* ◊ *adjective* ◊ *noun, plural* **likes**

> ***HISTORY* • like**[1]**, like**[2]
>
> **Like**[1] comes from an old English word that meant "to please, have a pleasing appearance." **Like**[2] comes from a related old English word that meant "similar, having the same appearance."

-like The suffix *-like* forms adjectives and means "similar to," "like," or "resembling." A person who takes *catlike* steps is a person who walks like a cat. A *lifelike* sculpture is a sculpture that looks like a living person or thing.

> ***VOCABULARY BUILDER* • -like**
>
> Many words that are formed with **-like** are not in this dictionary. But you can figure out what these words mean by looking up the meanings of the root words and the suffix. For example:
> **blisterlike** = resembling a blister
> **homelike** = like a home

likelihood *noun* The chance that a certain thing will happen: *In all likelihood we will still have the picnic.*
like·li·hood (līk′lē ho͝od′) ◊ *noun*

likeliness *noun* Likelihood.
like·li·ness (līk′lē nĭs) ◊ *noun*

likely *adjective* **1.** Having or showing a strong chance of happening: *It is likely to rain.* **2.** Seeming to be true; believable: *They have a likely excuse for their absence.* **3.** Showing promise; suitable: *This is a likely place to plant a tree.*
◊ *adverb* Probably: *Most likely it's none of my business.*
like·ly (līk′lē) ◊ *adjective* **likelier, likeliest** ◊ *adverb*

like-minded *adjective* Being of the same mind or having the same way of thinking: *We are like-minded sports fans.*
like-mind·ed (līk′mīn′dĭd) ◊ *adjective*

liken *verb* To describe as being like something else; compare: *Politics has often been likened to a game of chess.*
lik·en (lī′kən) ◊ *verb* **likened, likening**
‖*These sound alike:* **liken, lichen**

likeness *noun* **1.** The state of being similar: *There is a close likeness between parent and child.* **2.** A picture of a person.
like·ness (līk′nĭs) ◊ *noun, plural* **likenesses**

SYNONYMS

likeness, resemblance, similarity

I see a real *likeness* between the plots of those two stories. There is a clear *resemblance* in appearance between you and your cousin. The *similarity* between those two ideas is not that close.

likewise *adverb* **1.** In a similar manner: *The kittens watched the mother cat climb the tree and did likewise.* **2.** In addition; also: *The football player is likewise a good student.*
like·wise (līk′wīz′) ◊ *adverb*

liking *noun* A feeling of fondness or affection: *I have a special liking for horses.*
lik·ing (lī′kĭng) ◊ *noun, plural* **likings**

lilac *noun* A shrub having clusters of fragrant purplish or white flowers.
li·lac (lī′lək) ◊ *noun, plural* **lilacs**

lilt *noun* **1.** A lively song or tune. **2.** A smoothly flowing motion or rhythm.
lilt (lĭlt) ◊ *noun, plural* **lilts**

lilting *adjective* Having a pleasant, lively rhythm: *That is a happy, lilting tune.*
lilt·ing (lĭl′tĭng) ◊ *adjective*

lily *noun* Any of several related plants that grow from bulbs and have tall, leafy stems and white or brightly colored flowers shaped like trumpets.
lil·y (lĭl′ē) ◊ *noun, plural* **lilies**

lily of the valley *noun* A low-growing plant related to the lilies that has a slender cluster of white, sweet-smelling, bell-shaped flowers.
lily of the valley ◊ *noun, plural* **lilies of the valley**

▲ **lily of the valley**

lima bean *noun* A plant with flat pods that hold large, light-green, edible beans.
li·ma bean (lī′mə) ◊ *noun, plural* **lima beans**

limb *noun* **1.** A paired and jointed animal part, such as a leg, arm, wing, or flipper. **2.** One of the larger branches of a tree.
limb (lĭm) ◊ *noun, plural* **limbs**

lime¹ *noun* **1.** A small green citrus fruit that is related to the lemon. Limes have sour juice that is used as flavoring. **2.** A tree that bears this fruit.
lime¹ (līm) ◊ *noun, plural* **limes**

lime² *noun* A white powder that is made by heating limestone. Lime is used in making cement and as a fertilizer.
lime² (līm) ◊ *noun*

***HISTORY* • lime¹, lime²**

Lime¹ comes from the Arabic name for this fruit. **Lime²** comes from an old English word that meant "something sticky."

limerick *noun* An amusing poem of five lines.
lim·er·ick (lĭm′ər ĭk) ◊ *noun, plural* **limericks**

limestone *noun* A rock formed especially from shells or coral that is used in building and in making lime and cement.
lime·stone (līm′stōn′) ◊ *noun*

limit *noun* **1.** A point beyond which someone or something cannot go: *The speed limit is 55 miles per hour.* **2.** Often **limits** The boundary

ă	pat	ĭ	pit	oi	oil	th	bath
ā	pay	ī	ride	o͝o	book	*th*	bathe
â	care	î	fierce	o͞o	boot	ə	ago, item
ä	father	ŏ	pot	ou	out		pencil
ĕ	pet	ō	go	ŭ	cut		atom
ē	be	ô	paw, for	û	fur		circus

surrounding an area: *We live within the city limits.*
◊ *verb* To place a limit on.
lim·it (lĭm′ĭt) ◊ *noun, plural* **limits** ◊ *verb* **limited, limiting**

limp *verb* To walk in an uneven way.
◊ *noun* An uneven walk.
◊ *adjective* Not stiff, crisp, or firm: *Lettuce gets limp if it is not refrigerated.*
limp (lĭmp) ◊ *verb* **limped, limping** ◊ *noun, plural* **limps** ◊ *adjective* **limper, limpest**

linden *noun* A shade tree with heart-shaped leaves and yellowish, sweet-smelling flowers.
lin·den (lĭn′dən) ◊ *noun, plural* **lindens**

▲ **linden**

line¹ *noun* **1.** A set of points that extend indefinitely in opposite directions in a straight or curved path. **2.** A long, thin mark, as one made by a pencil. **3.** A border or boundary: *This sign marks the county line.* **4.** A group of people or things arranged in a row. **5.** Often **lines** An outline or contour, as of a car. **6.** A row of words printed or written across a page or column. **7. lines** The words of a part in a play: *We are busy learning our lines.* **8.** A wrinkle or crease on the skin. **9.** A long, thin rope, string, or cord: *Our fishing lines are tangled.* **10.** The path of something in motion: *We watched the line of flight of the geese.* **11.** A certain way of making or doing something: *We planned our trip along these lines.* **12.** A system of transportation. **13.** A system of wires used to carry communications or electricity over long distances for a telephone or power company. **14.** A pipe or system of pipes used to carry a fluid, such as water, oil, or sewage. **15.** A short letter; note. **16.** A family of persons or animals descended from a common ancestor. **17.** A range of merchandise: *This store carries the newest line of sports equipment.*
◊ *verb* **1.** To mark with lines: *I lined my paper with a ruler.* **2.** To form a line along: *People lined the sidewalks.*
line¹ (līn) ◊ *noun, plural* **lines** ◊ *verb* **lined, lining**

line² *verb* To cover the inside surface of: *I lined the coat with silk.*
line² (līn) ◊ *verb* **lined, lining**

***HISTORY* • line¹, line²**

Line¹ and **line²** both go back to the Latin name for **flax**, a plant used to make thread and cloth. **Line¹** came from the Latin for "flax thread." **Line²** came from a verb meaning "to attach flax cloth to a garment."

linen *noun* **1.** Strong, smooth cloth made of flax fibers. **2.** Often **linens** Clothing or household articles made of linen.
lin·en (lĭn′ən) ◊ *noun, plural* **linens**

line segment *noun* The part of a line lying between two points chosen to be its ends.
line segment ◊ *noun, plural* **line segments**

lineup *noun* The members of a team who play in a game: *Our best hitter was not in the starting lineup.*
line·up (līn′ŭp′) ◊ *noun, plural* **lineups**

linger *verb* To stay in a place longer than usual: *The guests lingered until very late.*
lin·ger (lĭng′gər) ◊ *verb* **lingered, lingering**

link *noun* **1.** One of the rings or loops forming a chain. **2.** Something that joins or connects: *That old church is our town's link with the past.*
◊ *verb* To bring together; join: *Train service links the two cities.*
link (lĭngk) ◊ *noun, plural* **links** ◊ *verb* **linked, linking**

linking verb *noun* A verb that joins the subject of the sentence with a word or phrase that tells something about the subject. In the

L

sentence, *I am happy*, the word *am* is a linking verb. *Am* joins the subject *I* with the word *happy*, which tells how the subject is feeling.
linking verb ◊ *noun, plural* **linking verbs**

linoleum *noun* A sturdy, washable material made in sheets and used for covering floors and counters.
li·no·le·um (lĭ **nō′** lē əm) ◊ *noun, plural* **linoleums**

lint *noun* Bits of fiber and fluff from cloth.
lint (lĭnt) ◊ *noun*

lion *noun* A very large light-brown wild cat of Africa and India. The male has a shaggy mane around the head and shoulders.
li·on (lī′ ən) ◊ *noun, plural* **lions**

▲ **lion**

lioness *noun* A female lion.
li·on·ess (lī′ ə nĭs) ◊ *noun, plural* **lionesses**

lip *noun* **1.** Either of the fleshy, muscular folds of tissue that surround the mouth. **2.** The edge of a container; rim.
lip (lĭp) ◊ *noun, plural* **lips**

lipstick *noun* A stick of waxy material used to color the lips.
lip·stick (**lĭp′** stĭk′) ◊ *noun, plural* **lipsticks**

ă	pat	ĭ	pit	oi	**oil**	th	**bath**
ā	pay	ī	ride	ŏŏ	**book**	*th*	**bathe**
â	care	î	fierce	ōō	**boot**	ə	ago, item
ä	father	ŏ	pot	ou	**out**		pencil
ĕ	pet	ō	go	ŭ	cut		atom
ē	be	ô	paw, for	û	fur		circus

liquefy *verb* To make or become liquid.
liq·ue·fy (**lĭk′** wə fī′) ◊ *verb* **liquefied, liquefying**

liquid *noun* A substance that flows easily and that is hard to compress. Water, milk, and juice are liquids.
◊ *adjective* Of or being a liquid; flowing like water.
liq·uid (**lĭk′** wĭd) ◊ *noun, plural* **liquids** ◊ *adjective*

liquor *noun* A strong alcoholic beverage.
liq·uor (**lĭk′** ər) ◊ *noun, plural* **liquors**

lisp *noun* A way of speaking in which the sounds *s* and *z* are pronounced like the *th* in the word *thick*.
◊ *verb* To speak with a lisp.
lisp (lĭsp) ◊ *noun, plural* **lisps** ◊ *verb* **lisped, lisping**

list¹ *noun* A series of names or items, written one after the other: *Let's make a shopping list.*
◊ *verb* **1.** To make a list of: *List what you want from the store.* **2.** To include in a list: *Why aren't you listed in the phone book?*
list¹ (lĭst) ◊ *noun, plural* **lists** ◊ *verb* **listed, listing**

list² *noun* A tilt to one side, as of a ship.
◊ *verb* To tilt to one side.
list² (lĭst) ◊ *noun, plural* **lists** ◊ *verb* **listed, listing**

***HISTORY* • list¹, list²**

List¹ comes from an old French word that meant "edge, strip of paper." The origin of **list²** is not known for certain.

listen *verb* **1.** To try to hear something: *If you listen, you can hear the ocean.* **2.** To pay attention; heed: *Now listen to me!*
lis·ten (**lĭs′** ən) ◊ *verb* **listened, listening**

listless *adjective* Too tired or too weak to want to do anything.
list·less (**lĭst′** lĭs) ◊ *adjective*

lit *verb* A past tense and a past participle of **light¹** and **light²**.
lit (lĭt) ◊ *verb*

liter *noun* A unit of capacity for liquids in the metric system. A liter is equal to about 1.056 liquid quarts.
li·ter (**lē′** tər) ◊ *noun, plural* **liters**

literacy *noun* **1.** The ability to read and write. **2.** Good understanding of a certain field, such as computers.
lit·er·a·cy (lĭt′ər ə sē) ◊ *noun*

literally *adverb* Word for word: *I translated the speech literally from French into English for the audience.*
lit·er·al·ly (lĭt′ər ə lē) ◊ *adverb*

literate *adjective* Able to read and write.
lit·er·ate (lĭt′ər ĭt) ◊ *adjective*

literature *noun* **1.** Written works that have lasting value and interest. **2.** Printed material of any kind: *I read the campaign literature.*
lit·er·a·ture (lĭt′ər ə chŏŏr′) ◊ *noun*

litmus paper *noun* Small strips of paper coated with a special dye. Litmus paper changes from blue to red in an acid solution and from red to blue in a base solution.
lit·mus paper (lĭt′məs) ◊ *noun*

litter *noun* **1.** Pieces of paper, empty cans and bottles, and other waste material left lying around. **2.** Young animals that are born at one time. **3.** A stretcher that is used to carry a sick or wounded person. **4.** A couch on horizontal poles that is used to carry a person from place to place.
◊ *verb* **1.** To make messy by leaving trash around: *Don't litter the picnic area.* **2.** To cover with scattered things: *Papers and open books littered the desk.*
lit·ter (lĭt′ər) ◊ *noun, plural* **litters** ◊ *verb* **littered, littering**

▲ **litter**

little *adjective* **1.** Small in size or quantity: *Dolls look like little people. We have little food to waste.* **2.** Young: *The little children went to bed early.* **3.** Short in time or distance; brief: *We waited for a little while.*
◊ *adverb* To a limited degree or extent: *I was a little frightened.*
◊ *noun* **1.** A small amount or quantity: *Please give me a little of your fruit.* **2.** A short time: *It's a little after four o'clock.*
lit·tle (lĭt′l) ◊ *adjective* **littler** *or* **less, littlest** *or* **least** ◊ *adverb* **less, least** ◊ *noun*

SYNONYMS

little, miniature, small, tiny

My mother sewed a *little* dress for my doll. I made a *miniature* model of our house. That is a *small* car for so many people. Babies have such *tiny* hands.
Antonym: *big*

live¹ *verb* **1.** To be alive; exist: *Fish cannot live long out of water.* **2.** To continue to remain alive: *My great-grandparents have lived almost a century.* **3.** To support oneself; maintain one's life: *They live on what they earn.* **4.** To make one's home; dwell: *Where do you live?* **5.** To pass one's life in a certain way: *They live happily in the country.*
live¹ (lĭv) ◊ *verb* **lived, living**

live² *adjective* **1.** Having life; living: *The zoo has live animals.* **2.** Glowing; burning: *There are live coals in the fireplace.* **3.** Carrying an electric current: *Don't touch that live wire.* **4.** Not exploded. **5.** Broadcast while actually being performed: *A live concert is on television tonight.*
live² (līv) ◊ *adjective*

***HISTORY* • live¹, live²**

Live¹ comes from an old English word that meant "to be alive." **Live²** is shortened from **alive.**

livelihood *noun* The way in which a person earns a living: *Practicing medicine is my parents' livelihood.*
live·li·hood (līv′lē hŏŏd′) ◊ *noun, plural* **livelihoods**

L

lively *adjective* **1.** Full of life; energetic: *Lively children need space and plenty of fresh air.* —See Synonyms at **active. 2.** Bright; vivid: *Red is a lively color.*
live·ly (līv′lē) ◊ *adjective* **livelier, liveliest**

liven *verb* To make or become lively.
liv·en (lī′vən) ◊ *verb* **livened, livening**

live oak *noun* An evergreen oak tree of the southern United States.
live oak (līv) ◊ *noun, plural* **live oaks**

liver *noun* **1.** A large organ found in the abdomen of human beings and animals. The liver makes bile and helps the body to absorb food. **2.** The liver of an animal, used as food.
liv·er (lĭv′ər) ◊ *noun, plural* **livers**

livery *noun* **1.** A uniform worn by the male servants of a household. **2.** A uniform or distinctive clothing worn by a group or profession. **3.** The shelter and care of horses for a fee.
liv·er·y (lĭv′ə rē) ◊ *noun, plural* **liveries**

lives *noun* Plural of **life.**
lives (līvz) ◊ *noun*

livestock *noun* Animals that are raised on a farm or ranch.
live·stock (līv′stŏk′) ◊ *noun*

living *adjective* **1.** Having life; alive. **2.** Now in use: *Spanish is a living language.*
◊ *noun* **1.** The condition of having or maintaining life: *The cost of living is high in the city.* **2.** A manner or style of life: *Our family believes in plain living.* **3.** A way of maintaining life; livelihood: *The early settlers made a living by hunting, trapping, and trading.*
liv·ing (lĭv′ĭng) ◊ *adjective* ◊ *noun, plural* **livings**

living room *noun* A room in a home for general use and for entertaining guests.
living room ◊ *noun, plural* **living rooms**

lizard *noun* Any of a group of reptiles that have a scaly, often slender body, four legs, and a long tail. Most lizards live in warm regions.
liz·ard (lĭz′ərd) ◊ *noun, plural* **lizards**

ă	pat	ĭ	pit	oi	oil	th	bath
ā	pay	ī	ride	ŏŏ	book	*th*	bathe
â	care	î	fierce	ōō	boot	ə	ago, item
ä	father	ŏ	pot	ou	out		pencil
ĕ	pet	ō	go	ŭ	cut		atom
ē	be	ô	paw, for	û	fur		circus

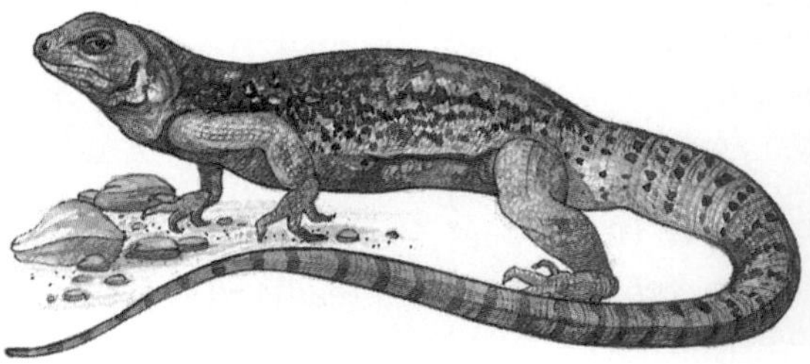

▲ **lizard**

llama *noun* A South American animal that is related to the camel. The llama has a thick, fleecy coat. It is raised for its wool and is also used for carrying loads.
lla·ma (lä′mə) ◊ *noun, plural* **llamas**

▲ **llama**

load *noun* **1.** Something that is carried, lifted, or supported; burden. **2.** An amount carried: *The wagon had a full load of hay.* **3.** An amount of work to be done: *We have a heavy load of homework.* **4.** A single charge of ammunition for a gun. **5. loads** A great number or amount: *I have loads of homework.*
◊ *verb* **1.** To put into a vehicle or structure for carrying: *The dock workers loaded grain onto the ship. We loaded the back of the car with groceries.* **2.** To provide or fill nearly to overflowing: *We loaded the table with food.*

3. To put needed materials into a machine or other device: *Load the camera with film.*
load (lōd) ◊ *noun, plural* **loads** ◊ *verb* **loaded, loading**
‖*These sound alike:* **load, lode**

loaf[1] *noun* **1.** A mass of bread that is shaped and then baked in one piece. **2.** A rounded mass of food: *Let's cook a meat loaf.*
loaf[1] (lōf) ◊ *noun, plural* **loaves**

loaf[2] *verb* To spend time lazily or aimlessly; idle: *Don't loaf; please get the job done.*
loaf[2] (lōf) ◊ *verb* **loafed, loafing**

***HISTORY* • loaf[1], loaf[2]**

Loaf[1] comes from an old English word that meant "bread." The verb **loaf[2]** probably came from the noun **loafer.** This word may have come from a German word that means "wanderer, tramp."

loafer *noun* **1.** A lazy person. **2.** A shoe without laces that is shaped like a moccasin.
loaf·er (lō′fər) ◊ *noun, plural* **loafers**

loam *noun* Fertile soil that contains sand, clay, and decayed plant matter.
loam (lōm) ◊ *noun, plural* **loams**

loan *noun* **1.** The act of lending. **2.** The condition or arrangement of being lent: *Some of our library books are on loan from other schools.* **3.** Something borrowed. **4.** A sum of money lent.
loan (lōn) ◊ *noun, plural* **loans**
‖*These sound alike:* **loan, lone**

loathe *verb* To feel great dislike for; hate.
loathe (lō*th*) ◊ *verb* **loathed, loathing**

loathsome *adjective* Extremely unpleasant; disgusting.
loath·some (**lō*th*′**səm) ◊ *adjective*

loaves *noun* Plural of **loaf[1]**.
loaves (lōvz) ◊ *noun*

lobby *noun* **1.** An entrance area in a hotel, apartment house, or theater. **2.** A person or group that tries to influence legislators.
◊ *verb* To try to influence legislators.
lob·by (**lŏb′**ē) ◊ *noun, plural* **lobbies** ◊ *verb* **lobbied, lobbying**

lobster *noun* **1.** A sea animal that has a long, hard-shelled body. A lobster has five pairs of legs, of which the front pair are large, heavy claws. **2.** The meat of a lobster, used as food.
lob·ster (**lŏb′**stər) ◊ *noun, plural* **lobsters**

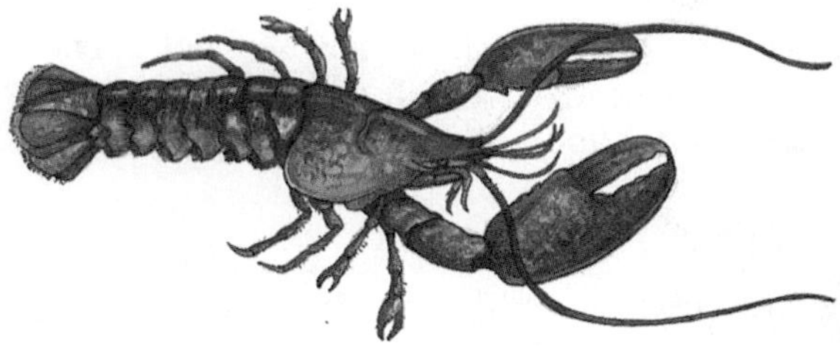

▲ **lobster**

local *adjective* **1.** Of a certain limited area or place: *The town has its own local government.* **2.** Making many stops: *Only the local train stops at my station.* **3.** Of one part of the body rather than the entire system.
◊ *noun* A train or bus that makes many stops.
lo·cal (**lō′**kəl) ◊ *adjective* ◊ *noun, plural* **locals**

locality *noun* A particular place, region, or neighborhood.
lo·cal·i·ty (lō **kăl′**ĭ tē) ◊ *noun, plural* **localities**

locate *verb* **1.** To find and show the position of: *Can you locate Austria on the map?* **2.** To find by searching: *The animals had trouble locating food last winter.* **3.** To place or situate: *Locate your vegetable garden in a fertile area.* **4.** To go and live somewhere: *The family has located in Iowa.*
lo·cate (**lō′**kāt′) ◊ *verb* **located, locating**

location *noun* **1.** A place where something is located; position: *We finally found the location of the airport.* **2.** The act or process of locating: *Location of a hotel is our first task.* **3.** A place away from a movie or television studio at which a scene is filmed.
lo·ca·tion (lō **kā′**shən) ◊ *noun, plural* **locations**

lock[1] *noun* **1.** A device used to hold something shut, usually needing a key to open it. **2.** A section of a canal closed off with gates. A ship can be raised or lowered in a lock by pumping water in or out.
◊ *verb* **1.** To shut or secure with a lock or

L

locks: *Close the door and lock it.* **2.** To hold, fasten, or bind securely in place: *The brakes locked the wheels.* **3.** To link together; intertwine: *They locked arms and walked off.*
lock¹ (lŏk) ◊ *noun, plural* **locks** ◊ *verb* **locked, locking**

lock² *noun* **1.** A curl of hair. **2. locks** The hair of the head.
lock² (lŏk) ◊ *noun, plural* **locks**

***HISTORY* • lock¹, lock²**

Lock¹ comes from an old English word that meant "a device for fastening a door." **Lock²** comes from a different but probably related old English word that referred to a curl of hair.

locker *noun* A small closet or trunk for locking up clothes and valuables.
lock·er (lŏk′ər) ◊ *noun, plural* **lockers**

locket *noun* A small ornamental metal case for a picture or other keepsake. A locket is often worn on a chain around the neck.
lock·et (lŏk′ĭt) ◊ *noun, plural* **lockets**

lockjaw *noun* Tetanus.
lock·jaw (lŏk′jô′) ◊ *noun*

locknut *noun* A thin nut that is screwed down on another nut to keep it from turning.
lock·nut (lŏk′nŭt′) ◊ *noun, plural* **locknuts**

locksmith *noun* A person who makes or repairs locks and keys.
lock·smith (lŏk′smĭth′) ◊ *noun, plural* **locksmiths**

lock step *noun* A way of marching in which the marchers follow each other closely.

locomotion *noun* The act of moving or the ability to move from one place to another.
lo·co·mo·tion (lō′kə mō′shən) ◊ *noun*

locomotive *noun* An engine used to pull or push railroad cars along a track.
lo·co·mo·tive (lō′kə mō′tĭv) ◊ *noun, plural* **locomotives**

ă	pat	ĭ	pit	oi	**oil**	th	ba**th**
ā	pay	ī	ride	o͝o	book	*th*	ba*th*e
â	care	î	fierce	o͞o	boot	ə	ago, item
ä	father	ŏ	pot	ou	**out**		pencil
ĕ	pet	ō	go	ŭ	cut		atom
ē	be	ô	paw, for	û	fur		circus

▲ **locomotive**

locust *noun* **1.** A grasshopper that travels in a large swarm. Locusts often do great damage to crops. **2.** A tree with feathery leaves, clusters of sweet-smelling white flowers, and pods like beans.
lo·cust (lō′kəst) ◊ *noun, plural* **locusts**

lode *noun* A deposit of rock that has valuable metal in it: *Miners struck a lode of silver.*
lode (lōd) ◊ *noun, plural* **lodes**
‖*These sound alike:* **lode, load**

lodestone *noun* A piece of iron ore that acts as a magnet.
lode·stone (lōd′stōn′) ◊ *noun, plural* **lodestones**

lodge *noun* **1.** A cottage or cabin, especially one used as a temporary place to stay. **2.** A local branch or meeting place of an organization, such as a club.
◊ *verb* **1.** To provide with a place to sleep: *We lodged our guest in a spare room.* **2.** To live in a place, especially a rented room: *They lodged in a hotel for the night.* **3.** To become stuck or caught: *A splinter lodged in my heel.*
lodge (lŏj) ◊ *noun, plural* **lodges** ◊ *verb* **lodged, lodging**

lodger *noun* A person who rents a room.
lodg·er (lŏj′ər) ◊ *noun, plural* **lodgers**

lodging *noun* **1.** A place to stay for a short time. **2. lodgings** A rented room or rooms.
lodg·ing (lŏj′ĭng) ◊ *noun, plural* **lodgings**

loft *noun* **1.** A large, often open floor in a commercial building. Lofts are usually used for

storage or as work areas. **2.** An open space under a roof; attic. **3.** A balcony in an auditorium or hall.
loft (lôft) ◊ *noun, plural* **lofts**

lofty *adjective* **1.** Very tall; towering. **2.** Arrogant; haughty: *I don't like your lofty manner.*
loft·y (lôf′tē) ◊ *adjective* **loftier, loftiest**

log *noun* **1.** A large trunk of a tree that has fallen or been cut down. **2.** A cut piece of a tree trunk, used for building, firewood, or lumber. **3.** An official record of speed, progress, and important events that is kept for a ship or aircraft.
◊ *verb* To cut down trees, trim them, and haul the pieces away.
log (lôg) ◊ *noun, plural* **logs** ◊ *verb* **logged, logging**

loganberry *noun* A large, dark-red berry that grows on a prickly plant. The loganberry is a cross between the blackberry and the raspberry.
lo·gan·ber·ry (lō′gən bĕr′ē) ◊ *noun, plural* **loganberries**

▲ **loganberry**

logger *noun* A person who cuts down trees and trims them into logs; lumberjack.
log·ger (lôg′ər) ◊ *noun, plural* **loggers**

loggerhead *noun* A large sea turtle of warm waters. It has a large beaked head.
log·ger·head (lŏg′ər hĕd′) ◊ *noun, plural* **loggerheads**

logic *noun* **1.** The study of the principles of sound reasoning. **2.** Rational thought; sound reasoning. **3.** A way of thinking or reasoning.
log·ic (lŏj′ĭk) ◊ *noun*

logical *adjective* **1.** Of, using, or agreeing with the principles of sound reasoning: *Your argument is logical.* **2.** Able to reason clearly and rationally: *It is easy to see that you have a logical mind.*
log·i·cal (lŏj′ĭ kəl) ◊ *adjective*

LOGO *noun* A computer programming language for use by young people.
LO·GO (lō′gō′) ◊ *noun*

logy *adjective* Not being alert; sluggish: *The flu left me feeling logy.*
lo·gy (lō′gē) ◊ *adjective* **logier, logiest**

loin *noun* **1. loins** The part of the sides and back of the body between the ribs and hip. **2.** A cut of meat from this part of an animal.
loin (loin) ◊ *noun, plural* **loins**

loiter *verb* To stand around, doing nothing.
loi·ter (loi′tər) ◊ *verb* **loitered, loitering**

loll *verb* To sit or lie in a relaxed or lazy way.
loll (lŏl) ◊ *verb* **lolled, lolling**

lollipop *noun* A piece of hard candy on the end of a stick.
lol·li·pop (lŏl′ē pŏp′) ◊ *noun, plural* **lollipops**

lone *adjective* **1.** Without others; single: *A lone sailor stood watch.* **2.** By itself; solitary: *A lone tree stood in the meadow.*
lone (lōn) ◊ *adjective*
‖ *These sound alike:* **lone, loan**

lonely *adjective* **1.** Sad at being alone: *The lonely child had no friends.* —See Synonyms at **alone. 2.** Without a companion; lone. **3.** Not often visited; remote: *We drove along a lonely mountain road.*
lone·ly (lōn′lē) ◊ *adjective* **lonelier, loneliest**

lonesome *adjective* Sad at being alone.
lone·some (lōn′səm) ◊ *adjective* **lonesomer, lonesomest**

long[1] *adjective* **1.** Measuring a large amount from end to end; having great length: *The Mississippi is a long river.* **2.** Lasting for a large amount of time: *The candidate gave a long speech.* **3.** Of a certain extent or duration: *The movie was two hours long.* **4.** Having a sound like one of the vowel sounds (ā), (ē), (ī), (ō), or (o͞o): *The "a" in "pane" is a long vowel, but the "a" in "pan" is short.*
◊ *adverb* **1.** During or for a large amount of time: *Stay as long as you like.* **2.** For the whole time: *We stayed up all night long.* **3.** At a time far in the past: *These events took place long ago.*
long[1] (lông) ◊ *adjective, adverb* **longer, longest**

L

long² *verb* To wish or want very much.
long² (lông) ◊ *verb* **longed, longing**

> ***HISTORY*** **• long¹, long²**
>
> **Long¹** comes from an old English word that meant "large in measurement from end to end." **Long²** comes from a related old English word that meant "to grow longer." When you long for something, time seems to grow longer.

longhand *noun* Ordinary handwriting.
long·hand (**lông′** hănd′) ◊ *noun, plural* **longhands**

longhorn *noun* One of a breed of cattle with long, spreading horns.
long·horn (**lông′** hôrn′) ◊ *noun, plural* **longhorns**

▲ **longhorn**

longitude *noun* Distance measured in degrees east or west of the meridian at Greenwich, a city in southeastern England.
lon·gi·tude (**lŏn′** jĭ to͞od′ *or* **lŏn′** jĭ tyo͞od′) ◊ *noun, plural* **longitudes**

ă	pat	ĭ	pit	oi	**oil**	th	**bath**
ā	pay	ī	ride	o͝o	**book**	*th*	**bathe**
â	care	î	fierce	o͞o	**boot**	ə	ago, item
ä	father	ŏ	pot	ou	**out**		pencil
ĕ	pet	ō	go	ŭ	cut		atom
ē	be	ô	paw, for	û	fur		circus

long-range *adjective* Involving a lengthy period of time or long distances: *What are your long-range plans?*
long-range (**lông′ rānj′**) ◊ *adjective*

look *verb* **1.** To use the eyes to see: *I looked everywhere for the missing key.* **2.** To focus one's gaze or attention: *Please look at the camera.* —See Synonyms at **watch. 3.** To appear to be; seem: *These bananas look ripe. It looks stormy.* **4.** To face in a certain direction: *The house looks onto the ocean.*
◊ *noun* **1.** An act of looking; glance: *I took a quick look at my watch.* **2.** An inspection; examination: *Our parents took a careful look at the whole house before buying it.* **3.** An expression, as on a person's face. **4. looks** Personal appearance.
◊ *idioms* **look after** To take care of: *I looked after the baby while my parents were shopping.* **look down on** To think of oneself as superior to: *Don't look down on the younger children.* **look forward to** To wait for with pleasure: *I'm looking forward to learning new things.* **look out** To be on guard: *Look out for ice on the road.* **look up** To search for, especially in a reference book: *If you can't spell the word, look it up in the dictionary.*
look (lo͝ok) ◊ *verb* **looked, looking** ◊ *noun, plural* **looks**

looking glass *noun* A mirror.
looking glass ◊ *noun, plural* **looking glasses**

lookout *noun* **1.** A person whose job is to watch for something. **2.** The action of waiting and watching.
look·out (**lo͝ok′** out′) ◊ *noun, plural* **lookouts**

loom¹ *verb* **1.** To come into view, often with a threatening appearance: *Storm clouds loomed on the horizon.* **2.** To seem close at hand: *The day of the big test loomed before us.*
loom¹ (lo͞om) ◊ *verb* **loomed, looming**

loom² *noun* A machine or frame on which thread or yarn is woven to make cloth.
loom² (lo͞om) ◊ *noun, plural* **looms**

> ***HISTORY*** **• loom¹, loom²**
>
> **Loom¹** first appeared in written English about 450 years ago. Its history before that is not known for certain. **Loom²** comes from an old English word that meant "a tool, utensil."

loon *noun* A large diving bird with a dark, speckled back. The cry of the loon sounds like a wild laugh.
loon (lo͞on) ◊ *noun, plural* **loons**

▲ **loon**

loop *noun* **1.** A circular form made when something long and flexible, such as rope or wire, turns and crosses itself. **2.** A circular path or pattern: *The car made a loop around the town.*
◊ *verb* To make or form into a loop or loops.
loop (lo͞op) ◊ *noun, plural* **loops** ◊ *verb* **looped, looping**

loose *adjective* **1.** Not fastened tightly: *Your shoelaces are loose.* **2.** Not confined or tied up; free: *Chickens were loose in the yard.* **3.** Not fitting tightly: *I put on a loose sweater.* **4.** Not bound, bundled, or joined together: *Some loose pages fell out of the book.* **5.** Not placed or packed closely together: *Loose gravel was scattered on the road.*
◊ *adverb* In a loose way: *My hair hung loose.*
◊ *verb* **1.** To set free; release. **2.** To make less tight; loosen.
loose (lo͞os) ◊ *adjective, adverb* **looser, loosest** ◊ *verb* **loosed, loosing**

loose-leaf *adjective* Designed so that pages can be put in and taken out: *Keep your class notes in a loose-leaf notebook.*
loose-leaf (lo͞os′lēf′) ◊ *adjective*

loosen *verb* **1.** To make or become loose or looser: *Loosen the belt a notch.* **2.** To free, untie, or release; let loose: *We loosened the dog from its leash.*
loos·en (lo͞o′sən) ◊ *verb* **loosened, loosening**

loot *noun* Stolen goods.
◊ *verb* To rob of valuable things.
loot (lo͞ot) ◊ *noun* ◊ *verb* **looted, looting**
‖*These sound alike:* **loot, lute**

lop *verb* To cut off a part from; trim.
lop (lŏp) ◊ *verb* **lopped, lopping**

lope *verb* To run with long, smooth strides.
◊ *noun* A gait with long, smooth strides.
lope (lōp) ◊ *verb* **loped, loping** ◊ *noun, plural* **lopes**

lopsided *adjective* Being heavier, larger, or higher on one side than on the other: *The pumpkin was lopsided.*
lop·sid·ed (lŏp′sī′dĭd) ◊ *adjective*

lord *noun* **1.** A person who has great authority or power, such as an owner of an estate. **2.** A man of noble rank in Great Britain. **3. Lord** A title for a man of noble rank.
lord (lôrd) ◊ *noun, plural* **lords**

lose *verb* **1.** To miss from one's possession; fail to find: *I lost my spelling book.* **2.** To be unable to keep: *I lost my balance and fell.* **3.** To give up in a natural process; shed: *Many trees lose their leaves in the fall.* **4.** To fail to win: *We lost both games.* **5.** To fail to take advantage of; waste: *We'll lose time if we stop to eat.* **6.** To stop seeing; miss: *We finally lost the balloon in the clouds.*
lose (lo͞oz) ◊ *verb* **lost, losing**

loss *noun* **1.** The act or fact of losing something: *The accident victim suffered a loss of memory. The team had two wins and three losses.* **2.** The pain or hardship caused by losing something or someone: *We all felt the loss of our dog.*
loss (lôs) ◊ *noun, plural* **losses**

lost *adjective* **1.** Misplaced or missing: *We never found the lost ring.* **2.** Not won or likely to be won: *Don't waste your efforts on a lost cause.* **3.** Having the mind fully occupied; absorbed: *I was lost in the book.* **4.** Not able to find one's way: *We took a wrong turn, and soon we were lost.*
◊ *verb* Past tense and past participle of **lose.**
lost (lôst) ◊ *adjective* ◊ *verb*

lot *noun* **1.** A large amount or number: *I have a lot of work to do.* **2.** A number of people or things of a kind: *This apple is the best of the lot.* **3.** A kind, type, or sort: *Pirates are a bad lot.* **4.** A piece of land: *There's a vacant lot behind our house.* **5.** Fortune in life; fate: *It was our lot to get the blame.*
lot (lŏt) ◊ *noun, plural* **lots**

L

lotion *noun* A liquid that is used to heal, cleanse, or soften the skin.
lo·tion (lō′shən) ◊ *noun, plural* **lotions**

lotus *noun* A water plant with large, usually pink or white flowers.
lo·tus (lō′təs) ◊ *noun, plural* **lotuses**

▲ **lotus**

loud *adjective* **1.** Having a high volume of sound: *We heard a loud crash.* **2.** Too bright: *That outfit is too loud to wear to school.*
◊ *adverb* In a loud manner: *Speak louder.*
loud (loud) ◊ *adjective, adverb* **louder, loudest**

loudspeaker *noun* A device that changes an electrical signal into sound and makes the sound louder.
loud·speak·er (**loud**′spē′kər) ◊ *noun, plural* **loudspeakers**

lounge *verb* To stand, sit, or lie in a lazy or relaxed way.
◊ *noun* A room with comfortable chairs where people can relax.
lounge (lounj) ◊ *verb* **lounged, lounging** ◊ *noun, plural* **lounges**

louse *noun* A small, wingless insect that often lives on the bodies of various animals and human beings. Lice bite and suck blood.
louse (lous) ◊ *noun, plural* **lice**

lovable *adjective* Having qualities that attract affection.
lov·a·ble (**lŭv**′ə bəl) ◊ *adjective*

love *noun* **1.** Strong affection and warm feeling for another. **2.** Affectionate regards: *Give them my love.* **3.** Strong fondness for or devotion to something.
◊ *verb* **1.** To feel love or strong affection for. **2.** To have a great enthusiasm or liking for: *I love to play hockey.*
love (lŭv) ◊ *noun, plural* **loves** ◊ *verb* **loved, loving**

ă pat	ĭ pit	oi	**oil**	th	ba**th**		
ā pay	ī ride	o͝o	book	*th*	ba*th*e		
â care	î fierce	o͞o	boot	ə	ago, item		
ä father	ŏ pot	ou	**out**		pencil		
ĕ pet	ō go	ŭ	cut		atom		
ē be	ô paw, for	û	fur		circus		

lovely *adjective* **1.** Inspiring love and affection: *You are a lovely, generous person.* **2.** Having pleasing or attractive qualities: *Their garden is lovely in spring.* —See Synonyms at **beautiful.**
love·ly (**lŭv**′lē) ◊ *adjective* **lovelier, loveliest**

loving *adjective* Feeling or showing love.
lov·ing (**lŭv**′ĭng) ◊ *adjective*

low¹ *adjective* **1.** Not high or tall: *We walked over the low hill.* **2.** Of less than the usual depth; shallow: *The river is low in late summer.* **3.** Near or at the horizon: *The moon was low in the sky.* **4.** Below average, as in amount, degree, or intensity: *These are low temperatures for June.* **5.** Having deep tones: *The tuba can play very low notes.* **6.** Not loud; hushed: *They spoke in low voices.* **7.** Less than the usual amount; short: *Our supplies are low.* **8.** Not happy or lively: *The coach was low after we lost the game.* **9.** Not favorable: *I have a low opinion of your friend.*
◊ *adverb* **1.** At, in, or to a low position or level: *The bird flew low over the ground.* **2.** With a low pitch: *A cello plays lower than a violin.* **3.** Not loudly: *Speak low; don't yell.*
low¹ (lō) ◊ *adjective, adverb* **lower, lowest**

low² *noun* The deep, long sound made by cattle; moo.
◊ *verb* To make this sound; moo.
low² (lō) ◊ *noun, plural* **lows** ◊ *verb* **lowed, lowing**

HISTORY **• low¹, low²**

Low¹ comes from an old Scandinavian word that meant "not high or tall." **Low²** goes back to an old English word for the sound made by cattle.

lower *verb* **1.** To let, bring, or move down to a level beneath the present level: *We lowered the flag at sunset.* **2.** To make or become less in value, degree, or quality: *The store owners lowered their prices.* **3.** To make less loud: *Please lower your voices in the hallways during school hours.*
low·er (lō′ər) ◊ *verb* **lowered, lowering**

lowland *noun* An area of low, flat land.
low·land (lō′lənd) ◊ *noun, plural* **lowlands**

▲ **lowland**

low tide *noun* The time at which the ocean is at its lowest level on the shore.
low tide ◊ *noun, plural* **low tides**

loyal *adjective* Firm in supporting a person, country, or cause; faithful.
loy·al (loi′əl) ◊ *adjective*

loyalty *noun* Firm, faithful support.
loy·al·ty (loi′əl tē) ◊ *noun, plural* **loyalties**

Lt. The abbreviation for *Lieutenant.*

lubricant *noun* A slippery substance, such as oil or grease, used to lubricate moving machine parts.
lu·bri·cant (lo͞o′brĭ kənt) ◊ *noun, plural* **lubricants**

lubricate *verb* To apply a lubricant to moving machine parts in order to reduce wear: *We lubricated the engine of our car.*
lu·bri·cate (lo͞o′brĭ kāt′) ◊ *verb* **lubricated, lubricating**

luck *noun* **1.** The chance happening of good or bad events; fortune: *Good luck seemed to favor the other team, and we lost the game.* **2.** Good fortune; success.
luck (lŭk) ◊ *noun*

luckily *adverb* By or with good luck.
luck·i·ly (lŭk′ə lē) ◊ *adverb*

lucky *adjective* **1.** Having good luck: *A lucky person won the contest.* **2.** Bringing good luck: *I always carry my lucky penny.*
luck·y (lŭk′ē) ◊ *adjective* **luckier, luckiest**

lug *verb* To haul or carry with great difficulty: *I had to lug ten books to school.*
lug (lŭg) ◊ *verb* **lugged, lugging**

luggage *noun* Bags and suitcases that a person takes on a trip; baggage.
lug·gage (lŭg′ĭj) ◊ *noun*

lukewarm *adjective* **1.** Neither hot nor cold; mildly warm: *Wash delicate things in lukewarm water.* **2.** Lacking enthusiasm: *I wanted to go on a bicycle trip, but my parents were lukewarm toward the idea.*
luke·warm (lo͝ok′wôrm′) ◊ *adjective*

lull *verb* To calm, quiet, and soothe: *Rocking the cradle will lull the baby to sleep.*
◊ *noun* A temporary period of quiet or calm: *There was a lull in the storm.*
lull (lŭl) ◊ *verb* **lulled, lulling** ◊ *noun, plural* **lulls**

lullaby *noun* A soothing song meant to lull a child to sleep.
lull·a·by (lŭl′ə bī′) ◊ *noun, plural* **lullabies**

lumber *noun* Timber that is sawed into boards and planks.
lum·ber (lŭm′bər) ◊ *noun*

lumberjack *noun* A person who chops down trees and hauls the logs to a sawmill.
lum·ber·jack (lŭm′bər jăk′) ◊ *noun, plural* **lumberjacks**

luminous *adjective* Giving off light; shining.
lu·mi·nous (lo͞o′mə nəs) ◊ *adjective*

lump *noun* **1.** A mass or piece that has a rough, irregular shape: *The artist started with a big lump of clay.* **2.** A swelling or bump: *The blow on my head raised quite a lump.*
◊ *adjective* Not divided into parts; whole: *I would like my allowance in a lump sum.*
◊ *verb* To form or cause to form lumps.
lump (lŭmp) ◊ *noun, plural* **lumps** ◊ *adjective* ◊ *verb* **lumped, lumping**

luna moth *noun* A large, pale-green North American moth.
lu·na moth (lo͞o′nə) ◊ *noun, plural* **luna moths**

lunar *adjective* **1.** Of, on, or having to do with the moon: *The spacecraft made a perfect lunar landing.* **2.** Measured or determined by motions of the moon.
lu·nar (lo͞o′nər) ◊ *adjective*

L

lunar module *noun* A small space vehicle designed to take astronauts from an orbiting spacecraft to the moon's surface and back.
lunar mod·ule (mŏj′ o͞ol) ◊ *noun, plural* **lunar modules**

▲ **lunar module**

lunch *noun* A meal eaten at midday.
◊ *verb* To eat a midday meal.
lunch (lŭnch) ◊ *noun, plural* **lunches** ◊ *verb* **lunched, lunching**

luncheon *noun* A midday meal; lunch.
lunch·eon (**lŭn′** chən) ◊ *noun, plural* **luncheons**

lung *noun* Either of two spongy, baglike organs that are used for breathing and that are found in the chests of human beings and most animals. The lungs take in air, absorb oxygen, and give off carbon dioxide.
lung (lŭng) ◊ *noun, plural* **lungs**

lunge *noun* A sudden, forceful movement forward: *The player made a lunge for the ball.*
◊ *verb* To make a sudden movement forward: *The player lunged at the ball.*
lunge (lŭnj) ◊ *noun, plural* **lunges** ◊ *verb* **lunged, lunging**

ă	pat	ĭ	pit	oi	**oil**	th	ba**th**
ā	pay	ī	ride	o͝o	**book**	*th*	ba**the**
â	care	î	fierce	o͞o	**boot**	ə	ago, item
ä	father	ŏ	pot	ou	**out**		pencil
ĕ	pet	ō	go	ŭ	**cut**		atom
ē	be	ô	paw, for	û	**fur**		circus

lurch *noun* A sudden, heavy, unsteady movement to one side or forward.
◊ *verb* To move with a lurch; stagger.
lurch (lûrch) ◊ *noun, plural* **lurches** ◊ *verb* **lurched, lurching**

lure *noun* **1.** Something that attracts, especially with the promise of pleasure or a reward. **2.** An artificial bait used to attract and catch fish.
◊ *verb* To attract by offering something tempting.
lure (lo͝or) ◊ *noun, plural* **lures** ◊ *verb* **lured, luring**

lush *adjective* **1.** Growing thick and very green, as grass or lawns. **2.** Covered with plant growth: *We passed lush banks of ivy.* **3.** Splendid and comfortable; luxurious.
lush (lŭsh) ◊ *adjective* **lusher, lushest**

luster *noun* A shine or glow of soft reflected light: *I admire the luster of polished wood.*
lus·ter (**lŭs′** tər) ◊ *noun*

lustrous *adjective* Having luster; shining.
lus·trous (**lŭs′** trəs) ◊ *adjective*

lusty *adjective* Full of energy, strength, and power; robust.
lust·y (**lŭs′** tē) ◊ *adjective* **lustier, lustiest**

lute *noun* A stringed musical instrument that has a pear-shaped body and usually a bent neck.
lute (lo͞ot) ◊ *noun, plural* **lutes**
‖ *These sound alike:* **lute, loot**

luxuriant *adjective* Growing or producing abundantly; lush: *The horses grazed in luxuriant meadows.*
lux·u·ri·ant (lŭg **zho͝or′** ē ənt) ◊ *adjective*

luxurious *adjective* **1.** Very fond of pleasure and luxury. **2.** Very splendid and comfortable: *They live in a luxurious apartment.*
lux·u·ri·ous (lŭg **zho͝or′** ē əs) ◊ *adjective*

luxury *noun* **1.** Something that is not really needed but that gives great pleasure, enjoyment, or comfort: *A luxury is often expensive or hard to get.* **2.** A splendid, pleasing, and comfortable environment: *They have always lived in luxury.*
lux·u·ry (**lŭg′** zhə rē *or* **lŭk′** shə rē) ◊ *noun, plural* **luxuries**

-ly[1] The suffix *-ly[1]* forms adjectives and means "like" or "having the characteristics of." A *friendly* smile shows or encourages friendship.

VOCABULARY BUILDER • –ly¹

Many words that are formed with **–ly¹** are not entries in this dictionary. But you can figure out what these words mean by looking up the meanings of the root words and the suffix. For example:
cowardly = like a coward
knightly = having the characteristics of a knight

–ly² The suffix *-ly²* forms adverbs and means "in a certain way." When something happens *accidentally,* it happens in an accidental way. When a person smiles *happily,* he or she smiles in a happy way. When someone does something *simply,* he or she does it in a simple way.

VOCABULARY BUILDER • –ly²

Many words that are formed with **–ly²** are not entries in this dictionary. But you can figure out what these words mean by looking up the meanings of the root words and the suffix. For example:
boldly = in a bold way
quickly = in a quick way

lye *noun* A very strong cleaning solution made by allowing water to pass through wood ashes.
lye (lī) ◊ *noun*
‖*These sound alike:* **lye, lie**

lymph *noun* A clear liquid that carries nourishment to bodily tissues and returns wastes to the bloodstream.
lymph (lĭmf) ◊ *noun*

lymphatic *adjective* Of or having to do with lymph.
lym·phat·ic (lĭm **făt**′ĭk) ◊ *adjective*

lynx *noun* A wild cat with thick, soft fur, tufts of hair on its ears, and a short tail.
lynx (lĭngks) ◊ *noun, plural* **lynx** *or* **lynxes**

▲ **lynx**

lyre *noun* An ancient stringed instrument that is related to the harp.
lyre (līr) ◊ *noun, plural* **lyres**

lyric *or* **lyrical** *adjective* Like a song or fit for singing.
lyr·ic (lĭr′ĭk) *or* **lyr·i·cal** (lĭr′ĭ kəl) ◊ *adjective*

lyrics *plural noun* The words of a song.
lyr·ics (lĭr′ĭks) ◊ *plural noun*

Mouse

Mm

M is the thirteenth letter of the English alphabet. Did you know that it has a long history?

Over 3,500 years ago, people in the Middle East were using symbols that became the letters of our alphabet. This ancient Middle Eastern symbol is a form of the letter that became our letter *M*.

M

The ancient Greeks borrowed their alphabet from people in the Middle East. Here is a form of the Greek letter that became our letter *M*.

M

The ancient Romans borrowed their alphabet from a people who had taken their own letter symbols from the Greeks. Here is a form of the Roman letter *M* that was used for carving letters into stone. These letters became the model for our printed capital letters.

m

As people wrote quickly, especially with pens, the capital letters began to take the shapes of small letters. Here is a small-letter *m* that was developed about 1,200 years ago.

Mm *Mm*	Mm	Mm	Mm
Handwriting	Sans Serif Type	Serif Type	Computer Printing

m *or* **M** *noun* **1.** The thirteenth letter of the English alphabet. **2.** The Roman numeral for the number 1,000.
m *or* **M** (ĕm) ◊ *noun, plural* **m's** *or* **M's**

m The abbreviation for *meter.*

MA The abbreviation for *Massachusetts* used with a Zip Code.

ma'am *noun* Madam.
ma'am (măm) ◊ *noun*

macaroni *noun* A food made of flour paste that is dried and shaped into hollow tubes.
mac·a·ro·ni (măk′ə **rō′** nē) ◊ *noun, plural* **macaronis** *or* **macaronies**

macaw *noun* A large, often brightly colored tropical American parrot with a long tail, a powerful curved bill, and a harsh cry.
ma·caw (mə **kô′**) ◊ *noun, plural* **macaws**

ă	pat	ĭ	pit	oi	**oil**	th	ba**th**
ā	pay	ī	ride	o͝o	**book**	*th*	ba*th*e
â	care	î	fierce	o͞o	**boot**	ə	ago, item
ä	father	ŏ	pot	ou	**out**		pencil
ĕ	pet	ō	go	ŭ	cut		atom
ē	be	ô	paw, for	û	fur		circus

machine *noun* **1.** A combination of mechanical parts that operate together to perform a certain task: *Vacuum cleaners are machines that make housework easier.* **2.** A simple device, as a pulley, for applying power, creating motion, or changing direction.
ma·chine (mə **shēn′**) ◊ *noun, plural* **machines**

machine gun *noun* A rifle that fires rapidly while the trigger is being pressed.
machine gun ◊ *noun, plural* **machine guns**

machinery *noun* **1.** A group of machines. **2.** The working parts of a particular machine. **3.** A system with related elements that work together: *We are studying the complicated machinery of our government.*
ma·chin·er·y (mə **shē′** nə rē) ◊ *noun*

machinist *noun* A person who is skilled in using machine-operated tools.
ma·chin·ist (mə **shē′** nĭst) ◊ *noun, plural* **machinists**

mackerel *noun* An ocean food fish with a silvery body and dark bars on its back.
mack·er·el (**măk′** ər əl) ◊ *noun, plural* **mackerel** *or* **mackerels**

mackinaw *noun* A short coat made of heavy woolen material.
mack·i·naw (**măk′** ə-nô′) ◊ *noun, plural* **mackinaws**

▲ **mackinaw**

macron *noun* A mark (¯) that is placed over a vowel to show that it has a long sound. In the pronunciation of the word *make* (māk), the macron is placed over the *ā*.
ma·cron (**mā′** krŏn′) ◊ *noun, plural* **macrons**

mad *adjective* **1.** Mentally ill; insane. **2.** Very angry: *You make me mad by interrupting all the time.* **3.** Very enthusiastic: *I am really mad about basketball.* **4.** Wildly excited or uncontrolled: *There was a mad scramble to get on the bus.*
mad (măd) ◊ *adjective* **madder, maddest**

madam *noun* A polite form of address used for a woman: *May I help you, madam?*
mad·am (**măd′** əm) ◊ *noun*

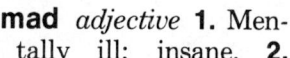

> ***HISTORY*** • **madam**
>
> **Madam** comes from the French phrase *ma dame,* meaning "my lady."

madden *verb* To make very angry.
mad·den (**măd′** n) ◊ *verb* **maddened, maddening**

made *verb* Past tense and past participle of **make.**
made (mād) ◊ *verb*
‖*These sound alike:* **made, maid**

made-up *adjective* Not real; invented: *We told made-up stories about ghosts.*
made-up (**mād′ ŭp′**) ◊ *adjective*

madhouse *noun* **1.** An asylum for insane people. **2.** A place of total confusion.
mad·house (**măd′** hous′) ◊ *noun, plural* **madhouses**

magazine *noun* **1.** A publication that is issued regularly, as every week or month. **2.** A building for storing military supplies. **3.** A storage place for ammunition in a fort or ship. **4.** A container in a gun where the cartridges are held.
mag·a·zine (**măg′** ə zēn′ *or* măg′ə **zēn′**) ◊ *noun, plural* **magazines**

> ***HISTORY*** • **magazine**
>
> **Magazine** comes from an Arabic word meaning "storehouse." A **magazine** is a "storehouse" of information.

maggot *noun* The soft, thick, legless larva of a fly that has recently hatched.
mag·got (**măg′** ət) ◊ *noun, plural* **maggots**

magic *noun* **1.** The pretended art of controlling natural forces by using charms or spells. **2.** The art of creating entertaining and mysterious effects as if by magic. **3.** A special charm or enchantment: *I love the magic of rainbows.* ◊ *adjective* **1.** Of or relating to the practice of magic. **2.** Done by or as if by magic. **3.** Charming; enchanting.
mag·ic (**măj′** ĭk) ◊ *noun* ◊ *adjective*

magical *adjective* **1.** Of or produced by magic. **2.** Having a mysterious or enchanting quality.
mag·i·cal (**măj′** ĭ kəl) ◊ *adjective*

magician *noun* **1.** A person who uses magic; wizard. **2.** An entertainer who performs magic tricks.
ma·gi·cian (mə **jĭsh′** ən) ◊ *noun, plural* **magicians**

magistrate *noun* **1.** A government official who has the power to put laws into effect. **2.** A local law official, such as the judge of a police court.
mag·is·trate (**măj′** ĭ strāt′) ◊ *noun, plural* **magistrates**

magnesium *noun* A very lightweight silver-white chemical element that is used in many alloys and in fireworks.
mag·ne·si·um (măg **nē′** zē əm) ◊ *noun*

magnet *noun* A piece of material, such as metal or an ore, that attracts iron and steel.
mag·net (**măg′** nĭt) ◊ *noun, plural* **magnets**

magnetic *adjective* **1.** Of or relating to magnetism or magnets. **2.** Able to attract iron and

M

steel. **3.** Able to attract or fascinate other people.
mag·net·ic (măg **nĕt′**ĭk) ◊ *adjective*

magnetic field *noun* The space around a magnet within which magnetic power can be detected.
magnetic field ◊ *noun, plural* **magnetic fields**

magnetic pole *noun* **1.** Either of the poles of a magnet where the magnetic field is strongest. **2.** Either of two points on the surface of the earth, near the North and South Poles, where the earth's magnetic field is strongest.
magnetic pole ◊ *noun, plural* **magnetic poles**

magnetism *noun* **1.** The power to attract iron and steel as a magnet does. **2.** The force that is produced by a magnetic field. **3.** The ability to attract or fascinate others.
mag·net·ism (**măg′**nĭ tĭz′əm) ◊ *noun*

magnetize *verb* To make magnetic.
mag·net·ize (**măg′**nĭ tīz′) ◊ *verb* **magnetized, magnetizing**

magnificence *noun* The quality or condition of being magnificent.
mag·nif·i·cence (măg **nĭf′**ĭ səns) ◊ *noun*

magnificent *adjective* Superb; splendid: *We visited a magnificent castle.* —See Synonyms at **grand.**
mag·nif·i·cent (măg **nĭf′**ĭ sənt) ◊ *adjective*

magnify *verb* **1.** To cause to appear greater or more important; exaggerate: *Don't magnify small problems.* **2.** To enlarge the appearance of: *A microscope magnifies bacteria.*
mag·ni·fy (**măg′**nə fī′) ◊ *verb* **magnified, magnifying**

magnifying glass *noun* A lens that magnifies objects seen through it.
magnifying glass ◊ *noun, plural* **magnifying glasses**

magnitude *noun* **1.** Great size or extent. **2.** Importance; significance: *This is a problem of the first magnitude.*
mag·ni·tude (**măg′**nĭ to͞od′ *or* **măg′**nĭ tyo͞od′) ◊ *noun*

ă	pat	ĭ	pit	oi	**oi**l	th	ba**th**
ā	pay	ī	ride	o͝o	b**oo**k	*th*	ba**th**e
â	care	î	fierce	o͞o	b**oo**t	ə	ago, item
ä	father	ŏ	pot	ou	**ou**t		pencil
ĕ	pet	ō	go	ŭ	c**u**t		atom
ē	be	ô	paw, for	û	f**u**r		circus

magnolia *noun* A tree or tall shrub that has large, usually white, pink, purple, or yellow flowers.
mag·no·lia (măg **nōl′**yə) ◊ *noun, plural* **magnolias**

HISTORY • magnolia

The **magnolia** was named after Pierre *Magnol*, a French professor of botany who lived about 300 years ago.

▲ **magnolia**

magpie *noun* A noisy, black and white bird related to the crows and jays.
mag·pie (**măg′**pī′) ◊ *noun, plural* **magpies**

mahogany *noun* A tropical American tree with hard, reddish-brown wood that is used for making furniture.
ma·hog·a·ny (mə **hŏg′**ə nē) ◊ *noun, plural* **mahoganies**

maid *noun* **1.** A girl or unmarried woman. **2.** A woman servant.
maid (mād) ◊ *noun, plural* **maids**
‖*These sound alike:* **maid, made**

maiden *noun* An unmarried girl or young woman.
◊ *adjective* **1.** Not married. **2.** First or earliest: *The ship sailed on its maiden voyage.*
maid·en (**mād′**n) ◊ *noun, plural* **maidens**
◊ *adjective*

maidenhood *noun* The state or time of being a maiden.
maid·en·hood (**mād′**n ho͝od′) ◊ *noun*

maiden name *noun* A woman's family name before she marries.
maiden name ◊ *noun, plural* **maiden names**

maid of honor *noun* An unmarried woman who is a bride's chief attendant.
maid of honor ◊ *noun, plural* **maids of honor**

mail¹ *noun* **1.** Material, such as letters, that is handled in a country's postal system. **2.** A delivery of mail: *What did we get in the mail today?* **3.** The government system by which mail is sent and delivered.
◊ *verb* To send by mail.
mail¹ (māl) ◊ *noun, plural* **mails** ◊ *verb* **mailed, mailing**
‖*These sound alike:* **mail, male**

mail² *noun* Flexible armor made especially of metal rings connected together.
mail² (māl) ◊ *noun*
‖*These sound alike:* **mail, male**

***HISTORY* • mail¹, mail²**

Mail¹ used to mean "a bag for carrying letters." It comes from an old French word that meant "bag, pouch." **Mail²** comes from an old French word that meant "mesh." The French word in turn came from a Latin word that meant both "spot" and "mesh."

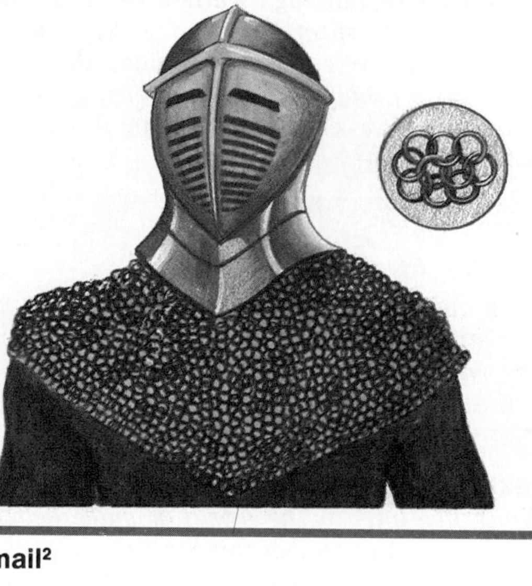

▲ **mail²**

mailbox *noun* **1.** A public box in which to place letters being sent by mail. **2.** A private box for mail delivered to a home or business.
mail·box (**māl**′bŏks′) ◊ *noun, plural* **mailboxes**

mail carrier *noun* A person who delivers mail or collects it from mailboxes.
mail carrier ◊ *noun, plural* **mail carriers**

mailman *noun* A mail carrier.
mail·man (**māl**′măn′) ◊ *noun, plural* **mailmen**

maim *verb* To disable badly; cripple.
maim (mām) ◊ *verb* **maimed, maiming**

main *adjective* Most important; chief: *Look for the main idea in each paragraph.*
◊ *noun* **1.** A large pipe, duct, or line used to carry water, oil, gas, or electricity. **2.** The open sea.
main (mān) ◊ *adjective* ◊ *noun, plural* **mains**
‖*These sound alike:* **main, mane**

mainland *noun* The main part of a country, territory, or continent as opposed to its islands or, sometimes, its peninsulas.
main·land (**mān**′lănd′) ◊ *noun, plural* **mainlands**

mainly *adverb* For the most part; chiefly.
main·ly (**mān**′lē) ◊ *adverb*

mainmast *noun* The tallest mast of a sailing ship.
main·mast (**mān**′măst′ *or* **mān**′məst) ◊ *noun, plural* **mainmasts**

mainsail *noun* The largest sail on the mainmast of a sailing ship.
main·sail (**mān**′sāl′ *or* **mān**′səl) ◊ *noun, plural* **mainsails**

mainspring *noun* The principal spring of a clock or watch.
main·spring (**mān**′sprĭng′) ◊ *noun, plural* **mainsprings**

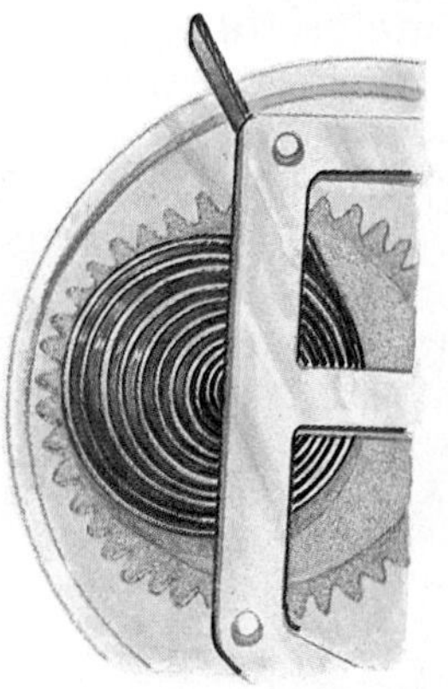

▲ **mainspring**

mainstay *noun* **1.** A strong rope or cable that holds a mainmast in place. **2.** A main support: *You are the mainstay of our team.*
main·stay (**mān**′stā′) ◊ *noun, plural* **mainstays**

maintain *verb* **1.** To carry on; continue: *They maintained their habit of exercising.* **2.** To keep in a desirable condition: *Road crews maintain our highways.* **3.** To provide for the upkeep of: *We maintain an apartment*

M

in the city. **4.** To uphold by using sound arguments; defend: *He maintained his opinion firmly.* **5.** To declare to be true: *She maintained that her friend was innocent.*
main·tain (mān **tān′**) ◊ *verb* **maintained, maintaining**

maintenance *noun* **1.** The act of maintaining or the condition of being maintained. **2.** The work involved in maintaining; upkeep. **3.** Means of support or livelihood.
main·te·nance (**mān′** tə nəns) ◊ *noun*

maize *noun* The corn plant or its kernels.
maize (māz) ◊ *noun*
‖*These sound alike:* **maize, maze**

Maj. The abbreviation for *Major.*

majestic *adjective* Stately and dignified: *The monarch gave a majestic wave.* —See Synonyms at **grand.**
ma·jes·tic (mə **jĕs′** tĭk) ◊ *adjective*

majesty *noun* **1.** Royal power, greatness, and dignity. **2.** The quality or condition of being majestic. **3. Majesty** A title used in speaking of or to a king, queen, emperor, or empress.
maj·es·ty (**măj′** ĭ stē) ◊ *noun, plural* **majesties**

major *adjective* Larger, greater, or more important: *Students spend the major part of the day in school.*
◊ *noun* An Army, Air Force, or Marine Corps officer ranking above a captain.
ma·jor (**mā′** jər) ◊ *adjective* ◊ *noun, plural* **majors**

majorette *noun* A drum majorette.
ma·jor·ette (mā′jə **rĕt′**) ◊ *noun, plural* **majorettes**

majority *noun* **1.** The greater number or part: *Girls make up the majority of the class.* **2.** The amount by which one number is greater than another: *He won by 12,000 votes to 7,000, which gives him a majority of 5,000.* **3.** Legal voting age.
ma·jor·i·ty (mə **jôr′** ĭ tē) ◊ *noun, plural* **majorities**

ă	pat	ĭ	pit	oi	oil	th	bath
ā	pay	ī	ride	ŏŏ	book	*th*	bathe
â	care	î	fierce	ōō	boot	ə	ago, item
ä	father	ŏ	pot	ou	out		pencil
ĕ	pet	ō	go	ŭ	cut		atom
ē	be	ô	paw, for	û	fur		circus

make *verb* **1.** To form, shape, or put together out of material or parts: *I made a shirt.* **2.** To cause to happen; bring about: *Don't make so much noise.* **3.** To cause to be or become: *That song makes me sad.* **4.** To force; compel: *Make them clean their rooms.* **5.** To carry out, engage in, or perform: *You should make an attempt to study.* **6.** To serve as: *This makes a good hiding place.* **7.** To produce by thought or action: *I made a mistake.* **8.** To get or gain; acquire: *You make friends easily. We need to make some money.* **9.** To amount to; equal: *Ten dimes make a dollar.* **10.** To set up or in order; prepare: *Please make your bed.*
◊ *noun* **1.** The style or way in which something is made. **2.** A particular kind or brand: *They have an expensive make of car.*
◊ *idioms* **make believe** To pretend; imagine. **make good 1.** To fulfill or accomplish: *He made good his promise.* **2.** To do well; succeed: *She made good in her new job.* **make out 1.** To see and identify: *I can just make out a sign ahead.* **2.** To understand: *Can you make out the words?* **3.** To write out: *He made out a list.* **4.** To get along: *How did you make out in school?* **make up 1.** To create by using the imagination: *She enjoys making up stories.* **2.** To form by putting together; compose: *The band is made up of boys and girls.* **make up one's mind** To reach a decision; decide: *I made up my mind to buy a camera.*
make (māk) ◊ *verb* **made, making** ◊ *noun, plural* **makes**

SYNONYMS

make, form, manufacture

We *made* a little house out of old boards. They *formed* figures out of clay. How many television sets are *manufactured* each year?

make-believe *noun* A playful pretending: *Elves live only in the world of make-believe.*
◊ *adjective* Pretended; imaginary.
make-be·lieve (**māk′** bĭ lēv′) ◊ *noun* ◊ *adjective*

makeshift *noun* Something that is used as a temporary substitute for something else.
make·shift (**māk′** shĭft′) ◊ *noun, plural* **makeshifts**

make-up *or* **makeup** *noun* **1.** The way in which something is put together; composition. **2.** The basic nature or disposition of someone. **3.** Materials that are applied to the face or body for a theatrical role. **4.** Cosmetics, such as lipstick.
make-up *or* **make·up** (māk′ŭp′) ◊ *noun, plural* **make-ups** *or* **makeups**

▲ **make-up**
Applying clown make-up

malady *noun* A disease or ailment.
mal·a·dy (măl′ə dē) ◊ *noun, plural* **maladies**

malaria *noun* A severe disease marked by chills, fever, and sweating. Malaria is spread by the bite of a certain kind of mosquito.
ma·lar·i·a (mə lâr′ē ə) ◊ *noun*

male *adjective* **1.** Of, relating to, or being the sex that can fertilize female egg cells. **2.** Of, relating to, or typical of a man or boy.
◊ *noun* A male individual.
male (māl) ◊ *adjective* ◊ *noun, plural* **males**
‖*These sound alike:* **male, mail**

malice *noun* A desire to hurt others or see others suffer; spite.
mal·ice (măl′ĭs) ◊ *noun*

malicious *adjective* Feeling or showing malice; spiteful.
ma·li·cious (mə lĭsh′əs) ◊ *adjective*

malign *verb* To speak in an evil way about; slander.
ma·lign (mə līn′) ◊ *verb* **maligned, maligning**

malignant *adjective* **1.** Having or showing ill will; malicious. **2.** Threatening to life and health; deadly: *Cancer is a malignant disease.*
ma·lig·nant (mə lĭg′nənt) ◊ *adjective*

mall *noun* **1.** A public walk lined with trees. **2.** A street lined with shops and closed to motor vehicles. **3.** A shopping center.
mall (môl) ◊ *noun, plural* **malls**
‖*These sound alike:* **mall, maul**

mallard *noun* A wild duck of North America, Europe, and northern Asia.
mal·lard (măl′ərd) ◊ *noun, plural* **mallards**

malleable *adjective* Capable of being shaped or formed by pressure or hammering: *Silver is a malleable metal.*
mal·le·a·ble (măl′ē ə bəl) ◊ *adjective*

mallet *noun* A long-handled club with a wooden head that is used especially in playing croquet.
mal·let (măl′ĭt) ◊ *noun, plural* **mallets**

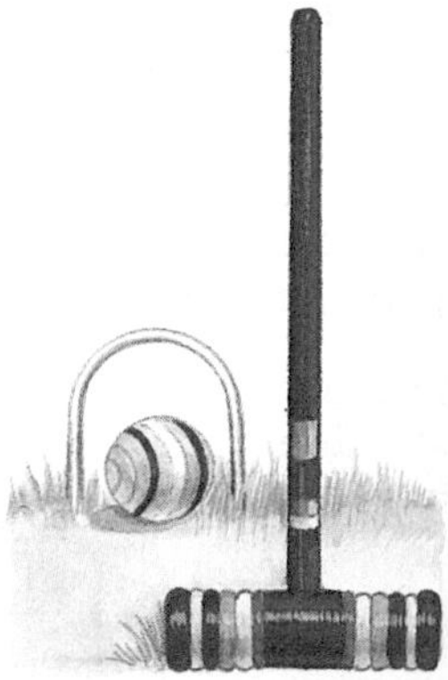

▲ **mallet**

malnutrition *noun* A condition that has been caused by having too little food to eat or by eating the wrong kinds of food.
mal·nu·tri·tion (măl′no͞o **trĭsh′**ən *or* măl′nyo͞o **trĭsh′**ən) ◊ *noun*

malt *noun* **1.** Grain, especially barley, that has been soaked in water and allowed to sprout. **2.** A malted milk.
malt (môlt) ◊ *noun, plural* **malts**

malted milk *noun* A drink made of milk, a powder containing malt, and flavoring.
malted milk ◊ *noun, plural* **malted milks**

maltreat *verb* To treat in a rough or cruel way; abuse.
mal·treat (măl **trēt′**) ◊ *verb* **maltreated, maltreating**

maltreatment *noun* Bad treatment; abuse.
mal·treat·ment (măl **trēt′**mənt) ◊ *noun*

mama *noun* Mother.
ma·ma (mä′mə) ◊ *noun, plural* **mamas**

mammal *noun* A warm-blooded animal, as a human being, cat, elephant, or whale, that has a backbone and usually has some hair or fur on its body. Mammals produce milk for feeding their young.
mam·mal (măm′əl) ◊ *noun, plural* **mammals**

M

mammoth *noun* A very large elephant with long curved tusks and thick hair. Mammoths no longer exist.
◊ *adjective* Huge; gigantic.
mam·moth (**măm′** əth) ◊ *noun, plural* **mammoths** ◊ *adjective*

▲ **mammoth**

man *noun* **1.** A fully grown male human being. **2.** Any human being; person. **3.** Human beings in general; mankind. **4.** A male servant or employee. **5.** A piece used in a game such as chess.
◊ *verb* **1.** To work at operating: *Who will man the oars?* **2.** To take one's post at: *The first mate manned the bridge.* **3.** To supply with crew members.
man (măn) ◊ *noun, plural* **men** ◊ *verb* **manned, manning**

Man. The abbreviation for *Manitoba,* Canada.

manage *verb* **1.** To have control over; direct: *Who will manage the business while your parents are away?* **2.** To succeed in doing something: *I managed to finish my work. We have to manage somehow.*
man·age (**măn′** ĭj) ◊ *verb* **managed, managing**

management *noun* **1.** The act or process of managing. **2.** A group of people who manage something, such as a business.
man·age·ment (**măn′** ĭj mənt) ◊ *noun*

manager *noun* A person who manages.
man·ag·er (**măn′** ĭ jər) ◊ *noun, plural* **managers**

mandarin *noun* A high public official in the days of the Chinese empire.
man·da·rin (**măn′** də rĭn) ◊ *noun, plural* **mandarins**

mandate *noun* **1.** An order that is issued by an authority, such as a court of law. **2.** An instruction that is given by public voters to an elected official.
man·date (**măn′** dāt′) ◊ *noun, plural* **mandates**

mandible *noun* **1.** A jaw, especially the lower jaw. **2.** One of a pair of small mouth parts in some insects for gripping and biting.
man·di·ble (**măn′** də bəl) ◊ *noun, plural* **mandibles**

mandolin *noun* A musical instrument that has a pear-shaped body, a long neck, and usually four pairs of strings.
man·do·lin (măn′də **lĭn′**) ◊ *noun, plural* **mandolins**

mane *noun* The long, heavy hair growing from the neck and head of an animal such as a horse or a male lion.
mane (mān) ◊ *noun, plural* **manes**
‖*These sound alike:* **mane, main**

maneuver *noun* **1.** A skillful or clever action or plan of action. **2.** A planned movement, as of troops or warships. **3.** **maneuvers** A military training exercise.
◊ *verb* **1.** To move or guide in a skillful way. **2.** To use or get by using skillful plans or clever tricks. **3.** To carry out maneuvers.
ma·neu·ver (mə **no͞o′** vər *or* mə **nyo͞o′** vər) ◊ *noun, plural* **maneuvers** ◊ *verb* **maneuvered, maneuvering**

manganese *noun* A brittle, grayish chemical element that is used especially to strengthen steel alloys.
man·ga·nese (**măng′** gə nēz′) ◊ *noun*

manger *noun* A trough or open box in which feed for horses or cattle is placed.
man·ger (**mān′** jər) ◊ *noun, plural* **mangers**

mangle *verb* To injure by cutting, tearing, or crushing.
man·gle (**măng′** gəl) ◊ *verb* **mangled, mangling**

ă	pat	ĭ	pit	oi	**oil**	th	ba**th**
ā	pay	ī	ride	o͝o	book	*th*	bathe
â	care	î	fierce	o͞o	boot	ə	ago, item
ä	father	ŏ	pot	ou	**out**		pencil
ĕ	pet	ō	go	ŭ	cut		atom
ē	be	ô	paw, for	û	fur		circus

mango *noun* A tropical fruit with a smooth rind and sweet, juicy, yellow-orange flesh.
man·go (măng′ gō) ◊ *noun, plural* **mangoes** *or* **mangos**

▲ **mango**

manhole *noun* A covered hole, as in a street, through which a worker can enter to make repairs.
man·hole (măn′hōl′) ◊ *noun, plural* **manholes**

manhood *noun* **1.** The condition or time of being an adult male. **2.** Adult males as a group.
man·hood (măn′hŏŏd′) ◊ *noun*

mania *noun* **1.** A form of mental illness marked by excited and sometimes violent activity. **2.** Great enthusiasm: *They have a mania for model airplanes.*
ma·ni·a (mā′nē ə) ◊ *noun, plural* **manias**

manicure *noun* A cosmetic treatment for the hands and fingernails.
◊ *verb* To give a manicure to.
man·i·cure (măn′ĭ kyŏŏr′) ◊ *noun, plural* **manicures** ◊ *verb* **manicured, manicuring**

manifest *adjective* Easy to see; obvious.
man·i·fest (măn′ə fĕst′) ◊ *adjective*

manifestation *noun* **1.** The act of showing openly. **2.** Something that gives proof: *Sneezing often seems to be the first manifestation of a cold.*
man·i·fes·ta·tion (măn′ə fə **stā′**shən) ◊ *noun, plural* **manifestations**

manipulate *verb* **1.** To operate with the hands, especially in a skillful way: *The pilot manipulates the controls on an airplane.* **2.** To influence or manage cleverly and often in order to deceive: *Don't try to manipulate the teacher to get a good grade.*
ma·nip·u·late (mə **nĭp′**yə lāt′) ◊ *verb* **manipulated, manipulating**

mankind *noun* Human beings as a group.
man·kind (măn′kīnd′) ◊ *noun*

manly *adjective* **1.** Having qualities, such as physical strength, that are traditionally thought of as appropriate to a man. **2.** Of or relating to a man or men: *Some people don't think of knitting as a manly activity.*
man·ly (măn′lē) ◊ *adjective* **manlier, manliest**

manmade *adjective* Made by human beings rather than by nature; synthetic: *Nylon is a manmade fiber.*
man·made (măn′**mād′**) ◊ *adjective*

manner *noun* **1.** A way or style of doing things: *Work in a careful manner.* **2.** A style of personal behavior: *Your pleasant manner makes us like you.* **3. manners** Behavior toward or in the company of others: *Their parents taught them good manners.* **4.** Kind; sort: *What manner of person are you?*
man·ner (măn′ər) ◊ *noun, plural* **manners**
‖*These sound alike:* **manner, manor**

mannerism *noun* A way of behaving that has become a habit.
man·ner·ism (măn′ər ĭz′əm) ◊ *noun, plural* **mannerisms**

mannerly *adjective* Having or showing good manners; polite.
man·ner·ly (măn′ər lē) ◊ *adjective*

man-of-war *noun* A warship.
man-of-war (măn′əv **wôr′**) ◊ *noun, plural* **men-of-war**

manor *noun* **1.** A lord's estate in the Middle Ages. **2.** A large estate.
man·or (măn′ər) ◊ *noun, plural* **manors**
‖*These sound alike:* **manor, manner**

mansion *noun* A large, stately house.
man·sion (măn′shən) ◊ *noun, plural* **mansions**

manslaughter *noun* The unlawful act of killing a person without intending to do so.
man·slaugh·ter (măn′slô′tər) ◊ *noun*

mantel *noun* **1.** The structure that surrounds a fireplace. **2.** A mantelpiece.
man·tel (măn′tl) ◊ *noun, plural* **mantels**
‖*These sound alike:* **mantel, mantle**

mantelpiece *noun* The shelf over a fireplace.
man·tel·piece (măn′tl pēs′) ◊ *noun, plural* **mantelpieces**

M

mantis *noun* A large insect related to the grasshopper. A mantis feeds on other insects that it grasps in its folded front legs.
man·tis (măn′tĭs) ◊ *noun, plural* **mantises**

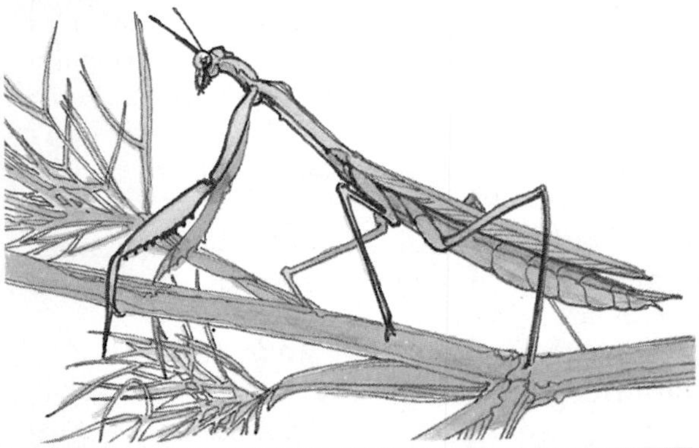

▲ **mantis**

mantle *noun* **1.** A loose outer cloak without sleeves. **2.** Something that covers or conceals like a mantle: *A white mantle of snow covered the ground.*
man·tle (măn′tl) ◊ *noun, plural* **mantles**
‖*These sound alike:* **mantle, mantel**

manual *adjective* **1.** Of or relating to the hands: *I have no manual skill.* **2.** Used by or operated with the hands: *The typewriter has a manual keyboard.*
◊ *noun* A book of instructions; handbook.
man·u·al (măn′yo͞o əl) ◊ *adjective* ◊ *noun, plural* **manuals**

manufacture *verb* To make, especially by using machinery: *The town's biggest factory manufactures cars.* —See Synonyms at **make.**
◊ *noun* The act or process of manufacturing: *Their business is the manufacture of toys.*
man·u·fac·ture (măn′yə **făk′**chər) ◊ *verb* **manufactured, manufacturing** ◊ *noun*

manure *noun* Animal waste that is used as a fertilizer.
ma·nure (mə **no͝or′** *or* mə **nyo͝or′**) ◊ *noun*

manuscript *noun* Something, such as a book or magazine article, that is written by hand or on a typewriter.
man·u·script (măn′yə skrĭpt′) ◊ *noun, plural* **manuscripts**

many *adjective* **1.** Adding up to a large number; numerous: *Our club has many rules.* **2.** Being one of a large number: *Many a day passed before the weather changed.*
◊ *pronoun* A large number of persons or things: *Many were invited.*
man·y (mĕn′ē) ◊ *adjective* **more, most** ◊ *pronoun*

SYNONYMS

many, numerous, several

I don't know how *many* times I've wanted to go there. *Numerous* people were at the parade. The phone rang *several* times before I could answer it.
Antonym: *few*

map *noun* **1.** A drawing or chart of all or part of the earth's surface that shows features such as rivers and mountains. **2.** A drawing or chart of the sky that shows the positions of heavenly bodies.
◊ *verb* **1.** To make a map of: *Scientists are using sonar to map the ocean floor.* **2.** To plan in detail: *We mapped a full schedule.*
map (măp) ◊ *noun, plural* **maps** ◊ *verb* **mapped, mapping**

maple *noun* A tree that has leaves with deep notches, seeds that grow in pairs and look like wings, and hard wood. One kind of maple has sap that is boiled to produce syrup and sugar.
ma·ple (mā′pəl) ◊ *noun, plural* **maples**

mar *verb* To spoil the beauty or pleasure of; ruin: *Rain marred their vacation.* —See Synonyms at **harm.**
mar (mär) ◊ *verb* **marred, marring**

Mar. The abbreviation for *March.*

marabou *noun* A large African stork.
mar·a·bou (măr′ə bo͞o) ◊ *noun, plural* **marabous**

maraca *noun* A musical instrument that is made of a hollow gourd that contains seeds or pebbles. Maracas are usually played in pairs by shaking them.
ma·ra·ca (mə **rä′**kə) ◊ *noun, plural* **maracas**

ă	pat	ĭ	pit	oi	**oil**	th	ba**th**
ā	pay	ī	ride	o͝o	**book**	*th*	ba**the**
â	care	î	fierce	o͞o	**boot**	ə	ago, item
ä	father	ŏ	pot	ou	**out**		pencil
ĕ	pet	ō	go	ŭ	**cut**		atom
ē	be	ô	paw, for	û	**fur**		circus

marathon *noun* **1.** A race for runners over a distance of 26 miles, 385 yards. **2.** A very long race or contest.
mar·a·thon (măr′ə thŏn′) ◊ *noun, plural* **marathons**

> ***HISTORY* • marathon**
>
> The ancient Greeks won a major battle on the plain of *Marathon.* A messenger then ran a long way to announce their victory. The modern **marathon** was named in honor of this ancient runner's accomplishment.

marble *noun* **1.** A limestone that can be highly polished. Marble is widely used for buildings and sculpture. **2.** A little ball, usually made of glass, that is used in a children's game. **3. marbles** (*used with a singular verb*) A children's game played with marbles.
mar·ble (mär′bəl) ◊ *noun, plural* **marbles**

march *verb* **1.** To walk or cause to walk with regular and measured steps, often in a group, as soldiers do: *The mayor marched in a parade honoring veterans.* —See Synonyms at **walk. 2.** To move or advance in a steady way: *Time marches on.*
◊ *noun* **1.** The act of marching. **2.** The distance covered by marching: *The city was only two days' march away.* **3.** A piece of music with a strong beat to which people can march.
march (märch) ◊ *verb* **marched, marching**
◊ *noun, plural* **marches**

March *noun* The third month of the year. March has 31 days.
March (märch) ◊ *noun*

mare *noun* A female horse or a related animal, such as a zebra.
mare (mâr) ◊ *noun, plural* **mares**

margarine *noun* A substitute for butter that is made of vegetable oils.
mar·ga·rine (mär′jər ĭn) ◊ *noun*

margin *noun* **1.** An edge or border: *Weeds grew around the margin of the pond.* **2.** The space between the edge of a page and the printing on the page. —See Synonyms at **border. 3.** An extra amount, as of time, allowed beyond what is needed: *We have a margin of an hour to catch the plane.*
mar·gin (mär′jĭn) ◊ *noun, plural* **margins**

marigold *noun* A garden plant that has orange, yellow, or reddish flowers.
mar·i·gold (măr′ĭ gōld′) ◊ *noun, plural* **marigolds**

▲ **marigold**

marine *adjective* **1.** Of, relating to, or living in the sea: *We studied marine plants and animals.* **2.** Of or relating to ships, shipping, or navigation: *My parents sell marine insurance.*
◊ *noun* **Marine** A member of the United States Marine Corps.
ma·rine (mə rēn′) ◊ *adjective* ◊ *noun, plural* **Marines**

Marine Corps *noun* A branch of the United States armed forces whose troops operate on ships and on land.

mariner *noun* A sailor.
mar·i·ner (măr′ə nər) ◊ *noun, plural* **mariners**

marionette *noun* A puppet that is moved by strings or wires attached to it and held from above.
mar·i·o·nette (măr′ē ə nĕt′) ◊ *noun, plural* **marionettes**

▲ **marionette**

maritime *adjective* **1.** Located on or living near the sea: *People in many maritime countries fish for a living.* **2.** Of or relating to shipping or navigation: *I'm reading a book on American and British maritime history.*
mar·i·time (măr′ĭ tīm′) ◊ *adjective*

mark *noun* **1.** A flaw, such as a scratch or dent on a surface: *The cat left claw marks on the table.* **2.** A written symbol: *The comma is used as a punctuation mark.* **3.** Something, such as a line, that shows position: *The red sign is the halfway mark in the road race.*

M

4. An indication of a quality or condition: *Your good questions are a mark of intelligence.* **5.** Something that is aimed at; target: *The arrow found its mark.* **6.** A grade showing how well a student has performed: *Try to get better marks in arithmetic.* **7.** The starting line or position in a race.
◊ *verb* **1.** To make a mark on: *Books are school property; please don't mark them.* **2.** To show by making or being a mark: *The fence marks the border of our property.* **3.** To give clear evidence of: *Falling leaves marked the end of summer.* **4.** To pay attention to; heed: *Mark my words, you're in for trouble.* **5.** To give a mark to; grade: *The teacher has marked our tests.*
mark (märk) ◊ *noun, plural* **marks** ◊ *verb* **marked, marking**

market *noun* **1.** A public place where people buy and sell goods: *We took our fruits and vegetables to market.* **2.** A store that sells a particular type of merchandise: *I bought lamb chops at the meat market.* **3.** A region or country where goods may be sold: *There's a large foreign market for American products.* **4.** A desire to buy; demand: *There is a big market for our books.*
◊ *verb* To sell or offer for sale: *My friends market their pottery through two stores and have done very well.*
mar·ket (**mär′** kĭt) ◊ *noun, plural* **markets** ◊ *verb* **marketed, marketing**

marketplace *noun* A place, such as a public square, where a market is set up.
mar·ket·place (**mär′** kĭt plās′) ◊ *noun, plural* **marketplaces**

marking *noun* A mark: *The bird had red and green markings on its wings.*
mark·ing (**mär′** kĭng) ◊ *noun, plural* **markings**

marksman *noun* A person who is skilled at shooting.
marks·man (**märks′** mən) ◊ *noun, plural* **marksmen**

ă	pat	ĭ	pit	oi	oil	th	bath
ā	pay	ī	ride	o͝o	book	*th*	bathe
â	care	î	fierce	o͞o	boot	ə	ago, item
ä	father	ŏ	pot	ou	out		pencil
ĕ	pet	ō	go	ŭ	cut		atom
ē	be	ô	paw, for	û	fur		circus

marmalade *noun* A preserve made from the pulp and rind of fruits, such as oranges.
mar·ma·lade (**mär′** mə lād′) ◊ *noun, plural* **marmalades**

maroon[1] *verb* To be abandoned on a deserted shore or island with little hope of escaping or of being rescued.
ma·roon[1] (mə **ro͞on′**) ◊ *verb* **marooned, marooning**

maroon[2] *noun* A dark purplish red.
ma·roon[2] (mə **ro͞on′**) ◊ *noun*

***HISTORY* • maroon[1], maroon[2]**

Maroon[1] goes back to a Spanish word that meant "wild." It was first used to describe slaves who had escaped into the wild. Later it came to mean also "to put someone in a wild area." **Maroon[2]** comes from the French word for chestnut.

marquis *noun* A nobleman ranking below a duke and above an earl or count.
mar·quis (**mär′** kwĭs *or* mär **kē′**) ◊ *noun, plural* **marquis** *or* **marquises**

marquise *noun* **1.** The wife of a marquis. **2.** A woman who holds a rank equal to that of a marquis in her own right.
mar·quise (mär **kēz′**) ◊ *noun, plural* **marquises**

marriage *noun* **1.** The condition of living together as husband and wife. **2.** The act or ceremony that unites people as husband and wife; wedding.
mar·riage (**măr′** ĭj) ◊ *noun, plural* **marriages**

marrow *noun* The soft material that fills the cavities inside bones.
mar·row (**măr′** ō) ◊ *noun*

marry *verb* **1.** To take as husband or wife: *He married my sister.* **2.** To enter into marriage: *She has no plans to marry.* **3.** To unite as husband and wife: *The rabbi married them at home.* **4.** To give in marriage: *They have married off four of their children.*
mar·ry (**măr′** ē) ◊ *verb* **married, marrying**

Mars *noun* The planet that is fourth in distance from the sun.
Mars (märz) ◊ *noun*

marsh *noun* Low, wet land; swamp.
marsh (märsh) ◊ *noun, plural* **marshes**

marshal *noun* **1.** A federal officer who carries out court orders and performs duties similar to those of a sheriff. **2.** An investigator for a fire department. **3.** A person in charge of a ceremony or parade.
◊ *verb* To place in proper order; organize: *The team marshaled facts for the debate.*
mar·shal (**mär'** shəl) ◊ *noun, plural* **marshals** ◊ *verb* **marshaled, marshaling**
‖*These sound alike:* **marshal, martial**

marshmallow *noun* A soft, white candy with a spongy texture.
marsh·mal·low (**märsh'** mĕl'ō) ◊ *noun, plural* **marshmallows**

marshy *adjective* Wet and swampy.
marsh·y (**mär'** shē) ◊ *adjective* **marshier, marshiest**

marsupial *noun* An animal, such as a kangaroo or an opossum, that carries its newborn young in a pouch on the outside of the mother's body.
mar·su·pi·al (mär **sōō'** pē əl) ◊ *noun, plural* **marsupials**

marten *noun* An animal that is related to the weasel and has thick, soft brown fur.
mar·ten (**mär'** tn) ◊ *noun, plural* **martens**
‖*These sound alike:* **marten, martin**

martial *adjective* Of or relating to war.
mar·tial (**mär'** shəl) ◊ *adjective*
‖*These sound alike:* **martial, marshal**

Martian *adjective* Of or relating to Mars.
Mar·tian (**mär'** shən) ◊ *adjective*

martin *noun* A bird that is related to the swallows and has a forked tail.
mar·tin (**mär'** tn) ◊ *noun, plural* **martins**
‖*These sound alike:* **martin, marten**

▲ **martin**

martyr *noun* A person who chooses to die or suffer greatly rather than give up a religion or other belief.
◊ *verb* To make a martyr of.
mar·tyr (**mär'** tər) ◊ *noun, plural* **martyrs** ◊ *verb* **martyred, martyring**

marvel *noun* Someone or something that causes surprise, astonishment, or wonder: *The computer is a marvel of technology.*
◊ *verb* To be filled with surprise, astonishment, or wonder: *We marveled at the beauty of the mountain scenery.*
mar·vel (**mär'** vəl) ◊ *noun, plural* **marvels** ◊ *verb* **marveled, marveling**

marvelous *adjective* **1.** Causing surprise, astonishment, or wonder: *You have a marvelous gift for science.* **2.** Of the highest or best kind or quality: *I just read a marvelous biography.*
mar·vel·ous (**mär'** və ləs) ◊ *adjective*

mascot *noun* Someone or something believed to bring good luck: *The mascot of the football team is a donkey.*
mas·cot (**măs'** kŏt') ◊ *noun, plural* **mascots**

masculine *adjective* Of, relating to, or belonging to men or boys.
mas·cu·line (**măs'** kyə lĭn) ◊ *adjective*

mash *noun* **1.** A mixture of crushed grain and water that is used to feed livestock. **2.** A soft mixture or mass.
◊ *verb* To crush or grind into mash.
mash (măsh) ◊ *noun, plural* **mashes** ◊ *verb* **mashed, mashing**

mask *noun* **1.** A covering worn over the face to disguise or protect: *Put on your clown masks and let's go to the party.* **2.** Something that disguises or conceals: *Telling jokes is often a mask for shyness.*
◊ *verb* **1.** To cover or hide; conceal: *Big hedges masked the yard.* **2.** To put a mask on.
mask (măsk) ◊ *noun, plural* **masks** ◊ *verb* **masked, masking**

mason *noun* A person who builds or works with stone, cement, or bricks.
ma·son (**mā'** sən) ◊ *noun, plural* **masons**

masonry *noun* **1.** A mason's trade or work. **2.** Something, such as a fireplace, that is made of stone, cement, or bricks.
ma·son·ry (**mā'** sən rē) ◊ *noun*

masquerade *noun* **1.** A party or dance at which people wear masks and fancy costumes. **2.** A false outward show.

M

◊ *verb* **1.** To wear a mask or disguise. **2.** To pretend to be something one is not.
mas·quer·ade (măs′kə **rād′**) ◊ *noun, plural* **masquerades** ◊ *verb* **masqueraded, masquerading**

▲ **masquerade**

mass *noun* **1.** A lump or pile of matter without any definite shape: *The child played with a mass of clay.* **2.** A large amount or number: *I put a mass of flowers in the vase.* **3.** The largest part: *The mass of voters didn't like either candidate.* **4.** Bulk; size: *The sheer mass of the whale was amazing.*
◊ *verb* To gather into or assemble in a mass.
◊ *adjective* **1.** Of, involving, or attended by large numbers of people: *A mass meeting was held to discuss construction of the highway.* **2.** Done on a large scale: *Mass production of cars has resulted in many new jobs.*
mass (măs) ◊ *noun, plural* **masses** ◊ *verb* **massed, massing** ◊ *adjective*

Mass *noun* The main religious service in the Roman Catholic Church and in many other churches.
Mass (măs) ◊ *noun, plural* **Masses**

ă	pat	ĭ	pit	oi	oil	th	bath
ā	pay	ī	ride	o͝o	book	*th*	bathe
â	care	î	fierce	o͞o	boot	ə	ago, item
ä	father	ŏ	pot	ou	out		pencil
ĕ	pet	ō	go	ŭ	cut		atom
ē	be	ô	paw, for	û	fur		circus

Mass. An abbreviation for *Massachusetts.*

massacre *noun* The brutal killing of many people or animals.
◊ *verb* To kill in a massacre.
mas·sa·cre (**măs′** ə kər) ◊ *noun, plural* **massacres** ◊ *verb* **massacred, massacring**

massage *noun* The rubbing of parts of the body to relax the muscles and improve blood circulation.
◊ *verb* To give a massage to: *Massaging your leg will ease the cramp.*
mas·sage (mə **säzh′**) ◊ *noun, plural* **massages** ◊ *verb* **massaged, massaging**

massive *adjective* Large, heavy, and solid; bulky: *A massive elephant stood at the center of the circus ring.* —See Synonyms at **heavy.**
mas·sive (**măs′** ĭv) ◊ *adjective*

mast *noun* **1.** An upright pole that supports the sails and rigging of a ship or boat. **2.** A tall upright pole, as on a derrick or crane.
mast (măst) ◊ *noun, plural* **masts**

master *noun* **1.** A person who has power, control, or authority over another: *The dog ran to its master.* **2.** A man who teaches, especially in a private school. **3.** A person of great learning, skill, or ability; expert: *The artist was a master at painting water colors.* **4. Master** The form of address used for a boy who is not old enough to be called *Mister.*
◊ *adjective* **1.** Very skilled; expert: *A master carpenter built the new shelves in the living room.* **2.** Most important or largest; main: *The master bedroom has its own bath.*
◊ *verb* **1.** To bring under control; overcome: *No matter how hard he tried, he couldn't master his fear of heights.* **2.** To become skilled in: *In just a few lessons she mastered photography.*
mas·ter (**măs′** tər) ◊ *noun, plural* **masters** ◊ *adjective* ◊ *verb* **mastered, mastering**

masterful *adjective* **1.** Tending to act like a master; forceful and domineering. **2.** Highly skilled; expert: *The pianist gave a masterful performance.*
mas·ter·ful (**măs′** tər fəl) ◊ *adjective*

masterpiece *noun* An outstanding piece of work, especially an artist's greatest work.
mas·ter·piece (**măs′** tər pēs′) ◊ *noun, plural* **masterpieces**

mastery *noun* **1.** The power, control, or authority of a master. **2.** Victory: *The team*

gained mastery over its opponent. **3.** Great skill, knowledge, or technique: *The student showed a mastery of the subject.*
mas·ter·y (**măs'** tə rē) ◊ *noun*

mastiff *noun* A large dog with a short, brownish coat and short, square jaws.
mas·tiff (**măs'** tĭf) ◊ *noun, plural* **mastiffs**

mat *noun* **1.** A flat piece of material used as a floor or seat covering. **2.** A small rug, as one used to wipe the shoes on. **3.** A small piece of material put under an object, as a dish or lamp, for protection or decoration. **4.** A pad or mattress used for tumbling, wrestling, or acrobatics. **5.** A thick, tangled, or twisted mass, as of hair.
◊ *verb* To form into a thick, tangled, or twisted mass: *The cat's wet fur was matted.*
mat (măt) ◊ *noun, plural* **mats** ◊ *verb* **matted, matting**

match[1] *noun* **1.** Someone or something that is similar to or identical with another: *Find the match for this color.* **2.** Someone or something that goes well with another: *This tie is a good match for your striped shirt.* **3.** Something or someone that is equal or nearly equal to another: *By the second round we knew the boxer had met his match.* **4.** A sports contest: *The whole family attended the tennis match.*
◊ *verb* **1.** To be alike: *The two colors match exactly.* **2.** To do as well as; equal: *Can you match her score at darts?* **3.** To go well with: *The shirt matches the slacks.* **4.** To put two like or similar things together; pair: *Match up your socks.* **5.** To put into competition: *The teacher matched one half of the class against the other in a spelling bee.*
match[1] (măch) ◊ *noun, plural* **matches** ◊ *verb* **matched, matching**

match[2] *noun* A strip of wood, cardboard, or wax coated at one end with a substance that catches fire when it is rubbed on a rough surface or on a specially treated surface.
match[2] (măch) ◊ *noun, plural* **matches**

HISTORY • match[1], match[2]

Match[1] comes from an old English word that meant "companion, one of a pair." **Match[2]** originally meant "the wick of a candle or a lamp" and was borrowed from French.

mate *noun* **1.** One of a pair: *Find the mate to this glove.* **2.** A husband or wife. **3.** The male or female of a pair of animals or birds. **4.** An officer on a ship.
◊ *verb* To join closely; pair.
mate (māt) ◊ *noun, plural* **mates** ◊ *verb* **mated, mating**

material *noun* **1.** The substance from which something is or can be made: *Hemp is often used as material for rope.* **2.** Cloth or fabric. **3. materials** The things, such as tools, that are needed for doing a certain job: *Your writing materials are in the top drawer of your desk.*
◊ *adjective* **1.** Of, relating to, or in the form of matter; physical: *A watch is a material object.* **2.** Of or affecting the well-being of the body: *A warm house and good food are material comforts.*
ma·te·ri·al (mə **tîr'** ē əl) ◊ *noun, plural* **materials** ◊ *adjective*

materialize *verb* To become real or actual: *The help they promised never materialized.*
ma·te·ri·al·ize (mə **tîr'** ē ə līz') ◊ *verb* **materialized, materializing**

maternal *adjective* **1.** Of, relating to, or like a mother. **2.** Related through one's mother.
ma·ter·nal (mə **tûr'** nəl) ◊ *adjective*

math *noun* Mathematics.
math (măth) ◊ *noun*

mathematical *adjective* Of or having to do with mathematics.
math·e·mat·i·cal (măth'ə **măt'** ĭ kəl) ◊ *adjective*

mathematician *noun* A person who specializes in mathematics.
math·e·ma·ti·cian (măth'ə mə **tĭsh'** ən) ◊ *noun, plural* **mathematicians**

mathematics *noun* (*used with a singular verb*) The study of numbers, shapes, and measurements and of their relationships and properties.
math·e·mat·ics (măth'ə **măt'** ĭks) ◊ *noun*

matinee *noun* A dramatic or musical performance that is given in the afternoon.
mat·i·nee (măt'n **ā'**) ◊ *noun, plural* **matinees**

matriarch *noun* **1.** The female leader of a family or tribe. **2.** An old and respected woman.
ma·tri·arch (**mā'** trē ärk') ◊ *noun, plural* **matriarchs**

M

matrimony *noun* The condition of being married; marriage.
mat·ri·mo·ny (**măt′** rə mō′nē) ◊ *noun*

matron *noun* **1.** A married woman. **2.** A woman official in a public institution, such as a hospital.
ma·tron (**mā′** trən) ◊ *noun, plural* **matrons**

matter *noun* **1.** Something that takes up space and has weight. **2.** Substance or content; material: *The flood was the subject matter of the newscast.* **3.** A subject of interest or concern: *I refuse to discuss the matter.* **4.** A problem; difficulty: *What's the matter with you?* **5.** Something written or printed.
◊ *verb* To be important: *We tried to pretend that it didn't matter.*
mat·ter (**măt′** ər) ◊ *noun, plural* **matters**
◊ *verb* **mattered, mattering**

matter-of-fact *adjective* Concerned with or conforming just to the facts: *They gave a matter-of-fact answer to the question.*
mat·ter-of-fact (**măt′** ər əv **făkt′**) ◊ *adjective*

mattress *noun* A pad of heavy cloth filled with soft material that is used on or as a bed.
mat·tress (**măt′** rĭs) ◊ *noun, plural* **mattresses**

mature *adjective* **1.** Fully grown or developed: *The plant blooms when it is mature.* **2.** Of or like an adult: *You are very mature for your age.*
◊ *verb* To grow up or develop fully.
ma·ture (mə **tŏŏr′** *or* mə **tyŏŏr′**) ◊ *adjective* **maturer, maturest** ◊ *verb* **matured, maturing**

SYNONYMS

mature, adult, grown-up

Thanking your uncle for the gift without being asked was a *mature* thing to do. *Adult* education programs offer courses in computer science. Sometimes my little sister acts in a very *grown-up* way.
Antonyms: *childish, immature*

ă	pat	ĭ	pit	oi	**oi**l	th	ba**th**
ā	pay	ī	ride	ŏŏ	b**oo**k	*th*	ba**th**e
â	care	î	fierce	ōō	b**oo**t	ə	ago, item
ä	father	ŏ	pot	ou	**ou**t		pencil
ĕ	pet	ō	go	ŭ	c**u**t		atom
ē	be	ô	paw, for	û	f**u**r		circus

maturity *noun* The condition of being mature; full growth or development.
ma·tur·i·ty (mə **tŏŏr′** ĭ tē *or* mə **tyŏŏr′** ĭ tē) ◊ *noun*

maul *noun* A heavy hammer, as one used for driving posts into the ground.
◊ *verb* To injure or damage by beating, tearing, or handling roughly.
maul (môl) ◊ *noun, plural* **mauls** ◊ *verb* **mauled, mauling**
‖*These sound alike:* **maul, mall**

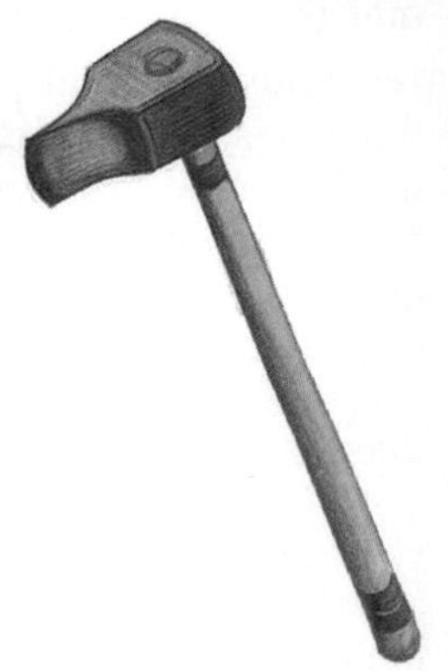
▲ **maul**

maximum *noun* The greatest or highest possible quantity, degree, or number: *The temperature reached its maximum at noon.*
◊ *adjective* Being a maximum: *The train's maximum speed is 80 miles per hour.*
max·i·mum (**măk′** sə məm) ◊ *noun, plural* **maximums** ◊ *adjective*

may *auxiliary verb* Used to show or express: **1.** Possibility: *It may rain this afternoon.* **2.** A request for or granting of permission: *May I take a swim? You may.* **3.** Hope or wish: *May you never be lonesome again.*
may (mā) ◊ *auxiliary verb, past tense* **might**

May *noun* The fifth month of the year. May has 31 days.
May (mā) ◊ *noun*

maybe *adverb* Possibly; perhaps: *Maybe we can go sailing tomorrow.*
may·be (**mā′** bē) ◊ *adverb*

mayonnaise *noun* A thick dressing, as for salad, that is made of beaten raw egg yolk, oil, and lemon juice or vinegar.
may·on·naise (mā′ə **nāz′**) ◊ *noun*

mayor *noun* The chief government official of a city or town.
may·or (**mā′** ər) ◊ *noun, plural* **mayors**

maze *noun* A complicated network of passages or paths.
maze (māz) ◊ *noun, plural* **mazes**
‖*These sound alike:* **maze, maize**

MD The abbreviation for *Maryland* used with a Zip Code.

Md. An abbreviation for *Maryland.*

M.D. The abbreviation for *Doctor of Medicine.*

me *pronoun* The objective case of **I:** *Can you hear me? They sent me a book for my birthday. Don't wait for me.*
me (mē) ◊ *pronoun*
‖ *These sound alike:* **me, mi**

ME The abbreviation for *Maine* used with a Zip Code.

Me. An abbreviation for *Maine.*

meadow *noun* An area of grassy ground, as one used as a pasture.
mead·ow (mĕd′ō) ◊ *noun, plural* **meadows**

meadowlark *noun* A North American songbird with a brownish back and a yellow breast that has a black marking on it.
mead·ow·lark (mĕd′ō-lärk′) ◊ *noun, plural* **meadowlarks**

▲ **meadowlark**

meager *adjective* Not enough; insufficient: *You gave me a meager serving of food.*
mea·ger (mē′gər) ◊ *adjective*

meal¹ *noun* Grain that has been ground.
meal¹ (mēl) ◊ *noun*

meal² *noun* **1.** The food that is served and eaten at one time. **2.** The time for eating: *Please don't eat between meals.*
meal² (mēl) ◊ *noun, plural* **meals**

***HISTORY* • meal¹, meal²**

Meal¹ comes from an old English word that meant "flour, ground grain." **Meal²** comes from a completely different old English word that meant "period of time" and "a time for eating."

mean¹ *verb* **1.** To have as its meaning: *What does this word mean?* **2.** To have as a purpose; intend: *She meant no harm.* **3.** To be important; matter: *His friendship means a great deal to us.*
mean¹ (mēn) ◊ *verb* **meant, meaning**
‖ *These sound alike:* **mean, mien**

mean² *adjective* **1.** Not kind or good; cruel: *Hiding the child's bicycle was a mean trick.* **2.** Common, ordinary, or low, as in quality or value: *The poor family lived in a mean cottage.* **3.** Stingy: *Are you too mean to give money to charity?*
mean² (mēn) ◊ *adjective* **meaner, meanest**
‖ *These sound alike:* **mean, mien**

mean³ *noun* **1.** Something in the middle between two extremes: *Comfort is a pleasant mean between wealth and poverty.* **2. means** Something used to help reach a goal; method. **3. means** Wealth.
◊ *adjective* Being in the middle between two extremes; average: *The mean temperature for the day was 62° Fahrenheit.*
mean³ (mēn) ◊ *noun, plural* **means** ◊ *adjective*
‖ *These sound alike:* **mean, mien**

***HISTORY* • mean¹, mean², mean³**

Mean¹ comes from an old English word that meant "intend, tell." **Mean²** comes from a different old English word that first meant "common, shared by all," but later came to mean "ordinary" and "inferior." **Mean³** comes from an old French word that came from a Latin word meaning "middle."

meander *verb* To go along a winding course: *The river meanders through the town.*
me·an·der (mē ăn′dər) ◊ *verb* **meandered, meandering**

meaning *noun* **1.** What is meant or signified, as by a word; sense: *I don't understand the meaning of that paragraph.* **2.** Something that a person wants to convey or indicate: *What was the meaning of your action?*
mean·ing (mē′nĭng) ◊ *noun, plural* **meanings**

SYNONYMS

meaning, sense, significance

What is the *meaning* of all this? Some words have only one *sense.* We didn't understand the *significance* of the speech at first.

M

meant *verb* Past tense and past participle of **mean[1]**.
meant (mĕnt) ◊ *verb*

meantime *noun* The time between one event and another.
mean·time (**mēn′** tīm′) ◊ *noun*

meanwhile *adverb* **1.** During the time between; meantime. **2.** At the same time.
mean·while (**mēn′** hwīl′) ◊ *adverb*

measles *noun* (*used with a singular or plural verb*) A contagious disease marked by fever and many red spots on the skin.
mea·sles (**mē′** zəlz) ◊ *noun*

measure *verb* **1.** To find the size, amount, capacity, or degree of: *We measured the room twice.* **2.** To be a unit of size, amount, capacity, or degree: *Yards and meters measure length.* **3.** To have as a measurement: *The paper measures 8 by 10 inches.* **4.** To estimate by comparing or evaluating: *How can you measure an athlete's skill?*
◊ *noun* **1.** The size, amount, capacity, or degree of something that is figured out by measuring: *I took the measure of the child's waist with a piece of string.* **2.** A unit used in measuring: *The pint is a measure of liquid capacity.* **3.** Something, such as a scale, that is used in measuring. **4.** Extent, amount, or degree: *Try to have a measure of understanding of other people's problems.* **5.** An action taken for a reason: *The teacher took measures to stop the noise.* **6.** A bill or act that may become law: *The Senate is considering a measure to raise taxes.* **7.** The unit of music between two bars on a musical staff.
meas·ure (**mĕzh′** ər) ◊ *verb* **measured, measuring** ◊ *noun, plural* **measures**

measurement *noun* **1.** The act of measuring. **2.** A system of measuring: *Metric measurement is used in Europe.* **3.** The size, amount, capacity, or degree found by measuring.
meas·ure·ment (**mĕzh′** ər mənt) ◊ *noun, plural* **measurements**

ă	pat	ĭ	pit	oi	oil	th	bath
ā	pay	ī	ride	ŏŏ	book	*th*	bathe
â	care	î	fierce	ōō	boot	ə	ago, item
ä	father	ŏ	pot	ou	out		pencil
ĕ	pet	ō	go	ŭ	cut		atom
ē	be	ô	paw, for	û	fur		circus

measuring worm *noun* An inchworm.
measuring worm ◊ *noun, plural* **measuring worms**

meat *noun* **1.** The flesh of an animal eaten as food. **2.** The edible part of a nut or fruit. **3.** The most important part of something: *Now we're getting to the meat of the story and it's getting exciting.*
meat (mēt) ◊ *noun, plural* **meats**
‖*These sound alike:* **meat, meet, mete**

> ***HISTORY* • meat**
>
> **Meat** is a native English word that first meant "food in general" and then came to mean "animal flesh eaten as food."

meatball *noun* A small ball of ground meat combined with other ingredients and cooked.
meat·ball (**mēt′** bôl′) ◊ *noun, plural* **meatballs**

mechanic *noun* A person who is skilled in making or repairing machines.
me·chan·ic (mə **kăn′** ĭk) ◊ *noun, plural* **mechanics**

mechanical *adjective* **1.** Of or relating to machines or tools: *It takes mechanical skill to repair a clock.* **2.** Operated or performed by a machine: *The garage has a mechanical door that opens when you press a button.* **3.** Acting or done as if by a machine: *After a while stringing beads becomes a mechanical job.*
me·chan·i·cal (mə **kăn′** ĭ kəl) ◊ *adjective*

mechanics *noun* **1.** (*used with a singular verb*) The scientific study of the action of forces on solids, liquids, and gases. **2.** (*used with a plural verb*) The way something works or the way parts of something are related to each other: *The keyboard, screen, and memory are part of the mechanics of a computer.*
me·chan·ics (mə **kăn′** ĭks) ◊ *noun*

mechanism *noun* **1.** A mechanical device; machine. **2.** The parts that make a machine work: *The glass cover of the watch was broken, but the mechanism was not damaged.*
mech·a·nism (**mĕk′** ə nĭz′əm) ◊ *noun, plural* **mechanisms**

mechanize *verb* To equip with machinery: *After the bakery was mechanized, the bread was cheaper but not as tasty.*
mech·a·nize (**mĕk′** ə nīz′) ◊ *verb* **mechanized, mechanizing**

medal *noun* A small, flat, often circular piece of metal with a design. A medal may be awarded to honor a person, an action, an accomplishment, or an event.
med·al (mĕd′l) ◊ *noun, plural* **medals**
‖*These sound alike:* **medal, meddle**

▲ **medal**

medallion *noun* **1.** A large medal. **2.** A round ornament or design.
me·dal·lion (mə dăl′yən) ◊ *noun, plural* **medallions**

meddle *verb* To interfere in other people's business: *When I tried to settle the argument, my friends told me not to meddle.*
med·dle (mĕd′l) ◊ *verb* **meddled, meddling**
‖*These sound alike:* **meddle, medal**

meddlesome *adjective* Inclined to meddle.
med·dle·some (mĕd′l səm) ◊ *adjective*

media *noun* A plural of **medium.**
me·di·a (mē′dē ə) ◊ *noun*

medical *adjective* Of or relating to the study or practice of medicine: *She went to medical school. The boy needs medical treatment.*
med·i·cal (mĕd′ĭ kəl) ◊ *adjective*

medicate *verb* To treat with medicine.
med·i·cate (mĕd′ĭ kāt′) ◊ *verb* **medicated, medicating**

medication *noun* **1.** The act of medicating. **2.** A medicine.
med·i·ca·tion (mĕd′ĭ **kā′**shən) ◊ *noun, plural* **medications**

medicinal *adjective* Of, relating to, or like a medicine.
me·dic·i·nal (mə **dĭs′**ə nəl) ◊ *adjective*

medicine *noun* **1.** The scientific study of diseases and of methods for discovering, treating, and preventing them. **2.** A substance used to treat a disease or relieve pain.
med·i·cine (mĕd′ĭ sĭn) ◊ *noun, plural* **medicines**

medicine man *noun* A person who is believed to have magic powers for treating and curing illnesses.
medicine man ◊ *noun, plural* **medicine men**

medieval *adjective* Of, relating to, or characteristic of the Middle Ages.
me·di·e·val (mē′dē **ē′**vəl) ◊ *adjective*

mediocre *adjective* Neither good nor bad; ordinary: *The food at the cafeteria was just mediocre.*
me·di·o·cre (mē′dē **ō′**kər) ◊ *adjective*

meditate *verb* To think quietly; reflect.
med·i·tate (mĕd′ĭ tāt′) ◊ *verb* **meditated, meditating**

meditation *noun* The act or process of meditating.
med·i·ta·tion (mĕd′ĭ **tā′**shən) ◊ *noun*

medium *noun* **1.** Something, such as a point of view, that is in the middle between two extremes. **2.** A substance in which something lives, is kept, or is carried: *Sound waves travel through the medium of air.* **3.** A means by which something is done: *Drawing pictures is a medium of expression.* **4.** A means for communicating information to large numbers of people: *Radio is a good advertising medium.* ◊ *adjective* In the middle between two extremes; intermediate: *The blender can be used on low, medium, and high speeds.*
me·di·um (mē′dē əm) ◊ *noun, plural* **mediums** *or* **media** (for senses 2, 3, and 4) ◊ *adjective*

medley *noun* **1.** A mixture, as of sounds. **2.** A piece of music made up of different songs or melodies.
med·ley (mĕd′lē) ◊ *noun, plural* **medleys**

meek *adjective* **1.** Putting up with mistreatment without getting angry; patient and humble. **2.** Not resisting, struggling, or asserting oneself.
meek (mēk) ◊ *adjective* **meeker, meekest**

meet *verb* **1.** To come together; connect or touch: *The two rivers meet near the capital.* **2.** To come face to face; encounter: *The two friends shook hands when they met.* **3.** To come together with by appointment: *I'll meet you on the corner in ten minutes.* **4.** To be introduced: *We first met in school.* **5.** To have a meeting; confer: *Parents will meet with the teachers on Monday.* **6.** To be present at the arrival of: *I went to meet the train.* **7.** To deal or cope with: *Let's meet that problem when it comes up.* **8.** To provide enough to fill; satisfy: *The store's supply did not meet the demand.* **9.** To pay for: *With such a low*

M

allowance I can barely meet my expenses.
◊ *noun* A gathering for a sports competition: *The school held a track meet.*
meet (mēt) ◊ *verb* **met, meeting** ◊ *noun, plural* **meets**
‖*These sound alike:* **meet, meat, mete**

meeting *noun* **1.** The act or process of coming together. **2.** A gathering of people held at a fixed time and place: *I hate to miss a meeting of the chess club.*
meet·ing (mē′tĭng) ◊ *noun, plural* **meetings**

megaphone *noun* A device shaped like a long cone that is used to make the sound of the voice louder.
meg·a·phone (mĕg′ə fōn′) ◊ *noun, plural* **megaphones**

▲ **megaphone**

melancholy *noun* Low spirits; sadness.
◊ *adjective* Sad; gloomy.
mel·an·chol·y (mĕl′ən kŏl′ē) ◊ *noun* ◊ *adjective*

mellow *adjective* **1.** Soft, sweet, and fully ripe: *I had a mellow peach for dessert.* **2.** Soft, full, and soothing, as in sound: *We enjoyed listening to the mellow tones of the guitar.*
◊ *verb* To make or become mellow.
mel·low (mĕl′ō) ◊ *adjective* **mellower, mellowest** ◊ *verb* **mellowed, mellowing**

ă	pat	ĭ	pit	oi	**oil**	th	**bath**
ā	pay	ī	ride	o͝o	**book**	*th*	**bathe**
â	care	î	fierce	o͞o	**boot**	ə	**ago, item**
ä	father	ŏ	**pot**	ou	**out**		pencil
ĕ	pet	ō	**go**	ŭ	cut		atom
ē	be	ô	paw, for	û	fur		circus

melodious *adjective* Full of or making pleasing sounds: *You have a melodious voice.*
me·lo·di·ous (mə lō′dē əs) ◊ *adjective*

melody *noun* **1.** A pleasing series of musical tones; tune. **2.** A musical quality.
mel·o·dy (mĕl′ə dē) ◊ *noun, plural* **melodies**

melon *noun* A large fruit, such as a cantaloupe, that grows on a vine and has a hard rind and juicy flesh.
mel·on (mĕl′ən) ◊ *noun, plural* **melons**

▲ **melon**
Cantaloupe, watermelon, and honeydew melon

melt *verb* **1.** To change a solid to a liquid by heating: *Melt the butter in a pan. The snow melted in the sun.* **2.** To dissolve: *Sugar melts in water.* **3.** To lessen or fade gradually; vanish: *The crowd melted away.* **4.** To change or blend gradually: *The brown rabbit melted into the background of the forest.* **5.** To make or become gentler or milder; soften: *The look on the child's face melted our hearts.*
melt (mĕlt) ◊ *verb* **melted, melting**

SYNONYMS

melt, dissolve, thaw

Melt the butter before mixing it with the flour. *Dissolve* the tablet in water. The snow is beginning to *thaw*.

member *noun* **1.** A person or thing belonging to a group or organization: *The Senate has 100 members. The lion is a member of the cat family.* **2.** A part, such as an organ or a limb, of a person, animal, or plant.
mem·ber (mĕm′bər) ◊ *noun, plural* **members**

membership *noun* **1.** The condition or fact of being a member: *You need a card to prove your membership in the fan club.* **2.** The total number of members: *Unions increased their membership rapidly from 1937 to 1947.*
mem·ber·ship (**mĕm′** bər shĭp′) ◊ *noun, plural* **memberships**

membrane *noun* A thin, flexible layer of tissue in the body of an animal or plant. A membrane may line or cover a part of the body.
mem·brane (**mĕm′** brān′) ◊ *noun, plural* **membranes**

memo *noun* A memorandum.
mem·o (**mĕm′** ō) ◊ *noun, plural* **memos**

memorable *adjective* Worthy of being remembered; remarkable: *Memorable events are often pictured on postage stamps.*
mem·o·ra·ble (**mĕm′** ər ə bəl) ◊ *adjective*

memoranda *noun* A plural of **memorandum.**
mem·o·ran·da (mĕm′ə **răn′** də) ◊ *noun*

memorandum *noun* **1.** A short note that is written as a reminder. **2.** A written communication that is sent between members or offices of an organization.
mem·o·ran·dum (mĕm′ə **răn′** dəm) ◊ *noun, plural* **memorandums** *or* **memoranda**

memorial *noun* Something that is put up, kept, or done to help people continue to remember a person, group, or thing: *That stone arch is a war memorial.*
◊ *adjective* Serving to honor the memory of a person or event: *We went to a memorial service for our grandparents.*
me·mo·ri·al (mə **môr′** ē əl) ◊ *noun, plural* **memorials** ◊ *adjective*

▲ **memorial**
The Marine Corps Memorial

Memorial Day *noun* A holiday in honor of members of the United States armed forces who have died in wars. In most states Memorial Day is celebrated on the last Monday in May.

memorize *verb* To learn by heart.
mem·o·rize (**mĕm′** ə rīz′) ◊ *verb* **memorized, memorizing**

memory *noun* **1.** The power or ability to remember. **2.** The act or an example of remembering. **3.** Something that is remembered: *My earliest memory is of my third birthday party.* **4.** Honor and respect for someone or something in the past: *The statue is in memory of our first mayor.* **5.** The unit of a computer in which information is stored for later use.
mem·o·ry (**mĕm′** ə rē) ◊ *noun, plural* **memories**

men *noun* Plural of **man.**
men (mĕn) ◊ *noun*

menace *noun* A threat or danger.
◊ *verb* To put into danger: *An oil spill menaced the lives of birds, fish, and plants.*
men·ace (**mĕn′** əs) ◊ *noun, plural* **menaces** ◊ *verb* **menaced, menacing**

menagerie *noun* A collection of wild animals kept in cages or pens.
me·nag·er·ie (mə **năj′** ə rē) ◊ *noun, plural* **menageries**

mend *verb* **1.** To put back into good condition; repair: *I mended the rip in my jacket.* **2.** To become better; improve: *The dog's broken leg is mending slowly.*
◊ *noun* A place that has been mended.
◊ *idiom* **on the mend** Getting better; improving: *The patient is on the mend.*
mend (mĕnd) ◊ *verb* **mended, mending** ◊ *noun, plural* **mends**

> ***SYNONYMS***
>
> ***mend, patch, repair***
>
> I have the right color of thread to *mend* the hole in your shirt. I don't have the material to *patch* the roof. Do you think that the shop can *repair* our television set? **Antonyms:** *break, tear*

menial *adjective* Requiring little skill: *I ran errands and did other menial jobs.*
me·ni·al (**mē′** nē əl) ◊ *adjective*

M

men-of-war *noun* Plural of **man-of-war.**
men-of-war (mən′əv **wôr′**) ◊ *noun*

-ment The suffix *-ment* forms nouns and means "action" or "process." *Government* is the action or process of governing. The suffix *-ment* also means "the result of an action or process." A *measurement* is a result found by the action of measuring. The suffix *-ment* also means "condition." *Amazement* is the condition of being amazed.

***VOCABULARY BUILDER* • -ment**

Many words that are formed with **-ment** are not entries in this dictionary. But you can figure out what these words mean by looking up the meanings of the root words and the suffix. For example:
betterment = the result of the action of making better
bewilderment = the condition of being bewildered
encirclement = the action of encircling

mental *adjective* Of, relating to, or done in the mind: *Adding figures is a mental activity.*
men·tal (**mĕn′** tl) ◊ *adjective*

mentality *noun* Mental ability; intelligence.
men·tal·i·ty (mĕn **tăl′** ĭ tē) ◊ *noun, plural* **mentalities**

mentally *adverb* In or by using the mind.
men·tal·ly (**mĕn′** tl ē) ◊ *adverb*

mention *verb* To speak of or write about briefly: *I mentioned my idea during class.*
◊ *noun* A brief reference or remark: *There was no mention of the incident in the papers.*
men·tion (**mĕn′** shən) ◊ *verb* **mentioned, mentioning** ◊ *noun, plural* **mentions**

menu *noun* **1.** A list of foods and drinks available for a meal. **2.** A list of choices of functions and operations within a computer program.
men·u (**mĕn′** yo͞o) ◊ *noun, plural* **menus**

ă	pat	ĭ	pit	oi	**oi**l	th	ba**th**
ā	pay	ī	ride	o͝o	b**oo**k	*th*	ba***th***e
â	care	î	fierce	o͞o	b**oo**t	ə	ago, item
ä	father	ŏ	pot	ou	**ou**t		pencil
ĕ	pet	ō	go	ŭ	c**u**t		atom
ē	be	ô	paw, for	û	f**u**r		circus

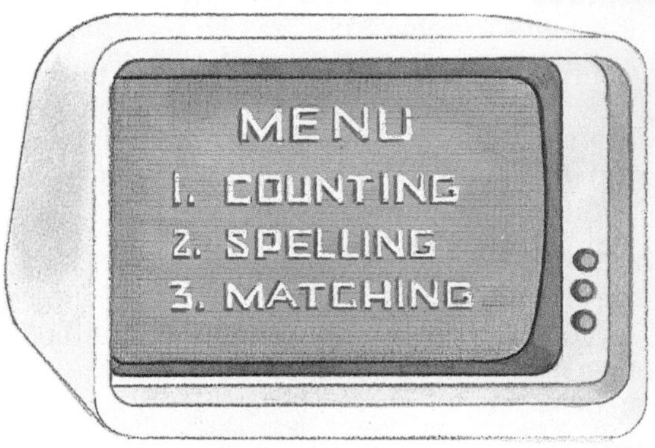

▲ **menu**

meow *noun* The sound that a cat makes.
◊ *verb* To make a meow.
me·ow (mē **ou′**) ◊ *noun, plural* **meows** ◊ *verb* **meowed, meowing**

mercenary *adjective* Concerned only with making money.
◊ *noun* A professional soldier who is hired to serve in a foreign army.
mer·ce·nar·y (**mûr′** sə nĕr′ē) ◊ *adjective* ◊ *noun, plural* **mercenaries**

merchandise *noun* Things that are bought and sold; goods.
mer·chan·dise (**mûr′** chən dīz′) ◊ *noun*

merchant *noun* A person who buys and sells goods, especially a person who runs a store.
◊ *adjective* Of or relating to trade or commerce: *Spices arrived in merchant ships from the Orient.*
mer·chant (**mûr′** chənt) ◊ *noun, plural* **merchants** ◊ *adjective*

merchant marine *noun* A nation's ships that carry goods and passengers from one country to another.
merchant marine ◊ *noun, plural* **merchant marines**

merciful *adjective* Having or showing mercy.
mer·ci·ful (**mûr′** sĭ fəl) ◊ *adjective*

merciless *adjective* Without mercy; cruel.
mer·ci·less (**mûr′** sĭ lĭs) ◊ *adjective*

mercury *noun* **1.** A silvery-white metal that is a liquid at room temperature. Mercury is one of the chemical elements. It is used in thermometers and barometers. **2. Mercury** The planet that is closest to the sun and has a diameter of about 3,000 miles.
mer·cu·ry (**mûr′** kyə rē) ◊ *noun*

mercy *noun* **1.** Kindness that goes beyond what can be expected. **2.** A fortunate act or occurrence; blessing: *It's a mercy that no one was hurt during the fire.*
mer·cy (**mûr′**sē) ◊ *noun, plural* **mercies**

mere *adjective* Being nothing more than: *He was a mere boy when he became king.*
mere (mîr) ◊ *adjective, superlative* **merest**

merely *adverb* Nothing more than; only.
mere·ly (**mîr′**lē) ◊ *adverb*

merge *verb* To bring or come together so as to form a single unit; unite: *The owners decided to merge the two companies. The rivers run parallel before they merge.*
merge (mûrj) ◊ *verb* **merged, merging**

meridian *noun* An imaginary half circle on the earth's surface running from the North Pole to the South Pole.
me·rid·i·an (mə **rĭd′**ē ən) ◊ *noun, plural* **meridians**

merino *noun* **1.** A sheep of a breed that has fine, soft wool. **2.** Cloth or yarn made from this wool.
me·ri·no (mə **rē′**nō) ◊ *noun, plural* **merinos**

merit *noun* **1.** The fact or condition of deserving good or bad: *Grades should be based on the student's merit.* **2.** A feature or quality that deserves praise: *We discussed the merits of the book.*
◊ *verb* To be worthy of; deserve: *Your suggestion merits our consideration.*
mer·it (**mĕr′**ĭt) ◊ *noun, plural* **merits** ◊ *verb* **merited, meriting**

mermaid *noun* An imaginary sea creature with the head and upper body of a woman and the tail of a fish.
mer·maid (**mûr′**mād′) ◊ *noun, plural* **mermaids**

merriment *noun* Laughter and fun; amusement and enjoyment.
mer·ri·ment (**mĕr′**ĭ mənt) ◊ *noun*

merry *adjective* Full of good humor and gaiety; jolly: *She whistled a merry tune as she walked home from school.*
mer·ry (**mĕr′**ē) ◊ *adjective* **merrier, merriest**

merry-go-round *noun* A round, revolving platform with seats shaped like animals on which people ride for fun.
mer·ry-go-round (**mĕr′**ē gō round′) ◊ *noun, plural* **merry-go-rounds**

▲ **merry-go-round**

merrymaking *noun* Fun and gaiety.
mer·ry·mak·ing (**mĕr′**ē mā′kĭng) ◊ *noun*

mesa *noun* A hill with steep sides and a broad flat top.
me·sa (**mā′**sə) ◊ *noun, plural* **mesas**

mesh *noun* **1.** One of the open spaces in a net or a screen. **2.** A material or structure made of threads, wires, or lines that cross each other with many small, open spaces: *I used a strainer with a fine mesh to sift the flour.*
◊ *verb* To fit together effectively or neatly: *The teeth of the gears didn't mesh. If our plans mesh, we will finish together.*
mesh (mĕsh) ◊ *noun, plural* **meshes** ◊ *verb* **meshed, meshing**

mesquite *noun* A thorny shrub or tree of southwestern North America that has feathery leaves and long, narrow pods. The pods are used as cattle feed.
mes·quite (mĕ **skēt′**) ◊ *noun, plural* **mesquites**

mess *noun* **1.** A cluttered and untidy state: *The twins left their room in a mess.* **2.** A dirty or untidy person, place, or thing: *The kitchen was a mess after dinner.* **3.** A complicated or troubling situation: *Who got us into this mess?* **4.** A meal served to a group of soldiers, sailors, or campers. **5.** A group of soldiers, sailors, or campers who eat together.
◊ *verb* **1.** To make dirty or untidy; clutter: *Please don't mess up the living room.* **2.** To handle or manage badly; ruin: *You shouldn't mess up your chance to get the best education available to you.*
mess (mĕs) ◊ *noun, plural* **messes** ◊ *verb* **messed, messing**

M

message *noun* **1.** Words that are sent from one person or group to another: *My friends were out, so I left a message for them.* **2.** A speech or other formal communication: *The President's message to Congress has to do with taxes.*
mes·sage (**mĕs′**ĭj) ◊ *noun, plural* **messages**

messenger *noun* A person who carries messages or does errands.
mes·sen·ger (**mĕs′** ən jər) ◊ *noun, plural* **messengers**

messy *adjective* Dirty and untidy.
mess·y (**mĕs′**ē) ◊ *adjective* **messier, messiest**

met *verb* Past tense and past participle of **meet.**
met (mĕt) ◊ *verb*

metabolism *noun* The processes by which living things change food into energy and living tissue and then dispose of waste material.
me·tab·o·lism (mə **tăb′** ə lĭz′əm) ◊ *noun*

metal *noun* A substance, such as copper, iron, silver, or gold, that is usually shiny and hard, conducts heat and electricity, and can be hammered or cast into a desired shape.
◊ *adjective* Made of a metal or metals.
met·al (**mĕt′**l) ◊ *noun, plural* **metals**
◊ *adjective*
‖*These sound alike:* **metal, mettle**

metallic *adjective* Of, relating to, like, or containing metal: *Tin is a metallic element.*
me·tal·lic (mə **tăl′**ĭk) ◊ *adjective*

metamorphic *adjective* Of or having to do with metamorphosis.
met·a·mor·phic (mĕt′ə **môr′** fĭk) ◊ *adjective*

metamorphoses *noun* Plural of **metamorphosis.**
met·a·mor·pho·ses (mĕt′ə **môr′** fə sēz′) ◊ *noun*

metamorphosis *noun* A complete change in appearance or form, as the one that occurs when a caterpillar becomes a butterfly.
met·a·mor·pho·sis (mĕt′ə **môr′** fə sĭs) ◊ *noun, plural* **metamorphoses**

ă	pat	ĭ	pit	oi	**oi**l	th	ba**th**
ā	pay	ī	ride	ŏŏ	b**oo**k	*th*	ba**th**e
â	care	î	fierce	ōō	b**oo**t	ə	ago, item
ä	father	ŏ	pot	ou	**ou**t		pencil
ĕ	pet	ō	go	ŭ	cut		atom
ē	be	ô	paw, for	û	fur		circus

▲ **metamorphosis**
The stages of a butterfly's development: egg, larva, pupa, and adult

mete *verb* To give out; distribute: *Our parents meted out rewards for good behavior.*
mete (mēt) ◊ *verb* **meted, meting**
‖*These sound alike:* **mete, meat, meet**

meteor *noun* A chunk of matter from outer space that enters the earth's atmosphere, quickly burns up, and often forms a streak of light.
me·te·or (**mē′** tē ər) ◊ *noun, plural* **meteors**

meteoric *adjective* **1.** Of, relating to, or made by a meteor or meteors. **2.** Like a meteor, as in speed or brilliance: *The movie star's rise to fame was meteoric.*
me·te·or·ic (mē′tē **ôr′** ĭk) ◊ *adjective*

meteorite *noun* A meteor that reaches the earth's surface without burning up beforehand.
me·te·or·ite (**mē′** tē ə rīt′) ◊ *noun, plural* **meteorites**

meteorologist *noun* A person who specializes in meteorology.
me·te·or·ol·o·gist (mē′tē ə **rŏl′** ə jĭst) ◊ *noun, plural* **meteorologists**

meteorology *noun* The scientific study of the atmosphere and weather.
me·te·or·ol·o·gy (mē′tē ə **rŏl′** ə jē) ◊ *noun*

meter[1] *noun* The basic unit of length in the metric system, equal to about 39.37 inches.
me·ter[1] (**mē′** tər) ◊ *noun, plural* **meters**

meter² *noun* An instrument for measuring and showing a quantity, as the amount of gas used to heat a building.
me·ter² (mē′tər) ◊ *noun, plural* **meters**

meter³ *noun* **1.** The arrangement of accents and beats used in a poem. **2.** The pattern of beats in each measure of a piece of music.
me·ter³ (mē′tər) ◊ *noun, plural* **meters**

HISTORY **• meter¹, meter², meter³**

These three words all go back to the same Greek word that had a basic meaning of "measure." **Meter¹** comes from a French word that goes back to this Greek word. **Meter²** was taken from the end of words like **thermometer** and **barometer,** which had been formed with this Greek word in mind. **Meter³** comes from a French word that came through Latin from this Greek word.

methane *noun* A colorless, odorless gas that burns easily. It is used as a fuel.
meth·ane (mĕth′ān′) ◊ *noun*

method *noun* A regular or deliberate way of doing something: *Broiling is a method of cooking.*
meth·od (mĕth′əd) ◊ *noun, plural* **methods**

methodical *adjective* **1.** Arranged or done according to a method: *They started a methodical search for the lost book.* **2.** Following or preferring a fixed method: *A methodical person gets up at the same time each morning.*
me·thod·i·cal (mə thŏd′ĭ kəl) ◊ *adjective*

meticulous *adjective* **1.** Very careful; precise: *Your work is meticulous.* **2.** Taking great care with details; scrupulous: *My cousin is a meticulous dresser.*
me·tic·u·lous (mə tĭk′yə ləs) ◊ *adjective*

metric *adjective* Of or relating to the metric system.
met·ric (mĕt′rĭk) ◊ *adjective*

metrical *adjective* Of or relating to poetic or musical meter.
met·ri·cal (mĕt′rĭ kəl) ◊ *adjective*

metric system *noun* A system of weights and measures in which the meter is the basic unit of length, the kilogram is the basic unit of mass or weight, and the liter is the basic unit of liquid volume.

metric ton *noun* A unit of mass and weight equal to 1,000 kilograms.
metric ton ◊ *noun, plural* **metric tons**

metronome *noun* A device that clicks to provide a student with a steady beat for practicing music.
met·ro·nome (mĕt′rə nōm′) ◊ *noun, plural* **metronomes**

metropolis *noun* **1.** A large city. **2.** The largest or most important city of a region.
me·trop·o·lis (mə trŏp′ə lĭs) ◊ *noun, plural* **metropolises**

metropolitan *adjective* Of, relating to, or from a metropolis: *We went downtown on the metropolitan bus system.*
met·ro·pol·i·tan (mĕt′rə pŏl′ĭ tən) ◊ *adjective*

mettle *noun* Strength of character or spirit.
met·tle (mĕt′l) ◊ *noun*
‖*These sound alike:* **mettle, metal**

mew *noun* A cry like the one made by a kitten or a bird such as the sea gull or catbird. ◊ *verb* To make this sound.
mew (myōō) ◊ *noun, plural* **mews** ◊ *verb* **mewed, mewing**

Mex. The abbreviation for *Mexico.*

Mexican *noun* A person who was born in or lives in Mexico.
◊ *adjective* Of or relating to Mexico or the Mexicans.
Mex·i·can (mĕk′sĭ kən) ◊ *noun, plural* **Mexicans** ◊ *adjective*

mg The abbreviation for *milligram.*

mi *noun* The third note of the musical scale.
mi (mē) ◊ *noun*
‖*These sound alike:* **mi, me**

MI The abbreviation for *Michigan* used with a Zip Code.

mi. The abbreviation for *mile.*

mica *noun* A mineral that splits easily into thin transparent sheets. Mica is used as an insulator in small electrical appliances.
mi·ca (mī′kə) ◊ *noun*

mice *noun* Plural of **mouse.**
mice (mīs) ◊ *noun*

Mich. An abbreviation for *Michigan.*

microbe *noun* A very tiny living organism; microorganism.
mi·crobe (mī′krōb′) ◊ *noun, plural* **microbes**

microchip *noun* A very tiny slice of material that is used in a computer. Many electronic

M

parts and their connections are imprinted on microchips.
mi·cro·chip (mī′krō chĭp′) ◊ *noun, plural* **microchips**

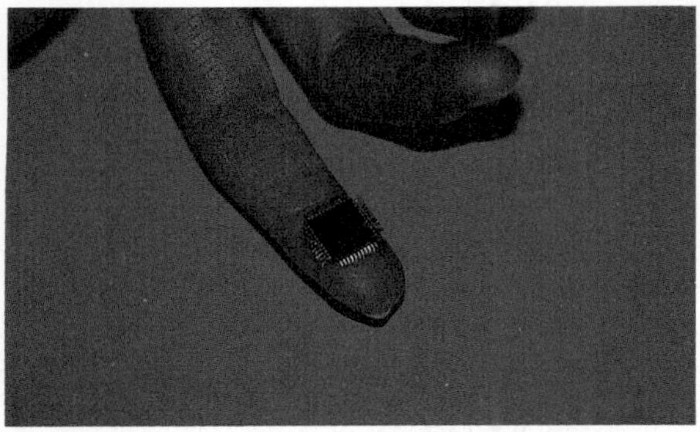

▲ **microchip**

microcomputer *noun* A very small computer that has less memory and a lower speed than a minicomputer.
mi·cro·com·put·er (mī′krō kəm pyo͞o′tər) ◊ *noun, plural* **microcomputers**

microfilm *noun* A film on which printed material or drawings can be photographed in a much smaller size.
mi·cro·film (mī′krə fĭlm′) ◊ *noun, plural* **microfilms**

microorganism *noun* An organism, as a bacterium, so small that it can be seen only by using a microscope.
mi·cro·or·gan·ism (mī′krō ôr′gə nĭz′əm) ◊ *noun, plural* **microorganisms**

microphone *noun* A device for magnifying or sending sound by means of electrical signals, as in radio and television.
mi·cro·phone (mī′krə fōn′) ◊ *noun, plural* **microphones**

microscope *noun* An instrument with a special lens or combination of lenses for making a very small object appear larger.
mi·cro·scope (mī′krə skōp′) ◊ *noun, plural* **microscopes**

ă	pat	ĭ	pit	oi	**oil**	th	**bath**
ā	pay	ī	ride	o͝o	**book**	*th*	**bathe**
â	care	î	fierce	o͞o	**boot**	ə	ago, item
ä	father	ŏ	pot	ou	**out**		pencil
ĕ	pet	ō	go	ŭ	cut		atom
ē	be	ô	paw, for	û	fur		circus

▲ **microscope**

microscopic *adjective* **1.** Capable of being seen only through a microscope; very small. **2.** Of, relating to, or using a microscope.
mi·cro·scop·ic (mī′krə skŏp′ĭk) ◊ *adjective*

microwave *noun* An energy wave that is shorter than a radio wave and longer than a light wave. Microwaves are used in radar and in microwave ovens.
mi·cro·wave (mī′krə wāv′) ◊ *noun, plural* **microwaves**

microwave oven *noun* An oven in which microwaves cook the food. Microwave ovens cook food very quickly. They can also be used to thaw frozen food quickly.
microwave oven ◊ *noun, plural* **microwave ovens**

mid *adjective* Being in the middle: *It was mid afternoon when we left.*
mid (mĭd) ◊ *adjective*

midday *noun* The middle of the day; noon.
mid·day (mĭd′dā′) ◊ *noun, plural* **middays**

middle *noun* A point or part that is the same distance from each side or end: *A deer stood in the middle of the road.* —See Synonyms at **center.**
◊ *adjective* **1.** At or in the middle: *I broke my middle finger.* **2.** Medium; average: *A beagle is a dog of middle size.*
mid·dle (mĭd′l) ◊ *noun, plural* **middles** ◊ *adjective*

middle-aged *adjective* Being between about 40 and 60 years of age.
mid·dle-aged (mĭd′l ājd′) ◊ *adjective*

Middle Ages *plural noun* The period in European history from about A.D. 500 to about 1450.

middle class *noun* The social class between the rich and the poor.
middle class ◊ *noun, plural* **middle classes**

middy *noun* **1.** A midshipman. **2.** A loose blouse with a wide collar that is V-shaped in front and square in back.
mid·dy (mĭd′ē) ◊ *noun, plural* **middies**

midget *noun* A very small person or thing.
midg·et (mĭj′ĭt) ◊ *noun, plural* **midgets**

midland *noun* The middle or interior part of a country or region.
mid·land (mĭd′lənd) ◊ *noun, plural* **midlands**

midnight *noun* The middle of the night; twelve o'clock at night.
mid·night (mĭd′nīt′) ◊ *noun, plural* **midnights**

midrib *noun* The main or central vein of a leaf.
mid·rib (mĭd′rĭb′) ◊ *noun, plural* **midribs**

midshipman *noun* A student who is training to be a commissioned officer at a naval or coast guard academy.
mid·ship·man (mĭd′shĭp′mən) ◊ *noun, plural* **midshipmen**

midst *noun* **1.** The middle position or part: *There was a willow tree in the midst of the garden.* **2.** The condition of being surrounded: *You stayed calm in the midst of all the trouble.* **3.** A position among others in a group: *We noticed a new guest in our midst.* ◊ *preposition* In the midst of.
midst (mĭdst) ◊ *noun* ◊ *preposition*

midstream *noun* The part of a stream farthest from the banks.
mid·stream (mĭd′strēm′) ◊ *noun*

midsummer *noun* **1.** The middle of the summer. **2.** The time about June 21.
mid·sum·mer (mĭd′sŭm′ər) ◊ *noun*

midway *adverb & adjective* In the middle of a distance, way, or period of time.
◊ *noun* The area of a fair, carnival, or circus in which rides and amusements are located.
mid·way (mĭd′wā′) ◊ *adverb & adjective* ◊ *noun, plural* **midways**

midwinter *noun* **1.** The middle of the winter. **2.** The time about December 22.
mid·win·ter (mĭd′wĭn′tər) ◊ *noun*

mien *noun* A person's way of looking or behaving; bearing.
mien (mēn) ◊ *noun, plural* **miens**
‖*These sound alike:* **mien, mean**

might[1] *noun* Power or force; strength.
might[1] (mīt) ◊ *noun*
‖*These sound alike:* **might, mite**

might[2] *verb* Past tense of **may.**
might[2] (mīt) ◊ *verb*
‖*These sound alike:* **might, mite**

mighty *adjective* **1.** Having or showing great power, strength, or force: *Once a mighty empire ruled the world.* **2.** Great in size, importance, or effect: *Mighty mountains rose above the plain.*
might·y (mī′tē) ◊ *adjective* **mightier, mightiest**

migrant *noun* A person or animal that migrates.
mi·grant (mī′grənt) ◊ *noun, plural* **migrants**

migrate *verb* **1.** To move from one country or region and settle in another. **2.** To move regularly from one region or climate to another: *Many birds migrate south in the fall.*
mi·grate (mī′grāt′) ◊ *verb* **migrated, migrating**

migration *noun* **1.** The act or an example of migrating. **2.** A group migrating together.
mi·gra·tion (mī **grā′**shən) ◊ *noun, plural* **migrations**

mild *adjective* **1.** Gentle in manner. **2.** Moderate in action or effect: *We had a mild winter. The taste of this cheese is very mild.*
mild (mīld) ◊ *adjective* **milder, mildest**

mildew *noun* **1.** A fungus that forms a white or grayish coating, as on fabric, paper, or plants. **2.** The coating formed by mildew.
◊ *verb* To become covered with mildew.
mil·dew (mĭl′do͞o′ *or* mĭl′dyo͞o′) ◊ *noun, plural* **mildews** ◊ *verb* **mildewed, mildewing**

mile *noun* **1.** A unit of length equal to 5,280 feet or 1,760 yards. **2.** A unit of length used in air or sea travel that is equal to about 6,076 feet.
mile (mīl) ◊ *noun, plural* **miles**

> ***HISTORY* • mile**
>
> **Mile** goes back to a Latin phrase that meant "a thousand paces."

mileage *noun* Distance measured in miles.
mile·age (mī′lĭj) ◊ *noun, plural* **mileages**

milestone *noun* **1.** A stone marker that indicates the distance in miles to a certain point.

2. An important event or point: *Graduation is a milestone in a student's life.*
mile·stone (**mīl′**stōn′) ◊ *noun, plural* **milestones**

▲ **milestone**

military *adjective* Of or relating to soldiers, the armed forces, or war.
◊ *noun* A nation's armed forces.
mil·i·tar·y (**mĭl′**ĭ tĕr′ē) ◊ *adjective* ◊ *noun*

militia *noun* A group of citizens who receive military training but who are on call only for emergencies.
mi·li·tia (mə **lĭsh′** ə) ◊ *noun, plural* **militias**

milk *noun* **1.** A whitish liquid that is produced by female mammals for feeding their young. **2.** The milk of cows and sometimes goats used as food by human beings. **3.** A milklike liquid, as the juice of a plant.
◊ *verb* To squeeze or draw milk from a cow or goat.
milk (mĭlk) ◊ *noun* ◊ *verb* **milked, milking**

milk shake *noun* A beverage made of milk, flavoring, and usually ice cream that is shaken or mixed.
milk shake ◊ *noun, plural* **milk shakes**

milkweed *noun* A plant with clusters of purplish flowers, milky juice, and large pods that split open to release downy seeds.
milk·weed (**mĭlk′**wēd′) ◊ *noun*

ă	pat	ĭ	pit	oi	**oil**	th	ba**th**
ā	pay	ī	ride	o͝o	book	*th*	ba**th**e
â	care	î	fierce	o͞o	boot	ə	ago, item
ä	father	ŏ	pot	ou	**out**		pencil
ĕ	pet	ō	go	ŭ	cut		atom
ē	be	ô	paw, for	û	fur		circus

▲ **milkweed**

milky *adjective* **1.** Like milk in color or texture. **2.** Full of or containing milk.
milk·y (**mĭl′**kē) ◊ *adjective* **milkier, milkiest**

Milky Way *noun* **1.** A broad band of white light across the night sky that is caused by countless numbers of faint stars. **2.** The galaxy in which the sun and solar system are located and which contains the stars of the Milky Way.

mill *noun* **1.** A machine that grinds or crushes something, such as coffee beans, into powder or fine grains. **2.** A building equipped with machines for grinding grain into flour or meal. **3.** A building or factory equipped with machinery for processing a material, such as paper, textiles, or steel.
◊ *verb* **1.** To grind or crush into powder or fine grains. **2.** To move around in a confused or disorderly way: *A crowd was milling about in front of the stadium.*
mill (mĭl) ◊ *noun, plural* **mills** ◊ *verb* **milled, milling**

miller *noun* **1.** A person who works in, operates, or owns a flour mill. **2.** A moth whose wings and body are covered with a whitish, flourlike powder.
mill·er (**mĭl′**ər) ◊ *noun, plural* **millers**

millet *noun* A grass that is grown for its edible seeds and is used as hay.
mil·let (**mĭl′**ĭt) ◊ *noun*

milligram *noun* A unit of mass and weight in the metric system equal to 1/1000 gram.
mil·li·gram (**mĭl′**ĭ grăm′) ◊ *noun, plural* **milligrams**

milliliter *noun* A unit of capacity for liquids in the metric system equal to 1/1000 liter.

mil·li·li·ter (mĭl′ə lē′tər) ◊ *noun, plural* **milliliters**

millimeter *noun* A unit of length in the metric system equal to 1/1000 meter.
mil·li·me·ter (mĭl′ə mē′tər) ◊ *noun, plural* **millimeters**

million *noun* **1.** One thousand thousands; 1,000,000. **2.** Often **millions** A very large number: *Millions of things can go wrong.*
◊ *adjective* Being equal to a thousand thousands in number.
mil·lion (mĭl′yən) ◊ *noun, plural* **million** *or* **millions** ◊ *adjective*

millionaire *noun* A person who has at least a million dollars.
mil·lion·aire (mĭl′yə **nâr′**) ◊ *noun, plural* **millionaires**

millionth *noun* **1.** The number in a series that matches the number 1,000,000. **2.** One of a million equal parts, written 1/1,000,000.
◊ *adjective* Coming after the 999,999th.
mil·lionth (mĭl′yənth) ◊ *noun, plural* **millionths** ◊ *adjective*

millstone *noun* One of a pair of large round stones used to grind grain.
mill·stone (mĭl′stōn′) ◊ *noun, plural* **millstones**

mill wheel *noun* A wheel, usually driven by moving water, that supplies power to a mill.
mill wheel ◊ *noun, plural* **mill wheels**

▲ **mill wheel**

mimeograph *noun* A machine that makes copies of written, drawn, or typed material by means of a stencil that is fitted around an inked drum.
mim·e·o·graph (mĭm′ē ə grăf′) ◊ *noun, plural* **mimeographs**

mimic *verb* **1.** To copy or imitate closely; ape. **2.** To make fun of by imitating; mock.
◊ *noun* One that imitates another.
mim·ic (mĭm′ĭk) ◊ *verb* **mimicked, mimicking** ◊ *noun, plural* **mimics**

min. The abbreviation for *minute.*

minaret *noun* A tower on a mosque from which the people are called to prayer.
min·a·ret (mĭn′ə **rĕt′**) ◊ *noun, plural* **minarets**

▲ **minaret**

mince *verb* To cut or chop into very small pieces.
mince (mĭns) ◊ *verb* **minced, mincing**

mincemeat *noun* A mixture of very finely chopped fruit, spices, suet, and sometimes meat, used especially as a pie filling.
mince·meat (mĭns′mēt′) ◊ *noun*

mind *noun* **1.** The part of a human being that thinks, feels, understands, remembers, and reasons: *The mathematician has a brilliant mind.* **2.** Center of thought; attention: *Keep your mind on your work.* **3.** Memory; recall: *It completely slipped my mind.* **4.** Opinion or point of view: *You spoke your mind.* **5.** Intention; purpose: *I changed my mind.*
◊ *verb* **1.** To object to or dislike: *Would you mind if I sat down?* **2.** To be concerned about: *Never mind the broken glass.* **3.** To listen to and obey: *Mind your parents.* —See Synonyms at **obey.** **4.** To take charge of; look after: *We stayed home to mind the baby.* **5.** To pay attention to: *Mind your own business.*

M

6. To be careful about: *Mind your manners.*
mind (mīnd) ◊ *noun, plural* **minds** ◊ *verb* **minded, minding**

SYNONYMS

mind, brains, intelligence

He has a good *mind* for mathematics. My sister has the *brains* in our family. Just use your *intelligence* and you'll figure out the answer.

mindful *adjective* Bearing in mind; aware: *We are always mindful of the danger of fire.*
mind·ful (**mīnd′**fəl) ◊ *adjective*

mine¹ *noun* **1.** An underground hole or tunnel from which minerals such as coal, iron, salt, or gold can be taken. **2.** An abundant supply or source: *The encyclopedia is a mine of information.* **3.** An explosive device that can be buried in the ground or placed underwater.
◊ *verb* **1.** To dig, tunnel, or work in a mine. **2.** To get minerals from a mine. **3.** To place explosive mines in or under.
mine¹ (mīn) ◊ *noun, plural* **mines** ◊ *verb* **mined, mining**

mine² *pronoun* The one or ones that belong to me: *The red scarf on the chair is mine. They needed extra dishes for the party, so I lent them mine.*
mine² (mīn) ◊ *pronoun*

HISTORY **• mine¹, mine²**

Mine¹ comes from an old French word that meant "to dig for ore." **Mine²** is a native English word related to **my.**

miner *noun* A person who works in a mine.
min·er (**mī′**nər) ◊ *noun, plural* **miners**
‖*These sound alike:* **miner, minor**

mineral *noun* **1.** A natural substance, such as a diamond, that is not of plant or animal origin. **2.** A natural substance, such as ore, coal, or petroleum, that is mined for human use.
◊ *adjective* Containing minerals: *Mineral water is good for the health.*
min·er·al (**mĭn′** ər əl) ◊ *noun, plural* **minerals** ◊ *adjective*

mingle *verb* **1.** To mix or become mixed; combine: *The sound of chimes mingled with the ringing of the doorbell.* —See Synonyms at **mix. 2.** To join in company with others: *We mingled with the crowd during the play's intermission.*
min·gle (**mĭng′** gəl) ◊ *verb* **mingled, mingling**

miniature *adjective* Much smaller than the usual size: *We have a miniature train.* —See Synonyms at **little.**
◊ *noun* **1.** A very small copy or model of something else: *I bought a miniature of the White House.* **2.** A very small painting, especially a portrait.
min·i·a·ture (**mĭn′** ē ə chər) ◊ *adjective* ◊ *noun, plural* **miniatures**

minicomputer *noun* A small computer with more memory and higher speed than a microcomputer.
min·i·com·put·er (mĭn′ē kəm **pyōō′** tər) ◊ *noun, plural* **minicomputers**

▲ **minicomputer**

minimum *noun* The smallest possible quantity or degree: *In the story the author gets across complex ideas with a minimum of words.*
◊ *adjective* Being the lowest possible: *Sixteen is the minimum age for getting a driver's license.*
min·i·mum (**mĭn′** ə məm) ◊ *noun, plural* **minimums** ◊ *adjective*

ă	pat	ĭ	pit	oi	oil	th	bath
ā	pay	ī	ride	ŏŏ	book	*th*	bathe
â	care	î	fierce	ōō	boot	ə	ago, item
ä	father	ŏ	pot	ou	out		pencil
ĕ	pet	ō	go	ŭ	cut		atom
ē	be	ô	paw, for	û	fur		circus

mining *noun* The work, process, or business of taking minerals from the earth.
min·ing (mī′nĭng) ◊ *noun*

minister *noun* **1.** A pastor of a church, especially a Protestant church. **2.** A person who is in charge of a department, such as the treasury, in a country's government. **3.** An official who represents his or her government in a foreign country.
min·is·ter (mĭn′ĭ stər) ◊ *noun, plural* **ministers**

mink *noun* **1.** An animal that resembles a weasel and has thick, soft, brown fur. **2.** The fur of the mink.
mink (mĭngk) ◊ *noun, plural* **mink** *or* **minks**

▲ **mink**

Minn. An abbreviation for *Minnesota.*

minnow *noun* A very small freshwater fish that is often used as bait.
min·now (mĭn′ō) ◊ *noun, plural* **minnows**

minor *adjective* Smaller in amount, size, extent, or importance: *My neighbor is a minor official in state government.*
◊ *noun* A person too young to take on the rights and duties of an adult.
mi·nor (mī′nər) ◊ *adjective* ◊ *noun, plural* **minors**
‖ *These sound alike:* **minor, miner**

minority *noun* **1.** The smaller of two groups forming a whole: *Only a minority of the class voted for the plan.* **2.** A group of people that differs, as in race, from the larger population of which it is a part.
mi·nor·i·ty (mĭ nôr′ĭ tē) ◊ *noun, plural* **minorities**

minstrel *noun* A musician of the Middle Ages who traveled from place to place, singing and reciting poetry.
min·strel (mĭn′strəl) ◊ *noun, plural* **minstrels**

mint¹ *noun* **1.** A plant with leaves that have a strong, pleasant smell and taste. **2.** A candy flavored with mint.
mint¹ (mĭnt) ◊ *noun, plural* **mints**

mint² *noun* **1.** A place where coins are made by a government. **2.** A large amount of money: *The diamond necklace cost a mint.*
◊ *verb* To coin money.
mint² (mĭnt) ◊ *noun, plural* **mints** ◊ *verb* **minted, minting**

***HISTORY* • mint¹, mint²**

Mint¹ goes back to a Greek word for this plant. **Mint²** goes back to a Latin word that meant both "money" and "a place where money is coined."

minuend *noun* A number from which another number is to be subtracted. In the example 8 − 5 = 3, 8 is the minuend.
min·u·end (mĭn′yo͞o ĕnd′) ◊ *noun, plural* **minuends**

minuet *noun* **1.** A slow, stately dance. **2.** Music written to accompany a minuet.
min·u·et (mĭn′yo͞o **ĕt′**) ◊ *noun, plural* **minuets**

minus *preposition* Made less by the subtraction of: *Seven minus four equals three.*
◊ *adjective* Slightly lower or less than: *In the exam I got a grade of A minus.*
◊ *noun* The sign (−) used to show that the number following is to be subtracted, as in 7 − 2 = 5, or that it has a negative value, as in −6.
mi·nus (mī′nəs) ◊ *preposition* ◊ *adjective* ◊ *noun, plural* **minuses**

minute¹ *noun* **1.** A unit of time equal to 60 seconds. **2.** A short time: *Wait just a minute.* —See Synonyms at **moment. 3.** A specific point in time: *We are leaving this very minute.* **4. minutes** An official record of what happened at a meeting.
min·ute¹ (mĭn′ĭt) ◊ *noun, plural* **minutes**

minute² *adjective* **1.** Extremely small; tiny: *The wind blew a minute speck of dirt into my eye.* **2.** Marked by careful study of small details: *The inspector made a minute check of*

M

the wiring to be sure it was put in properly.
mi·nute² (mī **nōōt′** *or* mī **nyōōt′**) ◊ *adjective*

HISTORY • minute¹, minute²

Minute¹ comes from a Latin word that meant "a small part." **Minute²** comes from a related Latin word that meant "small."

miracle *noun* **1.** An event that seems impossible because it cannot be explained by the laws of nature. **2.** Something amazing and marvelous: *The moon landings were miracles of modern technology.*
mir·a·cle (**mĭr′** ə kəl) ◊ *noun, plural* **miracles**

miraculous *adjective* Of or like a miracle.
mi·rac·u·lous (mĭ **răk′** yə ləs) ◊ *adjective*

mirage *noun* An optical illusion in which something that is not really there appears to be seen in the distance: *In the desert we saw a mirage that looked like a lake.*
mi·rage (mĭ **räzh′**) ◊ *noun, plural* **mirages**

mire *noun* **1.** An area of wet, muddy ground. **2.** Deep, slimy soil or mud.
◊ *verb* To cause to sink or become stuck in or as if in mire.
mire (mīr) ◊ *noun* ◊ *verb* **mired, miring**

mirror *noun* **1.** A surface, as of glass, that reflects the image of an object placed in front of it. **2.** Something that gives an accurate picture: *The book is a mirror of life in the city.*
◊ *verb* To reflect in or as if in a mirror.
mir·ror (**mĭr′** ər) ◊ *noun, plural* **mirrors** ◊ *verb* **mirrored, mirroring**

mirth *noun* Gaiety and laughter.
mirth (mûrth) ◊ *noun*

mirthful *adjective* Full of mirth; merry.
mirth·ful (**mûrth′** fəl) ◊ *adjective*

mis– The prefix *mis–* means "bad" or "wrong." *Misconduct* is bad conduct. The prefix *mis–* also means "badly" or "wrongly." If you *misspell* a word, you spell it wrong.

ă	pat	ĭ	pit	oi	**oil**	th	**bath**
ā	pay	ī	ride	ŏŏ	**book**	*th*	**bathe**
â	care	î	fierce	ōō	**boot**	ə	**ago, item**
ä	father	ŏ	pot	ou	**out**		pencil
ĕ	pet	ō	**go**	ŭ	**cut**		atom
ē	be	ô	**paw, for**	û	**fur**		circus

VOCABULARY BUILDER • mis–

Many words that are formed with **mis–** are not entries in this dictionary. But you can figure out what these words mean by looking up the meanings of the root words and the prefix. For example:
misgovern = to govern badly
mispronunciation = a wrong pronunciation

misbehave *verb* To behave badly.
mis·be·have (mĭs′bĭ **hāv′**) ◊ *verb* **misbehaved, misbehaving**

miscellaneous *adjective* Made up of different kinds of things.
mis·cel·la·ne·ous (mĭs′ə **lā′** nē əs) ◊ *adjective*

mischief *noun* **1.** Naughty or bad behavior. **2.** Harm or damage caused by someone or something.
mis·chief (**mĭs′** chĭf) ◊ *noun*

mischievous *adjective* **1.** Full of mischief; naughty: *Newborn kittens can be mischievous.* **2.** Playful or teasing: *There's a mischievous look on your face.* **3.** Causing harm or damage.
mis·chie·vous (**mĭs′** chə vəs) ◊ *adjective*

misconduct *noun* Improper or unlawful conduct: *The judge was removed for misconduct in office.*
mis·con·duct (mĭs **kŏn′** dŭkt′) ◊ *noun*

miscount *verb* To count wrongly.
◊ *noun* A wrong count.
mis·count ◊ *verb* (mĭs **kount′**) **miscounted, miscounting** ◊ *noun* (**mĭs′** kount′), *plural* **miscounts**

miser *noun* A stingy person.
mi·ser (**mī′** zər) ◊ *noun, plural* **misers**

miserable *adjective* **1.** Very unhappy: *I was miserable on my first night at camp.* **2.** Causing real unhappiness or discomfort: *We had miserable weather last winter.* **3.** Very poor; inferior: *They live in a miserable shack in the woods.*
mis·er·a·ble (**mĭz′** ər ə bəl) ◊ *adjective*

misery *noun* **1.** Great pain or distress: *I was in misery with a strained muscle.* **2.** Miserable conditions of life: *The family lives in misery in a slum.*
mis·er·y (**mĭz′** ə rē) ◊ *noun, plural* **miseries**

misfortune *noun* **1.** Bad luck: *I had the misfortune to lose my watch.* **2.** An unfortunate happening: *The hurricane was a great misfortune for many people in the area.*
mis·for·tune (mĭs **fôr′** chən) ◊ *noun, plural* **misfortunes**

misgiving *noun* A feeling of doubt or concern: *My parents had misgivings about getting me a horse.*
mis·giv·ing (mĭs **gĭv′**ĭng) ◊ *noun, plural* **misgivings**

mishap *noun* An unfortunate accident: *The trip ended without a mishap.*
mis·hap (**mĭs′**hăp′) ◊ *noun, plural* **mishaps**

mislaid *verb* Past tense and past participle of **mislay.**
mis·laid (mĭs **lād′**) ◊ *verb*

mislay *verb* To put down in a place that is afterward forgotten: *I mislaid my glasses.*
mis·lay (mĭs **lā′**) ◊ *verb* **mislaid, mislaying**

mislead *verb* **1.** To lead in the wrong direction: *The map misled us.* **2.** To give the wrong idea to; deceive: *The candidate's promises misled many voters.*
mis·lead (mĭs **lēd′**) ◊ *verb* **misled, misleading**

misled *verb* Past tense and past participle of **mislead.**
mis·led (mĭs **lĕd′**) ◊ *verb*

misplace *verb* **1.** To put in a wrong place: *I misplaced my math book in my locker.* **2.** To lose; mislay: *I misplaced my keys.*
mis·place (mĭs **plās′**) ◊ *verb* **misplaced, misplacing**

misprint *noun* An error in printing.
mis·print (**mĭs′**prĭnt′) ◊ *noun, plural* **misprints**

mispronounce *verb* To pronounce incorrectly: *Try not to mispronounce my name.*
mis·pro·nounce (mĭs′prə **nouns′**) ◊ *verb* **mispronounced, mispronouncing**

miss *verb* **1.** To fail to hit, reach, catch, meet, or get: *The arrow missed the target. We missed the train. The catcher missed the ball.* **2.** To fail to attend or be present for: *We missed three days of school.* **3.** To let slip by: *I wasn't paying attention, so I missed my turn.* **4.** To notice or feel the absence or loss of: *It was only after we left the theater that I missed my wallet.* **5.** To avoid or escape: *If you leave early, you'll miss most of the traffic.*
◊ *noun* A failure to hit, reach, catch, meet, or get.
miss (mĭs) ◊ *verb* **missed, missing** ◊ *noun, plural* **misses**

Miss *noun* A form of address used for an unmarried woman: *Miss Smith.*
Miss (mĭs) ◊ *noun*

Miss. An abbreviation for *Mississippi.*

missile *noun* An object, such as a weapon, that is thrown, fired, dropped, or launched at a target.
mis·sile (**mĭs′**əl) ◊ *noun, plural* **missiles**

missing *adjective* Not to be found; lost or lacking: *The book has several missing pages.*
miss·ing (**mĭs′**ĭng) ◊ *adjective*

mission *noun* **1.** An assignment to be carried out; task: *Our mission is to send food to needy people.* **2.** A group of persons sent to carry out a mission: *My parents joined an international rescue mission.* **3.** A place at which missionaries live or work.
mis·sion (**mĭsh′**ən) ◊ *noun, plural* **missions**

missionary *noun* A person sent, as to a foreign land, to spread a religion and do good works.
mis·sion·ar·y (**mĭsh′**ə nĕr′ē) ◊ *noun, plural* **missionaries**

misspell *verb* To spell incorrectly.
mis·spell (mĭs **spĕl′**) ◊ *verb* **misspelled** *or* **misspelt, misspelling**

misspelt *verb* A past tense and a past participle of **misspell.**
mis·spelt (mĭs **spĕlt′**) ◊ *verb*

mist *noun* **1.** A mass of tiny drops of water in the air. **2.** Something that dims or obscures the sight.
◊ *verb* **1.** To be or become misty: *My glasses misted in the cold air.* **2.** To become or cause to become clouded as if with mist: *Their eyes misted with tears.*
mist (mĭst) ◊ *noun, plural* **mists** ◊ *verb* **misted, misting**

mistake *noun* Something that is thought up, done, or figured out in an incorrect way: *I made a mistake in arithmetic.* —See Synonyms at **error.**
◊ *verb* **1.** To misunderstand. **2.** To recognize or identify incorrectly: *I mistook you for your cousin.*
mis·take (mĭ **stāk′**) ◊ *noun, plural* **mistakes** ◊ *verb* **mistook, mistaken, mistaking**

M

mistaken *adjective* **1.** Having made a mistake: *If I'm not mistaken, you did go.* **2.** Based on a mistake; wrong: *Don't get any mistaken ideas about winning without practicing.*
◊ *verb* Past participle of **mistake.**
mis·tak·en (mĭ **stā′** kən) ◊ *adjective* ◊ *verb*

Mister *noun* A form of address, usually written *Mr.*, used for a man: *Mr. Smith.*
Mis·ter (**mĭs′** tər) ◊ *noun*

mistletoe *noun* A plant with evergreen leaves and white berries that grows as a parasite on trees.
mis·tle·toe (**mĭs′** əl tō′) ◊ *noun*

▲ **mistletoe**

mistook *verb* Past tense of **mistake.**
mis·took (mĭ **stŏŏk′**) ◊ *verb*

mistreat *verb* To treat badly.
mis·treat (mĭs **trēt′**) ◊ *verb* **mistreated, mistreating**

mistress *noun* A woman in a position of authority, control, or ownership.
mis·tress (**mĭs′** trĭs) ◊ *noun, plural* **mistresses**

mistrust *noun* Lack of trust; suspicion.
◊ *verb* To have no trust in; doubt: *I mistrust your promises.*
mis·trust (mĭs **trŭst′**) ◊ *noun* ◊ *verb* **mistrusted, mistrusting**

ă	pat	ĭ	pit	oi	oil	th	bath
ā	pay	ī	ride	ŏŏ	book	*th*	bathe
â	care	î	fierce	ōō	boot	ə	ago, item
ä	father	ŏ	pot	ou	out		pencil
ĕ	pet	ō	go	ŭ	cut		atom
ē	be	ô	paw, for	û	fur		circus

misty *adjective* **1.** Consisting of, filled with, or covered by mist: *Yesterday we had a misty morning.* **2.** Obscured or blurred by or as if by mist; dim: *I have only misty memories of my early childhood.*
mist·y (**mĭs′** tē) ◊ *adjective* **mistier, mistiest**

misunderstand *verb* To understand incorrectly: *My story was misunderstood.*
mis·un·der·stand (mĭs′ŭn dər **stănd′**) ◊ *verb* **misunderstood, misunderstanding**

misunderstanding *noun* **1.** A failure to understand. **2.** A quarrel or disagreement.
mis·un·der·stand·ing (mĭs′ŭn dər **stăn′** dĭng) ◊ *noun, plural* **misunderstandings**

misunderstood *verb* Past tense and past participle of **misunderstand.**
mis·un·der·stood (mĭs′ŭn dər **stŏŏd′**) ◊ *verb*

misuse *verb* **1.** To use wrongly or incorrectly: *I misused the word.* **2.** To make improper use of: *It is wrong to misuse our natural resources.*
◊ *noun* Wrong or improper use.
mis·use ◊ *verb* (mĭs **yōōz′**) **misused, misusing** ◊ *noun* (mĭs **yōōs′**), *plural* **misuses**

mite *noun* A very small animal related to the spiders that often lives as a parasite on plants or other animals.
mite (mīt) ◊ *noun, plural* **mites**
‖*These sound alike:* **mite, might**

mitt *noun* A large, padded leather glove that is worn to protect the hand when catching a baseball.
mitt (mĭt) ◊ *noun, plural* **mitts**

mitten *noun* A warm covering for the hand that has a separate section for the thumb.
mit·ten (**mĭt′** n) ◊ *noun, plural* **mittens**

▲ **mitt**

mix *verb* **1.** To blend or combine into a single mass or substance: *Mix the flour, water, and eggs to form dough.* **2.** To make by combining ingredients: *I'm going to mix some lemonade.*
◊ *noun* Something formed by mixing; mix-

ture: *We decided to try a new cake mix.* ◊ *idiom* **mix up** To confuse: *Try not to mix up the words "principal" and "principle."*
mix (mĭks) ◊ *verb* **mixed, mixing** ◊ *noun, plural* **mixes**

> ***SYNONYMS***
>
> ***mix, blend, mingle***
>
> Anger and friendship don't *mix* well. The two fragrances *blended* into one. The author *mingles* happy events and sad events in this story. **Antonym:** *separate*

mixed *adjective* Made up of different things or kinds: *We had a mixed salad for lunch.*
mixed (mĭkst) ◊ *adjective*

mixed number *noun* A number made up of a whole number and a fraction. An example of a mixed number is $1\frac{1}{2}$.
mixed number ◊ *noun, plural* **mixed numbers**

mixer *noun* A device that mixes.
mix·er (**mĭk'** sər) ◊ *noun, plural* **mixers**

mixture *noun* **1.** Something that is made by mixing: *For paste we used a mixture of flour and water.* **2.** The act or process of mixing or the condition of being mixed.
mix·ture (**mĭks'** chər) ◊ *noun, plural* **mixtures**

mix-up *noun* A confused situation: *There was a mix-up over the time of the game.*
mix-up (**mĭks'** ŭp') ◊ *noun, plural* **mix-ups**

ml The abbreviation for *milliliter.*

mm The abbreviation for *millimeter.*

MN The abbreviation for *Minnesota* used with a Zip Code.

MO The abbreviation for *Missouri* used with a Zip Code.

mo. The abbreviation for *month.*

Mo. An abbreviation for *Missouri.*

moan *noun* A long, low sound, as of sorrow. ◊ *verb* **1.** To utter a moan. **2.** To make a sound like a moan: *The wind moaned in the chimney.*
moan (mōn) ◊ *noun, plural* **moans** ◊ *verb* **moaned, moaning**
‖*These sound alike:* **moan, mown**

moat *noun* A deep, wide ditch, as one going around a castle. A moat is usually filled with water.
moat (mōt) ◊ *noun, plural* **moats**

▲ **moat**

mob *noun* **1.** A large, disorderly crowd. **2.** A large group of people; crowd: *A mob waited at the airport to welcome the astronauts.* ◊ *verb* To crowd around and jostle or annoy: *Fans mobbed the movie star.*
mob (mŏb) ◊ *noun, plural* **mobs** ◊ *verb* **mobbed, mobbing**

mobile *adjective* Capable of moving or being moved: *Mobile cameras filmed the parade.* ◊ *noun* A type of sculpture consisting of parts that sway in a breeze.
mo·bile ◊ *adjective* (**mō'** bəl) ◊ *noun* (mō-**bēl'**), *plural* **mobiles**

mobile home *noun* A trailer that is used as a permanent home.
mobile home ◊ *noun, plural* **mobile homes**

moccasin *noun* **1.** A soft leather slipper or shoe without a heel. **2.** The water moccasin.
moc·ca·sin (**mŏk'** ə sĭn) ◊ *noun, plural* **moccasins**

mock *verb* **1.** To treat with scorn: *Some people mock customs that they don't understand.* **2.** To imitate, especially in a way that insults. ◊ *adjective* Not real; false: *I wore a mock pearl ring.*
mock (mŏk) ◊ *verb* **mocked, mocking** ◊ *adjective*

mockery *noun* **1.** Action or speech that mocks or ridicules. **2.** A bad imitation: *The trial was a mockery of justice.*
mock·er·y (**mŏk'** ə rē) ◊ *noun, plural* **mockeries**

M

mockingbird *noun* A gray and white American songbird that often imitates other birds' songs.
mock·ing·bird (**mŏk′**ĭng bûrd′) ◊ *noun, plural* **mockingbirds**

▲ **mockingbird**

mode *noun* A way or style of doing, acting, or speaking: *Jet planes are a modern mode of transportation.*
mode (mōd) ◊ *noun, plural* **modes**

model *noun* **1.** A small copy: *I built a model of a sailboat.* **2.** A style, type, or design: *This car is last year's model.* **3.** A person or thing that is a good example: *The farm is a model of efficient management.* **4.** A person hired to display merchandise, such as clothing, that is for sale. **5.** A person who poses for an artist or a photographer.
◊ *verb* **1.** To make, shape, or build, as out of wax: *In art class I modeled animals in clay.* **2.** To form after a model or pattern: *The library was modeled on a famous building.* **3.** To display by wearing.
◊ *adjective* **1.** Serving as a model: *Since we have to move, we looked at a number of model homes.* **2.** Worthy of imitation: *You are a model student.*
mod·el (**mŏd′**l) ◊ *noun, plural* **models** ◊ *verb* **modeled, modeling** ◊ *adjective*

ă	pat	ĭ	pit	oi	**oi**l	th	ba**th**
ā	pay	ī	ride	ŏŏ	b**oo**k	*th*	ba**the**
â	care	î	fierce	ōō	b**oo**t	ə	**a**go, it**e**m
ä	father	ŏ	pot	ou	**ou**t		penc**i**l
ĕ	pet	ō	go	ŭ	c**u**t		at**o**m
ē	be	ô	paw, for	û	f**u**r		circ**u**s

moderate *adjective* **1.** Not too much or too little: *My parents always drive at moderate speeds.* **2.** Of medium amount, extent, or quality: *My friend earns a moderate income.* **3.** Neither too hot nor too cold; temperate: *North Carolina has a moderate climate.*
◊ *verb* To make or become less extreme.
mod·er·ate ◊ *adjective* (**mŏd′** ər ĭt) ◊ *verb* (**mŏd′** ə rāt′) **moderated, moderating**

modern *adjective* **1.** Of or relating to the present or recent past: *The transistor is a modern invention.* **2.** Advanced, as in style; up-to-date: *My parents work in a modern office building.* —See Synonyms at **new.**
mod·ern (**mŏd′** ərn) ◊ *adjective*

modest *adjective* **1.** Not thinking too highly of one's own talents, abilities, or accomplishments: *We were surprised at how modest the famous artist was.* —See Synonyms at **shy.** **2.** Retiring in manner: *The woman was delighted by her grandchild's quiet, modest behavior.* **3.** Moderate in size or amount; not large: *My brother makes a modest salary.*
mod·est (**mŏd′**ĭst) ◊ *adjective*

modification *noun* **1.** The act or process of modifying. **2.** The result of modifying: *The design is a modification of the original one.*
mod·i·fi·ca·tion (mŏd′ə fĭ **kā′**shən) ◊ *noun, plural* **modifications**

modifier *noun* A word, as an adjective or adverb, that limits the meaning of another word. In the sentence *It is a hot day,* the word *hot* is a modifier of *day.*
mod·i·fi·er (**mŏd′** ə fī′ər) ◊ *noun, plural* **modifiers**

modify *verb* **1.** To change somewhat; alter: *The architect modified the plans for the house so as to include three more rooms.* **2.** To limit the meaning of. In the phrase *very pretty,* the word *very* modifies *pretty.*
mod·i·fy (**mŏd′** ə fī′) ◊ *verb* **modified, modifying**

Mohammed *noun* A.D. 570?–632. The Arab prophet who founded the religion of Islam.
Mo·ham·med (mō **hăm′**ĭd) ◊ *noun*

moist *adjective* Slightly wet; damp: *I tried to remove the stain with a moist towel.*
moist (moist) ◊ *adjective* **moister, moistest**

moisten *verb* To make moist.
moist·en (**moi′**sən) ◊ *verb* **moistened, moistening**

moisture *noun* Liquid, as water, that is present in the air or in the ground or that forms tiny drops on a surface.
mois·ture (mois′chər) ◊ *noun*

molar *noun* A large tooth in the back of the mouth with a wide, flat top for grinding food.
mo·lar (mō′lər) ◊ *noun, plural* **molars**

molasses *noun* A thick, sweet syrup that is produced when sugar cane is made into sugar.
mo·las·ses (mə lăs′ĭz) ◊ *noun*

mold[1] *noun* **1.** A hollow container in which a liquid or soft substance, such as wax or plaster, can be shaped. **2.** Something shaped in a mold: *We had a gelatin mold for dessert.* ◊ *verb* To shape or form in or as if in a mold.
mold[1] (mōld) ◊ *noun, plural* **molds** ◊ *verb* **molded, molding**

mold[2] *noun* **1.** A type of fungus that forms a fuzzy coating on the surface of damp or decaying substances. **2.** The coating itself. ◊ *verb* To become moldy.
mold[2] (mōld) ◊ *noun, plural* **molds** ◊ *verb* **molded, molding**

> ***HISTORY* • mold**[1]**, mold**[2]
>
> **Mold**[1] goes back to a Latin word that meant "measure, model." **Mold**[2] may have come from an old Scandinavian word for this fungus.

molding *noun* An ornamental strip, as of wood or plaster, used to decorate a surface.
mold·ing (mōl′dĭng) ◊ *noun, plural* **moldings**

moldy *adjective* Of, like, or being covered with mold.
mold·y (mōl′dē) ◊ *adjective* **moldier, moldiest**

mole[1] *noun* A small, slightly raised, usually dark growth on the human skin.
mole[1] (mōl) ◊ *noun, plural* **moles**

mole[2] *noun* A small burrowing animal with very small eyes and short, silky fur.
mole[2] (mōl) ◊ *noun, plural* **moles**

> ***HISTORY* • mole**[1]**, mole**[2]
>
> **Mole**[1] comes from an old English word that meant "spot, blemish." **Mole**[2] comes from an old Dutch name for this animal.

molecule *noun* The smallest and most basic particle into which a substance can be divided and still be the same substance.
mol·e·cule (mŏl′ĭ kyōōl′) ◊ *noun, plural* **molecules**

mollusk *noun* One of a large group of animals, as clams and snails, that usually live in water and have a hard outer shell.
mol·lusk (mŏl′əsk) ◊ *noun, plural* **mollusks**

▲ **mollusk**
Clams and snails are kinds of mollusks.

molt *verb* To shed an outer covering, as skin, feathers, or hair, that is replaced by new growth.
molt (mōlt) ◊ *verb* **molted, molting**

molten *adjective* Melted by heat.
mol·ten (mōl′tən) ◊ *adjective*

mom *noun* Mother.
mom (mŏm) ◊ *noun, plural* **moms**

moment *noun* A very short period of time; instant: *Wait a moment while I wash my hands.*
mo·ment (mō′mənt) ◊ *noun, plural* **moments**

> ***SYNONYMS***
>
> ***moment, instant, jiffy, minute***[1]
>
> That was an important *moment* in my life. I ran to help the *instant* I heard the cry. I'll be with you in a *jiffy*. In a *minute* we'll be done with this job.

M

momentary *adjective* Lasting only for a moment: *I caught a momentary glimpse of them.*
mo·men·tar·y (**mō′** mən tĕr′ē) ◊ *adjective*

momentous *adjective* Very important; significant: *The signing of the treaty was a momentous event.*
mo·men·tous (mō **mĕn′** təs) ◊ *adjective*

momentum *noun* The force or speed that an object has when it moves.
mo·men·tum (mō **mĕn′** təm) ◊ *noun*

Mon. The abbreviation for *Monday.*

monarch *noun* **1.** A ruler, as a king or queen. **2.** A large orange and black butterfly.
mon·arch (**mŏn′** ərk) ◊ *noun, plural* **monarchs**

monarchy *noun* **1.** Government by a monarch. **2.** A country ruled by a monarch.
mon·ar·chy (**mŏn′** ər kē) ◊ *noun, plural* **monarchies**

monastery *noun* A place where a group of monks live and work.
mon·as·ter·y (**mŏn′** ə stĕr′ē) ◊ *noun, plural* **monasteries**

Monday *noun* The second day of the week.
Mon·day (**mŭn′** dē) ◊ *noun, plural* **Mondays**

***HISTORY* • Monday**

Three of the seven days of the week were named after planets or heavenly bodies. **Monday** was named after the **moon.**

money *noun* **1.** Coins and bills issued by a government for use in buying or paying for goods and services; currency. **2.** Wealth; riches: *Their family has money.*
mon·ey (**mŭn′** ē) ◊ *noun*

mongoose *noun* An animal with a long, narrow body and a long tail. A mongoose can kill poisonous snakes.
mon·goose (**mŏng′** go͞os′) ◊ *noun, plural* **mongooses**

ă	pat	ĭ	pit	oi	oil	th	bath
ā	pay	ī	ride	o͝o	book	*th*	bathe
â	care	î	fierce	o͞o	boot	ə	ago, item
ä	father	ŏ	pot	ou	out		pencil
ĕ	pet	ō	go	ŭ	cut		atom
ē	be	ô	paw, for	û	fur		circus

▲ **mongoose**

mongrel *noun* An animal or plant, especially a dog, that is a mixture of different breeds.
mon·grel (**mŭng′** grəl *or* **mŏng′** grəl) ◊ *noun, plural* **mongrels**

monitor *noun* **1.** A student who does a special job to help a teacher in school. **2.** A device used to record or control a process or activity: *A monitor kept track of the patient's heartbeats during surgery.*
◊ *verb* To keep watch over, record, or control, especially with a technical device: *The police used radar to monitor traffic.*
mon·i·tor (**mŏn′** ĭ tər) ◊ *noun, plural* **monitors** ◊ *verb* **monitored, monitoring**

monk *noun* A man who belongs to a religious order and promises to observe its rules and practices.
monk (mŭngk) ◊ *noun, plural* **monks**

monkey *noun* Any of a group of animals that have long arms and legs, and hands and feet that are adapted for climbing and grasping objects. Monkeys, and especially the smaller ones, have long tails.
◊ *verb* **1.** To behave in a silly or careless way: *We were told not to monkey around during the assembly.* **2.** To tamper; fool: *The child monkeyed with the TV until it broke.*
mon·key (**mŭng′** kē) ◊ *noun, plural* **monkeys** ◊ *verb* **monkeyed, monkeying**

monkey wrench *noun* A tool with a jaw that adjusts to fit different sizes of nuts.
monkey wrench ◊ *noun, plural* **monkey wrenches**

monogram *noun* A design made by combining the initials of a person's name.
mon·o·gram (**mŏn′** ə grăm′) ◊ *noun, plural* **monograms**

monologue *noun* A long speech given by an actor or made by one person in a group.
mon·o·logue (**mŏn′** ə lôg′) ◊ *noun, plural* **monologues**

monopolize *verb* To have all to oneself: *They monopolized the conversation.*
mo·nop·o·lize (mə **nŏp′** ə līz′) ◊ *verb* **monopolized, monopolizing**

monopoly *noun* **1.** Complete control over a product or service: *The electric company has a monopoly on electricity.* **2.** A group or person having a monopoly.
mo·nop·o·ly (mə **nŏp′** ə lē) ◊ *noun, plural* **monopolies**

monorail *noun* **1.** A single rail on which a train travels. **2.** A vehicle that travels on a monorail.
mon·o·rail (**mŏn′** ə rāl′) ◊ *noun, plural* **monorails**

▲ **monorail**

monosyllable *noun* A word that has one syllable. The word *buy* is a monosyllable.
mon·o·syl·la·ble (mŏn′ə **sĭl′** ə bəl) ◊ *noun, plural* **monosyllables**

monotone *noun* A succession of sounds or words uttered in a single tone of voice.
mon·o·tone (**mŏn′** ə tōn′) ◊ *noun*

monotonous *adjective* Dull because of being always the same: *The explorers lived on a monotonous diet of beans and rice.*
mo·not·o·nous (mə **nŏt′**n əs) ◊ *adjective*

monotony *noun* Boring lack of variety.
mo·not·o·ny (mə **nŏt′**n ē) ◊ *noun*

monsoon *noun* **1.** A wind in southern Asia that changes direction with the seasons. **2.** The rainy summer season brought by the monsoon.
mon·soon (mŏn **sōōn′**) ◊ *noun, plural* **monsoons**

monster *noun* **1.** An imaginary creature that is huge and frightening. **2.** A very large animal, person, or thing: *Fish range from tiny animals to monsters many feet long.* **3.** A very evil or cruel person.
mon·ster (**mŏn′** stər) ◊ *noun, plural* **monsters**

monstrous *adjective* **1.** Extremely large; enormous: *The monstrous oil tanker could not fit into the canal.* **2.** Very ugly: *The ancient statue was of a monstrous creature, part lion, part bird, and part person.* **3.** Very evil, cruel, or wrong.
mon·strous (**mŏn′** strəs) ◊ *adjective*

Mont. An abbreviation for *Montana.*

month *noun* One of the 12 periods that make up a year.
month (mŭnth) ◊ *noun, plural* **months**

monthly *adjective* **1.** Happening, appearing, or to be paid once every month: *The student council has monthly meetings.* **2.** Covering a period of a month: *The average monthly rainfall in our town is about three inches.* ◊ *adverb* Every month; once a month.
month·ly (**mŭnth′** lē) ◊ *adjective* ◊ *adverb*

monument *noun* Something, as a statue or building, put up to help people continue to remember a person, group, or thing.
mon·u·ment (**mŏn′** yə mənt) ◊ *noun, plural* **monuments**

▲ **monument**
The Washington Monument

M

moo *noun* The sound a cow makes.
◊ *verb* To make this sound.
moo (mo͞o) ◊ *noun, plural* **moos** ◊ *verb* **mooed, mooing**

LANGUAGE DETECTIVE

moo

In the South and in southern New England if you refer to the sound made by cows, you might say that cows *low* (lō). In the rest of the country you probably say that cows *moo* (mo͞o). Cows sound pretty much the same all over the country, but people who live in different areas use these two different words to talk about the sounds their cattle make.

mood *noun* A person's state of mind: *Playing with my friends puts me in a happy mood.*
mood (mo͞od) ◊ *noun, plural* **moods**

moodily *adverb* In a moody manner.
mood·i·ly (**mo͞o′** də lē) ◊ *adverb*

moody *adjective* **1.** Tending to have frequent changes in mood. **2.** Being in or showing a bad mood; gloomy.
mood·y (**mo͞o′** dē) ◊ *adjective* **moodier, moodiest**

moon *noun* **1.** The heavenly body that revolves around the earth in 29 days, 12 hours, and 44 minutes and that reflects the sun's light. **2.** A heavenly body that revolves around a planet; satellite.
moon (mo͞on) ◊ *noun, plural* **moons**

moonbeam *noun* A ray of moonlight.
moon·beam (**mo͞on′** bēm′) ◊ *noun, plural* **moonbeams**

moonlight *noun* The light of the moon.
moon·light (**mo͞on′** līt′) ◊ *noun*

moonscape *noun* A view or picture of the moon's surface.
moon·scape (**mo͞on′** skāp′) ◊ *noun, plural* **moonscapes**

ă	pat	ĭ	pit	oi	**oi**l	th	ba**th**
ā	pay	ī	ride	o͝o	b**oo**k	*th*	ba**the**
â	care	î	fierce	o͞o	b**oo**t	ə	ago, item
ä	father	ŏ	pot	ou	**ou**t		pencil
ĕ	pet	ō	go	ŭ	c**u**t		atom
ē	be	ô	paw, for	û	f**u**r		circus

moor¹ *verb* To fasten in place by using ropes, cables, or anchors: *We moored the rowboat at the dock.*
moor¹ (mo͝or) ◊ *verb* **moored, mooring**

moor² *noun* A broad stretch of open land, often with marshes and areas of shrubs.
moor² (mo͝or) ◊ *noun, plural* **moors**

***HISTORY* • moor¹, moor²**

Moor¹ comes from an old German word that meant "to anchor." **Moor²** came from an old English word that meant "land that is not cultivated or lived on."

mooring *noun* **1.** A place where a ship or an aircraft can be moored. **2.** A rope, chain, or cable for mooring a ship or an aircraft.
moor·ing (**mo͝or′** ĭng) ◊ *noun, plural* **moorings**

moose *noun* A large animal with big broad antlers that is related to the deer. Moose live in the forests of northern North America, Europe, and Asia.
moose (mo͞os) ◊ *noun, plural* **moose**

▲ **moose**

mop *noun* **1.** A cleaning tool that has a handle attached to material, as sponge for soaking up liquid or yarn for picking up dust. **2.** A thick mass like a mop: *You have quite a mop of hair.*
◊ *verb* To clean or wipe with or as if with a mop: *I mopped and waxed the floor.*
mop (mŏp) ◊ *noun, plural* **mops** ◊ *verb* **mopped, mopping**

mope *verb* To be gloomy and often silent.
mope (mōp) ◊ *verb* **moped, moping**

moral *adjective* **1.** Concerned with what is right and wrong. **2.** Good and just; virtuous: *Is it moral to waste food when others in the world are starving?*
◊ *noun* **1.** The lesson taught by a story, experience, or event. **2. morals** Behavior with respect to right and wrong: *Children should learn good morals from grownups.*
mor·al (**môr′** əl) ◊ *adjective* ◊ *noun, plural* **morals**

morale *noun* The state of mind of a person or group: *The team's morale was high.*
mo·rale (mə **răl′**) ◊ *noun*

morality *noun* **1.** The quality of being moral; goodness. **2.** Moral behavior; virtue.
mo·ral·i·ty (mə **răl′** ĭ tē) ◊ *noun*

morass *noun* An area of low, soggy ground; marsh.
mo·rass (mə **răs′**) ◊ *noun, plural* **morasses**

moray *noun* Any of several eels that have very sharp teeth. Morays are found in warm ocean waters and can be dangerous to swimmers.
mo·ray (**môr′** ā) ◊ *noun, plural* **morays**

more *adjective* **1.** Greater, as in number, size, extent, or degree: *Our class does more work than any of the others.* **2.** Additional; extra: *We brought more food along, just in case.*
◊ *noun* A greater or additional quantity, number, degree, or amount: *I ordered some more.*
◊ *adverb* **1.** Often used to form the comparative of adjectives and adverbs that do not form comparatives by adding *-er*: *The test was more difficult than I had expected. A cat moves more quietly than a dog.* **2.** In addition; again: *What more do you want?*
more (môr) ◊ *adjective* ◊ *noun* ◊ *adverb*

moreover *adverb* Beyond what has already been said; furthermore: *I'm willing to paint my room, and moreover I'd enjoy doing it.*
more·o·ver (môr **ō′** vər) ◊ *adverb*

morn *noun* Morning.
morn (môrn) ◊ *noun, plural* **morns**
‖*These sound alike:* **morn, mourn**

morning *noun* The early part of the day, from midnight to noon or from sunrise to noon.
morn·ing (**môr′** nĭng) ◊ *noun, plural* **mornings**
‖*These sound alike:* **morning, mourning**

morning-glory *noun* A climbing vine with funnel-shaped flowers that usually close in the afternoon.
mor·ning-glo·ry (**môr′** nĭng glôr′ē) ◊ *noun, plural* **morning-glories**

▲ **morning-glory**

morsel *noun* A small piece, especially of food; bit.
mor·sel (**môr′** səl) ◊ *noun, plural* **morsels**

mortal *adjective* **1.** Certain to die: *All human beings are mortal beings.* **2.** Causing death; fatal. **3.** Extremely hostile: *Those two are mortal enemies.* **4.** Very great; extreme: *They live in mortal fear of earthquakes.*
◊ *noun* A human being.
mor·tal (**môr′** tl) ◊ *adjective* ◊ *noun, plural* **mortals**

mortar *noun* **1.** A bowl in which substances can be crushed or ground with a pestle. **2.** A building material that is made of sand, water, lime, and often cement. Mortar is used to hold bricks or stones together. **3.** A short, light muzzle-loading cannon used to fire shells in a high arc.
mor·tar (**môr′** tər) ◊ *noun, plural* **mortars**

mosaic *noun* A design on a surface made by fitting and cementing together small pieces of hard material, such as colored glass or tile.
mo·sa·ic (mō **zā′** ĭk) ◊ *noun, plural* **mosaics**

▲ **mosaic**

M

Moslem *noun* A person who believes in or follows the religion of Islam.
◊ *adjective* Of or relating to Islam.
Mos·lem (**mŏz**′ləm) ◊ *noun, plural* **Moslems** ◊ *adjective*

mosque *noun* A Moslem house of worship.
mosque (mŏsk) ◊ *noun, plural* **mosques**

mosquito *noun* A small flying insect. The female mosquito bites and sucks blood from animals and human beings.
mos·qui·to (mə **skē**′tō) ◊ *noun, plural* **mosquitoes** *or* **mosquitos**

moss *noun* One of a group of small green plants that do not produce flowers and that often form a dense growth on damp ground, rocks, or tree trunks.
moss (môs) ◊ *noun, plural* **mosses**

mossy *adjective* Of, like, or covered with moss: *We sat on a mossy rock.*
moss·y (**mô**′sē) ◊ *adjective* **mossier, mossiest**

most *adjective* **1.** Greatest, as in number, size, extent, or degree: *The player with the most skill won the game.* **2.** The majority of: *Most birds can fly.*
◊ *noun* The greatest number, quantity, degree, or amount: *Most of the houses in our neighborhood are old.*
◊ *adverb* **1.** Often used to form the superlative of adjectives and adverbs that do not form superlatives by adding *-est*: *He is the most generous person that I know. She gave money most generously.* **2.** To a high degree; very: *It was a most impressive piece of work.*
most (mōst) ◊ *adjective* ◊ *noun* ◊ *adverb*

mostly *adverb* For the greatest part; mainly: *Lizards live mostly in warm climates.*
most·ly (**mōst**′lē) ◊ *adverb*

motel *noun* A hotel for motorists with rooms usually next to parking spaces.
mo·tel (mō **tĕl**′) ◊ *noun, plural* **motels**

moth *noun* A flying insect that is usually active at night and has feathery antennae. A moth is like a butterfly but it usually has a stouter body. The larvae of some moths damage cloth and fur.
moth (môth) ◊ *noun, plural* **moths**

mother *noun* **1.** A female parent. **2.** Source; origin: *The state of Virginia is called the Mother of Presidents.*
◊ *adjective* **1.** Of, relating to, or being a mother: *The mother hen fed her chicks.* **2.** Having a relationship with others like that of a mother: *The sailors longed to return to their mother country.*
◊ *verb* To take care of as or like a mother.
moth·er (**mŭth**′ər) ◊ *noun, plural* **mothers** ◊ *adjective* ◊ *verb* **mothered, mothering**

motherhood *noun* The condition of being a mother.
moth·er·hood (**mŭth**′ər ho͝od′) ◊ *noun*

mother-in-law *noun* The mother of one's wife or husband.
moth·er-in-law (**mŭth**′ər ĭn lô′) ◊ *noun, plural* **mothers-in-law**

motherly *adjective* Of, relating to, or like a mother; maternal.
moth·er·ly (**mŭth**′ər lē) ◊ *adjective*

mother-of-pearl *noun* A hard, shiny material on the inside of certain mollusk shells that is used to make buttons and jewelry.
moth·er-of-pearl (mŭth′ər əv **pûrl**′) ◊ *noun*

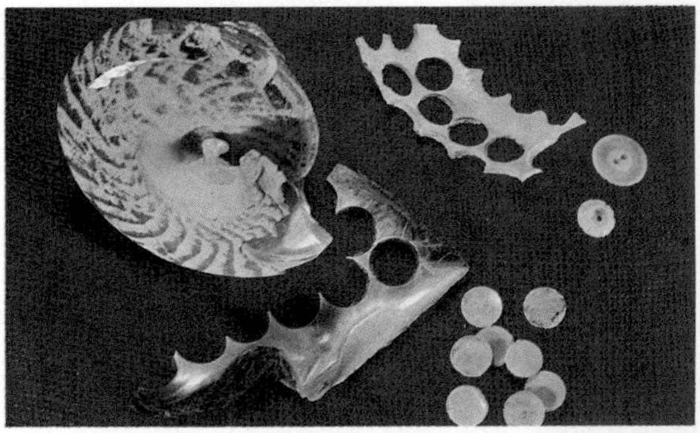

▲ **mother-of-pearl**

motion *noun* The act or process of moving; movement or gesture.
◊ *verb* To signal or direct by a motion, such as a wave of the hand.
mo·tion (**mō**′shən) ◊ *noun, plural* **motions** ◊ *verb* **motioned, motioning**

ă	pat	ĭ	pit	oi	**oil**	th	ba**th**
ā	pay	ī	ride	o͝o	**book**	*th*	ba**the**
â	care	î	fierce	o͞o	**boot**	ə	ago, item
ä	father	ŏ	pot	ou	**out**		pencil
ĕ	pet	ō	go	ŭ	cut		atom
ē	be	ô	paw, for	û	fur		circus

motion picture *noun* A series of pictures projected on a screen so quickly that the objects in the pictures seem to move as they would in life; movie.
motion picture ◊ *noun, plural* **motion pictures**

motive *noun* A reason that causes a person to act: *My motive in speaking to the new students was a wish to get to know them.*
mo·tive (mō′tĭv) ◊ *noun, plural* **motives**

motley *adjective* **1.** Having many different colors: *The clown wore a motley costume.* **2.** Made up of a number of different types or members.
mot·ley (mŏt′lē) ◊ *adjective*

motor *noun* A device that provides the power to make something move or run; engine: *An electric motor drives the fan.*
◊ *adjective* **1.** Driven on roads by motors: *Cars, trucks, and buses are motor vehicles.* **2.** Of or relating to nerves or muscles that control body movements.
mo·tor (mō′tər) ◊ *noun, plural* **motors**
◊ *adjective*

motorboat *noun* A boat driven by an engine.
mo·tor·boat (mō′tər bōt′) ◊ *noun, plural* **motorboats**

motorcycle *noun* A vehicle with two wheels that is driven by an engine.
mo·tor·cy·cle (mō′tər sī′kəl) ◊ *noun, plural* **motorcycles**

motorist *noun* A person who drives or rides in a motor vehicle.
mo·tor·ist (mō′tər ĭst) ◊ *noun, plural* **motorists**

mottled *adjective* Having spots or small patches of different colors: *The back of my hand is mottled lightly with freckles.*
mot·tled (mŏt′əld) ◊ *adjective*

motto *noun* **1.** A saying that is inscribed on something, as a coin or seal, to show its purpose. **2.** A brief expression of a guiding principle; slogan: *Their motto was "All for one and one for all."*
mot·to (mŏt′ō) ◊ *noun, plural* **mottoes** *or* **mottos**

mound *noun* A pile of material such as earth or sand: *There is a big mound of dirt by the excavation site.*
mound (mound) ◊ *noun, plural* **mounds**

mount¹ *verb* **1.** To go up; climb: *We mounted the stairs.* **2.** To get up on: *The sheriff mounted a fresh horse and rode off.* **3.** To increase rapidly; rise: *As the sun got stronger the temperature mounted.* **4.** To put in a suitable place for use or display.
◊ *noun* **1.** An animal, especially a horse, on which to ride. **2.** A structure for holding something else that is to be displayed or used.
mount¹ (mount) ◊ *verb* **mounted, mounting**
◊ *noun, plural* **mounts**

mount² *noun* A mountain.
mount² (mount) ◊ *noun, plural* **mounts**

> ***HISTORY* • mount¹, mount²**
>
> **Mount¹** goes back to a Latin word that meant "to climb a mountain." **Mount²** goes back to a related Latin word that meant "mountain." Both words passed through French before they came into English.

mountain *noun* **1.** An area of land that rises to a great height. **2.** A large heap or quantity.
moun·tain (moun′tən) ◊ *noun, plural* **mountains**

mountaineer *noun* **1.** A person who lives in a mountainous area. **2.** A person who climbs mountains for sport.
moun·tain·eer (moun′tə **nîr′**) ◊ *noun, plural* **mountaineers**

mountain goat *noun* A goatlike animal that has a thick white coat and short black horns and lives in the mountains of northwestern North America.
mountain goat ◊ *noun, plural* **mountain goats**

▲ **mountain goat**

M

mountain lion *noun* A large, tawny animal that belongs to the cat family. It lives in western North America and South America.
mountain lion ◊ *noun, plural* **mountain lions**

mountainous *adjective* Having many mountains: *Colorado is a mountainous state.*
moun·tain·ous (**moun′** tə nəs) ◊ *adjective*

mourn *verb* To express or feel sorrow, especially for a death; grieve.
mourn (môrn) ◊ *verb* **mourned, mourning**
‖*These sound alike:* **mourn, morn**

mournful *adjective* Feeling, showing, or causing grief; sad.
mourn·ful (**môrn′** fəl) ◊ *adjective*

mourning *noun* **1.** The act of feeling or expressing grief. **2.** A sign, as the wearing of dark, plain clothes, of grief over a person's death.
mourn·ing (**môr′** nĭng) ◊ *noun*
‖*These sound alike:* **mourning, morning**

mouse *noun* **1.** A small furry animal with a thin, almost hairless tail. Some kinds live in or near houses of human beings. **2.** A small device on some computers that is held in the hand and used to move the cursor.
mouse (mous) ◊ *noun, plural* **mice**

moustache *noun* Another spelling for **mustache.**
mous·tache (**mŭs′** tăsh′) ◊ *noun, plural* **moustaches**

mouth *noun* **1.** The opening through which an animal takes in food. The human mouth contains the teeth and tongue. **2.** The part of a body of water, such as a river, that empties into a larger body of water. **3.** An opening: *We looked into the mouth of the cave.*
mouth (mouth) ◊ *noun, plural* **mouths**

mouthful *noun* An amount taken into the mouth at one time.
mouth·ful (**mouth′** fo͝ol′) ◊ *noun, plural* **mouthfuls**

mouth organ *noun* A harmonica.
mouth organ ◊ *noun, plural* **mouth organs**

ă	pat	ĭ	pit	oi	**oil**	th	**bath**
ā	pay	ī	ride	o͝o	**book**	*th*	**bathe**
â	care	î	fierce	o͞o	**boot**	ə	**ago, item**
ä	father	ŏ	pot	ou	**out**		pencil
ĕ	pet	ō	go	ŭ	cut		atom
ē	be	ô	paw, for	û	fur		circus

mouthpiece *noun* The part of a device that is put into or near the mouth: *Blow into the mouthpiece of the clarinet.*
mouth·piece (**mouth′** pēs′) ◊ *noun, plural* **mouthpieces**

movable *adjective* **1.** Capable of being moved: *The speaker stood on a movable platform.* **2.** Changing date from year to year: *Easter is a movable holiday.*
mov·a·ble (**mo͞o′** və bəl) ◊ *adjective*

move *verb* **1.** To change or cause to change position: *Don't move while I take your picture. Move your chair closer to the window.* **2.** To change the place where one lives or works: *My grandparents moved to Florida.* **3.** To arouse strong feelings in: *The sad story moved us deeply.* **4.** To act or cause to act: *What moved you to enlist in the army?* —See Synonyms at **affect. 5.** To set or keep in motion: *I moved my arm.* **6.** To make a formal suggestion or proposal: *One council member moved that the meeting be adjourned.*
◊ *noun* **1.** The act of moving; movement. **2.** An action planned and carried out to accomplish something: *In a move to win votes the candidate promised lower taxes.* **3.** The act of moving a piece during a board game. **4.** A player's turn to move a piece: *It's your move.*
move (mo͞ov) ◊ *verb* **moved, moving** ◊ *noun, plural* **moves**

movement *noun* **1.** The act or process of moving: *The player snatched up the ball in a quick movement.* **2.** The activities, membership, or cause of a group of people who are trying to achieve a goal: *We are active in the movement for a cleaner and safer environment.* **3.** The moving parts of a machine or device: *The movement of my watch is broken.* **4.** A section of a longer piece of music, as a symphony.
move·ment (**mo͞ov′** mənt) ◊ *noun, plural* **movements**

mover *noun* A person or company that is hired to move belongings, as furniture.
mov·er (**mo͞o′** vər) ◊ *noun, plural* **movers**

movie *noun* **1.** A motion picture. **2. movies** A showing of a motion picture.
mov·ie (**mo͞o′** vē) ◊ *noun, plural* **movies**

moving *adjective* **1.** Changing or capable of changing position: *The moving parts of a ma-*

chine should be oiled. **2.** Affecting the emotions; stirring: *The book told a moving story of love and courage.*
mov·ing (mo͞o′vĭng) ◊ *adjective*

moving picture *noun* A motion picture.
moving picture ◊ *noun, plural* **moving pictures**

mow *verb* **1.** To cut down grass or grain: *Mow the grass before it gets too high.* **2.** To cut grass or grain from: *We mow the lawn every two weeks.*
mow (mō) ◊ *verb* **mowed, mowed** *or* **mown, mowing**

mown *verb* A past participle of **mow.**
mown (mōn) ◊ *verb*
‖*These sound alike:* **mown, moan**

m.p.g. *or* **mpg** Abreviations for *miles per gallon.*

m.p.h. *or* **mph** Abbreviations for *miles per hour.*

Mr. A form of address used before a man's name: *Mr. Smith.*

Mrs. A form of address used before a married woman's name: *Mrs. Smith.*

MS The abbreviation for *Mississippi* used with a Zip Code.

Ms. *or* **Ms** A form of address used before a woman's name: *Ms. Judy Smith.*

MT The abbreviation for *Montana* used with a Zip Code.

Mt. The abbreviation for *Mount* or *Mountain.*

much *adjective* Great in quantity, degree, or extent: *How much money will it cost?*
◊ *adverb* **1.** To a great degree or extent: *The test was much harder than I thought.* **2.** Just about; almost: *The jungle looked much as I expected it to.*
◊ *noun* A great quantity, degree, or extent: *Much of the work is done.*
much (mŭch) ◊ *adjective, adverb* **more, most** ◊ *noun*

mucilage *noun* A glue, especially one made from the natural gum of plants.
mu·ci·lage (myo͞o′sə lĭj) ◊ *noun*

muck *noun* A moist, sticky, messy substance, such as mud or manure.
muck (mŭk) ◊ *noun*

mud *noun* Wet, sticky, soft earth.
mud (mŭd) ◊ *noun*

muddle *verb* **1.** To make confused; mix up. **2.** To perform in a bad or clumsy way; make a mess of: *By not planning well we muddled the job.*
◊ *noun* A confused situation or condition.
mud·dle (mŭd′l) ◊ *verb* **muddled, muddling** ◊ *noun, plural* **muddles**

muddy *adjective* Covered or soiled with mud.
◊ *verb* To cover or soil with mud.
mud·dy (mŭd′ē) ◊ *adjective* **muddier, muddiest** ◊ *verb* **muddied, muddying**

muff *noun* A tube of fur or cloth with open ends into which the hands can be put for warmth.
muff (mŭf) ◊ *noun, plural* **muffs**

muffin *noun* A small, cup-shaped bread.
muf·fin (mŭf′ĭn) ◊ *noun, plural* **muffins**

muffle *verb* **1.** To wrap up in clothing or coverings: *I muffled myself up in a heavy coat.* **2.** To deaden the sound of: *The thick rug muffled our footsteps.*
muf·fle (mŭf′əl) ◊ *verb* **muffled, muffling**

muffler *noun* **1.** A scarf worn around the neck for warmth. **2.** A device that deadens the noise of a motor vehicle's engine.
muf·fler (mŭf′lər) ◊ *noun, plural* **mufflers**

▲ **muffler**

mug *noun* A large, heavy drinking cup.
mug (mŭg) ◊ *noun, plural* **mugs**

muggy *adjective* Hot and humid: *It gets muggy in August.*
mug·gy (mŭg′ē) ◊ *adjective* **muggier, muggiest**

mulberry *noun* A sweet purplish or white fruit that grows on a tree with irregularly shaped leaves.
mul·ber·ry (mŭl′bĕr′ē) ◊ *noun, plural* **mulberries**

mulch *noun* A covering, as of leaves or straw, placed around growing plants to protect them against cold or to keep the soil moist.
◊ *verb* To cover with a mulch.
mulch (mŭlch) ◊ *noun, plural* **mulches** ◊ *verb* **mulched, mulching**

M

mule *noun* **1.** An animal that is the offspring of a male donkey and a female horse. **2.** A stubborn person.
mule (myo͞ol) ◊ *noun, plural* **mules**

▲ **mule**

mulish *adjective* Hard to change or persuade; stubborn.
mul·ish (**myo͞o′** lĭsh) ◊ *adjective*

mullet *noun* A fish found in warm waters and caught for food. Mullet are gray or red in color.
mul·let (**mŭl′** ĭt) ◊ *noun, plural* **mullet** *or* **mullets**

multiple *adjective* Having or being more than one: *We took a multiple choice test.*
◊ *noun* A number that contains another number a certain number of times without any amount left over; for example, 4 is a multiple of 2 because it contains 2 exactly two times.
mul·ti·ple (**mŭl′** tə pəl) ◊ *adjective* ◊ *noun, plural* **multiples**

multiplicand *noun* A number that is to be multiplied by another number. In the example 16 multiplied by 5, the multiplicand is 16.
mul·ti·pli·cand (mŭl′tə plĭ **kănd′**) ◊ *noun, plural* **multiplicands**

multiplication *noun* A mathematical operation that is a short way of adding a certain number to itself the number of times indicated by a second number. For example, $3 \times 4 = 12$ is the same as $3 + 3 + 3 + 3 = 12$.
mul·ti·pli·ca·tion (mŭl′tə plĭ **kā′** shən) ◊ *noun*

multiplier *noun* A number by which another number is to be multiplied. In the example 16 multiplied by 9, the multiplier is 9.
mul·ti·pli·er (**mŭl′** tə plī′ər) ◊ *noun, plural* **multipliers**

multiply *verb* **1.** To make or become more; increase in number: *Getting a good education multiplies the number of jobs open to you.* **2.** To perform multiplication on: *Can you multiply 13 by 7 in your head?*
mul·ti·ply (**mŭl′** tə plī′) ◊ *verb* **multiplied, multiplying**

multitude *noun* A large number: *On a clear night you can see a multitude of stars.*
mul·ti·tude (**mŭl′** tĭ to͞od′ *or* **mŭl′** tĭ tyo͞od′) ◊ *noun, plural* **multitudes**

mumble *verb* To speak in an unclear way, as with the lips partly closed: *I can't understand you when you mumble.*
◊ *noun* The act or sound of mumbling.
mum·ble (**mŭm′** bəl) ◊ *verb* **mumbled, mumbling** ◊ *noun, plural* **mumbles**

mummy *noun* The body of a person that has been preserved from decay after death. Ancient Egyptian mummies were wrapped in specially treated cloth, placed in cases, and sealed in tombs.
mum·my (**mŭm′** ē) ◊ *noun, plural* **mummies**

mumps *noun* (*used with a singular or plural verb*) A contagious disease that causes swelling and soreness of the glands at the back of the jaw.
mumps (mŭmps) ◊ *noun*

munch *verb* To chew steadily with a crunching sound: *The rabbit munched on the fresh carrots.*
munch (mŭnch) ◊ *verb* **munched, munching**

municipal *adjective* Of or relating to a city or town or its government: *A municipal election will be held to choose a new mayor.*
mu·nic·i·pal (myo͞o **nĭs′** ə pəl) ◊ *adjective*

munitions *plural noun* Supplies for warfare, especially guns and ammunition.
mu·ni·tions (myo͞o **nĭsh′** ənz) ◊ *plural noun*

mural *noun* A painting that is done on a wall or ceiling.
mu·ral (**myo͝or′** əl) ◊ *noun, plural* **murals**

ă	pat	ĭ	pit	oi	**oi**l	th	ba**th**
ā	pay	ī	ride	o͝o	b**oo**k	*th*	ba**the**
â	care	î	fierce	o͞o	b**oo**t	ə	**a**go, it**e**m
ä	father	ŏ	pot	ou	**ou**t		penc**i**l
ĕ	pet	ō	go	ŭ	cut		at**o**m
ē	be	ô	paw, for	û	fur		circ**u**s

▲ mural

murder *noun* The unlawful and deliberate killing of a person.
◊ *verb* To kill a person unlawfully and deliberately.
mur·der (mûr′ dər) ◊ *noun, plural* **murders** ◊ *verb* **murdered, murdering**

murderer *noun* A person who commits a murder.
mur·der·er (mûr′ dər ər) ◊ *noun, plural* **murderers**

murderous *adjective* Guilty of, capable of, or intent on murder.
mur·der·ous (mûr′ dər əs) ◊ *adjective*

murk *noun* Darkness; gloom.
murk (mûrk) ◊ *noun*

murky *adjective* Very dark or gloomy: *We could not see the sunken boat in the murky waters of the lake.*
murk·y (mûr′ kē) ◊ *adjective* **murkier, murkiest**

murmur *noun* **1.** A low, continuous sound: *We could hear a murmur of voices from the next room.* **2.** A mumbled complaint: *I paid the library fine without a murmur.*
◊ *verb* **1.** To make a murmur. **2.** To say in a low, soft voice: *I shyly murmured an answer to my parents' friend.*
mur·mur (mûr′ mər) ◊ *noun, plural* **murmurs** ◊ *verb* **murmured, murmuring**

muscle *noun* **1.** A type of body tissue that can be contracted and relaxed to cause movement or exert force. **2.** A mass of muscle that moves a particular part of the body: *I have strong muscles in my arms.*
mus·cle (mŭs′ əl) ◊ *noun, plural* **muscles**
‖*These sound alike:* **muscle, mussel**

HISTORY • muscle

Muscle goes back to a Latin word that meant "little mouse." The movement of arm and leg muscles probably reminded people of a little mouse moving under the skin.

muscle-bound *adjective* Having some muscles that are overdeveloped and stiff.
mus·cle-bound (mŭs′ əl bound′) ◊ *adjective*

muscular *adjective* **1.** Of, relating to, or consisting of muscle: *The heart is a muscular organ.* **2.** Having strong muscles: *I have muscular legs from riding my bicycle every single day.*
mus·cu·lar (mŭs′ kyə lər) ◊ *adjective*

musculature *noun* The system of muscles of an animal or body part.
mus·cu·la·ture (mŭs′ kyə lə chər) ◊ *noun*

muse *verb* To think deeply: *I like to muse about what I will do when I grow up.*
muse (myōōz) ◊ *verb* **mused, musing**

museum *noun* A building in which objects of artistic, historical, or scientific interest are displayed.
mu·se·um (myōō zē′ əm) ◊ *noun, plural* **museums**

SYNONYMS

museum, gallery, library

I like looking at the mummies in the *museum.* My parents bought a painting at the art *gallery.* There was an exhibit of rare books at the *library.*

mush *noun* **1.** Cornmeal boiled in water or milk. **2.** A thick, soft mass: *The snow turned to mush in the rain.*
mush (mŭsh) ◊ *noun*

mushroom *noun* A small fungus with a stalk that is topped by a fleshy, umbrella-shaped cap. Some mushrooms are edible, but others are poisonous.
◊ *verb* To grow, multiply, or spread quickly:

M

Factories mushroomed at the edge of town.
mush·room (**mŭsh′** rōōm′ *or* **mŭsh′** rŏŏm′) ◊ *noun, plural* **mushrooms** ◊ *verb* **mushroomed, mushrooming**

▲ **mushroom**
Several kinds of mushrooms

music *noun* **1.** The art of combining tones or sounds in a pleasing or meaningful way. **2.** Vocal or instrumental sounds that have rhythm, melody, and harmony. **3.** The written or printed form of a musical composition: *I play the piano but I can't read music.* **4.** A pleasing sound or combination of sounds.
mu·sic (**myōō′** zĭk) ◊ *noun*

musical *adjective* **1.** Of or relating to music: *The violin is a musical instrument.* **2.** Given a musical accompaniment: *They performed a musical play.* **3.** Devoted to or skilled in music: *She comes from a musical family.* **4.** Pleasing to the ear: *He has a musical speaking voice.*
◊ *noun* A play that has songs and dances as well as spoken lines.
mu·si·cal (**myōō′** zĭ kəl) ◊ *adjective* ◊ *noun, plural* **musicals**

music box *noun* A box containing an automatic mechanical device that makes musical sounds.
music box ◊ *noun, plural* **music boxes**

ă	pat	ĭ	pit	oi	**oi**l	th	ba**th**
ā	pay	ī	ride	ŏŏ	b**oo**k	*th*	ba**th**e
â	care	î	fierce	ōō	b**oo**t	ə	ago, item
ä	father	ŏ	pot	ou	**ou**t		pencil
ĕ	pet	ō	go	ŭ	c**u**t		atom
ē	be	ô	paw, for	û	f**u**r		circus

musician *noun* A person who is skilled in music, especially as a professional composer or performer.
mu·si·cian (myōō **zĭsh′** ən) ◊ *noun, plural* **musicians**

musk *noun* A strong-smelling substance from a gland of a kind of deer. Musk is used in making perfume.
musk (mŭsk) ◊ *noun*

musket *noun* An old type of gun with a long barrel. Muskets were used before the invention of the rifle.
mus·ket (**mŭs′** kĭt) ◊ *noun, plural* **muskets**

musketeer *noun* A soldier armed with a musket.
mus·ket·eer (mŭs′kĭ **tîr′**) ◊ *noun, plural* **musketeers**

muskmelon *noun* A small oval or round melon, as the cantaloupe, that has a hard rind and sweet, juicy flesh.
musk·mel·on (**mŭsk′** mĕl′ən) ◊ *noun, plural* **muskmelons**

musk ox *noun* A large animal of northern North America and Greenland, that has dark, shaggy hair and curved horns.
musk ox ◊ *noun, plural* **musk oxen**

▲ **musk ox**

muskrat *noun* **1.** A small North American animal related to rats that lives in or near water and has thick, brown fur and a long, scaly tail. **2.** The fur of the muskrat.
musk·rat (**mŭs′** krăt′) ◊ *noun, plural* **muskrats**

muslin *noun* Cotton cloth that has a plain weave. Muslin is used for sheets and curtains.
mus·lin (**mŭz′**lĭn) ◊ *noun*

muss *verb* To make untidy or messy: *The wind mussed my hair.*
muss (mŭs) ◊ *verb* **mussed, mussing**

mussel *noun* A saltwater or freshwater mollusk with narrow, dark-blue shells.
mus·sel (**mŭs′** əl) ◊ *noun, plural* **mussels**
‖*These sound alike:* **mussel, muscle**

must *auxiliary verb* Used to show: **1.** Necessity or obligation: *If you want to get good marks, you must do your homework.* **2.** Something that is very likely: *It must be about time for supper.*
must (mŭst) ◊ *auxiliary verb*

mustache *or* **moustache** *noun* The hair growing on a man's upper lip.
mus·tache *or* **mous·tache** (**mŭs′**tăsh′)
◊ *noun, plural* **mustaches** *or* **moustaches**

mustang *noun* A small wild horse of the plains of western North America.
mus·tang (**mŭs′**tăng′) ◊ *noun, plural* **mustangs**

mustard *noun* A spicy yellow or light brown paste or powder made from the sharp-tasting seeds of a plant and used as a seasoning for food.
mus·tard (**mŭs′**tərd) ◊ *noun*

muster *verb* **1.** To gather together for inspection, roll call, or service. **2.** To call forth: *I mustered the courage to admit my mistake.*
◊ *noun* A gathering, especially of troops, as for inspection, roll call, or service.
mus·ter (**mŭs′**tər) ◊ *verb* **mustered, mustering** ◊ *noun, plural* **musters**

mustn't Contraction of "must not."
must·n't (**mŭs′**ənt) ◊ *contraction*

musty *adjective* Having a smell of dampness or decay.
must·y (**mŭs′**tē) ◊ *adjective* **mustier, mustiest**

mutate *verb* To undergo or cause to undergo change, especially by mutation.
mu·tate (**myo͞o′**tāt′) ◊ *verb* **mutated, mutating**

mutation *noun* A change in the genes or chromosomes of a living thing that can be inherited by its offspring.
mu·ta·tion (myo͞o **tā′**shən) ◊ *noun, plural* **mutations**

mute *adjective* **1.** Not able to speak; dumb. **2.** Not speaking or spoken; silent: *I nodded my head in mute agreement.*
◊ *noun* **1.** A person who cannot speak. **2.** A device used to soften, muffle, or change the tone of a musical instrument.
◊ *verb* To muffle or soften the sound of: *We mute our voices in the library.*
mute (myo͞ot) ◊ *adjective* **muter, mutest**
◊ *noun, plural* **mutes** ◊ *verb* **muted, muting**

mutilate *verb* To damage badly by cutting, tearing, or removing a part: *Someone mutilated the book by tearing out the illustrations.*
mu·ti·late (**myo͞ot′**l āt′) ◊ *verb* **mutilated, mutilating**

mutineer *noun* A person who takes part in a mutiny.
mu·ti·neer (myo͞ot′n **îr′**) ◊ *noun, plural* **mutineers**

mutinous *adjective* Engaged in mutiny.
mu·ti·nous (**myo͞ot′**n əs) ◊ *adjective*

mutiny *noun* Open rebellion against authority, especially of soldiers or sailors against their officers.
◊ *verb* To commit mutiny.
mu·ti·ny (**myo͞ot′**n ē) ◊ *noun, plural* **mutinies**
◊ *verb* **mutinied, mutinying**

mutt *noun* A dog of mixed breed; mongrel.
mutt (mŭt) ◊ *noun, plural* **mutts**

mutter *verb* **1.** To speak in a low voice with the lips barely moving. **2.** To complain or grumble: *People are muttering about the high price of food.*
◊ *noun* The act or sound of muttering.
mut·ter (**mŭt′**ər) ◊ *verb* **muttered, muttering**
◊ *noun, plural* **mutters**

mutton *noun* The meat of an adult sheep.
mut·ton (**mŭt′**n) ◊ *noun*

mutual *adjective* **1.** Having the same relationship to each other: *The two countries are mutual allies.* **2.** Shared in common: *My friend and I have a mutual interest in astronomy.* **3.** Given and received equally: *We have mutual respect for each other.*
mu·tu·al (**myo͞o′**cho͞o əl) ◊ *adjective*

mutually *adverb* In a mutual way.
mu·tu·al·ly (**myo͞o′**cho͞o ə lē) ◊ *adverb*

muumuu *noun* A dress that hangs loose from the shoulders. Muumuus were originally made in Hawaii.
muu·muu (**mo͞o′**mo͞o′) ◊ *noun, plural* **muumuus**

M

muzzle *noun* **1.** The projecting part of the head of certain animals, such as dogs and horses, containing the nose and jaws. **2.** A set of straps or wires fitted over an animal's nose and jaws to keep it from biting. **3.** The front of a gun barrel.
◊ *verb* To put a muzzle on: *I muzzle my dog when I take it for walks.*
muz·zle (**mŭz**′ əl) ◊ *noun, plural* **muzzles** ◊ *verb* **muzzled, muzzling**

▲ **muzzle**

my *adjective* Relating or belonging to me: *Where did I put my glasses?*
my (mī) ◊ *adjective*

myriad *adjective* Of an extremely great number; countless: *The moon, sun, and myriad stars can be seen in the heavens.*
◊ *noun* A very great number.
myr·i·ad (**mîr**′ ē əd) ◊ *adjective* ◊ *noun, plural* **myriads**

myrtle *noun* A shrub with evergreen leaves, white or pinkish flowers, and blackish berries.
myr·tle (**mûr**′ tl) ◊ *noun, plural* **myrtles**

ă	pat	ĭ	pit	oi	**oi**l	th	ba**th**
ā	pay	ī	ride	o͝o	b**oo**k	*th*	ba**the**
â	care	î	fierce	o͞o	b**oo**t	ə	**a**go, it**e**m
ä	father	ŏ	pot	ou	**ou**t		penc**i**l
ĕ	pet	ō	go	ŭ	cut		at**o**m
ē	be	ô	paw, for	û	fur		circ**u**s

myself *pronoun* My own self: *I cut myself when I sliced the bread. I myself could not answer the question.*
my·self (mī **sĕlf**′) ◊ *pronoun*

mysterious *adjective* Very hard to explain or understand: *A mysterious light came from the deserted house.*
mys·te·ri·ous (mĭ **stîr**′ ē əs) ◊ *adjective*

mystery *noun* **1.** Something that is not fully understood or is kept secret: *That person's identity remains a mystery.* **2.** A mysterious quality. **3.** A piece of fiction dealing with a puzzling crime.
mys·te·ry (**mĭs**′ tə rē) ◊ *noun, plural* **mysteries**

mystify *verb* To confuse; bewilder: *The unexpected results of the experiment mystified the scientists.*
mys·ti·fy (**mĭs**′ tə fī′) ◊ *verb* **mystified, mystifying**

myth *noun* **1.** A story that tries to give the reasons for the beliefs and practices of a group of people, tells of gods and heroes, or tries to explain natural events such as the weather: *The myth told how thunder was made by the gods.* **2.** A made-up or imaginary story, person, or thing: *It's a myth that elephants are afraid of mice.*
myth (mĭth) ◊ *noun, plural* **myths**

mythical *adjective* **1.** Relating to or existing only in myths: *A unicorn is a mythical creature.* **2.** Not based on fact; imaginary: *The superiority of their team is mythical.*
myth·i·cal (**mĭth**′ ĭ kəl) ◊ *adjective*

mythology *noun* A collection of myths.
my·thol·o·gy (mĭ **thŏl**′ ə jē) ◊ *noun, plural* **mythologies**

Newt

Nn

N is the fourteenth letter of the English alphabet. Did you know that it has a long history?

Over 3,500 years ago, people in the Middle East were using symbols that became the letters of our alphabet. This ancient Middle Eastern symbol is a form of the letter that became our letter *N*.

N

The ancient Greeks borrowed their alphabet from people in the Middle East. Here is a form of the Greek letter that became our letter *N*.

N

The ancient Romans borrowed their alphabet from a people who had taken their own letter symbols from the Greeks. Here is a form of the Roman letter *N* that was used for carving letters into stone. These letters became the model for our printed capital letters.

n

As people wrote quickly, especially with pens, the capital letters began to take the shapes of small letters. Here is a small-letter *n* that was developed about 1,200 years ago.

Nn *Nn*	Nn	Nn	Nn
Handwriting	Sans Serif Type	Serif Type	Computer Printing

n *or* **N** *noun* The fourteenth letter of the English alphabet.
n *or* **N** (ĕn) ◊ *noun, plural* **n's** *or* **N's**

N. *or* **N** Abbreviations for *North.*

nag[1] *verb* To pester or annoy by complaining, scolding, or criticizing all the time.
nag[1] (năg) ◊ *verb* **nagged, nagging**

nag[2] *noun* A horse, especially an old or worn-out horse.
nag[2] (năg) ◊ *noun, plural* **nags**

> ***HISTORY* • nag[1], nag[2]**
>
> **Nag[1]** originally meant "to bite at" and comes from an old Scandinavian word. **Nag[2]** is from an old Dutch word meaning "horse."

nail *noun* **1.** A thin, pointed piece of metal. People hammer nails into pieces of wood to hold them together. **2.** The thin, hard covering at the end of a finger or toe.
◊ *verb* To fasten with or as if with nails.
nail (nāl) ◊ *noun, plural* **nails** ◊ *verb* **nailed, nailing**

naked *adjective* **1.** Wearing no clothing. **2.** Lacking the usual covering: *In winter many trees have naked branches.* **3.** Not helped by an optical instrument: *Some planets can be seen with the naked eye.*
na•ked (nā′kĭd) ◊ *adjective*

name *noun* **1.** A word or words by which a person, animal, thing, or place is known. **2.** General reputation: *Your pranks have given you a bad name.*
◊ *verb* **1.** To give a name to: *We named our cat Cleo.* **2.** To identify or refer to by name: *Name the 50 states.* **3.** To settle on or choose: *Have they named the day for the wedding?* **4.** To nominate or appoint: *I was named captain of the basketball team.*
name (nām) ◊ *noun, plural* **names** ◊ *verb* **named, naming**

nameless *adjective* **1.** Having no name. **2.** Unknown by name: *The contributor wants to remain nameless.* **3.** Undescribable: *A*

nameless fear gripped us.
name·less (**nām′**lĭs) ◊ *adjective*

namely *adverb* That is to say: *We get vitamin C from citrus fruits, namely, oranges, lemons, limes, and grapefruit.*
name·ly (**nām′**lē) ◊ *adverb*

namesake *noun* A person or thing named after another.
name·sake (**nām′**sāk′) ◊ *noun, plural* **namesakes**

nap[1] *noun* A short, light sleep, usually during the day.
◊ *verb* To sleep for a short time; doze.
nap[1] (năp) ◊ *noun, plural* **naps** ◊ *verb* **napped, napping**

nap[2] *noun* A soft or fuzzy surface on certain kinds of cloth or leather.
nap[2] (năp) ◊ *noun, plural* **naps**

***HISTORY* • nap[1], nap[2]**

Nap[1] comes from an old English word that meant "to doze." **Nap**[2] was borrowed from a Dutch word and first appeared in written English about 550 years ago.

nape *noun* The back of the neck.
nape (nāp) ◊ *noun, plural* **napes**

naphtha *noun* A flammable liquid obtained from petroleum. Naphtha is used as a cleaning fluid and in making gasoline.
naph·tha (**năf′**thə *or* **năp′**thə) ◊ *noun*

napkin *noun* A piece of cloth or soft paper used while eating to protect the clothes or to wipe the mouth and fingers.
nap·kin (**năp′**kĭn) ◊ *noun, plural* **napkins**

narcissus *noun* A garden plant that is related to the daffodil. It has sweet-smelling white or yellow flowers with cup-shaped central parts.
nar·cis·sus (när **sĭs′**əs) ◊ *noun, plural* **narcissuses**

ă	pat	ĭ	pit	oi	**oil**	th	ba**th**
ā	pay	ī	ride	o͝o	**book**	*th*	ba*th*e
â	care	î	fierce	o͞o	**boot**	ə	ago, item
ä	father	ŏ	pot	ou	**out**		pencil
ĕ	pet	ō	go	ŭ	cut		atom
ē	be	ô	paw, for	û	fur		circus

▲ **narcissus**

narrate *verb* To tell the story of in speech or writing.
nar·rate (**năr′**āt′) ◊ *verb* **narrated, narrating**

narration *noun* **1.** The act of telling a story. **2.** An account or story.
nar·ra·tion (nă **rā′**shən) ◊ *noun, plural* **narrations**

narrative *noun* A story or description: *We read the exciting narrative about the discovery of the South Pole.*
◊ *adjective* Telling a story: *"A Visit from Saint Nicholas" is a narrative poem.*
nar·ra·tive (**năr′**ə tĭv) ◊ *noun, plural* **narratives** ◊ *adjective*

narrow *adjective* **1.** Small or slender in width: *The road was long and narrow.* **2.** Limited in size, variety, or extent: *She has only a narrow circle of friends.* **3.** Rigid in one's opinions and ideas: *People with narrow minds are often intolerant of other people's problems.* **4.** Barely successful; uncomfortably close: *He had a narrow escape from the burning building. The candidate won by a narrow margin of votes.*
◊ *verb* To make or become narrow: *The river narrows below the dam.*
nar·row (**năr′**ō) ◊ *adjective* **narrower, narrowest** ◊ *verb* **narrowed, narrowing**

narrows *plural noun* A narrow body of water that connects two larger ones.
nar·rows (**năr′**ōz) ◊ *plural noun*

nasal *adjective* **1.** Of or involving the nose: *Allergies can cause nasal congestion.* **2.** Spoken through the nose rather than the mouth: *M, n, and ng are nasal sounds.*
na·sal (**nā′**zəl) ◊ *adjective*

nasturtium *noun* A garden plant with orange, yellow, or red flowers and rounded leaves that have a strong taste.
na·stur·tium (nə stûr′shəm) ◊ *noun, plural* **nasturtiums**

▲ **nasturtium**

nasty *adjective* **1.** Mean; spiteful: *Scrooge was a nasty man.* **2.** Dirty, disgusting, or offensive. **3.** Very unpleasant: *The nasty winter weather forced us to stay indoors.* **4.** Very harmful; severe: *I got a nasty cut on my foot while playing on the beach.*
nas·ty (năs′tē) ◊ *adjective* **nastier, nastiest**

nation *noun* **1.** A group of people who share the same territory and are organized under a single government; country: *The United States is a nation.* **2.** The land occupied by a country: *All across the nation new computer industries are developing.*
na·tion (nā′shən) ◊ *noun, plural* **nations**

national *adjective* Of, having to do with, or belonging to a nation: *Yellowstone and Yosemite are national parks.*
◊ *noun* A citizen of a particular nation.
na·tion·al (năsh′ə nəl) ◊ *adjective* ◊ *noun, plural* **nationals**

nationalism *noun* Great loyalty to the interests of one's country.
na·tion·al·ism (năsh′ə nə lĭz′əm) ◊ *noun*

nationality *noun* **1.** The condition of belonging to a particular nation: *Children born in the United States are of American nationality.* **2.** A group of people having common origins, traditions, and usually language: *Many nationalities have settled in America.*
na·tion·al·i·ty (năsh′ə năl′ĭ tē) ◊ *noun, plural* **nationalities**

nationwide *adjective* Throughout a whole nation.
na·tion·wide (nā′shən wīd′) ◊ *adjective*

native *adjective* **1.** Belonging to a person by nature; natural: *That student has a good deal of native intelligence.* **2.** Born in a particular place or country: *Thomas Jefferson was a native Virginian.* **3.** Belonging to a person because of the person's place of birth: *Spanish is my native language.* **4.** Living, growing, or produced in a certain place: *The redwood tree is native to California.* **5.** Of or belonging to the people first known to have lived in a place. **6.** Belonging to the original body of words in a language and not borrowed from another language.
◊ *noun* **1.** A person born in a certain place or country: *I am a native of New England.* **2.** A member of a group of people first known to have lived in a place; aborigine. **3.** A person who lives in a place all the time. **4.** An animal or plant originally living or growing in a certain place: *The kangaroo is a native of Australia.*
na·tive (nā′tĭv) ◊ *adjective* ◊ *noun, plural* **natives**

Native American *noun* A descendant of one of the peoples who lived in North America long before European explorers and colonists arrived
Native American ◊ *noun, plural* **Native Americans**

LANGUAGE DETECTIVE

Native American

Native American is the term that many people prefer to use when they refer to the original inhabitants of North America. Usage, however, varies according to tribe and region. For example, in Canada and Alaska, *American Indian* is still the preferred term for all original inhabitants other than Eskimos.

natural *adjective* **1.** Found in or produced by nature; not artificial or manmade. **2.** Of or having to do with nature and all the objects, living things, and events that make up parts of it: *Biology is a natural science.* **3.** Being what is expected or usual in nature: *I had a*

N

natural recovery from my illness. **4.** Present from birth: *Kittens have a natural ability to climb and jump.* **5.** Closely imitating nature; lifelike: *The flowers in this drawing look very natural.*
◊ *noun* Someone or something that is perfectly suited for an activity because of ability that is present from birth: *You are a natural as an athlete.*
nat·u·ral (năch′ər əl) ◊ *adjective* ◊ *noun, plural* **naturals**

natural gas *noun* A gas that is found in the earth with petroleum deposits. It is used for cooking and heating.

naturalist *noun* A person who studies plants and animals.
nat·u·ral·ist (năch′ər ə lĭst) ◊ *noun, plural* **naturalists**

naturalize *verb* To give full citizenship to someone who was born in another country.
nat·u·ral·ize (năch′ər ə līz′) ◊ *verb* **naturalized, naturalizing**

naturally *adverb* **1.** In a natural way: *Be yourself and behave naturally.* **2.** By nature: *I wish I had naturally curly hair.* **3.** As might be expected; without a doubt: *Naturally if you invite me, I'll come to your party.*
nat·u·ral·ly (năch′ər ə lē) ◊ *adverb*

natural resource *noun* Something found in nature that is necessary or useful to people. Water, forests, and mineral deposits are natural resources.
natural resource ◊ *noun, plural* **natural resources**

nature *noun* **1.** The physical world and all the living things, objects, and events that are part of it. **2.** The world of living things and the outdoors; wildlife and natural scenery: *We camped beside a lake to enjoy the beauties of nature.* **3.** The basic character or quality of a person or thing: *My cousin has a generous nature.*
na·ture (nā′chər) ◊ *noun, plural* **natures**

ă	pat	ĭ	pit	oi	oil	th	bath
ā	pay	ī	ride	o͝o	book	*th*	bathe
â	care	î	fierce	o͞o	boot	ə	ago, item
ä	father	ŏ	pot	ou	out		pencil
ĕ	pet	ō	go	ŭ	cut		atom
ē	be	ô	paw, for	û	fur		circus

naught *or* **nought** *noun* **1.** Nothing: *All their dreams came to naught.* **2.** The digit 0; zero.
naught *or* **nought** (nôt) ◊ *noun, plural* **naughts** *or* **noughts**

naughty *adjective* Behaving in a disobedient or mischievous way; bad.
naugh·ty (nô′tē) ◊ *adjective* **naughtier, naughtiest**

nausea *noun* A feeling of sickness in the stomach and of the need to vomit.
nau·se·a (nô′zē ə *or* nô′shə) ◊ *noun*

nautical *adjective* Having to do with ships, sailors, or navigation.
nau·ti·cal (nô′tĭ kəl) ◊ *adjective*

naval *adjective* **1.** Of, for, or relating to a navy or warships. **2.** Having a navy: *The United States is a great naval power.*
na·val (nā′vəl) ◊ *adjective*
‖*These sound alike:* **naval, navel**

nave *noun* The long, central part of a church, flanked by the aisles on the sides.
nave (nāv) ◊ *noun, plural* **naves**

navel *noun* A small scar or hollow in the middle of the abdomen.
na·vel (nā′vəl) ◊ *noun, plural* **navels**
‖*These sound alike:* **navel, naval**

navigable *adjective* Deep or wide enough to allow ships to pass through.
nav·i·ga·ble (năv′ĭ gə bəl) ◊ *adjective*

navigate *verb* **1.** To direct the course of a ship or aircraft. **2.** To travel over or across: *They navigated the rapids in a canoe.*
nav·i·gate (năv′ĭ gāt′) ◊ *verb* **navigated, navigating**

navigation *noun* **1.** The act or practice of navigating. **2.** The science of charting a course for a ship or aircraft.
nav·i·ga·tion (năv′ĭ gā′shən) ◊ *noun*

navigator *noun* A crew member who plots the course of a ship or aircraft.
nav·i·ga·tor (năv′ĭ gā′tər) ◊ *noun, plural* **navigators**

navy *noun* **1.** All of a nation's warships. **2.** Often **Navy** A nation's entire organization for sea warfare, including ships, aircraft, weapons, personnel, and bases on shore. **3.** A dark blue color.
◊ *adjective* Dark blue.
na·vy (nā′vē) ◊ *noun, plural* **navies** ◊ *adjective*

navy blue *noun* A dark blue color.

nay *adverb* No.
◊ *noun* A vote or voter against something.
nay (nā) ◊ *adverb* ◊ *noun, plural* **nays**
‖*These sound alike:* **nay, neigh**

N.B. The abbreviation for *New Brunswick,* Canada.

NC The abbreviation for *North Carolina* used with a Zip Code.

N.C. An abbreviation for *North Carolina.*

ND The abbreviation for *North Dakota* used with a Zip Code.

N.Dak. An abbreviation for *North Dakota.*

NE The abbreviation for *Nebraska* used with a Zip Code.

N.E. *or* **NE** Abbreviations for *Northeast.*

near *adverb* To, at, or within a short distance or time: *The deer ran off as we came near.*
◊ *adjective* **1.** Close in distance or time: *I'll see you in the near future.* **2.** Closely related or associated: *She is his nearest living relative.* **3.** Achieved or missed by a narrow margin; close: *They had a near escape from the fire.* **4.** Short and direct: *Take the nearest route to the airport.*
◊ *preposition* Close to: *Stay near me when we explore the cave.*
◊ *verb* To draw near; approach: *The ship neared the port.*
near (nîr) ◊ *adverb* ◊ *adjective* **nearer, nearest** ◊ *preposition* ◊ *verb* **neared, nearing**

nearby *adverb* Not far away; close at hand.
◊ *adjective* Located a short distance away: *The children play in a nearby park.*
near·by (**nîr′** **bī′**) ◊ *adverb* ◊ *adjective*

nearly *adverb* Almost but not quite: *We nearly missed the school bus.*
near·ly (**nîr′** lē) ◊ *adverb*

nearsighted *adjective* Unable to see distant objects clearly.
near·sight·ed (**nîr′** sī′tĭd) ◊ *adjective*

neat *adjective* **1.** Clean and tidy: *You keep a very neat room.* **2.** Orderly and precise: *Write the figures in neat columns.* **3.** Done in a clever way: *That was a neat trick.*
neat (nēt) ◊ *adjective* **neater, neatest**

Neb. *or* **Nebr.** Abbreviations for *Nebraska.*

necessarily *adverb* **1.** As a necessary result: *A cloudy sky does not necessarily mean it will rain.* **2.** By or of necessity: *You don't necessarily have to attend the club meeting.*
nec·es·sar·i·ly (nĕs′ĭ **sâr′** ə lē) ◊ *adverb*

necessary *adjective* **1.** Having to be done; required: *Fill out the necessary forms.* **2.** Happening as a result: *Poor grades are the necessary consequence of not studying.*
◊ *noun* Something that is needed; essential: *Food and water are necessaries of life.*
nec·es·sa·ry (**nĕs′** ĭ sĕr′ē) ◊ *adjective* ◊ *noun, plural* **necessaries**

necessity *noun* **1.** Something that has to be done or must be included; requirement: *Proper food is a necessity for good health. We packed a few necessities for the trip.* **2.** The fact of being necessary: *We recognize the necessity of eating properly.* **3.** Great or urgent need: *Necessity forced us to ask for help.*
ne·ces·si·ty (nə **sĕs′** ĭ tē) ◊ *noun, plural* **necessities**

neck *noun* **1.** The part of the body that connects the head and the shoulders. **2.** The part of a garment that fits around the neck. **3.** A narrow or connecting part like a neck: *Pick up the bottle by the neck.*
neck (nĕk) ◊ *noun, plural* **necks**

neckerchief *noun* A scarf or square of cloth worn around the neck.
neck·er·chief (**nĕk′** ər chĭf) ◊ *noun, plural* **neckerchiefs**

▲ **neckerchief**

necklace *noun* An ornament, such as a string of beads, worn around the neck.
neck·lace (**nĕk′** ləs) ◊ *noun, plural* **necklaces**

neckline *noun* The outline formed by the edge of a garment at or below the neck.
neck·line (**nĕk'** līn') ◊ *noun, plural* **necklines**

necktie *noun* A narrow band of cloth worn around the neck under the shirt collar and tied in front.
neck·tie (**nĕk'** tī') ◊ *noun, plural* **neckties**

nectar *noun* A sweet liquid found in many flowers. Bees gather nectar and make honey from it.
nec·tar (**nĕk'** tər) ◊ *noun, plural* **nectars**

nectarine *noun* A kind of peach that has smooth skin.
nec·tar·ine (nĕk'tə **rēn'**) ◊ *noun, plural* **nectarines**

need *noun* **1.** A lack of something required or desirable: *Their crops are in need of water.* **2.** Something required or wanted: *We are people of modest needs.* **3.** Necessity or obligation: *There is no need for you to leave.* **4.** Poverty or misfortune.
◊ *verb* **1.** To have to: *I need to return the book today.* **2.** To have need of; require: *This toaster needs repair.*
need (nēd) ◊ *noun, plural* **needs** ◊ *verb* **needed, needing**
‖ *These sound alike:* **need, knead**

needful *adjective* Needed; necessary: *The children received everything needful.*
need·ful (**nēd'** fəl) ◊ *adjective*

needle *noun* **1.** A small, slender tool for sewing, usually made of polished steel. It has a sharp point at one end and an eye at the other end through which thread is passed. **2.** A slender, pointed rod used in knitting. **3.** The pointer on a dial or compass. **4.** A pointed, thin, hollow tube that is used especially by doctors and nurses to give shots. **5.** A stiff, needle-shaped leaf, such as one on a pine tree.
◊ *verb* To tease or provoke with annoying remarks: *Why are you always needling me about my glasses?*
nee·dle (**nēd'** l) ◊ *noun, plural* **needles** ◊ *verb* **needled, needling**

ă pat	ĭ pit	oi	**oil**	th	**bath**		
ā pay	ī ride	o͝o	**book**	*th*	**bathe**		
â care	î fierce	o͞o	**boot**	ə	ago, item		
ä father	ŏ pot	ou	**out**		pencil		
ĕ pet	ō go	ŭ	**cut**		atom		
ē be	ô paw, for	û	**fur**		circus		

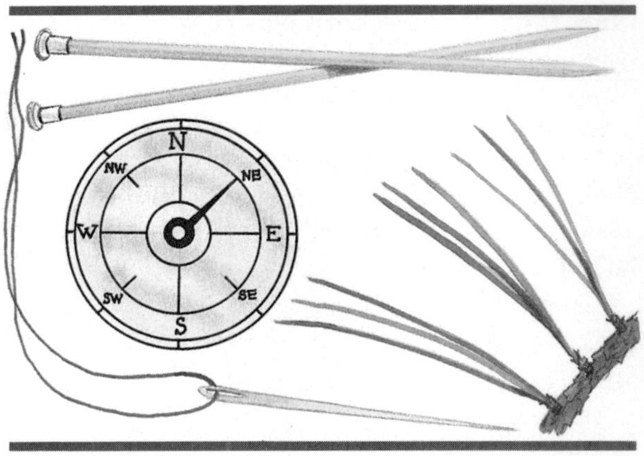

▲ **needle**

needlepoint *noun* Embroidery done with even stitches on canvas. Needlepoint looks like a woven tapestry.
nee·dle·point (**nēd'** l-point') ◊ *noun*

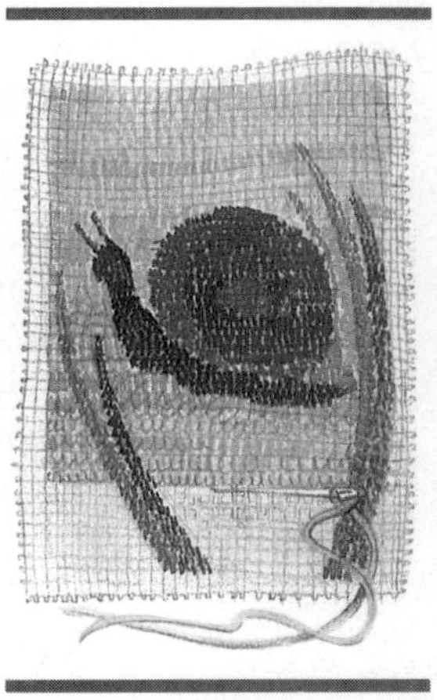
▲ **needlepoint**

needless *adjective* Not needed; unnecessary: *A third car was a needless expense.*
need·less (**nēd'** lĭs) ◊ *adjective*

needlework *noun* Work such as embroidery or sewing that is done with a needle.
nee·dle·work (**nēd'** l-wûrk') ◊ *noun*

needn't Contraction of "need not."
need·n't (**nēd'** nt) ◊ *contraction*

needy *adjective* Very poor.
need·y (**nē'** dē) ◊ *adjective* **needier, neediest**

negative *adjective* **1.** Expressing a refusal or denial; saying no: *They gave a negative answer to my request.* **2.** Lacking in positive qualities such as optimism and enthusiasm: *Your negative attitude is not helping you to make friends.* **3.** Showing that a particular disease, condition, or germ is not present: *The blood test was negative.* **4.** Less than zero: *An example of a negative number is* -2. **5.** Having one of two opposite electrical charges and tending to repel electrons.
◊ *noun* **1.** A word or expression that says "no" or denies something. The words *no* and *not* are negatives. **2.** A photographic image in

which the areas that are normally light and those that are normally dark are reversed.
neg·a·tive (nĕg′ə tĭv) ◊ *adjective* ◊ *noun, plural* **negatives**

neglect *verb* **1.** To fail to give proper care and attention to: *Don't neglect your teeth. A good student doesn't neglect homework.* **2.** To fail to do, as through carelessness: *The cake burned because you neglected to turn off the oven.*
◊ *noun* **1.** The act of neglecting: *Neglect of your homework may result in bad grades.* **2.** The condition of being neglected: *The garden has fallen into neglect.*
ne·glect (nĭ **glĕkt′**) ◊ *verb* **neglected, neglecting** ◊ *noun*

negligence *noun* A failing to act with proper care or concern: *The accident was caused by the driver's negligence.*
neg·li·gence (**nĕg′** lĭ jəns) ◊ *noun*

negligent *adjective* Not acting with proper care or concern; careless.
neg·li·gent (**nĕg′** lĭ jənt) ◊ *adjective*

negotiate *verb* **1.** To have a discussion with another in order to reach an agreement: *The union is willing to negotiate with the company's management.* **2.** To arrange for by discussing: *I negotiated a fair trade.*
ne·go·ti·ate (nĭ **gō′** shē āt′) ◊ *verb* **negotiated, negotiating**

neigh *noun* The long, high-pitched sound made by a horse.
◊ *verb* To make such a sound.
neigh (nā) ◊ *noun, plural* **neighs** ◊ *verb* **neighed, neighing**
‖*These sound alike:* **neigh, nay**

neighbor *noun* **1.** A person who lives next door to or near another. **2.** Someone or something that is next to or near another: *The nearest neighbor to the earth is the moon.* **3.** A fellow human being: *Have respect for your neighbor.*
neigh·bor (**nā′** bər) ◊ *noun, plural* **neighbors**

neighborhood *noun* **1.** An area or section of a city or town. **2.** The people who live near one another.
neigh·bor·hood (**nā′** bər ho͝od′) ◊ *noun, plural* **neighborhoods**

neighboring *adjective* Living near or located close by; bordering.
neigh·bor·ing (**nā′** bər ĭng) ◊ *adjective*

neighborly *adjective* Of or like a friendly neighbor.
neigh·bor·ly (**nā′** bər lē) ◊ *adjective*

neither *adjective* Not either; not one or the other: *Neither shoe fits comfortably.*
◊ *pronoun* Not either one; not the one and not the other: *Neither of you replied.*
◊ *conjunction* **1.** Used with *nor* to show two negative alternatives: *Neither Sue nor Bill wants to go.* **2.** Also not; nor: *I haven't seen them and neither has the teacher.*
nei·ther (**nē′** *th*ər *or* **nī′** *th*ər) ◊ *adjective* ◊ *pronoun* ◊ *conjunction*

neon *noun* A colorless, odorless gas found in very small amounts in the air. Neon is one of the chemical elements. Tubes filled with neon are often used in electric signs.
ne·on (**nē′** ŏn′) ◊ *noun*

> ***HISTORY* • neon**
>
> **Neon** was named from the Greek word for "new." The gas was "new" to science when it was first discovered in 1898.

N

nephew *noun* **1.** The son of one's brother or sister. **2.** The son of one's brother-in-law or sister-in-law.
neph·ew (**nĕf′** yo͞o) ◊ *noun, plural* **nephews**

Neptune *noun* The eighth planet in order of distance from the sun. It is the fourth largest planet in the solar system.
Nep·tune (**nĕp′** to͞on′ *or* **nĕp′** tyo͞on′) ◊ *noun*

nerve *noun* **1.** Any of the bundles of fibers that carry messages between the brain or spinal cord and other parts of the body. **2.** Courage or daring: *It took all my nerve to jump that high fence.* **3.** Insolent boldness: *They had nerve coming to the birthday party without being asked.*
nerve (nûrv) ◊ *noun, plural* **nerves**

nervous *adjective* **1.** Of or relating to the nerves. **2.** Easily excited or upset; tense. **3.** Anxious; fearful: *I was nervous about going to the dentist.*
nerv·ous (**nûr′** vəs) ◊ *adjective*

nervous system *noun* The system in the body that controls all of its actions. The nervous system includes the brain, the spinal cord, and the nerves.

-ness The suffix *-ness* forms nouns and means "condition" or "quality." *Kindness* is the condition or quality of being kind.

VOCABULARY BUILDER • -ness

Many words that are formed with **-ness** are not entries in this dictionary. But you can figure out what these words mean by looking up the meanings of the root words and the suffix. For example:
brightness = the condition or quality of being bright
lateness = the condition or quality of being late

nest *noun* **1.** A container or shelter made by birds for holding their eggs and young while they are helpless. **2.** A similar shelter made by insects, fish, or animals such as mice or squirrels. **3.** A group, as of birds or insects, in such a shelter: *The nest of hornets buzzed loudly.* **4.** A snug, cozy place.
◊ *verb* **1.** To build or stay in a nest: *Robins nested in the willow tree.* **2.** To fit snugly together or inside one another: *We'll nest these boxes for storage.*
nest (nĕst) ◊ *noun, plural* **nests** ◊ *verb* **nested, nesting**

▲ **nest**

ă	pat	ĭ	pit	oi	**oil**	th	**bath**
ā	pay	ī	ride	o͝o	book	*th*	**bathe**
â	care	î	fierce	o͞o	boot	ə	ago, item
ä	father	ŏ	pot	ou	**out**		pencil
ĕ	pet	ō	go	ŭ	cut		atom
ē	be	ô	paw, for	û	fur		circus

nest egg *noun* A sum of money saved for future use; savings.
nest egg ◊ *noun, plural* **nest eggs**

nestle *verb* **1.** To settle down snugly and comfortably: *The children nestled in their beds.* **2.** To press or snuggle close: *The kitten nestled up to its mother.*
nes·tle (nĕs′əl) ◊ *verb* **nestled, nestling**

nestling *noun* A bird that is too young to leave its nest.
nest·ling (nĕst′lĭng) ◊ *noun, plural* **nestlings**

net[1] *noun* **1.** A fabric that has holes in a regular pattern. Net is made of threads, cords, or ropes. **2.** Something made of net. A net can be used to catch fish or hold hair in place.
◊ *verb* To catch in or as if in a net: *They netted rare butterflies on their expedition into the jungle.*
net[1] (nĕt) ◊ *noun, plural* **nets** ◊ *verb* **netted, netting**

net[2] *adjective* Remaining after all necessary subtractions have been made: *My net profit after paying the money I owed was $12.*
◊ *verb* To bring in or get as profit.
net[2] (nĕt) ◊ *adjective* ◊ *verb* **netted, netting**

HISTORY • net[1], net[2]

Net[1] comes from an old English word that meant both "net" and "spider web." **Net[2]** comes from an old French word that meant "simple, neat."

nethermost *adjective* Lowest.
neth·er·most (nĕ*th*′ər mōst′) ◊ *adjective*

nettle *noun* A plant with sharp or prickly hairs that give a sting when touched.
◊ *verb* To make impatient, angry, or disturbed: *I was nettled by their bragging.*
net·tle (nĕt′l) ◊ *noun, plural* **nettles** ◊ *verb* **nettled, nettling**

network *noun* **1.** A fabric or structure made in the pattern of a net. **2.** A system or pattern, as of lines or routes that cross: *The United States has a large network of roads.* **3.** A group of related radio or television stations that share programs. **4.** A group of friends or associates who help one another.
net·work (nĕt′wûrk′) ◊ *noun, plural* **networks**

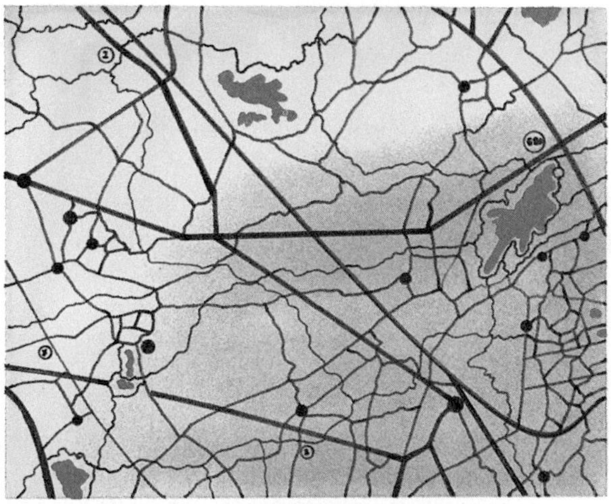

▲ **network**
A network of roads on a map

neutral *adjective* **1.** Not taking sides in a war, quarrel, or contest. **2.** Having little color: *Gray is a neutral shade.*
◊ *noun* **1.** A person or nation that does not take sides in a war or dispute. **2.** The arrangement of a set of gears in which no power can be transmitted: *Leave the car in neutral.*
neu·tral (**nōō'** trəl *or* **nyōō'** trəl) ◊ *adjective* ◊ *noun, plural* **neutrals**

neutron *noun* A tiny particle that is present in the nucleus of all atoms except hydrogen. A neutron has about the same mass as a proton and no electrical charge.
neu·tron (**nōō'** trŏn' *or* **nyōō'** trŏn') ◊ *noun, plural* **neutrons**

Nev. An abbreviation for *Nevada.*

never *adverb* **1.** At no time; not ever: *I have never been here before.* **2.** Not at all; in no way: *Never mind.*
nev·er (**nĕv'** ər) ◊ *adverb*

nevermore *adverb* Never again.
nev·er·more (nĕv'ər **môr'**) ◊ *adverb*

nevertheless *adverb* All the same; in spite of that: *The plan may fail, but we must try it nevertheless.*
nev·er·the·less (nĕv'ər *thə* **lĕs'**) ◊ *adverb*

new *adjective* **1.** Having lately come into being: *The new supermarket just opened.* **2.** Just found, discovered, or learned about: *The scientists were excited about the new star.* **3.** Never used or worn before. **4.** Coming after or taking the place of one that came before: *The new librarian once managed a bookstore.* **5.** Starting over again: *The new year begins on January 1.* **6.** Not known before; unfamiliar: *Try to learn a new word every day.* **7.** Recently arrived or established in a place, position, or relationship: *The new student moved here from Canada.*
new (nōō *or* nyōō) ◊ *adjective* **newer, newest**
‖*These sound alike:* **new, gnu, knew**

> ***SYNONYMS***
>
> ***new, fresh, modern, original***
>
> Are those *new* clothes? I love the taste of *fresh* vegetables. That house is built in a *modern* style of architecture. They had the *original* idea. **Antonym:** *old*

newborn *adjective* **1.** Only just born. **2.** Made stronger: *With newborn interest we made a fresh start.*
new·born (**nōō'** bôrn' *or* **nyōō'** bôrn') ◊ *adjective*

newcomer *noun* A person, animal, or thing that has only recently arrived in a new place or situation.
new·com·er (**nōō'** kŭm'ər *or* **nyōō'** kŭm'ər) ◊ *noun, plural* **newcomers**

Newf. An abbreviation for *Newfoundland,* Canada.

newfangled *adjective* Very new and different: *I love newfangled appliances.*
new·fan·gled (**nōō' făng'** gəld *or* **nyōō' făng'** gəld) ◊ *adjective*

newly *adverb* Just recently: *We went to see the newly opened playground.*
new·ly (**nōō'** lē *or* **nyōō'** lē) ◊ *adverb*

news *noun* (*used with a singular verb*) **1.** Information about recent events. News is passed on from person to person or reported by newspapers, magazines, radio, or television. **2.** A fact or an event that is interesting enough to be reported.
news (nōōz *or* nyōōz) ◊ *noun*

newsboy *noun* A boy who delivers or sells newspapers.
news·boy (**nōōz'** boi' *or* **nyōōz'** boi') ◊ *noun, plural* **newsboys**

newscast *noun* A broadcast of news on radio or television.

N

news·cast (**nōōz'**kăst' *or* **nyōōz'**kăst') ◊ *noun, plural* **newscasts**

newsgirl *noun* A girl who delivers or sells newspapers.
news·girl (**nōōz'**gûrl' *or* **nyōōz'**gûrl') ◊ *noun, plural* **newsgirls**

newspaper *noun* A printed paper that is usually issued every day and contains news, articles, and advertisements.
news·pa·per (**nōōz'**pā'pər *or* **nyōōz'**pā'pər) ◊ *noun, plural* **newspapers**

newsreel *noun* A short motion picture about recent news events.
news·reel (**nōōz'**rēl' *or* **nyōōz'**rēl') ◊ *noun, plural* **newsreels**

newsstand *noun* A place where newspapers and magazines are sold.
news·stand (**nōōz'**stănd' *or* **nyōōz'**stănd') ◊ *noun, plural* **newsstands**

newt *noun* A small salamander that lives on land and in the water.
newt (nōōt *or* nyōōt) ◊ *noun, plural* **newts**

▲ newt

New World *noun* The Western Hemisphere; North, Central, and South America.

New Year's Day *noun* January 1, the first day of the year, a holiday in many parts of the world.

next *adjective* Coming right before or after, as in space or time: *The next day was sunny.*
◊ *adverb* In the time, position, or order closest or following right after: *What comes next?*
next (nĕkst) ◊ *adjective* ◊ *adverb*

next door *adverb* In, to, or at the next building, apartment, or room.

ă	pat	ĭ	pit	oi	oil	th	bath
ā	pay	ī	ride	ŏŏ	book	*th*	bathe
â	care	î	fierce	ōō	boot	ə	ago, item
ä	father	ŏ	pot	ou	out		pencil
ĕ	pet	ō	go	ŭ	cut		atom
ē	be	ô	paw, for	û	fur		circus

next-door *adjective* Located next door.
next-door (**nĕkst'**dôr') ◊ *adjective*

Nfld. An abbreviation for *Newfoundland,* Canada.

NH The abbreviation for *New Hampshire* used with a Zip Code.

N.H. An abbreviation for *New Hampshire.*

nibble *verb* **1.** To eat with small, quick bites. **2.** To bite at gently: *The fish nibbled my bait.*
◊ *noun* A small or gentle bite.
nib·ble (**nĭb'**əl) ◊ *verb* **nibbled, nibbling** ◊ *noun, plural* **nibbles**

nice *adjective* **1.** Pleasing; agreeable: *It was a nice party. You look nice in your new outfit.* **2.** Courteous and polite; well-mannered. **3.** Very particular about proper dress, food, or manners. **4.** Very sensitive to small differences: *The artist has a nice eye for shades of color.*
nice (nīs) ◊ *adjective* **nicer, nicest**

niche *noun* **1.** A hollow place in a wall, as for holding a statue. **2.** A job or activity specially suited for someone.
niche (nĭch) ◊ *noun, plural* **niches**

nick *noun* A small cut, notch, or chip in a surface or edge.
◊ *verb* To make a nick in.
◊ *idiom* **in the nick of time** At the last moment; just in time.
nick (nĭk) ◊ *noun, plural* **nicks** ◊ *verb* **nicked, nicking**

nickel *noun* **1.** A hard, silvery metal that is used in alloys. Nickel is a chemical element. **2.** A United States or Canadian coin worth five cents.
nick·el (**nĭk'**əl) ◊ *noun, plural* **nickels**

nickname *noun* **1.** A descriptive name used instead of or along with the real name of a person, place, or thing. **2.** A familiar or shortened form of a proper name: *Beth and Liz are nicknames for Elizabeth.*
◊ *verb* To call by a nickname.
nick·name (**nĭk'**nām') ◊ *noun, plural* **nicknames** ◊ *verb* **nicknamed, nicknaming**

***HISTORY* • nickname**

Nickname comes from an earlier English phrase *an eke name,* which meant "an additional name."

niece *noun* **1.** The daughter of one's brother or sister. **2.** The daughter of one's brother-in-law or sister-in-law.
niece (nēs) ◊ *noun, plural* **nieces**

night *noun* **1.** The period between sunset and sunrise, especially the hours of darkness. **2.** Nightfall: *We work from morning to night.*
night (nīt) ◊ *noun, plural* **nights**
‖*These sound alike:* **night, knight**

night crawler *noun* An earthworm that comes out of the ground at night. Night crawlers are used for fishing bait.
night crawler ◊ *noun, plural* **night crawlers**

nightfall *noun* The coming of darkness at the end of the day.
night·fall (**nīt′**fôl′) ◊ *noun*

nightgown *noun* A loose garment worn while sleeping.
night·gown (**nīt′**goun′) ◊ *noun, plural* **nightgowns**

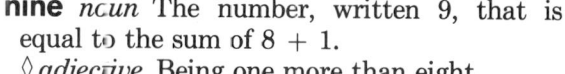

nightingale *noun* A brownish bird of Europe and Asia that has a very sweet song and often sings at night.
night·in·gale (**nīt′**n-gāl′ *or* **nī′**tĭng gāl′) ◊ *noun, plural* **nightingales**

▲ **nightingale**

nightly *adjective* Taking place, done, or used at night or every night.
◊ *adverb* **1.** Every night. **2.** At night.
night·ly (**nīt′**lē) ◊ *adjective* ◊ *adverb*

nightmare *noun* **1.** A bad dream: *The nightmare woke me up.* **2.** A frightening or horrible experience.
night·mare (**nīt′**mâr′) ◊ *noun, plural* **nightmares**

nighttime *noun* The time between nightfall and dawn; night.
night·time (**nīt′**tīm′) ◊ *noun, plural* **nighttimes**

nimble *adjective* **1.** Moving quickly, lightly, and easily. **2.** Quick and clever in thinking, learning, or answering: *The child has a nimble mind.*
nim·ble (**nĭm′**bəl) ◊ *adjective* **nimbler, nimblest**

nine *noun* The number, written 9, that is equal to the sum of 8 + 1.
◊ *adjective* Being one more than eight.
nine (nīn) ◊ *noun, plural* **nines** ◊ *adjective*

nineteen *noun* The number, written 19, that is equal to the sum of 18 + 1.
◊ *adjective* Being one more than eighteen.
nine·teen (nīn **tēn′**) ◊ *noun, plural* **nineteens** ◊ *adjective*

nineteenth *noun* **1.** The number in a series that matches the number nineteen. **2.** One of nineteen equal parts, written 1/19.
◊ *adjective* Coming after the eighteenth.
nine·teenth (nīn **tēnth′**) ◊ *noun, plural* **nineteenths** ◊ *adjective*

ninetieth *noun* **1.** The number in a series that matches the number ninety. **2.** One of ninety equal parts, written 1/90.
◊ *adjective* Coming after the eighty-ninth.
nine·ti·eth (**nīn′**tē ĭth) ◊ *noun, plural* **ninetieths** ◊ *adjective*

ninety *noun* The number, written 90, that is equal to the product of 9 × 10.
◊ *adjective* Being equal to ten times nine.
nine·ty (**nīn′**tē) ◊ *noun, plural* **nineties** ◊ *adjective*

ninth *noun* **1.** The number in a series that matches the number nine. **2.** One of nine equal parts, written 1/9.
◊ *adjective* Coming after the eighth.
ninth (nīnth) ◊ *noun, plural* **ninths** ◊ *adjective*

nip *verb* **1.** To bite or squeeze sharply but not hard: *One puppy playfully nipped the other.* **2.** To remove by biting, pinching, or snipping: *The rabbit nipped off the lettuce leaf.* **3.** To sting or chill, as cold air does: *The freezing weather nipped our ears.*
◊ *noun* **1.** A small, sharp bite or pinch. **2.** Sharp, biting cold: *There's a nip in the air tonight.*
nip (nĭp) ◊ *verb* **nipped, nipping** ◊ *noun, plural* **nips**

nitrogen *noun* A colorless, odorless gas that is a chemical element and that makes up about four-fifths of the atmosphere. All plants and animals need nitrogen.
ni·tro·gen (**nī′**trə jən) ◊ *noun*

NJ The abbreviation for *New Jersey* used with a Zip Code.

N.J. An abbreviation for *New Jersey.*

N

NM The abbreviation for *New Mexico* used with a Zip Code.

N.Mex. An abbreviation for *New Mexico.*

no *adverb* **1.** Not so: *No, I'm not going.* **2.** Not at all; not any: *Be there no later than noon.* **3.** In no way: *No—it can't be true!*
◊ *adjective* **1.** Not any: *There are no tickets left for the play.* **2.** Not a: *My friend is no fool.*
◊ *noun* **1.** A negative response; denial or refusal: *My suggestion met with a chorus of noes.* **2.** A negative vote or voter.
no (nō) ◊ *adverb* ◊ *adjective* ◊ *noun, plural* **noes**
‖*These sound alike:* **no, know**

no. The abbreviation for *number.*

nobility *noun* **1.** A social class marked by high birth or rank. **2.** Noble rank. **3.** Noble nature, character, or quality.
no·bil·i·ty (nō **bĭl′**ĭ tē) ◊ *noun, plural* **nobilities**

noble *adjective* **1.** Of or belonging to the nobility. **2.** Having or showing high moral character, courage, generosity, or self-sacrifice. **3.** Worthy of admiration; excellent: *To wipe out world hunger is a noble ideal.* **4.** Grand; majestic: *Noble mountain peaks towered above us.*
◊ *noun* A person of noble birth or rank.
no·ble (**nō′**bəl) ◊ *adjective* **nobler, noblest** ◊ *noun, plural* **nobles**

nobleman *noun* A man of noble rank.
no·ble·man (**nō′**bəl mən) ◊ *noun, plural* **noblemen**

noblewoman *noun* A woman of noble rank.
no·ble·wom·an (**nō′**bəl wŏŏm′ən) ◊ *noun, plural* **noblewomen**

nobody *pronoun* No person; no one: *Nobody was looking.*
◊ *noun* A person of no importance.
no·bod·y (**nō′**bŏd′ē) ◊ *pronoun* ◊ *noun, plural* **nobodies**

nocturnal *adjective* **1.** Of or happening at night. **2.** Active at night: *Owls are nocturnal birds.*
noc·tur·nal (nŏk **tûr′**nəl) ◊ *adjective*

nod *verb* **1.** To move the head down and then up in a quick motion, as when saying yes, giving a greeting or signal, or getting sleepy. **2.** To show by nodding: *I nodded my approval.* **3.** To droop, sway, or bend downward: *Lilies nodded in the garden.*
◊ *noun* A nodding motion.
nod (nŏd) ◊ *verb* **nodded, nodding** ◊ *noun, plural* **nods**

noise *noun* **1.** A loud or unpleasant sound. **2.** Sound of any kind: *The only noise was the wind in the pines.*
noise (noiz) ◊ *noun, plural* **noises**

noisy *adjective* **1.** Making a lot of noise: *The audience was restless and noisy.* **2.** Full of noise: *We live on a busy, noisy street.*
nois·y (**noi′**zē) ◊ *adjective* **noisier, noisiest**

nomad *noun* **1.** A member of a people who move about from place to place in search of food, water, and grazing land for their livestock. **2.** A wanderer.
no·mad (**nō′**măd′) ◊ *noun, plural* **nomads**

nominate *verb* To select as a candidate for election, appointment to office, or an honor.
nom·i·nate (**nŏm′**ə nāt′) ◊ *verb* **nominated, nominating**

nomination *noun* **1.** The act or an example of nominating. **2.** Appointment to a position, office, or honor.
nom·i·na·tion (nŏm′ə **nā′**shən) ◊ *noun, plural* **nominations**

nominee *noun* A person who is nominated for an office or honor.
nom·i·nee (nŏm′ə **nē′**) ◊ *noun, plural* **nominees**

non– The prefix *non–* means "not." If a book is *nonfiction,* it is not fiction. If a material is *nonflammable,* it will not catch fire easily.

***VOCABULARY BUILDER* • non–**

Many words formed with the prefix **non–** are not entries in this dictionary. But you can figure out what these words mean by looking up the meanings of the root words and the prefix. For example:
nongreasy = not greasy
nonstandard = not standard

ă	pat	ĭ	pit	oi	**oi**l	th	ba**th**
ā	pay	ī	ride	ŏŏ	b**oo**k	*th*	ba**the**
â	care	î	fierce	ōō	b**oo**t	ə	ago, item
ä	father	ŏ	pot	ou	**ou**t		pencil
ĕ	pet	ō	go	ŭ	cut		atom
ē	be	ô	paw, for	û	fur		circus

nonchalant *adjective* Confident and carefree; unconcerned: *I pretended to be nonchalant but I was really very nervous.*
non·cha·lant (nŏn′shə **länt′**) ◊ *adjective*

nonconductor *noun* A substance that does not easily conduct electricity, heat, or sound.
non·con·duc·tor (nŏn′kən **dŭk′** tər) ◊ *noun, plural* **nonconductors**

nondescript *adjective* Not having distinctive qualities and thus being difficult to describe: *The outfit was so nondescript that I can't remember a thing about it.*
non·de·script (nŏn′dĭ **skrĭpt′**) ◊ *adjective*

none *pronoun* **1.** Not any: *None of the water spilled.* **2.** Not one: *None dared to try it.*
◊ *adverb* Not at all: *Your room is none too tidy.*
none (nŭn) ◊ *pronoun* ◊ *adverb*
‖*These sound alike:* **none, nun**

nonentity *noun* A person or thing of no importance or significance.
non·en·ti·ty (nŏn **ĕn′** tĭ tē) ◊ *noun, plural* **nonentities**

nonfiction *noun* Writings that are not fiction, especially books that discuss facts and give general information. The story of a person's life, called a biography, is an example of nonfiction.
non·fic·tion (nŏn **fĭk′** shən) ◊ *noun*

nonflammable *adjective* Not tending to catch fire easily or burn rapidly; not flammable: *Firefighters wear nonflammable coats, hats, and gloves.*
non·flam·ma·ble (nŏn **flăm′** ə bəl) ◊ *adjective*

nonsense *noun* **1.** Foolish talk, writing, or behavior. **2.** Something that is unimportant or useless.
non·sense (**nŏn′** sĕns′) ◊ *noun*

nonstop *adverb & adjective* Without a stop: *We flew nonstop from Miami to Chicago. It was a nonstop flight.*
non·stop (**nŏn′** **stŏp′**) ◊ *adverb & adjective*

noodle *noun* A flat strip of dried dough, usually made of eggs, flour, and water.
noo·dle (**nōōd′** l) ◊ *noun, plural* **noodles**

nook *noun* **1.** A small separate place usually formed by two walls in a room: *We studied in a nook in the library.* **2.** A cozy or hidden spot: *We found a shady nook by the side of the stream for our picnic.*
nook (nŏŏk) ◊ *noun, plural* **nooks**

▲ **nook**

noon *noun* The middle of the day; twelve o'clock in the daytime.
noon (nōōn) ◊ *noun, plural* **noons**

noonday *noun* Noon.
noon·day (**nōōn′** dā′) ◊ *noun, plural* **noondays**

no one *pronoun* No person; nobody.

noontime *noun* Noon.
noon·time (**nōōn′** tīm′) ◊ *noun, plural* **noontimes**

noose *noun* A loop formed in a rope by means of a knot that lets the loop tighten.
noose (nōōs) ◊ *noun, plural* **nooses**

nor *conjunction* Or not: *We are neither rich nor poor.*
nor (nôr) ◊ *conjunction*

normal *adjective* **1.** Of the usual or regular kind: *My weight is normal for my height.* **2.** Happening in a natural, healthy way: *The baby has a normal heartbeat.* **3.** Having average intelligence.
◊ *noun* The usual or expected condition.
nor·mal (**nôr′** məl) ◊ *adjective* ◊ *noun*

SYNONYMS

normal, regular, standard, typical

That is not the *normal* way to ride a bike. Show me the *regular* way to throw a baseball. That is not the *standard* price for such toys. This book is not *typical* of the other books in the series.

N

Norse *noun* **1.** (*used with a plural verb*) The people of ancient Scandinavia. **2.** The language of the Norse.
◊ *adjective* Of or relating to ancient Scandinavia, its people, or their language.
Norse (nôrs) ◊ *noun* ◊ *adjective*

north *noun* **1.** The direction to the right of a person who faces the sunset. **2.** Often **North** A region in this direction. **3.** **North** The northern part of the United States, especially the states north of Maryland, West Virginia, Kentucky, and Missouri.
◊ *adjective* **1.** Of, in, or toward the north: *We camped on the north side of the lake.* **2.** Coming from the north: *A north wind blew all day.*
◊ *adverb* Toward the north: *We drove north.*
north (nôrth) ◊ *noun* ◊ *adjective* ◊ *adverb*

North American *noun* A person who was born in or lives in North America. People who live in Canada, the United States, and Mexico are North Americans.
◊ *adjective* Of or relating to North America or North Americans.
North American ◊ *noun, plural* **North Americans** ◊ *adjective*

northeast *noun* **1.** The direction that is halfway between north and east. **2.** Often **Northeast** A region in this direction.
◊ *adjective* **1.** Of, in, or toward the northeast. **2.** Coming from the northeast: *The cold northeast wind made us shiver.*
◊ *adverb* Toward the northeast: *The border runs northeast along the mountains.*
north·east (nôrth **ēst′**) ◊ *noun* ◊ *adjective* ◊ *adverb*

northerly *adjective & adverb* **1.** In or toward the north. **2.** From the north: *We were blown off course by northerly winds.*
north·er·ly (**nôr′** *th*ər lē) ◊ *adjective & adverb*

northern *adjective* **1.** Often **Northern** Of, in, or toward the north. **2.** Coming from the north.
north·ern (**nôr′** *th*ərn) ◊ *adjective*

ă	pat	ĭ	pit	oi	**oi**l	th	ba**th**
ā	pay	ī	ride	o͝o	b**oo**k	*th*	ba**the**
â	care	î	fierce	o͞o	b**oo**t	ə	**a**go, it**e**m
ä	father	ŏ	pot	ou	**ou**t		penc**i**l
ĕ	pet	ō	go	ŭ	c**u**t		at**o**m
ē	be	ô	paw, for	û	f**u**r		circ**u**s

northern lights *plural noun* The aurora borealis.

North Pole *noun* The most northern point of the earth.

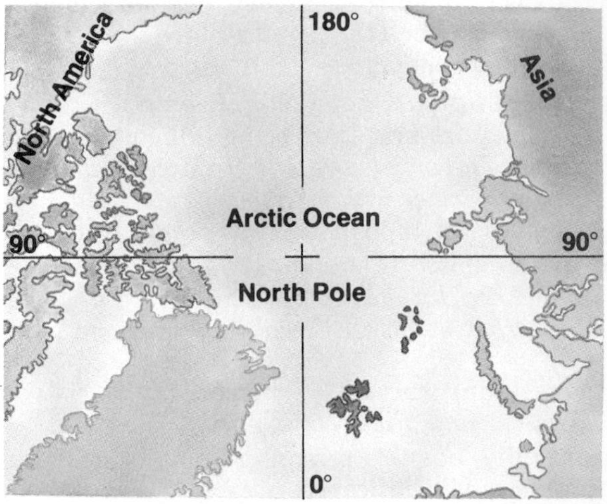

▲ **North Pole**

northward *adverb* To or toward the north.
◊ *adjective* Moving to or toward the north: *We began our northward journey at dawn.*
north·ward (**nôrth′** wərd) ◊ *adverb* ◊ *adjective*

northwards *adverb* Northward.
north·wards (**nôrth′** wərdz) ◊ *adverb*

northwest *noun* **1.** The direction that is halfway between north and west. **2.** Often **Northwest** A region in this direction.
◊ *adjective* **1.** Of, in, or toward the northwest. **2.** Coming from the northwest: *We're expecting a northwest wind tomorrow.*
◊ *adverb* Toward the northwest: *We sailed northwest to the island for a picnic.*
north·west (nôrth **wĕst′**) ◊ *noun* ◊ *adjective* ◊ *adverb*

Norwegian *noun* **1.** A person who was born in or lives in Norway. **2.** The language of the Norwegians.
◊ *adjective* Of or relating to Norway, the Norwegians, or their language.
Nor·we·gian (nôr **wē′** jən) ◊ *noun, plural* **Norwegians** ◊ *adjective*

nose *noun* **1.** The part of the human face or an animal's head that contains the nostrils and organs of smell. **2.** The sense of smell: *The dog's nose told it that food was being*

cooked. **3.** Something, as the forward end of an airplane, rocket, or submarine that looks somewhat like a nose.
◊ *verb* **1.** To perceive by or as if by smell: *The dog nosed out the scent of the fox.* **2.** To touch, push, or examine with the nose; nuzzle. **3.** To pry into other people's business. **4.** To move forward cautiously: *The barge nosed past the dock.*
nose (nōz) ◊ *noun, plural* **noses** ◊ *verb* **nosed, nosing**

nosebleed *noun* A bleeding from the nose.
nose·bleed (nōz′blēd′) ◊ *noun, plural* **nosebleeds**

nose cone *noun* The cone-shaped front end of a rocket or missile.
nose cone ◊ *noun, plural* **nose cones**

▲ **nose cone**

nostril *noun* Either of the outer openings of the nose.
nos·tril (nŏs′trəl) ◊ *noun, plural* **nostrils**

nosy *adjective* Prying into other people's business.
nos·y (nō′zē) ◊ *adjective* **nosier, nosiest**

not *adverb* Used to make a word or group of words negative: *I will not go.*
not (nŏt) ◊ *adverb*
‖*These sound alike:* **not, knot**

notable *adjective* Worthy of notice: *Our team had notable success at the spelling bee.*
◊ *noun* A well-known person.
no·ta·ble (nō′tə bəl) ◊ *adjective* ◊ *noun, plural* **notables**

notation *noun* **1.** A system of symbols or figures used to represent things such as numbers or musical tones. **2.** A short note: *I made a notation of the date on my calendar.*
no·ta·tion (nō tā′shən) ◊ *noun, plural* **notations**

notch *noun* **1.** A cut shaped like a V. **2.** A deep, narrow opening between mountains.
◊ *verb* To cut a notch in.
notch (nŏch) ◊ *noun, plural* **notches** ◊ *verb* **notched, notching**

note *noun* **1.** A short letter or message: *My parents sent a note to the teacher.* **2.** A brief record of facts written down as a help in remembering something: *I took notes during the class.* **3.** A printed explanation or comment on a part of a printed text. **4.** A paper that promises that a debt will be paid back. **5.** A musical tone or a symbol that represents a musical tone. **6.** A key of an instrument keyboard, as a piano. **7.** The call or cry of a bird: *We heard the clear note of a cardinal.* **8.** A sign that reveals a certain quality: *There was a note of hope in your voice.*
◊ *verb* **1.** To observe with care; notice: *Have you noted that your necktie and handkerchief don't match?* **2.** To make a written record of.
note (nōt) ◊ *noun, plural* **notes** ◊ *verb* **noted, noting**

notebook *noun* A book with blank pages to write on.
note·book (nōt′bo͝ok′) ◊ *noun, plural* **notebooks**

noted *adjective* Well known; famous: *His mother is a noted musician.*
not·ed (nō′tĭd) ◊ *adjective*

noteworthy *adjective* Worthy of notice.
note·wor·thy (nōt′wûr′*th*ē) ◊ *adjective*

nothing *pronoun* **1.** Not anything: *I have nothing to say.* **2.** Someone or something of little or no importance or interest: *There's nothing on television tonight.*
◊ *noun* Zero: *We had two points and they had nothing.*
◊ *adverb* Not at all: *You look nothing like your cousin.*
noth·ing (nŭth′ĭng) ◊ *pronoun* ◊ *noun* ◊ *adverb*

notice *verb* To take note of; pay attention to: *I sat in the last row and hoped nobody would notice me.*

N

◊ *noun* **1.** The fact of being noticed; observation or attention: *They escaped notice by wearing disguises.* **2.** A published or printed announcement: *The newspaper had a notice about the school play.* **3.** An announcement of purpose, especially of one's intention to leave a job: *I gave my employer a week's notice.* **4.** A warning of something to come: *Two visitors came to our house without notice.*
no·tice (nō′tĭs) ◊ *verb* **noticed, noticing** ◊ *noun, plural* **notices**

noticeable *adjective* **1.** Easily noticed; evident. **2.** Worth noting.
no·tice·a·ble (nō′tĭ sə bəl) ◊ *adjective*

notify *verb* To give notice to; inform: *The school notified me that I had passed my test.*
no·ti·fy (nō′tə fī′) ◊ *verb* **notified, notifying**

notion *noun* **1.** Something that exists in the mind; idea: *Do you have any notion of what the announcement means?* **2.** A sudden inclination or impulse; whim: *I had a notion to sing.* **3. notions** Small useful items, such as needles, buttons, thread, or ribbons.
no·tion (nō′shən) ◊ *noun, plural* **notions**

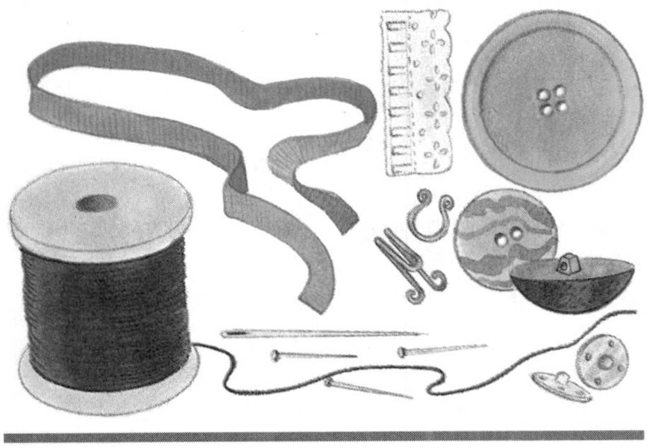

▲ **notion**
Sewing notions

notorious *adjective* Well known for something bad or unpleasant.
no·to·ri·ous (nō **tôr′**ē əs) ◊ *adjective*

ă	pat	ĭ	pit	oi	**oi**l	th	ba**th**
ā	pay	ī	ride	o͝o	b**oo**k	*th*	ba**th**e
â	care	î	fierce	o͞o	b**oo**t	ə	ago, item
ä	father	ŏ	pot	ou	**ou**t		pencil
ĕ	pet	ō	go	ŭ	c**u**t		atom
ē	be	ô	paw, for	û	f**u**r		circus

nought *noun* Another spelling for **naught.**
nought (nôt) ◊ *noun, plural* **noughts**

noun *noun* A word that is used to name a person, place, or thing. In the sentence *We found a boat on the beach,* the words *boat* and *beach* are nouns.
noun (noun) ◊ *noun, plural* **nouns**

nourish *verb* To provide with what is needed for growth and development; feed: *Human babies are nourished with milk.*
nour·ish (**nûr′**ĭsh) ◊ *verb* **nourished, nourishing**

nourishment *noun* **1.** The act of nourishing or the condition of being nourished. **2.** Something that nourishes; food.
nour·ish·ment (**nûr′**ĭsh mənt) ◊ *noun*

Nov. The abbreviation for *November.*

novel¹ *adjective* Very new, unusual, or different: *The hang glider is a novel way to fly.*
nov·el¹ (**nŏv′**əl) ◊ *adjective*

novel² *noun* A story that is long enough to fill a book and that is about made-up characters and events.
nov·el² (**nŏv′**əl) ◊ *noun, plural* **novels**

HISTORY **• novel¹, novel²**

Novel¹ and **novel²** both go back to a Latin word that meant "new." But **novel²** came to English by way of Italian, where it was used to describe a "new" form of short story.

novelist *noun* A person who writes novels.
nov·el·ist (**nŏv′**ə lĭst) ◊ *noun, plural* **novelists**

novelty *noun* **1.** The quality or condition of being unusual: *The novelty of swimming in the ocean soon wore off.* **2.** Something new and unusual: *At first the light bulb was just an interesting novelty.* **3.** A small inexpensive article for sale.
nov·el·ty (**nŏv′**əl tē) ◊ *noun, plural* **novelties**

November *noun* The eleventh month of the year. November has 30 days.
No·vem·ber (nō **vĕm′**bər) ◊ *noun*

now *adverb* **1.** At the present time: *He's eating and can't answer the telephone now.* **2.** At once; immediately: *We'd better start now.* **3.** Very recently: *She left just now.* **4.** In

these circumstances; as things are: *Now we won't be able to go.* **5.** At the time spoken of: *Now the ship began to sink.* **6.** Used especially to introduce a command or request: *Now listen to me.*
◊ *conjunction* Seeing that; since: *Now that we've finished eating, let's go to the movie.*
◊ *noun* The present: *You should have been home by now.*
now (nou) ◊ *adverb* ◊ *conjunction* ◊ *noun*

nowadays *adverb* During the present time.
now·a·days (**nou′** ə dāz′) ◊ *adverb*

nowhere *adverb* In, at, or to no place; not anywhere: *My friend was nowhere to be seen.*
no·where (**nō′** hwâr′) ◊ *adverb*

nozzle *noun* A projecting spout, as one on the end of a hose, that forms an outlet for a liquid forced out under pressure.
noz·zle (**nŏz′** əl) ◊ *noun, plural* **nozzles**

N.S. The abbreviation for *Nova Scotia,* Canada.

nuclear *adjective* **1.** Of, relating to, or forming a nucleus. **2.** Of, relating to, or using energy that comes from the nuclei of atoms. **3.** Of, relating to, having, or using atomic or hydrogen bombs.
nu·cle·ar (**nōō′** klē ər *or* **nyōō′** klē ər) ◊ *adjective*

nuclei *noun* A plural of **nucleus.**
nu·cle·i (**nōō′** klē ī′ *or* **nyōō′** klē ī′) ◊ *noun*

nucleus *noun* **1.** A central or essential part around which other parts are grouped; core: *The three children were the nucleus of our school's baseball team.* **2.** A structure within a living cell that controls functions such as growth and reproduction. **3.** The central core of an atom, made up of protons and neutrons.
nu·cle·us (**nōō′** klē əs *or* **nyōō′** klē əs) ◊ *noun, plural* **nuclei** *or* **nucleuses**

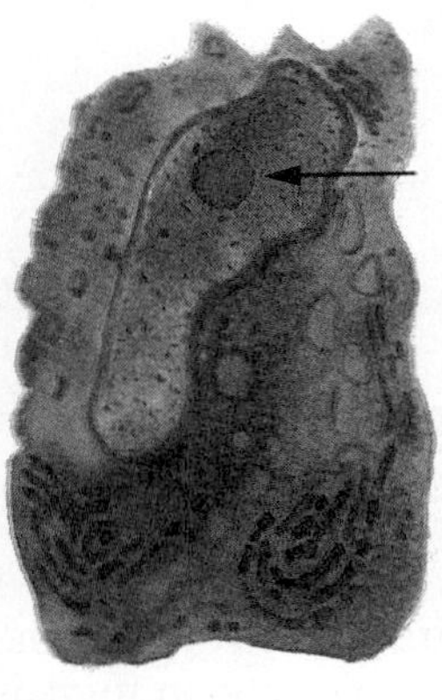

▲ **nucleus**

nudge *verb* To push in a gentle way, especially in order to attract attention.
◊ *noun* A gentle push.
nudge (nŭj) ◊ *verb* **nudged, nudging** ◊ *noun, plural* **nudges**

nugget *noun* A hard lump, especially of a precious metal, such as gold.
nug·get (**nŭg′** ĭt) ◊ *noun, plural* **nuggets**

nuisance *noun* Someone or something that is annoying.
nui·sance (**nōō′** səns *or* **nyōō′** səns) ◊ *noun, plural* **nuisances**

numb *adjective* **1.** Lacking the power to feel or move: *My fingers were numb with cold.* **2.** Stunned, as from strong emotion: *I was too numb with astonishment even to speak.*
◊ *verb* To make or become numb.
numb (nŭm) ◊ *adjective* **number, numbest** ◊ *verb* **numbed, numbing**

number *noun* **1.** A symbol or word used in counting: *Six is a number.* **2.** A numeral given to something to identify it: *What is your house number?* **3.** A quantity that is the sum of all the units or members; total: *What is the number of feet in a mile?* **4.** An amount or quantity that is not counted exactly: *I said no for a number of reasons.*
◊ *verb* **1.** To count one by one: *Can you number from one to ten in Spanish?* **2.** To amount to; total: *The audience numbered nearly a thousand.* **3.** To give a number to: *The houses on that road are not numbered.* **4.** To include in a group or category: *We number you among the school's best students.* **5.** To limit in number: *The days before cold weather sets in are numbered.*
num·ber (**nŭm′** bər) ◊ *noun, plural* **numbers** ◊ *verb* **numbered, numbering**

numberless *adjective* Being too many to be counted; countless.
num·ber·less (**nŭm′** bər lĭs) ◊ *adjective*

numeral *noun* A symbol or a group of symbols used to represent a number.
nu·mer·al (**nōō′** mər əl *or* **nyōō′** mər əl) ◊ *noun, plural* **numerals**

numerator *noun* The number written above the line in a fraction: *In the fraction* $^2/_7$ *the numerator is 2.*
nu·mer·a·tor (**nōō′** mə rā′tər *or* **nyōō′** mə-rā′tər) ◊ *noun, plural* **numerators**

numerical *adjective* Of, relating to, or expressed as a number or series of numbers.
nu·mer·i·cal (nōō **mĕr′** ĭ kəl *or* nyōō **mĕr′** ĭ-kəl) ◊ *adjective*

N

numerous *adjective* Including or made up of a large number: *They have numerous problems.* —See Synonyms at **many.**
nu·mer·ous (**nōō′** mər əs *or* **nyōō′** mər əs) ◊ *adjective*

nun *noun* A woman who is a member of a religious order.
nun (nŭn) ◊ *noun, plural* **nuns**
‖*These sound alike:* **nun, none**

nurse *noun* **1.** A person who cares for or is trained to care for sick people. **2.** A woman who is employed to take care of a young child or children.
◊ *verb* **1.** To be a nurse for, as for a sick person. **2.** To take special care of: *I nursed the house plants through a long winter.*
nurse (nûrs) ◊ *noun, plural* **nurses** ◊ *verb* **nursed, nursing**

nursery *noun* **1.** A room or place set apart for babies or young children. **2.** A place where plants and young trees are raised, often to be sold.
nurs·er·y (**nûr′** sə rē) ◊ *noun, plural* **nurseries**

▲ **nursery**
A nursery for infants

ă	pat	ĭ	pit	oi	**oil**	th	**bath**
ā	pay	ī	ride	ŏŏ	**book**	*th*	**bathe**
â	care	î	fierce	ōō	**boot**	ə	**ago, item**
ä	father	ŏ	pot	ou	**out**		pencil
ĕ	pet	ō	go	ŭ	**cut**		atom
ē	be	ô	paw, for	û	**fur**		circus

nut *noun* **1.** A fruit or seed with a hard shell and usually a single kernel. **2.** The often edible kernel of a nut. **3.** A piece of metal or wood that has a hole in it with spiral grooves. A nut is designed to screw onto and hold a bolt or screw.
nut (nŭt) ◊ *noun, plural* **nuts**

nutcracker *noun* **1.** A device for cracking the shells of nuts. **2.** A gray and white bird with a sharp bill.
nut·crack·er (**nŭt′** krăk′ər) ◊ *noun, plural* **nutcrackers**

nuthatch *noun* A small gray bird with a sharp bill. Nuthatches climb up and down tree trunks.
nut·hatch (**nŭt′** hăch′) ◊ *noun, plural* **nuthatches**

nutmeg *noun* The hard seed of a tropical tree. Nutmeg is ground up and used as a spice.
nut·meg (**nŭt′** mĕg′) ◊ *noun, plural* **nutmegs**

▲ **nutmeg**

nutria *noun* A beaverlike South American animal that has thick brownish fur.
nu·tri·a (**nōō′** trē ə *or* **nyōō′** trē ə) ◊ *noun, plural* **nutrias**

nutrient *noun* Something that nourishes, especially an ingredient in a food.
nu·tri·ent (**nōō′** trē ənt *or* **nyōō′** trē ənt) ◊ *noun, plural* **nutrients**

nutriment *noun* Nourishment; food.
nu·tri·ment (**nōō′** trə mənt *or* **nyōō′** trə mənt) ◊ *noun, plural* **nutriments**

nutrition *noun* **1.** The process of nourishing or being nourished. **2.** The processes by which a living thing takes in and uses food.
nu·tri·tion (no͞o **trĭsh′**ən *or* nyo͞o **trĭsh′**ən) ◊ *noun*

nutritional *adjective* **1.** Of or relating to the processes of taking in and using food. **2.** Of, relating to, or necessary to proper diet: *Junk food has no nutritional value.*
nu·tri·tion·al (no͞o **trĭsh′**ə nəl *or* nyo͞o-**trĭsh′**ə nəl) ◊ *adjective*

nutritious *adjective* Providing nourishment.
nu·tri·tious (no͞o **trĭsh′**əs *or* nyo͞o **trĭsh′**əs) ◊ *adjective*

nutshell *noun* The hard shell that holds the kernel of a nut.
nut·shell (**nŭt′**shĕl′) ◊ *noun, plural* **nutshells**

nutty *adjective* **1.** Full of or tasting like nuts. **2.** Crazy or silly; eccentric: *That was a nutty thing to do.*
nut·ty (**nŭt′**ē) ◊ *adjective* **nuttier, nuttiest**

nuzzle *verb* To rub or touch with the nose: *The calf nuzzled the cow.*
nuz·zle (**nŭz′**əl) ◊ *verb* **nuzzled, nuzzling**

NV The abbreviation for *Nevada* used with a Zip Code.

NW The abbreviation for *Northwest.*

N.W.T. The abbreviation for *Northwest Territories,* Canada.

NY The abbreviation for *New York* used with a Zip Code.

N.Y. An abbreviation for *New York.*

nylon *noun* A very strong elastic synthetic material that is used to make cloth, yarn, and plastics.
ny·lon (**nī′**lŏn′) ◊ *noun, plural* **nylons**

nymph *noun* **1.** A graceful, legendary female spirit or goddess that lives in the woods and in the water. **2.** A young insect, such as a grasshopper, that has not yet developed into its adult stage.
nymph (nĭmf) ◊ *noun, plural* **nymphs**

N

Octopus

Oo

O is the fifteenth letter of the English alphabet. Did you know that it has a long history?

Over 3,500 years ago, people in the Middle East were using symbols that became the letters of our alphabet. This ancient Middle Eastern symbol is a form of the letter that became our letter *O*.

The ancient Greeks borrowed their alphabet from people in the Middle East. Here is a form of the Greek letter that became our letter *O*.

The ancient Romans borrowed their alphabet from a people who had taken their own letter symbols from the Greeks. Here is a form of the Roman letter *O* that was used for carving letters into stone. These letters became the model for our printed capital letters.

As people wrote quickly, especially with pens, the capital letters began to take the shapes of small letters. Here is a small-letter *o that* was developed about 1,200 years ago.

Oo *Oo* — Handwriting | Oo — Sans Serif | Oo — Serif | Oo — Computer Printing

o *or* **O** *noun* The fifteenth letter of the English alphabet.
o *or* **O** (ō) ◊ *noun, plural* **o's** *or* **O's**

O. 1. The abbreviation for *Ocean.* **2.** An abbreviation for *Ohio.*

oak *noun* A tree that has leaves with uneven notches along the edges, bears acorns, and yields a hard wood.
oak (ōk) ◊ *noun, plural* **oaks**

oar *noun* A long pole with a blade at one end that is used to row or steer a boat.
oar (ôr) ◊ *noun, plural* **oars**

oasis *noun* A fertile spot or area in a desert, watered by a spring, stream, or well.
o·a·sis (ō **ā′** sĭs) ◊ *noun, plural* **oases**

ă	pat	ĭ	pit	oi	**oil**	th	ba**th**
ā	pay	ī	ride	ŏŏ	book	*th*	ba**th**e
â	care	î	fierce	ōō	boot	ə	ago, item
ä	father	ŏ	pot	ou	**out**		pencil
ĕ	pet	ō	go	ŭ	cut		atom
ē	be	ô	paw, for	û	fur		circus

oat *noun* A grass grown for its seeds that are used as food and as fodder for animals.
oat (ōt) ◊ *noun, plural* **oats**

oath *noun* A statement or promise that a person swears is true: *The witness made an oath to tell the truth.*
oath (ōth) ◊ *noun, plural* **oaths**

oatmeal *noun* **1.** Meal made from oats that have been ground or pressed flat by rollers. **2.** A hot cereal that is made from oatmeal.
oat·meal (**ōt′** mēl′) ◊ *noun*

obedient *adjective* Doing what is asked, ordered, or required; willing to obey: *An obedient dog comes when it is called.*
o·be·di·ent (ō **bē′** dē ənt) ◊ *adjective*

obelisk *noun* A shaft with four sides that tapers to a point.
ob·e·lisk (**ŏb′** ə lĭsk′) ◊ *noun, plural* **obelisks**

obey *verb* **1.** To carry out; fulfill: *You didn't obey the instructions.* **2.** To do what is commanded or requested by: *Always obey your parents.*
o·bey (ō **bā′**) ◊ *verb* **obeyed, obeying**

SYNONYMS

obey, follow, mind

Be sure to *obey* the law. I *followed* the instructions carefully. Toddlers do not always *mind* their parents.
Antonym: *disobey*

object *noun* **1.** Something that has shape and can be felt or seen: *There were several objects on the table.* **2.** Someone or something toward which attention is directed; target. **3.** A purpose or goal: *The object of the game is to drive the ball through the hoop.* **4.** A noun or word functioning like a noun that receives the action of a verb or follows a preposition. In the sentence *We flew kites,* the word *kites* is the object of the verb *flew.* In the phrase *between us,* the word *us* is the object of the preposition *between.*
◊ *verb* To express an objection: *The students objected that giving a surprise test was unfair.*
ob·ject ◊ *noun* (ŏb′jĭkt), *plural* **objects** ◊ *verb* (əb **jĕkt′**) **objected, objecting**

objection *noun* **1.** The expression of an opposing view or argument: *You should have made your objection when we first mentioned the idea.* **2.** A feeling of opposition or dislike: *My parents had no objection to the extra classes I wanted to take.*
ob·jec·tion (əb **jĕk′**shən) ◊ *noun, plural* **objections**

objective *adjective* Not influenced by feelings or prejudice; impartial; fair: *A judge must be objective.*
◊ *noun* Something that one tries to achieve or reach; goal or purpose.
ob·jec·tive (əb **jĕk′**tĭv) ◊ *adjective* ◊ *noun, plural* **objectives**

objective case *noun* The form of a noun or pronoun that functions as the object of a verb or preposition.

obligation *noun* **1.** Something, such as a promise, that requires a person to do something: *Our parents fulfilled their obligation to support us.* **2.** The binding power of a law, promise, contract, or sense of duty: *We were under obligation to finish the work in a satisfactory way.*
ob·li·ga·tion (ŏb′lĭ **gā′**shən) ◊ *noun, plural* **obligations**

oblige *verb* **1.** To force to act in a certain way: *The weather obliged us to cancel our trip.* **2.** To make grateful or thankful: *I am obliged to you for helping me.*
o·blige (ə **blīj′**) ◊ *verb* **obliged, obliging**

oblique *adjective* **1.** Slanting or sloping. **2.** Neither parallel nor perpendicular. **3.** Not straightforward; indirect or evasive: *I can't understand your oblique answer.*
o·blique (ə **blēk′**) ◊ *adjective*

oblique angle *noun* An acute angle or an obtuse angle.
oblique angle ◊ *noun, plural* **oblique angles**

oblong *adjective* Greater in length than in width.
◊ *noun* An oblong object or figure.
ob·long (ŏb′lông′) ◊ *adjective* ◊ *noun, plural* **oblongs**

obnoxious *adjective* Extremely unpleasant.
ob·nox·ious (əb **nŏk′**shəs) ◊ *adjective*

obnoxiously *adverb* In an obnoxious manner or way; unpleasantly.
ob·nox·ious·ly (əb **nŏk′**shəs lē) ◊ *adverb*

oboe *noun* A musical instrument that is shaped like a slender tapering tube. An oboe is played by blowing into a mouthpiece made of two thin pieces of reed. It is a hard instrument to play.
o·boe (ō′bō) ◊ *noun, plural* **oboes**

▲ **oboe**

obscure *adjective* **1.** Hard to understand: *The reason for the problem is obscure.* **2.** Not easy to see or figure out: *Your handwriting is too obscure.* **3.** Not well known: *We bought a cottage in an obscure village.*
◊ *verb* To make obscure: *Clouds obscured the stars.*
ob·scure (əb **skyŏŏr′**) ◊ *adjective* **obscurer, obscurest** ◊ *verb* **obscured, obscuring**

observation *noun* **1.** The act, process, or practice of observing. **2.** The fact of being observed. **3.** Something that has been observed; a comment or remark: *The teacher made an*

observation about the weather.
ob·ser·va·tion (ŏb′zûr **vā′**shən) ◊ *noun, plural* **observations**

observatory *noun* A place designed and equipped for making observations, as of the the stars and planets or of the weather.
ob·ser·va·to·ry (əb **zûr′**və tôr′ē) ◊ *noun, plural* **observatories**

▲ **observatory**

observe *verb* **1.** To see and pay attention to; watch: *They observed a bird on the ledge.* **2.** To make a remark; comment: *I observed that it would soon be time for our vacation.* **3.** To act in accordance with; obey: *Always observe the speed limit.*
ob·serve (əb **zûrv′**) ◊ *verb* **observed, observing**

obstacle *noun* Something that blocks or stands in the way: *Fallen rocks and other obstacles made it impossible to use the road.*
ob·sta·cle (**ŏb′**stə kəl) ◊ *noun, plural* **obstacles**

obstinate *adjective* **1.** Stubbornly holding to an attitude or opinion. **2.** Hard to manage, control, or cure: *That is an obstinate cough.*
ob·sti·nate (**ŏb′**stə nĭt) ◊ *adjective*

ă	pat	ĭ	pit	oi	oil	th	bath
ā	pay	ī	ride	ŏŏ	book	*th*	bathe
â	care	î	fierce	ōō	boot	ə	ago, item
ä	father	ŏ	pot	ou	out		pencil
ĕ	pet	ō	go	ŭ	cut		atom
ē	be	ô	paw, for	û	fur		circus

SYNONYMS

obstinate, headstrong, stubborn

No matter what I said they remained *obstinate* about going. She was so *headstrong* that she went swimming in spite of the warning. He has always been very *stubborn.*

obstruct *verb* **1.** To close up with an obstacle; block: *Fallen rocks obstructed the mountain pass.* **2.** To be or get in the way of; hinder: *The tall building obstructs our view of the river.*
ob·struct (əb **strŭkt′**) ◊ *verb* **obstructed, obstructing**

obstruction *noun* **1.** Something that obstructs. **2.** The act of obstructing or the condition of being obstructed.
ob·struct·ion (əb **strŭk′**shən) ◊ *noun, plural* **obstructions**

obtain *verb* To gain or get by means of planning or effort; acquire: *I obtained a copy of the report.* —See Synonyms at **get**.
ob·tain (əb **tān′**) ◊ *verb* **obtained, obtaining**

obtuse angle *noun* An angle that is greater than 90 degrees and less than 180 degrees.
ob·tuse angle (əb-**tōōs′** *or* əb **tyōōs′**) ◊ *noun, plural* **obtuse angles**

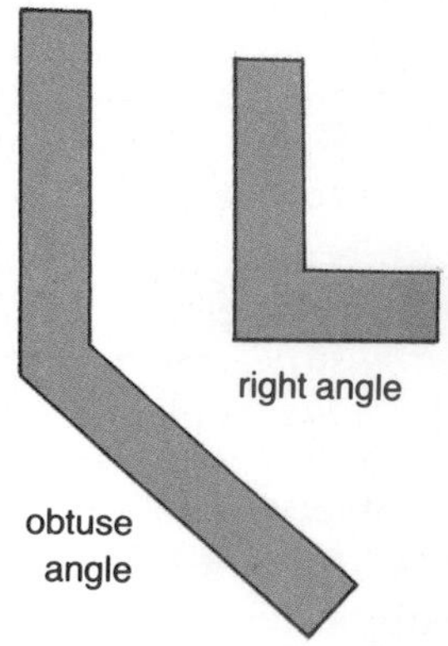

▲ **obtuse angle**

obvious *adjective* Easily noticed or understood: *The student made an obvious mistake in subtraction.*
ob·vi·ous (**ŏb′**vē əs) ◊ *adjective*

occasion *noun* **1.** A very important event: *Thanksgiving is a great occasion.* **2.** The time when something takes place: *They met on the occasion of my friend's wedding.* **3.** An opportunity: *We never miss an occasion to visit our parents.*
oc·ca·sion (ə **kā′**zhən) ◊ *noun, plural* **occasions**

occasional *adjective* Happening or encountered from time to time: *Except for an occa-*

sional cold, I have been well this winter.
oc·ca·sion·al (ə **kā′**zhə nəl) ◊ *adjective*

occupant *noun* Someone or something that occupies a place or position: *Squirrels and mice were the only occupants of the old barn.*
oc·cu·pant (**ŏk′**yə pənt) ◊ *noun, plural* **occupants**

occupation *noun* **1.** A profession, business, or job: *Our neighbor is a teacher by occupation.* **2.** The act of taking possession and control of a place or an area.
oc·cu·pa·tion (ŏk′yə **pā′**shən) ◊ *noun, plural* **occupations**

occupy *verb* **1.** To live in; inhabit: *They occupy a small cabin.* **2.** To take up; fill: *Reading occupies much of my free time.* **3.** To take possession and control of: *Troops invaded and occupied the city.* **4.** To have and control: *My cousin occupies the office of class president.* **5.** To keep busy: *We occupied ourselves with several small tasks.*
oc·cu·py (**ŏk′**yə pī′) ◊ *verb* **occupied, occupying**

occur *verb* **1.** To take place; happen: *Many accidents occur in the home.* **2.** To be found to exist; live, grow, or appear: *This plant occurs mainly near the ocean.* **3.** To come to mind: *It occurred to us that they could go too.*
oc·cur (ə **kûr′**) ◊ *verb* **occurred, occurring**

occurrence *noun* **1.** The act, fact, or process of occurring: *The occurrence of an accident closed the road to traffic.* **2.** Something that occurs; event: *A strange occurrence was reported in the newspaper.*
oc·cur·rence (ə **kûr′**əns) ◊ *noun, plural* **occurrences**

ocean *noun* **1.** The great mass of salt water that covers about 72 percent of the earth's surface. **2.** One of the four main divisions of this mass of salt water: *The Arctic Ocean surrounds the North Pole.*
o·cean (**ō′**shən) ◊ *noun, plural* **oceans**

oceanography *noun* The study and exploration of the ocean and the plants and animals that live in it.
o·cean·og·ra·phy (ō′shə **nŏg′**rə fē) ◊ *noun*

ocelot *noun* A wild cat of Mexico, Central America, and South America that has a yellowish coat spotted with black.
oc·e·lot (**ŏs′**ə lŏt′ *or* **ō′**sə lŏt′) ◊ *noun, plural* **ocelots**

o'clock *adverb* Of or according to the clock: *When the bell rings, it will be 11 o'clock.*
o'clock (ə **klŏk′**) ◊ *adverb*

Oct. The abbreviation for *October.*

octagon *noun* A figure having eight sides and eight angles.
oc·ta·gon (**ŏk′**tə gŏn′) ◊ *noun, plural* **octagons**

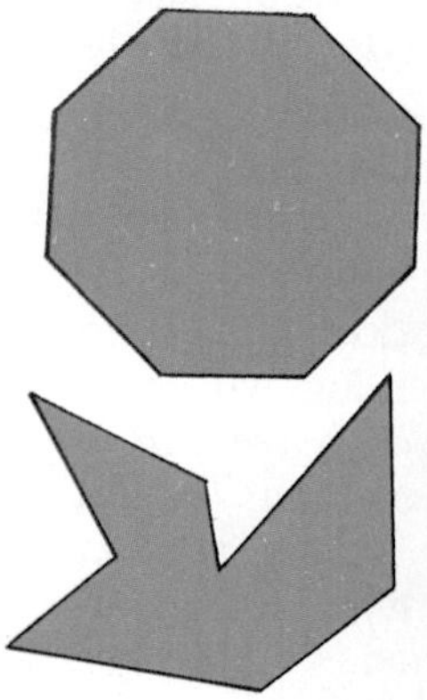
▲ **octagon**

octave *noun* **1.** The musical interval that is between two tones, one of which with twice as many vibrations per second as the other. **2.** A series of tones that make up an octave.
oc·tave (**ŏk′**tĭv) ◊ *noun, plural* **octaves**

October *noun* The tenth month of the year. The month of October has 31 days.
Oc·to·ber (ŏk **tō′**bər) ◊ *noun*

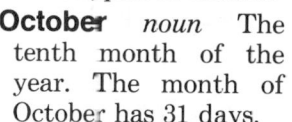

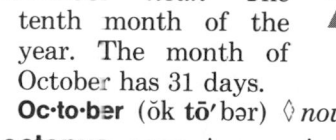

octopus *noun* A sea animal that has a large head, a soft, rounded body, and eight long arms. The undersides of the arms have sucking disks used for grasping and holding.
oc·to·pus (**ŏk′**tə pəs) ◊ *noun, plural* **octopuses**

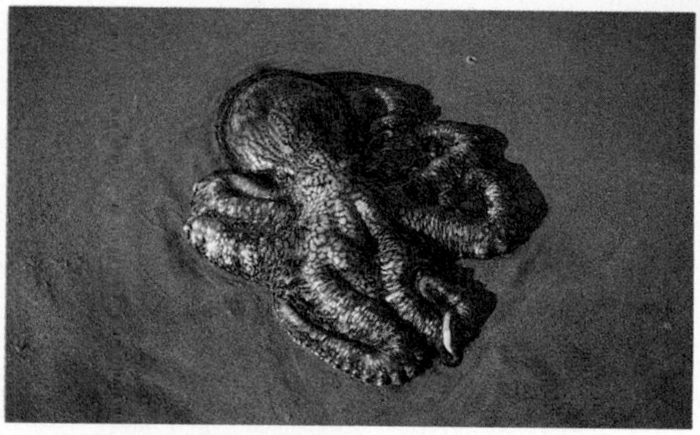
▲ **octopus**

odd *adjective* **1.** Not ordinary or usual; peculiar: *The car is making an odd noise.* **2.** Being the only one left of a set or pair: *I found an odd mitten in the drawer.* **3.** Remaining after others are paired or grouped: *They formed two teams, leaving one odd player.* **4.** Not

O

regular, planned, or expected: *We earn extra money by doing odd jobs.* **5.** Leaving a remainder of one when divided by two: *Five and nine are odd numbers.*
odd (ŏd) ◊ *adjective* **odder, oddest**

oddity *noun* Someone or something that seems unusual or strange.
odd·i·ty (ŏd′ĭ tē) ◊ *noun, plural* **oddities**

oddment *noun* Often **oddments** Something that is left over.
odd·ment (ŏd′mənt) ◊ *noun, plural* **oddments**

odds *plural noun* The likelihood that one thing will occur rather than another: *The odds are that it will rain tomorrow. The odds are that the champion will win.*
◊ *idiom* **at odds** In disagreement: *My parents and I are at odds over my allowance.*
odds (ŏdz) ◊ *plural noun*

odious *adjective* Very unpleasant and disgusting; hateful.
o·di·ous (ō′dē əs) ◊ *adjective*

odor *noun* Smell; scent: *The odor of roses was in the air.*
o·dor (ō′dər) ◊ *noun, plural* **odors**

of *preposition* **1.** Belonging to or connected with: *The walls of the room are white.* **2.** From the total or group making up: *Most of the students are here.* **3.** Made from: *We built a house of wood.* **4.** Having; with: *It is a matter of importance.* **5.** Containing: *We carried the bag of groceries home.* **6.** Named: *I visited the city of San Francisco.* **7.** Concerning; about: *We spoke of you last night.*
of (ŭv *or* ŏv) ◊ *preposition*

off *adverb* **1.** Away from a place or position: *The car drove off.* **2.** So as to be no longer on, attached, or connected: *Take your coat off.* **3.** So as to be no longer operating or functioning: *Turn the radio off.* **4.** So as to be away from work or duty: *I took the day off.*
◊ *adjective* **1.** Not operating or functioning: *The radio is off.* **2.** Not taking place; canceled: *The meeting is off.* **3.** In error: *Your estimate was off by several inches.*
◊ *preposition* So as to be no longer on or in contact with: *The book fell off the table.*
off (ôf) ◊ *adverb* ◊ *adjective* ◊ *preposition*

offend *verb* To cause hurt feelings, anger, or annoyance; insult: *Those rude remarks offended our guest.*
of·fend (ə fĕnd′) ◊ *verb* **offended, offending**

offense *noun* **1.** The act of offending or the condition of being offended: *No offense was intended by my remark.* **2.** The act of breaking the law or committing a sin: *Driving through a red light is a traffic offense.* **3.** Something that offends: *The rude remark was an offense to everyone in the room.*
of·fense (ə fĕns′) ◊ *noun, plural* **offenses**

offensive *adjective* **1.** Unpleasant to the senses; disgusting: *An offensive smell came from the swamp.* **2.** Causing hurt feelings, anger, or annoyance. **3.** Of, relating to, or designed for attacking: *Offensive teams try to score touchdowns in football.*
◊ *noun* The attitude or position of one who is attacking: *If you take the offensive, they may back down.*
of·fen·sive (ə fĕn′sĭv) ◊ *adjective* ◊ *noun, plural* **offensives**

offer *verb* **1.** To put forward to be accepted or refused: *They offered us some soup. They offered their services.* **2.** To present for consideration; propose: *The editor offered some suggestions for improving the story.* **3.** To provide; afford: *This job offers many opportunities.*
◊ *noun* **1.** The act of offering: *We appreciate the offer of help.* **2.** Something offered: *They made an offer of $65,000 for the house.*
of·fer (ô′fər) ◊ *verb* **offered, offering** ◊ *noun, plural* **offers**

office *noun* **1.** A place, as a room or series of rooms, in which the work of a business or profession is carried on. **2.** The people who work in such a place: *The office gave the boss a surprise party.* **3.** A position of authority or trust, especially one in government: *The executive has decided to run for public office.*
of·fice (ô′fĭs) ◊ *noun, plural* **offices**

officer *noun* **1.** A person who holds a position of authority or trust in a government, corporation, club, or other institution. **2.** A person

ă	pat	ĭ	pit	oi	oil	th	bath
ā	pay	ī	ride	o͝o	book	*th*	bathe
â	care	î	fierce	o͞o	boot	ə	ago, item
ä	father	ŏ	pot	ou	out		pencil
ĕ	pet	ō	go	ŭ	cut		atom
ē	be	ô	paw, for	û	fur		circus

who holds a commission in the armed forces. **3.** A member of a police force.
of·fi·cer (ô′fĭ sər) ◊ *noun, plural* **officers**

official *adjective* **1.** Of or having to do with a position of authority: *They are on official business.* **2.** Coming from the proper authority: *This is an official document.* **3.** Meeting the requirements set by authority: *Spanish is the official language of Mexico.*
◊ *noun* A person in a position of authority.
of·fi·cial (ə **fĭsh′**əl) ◊ *adjective* ◊ *noun, plural* **officials**

offshoot *noun* A shoot that branches out from the main stem of a plant.
off·shoot (**ôf′**shōōt′) ◊ *noun, plural* **offshoots**

offshore *adjective* **1.** Moving away from the shore: *An offshore breeze was blowing.* **2.** Located or taking place in waters away from shore: *They are doing offshore drilling for oil.*
◊ *adverb* **1.** In a direction away from shore: *The breeze was blowing offshore.* **2.** At a distance from shore: *We saw a huge whale a mile offshore.*
off·shore (**ôf′ shôr′**) ◊ *adjective* ◊ *adverb*

offspring *noun* The young of a person, animal, or plant: *Rabbits have many offspring.*
off·spring (**ôf′**sprĭng′) ◊ *noun, plural* **offspring**

often *adverb* Many times; frequently: *I often read before going to sleep.*
of·ten (**ô′**fən) ◊ *adverb*

ogre *noun* One of a race of man-eating giants in folklore.
o·gre (**ō′**gər) ◊ *noun, plural* **ogres**

oh *interjection* An expression used to show strong feeling, such as surprise, happiness, anger, or pain: *Oh, hush!*
oh (ō) ◊ *interjection*
‖*These sound alike:* **oh, owe**

OH The abbreviation for *Ohio* used with a Zip Code.

oil *noun* **1.** Any of a large group of greasy, usually liquid substances that burn easily and do not mix with water. Oils may come from plant, animal, or mineral sources. They are commonly used as fuel, lubricants, and food. **2. oils** Artists' paints made from pigments mixed with oil. **3.** A painting done in oils.
◊ *verb* To put oil on or in.
oil (oil) ◊ *noun, plural* **oils** ◊ *verb* **oiled, oiling**

oil slick *noun* A thin film of oil on water.
oil slick ◊ *noun, plural* **oil slicks**

oily *adjective* **1.** Of or like oil: *The bottle contained an oily liquid.* **2.** Covered or soaked with oil: *Oily rags can cause a fire.*
oil·y (**oi′**lē) ◊ *adjective* **oilier, oiliest**

ointment *noun* A thick, often greasy substance rubbed on the skin to heal, soothe, or protect it.
oint·ment (**oint′**mənt) ◊ *noun, plural* **ointments**

OK The abbreviation for *Oklahoma* used with a Zip Code.

OK *or* **O.K.** *interjection* All right: *OK, let's go!*
◊ *adjective* All right; acceptable or fine: *The plan is OK with me.*
◊ *adverb* Well; fine: *The team's doing OK.*
◊ *noun* Approval: *Get your parent's OK before we start on the trip.*
◊ *verb* To approve; agree to: *The principal OK'd the plans for a new library.*
OK *or* **O.K.** (ō **kā′**) ◊ *interjection* ◊ *adjective* ◊ *adverb* ◊ *noun, plural* **OK's** *or* **O.K.'s** ◊ *verb* **OK'd, OK'ing** *or* **O.K.'d, O.K.'ing**

Okla. An abbreviation for *Oklahoma.*

okra *noun* A tall plant with narrow, sticky seed pods that are used in soups or stews.
o·kra (**ō′**krə) ◊ *noun*

▲ **okra**

old *adjective* **1.** Having lived or been in existence for a long time: *Old people often have interesting stories to tell.* **2.** Of a certain age: *The child is ten years old.* **3.** Showing signs of age, use, or neglect: *We have replaced our old rug with a new one.* **4.** Of or belonging to a long time ago; ancient: *We still practice the old customs.* **5.** Continuing from an earlier time: *Old friendships are best.* **6.** Former: *I saw my old classmates. Who lives in your old house?*
◊ *noun* A time long ago; former times: *Knights killed dragons in tales of old.*
old (ōld) ◊ *adjective* **older, oldest** ◊ *noun*

O

SYNONYMS

old, ancient, antique, old-fashioned

That building was *old* in your grandparents' time. We studied the *ancient* civilizations of the Greeks and Romans. We have an *antique* table that has belonged to my family for years. People don't wear *old-fashioned* clothes like that anymore.
Antonym: *new*

old-fashioned *adjective* **1.** Of the style of an earlier time and no longer fashionable: *The children found some old-fashioned clothes in a trunk.* —See Synonyms at **old. 2.** Keeping to the ways or ideas of an earlier time: *We come from an old-fashioned family.*
old-fash·ioned (**ōld′ făsh′** ənd) ◊ *adjective*

Old Testament *noun* A collection of writings that make up the Jewish Bible and the first of the two parts of the Christian Bible.

old-time *adjective* Of a time in the past: *That is the wreck of an old-time whaling ship.*
old-time (**ōld′ tīm′**) ◊ *adjective*

Old World *noun* The Eastern Hemisphere; Europe, Asia, and Africa.

oleomargarine *noun* Margarine.
o·le·o·mar·ga·rine (ō′lē ō **mär′** jər ĭn) ◊ *noun, plural* **oleomargarines**

olive *noun* The small, oval fruit of an evergreen tree that grows in warm regions. Olives are eaten green or ripe as a relish or are pressed to yield olive oil.
ol·ive (**ôl′** ĭv) ◊ *noun, plural* **olives**

olive oil *noun* A yellowish oil pressed from olives. It is used for cooking, in salad dressings, and in soaps.

Olympic games *plural noun* **1.** An ancient Greek festival consisting of contests in athletics, poetry, and dancing. **2.** A modern international athletic competition held every four years in a different country.
O·lym·pic games (ō **lĭm′** pĭk) ◊ *plural noun*

▲ **Olympic games**
Opening ceremonies of the summer Olympic games

omelet *noun* A dish made of beaten eggs that are cooked and folded over.
om·e·let (**ŏm′** ə lĭt *or* **ŏm′** lĭt) ◊ *noun, plural* **omelets**

omen *noun* Something that is thought to be a sign of a good or bad event to come.
o·men (**ō′** mən) ◊ *noun, plural* **omens**

omit *verb* To leave out; not include: *I decided to omit sweets from my meals.*
o·mit (ō **mĭt′**) ◊ *verb* **omitted, omitting**

on *preposition* **1.** Supported by and touching: *The dishes are on the table.* **2.** Located at, near, or along: *Our city is on a river.* **3.** In contact with: *Hang the picture on the wall.* **4.** At the time of; during: *We leave on Tues-*

ă	pat	ĭ	pit	oi	**oil**	th	ba**th**
ā	pay	ī	ride	ŏŏ	**book**	*th*	ba**the**
â	care	î	fierce	ōō	**boot**	ə	ago, item
ä	father	ŏ	pot	ou	**out**		pencil
ĕ	pet	ō	go	ŭ	**cut**		atom
ē	be	ô	paw, for	û	**fur**		circus

day. **5.** In the state, condition, or process of: *The house was on fire.* **6.** About: *I bought a new book on dinosaurs.*
◊ *adverb* **1.** In or into contact with something: *Put the coffee on.* **2.** In or into action or operation: *Turn the television on.*
◊ *adjective* **1.** In use or operation: *The lights are on.* **2.** Taking place: *The game was on when we arrived.* **3.** Planned: *We have nothing on for this weekend.*
◊ *idiom* **on and on** Without stopping: *The music went on and on.*
on (ŏn) ◊ *preposition* ◊ *adverb* ◊ *adjective*

once *adverb* **1.** One time only: *We feed our dog once a day.* **2.** At a time in the past; formerly: *I was once a child, too.*
◊ *noun* One single time: *Let me go there just this once.*
◊ *conjunction* As soon as; when: *Once they leave, we can clean up.*
◊ *idiom* **at once 1.** At the same time: *Everyone was talking at once.* **2.** Immediately: *We must leave at once.*
once (wŭns) ◊ *adverb* ◊ *noun* ◊ *conjunction*

oncoming *adjective* Coming nearer: *We got ready for the oncoming winter.*
on·com·ing (ŏn′kŭm′ĭng) ◊ *adjective*

one *noun* **1.** The number that indicates a single unit. A number that is multiplied by one will not change. **2.** A single person or thing.
◊ *adjective* **1.** Being a single person or thing. **2.** Some: *One day I plan to go to India.*
◊ *pronoun* **1.** A certain person or thing: *My hat didn't fit so I got a new one.* **2.** Any person: *Where can one buy tickets for the game?*
one (wŭn) ◊ *noun, plural* **ones** ◊ *adjective* ◊ *pronoun, plural* **ones**
‖*These sound alike:* **one, won**

oneself *pronoun* One's own self: *One should try to have confidence in oneself.*
one·self (wŭn **sĕlf′**) ◊ *pronoun*

one-sided *adjective* **1.** Favoring one side or group; partial: *They gave a one-sided account of the argument.* **2.** Not equal or even: *With all the strong players on one team, it was a one-sided contest.*
one-sid·ed (**wŭn′ sī′**dĭd) ◊ *adjective*

one-way *adjective* Moving or allowing movement in one direction only: *This is a one-way street.*
one-way (**wŭn′ wā′**) ◊ *adjective*

onion *noun* A plant with an edible bulb that is widely grown as a vegetable. The bulb has a strong smell and a sharp taste.
on·ion (**ŭn′** yən) ◊ *noun, plural* **onions**

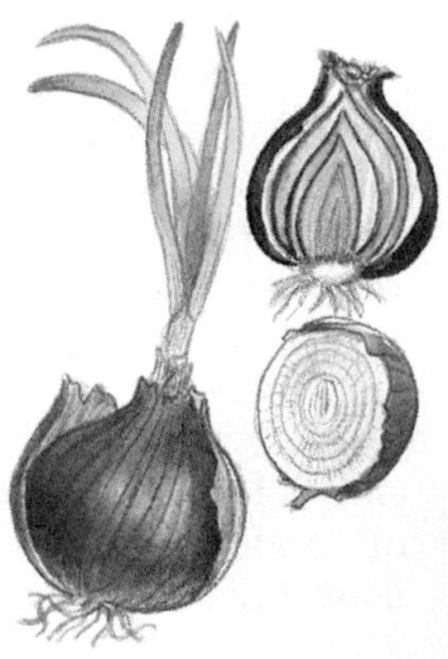

▲ **onion**

onlooker *noun* A person who watches or looks on; spectator.
on·look·er (**ŏn′** lŏŏk′ər) ◊ *noun, plural* **onlookers**

only *adjective* **1.** One and no more: *It was our only reason for going.* **2.** Best or most suitable of all: *You are my only friend.*
◊ *adverb* **1.** And no one else; and nothing more: *I'm only following the rules.* **2.** In the end; as a result: *If you don't prepare for the test, you will only fail again.* **3.** As recently as: *I saw them only yesterday.*
on·ly (**ōn′** lē) ◊ *adjective* ◊ *adverb*

onset *noun* **1.** A beginning; start: *A high fever often accompanies the onset of flu.* **2.** An attack: *The onset of the hurricane caught us by surprise.*
on·set (**ŏn′** sĕt′) ◊ *noun, plural* **onsets**

onshore *adjective* Toward or on the shore: *The onshore breeze lowered the temperature.*
◊ *adverb* In a direction toward the shore: *The wind shifted onshore.*
on·shore (**ŏn′ shôr′**) ◊ *adjective* ◊ *adverb*

Ont. The abbreviation for *Ontario,* Canada.

onto *preposition* To a position on or upon: *We climbed onto the train.*
on·to (**ŏn′** tōō′) ◊ *preposition*

onward *adverb* Toward a position that is ahead in space or time; forward: *The explorers plodded onward through the mountains.*
◊ *adjective* Directed toward a position that is ahead in space or time: *They continued their onward march.*
on·ward (**ŏn′** wərd) ◊ *adverb* ◊ *adjective*

onwards *adverb* Onward.
on·wards (**ŏn′** wərdz) ◊ *adverb*

ooze *verb* To flow or leak out slowly: *Mud oozed between my toes.*
ooze (ōōz) ◊ *verb* **oozed, oozing**

O

opal *noun* A mineral of many colors, often used as a gem.
o·pal (ō′pəl) ◊ *noun, plural* **opals**

opaque *adjective* Not capable of letting light pass through: *Fog is opaque.*
o·paque (ō **pāk′**) ◊ *adjective*

▲ **opal**

open *adjective* **1.** Not shut, closed, fastened, or sealed: *An open book lay on the desk. The door is open.* **2.** Not covered or protected; exposed: *We cooked over an open fire.* **3.** Allowing free passage or view: *They sailed the open seas.* **4.** Able to be used, entered, or attended by all: *The city council holds open meetings.* **5.** Not filled or decided: *The job is still open.* **6.** Ready for business: *The stores are open.* **7.** Spread out: *The umbrella is open.* **8.** Able to take in new ideas; objective: *You should keep an open mind.* **9.** Not hidden or secret.
◊ *verb* **1.** To make or become no longer shut, closed, fastened, or sealed: *The door opened suddenly.* **2.** To spread apart; unfold: *The buds will open in the spring.* **3.** To begin: *Read the sentence that opens the chapter.* **4.** To make or become available for use: *The stores open at nine.*
◊ *noun* **1.** An open or clear space: *The deer stepped into the open.* **2.** The outdoors: *Shepherds are used to living in the open.*
o·pen (ō′pən) ◊ *adjective* ◊ *verb* **opened, opening** ◊ *noun*

opener *noun* **1.** A device that is used to cut open cans or pry off bottle caps. **2.** The first in a series.
o·pen·er (ō′pə nər) ◊ *noun, plural* **openers**

opening *noun* **1.** The act of becoming open or being made to open: *The railroads cleared the way for the opening of the West.* **2.** An open space or clearing. **3.** The beginning of something: *The opening of the story is set in Japan.* **4.** The first occasion of something, especially of a play. **5.** An unfilled position; vacancy: *There are two openings on the team.*
o·pen·ing (ō′pə nĭng) ◊ *noun, plural* **openings**

opera *noun* A play in which most of the words are sung to music and an orchestra accompanies the singing.
op·er·a (**ŏp′**ər ə) ◊ *noun, plural* **operas**

operate *verb* **1.** To work or run: *This machine operates well.* **2.** To control the running or functioning of something: *The students are learning how to operate a computer.* **3.** To perform surgery.
op·er·ate (**ŏp′**ə rāt′) ◊ *verb* **operated, operating**

operation *noun* **1.** The act, process, or way of operating: *We are learning the operation of a computer.* **2.** The condition of being able to operate: *This machine is no longer in operation.* **3.** A procedure that treats disorders of the body by surgery.
op·er·a·tion (ŏp′ə **rā′**shən) ◊ *noun, plural* **operations**

operator *noun* **1.** A person who operates a machine or other device: *Ask the telephone operator for the number.* **2.** A person who owns or runs something, such as a business.
op·er·a·tor (**ŏp′**ə rā′tər) ◊ *noun, plural* **operators**

operetta *noun* A short, amusing musical work similar to an opera but containing some spoken parts.
op·er·et·ta (ŏp′ə **rĕt′**ə) ◊ *noun, plural* **operettas**

opinion *noun* **1.** A belief based on what one thinks or feels although not based on actual facts: *It is my opinion that the winters are getting colder.* **2.** A judgment based on special knowledge and given by an expert: *We got our lawyer's opinion and bought the house.*
o·pin·ion (ə **pĭn′**yən) ◊ *noun, plural* **opinions**

opossum *noun* A furry animal that lives mostly in trees and carries its young in a pouch.
o·pos·sum (ə **pŏs′**əm) ◊ *noun, plural* **opossums**

ă	pat	ĭ	pit	oi	**oi**l	th	ba**th**
ā	pay	ī	ride	ŏŏ	b**oo**k	*th*	ba**the**
â	care	î	fierce	ōō	b**oo**t	ə	ago, item
ä	father	ŏ	pot	ou	**ou**t		pencil
ĕ	pet	ō	go	ŭ	cut		atom
ē	be	ô	paw, for	û	fur		circus

HISTORY • opossum

Opossum comes from a Native American name for this animal. The early settlers often adopted such names for the new animals they encountered in America. Other examples include **chipmunk** and **skunk.**

SYNONYMS

opposite, contradictory, contrary

We live on *opposite* sides of the street. I can't decide which of these two *contradictory* opinions is correct. The two countries have *contrary* ideas about who should control the territory.

▲ **opossum**

opponent *noun* A person who is against another in a fight, contest, or debate.
op·po·nent (ə **pō′** nənt) ◊ *noun, plural* **opponents**

opportunity *noun* **1.** A favorable time or occasion for doing something: *I hope to have the opportunity to go to camp.* **2.** A good chance, as to advance oneself: *That summer job offers many opportunities.*
op·por·tu·ni·ty (ŏp′ər **to͞o′** nĭ tē *or* ŏp′ər-**tyo͞o′** nĭ tē) ◊ *noun, plural* **opportunities**

oppose *verb* **1.** To be or fight against; resist: *They opposed the plan to raise taxes.* **2.** To be or place in contrast: *Love is opposed to hate.*
op·pose (ə **pōz′**) ◊ *verb* **opposed, opposing**

opposite *adjective* **1.** Placed or located directly across from something else or from each other: *We sat on opposite sides of the room.* **2.** Moving or facing away from each other: *They went off in opposite directions.* **3.** Completely different from another: *I came to the opposite conclusion.*
◊ *noun* Someone or something that is completely different from another.
op·po·site (**ŏp′** ə zĭt) ◊ *adjective* ◊ *noun, plural* **opposites**

opposition *noun* The act or condition of opposing or being against: *The citizens joined in opposition to the new tax program.*
op·po·si·tion (ŏp′ə **zĭsh′** ən) ◊ *noun*

optical *adjective* **1.** Of or having to do with sight: *A mirage in the desert is an optical illusion.* **2.** Designed to assist sight: *Microscopes and telescopes are optical instruments.*
op·ti·cal (**ŏp′** tĭ kəl) ◊ *adjective*

optimistic *adjective* Tending to take a hopeful or cheerful view of things: *I am optimistic about our chances for success.*
op·ti·mis·tic (ŏp′tə **mĭs′** tĭk) ◊ *adjective*

optional *adjective* Not required: *Attendance at study hall is optional.*
op·tion·al (**ŏp′** shə nəl) ◊ *adjective*

optometrist *noun* A person who examines eyes and prescribes eyeglasses.
op·tom·e·trist (ŏp **tŏm′** ĭ trĭst) ◊ *noun, plural* **optometrists**

or *conjunction* Used between words or groups of words to indicate a choice: *I don't know whether to laugh or cry.*
or (ôr) ◊ *conjunction*
‖*These sound alike:* **or, oar, ore**

OR The abbreviation for *Oregon* used with a Zip Code.

oral *adjective* **1.** Not written; spoken: *Each student gave an oral book report.* **2.** Of, used in, or taken through the mouth: *The nurse checked for fever with an oral thermometer.*
o·ral (**ôr′** əl) ◊ *adjective*

orange *noun* **1.** A round, juicy fruit with a reddish-yellow rind. Oranges grow in warm regions on evergreen trees that have fragrant white flowers. **2.** A reddish yellow color.
or·ange (**ôr′** ĭnj) ◊ *noun, plural* **oranges**

orangeade ◊ *noun* A drink made of orange juice, sugar, and water.
or·ange·ade (ôr′ĭn **jād′**) ◊ *noun, plural* **orangeades**

O

orangutan *noun* A large ape that lives in trees on islands in Southeast Asia. Orangutans have long arms and shaggy reddish-brown hair.
o·rang·u·tan (ō **răng′** ə tăn′) ◊ *noun, plural* **orangutans**

▲ **orangutan**

orator *noun* A skilled public speaker.
or·a·tor (**ôr′** ə tər) ◊ *noun, plural* **orators**

orbit *noun* The path of a heavenly body or manmade satellite as it circles around another body. The earth is in orbit around the sun. ◊ *verb* **1.** To put into orbit: *They orbited a satellite around the earth.* **2.** To move in an orbit around: *The moon orbits the earth.*
or·bit (**ôr′** bĭt) ◊ *noun, plural* **orbits** ◊ *verb* **orbited, orbiting**

orchard *noun* A piece of land where fruit trees are grown.
or·chard (**ôr′** chərd) ◊ *noun, plural* **orchards**

orchestra *noun* **1.** A usually large group of musicians who play together on various instruments. **2.** The main floor of a theater.
or·ches·tra (**ôr′** kĭ strə) ◊ *noun, plural* **orchestras**

ă	pat	ĭ	pit	oi	oil	th	bath
ā	pay	ī	ride	ŏŏ	book	*th*	bathe
â	care	î	fierce	ōō	boot	ə	ago, item
ä	father	ŏ	pot	ou	out		pencil
ĕ	pet	ō	go	ŭ	cut		atom
ē	be	ô	paw, for	û	fur		circus

▲ **orchestra**

orchid *noun* **1.** A plant with often large and brightly colored flowers. **2.** A light purple color.
or·chid (**ôr′** kĭd) ◊ *noun, plural* **orchids**

ordain *verb* **1.** To install as a minister, priest, or rabbi by a special ceremony. **2.** To decide by law; decree: *The Constitution ordains freedom of speech.*
or·dain (ôr **dān′**) ◊ *verb* **ordained, ordaining**

ordeal *noun* A very difficult or painful experience or test.
or·deal (ôr **dēl′**) ◊ *noun, plural* **ordeals**

order *noun* **1.** A condition in which everything is as it should be: *I always keep my room in order.* **2.** An arrangement of things one after another: *List the names in alphabetical order.* **3.** A condition in which rules, laws, or customs are observed: *The sheriffs brought law and order to the frontier.* **4.** A command or rule: *Soldiers are expected to follow orders.* **5.** A request for items to be supplied: *The teachers placed an order for 20 arithmetic books.* **6.** A portion of food in a restaurant: *I requested an extra order of salad.* **7.** A group of people who live under the same religious rules or belong to the same organization: *Monks and nuns are members of orders.* **8.** A group of animals or plants that are similar in many ways. Rodents such as rats, mice, hamsters, and beavers belong to the same order.
◊ *verb* **1.** To give an order or instruction to:

The teacher ordered the class to open their books. —See Synonyms at **command. 2.** To place an order for: *We ordered a new washing machine.* **3.** To arrange things one after another: *We ordered the books on the shelf according to the authors' names.*
◊ *idioms* **in order to** For the purpose of; so as to be able to: *We stayed on after class in order to work on our project.* **out of order** Not working properly or at all: *Our telephone is out of order.*
or·der (ôr′ dər) ◊ *noun, plural* **orders** ◊ *verb* **ordered, ordering**

orderly *adjective* **1.** Arranged in a neat and tidy way: *Let's all help to keep the kitchen orderly.* **2.** Not causing trouble; well-behaved: *The children lined up in an orderly manner and marched out of the room.*
◊ *noun* **1.** A hospital worker who does cleaning and other general tasks. **2.** A soldier assigned to an officer to carry messages or perform other duties.
or·der·ly (ôr′ dər lē) ◊ *adjective* ◊ *noun, plural* **orderlies**

ordinal number *noun* A number, as first or tenth, showing the position of an element in a series.
or·di·nal number (ôr′ dn əl) ◊ *noun, plural* **ordinal numbers**

ordinance *noun* A regulation or law, especially of a town or city.
or·di·nance (ôr′ dn əns) ◊ *noun, plural* **ordinances**

ordinarily *adverb* As a rule; usually: *I ordinarily leave for school at seven o'clock.*
or·di·nar·i·ly (ôr′dn **âr′** ə lē) ◊ *adverb*

ordinary *adjective* **1.** Commonly met with; usual: *After the flood the river returned to its ordinary course.* —See Synonyms at **common. 2.** Not distinguished in any way; average: *This bread you baked is much tastier than ordinary bread.*
or·di·nar·y (ôr′ dn ĕr′ē) ◊ *adjective*

ore *noun* A mineral from which a valuable substance, such as gold, can be mined.
ore (ôr) ◊ *noun, plural* **ores**
‖*These sound alike:* **ore, oar, or**

Ore. *or* **Oreg.** Abbreviations for *Oregon.*

organ *noun* **1.** A musical instrument with one or more keyboards that control the flow of air to pipes. The pipes sound tones when supplied with air. **2.** A part of an animal or plant that is adapted to perform a certain function: *The stomach is an organ of digestion.*
or·gan (ôr′ gən) ◊ *noun, plural* **organs**

▲ **organ**

organic *adjective* **1.** Of or relating to an organ of a living thing. **2.** Of, relating to, or obtained from living things: *Decaying leaves and animal manure are organic fertilizers.*
or·gan·ic (ôr **găn′** ĭk) ◊ *adjective*

organism *noun* A living individual; plant or animal: *We studied sea organisms this year.*
or·gan·ism (ôr′ gə nĭz′əm) ◊ *noun, plural* **organisms**

organization *noun* **1.** The act or process of organizing: *We began with the organization of rides to the fair for all of the children.* **2.** The condition of being organized: *A busy classroom needs a high degree of organization.* **3.** The way in which something is organized: *Our class is studying the organization of the American government.* **4.** A number of persons united for a certain purpose: *My parents are active in a political organization.*
or·gan·i·za·tion (ôr′gə nĭ **zā′** shən) ◊ *noun, plural* **organizations**

organize *verb* **1.** To put together or arrange in an orderly way: *I tried to organize my thoughts before speaking.* **2.** To form as or into a group, especially in order to work together for a certain purpose.
or·gan·ize (ôr′ gə nīz′) ◊ *verb* **organized, organizing**

O

Orient *noun* The countries of Asia, especially eastern Asia. China, Japan, and Korea are in the Orient.
O·ri·ent (ôr′ē ənt) ◊ *noun*

origami *noun* The Japanese art of folding paper into complicated designs and shapes.
o·ri·ga·mi (ôr′i **gä′** mē) ◊ *noun*

origin *noun* **1.** The beginning or rise of something: *Our teacher told us about the origin of fire departments in the United States.* **2.** The original source of something: *What was the origin of that argument?* **3.** Line of descent: *My parents are of Hispanic origin.*
or·i·gin (ôr′ə jĭn) ◊ *noun, plural* **origins**

original *adjective* **1.** Of, relating to, or existing from the origin; first: *The painting still has its original gold frame.* **2.** Fresh and newly created; not copied or based on something else: *I wrote an original poem.* —See Synonyms at **new. 3.** Capable of thinking up new ideas: *Inventors are original thinkers.*
◊ *noun* A thing from which copies are made: *I have a photograph of the drawing; the original is in a museum.*
o·rig·i·nal (ə **rĭj′** ə nəl) ◊ *adjective* ◊ *noun, plural* **originals**

originality *noun* The quality or condition of being original: *The clay figure is a work of great originality.*
o·rig·i·nal·i·ty (ə rĭj′ə **năl′** ĭ tē) ◊ *noun*

originally *adverb* **1.** In the beginning; at first: *The house was originally painted dark red.* **2.** With reference to origin: *We are originally Dutch but have lived here for years.*
o·rig·i·nal·ly (ə **rĭj′** ə nə lē) ◊ *adverb*

originate *verb* To bring or come into being: *That game originated at my school.*
o·rig·i·nate (ə **rĭj′** ə nāt′) ◊ *verb* **originated, originating**

oriole *noun* A songbird that has black and yellow or black and orange feathers. Orioles often build hanging nests.
o·ri·ole (ôr′ē ōl′) ◊ *noun, plural* **orioles**

ă	pat	ĭ	pit	oi	**oi**l	th	ba**th**
ā	pay	ī	ride	ŏŏ	b**oo**k	*th*	ba**th**e
â	care	î	fierce	ōō	b**oo**t	ə	**a**go, it**e**m
ä	father	ŏ	pot	ou	**ou**t		penc**i**l
ĕ	pet	ō	go	ŭ	c**u**t		at**o**m
ē	be	ô	paw, for	û	f**u**r		circ**u**s

ornament *noun* Something that decorates or makes more beautiful.
◊ *verb* To supply with something beautiful or decorative: *Flowers ornamented the room.*
or·na·ment ◊ *noun* (ôr′ nə mənt), *plural* **ornaments** ◊ *verb* (ôr′ nə mĕnt′) **ornamented, ornamenting**

ornamental *adjective* Used as an ornament.
or·na·men·tal (ôr′nə **mĕn′** tl) ◊ *adjective*

orphan *noun* A child whose parents are dead.
◊ *verb* To make an orphan of: *The fire orphaned the children.*
or·phan (ôr′ fən) ◊ *noun, plural* **orphans**
◊ *verb* **orphaned, orphaning**

orphanage *noun* An institution or home for the care of orphans.
or·phan·age (ôr′ fə nĭj) ◊ *noun, plural* **orphanages**

orthodontist *noun* A dentist who specializes in straightening teeth.
or·tho·don·tist (ôr′thə **dŏn′** tĭst) ◊ *noun, plural* **orthodontists**

orthodox *adjective* **1.** Of, relating to, or following accepted or established beliefs or doctrines: *My political views are very orthodox.* **2.** Of, relating to, or in accordance with what is considered proper or usual; conventional.
or·tho·dox (ôr′ thə dŏks′) ◊ *adjective*

ostrich *noun* A large African bird that cannot fly but can run very fast. Ostriches have long, soft plumes.
os·trich (ôs′ trĭch) ◊ *noun, plural* **ostriches**

▲ **ostrich**

other *adjective* **1.** Being the remaining one or ones: *Let me have my other shoe. My other friends are away on vacation.* **2.** Different: *Call me some other time.* **3.** Additional, extra: *I have no other clothes to wear.*
◊*pronoun* A different or additional person or thing: *One is here and the other is there.*
oth·er (ŭ*th*′ər) ◊*adjective* ◊*pronoun, plural* **others**

otherwise *adverb* **1.** In another way; differently: *They could not behave otherwise.* **2.** Under other circumstances: *I studied hard, because otherwise I might have failed the test.* **3.** In other respects: *It was windy but an otherwise beautiful day.*
oth·er·wise (ŭ*th*′ər wīz′) ◊*adverb*

otter *noun* An animal with webbed feet that lives in or near water. Otters have thick, dark-brown fur and are good swimmers.
ot·ter (ŏt′ər) ◊*noun, plural* **otters**

▲ **otter**

ouch *interjection* An expression that is used to show pain: *Ouch! I cut my finger.*
ouch (ouch) ◊*interjection*

ought *auxiliary verb* Used to show: **1.** Obligation or duty: *We ought to try to help them.* **2.** What is wise: *The doctor said I ought to get plenty of rest.* **3.** What is expected or likely: *Dinner ought to be ready by this time.*
ought (ôt) ◊*auxiliary verb*

ounce *noun* A unit of weight and mass equal to 1/16 pound.
ounce (ouns) ◊*noun, plural* **ounces**

our *adjective* Relating or belonging to us: *Our car is being repaired.*
our (our) ◊*adjective*
‖*These sound alike:* **our, hour**

ours *pronoun* The one or ones that belong to us: *They are friends of ours.*
ours (ourz) ◊*pronoun*

ourselves *pronoun* Our own selves: *Let's keep our plans to ourselves.*
our·selves (our sĕlvz′) ◊*pronoun*

–ous The suffix *–ous* forms adjectives and means "full of" or "having the qualities of." If I am *joyous,* I am full of joy. If a substance is *poisonous,* it has the qualities of poison.

VOCABULARY BUILDER • –ous

Many words that are formed with **–ous** are not entries in this dictionary. But you can figure out what these words mean by looking up the meanings of the root words and the suffix. For example:
gelatinous = having the qualities of gelatin
vaporous = full of vapor

oust *verb* To force out; eject: *They ousted the dictator from office.*
oust (oust) ◊*verb* **ousted, ousting**

out *adverb* **1.** Away from the inside or center: *I went out for fresh air. The troops spread out.* **2.** Away from work, home, or the usual place: *They must have stepped out for a minute.* **3.** So as to be no longer available or no longer active: *The fire finally went out.* **4.** Into view: *The stars came out.* **5.** So as to be heard; aloud: *They called out to me.*
◊*adjective* **1.** Being outside or away: *You're always out when I call.* **2.** No longer working or being used: *The bridge is out because of the flood.* **3.** Not allowed to continue to bat or run in baseball.
◊*preposition* Forth from; through: *I walked out the door.*
◊*noun* A play that causes a baseball batter or base runner to be out.
out (out) ◊*adverb* ◊*adjective* ◊*preposition* ◊*noun, plural* **outs**

out– The prefix *out–* means "outward," "forth," or "away." When someone has an *outburst* of laughter, that person's laughter bursts forth from inside. The prefix *out–* also means "to do better than or go beyond." To *outdo* someone in a sport is to do better in a sport than the other person.

O

VOCABULARY BUILDER • out–

Many words that are formed with **out–** are not entries in this dictionary. But you can figure out what these words mean by looking up the meanings of the root words and the prefix. For example:
outbargain = to do better than someone else in bargaining
outflow = the act of flowing out

outboard motor *noun* A gasoline engine with a propeller that can be attached to the stern of a small boat.
out·board motor (**out′**bôrd′) ◊ *noun, plural* **outboard motors**

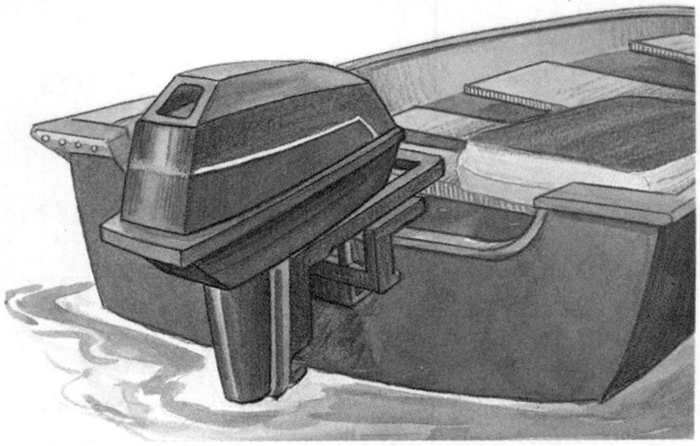

▲ **outboard motor**

outbound *adjective* Outward bound; headed away: *I took the outbound train.*
out·bound (**out′**bound′) ◊ *adjective*

outbreak *noun* A sudden breaking out: *We had an outbreak of flu at our school.*
out·break (**out′**brāk′) ◊ *noun, plural* **outbreaks**

outburst *noun* A sudden display or expression, as of emotion: *I was a little surprised at the audience's outburst of laughter.*
out·burst (**out′**bûrst′) ◊ *noun, plural* **outbursts**

ă	pat	ĭ	pit	oi	oil	th	bath
ā	pay	ī	ride	o͝o	book	*th*	bathe
â	care	î	fierce	o͞o	boot	ə	ago, item
ä	father	ŏ	pot	ou	out		pencil
ĕ	pet	ō	go	ŭ	cut		atom
ē	be	ô	paw, for	û	fur		circus

outcome *noun* Something that happens as a result: *The outcome of the class election disappointed some of us.*
out·come (**out′**kŭm′) ◊ *noun, plural* **outcomes**

outcry *noun* **1.** A loud cry. **2.** A strong protest: *There was a loud public outcry over the rise in gasoline prices.*
out·cry (**out′**krī′) ◊ *noun, plural* **outcries**

outdated *adjective* No longer used or useful; out-of-date.
out·dat·ed (out **dā′**tĭd) ◊ *adjective*

outdid *verb* Past tense of **outdo.**
out·did (out **dĭd′**) ◊ *verb*

outdo *verb* To do better than; excel.
out·do (out **do͞o′**) ◊ *verb* **outdid, outdone, outdoing**

outdone *verb* Past participle of **outdo.**
out·done (out **dŭn′**) ◊ *verb*

outdoor *adjective* Being, used, or done outdoors: *Football is an outdoor sport.*
out·door (**out′**dôr′) ◊ *adjective*

outdoors *adverb* In or into the open air; outside: *In summer we often eat outdoors.*
◊ *noun* **1.** An area away from where people live. **2.** The open air.
out·doors (out **dôrz′**) ◊ *adverb* ◊ *noun*

outer *adjective* Located on the outside; external: *A coat is an outer garment.*
out·er (**ou′**tər) ◊ *adjective*

outer space *noun* The space beyond the earth's atmosphere.

outfield *noun* The playing area that extends outward from a baseball diamond and is divided into right, center, and left fields.
out·field (**out′**fēld′) ◊ *noun, plural* **outfields**

outfit *noun* **1.** The equipment for a certain activity or purpose: *I bought a hiking outfit.* **2.** A set of clothes and accessories that go together: *You are wearing a nice outfit.* **3.** A group of people who form a unit, as for working together; association.
◊ *verb* To provide with an outfit; equip.
out·fit (**out′**fĭt′) ◊ *noun, plural* **outfits** ◊ *verb* **outfitted, outfitting**

outgoing *adjective* **1.** Going out; leaving: *I have to catch an outgoing train at three o'clock.* **2.** Friendly; sociable: *Your friend has an outgoing personality.*
out·go·ing (**out′**gō′ĭng) ◊ *adjective*

outing *noun* An often short outdoor trip taken for pleasure: *We enjoy outings in the country on Sundays.*
out·ing (ou′tĭng) ◊ *noun, plural* **outings**

outlaw *noun* A person who acts against the law; criminal.
◊ *verb* To make illegal.
out·law (out′lô′) ◊ *noun, plural* **outlaws**
◊ *verb* **outlawed, outlawing**

outlet *noun* **1.** A passage or opening for letting something out: *The river has no outlet to the sea.* **2.** A device, especially one mounted in a wall, that is connected to a supply of electric power. An outlet is equipped with a socket for a plug.
out·let (out′lĕt′) ◊ *noun, plural* **outlets**

outline *noun* **1.** A line that forms the outer edge, limit, or boundary of something and shows its shape: *We saw the outline of the skyscraper against the twilight sky.* **2.** A picture or drawing that consists only of the outline of something: *The teacher told me to trace an outline of California from the map.* **3.** A short description or account; summary: *I handed in an outline of my book report.*
◊ *verb* **1.** To draw the outline of. **2.** To prepare or give an outline of; summarize: *I outlined our plans for the camping trip.*
out·line (out′līn′) ◊ *noun, plural* **outlines**
◊ *verb* **outlined, outlining**

outlook *noun* **1.** A way of looking at things; attitude: *My friend's outlook on life is happy.* **2.** The situation that seems likely to be ahead: *The outlook for tomorrow's weather is gloomy.*
out·look (out′lo͝ok′) ◊ *noun, plural* **outlooks**

outlying *adjective* Being at a distance from a center: *We live in the outlying suburbs.*
out·ly·ing (out′lī′ĭng) ◊ *adjective*

out-of-date *adjective* Outdated.
out-of-date (out′əv **dāt′**) ◊ *adjective*

outpost *noun* **1.** A soldier or group of soldiers stationed away from a camp or main body of troops to warn of or stop a surprise attack. **2.** The place where an outpost is stationed.
out·post (out′pōst′) ◊ *noun, plural* **outposts**

output *noun* **1.** An amount produced: *The output of the mine is less this month than last.* **2.** Information processed and printed out by a computer.
out·put (out′po͝ot′) ◊ *noun, plural* **outputs**

outrage *noun* Anger caused by a violent, wicked, or offensive act.
◊ *verb* To fill with anger or resentment.
out·rage (out′rāj′) ◊ *noun* ◊ *verb* **outraged, outraging**

outrigger *noun* A long float attached parallel to a canoe by means of a framework. It prevents the canoe from capsizing.
out·rig·ger (out′rĭg′ər) ◊ *noun, plural* **outriggers**

▲ **outrigger**

outright *adjective* Without conditions or restrictions; complete: *They gave us an outright refusal*
◊ *adverb* **1.** Completely: *I accepted the offer outright.* **2.** Without restraint: *I decided to tell them the news outright.*
out·right (out′rīt′) ◊ *adjective* ◊ *adverb*

outside *noun* An outer surface, side, or part; exterior: *I wrote my friend's name on the outside of the envelope.*
◊ *adjective* Of, relating to, or located on the outside: *We came in through the outside door.*
◊ *adverb* On or to the outside: *The children went outside to play.*
◊ *preposition* On or to the outside of: *I put up a thermometer outside my window.*
out·side (out **sīd′**) ◊ *noun, plural* **outsides**
◊ *adjective* ◊ *adverb* ◊ *preposition*

outskirts *plural noun* The areas away from a central district: *They built a house on the outskirts of town.*
out·skirts (out′skûrts′) ◊ *plural noun*

O

outspoken *adjective* Not speaking or spoken with reserve; frank and honest: *You are too outspoken about your political views.*
out·spo·ken (out **spō′**kən) ◊ *adjective*

outstanding *adjective* **1.** Standing out from others, especially because of superiority: *My cousin is one of the outstanding musicians in the school band.* **2.** Not paid or settled: *Please pay your outstanding debts.*
out·stand·ing (out **stăn′**dĭng) ◊ *adjective*

outward *adverb* Away from a center: *The screen door opens outward.*
◊ *adjective* **1.** Moving or directed toward the outside: *The outward trip from the city was slow.* **2.** Visible on the surface: *I gave no outward sign that I had seen them.*
out·ward (**out′**wərd) ◊ *adverb* ◊ *adjective*

outwards *adverb* Outward.
out·wards (**out′**wərdz) ◊ *adverb*

outweigh *verb* **1.** To weigh more than. **2.** To be of greater importance than.
out·weigh (out **wā′**) ◊ *verb* **outweighed, outweighing**

outwit *verb* To get the better of with cunning or cleverness.
out·wit (out **wĭt′**) ◊ *verb* **outwitted, outwitting**

oval *adjective* Shaped like an egg or ellipse.
◊ *noun* An oval figure, form, or structure.
o·val (**ō′**vəl) ◊ *adjective* ◊ *noun, plural* **ovals**

***HISTORY* • oval**

The word **oval**, which means "egg-shaped," goes back to the Latin word for "egg."

ovary *noun* **1.** A part of a female animal in which egg cells are produced. **2.** A plant part in which seeds are formed.
o·va·ry (**ō′**və rē) ◊ *noun, plural* **ovaries**

oven *noun* An enclosed chamber, as in a stove, used for baking, heating, or drying.
ov·en (**ŭv′**ən) ◊ *noun, plural* **ovens**

ă	pat	ĭ	pit	oi	**oi**l	th	ba**th**
ā	pay	ī	ride	o͝o	b**oo**k	*th*	ba**th**e
â	care	î	fierce	o͞o	b**oo**t	ə	ago, item
ä	father	ŏ	pot	ou	**ou**t		pencil
ĕ	pet	ō	go	ŭ	cut		atom
ē	be	ô	paw, for	û	fur		circus

over *preposition* **1.** Higher than; above: *A sign was hanging over the door.* **2.** From one side to the other side of; across: *I jumped over the fence.* **3.** Across or along the surface of; upon: *I spilled milk all over the floor.*
◊ *adverb* **1.** Across a space between two points: *Come over after school.* **2.** Across the edge or brim: *The juice spilled over.* **3.** From an upright position: *The lamp fell over.* **4.** To a position with the underside up: *Turn the book over.* **5.** One more time; again: *We had to do our homework over.*
◊ *adjective* Being at an end; finished: *The movie is over.*
o·ver (**ō′**vər) ◊ *preposition* ◊ *adverb* ◊ *adjective*

over– The prefix *over–* means "too" or "too much." If you *overdo* it when you exercise, you exercise too much. The prefix *over–* also means "above" or "on top of." When a plane passes *overhead,* it passes above your head. The prefix *over–* also means "worn above or over." *Overshoes* are worn over your shoes.

***VOCABULARY BUILDER* • over–**

Many words that are formed with **over–** are not entries in this dictionary. But you can figure out what these words mean by looking up the meanings of the root words and the prefix. For example:
overcrowded = too crowded
overpass = to pass over
overskirt = a skirt worn over the main skirt

overalls *plural noun* Loose trousers with a top part covering the chest. Overalls are often worn over other clothes to protect them.
o·ver·alls (**ō′**vər ôlz′) ◊ *plural noun*

overboard *adverb* Over the side of a boat: *The sailor fell overboard.*
o·ver·board (**ō′**vər bôrd′) ◊ *adverb*

overcame *verb* Past tense of **overcome.**
o·ver·came (ō′vər **kām′**) ◊ *verb*

overcast *adjective* Covered with clouds.
o·ver·cast (**ō′**vər kăst′) ◊ *adjective*

overcoat *noun* A heavy coat worn over ordinary clothing, especially in cold weather.
o·ver·coat (**ō′**vər kōt′) ◊ *noun, plural* **overcoats**

overcome *verb* **1.** To get the better of; conquer: *I overcame my fear of diving.* **2.** To affect deeply, as with emotion; overpower.
o·ver·come (ō′vər **kŭm′**) ◊ *verb* **overcame, overcome, overcoming**

overdid *verb* Past tense of **overdo.**
o·ver·did (ō′vər **dĭd′**) ◊ *verb*

overdo *verb* **1.** To do too much: *Don't overdo the exercise.* **2.** To carry too far; exaggerate: *They overdid the jokes.*
o·ver·do (ō′vər **do͞o′**) ◊ *verb* **overdid, overdone, overdoing**

overdone *verb* Past participle of **overdo.**
o·ver·done (ō′vər **dŭn′**) ◊ *verb*

overdose *noun* Too large a dose, as of a medicine.
o·ver·dose (**ō′**vər dōs′) ◊ *noun, plural* **overdoses**

overdress *verb* To dress up in too fancy a way for the occasion.
o·ver·dress (ō′vər **drĕs′**) ◊ *verb* **overdressed, overdressing**

overdue *adjective* **1.** Not paid on time: *The payment for your magazine subscription is overdue.* **2.** Later than scheduled or expected: *The train was two hours overdue.*
o·ver·due (ō′vər **dō′** *or* ō′vər **dyo͞o′**) ◊ *adjective*

overflow *verb* **1.** To flow over the top or brim of: *The river overflows its banks every spring.* **2.** To flow over limits: *Heavy rains caused the river to overflow.*
o·ver·flow (ō′vər **flō′**) ◊ *verb* **overflowed, overflowing**

overhand *adjective* Being done with the hand above the level of the shoulder: *The baseball player threw an overhand pitch.*
◊ *adverb* With an overhand motion.
o·ver·hand (**ō′**vər hănd′) ◊ *adjective* ◊ *adverb*

overhanded *adjective & adverb* Overhand.
o·ver·hand·ed (**ō′**vər hăn′dĭd) ◊ *adjective & adverb*

overhaul *verb* To examine and repair or make changes in: *The mechanic overhauled our car's engine.*
o·ver·haul (ō′vər **hôl′**) ◊ *verb* **overhauled, overhauling**

overhead *adverb* Above one's head: *Birds flew overhead.*
◊ *adjective* Located overhead: *We turned on the overhead light.*
◊ *noun* A business's general expenses, as for wages, rent, insurance, or heating.
o·ver·head ◊ *adverb* (ō′vər **hĕd′**) ◊ *adjective* (**ō′**vər hĕd′) ◊ *noun* (**ō′**vər hĕd′), *plural* **overheads**

overhear *verb* To hear when one is not supposed to hear.
o·ver·hear (ō′vər **hîr′**) ◊ *verb* **overheard, overhearing**

overheard *verb* Past tense and past participle of **overhear.**
o·ver·heard (ō′vər **hûrd′**) ◊ *verb*

overland *adjective* Proceeding or carried on over or across land: *They took the overland route from the Atlantic to the Pacific.*
o·ver·land (**ō′**vər lănd′) ◊ *adjective*

overlap *verb* To extend over and cover a part of something else: *The scales of a fish overlap.*
o·ver·lap (ō′vər **lăp′**) ◊ *verb* **overlapped, overlapping**

overlook *verb* **1.** To look down on from a higher place: *The porch overlooks the sea.* **2.** To fail to notice or consider; miss: *We overlooked an important detail.*
o·ver·look (ō′vər **lo͝ok′**) ◊ *verb* **overlooked, overlooking**

overnight *adjective* **1.** Lasting for a night: *I took an overnight trip.* **2.** For use on short trips: *I need an overnight bag.*
◊ *adverb* During or for the length of a night: *Soak the beans overnight.*
o·ver·night ◊ *adjective* (**ō′**vər nīt′) ◊ *adverb* (ō′vər **nīt′**)

overpower *verb* **1.** To get the better of by superior force: *Our hockey team overpowered the other school's team.* **2.** To be too much for; overcome: *Heat overpowered the hikers.*
o·ver·pow·er (ō′vər **pou′**ər) ◊ *verb* **overpowered, overpowering**

overrate *verb* To value too highly.
o·ver·rate (ō′vər **rāt′**) ◊ *verb* **overrated, overrating**

overrule *verb* To decide against: *The judge overruled the lawyer's objections.*
o·ver·rule (ō′vər **ro͞ol′**) ◊ *verb* **overruled, overruling**

overseas *adverb* Across the sea; abroad: *My best friend moved overseas.*
◊ *adjective* Of, relating to, or situated across the sea: *The airline offers overseas flights.*
o·ver·seas (ō′vər **sēz′**) ◊ *adverb* ◊ *adjective*

O

overshoe *noun* A shoe, often of rubber or plastic, worn over another for protection in wet or cold weather.
o·ver·shoe (ō′vər sho͞o′) ◊ *noun, plural* **overshoes**

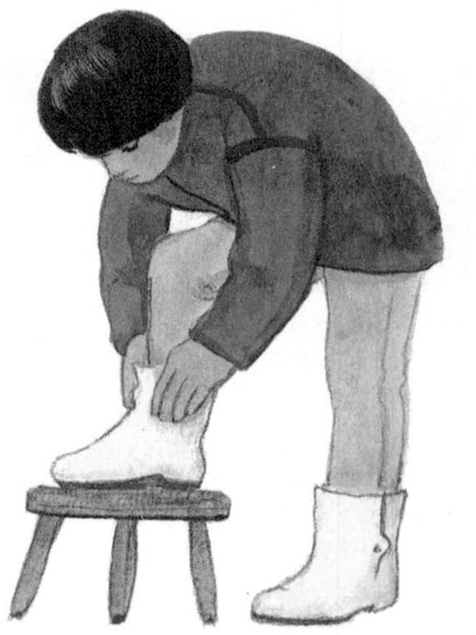

▲ **overshoe**

oversight *noun* A careless mistake.
o·ver·sight (ō′vər sīt′) ◊ *noun, plural* **oversights**

overtake *verb* **1.** To catch up with: *A rider on horseback overtook us on the mountain road.* **2.** To come upon suddenly or by surprise: *A thunderstorm overtook the campers.*
o·ver·take (ō′vər **tāk′**) ◊ *verb* **overtook, overtaken, overtaking**

overtaken *verb* Past participle of **overtake.**
o·ver·tak·en (ō′vər **tā′**kən) ◊ *verb*

overthrew *verb* Past tense of **overthrow.**
o·ver·threw (ō′vər **thro͞o′**) ◊ *verb*

overthrow *verb* To cause the fall or destruction of: *The rebels overthrew the government.*
◊ *noun* The act of overthrowing.
o·ver·throw ◊ *verb* (ō′vər **thrō′**) **overthrew, overthrown, overthrowing** ◊ *noun* (ō′vər-thrō′), *plural* **overthrows**

ă	pat	ĭ	pit	oi	**oil**	th	ba**th**
ā	pay	ī	ride	o͝o	**book**	*th*	ba**the**
â	care	î	fierce	o͞o	**boot**	ə	ago, item
ä	father	ŏ	pot	ou	**out**		pencil
ĕ	pet	ō	go	ŭ	cut		atom
ē	be	ô	paw, for	û	fur		circus

overthrown *verb* Past participle of **overthrow.**
o·ver·thrown (ō′vər **thrōn′**) ◊ *verb*

overtime *noun* Time that is beyond a set limit: *The game went into overtime.*
◊ *adverb* Beyond a set time limit: *The employees were expected to work overtime.*
o·ver·time (ō′vər tīm′) ◊ *noun* ◊ *adverb*

overtook *verb* Past tense of **overtake.**
o·ver·took (ō′vər **to͝ok′**) ◊ *verb*

overture *noun* A musical work that is played by an orchestra before a larger work, such as an opera or ballet.
o·ver·ture (ō′vər chər) ◊ *noun, plural* **overtures**

overturn *verb* To turn over; upset: *I overturned a glass of water.*
o·ver·turn (ō′vər **tûrn′**) ◊ *verb* **overturned, overturning**

overweight *adjective* Weighing more than is normal, necessary, or allowed.
o·ver·weight (ō′vər **wāt′**) ◊ *adjective*

overwhelm *verb* **1.** To overpower: *The terrible heat and humidity overwhelmed me.* **2.** To cover with or as if with water: *The village was overwhelmed by ash from the volcano.*
o·ver·whelm (ō′vər **hwĕlm′**) ◊ *verb* **overwhelmed, overwhelming**

owe *verb* **1.** To have to pay or repay: *We owe the store $20.* **2.** To have to give: *I owe you an apology.* **3.** To be obliged for: *We owe the discovery of polio vaccine to a famous scientist.*
owe (ō) ◊ *verb* **owed, owing**
‖*These sound alike:* **owe, oh**

owl *noun* A bird that has a large head, large eyes, and a short, hooked bill. Owls fly at night and hunt small animals and birds.
owl (oul) ◊ *noun, plural* **owls**

▲ **owl**

own *adjective* Of or belonging to oneself or itself: *The typewriter came with its own carrying case.*
◊ *verb* To have or possess: *Do you own a compact car?*
own (ōn) ◊ *adjective* ◊ *verb* **owned, owning**

ox *noun* **1.** An adult male of domestic cattle. **2.** Any of several animals that are related to domestic cattle.
ox (ŏks) ◊ *noun, plural* **oxen**

▲ **ox**

oxbow *noun* A bend in a river that is shaped like the letter U.
ox·bow (**ŏks′**bō′) ◊ *noun, plural* **oxbows**

oxcart *noun* A cart that is pulled by oxen.
ox·cart (**ŏks′**kärt′) ◊ *noun, plural* **oxcarts**

oxen *noun* Plural of **ox.**
ox·en (**ŏk′**sən) ◊ *noun*

oxeye daisy *noun* The common daisy of North America that has flowers with a yellow center and white petals.
ox·eye daisy (**ŏks′**ī′) ◊ *noun, plural* **oxeye daisies**

oxygen *noun* A colorless, odorless, tasteless gas that is needed by animals and plants to live. Oxygen is a chemical element.
ox·y·gen (**ŏk′**sĭ jən) ◊ *noun*

oyster *noun* A sea animal that lives in shallow waters and has an edible soft body with a shell made up of two hinged parts. Some kinds produce pearls inside their shells.
oy·ster (**oi′**stər) ◊ *noun, plural* **oysters**

oz. The abbreviation for *ounce* or *ounces.*

O

Peacock

Pp

P is the sixteenth letter of the English alphabet. Did you know that it has a long history?

Over 3,500 years ago, people in the Middle East were using symbols that became the letters of our alphabet. This ancient Middle Eastern symbol is a form of the letter that became our letter *P*.

The ancient Greeks borrowed their alphabet from people in the Middle East. Here is a form of the Greek letter that became our letter *P*.

P

The ancient Romans borrowed their alphabet from a people who had taken their own letter symbols from the Greeks. Here is a form of the Roman letter *P* that was used for carving letters into stone. These letters became the model for our printed capital letters.

p

As people wrote quickly, especially with pens, the capital letters began to take the shapes of small letters. Here is a small-letter *p* that was developed about 1,200 years ago.

Pp Pp	Pp	Pp	Pp
Handwriting	Sans Serif Type	Serif Type	Computer Printing

p *or* **P** *noun* The sixteenth letter of the English alphabet.
p *or* **P** (pē) ◊ *noun, plural* **p's** *or* **P's**

p. An abbreviation for *page.*

PA The abbreviation for *Pennsylvania* used with a Zip Code.

Pa. An abbreviation for *Pennsylvania.*

pace *noun* **1.** A step that is taken in walking or running. **2.** The length of a pace. **3.** Speed of motion or progress: *I love the fast pace of city life.* **4.** A horse's gait in which both feet on one side leave and return to the ground together.
◊ *verb* **1.** To walk up and down or back and forth across: *I paced the floor impatiently.* **2.** To measure by paces: *We paced off the length of the driveway.* **3.** To regulate or set the pace of: *I try to pace myself running.*
pace (pās) ◊ *noun, plural* **paces** ◊ *verb* **paced, pacing**

pacify *verb* To cause to be quiet or calm; soothe: *I gave the baby a bottle to pacify it.*
pac·i·fy (păs′ ə fī′) ◊ *verb* **pacified, pacifying**

pack *noun* **1.** A group of things tied or wrapped together for carrying; bundle. **2.** A group of similar or related persons, animals, or things: *We keep a pack of hounds.*
◊ *verb* **1.** To put into a container: *We packed the books before we moved.* **2.** To fill with things: *I packed my suitcase.* **3.** To fill full: *A crowd packed the stadium.* **4.** To cause to go: *We packed the kids off to camp.*
pack (păk) ◊ *noun, plural* **packs** ◊ *verb* **packed, packing**

package *noun* **1.** A bundle of things packed together; parcel. **2.** A container in which something is stored, shipped, or delivered.
pack·age (păk′ĭj) ◊ *noun, plural* **packages**

ă	pat	ĭ	pit	oi	**oil**	th	ba**th**
ā	pay	ī	ride	o͝o	book	*th*	ba*th*e
â	care	î	fierce	o͞o	boot	ə	ago, item
ä	father	ŏ	pot	ou	**out**		pencil
ĕ	pet	ō	go	ŭ	cut		atom
ē	be	ô	paw, for	û	fur		circus

pact *noun* A formal agreement, as one between nations; treaty.
pact (păkt) ◊ *noun, plural* **pacts**

pad *noun* **1.** A mass of soft, firmly packed material used for stuffing, lining, or protection; cushion. **2.** A piece of absorbent material placed in a container and used to hold ink for stamping. **3.** A number of sheets of paper of the same size stacked one on top of the other and glued together at one end. **4.** A broad, floating leaf, as of a water lily. **5.** A part that is like a small cushion on the bottom of the feet of many animals.
◊ *verb* **1.** To line, stuff, or cover with soft, firmly packed material: *We padded the sleeve of the winter jacket.* **2.** To lengthen with unnecessary material: *Some students pad their term papers.*
pad (păd) ◊ *noun, plural* **pads** ◊ *verb* **padded, padding**

paddle *noun* **1.** A short oar with a flat blade at one or both ends that is used to move and steer a small boat, as a canoe. **2.** A tool with a flat blade used for stirring, mixing, or beating. **3.** A board on the edge of a paddle wheel.
◊ *verb* **1.** To move and steer with a paddle. **2.** To spank with or as if with a paddle.
pad·dle (păd′l) ◊ *noun, plural* **paddles** ◊ *verb* **paddled, paddling**

paddle wheel *noun* A wheel with paddles around its rim that is used to move a boat.
paddle wheel ◊ *noun, plural* **paddle wheels**

▲ **paddle wheel**

paddock *noun* A fenced field or area where horses graze and exercise.
pad·dock (păd′ək) ◊ *noun, plural* **paddocks**

paddy *noun* A flooded or irrigated field where rice is grown.
pad·dy (păd′ē) ◊ *noun, plural* **paddies**

padlock *noun* A lock that has a hinged bar shaped like the letter U that can be put through a ring or link and snapped shut.
◊ *verb* To lock with a padlock.
pad·lock (păd′lŏk′) ◊ *noun, plural* **padlocks** ◊ *verb* **padlocked, padlocking**

pagan *noun* A person who is not a Christian, Moslem, or Jew.
pa·gan (pā′gən) ◊ *noun, plural* **pagans**

page[1] *noun* One side of a printed or written sheet of paper, as in a book or newspaper.
page[1] (pāj) ◊ *noun, plural* **pages**

page[2] *noun* **1.** A boy training to become a knight in the Middle Ages. **2.** A person who runs errands, carries messages, or acts as a guide, as in a legislature.
◊ *verb* To summon or call by name in a public place: *The nurse paged the doctor on the loudspeaker.*
page[2] (pāj) ◊ *noun, plural* **pages** ◊ *verb* **paged, paging**

***HISTORY* • page[1], page[2]**

Page[1] goes back to a Latin word that meant "a sheet of writing." **Page**[2] comes from an old French word that meant "a boy training to be a knight." The French word may have come from a Greek word that meant "boy."

pageant *noun* **1.** A play or dramatic spectacle that is often based on an event in history: *Our community puts on an annual Thanksgiving pageant.* **2.** A parade, procession, or celebration.
pag·eant (păj′ənt) ◊ *noun, plural* **pageants**

pagoda *noun* A Buddhist tower with many stories, usually built as a memorial or shrine.
pa·go·da (pə gō′də) ◊ *noun, plural* **pagodas**

paid *verb* Past tense and past participle of **pay.**
paid (pād) ◊ *verb*

pail *noun* **1.** A round container with a handle that is used especially for carrying water and

P

sand; bucket. **2.** The amount that a pail holds: *The horse drank two pails of water.*
pail (pāl) ◊ *noun, plural* **pails**
‖*These sound alike:* **pail, pale**

pain *noun* **1.** Physical suffering caused by injury or sickness. **2.** Mental or emotional suffering; distress. **3.** **pains** Trouble, care, or effort: *Take great pains to do the job right.*
◊ *verb* To feel or cause to feel pain.
pain (pān) ◊ *noun, plural* **pains** ◊ *verb* **pained, paining**
‖*These sound alike:* **pain, pane**

SYNONYMS

pain, ache, stitch

When I cut myself I felt *pain.* I have an *ache* in my right leg from all that walking. I stopped running because I had a *stitch* in my side.

painless *adjective* Without pain.
pain·less (**pān′** lĭs) ◊ *adjective*

paint *noun* A mixture of solid coloring matter and a liquid put onto surfaces to protect or decorate them.
◊ *verb* **1.** To coat or decorate with paint: *We painted the porch.* **2.** To produce with paints: *I painted a picture of a horse.*
paint (pānt) ◊ *noun, plural* **paints** ◊ *verb* **painted, painting**

paintbrush *noun* A brush for applying paint.
paint·brush (**pānt′**brŭsh′) ◊ *noun, plural* **paintbrushes**

painter *noun* A person who paints.
paint·er (**pān′** tər) ◊ *noun, plural* **painters**

painting *noun* **1.** The art, process, or job of working with paints. **2.** A picture or design done with paint.
paint·ing (**pān′** tĭng) ◊ *noun, plural* **paintings**

pair *noun* **1.** A set of two identical or matched things that are usually used together: *I lost a pair of shoes.* **2.** One thing that is made up of two connected parts: *I used a pair of scissors to cut the fabric.* **3.** Two persons or animals; couple: *A pair of dancers circled the ballroom floor.*
◊ *verb* To arrange in or form pairs.
pair (pâr) ◊ *noun, plural* **pairs** ◊ *verb* **paired, pairing**
‖*These sound alike:* **pair, pare, pear**

pajamas *plural noun* A loose jacket and trousers worn especially during sleep.
pa·ja·mas (pə **jä′**məz *or* pə **jăm′** əz) ◊ *plural noun*

pal *noun* A close friend; chum.
pal (păl) ◊ *noun, plural* **pals**

palace *noun* A ruler's official residence.
pal·ace (**păl′**ĭs) ◊ *noun, plural* **palaces**

▲ **palace**

palate *noun* The roof of the mouth, consisting of a bony front part, the hard palate, and a soft movable back part, the soft palate.
pal·ate (**păl′**ĭt) ◊ *noun, plural* **palates**
‖*These sound alike:* **palate, palette, pallet**

pale *adjective* **1.** Having skin that is lighter than usual, often because of illness. **2.** Containing a large amount of white; light in color.
◊ *verb* To become or cause to become pale.
pale (pāl) ◊ *adjective* **paler, palest** ◊ *verb* **paled, paling**
‖*These sound alike:* **pale, pail**

palette *noun* A thin board with a hole for the thumb, on which an artist mixes colors.
pal·ette (**păl′**ĭt) ◊ *noun, plural* **palettes**
‖*These sound alike:* **palette, palate, pallet**

ă	pat	ĭ	pit	oi	**oil**	th	ba**th**
ā	pay	ī	ride	ŏŏ	**book**	*th*	ba**the**
â	care	î	fierce	ōō	**boot**	ə	**a**go, it**e**m
ä	father	ŏ	pot	ou	**out**		penc**i**l
ĕ	pet	ō	go	ŭ	cut		at**o**m
ē	be	ô	paw, for	û	fur		circ**u**s

palisade *noun* **1.** A fence of pointed stakes to protect against attack. **2.** A line of high cliffs, often along a river.
pal·i·sade (păl′ĭ **sād′**) ◊ *noun, plural* **palisades**

pallet *noun* A narrow, hard bed or mattress filled with straw.
pal·let (**păl′**ĭt) ◊ *noun, plural* **pallets**
‖*These sound alike:* **pallet, palate, palette**

palm¹ *noun* The inner surface of the hand between the wrist and the fingers.
palm¹ (päm) ◊ *noun, plural* **palms**

palm² *noun* Any of many related trees of the tropics or warm regions that usually have a trunk without branches and large leaves shaped like feathers or fans at the top.
palm² (päm) ◊ *noun, plural* **palms**

HISTORY **• palm¹, palm²**

Palm¹ and **palm²** both go back to the same Latin word. This word first meant "palm of the hand." Later the same word came to mean also **palm²**, because the leaves of the tree were thought to resemble a hand with its fingers spread apart.

palmetto *noun* A palm tree with leaves shaped like fans.
pal·met·to (păl **mĕt′**ō *or* päl **mĕt′**ō) ◊ *noun, plural* **palmettos** *or* **palmettoes**

▲ **palmetto**

palomino *noun* A horse with a light tan coat and a whitish mane and tail.
pal·o·mi·no (păl′ə **mē′**nō) ◊ *noun, plural* **palominos**

▲ **palomino**

pamper *verb* To give in to the wishes or demands of; coddle.
pam·per (**păm′**pər) ◊ *verb* **pampered, pampering**

SYNONYMS

pamper, baby, indulge, spoil

You *pampered* me by giving me breakfast in bed. Please don't *baby* me by tying my shoes. They *indulged* our craving for walnuts by buying us some. Is it possible to *spoil* children by giving them too many presents?

P

pamphlet *noun* A short printed work with a paper cover and no binding.
pam·phlet (**păm′**flĭt) ◊ *noun, plural* **pamphlets**

pan *noun* **1.** A wide, shallow, open container used for holding liquids and for cooking. **2.** A container like a pan, such as one used to separate gold from gravel or earth by washing.
◊ *verb* To wash earth or gravel in a pan in search of gold.
◊ *idiom* **pan out** To turn out well; succeed.
pan (păn) ◊ *noun, plural* **pans** ◊ *verb* **panned, panning**

pancake *noun* A thin, flat cake of batter cooked on a hot griddle or in a skillet.
pan·cake (**păn′**kāk′) ◊ *noun, plural* **pancakes**

pancreas *noun* A gland behind the stomach that gives off juices that help digestion.
pan·cre·as (**păng′**krē əs) ◊ *noun*

panda *noun* **1.** An animal that looks like a bear and has long, thick fur with black and white markings. Pandas live in the mountains of China. **2.** A small animal that looks like a raccoon but has reddish fur and a long, ringed tail and lives in northeastern Asia.
pan·da (**păn′**də) ◊ *noun, plural* **pandas**

▲ **panda**

pane *noun* A sheet of glass, as in a door.
pane (pān) ◊ *noun, plural* **panes**
‖*These sound alike:* **pane, pain**

panel *noun* **1.** A piece, as a wooden board, that forms part of a surface or that lies over it. **2.** A board on which instruments or controls, as for a vehicle, are mounted. **3.** A group of persons selected to serve on a jury. **4.** A group of persons gathered together to take part in a discussion or a game show, as on television.
◊ *verb* To cover or decorate with panels: *We decided to panel the den with pine.*
pan·el (**păn′**əl) ◊ *noun, plural* **panels** ◊ *verb* **paneled, paneling**

ă	pat	ĭ	pit	oi	**oi**l	th	ba**th**
ā	pay	ī	ride	o͝o	b**oo**k	*th*	ba**the**
â	care	î	fierce	o͞o	b**oo**t	ə	ago, item
ä	father	ŏ	pot	ou	**ou**t		pencil
ĕ	pet	ō	go	ŭ	c**u**t		atom
ē	be	ô	paw, for	û	f**u**r		circus

pang *noun* A sudden sharp feeling, as of pain or strong emotion: *I had a pang of regret when we moved.*
pang (păng) ◊ *noun, plural* **pangs**

panic *noun* A sudden feeling of great fear, especially without a clear cause.
◊ *verb* **1.** To feel panic. **2.** To cause panic in: *Thunder and lightning can panic cattle.*
pan·ic (**păn′**ĭk) ◊ *noun, plural* **panics** ◊ *verb* **panicked, panicking**

panorama *noun* A view or picture of everything that can be seen over a wide area: *We admired the panorama of mountain scenery.*
pan·o·ram·a (păn′ə **răm′**ə *or* păn′ə **rä′**mə) ◊ *noun, plural* **panoramas**

pansy *noun* A garden flower with rounded petals that look like velvet and are often purple and yellow.
pan·sy (**păn′**zē) ◊ *noun, plural* **pansies**

pant *verb* **1.** To breathe in short, quick gasps. **2.** To say while panting: *"Are we nearly at the end of our climb?" I panted.*
◊ *noun* A short, quick gasp.
pant (pănt) ◊ *verb* **panted, panting** ◊ *noun, plural* **pants**

panther *noun* A large wild cat, especially the leopard in its black form or the mountain lion.
pan·ther (**păn′**thər) ◊ *noun, plural* **panthers**

pantomime *noun* **1.** A play or entertainment in which a story is told with gestures and body movements rather than words. **2.** Movements of the face and body used in place of words to express a message or meaning.
pan·to·mime (**păn′**tə mīm′) ◊ *noun, plural* **pantomimes**

pantry *noun* A small room where food, dishes, and utensils are kept.
pan·try (**păn′**trē) ◊ *noun, plural* **pantries**

pants *plural noun* Trousers or slacks.
pants (pănts) ◊ *plural noun*

papa *noun* Father.
pa·pa (**pä′**pə) ◊ *noun, plural* **papas**

papaya *noun* The large, sweet yellow fruit of a tropical American tree.
pa·pa·ya (pə **pä′**yə) ◊ *noun, plural* **papayas**

paper *noun* **1.** A material made in thin sheets of pulp, especially from wood and rags. It is used for writing, printing, drawing, wrapping, and covering walls. **2.** A single sheet of paper. **3.** A sheet of paper with writing or printing on

it; document. **4.** A newspaper. **5.** A report or essay that is assigned in school.
◊ *verb* To cover with wallpaper.
pa·per (pā′pər) ◊ *noun, plural* **papers** ◊ *verb* **papered, papering**

paperback *noun* A book with a paper cover.
pa·per·back (pā′pər băk′) ◊ *noun, plural* **paperbacks**

paper clip *noun* A bent piece of wire that is used to hold loose papers together.
paper clip ◊ *noun, plural* **paper clips**

papoose *noun* A Native American baby.
pa·poose (pă **po͞os′**) ◊ *noun, plural* **papooses**

paprika *noun* A mild red spice made from powdered sweet red peppers.
pa·pri·ka (pă **prē′**kə *or* **păp′**rĭ kə) ◊ *noun*

papyrus *noun* **1.** A tall water plant of northern Africa and nearby regions. **2.** A paper made from the stems and pith of the papyrus.
pa·py·rus (pə **pī′**rəs) ◊ *noun, plural* **papyruses**

par *noun* **1.** An accepted or normal average: *Most athletes are above par in physical condition.* **2.** A level of equality.
par (pär) ◊ *noun*

parachute *noun* A folding device shaped like an umbrella that is used to slow the fall of persons or objects from the sky.
◊ *verb* To descend or transport by parachute.
par·a·chute (**păr′**ə sho͞ot′) ◊ *noun, plural* **parachutes** ◊ *verb* **parachuted, parachuting**

▲ **parachute**

parade *noun* **1.** A festive public event in which people or vehicles pass by spectators: *Our town always has a Fourth of July parade.* **2.** A large number of people walking: *Photographers took pictures of the Easter parade.* **3.** A great show or display: *We watched the parade of autumn colors.*
◊ *verb* **1.** To take part in a parade. **2.** To make a great show or display of.
pa·rade (pə **rād′**) ◊ *noun, plural* **parades** ◊ *verb* **paraded, parading**

paradise *noun* A place or condition of great happiness.
par·a·dise (**păr′**ə dīs′ *or* **păr′**ə dīz′) ◊ *noun*

paraffin *noun* A white or colorless substance that is like wax. Paraffin is used in making candles and in sealing jars.
par·af·fin (**păr′**ə fĭn) ◊ *noun*

paragraph *noun* A division of a piece of writing that consists of one or more sentences on a single subject or idea.
par·a·graph (**păr′**ə grăf′) ◊ *noun, plural* **paragraphs**

parakeet *noun* A small parrot with a long, pointed tail.
par·a·keet (**păr′**ə kēt′) ◊ *noun, plural* **parakeets**

parallel *adjective* **1.** Lying in the same plane but not touching at any point: *Draw two parallel lines.* **2.** Similar; like: *My two friends have parallel likes and dislikes.*
◊ *noun* **1.** A parallel curve, line, or surface. **2.** Close comparison between two different things: *Space exploration has no parallel.* **3.** An imaginary line that encircles the earth parallel to the equator and represents degrees of latitude.
◊ *verb* **1.** To be or extend parallel to: *The town's main street paralleled a canal.* **2.** To be like; resemble: *Her career in medicine paralleled that of her father.*
par·al·lel (**păr′**ə lĕl′) ◊ *adjective* ◊ *noun, plural* **parallels** ◊ *verb* **paralleled, paralleling**

paralysis *noun* Complete or partial loss of the ability to feel or to move.
pa·ral·y·sis (pə **răl′**ĭ sĭs) ◊ *noun*

paralyze *verb* **1.** To cause paralysis in. **2.** To make helpless or unable to function: *The blizzard paralyzed the city.*
par·a·lyze (**păr′**ə līz′) ◊ *verb* **paralyzed, paralyzing**

P

paramecium *noun* A tiny organism consisting of only one cell that is shaped like an oval or a slipper.
par·a·me·ci·um (păr′ə **mē′**shē əm *or* păr′ə-**mē′**sē əm) ◊ *noun, plural* **parameciums**

paramount *adjective* Of highest rank, power, or importance.
par·a·mount (**păr′** ə mount′) ◊ *adjective*

parasite *noun* **1.** A plant or animal that lives in or on a different kind of plant or animal and gets its food from that plant or animal. **2.** A person who gets money, shelter, and care from others without doing anything in return.
par·a·site (**păr′** ə sīt′) ◊ *noun, plural* **parasites**

parasol *noun* A small, light umbrella used as a protection against the sun.
par·a·sol (**păr′** ə sôl′) ◊ *noun, plural* **parasols**

paratrooper *noun* A soldier trained to parachute from airplanes.
par·a·troop·er (**păr′** ə trōō′pər) ◊ *noun, plural* **paratroopers**

parcel *noun* **1.** A bundle; package. **2.** A section of land; plot.
◊ *verb* To divide into parts and distribute: *My parents parceled out the chores to us.*
par·cel (**pär′**səl) ◊ *noun, plural* **parcels**
◊ *verb* **parceled, parceling**

parch *verb* **1.** To make or become very dry: *A constant south wind parched the soil.* **2.** To make or become thirsty.
parch (pärch) ◊ *verb* **parched, parching**

parchment *noun* **1.** The skin of a sheep or goat that is prepared as a material to write on. **2.** Paper that looks like parchment.
parch·ment (**pärch′**mənt) ◊ *noun, plural* **parchments**

pardon *verb* **1.** To release from punishment. **2.** To excuse or overlook.
◊ *noun* **1.** Release from punishment. **2.** The act of forgiving or the state of being forgiven.
par·don (**pär′**dn) ◊ *verb* **pardoned, pardoning** ◊ *noun, plural* **pardons**

ă	pat	ĭ	pit	oi	**oil**	th	bath
ā	pay	ī	ride	ŏŏ	**book**	*th*	bathe
â	care	î	fierce	ōō	**boot**	ə	ago, item
ä	father	ŏ	pot	ou	**out**		pencil
ĕ	pet	ō	go	ŭ	cut		atom
ē	be	ô	paw, for	û	fur		circus

SYNONYMS

pardon, excuse, forgive

The governor *pardoned* the prisoner.
Excuse me for stepping on your foot.
Forgive your enemies. **Antonym:** *punish*

pare *verb* **1.** To remove the skin or rind of with or as if with a knife; peel: *We pared potatoes.* **2.** To make smaller as if by cutting: *We were asked to pare our budget.*
pare (pâr) ◊ *verb* **pared, paring**
‖*These sound alike:* **pare, pair, pear**

parent *noun* **1.** A father or mother. **2.** A plant or animal that produces another of its own kind.
par·ent (**păr′** ənt) ◊ *noun, plural* **parents**

parental *adjective* Of or relating to a parent: *You need parental approval to go on the trip.*
pa·ren·tal (pə **rĕn′** tl) ◊ *adjective*

parentheses *noun* Plural of **parenthesis.**
pa·ren·the·ses (pə **rĕn′** thĭ sēz′) ◊ *noun*

parenthesis *noun* One of a pair of curved lines, ( ), used in printing or writing to enclose a word or phrase.
pa·ren·the·sis (pə **rĕn′** thĭ sĭs) ◊ *noun, plural* **parentheses**

parish *noun* **1.** A district with its own church and clergy. **2.** The people who belong to a parish. **3.** A district in Louisiana that is like a county in other states.
par·ish (**păr′**ĭsh) ◊ *noun, plural* **parishes**

park *noun* **1.** An area of land used for recreation. **2.** An area of land set apart by a government to be kept in its natural state.
◊ *verb* To stop and leave a vehicle for a time: *We parked by the road and ate lunch in the meadow.*
park (pärk) ◊ *noun, plural* **parks** ◊ *verb* **parked, parking**

parka *noun* A warm jacket with a hood.
par·ka (**pär′** kə) ◊ *noun, plural* **parkas**

parkway *noun* A broad highway planted in certain areas with grass, bushes, and trees.
park·way (**pärk′** wā′) ◊ *noun, plural* **parkways**

parliament *noun* A legislature of a nation such as Great Britain.
par·lia·ment (**pär′** lə mənt) ◊ *noun, plural* **parliaments**

parlor *noun* **1.** A room for entertaining visitors. **2.** A room or building for a special use or business: *We own a beauty parlor.*
par·lor (pär′lər) ◊ *noun, plural* **parlors**

parochial *adjective* Of or relating to a church parish: *I attend a parochial school.*
pa·ro·chi·al (pə **rō′** kē əl) ◊ *adjective*

parrot *noun* A tropical bird with a hooked bill and brightly colored feathers. Parrots can be taught to imitate spoken words.
par·rot (păr′ət) ◊ *noun, plural* **parrots**

▲ **parrot**

parsley *noun* A plant with divided leaves that are used to flavor or decorate food.
pars·ley (pär′slē) ◊ *noun*

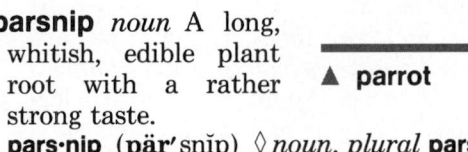

parsnip *noun* A long, whitish, edible plant root with a rather strong taste.
pars·nip (pär′snĭp) ◊ *noun, plural* **parsnips**

parson *noun* A minister.
par·son (pär′sən) ◊ *noun, plural* **parsons**

part *noun* **1.** A portion or division of a whole: *We arrived late and missed part of the movie.* **2.** A piece in a machine or mechanism: *I need a new part for my radio.* **3.** A proper or expected share in a responsibility or task: *When there's work to be done, it's only fair to do your part.* **4.** A role, as in a play or movie. **5.** A side in a dispute or argument: *Although you didn't completely agree with me, you took my part.* **6.** A dividing line formed when the hair is combed.
◊ *verb* **1.** To divide into parts; split. —See Synonyms at **separate. 2.** To go away from someone: *They parted at the corner.* **3.** To come apart.
◊ *adjective* Not full; partial: *My parents have part ownership in a restaurant.*
◊ *adverb* In part: *The dog is part brown.*
◊ *idiom* **take part** To join with others in something; participate: *The entire class took part in the fair.*
part (pärt) ◊ *noun, plural* **parts** ◊ *verb* **parted, parting** ◊ *adjective* ◊ *adverb*

SYNONYMS

part, piece, portion, section

They live in one *part* of the house; we live in the other. Please give me another *piece* of chicken. I asked for a bigger *portion* of food. I wish we could sit in a *section* of the stadium closer to the field.
Antonym: *whole*

partial *adjective* **1.** Being a part; not total: *The play was only a partial success.* **2.** Favoring one side over another; prejudiced: *A judge must not be partial.* **3.** Especially fond: *I'm partial to summer sports.*
par·tial (pär′shəl) ◊ *adjective*

participate *verb* To join with others: *We participated in the athletic program.*
par·tic·i·pate (pär **tĭs′** ə pāt′) ◊ *verb* **participated, participating**

participation *noun* The act or fact of participating.
par·tic·i·pa·tion (pär tĭs′ə **pā′**shən) ◊ *noun*

participle *noun* A verb form that functions as an adjective and is used with auxiliary verbs to show certain tenses. In the sentence *The child is running,* the word *running* is a present participle. In the sentence *I had left before you arrived,* the word *left* is a past participle.
par·ti·ci·ple (pär′ tĭ sĭp′əl) ◊ *noun, plural* **participles**

particle *noun* A very small piece or amount; speck: *Particles of dust floated in the air.*
par·ti·cle (pär′ tĭ kəl) ◊ *noun, plural* **particles**

particular *adjective* **1.** Of, relating to, or for a single person or thing: *This plan has a particular advantage.* **2.** Distinct from others; specific: *At that particular time I was busy.* **3.** Special or unusual: *Pay particular attention to this lesson.* **4.** Giving or requiring close attention to details; fussy.
◊ *noun* A single item, fact, or detail: *Your homework is correct in every particular.*
par·tic·u·lar (pər **tĭk′** yə lər) ◊ *adjective* ◊ *noun, plural* **particulars**

partition *noun* Something, as a partial wall, that divides up a room or space.
◊ *verb* To divide with partitions.
par·ti·tion (pär **tĭsh′** ən) ◊ *noun, plural* **partitions** ◊ *verb* **partitioned, partitioning**

partly *adverb* To some extent; in part: *We went partly by subway and partly by bus.*
part·ly (pärt′lē) ◊ *adverb*

partner *noun* **1.** One of two or more persons associated in a business. **2.** Either of a pair of persons dancing together. **3.** Either of two persons on the same side in a game or sport.
part·ner (pärt′nər) ◊ *noun, plural* **partners**

partnership *noun* The condition of being a partner.
part·ner·ship (pärt′nər shĭp′) ◊ *noun, plural* **partnerships**

part of speech *noun* A grammatical class, such as a noun, pronoun, verb, adjective, adverb, preposition, conjunction, or interjection, into which a word can be placed according to the way it is used in a phrase or sentence.
part of speech ◊ *noun, plural* **parts of speech**

partridge *noun* A game bird with a plump body and brownish feathers.
par·tridge (pär′trĭj) ◊ *noun, plural* **partridges**

▲ **partridge**

part-time *adjective* For or during only part of the usual time: *I got a part-time job.*
part-time (pärt′tīm′) ◊ *adjective*

party *noun* **1.** A gathering of people for pleasure or entertainment: *We went to a birthday party.* **2.** A group of people who join together in an activity: *A search party is looking for the child.* **3.** A group of people who are organized for political activity: *Which party do your parents belong to?*
par·ty (pär′tē) ◊ *noun, plural* **parties**

pass *verb* **1.** To move on; proceed: *Shoppers passed from store to store.* **2.** To go by: *We counted the railroad cars as they passed.* **3.** To catch up with and move past: *The truck passed us.* **4.** To die: *Our old friend passed away.* **5.** To remove or shift from one condition or place to another: *The house passed into the children's hands.* **6.** To come to an end: *The storm finally passed.* **7.** To hand or throw to another person: *Pass your plate.* **8.** To complete with satisfactory results: *I passed my history test.* **9.** To make into or become a law: *The senate passed the tax bill.* ◊ *noun* **1.** The act of passing. **2.** A narrow passage in a mountain range. **3.** Written or printed permission: *The soldier had a three-day pass.* **4.** A free ticket: *I won two passes to the concert.*
pass (păs) ◊ *verb* **passed, passing** ◊ *noun, plural* **passes**

passage *noun* **1.** The act or process of passing: *The river is deep enough for safe passage.* **2.** A journey, especially by water or air: *We had a rough passage across the Atlantic.* **3.** The right to travel, as on a ship: *We booked passage on an ocean liner.* **4.** A narrow path or channel: *An underground passage connects the two buildings.* **5.** Approval of law by a legislative body: *Passage of the bill seems sure.* **6.** A part of a written work or a piece of music.
pas·sage (păs′ĭj) ◊ *noun, plural* **passages**

passenger *noun* A person riding in a vehicle, as a car or airplane.
pas·sen·ger (păs′ən jər) ◊ *noun, plural* **passengers**

passenger pigeon *noun* A pigeon that used to be common in North America.
passenger pigeon ◊ *noun, plural* **passenger pigeons**

▲ **passenger pigeon**

ă	pat	ĭ	pit	oi	oil	th	bath
ā	pay	ī	ride	o͝o	book	*th*	bathe
â	care	î	fierce	o͞o	boot	ə	ago, item
ä	father	ŏ	pot	ou	out		pencil
ĕ	pet	ō	go	ŭ	cut		atom
ē	be	ô	paw, for	û	fur		circus

passer-by *noun* A person who happens to be passing by.
pass·er-by (păs′ər bī′) ◊ *noun, plural* **passers-by**

passing *adjective* **1.** Going by: *We counted the cars of the passing freight train.* **2.** Not lasting long; temporary: *They had a passing interest in music.* **3.** Said or done quickly; casual: *I made passing mention of the weather.* **4.** Satisfactory: *I got a passing mark.*
◊ *noun* The act of going by or past.
pass·ing (păs′ĭng) ◊ *adjective* ◊ *noun, plural* **passings**

passion *noun* **1.** A powerful feeling, as love or hatred. **2.** Great enthusiasm: *They have a passion for art.* **3.** The object of great enthusiasm: *Baseball is my passion.*
pas·sion (păsh′ən) ◊ *noun, plural* **passions**

passionate *adjective* Having or showing intense feelings.
pas·sion·ate (păsh′ə nĭt) ◊ *adjective*

passive *adjective* Not taking an active part: *They're passive bystanders.*
pas·sive (păs′ĭv) ◊ *adjective*

passkey *noun* A key that opens more than one lock.
pass·key (păs′kē′) ◊ *noun, plural* **passkeys**

Passover *noun* A Jewish holiday that is celebrated in the spring in honor of the Jews' escape from slavery in Egypt.
Pass·o·ver (păs′ō′vər) ◊ *noun*

passport *noun* A government document that gives a citizen permission to travel in foreign countries.
pass·port (păs′pôrt′) ◊ *noun, plural* **passports**

password *noun* A secret word or phrase that a person must use to pass a guard or sentry.
pass·word (păs′wûrd′) ◊ *noun, plural* **passwords**

past *adjective* **1.** Of or relating to a time before the present: *I've been sick for the past week.* **2.** Having formerly served: *I am a past president of the club.* **3.** Expressing a time gone by: *"Picked" is the past tense of "pick."*
◊ *noun* **1.** A time before the present: *We have pleasant memories of the past.* **2.** A past history: *Our city has a distinguished past.*
◊ *preposition* **1.** Alongside and then beyond: *The river flows past the city.* **2.** Beyond: *It is well past midnight.*
◊ *adverb* So as to go beyond: *We tooted the horn as we drove past.*
past (păst) ◊ *adjective* ◊ *noun, plural* **pasts** ◊ *preposition* ◊ *adverb*

paste *noun* **1.** A substance, as a mixture of flour and water, used to stick things together. **2.** A food that has been made soft and creamy by pounding or grinding.
◊ *verb* To stick with paste.
paste (pāst) ◊ *noun, plural* **pastes** ◊ *verb* **pasted, pasting**

pasteboard *noun* A firm board made of wood pulp or sheets of paper pasted together.
paste·board (pāst′bôrd′) ◊ *noun*

pastel *noun* **1.** A crayon similar to chalk that is used in drawing or marking. **2.** A picture drawn or painted with pastels. **3.** A light, delicate color.
pas·tel (pă stĕl′) ◊ *noun, plural* **pastels**

pasteurize *verb* To heat a liquid, such as milk, in order to kill harmful germs.
pas·teur·ize (păs′chə rīz′) ◊ *verb* **pasteurized, pasteurizing**

> ***HISTORY* • pasteurize**
>
> The process of **pasteurizing** milk was invented by and named for Louis *Pasteur*, a French chemist who lived about a hundred years ago.

pastime *noun* An activity that occupies one's time pleasantly.
pas·time (păs′tīm′) ◊ *noun, plural* **pastimes**

pastor *noun* A member of the Christian clergy.
pas·tor (păs′tər) ◊ *noun, plural* **pastors**

pastoral *adjective* **1.** Of or relating to shepherds or country life. **2.** Of or relating to a pastor.
pas·tor·al (păs′tər əl) ◊ *adjective*

pastry *noun* **1.** Dough, as of flour, water, and shortening, used for baked crusts, as of pies. **2.** Baked goods made with pastry.
pas·try (pā′strē) ◊ *noun, plural* **pastries**

pasture *noun* **1.** Plants eaten by grazing animals. **2.** Ground where animals graze.
◊ *verb* To herd into a pasture to graze: *We pastured the cattle in the south field.*
pas·ture (păs′chər) ◊ *noun, plural* **pastures** ◊ *verb* **pastured, pasturing**

P

pat *verb* To stroke or tap gently with the open hand: *We patted the kitten.*
◊ *noun* **1.** The act or sound of patting. **2.** A small, flat piece, as of butter.
pat (păt) ◊ *verb* **patted, patting** ◊ *noun, plural* **pats**

patch *noun* **1.** A piece of material used to cover or mend a hole, rip, or worn place. **2.** A protective pad, dressing, or bandage worn over a wound or injury. **3.** A small cloth badge sewn onto a sleeve or shirt front. **4.** A small area that differs from or contrasts with what surrounds it: *There is a patch of snow on the ground.*
◊ *verb* To cover or mend with a patch. —See Synonyms at **mend.**
◊ *idiom* **patch up** To settle or smooth over: *They patched up their quarrel.*
patch (păch) ◊ *noun, plural* **patches** ◊ *verb* **patched, patching**

patchwork *noun* Pieces of cloth of various colors, shapes, and sizes sewn together.
patch·work (**păch′**wûrk′) ◊ *noun*

▲ **patchwork**

patent *noun* An official paper that gives an inventor the right to be the only one to make, use, and sell an invention for a certain period of time.
pat·ent (**păt′**nt) ◊ *noun, plural* **patents**

ă	pat	ĭ	pit	oi	**oil**	th	bath
ā	pay	ī	ride	o͝o	book	*th*	bathe
â	care	î	fierce	o͞o	boot	ə	ago, item
ä	father	ŏ	pot	ou	**out**		pencil
ĕ	pet	ō	go	ŭ	cut		atom
ē	be	ô	paw, for	û	fur		circus

patent leather *noun* Leather with a smooth, hard, shiny surface that is used to make shoes, belts, and pocketbooks.

paternal *adjective* **1.** Of, relating to, or like a father: *He has a paternal concern for the student.* **2.** Of or on a father's side of a family: *She visited her paternal grandparents.*
pa·ter·nal (pə **tûr′**nəl) ◊ *adjective*

path *noun* **1.** A track made by or for walking: *I shoveled a path through the snow.* **2.** The route or course along which something moves: *Our town was in the path of the hurricane.*
path (păth) ◊ *noun, plural* **paths**

pathetic *adjective* Causing one to feel pity, sorrow, or sympathy.
pa·thet·ic (pə **thĕt′**ĭk) ◊ *adjective*

pathway *noun* A path.
path·way (**păth′**wā′) ◊ *noun, plural* **pathways**

patience *noun* The quality of being patient.
pa·tience (**pā′**shəns) ◊ *noun*

patient *adjective* Able to put up with trouble, hardship, annoyance, or delay without complaining.
◊ *noun* A person who is receiving medical treatment.
pa·tient (**pā′**shənt) ◊ *adjective* ◊ *noun, plural* **patients**

patio *noun* A paved space next to a building for eating or recreation.
pat·i·o (**păt′**ē ō′) ◊ *noun, plural* **patios**

patriarch *noun* **1.** The male leader of a family or tribe. **2.** An old and respected man.
pa·tri·arch (**pā′**trē ärk′) ◊ *noun, plural* **patriarchs**

patriot *noun* A person who loves, supports, and defends his or her country.
pa·tri·ot (**pā′**trē ət) ◊ *noun, plural* **patriots**

patriotic *adjective* Feeling or expressing patriotism: *We sang patriotic songs.*
pa·tri·ot·ic (pā′trē **ŏt′**ĭk) ◊ *adjective*

patriotism *noun* Love of and support for one's country.
pa·tri·ot·ism (**pā′**trē ə tĭz′əm) ◊ *noun*

patrol *verb* To move about an area in order to watch or guard.
◊ *noun* **1.** The act of patrolling. **2.** A person or group carrying out a patrol: *The highway patrol helps drivers in trouble.*
pa·trol (pə **trōl′**) ◊ *verb* **patrolled, patrolling** ◊ *noun, plural* **patrols**

patron *noun* **1.** A person who supports or helps another person, an activity, or an institution: *My parents are patrons of the symphony orchestra.* **2.** A regular customer: *I have been a patron of this store for ten years.*
pa·tron (pā′ trən) ◊ *noun, plural* **patrons**

patronage *noun* **1.** The support or encouragement of a patron. **2.** The business given, as to a store, by its customers. **3.** The customers of a business. **4.** The power to give out jobs or positions in government.
pa·tron·age (pā′ trə nĭj) ◊ *noun*

patronize *verb* **1.** To act as a patron to. **2.** To be a regular customer of: *I patronize the store around the corner.*
pa·tron·ize (pā′ trə nīz′) ◊ *verb* **patronized, patronizing**

patter *verb* **1.** To make quick, light taps: *Rain pattered on the roof.* **2.** To walk or run softly and quickly.
◊ *noun* A series of quick, light sounds: *We could hear the patter of feet upstairs.*
pat·ter (păt′ ər) ◊ *verb* **pattered, pattering** ◊ *noun, plural* **patters**

pattern *noun* **1.** An artistic design used for decoration: *The wallpaper has a pattern of flowers.* **2.** A model or guide for making something: *Use a pattern for cutting out the dress.*
◊ *verb* To form or design according to a pattern: *That country's constitution is patterned after ours.*
pat·tern (păt′ ərn) ◊ *noun, plural* **patterns** ◊ *verb* **patterned, patterning**

patty *noun* A small, flat piece of chopped or ground food.
pat·ty (păt′ ē) ◊ *noun, plural* **patties**

pauper *noun* A very poor person.
pau·per (pô′ pər) ◊ *noun, plural* **paupers**

pause *noun* A brief stop.
◊ *verb* To stop briefly.
pause (pôz) ◊ *noun, plural* **pauses** ◊ *verb* **paused, pausing**

pave *verb* To cover with a hard surface of concrete or asphalt.
pave (pāv) ◊ *verb* **paved, paving**

pavement *noun* A paved surface.
pave·ment (pāv′ mənt) ◊ *noun*

pavilion *noun* **1.** A large tent. **2.** A building with open sides that is used at parks or fairs.
pa·vil·ion (pə vĭl′ yən) ◊ *noun, plural* **pavilions**

▲ **pavilion**

paw *noun* The foot of a four-footed animal that has claws.
◊ *verb* **1.** To touch or strike with a paw. **2.** To handle in a clumsy way.
paw (pô) ◊ *noun, plural* **paws** ◊ *verb* **pawed, pawing**

pawn¹ *verb* To give or leave as a guarantee to pay back borrowed money: *They had to pawn their TV to pay for food.*
pawn¹ (pôn) ◊ *verb* **pawned, pawning**

pawn² *noun* A chess piece.
pawn² (pôn) ◊ *noun, plural* **pawns**

***HISTORY* • pawn¹, pawn²**

Pawn¹ comes from an old French word that meant "a pledge." **Pawn²** goes back to a Latin word that meant "foot soldier, infantryman."

pay *verb* **1.** To give money in exchange for goods or for work done: *Pay the waiter. I paid for my ticket.* **2.** To give the required amount for: *We have to pay taxes.* **3.** To be worthwhile or helpful: *It pays to study.* **4.** To give or express: *Pay attention.*
◊ *noun* Money paid for work done; salary.
pay (pā) ◊ *verb* **paid, paying** ◊ *noun*

payment *noun* **1.** The action of paying. **2.** Something paid: *We make monthly payments on the car.*
pay·ment (pā′ mənt) ◊ *noun, plural* **payments**

P

pea *noun* A vegetable that is the round green seed in the pods of a garden plant.
pea (pē) ◊ *noun, plural* **peas**

peace *noun* **1.** The absence of war or fighting. **2.** Freedom from mental or emotional upset: *I need peace and quiet.* **3.** Public security; law and order.
peace (pēs) ◊ *noun*
‖*These sound alike:* **peace, piece**

peaceable *adjective* Peaceful.
peace·a·ble (pē′sə bəl) ◊ *adjective*

peaceful *adjective* **1.** Not likely to go to war or to fight: *We live in a peaceful nation.* **2.** Marked by peace and calmness. —See Synonyms at **calm.**
peace·ful (pēs′fəl) ◊ *adjective*

peace pipe *noun* A pipe smoked by Native Americans, especially as a sign of peace.
peace pipe ◊ *noun, plural* **peace pipes**

peach *noun* **1.** A sweet, round, juicy fruit with fuzzy yellow or pink skin and a pit with a hard shell. **2.** A light yellowish pink color.
peach (pēch) ◊ *noun, plural* **peaches**

peacock *noun* A large bird that has brilliant blue or green feathers. A peacock has long, brightly colored tail feathers that can be spread out like a large fan.
pea·cock (pē′kŏk′) ◊ *noun, plural* **peacocks**

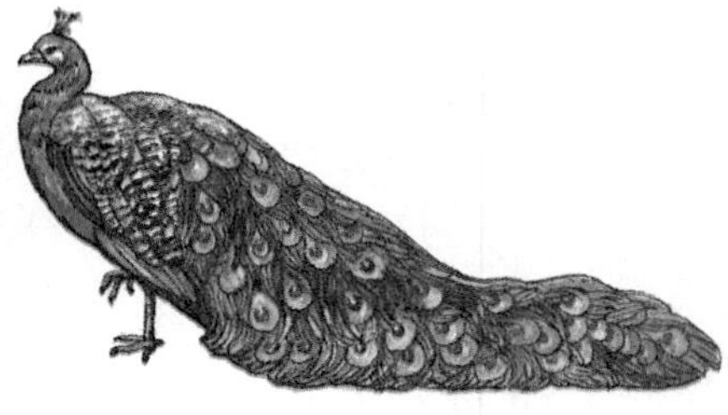

▲ **peacock**

ă	pat	ĭ	pit	oi	oil	th	bath
ā	pay	ī	ride	o͝o	book	*th*	bathe
â	care	î	fierce	o͞o	boot	ə	ago, item
ä	father	ŏ	pot	ou	out		pencil
ĕ	pet	ō	go	ŭ	cut		atom
ē	be	ô	paw, for	û	fur		circus

peak *noun* **1.** The top of a mountain. **2.** A mountain. **3.** A pointed top or end: *I touched the peak of my cap.* **4.** The point of greatest development or intensity.
peak (pēk) ◊ *noun, plural* **peaks**
‖*These sound alike:* **peak, peek**

peal *noun* **1.** The sound of ringing bells. **2.** A loud noise or series of noises: *We heard peals of laughter.*
◊ *verb* To sound in peals; ring: *The bells pealed.*
peal (pēl) ◊ *noun, plural* **peals** ◊ *verb* **pealed, pealing**
‖*These sound alike:* **peal, peel**

peanut *noun* **1.** A vine similar to the pea that bears oily, edible, light-brown seeds enclosed in pods that ripen underground. **2.** The seed of the peanut.
pea·nut (pē′nŭt′) ◊ *noun, plural* **peanuts**

peanut butter *noun* A spread that is made of crushed peanuts.

pear *noun* A fruit with a rounded base and a tapering end at the stem. Pears grow on trees.
pear (pâr) ◊ *noun, plural* **pears**
‖*These sound alike:* **pear, pair, pare**

▲ **pear**

pearl *noun* A smooth, rounded, white or grayish growth formed inside the shells of oysters and used as a gem.
pearl (pûrl) ◊ *noun, plural* **pearls**

peasant *noun* A small farmer or farm laborer in Europe.
peas·ant (pĕz′ənt) ◊ *noun, plural* **peasants**

peat *noun* A material made up of decaying plants that is found in swamps. Peat is used as a fuel and as a fertilizer.
peat (pēt) ◊ *noun*

pebble *noun* A small round stone.
peb·ble (pĕb′əl) ◊ *noun, plural* **pebbles**

pebbly *adjective* Covered with pebbles.
peb·bly (pĕb′lē) ◊ *adjective*

pecan *noun* **1.** An edible nut with a smooth, oval shell. **2.** A tree that bears pecans.
pe·can (pĭ **kän′** *or* pĭ **kăn′**) ◊ *noun, plural* **pecans**

peck¹ *verb* **1.** To strike with a beak or sharp instrument. **2.** To cut, make a hole in, or open by striking with or as if with a beak.
◊ *noun* A stroke or light blow with a beak.
peck¹ (pĕk) ◊ *verb* **pecked, pecking** ◊ *noun, plural* **pecks**

peck² *noun* A unit of capacity for dry things equal to eight quarts.
peck² (pĕk) ◊ *noun, plural* **pecks**

***HISTORY* • peck¹, peck²**

Peck¹ was probably borrowed from an old German word that meant "to strike with the beak." **Peck²** comes from an old French word that meant "a measure of grain."

peculiar *adjective* **1.** Not usual. **2.** Characteristic of a particular person, place, or thing: *Speech is peculiar to human beings.*
pe·cu·liar (pĭ **kyo͞ol′**yər) ◊ *adjective*

peculiarity *noun* **1.** The quality or condition of being peculiar. **2.** Something peculiar.
pe·cu·li·ar·i·ty (pĭ kyo͞o′lē **ăr′**ĭ tē) ◊ *noun, plural* **peculiarities**

pedal *noun* A lever, as on a piano, that is worked by the foot.
◊ *verb* **1.** To use or operate a pedal. **2.** To ride a bicycle or tricycle.
ped·al (**pĕd′**l) ◊ *noun, plural* **pedals** ◊ *verb* **pedaled, pedaling**
‖*These sound alike:* **pedal, peddle**

peddle *verb* To travel about while selling: *I can make money peddling magazines.*
ped·dle (**pĕd′**l) ◊ *verb* **peddled, peddling**
‖*These sound alike:* **peddle, pedal**

pedestal *noun* A base or support, as for a column or a statue.
ped·es·tal (**pĕd′**ĭ stəl) ◊ *noun, plural* **pedestals**

pedestrian *noun* A person traveling on foot.
pe·des·tri·an (pə **dĕs′**trē ən) ◊ *noun, plural* **pedestrians**

pediatrician *noun* A medical doctor who treats the diseases of children and babies.
pe·di·a·tri·cian (pē′dē ə **trĭsh′**ən) ◊ *noun, plural* **pediatricians**

pedigree *noun* A line or list of ancestors.
ped·i·gree (**pĕd′**ĭ grē′) ◊ *noun, plural* **pedigrees**

peek *verb* To glance or look quickly or secretly.
◊ *noun* A quick, secret glance or look.
peek (pēk) ◊ *verb* **peeked, peeking** ◊ *noun, plural* **peeks**
‖*These sound alike:* **peek, peak**

peel *noun* The skin or rind of a fruit such as an orange or a banana.
◊ *verb* **1.** To remove the skin or rind from. **2.** To strip away; pull off: *We peeled the label from the jar.* **3.** To come off in strips or layers: *The paint peeled from the walls.*
peel (pēl) ◊ *noun, plural* **peels** ◊ *verb* **peeled, peeling**
‖*These sound alike:* **peel, peal**

peep¹ *noun* A weak, high-pitched sound.
◊ *verb* To make this sound.
peep¹ (pēp) ◊ *noun, plural* **peeps** ◊ *verb* **peeped, peeping**

peep² *verb* To look secretly, especially from a hidden place; peek.
◊ *noun* A quick look; peek.
peep² (pēp) ◊ *verb* **peeped, peeping** ◊ *noun, plural* **peeps**

***HISTORY* • peep¹, peep²**

Peep¹ is a word made up to imitate the sound it describes. **Peep²** seems to be a different form of the word **peek.**

peer¹ *verb* To look intently or with difficulty.
peer¹ (pîr) ◊ *verb* **peered, peering**
‖*These sound alike:* **peer, pier**

peer² *noun* **1.** A member of the British nobility, such as a duke. **2.** A person of the same age, rank, or standing as another; equal.
peer² (pîr) ◊ *noun, plural* **peers**
‖*These sound alike:* **peer, pier**

P

HISTORY • peer[1], peer[2]

Peer[1] may have been shortened from **appear. Peer[2]** comes from an old French word that came from a Latin word meaning "equal."

peg *noun* A pin, often of wood, used especially to fasten things or to plug a hole. ◊ *verb* To fasten down or plug with a peg.
peg (pĕg) ◊ *noun, plural* **pegs** ◊ *verb* **pegged, pegging**

P.E.I. The abbreviation for *Prince Edward Island,* Canada.

Pekingese *noun* A small dog with short legs, long hair, and a flat nose.
Pe·king·ese (pē′kĭ nēz′) ◊ *noun, plural* **Pekingese**

pelican *noun* A bird with a long bill, webbed feet, and a large pouch under the lower bill in which it holds the fish it catches.
pel·i·can (pĕl′ĭ kən) ◊ *noun, plural* **pelicans**

▲ **pelican**

pellet *noun* A small ball, as of medicine.
pel·let (pĕl′ĭt) ◊ *noun, plural* **pellets**

pell-mell *adverb* In a confused way: *The crowd rushed out pell-mell from the arena.*
pell-mell (pĕl′mĕl′) ◊ *adverb*

pelt[1] *noun* An animal skin, especially with the hair or fur still on it.
pelt[1] (pĕlt) ◊ *noun, plural* **pelts**

pelt[2] *verb* To strike or beat against again and again: *We pelted our friends with snowballs. The rain pelted down.*
pelt[2] (pĕlt) ◊ *verb* **pelted, pelting**

ă	pat	ĭ	pit	oi	**oi**l	th	ba**th**
ā	pay	ī	ride	ŏŏ	book	*th*	ba**th**e
â	care	î	fierce	ōō	boot	ə	ago, item
ä	father	ŏ	pot	ou	**ou**t		pencil
ĕ	pet	ō	go	ŭ	cut		atom
ē	be	ô	paw, for	û	fur		circus

HISTORY • pelt[1], pelt[2]

Pelt[1] is probably related to a Latin word meaning "skin." **Pelt[2]** may have been shortened from a verb form of **pellet,** meaning "to strike with pellets."

pen[1] *noun* An instrument used for writing with ink.
pen[1] (pĕn) ◊ *noun, plural* **pens**

pen[2] *noun* A small, fenced-in area, especially one in which animals are kept. ◊ *verb* To keep in or as if in a pen.
pen[2] (pĕn) ◊ *noun, plural* **pens** ◊ *verb* **penned, penning**

HISTORY • pen[1], pen[2]

Pen[1] goes back to a Latin word that meant "feather." The earliest pens were made from the central parts of feathers. **Pen[2]** comes from an old English word that meant "an enclosure for animals."

penalize *verb* To give a penalty to. —See Synonyms at **punish.**
pe·nal·ize (pē′nə līz′ *or* pĕn′ə līz′) ◊ *verb* **penalized, penalizing**

penalty *noun* **1.** Punishment for a crime or offense. **2.** Something that must be given up for breaking a rule in a game or sport.
pen·al·ty (pĕn′əl tē) ◊ *noun, plural* **penalties**

pencil *noun* A thin stick of black or colored material used for writing or drawing. ◊ *verb* To write or draw with a pencil.
pen·cil (pĕn′səl) ◊ *noun, plural* **pencils** ◊ *verb* **penciled, penciling**

pendant *noun* A hanging ornament, as one on a necklace.
pen·dant (pĕn′dənt) ◊ *noun, plural* **pendants**

pendulum *noun* A weight hung, as in a clock, so that it can swing back and forth.
pen·du·lum (pĕn′jə ləm *or* pĕn′dyə ləm) ◊ *noun, plural* **pendulums**

penetrate *verb* **1.** To pass into or through; pierce: *Very little light penetrated the forest.* **2.** To come to an understanding of: *I can't penetrate the mystery.*
pen·e·trate (pĕn′ĭ trāt′) ◊ *verb* **penetrated, penetrating**

penetration *noun* **1.** The act or process of penetrating. **2.** Complete understanding.
pen·e·tra·tion (pĕn′ĭ **trā′**shən) ◊ *noun*

penguin *noun* A sea bird that lives in or near Antarctica, has webbed feet, and cannot fly.
pen·guin (**pĕn′**gwĭn *or* **pĕng′**gwĭn) ◊ *noun, plural* **penguins**

penicillin *noun* Any of a group of antibiotic drugs made from mold. Penicillin is used to treat diseases and infections.
pen·i·cil·lin (pĕn′ĭ **sĭl′**ĭn) ◊ *noun*

peninsula *noun* A piece of land that sticks out into water from a larger land mass.
pen·in·su·la (pə **nĭn′**syə lə *or* pə **nĭn′**sə lə) ◊ *noun, plural* **peninsulas**

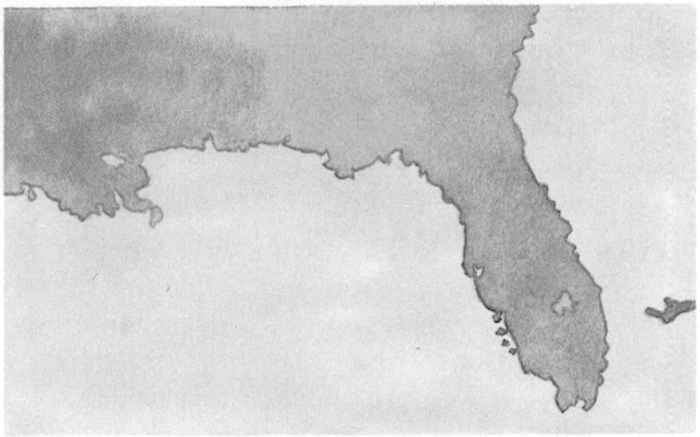

▲ **peninsula**

penitentiary *noun* A prison.
pen·i·ten·tia·ry (pĕn′ĭ **tĕn′**shə rē) ◊ *noun, plural* **penitentiaries**

penknife *noun* A small pocketknife.
pen·knife (**pĕn′**nīf′) ◊ *noun, plural* **penknives**

penmanship *noun* The art, skill, style, or manner of handwriting.
pen·man·ship (**pĕn′**mən shĭp′) ◊ *noun*

Penn. *or* **Penna.** Abbreviations for *Pennsylvania.*

pennant *noun* A long, tapering flag used for signaling or identification.
pen·nant (**pĕn′**ənt) ◊ *noun, plural* **pennants**

penniless *adjective* Having no money.
pen·ni·less (**pĕn′**ē lĭs) ◊ *adjective*

penny *noun* A coin used in the United States and Canada; cent. One hundred pennies equal one dollar.
pen·ny (**pĕn′**ē) ◊ *noun, plural* **pennies**

pension *noun* A sum of money that is paid regularly to a person who has retired from work.
pen·sion (**pĕn′**shən) ◊ *noun, plural* **pensions**

pentagon *noun* A figure with five sides and five angles.
pen·ta·gon (**pĕn′**tə gŏn′) ◊ *noun, plural* **pentagons**

▲ **pentagon**

penthouse *noun* An apartment on the top floor of a building.
pent·house (**pĕnt′**hous′) ◊ *noun, plural* **penthouses**

peony *noun* A plant with large pink, red, or white flowers.
pe·o·ny (**pē′**ə nē) ◊ *noun, plural* **peonies**

people *noun* **1.** Human beings. **2.** A group of persons living in the same country under one government. **3.** A group of persons sharing a common religion, culture, language, or way of life. **4.** Family, relatives, or ancestors: *My people are farmers.*
◊ *verb* To populate.
peo·ple (**pē′**pəl) ◊ *noun, plural* **people** (for senses 1, 2, and 4) *or* **peoples** (for sense 3) ◊ *verb* **peopled, peopling**

pep *noun* High spirits or energy.
pep (pĕp) ◊ *noun*

pepper *noun* **1.** A strong seasoning made from the dried, blackish berries of an Asian vine. **2.** A hollow green or red vegetable that is eaten raw or cooked and is often used as a seasoning.
pep·per (**pĕp′**ər) ◊ *noun, plural* **peppers**

peppermint *noun* A plant with leaves that yield a strong oil used especially to flavor candy.
pep·per·mint (**pĕp′**ər mĭnt′) ◊ *noun, plural* **peppermints**

per *preposition* For or to every: *We paid $1.00 per gallon for gasoline.*
per (pûr *or* pər) ◊ *preposition*

perceive *verb* **1.** To be aware of through the senses, especially the senses of sight or hearing. **2.** To understand.
per·ceive (pər **sēv′**) ◊ *verb* **perceived, perceiving**

P

percent *or* **per cent** *noun* One part in a hundred: *Twenty-five percent of the members voted against the amendment.*
per·cent *or* **per cent** (pər **sĕnt′**) ◊ *noun*

percentage *noun* **1.** A fraction with 100 as its denominator. **2.** A share in relation to a whole: *Each of them got a percentage of the profits.*
per·cent·age (pər **sĕn′**tĭj) ◊ *noun, plural* **percentages**

perception *noun* **1.** The act or process of perceiving. **2.** The ability to perceive or understand. **3.** Something perceived.
per·cep·tion (pər **sĕp′**shən) ◊ *noun, plural* **perceptions**

perch[1] *noun* **1.** A branch or rod on which a bird can sit. **2.** A place where a person can sit.
◊ *verb* To rest or sit on or as if on a perch.
perch[1] (pûrch) ◊ *noun, plural* **perches** ◊ *verb* **perched, perching**

perch[2] *noun* A freshwater food fish.
perch[2] (pûrch) ◊ *noun, plural* **perch** *or* **perches**

***HISTORY* • perch[1], perch[2]**

Perch[1] goes back to a Latin word that meant "pole." **Perch**[2] goes back to a Greek word for this fish. **Perch**[2] passed through Latin and French before arriving in English.

percussion *noun* **1.** The striking together of two things, especially when it creates noise. **2.** A sound, vibration, or shock produced by percussion. **3.** Percussion instruments as a group.
per·cus·sion (pər **kŭsh′**ən) ◊ *noun, plural* **percussions**

percussion instrument *noun* A musical instrument, such as a drum or tambourine, that is sounded by striking or shaking.
percussion instrument ◊ *noun, plural* **percussion instruments**

ă	pat	ĭ	pit	oi	oil	th	bath
ā	pay	ī	ride	ŏŏ	book	*th*	bathe
â	care	î	fierce	ōō	boot	ə	ago, item
ä	father	ŏ	pot	ou	out		pencil
ĕ	pet	ō	go	ŭ	cut		atom
ē	be	ô	paw, for	û	fur		circus

perennial *adjective* **1.** Living, growing, and flowering and producing seeds for several or many years: *Roses are perennial plants.* **2.** Lasting indefinitely; never ending: *I seem to have perennial health problems.*
◊ *noun* A perennial plant.
per·en·ni·al (pə **rĕn′**ē əl) ◊ *adjective* ◊ *noun, plural* **perennials**

perfect *adjective* **1.** Lacking nothing; complete: *My friend has perfect knowledge of German.* **2.** Having no flaws, mistakes, or defects: *My drawing is a perfect copy of yours.* **3.** Completely qualified or skilled: *You are the perfect actor for the part.* **4.** Excellent in every way: *This is perfect weather.*
◊ *verb* To make perfect.
per·fect ◊ *adjective* (**pûr′**fĭkt) ◊ *verb* (pər-**fĕkt′**), **perfected, perfecting**

perfection *noun* **1.** The act or process of perfecting. **2.** The quality or condition of being perfect.
per·fec·tion (pər **fĕk′**shən) ◊ *noun*

perforate *verb* **1.** To make a hole in; pierce: *Perforate the top of the pie to let the steam escape.* **2.** To make rows of holes in to allow easy separation: *The pages are perforated.*
per·fo·rate (**pûr′**fə rāt′) ◊ *verb* **perforated, perforating**

perform *verb* **1.** To carry out; do: *We will perform an experiment in class.* **2.** To present, especially before an audience: *The fifth graders performed a play.*
per·form (pər **fôrm′**) ◊ *verb* **performed, performing**

SYNONYMS

perform, accomplish, fulfill

Dogs can *perform* amazing tricks. I have a lot to *accomplish* today. You have *fulfilled* your responsibilities.

performance *noun* **1.** The act, process, or manner of performing. **2.** A public presentation of something, such as a play.
per·form·ance (pər **fôr′**məns) ◊ *noun, plural* **performances**

perfume *noun* **1.** A pleasant-smelling liquid made especially from flowers. **2.** A pleasing scent or odor.
◊ *verb* To fill with perfume: *The smell of*

flowers perfumed the house.
per·fume ◊ *noun* (**pûr′**fyo͞om′ *or* pər-**fyo͞om′**), *plural* **perfumes** ◊ *verb* (pər-**fyo͞om′**) **perfumed, perfuming**

perhaps *adverb* Maybe but not definitely; possibly: *Perhaps you'll come with us.*
per·haps (pər **hăps′**) ◊ *adverb*

peril *noun* **1.** The condition of being in danger: *The diver's life is in peril.* **2.** Something dangerous.
per·il (**pĕr′** əl) ◊ *noun, plural* **perils**

perilous *adjective* Full of peril; dangerous.
per·il·ous (**pĕr′** ə ləs) ◊ *adjective*

perimeter *noun* The distance around the sides of a flat space or a geometric figure.
pe·rim·e·ter (pə **rĭm′**ĭ tər) ◊ *noun, plural* **perimeters**

period *noun* **1.** An interval or portion of time: *A year is a period of 12 months.* **2.** A punctuation mark (.) used to indicate the end of a sentence or an abbreviation.
pe·ri·od (**pîr′** ē əd) ◊ *noun, plural* **periods**

periodic *adjective* Happening or repeating at regular intervals: *There have been periodic outbreaks of flu all winter.*
pe·ri·od·ic (pîr′ē **ŏd′**ĭk) ◊ *adjective*

periodical *noun* A publication, especially a magazine, that appears at regular intervals.
pe·ri·od·i·cal (pîr′ē **ŏd′**ĭ kəl) ◊ *noun, plural* **periodicals**

periscope *noun* An instrument with mirrors or prisms that allows a person, as on a submarine, to see objects that would otherwise be blocked from view.
per·i·scope (**pĕr′**ĭ skōp′) ◊ *noun, plural* **periscopes**

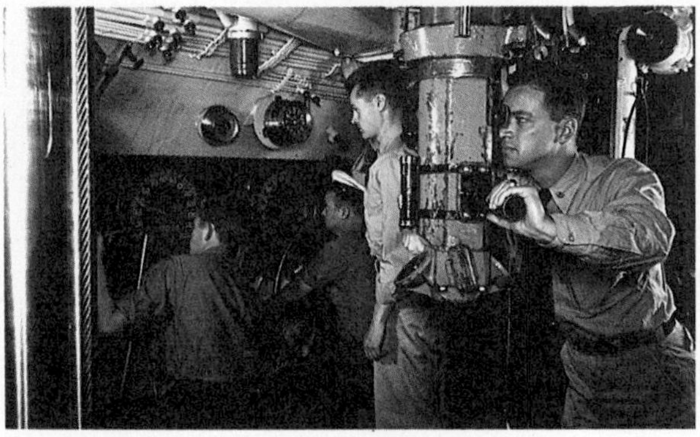

▲ **periscope**

perish *verb* To come to an end; die: *Entire towns perished in the earthquake.*
per·ish (**pĕr′**ĭsh) ◊ *verb* **perished, perishing**

perishable *adjective* Being likely to decay or spoil: *Milk is perishable.*
per·ish·a·ble (**pĕr′**ĭ shə bəl) ◊ *adjective*

periwinkle *noun* A small sea snail that is sometimes eaten as food.
per·i·win·kle (**pĕr′**ĭ wĭng′kəl) ◊ *noun, plural* **periwinkles**

perk *verb* To lift in a brisk, bold, or alert way: *The dog perked its ears.*
◊ *idiom* **perk up** To become or cause to become lively or bright again, as after depression: *We perked up at the good news.*
perk (pûrk) ◊ *verb* **perked, perking**

perky *adjective* Cheerful and brisk.
perk·y (**pûr′**kē) ◊ *adjective* **perkier, perkiest**

permanent *adjective* Lasting or meant to last for a long time: *The Arctic is a land of permanent ice and snow.*
per·ma·nent (**pûr′** mə nənt) ◊ *adjective*

permeate *verb* **1.** To spread or flow throughout: *The smell of cabbage permeated the house.* **2.** To pass through the pores or substance of: *Water permeates gravel.*
per·me·ate (**pûr′**mē āt′) ◊ *verb* **permeated, permeating**

permission *noun* Consent granted by someone in authority: *Our parents gave us permission to go to the movies.*
per·mis·sion (pər **mĭsh′**ən) ◊ *noun*

permit *verb* **1.** To give permission to; allow: *Smoking is not permitted in elevators.* —See Synonyms at **let. 2.** To afford an opportunity; make possible: *If the weather permits, we will have a softball game.*
◊ *noun* A written certificate of permission.
per·mit ◊ *verb* (pər **mĭt′**) **permitted, permitting** ◊ *noun* (**pûr′**mĭt′ *or* pər **mĭt′**), *plural* **permits**

pernicious *adjective* Very harmful or destructive.
per·ni·cious (pər **nĭsh′**əs) ◊ *adjective*

perpendicular *adjective* **1.** Crossing at or forming a right angle: *In geometry class we drew perpendicular lines.* **2.** Being at right angles to the horizontal. —See Synonyms at **vertical.**
per·pen·dic·u·lar (pûr′pən **dĭk′** yə lər) ◊ *adjective*

P

perpetrate *verb* To carry through; commit: *They perpetrated a crime.*
per·pe·trate (pûr′ pĭ trāt′) ◊ *verb* **perpetrated, perpetrating**

perpetual *adjective* **1.** Lasting forever: *The mountain is covered with perpetual snow.* **2.** Continuing without interruption; constant: *Stop your perpetual complaining.*
per·pet·u·al (pər **pĕch′** o͞o əl) ◊ *adjective*

perpetuate *verb* To cause to be perpetual: *The nation perpetuated the hero's memory by erecting a memorial to him.*
per·pet·u·ate (pər **pĕch′** o͞o āt′) ◊ *verb* **perpetuated, perpetuating**

perplex *verb* To cause mental confusion in; puzzle: *Parts of her story perplex me.*
per·plex (pər **plĕks′**) ◊ *verb* **perplexed, perplexing**

perplexity *noun* **1.** The condition of being perplexed. **2.** Something that perplexes.
per·plex·i·ty (pər **plĕk′** sĭ tē) ◊ *noun, plural* **perplexities**

persecute *verb* To cause constant suffering to, as because of political beliefs; oppress.
per·se·cute (**pûr′** sĭ kyo͞ot′) ◊ *verb* **persecuted, persecuting**

persecution *noun* **1.** The act of persecuting. **2.** The condition or fact of being persecuted.
per·se·cu·tion (pûr′sĭ **kyo͞o′** shən) ◊ *noun, plural* **persecutions**

perseverance *noun* The act or quality of persevering.
per·se·ver·ance (pûr′sə **vîr′** əns) ◊ *noun*

persevere *verb* To continue to try to do something despite obstacles or difficulties: *We persevered in our efforts to learn to sew.*
per·se·vere (pûr′sə **vîr′**) ◊ *verb* **persevered, persevering**

persimmon *noun* An orange-red fruit with sweet pulp that can be eaten only when it is fully ripe.
per·sim·mon (pər **sĭm′** ən) ◊ *noun, plural* **persimmons**

ă	pat	ĭ	pit	oi	**oil**	th	bath
ā	pay	ī	ride	o͝o	**book**	*th*	bathe
â	care	î	fierce	o͞o	**boot**	ə	ago, item
ä	father	ŏ	pot	ou	**out**		pencil
ĕ	pet	ō	go	ŭ	cut		atom
ē	be	ô	paw, for	û	fur		circus

▲ **persimmon**

persist *verb* **1.** To continue stubbornly to say or do something: *Why do you persist in going to bed so late?* **2.** To continue to happen or exist; last: *Snow persisted most of the week.*
per·sist (pər **sĭst′**) ◊ *verb* **persisted, persisting**

persistence *noun* **1.** The act or fact of persisting. **2.** The quality of being persistent.
per·sist·ence (pər **sĭs′** təns) ◊ *noun*

persistent *adjective* **1.** Refusing to give up or let go: *A persistent salesperson finally sold them the car.* **2.** Lasting for a long time: *A persistent cough kept me awake all night.*
per·sist·ent (pər **sĭs′** tənt) ◊ *adjective*

person *noun* **1.** A human being; individual: *Any person who wants to can come.* **2.** The living body of a human being: *He had a lot of money on his person.* **3.** A pronoun or verb form that refers to the speaker or speakers (*first person*), the one or ones spoken to (*second person*), or the one or ones spoken of (*third person*).
◊ *idiom* **in person** With or by means of one's own physical presence: *I applied for the job in person.*
per·son (**pûr′** sən) ◊ *noun, plural* **persons**

personal *adjective* **1.** Of, relating to, or belonging to a person; private: *My clothes are my personal property.* **2.** Of or relating to a particular person and his or her character: *Personal comments about others are often impolite.* **3.** Done or made in person: *The writer gave a personal interview.* **4.** Of the body or physical being: *Our parents teach us personal tidiness.*
per·son·al (**pûr′** sə nəl) ◊ *adjective*

personality *noun* **1.** All the qualities and traits, as of character, that distinguish one person from others: *My teacher has a pleasing personality.* **2.** A person's appealing qualities: *The candidate won on personality.* **3.** An important or famous person: *Many television personalities attended the play.*
per·son·al·i·ty (pûr′sə **năl′** ĭ tē) ◊ *noun, plural* **personalities**

personally *adverb* **1.** Without the help of another; in person: *I thanked her personally.* **2.** As far as oneself is concerned: *Personally I can't stand figs.* **3.** As a person: *I don't know him personally.*
per·son·al·ly (**pûr′** sə nə lē) ◊ *adverb*

personnel *noun* The body of persons employed by an organization or a business.
per·son·nel (pûr′sə **nĕl′**) ◊ *noun*

perspective *noun* **1.** The art of representing objects on a flat surface so that they seem to be the same as in real life. **2.** The relationship of objects or events to each other and to a whole: *Put your problems into proper perspective; after all, they are very minor.*
per·spec·tive (pər **spĕk′** tĭv) ◊ *noun, plural* **perspectives**

perspiration *noun* **1.** Salty moisture given off through the skin by the sweat glands; sweat. **2.** The act or process of perspiring.
per·spi·ra·tion (pûr′spə **rā′** shən) ◊ *noun*

perspire *verb* To give off perspiration.
per·spire (pər **spīr′**) ◊ *verb* **perspired, perspiring**

persuade *verb* To cause to do or believe something, as by arguing; convince: *We finally persuaded them that they were wrong.*
per·suade (pər **swād′**) ◊ *verb* **persuaded, persuading**

persuasion *noun* **1.** The act of persuading. **2.** The ability to persuade: *Some lawyers lack persuasion.* **3.** A form or kind of belief: *People of all persuasions listened to the speech.*
per·sua·sion (pər **swā′** zhən) ◊ *noun, plural* **persuasions**

pertain *verb* To have reference; relate: *This lesson pertains to marine animals.*
per·tain (pər **tān′**) ◊ *verb* **pertained, pertaining**

pertinent *adjective* Related to the matter being discussed or considered.
per·ti·nent (**pûr′** tn ənt) ◊ *adjective*

perturb *verb* To make uneasy in the mind.
per·turb (pər **tûrb′**) ◊ *verb* **perturbed, perturbing**

pervade *verb* To spread or be present throughout; permeate.
per·vade (pər **vād′**) ◊ *verb* **pervaded, pervading**

perverse *adjective* Stubbornly doing or determined to do the opposite of what is right, expected, or desired; contrary.
per·verse (pər **vûrs′**) ◊ *adjective*

peso *noun* A unit of money used in Mexico, the Philippines, and many countries of Latin America.
pe·so (**pā′** sō) ◊ *noun, plural* **pesos**

pessimistic *adjective* Likely to take the gloomiest or least hopeful view of a situation.
pes·si·mis·tic (pĕs′ə **mĭs′** tĭk) ◊ *adjective*

pest *noun* **1.** An annoying person. **2.** An animal or a plant that is harmful or troublesome to human beings.
pest (pĕst) ◊ *noun, plural* **pests**

pester *verb* To annoy repeatedly.
pes·ter (**pĕs′** tər) ◊ *verb* **pestered, pestering**

pesticide *noun* A chemical used to kill harmful pests, such as insects.
pes·ti·cide (**pĕs′** tĭ sīd′) ◊ *noun, plural* **pesticides**

pestle *noun* A tool with a rounded end for crushing or mashing substances in a mortar.
pes·tle (**pĕs′** əl) ◊ *noun, plural* **pestles**

▲ **pestle**

pet *noun* **1.** A tame animal kept for companionship or pleasure. **2.** Someone or something that one is especially fond of; favorite: *The youngest child was the pet of the family.*
◊ *adjective* **1.** Treated or kept as a pet: *My pet cat sleeps on my bed.* **2.** Being a favorite: *That is the scientist's pet theory. That is my pet peeve.*
◊ *verb* To stroke or pat in a gentle manner.
pet (pĕt) ◊ *noun, plural* **pets** ◊ *adjective* ◊ *verb* **petted, petting**

P

petal *noun* One of the usually brightly colored leaflike parts of a flower.
pet·al (pĕt′l) ◊ *noun, plural* **petals**

petition *noun* **1.** A solemn request, especially to a person or group in authority. **2.** A written document making a request.
◊ *verb* **1.** To address a petition to. **2.** To make a petition.
pe·ti·tion (pə **tĭsh′**ən) ◊ *noun, plural* **petitions** ◊ *verb* **petitioned, petitioning**

petrel *noun* A sea bird that flies over the open ocean far from land.
pet·rel (pĕt′rəl) ◊ *noun, plural* **petrels**

petrify *verb* **1.** To turn organic material, such as wood, into a stonelike substance: *I found petrified fish in the desert.* **2.** To terrify.
pet·ri·fy (pĕt′rə fī′) ◊ *verb* **petrified, petrifying**

petroleum *noun* A thick, yellowish-black oil that occurs naturally below the surface of the earth. It is the source of gasoline, paraffin, and kerosene.
pe·tro·le·um (pə **trō′**lē əm) ◊ *noun*

petticoat *noun* A skirt worn by girls and women as an undergarment.
pet·ti·coat (**pĕt′**ē kōt′) ◊ *noun, plural* **petticoats**

petty *adjective* **1.** Small and unimportant; trivial: *Don't bother the teacher with petty complaints.* **2.** Mean in small ways.
pet·ty (**pĕt′**ē) ◊ *adjective* **pettier, pettiest**

petty officer *noun* A Navy or Coast Guard officer appointed from enlisted personnel.
petty officer ◊ *noun, plural* **petty officers**

petunia *noun* A garden plant with brightly colored flowers shaped like funnels.
pe·tu·nia (pə **to͞o′**nyə *or* pə **tyo͞o′**nyə) ◊ *noun, plural* **petunias**

pew *noun* A bench that people sit on in church.
pew (pyo͞o) ◊ *noun, plural* **pews**

pewee *noun* A small, brownish bird with a call that sounds like its name.
pe·wee (**pē′**wē′) ◊ *noun, plural* **pewees**

ă	pat	ĭ	pit	oi	**oi**l	th	ba**th**
ā	pay	ī	ride	o͝o	b**oo**k	*th*	ba**the**
â	care	î	fierce	o͞o	b**oo**t	ə	**a**go, it**e**m
ä	father	ŏ	pot	ou	**ou**t		penc**i**l
ĕ	pet	ō	go	ŭ	cut		at**o**m
ē	be	ô	paw, for	û	fur		circ**u**s

pewter *noun* **1.** An alloy of tin mixed with copper and lead that is used for making utensils, such as candlesticks and pitchers. **2.** Utensils made of pewter.
pew·ter (**pyo͞o′**tər) ◊ *noun*

pg. An abbreviation for *page.*

phantom *noun* A ghost.
phan·tom (**făn′**təm) ◊ *noun, plural* **phantoms**

pharaoh *noun* A king of ancient Egypt.
phar·aoh (**fâr′**ō) ◊ *noun, plural* **pharaohs**

pharmaceutical *adjective* Of or having to do with pharmacy or pharmacists.
phar·ma·ceu·ti·cal (fär′mə **so͞o′**tĭ kəl) ◊ *adjective*

pharmacist *noun* A person who specializes in pharmacy; druggist.
phar·ma·cist (**fär′**mə sĭst) ◊ *noun, plural* **pharmacists**

pharmacy *noun* **1.** The methods, techniques, or profession of preparing medicines and drugs. **2.** A place where medicines and drugs are sold; drugstore.
phar·ma·cy (**fär′**mə sē) ◊ *noun, plural* **pharmacies**

phase *noun* **1.** A stage of development: *A new phase of my life began when I entered school.* **2.** A part; aspect: *Have you considered every phase of the problem?* **3.** The shape and appearance of the moon or a planet at a certain time in its cycle of changes.
phase (fāz) ◊ *noun, plural* **phases**

pheasant *noun* A large, brightly colored game bird with a long tail.
pheas·ant (**fĕz′**ənt) ◊ *noun, plural* **pheasants**

▲ **pheasant**

phenomena *noun* A plural of **phenomenon**.
phe·nom·e·na (fĭ **nŏm′**ə nə) ◊ *noun*

phenomenal *adjective* Remarkable; extraordinary: *She ran at a phenomenal speed.*
phe·nom·e·nal (fĭ **nŏm′**ə nəl) ◊ *adjective*

phenomenon *noun* **1.** An event or fact that can be felt by the senses or taken in by the mind: *Floods are natural phenomena.* **2.** Someone or something that is very unusual: *As a musician he's a phenomenon.*
phe·nom·e·non (fĭ **nŏm′**ə nŏn′) ◊ *noun, plural* **phenomena** *or* **phenomenons**

philanthropist *noun* A person who helps other people by making generous gifts.
phi·lan·thro·pist (fĭ **lăn′**thrə pĭst) ◊ *noun, plural* **philanthropists**

philanthropy *noun* **1.** An effort to help other people. **2.** A charitable gift. **3.** An institution that distributes or receives charitable gifts.
phi·lan·thro·py (fĭ **lăn′**thrə pē) ◊ *noun, plural* **philanthropies**

philodendron *noun* A climbing plant with glossy evergreen leaves that is often grown as a house plant.
phil·o·den·dron (fĭl′ə **dĕn′**drən) ◊ *noun, plural* **philodendrons**

philosopher *noun* **1.** A student of or expert in philosophy. **2.** A person who is calm and patient under difficult circumstances.
phi·los·o·pher (fĭ **lŏs′**ə fər) ◊ *noun, plural* **philosophers**

philosophical *or* **philosophic** *adjective* **1.** Of or relating to philosophy. **2.** Calm and patient under difficult circumstances.
phil·o·soph·i·cal (fĭl′ə **sŏf′**ĭ kəl) *or* **phil·o·soph·ic** (fĭl′ə **sŏf′**ĭk) ◊ *adjective*

philosophically *adverb* In a calm and patient way or manner.
phil·o·soph·i·cal·ly (fĭl′ə **sŏf′**ĭk lē) ◊ *adverb*

philosophy *noun* **1.** The study of the basic truths and ideas about the universe. **2.** A system of ideas and principles that govern an individual's life. **3.** A personal set of opinions about life and the world. **4.** Calmness and patience under difficult circumstances.
phi·los·o·phy (fĭ **lŏs′**ə fē) ◊ *noun, plural* **philosophies**

phlox *noun* A plant with clusters of red, purple, or white flowers.
phlox (flŏks) ◊ *noun, plural* **phlox** *or* **phloxes**

▲ **phlox**

phone *noun* A telephone.
◊ *verb* To telephone.
phone (fōn) ◊ *noun, plural* **phones** ◊ *verb* **phoned, phoning**

phonetic *adjective* Of, relating to, or representing the sounds of speech.
pho·net·ic (fə **nĕt′**ĭk) ◊ *adjective*

phonograph *noun* A device that reproduces sound from a groove cut into a record.
pho·no·graph (**fō′**nə grăf′) ◊ *noun, plural* **phonographs**

phony *adjective* Not genuine; fake: *This is a phony diamond.*
◊ *noun* An insincere person; fake. —See Synonyms at **impostor**.
pho·ny (**fō′**nē) ◊ *adjective* ◊ *noun, plural* **phonies**

phosphorescence *noun* **1.** Generation of light by a living thing: *We studied the phosphorescence of certain insects and fish.* **2.** The light that is given off by a living thing.
phos·pho·res·cence (fŏs′fə **rĕs′**əns) ◊ *noun*

phosphorus *noun* A poisonous white or yellow substance that glows in the dark and is used in making matches, detergents, and fertilizers. Phosphorus is a chemical element.
phos·pho·rus (**fŏs′**fər əs) ◊ *noun*

photo *noun* A photograph.
pho·to (**fō′**tō) ◊ *noun, plural* **photos**

photograph *noun* An image formed on film by a camera and developed by chemicals to produce a print.
◊ *verb* To make a photograph of.
pho·to·graph (**fō′**tə grăf′) ◊ *noun, plural* **photographs** ◊ *verb* **photographed, photographing**

P

photographer *noun* A person who takes photographs, especially as an occupation.
pho·tog·ra·pher (fə **tŏg′** rə fər) ◊ *noun, plural* **photographers**

photographic *adjective* Of, relating to, or used in photography.
pho·to·graph·ic (fō′tə **grăf′** ĭk) ◊ *adjective*

photography *noun* The act, process, art, or profession of making photographs.
pho·tog·ra·phy (fə **tŏg′** rə fē) ◊ *noun*

phrase *noun* **1.** A group of words, as *on the table,* that has meaning but is not a complete sentence. **2.** A brief expression.
◊ *verb* To express in spoken or written words.
phrase (frāz) ◊ *noun, plural* **phrases** ◊ *verb* **phrased, phrasing**

physical *adjective* **1.** Of or relating to the body: *I exercise daily for physical fitness.* **2.** Of or relating to matter; material: *A rock is a physical object.* **3.** Of or relating to matter that is not living and to energy rather than living phenomena: *Chemistry is one of the physical sciences.*
phys·i·cal (**fĭz′** ĭ kəl) ◊ *adjective*

physician *noun* A person who has a license to practice medicine; doctor.
phy·si·cian (fĭ **zĭsh′** ən) ◊ *noun, plural* **physicians**

physicist *noun* A scientist who specializes in physics.
phys·i·cist (**fĭz′** ĭ sĭst) ◊ *noun, plural* **physicists**

physics *noun* (*used with a singular verb*) A science that deals with matter and energy and includes light, motion, sound, heat, electricity, and force.
phys·ics (**fĭz′** ĭks) ◊ *noun*

physique *noun* The proportions, development, and appearance of a person's body.
phy·sique (fĭ **zēk′**) ◊ *noun, plural* **physiques**

pianist *noun* A person who plays the piano.
pi·an·ist (pē **ăn′** ĭst *or* **pē′** ə nĭst) ◊ *noun, plural* **pianists**

ă pat	ĭ pit	oi	**oil**	th	**bath**		
ā pay	ī ride	o͝o	book	*th*	bathe		
â care	î fierce	o͞o	boot	ə	ago, item		
ä father	ŏ pot	ou	**out**		pencil		
ĕ pet	ō go	ŭ	cut		atom		
ē be	ô paw, for	û	fur		circus		

piano *noun* A keyboard instrument in which a hammer covered with felt strikes a metal string to produce a tone.
pi·an·o (pē **ăn′** ō) ◊ *noun, plural* **pianos**

piccolo *noun* A small flute with tones an octave above those of the ordinary flute.
pic·co·lo (**pĭk′** ə lō′) ◊ *noun, plural* **piccolos**

▲ **piccolo**

pick¹ *verb* **1.** To select from a group; choose: *I picked the material.* **2.** To gather with the fingers: *I enjoy picking blueberries.* **3.** To remove little by little: *We picked the meat from the bones to make turkey hash.* **4.** To break up or dig at with something pointed: *Chickens picked at the gravel in the driveway.* **5.** To cause deliberately; provoke: *Are you trying to pick a fight?* **6.** To open without using a key: *I picked the lock on my diary.* **7.** To play by plucking with the fingers or a pick: *I picked a tune on my ukulele.*
◊ *noun* **1.** An act of choosing; choice: *We took our pick of the tomatoes.* **2.** The best one: *This puppy is the pick of the litter.*
◊ *idioms* **pick on** To nag at constantly; tease: *Stop picking on me.* **pick up 1.** To grasp and lift: *I picked up my suitcase.* **2.** To get in a casual way or by chance: *I picked up a beautiful suit at a sale.* **3.** To change for the better; improve: *Business is sure to pick up soon.* **4.** To be able to perceive or receive: *The Coast Guard picked up radio signals from a ship in distress.* **5.** To learn without great effort: *I picked up several foreign languages when we lived in Europe.*
pick¹ (pĭk) ◊ *verb* **picked, picking** ◊ *noun, plural* **picks**

pick² *noun* **1.** A pickax. **2.** A device, such as a toothpick, that is used for picking.
pick² (pĭk) ◊ *noun, plural* **picks**

HISTORY • pick¹, pick²

Pick¹ probably comes from an old English word that meant "to prick." **Pick²** is probably related to *pike,* an older English name for this tool.

pickax *or* **pickaxe** *noun* A tool for loosening or breaking up soil. A pickax consists of a slightly curved bar sharpened at one or both ends and fitted onto a long wooden handle.
pick·ax *or* **pick·axe** (**pĭk′**ăks′) ◊ *noun, plural* **pickaxes**

pickerel *noun* A freshwater fish that has a long, pointed head. The pickerel looks like the pike but is smaller.
pick·er·el (**pĭk′** ər əl) ◊ *noun, plural* **pickerel** *or* **pickerels**

picket *noun* **1.** A pointed stake or spike. A picket can be driven into the ground to support a fence. **2.** A soldier or group of soldiers posted as guards. **3.** A person stationed outside a place of work, as a factory, where a strike is going on. Pickets carry signs that express their complaints.
◊ *verb* **1.** To fasten with a picket. **2.** To post or act as a picket during a strike.
pick·et (**pĭk′**ĭt) ◊ *noun, plural* **pickets** ◊ *verb* **picketed, picketing**

pickle *noun* **1.** A liquid for preserving food that is prepared with vinegar or brine. **2.** A food, as a cucumber, that has been preserved and flavored in vinegar or brine.
◊ *verb* To preserve or flavor in a pickle.
pick·le (**pĭk′** əl) ◊ *noun, plural* **pickles** ◊ *verb* **pickled, pickling**

pickup *noun* **1.** The act or process of picking up. **2.** Ability to accelerate rapidly: *My friend's car has good pickup.* **3.** A small, light truck with an open body and low sides.
pick·up (**pĭk′**ŭp′) ◊ *noun, plural* **pickups**

picnic *noun* A party in which those taking part carry their food with them and then eat it outdoors.
◊ *verb* To go on or take part in a picnic.
pic·nic (**pĭk′**nĭk′) ◊ *noun, plural* **picnics** ◊ *verb* **picnicked, picnicking**

pictorial *adjective* **1.** Of, relating to, or expressed in pictures: *The ancient Egyptians used pictorial writing.* **2.** Containing or illustrated by pictures: *I bought a pictorial history of our country.*
pic·to·ri·al (pĭk **tôr′** ē əl) ◊ *adjective*

picture *noun* **1.** A painting, drawing, or photograph of a person or thing. **2.** Someone or something that looks like another: *You are a picture of your cousin.* **3.** An image on a television screen. **4.** A motion picture; movie.
◊ *verb* **1.** To make a picture of. **2.** To form a mental image of; imagine.
pic·ture (**pĭk′** chər) ◊ *noun, plural* **pictures** ◊ *verb* **pictured, picturing**

picturesque *adjective* Like, suggesting, or suitable for a picture: *We drove through several picturesque mountain villages.*
pic·tur·esque (pĭk′chə **rĕsk′**) ◊ *adjective*

pie *noun* A food consisting of a filling, as of fruit or meat, baked in a pastry shell and often covered with a crust.
pie (pī) ◊ *noun, plural* **pies**

piece *noun* **1.** A portion of something larger: *We bought a piece of land in the country.* **2.** A part that has been broken, torn, or cut from a whole: *Put a piece of pie on my plate.* —See Synonyms at **part. 3.** A part of a set or group: *They got a set of china with 60 pieces.* **4.** An artistic, musical, or literary work: *I played the piece I had learned on the piano.* **5.** An item or example: *That's a fine piece of work.* **6.** A coin: *I found a 50-cent piece.*
◊ *verb* To complete by uniting the pieces of: *We sat and pieced the puzzle together.*
piece (pēs) ◊ *noun, plural* **pieces** ◊ *verb* **pieced, piecing**
‖*These sound alike:* **piece, peace**

pied *adjective* Having patches of color.
pied (pīd) ◊ *adjective*

pier *noun* **1.** A platform that extends into water. A pier can be used to protect a harbor or serve as a landing place for ships and boats. **2.** A structure that supports a bridge.
pier (pîr) ◊ *noun, plural* **piers**
‖*These sound alike:* **pier, peer**

pierce *verb* **1.** To make a hole or opening in or through: *A nail pierced the tire.* **2.** To pass into or through: *Icy wind pierced my jacket.* **3.** To make a way into or through.
pierce (pîrs) ◊ *verb* **pierced, piercing**

P

pig *noun* An animal that has hoofs, short legs, a stout body, bristles, and a blunt snout.
pig (pĭg) ◊ *noun, plural* **pigs**

pigeon *noun* A bird with short legs, a plump body, and a small head.
pi·geon (pĭj′ĭn) ◊ *noun, plural* **pigeons**

piggyback *adverb* On the shoulders or back.
pig·gy·back (pĭg′ē băk′) ◊ *adverb*

▲ **piggyback**

pigment *noun* **1.** A substance that gives color to something else. **2.** A substance in plant or animal tissues that gives them their characteristic color.
pig·ment (pĭg′mənt) ◊ *noun, plural* **pigments**

pigpen *noun* **1.** A pen where pigs are kept. **2.** A dirty or messy place.
pig·pen (pĭg′pĕn′) ◊ *noun, plural* **pigpens**

pigsty *noun* A pigpen.
pig·sty (pĭg′stī′) ◊ *noun, plural* **pigsties**

pigtail *noun* A braid of hair at the back of the head.
pig·tail (pĭg′tāl′) ◊ *noun, plural* **pigtails**

pike *noun* A large freshwater fish with a narrow body and a long snout.
pike (pīk) ◊ *noun, plural* **pike** *or* **pikes**

ă	pat	ĭ	pit	oi	**oil**	th	**bath**
ā	pay	ī	ride	o͝o	**book**	*th*	**bathe**
â	care	î	fierce	o͞o	**boot**	ə	ago, item
ä	father	ŏ	pot	ou	**out**		pencil
ĕ	pet	ō	go	ŭ	**cut**		atom
ē	be	ô	paw, for	û	**fur**		circus

pile¹ *noun* A mass of objects heaped together: *A pile of old magazines lay in the attic.*
◊ *verb* **1.** To place or heap in a pile: *Just pile the dishes in the sink.* **2.** To heap in great quantities: *I piled my plate with food.* **3.** To move, often in haste, in a group or mass.
pile¹ (pīl) ◊ *noun, plural* **piles** ◊ *verb* **piled, piling**

pile² *noun* A heavy beam, as of wood or steel, driven into the ground as a foundation or support for a structure.
pile² (pīl) ◊ *noun, plural* **piles**

pile³ *noun* A soft, velvety nap made of loops of yarn: *We bought a rug with a shaggy pile.*
pile³ (pīl) ◊ *noun, plural* **piles**

HISTORY **• pile¹, pile², pile³**

Pile¹ comes from an old French word that meant "heap of stone." **Pile²** was borrowed long ago from a Latin word for a type of spear. **Pile³** goes back to the Latin word for "hair."

pilfer *verb* To steal things of little value.
pil·fer (pĭl′fər) ◊ *verb* **pilfered, pilfering**

pilgrim *noun* **1.** A person who travels to a sacred place. **2. Pilgrim** One of the English settlers who founded Plymouth Colony in New England in 1620.
pil·grim (pĭl′grĭm) ◊ *noun, plural* **pilgrims**

▲ **pilgrim**
The Pilgrims at Plimoth Plantation

piling *noun* A structure made up of several piles driven into the earth.
pil·ing (pī′lĭng) ◊ *noun, plural* **pilings**

pill *noun* A small ball or tablet of medicine to be taken by mouth.
pill (pĭl) ◊ *noun, plural* **pills**

pillage *verb* To rob by force; plunder.
pil·lage (pĭl′ĭj) ◊ *verb* **pillaged, pillaging**

pillar *noun* **1.** An upright structure that serves as a support or stands alone as a monument; column. **2.** Something that is like a pillar: *A pillar of flame rose from the volcano.*
pil·lar (pĭl′ər) ◊ *noun, plural* **pillars**

pillory *noun* A wooden frame in a public place with holes in which the head and hands were locked as punishment.
pil·lo·ry (pĭl′ə rē) ◊ *noun, plural* **pillories**

pillow *noun* A case filled with soft material, as down, and used to cushion a person's head during rest or sleep.
pil·low (pĭl′ō) ◊ *noun, plural* **pillows**

pillowcase *noun* A cloth cover for a pillow.
pil·low·case (pĭl′ō kās′) ◊ *noun, plural* **pillowcases**

pilot *noun* **1.** A person who operates an aircraft in flight. **2.** A person who steers a ship, especially a person who steers large ships into and out of harbors or in dangerous waters.
◊ *verb* To serve as the pilot of.
pi·lot (pī′lət) ◊ *noun, plural* **pilots** ◊ *verb* **piloted, piloting**

pimiento *or* **pimento** *noun* A red pepper that has a mild taste.
pi·mien·to *or* **pi·men·to** (pĭ mĕn′tō) ◊ *noun, plural* **pimientos** *or* **pimentos**

▲ **pimiento**

pimple *noun* A small swelling on the skin that is often full of pus.
pim·ple (pĭm′pəl) ◊ *noun, plural* **pimples**

pin *noun* **1.** A short, straight, stiff piece of wire with a head at one end and a sharp point at the other. A pin is used to fasten one thing to another. **2.** Something that is shaped or used like a pin. **3.** An ornament or badge fastened to the clothing with a pin or clasp. **4.** One of the ten wooden clubs serving as the target in bowling.
◊ *verb* **1.** To fasten or attach with a pin. **2.** To hold fast: *The tree fell and pinned the lumberjack to the ground.*
pin (pĭn) ◊ *noun, plural* **pins** ◊ *verb* **pinned, pinning**

pinafore *noun* A sleeveless garment that is worn as or over a dress.
pin·a·fore (pĭn′ə fôr′) ◊ *noun, plural* **pinafores**

pinch *verb* **1.** To squeeze between the thumb and a finger or between edges. **2.** To squeeze or press so hard as to cause pain: *The shoes pinched my feet.* **3.** To cause to seem shriveled or shrunken: *Their faces were pinched with cold.*
◊ *noun* **1.** The act of pinching. **2.** The amount that can be held between the thumb and a finger: *This soup needs a pinch of pepper.* **3.** A time of trouble or difficulty: *In a pinch I can take over your paper route.*
pinch (pĭnch) ◊ *verb* **pinched, pinching** ◊ *noun, plural* **pinches**

pincushion *noun* A small, firm cushion in which pins can be stuck when not in use.
pin·cush·ion (pĭn′ko͝osh′ən) ◊ *noun, plural* **pincushions**

pine *noun* An evergreen tree that has cones, leaves that look like needles, and wood used for lumber.
pine (pīn) ◊ *noun, plural* **pines**

pineapple *noun* A large, juicy tropical fruit with a thorny skin and stiff leaves.
pine·ap·ple (pīn′ăp′əl) ◊ *noun, plural* **pineapples**

Ping-Pong *noun* A trademark for the equipment used in the game of table tennis.
Ping-Pong (pĭng′pông′) ◊ *noun*

pink *noun* **1.** A pale red color. **2.** A garden plant that has flowers with a spicy fragrance.
◊ *adjective* Of the color pink.
pink (pĭngk) ◊ *noun, plural* **pinks** ◊ *adjective* **pinker, pinkest**

pinkeye *or* **pink eye** *noun* A very contagious disease of the eyes in which the inside of the eyelid becomes sore and red.
pink·eye *or* **pink eye** (pĭngk′ī′) ◊ *noun*

pinkish *adjective* Somewhat pink.
pink·ish (pĭng′kĭsh) ◊ *adjective*

P

pinpoint *verb* To locate or find exactly: *We tried to pinpoint the problem.*
pin·point (pĭn′point′) ◊ *verb* **pinpointed, pinpointing**

pint *noun* A unit of capacity equal to ½ quart or 16 fluid ounces.
pint (pīnt) ◊ *noun, plural* **pints**

pinto *noun* A horse with irregular spots or patches of color on its coat.
pin·to (pĭn′tō) ◊ *noun, plural* **pintos**

▲ **pinto**

pioneer *noun* **1.** A person who is first to settle in a region. **2.** A person who does something first in an area of research or activity, leading the way for others.
◊ *verb* To act as a pioneer.
pi·o·neer (pī′ə **nîr′**) ◊ *noun, plural* **pioneers** ◊ *verb* **pioneered, pioneering**

pious *adjective* Having or showing religious respect or reverence.
pi·ous (pī′əs) ◊ *adjective*

pipe *noun* **1.** A tube or hollow cylinder that a liquid or gas can flow through. **2.** A tube with a small bowl at the end, for smoking tobacco or blowing bubbles. **3.** A musical instrument or part of a musical instrument shaped like a tube that is played by blowing.
◊ *verb* **1.** To carry or send by means of pipes: *We piped water into our fields.* **2.** To play on a pipe: *I piped a lively tune.*
pipe (pīp) ◊ *noun, plural* **pipes** ◊ *verb* **piped, piping**

pipeline *noun* A line of pipes for carrying substances such as oil over long distances.
pipe·line (pīp′līn′) ◊ *noun, plural* **pipelines**

piracy *noun* Armed robbery on the high seas.
pi·ra·cy (pī′rə sē) ◊ *noun, plural* **piracies**

pirate *noun* A person who robs ships at sea.
pi·rate (pī′rĭt) ◊ *noun, plural* **pirates**

pistil *noun* The part of a flower in which seeds develop.
pis·til (pĭs′təl) ◊ *noun, plural* **pistils**
‖*These sound alike:* **pistil, pistol**

pistol *noun* A gun that can be held and fired with one hand.
pis·tol (pĭs′təl) ◊ *noun, plural* **pistols**
‖*These sound alike:* **pistol, pistil**

piston *noun* A circular block or disk that moves back and forth in a large cylinder. In motor vehicles pistons are moved by the ignition of fuel.
pis·ton (pĭs′tən) ◊ *noun, plural* **pistons**

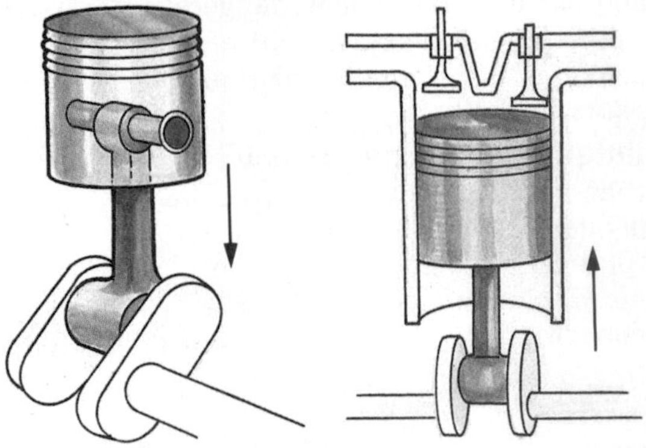

▲ **piston**

pit¹ *noun* **1.** A hole in the ground: *We roasted our dinner in the barbecue pit.* **2.** A hollow area or depression on a surface, as of the skin.
◊ *verb* **1.** To mark or become marked with pits or scars. **2.** To set against another in a contest or competition; match: *This tournament pits our school against yours.*
pit¹ (pĭt) ◊ *noun, plural* **pits** ◊ *verb* **pitted, pitting**

ă	pat	ĭ	pit	oi	oil	th	bath
ā	pay	ī	ride	o͝o	book	*th*	bathe
â	care	î	fierce	o͞o	boot	ə	ago, item
ä	father	ŏ	pot	ou	out		pencil
ĕ	pet	ō	go	ŭ	cut		atom
ē	be	ô	paw, for	û	fur		circus

pit² *noun* The single hard seed of a fruit, such as a peach or cherry; stone.
◊ *verb* To remove the pits from.
pit² (pĭt) ◊ *noun, plural* **pits** ◊ *verb* **pitted, pitting**

HISTORY • pit¹, pit²

Pit¹ comes from an old English word that meant "a hole in the ground." **Pit²** comes from an old Dutch word distantly related to **pith.**

pitch¹ *noun* A sticky, dark, thick substance made from tar or petroleum and used in making roofs waterproof and in paving.
pitch¹ (pĭch) ◊ *noun*

pitch² *verb* **1.** To throw, hurl, or toss, as in baseball or horseshoes. **2.** To set up and fix firmly: *I pitched a tent by the river.* **3.** To fall forward; plunge: *I lost my footing and pitched down the stairs.* **4.** To move so that one end goes down while the other end goes up: *The ship pitched in the heavy storm.*
◊ *noun* **1.** An act of pitching. **2.** A throw of the baseball by a pitcher to a batter. **3.** A degree or level: *The game reached a high pitch of excitement.* **4.** A degree of slant; slope: *The roof had a steep pitch.* **5.** The highness or lowness of a musical sound.
pitch² (pĭch) ◊ *verb* **pitched, pitching** ◊ *noun, plural* **pitches**

HISTORY • pitch¹, pitch²

Pitch¹ goes back to a Latin word meaning "sticky substance." **Pitch²** probably comes from an old English word that meant "to thrust."

pitch-black *adjective* Extremely black.
pitch-black (pĭch′blăk′) ◊ *adjective*

pitch-dark *adjective* Very dark.
pitch-dark (pĭch′därk′) ◊ *adjective*

pitcher¹ *noun* A baseball player who pitches the ball to the batter.
pitch·er¹ (pĭch′ər) ◊ *noun, plural* **pitchers**

pitcher² *noun* A container, usually with a handle and a lip or spout, for holding and pouring out liquids.
pitch·er² (pĭch′ər) ◊ *noun, plural* **pitchers**

HISTORY • pitcher¹, pitcher²

Pitcher¹ was formed from **pitch²** plus the ending **-er,** which together mean "someone who pitches." **Pitcher²** goes back to a Greek word that meant "jar." The word passed through Latin and French before arriving in English.

pitchfork *noun* A large fork with a long handle used especially for lifting hay.
pitch·fork (pĭch′fôrk′) ◊ *noun, plural* **pitchforks**

pitfall *noun* **1.** A hidden pit in the ground used as a trap for animals or people. **2.** A hidden or unexpected danger or difficulty.
pit·fall (pĭt′fôl′) ◊ *noun, plural* **pitfalls**

pith *noun* The soft, spongy substance in the center of the stems of many plants.
pith (pĭth) ◊ *noun*

pitiful *adjective* **1.** Causing others to feel pity: *The wet, cold puppy was a pitiful sight.* **2.** Deserving pity: *I earned a pitiful salary.*
pit·i·ful (pĭt′ĭ fəl) ◊ *adjective*

pity *noun* **1.** A feeling of sorrow or sympathy for the suffering of another. **2.** A reason for pity or regret: *It's a pity you're sick.*
◊ *verb* To feel pity for.
pit·y (pĭt′ē) ◊ *noun, plural* **pities** ◊ *verb* **pitied, pitying**

pivot *noun* A rod or pin on which something else turns.
◊ *verb* To turn or swing on or as if on a pivot.
piv·ot (pĭv′ət) ◊ *noun, plural* **pivots** ◊ *verb* **pivoted, pivoting**

pizza *noun* An open pie made up of a flat crust covered usually with a seasoned tomato sauce and toppings such as cheese or pieces of sausage.
piz·za (pēt′sə) ◊ *noun, plural* **pizzas**

place *noun* **1.** An area; region: *We visited many places along the coast.* **2.** A particular location, as a city: *In what place were you born?* **3.** A portion of space where a person lives; dwelling. **4.** A short city street or a public square. **5.** An area, as a building, set aside for a particular purpose: *A school is a place of learning.* **6.** A space for one person to sit or stand: *Save a place for me at the movies.* **7.** Position in a series or sequence; rank: *My*

P

friend's flowers won first place at the fair. **8.** The proper or usual position, order, or function: *Everything is in its place on the kitchen counter.*
◊ *verb* **1.** To put in a particular place or order: *I placed cups and saucers on the table.* **2.** To identify by remembering how someone or something was seen or met before: *I can't place your face.*
◊ *idiom* **take place** To happen; occur: *Sometimes changes take place very slowly.*
place (plās) ◊ *noun, plural* **places** ◊ *verb* **placed, placing**

placid *adjective* Pleasantly peaceful or calm: *You have a placid disposition.*
plac·id (plăs′ĭd) ◊ *adjective*

plague *noun* **1.** A very contagious disease that often causes death. **2.** Something that causes misery: *A plague of locusts destroyed the farmer's crops.*
◊ *verb* **1.** To torment with disease or misery. **2.** To annoy or bother; pester.
plague (plāg) ◊ *noun, plural* **plagues** ◊ *verb* **plagued, plaguing**

plaid *noun* **1.** A pattern of squares formed by stripes of different widths and colors that cross each other. **2.** A fabric that has a plaid pattern.
plaid (plăd) ◊ *noun, plural* **plaids**

plain *adjective* **1.** Open to the sight: *The wallet was in plain view.* **2.** Easy to understand; obvious: *The meaning of the sentence is very plain.* **3.** Not fancy; simple: *We ate plain food.* **4.** Without a pattern or design: *They put up plain wallpaper.* **5.** Ordinary; average: *My parents are plain people.* **6.** Not beautiful or handsome: *The child has a plain face.* **7.** Honest and sincere; frank: *The teacher was perfectly plain with us.*
◊ *noun* A large, flat area of land without any trees.
plain (plān) ◊ *adjective* **plainer, plainest** ◊ *noun, plural* **plains**
‖ *These sound alike:* **plain, plane**

ă	pat	ĭ	pit	oi	**oil**	th	**bath**
ā	pay	ī	ride	ŏŏ	**book**	*th*	**bathe**
â	care	î	fierce	ōō	**boot**	ə	**ago, item**
ä	father	ŏ	pot	ou	**out**		pencil
ĕ	pet	ō	go	ŭ	cut		atom
ē	be	ô	paw, for	û	fur		circus

plain-spoken *adjective* Frank and straightforward.
plain-spo·ken (plān′spō′kən) ◊ *adjective*

plaintive *adjective* Sad and mournful.
plain·tive (plān′tĭv) ◊ *adjective*

plait *noun* A braid of hair.
◊ *verb* To braid hair.
plait (plāt) ◊ *noun, plural* **plaits** ◊ *verb* **plaited, plaiting**
‖ *These sound alike:* **plait, plate**

plan *noun* **1.** A method for doing something that has been thought out ahead of time: *What are your plans for the evening?* **2.** A drawing or diagram showing how the parts of something are arranged or put together.
◊ *verb* **1.** To decide on a plan for or of: *We like to plan our summer vacation during the winter.* —See Synonyms at **think.** **2.** To have in mind; intend: *We plan to go to Europe this summer.*
plan (plăn) ◊ *noun, plural* **plans** ◊ *verb* **planned, planning**

plane¹ *noun* **1.** A smooth, flat surface. **2.** A stage of development: *That student's work is on a high plane.* **3.** An airplane.
◊ *adjective* Smooth and flat; level: *This road has a plane surface.*
plane¹ (plān) ◊ *noun, plural* **planes** ◊ *adjective*
‖ *These sound alike:* **plane, plain**

plane² *noun* A hand tool with a sharp blade that is used to smooth wood surfaces.
◊ *verb* To smooth or level with or as if with a plane.
plane² (plān) ◊ *noun, plural* **planes** ◊ *verb* **planed, planing**
‖ *These sound alike:* **plane, plain**

HISTORY • plane¹, plane²

Plane¹ and **plane²** both go back to a Latin word that meant "flat, smooth." The Latin word formed a noun, meaning "a flat surface," from which we get **plane¹**. The Latin word also formed a verb, meaning "to smooth," from which we get **plane²**.

planet *noun* A heavenly body that moves in an orbit around a star, such as the sun.
plan·et (plăn′ĭt) ◊ *noun, plural* **planets**

▲ **planet**
Earth, as seen from a space shuttle

planetarium *noun* A building in which special equipment projects images of the sun, moon, planets, and stars.
plan·e·tar·i·um (plăn′ĭ **târ′**ē əm) ◊ *noun, plural* **planetariums**

plank *noun* A long board.
plank (plăngk) ◊ *noun, plural* **planks**

plankton *noun* Very tiny plants and animals that float on bodies of water.
plank·ton (**plăngk′**tən) ◊ *noun*

plant *noun* **1.** A living thing, as a flower, tree, fern, or mushroom, that is not an animal, that cannot usually move from place to place, but can usually make its own food. **2.** A kind of plant that has a soft stem and is small compared with a tree or shrub. **3.** The buildings and equipment used in making a product; factory.
◊ *verb* **1.** To put in the ground or in soil to grow: *We planted marigold seeds in pots.* **2.** To place or set firmly; fix: *I planted my feet on the ground.* **3.** To cause to take hold or develop; introduce: *The teacher planted interesting new ideas in our minds.*
plant (plănt) ◊ *noun, plural* **plants** ◊ *verb* **planted, planting**

plantation *noun* **1.** A large farm or estate on which crops, especially cotton, are cared for and harvested by workers who often live there. **2.** A group of plants or trees planted and cared for.
plan·ta·tion (plăn **tā′**shən) ◊ *noun, plural* **plantations**

planter *noun* **1.** A person, tool, or machine that plants seeds. **2.** The owner of a plantation. **3.** A container in which plants are grown.
plant·er (**plăn′**tər) ◊ *noun, plural* **planters**

plasma *noun* The clear, yellowish liquid part of blood in which cells are suspended.
plas·ma (**plăz′**mə) ◊ *noun*

plaster *noun* A mixture, usually of sand, lime, and water, that hardens when it dries and is used for coating walls and ceilings.
◊ *verb* To cover or coat with or as if with plaster: *We plastered the wall with snapshots.*
plas·ter (**plăs′**tər) ◊ *noun, plural* **plasters** ◊ *verb* **plastered, plastering**

plastic *noun* Any of a large number of materials that are made from chemicals. Plastic can be formed into films, molded into objects, or made into fibers.
◊ *adjective* **1.** Capable of being shaped or molded: *Clay is a plastic material.* **2.** Made of plastic: *The baby played with a plastic duck.*
plas·tic (**plăs′**tĭk) ◊ *noun, plural* **plastics** ◊ *adjective*

plate *noun* **1.** A shallow, usually circular dish. **2.** The food on a plate: *Finish your plate before you leave the table.* **3.** A thin, flat sheet or piece of material, as metal: *The carpenter put a glass plate in the door.* **4.** A piece of flat metal or plastic on which something is stamped or engraved: *I ordered a name plate for my desk.* **5.** Home base in baseball.
◊ *verb* To coat with a thin layer of metal, as silver or gold.
plate (plāt) ◊ *noun, plural* **plates** ◊ *verb* **plated, plating**
‖*These sound alike:* **plate, plait**

plateau *noun* An area of flat land that is higher than the land around it.
pla·teau (plă **tō′**) ◊ *noun, plural* **plateaus**

platform *noun* **1.** A raised floor or surface, as for a speaker or performer. **2.** A formal statement of principles or policy, as of a political party.
plat·form (**plăt′**fôrm′) ◊ *noun, plural* **platforms**

platinum *noun* A valuable silver-white metal that is used especially in jewelry. Platinum is one of the chemical elements.
plat·i·num (**plăt′**n əm) ◊ *noun*

platoon *noun* A group of soldiers made up of two or more squads.
pla·toon (plə **to͞on′**) ◊ *noun, plural* **platoons**

P

platter *noun* A large, shallow plate for serving food.
plat·ter (plăt′ər) ◊ *noun, plural* **platters**

platypus *noun* A furry brown mammal of Australia that has webbed feet and a bill like a duck's. The female platypus lays eggs.
plat·y·pus (plăt′ə pəs) ◊ *noun, plural* **platypuses**

▲ **platypus**

play *verb* **1.** To amuse oneself: *The children went out to play.* **2.** To take part in a game of: *Let's play baseball.* **3.** To compete against in a game: *We played the visiting team last night.* **4.** To act a dramatic part or role: *I played a ghost in our Halloween show.* **5.** To act or behave: *You're not playing fair. The opossum played dead.* **6.** To perform or do: *The stomach plays an important part in digestion.* **7.** To make or cause to make sound or music: *I play the trumpet.*
◊ *noun* **1.** A story written and acted or to be acted on the stage. **2.** Activity taken part in for pleasure: *All work and no play is no fun.* **3.** A move, turn, or action in a game: *The athlete made a tricky play.* **4.** Action; use: *We brought all our energy into play to win.*
play (plā) ◊ *verb* **played, playing** ◊ *noun, plural* **plays**

player *noun* **1.** A person who takes part in a game or sport. **2.** A person who plays a role or part in a drama; actor. **3.** A person who plays a musical instrument. **4.** A machine that reproduces sound.
play·er (plā′ər) ◊ *noun, plural* **players**

playful *adjective* **1.** Full of high spirits; lively. **2.** Said or done in fun; humorous.
play·ful (plā′fəl) ◊ *adjective*

playground *noun* An outdoor area for play, sports, and games.
play·ground (plā′ground′) ◊ *noun, plural* **playgrounds**

playmate *noun* A companion in play.
play·mate (plā′māt′) ◊ *noun, plural* **playmates**

playpen *noun* A small enclosure for a baby or young child to play in.
play·pen (plā′pĕn′) ◊ *noun, plural* **playpens**

plaything *noun* A toy.
play·thing (plā′thĭng′) ◊ *noun, plural* **playthings**

playwright *noun* A person who writes plays.
play·wright (plā′rīt′) ◊ *noun, plural* **playwrights**

plaza *noun* A public square in a town or city.
pla·za (plăz′ə *or* plä′zə) ◊ *noun, plural* **plazas**

plea *noun* **1.** An urgent request. **2.** The answer that an accused person gives in a court of law to the charges against him or her.
plea (plē) ◊ *noun, plural* **pleas**

plead *verb* **1.** To make an urgent request; appeal: *They were pleading with us to return.* **2.** To offer a plea of in a court of law: *I plead guilty.*
plead (plēd) ◊ *verb* **pleaded** *or* **pled, pleading**

pleasant *adjective* **1.** Giving pleasure; agreeable: *Our state has a pleasant climate.* **2.** Pleasing in manner; friendly: *Our teacher is a pleasant person.*
pleas·ant (plĕz′ənt) ◊ *adjective* **pleasanter, pleasantest**

ă	pat	ĭ	pit	oi	oil	th	bath
ā	pay	ī	ride	ŏŏ	book	*th*	bathe
â	care	î	fierce	ōō	boot	ə	ago, item
ä	father	ŏ	pot	ou	out		pencil
ĕ	pet	ō	go	ŭ	cut		atom
ē	be	ô	paw, for	û	fur		circus

SYNONYMS

pleasant, agreeable, pleasing, welcome
We had a *pleasant* afternoon together. Your participation will be *agreeable* to me. The gift was *pleasing* to me. Warm weather will be a *welcome* change.

please *verb* **1.** To give pleasure or enjoyment: *The movie pleased the audience.* **2.** To be willing to: *Please tell us a story.* **3.** To wish or prefer: *They can do exactly as they please.*
please (plēz) ◊ *verb* **pleased, pleasing**

pleasing *adjective* Giving pleasure; agreeable: *He had a pleasing way of doing things. Her smile was pleasing.* —See Synonyms at **pleasant.**
pleas·ing (plē′zing) ◊ *adjective*

pleasure *noun* **1.** A feeling of happiness or enjoyment; delight: *She smiled with pleasure.* —See Synonyms at **joy. 2.** Something that pleases or gives enjoyment: *Reading is his main pleasure.*
pleas·ure (plĕzh′ər) ◊ *noun, plural* **pleasures**

pleat *noun* A flat fold, as in cloth, that is made by doubling fabric on itself.
◊ *verb* To form or arrange in pleats.
pleat (plēt) ◊ *noun, plural* **pleats** ◊ *verb* **pleated, pleating**

pled *verb* A past tense and a past participle of **plead.**
pled (plĕd) ◊ *verb*

pledge *noun* **1.** A formal promise; vow: *They made a pledge to do their duty.* **2.** Something that is given or held to make sure that a loan is paid back. **3.** A token or symbol: *They exchanged pictures as a pledge of friendship.*
◊ *verb* **1.** To make a pledge. **2.** To leave or hold something as a pledge.
pledge (plĕj) ◊ *noun, plural* **pledges** ◊ *verb* **pledged, pledging**

plentiful *adjective* Being more than enough; abundant: *Food was plentiful at harvest time.*
plen·ti·ful (plĕn′tĭ fəl) ◊ *adjective*

plenty *noun* A full supply or amount: *Children need plenty of exercise.*
plen·ty (plĕn′tē) ◊ *noun*

pliable *adjective* **1.** Easily bent or shaped without breaking; flexible: *The bow was made of pliable wood.* **2.** Easily influenced.
pli·a·ble (plī′ə bəl) ◊ *adjective*

pliers *plural noun* A tool consisting of a pair of pivoted jaws and a pair of handles, used for holding, bending, or cutting wire.
pli·ers (plī′ərz) ◊ *plural noun*

plod *verb* To walk heavily or with effort; trudge: *We plodded home through the snow.*
plod (plŏd) ◊ *verb* **plodded, plodding**

plot *noun* **1.** A small piece of ground: *We have a plot of good land for our garden.* **2.** The actions or events of a story. **3.** A secret plan, especially to do something wrong.
◊ *verb* **1.** To mark or note the position of on a map or chart: *We plotted our route on the map.* **2.** To plan secretly; scheme.
plot (plŏt) ◊ *noun, plural* **plots** ◊ *verb* **plotted, plotting**

plover *noun* A shore bird with a short bill, short tail, and long, pointed wings.
plov·er (plŭv′ər *or* plō′vər) ◊ *noun, plural* **plovers**

▲ **plover**

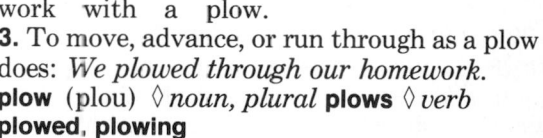

plow *noun* **1.** A piece of farm equipment used to break up and turn over soil. **2.** A device used to remove matter, as snow, from roads, sidewalks, or railroad tracks.
◊ *verb* **1.** To break up and turn over with a plow. **2.** To remove or work with a plow. **3.** To move, advance, or run through as a plow does: *We plowed through our homework.*
plow (plou) ◊ *noun, plural* **plows** ◊ *verb* **plowed, plowing**

pluck *verb* **1.** To remove by pulling off or out; pick: *I plucked a peach from the branch.* **2.** To pull out the feathers or hair of: *The butcher plucked the chicken.* **3.** To pull or tug; snatch: *I plucked at my friend's sleeve.* **4.** To pull at and let go: *We plucked the guitar strings.*
◊ *noun* **1.** A sharp pull; tug. **2.** Courage and boldness.
pluck (plŭk) ◊ *verb* **plucked, plucking** ◊ *noun, plural* **plucks**

plucky *adjective* Showing courage.
pluck·y (plŭk′ē) ◊ *adjective* **pluckier, pluckiest**

plug *noun* **1.** A piece, as of cork, used to stop up a hole or leak; stopper. **2.** A device at the end of a wire that makes an electrical connection by means of metal prongs that fit into a matching socket.
◊ *verb* **1.** To stop up tightly with or as if with

P

a plug. **2.** To make an electrical connection by means of a plug. **3.** To work in a slow and steady way: *I keep plugging away at my assignments.*
plug (plŭg) ◊ *noun, plural* **plugs** ◊ *verb* **plugged, plugging**

plum *noun* A small, edible fruit with a pit and red, purple, or yellow skin. Plums grow on small trees.
plum (plŭm) ◊ *noun, plural* **plums**
‖*These sound alike:* **plum, plumb**

▲ **plum**

plumage *noun* The feathers of a bird.
plum·age (**plo͞o′**mĭj) ◊ *noun*

plumb *noun* A weight on the end of a line. A plumb is used to measure depth or to show whether something is straight up and down.
◊ *verb* To test with or as if with a plumb.
plumb (plŭm) ◊ *noun, plural* **plumbs** ◊ *verb* **plumbed, plumbing**
‖*These sound alike:* **plumb, plum**

plumber *noun* A person whose work is putting in and repairing pipes and plumbing.
plumb·er (**plŭm′**ər) ◊ *noun, plural* **plumbers**

plumbing *noun* **1.** The equipment, as pipes and fixtures, through which water, sewage, or gas flows in a building. **2.** A plumber's work.
plumb·ing (**plŭm′**ĭng) ◊ *noun*

plume *noun* A feather, especially a large and showy one used for decoration.
plume (plo͞om) ◊ *noun, plural* **plumes**

plump *adjective* Rounded and full in shape.
◊ *verb* To make or become plump: *We plumped up the pillows.*
plump (plŭmp) ◊ *adjective* **plumper, plumpest** ◊ *verb* **plumped, plumping**

ă	pat	ĭ	pit	oi	**oi**l	th	ba**th**
ā	pay	ī	ride	o͝o	b**oo**k	*th*	ba**th**e
â	care	î	fierce	o͞o	b**oo**t	ə	**a**go, it**e**m
ä	father	ŏ	pot	ou	**ou**t		penc**i**l
ĕ	pet	ō	go	ŭ	c**u**t		at**o**m
ē	be	ô	paw, for	û	f**u**r		circ**u**s

plunder *verb* To rob by force: *Pirates plundered the city on the coast.*
◊ *noun* Property stolen by plundering.
plun·der (**plŭn′**dər) ◊ *verb* **plundered, plundering** ◊ *noun*

plunge *verb* **1.** To throw oneself suddenly into or as if into water: *We plunged into the swimming pool.* **2.** To thrust suddenly or with force: *The farmer plunged the pitchfork into the hay.* **3.** To enter or cause to enter suddenly or violently: *Those events plunged the world into war.* **4.** To descend sharply: *The temperature plunged.*
◊ *noun* An act of plunging.
plunge (plŭnj) ◊ *verb* **plunged, plunging** ◊ *noun, plural* **plunges**

plural *adjective* Of, relating to, or being the form of a word that is used to show more than one person or thing.
◊ *noun* The form of a word used to show that the word means more than one person or thing. For example, *birds* is the plural of *bird.*
plu·ral (**plo͝or′**əl) ◊ *adjective* ◊ *noun, plural* **plurals**

plus *preposition* Added to; increased by: *Two plus three equals five.*
◊ *adjective* Slightly more than: *My essay got a grade of C plus.*
◊ *noun* A sign (+) used to show addition.
plus (plŭs) ◊ *preposition* ◊ *adjective* ◊ *noun, plural* **pluses**

Pluto *noun* The planet of the solar system that is farthest from the sun.
Plu·to (**plo͞o′**tō) ◊ *noun*

plutonium *noun* A silvery, radioactive metal that can be made artificially from uranium and is used to produce atomic energy. Plutonium is one of the chemical elements.
plu·to·ni·um (plo͞o **tō′**nē əm) ◊ *noun*

plywood *noun* A kind of board made of thin layers of wood glued and pressed together.
ply·wood (**plī′**wo͝od′) ◊ *noun*

p.m. *or* **P.M.** Abbreviations for the Latin words *post meridiem,* which mean "after noon."

pneumatic *adjective* **1.** Of or relating to a gas, as air. **2.** Operated by air: *Pneumatic drills are noisy.*
pneu·mat·ic (no͞o **măt′**ĭk *or* nyo͞o **măt′**ĭk) ◊ *adjective*

pneumonia *noun* A serious disease that

causes the lungs to become inflamed.
pneu·mo·nia (no͝o **mōn′** yə *or* nyo͝o **mōn′** yə) ◊ *noun*

P.O. The abbreviation for *Post Office.*

poach *verb* To cook in gently boiling liquid.
poach (pōch) ◊ *verb* **poached, poaching**

pocket *noun* **1.** A small pouch, open at the side or top, that is sewn into or onto a garment for carrying small items. **2.** Something like a pocket in appearance or use: *There are pockets of ore in the mountain.*
◊ *adjective* Small enough to be carried in a pocket: *I bought a pocket dictionary.*
◊ *verb* To place in a pocket: *I picked up my coins and pocketed them.*
pock·et (**pŏk′** ĭt) ◊ *noun, plural* **pockets** ◊ *adjective* ◊ *verb* **pocketed, pocketing**

pocketbook *noun* A handbag or wallet.
pock·et·book (**pŏk′** ĭt bo͝ok′) ◊ *noun, plural* **pocketbooks**

pocketknife *noun* A small knife with a blade or blades that fold into the handle.
pock·et·knife (**pŏk′** ĭt nīf′) ◊ *noun, plural* **pocketknives**

pod *noun* A seedcase, as of a pea or bean plant, that splits open to release the enclosed seeds when it is ripe.
pod (pŏd) ◊ *noun, plural* **pods**

poem *noun* A piece of writing, often in rhyme, in which words are chosen for their sound and beauty as well as meaning.
po·em (**pō′** əm) ◊ *noun, plural* **poems**

poet *noun* A writer of poems.
po·et (**pō′** ĭt) ◊ *noun, plural* **poets**

poetic *adjective* Of, relating to, or like poetry: *Poetic language is beautiful.*
po·et·ic (pō **ĕt′** ĭk) ◊ *adjective*

poetry *noun* **1.** The art or works of a poet. **2.** Poems thought of as a part of literature.
po·et·ry (**pō′** ĭ trē) ◊ *noun*

poignant *adjective* Affecting the feelings in a strong, often sad way.
poign·ant (**poin′** yənt) ◊ *adjective*

poinsettia *noun* A tropical plant with bright-red, pink, or white leaves that look like petals growing around its small yellowish flowers. Poinsettias are used as Christmas decorations.
poin·set·ti·a (poin **sĕt′** ē ə *or* poin **sĕt′** ə) ◊ *noun, plural* **poinsettias**

▲ **poinsettia**

point *noun* **1.** A sharp end, as of a pin. **2.** A piece of land that juts out into a body of water. **3.** A dot in writing or printing; period. **4.** A certain place or position: *The tower is on the highest point in the city.* **5.** One of the 32 directions marked on a compass. **6.** A geometric element having position, but no width, length, or height: *Draw a straight line between two points.* **7.** A particular condition or degree: *The milk was close to the boiling point.* **8.** An instant in time; moment: *At that point we all started to laugh.* **9.** The most important idea or part: *Please come to the point.* **10.** A purpose or reason: *There's no point in crying.* **11.** A quality or characteristic; feature: *Our new neighbor has good points and bad points.* **12.** Something that a person wants to say or communicate: *The speaker made three points.* **13.** A unit that counts in scoring a game or test: *Our team won the game by 12 points.*
◊ *verb* **1.** To direct; aim: *I pointed the flashlight into the closet.* **2.** To call attention to something with or as if with the finger: *The librarian pointed to the sign that said "Quiet."* **3.** To be turned or directed: *The compass needle points north.*
point (point) ◊ *noun, plural* **points** ◊ *verb* **pointed, pointing**

pointer *noun* **1.** A device, as an arrow, that points or is used for pointing. **2.** A piece of helpful advice; hint. **3.** A hunting dog with a short, smooth coat.
point·er (**poin′** tər) ◊ *noun, plural* **pointers**

point of view *noun* A way of looking at things; attitude.
point of view ◊ *noun, plural* **points of view**

P

poise *verb* To balance or be balanced: *The horse poised for the jump.*
◊ *noun* **1.** The condition of being balanced. **2.** Sureness and confidence of manner: *The child recited the poem with poise.*
poise (poiz) ◊ *verb* **poised, poising** ◊ *noun*

poison *noun* A substance that, when swallowed or breathed, causes injury, sickness, or death.
◊ *verb* **1.** To harm or kill with poison. **2.** To put poison on or in.
poi·son (poi′zən) ◊ *noun, plural* **poisons** ◊ *verb* **poisoned, poisoning**

poison ivy *noun* A plant with leaflets in groups of three that can cause an itching skin rash if touched.

▲ **poison ivy**

poisonous *adjective* Containing or having effects like that of poison: *The rattlesnake has a poisonous bite.*
poi·son·ous (poi′zə nəs) ◊ *adjective*

poke *verb* **1.** To give a sudden sharp jab: *Why did you poke me in the ribs?* **2.** To push forward; thrust: *The dog poked its head out the window.* **3.** To make by poking: *We poked a hole through the ice to fish.* **4.** To move or search in a slow, casual way: *The old car is still poking along.*
◊ *noun* A sudden sharp jab.

ă	pat	ĭ	pit	oi	**oi**l	th	ba**th**
ā	pay	ī	ride	ŏŏ	b**oo**k	*th*	ba**the**
â	care	î	fierce	ōō	b**oo**t	ə	ago, item
ä	father	ŏ	pot	ou	**ou**t		pencil
ĕ	pet	ō	go	ŭ	cut		atom
ē	be	ô	paw, for	û	fur		circus

poke (pōk) ◊ *verb* **poked, poking** ◊ *noun, plural* **pokes**

poker¹ *noun* A metal rod used to stir a fire.
pok·er¹ (pō′kər) ◊ *noun, plural* **pokers**

poker² *noun* A card game in which the players bet on the value of their cards.
pok·er² (pō′kər) ◊ *noun*

***HISTORY* • poker¹, poker²**

Poker¹ was formed from **poke** plus the ending **–er,** which together mean "something that pokes." No one knows for certain how **poker²,** the card game, got its name.

polar *adjective* Of, relating to, or near the North Pole or the South Pole.
po·lar (pō′lər) ◊ *adjective*

polar bear *noun* A large white bear of far northern regions.
polar bear ◊ *noun, plural* **polar bears**

▲ **polar bear**

pole¹ *noun* **1.** Either of the two places where the earth's axis meets the earth's surface. **2.** Either end of a magnet. **3.** Either of the terminals of an electric battery.
pole¹ (pōl) ◊ *noun, plural* **poles**
‖*These sound alike:* **pole, Pole, poll**

pole² *noun* A long slender rod: *We used a branch as a fishing pole.*
pole² (pōl) ◊ *noun, plural* **poles**
‖*These sound alike:* **pole, Pole, poll**

HISTORY • pole[1], pole[2]

Pole[1] goes back to a Greek word that meant "axis." **Pole[2]** was borrowed long ago from a Latin word that meant "stake."

Pole *noun* A person who was born in or lives in Poland.
Pole (pōl) ◊ *noun, plural* **Poles**
‖*These sound alike:* **Pole, pole, poll**

polecat *noun* **1.** A skunk. **2.** A furry, dark-brown animal that looks like a weasel and is found in Europe and Asia.
pole·cat (pōl′kăt′) ◊ *noun, plural* **polecats**

pole vault *noun* An athletic contest in which a person tries to leap over a high bar with the help of a long pole.
pole vault ◊ *noun, plural* **pole vaults**

police *plural noun* The members of a police department.
◊ *verb* To guard or patrol so as to keep order or enforce the law: *Soldiers policed the airport until the president left.*
po·lice (pə lēs′) ◊ *plural noun* ◊ *verb* **policed, policing**

police department *noun* A department of government that keeps order, sees that laws are obeyed, and tries to solve crimes.
police department ◊ *noun, plural* **police departments**

policeman *noun* A man who is a member of a police department.
po·lice·man (pə lēs′mən) ◊ *noun, plural* **policemen**

police officer *noun* A member of a police department.
police officer ◊ *noun, plural* **police officers**

policewoman *noun* A woman who is a member of a police department.
po·lice·wom·an (pə lēs′wo͝om′ən) ◊ *noun, plural* **policewomen**

policy[1] *noun* A general plan or principle that is chosen to help people make decisions: *Honesty is the best policy.*
pol·i·cy[1] (pŏl′ĭ sē) ◊ *noun, plural* **policies**

policy[2] *noun* A written agreement between an insurance company and the person who is being insured.
pol·i·cy[2] (pŏl′ĭ sē) ◊ *noun, plural* **policies**

HISTORY • policy[1], policy[2]

Policy[1] goes back to a Greek word that meant "government." It passed into Latin and French before arriving in English. **Policy[2]** goes back to a Greek word that meant "proof." It passed into Latin, Italian, and French before arriving in English.

polio *noun* Poliomyelitis.
po·li·o (pō′lē ō′) ◊ *noun*

poliomyelitis *noun* A contagious virus disease, mainly affecting children, that can cause paralysis. Poliomyelitis is less common now than it once was because there is a vaccine that can prevent it.
po·li·o·my·e·li·tis (pō′lē ō mī′ə lī′tĭs) ◊ *noun*

polish *verb* **1.** To make smooth and shiny, especially by rubbing: *We polish the marble floor regularly.* **2.** To make smoother or more refined: *I took some time to polish my article before turning it in.*
◊ *noun* **1.** A substance used for polishing. **2.** A smooth and shiny surface; shine. **3.** Good or elegant manners; refinement.
pol·ish (pŏl′ĭsh) ◊ *verb* **polished, polishing** ◊ *noun, plural* **polishes**

Polish *noun* The language of the Poles.
◊ *adjective* Of or relating to Poland, the Poles, or their language.
Po·lish (pō′lĭsh) ◊ *noun* ◊ *adjective*

polite *adjective* Having or showing good manners; courteous.
po·lite (pə līt′) ◊ *adjective* **politer, politest**

SYNONYMS

polite, civil, courteous

I said I could not go but thanked them in a *polite* way for the invitation. Though I do not like him, I will at least be *civil* to him. She was *courteous* and held the door open for me. **Antonym:** *rude*

political *adjective* **1.** Of or relating to the structure or activities of government: *Democracy is one kind of political system.* **2.** Of or relating to politics or politicians.
po·lit·i·cal (pə lĭt′ĭ kəl) ◊ *adjective*

P

politician *noun* A person who runs for or holds an office in government.
pol·i·ti·cian (pŏl′ĭ **tĭsh′** ən) ◊ *noun, plural* **politicians**

politics *noun* **1.** (*used with a singular verb*) The science, art, or work of government. **2.** (*used with a singular verb*) The activities of politicians and political parties **3.** (*used with a plural verb*) A person's opinions about government and political policies and decisions.
pol·i·tics (**pŏl′** ĭ tĭks′) ◊ *noun*

polka *noun* A lively dance of central European origin.
pol·ka (**pōl′** kə) ◊ *noun, plural* **polkas**

polka dot *noun* One of many round dots that are repeated to form a pattern.
pol·ka dot (**pō′** kə) ◊ *noun, plural* **polka dots**

poll *noun* **1.** The casting and counting of votes in an election. **2.** Often **polls** The place where votes are cast. **3.** A survey made to find out what people think.
◊ *verb* **1.** To receive votes in an election. **2.** To ask for and record the opinions of.
poll (pōl) ◊ *noun, plural* **polls** ◊ *verb* **polled, polling**
‖*These sound alike:* **poll, pole, Pole**

pollen *noun* Tiny, usually yellow grains that fertilize the female cells of a plant to produce seeds. Some pollens cause allergies.
pol·len (**pŏl′** ən) ◊ *noun, plural* **pollens**

polliwog *noun* A tadpole.
pol·li·wog (**pŏl′** ē wŏg′) ◊ *noun, plural* **polliwogs**

pollute *verb* To make dirty or impure; contaminate: *Gasoline exhaust pollutes the air.*
pol·lute (pə **lo͞ot′**) ◊ *verb* **polluted, polluting**

pollution *noun* The act of polluting or condition of being polluted.
pol·lu·tion (pə **lo͞o′** shən) ◊ *noun*

polo *noun* A sport played by horseback riders who use mallets with long handles to drive a wooden ball through a goal.
po·lo (**pō′** lō) ◊ *noun*

ă	pat	ĭ	pit	oi	**oi**l	th	ba**th**
ā	p**ay**	ī	r**i**de	o͝o	b**oo**k	*th*	ba**th**e
â	c**a**re	î	f**i**erce	o͞o	b**oo**t	ə	**a**go, it**e**m
ä	f**a**ther	ŏ	p**o**t	ou	**ou**t		penc**i**l
ĕ	p**e**t	ō	g**o**	ŭ	c**u**t		at**o**m
ē	b**e**	ô	p**aw**, f**o**r	û	f**u**r		circ**u**s

polygon *noun* A flat, closed geometric figure with three or more straight sides.
pol·y·gon (**pŏl′** ĭ gŏn′) ◊ *noun, plural* **polygons**

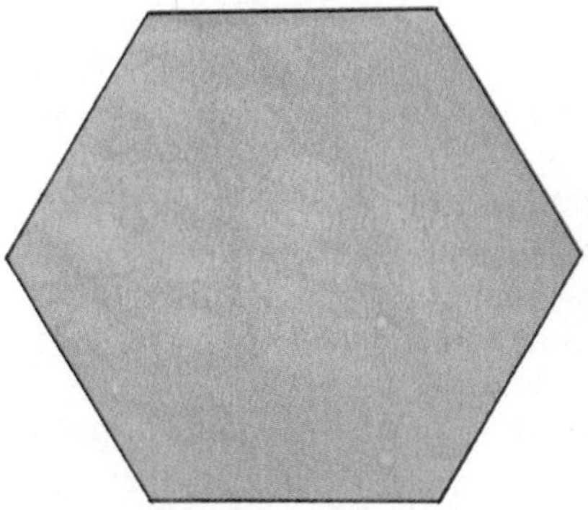

▲ **polygon**

polyp *noun* A small water animal that has a body shaped like a tube and a mouth surrounded by tentacles.
pol·yp (**pŏl′** ĭp) ◊ *noun, plural* **polyps**

pomegranate *noun* A round fruit with a tough, red rind and many small seeds enclosed in juicy red flesh with a slightly sour taste.
pome·gran·ate (**pŏm′** grăn′ĭt *or* **pŏm′** ĭ-grăn′ĭt) ◊ *noun, plural* **pomegranates**

pomp *noun* Splendid or stately display: *They crowned the monarch with great pomp.*
pomp (pŏmp) ◊ *noun*

pompom *noun* **1.** A ball of material, such as colored paper or feathers, that is waved by cheerleaders or sports fans. **2.** A flower with a rounded head that is worn as a decoration.
pom·pom (**pŏm′** pŏm′) ◊ *noun, plural* **pompoms**

poncho *noun* **1.** A cloak like a blanket with a hole in the center for the head, worn especially in Latin America. **2.** A waterproof poncho worn as a raincoat.
pon·cho (**pŏn′** chō) ◊ *noun, plural* **ponchos**

pond *noun* A body of water that is smaller than a lake.
pond (pŏnd) ◊ *noun, plural* **ponds**

ponder *verb* To think about carefully; consider: *I pondered the meaning of my dream.* —See Synonyms at **think.**
pon·der (**pŏn′** dər) ◊ *verb* **pondered, pondering**

ponderous *adjective* **1.** Heavy and often clumsy: *The elephant is a ponderous animal.* **2.** Boring; dull: *The study was lined with ponderous books.*
pon·der·ous (pŏn′ dər əs) ◊ *adjective*

pontoon *noun* **1.** A floating structure used to support a bridge or a dock. **2.** One of the floats that is attached to the bottom of a seaplane to support it on water.
pon·toon (pŏn **to͞on′**) ◊ *noun, plural* **pontoons**

pony *noun* A type or breed of horse that remains small when fully grown.
po·ny (pō′ nē) ◊ *noun, plural* **ponies**

pony express *noun* A system of carrying mail on horseback across the western United States that was used in 1860 and 1861.

poodle *noun* A dog with thick, curly hair.
poo·dle (po͞od′ l) ◊ *noun, plural* **poodles**

▲ **poodle**

pool¹ *noun* **1.** A small, still body of water. **2.** A tank of water, as one used for swimming. **3.** A small body of liquid; puddle: *There's a pool of oil on the garage floor.*
pool¹ (po͞ol) ◊ *noun, plural* **pools**

pool² *noun* **1.** A game played with balls and a cue on a table with six pockets. **2.** A collection of people, things, or money brought together for common use or a special purpose: *Our parents got together and formed a pool to drive us to soccer games.*
◊ *verb* To put together for common use or a special purpose: *My brother and I pooled our money and bought flowers for our aunt.*
pool² (po͞ol) ◊ *noun, plural* **pools** ◊ *verb* **pooled, pooling**

***HISTORY* • pool¹, pool²**

Pool¹ comes from an old English word that meant "a small pond." **Pool²** comes from an old French word that meant "chicken." It seems that **pool²** was named for an older game in which the prize was a chicken.

poor *adjective* **1.** Having little or no money or possessions. **2.** Low in quality or quantity: *Poor handwriting makes your papers hard to read.* **3.** Deserving pity; unfortunate: *The poor kitten is cold.*
poor (po͝or) ◊ *adjective* **poorer, poorest**

pop *noun* **1.** A sudden sharp sound: *The balloon burst with a pop.* **2.** A soft drink with bubbles of gas in it; soda.
◊ *verb* **1.** To make or cause to make a sound like a pop: *The fire crackled and popped.* **2.** To burst or cause to burst with a pop: *Be careful not to pop the balloon.* **3.** To appear casually or unexpectedly: *I just popped in to say hello.* **4.** To open wide suddenly: *The acrobat had everyone's eyes popping.*
pop (pŏp) ◊ *noun, plural* **pops** ◊ *verb* **popped, popping**

popcorn *noun* Corn that bursts and becomes white and puffy when heated.
pop·corn (**pŏp′** kôrn′) ◊ *noun*

pope *noun* The head of the Roman Catholic Church.
pope (pōp) ◊ *noun, plural* **popes**

poplar *noun* A tree with triangular leaves and soft, light-colored wood. The cottonwood is a kind of poplar.
pop·lar (**pŏp′** lər) ◊ *noun, plural* **poplars** *or* **poplar**

poppy *noun* A plant with bright, often red flowers, a hairy stem, and milky juice.
pop·py (**pŏp′** ē) ◊ *noun, plural* **poppies**

popular *adjective* **1.** Of, for, or by the people: *In a democracy representatives are elected by popular vote.* **2.** Enjoyed or liked by many or most people: *Running is a popular sport.*
pop·u·lar (**pŏp′** yə lər) ◊ *adjective*

P

popularity *noun* The quality or condition of being popular.
pop·u·lar·i·ty (pŏp′yə **lăr′** ĭ tē) ◊ *noun*

populate *verb* **1.** To supply with inhabitants. **2.** To live in; inhabit.
pop·u·late (**pŏp′** yə lāt′) ◊ *verb* **populated, populating**

population *noun* **1.** The people, plants, or animals living in a certain place. **2.** The total number of people living in a certain place.
pop·u·la·tion (pŏp′yə **lā′** shən) ◊ *noun, plural* **populations**

porcelain *noun* A hard, white material made by baking a fine clay. Porcelain is used especially to make dishes and cups.
por·ce·lain (**pôr′** sə lĭn) ◊ *noun*

porch *noun* A structure with a roof that is attached to the outside of a house.
porch (pôrch) ◊ *noun, plural* **porches**

porcupine *noun* An animal whose back and sides are covered with long, sharp quills.
por·cu·pine (**pôr′** kyə pīn′) ◊ *noun, plural* **porcupines**

***HISTORY* • porcupine**

Porcupine comes from an old French phrase that meant "spiny pig."

▲ **porcupine**

ă	pat	ĭ	pit	oi	**oi**l	th	ba**th**
ā	pay	ī	ride	o͝o	b**oo**k	*th*	ba**the**
â	care	î	fierce	o͞o	b**oo**t	ə	ago, item
ä	father	ŏ	pot	ou	**ou**t		pencil
ĕ	pet	ō	go	ŭ	cut		atom
ē	be	ô	paw, for	û	fur		circus

pore[1] *noun* A tiny opening, as in the skin or on the surface of a plant.
pore[1] (pôr) ◊ *noun, plural* **pores**
‖*These sound alike:* **pore, pour**

pore[2] *verb* To examine with great care and attention: *I pored over the magazine.*
pore[2] (pôr) ◊ *verb* **pored, poring**
‖*These sound alike:* **pore, pour**

***HISTORY* • pore[1], pore[2]**

Pore[1] goes back to a Greek word that meant "passage." **Pore[2]** first appeared in written English toward the end of the Middle Ages; its history before that is not known for certain.

pork *noun* The meat of a hog used as food.
pork (pôrk) ◊ *noun*

porous *adjective* Full of pores: *The water seeped down through the porous rock.*
po·rous (**pôr′** əs) ◊ *adjective*

porpoise *noun* A sea animal that swims like a fish but breathes air. A porpoise is related to the whale but is smaller and has a short, blunt snout.
por·poise (**pôr′** pəs) ◊ *noun, plural* **porpoise** *or* **porpoises**

▲ **porpoise**

porridge *noun* A food that is made by boiling meal, such as oatmeal, in water or milk until it is thick.
por·ridge (**pôr′** ĭj) ◊ *noun, plural* **porridges**

port[1] *noun* **1.** A town or city that has a harbor. **2.** A place along a body of water where ships can dock or anchor.
port[1] (pôrt) ◊ *noun, plural* **ports**

port² *noun* The left-hand side of a ship or aircraft.
port² (pôrt) ◊ *noun*

> ***HISTORY* • port¹, port²**
>
> **Port¹** comes from an old English word and an old French word. Both words go back to a Latin word that meant "harbor." **Port²** probably comes from **port¹**, possibly because the left side of a ship was the side turned toward the **port¹** when the ship was being loaded.

portable *adjective* Capable of being carried or moved: *We bought a portable radio.*
port·a·ble (**pôr′** tə bəl) ◊ *adjective*

portage *noun* The carrying of boats and supplies overland between waterways or around an obstruction such as a waterfall.
port·age (**pôr′** tĭj) ◊ *noun, plural* **portages**

portend *verb* To serve as a warning of: *Black clouds portended a storm.*
por·tend (pôr **tĕnd′**) ◊ *verb* **portended, portending**

portent *noun* A sign that something, usually something bad, is going to happen.
por·tent (**pôr′** tĕnt′) ◊ *noun, plural* **portents**

porter *noun* **1.** A person hired to carry baggage, as at a railroad station. **2.** A person who waits on passengers.
por·ter (**pôr′** tər) ◊ *noun, plural* **porters**

portfolio *noun* A flat case for carrying loose papers, documents, or drawings.
port·fo·li·o (pôrt **fō′** lē ō′) ◊ *noun, plural* **portfolios**

porthole *noun* An opening in a ship's side.
port·hole (**pôrt′** hōl′) ◊ *noun, plural* **portholes**

portico *noun* A porch or walkway with a roof that is supported by a row of columns.
por·ti·co (**pôr′** tĭ kō′) ◊ *noun, plural* **porticoes** *or* **porticos**

portion *noun* A part of a whole: *I ate two portions of stew.* —See Synonyms at **part.**
◊ *verb* To give out in portions; distribute.
por·tion (**pôr′** shən) ◊ *noun, plural* **portions** ◊ *verb* **portioned, portioning**

portrait *noun* A picture of someone's face or sometimes of the whole person.
por·trait (**pôr′** trĭt′) ◊ *noun, plural* **portraits**

portray *verb* **1.** To make a picture of. **2.** To picture with the use of words; describe: *The novel portrays life in a small town.* **3.** To play the part of: *In the movie the star portrays a young construction worker.*
por·tray (pôr **trā′**) ◊ *verb* **portrayed, portraying**

portrayal *noun* The act of portraying.
por·tray·al (pôr **trā′** əl) ◊ *noun, plural* **portrayals**

Portuguese *noun* **1.** A person who was born in or lives in Portugal. **2.** The language of Portugal and Brazil.
◊ *adjective* Of or relating to Portugal, the Portuguese, or the Portuguese language.
Por·tu·guese (**pôr′** chə gēz′) ◊ *noun, plural* **Portuguese** ◊ *adjective*

pose *verb* **1.** To take or put in a special position for a picture: *The children posed in front of the fireplace.* **2.** To pretend to be someone or something that one is not: *The reporter posed as a detective to get into the building.* **3.** To present or put forward: *I posed the question with care.*
◊ *noun* **1.** A position taken, especially for a portrait. **2.** A false appearance or way of acting: *My friend's outer cheerfulness was just a pose.*
pose (pōz) ◊ *verb* **posed, posing** ◊ *noun, plural* **poses**

position *noun* **1.** The place where someone or something is: *We changed the position of our beach blanket to get more sun.* **2.** The way a person or thing is placed or arranged: *Try not to sit in one position too long.* **3.** A personal situation: *Being praised for something I didn't do put me in an awkward position.* **4.** A way of thinking; point of view: *What is your position on the coming election?* **5.** A job: *My cousin holds an important position in the government.* **6.** The area that a particular player in a sport is responsible for.
po·si·tion (pə **zĭsh′** ən) ◊ *noun, plural* **positions**

positive *adjective* **1.** Showing consent or approval: *I got a positive answer to my request for help.* **2.** Wanting to improve or develop; constructive: *If you have a positive attitude, you'll succeed.* **3.** Having no doubts; sure: *I'm positive that we've met before.* **4.** Showing the presence of what is being looked for: *The test*

P

for anemia was positive. **5.** Greater than zero: *When you multiply positive numbers, the product is positive.* **6.** Having one of two opposite electrical charges: *A battery has positive and negative terminals.*
◊ *noun* A photographic image in which the areas of light and dark appear as they normally do.
pos·i·tive (pŏz′ĭ tĭv) ◊ *adjective* ◊ *noun, plural* **positives**

posse *noun* A group of citizens gathered together by a sheriff to help keep order or catch an outlaw.
pos·se (pŏs′ē) ◊ *noun, plural* **posses**

possess *verb* **1.** To have or own. **2.** To have or gain control over: *Anger possessed me.*
pos·sess (pə zĕs′) ◊ *verb* **possessed, possessing**

possession *noun* **1.** The fact or condition of having or owning something: *The teams fought for possession of the ball.* **2.** Something that is owned; belongings: *They fled the burning building, leaving their possessions behind.* **3.** A territory ruled by an outside power: *The Philippine Islands were once a possession of the United States.*
pos·ses·sion (pə zĕsh′ən) ◊ *noun, plural* **possessions**

possessive *adjective* Of, relating to, or being a word in the form that shows possession: *"Your" and "yours" are the possessive forms of "you." "Dog's" is the possessive form of "dog." "Farmers'" is the possessive form of "farmers." "Children's" is the possessive form of "children."*
◊ *noun* A word form that shows possession.
pos·ses·sive (pə zĕs′ĭv) ◊ *adjective* ◊ *noun, plural* **possessives**

possibility *noun* **1.** The fact or condition of being possible: *Scientists now doubt the possibility of life on Mars.* **2.** Something that may happen or exist: *Rain is a possibility today.*
pos·si·bil·i·ty (pŏs′ə **bĭl′**ĭ tē) ◊ *noun, plural* **possibilities**

ă	pat	ĭ	pit	oi	**oi**l	th	ba**th**
ā	pay	ī	ride	ŏŏ	b**oo**k	*th*	ba**th**e
â	care	î	fierce	ōō	b**oo**t	ə	**a**go, it**e**m
ä	father	ŏ	pot	ou	**ou**t		penc**i**l
ĕ	pet	ō	go	ŭ	c**u**t		at**o**m
ē	be	ô	paw, for	û	f**u**r		circ**u**s

possible *adjective* **1.** Capable of happening or being done: *It is possible to get to the airport by bus.* **2.** Capable of being used for a certain purpose: *That field is a possible site for the new school.*
pos·si·ble (pŏs′ə bəl) ◊ *adjective*

possibly *adverb* **1.** Perhaps; maybe: *Possibly you've read the book.* **2.** Under any circumstances; at all: *I can't possibly do it.*
pos·si·bly (pŏs′ə blē) ◊ *adverb*

possum *noun* An opossum.
pos·sum (pŏs′əm) ◊ *noun, plural* **possums**

post[1] *noun* An upright piece of wood or metal that serves as a support or marker.
◊ *verb* To put upon or as if on a post: *Winners' names will be posted on the bulletin board.*
post[1] (pōst) ◊ *noun, plural* **posts** ◊ *verb* **posted, posting**

post[2] *noun* **1.** A military base where troops are stationed. **2.** A place assigned to a guard or soldier. **3.** A position of employment; job.
◊ *verb* To assign to a post: *The police posted guards at all the exits.*
post[2] (pōst) ◊ *noun, plural* **posts** ◊ *verb* **posted, posting**

post[3] *noun* **1.** The transporting and delivering of mail. **2.** A delivery of mail.
◊ *verb* **1.** To mail a letter or package. **2.** To inform of events as they happen: *Keep me posted on what you're reading.*
post[3] (pōst) ◊ *noun, plural* **posts** ◊ *verb* **posted, posting**

> ***HISTORY* • post[1], post[2], post[3]**
>
> **Post**[1] was borrowed long ago from a Latin word that meant "wooden stake." **Post**[2] and **post**[3] go back to slightly different forms of a Latin word that meant "place."

postage *noun* The charge for mailing something.
post·age (pō′stĭj) ◊ *noun*

postage stamp *noun* A small printed piece of paper that is issued by a government and attached to letters and packages to show that the postage has been paid.
postage stamp ◊ *noun, plural* **postage stamps**

▲ **postage stamp**

postal *adjective* Of or relating to the post office or mail service: *Postal rates are rising.*
post·al (pō′stəl) ◊ *adjective*

post card *noun* A card used for sending a short message through the mail without an envelope. A post card usually has a picture on one side, with space on the other side for the address and a message.
post card ◊ *noun, plural* **post cards**

poster *noun* A large sheet with a picture or printing on it that is put up as an advertisement, notice, or decoration.
post·er (pō′stər) ◊ *noun, plural* **posters**

posterity *noun* Future generations: *The author left a rich body of fiction to posterity.*
pos·ter·i·ty (pŏ **stĕr′**ĭ tē) ◊ *noun*

postman *noun* A man who delivers mail.
post·man (**pōst′**mən) ◊ *noun, plural* **postmen**

postmark *noun* A mark stamped on a piece of mail especially to cancel the stamp.
post·mark (**pōst′**märk′) ◊ *noun, plural* **postmarks**

postmaster *noun* A man who is in charge of a post office.
post·mas·ter (**pōst′**măs′tər) ◊ *noun, plural* **postmasters**

postmistress *noun* A woman who is in charge of a post office.
post·mis·tress (**pōst′**mĭs′trĭs) ◊ *noun, plural* **postmistresses**

post office *noun* **1.** A government department or agency responsible for sending and delivering mail. **2.** A local office where mail is received, sorted, and sent out.
post office ◊ *noun, plural* **post offices**

postpone *verb* To put off until a later time: *Rain forced us to postpone the baseball game for a week.*
post·pone (pōst **pōn′**) ◊ *verb* **postponed, postponing**

postscript *noun* A message added at the end of a letter after the writer's signature.
post·script (**pōst′**skrĭpt′) ◊ *noun, plural* **postscripts**

posture *noun* The way in which a person holds or carries the body.
pos·ture (**pŏs′**chər) ◊ *noun, plural* **postures**

postwar *adjective* After a war.
post·war (**pōst′wôr′**) ◊ *adjective*

pot *noun* **1.** A deep, rounded container that is used especially in cooking, for holding food or liquid, and for growing plants. **2.** The amount that a pot holds: *Our guests drank two pots of tea.*
◊ *verb* **1.** To plant or put in a pot: *We potted the tulip bulbs.* **2.** To preserve food in a pot, jar, or can.
pot (pŏt) ◊ *noun, plural* **pots** ◊ *verb* **potted, potting**

potassium *noun* A soft, silvery, metallic chemical element that is used especially to make soaps and fertilizers.
po·tas·si·um (pə **tăs′**ē əm) ◊ *noun*

potato *noun* A vegetable that has firm white flesh. Potatoes grow underground and are the thick, rounded stems of a leafy plant.
po·ta·to (pə **tā′**tō) ◊ *noun, plural* **potatoes**

▲ **potato**

potential *adjective* Possible but not yet actual, definite, or real: *People who look in store windows are potential customers.*
po·ten·tial (pə **tĕn′**shəl) ◊ *adjective*

P

potion *noun* A drink of liquid, especially a medicine or a poison.
po·tion (pō′shən) ◊ *noun, plural* **potions**

potluck *noun* The food available, especially when offered to guests as a meal.
pot·luck (pŏt′lŭk′) ◊ *noun*

potter *noun* A person who makes pottery.
pot·ter (pŏt′ər) ◊ *noun, plural* **potters**

pottery *noun* **1.** Objects, such as pots, vases, or dishes, that are shaped from moist clay and hardened by heat. **2.** The art or work of a potter.
pot·ter·y (pŏt′ə rē) ◊ *noun*

pouch *noun* **1.** A bag of flexible material, such as leather, for holding or carrying various things. **2.** A part of an animal's body that is like a bag, as one in which the kangaroo carries its young. **3.** A loose or puffy fold of flesh: *I have pouches under my eyes.*
pouch (pouch) ◊ *noun, plural* **pouches**

poultry *noun* Birds, such as chickens, turkeys, ducks, or geese, that are raised for their eggs or meat.
poul·try (pōl′trē) ◊ *noun*

pounce *verb* To seize by or as if by swooping: *The kitten pounced on the ball.*
◊ *noun* The act of seizing with a swoop.
pounce (pouns) ◊ *verb* **pounced, pouncing** ◊ *noun, plural* **pounces**

pound[1] *noun* **1.** A unit of weight and mass equal to 16 ounces. **2.** A unit of money used in the United Kingdom, Ireland, and several other countries.
pound[1] (pound) ◊ *noun, plural* **pounds**

pound[2] *verb* **1.** To hit hard again and again: *The surf pounded against the rocks.* **2.** To beat rapidly or loudly: *My heart was pounding with excitement.* **3.** To crush to a powder or pulp: *I pounded the corn into meal.*
pound[2] (pound) ◊ *verb* **pounded, pounding**

pound[3] *noun* An enclosed place for keeping stray animals.
pound[3] (pound) ◊ *noun, plural* **pounds**

ă	pat	ĭ	pit	oi	oil	th	bath
ā	pay	ī	ride	ŏŏ	book	*th*	bathe
â	care	î	fierce	ōō	boot	ə	ago, item
ä	father	ŏ	pot	ou	out		pencil
ĕ	pet	ō	go	ŭ	cut		atom
ē	be	ô	paw, for	û	fur		circus

HISTORY • pound[1], pound[2], pound[3]

Pound[1] was borrowed long ago from a Latin word that meant "unit of weight." **Pound[2]** comes from an old English word that meant "to grind with a pestle." **Pound[3]** comes from a different old English word that meant "an enclosure for animals."

pour *verb* **1.** To flow or cause to flow in a steady stream: *When you pour the milk, pour slowly.* **2.** To rain hard: *It's pouring outside.* **3.** To express freely and fully: *I poured out my troubles to my friends.*
pour (pôr) ◊ *verb* **poured, pouring**
‖*These sound alike:* **pour, pore**

pout *verb* To push out the lips, especially as a sign that one is annoyed or angry.
◊ *noun* An act of pouting.
pout (pout) ◊ *verb* **pouted, pouting** ◊ *noun, plural* **pouts**

poverty *noun* **1.** The condition of being poor; lack of money and material goods. **2.** The condition of being of poor quality: *The farm is unsuccessful because of the poverty of the soil.*
pov·er·ty (pŏv′ər tē) ◊ *noun*

powder *noun* **1.** A dry substance consisting of many very small particles. **2.** Something, such as a cosmetic, in the form of powder.
◊ *verb* **1.** To turn into powder, as by grinding, crumbling, or drying. **2.** To cover or dust with or as if with powder: *I powdered my nose.*
pow·der (pou′dər) ◊ *noun, plural* **powders** ◊ *verb* **powdered, powdering**

powdery *adjective* Of, like, or easily made into powder.
pow·der·y (pou′də rē) ◊ *adjective*

power *noun* **1.** The force, strength, or ability to do or accomplish something: *It took all my power to open the door that was stuck. It is in our power to preserve the environment.* **2.** The ability or authority to control others: *The president has power over the armed forces.* **3.** A person, group, or nation that has great influence or control over others: *The world powers met to discuss their problems.* **4.** Energy that can be used for doing work: *The mill runs on water power.* **5.** Electricity: *The power failed during the storm.*

◊ *verb* To supply with power: *A gasoline engine powers the truck.*
pow·er (pou′ər) ◊ *noun, plural* **powers** ◊ *verb* **powered, powering**

SYNONYMS

power, authority, control

The president has a great deal of *power.* I don't have the *authority* to let you do that. A good conductor has *control* over the orchestra.

powerful *adjective* Having power, authority, or influence: *The United States of America is a powerful nation.*
pow·er·ful (pou′ər fəl) ◊ *adjective*

powerless *adjective* Lacking power.
pow·er·less (pou′ər lĭs) ◊ *adjective*

pp. The abbreviation for *pages.*

PR The abbreviation for *Puerto Rico* used with a Zip Code.

practical *adjective* **1.** Having or serving a useful purpose: *It's not easy to turn an idea into a practical invention.* **2.** Coming from experience, practice, or use rather than theory or study: *We got our practical training by working on a farm.*
prac·ti·cal (prăk′tĭ kəl) ◊ *adjective*

practical joke *noun* A mischievous trick done to make someone look or feel foolish.
practical joke ◊ *noun, plural* **practical jokes**

practically *adverb* **1.** Almost, but not quite; nearly: *It is practically five o'clock; I can leave then.* **2.** In a practical or useful way.
prac·ti·cal·ly (prăk′tĭk lē) ◊ *adverb*

practice *verb* **1.** To do or work over and over in order to acquire skill: *I practice the piano every day.* **2.** To make a habit of: *Learn to practice self-control.* **3.** To work at a profession: *I would like to practice medicine.*
◊ *noun* **1.** Action done over and over to develop, maintain, or improve skill: *He used to be a good skater, but lately he's had no practice.* **2.** Skill gained or maintained through practice: *She was out of practice at skiing.* **3.** A usual way of doing things; habit: *I make a practice of getting up early.* **4.** Actual performance: *Put into practice what you have learned in school.* **5.** The work of a profession: *My parents are in the practice of law.* **6.** The business built up by a professional person: *The doctor has a large practice.*
prac·tice (prăk′tĭs) ◊ *verb* **practiced, practicing** ◊ *noun, plural* **practices**

prairie *noun* A wide area of flat or rolling land with tall grass and few trees.
prai·rie (prâr′ē) ◊ *noun, plural* **prairies**

prairie dog *noun* A burrowing animal of the plains of central North America. Prairie dogs have a call like a bark and live underground in large colonies.
prairie dog ◊ *noun, plural* **prairie dogs**

▲ **prairie dog**

prairie schooner *noun* A large wagon with a canvas top used by pioneers for travel across the prairies.
prairie schooner ◊ *noun, plural* **prairie schooners**

praise *noun* Approval or admiration: *Praise from the coach meant a lot to me.*
◊ *verb* To express praise for: *Everyone has praised your good sense.*
praise (prāz) ◊ *noun* ◊ *verb* **praised, praising**

prance *verb* **1.** To rise on the hind legs and spring forward: *The circus ponies pranced in a circle.* **2.** To move, walk, or run in a proud way.
prance (prăns) ◊ *verb* **pranced, prancing**

prank *noun* A playful trick or joke.
prank (prăngk) ◊ *noun, plural* **pranks**

pray *verb* **1.** To say a prayer. **2.** To beg earnestly. **3.** To hope very much.
pray (prā) ◊ *verb* **prayed, praying**
‖*These sound alike:* **pray, prey**

prayer *noun* **1.** An expression of human thoughts, hopes, or needs when asking or giving thanks to God for divine help, favor, or forgiveness. **2.** The act of praying: *They clasped their hands in prayer.* **3.** A serious request: *Our prayers for rain were finally answered.*
prayer (prâr) ◊ *noun, plural* **prayers**

praying mantis *noun* A mantis.
praying mantis ◊ *noun, plural* **praying mantises**

P

pre– The prefix *pre–* means "earlier," "before," or "in advance." If I *prepay* my tickets to the baseball game, I pay for them in advance of the game.

VOCABULARY BUILDER • pre–

Many words that are formed with **pre–** are not entries in this dictionary. But you can figure out what these words mean by looking up the meanings of the root words and the prefix. For example:
prearrange = to arrange in advance
precook = to cook food before final cooking

preach *verb* **1.** To give a talk on a religious or moral subject. **2.** To teach and urge others to accept: *The leaders preach economy.*
preach (prēch) ◊ *verb* **preached, preaching**

preacher *noun* A person who preaches, especially a minister.
preach·er (**prē′** chər) ◊ *noun, plural* **preachers**

precaution *noun* An action or step that is taken to guard against possible danger, error, or accident: *Fastening your seat belt is a simple but important safety precaution.*
pre·cau·tion (prĭ **kô′** shən) ◊ *noun, plural* **precautions**

precede *verb* To go or come before, as in time, order, or rank: *A small surge of water precedes all geyser eruptions.*
pre·cede (prĭ **sēd′**) ◊ *verb* **preceded, preceding**

precedent *noun* A model or example that may be followed or referred to later.
prec·e·dent (**prĕs′** ĭ dənt) ◊ *noun, plural* **precedents**

precinct *noun* A section or district of a city or town.
pre·cinct (**prē′** sĭngkt′) ◊ *noun, plural* **precincts**

ă	pat	ĭ	pit	oi	oil	th	bath
ā	pay	ī	ride	o͝o	book	*th*	bathe
â	care	î	fierce	o͞o	boot	ə	ago, item
ä	father	ŏ	pot	ou	out		pencil
ĕ	pet	ō	go	ŭ	cut		atom
ē	be	ô	paw, for	û	fur		circus

precious *adjective* Having very great value: *Gold and silver are precious metals.* —See Synonyms at **valuable.**
pre·cious (**prĕsh′** əs) ◊ *adjective*

precipice *noun* A very steep mass of rock, as a cliff.
prec·i·pice (**prĕs′** ə pĭs) ◊ *noun, plural* **precipices**

▲ **precipice**

precipitate *verb* **1.** To cause to happen; bring on: *A vibration on the mountain slope precipitated an avalanche.* **2.** To change from vapor to water and fall as rain, snow, sleet, or hail.
pre·cip·i·tate (prĭ **sĭp′** ĭ tāt′) ◊ *verb* **precipitated, precipitating**

precipitation *noun* Water that falls to the earth as rain, snow, sleet, or hail.
pre·cip·i·ta·tion (prĭ sĭp′ĭ **tā′** shən) ◊ *noun*

precise *adjective* **1.** Being strictly defined or

stated: *Give me precise instructions.* **2.** Distinct from all others; particular: *I was standing on that precise spot.* **3.** Very accurate; exact: *Tell me how to get there, and please be precise.*
pre·cise (prĭ **sīs′**) ◊ *adjective*

precision *noun* The quality or condition of being precise: *Cutting a large diamond takes great precision.*
pre·ci·sion (prĭ **sĭzh′**ən) ◊ *noun*

precocious *adjective* Showing skills or abilities at an earlier age than is usual.
pre·co·cious (prĭ **kō′**shəs) ◊ *adjective*

predator *noun* An animal that lives by preying on other animals.
pred·a·tor (**prĕd′**ə tər) ◊ *noun, plural* **predators**

predecessor *noun* A person who has held an office or position before another.
pred·e·ces·sor (**prĕd′**ĭ sĕs′ər) ◊ *noun, plural* **predecessors**

predicament *noun* A difficult or embarrassing situation.
pre·dic·a·ment (prĭ **dĭk′**ə mənt) ◊ *noun, plural* **predicaments**

predicate *noun* The part of a sentence or clause that tells something about the subject or what the subject does: *Tastes good* is the predicate in the sentence *Milk tastes good.*
pred·i·cate (**prĕd′**ĭ kĭt) ◊ *noun, plural* **predicates**

predict *verb* To tell about in advance: *The weather report predicts showers.*
pre·dict (prĭ **dĭkt′**) ◊ *verb* **predicted, predicting**

prediction *noun* **1.** The act of predicting. **2.** Something predicted: *My optimistic predictions came true.*
pre·dic·tion (prĭ **dĭk′**shən) ◊ *noun, plural* **predictions**

preface *noun* Words that introduce the main part of a book or speech.
pref·ace (**prĕf′**ĭs) ◊ *noun, plural* **prefaces**

prefer *verb* To like better: *I prefer books to television.*
pre·fer (prĭ **fûr′**) ◊ *verb* **preferred, preferring**

preference *noun* **1.** The choosing of one thing over another: *We dress simply by preference.* **2.** A liking for one person or thing over another: *We don't show preference for our dog over our cat.* —See Synonyms at **choice. 3.** One that is preferred: *A window seat is my preference.*
pref·er·ence (**prĕf′**ər əns) ◊ *noun, plural* **preferences**

prefix *noun* A word part added to the beginning of a base word or root word. A prefix changes the meaning. The word *discomfort* is made up of the prefix *dis–* and the base word *comfort.*
pre·fix (**prē′**fĭks′) ◊ *noun, plural* **prefixes**

pregnant *adjective* Having offspring that are developing within the body.
preg·nant (**prĕg′**nənt) ◊ *adjective*

prehistoric *adjective* Of, relating to, or belonging to the time before people began to record events in writing.
pre·his·tor·ic (prē′hĭ **stôr′**ĭk) ◊ *adjective*

prejudice *noun* A strong feeling or opinion formed unfairly or without knowing all the facts; bias.
◊ *verb* To fill with prejudice; bias.
prej·u·dice (**prĕj′**ə dĭs) ◊ *noun, plural* **prejudices** ◊ *verb* **prejudiced, prejudicing**

preliminary *adjective* Coming before a main event or activity: *We made preliminary outlines before we wrote our reports.*
pre·lim·i·nar·y (prĭ **lĭm′**ə nĕr′ē) ◊ *adjective*

premature *adjective* Appearing, happening, or done before the usual time: *We had a premature snowstorm in September.*
pre·ma·ture (prē′mə **tŏŏr′** *or* prē′mə **tyŏŏr′**) ◊ *adjective*

premeditate *verb* To plan and think out in advance.
pre·med·i·tate (prĭ **mĕd′**ĭ tāt′) ◊ *verb* **premeditated, premeditating**

premier *noun* A prime minister.
pre·mier (prĭ **mîr′**) ◊ *noun, plural* **premiers**

premise *noun* **1.** A statement on which an argument is based or from which a conclusion is reached. **2. premises** A piece of property, including the buildings on it.
prem·ise (**prĕm′**ĭs) ◊ *noun, plural* **premises**

premium *noun* **1.** A prize given for quality or performance. **2.** An extra benefit; bonus: *The new store gave out gifts as premiums to its first customers.* **3.** A very high value: *Some coaches place a premium on winning.* **4.** An amount paid for an insurance policy.
pre·mi·um (**prē′**mē əm) ◊ *noun, plural* **premiums**

P

prepaid *verb* Past tense and past participle of **prepay.**
pre·paid (prē **pād′**) ◊ *verb*

preparation *noun* **1.** The act or process of preparing. **2.** An action by which a person prepares for something: *They finished the preparations for the party.* **3.** Something prepared for a certain use: *I used a preparation of herbs for seasoning the salad.*
prep·a·ra·tion (prĕp′ə **rā′**shən) ◊ *noun, plural* **preparations**

preparatory *adjective* Serving to prepare: *I did preparatory exercises before the race.*
pre·par·a·to·ry (prĭ **păr′** ə tôr′ē) ◊ *adjective*

prepare *verb* **1.** To make ready: *I have to prepare a book report.* **2.** To put together the ingredients of: *I prepared lunch.*
pre·pare (prĭ **pâr′**) ◊ *verb* **prepared, preparing**

prepay *verb* To pay for in advance.
pre·pay (prē **pā′**) ◊ *verb* **prepaid, prepaying**

preposition *noun* A word, such as *with,* that relates a noun or pronoun to some other word in the sentence.
prep·o·si·tion (prĕp′ə **zĭsh′** ən) ◊ *noun, plural* **prepositions**

prepositional *adjective* Of, relating to, or containing a preposition: *"With them" is a prepositional phrase.*
prep·o·si·tion·al (prĕp′ə **zĭsh′** ə nəl) ◊ *adjective*

prescribe *verb* **1.** To order or recommend the use of as a treatment: *The doctor prescribed rest.* **2.** To set down as a rule: *Good manners prescribe that we say thank you.*
pre·scribe (prĭ **skrīb′**) ◊ *verb* **prescribed, prescribing**

prescription *noun* **1.** A written instruction from a doctor indicating the medicine or treatment a patient is to receive. **2.** A medicine ordered by a doctor's prescription.
pre·scrip·tion (prĭ **skrĭp′**shən) ◊ *noun, plural* **prescriptions**

ă	pat	ĭ	pit	oi	oil	th	bath
ā	pay	ī	ride	o͝o	book	*th*	bathe
â	care	î	fierce	o͞o	boot	ə	ago, item
ä	father	ŏ	pot	ou	out		pencil
ĕ	pet	ō	go	ŭ	cut		atom
ē	be	ô	paw, for	û	fur		circus

presence *noun* **1.** The fact or condition of being present: *Your presence is not required.* **2.** Immediate nearness: *I get nervous in the presence of famous people.*
pres·ence (**prĕz′** əns) ◊ *noun*

present[1] *noun* A moment or period of time between the past and the future.
◊ *adjective* **1.** Being or happening now: *I can't visit you at the present time.* **2.** Being at hand: *All the fifth graders are present.* **3.** Expressing a time between the past and the future: *In the sentence "They are here," the verb "are" is in the present tense.*
pres·ent[1] (**prĕz′** ənt) ◊ *noun* ◊ *adjective*

present[2] *verb* **1.** To make a gift or award of or to: *We presented the trophy to the winners.* **2.** To introduce one person to another: *I would like to present my parents.* **3.** To take oneself into the presence of another: *We presented ourselves to the school committee.* **4.** To offer to the public: *The class presented a new play.*
◊ *noun* Something presented; gift: *I bought a birthday present for my cousin.*
pre·sent[2] ◊ *verb* (prĭ **zĕnt′**) **presented, presenting** ◊ *noun* **pres·ent** (**prĕz′** ənt), *plural* **presents**

> ***HISTORY* • present[1], present[2]**
>
> **Present[1]** and **present[2]** go back to slightly different forms of a Latin word that meant "to be in front of."

presentation *noun* **1.** The act of presenting. **2.** Something that is presented.
pres·en·ta·tion (prĕz′ən **tā′**shən *or* prē′zĕn-**tā′**shən) ◊ *noun, plural* **presentations**

presently *adverb* **1.** In a short time; soon: *I'll be leaving presently.* **2.** At this time; now: *An expedition is presently under way.*
pres·ent·ly (**prĕz′** ənt lē) ◊ *adverb*

preservation *noun* The act of preserving or the condition of being preserved.
pres·er·va·tion (prĕz′ər **vā′**shən) ◊ *noun*

preservative *noun* Something that is used to preserve, especially a chemical added to a food to keep it from spoiling. Some food preservatives are harmful to health.
pre·ser·va·tive (prĭ **zûr′** və tĭv) ◊ *noun, plural* **preservatives**

preserve *verb* **1.** To protect, as from injury or destruction: *We want to preserve our forests.* **2.** To maintain intact: *I preserved my calm attitude.* **3.** To protect food from spoiling, as by freezing, canning, or pickling.
◊ *noun* **1.** Often **preserves** Fruit cooked with sugar to keep it from spoiling. **2.** An area maintained for the protection of wildlife or natural resources.
pre·serve (prĭ **zûrv′**) ◊ *verb* **preserved, preserving** ◊ *noun, plural* **preserves**

preside *verb* **1.** To hold the position of chairperson at a meeting. **2.** To have authority: *Our parents preside at the dinner table.*
pre·side (prĭ **zīd′**) ◊ *verb* **presided, presiding**

presidency *noun* **1.** The office of president. **2.** The period during which a president is in office.
pres·i·den·cy (**prĕz′**ĭ dən sē) ◊ *noun, plural* **presidencies**

president *noun* **1.** The chief executive of a republic, such as the United States. **2.** The chief officer of a company, organization, or institution.
pres·i·dent (**prĕz′**ĭ dənt) ◊ *noun, plural* **presidents**

presidential *adjective* Of or relating to a president or presidency.
pres·i·den·tial (prĕz′ĭ **dĕn′**shəl) ◊ *adjective*

press *verb* **1.** To put steady force against: *Press the doorbell.* **2.** To squeeze out the juice or contents of: *We pressed apples to make cider.* **3.** To smooth by using heat and pressure; iron: *I will have to press this wrinkled shirt.* **4.** To try hard to persuade: *We pressed our relatives to stay for the holiday.*
◊ *noun* **1.** A machine or device used to squeeze or put pressure on something. **2.** A printing press. **3.** Printed matter, especially newspapers and magazines. **4.** The people who produce newspapers and magazines.
press (prĕs) ◊ *verb* **pressed, pressing** ◊ *noun, plural* **presses**

pressure *noun* **1.** The force applied by one body on another body that it is touching. **2.** A burden that causes distress; strain: *The pressure of taking tests makes me nervous.* **3.** A strong influence or force: *I'm under pressure to succeed.*
pres·sure (**prĕsh′**ər) ◊ *noun, plural* **pressures**

prestige *noun* Great respect or importance in the opinion of others.
pres·tige (prĕ **stēzh′**) ◊ *noun*

presume *verb* **1.** To suppose to be true; take for granted: *I presume you're happy.* **2.** To act without authority or permission: *They presumed to invite themselves to the party.*
pre·sume (prĭ **zo͞om′**) ◊ *verb* **presumed, presuming**

pretend *verb* **1.** To put on a false show of: *They pretended illness.* **2.** To make believe: *Let's pretend we're famous.* **3.** To claim falsely: *I don't pretend to be an art expert.*
pre·tend (prĭ **tĕnd′**) ◊ *verb* **pretended, pretending**

pretty *adjective* Pleasing, attractive, or appealing to the eye or ear. —See Synonyms at **beautiful**.
◊ *adverb* To a fair degree; somewhat: *We will leave pretty soon.*
pret·ty (**prĭt′**ē) ◊ *adjective* **prettier, prettiest** ◊ *adverb*

pretzel *noun* A hard salted cracker usually baked in the form of a loose knot.
pret·zel (**prĕt′**səl) ◊ *noun, plural* **pretzels**

prevail *verb* **1.** To win control; triumph: *Good prevailed over evil.* **2.** To be usual or common: *Cold winds prevail in winter.*
pre·vail (prĭ **vāl′**) ◊ *verb* **prevailed, prevailing**

prevalent *adjective* Existing, happening, or used widely: *Sickness is less prevalent in summer than in winter.*
prev·a·lent (**prĕv′**ə lənt) ◊ *adjective*

prevent *verb* **1.** To keep from happening: *Doctors would rather prevent illness than treat it.* **2.** To keep from doing something: *The loud music prevents me from sleeping.*
pre·vent (prĭ **vĕnt′**) ◊ *verb* **prevented, preventing**

prevention *noun* **1.** The act or an example of preventing: *Prevention of illness is very important.* **2.** Something that prevents: *Some people think that vitamin C is a prevention against colds.*
pre·ven·tion (prĭ **vĕn′**shən) ◊ *noun*

preventive *adjective* Serving to prevent.
pre·ven·tive (prĭ **vĕn′**tĭv) ◊ *adjective*

preview *noun* A showing of something, as a movie, to an invited audience before presenting it to the public.
pre·view (**prē′**vyo͞o′) ◊ *noun, plural* **previews**

P

previous *adjective* Existing or taking place earlier: *We read about plants in the previous chapter.*
pre·vi·ous (prē′ vē əs) ◊ *adjective*

prey *noun* **1.** An animal hunted or caught by another for food. **2.** Someone or something that is helpless, as against attack or trouble.
◊ *verb* **1.** To hunt for food: *Owls prey on mice.* **2.** To have a bad effect: *Worries prey on my mind.*
prey (prā) ◊ *noun* ◊ *verb* **preyed, preying**
‖*These sound alike:* **prey, pray**

price *noun* **1.** The amount of money asked or paid for something. **2.** The cost at which something is gotten: *The price of independence is often high.*
◊ *verb* **1.** To set a price for: *The squash was priced at 50¢ a pound.* **2.** To find out the price of: *Let's price the jacket in the window.*
price (prīs) ◊ *noun, plural* **prices** ◊ *verb* **priced, pricing**

SYNONYMS

price, charge, cost, expense
What is the *price* of the red cap? There is a *charge* for wrapping presents. The *cost* of this book is low. I paid the *expense* of the whole trip at one time.

priceless *adjective* Of great value; beyond price: *We saw priceless jewels at the museum.* —See Synonyms at **valuable.**
price·less (prīs′ lĭs) ◊ *adjective*

prick *verb* To make a small hole or mark with or as if with a pointed object: *I pricked my finger with a needle.*
◊ *noun* **1.** The act of piercing. **2.** The feeling of being pierced. **3.** A hole or mark left by piercing.
prick (prĭk) ◊ *verb* **pricked, pricking** ◊ *noun, plural* **pricks**

prickle *noun* **1.** A small, sharp point, such as a thorn. **2.** A tingling feeling.
◊ *verb* To have a tingling feeling.
prick·le (prĭk′ əl) ◊ *noun, plural* **prickles** ◊ *verb* **prickled, prickling**

prickly *adjective* **1.** Having thorns or prickles: *I bumped into a prickly cactus.* **2.** Tingling: *I had a prickly sensation in my foot.*
prick·ly (prĭk′ lē) ◊ *adjective* **pricklier, prickliest**

prickly pear *noun* A cactus with flat, spiny stems, usually yellow flowers, and edible oval fruit.
prickly pear ◊ *noun, plural* **prickly pears**

▲ **prickly pear**

pride *noun* **1.** A sense of one's own dignity or worth; self-respect. **2.** Pleasure or satisfaction in accomplishments or possessions: *My parents take pride in their children.* **3.** Too high an opinion of oneself; conceit.
◊ *verb* To be proud of oneself.
pride (prīd) ◊ *noun* ◊ *verb* **prided, priding**

priest *noun* A member of the clergy who has the authority to perform religious services or ceremonies.
priest (prēst) ◊ *noun, plural* **priests**

prim *adjective* Very proper and precise.
prim (prĭm) ◊ *adjective* **primmer, primmest**

primarily *adverb* In the first place; chiefly.
pri·mar·i·ly (prī **mĕr**′ ə lē) ◊ *adverb*

primary *adjective* **1.** Being first in time or sequence: *Our studies are in the primary stage.* **2.** First in importance, degree, or quality; chief: *The primary function of furniture is*

ă	pat	ĭ	pit	oi	**oi**l	th	ba**th**
ā	pay	ī	ride	o͝o	book	*th*	ba**th**e
â	care	î	fierce	o͞o	boot	ə	ago, item
ä	father	ŏ	pot	ou	**ou**t		pencil
ĕ	pet	ō	go	ŭ	cut		atom
ē	be	ô	paw, for	û	fur		circus

comfort. **3.** Being a fundamental part; basic: *Food is one of the primary needs of human beings and animals.*
◊ *noun* A primary election in which voters, usually the voters of each party, nominate candidates for office.
pri·mar·y (prī′mĕr′ē) ◊ *adjective* ◊ *noun, plural* **primaries**

primary color *noun* Any of the three colors, red, yellow, and blue, from which all other colors can be made.
primary color ◊ *noun, plural* **primary colors**

primary school *noun* A school that includes the first three or four grades and sometimes kindergarten.
primary school ◊ *noun, plural* **primary schools**

primary stress *noun* **1.** The strongest amount of stress or force that is used in pronouncing a word. The primary stress is on the first syllable of the word *flagpole* (**flăg′**pōl′). **2.** The mark (′) that is used to show which syllable of a word receives the strongest amount of stress.

prime *adjective* First in importance, degree, value, or significance: *My prime concern was to get home before the storm.*
prime (prīm) ◊ *adjective*

prime minister *noun* The chief minister of the government in some countries.
prime minister ◊ *noun, plural* **prime ministers**

primer *noun* **1.** A beginning reading textbook. **2.** A book that covers the basic elements of a subject.
prim·er (**prĭm′**ər) ◊ *noun, plural* **primers**

primitive *adjective* **1.** Of or in an early stage of development: *Bacteria are a primitive form of life.* **2.** Of or in an early stage in the development of human culture: *Some of the primitive cave people were skillful artists.* **3.** Simple or crude; not sophisticated: *We built a primitive form of rocket.*
prim·i·tive (**prĭm′**ĭ tĭv) ◊ *adjective*

primrose *noun* A plant that is often grown for its clusters of colored flowers.
prim·rose (**prĭm′**rōz′) ◊ *noun, plural* **primroses**

prince *noun* **1.** The son of a king or queen. **2.** A king. **3.** A nobleman of high rank. **4.** The husband of a queen.
prince (prĭns) ◊ *noun, plural* **princes**

princess *noun* **1.** The daughter of a king or queen. **2.** A queen. **3.** A noblewoman of high rank. **4.** The wife of a prince.
prin·cess (**prĭn′**sĭs *or* **prĭn′**sĕs′) ◊ *noun, plural* **princesses**

principal *adjective* First in rank, degree, or importance; chief: *The principal food in my cat's diet is fish.*
◊ *noun* **1.** A person in a leading position. **2.** The head of a school.
prin·ci·pal (**prĭn′**sə pəl) ◊ *adjective* ◊ *noun, plural* **principals**
‖*These sound alike:* **principal, principle**

principle *noun* **1.** A fundamental truth that forms the basis of other truths: *We studied the principles of mathematics.* **2.** A rule or standard of behavior: *A banker should be a person of high principle.* **3.** A rule or law about how a device or machine functions or operates: *The teacher explained the principle of the pulley.*
prin·ci·ple (**prĭn′**sə pəl) ◊ *noun, plural* **principles**
‖*These sound alike:* **principle, principal**

print *verb* **1.** To stamp onto or into a surface by using pressure: *The fabric was printed with a design of flowers.* **2.** To produce on a printing press: *The government prints money.* **3.** To offer in printed form; publish: *The newspaper refused to print the articles.* **4.** To write with the letters separated like those commonly used in books and newspapers.
◊ *noun* **1.** A mark made in or on a surface by using pressure. **2.** Letters produced by printing. **3.** A design or picture made from an engraved plate or a wood block. **4.** Cloth on which a dyed pattern has been stamped. **5.** A photograph made from a negative.
print (prĭnt) ◊ *verb* **printed, printing** ◊ *noun, plural* **prints**

printer *noun* **1.** A person whose job or business is printing. **2.** The part of a computer system that produces printed material.
print·er (**prĭn′**tər) ◊ *noun, plural* **printers**

printing *noun* **1.** The art, process, or business of producing printed matter, as books, on a printing press. **2.** All the copies of something, as a book, that are printed at one time. **3.** Writing in which the letters are like those commonly used in books and magazines.
print·ing (**prĭn′**tĭng) ◊ *noun, plural* **printings**

P

printing press *noun* A machine that prints letters, words, and designs by pressing sheets of paper onto an inked surface.
printing press ◊ *noun, plural* **printing presses**

printout *noun* Printed material, as a list or diagram, that is produced by a computer.
print·out (**prĭnt′** out′) ◊ *noun, plural* **printouts**

prior *adjective* Coming before in time or order; earlier: *Tell me about your prior grades.*
pri·or (**prī′** ər) ◊ *adjective*

priority *noun* The quality or condition of coming before in time, order, or importance: *Safety has high priority in factories.*
pri·or·i·ty (prī **ôr′** ĭ tē) ◊ *noun, plural* **priorities**

prism *noun* A transparent solid object that usually has triangular bases and rectangular sides. A prism breaks light up into bands of color like a rainbow.
prism (**prĭz′** əm) ◊ *noun, plural* **prisms**

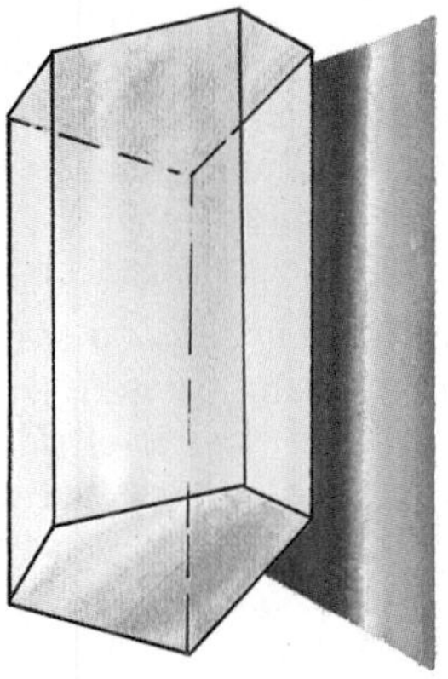

▲ **prism**

prison *noun* A place where persons convicted or accused of crimes are confined.
pris·on (**prĭz′** ən) ◊ *noun, plural* **prisons**

prisoner *noun* **1.** A person who is confined in a prison. **2.** A person who has been captured or is held by force.
pris·on·er (**prĭz′** ə nər) ◊ *noun, plural* **prisoners**

privacy *noun* **1.** The condition of being apart or away from others. **2.** The condition of being kept secret; secrecy.
pri·va·cy (**prī′** və sē) ◊ *noun*

private *adjective* **1.** Of, relating to, or for a particular person or group; not public: *We can't swim here; it's a private beach.* **2.** Hidden from public view or knowledge; secret: *They reached a private agreement.* **3.** Not holding public office: *The defeated governor is once again a private citizen.*
◊ *noun* An Army or Marine Corps enlisted person ranking below a corporal.
pri·vate (**prī′** vĭt) ◊ *adjective* ◊ *noun, plural* **privates**

privilege *noun* A special right or benefit that is granted to or enjoyed by some people and not by others. —See Synonyms at **right.**
priv·i·lege (**prĭv′** ə lĭj) ◊ *noun, plural* **privileges**

privileged *adjective* Having privileges.
priv·i·leged (**prĭv′** ə lĭjd) ◊ *adjective*

prize *noun* **1.** Something offered or won in a competition, a game, or a contest. **2.** Something worth having or working for.
◊ *adjective* **1.** Given as a prize: *I will use the prize money to help pay for my education.* **2.** Worthy of a prize: *The pet shop had a prize cat for sale.*
◊ *verb* To value highly; esteem: *I prize your friendship.*
prize (prīz) ◊ *noun, plural* **prizes** ◊ *adjective* ◊ *verb* **prized, prizing**

pro[1] *noun* An argument in favor of something.
◊ *adverb* In favor of something, as a vote: *We argued pro and con.*
pro[1] (prō) ◊ *noun, plural* **pros** ◊ *adverb*

pro[2] *noun* A professional.
◊ *adjective* Professional.
pro[2] (prō) ◊ *noun, plural* **pros** ◊ *adjective*

> ***HISTORY* • pro**[1]**, pro**[2]
>
> **Pro**[1] comes from a Latin word that means "in favor of." **Pro**[2] is short for **professional.**

probability *noun* **1.** The condition or quality of being probable: *There is a probability of snow today.* **2.** Something that is probable.
prob·a·bil·i·ty (prŏb′ə **bĭl′** ĭ tē) ◊ *noun, plural* **probabilities**

probable *adjective* Likely but not certain to happen or be true: *The probable reason for your success is that you work hard.*
prob·a·ble (**prŏb′** ə bəl) ◊ *adjective*

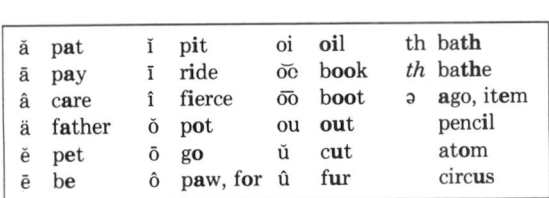

ă	pat	ĭ	pit	oi	oil	th	bath
ā	pay	ī	ride	ŏŏ	book	*th*	bathe
â	care	î	fierce	ōō	boot	ə	ago, item
ä	father	ŏ	pot	ou	out		pencil
ĕ	pet	ō	go	ŭ	cut		atom
ē	be	ô	paw, for	û	fur		circus

probably *adverb* Most likely: *I'll probably go to the party if I'm invited.*
prob·a·bly (**prŏb'** ə blē) ◊ *adverb*

probation *noun* A period of time during which a person's qualifications or willingness to work can be tested or determined.
pro·ba·tion (prō **bā'**shən) ◊ *noun*

probe *noun* **1.** A long, slender tool used to examine a wound or body cavity. **2.** A careful examination made as if with a probe.
◊ *verb* **1.** To explore or examine with or as if with a probe. **2.** To search into thoroughly: *The governor appointed a committee to probe the causes of the strike.*
probe (prōb) ◊ *noun, plural* **probes** ◊ *verb* **probed, probing**

problem *noun* **1.** A question that must be solved or thought about: *There were 12 problems on the arithmetic test.* **2.** Someone or something that is difficult to deal with or understand: *The teacher had the problem of keeping the class together while they took the subway to the museum.*
prob·lem (**prŏb'**ləm) ◊ *noun, plural* **problems**

procedure *noun* A way of doing something or getting something done, especially by a series of steps.
pro·ce·dure (prə **sē'**jər) ◊ *noun, plural* **procedures**

proceed *verb* **1.** To go forward or onward, especially after stopping: *The ship picked up passengers on the island and then proceeded to port.* **2.** To carry on an action or process: *The speaker told us about the actors and then proceeded to talk about the film.*
pro·ceed (prō **sēd'**) ◊ *verb* **proceeded, proceeding**

proceeds *plural noun* All of the money that comes from a business activity; profits.
pro·ceeds (**prō'**sēdz') ◊ *plural noun*

process *noun* A series of steps, actions, motions, or operations that bring about or lead to a result: *The farmer used a churn in the process of making butter.*
◊ *verb* To prepare or treat by a special process: *Milk is processed to kill certain germs.*
proc·ess (**prŏs'**ĕs' *or* **prō'**sĕs') ◊ *noun, plural* **processes** ◊ *verb* **processed, processing**

procession *noun* **1.** Orderly continuous forward motion: *The students walked in procession to the graduation ceremony.* **2.** A group of persons, vehicles, or objects moving along in orderly succession: *We watched the wedding procession march down the aisle.*
pro·ces·sion (prə **sĕsh'**ən) ◊ *noun, plural* **processions**

proclaim *verb* To announce publicly; declare: *The mayor proclaimed a holiday.*
pro·claim (prə **klām'**) ◊ *verb* **proclaimed, proclaiming**

proclamation *noun* **1.** The act of proclaiming. **2.** Something proclaimed.
proc·la·ma·tion (prŏk'lə **mā'**shən) ◊ *noun, plural* **proclamations**

procure *verb* **1.** To obtain; get: *We managed to procure tickets for the circus.* **2.** To bring about: *The city council is trying to procure a solution to the traffic problem.*
pro·cure (prə **kyŏŏr'**) ◊ *verb* **procured, procuring**

prod *verb* **1.** To poke with or as if with a pointed instrument: *She prodded me on the shoulder with her thumb.* **2.** To urge to action; stir: *My father had to prod me to do my homework.*
◊ *noun* **1.** Something used to prod. **2.** The act of prodding.
prod (prŏd) ◊ *verb* **prodded, prodding** ◊ *noun, plural* **prods**

prodigy *noun* A child with talents or abilities that are much higher than normal.
prod·i·gy (**prŏd'** ə jē) ◊ *noun, plural* **prodigies**

produce *verb* **1.** To bring forth; yield: *This plant produces flowers.* **2.** To make by working with raw materials; manufacture: *The factory produces tractors.* **3.** To bring forward; exhibit: *The child produced a frog from a little box.* **4.** To prepare and present to the public: *The fourth grade produced a play about a princess.*
◊ *noun* Farm products, as fruits or vegetables, raised for selling.
pro·duce ◊ *verb* (prə **dōōs'** *or* prə **dyōōs'**) **produced, producing** ◊ *noun* (**prŏd'**ōōs' *or* **prō'**dōōs')

producer *noun* Someone or something that produces.
pro·duc·er (prə **dōō'**sər *or* prə **dyōō'**sər) ◊ *noun, plural* **producers**

P

product *noun* **1.** Something produced, as by nature or thought: *The rumor is a product of your imagination.* **2.** The result obtained by multiplying two or more numbers: *The product of 3 and 2 is 6.*
prod·uct (prŏd′ əkt) ◊ *noun, plural* **products**

production *noun* **1.** The act or process of producing. **2.** Something produced: *This is the theater company's finest production so far.* **3.** The total amount that is produced.
pro·duc·tion (prə **dŭk′** shən) ◊ *noun, plural* **productions**

productive *adjective* Producing or likely to produce: *During the most productive time in her career, she wrote five books.*
pro·duc·tive (prə **dŭk′** tĭv) ◊ *adjective*

profess *verb* **1.** To declare openly: *They professed their innocence.* **2.** To make a show of; pretend: *He was sympathetic to my problems or at least professed to be.*
pro·fess (prə **fĕs′**) ◊ *verb* **professed, professing**

profession *noun* **1.** An occupation, as law, that requires training and special study. **2.** The group of persons practicing a profession. **3.** The act of declaring openly.
pro·fes·sion (prə **fĕsh′** ən) ◊ *noun, plural* **professions**

professional *adjective* **1.** Of or relating to a profession. **2.** Making money for doing something that other people do for pleasure or as a hobby.
◊ *noun* **1.** A person who works at a profession. **2.** A person who is paid for doing something that other people do for pleasure or as a hobby.
pro·fes·sion·al (prə **fĕsh′** ə nəl) ◊ *adjective* ◊ *noun, plural* **professionals**

professor *noun* A teacher, especially a teacher having the highest rank in a college or university.
pro·fes·sor (prə **fĕs′** ər) ◊ *noun, plural* **professors**

ă	pat	ĭ	pit	oi	**oi**l	th	ba**th**
ā	pay	ī	ride	o͝o	b**oo**k	*th*	ba**the**
â	care	î	fierce	o͞o	b**oo**t	ə	**a**go, it**e**m
ä	father	ŏ	pot	ou	**ou**t		penc**i**l
ĕ	pet	ō	go	ŭ	c**u**t		at**o**m
ē	be	ô	paw, for	û	f**u**r		circ**u**s

proficient *adjective* Very skillful through training or practice; expert.
pro·fi·cient (prə **fĭsh′** ənt) ◊ *adjective*

profile *noun* A side view or drawing of something, especially the human head.
pro·file (**prō′** fīl′) ◊ *noun, plural* **profiles**

profit *noun* **1.** An advantage gained from something; benefit: *There is no profit in complaining.* **2.** The amount of money left after all the costs of operating a business have been subtracted from all the money earned: *I made a profit of five cents on every newspaper I sold.*
◊ *verb* **1.** To gain an advantage or benefit: *You can profit from your own experience.* **2.** To be of help to; benefit: *It would profit you to pay closer attention.*
prof·it (**prŏf′** ĭt) ◊ *noun, plural* **profits** ◊ *verb* **profited, profiting**
‖ *These sound alike:* **profit, prophet**

profitable *adjective* Yielding profit: *The computer industry is very profitable.*
prof·it·a·ble (**prŏf′** ĭ tə bəl) ◊ *adjective*

profound *adjective* **1.** Having or showing much learning, understanding, or knowledge: *Our teacher has a very profound mind.* **2.** Coming from the depths of one's being; deep and intense: *We felt profound sadness when we moved away.*
pro·found (prə **found′**) ◊ *adjective* **profounder, profoundest**

profuse *adjective* Very abundant; plentiful.
pro·fuse (prə **fyo͞os′**) ◊ *adjective*

profusion *noun* A great amount; plenty.
pro·fu·sion (prə **fyo͞o′** zhən) ◊ *noun*

program *noun* **1.** A list of information, as the order of events and the names of those taking part in a public performance or presentation. **2.** A performance, especially before an audience: *Which television programs do you like?* **3.** A plan or set of plans for future action: *Landing a spaceship on the moon was one goal of the space program.* **4.** The set of instructions that a computer must carry out in solving a problem, answering a question, storing information, or retrieving information.
◊ *verb* To provide a computer with a program.
pro·gram (**prō′** grăm′) ◊ *noun, plural* **programs** ◊ *verb* **programmed, programming**

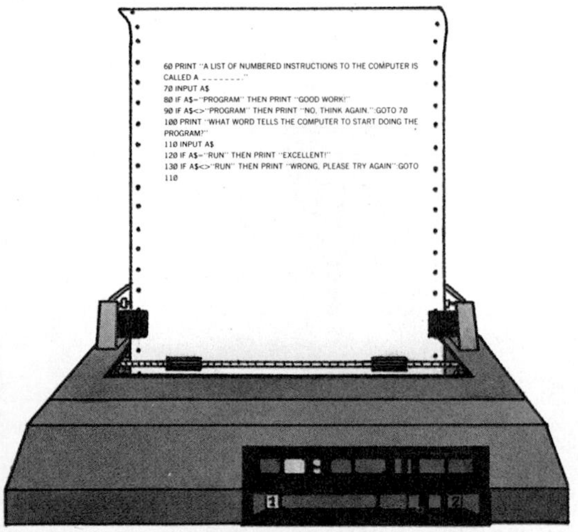

▲ **program**
Printout of a computer program

programmer *noun* A person who prepares programs for computers.
pro·gram·mer (**prō′** grăm′ər) ◊ *noun, plural* **programmers**

progress *noun* **1.** Movement toward a goal; advance: *Progress through the heavy traffic was slow.* **2.** Steady improvement.
◊ *verb* **1.** To move along; advance: *The construction of the swimming pool progresses slowly.* **2.** To make steady improvement.
prog·ress ◊ *noun* (**prŏg′** rĕs′) ◊ *verb* **pro·gress** (prə **grĕs′**) **progressed, progressing**

progressive *adjective* **1.** Happening or advancing in a steady way or step by step: *Weather caused the progressive erosion of the cliff.* **2.** Working for or favoring social progress or improvement; liberal.
pro·gres·sive (prə **grĕs′** ĭv) ◊ *adjective*

prohibit *verb* To forbid by law or authority: *Smoking is prohibited in most hospitals.*
pro·hib·it (prō **hĭb′** ĭt) ◊ *verb* **prohibited, prohibiting**

prohibition *noun* **1.** The act of prohibiting. **2.** The forbidding by law of the manufacture and sale of alcoholic beverages.
pro·hi·bi·tion (prō′ə **bĭsh′** ən) ◊ *noun, plural* **prohibitions**

project *noun* **1.** A plan for doing something; scheme: *The legislature approved the building project.* **2.** A special study or experiment carried on by students: *For our science project we built a model of an ant colony.* **3.** A group of houses or apartment buildings built as a unit.
◊ *verb* **1.** To extend forward or outward; stick out. **2.** To cause an image to appear on a surface: *We projected the color slides on the wall.*
proj·ect ◊ *noun* (**prŏj′** ĕkt′), *plural* **projects** ◊ *verb* **pro·ject** (prə **jĕkt′**) **projected, projecting**

projectile *noun* An object, such as a bullet or rocket, that is shot or thrown forward through the air or through space.
pro·jec·tile (prə **jĕk′** təl) ◊ *noun, plural* **projectiles**

projection *noun* **1.** The act or process of projecting an image on a surface. **2.** Something that sticks out.
pro·jec·tion (prə **jĕk′** shən) ◊ *noun, plural* **projections**

projector *noun* A machine that projects an image onto a screen.
pro·jec·tor (prə **jĕk′** tər) ◊ *noun, plural* **projectors**

prolific *adjective* **1.** Producing offspring or fruit in great numbers. **2.** Producing in abundance: *A prolific author is one who writes many books.*
pro·lif·ic (prə **lĭf′** ĭk) ◊ *adjective*

prolong *verb* To make longer; lengthen: *There's no need to prolong this argument.*
pro·long (prə **lông′**) ◊ *verb* **prolonged, prolonging**

prom *noun* A formal dance given by a school class.
prom (prŏm) ◊ *noun, plural* **proms**

promenade *noun* **1.** A walk that is taken for pleasure. **2.** A place for taking a walk.
prom·e·nade (prŏm′ə **nād′** *or* prŏm′ə **näd′**) ◊ *noun, plural* **promenades**

prominent *adjective* **1.** Sticking out: *I have a long, prominent nose.* **2.** Very easy to see: *The meat counter is in a prominent place in the supermarket.* **3.** Widely known: *Our neighbor is a prominent scientist.*
prom·i·nent (**prŏm′** ə nənt) ◊ *adjective*

promise *noun* **1.** A statement that one will do something; vow: *I kept my promise to write home.* **2.** A reason for expecting something, such as future success, excellence, or distinction: *The young dancer shows real promise.*
◊ *verb* **1.** To make a promise: *I promised to*

come home early. **2.** To give reasons for expecting: *The dark clouds promised rain.*
prom·ise (**prŏm′**ĭs) ◊ *noun, plural* **promises** ◊ *verb* **promised, promising**

promontory *noun* A high ridge of land or rock that juts out into a body of water.
prom·on·to·ry (**prŏm′**ən tôr′ē) ◊ *noun, plural* **promontories**

promote *verb* **1.** To help the progress, development, or growth of; further: *Regular exercise promotes physical fitness.* **2.** To raise to a higher rank, position, or class: *She was promoted to the sixth grade.*
pro·mote (prə **mōt′**) ◊ *verb* **promoted, promoting**

promotion *noun* **1.** The act of promoting; encouragement. **2.** Advancement in rank, position, or class: *If you want a promotion, you have to earn it.*
pro·mo·tion (prə **mō′**shən) ◊ *noun, plural* **promotions**

prompt *adjective* **1.** On time; punctual: *I try to be prompt for meals.* **2.** Done or given without delay: *I sent a prompt answer.* **3.** Ready and willing to act as needed: *My teacher was prompt to help me with the math problems.*
◊ *verb* **1.** To move to action: *The news of the birth of my new cousin prompted us to call.* **2.** To help by reminding of a forgotten word or supplying a cue: *I'll prompt you if you forget part of your speech.*
prompt (prŏmpt) ◊ *adjective* **prompter, promptest** ◊ *verb* **prompted, prompting**

prone *adjective* **1.** Lying or situated front or face downward. **2.** Having a tendency to act, feel, or be a certain way: *You are prone to overwork.*
prone (prōn) ◊ *adjective*

prong *noun* One of the pointed ends of an implement or a utensil, such as a fork.
prong (prông) ◊ *noun, plural* **prongs**

pronghorn *noun* An animal of western North America that has hoofs and short, forked horns and that runs swiftly.
prong·horn (**prông′**hôrn′) ◊ *noun, plural* **pronghorns**

▲ **pronghorn**

pronoun *noun* A word that can take the place of a noun. In the sentence *John takes the train when he travels,* the word *he* is a pronoun that takes the place of *John.*
pro·noun (**prō′**noun′) ◊ *noun, plural* **pronouns**

pronounce *verb* **1.** To produce the sounds of with the voice; articulate: *I don't know how to pronounce that word.* **2.** To declare in a formal or official way: *The doctor pronounced the patient cured.*
pro·nounce (prə **nouns′**) ◊ *verb* **pronounced, pronouncing**

pronounced *adjective* Strongly marked; distinct: *My dog has a pronounced limp.*
pro·nounced (prə **nounst′**) ◊ *adjective*

pronouncement *noun* A formal or official declaration.
pro·nounce·ment (prə **nouns′**mənt) ◊ *noun, plural* **pronouncements**

pronto *adverb* Right away; immediately: *We should leave pronto.*
pron·to (**prŏn′**tō) ◊ *adverb*

pronunciation *noun* The act or manner of pronouncing a word or words.
pro·nun·ci·a·tion (prə nŭn′sē **ā′**shən) ◊ *noun, plural* **pronunciations**

proof *noun* **1.** Evidence of truth or accuracy:

ă	pat	ĭ	pit	oi	**oi**l	th	ba**th**
ā	pay	ī	ride	o͝o	b**oo**k	*th*	ba**the**
â	care	î	fierce	o͞o	b**oo**t	ə	**a**go, it**e**m
ä	father	ŏ	pot	ou	**ou**t		penc**i**l
ĕ	pet	ō	go	ŭ	c**u**t		at**o**m
ē	be	ô	paw, for	û	f**u**r		circ**u**s

We have no proof that the money was stolen. **2.** The act or a way of testing the quality or nature of something: *I put my beliefs to the proof.* **3.** A test sheet of printed material to be checked for errors. **4.** A test print of a photograph.
proof (pro͞of) ◊ *noun, plural* **proofs**

–proof The suffix *-proof* forms adjectives and means "able to withstand" or "protected against." A *waterproof* coat protects against water coming through the coat.

VOCABULARY BUILDER • -proof

Many words that are formed with **-proof** are not entries in this dictionary. But you can figure out what these words mean by looking up the meanings of the root words and the suffix. For example:
heatproof = able to withstand heat
weatherproof = protected against the harmful effects of weather

proofread *verb* To read printed or written material and mark mistakes in it for correction.
proof·read (**pro͞of′**rĕd′) ◊ *verb* **proofread** (**pro͞of′**rĕd′), **proofreading**

prop *verb* To keep from falling by putting a support under or against: *I propped myself up on the bed with pillows.*
◊ *noun* Something used to give support.
prop (prŏp) ◊ *verb* **propped, propping**
◊ *noun, plural* **props**

propaganda *noun* **1.** The organized communication of information in order to help something such as a government or group. **2.** Such information that is spread in an organized way.
prop·a·gan·da (prŏp′ə **găn′**də) ◊ *noun*

propel *verb* To cause to move forward or onward: *A motor propelled the boat.* —See Synonyms at **push.**
pro·pel (prə **pĕl′**) ◊ *verb* **propelled, propelling**

propeller *noun* A device with blades that extend out from a hub. A propeller is driven by an engine and is used to propel an aircraft or a boat.
pro·pel·ler (prə **pĕl′**ər) ◊ *noun, plural* **propellers**

▲ **propeller**

proper *adjective* **1.** Right for a purpose or occasion; appropriate: *I don't have the proper tools for mending the roof.* **2.** Called for by or following social rules or conventions; correct: *I know the proper way to hold a fork.*
prop·er (**prŏp′**ər) ◊ *adjective*

properly *adverb* **1.** In a proper manner. **2.** In accordance with fact: *Properly speaking, shellfish are not fish.*
prop·er·ly (**prŏp′**ər lē) ◊ *adverb*

proper noun *noun* A noun that is the name of a specific person, place, or thing. The words *Lee Lawson, Grand Canyon,* and *Declaration of Independence* are proper nouns.
proper noun ◊ *noun, plural* **proper nouns**

property *noun* **1.** Something, as money, that is owned: *The farm is my parents' property.* **2.** An essential quality of a thing; characteristic: *Cold is a property of ice.* **3.** An object other than a costume or scenery that is used in a dramatic production, as a play.
prop·er·ty (**prŏp′**ər tē) ◊ *noun, plural* **properties**

prophecy *noun* **1.** Something that is said by a prophet. **2.** A declaration or warning of something to come; prediction.
proph·e·cy (**prŏf′**ĭ sē) ◊ *noun, plural* **prophecies**

prophesy *verb* **1.** To speak or utter as a prophet. **2.** To predict what will happen; foretell: *My friend prophesied that I would be successful.*

P

proph·e·sy (prŏf′ĭ sī′) ◊ *verb* **prophesied, prophesying**

prophet *noun* **1.** A person who is inspired by and speaks for God or a god. **2.** A person who predicts the future.
proph·et (prŏf′ĭt) ◊ *noun, plural* **prophets**
‖*These sound alike:* **prophet, profit**

proportion *noun* **1.** The size, amount, number, or extent of one thing as compared with that of another thing: *The proportion of students to teachers in our school is ten to one.* **2.** A pleasing, proper, or balanced relation between parts of a whole: *Your face is swollen out of all proportion because of your toothache.* **3. proportions** Relative size or extent: *The problem has reached great proportions.*
pro·por·tion (prə pôr′shən) ◊ *noun, plural* **proportions**

proposal *noun* **1.** The act of proposing; offer. **2.** A plan or scheme that is proposed for others to consider.
pro·pos·al (prə pō′ zəl) ◊ *noun, plural* **proposals**

propose *verb* **1.** To put forward for consideration; suggest: *I propose a trip to the museum.* **2.** To present or nominate a person for an office, position, or membership. **3.** To have as an intention; plan: *I propose to sell my bicycle.* **4.** To make an offer of marriage.
pro·pose (prə pōz′) ◊ *verb* **proposed, proposing**

proposition *noun* **1.** Something proposed; offer. **2.** A statement or idea to be discussed, studied, or proved.
prop·o·si·tion (prŏp′ə zĭsh′ən) ◊ *noun, plural* **propositions**

propriety *noun* **1.** The quality or condition of being proper. **2.** Proper manners or conduct.
pro·pri·e·ty (prə prī′ĭ tē) ◊ *noun, plural* **proprieties**

propulsion *noun* The act, process, or force of propelling.
pro·pul·sion (prə pŭl′shən) ◊ *noun*

prose *noun* Ordinary spoken or written language as opposed to verse or poetry. A short story is an example of prose.
prose (prōz) ◊ *noun*

prosecute *verb* To begin and carry on legal action against a person accused of an offense.
pros·e·cute (prŏs′ĭ kyōōt′) ◊ *verb* **prosecuted, prosecuting**

prosecution *noun* **1.** The act or process of prosecuting. **2.** The party, often a government, that brings a legal action against a person accused of an offense.
pros·e·cu·tion (prŏs′ĭ kyōō′shən) ◊ *noun, plural* **prosecutions**

prospect *noun* **1.** A scene; view: *A wide prospect of gardens stretched in front of the big house.* **2.** Something that is expected or looked forward to: *The prospect of a good dinner made us hurry home.* **3.** A possible customer or candidate.
◊ *verb* To explore, especially in search of mineral deposits, such as gold.
pros·pect (prŏs′pĕkt′) ◊ *noun, plural* **prospects** ◊ *verb* **prospected, prospecting**

prospective *adjective* **1.** Likely to happen: *The president spoke of prospective budget cuts.* **2.** Likely to be or become: *The prospective bride and groom received many gifts.*
pro·spec·tive (prə spĕk′tĭv) ◊ *adjective*

prospector *noun* A person who explores an area looking for valuable minerals.
pros·pec·tor (prŏs′pĕk′tər) ◊ *noun, plural* **prospectors**

▲ **prospector**

ă	pat	ĭ	pit	oi	oil	th	bath
ā	pay	ī	ride	ŏŏ	book	*th*	bathe
â	care	î	fierce	ōō	boot	ə	ago, item
ä	father	ŏ	pot	ou	out		pencil
ĕ	pet	ō	go	ŭ	cut		atom
ē	be	ô	paw, for	û	fur		circus

prosper *verb* To be fortunate or successful; thrive.
pros·per (prŏs′pər) ◊ *verb* **prospered, prospering**

prosperity *noun* The condition of being successful, especially in money matters.
pros·per·i·ty (prŏ **spĕr′**ĭ tē) ◊ *noun*

prosperous *adjective* Enjoying or marked by wealth or success: *My parents have built a prosperous business.*
pros·per·ous (**prŏs′**pər əs) ◊ *adjective*

protect *verb* To keep safe from harm, attack, or injury; guard: *We wore sunglasses to protect our eyes from the glare.*
pro·tect (prə **tĕkt′**) ◊ *verb* **protected, protecting**

protection *noun* **1.** The condition of being protected. **2.** The act of protecting. **3.** Someone or something that protects.
pro·tec·tion (prə **tĕk′**shən) ◊ *noun, plural* **protections**

protective *adjective* Intended to protect.
pro·tec·tive (prə **tĕk′**tĭv) ◊ *adjective*

protector *noun* Someone or something that protects.
pro·tec·tor (prə **tĕk′**tər) ◊ *noun, plural* **protectors**

protein *noun* A substance that contains nitrogen, occurs in all living plant and animal tissue, and is necessary to life. Meat, milk, cheese, eggs, and fish are sources of protein.
pro·tein (**prō′**tēn′) ◊ *noun, plural* **proteins**

protest *noun* A complaint or objection: *The residents sent a protest to the governor.*
◊ *verb* To express strong complaints about or objections to: *The customers protested the high prices.*
pro·test ◊ *noun* (**prō′**tĕst′), *plural* **protests** ◊ *verb* (prə **tĕst′**) **protested, protesting**

Protestant *noun* A Christian belonging to a church that broke away from the Roman Catholic Church.
◊ *adjective* Of or relating to Protestants or their religions.
Prot·es·tant (**prŏt′**ĭ stənt) ◊ *noun, plural* **Protestants** ◊ *adjective*

proton *noun* A tiny particle that is found in the nucleus of an atom and has a positive electrical charge.
pro·ton (**prō′**tŏn′) ◊ *noun, plural* **protons**

protoplasm *noun* A jellylike substance that forms the living matter in all plant and animal cells.
pro·to·plasm (**prō′**tə plăz′əm) ◊ *noun*

protract *verb* To draw out in time; prolong.
pro·tract (prō **trăkt′**) ◊ *verb* **protracted, protracting**

protrude *verb* To stick out from a surface: *We saw big rocks that protruded from the snow.*
pro·trude (prō **trōōd′**) ◊ *verb* **protruded, protruding**

proud *adjective* **1.** Feeling pleased and satisfied over something one owns, makes, does, or is a part of: *They were proud to be named to the Olympic team.* **2.** Full of self-respect and independence: *The new pupil was too proud to ask for help.* **3.** Thinking too highly of oneself; haughty.
proud (proud) ◊ *adjective* **prouder, proudest**

prove *verb* **1.** To show to be true by or as if by producing evidence or using convincing arguments: *The police could not prove that the person was guilty.* **2.** To turn out; test: *My estimate of the price proved low.*
prove (prōōv) ◊ *verb* **proved, proved** *or* **proven, proving**

SYNONYMS
prove, demonstrate, establish
I will try to *prove* that I didn't do it. This experiment *demonstrates* that air contains oxygen. It has been *established* that the earth is round.

proven *verb* A past participle of **prove.**
prov·en (**prōō′**vən) ◊ *verb*

proverb *noun* A short, common saying that tells a truth. "A rolling stone gathers no moss" is a proverb.
prov·erb (**prŏv′**ûrb′) ◊ *noun, plural* **proverbs**

proverbial *adjective* **1.** Of or referred to in a proverb or other well-known saying: *I slept like the proverbial log.* **2.** Widely known and spoken of; famous.
pro·ver·bi·al (prə **vûr′**bē əl) ◊ *adjective*

provide *verb* **1.** To give something needed or useful; supply: *The teacher provided paper and pencils for the test.* **2.** To take necessary measures in advance; make provisions: *We provided against emergencies by taking extra*

P

money and clothing. **3.** To set down as a rule or condition: *The constitution provides that citizens have the right to vote.*
pro·vide (prə vīd′) ◊ *verb* **provided, providing**

provided *conjunction* On the condition; if: *You may go, provided your work is done.*
pro·vid·ed (prə vī′dĭd) ◊ *conjunction*

province *noun* **1.** A political division that is like a state of the United States: *Ontario is a leading industrial province of Canada.* **2.** An area of knowledge, authority, or responsibility; scope: *Prescribing medicine is within the province of a doctor.*
prov·ince (prŏv′ĭns) ◊ *noun, plural* **provinces**

provincial *adjective* Of, relating to, or from a province.
pro·vin·cial (prə vĭn′shəl) ◊ *adjective*

provision *noun* **1.** The act of providing. **2.** Something done or put in place for future need: *We made provision for escape in case of fire.* **3. provisions** A supply of stored food. **4.** A part of an agreement, law, or document; condition: *A provision of the treaty forbids nuclear weapons.*
◊ *verb* To supply with provisions.
pro·vi·sion (prə vĭzh′ən) ◊ *noun, plural* **provisions** ◊ *verb* **provisioned, provisioning**

provisional *adjective* Serving for the time being; temporary: *This is a provisional government until the elections.*
pro·vi·sion·al (prə vĭzh′ən əl) ◊ *adjective*

provocation *noun* **1.** The act of provoking. **2.** An action that provokes.
prov·o·ca·tion (prŏv′ə kā′shən) ◊ *noun, plural* **provocations**

provoke *verb* **1.** To bring on; cause: *The comedian provoked steady laughter.* **2.** To make angry; annoy: *Their rudeness provoked me.*
pro·voke (prə vōk′) ◊ *verb* **provoked, provoking**

prow *noun* The pointed front of a ship; bow.
prow (prou) ◊ *noun, plural* **prows**

ă	pat	ĭ	pit	oi	oil	th	bath
ā	pay	ī	ride	o͝o	book	*th*	bathe
â	care	î	fierce	o͞o	boot	ə	ago, item
ä	father	ŏ	pot	ou	out		pencil
ĕ	pet	ō	go	ŭ	cut		atom
ē	be	ô	paw, for	û	fur		circus

▲ **prow**

prowl *verb* To move about secretly and quietly as if looking for prey: *City cats prowl through alleys at night.*
prowl (proul) ◊ *verb* **prowled, prowling**

prudence *noun* The quality, condition, or fact of being prudent.
pru·dence (pro͞od′ns) ◊ *noun*

prudent *adjective* Having or showing caution and good judgment; sensible: *A prudent person never swims alone.* —See Synonyms at **careful.**
pru·dent (pro͞od′nt) ◊ *adjective*

prune¹ *noun* A dried plum.
prune¹ (pro͞on) ◊ *noun, plural* **prunes**

prune² *verb* **1.** To cut outer or unwanted parts from a bush or tree; trim. **2.** To remove unwanted or unneeded parts from: *I pruned the essay down to two pages.*
prune² (pro͞on) ◊ *verb* **pruned, pruning**

***HISTORY* • prune¹, prune²**

Prune¹ goes back to a French word that came from a Latin word meaning "plum." **Prune²** comes from a Latin word that meant "to cut around."

pry¹ *verb* **1.** To raise, move, or force open with or as if with a lever: *I pried the lid off the box.* **2.** To get with difficulty: *We tried to pry the answer to the riddle out of them.*
pry¹ (prī) ◊ *verb* **pried, prying**

pry² *verb* To look curiously, often in a nosy way: *Stop prying into my business.*
pry² (prī) ◊ *verb* **pried, prying**

***HISTORY* • pry¹, pry²**

Pry¹ was shortened from *prize,* which means "to force open" and is a different word from the **prize** that means "something won." **Pry²** first appeared in written English about 700 years ago. Its history before that is not known for certain.

P.S. *or* **PS** Abbreviations for *postscript* or *Public School.*

psalm *noun* A sacred song or poem.
psalm (säm) ◊ *noun, plural* **psalms**

psychiatrist *noun* A medical doctor who treats mental or emotional disorders.
psy·chi·a·trist (sĭ **kī′**ə trĭst *or* sī **kī′**ə trĭst) ◊ *noun, plural* **psychiatrists**

psychologist *noun* A person who specializes in the mind and human behavior.
psy·chol·o·gist (sī **kŏl′**ə jĭst) ◊ *noun, plural* **psychologists**

pt. The abbreviation for *pint* or *pints.*

public *adjective* **1.** Of or relating to the people or the community: *The cracked sidewalk was a threat to public safety.* **2.** Supported by, used by, or open to all people; not private: *I used a public telephone to make the call.* **3.** Working for a government or community: *Senators and governors are public servants.* **4.** Known to many people: *The newspaper made the facts of the matter public.*
◊ *noun* All of the people: *The capitol is open to the public.*
◊ *idiom* **in public** In the presence of other people; not private.
pub·lic (**pŭb′**lĭk) ◊ *adjective* ◊ *noun*

publication *noun* **1.** The act or process of publishing. **2.** Something, such as a magazine, that is published.
pub·li·ca·tion (pŭb′lĭ **kā′**shən) ◊ *noun, plural* **publications**

publicity *noun* Information that is given out to let the public know about something or to get its approval: *The publicity for the new movie included television interviews with the star.*
pub·lic·i·ty (pŭ **blĭs′**ĭ tē) ◊ *noun*

public school *noun* A school in a community that students can attend free and that is paid for by taxes.
public school ◊ *noun, plural* **public schools**

publish *verb* To print and offer for public sale or distribution: *The newspaper published my letter.*
pub·lish (**pŭb′**lĭsh) ◊ *verb* **published, publishing**

publisher *noun* A person or company that publishes printed matter, such as books.
pub·lish·er (**pŭb′**lĭ shər) ◊ *noun, plural* **publishers**

puck *noun* A hard rubber disk that is used in ice hockey.
puck (pŭk) ◊ *noun, plural* **pucks**

pucker *verb* To gather together so that folds or wrinkles are formed.
◊ *noun* A small fold or wrinkle.
puck·er (**pŭk′**ər) ◊ *verb* **puckered, puckering** ◊ *noun, plural* **puckers**

pudding *noun* A sweet, smooth dessert that is like custard.
pud·ding (**po͝od′**ĭng) ◊ *noun, plural* **puddings**

puddle *noun* A small pool of liquid, especially of dirty or muddy water.
pud·dle (**pŭd′**l) ◊ *noun, plural* **puddles**

pueblo *noun* A village that consists of stone and adobe buildings built next to and on top of each other. Pueblos were built by Native Americans in the southwestern United States.
pueb·lo (**pwĕb′**lō) ◊ *noun, plural* **pueblos**

▲ **pueblo**

P

Puerto Rican *noun* A person who was born in or lives in Puerto Rico.
◊ *adjective* Of or relating to Puerto Rico or the Puerto Ricans.
Puer·to Ri·can (pwĕr′tə **rē′**kən) ◊ *noun, plural* **Puerto Ricans** ◊ *adjective*

puff *noun* **1.** A short quick gust of air, smoke, or steam: *Puffs of smoke rose from the chimney.* **2.** A mass that looks light and fluffy: *A few puffs of clouds floated in the sky.*
◊ *verb* **1.** To blow in short quick gusts: *A light breeze puffed across the meadow.* **2.** To come or send out in puffs: *Smoke puffed from the steam engine.* **3.** To breathe heavily; pant: *I began to puff from the hard climb.* **4.** To grow or cause to grow fuller and rounder; swell up: *The painful bruise puffed up.*
puff (pŭf) ◊ *noun, plural* **puffs** ◊ *verb* **puffed, puffing**

puffy *adjective* **1.** Puffed out; swollen. **2.** Full and rounded: *The dress had puffy sleeves.*
puff·y (**pŭf′**ē) ◊ *adjective* **puffier, puffiest**

pug *noun* A small dog with short hair, a short, flat nose, a wrinkled face, and a curled tail.
pug (pŭg) ◊ *noun, plural* **pugs**

▲ **pug**

pull *verb* **1.** To apply force to in order to draw toward the force; tug at: *A team of horses pulled the wagon.* **2.** To draw out or forth from a fixed position: *I pulled up all the weeds. The dentist pulled my tooth.* **3.** To move: *The car pulled off the road.* **4.** To draw apart; tear or break: *The puppy pulled the towel into bits.*
◊ *noun* **1.** The act of pulling; tug: *It took two pulls to open the door.* **2.** A force that draws things toward it; attraction: *The pull of the magnet made the can opener stick to the refrigerator door.* **3.** The steady effort used in or as if in pulling: *It was a long pull across the prairies to the West.*
pull (po͝ol) ◊ *verb* **pulled, pulling** ◊ *noun, plural* **pulls**

SYNONYMS
pull, drag, haul, tow
That car is *pulling* a trailer. I *dragged* the small tree over the snow. Dogs are *hauling* the sled. The tugboat *towed* the barge into the harbor. **Antonym:** *push*

pullet *noun* A young hen.
pul·let (**po͝ol′**ĭt) ◊ *noun, plural* **pullets**

pulley *noun* A freely turning wheel that has a groove around its edge through which a rope, chain, or belt moves. A pulley can be used to raise and lower heavy weights.
pul·ley (**po͝ol′**ē) ◊ *noun, plural* **pulleys**

▲ **pulley**

pulp *noun* **1.** The soft, juicy or fleshy part of fruit or vegetables. **2.** A wet mixture of ground-up wood or rags used to make paper. **3.** The soft inner part of a tooth.
pulp (pŭlp) ◊ *noun, plural* **pulps**

pulpit *noun* A raised platform in a church, from which a minister speaks to the congregation.
pul·pit (**po͝ol′**pĭt) ◊ *noun, plural* **pulpits**

pulse *noun* **1.** The rhythmic movement of the arteries as blood is pushed through them

ă	pat	ĭ	pit	oi	oil	th	bath
ā	pay	ī	ride	o͝o	book	*th*	bathe
â	care	î	fierce	o͞o	boot	ə	ago, item
ä	father	ŏ	pot	ou	out		pencil
ĕ	pet	ō	go	ŭ	cut		atom
ē	be	ô	paw, for	û	fur		circus

by the beating of the heart. **2.** A regular or rhythmic beat: *We heard the pulse of the ship's engine across the harbor.*
pulse (pŭls) ◊ *noun, plural* **pulses**

pulverize *verb* To pound, crush, or grind into a powder or dust.
pul·ver·ize (**pŭl'** və rīz') ◊ *verb* **pulverized, pulverizing**

puma *noun* A mountain lion.
pu·ma (**pyōō'** mə *or* **pōō'** mə) ◊ *noun, plural* **pumas**

pummel *verb* To hit again and again.
pum·mel (**pŭm'** əl) ◊ *verb* **pummeled, pummeling**

pump *noun* A device used to move a liquid or gas from one place or container to another: *I filled the balloons with a small air pump.*
◊ *verb* **1.** To raise or move a liquid or gas with a pump. **2.** To fill by means of a pump: *I pumped up the flat tire.* **3.** To empty of liquid or gas by means of a pump: *We had to pump out our flooded cellar.*
pump (pŭmp) ◊ *noun, plural* **pumps** ◊ *verb* **pumped, pumping**

pumpkin *noun* A large, round fruit with a thick, orange rind.
pump·kin (**pŭmp'** kĭn) ◊ *noun, plural* **pumpkins**

▲ **pumpkin**

pun *noun* A form of joking in which a person uses different words that sound alike or the same word in two senses. *The street is cross because you crossed it* is an example of a sentence containing a pun.
◊ *verb* To make a pun.
pun (pŭn) ◊ *noun, plural* **puns** ◊ *verb* **punned, punning**

punch[1] *noun* A tool for piercing or stamping.
◊ *verb* To pierce or stamp with a punch: *The conductor punched our train tickets.*
punch[1] (pŭnch) ◊ *noun, plural* **punches** ◊ *verb* **punched, punching**

punch[2] *verb* **1.** To hit with or as if with the fist. **2.** To move cattle; herd. **3.** To press in order to operate: *The workers punch the time clock when they get to the factory.*
◊ *noun* A blow with or as if with the fist.
punch[2] (pŭnch) ◊ *verb* **punched, punching** ◊ *noun, plural* **punches**

punch[3] *noun* A sweet drink made by mixing fruit juices, often with ginger ale and spices.
punch[3] (pŭnch) ◊ *noun, plural* **punches**

HISTORY **• punch[1], punch[2], punch[3]**

Punch[1] is from an old French word for a type of sharp tool. **Punch[2]** is from an old French word meaning "to prick, stamp." **Punch[3]** goes back to a word used in ancient India to mean "five." Perhaps the earliest **punch[3]** was made from five ingredients.

punctual *adjective* Acting or arriving on time; prompt.
punc·tu·al (**pŭngk'** chōō əl) ◊ *adjective*

punctuate *verb* To mark written or printed material with punctuation.
punc·tu·ate (**pŭngk'** chōō āt') ◊ *verb* **punctuated, punctuating**

punctuation *noun* Marks, such as periods, commas, and semicolons, that are used to make the meaning of written or printed material clear.
punc·tu·a·tion (pŭngk'chōō **ā'** shən) ◊ *noun*

punctuation mark *noun* One of the marks, as a comma or period, used in punctuating.
punctuation mark ◊ *noun, plural* **punctuation marks**

puncture *verb* To pierce with something sharp: *A nail punctured the bicycle tire.*
◊ *noun* A hole or wound made by puncturing.
punc·ture (**pŭngk'** chər) ◊ *verb* **punctured, puncturing** ◊ *noun, plural* **punctures**

pundit *noun* A learned person, especially an expert or authority.
pun·dit (**pŭn'** dĭt) ◊ *noun, plural* **pundits**

pungent *adjective* Biting or sharp to the

P

taste or smell: *The fire in the hearth burned with a pungent smoke.*
pun·gent (pŭn′jənt) ◊ *adjective*

punish *verb* To cause to suffer for a crime, fault, or misbehavior.
pun·ish (pŭn′ĭsh) ◊ *verb* **punished, punishing**

> ***SYNONYMS***
>
> ***punish, discipline, penalize***
>
> To *punish* me my parents took away my allowance. You will be *disciplined* if you don't learn to control your temper. Don't get *penalized* for coming to school late.

punishment *noun* **1.** A penalty for a crime or wrongdoing: *My punishment for littering was several hours of picking up trash.* **2.** The act of punishing.
pun·ish·ment (pŭn′ĭsh mənt) ◊ *noun, plural* **punishments**

punt *noun* A football play in which the ball is dropped and kicked before it touches the ground.
punt (pŭnt) ◊ *noun, plural* **punts**

puny *adjective* Being very small, weak, or unimportant.
pu·ny (pyo͞o′nē) ◊ *adjective* **punier, puniest**

pup *noun* **1.** A puppy. **2.** The young of such animals as the coyotes or seals.
pup (pŭp) ◊ *noun, plural* **pups**

pupa *noun* An insect, such as a moth, during a stage of its life cycle when it is changing from a larva into an adult. A pupa is protected by a covering such as a cocoon.
pu·pa (pyo͞o′pə) ◊ *noun, plural* **pupas**

pupil¹ *noun* A young person who is being taught in a school or by a private teacher.
pu·pil¹ (pyo͞o′pəl) ◊ *noun, plural* **pupils**

pupil² *noun* The opening in the center of the iris through which light enters the eye.
pu·pil² (pyo͞o′pəl) ◊ *noun, plural* **pupils**

ă	pat	ĭ	pit	oi	**oil**	th	ba**th**
ā	pay	ī	ride	o͝o	**book**	*th*	ba**the**
â	care	î	fierce	o͞o	**boot**	ə	ago, item
ä	father	ŏ	pot	ou	**out**		pencil
ĕ	pet	ō	go	ŭ	cut		atom
ē	be	ô	paw, for	û	fur		circus

> ***HISTORY* • pupil¹, pupil²**
>
> **Pupil¹** goes back to two Latin words, one for a boy orphan and one for a girl orphan. In English **pupil¹** came to mean "a student." **Pupil²** goes back to the Latin word for a girl orphan, which also meant the circular opening in the center of the eye. This meaning came from the fact that one can see a tiny image of a person in the **pupil** of the eye.

puppet *noun* A small figure that looks like a person or animal. A puppet is worked by hand or by strings or wires.
pup·pet (pŭp′ĭt) ◊ *noun, plural* **puppets**

▲ **puppet**

puppy *noun* A young dog.
pup·py (pŭp′ē) ◊ *noun, plural* **puppies**

purchase *verb* To get something by paying money. —See Synonyms at **buy.**
◊ *noun* **1.** Something bought: *The car was a wise purchase.* **2.** The act of purchasing: *We saved our money for the purchase of new sports equipment.*
pur·chase (pûr′chĭs) ◊ *verb* **purchased, purchasing** ◊ *noun, plural* **purchases**

pure *adjective* **1.** Not mixed with anything else: *The cup was made of pure silver.* **2.** Complete; utter: *A look of pure delight lit up the child's face.* **3.** Without sin; innocent.
pure (pyo͝or) ◊ *adjective* **purer, purest**

purebred *adjective* Coming from many generations of ancestors of the same breed or kind: *We raise purebred horses.*
pure·bred (pyŏŏr′ brĕd′) ◊ *adjective*

purify *verb* To make pure; cleanse: *This filter purifies the water that we drink.*
pu·ri·fy (pyŏŏr′ ə fī′) ◊ *verb* **purified, purifying**

Puritan *noun* In the sixteenth and seventeenth centuries, a person in England or America who wanted simple forms of worship.
Pu·ri·tan (pyŏŏr′ ĭ tn) ◊ *noun, plural* **Puritans**

purity *noun* The condition of being pure.
pu·ri·ty (pyŏŏr′ ĭ tē) ◊ *noun*

purple *noun* A color between blue and red.
◊ *adjective* Of the color purple.
pur·ple (pûr′ pəl) ◊ *noun, plural* **purples** ◊ *adjective*

purpose *noun* An intended or desired result; aim: *My purpose in going into town was to buy a newspaper.*
◊ *idiom* **on purpose** Not accidentally; deliberately: *You bumped into me on purpose.*
pur·pose (pûr′ pəs) ◊ *noun, plural* **purposes**

purposeful *adjective* Having a purpose.
pur·pose·ful (pûr′ pəs fəl) ◊ *adjective*

purposely *adverb* On purpose.
pur·pose·ly (pûr′ pə slē) ◊ *adverb*

purr *noun* The low, soft, buzzing sound made by a contented cat.
◊ *verb* To make a purr.
purr (pûr) ◊ *noun, plural* **purrs** ◊ *verb* **purred, purring**

purse *noun* **1.** A bag or pouch used to carry money. **2.** A handbag or pocketbook. **3.** A sum of money given as a gift or prize.
◊ *verb* To draw together; pucker: *I pursed my lips as I thought it over.*
purse (pûrs) ◊ *noun, plural* **purses** ◊ *verb* **pursed, pursing**

pursue *verb* **1.** To chase in order to catch: *The dog pursued the cat across the lawn.* **2.** To engage in or keep at an activity: *She's pursuing her studies at a medical school.* **3.** To keep trying to achieve: *Should I pursue my goal to become a lawyer?* **4.** To carry on; follow: *He is pursuing his own plan.*
pur·sue (pər sōō′) ◊ *verb* **pursued, pursuing**

pursuit *noun* **1.** The act of pursuing: *The cat ran off in pursuit of the mouse.* **2.** An activity that a person engages in; occupation: *Their weekends were filled with pursuits such as gardening.*
pur·suit (pər sōōt′) ◊ *noun, plural* **pursuits**

pus *noun* A thick, yellowish-white liquid that forms in an infected sore or wound.
pus (pŭs) ◊ *noun*

push *verb* **1.** To press against so as to move away: *I pushed the rock, but it wouldn't budge.* **2.** To move against resistance; thrust: *We pushed through the crowd.* **3.** To try hard to influence; put pressure on: *My family is pushing me to get a summer job.* **4.** To make a strong effort to do something.
◊ *noun* **1.** An act of pushing; shove: *We gave the sled a push.* **2.** A strong effort: *With a big push, we finished the project on time.*
push (pŏŏsh) ◊ *verb* **pushed, pushing** ◊ *noun, plural* **pushes**

SYNONYMS

push, shove, thrust

I *pushed* the chair across the floor.
Someone *shoved* me out of the way fast.
I *thrust* the spade into the ground.
Antonym: *pull*

pushup *noun* An exercise performed by resting on the hands and toes with the body straight and lowering and raising the body by bending the arms.
push·up (pŏŏsh′ ŭp′) ◊ *noun, plural* **pushups**

pussy willow *noun* A shrub that has small, gray, furry flower clusters in early spring.
puss·y willow (pŏŏs′ ē) ◊ *noun, plural* **pussy willows**

▲ **pussy willow**

P

put *verb* **1.** To cause to be in a particular position or condition: *Put the bowl on the table. Put the papers in order.* **2.** To cause to undergo something: *You put me to a lot of trouble.* **3.** To think of as having: *They put a high value on honesty.* **4.** To express in words; state: *To put it bluntly, I hate cartoons.* **5.** To apply: *We must put our minds to it.* **6.** To proceed; go: *The ship put into the harbor.*
◊ *idioms* **put off** To delay doing; postpone: *This is an urgent matter, so don't put it off.* **put on 1.** To dress oneself in: *If you're cold, put on a sweater.* **2.** To present on a stage: *Our class is putting on a play.* **3.** To pretend to have; assume: *They put on a show of friendship.* **put out 1.** To stop from burning or glowing; extinguish: *Put out the light and go to sleep.* **2.** To annoy; irritate: *I was put out by your phone call so late at night.* **put up 1.** To build; construct: *We're putting up a new school.* **2.** To provide; contribute: *Their parents put up the money for a new business.* **3.** To provide with or receive a place to sleep: *Can you put us up for the night?* **4.** To prepare or preserve for later use: *We put up cans of tomatoes for the winter.* **put up with** To endure; tolerate: *We can't put up with two noisy dogs in the house.*
put (po͝ot) ◊ *verb* **put, putting**

putter *verb* To work or move about without really accomplishing much: *We puttered around in the garden all day.*
put·ter (pŭt′ər) ◊ *verb* **puttered, puttering**

putty *noun* A soft cement that is used to hold panes of glass in place.
put·ty (pŭt′ē) ◊ *noun*

ă	pat	ĭ	pit	oi	**oil**	th	**bath**
ā	pay	ī	ride	o͝o	**book**	*th*	**bathe**
â	care	î	fierce	o͞o	**boot**	ə	ago, item
ä	father	ŏ	pot	ou	**out**		pencil
ĕ	pet	ō	go	ŭ	cut		atom
ē	be	ô	paw, for	û	fur		circus

puzzle *noun* **1.** Something that is hard to understand; mystery: *It's a puzzle to me how you can finish your work so fast.* **2.** A problem, toy, or game that makes one think and tests one's skill: *It took us all day to fit together the pieces of the jigsaw puzzle.*
◊ *verb* **1.** To cause to be uncertain; perplex: *Where insects go in winter puzzles me.* **2.** To think hard in trying to understand: *I puzzled over the strange words engraved on the monument.*
puz·zle (pŭz′əl) ◊ *noun, plural* **puzzles**
◊ *verb* **puzzled, puzzling**

pyramid *noun* **1.** A solid object with a flat base and three or more sides shaped like triangles that meet in a point at the top. **2.** A huge stone structure in the shape of a pyramid built especially in ancient Egypt as a tomb.
pyr·a·mid (pĭr′ə mĭd) ◊ *noun, plural* **pyramids**

▲ **pyramid**

python *noun* A very large snake of Africa, Asia, and Australia that coils around and crushes its prey.
py·thon (pī′thŏn′) ◊ *noun, plural* **pythons**

Quail

Qq

Q is the seventeenth letter of the English alphabet. Did you know that it has a long history?

Over 3,500 years ago, people in the Middle East were using symbols that became the letters of our alphabet. This ancient Middle Eastern symbol is a form of the letter that became our letter *Q*.

The ancient Greeks borrowed their alphabet from people in the Middle East. Here is a form of the Greek letter that became our letter *Q*.

The ancient Romans borrowed their alphabet from a people who had taken their own letter symbols from the Greeks. Here is a form of the Roman letter *Q* that was used for carving letters into stone. These letters became the model for our printed capital letters.

As people wrote quickly, especially with pens, the capital letters began to take the shapes of small letters. Here is a small-letter *q* that was developed about 1,200 years ago.

Qq Qq	Qq	Qq	Qq
Handwriting	Sans Serif Type	Serif Type	Computer Printing

q *or* **Q** *noun* The seventeenth letter of the English alphabet.
q *or* **Q** (kyōō) ◊ *noun, plural* **q's** *or* **Q's**

qt. The abbreviation for *quart* or *quarts.*

quack *noun* The sound made by a duck.
◊ *verb* To make a quack.
quack (kwăk) ◊ *noun, plural* **quacks** ◊ *verb* **quacked, quacking**

quadruped *noun* An animal, such as a horse, with four feet.
quad·ru·ped (**kwŏd′**rōō pĕd′) ◊ *noun, plural* **quadrupeds**

quadruplet *noun* One of four children born at a single birth.
quad·ru·plet (kwŏ **drŭp′**lĭt *or* kwŏ **drōō′**plĭt) ◊ *noun, plural* **quadruplets**

quahog *noun* A clam of the Atlantic coast of North America that has a hard, rounded shell. Quahogs are much used as food and their shells were used by Native Americans to make wampum.
qua·hog (**kwô′**hôg′ *or* **kō′**hôg′) *noun, plural* **quahogs**

> **LANGUAGE DETECTIVE**
>
> ***quahog***
>
> When you see the words *quahog* and *geoduck,* you might think of pigs and ducks and not of clams. But a kind of big clam found along the coast of New England is called a *quahog,* and another kind of big clam on the Pacific coast is called a *geoduck.* Both words are not what they seem because we took them into English from Native American languages. In those languages the parts of the words that look like *hog* and *duck* mean other things. The *hog* part of *quahog* means "shell," and the *duck* part of *geoduck* is related to a word meaning "something attached to something else."

quail *noun* A small, rather plump bird that has a short tail and brownish feathers.
quail (kwāl) ◊ *noun, plural* **quail** *or* **quails**

quaint *adjective* Old-fashioned, especially in a pleasing way: *We drove through a quaint old country village.*
quaint (kwānt) ◊ *adjective* **quainter, quaintest**

quake *verb* **1.** To shake, as from shock or lack of balance: *The ground quaked from the stampede of cattle.* **2.** To shiver or tremble, as from fear or cold: *I was so frightened that my legs quaked.* —See Synonyms at **shake.**
◊ *noun* **1.** An example of shaking or quivering. **2.** An earthquake.
quake (kwāk) ◊ *verb* **quaked, quaking**
◊ *noun, plural* **quakes**

qualification *noun* **1.** The act of qualifying or the condition of being qualified. **2.** A skill, accomplishment, or quality that makes a person fit for a particular job or task: *What are the qualifications for an airline pilot?* **3.** Something that limits or restricts: *The group accepted my plan without qualifications of any kind.*
qual·i·fi·ca·tion (kwŏl′ə fĭ **kā′**shən) ◊ *noun, plural* **qualifications**

qualify *verb* **1.** To make, be, or become fit for a particular position, purpose, or task: *Your grades qualify you for the honor society.* **2.** To limit the meaning of; modify: *Adjectives qualify nouns and adverbs qualify verbs.*
qual·i·fy (**kwŏl′**ə fī′) ◊ *verb* **qualified, qualifying**

quality *noun* **1.** A property or feature that makes someone or something what it is: *I used vinegar in the salad dressing because of its sour quality.* **2.** Degree or grade of merit: *Don't buy at that store; they sell fruits and vegetables of poor quality.*
qual·i·ty (**kwŏl′**ĭ tē) ◊ *noun, plural* **qualities**

quantity *noun* **1.** An amount or number of a thing or things: *Fresh fruits and vegetables contain vitamins in various quantities.* **2.** A large amount or number: *Restaurants buy bread in quantity.*
quan·ti·ty (**kwŏn′**tĭ tē) ◊ *noun, plural* **quantities**

ă	pat	ĭ	pit	oi	**oil**	th	ba**th**
ā	pay	ī	ride	o͝o	**book**	*th*	ba**th**e
â	care	î	fierce	o͞o	**boot**	ə	ago, item
ä	father	ŏ	pot	ou	**out**		pencil
ĕ	pet	ō	go	ŭ	cut		atom
ē	be	ô	paw, for	û	fur		circus

quarantine *noun* The prevention or tight control of the movement of people, animals, plants, or goods out of a place or region to keep pests or disease from spreading.
◊ *verb* To place or keep in quarantine.
quar·an·tine (**kwôr′**ən tēn′) ◊ *noun, plural* **quarantines** ◊ *verb* **quarantined, quarantining**

***HISTORY* • quarantine**

Quarantine comes from the Italian word meaning "forty." Traditionally a **quarantine** lasted forty days.

quarrel *noun* **1.** An angry argument; dispute: *The teacher tried to stop the students' quarrel.* —See Synonyms at **fight. 2.** A reason for argument or dispute: *I have no quarrel with what you say.*
◊ *verb* **1.** To engage in a quarrel: *They quarreled over the use of the tennis court.* **2.** To find fault: *You can't quarrel with that decision.*
quar·rel (**kwôr′**əl) ◊ *noun, plural* **quarrels**
◊ *verb* **quarreled, quarreling**

quarry *noun* An open pit from which stone, especially for building, is gotten by digging, cutting, or blasting.
quar·ry (**kwôr′**ē) ◊ *noun, plural* **quarries**

▲ **quarry**

quart *noun* A unit of capacity equal to two pints.
quart (kwôrt) ◊ *noun, plural* **quarts**

quarter *noun* **1.** Any of four equal parts into which something can be divided: *I cut the apple into quarters.* **2.** One fourth of the time it takes for the moon to revolve around the earth. **3.** A coin used in the United States or Canada that is worth 25 cents. **4.** One of the four time periods that make up a game, as in football. **5.** A district or section of a city. **6. quarters** A place in which to sleep or live: *Our summer quarters are at the seashore.*
◊ *verb* To cut or divide into four equal parts: *I'll quarter the apple for you and your friends.*
quar·ter (**kwôr′** tər) ◊ *noun, plural* **quarters** ◊ *verb* **quartered, quartering**

quarterback *noun* A football player who directs the offense and usually passes the ball.
quar·ter·back (**kwôr′** tər băk′) ◊ *noun, plural* **quarterbacks**

quarterly *adjective* Happening or coming every three months: *I receive quarterly interest on my bank account.*
◊ *adverb* Every three months: *Some employees were paid quarterly.*
quar·ter·ly (**kwôr′** tər lē) ◊ *adjective* ◊ *adverb*

quartet *noun* A group of four people or things.
quar·tet (kwôr **tĕt′**) ◊ *noun, plural* **quartets**

quartz *noun* A clear, hard mineral found in rocks. Quartz is often colorless and transparent but is sometimes brightly colored.
quartz (kwôrts) ◊ *noun*

quaver *verb* To shake; tremble.
qua·ver (**kwā′** vər) ◊ *verb* **quavered, quavering**

quay *noun* A stone wharf or reinforced landing place where ships are loaded or unloaded.
quay (kē) ◊ *noun, plural* **quays**
‖*These sound alike:* **quay, key**

Que. The abbreviation for *Quebec,* Canada.

queasy *adjective* **1.** Sick to one's stomach; nauseated. **2.** Easily nauseated.
quea·sy (**kwē′** zē) ◊ *adjective* **queasier, queasiest**

queen *noun* **1.** A woman who is the ruler of a country. **2.** The wife or widow of a king. **3.** A woman or thing that is outstanding, as in importance: *The moon is queen of the sky.* **4.** A chess piece. **5.** A large, specially developed female that lays eggs in a colony of bees, ants, or termites.
queen (kwēn) ◊ *noun, plural* **queens**

▲ **queen**

queer *adjective* Different in a strange way from what is usual or expected; odd.
queer (kwîr) ◊ *adjective* **queerer, queerest**

quench *verb* To put out a fire; bring to an end by extinguishing: *I quenched my thirst with a glass of cold water.*
quench (kwĕnch) ◊ *verb* **quenched, quenching**

query *noun* A question: *I hope you will be able to answer my queries.*
◊ *verb* **1.** To ask questions of: *Our friends queried us about our vacation plans.* **2.** To express doubt about; question: *I query the wisdom of your plan.*
que·ry (**kwîr′** ē) ◊ *noun, plural* **queries** ◊ *verb* **queried, querying**

question *noun* **1.** Something that is asked: *I don't understand your question.* **2.** A subject that is being discussed or debated: *The chairperson called for a vote on the question of building a new library.* **3.** A matter being or to be dealt with; problem: *It is only a question of how much money we can save.* **4.** Dispute or doubt: *There is no question about your ability to do the job.*
◊ *verb* **1.** To ask questions of: *My parents questioned me about my plans.* —See Synonyms at **ask. 2.** To have, show, or express doubt about; dispute: *No one questions the principal's decisions.*
ques·tion (**kwĕs′** chən) ◊ *noun, plural* **questions** ◊ *verb* **questioned, questioning**

Q

question mark *noun* A punctuation mark (?) used especially at the end of a sentence to show that a question is being asked.
question mark ◊ *noun, plural* **question marks**

queue *noun* A line, as of people, awaiting a turn: *The queue at the ticket window extended all the way to the corner of the street.*
queue (kyo͞o) ◊ *noun, plural* **queues**
‖*These sound alike:* **queue, cue**

quick *adjective* **1.** Very fast; rapid: *I turned on the light with a quick motion of my hand.* **2.** Thinking or learning fast and with ease; bright: *The child has a quick mind.*
◊ *adverb* In a quick manner; rapidly: *Come here quick!*
quick (kwĭk) ◊ *adjective, adverb* **quicker, quickest**

> **SYNONYMS**
>
> ***quick, fast¹, hasty, rapid***
>
> Be as *quick* as you can in putting on your coat. He is so *fast* that nobody can beat him. She was too *hasty* in doing her work and made several mistakes. The train made *rapid* progress down the hill. **Antonym:** *slow*

quicken *verb* **1.** To make or become quicker; accelerate: *We quickened our pace but had to slow down at the corner.* **2.** To make or become livelier or more intense: *Interest in the elections quickened.*
quick·en (**kwĭk′** ən) ◊ *verb* **quickened, quickening**

quicksand *noun* A soft, shifting mass of loose sand mixed with water. Quicksand swallows up objects resting on its surface.
quick·sand (**kwĭk′**săndʹ) ◊ *noun*

quick-witted *adjective* Mentally alert.
quick-wit·ted (**kwĭk′ wĭt′**ĭd) ◊ *adjective*

quiet *adjective* **1.** Marked by little or no noise; silent or nearly silent: *A library is a quiet place to study.* **2.** Not loud: *The teacher spoke in a quiet voice.* **3.** Free or nearly free from activity or motion; calm: *The sea was quiet after the storm.*
◊ *noun* The quality or condition of being quiet: *The speaker asked for quiet.*
◊ *verb* To make or become quiet: *The teacher quieted the class.*
qui·et (**kwī′**ĭt) ◊ *adjective* **quieter, quietest** ◊ *noun* ◊ *verb* **quieted, quieting**

quill *noun* **1.** A long, stiff feather. **2.** A writing pen made from a feather. **3.** One of the sharp hollow spines of a porcupine.
quill (kwĭl) ◊ *noun, plural* **quills**

▲ **quill**

quilt *noun* A bed covering made by stitching together two layers of fabric with an inner layer of cotton, wool, down, or feathers.
◊ *verb* **1.** To work on or make a quilt. **2.** To stitch together like a quilt, with an inner layer of padding.
quilt (kwĭlt) ◊ *noun, plural* **quilts** ◊ *verb* **quilted, quilting**

quintet *noun* A group of five people or things.
quin·tet (kwĭn **tĕt′**) ◊ *noun, plural* **quintets**

quintuplet *noun* One of five children born at a single birth.
quin·tu·plet (kwĭn **tŭp′**lĭt *or* kwĭn **to͞o′**plĭt) ◊ *noun, plural* **quintuplets**

quit *verb* **1.** To stop doing; cease: *I quit work at five o'clock.* **2.** To depart from: *They decided to quit the city and move to the country.*
quit (kwĭt) ◊ *verb* **quit, quitting**

quite *adverb* **1.** To the fullest extent; completely: *Plant cells are not quite the same as animal cells.* **2.** To a degree; rather: *Our own group of planets is quite small.*
quite (kwīt) ◊ *adverb*

quiver¹ *verb* To shake with a slight vibrating motion; tremble: *My voice quivered with excitement.*
◊ *noun* The act or motion of quivering.
quiv·er¹ (**kwĭv′** ər) ◊ *verb* **quivered, quivering** ◊ *noun, plural* **quivers**

ă	pat	ĭ	pit	oi	**oi**l	th	ba**th**
ā	pay	ī	ride	o͝o	bo**o**k	*th*	ba**th**e
â	care	î	fierce	o͞o	bo**o**t	ə	ago, item
ä	father	ŏ	pot	ou	**ou**t		pencil
ĕ	pet	ō	go	ŭ	c**u**t		atom
ē	be	ô	paw, for	û	f**u**r		circus

quiver² *noun* A case for holding and carrying arrows.
quiv·er² (**kwĭv′** ər) ◊ *noun, plural* **quivers**

HISTORY • quiver¹, quiver²

Quiver¹ is probably related to an old English word that meant "nimble." **Quiver²** comes from an old French word. This word in turn probably came from a Germanic word for an arrow case.

▲ **quiver²**

quiz *noun* A short written or oral test. ◊ *verb* **1.** To question closely. **2.** To test the knowledge of by asking questions.
quiz (kwĭz) ◊ *noun, plural* **quizzes** ◊ *verb* **quizzed, quizzing**

quizzical *adjective* Showing or suggesting puzzlement; perplexed.
quiz·zi·cal (**kwĭz′** ĭ kəl) ◊ *adjective*

quota *noun* An amount of something assigned to be done, made, or sold: *I sold my quota of tickets for the benefit concert.*
quo·ta (**kwō′** tə) ◊ *noun, plural* **quotas**

quotation *noun* **1.** The act of quoting. **2.** Something, as a passage from a book, that is quoted.
quo·ta·tion (kwō **tā′** shən) ◊ *noun, plural* **quotations**

quotation mark *noun* Either of a pair of punctuation marks (" ") used to mark the beginning and end of a quotation.
quotation mark ◊ *noun, plural* **quotation marks**

quote *verb* To repeat exactly the words of another: *The newspaper quoted the mayor.* ◊ *noun* A quotation.
quote (kwōt) ◊ *verb* **quoted, quoting** ◊ *noun, plural* **quotes**

quotient *noun* The number that results when one number is divided by another.
quo·tient (**kwō′** shənt) ◊ *noun, plural* **quotients**

Q

Raccoon

Rr

R is the eighteenth letter of the English alphabet. Did you know that it has a long history?

Over 3,500 years ago, people in the Middle East were using symbols that became the letters of our alphabet. This ancient Middle Eastern symbol is a form of the letter that became our letter *R*.

P

The ancient Greeks borrowed their alphabet from people in the Middle East. Here is a form of the Greek letter that became our letter *R*.

R

The ancient Romans borrowed their alphabet from a people who had taken their own letter symbols from the Greeks. Here is a form of the Roman letter *R* that was used for carving letters into stone. These letters became the model for our printed capital letters.

r

As people wrote quickly, especially with pens, the capital letters began to take the shapes of small letters. Here is a small-letter *r* that was developed about 1,200 years ago.

Rr *Rr*	Rr	Rr	Rr
Handwriting	Sans Serif Type	Serif Type	Computer Printing

r *or* **R** *noun* The eighteenth letter of the English alphabet.
r *or* **R** (är) ◊ *noun, plural* **r's** *or* **R's**

rabbi *noun* **1.** The leader of a Jewish congregation. **2.** A teacher of Jewish law.
rab·bi (**răb**′ī′) ◊ *noun, plural* **rabbis**

rabbit *noun* A burrowing animal with long ears, soft fur, and a short, furry tail.
rab·bit (**răb**′ĭt) ◊ *noun, plural* **rabbits**

rabies *noun* A disease of certain mammals, as dogs and wolves, that almost always causes death. A person can get rabies if bitten by an infected animal.
ra·bies (**rā**′bēz) ◊ *noun*

raccoon *noun* A North American animal with grayish-brown fur, black face markings that look like a mask, and a bushy tail with black rings.
rac·coon (ră **ko͞on**′) ◊ *noun, plural* **raccoons**

race[1] *noun* A contest of speed: *We watched the sailboat race from the dock.*
◊ *verb* **1.** To try to beat in a contest of speed. **2.** To rush at top speed: *I raced home when I heard the news.*
race[1] (rās) ◊ *noun, plural* **races** ◊ *verb* **raced, racing**

race[2] *noun* A large group of people who share certain physical characteristics that are passed on from one generation to another.
race[2] (rās) ◊ *noun, plural* **races**

ă	pat	ĭ	pit	oi	**oi**l	th	ba**th**
ā	pay	ī	ride	o͝o	b**oo**k	*th*	ba**th**e
â	care	î	fierce	o͞o	b**oo**t	ə	**a**go, it**e**m
ä	father	ŏ	pot	ou	**ou**t		penc**i**l
ĕ	pet	ō	go	ŭ	c**u**t		at**o**m
ē	be	ô	paw, for	û	f**u**r		circ**u**s

HISTORY • race[1], race[2]

Race[1] comes from an old Scandinavian word that meant "a fast current of water." **Race**[2] comes from an old French word that meant "a group of people."

racer *noun* **1.** Someone or something that takes part in or is used in races. **2.** A North American snake that can move very fast.
rac·er (rā′sər) ◊ *noun, plural* **racers**

racetrack *noun* A course on which races can be run.
race·track (rās′trăk′) ◊ *noun, plural* **racetracks**

racial *adjective* Of, relating to, or based on race.
ra·cial (rā′shəl) ◊ *adjective*

rack *noun* A stand or frame on which to hang, hold, or display things: *There is a coat rack in the hall.*
rack (răk) ◊ *noun, plural* **racks**

racket[1] *noun* A device consisting of a frame with tightly laced strings and a handle. It is used to strike the ball in a game like tennis.
rack·et[1] (răk′ĭt) ◊ *noun, plural* **rackets**

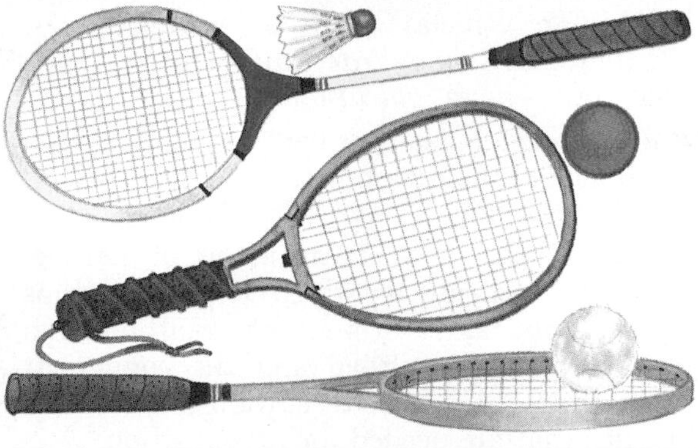

▲ **racket[1]**

racket[2] *noun* **1.** A loud, unpleasant noise. **2.** A dishonest scheme for getting money, as by using threats or violence.
rack·et[2] (răk′ĭt) ◊ *noun, pural* **rackets**

***HISTORY* • racket[1], racket[2]**

Racket[1] goes back to an Arabic word that meant "palm of the hand." **Racket[2]** may have been made up in imitation of the sound it describes.

racquetball *noun* A game played on an enclosed court with four walls. The players use short, metal rackets and a hollow rubber ball.
rac·quet·ball (răk′ĭt bôl′) ◊ *noun*

radar *noun* A device for finding the location and measuring the speed of distant objects, such as airplanes and rockets.
ra·dar (rā′där′) ◊ *noun*

▲ **radar**

radiant *adjective* **1.** Sending out rays of light. **2.** Filled with love or happiness; glowing: *The children had radiant smiles.*
ra·di·ant (rā′dē ənt) ◊ *adjective*

radiate *verb* **1.** To send out energy in rays or waves: *The sun radiates heat.* **2.** To be sent out in rays or waves: *Light radiates from stars.*
ra·di·ate (rā′dē āt′) ◊ *verb* **radiated, radiating**

radiation *noun* **1.** The act or process of radiating. **2.** Something, such as waves or particles, that is radiated.
ra·di·a·tion (rā′dē ā′shən) ◊ *noun*

radiator *noun* **1.** A device for heating air, as in a house. **2.** A device for cooling something, such as an automobile engine.
ra·di·a·tor (rā′dē ā′tər) ◊ *noun, plural* **radiators**

radical *adjective* **1.** Of, relating to, or affecting what is basic and essential; fundamental: *Leaving school and going to work was a radical change in my cousin's life.* **2.** Favoring extreme or rapid changes, especially in politics, law, or government.
◊ *noun* A person who favors rapid political changes.
rad·i·cal (răd′ĭ kəl) ◊ *adjective* ◊ *noun, plural* **radicals**

R

radio *noun* **1.** A way of using energy waves to carry signals between points without using wires. **2.** The equipment used to send or receive signals transmitted by radio.
◊ *verb* To send or communicate with by radio.
ra·di·o (rā′dē ō) ◊ *noun, plural* **radios** ◊ *verb* **radioed, radioing**

radioactive *adjective* Of, caused by, or showing radioactivity.
ra·di·o·ac·tive (rā′dē ō ăk′tĭv) ◊ *adjective*

radioactivity *noun* The process or property by which certain chemical elements, such as radium, give off energy in the form of rays when their atoms split apart.
ra·di·o·ac·tiv·i·ty (rā′dē ō ăk tĭv′ĭ tē) ◊ *noun*

radish *noun* A crisp, red or white edible root with a strong taste.
rad·ish (răd′ĭsh) ◊ *noun, plural* **radishes**

radium *noun* A white, highly radioactive metallic chemical element. Radium is used in treating cancer.
ra·di·um (rā′dē əm) ◊ *noun*

radius *noun* **1.** A line that extends straight from the center of a circle to its circumference or from the center of a sphere to its surface. **2.** A circular or almost circular area measured by its radius: *There are no buildings within a radius of 15 miles.*
ra·di·us (rā′dē əs) ◊ *noun, plural* **radiuses**

raft *noun* A floating platform made of material such as logs or rubber.
raft (răft) ◊ *noun, plural* **rafts**

rafter *noun* One of the sloping beams that hold up a roof.
raft·er (răf′tər) ◊ *noun, plural* **rafters**

rag *noun* **1.** A scrap of torn, frayed, or leftover cloth. **2. rags** Shabby, torn, or tattered clothing.
rag (răg) ◊ *noun, plural* **rags**

rage *noun* **1.** Violent anger; fury. **2.** Something that is popular only for a short time.
◊ *verb* **1.** To feel or show violent anger. **2.** To move with great violence: *A blizzard raged through the northern states.*
rage (rāj) ◊ *noun, plural* **rages** ◊ *verb* **raged, raging**

ă	pat	ĭ	pit	oi	oil	th	bath
ā	pay	ī	ride	o͝o	book	*th*	bathe
â	care	î	fierce	o͞o	boot	ə	ago, item
ä	father	ŏ	pot	ou	out		pencil
ĕ	pet	ō	go	ŭ	cut		atom
ē	be	ô	paw, for	û	fur		circus

ragged *adjective* **1.** Worn to rags; tattered: *We dressed in ragged old clothes to paint the house.* **2.** Dressed in tattered clothes. **3.** Rough or jagged in surface or outline; uneven: *The knife has a ragged edge and needs to be sharpened.*
rag·ged (răg′ĭd) ◊ *adjective*

ragweed *noun* A weed that produces pollen that is one of the main causes of hay fever.
rag·weed (răg′wēd′) ◊ *noun*

raid *noun* A sudden attack, as one made by police or soldiers.
◊ *verb* To carry out a raid on.
raid (rād) ◊ *noun, plural* **raids** ◊ *verb* **raided, raiding**

rail *noun* **1.** A bar, as of wood, supported by upright posts and forming a barrier or guard. **2.** A steel bar, usually one of a pair, forming a path for vehicles such as railroad cars. **3.** Railroad: *I enjoy traveling by rail.*
rail (rāl) ◊ *noun, plural* **rails**

railing *noun* A fence or banister that consists of rails and their supports.
rail·ing (rā′lĭng) ◊ *noun, plural* **railings**

railroad *noun* **1.** A path made of parallel pairs of steel rails on which vehicles, such as trains, run. **2.** A system of transportation consisting of a railroad and the equipment and property, such as stations, land, and trains, that are needed for its operation.
rail·road (rāl′rōd′) ◊ *noun, plural* **railroads**

railway *noun* **1.** A railroad. **2.** The tracks of a railroad.
rail·way (rāl′wā′) ◊ *noun, plural* **railways**

rain *noun* **1.** Water that falls from clouds to the earth in drops. **2.** A fall of rain.
◊ *verb* **1.** To fall in drops of water from the clouds: *It rained all day.* **2.** To send down or fall like rain: *Tears rained down my cheeks.*
rain (rān) ◊ *noun, plural* **rains** ◊ *verb* **rained, raining**
‖*These sound alike:* **rain, reign, rein**

rainbow *noun* An arc of color that is seen in the sky opposite the sun, especially after rain. It is caused by the sun's rays shining through tiny drops of water.
rain·bow (rān′bō′) ◊ *noun, plural* **rainbows**

▲ rainbow

raincoat *noun* A waterproof coat worn to protect against rain.
rain·coat (rān′kōt′) ◊ *noun, plural* **raincoats**

raindrop *noun* A drop of rain.
rain·drop (rān′drŏp′) ◊ *noun, plural* **raindrops**

rainfall *noun* **1.** A fall of rain; shower. **2.** The amount of water, as in the form of rain or snow, that falls over a given area during a given time.
rain·fall (rān′fôl′) ◊ *noun, plural* **rainfalls**

rainy *adjective* Marked by much rain: *Because it was a rainy afternoon, I stayed at home and read.*
rain·y (rā′nē) ◊ *adjective* **rainier, rainiest**

raise *verb* **1.** To move to a higher position: *I raised my arm and waved at my friend.* —See Synonyms at **lift. 2.** To make greater; increase: *The store lost customers when it raised prices.* **3.** To bring up and take care of: *My grandparents raised a large family.* **4.** To promote the growth and development of; grow or breed: *We raise and sell tulips.* **5.** To gather together; collect: *We're trying to raise money to build a new wing for the hospital.* **6.** To bring up; put forward: *Why do you even raise the question?*
◊ *noun* An increase in amount, as in wages.
raise (rāz) ◊ *verb* **raised, raising** ◊ *noun, plural* **raises**

raisin *noun* A sweet dried grape.
rai·sin (rā′zən) ◊ *noun, plural* **raisins**

rake *noun* A tool with a long handle and a bar with teeth or prongs at one end. A rake is used for working in gardens or on lawns.
◊ *verb* To gather, smooth, or remove with a rake: *We rake leaves often during the fall.*
rake (rāk) ◊ *noun, plural* **rakes** ◊ *verb* **raked, raking**

rally *verb* **1.** To bring or come together again: *The team rallied and won the game.* **2.** To gather or join together in support of a common cause: *Many people rallied to our defense.* **3.** To show an improvement in health, strength, or mental condition; revive.
◊ *noun* A large meeting held to support a cause or inspire enthusiasm.
ral·ly (răl′ē) ◊ *verb* **rallied, rallying** ◊ *noun, plural* **rallies**

ram *noun* A male sheep.
◊ *verb* **1.** To force by pushing hard; jam: *I rammed my hat onto my head.* **2.** To strike with great force.
ram (răm) ◊ *noun, plural* **rams** ◊ *verb* **rammed, ramming**

ramble *verb* **1.** To wander without direction or purpose: *We rambled around the park.* **2.** To speak or write without a clear sequence of thoughts.
◊ *noun* A leisurely walk taken for fun.
ram·ble (răm′bəl) ◊ *verb* **rambled, rambling** ◊ *noun, plural* **rambles**

ramp *noun* A sloping passage or roadway that leads from one level to another.
ramp (rămp) ◊ *noun, plural* **ramps**

▲ ramp

R

rampart *noun* A wall or bank raised around a place, as a fort, for protection against attack.
ram·part (**răm′**pärt′) ◊ *noun, plural* **ramparts**

ramrod *noun* **1.** A rod used to force ammunition into the muzzle of a gun. **2.** A rod used to clean a gun barrel.
ram·rod (**răm′**rŏd′) ◊ *noun, plural* **ramrods**

ran *verb* Past tense of **run.**
ran (răn) ◊ *verb*

ranch *noun* A large farm where cattle, sheep, or horses are raised.
◊ *verb* To work on or manage a ranch.
ranch (rănch) ◊ *noun, plural* **ranches** ◊ *verb* **ranched, ranching**

random *adjective* Lacking a definite plan, pattern, or purpose: *I made a few random remarks about the weather.*
ran·dom (**răn′**dəm) ◊ *adjective*

rang *verb* Past tense of **ring²**.
rang (răng) ◊ *verb*

range *noun* **1.** The extent to which something can vary: *Bicycles are available at a wide range of prices.* **2.** An extent of ability, knowledge, or understanding; scope: *I am always trying to widen the range of what I know about other countries.* **3.** The distance over which something, such as a signal or a ship, can travel: *The car has a range of 200 miles on a tank of gas.* **4.** A place for shooting at targets. **5.** An expanse of open land where livestock can wander and graze. **6.** A stove with spaces for cooking a number of things at the same time. **7.** A group of things in a row: *A range of mountains surrounds the valley.*
◊ *verb* **1.** To move between certain limits: *The ages of the children ranged from four to ten.* **2.** To travel or roam over: *We ranged the woods looking for a place to set up our tents.* **3.** To extend in a certain direction: *The road ranges westward from the lake.*
range (rānj) ◊ *noun, plural* **ranges** ◊ *verb* **ranged, ranging**

ă	pat	ĭ	pit	oi	**oil**	th	ba**th**
ā	pay	ī	ride	o͝o	book	*th*	ba**the**
â	care	î	fierce	o͞o	boot	ə	ago, item
ä	father	ŏ	pot	ou	**out**		pencil
ĕ	pet	ō	go	ŭ	cut		atom
ē	be	ô	paw, for	û	fur		circus

ranger *noun* **1.** A person who patrols a forest or park. **2.** One of a body of troops or police that patrols a region.
rang·er (**rān′**jər) ◊ *noun, plural* **rangers**

▲ **ranger**

rank¹ *noun* **1.** Position or standing on a scale or in a group: *My friend is in the first rank as an athlete.* **2.** Official position or grade: *Last month my cousin was promoted to the rank of colonel.* **3. ranks** Enlisted people in the armed forces.
◊ *verb* **1.** To take or hold a particular rank: *How does our state rank in size compared with other states?* **2.** To assign a rank to: *Sports writers rank the team second in the nation.*
rank¹ (răngk) ◊ *noun, plural* **ranks** ◊ *verb* **ranked, ranking**

rank² *adjective* **1.** Strong and unpleasant in odor or taste. **2.** Absolute; complete: *That musician is a rank amateur.*
rank² (răngk) ◊ *adjective* **ranker, rankest**

***HISTORY* • rank¹, rank²**

Rank¹ comes from an old French word that meant "row." **Rank²** comes from an old English word that meant "strong, proud, arrogant."

rankle *verb* To cause, have, or continue to have pain, anger, or annoyance.
ran·kle (**răng′**kəl) ◊ *verb* **rankled, rankling**

ransom *noun* **1.** The release of a person being held prisoner in exchange for money. **2.** The amount of money demanded or paid so that a person being held prisoner may be freed.
◊ *verb* To free a person being held prisoner by paying a ransom.
ran·som (răn′səm) ◊ *noun, plural* **ransoms** ◊ *verb* **ransomed, ransoming**

rap *verb* To strike a surface quickly and sharply; knock: *I rapped on the door.*
◊ *noun* A quick, sharp blow; knock.
rap (răp) ◊ *verb* **rapped, rapping** ◊ *noun, plural* **raps**
‖*These sound alike:* **rap, wrap**

rapid *adjective* Marked by speed; fast. —See Synonyms at **quick.**
rap·id (răp′ĭd) ◊ *adjective*

rapids *plural noun* A place in a river where the water flows very fast.
rap·ids (răp′ĭdz) ◊ *plural noun*

▲ **rapids**

rapport *noun* A relationship of mutual trust and understanding.
rap·port (ră pôr′) ◊ *noun*

rapture *noun* A feeling or condition of great joy, delight, or happiness.
rap·ture (răp′chər) ◊ *noun, plural* **raptures**

rapturous *adjective* Feeling rapture.
rap·tur·ous (răp′chər əs) ◊ *adjective*

rare[1] *adjective* **1.** Not often found, seen, or happening: *Our cat is a rare breed.* **2.** Unusually good; excellent: *The artist had a rare gift for painting.*
rare[1] (râr) ◊ *adjective* **rarer, rarest**

rare[2] *adjective* Not thoroughly cooked: *I like my steak rare.*
rare[2] (râr) ◊ *adjective* **rarer, rarest**

***HISTORY* • rare[1], rare[2]**

Rare[1] comes from a Latin word that meant "uncommon." **Rare[2]** comes from an old English word that meant "lightly boiled." The word has been used to describe lightly cooked meat only in the last few hundred years.

rarely *adverb* Not very often; seldom.
rare·ly (râr′lē) ◊ *adverb*

rascal *noun* **1.** A dishonest person. **2.** A person who misbehaves in a playful way.
ras·cal (răs′kəl) ◊ *noun, plural* **rascals**

rash[1] *adjective* Too hasty; reckless.
rash[1] (răsh) ◊ *adjective* **rasher, rashest**

rash[2] *noun* An outbreak of red spots on the skin, as in measles.
rash[2] (răsh) ◊ *noun, plural* **rashes**

***HISTORY* • rash[1], rash[2]**

Rash[1] first appeared in writing about 600 years ago and meant "too hasty, reckless." **Rash[1]** is probably related to an old English word that meant "to flash." **Rash[2]** may be related to a Latin word that meant "to scratch."

rasp *noun* A harsh, grating sound.
◊ *verb* To make a harsh, grating sound.
rasp (răsp) ◊ *noun, plural* **rasps** ◊ *verb* **rasped, rasping**

R

raspberry *noun* An edible berry that grows on a prickly plant with long, woody stems.
rasp·ber·ry (răz′bĕr′ē) ◊ *noun, plural* **raspberries**

▲ **raspberry**

rat *noun* A gnawing animal with a long tail. Rats look like mice but are larger.
rat (răt) ◊ *noun, plural* **rats**

rate *noun* **1.** An amount of one thing measured in relation to a unit of another thing: *The airplane could fly at a rate of 500 miles an hour.* **2.** A cost or price charged on the basis of a standard or scale: *Postal rates seem to go up every year.*
◊ *verb* **1.** To judge the quality or worth of; evaluate: *How do you rate this restaurant?* **2.** To have a particular position or rank on a scale: *Those players rate high in my opinion.*
◊ *idiom* **at any rate** Whatever happens; in any case.
rate (rāt) ◊ *noun, plural* **rates** ◊ *verb* **rated, rating**

rather *adverb* **1.** To a certain extent; somewhat: *I'm feeling rather sleepy.* **2.** More willingly: *I'd rather stay at home.* **3.** More properly, truly, or correctly: *I've done my work or, rather, I've done most of it.*
rath·er (răth′ər) ◊ *adverb*

ratify *verb* To make legal by officially approving: *The two countries ratified the peace treaty.*
rat·i·fy (răt′ə fī′) ◊ *verb* **ratified, ratifying**

ratio *noun* A relationship in amount, number, or size of two things. If there are ten students and one teacher in a room, the ratio of students to teachers is ten to one. There are ten times as many students as teachers in the room.
ra·tio (rā′shē ō′) ◊ *noun, plural* **ratios**

ration *noun* A fixed amount or portion, especially of food.
◊ *verb* To give out or make available in fixed, limited amounts: *During the drought the city council had to ration water.*
ra·tion (răsh′ən *or* rā′shən) ◊ *noun, plural* **rations** ◊ *verb* **rationed, rationing**

rational *adjective* **1.** Having the ability to think things through. **2.** Of or relating to reason: *Try to give me a rational explanation for what you did.*
ra·tion·al (răsh′ə nəl) ◊ *adjective*

rattle *verb* **1.** To make or cause to make a quick series of short, sharp sounds: *The wind rattled the windows.* **2.** To talk or say quickly and without pausing: *I rattled off the list of names.* **3.** To cause to be upset; disturb: *The size of my audience rattled me.*
◊ *noun* **1.** A quick series of short, sharp sounds. **2.** A device, as a baby's toy, that makes a rattling sound when it is shaken. **3.** The dry, horny rings at the end of a rattlesnake's tail.
rat·tle (răt′l) ◊ *verb* **rattled, rattling** ◊ *noun, plural* **rattles**

rattlesnake *noun* A poisonous American snake that has dry, horny rings at the end of its tail. When the snake shakes its tail, the rings make a rattling sound.
rat·tle·snake (răt′l snāk′) ◊ *noun, plural* **rattlesnakes**

ravage *verb* To be violently destructive to; devastate: *A hurricane ravaged the coast.*
rav·age (răv′ĭj) ◊ *verb* **ravaged, ravaging**

rave *verb* **1.** To talk in a wild, angry, or crazy way. **2.** To speak with great enthusiasm: *The guests raved about dinner.*
rave (rāv) ◊ *verb* **raved, raving**

ravel *verb* To separate into single loose threads: *The rug has raveled along the edges.*
rav·el (răv′əl) ◊ *verb* **raveled, raveling**

ă	pat	ĭ	pit	oi	oil	th	bath
ā	pay	ī	ride	o͝o	book	*th*	bathe
â	care	î	fierce	o͞o	boot	ə	ago, item
ä	father	ŏ	pot	ou	out		pencil
ĕ	pet	ō	go	ŭ	cut		atom
ē	be	ô	paw, for	û	fur		circus

raven *noun* A large black bird that resembles a crow and has a harsh cry.
ra•ven (rā′vən) ◊ *noun, plural* **ravens**

▲ **raven**

ravenous *adjective* Extremely hungry.
rav•en•ous (răv′ə nəs) ◊ *adjective*

ravine *noun* A deep, narrow valley that is similar to a canyon or gorge.
ra•vine (rə vēn′) ◊ *noun, plural* **ravines**

raw *adjective* **1.** Being in a natural condition; not treated, processed, or refined: *Wood pulp is the raw material from which we make paper.* **2.** Not cooked: *I made a salad of raw vegetables.* **3.** Lacking experience or training. **4.** Having the skin scraped off: *Let me put a bandage on your raw knee.* **5.** Unpleasantly damp and chilly: *It was a raw evening.*
raw (rô) ◊ *adjective* **rawer, rawest**

rawhide *noun* The hide of cattle before it has been tanned.
raw•hide (rô′hīd′) ◊ *noun*

ray *noun* **1.** A narrow beam of radiation, as light. **2.** A small amount; bit: *There isn't a ray of hope for their team.* **3.** One of several lines that extend from a common center. **4.** A part of a plant or animal that looks like a ray.
ray (rā) ◊ *noun, plural* **rays**
‖*These sound alike:* **ray, re**

rayon *noun* A fabric that is made from cellulose fibers.
ray•on (rā′ŏn′) ◊ *noun*

razor *noun* A sharp cutting instrument that is used to shave hair, especially on the face.
ra•zor (rā′zər) ◊ *noun, plural* **razors**

rd. The abbreviation for *rod.*

Rd. The abbreviation for *Road.*

re *noun* The second tone of the musical scale.
re (rā) ◊ *noun*
‖*These sound alike:* **re, ray**

re– The prefix *re–* means "again." If you *refill* a glass with water, you fill it again. The prefix *re–* also means "back" or "backward." If people are *recalled* to work, they are called back to work.

***VOCABULARY BUILDER* • re–**

Many words that are formed with **re–** are not entries in this dictionary. But you can figure out what these words mean by looking up the meanings of the root words and the prefix. For example:
rearrange = to arrange again
repay = to pay back

reach *verb* **1.** To go as far as; arrive at: *We managed to reach the house before it rained.* **2.** To stretch out; extend: *Nerves reach to every part of the body.* **3.** To touch or try to touch by extending a part of the body, as the hand: *I reached for a cup.* **4.** To get in touch with: *I tried to reach you by phone.*
◊ *noun* **1.** An act of reaching. **2.** The distance or extent of reaching: *I left the grapes within everyone's reach.*
reach (rēch) ◊ *verb* **reached, reaching**
◊ *noun, plural* **reaches**

SYNONYMS

reach, achieve, gain

Have we *reached* the right house yet? We have almost *achieved* the goal we set for raising money. Our team *gained* the victory in a very close game.

react *verb* To act in response, as to an experience or the behavior of another: *The audience reacted with pleasure to the play.*
re•act (rē ăkt′) ◊ *verb* **reacted, reacting**

reaction *noun* A response to something: *I developed a rash as a reaction to the medicine.*
re•ac•tion (rē ăk′shən) ◊ *noun, plural* **reactions**

reactor *noun* A device in which atoms are split under controlled conditions.
re•ac•tor (rē ăk′tər) ◊ *noun, plural* **reactors**

R

read *verb* **1.** To understand the meaning of written or printed words. **2.** To say aloud the words of something written or printed: *Our parents read to us every night.* **3.** To learn or become informed through written or printed material: *We're reading about the sun.* **4.** To show by letters or numbers: *The speedometer reads 50 miles per hour.*
read (rēd) ◊ *verb* **read** (rĕd), **reading**
‖ *These sound alike:* **read, reed**

readable *adjective* Capable of being read easily; legible.
read·a·ble (**rē′**də bəl) ◊ *adjective*

reader *noun* **1.** A person who reads. **2.** A textbook for learning or practicing reading.
read·er (**rē′**dər) ◊ *noun, plural* **readers**

readily *adverb* **1.** In a quick and willing manner: *They readily took our advice.* **2.** Without difficulty; easily: *The paints are readily available at a hardware store.*
read·i·ly (**rĕd′**l ē) ◊ *adverb*

reading *noun* **1.** The activity of getting knowledge and pleasure from written material. **2.** Material read or for reading. **3.** A reciting of written or printed material.
read·ing (**rē′**dĭng) ◊ *noun, plural* **readings**

ready *adjective* **1.** Prepared for action or use: *Are you getting ready for school?* **2.** Feeling inclined; willing: *They are ready to accept your offer.* **3.** Likely or about to do something: *I am ready to cry.* **4.** Showing quickness and ease: *You always have a ready answer for everything.* **5.** Close at hand; easily available: *Try to have some ready money in case of an emergency.*
◊ *verb* To make ready; prepare.
read·y (**rĕd′**ē) ◊ *adjective* **readier, readiest**
◊ *verb* **readied, readying**

real *adjective* **1.** Not imaginary or made up; actual: *This is a story about real people.* **2.** Not artificial; genuine: *A real cat was sitting next to a picture of one.*
re·al (**rē′**əl *or* rēl) ◊ *adjective*

ă	pat	ĭ	pit	oi	oil	th	bath
ā	pay	ī	ride	o͝o	book	*th*	bathe
â	care	î	fierce	o͞o	boot	ə	ago, item
ä	father	ŏ	pot	ou	out		pencil
ĕ	pet	ō	go	ŭ	cut		atom
ē	be	ô	paw, for	û	fur		circus

SYNONYMS

real, actual, genuine, true

Many things that a magician does appear to be *real,* but they are only illusions. The *actual* time it took me to get there was five minutes. This wallet is not made of *genuine* leather. I believe that what you tell me is *true.*

real estate *noun* Land and buildings that make up property.

realistic *adjective* **1.** Closely resembling real life or nature: *I tried to do a realistic drawing of the animals.* **2.** Aware of things as they actually are; practical.
re·al·is·tic (rē′ə **lĭs′**tĭk) ◊ *adjective*

reality *noun* **1.** The condition or quality of being real; actual existence: *The author makes us believe in the reality of the characters.* **2.** Something that is real: *They lived to see their dreams become realities.*
re·al·i·ty (rē **ăl′**ĭ tē) ◊ *noun, plural* **realities**

realization *noun* **1.** The act or fact of realizing. **2.** Something realized: *The house was perfect, the realization of all our dreams.*
re·al·i·za·tion (rē′ə lĭ **zā′**shən) ◊ *noun, plural* **realizations**

realize *verb* **1.** To be fully aware of; understand: *He suddenly realized he was lost.* **2.** To make real; achieve: *She finally realized her ambition to become a firefighter.*
re·al·ize (**rē′**ə līz′) ◊ *verb* **realized, realizing**

really *adverb* **1.** In actual truth or fact: *The horseshoe crab isn't really a crab.* **2.** Truly; certainly: *It's a really beautiful morning.*
re·al·ly (**rē′**ə lē *or* **rē′**lē) ◊ *adverb*

realm *noun* A kingdom.
realm (rĕlm) ◊ *noun, plural* **realms**

realtor *noun* A person who buys and sells real estate for a living.
re·al·tor (**rē′**əl tər) ◊ *noun, plural* **realtors**

ream *noun* **1.** A quantity of paper of the same size and quality. **2. reams** A large amount.
ream (rēm) ◊ *noun, plural* **reams**

reap *verb* **1.** To cut grain or gather a crop by hand or machine. **2.** To harvest a crop from: *The farm hands are reaping the field.*
reap (rēp) ◊ *verb* **reaped, reaping**

reaper *noun* A person or machine that cuts and gathers a crop.
reap·er (rē′ pər) ◊ *noun, plural* **reapers**

▲ **reaper**

reappear *verb* To come into view again.
re·ap·pear (rē′ə **pîr′**) ◊ *verb* **reappeared, reappearing**

rear[1] *noun* The area or direction closest to or at the back.
◊ *adjective* Being at or in the back.
rear[1] (rîr) ◊ *noun, plural* **rears** ◊ *adjective*

rear[2] *verb* **1.** To care for during the early years of growth and learning; bring up. **2.** To rise up on the hind legs: *The frightened horse reared.* **3.** To raise upright: *The dog reared its head and barked.*
rear[2] (rîr) ◊ *verb* **reared, rearing**

***HISTORY* • rear[1], rear[2]**

Rear[1] was probably shortened from *rearguard,* a word for the part of an army that defends against attacks from behind. **Rear**[2] comes from an old English word that meant "to raise, lift up."

rear admiral *noun* An officer in the United States Navy ranking above a captain.
rear admiral ◊ *noun, plural* **rear admirals**

reason *noun* **1.** A cause or motive for acting, thinking, or feeling in a certain way: *I have reasons for asking these questions.* **2.** An explanation for an act or belief: *These are my reasons for being late.* **3.** The ability to think clearly and sensibly.
◊ *verb* **1.** To use the ability to think clearly and sensibly. **2.** To talk so as to influence another: *The teacher tried to reason with the disappointed child.*
rea·son (rē′ zən) ◊ *noun, plural* **reasons**
◊ *verb* **reasoned, reasoning**

reasonable *adjective* **1.** Showing good judgment; sensible or logical: *We came up with a reasonable solution.* **2.** Not extreme; moderate: *That is not a reasonable price.*
rea·son·a·ble (rē′ zə nə bəl) ◊ *adjective*

reasoning *noun* The process of thinking in an orderly way or an example of such thinking.
rea·son·ing (rē′ zə nĭng) ◊ *noun, plural* **reasonings**

reassure *verb* To restore confidence to; make less fearful or worried.
re·as·sure (rē′ə **shŏŏr′**) ◊ *verb* **reassured, reassuring**

rebel *verb* **1.** To resist or fight against a government or an authority. **2.** To feel or show strong dislike or resentment.
◊ *noun* A person who resists authority.
re·bel ◊ *verb* (rĭ **bĕl′**) **rebelled, rebelling**
◊ *noun* **reb·el** (**rĕb′** əl), *plural* **rebels**

rebellion *noun* **1.** Open revolt against a government. **2.** Strong opposition toward any authority.
re·bel·lion (rĭ **bĕl′** yən) ◊ *noun, plural* **rebellions**

rebound *verb* To spring back or bounce away after hitting something.
◊ *noun* The act or an example of rebounding.
re·bound ◊ *verb* (rĭ **bound′**) **rebounded, rebounding** ◊ *noun* (**rē′** bound′), *plural* **rebounds**

recall *verb* **1.** To ask or order to return. **2.** To bring back to mind; remember: *I can't recall their telephone number.*
◊ *noun* The act of recalling.
re·call ◊ *verb* (rĭ **kôl′**) **recalled, recalling**
◊ *noun* (rĭ **kôl′** *or* **rē′** kôl′), *plural* **recalls**

recapture *verb* **1.** To capture again. **2.** To recall or find again: *We tried to recapture the happy days of summer.*
re·cap·ture (rē **kăp′** chər) ◊ *verb* **recaptured, recapturing**

R

recede *verb* To move back or away from a limit, point, or mark.
re·cede (rĭ **sēd′**) ◊ *verb* **receded, receding**

receipt *noun* **1.** A written statement that money has been paid or that merchandise has been received. **2. receipts** Something that has been received: *The box office receipts totaled $500.*
re·ceipt (rĭ **sēt′**) ◊ *noun, plural* **receipts**

receive *verb* **1.** To take or acquire something given, offered, or sent: *I receive an allowance every week.* **2.** To greet or welcome.
re·ceive (rĭ **sēv′**) ◊ *verb* **received, receiving**

receiver *noun* **1.** Someone or something that receives. **2.** The part of a communications device, such as a radio, telephone, or television set, that receives an incoming signal and changes it into sounds or pictures.
re·ceiv·er (rĭ **sē′** vər) ◊ *noun, plural* **receivers**

▲ **receiver**

recent *adjective* **1.** Of a time just before the present: *I am getting over my recent illness.* **2.** Having just come into being; new: *Have you read the recent issue of that magazine?*
re·cent (**rē′** sənt) ◊ *adjective*

receptacle *noun* An object that holds or contains something else; container.
re·cep·ta·cle (rĭ **sĕp′** tə kəl) ◊ *noun, plural* **receptacles**

reception *noun* **1.** The act or manner of receiving: *My family gave them a warm reception.* **2.** A social gathering honoring or introducing someone. **3.** The receiving of electrical signals by a radio or television set.
re·cep·tion (rĭ **sĕp′** shən) ◊ *noun, plural* **receptions**

ă	pat	ĭ	pit	oi	**oil**	th	ba**th**
ā	pay	ī	ride	ŏŏ	book	*th*	ba**the**
â	care	î	fierce	ōō	boot	ə	ago, item
ä	father	ŏ	pot	ou	**out**		pencil
ĕ	pet	ō	go	ŭ	cut		atom
ē	be	ô	paw, for	û	fur		circus

recess *noun* **1.** A short period for rest or relaxation. **2.** A small indented or hollow place, such as one in a wall.
◊ *verb* To stop an activity for a time.
re·cess (**rē′** sĕs′ *or* rĭ **sĕs′**) ◊ *noun, plural* **recesses** ◊ *verb* **recessed, recessing**

recession *noun* A usually temporary slowing down of buying and selling goods, construction, and other economic activities.
re·ces·sion (rĭ **sĕsh′** ən) ◊ *noun, plural* **recessions**

recipe *noun* A set of directions for making or preparing something, especially food.
rec·i·pe (**rĕs′** ə pē) ◊ *noun, plural* **recipes**

HISTORY • recipe

Recipe first referred to instructions for making medicine, and only later to cooking instructions. **Recipe** came from Latin, where it meant "take," and was the first word in phrases like "take one ounce of."

recital *noun* **1.** A detailed account or report: *The speaker gave a long recital of events in history.* **2.** A public performance, as of music.
re·cit·al (rĭ **sīt′** l) ◊ *noun, plural* **recitals**

recitation *noun* The reciting of something memorized in a public performance or as a classroom exercise.
rec·i·ta·tion (rĕs′ĭ **tā′** shən) ◊ *noun, plural* **recitations**

recite *verb* **1.** To repeat from memory, especially before an audience. **2.** To speak about a lesson that one has prepared or memorized. **3.** To tell about in detail.
re·cite (rĭ **sīt′**) ◊ *verb* **recited, reciting**

reckless *adjective* Not careful or cautious.
reck·less (**rĕk′** lĭs) ◊ *adjective*

reckon *verb* To think or assume: *I reckon the train will arrive soon.*
reck·on (**rĕk′** ən) ◊ *verb* **reckoned, reckoning**

reclaim *verb* **1.** To make land or soil usable, as by draining, irrigating, or fertilizing it. **2.** To obtain useful substances from refuse or waste products.
re·claim (rĭ **klām′**) ◊ *verb* **reclaimed, reclaiming**

recline *verb* To lie back or lie down.
re·cline (rĭ **klīn′**) ◊ *verb* **reclined, reclining**

recognition *noun* **1.** The act of recognizing. **2.** Attention or favorable notice; praise.
rec·og·ni·tion (rĕk′əg **nĭsh′**ən) ◊ *noun*

recognize *verb* **1.** To know and remember from past experience: *I recognized my old friend right away.* **2.** To admit the truth or existence of: *They recognize the need to study.*
rec·og·nize (**rĕk′**əg nīz′) ◊ *verb* **recognized, recognizing**

recoil *verb* **1.** To move or jerk backward, as a gun does when it is fired. **2.** To draw back in fear or dislike.
re·coil (rĭ **koil′**) ◊ *verb* **recoiled, recoiling**

recollect *verb* To remember.
rec·ol·lect (rĕk′ə **lĕkt′**) ◊ *verb* **recollected, recollecting**

recollection *noun* **1.** The act or power of remembering. **2.** Something remembered.
rec·ol·lec·tion (rĕk′ə **lĕk′**shən) ◊ *noun, plural* **recollections**

recommend *verb* **1.** To praise as being worthy: *The principal recommended the teacher for a promotion.* **2.** To advise: *I recommend that we forget the whole idea.*
rec·om·mend (rĕk′ə **mĕnd′**) ◊ *verb* **recommended, recommending**

recommendation *noun* **1.** The act of recommending. **2.** Something that recommends: *Will you write a recommendation for me?*
rec·om·men·da·tion (rĕk′ə mĕn **dā′**shən) ◊ *noun, plural* **recommendations**

reconsider *verb* To consider again, especially with the idea of making a change.
re·con·sid·er (rē′kən **sĭd′**ər) ◊ *verb* **reconsidered, reconsidering**

record *noun* **1.** Something written down to preserve facts or information: *Here is a record of what happened at the club meeting.* **2.** The known history of a person or thing: *A good school record can be important in getting a job.* **3.** The best performance officially known, as in a sport. **4.** A disk that can be played on a phonograph.
◊ *verb* **1.** To set down in writing: *Record the time you spent on each test question.* **2.** To register or indicate: *A thermometer records temperature.* **3.** To store sound or images permanently for later listening or viewing.
rec·ord ◊ *noun* (**rĕk′**ərd), *plural* **records** ◊ *verb* **re·cord** (rĭ **kôrd′**) **recorded, recording**

recorder *noun* **1.** A person or machine that records. **2.** A flute that has a whistlelike mouthpiece and eight finger holes.
re·cord·er (rĭ **kôr′**dər) ◊ *noun, plural* **recorders**

▲ **recorder**

recording *noun* Something, as a magnetic tape or a phonograph record, on which sound is recorded.
re·cord·ing (rĭ **kôr′**-dĭng) ◊ *noun, plural* **recordings**

recount *verb* To tell in detail; narrate.
re·count (rĭ **kount′**) ◊ *verb* **recounted, recounting**

re-count *verb* To count again.
re-count (rē **kount′**) ◊ *verb* **re-counted, re-counting**

recover *verb* **1.** To get back; regain: *The police recovered the stolen car.* **2.** To return to a normal condition, as of health. **3.** To make up for: *It's hard to recover lost time.*
re·cov·er (rĭ **kŭv′**ər) ◊ *verb* **recovered, recovering**

> ***SYNONYMS***
>
> ***recover, regain, retrieve***
>
> We *recovered* most of our stolen property. I have *regained* my health now. The dog *retrieved* the ball quickly.

recovery *noun* **1.** A return to a normal condition, as of health. **2.** The act of getting back or regaining something.
re·cov·er·y (rĭ **kŭv′**ə rē) ◊ *noun, plural* **recoveries**

recreation *noun* Mental or physical relaxation after work, as by walking or gardening.
rec·re·a·tion (rĕk′rē **ā′**shən) ◊ *noun*

recruit *verb* To get a person to join: *We're recruiting new members for the hiking club.*
◊ *noun* A new member of the armed forces or of an organization or group.
re·cruit (rĭ **kroot′**) ◊ *verb* **recruited, recruiting** ◊ *noun, plural* **recruits**

R

rectangle *noun* A geometric figure that has four sides and four right angles.
rec·tan·gle (**rĕk′**tăng′gəl) ◊ *noun, plural* **rectangles**

rectangular *adjective* Shaped like a rectangle: *The new rose garden we designed is rectangular.*
rec·tan·gu·lar (rĕk-**tăng′**gyə lər) ◊ *adjective*

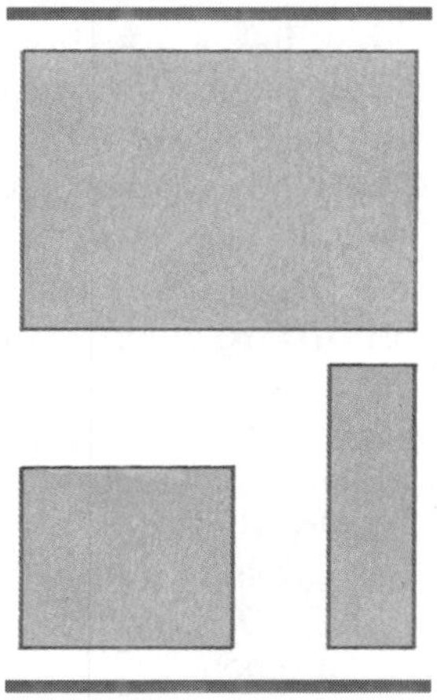

▲ **rectangle**

recur *verb* To appear or happen again: *They live in an area where earthquakes recur.*
re·cur (rĭ **kûr′**) ◊ *verb* **recurred, recurring**

recycle *verb* To treat materials that have been thrown away in order to use them again: *The city recycles glass, cans, and newspapers.*
re·cy·cle (rē **sī′**kəl) ◊ *verb* **recycled, recycling**

red *noun* The color of blood or of a ruby. ◊ *adjective* Of the color red.
red (rĕd) ◊ *noun, plural* **reds** ◊ *adjective* **redder, reddest**

red blood cell *noun* One of the reddish cells that are in the blood and contain hemoglobin. Red blood cells carry oxygen to the tissues.
red blood cell ◊ *noun, plural* **red blood cells**

redcoat *noun* A British soldier during the American Revolution and the War of 1812.
red·coat (**rĕd′**kōt′) ◊ *noun, plural* **redcoats**

red-handed *adverb* In the act of doing wrong: *They were caught red-handed.*
red-hand·ed (**rĕd′hăn′**dĭd) ◊ *adverb*

reduce *verb* **1.** To make or become smaller or less: *Stores often reduce prices after Christmas.* **2.** To lose body weight by dieting. —See Synonyms at **decrease.**
re·duce (rĭ **do͞os′** *or* rĭ **dyo͞os′**) ◊ *verb* **reduced, reducing**

ă	pat	ĭ	pit	oi	**oi**l	th	ba**th**
ā	pay	ī	ride	o͝o	b**oo**k	*th*	ba**th**e
â	care	î	fierce	o͞o	b**oo**t	ə	**a**go, it**e**m
ä	father	ŏ	pot	ou	**ou**t		penc**i**l
ĕ	pet	ō	go	ŭ	c**u**t		at**o**m
ē	be	ô	paw, for	û	f**u**r		circ**u**s

reduction *noun* **1.** The act or process of reducing. **2.** The amount by which something is reduced.
re·duc·tion (rĭ **dŭk′**shən) ◊ *noun, plural* **reductions**

redwood *noun* A very tall evergreen tree of northwestern California that has reddish-brown wood and bears cones.
red·wood (**rĕd′**wo͝od′) ◊ *noun, plural* **redwoods**

reed *noun* **1.** Any of several tall grasses with hollow stems that grow in wet places. **2.** A springy strip of cane or metal used in the mouthpiece of certain musical instruments. The reed vibrates when air passes over it. **3.** A musical instrument, such as an oboe or clarinet, that is played with a reed.
reed (rēd) ◊ *noun, plural* **reeds**
‖*These sound alike:* **reed, read**

reef *noun* A strip or ridge of rock, sand, or coral that rises to or close to the surface of a body of water.
reef (rēf) ◊ *noun, plural* **reefs**

reel[1] *noun* **1.** A spoollike device that is used for winding something flexible, such as fishing line or film. **2.** A fast, lively folk dance. ◊ *verb* **1.** To wind onto a reel. **2.** To pull in by winding on a reel: *I reeled in a fish that weighed 10 pounds.*
reel[1] (rēl) ◊ *noun, plural* **reels** ◊ *verb* **reeled, reeling**

▲ **reel[1]**

reel[2] *verb* **1.** To move or stand in an unsteady way: *I reeled when the ball hit me.* **2.** To whirl round and round: *The events of the day reeled in my mind.*
reel[2] (rēl) ◊ *verb* **reeled, reeling**

HISTORY • reel[1], reel[2]

Reel[1] comes from an old English word that meant "spool." **Reel[2]** may be a verb made from **reel[1]**.

re-elect *verb* To elect for another term.
re•e•lect (rē′ĭ **lĕkt′**) ◊ *verb* **re-elected, re-electing**

re-entry *noun* The return of a missile or spacecraft to the earth's atmosphere.
re-en•try (rē **ĕn′**trē) ◊ *noun, plural* **re-entries**

refer *verb* **1.** To direct a person or thing to for help or information: *The librarian referred us to the dictionary.* **2.** To turn for information: *Refer to the map on page 74.* **3.** To call or direct attention: *Are you referring to the comment I made?*
re•fer (rĭ **fûr′**) ◊ *verb* **referred, referring**

referee *noun* An official who enforces the rules in a sports contest.
◊ *verb* To judge or act as a referee.
ref•e•ree (rĕf′ə **rē′**) ◊ *noun, plural* **referees** ◊ *verb* **refereed, refereeing**

reference *noun* **1.** A mention: *They made many references to their trip to Europe.* **2.** A note in a book that directs the reader to another part of the book or to another source of information. **3.** A usually written statement about a person's character or ability.
◊ *idiom* **in** *or* **with reference to** In regard to: *Have you received an answer in reference to your question?*
ref•er•ence (**rĕf′**ər əns) ◊ *noun, plural* **references**

reference book *noun* A book, such as an encyclopedia or dictionary, that gives special information arranged according to a plan or system.
reference book ◊ *noun, plural* **reference books**

refill *verb* To fill again: *I used all the ice cubes and forgot to refill the tray.*
◊ *noun* A replacement for something that has been used up.
re•fill ◊ *verb* (rē **fĭl′**) **refilled, refilling** ◊ *noun* (**rē′**fĭl′), *plural* **refills**

refine *verb* To remove unwanted matter from a substance, such as oil or sugar.
re•fine (rĭ **fīn′**) ◊ *verb* **refined, refining**

refinery *noun* A factory for refining raw materials, such as oil, sugar, or metals.
re•fin•er•y (rĭ **fī′**nə rē) ◊ *noun, plural* **refineries**

reflect *verb* **1.** To send back light rays, heat, or sound from a surface: *The hood of a shiny new car reflects light.* **2.** To give back an image of, as a mirror does. **3.** To think seriously: *Be sure you reflect on the problem before deciding what to do.* **4.** To bring blame or discredit to: *A young person's bad behavior will often reflect on the parents.*
re•flect (rĭ **flĕkt′**) ◊ *verb* **reflected, reflecting**

reflection *noun* **1.** The act or process of reflecting light, heat, or sound from a surface. **2.** An image formed by reflected light: *The deer gazed at its reflection in the forest pool.* **3.** Something that brings blame or discredit: *Your saying that I lied is a reflection on my good name.* **4.** Serious thought: *After long reflection we decided to buy the electric train.*
re•flec•tion (rĭ **flĕk′**shən) ◊ *noun, plural* **reflections**

reflector *noun* A shiny surface or device for reflecting light or heat.
re•flec•tor (rĭ **flĕk′**tər) ◊ *noun, plural* **reflectors**

reflex *noun* An automatic response that occurs when a nerve or sense organ is stimulated. Blinking and sneezing are reflexes.
re•flex (**rē′**flĕks′) ◊ *noun, plural* **reflexes**

reforest *verb* To plant again with trees.
re•for•est (rē **fôr′**ĭst) ◊ *verb* **reforested, reforesting**

reform *verb* To make or become better by getting rid of faults: *Congress is working to reform the tax system.*
◊ *noun* An act, process, or example of making something better; improvement.
re•form (rĭ **fôrm′**) ◊ *verb* **reformed, reforming** ◊ *noun, plural* **reforms**

reformation *noun* The act of reforming or the condition of being reformed.
ref•or•ma•tion (rĕf′ər **mā′**shən) ◊ *noun, plural* **reformations**

refrain *noun* A phrase or verse that is repeated regularly in a song or poem.
re•frain (rĭ **frān′**) ◊ *noun, plural* **refrains**

refresh *verb* To make fresh again; renew.
re•fresh (rĭ **frĕsh′**) ◊ *verb* **refreshed, refreshing**

R

refreshment *noun* **1.** The act of refreshing or condition of being refreshed. **2. refreshments** Food and drink.
re·fresh·ment (rĭ **frĕsh′**mənt) ◊ *noun, plural* **refreshments**

refrigerate *verb* To make or keep food or beverages cool or cold.
re·frig·er·ate (rĭ **frĭj′**ə rāt′) ◊ *verb* **refrigerated, refrigerating**

refrigerator *noun* A container, machine, or room for keeping something cold.
re·frig·er·a·tor (rĭ **frĭj′**ə rā′tər) ◊ *noun, plural* **refrigerators**

refuge *noun* **1.** Protection or shelter from danger or trouble. **2.** A place of protection or shelter: *There are many animals in the wildlife refuge.*
ref·uge (**rĕf′**yo͞oj) ◊ *noun, plural* **refuges**

refugee *noun* A person who escapes to another place to find refuge.
ref·u·gee (rĕf′yo͝o **jē′**) ◊ *noun, plural* **refugees**

refund *verb* To pay back: *The store refunded the full price of the broken television set.*
◊ *noun* **1.** The refunding of an amount of money. **2.** An amount refunded.
re·fund ◊ *verb* (rĭ **fŭnd′**) **refunded, refunding** ◊ *noun* (**rē′**fŭnd′), *plural* **refunds**

refuse¹ *verb* **1.** To decline to do or give: *The cat refused to go out in the snow.* **2.** To decline to accept: *They refused my offer of help.*
re·fuse¹ (rĭ **fyo͞oz′**) ◊ *verb* **refused, refusing**

SYNONYMS

refuse¹, ignore, reject

I *refuse* to go with you. They *ignored* my request and walked away. We *reject* your suggestion and don't want to talk to you about it anymore.

refuse² *noun* Something to be thrown away.
ref·use² (**rĕf′**yo͞os) ◊ *noun*

ă	pat	ĭ	pit	oi	**oil**	th	**bath**
ā	pay	ī	ride	o͝o	**book**	*th*	**bathe**
â	care	î	fierce	o͞o	**boot**	ə	**ago, item**
ä	father	ŏ	pot	ou	**out**		pencil
ĕ	pet	ō	go	ŭ	cut		atom
ē	be	ô	paw, for	û	fur		circus

HISTORY • refuse¹, refuse²

Refuse¹ comes from an old French word that in turn came from a Latin word meaning "to pour back." **Refuse²** is a noun formed from the same French verb that gave us **refuse¹**.

regain *verb* **1.** To get back: *I regained my health after a long illness.* —See Synonyms at **recover. 2.** To manage to reach again: *I regained the shore in spite of the surf.*
re·gain (rĭ **gān′**) ◊ *verb* **regained, regaining**

regal *adjective* Of, like, or appropriate for a king or queen; royal.
re·gal (**rē′**gəl) ◊ *adjective*

regard *verb* **1.** To look at. **2.** To consider in a particular way: *I regard my cousin as a good friend.* **3.** To show consideration for: *We must regard the rights of others.*
◊ *noun* **1.** Esteem or affection: *I hold my parents in the highest regard.* **2.** Consideration: *Have you no regard for others' feelings?* **3. regards** Good wishes; greetings.
re·gard (rĭ **gärd′**) ◊ *verb* **regarded, regarding** ◊ *noun, plural* **regards**

regarding *preposition* Relating to; concerning: *There are rules regarding absences.*
re·gard·ing (rĭ **gär′**dĭng) ◊ *preposition*

regardless *adverb* In spite of everything.
re·gard·less (rĭ **gärd′**lĭs) ◊ *adverb*

regardless of *preposition* In spite of: *Our parents love us regardless of our mistakes.*

regatta *noun* A boat race or races, organized as a sports event.
re·gat·ta (rĭ **gä′**tə) ◊ *noun, plural* **regattas**

regiment *noun* A unit of troops made up of two or more battalions.
reg·i·ment (**rĕj′**ə mənt) ◊ *noun, plural* **regiments**

regimental *adjective* Of or belonging to a regiment: *The troops were wearing the regimental colors.*
reg·i·men·tal (rĕj′ə **mĕn′**tl) ◊ *adjective*

region *noun* **1.** A usually large area of the earth's surface. **2.** An area without distinct boundaries.
re·gion (**rē′**jən) ◊ *noun, plural* **regions**

register *noun* **1.** An official written record or list. **2.** A device that automatically records or

displays a number or quantity. **3.** A device that can be adjusted to control a flow of air. ◊ *verb* **1.** To record in an official register. **2.** To show automatically, as on a scale or device. **3.** To reveal by the face or body: *I tried hard not to register emotion.* **4.** To get special handling of by paying more postage.
reg·is·ter (rĕj′ĭ stər) ◊ *noun, plural* **registers** ◊ *verb* **registered, registering**

registered nurse *noun* A nurse who has graduated from a school of nursing and has passed an examination given by the state.
registered nurse ◊ *noun, plural* **registered nurses**

regret *verb* To feel sorry about.
◊ *noun* **1.** A sense of sorrow or distress over a past event or act. **2. regrets** A polite reply turning down an invitation: *I sent my regrets.*
re·gret (rĭ **grĕt′**) ◊ *verb* **regretted, regretting** ◊ *noun, plural* **regrets**

regretful *adjective* Full of regret: *I am excited about going abroad but I am regretful about leaving home*
re·gret·ful (rĭ **grĕt′**fəl) ◊ *adjective*

regular *adjective* **1.** Usual or normal; standard: *Those shirts are $5.00 below the regular price.* —See Synonyms at **normal. 2.** Appearing again and again; habitual: *I am a regular customer of that store.* **3.** Happening always at the same time: *We have regular meals.*
reg·u·lar (**rĕg′** yə lər) ◊ *adjective*

regulate *verb* **1.** To control or direct according to rules: *The government regulates the printing of money.* **2.** To put in good order: *I need to regulate my watch.*
reg·u·late (**rĕg′** yə lāt′) ◊ *verb* **regulated, regulating**

regulation *noun* **1.** The act of regulating or the condition of being regulated. **2.** A rule or law.
reg·u·la·tion (rĕg′yə **lā′**shən) ◊ *noun, plural* **regulations**

rehearsal *noun* A private practicing, as of a play, in preparation for a public performance.
re·hears·al (rĭ **hûr′**səl) ◊ *noun, plural* **rehearsals**

rehearse *verb* To practice in preparation for a public performance.
re·hearse (rĭ **hûrs′**) ◊ *verb* **rehearsed, rehearsing**

reign *noun* **1.** The power or rule of a monarch. **2.** The time when a monarch rules.
◊ *verb* **1.** To rule as a monarch. **2.** To be widespread: *Silence reigned in the forest.*
reign (rān) ◊ *noun, plural* **reigns** ◊ *verb* **reigned, reigning**
‖*These sound alike:* **reign, rain, rein**

rein *noun* **1.** Often **reins** A long, narrow, leather strap attached to the bit of a bridle and held by the rider or driver to control an animal. **2.** A restraining influence: *The teacher kept the class under a tight rein.* **3. reins** Power to control or guide.
◊ *verb* To guide or control by or as if by reins.
rein (rān) ◊ *noun, plural* **reins** ◊ *verb* **reined, reining**
‖*These sound alike:* **rein, rain, reign**

reindeer *noun* A deer of Arctic regions of Europe and Greenland that has large, spreading antlers in both the male and female.
rein·deer (**rān′** dîr′) ◊ *noun, plural* **reindeer**

▲ **reindeer**

reinforce *verb* To make stronger with more material, help, or support.
re·in·force (rē′ĭn **fôrs′**) ◊ *verb* **reinforced, reinforcing**

reject *verb* To refuse to accept or consider: *The school paper rejected my article.* —See Synonyms at **refuse.**
re·ject (rĭ **jĕkt′**) ◊ *verb* **rejected, rejecting**

rejoice *verb* To feel or express joy.
re·joice (rĭ **jois′**) ◊ *verb* **rejoiced, rejoicing**

R

relapse *noun* The act or result of falling back into a previous condition, especially a return to illness after a change for the better.
re·lapse (rĭ **lăps′**) ◊ *noun, plural* **relapses**

relate *verb* **1.** To tell or narrate: *I related the story of our trip.* **2.** To have a relationship or connection to: *Every sentence in a paragraph should relate to the topic that is discussed.*
re·late (rĭ **lāt′**) ◊ *verb* **related, relating**

related *adjective* Connected by family.
re·lat·ed (rĭ **lā′**tĭd) ◊ *adjective*

relation *noun* **1.** A connection or association between two or more things: *There is a close relation between good grades and hard work.* **2.** A person who belongs to the same family as another; relative. **3. relations** Dealings or associations with others: *Our government wants peaceful relations with all countries.*
re·la·tion (rĭ **lā′**shən) ◊ *noun, plural* **relations**

relationship *noun* **1.** The condition of being related. **2.** A connection or tie: *We learned about the relationship between the moon and the tides.*
re·la·tion·ship (rĭ **lā′**shən shĭp′) ◊ *noun, plural* **relationships**

relative *adjective* **1.** Having a relation; relating: *The teacher made some comments relative to our history essays.* **2.** Considered in comparison with something else.
◊ *noun* A person related to another by family.
rel·a·tive (**rĕl′**ə tĭv) ◊ *adjective* ◊ *noun, plural* **relatives**

relax *verb* **1.** To make or become less tight or tense: *Try to relax your muscles.* **2.** To make or become less severe or strict: *The principal relaxed playground rules.*
re·lax (rĭ **lăks′**) ◊ *verb* **relaxed, relaxing**

relay *noun* A crew, group, or team that relieves another; shift.
◊ *verb* To pass or send along: *The television station relayed the program to Europe.*
re·lay ◊ *noun* (**rē′**lā′), *plural* **relays** ◊ *verb* (**rē′**lā′ *or* rĭ **lā′**) **relayed, relaying**

ă	pat	ĭ	pit	oi	**oil**	th	ba**th**
ā	pay	ī	ride	ŏŏ	book	*th*	ba*th*e
â	care	î	fierce	ōō	boot	ə	ago, item
ä	father	ŏ	pot	ou	**out**		pencil
ĕ	pet	ō	go	ŭ	cut		atom
ē	be	ô	paw, for	û	fur		circus

relay race *noun* A race in which each team member goes a part of the total distance.
relay race ◊ *noun, plural* **relay races**

▲ **relay race**

release *verb* **1.** To set free; let go: *When will the students be released from class?* **2.** To make available to the public: *The film was released last summer.*
◊ *noun* The act of releasing or the condition of being released: *Lawyers worked for the release of the prisoner.*
re·lease (rĭ **lēs′**) ◊ *verb* **released, releasing** ◊ *noun, plural* **releases**

relent *verb* To become softened in attitude: *My parents finally relented and bought me a new bicycle.* —See Synonyms at **yield.**
re·lent (rĭ **lĕnt′**) ◊ *verb* **relented, relenting**

relevant *adjective* Relating to the matter or discussion at hand; pertinent.
rel·e·vant (**rĕl′**ə vənt) ◊ *adjective*

reliable *adjective* Able to be relied on; dependable: *We need a reliable clock.*
re·li·a·ble (rĭ lī′ ə bəl) ◊ *adjective*

relic *noun* Something that survives from long ago: *We saw relics of ancient civilizations in the museum.*
rel·ic (rĕl′ĭk) ◊ *noun, plural* **relics**

relief *noun* **1.** A lessening of pain, discomfort, or anxiety: *I took the medicine for relief of my cold.* **2.** Assistance and help: *Volunteers brought relief to the flood victims.* **3.** A release from a job or duty: *The divers worked in two-hour shifts with a one-hour relief.*
re·lief (rĭ lēf′) ◊ *noun, plural* **reliefs**

relief map *noun* A map that shows the physical features of land, as with contour lines, shading, or colors.
relief map ◊ *noun, plural* **relief maps**

relieve *verb* **1.** To lessen or reduce pain, discomfort, or anxiety; ease: *Did the medicine relieve your headache?* **2.** To release from a duty or position by being or providing a substitute: *The security guard was relieved at midnight.*
re·lieve (rĭ lēv′) ◊ *verb* **relieved, relieving**

religion *noun* **1.** A belief in and the worship of God or gods. **2.** A particular organized system of such belief.
re·lig·ion (rĭ lĭj′ən) ◊ *noun, plural* **religions**

religious *adjective* **1.** Of or relating to religion. **2.** Following the beliefs of a religion.
re·lig·ious (rĭ lĭj′ əs) ◊ *adjective*

relish *noun* **1.** A desire for something; appreciation or liking: *I have no relish for that game.* **2.** Great enjoyment; pleasure: *I began the book with relish.* **3.** A mixture of chopped vegetables, olives, chopped pickles, and other spicy foods. Relish is used to flavor foods and as a side dish.
◊ *verb* To get pleasure from; enjoy: *We relished working on our science fair.*
rel·ish (rĕl′ĭsh) ◊ *noun, plural* **relishes** ◊ *verb* **relished, relishing**

reluctant *adjective* Not having an inclination; not willing: *We were reluctant to leave before the end of the movie.*
re·luc·tant (rĭ lŭk′ tənt) ◊ *adjective*

rely *verb* To have confidence: *Don't rely on others to do your work. We rely on your judgment.*
re·ly (rĭ lī′) ◊ *verb* **relied, relying**

> ***SYNONYMS***
>
> ***rely, depend, trust***
>
> We *rely* on them to help us around the house. You can *depend* on me even if other people let you down. I know you're telling the truth because I *trust* you.

remain *verb* **1.** To continue to be; go on being: *We remained friends even after I moved away.* **2.** To stay in the same place: *Please remain in your seats.* **3.** To be left: *Much work remains to be done.*
re·main (rĭ mān′) ◊ *verb* **remained, remaining**

remainder *noun* **1.** The remaining part; rest: *We'll spend the remainder of the year in the country.* **2.** The number left over when one number is subtracted from another: *If you subtract 17 from 19, you get a remainder of 2.* **3.** The number left over when one number cannot be divided evenly by another: *I divided 5 by 2 and got a remainder of 1.*
re·main·der (rĭ mān′ dər) ◊ *noun, plural* **remainders**

remains *plural noun* **1.** Something that is left over: *We ate the remains of the Thanksgiving turkey for a week.* **2.** A dead body.
re·mains (rĭ mānz′) ◊ *plural noun*

remark *noun* A casual statement; comment: *Your remarks about my performance were very complimentary.*
◊ *verb* To say or write casually; mention: *They remarked about the weather.*
re·mark (rĭ märk′) ◊ *noun, plural* **remarks** ◊ *verb* **remarked, remarking**

remarkable *adjective* That is worthy of notice; extraordinary: *The landing on the moon was a remarkable achievement.*
re·mark·a·ble (rĭ mär′ kə bəl) ◊ *adjective*

remedy *noun* Something used to relieve pain or cure a disease.
rem·e·dy (rĕm′ ĭ dē) ◊ *noun, plural* **remedies**

remember *verb* **1.** To bring back to the mind; think of again: *I could not remember how to stop the machine.* **2.** To keep carefully in one's memory: *Remember that we have to leave early tonight.* **3.** To give someone a gift or tip.
re·mem·ber (rĭ mĕm′ bər) ◊ *verb* **remembered, remembering**

R

remind *verb* To cause someone to remember or think of something: *Remind me to water the plants.*
re·mind (rĭ **mīnd′**) ◊ *verb* **reminded, reminding**

remote *adjective* **1.** Far away; not near: *The cruise ship sails to remote islands.* **2.** Distant in time or relationship: *The novel dealt with the remote past.* **3.** Extremely small; slight: *I haven't even a remote idea of what you are talking about.*
re·mote (rĭ **mōt′**) ◊ *adjective* **remoter, remotest**

remote control *noun* The control of an activity, process, or machine from a distance, especially by radio or electricity.

removal *noun* The act of removing or the condition of being removed: *I bought a special cleaner for the removal of spots.*
re·mov·al (rĭ **mo͞o′**vəl) ◊ *noun, plural* **removals**

remove *verb* **1.** To move or take from a position or place: *Remove the fruit from the box.* **2.** To take off or away: *The new cleaner removed the stains from my coat.*
re·move (rĭ **mo͞ov′**) ◊ *verb* **removed, removing**

render *verb* **1.** To cause to become; make: *The hail rendered the crop worthless.* **2.** To give or make available: *It's nice to render service to a friend.*
ren·der (**rĕn′**dər) ◊ *verb* **rendered, rendering**

renew *verb* **1.** To make new again; restore: *Fresh paint renewed the old barn.* **2.** To begin or take up again: *They renewed their old friendship.* **3.** To arrange for an extension of: *We renewed our lease for a year.*
re·new (rĭ **no͞o′** *or* rĭ **nyo͞o′**) ◊ *verb* **renewed, renewing**

rent *noun* A payment made at regular times for the use of something: *How much rent do your parents pay each month for your apartment?*
◊ *verb* **1.** To occupy or use another's property in return for regular payment: *I'm going to rent a bicycle for the day.* **2.** To let someone else use one's own property in return for regular payments: *We rented our house to the young couple.* **3.** To be for rent: *The house rents for a lot more in the summer months.*
rent (rĕnt) ◊ *noun, plural* **rents** ◊ *verb* **rented, renting**

repair *verb* To put back into proper or useful condition; fix. —See Synonyms at **mend.**
◊ *noun* **1.** The act or work of repairing: *Those cars are in need of repair.* **2.** The general operating condition of a machine or system: *They keep their truck in good repair.*
re·pair (rĭ **pâr′**) ◊ *verb* **repaired, repairing** ◊ *noun, plural* **repairs**

repeal *verb* To do away with officially or formally: *The senator voted to repeal the law.*
re·peal (rĭ **pēl′**) ◊ *verb* **repealed, repealing**

repeat *verb* **1.** To say, do, or go through again: *Please repeat your question.* **2.** To recite from memory: *Can you repeat the poem?*
◊ *noun* Something repeated: *This television program is a repeat.*
re·peat (rĭ **pēt′**) ◊ *verb* **repeated, repeating** ◊ *noun, plural* **repeats**

repel *verb* **1.** To drive off, force back, or keep away: *The knights repelled the attack.* **2.** To cause a feeling of dislike in; disgust: *Rude behavior repels me.*
re·pel (rĭ **pĕl′**) ◊ *verb* **repelled, repelling**

repent *verb* To feel sorry for what one has done or failed to do.
re·pent (rĭ **pĕnt′**) ◊ *verb* **repented, repenting**

repetition *noun* The act or process of repeating: *We learn many new words by repetition.*
rep·e·ti·tion (rĕp′ĭ **tĭsh′**ən) ◊ *noun, plural* **repetitions**

replace *verb* **1.** To take or fill the place of: *Automobiles replaced the horse and buggy.* **2.** To provide a substitute for: *We have to replace the broken window.* **3.** To put back in place: *I replaced the dishes in the cabinet.*
re·place (rĭ **plās′**) ◊ *verb* **replaced, replacing**

reply *verb* To say or give an answer: *I replied that I would go.*
◊ *noun* An answer or response: *I didn't hear your reply to my question.*
re·ply (rĭ **plī′**) ◊ *verb* **replied, replying** ◊ *noun, plural* **replies**

ă	pat	ĭ	pit	oi	**oil**	th	ba**th**
ā	pay	ī	ride	o͝o	book	*th*	ba*th*e
â	care	î	fierce	o͞o	boot	ə	ago, item
ä	father	ŏ	pot	ou	**out**		pencil
ĕ	pet	ō	go	ŭ	cut		atom
ē	be	ô	paw, for	û	fur		circus

report *noun* A spoken or written description of something: *I heard the weather report.* ◊ *verb* **1.** To present an account of: *We reported the accident to the school nurse.* **2.** To provide an account for publication or broadcast. **3.** To present oneself: *We report for school in September.*
re·port (rĭ **pôrt′**) ◊ *noun, plural* **reports** ◊ *verb* **reported, reporting**

report card *noun* A report of a student's grades and behavior. It is sent regularly to a parent or guardian by a school.
report card ◊ *noun, plural* **report cards**

reporter *noun* A person who gathers and reports news for a newspaper or magazine or for a radio or television station.
re·port·er (rĭ **pôr′**tər) ◊ *noun, plural* **reporters**

represent *verb* **1.** To stand for; take the place of: *The Romans used the symbol C to represent 100.* **2.** To act for: *They represent our state in Congress.*
rep·re·sent (rĕp′rĭ **zĕnt′**) ◊ *verb* **represented, representing**

representative *noun* **1.** A person or thing that is typical of others of the same class: *That building is a good representative of modern architecture.* **2.** A person who is chosen or elected to represent others: *I was our class representative on the student council.* ◊ *adjective* **1.** Made up of elected representatives: *A democracy is a representative government.* **2.** Being a typical example.
rep·re·sen·ta·tive (rĕp′rĭ **zĕn′**tə tĭv) ◊ *noun, plural* **representatives** ◊ *adjective*

reproduce *verb* **1.** To make a copy of: *This machine can reproduce a photograph in seconds.* **2.** To produce offspring.
re·pro·duce (rē′prə **do͞os′** *or* rē′prə **dyo͞os′**) ◊ *verb* **reproduced, reproducing**

reproduction *noun* **1.** The act or process of reproducing: *The reproduction of sound has improved immensely because of modern technology.* **2.** Something that is reproduced; copy: *I bought a reproduction of a famous painting for my room.* **3.** The process by which living things produce offspring.
re·pro·duc·tion (rē′prə **dŭk′**shən) ◊ *noun, plural* **reproductions**

reptile *noun* Any of a group of cold-blooded animals that creep or crawl on the ground. Reptiles have backbones and are usually covered with scaly skin. Snakes, turtles, and lizards are reptiles.
rep·tile (**rĕp′**tīl′) ◊ *noun, plural* **reptiles**

▲ **reptile**
Snakes and turtles are reptiles.

republic *noun* **1.** A form of government in which power lies with the voters. The voters elect representatives to manage the government. **2.** A country that has such a form of government. The United States is a republic.
re·pub·lic (rĭ **pŭb′**lĭk) ◊ *noun, plural* **republics**

republican *adjective* **1.** Of, like, or in favor of a republic: *After ten years under a dictator, the people of the country demanded a republican form of government.* **2. Republican** Of or relating to the Republican Party. ◊ *noun* **Republican** A member of the Republican Party.
re·pub·li·can (rĭ **pŭb′**lĭ kən) ◊ *adjective* ◊ *noun, plural* **Republicans**

Republican Party *noun* One of the two major political parties of the United States.

reputation *noun* The general worth or quality of someone or something as judged by others: *The senator has a good reputation.*
rep·u·ta·tion (rĕp′yə **tā′**shən) ◊ *noun, plural* **reputations**

request *verb* To ask for: *The teacher requested the children to sit down.* ◊ *noun* **1.** The act of asking for something: *Other sizes are available on request.* **2.** Something that is asked for: *We have received many requests for that toy.*
re·quest (rĭ **kwĕst′**) ◊ *verb* **requested, requesting** ◊ *noun, plural* **requests**

R

require *verb* **1.** To call for or need: *Tightrope walking requires considerable practice.* **2.** To demand; order: *The rules require us to take arithmetic, science, social studies, and language arts.*
re·quire (rĭ **kwīr′**) ◊ *verb* **required, requiring**

required *adjective* Called for or needed.
re·quired (rĭ **kwīrd′**) ◊ *adjective*

requirement *noun* Something needed or demanded: *Hard work is a requirement for success in school.*
re·quire·ment (rĭ **kwīr′**mənt) ◊ *noun, plural* **requirements**

rescue *verb* To save from danger or harm: *Lifeguards learn how to rescue swimmers.*
◊ *noun* An act of rescuing or saving.
res·cue (**rĕs′**kyo͞o) ◊ *verb* **rescued, rescuing** ◊ *noun, plural* **rescues**

▲ **rescue**

research *noun* Careful study of a subject or problem: *Medical research has saved many lives.*
◊ *verb* To do research on: *I am researching ancient Roman customs for my school paper.*
re·search (rĭ **sûrch′** *or* **rē′**sûrch′) ◊ *noun, plural* **researches** ◊ *verb* **researched, researching**

resemblance *noun* Similarity in looks: *The children have a great resemblance to their parents.* —See Synonyms at **likeness.**
re·sem·blance (rĭ **zĕm′**bləns) ◊ *noun, plural* **resemblances**

resemble *verb* To be similar to; be like: *This house resembles our last one.*
re·sem·ble (rĭ **zĕm′**bəl) ◊ *verb* **resembled, resembling**

resent *verb* To feel angry or bitter about: *I resent those remarks about my clumsiness.*
re·sent (rĭ **zĕnt′**) ◊ *verb* **resented, resenting**

resentment *noun* An angry or bitter feeling.
re·sent·ment (rĭ **zĕnt′**mənt) ◊ *noun, plural* **resentments**

reservation *noun* **1.** The act of reserving something, such as a hotel room or a seat on an airplane, in advance. **2.** Something that limits, restricts, or causes doubt: *I want to believe you, but I have some reservations about your story.* **3.** Land set apart by the government for a certain purpose: *My parents took me to see a wildlife reservation last summer.*
res·er·va·tion (rĕz′ər **vā′**shən) ◊ *noun, plural* **reservations**

reserve *verb* **1.** To set aside for a special purpose or for later use: *We reserve our best tablecloth for holiday dinners.* —See Synonyms at **keep. 2.** To arrange to buy or use in advance: *I reserved two seats for the concert next week.*
◊ *noun* **1.** A supply of something saved for later use: *We have a large fuel reserve for next winter.* **2.** A tendency to say little and keep one's feelings to oneself: *My parents are people of great reserve.* **3. reserves** The part of a country's armed forces not on active duty but ready to be called up in an emergency.
re·serve (rĭ **zûrv′**) ◊ *verb* **reserved, reserving** ◊ *noun, plural* **reserves**

reservoir *noun* A place where a large amount of water has been collected and stored for use.
res·er·voir (**rĕz′**ər vwär′) ◊ *noun, plural* **reservoirs**

reside *verb* To make one's home; live: *We reside in Los Angeles.*
re·side (rĭ **zīd′**) ◊ *verb* **resided, residing**

residence *noun* **1.** The house or other building that a person lives in. **2.** The act or fact of

ă	pat	ĭ	pit	oi	**oil**	th	**bath**
ā	pay	ī	ride	o͝o	**book**	*th*	**bathe**
â	care	î	fierce	o͞o	**boot**	ə	**ago, item**
ä	father	ŏ	pot	ou	**out**		pencil
ĕ	pet	ō	go	ŭ	cut		atom
ē	be	ô	paw, for	û	fur		circus

living somewhere: *I learned Spanish during my residence in Mexico.*
res·i·dence (rĕz′ĭ dəns) ◊ *noun, plural* **residences**

resident *noun* A person who lives in a particular place.
res·i·dent (rĕz′ĭ dənt) ◊ *noun, plural* **residents**

residential *adjective* Of or containing homes; suitable for residences: *Factories are usually not located in residential neighborhoods.*
res·i·den·tial (rĕz′ĭ **dĕn′**shəl) ◊ *adjective*

resign *verb* To give up or quit a position: *The treasurer resigned after twenty years with the firm.*
re·sign (rĭ **zīn′**) ◊ *verb* **resigned, resigning**

resignation *noun* The act of giving up or quitting a position: *The mayor announced the fire commissioner's resignation.*
res·ig·na·tion (rĕz′ĭg **nā′**shən) ◊ *noun, plural* **resignations**

resin *noun* A yellowish or brownish substance that oozes from certain trees and plants. Resin is used in making varnishes, lacquers, plastics, and many other products.
res·in (**rĕz′**ĭn) ◊ *noun, plural* **resins**

resist *verb* **1.** To work against; oppose: *The lock resisted our efforts to open it.* **2.** To withstand the effect of: *A plastic that resists heat was used in the machine.* **3.** To keep from giving in to: *I resisted the temptation to eat too much.*
re·sist (rĭ **zĭst′**) ◊ *verb* **resisted, resisting**

resistance *noun* The act or capability of resisting: *I catch colds frequently because my resistance is low.*
re·sis·tance (rĭ **zĭs′**təns) ◊ *noun*

resolution *noun* **1.** The quality of having strong will and determination: *The hikers began the trip with enthusiasm and resolution.* **2.** A vow or pledge to do something or to keep from doing it: *My New Year's resolution was to finish my homework on time.*
res·o·lu·tion (rĕz′ə **lo͞o′**shən) ◊ *noun, plural* **resolutions**

resolve *verb* **1.** To make a firm decision: *He resolved to study harder.* —See Synonyms at **decide. 2.** To find a solution to; solve; settle: *She resolved the problem by herself.*
re·solve (rĭ **zŏlv′**) ◊ *verb* **resolved, resolving**

resort *verb* To go or turn for help or as a means of achieving something: *Don't resort to tears to get your own way.*
◊ *noun* **1.** A place where people go for rest or recreation: *I went to a ski resort last winter.* **2.** A person or thing one turns to for help: *I would ask them to lend me money only as a last resort.*
re·sort (rĭ **zôrt′**) ◊ *verb* **resorted, resorting** ◊ *noun, plural* **resorts**

resound *verb* **1.** To be filled with sound: *The stadium resounded with cheers from the crowd.* **2.** To make a loud sound: *The music resounded through the hall.*
re·sound (rĭ **zound′**) ◊ *verb* **resounded, resounding**

resource *noun* **1.** Something that one can turn to for support or help. **2. resources** Money that is available or on hand: *We pooled our resources to buy the present.* **3.** Something that is a source of wealth to a country: *Forests are a great natural resource.*
re·source (**rē′**sôrs′ *or* rĭ **sôrs′**) ◊ *noun, plural* **resources**

respect *noun* **1.** A feeling of honor or esteem: *The children showed great respect for their elders.* **2.** Regard or consideration: *Good manners demand respect for other people's feelings.* **3. respects** Polite expressions of consideration or regard: *Please give your family my respects.* **4.** A particular detail or feature: *The two plans differ in one major respect.*
◊ *verb* To have or show respect for: *I respect your opinion even if I do not agree with it.*
re·spect (rĭ **spĕkt′**) ◊ *noun, plural* **respects** ◊ *verb* **respected, respecting**

respectable *adjective* **1.** Proper in behavior, character, or appearance: *Our new neighbors are very respectable people.* **2.** Worthy of respect: *Our team made a respectable showing even though we lost.*
re·spect·a·ble (rĭ **spĕk′**tə bəl) ◊ *adjective*

respectful *adjective* Showing proper respect: *I replied to the teacher's questions in a respectful manner.*
re·spect·ful (rĭ **spĕkt′**fəl) ◊ *adjective*

respectively *adverb* As regards each one in the order given: *Albany, Atlanta, and Augusta are, respectively, the capitals of New York, Georgia, and Maine.*
re·spec·tive·ly (rĭ **spĕk′**tĭv lē) ◊ *adverb*

R

respiration *noun* The act or process of inhaling and exhaling; breathing.
res·pi·ra·tion (rĕs′pə **rā′**shən) ◊ *noun*

respiratory system *noun* The system of air passages through which a living thing breathes. In human beings and land animals with backbones, these passages connect the nose and mouth with the lungs.
res·pi·ra·to·ry system (**rĕs′**pər ə tôr′ē) ◊ *noun, plural* **respiratory systems**

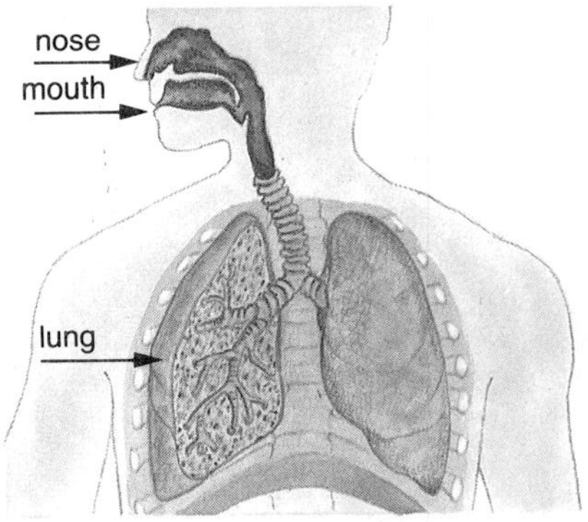

▲ **respiratory system**

respond *verb* **1.** To make a reply; answer: *I'll respond to your question in a minute.* **2.** To act in return or in answer: *How did our team respond to the challenge?*
re·spond (rĭ **spŏnd′**) ◊ *verb* **responded, responding**

response *noun* An answer or reply: *I haven't received a response to my letter yet.*
re·sponse (rĭ **spŏns′**) ◊ *noun, plural* **responses**

responsibility *noun* **1.** The quality or condition of being responsible: *You should accept responsibility for your actions.* **2.** Something that a person is responsible for: *Older brothers and sisters have more responsibilities than the young children do.*
re·spon·si·bil·i·ty (rĭ spŏn′sə **bĭl′**ĭ tē) ◊ *noun, plural* **responsibilities**

responsible *adjective* **1.** Having a certain duty or obligation: *We are responsible for cleaning our rooms.* **2.** Being the cause or source of something: *Viruses are responsible for many diseases.* **3.** Dependable; reliable; trustworthy: *A responsible student helps the teacher.* **4.** Involving important duties or obligations: *My cousin has a very responsible job in the government.*
re·spon·si·ble (rĭ **spŏn′**sə bəl) ◊ *adjective*

rest¹ *noun* **1.** A period when one stops doing something, relaxes, or sleeps: *The hikers stopped for a brief rest.* **2.** Sleep, ease, or relaxation resulting from this: *Be sure to get plenty of rest.* **3.** An absence of motion or an end to motion: *The kite came to a rest on the ground.* **4.** A pause in music.
◊ *verb* **1.** To stop doing something, relax, or sleep: *I like to rest after dinner.* **2.** To allow to relax: *Take off your shoes and rest your feet.* **3.** To place, lay, or lean on or against something else for support: *Rest the suitcase on the ground.* **4.** To lie or lean on a support: *My head rested on the pillow.* **5.** To fall or land: *Our gaze rested on the beautiful sunset.*
rest¹ (rĕst) ◊ *noun, plural* **rests** ◊ *verb* **rested, resting**

rest² *noun* **1.** The part that is left over; remainder: *I'll eat the rest of the fruit later.* **2.** (*used with a plural verb*) Those who remain; others: *We are staying, but the rest are going.*
rest² (rĕst) ◊ *noun*

***HISTORY* • rest¹, rest²**

Rest¹ comes from an old English word that meant both "sleep" and "a place for sleeping, a bed." **Rest²** goes back to a Latin word that meant "to stay behind."

restaurant *noun* A place where meals are served to the public.
res·tau·rant (**rĕs′**tər ənt) ◊ *noun, plural* **restaurants**

restless *adjective* **1.** Without rest or sleep: *I*

ă	pat	ĭ	pit	oi	**oil**	th	**bath**
ā	pay	ī	ride	ŏŏ	**book**	*th*	**bathe**
â	care	î	fierce	ōō	**boot**	ə	ago, item
ä	father	ŏ	pot	ou	**out**		pencil
ĕ	pet	ō	go	ŭ	cut		atom
ē	be	ô	paw, for	û	fur		circus

had a restless night and couldn't get to sleep. **2.** Unable to rest, relax, or be still: *The baby is restless.*
rest·less (rĕst′lĭs) ◊ *adjective*

restore *verb* **1.** To bring back into existence: *Their kindness restores my faith in people.* **2.** To bring back to an original condition: *Patient care restored the child to health.*
re·store (rĭ stôr′) ◊ *verb* **restored, restoring**

restrain *verb* **1.** To hold back by physical force: *The police restrained the enthusiastic crowds at the parade.* **2.** To hold back; check: *I managed to restrain my laughter.*
re·strain (rĭ strān′) ◊ *verb* **restrained, restraining**

restrict *verb* To keep within certain limits; confine: *We restrict our dog to the yard.*
re·strict (rĭ strĭkt′) ◊ *verb* **restricted, restricting**

restriction *noun* **1.** The act of limiting or restricting: *The swimming club is open to families in the neighborhood without restriction.* **2.** Something that limits or restricts: *Certain restrictions apply to all students.*
re·stric·tion (rĭ strĭk′shən) ◊ *noun, plural* **restrictions**

result *noun* Something that happens because of something else; consequence: *All this damage is a result of the tornado.* —See Synonyms at **effect.**
◊ *verb* **1.** To come about as a result of something: *Floods resulted from the hurricane.* **2.** To lead to a certain result: *Hard work results in success.*
re·sult (rĭ zŭlt′) ◊ *noun, plural* **results** ◊ *verb* **resulted, resulting**

resume *verb* To begin again, continue: *The play resumed after an intermission.*
re·sume (rĭ zo͞om′) ◊ *verb* **resumed, resuming**

retail *noun* The sale of goods directly to customers.
◊ *adjective* Of, relating to, or engaged in selling goods directly to customers.
re·tail (rē′tāl′) ◊ *noun* ◊ *adjective*

retain *verb* **1.** To continue to have: *Our team retained the championship this year.* —See Synonyms at **keep. 2.** To keep or hold in a particular place or position: *Certain plants retain much moisture in their leaves.*
re·tain (rĭ tān′) ◊ *verb* **retained, retaining**

retina *noun* A lining on the inside of the eyeball that is sensitive to light. The retina is connected to the brain by means of a nerve that carries images of things to the brain.
ret·i·na (rĕt′n ə) ◊ *noun, plural* **retinas**

retire *verb* **1.** To give up one's work, usually on reaching a certain age: *The player retired from baseball after a very successful career.* **2.** To go to bed.
re·tire (rĭ tīr′) ◊ *verb* **retired, retiring**

retiring *adjective* Shy and reserved: *The child is retiring in the presence of guests.*
re·tir·ing (rĭ tī′rĭng) ◊ *adjective*

retreat *verb* To move back in the face of an enemy attack; withdraw: *The soldiers retreated into the hills.*
◊ *noun* **1.** The act of withdrawing under enemy attack. **2.** The signal for such an act, made on a drum or trumpet. **3.** A quiet, private place: *My parents have a retreat in the country for summer vacations.*
re·treat (rĭ trēt′) ◊ *verb* **retreated, retreating** ◊ *noun, plural* **retreats**

retrieve *verb* **1.** To get back: *The player retrieved the ball from the opposing team.* —See Synonyms at **recover. 2.** To locate data or information in a file, library, or storage area and make it available for use, especially by means of a computer. **3.** To find and bring back game that has been shot.
re·trieve (rĭ trēv′) ◊ *verb* **retrieved, retrieving**

retriever *noun* A dog that can be trained to find and bring back game that has been shot.
re·triev·er (rĭ trē′vər) ◊ *noun, plural* **retrievers**

▲ **retriever**
A golden retriever

R

retrorocket *noun* A rocket engine used to slow, stop, or reverse the motion of an aircraft, spacecraft, or missile.
ret·ro·rock·et (rĕt′rō rŏk′ĭt) ◊ *noun, plural* **retrorockets**

return *verb* **1.** To go or come back: *We returned home after two weeks in Canada.* **2.** To bring, take, send, put, or give back: *I returned the book to him.* **3.** To give back in exchange for or as a reaction to something: *The baby returned my smile.* **4.** To appear or happen again: *Summer returns every year.*
◊ *noun* **1.** The act of returning: *We look forward to the return of the baseball season.* **2.** Interest or profit that is earned: *They received a good return on their investments.*
re·turn (rĭ tûrn′) ◊ *verb* **returned, returning** ◊ *noun, plural* **returns**

reunion *noun* A gathering of the members of a group who have been separated: *Our family has a yearly reunion.*
re·un·ion (rē yo͞on′yən) ◊ *noun, plural* **reunions**

reveal *verb* **1.** To make known; disclose: *Please don't reveal my secret.* **2.** To bring to view: *Your behavior reveals a lot about your character.*
re·veal (rĭ vēl′) ◊ *verb* **revealed, revealing**

revenge *verb* To injure or harm in return for an earlier injury or harm.
◊ *noun* **1.** The act or an example of revenging. **2.** An opportunity or wish to revenge.
re·venge (rĭ vĕnj′) ◊ *verb* **revenged, revenging** ◊ *noun*

revenue *noun* Money that a government collects, as through taxes.
rev·e·nue (rĕv′ə no͞o′ *or* rĕv′ə nyo͞o′) ◊ *noun, plural* **revenues**

reverence *noun* A feeling of awe and respect mixed with love.
rev·er·ence (rĕv′ər əns) ◊ *noun*

reverse *adjective* Being opposite in order, direction, position, or character: *Look at the reverse side of the page for the answer.*
◊ *noun* **1.** The opposite of something: *What you did is the reverse of what I told you to do.* **2.** The back or rear of something: *The picture is on the reverse of the page.* **3.** The mechanism, as a gear in a motor vehicle, that allows it to move backward.
◊ *verb* **1.** To turn or cause to turn in the opposite direction: *The band marched down the field, then reversed and marched back.* **2.** To turn inside out or upside down: *I reversed the fabric so I could iron the seams.*
re·verse (rĭ vûrs′) ◊ *adjective* ◊ *noun, plural* **reverses** ◊ *verb* **reversed, reversing**

review *verb* **1.** To examine or study another time: *Let's review the chapter before we take the test.* **2.** To write or give a critical report about. **3.** To make a formal inspection of: *The president reviewed the honor guard.*
◊ *noun* **1.** The act or process of studying again. **2.** The act or process of looking back on something; survey: *We listened to a review of the week's news.* **3.** A report that tries to determine the worth of something, as a book. **4.** A formal military inspection.
re·view (rĭ vyo͞o′) ◊ *verb* **reviewed, reviewing** ◊ *noun, plural* **reviews**

revise *verb* **1.** To look over and change in order to improve or correct: *Some textbooks are revised every two years.* **2.** To change or modify: *We had to revise our plans.*
re·vise (rĭ vīz′) ◊ *verb* **revised, revising**

revival *noun* **1.** The act or process of reviving or condition of being revived. **2.** A new presentation of an old movie or play.
re·viv·al (rĭ vī′vəl) ◊ *noun, plural* **revivals**

revive *verb* **1.** To bring or come back to life, consciousness, or strength: *When I listen to music my spirits revive.* **2.** To bring or come back into use: *The producer revived the old movie.*
re·vive (rĭ vīv′) ◊ *verb* **revived, reviving**

revolt *verb* **1.** To take part in a rebellion against a state, government, or ruler: *The colonies revolted against foreign rule.* **2.** To fill with disgust: *The smell of air pollution revolted us.*
◊ *noun* An act of revolting; rebellion.
re·volt (rĭ vōlt′) ◊ *verb* **revolted, revolting** ◊ *noun, plural* **revolts**

revolution *noun* **1.** A complete change in

ă	pat	ĭ	pit	oi	oil	th	bath
ā	pay	ī	ride	o͝o	book	*th*	bathe
â	care	î	fierce	o͞o	boot	ə	ago, item
ä	father	ŏ	pot	ou	out		pencil
ĕ	pet	ō	go	ŭ	cut		atom
ē	be	ô	paw, for	û	fur		circus

government or rule: *In the American Revolution we gained independence from England.* **2.** A sudden, complete change: *The invention of nylon caused a revolution in the textile industry.* **3.** Movement of one object around another: *How long does one revolution of the earth around the sun take?*
rev·o·lu·tion (rĕv′ə lo͞o′shən) ◊ *noun, plural* **revolutions**

revolutionary *adjective* **1.** Of, relating to, or connected with revolution: *Many of our ancestors fought in the revolutionary war.* **2.** Of, relating to, or marked by radical change: *The computer is a revolutionary device.*
rev·o·lu·tion·ar·y (rĕv′ə lo͞o′shə nĕr′ē) ◊ *adjective*

revolve *verb* **1.** To move in an orbit: *The earth revolves around the sun.* **2.** To turn or cause to turn on an axis; rotate.
re·volve (rĭ vŏlv′) ◊ *verb* **revolved, revolving**

revolver *noun* A pistol with a revolving cylinder that places the bullets in a position to be fired one at a time.
re·volv·er (rĭ vŏl′vər) ◊ *noun, plural* **revolvers**

reward *noun* Something that is offered, given, or received in return for a worthy act, service, or accomplishment: *You deserve a medal as a reward for your bravery.*
◊ *verb* To give a reward for or to.
re·ward (rĭ wôrd′) ◊ *noun, plural* **rewards** ◊ *verb* **rewarded, rewarding**

R.F.D. Abbreviation for *Rural Free Delivery.*

rheumatism *noun* A disease that causes pain and swelling in the muscles, bones, or joints.
rheu·ma·tism (ro͞o′mə tĭz′əm) ◊ *noun*

rhinoceros *noun* A large animal of Africa and Asia that has short legs, thick, tough skin, and one or two upright horns on its snout.
rhi·noc·er·os (rī nŏs′ər əs) ◊ *noun, plural* **rhinoceros** *or* **rhinoceroses**

HISTORY • rhinoceros

Rhinoceros comes into English through Latin from a Greek word for this animal. One part of the Greek word means "nose" and the other means "horn." This is not surprising since the outstanding thing about the *rhinoceros* is the one or two large horns on its nose.

▲ **rhinoceros**

rhododendron *noun* A shrub with evergreen leaves and clusters of white, pink, or purple flowers.
rho·do·den·dron (rō′də dĕn′drən) ◊ *noun, plural* **rhododendrons**

rhubarb *noun* A plant with large leaves and long reddish or green stalks that are cooked and used as food. The leaves of the rhubarb are poisonous.
rhu·barb (ro͞o′bärb′) ◊ *noun*

▲ **rhubarb**

rhyme *noun* **1.** Agreement in the final sounds of two or more words, syllables, or final lines of verse. **2.** A poem that has the same or similar sounds at the ends of lines.
◊ *verb* **1.** To agree or correspond in sound: *"Hour" rhymes with "power."* **2.** To make use of or have rhymes: *Not all poetry rhymes.*
rhyme (rīm) ◊ *noun, plural* **rhymes** ◊ *verb* **rhymed, rhyming**

rhythm *noun* **1.** A movement, action, or condition that repeats in regular sequence: *Notice the rhythm of the tides.* **2.** A musical pattern with a series of regularly accented beats.
rhythm (rĭth′əm) ◊ *noun, plural* **rhythms**

R

rhythmic *or* **rhythmical** *adjective* Of, relating to, or having rhythm.
rhyth·mic (rĭ*th*′mĭk) *or* **rhyth·mi·cal** (rĭ*th*′mĭ kəl) ◊ *adjective*

RI The abbreviation for *Rhode Island* used with a Zip Code.

R.I. An abbreviation for *Rhode Island.*

rib *noun* **1.** One of the pairs of long curved bones that extend from the spine toward the breastbone. The ribs enclose the chest cavity of human beings and most other vertebrates. **2.** Something, such as a curved timber in a ship's frame, that looks or functions like a rib.
rib (rĭb) ◊ *noun, plural* **ribs**

ribbon *noun* **1.** A narrow strip of fabric that is used to decorate or to trim things or tie packages. **2.** A long narrow band that is like a ribbon: *I had to change the typewriter ribbon.*
rib·bon (rĭb′ən) ◊ *noun, plural* **ribbons**

rice *noun* The grain from a cereal grass that grows in warm regions. Rice is an important food crop.
rice (rīs) ◊ *noun*

rich *adjective* **1.** Having much money or property. **2.** Consisting of, made of, or decorated with rare or expensive materials: *The curtains were made of rich brocade.* **3.** Abundantly supplied; plentiful: *Milk is rich in calcium.* **4.** Having many natural resources: *Texas and Oklahoma are states rich in oil and natural gas.* **5.** Producing abundantly; fertile: *We planted potatoes in the rich soil near the river.* **6.** Containing a large amount of fat or sugar: *Chocolate is richer than cocoa.*
rich (rĭch) ◊ *adjective* **richer, richest**

riches *plural noun* Great wealth in the form of money, land, or valuable possessions.
rich·es (rĭch′ĭz) ◊ *plural noun*

rickety *adjective* That is likely to fall apart or break: *Don't sit in that rickety old chair.*
rick·et·y (rĭk′ĭ tē) ◊ *adjective* **ricketier, ricketiest**

ricksha *noun* A small passenger carriage that has two wheels and is usually pulled by one person. Rickshas are used in the Orient.
rick·sha (rĭk′shô′) ◊ *noun, plural* **rickshas**

rid *verb* To free from something that is not wanted: *I tried to rid the house of dust.*
rid (rĭd) ◊ *verb* **rid** *or* **ridded, ridding**

ridden *verb* Past participle of **ride.**
rid·den (rĭd′n) ◊ *verb*

riddle *noun* A question or statement that is worded in a deliberately puzzling way so that it requires thought to figure out the answer.
rid·dle (rĭd′l) ◊ *noun, plural* **riddles**

ride *verb* **1.** To sit on and cause to move: *I ride my bicycle to school.* **2.** To be carried in a vehicle or on the back of an animal: *I'll drive the scooter; you can ride with me.* **3.** To be supported or carried on: *The swimmers rode the waves in to the shore.*
◊ *noun* **1.** A journey on the back of an animal or in a vehicle. **2.** A machine or device, as a roller coaster, that people ride on or in for fun.
ride (rīd) ◊ *verb* **rode, ridden, riding** ◊ *noun, plural* **rides**

ridge *noun* **1.** The line formed by two sloping surfaces that meet; crest: *A bird perched on the ridge of the roof.* **2.** A long, narrow chain of mountains or hills. **3.** A narrow raised strip, as in corduroy.
ridge (rĭj) ◊ *noun, plural* **ridges**

ridicule *noun* Words or actions intended to make fun of someone or something.
◊ *verb* To make fun of; mock.
rid·i·cule (rĭd′ĭ kyo͞ol′) ◊ *noun* ◊ *verb* **ridiculed, ridiculing**

ridiculous *adjective* Deserving or inspiring ridicule: *The clown's costume was so ridiculous that I couldn't help laughing.*
ri·dic·u·lous (rĭ dĭk′yə ləs) ◊ *adjective*

rifle *noun* A gun that has a long barrel.
ri·fle (rī′fəl) ◊ *noun, plural* **rifles**

rig *verb* **1.** To fit out; equip: *We rigged the barn window with canvas to keep the rain out.* **2.** To equip a ship with rigging. **3.** To make or build in a hurry or by using materials at hand: *We rigged up a tent with an old blanket.*
◊ *noun* **1.** The arrangement of masts, lines, and sails on a sailing vessel. **2.** Equipment for a special purpose; gear: *Our camping rig includes cooking pots and sleeping bags.*
rig (rĭg) ◊ *verb* **rigged, rigging** ◊ *noun, plural* **rigs**

ă	pat	ĭ	pit	oi	**oil**	th	ba**th**
ā	pay	ī	ride	o͝o	book	*th*	ba*th*e
â	care	î	fierce	o͞o	boot	ə	ago, item
ä	father	ŏ	pot	ou	**out**		pencil
ĕ	pet	ō	go	ŭ	cut		atom
ē	be	ô	paw, for	û	fur		circus

rigging *noun* The system of ropes, chains, and tackle used to support and control the masts, sails, and yards of a sailing vessel.
rig·ging (rĭg′ĭng) ◊ *noun*

▲ **rigging**

right *noun* **1.** The side or direction opposite the left: *The number 3 is on the right of the face of a clock.* **2.** Something that is correct, just, moral, or honorable: *People must be taught the difference between right and wrong.* **3.** A claim that is legal: *Citizens have the right to vote.*
◊ *adjective* **1.** Located on or directed toward the right: *I cannot write with my right hand.* **2.** In accordance with fact, reason, or truth; accurate: *I tried to think of the right answer.* —See Synonyms at **correct.** **3.** In accordance with what is correct or proper in a moral sense: *I always make an effort to do the right thing.* **4.** Appropriate; suitable: *The director found an actor who is just right for the part.*
◊ *adverb* **1.** To or toward the right: *Turn right here.* **2.** In a straight line; directly: *They walked right up to me.* **3.** In a correct manner; properly: *My watch isn't working right.* **4.** In the exact position or place; just: *The ball landed right where we were standing.* **5.** At once: *They left right after breakfast.*
◊ *verb* To bring or come back into an upright or proper position: *We righted the canoe.*
right (rīt) ◊ *noun, plural* **rights** ◊ *adjective* ◊ *adverb* ◊ *verb* **righted, righting**
‖*These sound alike:* **right, write**

SYNONYMS
right, privilege, title
In the United States we have the *right* of free speech. Only members of the club have the *privilege* of swimming in the pool. My parents have a *title* to several acres of land near here.

right angle *noun* An angle that is formed by two lines that are perpendicular.
right angle ◊ *noun, plural* **right angles**

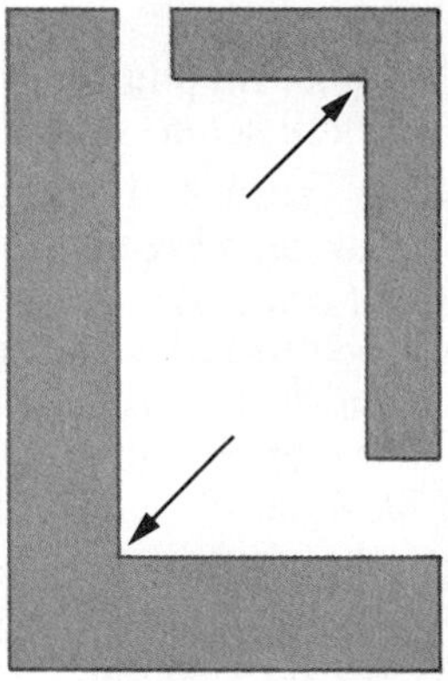

▲ **right angle**

rightful *adjective* Having a just, proper, or legal claim: *I am the rightful owner of that new bicycle.*
right·ful (rīt′fəl) ◊ *adjective*

right-hand *adjective* **1.** Being on the right: *All the pictures are in the right-hand margin of the page.* **2.** On or to the right: *The driver signaled for a right-hand turn.*
right-hand (rīt′hănd′) ◊ *adjective*

right-handed *adjective* **1.** Using the right hand more easily or naturally than the left. **2.** Done with or made for the right hand.
right-hand·ed (rīt′hăn′dĭd) ◊ *adjective*

right triangle *noun* A triangle that contains a right angle.
right triangle ◊ *noun, plural* **right triangles**

rigid *adjective* **1.** Not bending; stiff: *When you salute, keep your arm rigid.* **2.** Very closely enforced; strict.
rig·id (rĭj′ĭd) ◊ *adjective*

rigidly *adverb* In a stiff manner or way.
rig·id·ly (rĭj′ĭd lē) ◊ *adverb*

rile *verb* To anger or irritate; vex.
rile (rīl) ◊ *verb* **riled, riling**

rill *noun* A small brook.
rill (rĭl) ◊ *noun, plural* **rills**

rim *noun* The outside edge: *The rim of the antique bowl was chipped.* —See Synonyms at **border.**
rim (rĭm) ◊ *noun, plural* **rims**

R

rime *noun* A frost or coating of grains of ice, as on grass or trees.
rime (rīm) ◊ *noun, plural* **rimes**

rind *noun* A tough outer covering or layer, as of a lemon.
rind (rīnd) ◊ *noun, plural* **rinds**

ring¹ *noun* **1.** A circular band that is worn on a finger or is used to encircle or hold something. **2.** Something shaped like a circle: *Hold hands and form a ring.* **3.** An area where exhibitions or sports contests take place.
◊ *verb* To surround with a ring; encircle.
ring¹ (rĭng) ◊ *noun, plural* **rings** ◊ *verb* **ringed, ringing**
‖*These sound alike:* **ring, wring**

ring² *verb* **1.** To make or cause to give forth a clear piercing sound when struck: *The doorbell rang. We rang the doorbell.* **2.** To sound a bell in order to summon someone: *Ring for service at this counter.* **3.** To hear a persistent buzzing or humming: *My ears rang from the blast.* **4.** To call by telephone: *Don't ring me before breakfast.*
◊ *noun* **1.** The clear piercing sound made by a bell. **2.** A sound that resembles the ring of a bell. **3.** A telephone call.
ring² (rĭng) ◊ *verb* **rang, rung, ringing** ◊ *noun, plural* **rings**
‖*These sound alike:* **ring, wring**

HISTORY • **ring¹, ring²**

Ring¹ comes from an old English word for a circular object. **Ring²** comes from an old English word that was made up to imitate the sound it describes. **Ring²** was originally used most often to describe sounds like the clanking of armor.

ringlet *noun* A long curl of hair.
ring·let (rĭng′lĭt) ◊ *noun, plural* **ringlets**

rink *noun* An area with a smooth surface for skating.
rink (rĭngk) ◊ *noun, plural* **rinks**

ă	pat	ĭ	pit	oi	**oil**	th	ba**th**
ā	pay	ī	ride	ŏŏ	book	*th*	ba*th*e
â	care	î	fierce	ōō	boot	ə	ago, item
ä	father	ŏ	pot	ou	**out**		pencil
ĕ	pet	ō	go	ŭ	cut		atom
ē	be	ô	paw, for	û	fur		circus

▲ **rink**

rinse *verb* **1.** To wash lightly with water: *Rinse the dishes before putting them in the dishwasher.* **2.** To clear with a liquid, as water: *Rinse out your mouth after you brush your teeth.*
◊ *noun* The act or an example of rinsing.
rinse (rĭns) ◊ *verb* **rinsed, rinsing** ◊ *noun, plural* **rinses**

riot *noun* Disturbance created by a large number of people.
◊ *verb* To cause or take part in a riot.
ri·ot (rī′ət) ◊ *noun, plural* **riots** ◊ *verb* **rioted, rioting**

rip *verb* **1.** To tear or cut apart: *The sleeve ripped along the seam.* **2.** To remove by pulling or tearing roughly: *I ripped out the seams in the shirt.*
◊ *noun* A torn place.
rip (rĭp) ◊ *verb* **ripped, ripping** ◊ *noun, plural* **rips**

ripe *adjective* Fully grown and developed: *We ate ripe peaches for dessert.*
ripe (rīp) ◊ *adjective* **riper, ripest**

ripen *verb* To make or become ripe.
rip·en (rī′pən) ◊ *verb* **ripened, ripening**

ripple *noun* **1.** A small wave that forms when the surface of water is disturbed. **2.** A mark or motion that looks like a ripple: *When the horse ran, we could see the ripple of its muscles.* **3.** A sound like that of small waves: *We heard a ripple of laughter in the audience.*
◊ *verb* To form or cause to form ripples: *The*

wind rippled the hot desert sand.
rip·ple (rĭp′əl) ◊ *noun, plural* **ripples** ◊ *verb* **rippled, rippling**

rise *verb* **1.** To go up; ascend: *Hot air rises.* **2.** To get up from a sitting, kneeling, or lying position; stand up: *We all rose when the principal came in.* **3.** To get out of bed: *I rise at dawn every day.* **4.** To increase in number, amount, price, or value: *The temperature rose to 101 degrees.* **5.** To increase in intensity, force, or speed: *I could feel the wind rising.* **6.** To move ahead in position, rank, or importance: *Education will help you rise in the world.* **7.** To slope or extend upward: *The mountain rose thousands of feet above them.* **8.** To become visible above the horizon: *Each morning in the fall the sun rises a little later.* **9.** To resist authority; rebel: *The colonies rose against the empire.* **10.** To come into existence; originate: *Many streams rise in the mountains.* **11.** To puff up; swell: *Bread dough rises in a warm place.*
◊ *noun* **1.** An act or example of rising: *The senator's rise to power surprised us.* **2.** An increase in number, amount, value, or intensity. **3.** A gentle upward slope; hill.
rise (rīz) ◊ *verb* **rose, risen, rising** ◊ *noun, plural* **rises**

SYNONYMS

rise, climb, leap

Warm air *rises*. The airplane *climbed* rapidly in the sky. The basketball player *leaped* into the air for the rebound.
Antonym: *fall*

risen *verb* Past participle of **rise.**
ris·en (rĭz′ən) ◊ *verb*

risk *noun* The possibility of suffering harm or loss. —See Synonyms at **danger.**
◊ *verb* **1.** To expose to harm or loss: *I risked my life to save the drowning dog.* **2.** To take the risk of: *You risk an accident when you cross the street without looking both ways.*
risk (rĭsk) ◊ *noun, plural* **risks** ◊ *verb* **risked, risking**

ritual *noun* A system or form of ceremonies: *The ritual of inaugurating a new president is very grand.*
rit·u·al (rĭch′o͞o əl) ◊ *noun, plural* **rituals**

rival *noun* Someone who tries to do as well as or better than another; competitor.
◊ *adjective* Being a rival; competing.
◊ *verb* **1.** To compete or compete with: *Three candidates rivaled for the office of president.* **2.** To be the equal of: *Your talents rival your good looks.*
ri·val (rī′vəl) ◊ *noun, plural* **rivals** ◊ *adjective* ◊ *verb* **rivaled, rivaling**

river *noun* **1.** A large natural stream of water that is often fed by smaller streams flowing into it. **2.** A stream of liquid that looks like a river: *Rivers of lava flowed down the side of the volcano.*
riv·er (rĭv′ər) ◊ *noun, plural* **rivers**

rivet *noun* A metal bolt with a head at one end that is used to join two or more plates, pieces, or objects. A rivet is passed through a hole in each piece, and the plain end is hammered or compressed to form another head.
◊ *verb* To fasten with or as if with a rivet.
riv·et (rĭv′ĭt) ◊ *noun, plural* **rivets** ◊ *verb* **riveted, riveting**

roach *noun* A cockroach.
roach (rōch) ◊ *noun, plural* **roaches**

road *noun* An open way for vehicles, persons, or animals to pass along or through.
road (rōd) ◊ *noun, plural* **roads**
‖*These sound alike:* **road, rode**

roadside *noun* The area along the side of a road.
road·side (rōd′sīd′) ◊ *noun, plural* **roadsides**

roadway *noun* A road, especially the surface that vehicles travel on.
road·way (rōd′wā′) ◊ *noun, plural* **roadways**

roam *verb* To move around without a purpose or goal; wander.
roam (rōm) ◊ *verb* **roamed, roaming**

roar *noun* **1.** A loud, deep cry or sound, as that made by a lion. **2.** A loud, deep noise: *We heard the roar of a jet engine.*
◊ *verb* **1.** To utter or make a roar. **2.** To laugh very loudly.
roar (rôr) ◊ *noun, plural* **roars** ◊ *verb* **roared, roaring**

roast *verb* **1.** To cook or brown with dry heat, as in an oven. **2.** To make or be extremely hot: *We roasted in the desert sun.*
◊ *noun* A cut of meat for roasting.
roast (rōst) ◊ *verb* **roasted, roasting** ◊ *noun, plural* **roasts**

rob *verb* To take property or valuables from a person or place unlawfully and especially by force.
rob (rŏb) ◊ *verb* **robbed, robbing**

robbery *noun* The act or crime of robbing.
rob·ber·y (**rŏb′** ə rē) ◊ *noun, plural* **robberies**

robe *noun* **1.** A loose, flowing garment: *A judge's robe is usually black.* **2.** A dressing gown or bathrobe. **3.** A blanket, especially for the lap and legs.
◊ *verb* To dress in or as if in a robe.
robe (rōb) ◊ *noun, plural* **robes** ◊ *verb* **robed, robing**

robin *noun* A North American songbird with a rust-red breast and a dark gray back.
rob·in (**rŏb′**ĭn) ◊ *noun, plural* **robins**

robot *noun* A machine that can perform human tasks or imitate human actions. Robots sometimes look like human beings.
ro·bot (**rō′**bət) ◊ *noun, plural* **robots**

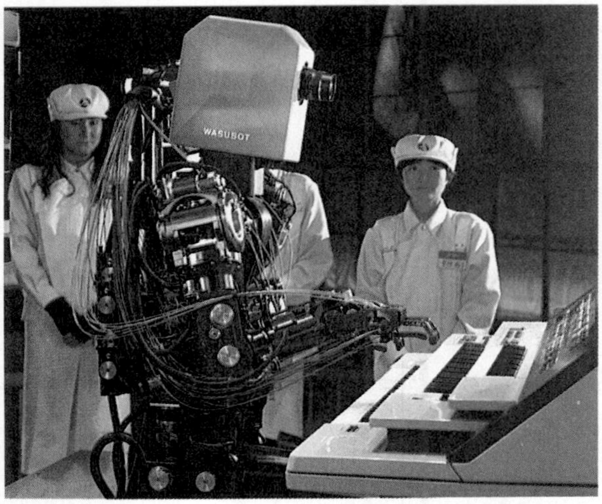

▲ **robot**

robust *adjective* Full of health and energy.
ro·bust (rō **bŭst′** *or* **rō′**bŭst′) ◊ *adjective*

rock¹ *noun* **1.** A hard, naturally occurring deposit of mineral. **2.** A large mass of stone. **3.** Naturally formed mineral matter that makes up an important part of the earth's crust.
rock¹ (rŏk) ◊ *noun, plural* **rocks**

rock² *verb* **1.** To move back and forth or from side to side: *A breeze rocked the hammock.* **2.** To shake violently, as from a shock or blow: *The earthquake rocked nearby villages.*
◊ *noun* **1.** A rocking motion. **2.** Rock 'n' roll.
rock² (rŏk) ◊ *verb* **rocked, rocking** ◊ *noun, plural* **rocks**

***HISTORY* • rock¹, rock²**

Rock¹ comes from an old French word for "a stone." **Rock²** comes from an old English word that meant "to move something from side to side."

rocker *noun* **1.** One of the curved pieces on which something, as a cradle or rocking chair, rocks. **2.** A rocking chair.
rock·er (**rŏk′** ər) ◊ *noun, plural* **rockers**

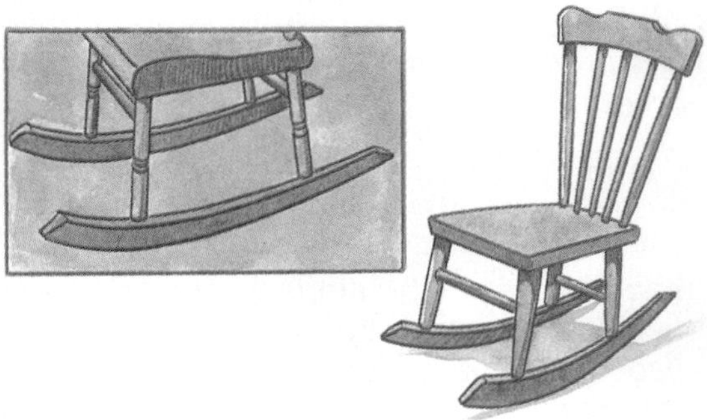
▲ **rocker**

rocket *noun* A device that is driven through the air by an explosive or by rapidly burning liquid or solid fuel. A rocket is tube-shaped, with one end open. Gases from the explosive or fuel escape from the open end. Large rockets carry space capsules into space.
◊ *verb* To travel very fast in or as if in a rocket: *The train rocketed by.*
rock·et (**rŏk′**ĭt) ◊ *noun, plural* **rockets** ◊ *verb* **rocketed, rocketing**

rocking chair *noun* A chair that is mounted on rockers.
rocking chair ◊ *noun, plural* **rocking chairs**

ă	pat	ĭ	pit	oi	**oi**l	th	ba**th**
ā	pay	ī	ride	o͝o	b**oo**k	*th*	ba**the**
â	care	î	fierce	o͞o	b**oo**t	ə	ago, item
ä	father	ŏ	pot	ou	**ou**t		pencil
ĕ	pet	ō	go	ŭ	cut		atom
ē	be	ô	paw, for	û	fur		circus

rock 'n' roll *noun* A form of popular music with a strongly accented beat and often very simple lyrics.
rock 'n' roll (rŏk′ ən **rōl′**) ◊ *noun*

rod *noun* **1.** A slender, stiff bar or stick. **2.** A rod used with a line for catching fish. **3.** A branch or stick used for whipping. **4.** A unit of length equal to 16½ feet.
rod (rŏd) ◊ *noun, plural* **rods**

rode *verb* Past tense of **ride.**
rode (rōd) ◊ *verb*
‖*These sound alike:* **rode, road**

rodent *noun* Any of several related animals, such as mice, rats, squirrels, and beavers, that have large front teeth used for gnawing.
ro·dent (**rōd′**nt) ◊ *noun, plural* **rodents**

rodeo *noun* A show in which cowboys and cowgirls display their skill in riding horses and steers and compete in events such as roping cattle.
ro·de·o (**rō′**dē ō′ *or* rō **dā′**ō) ◊ *noun, plural* **rodeos**

***HISTORY* • rodeo**

Rodeo comes from a Spanish word that meant "to go around." The word was first used as a term for a cattle roundup and only later as a term for an exhibition of riding and roping skills.

roe *noun* The eggs of a fish.
roe (rō) ◊ *noun*
‖*These sound alike:* **roe, row[1], row[2]**

rogue *noun* **1.** A tricky or dishonest person. **2.** A person who is playfully mischievous.
rogue (rōg) ◊ *noun, plural* **rogues**

role *noun* **1.** A part played by an actor: *I tried out for the role of the hero in the class play.* **2.** A part performed by a person or thing in real life: *I am busy in my role as a student.*
role (rōl) ◊ *noun, plural* **roles**
‖*These sound alike:* **role, roll**

roll *verb* **1.** To move along on a surface while turning over and over: *The coin rolled across the sidewalk.* **2.** To move along on wheels, on rollers, or in a vehicle with wheels: *Roll the wheelbarrow into the tool shed.* **3.** To turn over: *The dog rolled over onto its side. Pigs like to roll in the mud.* **4.** To wrap round and round; wind: *Roll the yarn into a ball.* **5.** To make flat or even by or as if by using a roller: *Dough must be rolled to make biscuits.* **6.** To move or flow in a steady stream: *Fog is rolling in from the ocean.* **7.** To sway or cause to sway from side to side: *The little sailboat rolled in the storm.* **8.** To make or cause to make a long, deep sound or a rapid, continuous beating sound: *Thunder rolled in the sky.* ◊ *noun* **1.** A rolling or swaying movement: *We felt the comforting roll of the ship.* **2.** Something that is rolled up into a cylinder or tube: *I bought a roll of paper towels.* **3.** A list of the names of the members of a group: *The teacher called the roll.* **4.** A rounded part, as a piece of baked bread dough. **5.** A long, deep sound or a rapid, continuous beating sound.
roll (rōl) ◊ *verb* **rolled, rolling** ◊ *noun, plural* **rolls**
‖*These sound alike:* **roll, role**

roller *noun* **1.** A small wheel, as on a roller skate. **2.** A cylinder around which something is passed or rolled: *We hung the kitchen towel on a roller.* **3.** A cylinder that is used to flatten, crush, or squeeze something. **4.** A cylinder for applying paint or ink onto a surface. **5.** A large wave that breaks along a shore.
roll·er (**rō′**lər) ◊ *noun, plural* **rollers**

roller coaster *noun* An elevated railway in an amusement park with steep slopes and sharp turns.
roller coaster ◊ *noun, plural* **roller coasters**

▲ **roller coaster**

R

roller skate *noun* A skate with four small wheels. Roller skates are used for skating on hard surfaces, such as pavement or floors.
roller skate ◊ *noun, plural* **roller skates**

roller-skate *verb* To skate on roller skates.
rol·ler-skate (**rō′**lər skāt′) ◊ *verb* **roller-skated, roller-skating**

rolling pin *noun* A cylinder, often of wood, that is used for rolling out dough.
rolling pin ◊ *noun, plural* **rolling pins**

Roman *noun* **1.** A citizen of the empire ruled by ancient Rome. **2.** A person who was born in or lives in modern Rome, Italy. **3. roman** A style of type with upright letters. The words in this sentence are printed in roman. ◊ *adjective* **1.** Of or relating to Rome, its people, or their culture. **2. roman** Of or printed in roman.
Ro·man (**rō′**mən) ◊ *noun, plural* **Romans** ◊ *adjective*

Roman Catholic *noun* A member of the Roman Catholic Church, a church that has ranks of priests and bishops and that is headed by the pope.
Roman Cath·o·lic (**kăth′**ə lĭk) ◊ *noun, plural* **Roman Catholics**

romance *noun* **1.** A long poem or story about the adventures of heroes and heroines. **2.** A quality of adventure, mystery, or excitement: *Jet planes have taken the romance out of traveling by air.*
ro·mance (rō **măns′** *or* **rō′**măns′) ◊ *noun, plural* **romances**

Romance language *noun* A language that developed from Latin. French, Italian, and Spanish are Romance languages.
Romance language ◊ *noun, plural* **Romance languages**

Roman numeral *noun* One of the numerals in the numbering system used by the ancient Romans. In this system symbols stand for numbers: I = 1, V = 5, X = 10, L = 50, C = 100, D = 500, and M = 1,000.
Roman numeral ◊ *noun, plural* **Roman numerals**

romantic *adjective* **1.** Of, relating to, or marked by romance: *I read a romantic novel.* **2.** Full of the quality or spirit of romance.
ro·man·tic (rō **măn′**tĭk) ◊ *adjective*

romp *verb* To play in a lively way; frolic. ◊ *noun* Lively play; frolic.
romp (rŏmp) ◊ *verb* **romped, romping** ◊ *noun, plural* **romps**

roof *noun* **1.** The outside top covering of a building. **2.** Something that is like a roof in form, position, or use. ◊ *verb* To cover with a roof.
roof (ro͞of *or* ro͝of) ◊ *noun, plural* **roofs** ◊ *verb* **roofed, roofing**

LANGUAGE DETECTIVE

roof

People all over the United States pronounce *roof* with the same vowel sound as in *tooth.* However, in some parts of the North a more common pronunciation of *roof* uses the same vowel sound as in *good.* If you live in the southern United States, you won't hear this second pronunciation very often. Other words with pronunciations like *roof* are *broom, hoop, room,* and *root.*

rook *noun* A chess piece; castle.
rook (ro͝ok) ◊ *noun, plural* **rooks**

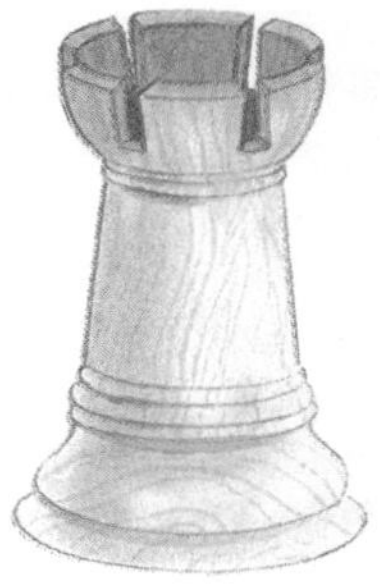
▲ **rook**

rookie *noun* **1.** A recruit who lacks training. **2.** A beginner.
rook·ie (**ro͝ok′**ē) ◊ *noun, plural* **rookies**

room *noun* **1.** Space that is or may be occupied: *There's room in our new car for five people.* **2.** An area of a building that is divided off by walls or partitions. **3.** An opportunity or chance to do something: *There's plenty of room for improvement in your work.*
room (ro͞om *or* ro͝om) ◊ *noun, plural* **rooms**

ă	pat	ĭ	pit	oi	oil	th	bath
ā	pay	ī	ride	o͝o	book	*th*	bathe
â	care	î	fierce	o͞o	boot	ə	ago, item
ä	father	ŏ	pot	ou	out		pencil
ĕ	pet	ō	go	ŭ	cut		atom
ē	be	ô	paw, for	û	fur		circus

roommate *noun* A person who shares a room or apartment with another or others.
room·mate (rōōm′māt′ *or* rŏŏm′māt′) ◊ *noun, plural* **roommates**

roomy *adjective* Providing plenty of room.
room·y (rōō′mē *or* rŏŏm′ē) ◊ *adjective* **roomier, roomiest**

roost *noun* A resting place, as a branch or rod, on which birds perch.
◊ *verb* To perch or settle on or as if on a roost.
roost (rōōst) ◊ *noun, plural* **roosts** ◊ *verb* **roosted, roosting**

rooster *noun* A fully grown male chicken.
roost·er (rōō′stər) ◊ *noun, plural* **roosters**

root¹ *noun* **1.** The part of a plant that usually grows down into the soil and that takes in water and minerals from the soil, stores food, and holds the plant in place. **2.** Something that is like a root in shape, position, or function. **3.** The point of origin or cause of something; source: *The root of our problem is lack of money.* **4.** A word or word element from which other words are formed by adding a suffix, prefix, or ending. *Hope* is the root of *hopeful. Fresh* is the root of *refresh. Bench* is the root of *benches.*
◊ *verb* **1.** To send out or start the growth of roots. **2.** To fix in place by or as if by roots: *I was rooted to the spot by surprise.*
root¹ (rōōt *or* rŏŏt) ◊ *noun, plural* **roots** ◊ *verb* **rooted, rooting**

root² *verb* To dig, dig up, or dig around with or as if with the snout: *Pigs root in mud.*
root² (rōōt *or* rŏŏt) ◊ *verb* **rooted, rooting**

root³ *verb* To encourage by or as if by cheering: *We rooted for the home team.*
root³ (rōōt *or* rŏŏt) ◊ *verb* **rooted, rooting**

***HISTORY* • root¹, root², root³**

Root¹ comes from an old Scandinavian word that had much the same meaning as it does today. **Root²** comes from an old English word meaning "to turn up soil with the snout." **Root³** is a fairly new word. It may be related to a Scandinavian word meaning "to roar."

rope *noun* **1.** A strong, thick cord made of braided or twisted strands, as of hemp or wire. **2.** A length or string, as of hair or beads, braided, twisted, or twined together: *I bought a beautiful rope of pearls.*
◊ *verb* **1.** To tie or fasten with a rope. **2.** To catch with a throw of a lasso: *We roped the calf.* **3.** To divide or set off with ropes: *The police roped off the playing field to keep back the crowd.*
rope (rōp) ◊ *noun, plural* **ropes** ◊ *verb* **roped, roping**

rose¹ *noun* **1.** Any of several prickly shrubs or vines with fragrant, usually red, pink, white, or yellow flowers. **2.** A deep pink color.
◊ *adjective* Deep pink.
rose¹ (rōz) ◊ *noun, plural* **roses** ◊ *adjective*

▲ **rose¹**

rose² *verb* Past tense of **rise**.
rose² (rōz) ◊ *verb*

Rosh Hashanah *or* **Rosh Hashana** *noun* The Jewish New Year, celebrated in September or October.
Rosh Ha·sha·nah *or* **Rosh Ha·sha·na** (rŏsh hə-shä′nə) ◊ *noun*

rosy *adjective* **1.** Having a deep pink color. **2.** Bright and cheerful; promising.
ros·y (rō′zē) ◊ *adjective* **rosier, rosiest**

rot *verb* To become or cause to become rotten; decay: *Meat rots if it is not refrigerated.*
◊ *noun* **1.** The process of rotting or the condition of being rotten. **2.** A destructive plant disease caused by certain fungi or bacteria.
rot (rŏt) ◊ *verb* **rotted, rotting** ◊ *noun*

rotate *verb* **1.** To turn on or as if on an axis; revolve: *The earth rotates once every day.* **2.** To take or cause to take turns: *The farmer rotated the crops in the field.*
ro·tate (rō′tāt′) ◊ *verb* **rotated, rotating**

R

rotation *noun* **1.** The act of rotating around a central point or axis: *The sun appears to rise and set because of the earth's rotation.* **2.** The changing of something, as crops or duties, by turns: *The rotation of kitchen chores meant that we each washed the dishes once a week.*
ro·ta·tion (rō tā′shən) ◊ *noun, plural* **rotations**

rotor *noun* **1.** A part of a machine that rotates. **2.** A system of rotating blades that enables a helicopter to fly.
ro·tor (rō′tər) ◊ *noun, plural* **rotors**

rotten *adjective* **1.** In a condition of decay; spoiled. **2.** Very bad or unpleasant; awful: *We had rotten weather for the picnic.*
rot·ten (rŏt′n) ◊ *adjective* **rottener, rottenest**

rouble *noun* A unit of money used in the Soviet Union.
rou·ble (ro͞o′bəl) ◊ *noun, plural* **roubles**

rouge *noun* A pink or red cosmetic used to color the cheeks or lips.
rouge (ro͞ozh) ◊ *noun, plural* **rouges**

rough *adjective* **1.** Bumpy or uneven; not smooth: *Hickory trees have rough bark.* **2.** Not perfectly made or finished; crude: *They built a rough model out of sticks and wire.* **3.** Not exact; approximate: *We made a rough guess that 300 people were at the game.* **4.** Not gentle or careful; rowdy: *Rough play can cause accidents.* **5.** Not calm; stormy: *The ship tossed on the rough seas.* **6.** Difficult or unpleasant: *I had a rough time during my first day at the new school.*
rough (rŭf) ◊ *adjective* **rougher, roughest**
‖*These sound alike:* **rough, ruff**

round *adjective* **1.** Shaped like a ball, circle, or cylinder. **2.** Having a curved surface or outline: *We sanded the corners of the board until they were round and smooth.* **3.** Expressed as an approximate amount: *They gave us an estimated price in round numbers.*
◊*noun* **1.** Something round in shape: *I sliced the carrots into rounds.* **2.** A regular course of places visited or duties performed: *Doctors make daily rounds of their patients.* **3.** A series of similar events or repeated acts: *There was a round of parties during the holidays.* **4.** Ammunition for a single shot from a gun. **5.** A period of play or competition in a sport or contest: *I won the first round in the tennis tournament.* **6.** A song for two or more voices in which each voice begins at a different time with the same melody.
◊*verb* **1.** To make or become round: *I rounded my lips to blow out the candles.* **2.** To go all or part way around: *They rounded the corner and disappeared.*
◊*adverb* About so as to face in the other direction; around: *The dancers spun round and round.* —See Synonyms at **around.**
◊*preposition* In a circle surrounding; around: *The children stood round the campfire and sang songs.*
◊*idiom* **round up 1.** To herd cattle or horses into a group. **2.** To look around for and bring together: *They rounded us up for lunch.*
round (round) ◊ *adjective* **rounder, roundest** ◊ *noun, plural* **rounds** ◊ *verb* **rounded, rounding** ◊ *adverb* ◊ *preposition*

round trip *noun* A trip to a place and back again.
round trip ◊ *noun, plural* **round trips**

roundup *noun* The herding together of cattle for branding or shipping to market.
round·up (round′ŭp′) ◊ *noun, plural* **roundups**

▲ **roundup**

ă	pat	ĭ	pit	oi	**oil**	th	**bath**
ā	pay	ī	ride	o͝o	**book**	*th*	**bathe**
â	care	î	fierce	o͞o	**boot**	ə	**ago, item**
ä	father	ŏ	pot	ou	**out**		pencil
ĕ	pet	ō	go	ŭ	cut		atom
ē	be	ô	paw, for	û	fur		circus

rouse *verb* **1.** To wake up; awaken. **2.** To stir up; excite.
rouse (rouz) ◊ *verb* **roused, rousing**

rout *noun* A big defeat.
◊ *verb* To defeat totally; crush: *We routed them by a score of 30–0.*
rout (rout) ◊ *noun, plural* **routs** ◊ *verb* **routed, routing**

route *noun* **1.** A road or lane of travel between two places. **2.** A series of places or customers visited regularly: *Twenty houses are on my paper route.*
◊ *verb* To send or pass on by a certain route: *We routed the package through Chicago.*
route (ro͞ot *or* rout) ◊ *noun, plural* **routes** ◊ *verb* **routed, routing**

routine *noun* A series of regular or usual activities; standard procedure: *Walking the dog is part of my daily routine.*
◊ *adjective* **1.** Done as part of a regular procedure: *I went to the dentist for a routine checkup.* **2.** Not special; ordinary: *We were tired of the routine food at camp.*
rou·tine (ro͞o **tēn′**) ◊ *noun, plural* **routines** ◊ *adjective*

row¹ *noun* **1.** A number of people or things arranged in a line. **2.** A line of seats, as in a classroom or theater.
row¹ (rō) ◊ *noun, plural* **rows**
‖ *These sound alike:* **row¹, roe, row²**

row² *verb* **1.** To move a boat with oars. **2.** To carry in a rowboat: *I rowed them to shore.*
◊ *noun* A trip in a rowboat.
row² (rō) ◊ *verb* **rowed, rowing** ◊ *noun, plural* **rows**
‖ *These sound alike:* **row², roe, row¹**

row³ *noun* A noisy quarrel or disturbance.
row³ (rou) ◊ *noun, plural* **rows**

HISTORY • row¹, row², row³

Row¹ comes from an old English word that meant "a line." **Row²** comes from a different old English word that meant "to use oars." **Row³** is a fairly new word. It may have been made up by British students a few hundred years ago.

rowboat *noun* A small boat moved by oars.
row·boat (rō′bōt′) ◊ *noun, plural* **rowboats**

▲ **rowboat**

royal *adjective* **1.** Of or having to do with a monarch: *The royal family led the procession.* **2.** Fit for a monarch; splendid: *We gave our team a royal welcome after their victory.*
roy·al (**roi′**əl) ◊ *adjective*

royalty *noun* **1.** Members of a royal family. Kings, queens, princes, and princesses are royalty. **2.** The rank or power of a monarch: *The crown is a symbol of royalty.*
roy·al·ty (**roi′**əl tē) ◊ *noun, plural* **royalties**

r.p.m. *or* **rpm** Abbreviations for *revolutions per minute.*

R.R. *or* **RR** Abbreviations for *Railroad.*

Rte. The abbreviation for *Route.*

rub *verb* **1.** To move back and forth against a surface: *The cat rubbed its back against my leg.* **2.** To press something against a surface and move it back and forth: *We rubbed the table with a clean cloth.* **3.** To put or spread on by rubbing: *Rub some stain on the boards.*
◊ *noun* An act of rubbing.
rub (rŭb) ◊ *verb* **rubbed, rubbing** ◊ *noun, plural* **rubs**

rubber *noun* **1.** A strong, elastic substance made from the milky sap of certain tropical plants. Rubber is waterproof and airtight. **2.** A low overshoe made of rubber.
rub·ber (**rŭb′**ər) ◊ *noun, plural* **rubbers**

rubber band *noun* An elastic loop of rubber that is used to hold objects together.
rubber band ◊ *noun, plural* **rubber bands**

rubber stamp *noun* A stamp made of rubber. It is pressed onto an ink pad and is used to print an image on paper.
rubber stamp ◊ *noun, plural* **rubber stamps**

R

rubbish *noun* **1.** Discarded or worthless material; trash. **2.** Silly talk or ideas; nonsense.
rub·bish (rŭb′ĭsh) ◊ *noun*

rubble *noun* Broken or crumbled material, as brick, that is left when a building falls down.
rub·ble (rŭb′əl) ◊ *noun*

ruby *noun* **1.** A deep-red precious stone. **2.** A deep red color.
◊ *adjective* Deep red.
ru·by (ro͞o′bē) ◊ *noun, plural* **rubies** ◊ *adjective*

rudder *noun* **1.** A movable board or plate that is mounted at the rear of a boat. The rudder is used in steering the boat. **2.** A movable piece in the tail of an aircraft that is used to steer it.
rud·der (rŭd′ər) ◊ *noun, plural* **rudders**

ruddy *adjective* Having a healthy pink or reddish color.
rud·dy (rŭd′ē) ◊ *adjective* **ruddier, ruddiest**

rude *adjective* **1.** Not considerate of others; impolite. **2.** Roughly or crudely made; primitive: *They built a rude boat out of logs.*
rude (ro͞od) ◊ *adjective* **ruder, rudest**

ruff *noun* **1.** A wide, round collar made of stiff cloth. **2.** A growth of long hair or feathers around the neck of an animal or bird.
ruff (rŭf) ◊ *noun, plural* **ruffs**
‖*These sound alike:* **ruff, rough**

ruffle *noun* A strip of gathered or pleated material, as ribbon or lace, used as a trimming.
◊ *verb* To disturb; upset: *The breeze ruffled the long grass. The shouting crowd didn't ruffle the pitcher.*
ruf·fle (rŭf′əl) ◊ *noun, plural* **ruffles** ◊ *verb* **ruffled, ruffling**

rug *noun* A piece of thick, heavy fabric used as a floor covering.
rug (rŭg) ◊ *noun, plural* **rugs**

rugged *adjective* **1.** Having a rough surface or jagged outline: *We flew over the rugged mountain peaks.* **2.** Very strong or durable; tough: *You need a rugged truck on these back roads.* **3.** Difficult; harsh: *Drilling oil wells is rugged work.*
rug·ged (rŭg′ĭd) ◊ *adjective*

ă	pat	ĭ	pit	oi	**oil**	th	ba**th**
ā	pay	ī	ride	o͝o	**book**	*th*	ba**th**e
â	care	î	fierce	o͞o	**boot**	ə	ago, item
ä	father	ŏ	pot	ou	**out**		pencil
ĕ	pet	ō	go	ŭ	cut		atom
ē	be	ô	paw, for	û	fur		circus

ruin *noun* **1.** Great damage or destruction; collapse. **2.** Total loss of one's money or social position. **3.** Often **ruins** The remains of something that has collapsed or has been destroyed: *We visited the ruins of the temple.*
◊ *verb* To damage beyond repair; wreck.
ru·in (ro͞o′ĭn) ◊ *noun, plural* **ruins** ◊ *verb* **ruined, ruining**

> ***SYNONYMS***
>
> ***ruin, destroy, wreck***
>
> You *ruined* my phonograph record by scratching it. The fire *destroyed* the house. We *wrecked* our sled when we hit the tree.

rule *noun* **1.** A statement or principle that controls behavior or action: *The school has a rule against running in the halls.* **2.** Something that is usually true; custom: *It is the rule among many farmers to get up before dawn.* **3.** The act or power of governing: *Democracy means rule by the people.*
◊ *verb* **1.** To have power or authority over: *The king and queen ruled the land for many years.* —See Synonyms at **govern. 2.** To make an official decision: *The judge ruled that the witness should testify.*
rule (ro͞ol) ◊ *noun, plural* **rules** ◊ *verb* **ruled, ruling**

ruler *noun* **1.** A person, as a king or queen, who governs a country. **2.** A thin strip of wood, metal, or plastic that is marked off into units of length. A ruler is used for drawing straight lines or for measuring.
rul·er (ro͞o′lər) ◊ *noun, plural* **rulers**

rumble *verb* To make or move with a deep, long rolling sound: *Thunder rumbled.*
◊ *noun* A deep, long rolling sound.
rum·ble (rŭm′bəl) ◊ *verb* **rumbled, rumbling** ◊ *noun, plural* **rumbles**

rummage *verb* To search thoroughly by turning things over or moving them around: *I rummaged in my desk for some paper clips.*
◊ *noun* A thorough search.
rum·mage (rŭm′ĭj) ◊ *verb* **rummaged, rummaging** ◊ *noun, plural* **rummages**

rumor *noun* A statement or story that is spread from one person to another and is believed to be true even though there is nothing to prove it: *I heard a rumor that you're moving away.*
◊ *verb* To tell or spread by rumors.
ru·mor (ro͞o′mər) ◊ *noun, plural* **rumors**
◊ *verb* **rumored, rumoring**

rump *noun* **1.** The fleshy part of an animal's body where the legs meet the back. **2.** A cut of meat, especially beef, from the rump.
rump (rŭmp) ◊ *noun, plural* **rumps**

run *verb* **1.** To move on foot at a pace faster than a walk. **2.** To carry while or as if while running: *The football player ran the ball six yards.* **3.** To move or travel quickly on foot or in a vehicle: *Run down to the store and pick up some fruit.* **4.** To move about freely; roam: *We let the dog run in the yard.* **5.** To leave in a hurry; flee: *I ran from the house.* **6.** To go from place to place on a regular route or schedule: *The trains are running slow today.* **7.** To cause to go; drive or chase: *The sheriff ran the outlaw out of town.* **8.** To be a candidate for elected office: *I decided to run for class president.* **9.** To pass through, over, or along: *I ran my fingers through my hair.* **10.** To get through or past: *The ship ran the blockade.* **11.** To do or accomplish by or as if by running: *I have to run some errands.* **12.** To flow or cause to flow in a steady stream: *Melted wax ran over the candlestick. The ink ran when the paper got wet.* **13.** To extend in space or time; stretch: *The road runs down to the lake. The president's term of office runs for four years.* **14.** To function or cause to function: *We bought a car with an engine that runs well.* **15.** To manage or direct; control: *Who's running the store?* **16.** To tear or ravel along a line: *The stocking ran.*
◊ *noun* **1.** A pace faster than a walk. **2.** An act or period of running: *We went for a run in the park.* **3.** A journey or the distance covered in a journey, especially one on a regular or scheduled route. **4.** A slope or track, as one on which people ski. **5.** Freedom to move about or use a place: *We had the run of the kitchen.* **6.** A continuous extent, series, or sequence: *The team had a run of nine victories.* **7.** A length of raveled or torn stitches in fabric: *I have a run in my stocking.*
◊ *idioms* **run across** To meet or find by chance: *I ran across my friend at the library.* **run into** To run across: *I ran into an old friend.* **run out** To become used up; be exhausted: *Our fuel ran out.*
run (rŭn) ◊ *verb* **ran, run, running** ◊ *noun, plural* **runs**

runaway *noun* A person who has run away, as from home.
◊ *adjective* Running or having run away.
run·a·way (rŭn′ə wā′) ◊ *noun, plural* **runaways** ◊ *adjective*

run-down *adjective* **1.** Badly maintained and in poor condition: *The new owner fixed up the run-down tenement.* **2.** Lacking energy; exhausted: *I feel run-down from overwork.*
run-down (rŭn′doun′) ◊ *adjective*

rung[1] *noun* **1.** A bar that forms a step of a ladder. **2.** A shaped piece that connects and supports the legs of a chair.
rung[1] (rŭng) ◊ *noun, plural* **rungs**
‖*These sound alike:* **rung, wrung**

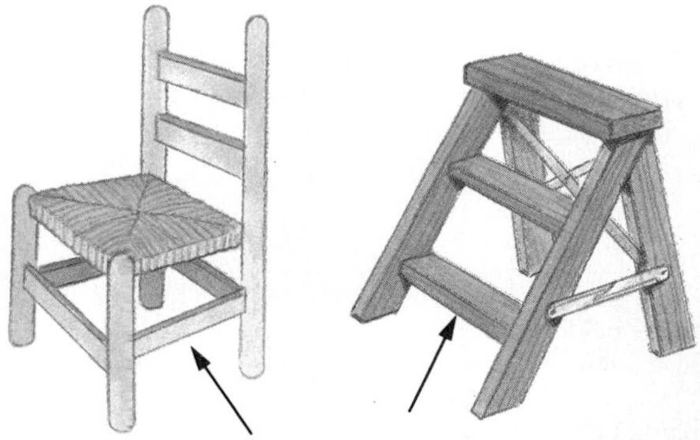

▲ **rung**[1]

rung[2] *verb* Past participle of **ring**[2].
rung[2] (rŭng) ◊ *verb*
‖*These sound alike:* **rung, wrung**

runner *noun* **1.** Someone or something that runs. **2.** A part, as a blade of an ice skate, on or in which something slides. **3.** A creeping stem of a plant that sends out roots to produce new plants. **4.** A long, narrow carpet, as one for covering a flight of stairs.
run·ner (rŭn′ər) ◊ *noun, plural* **runners**

runner-up *noun* A contestant that takes second place, as in an election or a race.
run·ner-up (rŭn′ər ŭp′) ◊ *noun, plural* **runners-up** *or* **runner-ups**

R

runt *noun* Something, as an animal or plant, that is smaller than usual.
runt (rŭnt) ◊ *noun, plural* **runts**

runway *noun* A strip of level ground, usually paved, on which aircraft take off and land.
run·way (**rŭn′** wā′) ◊ *noun, plural* **runways**

rupture *noun* The act or process of breaking open or bursting.
◊ *verb* To break, burst, or break off.
rup·ture (**rŭp′** chər) ◊ *noun, plural* **ruptures**
◊ *verb* **ruptured, rupturing**

rural *adjective* Of, relating to, or characteristic of the country, country people, or life in the country: *Our family lives in a rural area.*
ru·ral (**ro͝or′** əl) ◊ *adjective*

rush *verb* **1.** To move or act quickly; hurry: *Fire engines rushed past us.* **2.** To act or cause to act too quickly: *Don't rush into a decision yet.* **3.** To force, push, or send with speed or haste: *We rushed supplies to the scene of the accident.*
◊ *noun* **1.** The act of rushing. **2.** A flurry of speed or activity: *You left in such a rush that you forgot your wallet.*
◊ *adjective* Requiring or done with speed: *We received a rush order for the books.*
rush (rŭsh) ◊ *verb* **rushed, rushing** ◊ *noun, plural* **rushes** ◊ *adjective*

ă	pat	ĭ	pit	oi	**oil**	th	ba**th**
ā	pay	ī	ride	o͝o	b**oo**k	*th*	ba**th**e
â	care	î	fierce	o͞o	b**oo**t	ə	ago, item
ä	father	ŏ	pot	ou	**out**		pencil
ĕ	pet	ō	go	ŭ	cut		atom
ē	be	ô	paw, for	û	fur		circus

Russian *noun* **1.** A person who was born in or lives in the Soviet Union. **2.** The language of the Russians.
◊ *adjective* Of or relating to the Soviet Union, Russia, the Russians, or their language.
Rus·sian (**rŭsh′** ən) ◊ *noun, plural* **Russians**
◊ *adjective*

rust *noun* **1.** A reddish-brown coating that forms on metal, such as iron, when it is exposed to air and moisture. **2.** A plant disease in which reddish or brownish spots form on leaves and stems.
◊ *verb* To become or cause to become rusty.
rust (rŭst) ◊ *noun* ◊ *verb* **rusted, rusting**

rustle *verb* **1.** To make, cause to make, or move with a soft fluttering sound: *The leaves rustled in the wind.* **2.** To steal cattle.
◊ *noun* A soft fluttering sound.
rus·tle (**rŭs′** əl) ◊ *verb* **rustled, rustling**
◊ *noun, plural* **rustles**

rusty *adjective* **1.** Covered or coated with rust: *I found a rusty iron box.* **2.** Weaker, slower, or less skilled because of lack of use or practice: *My French is rusty.*
rust·y (**rŭs′** tē) ◊ *adjective* **rustier, rustiest**

rut *noun* **1.** A track, as in a dirt road, made especially by the passage of vehicles with wheels. **2.** A habitual or usual way of acting, doing, or living; routine.
rut (rŭt) ◊ *noun, plural* **ruts**

ruthless *adjective* Having or showing no pity; cruel.
ruth·less (**ro͞oth′** lĭs) ◊ *adjective*

rye *noun* A cereal grass whose seeds are used for making flour.
rye (rī) ◊ *noun*

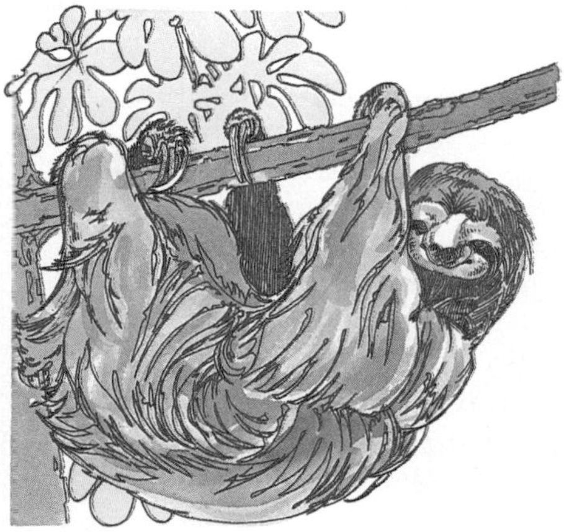

Sloth

Ss

S is the nineteenth letter of the English alphabet. Did you know that it has a long history?

W Over 3,500 years ago, people in the Middle East were using symbols that became the letters of our alphabet. This ancient Middle Eastern symbol is a form of the letter that became our letter *S*.

Σ The ancient Greeks borrowed their alphabet from people in the Middle East. Here is a form of the Greek letter that became our letter *S*.

S The ancient Romans borrowed their alphabet from a people who had taken their own letter symbols from the Greeks. Here is a form of the Roman letter *S* that was used for carving letters into stone. These letters became the model for our printed capital letters.

s As people wrote quickly, especially with pens, the capital letters began to take the shapes of small letters. Here is a small-letter *s* that was developed about 1,200 years ago.

Ss *Ss*	Ss	Ss	Ss
Handwriting	Sans Serif Type	Serif Type	Computer Printing

S *or* **S** *noun* The nineteenth letter of the English alphabet.
s *or* **S** (ĕs) ◊ *noun, plural* **s's** *or* **S's**

S. *or* **S** Abbreviations for *South.*

Sabbath *noun* A day of the week devoted to rest and worship. The Sabbath is Sunday for most Christians and Saturday for Jews.
Sab·bath (săb′əth) ◊ *noun, plural* **Sabbaths**

saber *noun* A heavy cavalry sword that has a slightly curved blade with a single edge.
sa·ber (sā′bər) ◊ *noun, plural* **sabers**

sable *noun* An animal of northern Europe and Asia with soft, dark, valuable fur.
sa·ble (sā′bəl) ◊ *noun, plural* **sables**

sabotage *noun* The deliberate destruction of enemy property in time of war.
◊ *verb* To damage by sabotage.
sab·o·tage (săb′ə täzh′) ◊ *noun* ◊ *verb* **sabotaged, sabotaging**

sac *noun* An animal or plant part that is like a bag or pouch.
sac (săk) ◊ *noun, plural* **sacs**
‖ *These sound alike:* **sac, sack**

sack[1] *noun* A bag of strong material.
◊ *verb* To put into a sack.
sack[1] (săk) ◊ *noun, plural* **sacks** ◊ *verb* **sacked, sacking**
‖ *These sound alike:* **sack, sac**

sack[2] *verb* To rob a captured place; loot.
◊ *noun* The robbing of a captured place.
sack[2] (săk) ◊ *verb* **sacked, sacking** ◊ *noun, plural* **sacks**
‖ *These sound alike:* **sack, sac**

***HISTORY* • sack**[1]**, sack**[2]

Sack[1] was borrowed long ago from a Latin word meaning "a large bag." The same Latin word passed into Italian and was used in a phrase meaning "to put into a bag, to steal." This meaning was borrowed into French and then English as **sack**[2].

sacred *adjective* **1.** Of or coming from God or a god; holy. **2.** For a religious use.
sa·cred (sā′krĭd) ◊ *adjective*

S

sacrifice *noun* **1.** The act of offering something to God or a god. **2.** The act of giving up something valuable for something else.
◊ *verb* **1.** To offer as a sacrifice to God or a god. **2.** To give up something valuable for the sake of someone or something else.
sac·ri·fice (**săk′** rə fīs′) ◊ *noun, plural* **sacrifices** ◊ *verb* **sacrificed, sacrificing**

sad *adjective* Showing, filled with, or causing sorrow or unhappiness.
sad (săd) ◊ *adjective* **sadder, saddest**

sadden *verb* To make or become sad.
sad·den (**săd′**n) ◊ *verb* **saddened, saddening**

saddle *noun* **1.** A seat for a rider, as of a horse or bicycle. **2.** Something that is like a saddle in shape.
◊ *verb* **1.** To put a saddle on. **2.** To load down; burden.
sad·dle (**săd′**l) ◊ *noun, plural* **saddles** ◊ *verb* **saddled, saddling**

▲ **saddle**
Left: An English saddle
Center: A bicycle saddle
Right: A Western saddle

safari *noun* A hunting trip in Africa.
sa·fa·ri (sə **fä′** rē) ◊ *noun, plural* **safaris**

safe *adjective* **1.** Secure or free from danger, risk, or harm. **2.** Providing protection: *Let's put the silver in a safe place.* **3.** Not likely to cause harm. **4.** Showing caution; careful: *His sister is a safe driver.* **5.** In baseball, having reached a base without being put out.
◊ *noun* A metal container in which valuable things are kept for protection.
safe (sāf) ◊ *adjective* **safer, safest** ◊ *noun, plural* **safes**

safeguard *verb* To keep safe; guard.
◊ *noun* A protection or defense: *Brushing the teeth is a safeguard against tooth decay.*
safe·guard (**sāf′** gärd′) ◊ *verb* **safeguarded, safeguarding** ◊ *noun, plural* **safeguards**

safety *noun* Freedom from danger or harm.
safe·ty (**sāf′** tē) ◊ *noun*

sag *verb* **1.** To curve or sink downward, especially in the middle: *The heavy snow made the barn roof sag.* **2.** To lose strength: *My spirits sagged when I lost the race.*
sag (săg) ◊ *verb* **sagged, sagging**

saga *noun* A story about heroic deeds.
sa·ga (**sä′** gə) ◊ *noun, plural* **sagas**

sage[1] *noun* A very wise person.
◊ *adjective* Having or showing wisdom.
sage[1] (sāj) ◊ *noun, plural* **sages** ◊ *adjective* **sager, sagest**

sage[2] *noun* **1.** A plant with leaves used as flavoring in cooking. **2.** Sagebrush.
sage[2] (sāj) ◊ *noun*

HISTORY • **sage**[1], **sage**[2]

Sage[1] is from an old French word that means "wise," which goes back to a Latin word meaning "to be wise." **Sage**[2] is from an old French word that came from a Latin word for the same plant.

sagebrush *noun* A shrub that grows in dry regions of western North America.
sage·brush (**sāj′** brŭsh′) ◊ *noun*

said *verb* Past tense and past participle of **say.**
said (sĕd) ◊ *verb*

sail *noun* **1.** A piece of strong fabric, such as canvas, that is stretched out to catch the wind and move a ship or boat through the water. **2.** A trip in a ship or boat that is propelled by sails.
◊ *verb* **1.** To travel on a ship or boat propelled by sails. **2.** To travel on, over, or across water. **3.** To guide or steer a ship or boat moved by

ă	pat	ĭ	pit	oi	**oil**	th	ba**th**
ā	pay	ī	ride	o͝o	book	*th*	ba**th**e
â	care	î	fierce	o͞o	boot	ə	ago, item
ä	father	ŏ	pot	ou	**out**		pencil
ĕ	pet	ō	go	ŭ	cut		atom
ē	be	ô	paw, for	û	fur		circus

sails. **4.** To begin a voyage on water: *The fleet sails at dawn.* **5.** To move smoothly; glide: *The balloon sailed away.*
sail (sāl) ◊ *noun, plural* **sails** ◊ *verb* **sailed, sailing**
‖*These sound alike:* **sail, sale**

sailboat *noun* A boat propelled by sails.
sail·boat (sāl′bōt′) ◊ *noun, plural* **sailboats**

sailor *noun* A person who sails, especially as a member of a ship's crew.
sail·or (sā′lər) ◊ *noun, plural* **sailors**

saint *noun* **1.** A very good and holy person, especially one who has been officially recognized as being worthy of special respect. **2.** A very patient, unselfish person.
saint (sānt) ◊ *noun, plural* **saints**

Saint Bernard *noun* A large, strong dog that was originally used to rescue lost travelers in the mountains of Switzerland.
Saint Ber·nard (bər **närd′**) ◊ *noun, plural* **Saint Bernards**

saintly *adjective* Of, like, or fit for a saint.
saint·ly (sānt′lē) ◊ *adjective* **saintlier, saintliest**

sake *noun* **1.** Reason or purpose: *Use a pen for the sake of neatness.* **2.** Benefit; good: *They work hard for their children's sake.*
sake (sāk) ◊ *noun, plural* **sakes**

salad *noun* A cold dish of raw vegetables, often served with a dressing. Sometimes fruit or other food is used instead.
sal·ad (săl′əd) ◊ *noun, plural* **salads**

salamander *noun* An animal that looks like a lizard but is related to the frog.
sal·a·man·der (săl′ə măn′dər) ◊ *noun, plural* **salamanders**

salary *noun* A fixed sum of money that is paid to a person for doing a job.
sal·a·ry (săl′ə rē) ◊ *noun, plural* **salaries**

sale *noun* **1.** The act of selling. **2.** A selling of goods at reduced prices.
sale (sāl) ◊ *noun, plural* **sales**
‖*These sound alike:* **sale, sail**

salesman *noun* A man who sells goods or services.
sales·man (sālz′mən) ◊ *noun, plural* **salesmen**

salesperson *noun* A person who sells goods or services.
sales·per·son (sālz′pûr′sən) ◊ *noun, plural* **salespersons**

sales tax *noun* A tax on the sale of goods or services.

saleswoman *noun* A woman who sells goods or services.
sales·wom·an (sālz′wo͝om′ən) ◊ *noun, plural* **saleswomen**

saliva *noun* The watery fluid discharged into the mouth by glands in the mouth. Saliva helps in chewing and swallowing food.
sa·li·va (sə lī′və) ◊ *noun*

sallow *adjective* Of a pale yellowish color.
sal·low (săl′ō) ◊ *adjective* **sallower, sallowest**

salmon *noun* A large food fish of northern waters that has pinkish flesh.
salm·on (săm′ən) ◊ *noun, plural* **salmon**

▲ **salmon**

salt *noun* **1.** A white substance that is found in deposits in the earth and in sea water and is used to season and preserve food. **2.** A chemical compound that is formed, along with water, by the reaction of an acid with a base. ◊ *adjective* Containing or preserved with salt. ◊ *verb* **1.** To season or sprinkle with or as if with salt. **2.** To preserve with salt.
salt (sôlt) ◊ *noun, plural* **salts** ◊ *adjective* ◊ *verb* **salted, salting**

saltwater *adjective* Of or living in salt water: *The shark is a saltwater fish.*
salt·wa·ter (sôlt′wô′tər) ◊ *adjective*

salty *adjective* Containing or tasting of salt.
salt·y (sôl′tē) ◊ *adjective* **saltier, saltiest**

salutation *noun* The words used at the beginning of a letter. For example, *Dear Ms. Smith* is a salutation.
sal·u·ta·tion (săl′yə **tā′**shən) ◊ *noun, plural* **salutations**

salute *verb* **1.** To show respect by raising the

S

right hand stiffly to the forehead or by firing guns. **2.** To greet with a polite gesture.
◊ *noun* An act of saluting.
sa·lute (sə lo͞ot′) ◊ *verb* **saluted, saluting** ◊ *noun, plural* **salutes**

salvage *verb* To save or rescue something that would otherwise be lost or destroyed.
◊ *noun* The rescue of property from loss.
sal·vage (săl′vĭj) ◊ *verb* **salvaged, salvaging** ◊ *noun*

salvation *noun* **1.** The act of saving or the condition of being saved; rescue. **2.** Someone or something that saves or rescues.
sal·va·tion (săl **vā′**shən) ◊ *noun*

salve *noun* **1.** A soothing ointment that is put on wounds, burns, or sores. **2.** Something soothing.
salve (săv) ◊ *noun, plural* **salves**

same *adjective* **1.** Exactly alike; identical: *These books are the same size.* **2.** Being the very one or ones: *This is the same seat I had yesterday.* **3.** Not changed or different: *You're the same kind person you always were.*
◊ *pronoun* The identical person or thing: *We asked the waiter to bring more of the same.*
same (sām) ◊ *adjective* ◊ *pronoun*

SYNONYMS

same, equal, identical

That is the *same* book that I read. Be sure everyone gets an *equal* amount of work. Are you sure that these two chairs are *identical?* **Antonym:** *different*

sample *noun* **1.** A part or piece that shows what the whole thing is like; specimen: *The astronauts brought back samples of moon rocks and soil.* **2.** An example or typical instance of something.
◊ *verb* To take or try a sample.
sam·ple (săm′pəl) ◊ *noun, plural* **samples** ◊ *verb* **sampled, sampling**

sample sentence *noun* A sentence in a dictionary entry that makes the meaning of an entry word clear by showing its use.
sample sentence ◊ *noun, plural* **sample sentences**

sanction *noun* Permission or approval.
◊ *verb* To give approval to.
sanc·tion (**săngk′**shən) ◊ *noun, plural* **sanctions** ◊ *verb* **sanctioned, sanctioning**

sanctuary *noun* **1.** A holy place, such as a church. **2.** Safety or protection. **3.** An area where animals and birds are protected.
sanc·tu·ar·y (**săngk′**cho͞o ĕr′ē) ◊ *noun, plural* **sanctuaries**

sand *noun* Loose grains of worn rock.
◊ *verb* **1.** To sprinkle or cover with sand. **2.** To rub with sand or sandpaper.
sand (sănd) ◊ *noun, plural* **sands** ◊ *verb* **sanded, sanding**

sandal *noun* A shoe made of a sole and straps used to fasten it to the foot.
san·dal (**săn′**dl) ◊ *noun, plural* **sandals**

sandbar *noun* A mass of sand built up in the water near a shore or beach.
sand·bar (**sănd′**bär′) ◊ *noun, plural* **sandbars**

▲ **sandbar**

sandbox *noun* An enclosed area filled with sand for children to play in.
sand·box (**sănd′**bŏks′) ◊ *noun, plural* **sandboxes**

sandpaper *noun* Heavy paper coated with sand, used for smoothing surfaces.
sand·pa·per (**sănd′**pā′pər) ◊ *noun*

sandpiper *noun* A small shore bird with a slender, pointed bill.
sand·pi·per (**sănd′**pī′pər) ◊ *noun, plural* **sandpipers**

ă	pat	ĭ	pit	oi	**oi**l	th	ba**th**
ā	pay	ī	ride	o͝o	b**oo**k	*th*	ba**th**e
â	care	î	fierce	o͞o	b**oo**t	ə	**a**go, it**e**m
ä	father	ŏ	pot	ou	**ou**t		penc**i**l
ĕ	pet	ō	go	ŭ	c**u**t		at**o**m
ē	be	ô	paw, for	û	f**u**r		circ**u**s

sandstone *noun* A kind of rock that is formed mostly from sand.
sand·stone (**sănd**′stōn′) ◊ *noun*

sandwich *noun* Two or more slices of bread with a filling of food put between them.
sand·wich (**sănd**′wĭch) ◊ *noun, plural* **sandwiches**

sandy *adjective* **1.** Of, full of, or covered with sand. **2.** Yellowish red in color.
sand·y (**săn**′dē) ◊ *adjective* **sandier, sandiest**

sane *adjective* **1.** Having a sound, healthy mind. **2.** Showing good judgment; sensible.
sane (sān) ◊ *adjective* **saner, sanest**

sang *verb* A past tense of **sing.**
sang (săng) ◊ *verb*

sanitary *adjective* **1.** Of or used for preventing disease and preserving good health. **2.** Free of dirt and germs; clean.
san·i·tar·y (**săn**′ĭ tĕr′ē) ◊ *adjective*

sanitation *noun* **1.** The study and use of procedures and rules intended to protect the public health. **2.** Disposal of wastes.
san·i·ta·tion (săn′ĭ **tā**′shən) ◊ *noun*

sanity *noun* Good mental health.
san·i·ty (**săn**′ĭ tē) ◊ *noun*

sank *verb* A past tense of **sink.**
sank (săngk) ◊ *verb*

sap *noun* The liquid that flows through plant tissues, carrying food to plant parts.
sap (săp) ◊ *noun, plural* **saps**

sapling *noun* A young tree.
sap·ling (**săp**′lĭng) ◊ *noun, plural* **saplings**

sapphire *noun* A hard, deep-blue precious stone that is valued as a gem.
sap·phire (**săf**′īr′) ◊ *noun, plural* **sapphires**

sarcasm *noun* **1.** A mocking or sneering remark. **2.** The use of such remarks.
sar·casm (**sär**′kăz′əm) ◊ *noun*

sarcastic *adjective* Characterized by mocking, sneering remarks.
sar·cas·tic (sär **kăs**′tĭk) ◊ *adjective*

sardine *noun* A small fish, often canned in oil for use as food.
sar·dine (sär **dēn**′) ◊ *noun, plural* **sardines**

sari *noun* An outer garment worn by women of India and Pakistan. A sari consists of a length of cloth with one end wrapped around the waist to form a long skirt and the other end draped over the shoulder.
sa·ri (**sä**′rē) ◊ *noun, plural* **saris**

▲ **sari**

sash¹ *noun* A band worn around the waist or over the shoulder as an ornament or symbol of rank.
sash¹ (săsh) ◊ *noun, plural* **sashes**

sash² *noun* A frame in which the panes of a window or door are set.
sash² (săsh) ◊ *noun, plural* **sashes**

HISTORY **• sash¹, sash²**

Sash¹ comes from an Arabic word that meant "muslin," a type of cloth. **Sash²** comes from an old French word that meant "frame."

Sask. The abbreviation for *Saskatchewan,* Canada.

sass *noun* Impudent talk.
◊ *verb* To talk in an impudent way to.
sass (săs) ◊ *noun* ◊ *verb* **sassed, sassing**

sat *verb* Past tense and past participle of **sit.**
sat (săt) ◊ *verb*

Sat. The abbreviation for *Saturday.*

satchel *noun* A small bag that is used to carry books or clothes.
satch·el (**săch**′əl) ◊ *noun, plural* **satchels**

satellite *noun* **1.** A heavenly body that travels in an orbit around a larger heavenly body. **2.** An object launched by a rocket in order to orbit and perhaps study a heavenly body.
sat·el·lite (**săt**′l īt′) ◊ *noun, plural* **satellites**

S

▲ **satellite**
A manmade satellite

satin *noun* A smooth, shiny fabric.
sat·in (săt′n) ◊ *noun, plural* **satins**

satisfaction *noun* The condition of being satisfied; fulfillment.
sat·is·fac·tion (săt′ĭs **făk′**shən) ◊ *noun*

satisfactory *adjective* Good enough but not the best; adequate: *I got a satisfactory grade.*
sat·is·fac·to·ry (săt′ĭs **făk′**tə rē) ◊ *adjective*

satisfy *verb* **1.** To fulfill or gratify: *We ate just enough to satisfy our hunger.* **2.** To set free of doubt; convince.
sat·is·fy (**săt′**ĭs fī′) ◊ *verb* **satisfied, satisfying**

saturate *verb* To soak or become soaked.
sat·u·rate (**săch′**ə rāt′) ◊ *verb* **saturated, saturating**

Saturday *noun* The seventh day of the week.
Sat·ur·day (**săt′**ər dē) ◊ *noun, plural* **Saturdays**

***HISTORY* • Saturday**

Three of the seven days of the week were named after planets or heavenly bodies. **Saturday** was named after the planet **Saturn.**

Saturn *noun* The planet that is sixth in distance from the sun. Saturn has many rings around it and is the second-largest planet.
Sat·urn (**săt′**ərn) ◊ *noun*

sauce *noun* A liquid dressing or relish served with food.
sauce (sôs) ◊ *noun, plural* **sauces**

saucepan *noun* A small cooking pan.
sauce·pan (**sôs′**păn′) ◊ *noun, plural* **saucepans**

saucer *noun* A small flat dish for a cup.
sau·cer (**sô′**sər) ◊ *noun, plural* **saucers**

saunter *verb* To walk leisurely; stroll.
saun·ter (**sôn′**tər) ◊ *verb* **sauntered, sauntering**

sausage *noun* Chopped and seasoned meat stuffed into a thin, tube-shaped casing.
sau·sage (**sô′**sĭj) ◊ *noun, plural* **sausages**

savage *adjective* **1.** Not cultivated; wild: *The explorers discovered savage lands.* **2.** Not civilized; primitive. **3.** Ferocious; fierce: *Savage lions roamed the plains.*
◊ *noun* **1.** A person untouched by civilization. **2.** A fierce or ferocious person or animal.
sav·age (**săv′**ĭj) ◊ *adjective* ◊ *noun, plural* **savages**

save *verb* **1.** To rescue from danger or loss. **2.** To keep from or avoid wasting or spending: *You can save money at a sale.* **3.** To make unnecessary: *A call saved a trip to the store.* **4.** To keep for future use; store.
save (sāv) ◊ *verb* **saved, saving**

saving *noun* **1.** An amount saved. **2. savings** Money saved.
sav·ing (**sā′**vĭng) ◊ *noun, plural* **savings**

savor *noun* The taste or smell of something.
sa·vor (**sā′**vər) ◊ *noun, plural* **savors**

saw[1] *noun* A tool that has a thin metal blade with sharp teeth for cutting hard material.
◊ *verb* To cut with or use a saw.
saw[1] (sô) ◊ *noun, plural* **saws** ◊ *verb* **sawed, sawed** *or* **sawn, sawing**

saw[2] *verb* Past tense of **see.**
saw[2] (sô) ◊ *verb*

sawdust *noun* The small pieces of wood that fall off when lumber is cut and sawed.
saw·dust (**sô′**dŭst′) ◊ *noun*

sawmill *noun* A place where lumber is cut.
saw·mill (**sô′**mĭl′) ◊ *noun, plural* **sawmills**

sawn *verb* A past participle of **saw**[1]**.**
sawn (sôn) ◊ *verb*

ă	pat	ĭ	pit	oi	**oi**l	th	ba**th**
ā	pay	ī	ride	o͝o	b**oo**k	*th*	ba**th**e
â	care	î	fierce	o͞o	b**oo**t	ə	ago, item
ä	father	ŏ	pot	ou	**ou**t		pencil
ĕ	pet	ō	go	ŭ	c**u**t		atom
ē	be	ô	paw, for	û	f**u**r		circ**u**s

saxophone *noun* A musical wind instrument with a reed mouthpiece, a curved metal body, and keys for the fingers.
sax·o·phone (săk′sə-fōn′) ◊ *noun, plural* **saxophones**

▲ **saxophone**

say *verb* **1.** To utter aloud; speak: *"Hello," my friend said.* **2.** To express in words; state: *The book says that the treaty was signed in 1945.* **3.** To communicate. **4.** To suppose; assume: *Let's say it will take us more than an hour to finish the job.*
◊ *noun* A chance to speak: *You can have your say at the meeting.*
say (sā) ◊ *verb* **said, saying** ◊ *noun*

SYNONYMS

say, communicate, state, tell

I *said* that I wanted to go. We *communicated* the information to them with our walkie-talkies. The judge *stated* her decision. *Tell* him a story.

saying *noun* A wise or humorous statement.
say·ing (sā′ĭng) ◊ *noun, plural* **sayings**

SC The abbreviation for *South Carolina* used with a Zip Code.

S.C. An abbreviation for *South Carolina.*

scab *noun* A crust over a healing wound.
scab (skăb) ◊ *noun, plural* **scabs**

scabbard *noun* A case for the blade of a sword, dagger, or bayonet.
scab·bard (skăb′ərd) ◊ *noun, plural* **scabbards**

scaffold *noun* A temporary platform used for supporting workers and their materials.
scaf·fold (skăf′əld) ◊ *noun, plural* **scaffolds**

scald *verb* To burn with hot liquid or steam.
scald (skôld) ◊ *verb* **scalded, scalding**

scale[1] *noun* **1.** One of the small, thin, platelike parts that cover a fish or reptile. **2.** A dry, thin flake or crust, as of rust.
◊ *verb* To remove scales from.
scale[1] (skāl) ◊ *noun, plural* **scales** ◊ *verb* **scaled, scaling**

scale[2] *noun* **1.** A series of marks placed at fixed distances, used for measuring. **2.** The relationship between the actual size of something and the size of a model or drawing that represents it: *This map is drawn to a scale of 1 inch to 50 miles.* **3.** A series of steps, degrees, or stages. **4.** The relative size or extent of something: *It is hard to imagine the scale of the universe.* **5.** A series of musical tones that goes up or down in pitch.
◊ *verb* **1.** To climb up to the top of or over. **2.** To draw or arrange in a given proportion.
scale[2] (skāl) ◊ *noun, plural* **scales** ◊ *verb* **scaled, scaling**

scale[3] *noun* An instrument for weighing.
scale[3] (skāl) ◊ *noun, plural* **scales**

HISTORY • **scale**[1], **scale**[2], **scale**[3]

Scale[1] comes from an old French word that meant "shell, husk." **Scale**[2] comes from a Latin word that meant "ladder." **Scale**[3] comes from an old Scandinavian word that meant "bowl" and also "one of the pans of a balance."

scallop *noun* **1.** A shellfish that has a soft body and a fan-shaped shell. The large muscle that opens and closes the shell of some scallops is edible. **2.** One of a series of curves forming a border.
scal·lop (skŏl′əp) ◊ *noun, plural* **scallops**

▲ **scallop**

scalp *noun* The skin that covers the top of the human head.
scalp (skălp) ◊ *noun, plural* **scalps**

scaly *adjective* Covered with scales.
scal·y (skā′lē) ◊ *adjective* **scalier, scaliest**

scan *verb* **1.** To examine closely: *I scanned the horizon for a sail.* **2.** To look over quickly: *I scanned the list to find my name.*
scan (skăn) ◊ *verb* **scanned, scanning**

S

scandal *noun* **1.** A wrong or immoral act that shocks people. **2.** Harmful gossip.
scan·dal (**skăn′**dl) ◊ *noun, plural* **scandals**

Scandinavian *noun* **1.** A person who was born in or lives in Denmark, Norway, and Sweden. **2.** A group of languages that are related to English and German. The languages include Danish, Norwegian, and Swedish.
◊ *adjective* Of or relating to the Scandinavians or their languages.
Scan·di·na·vi·an (skăn′də **nā′** vē ən) ◊ *noun, plural* **Scandinavians** ◊ *adjective*

scant *adjective* **1.** Not enough in amount or size. **2.** Not quite full: *Use a scant cup of flour.*
scant (skănt) ◊ *adjective* **scanter, scantest**

scanty *adjective* Barely enough: *The scanty meal left me still hungry.*
scant·y (**skăn′** tē) ◊ *adjective* **scantier, scantiest**

scar *noun* **1.** A mark left on the skin by a healed wound. **2.** A sign of damage.
◊ *verb* To mark with or form a scar.
scar (skär) ◊ *noun, plural* **scars** ◊ *verb* **scarred, scarring**

scarce *adjective* Not enough to meet a demand: *Food is scarce in some countries.*
scarce (skârs) ◊ *adjective* **scarcer, scarcest**

scarcely *adverb* **1.** Almost not at all; hardly: *I could scarcely breathe because of the tropical heat.* **2.** Certainly not: *We can scarcely ask for their help now.*
scarce·ly (**skârs′**lē) ◊ *adverb*

scare *verb* **1.** To frighten or become frightened. **2.** To frighten or drive away. —See Synonyms at **frighten.**
◊ *noun* A sensation of fear.
scare (skâr) ◊ *verb* **scared, scaring** ◊ *noun, plural* **scares**

scarecrow *noun* A crude figure set up in a field to scare birds away from crops.
scare·crow (**skâr′**krō′) ◊ *noun, plural* **scarecrows**

ă pat	ĭ pit	oi	**oil**	th	**bath**		
ā pay	ī ride	o͝o	book	*th*	ba**th**e		
â care	î fierce	o͞o	boot	ə	ago, item		
ä father	ŏ pot	ou	**out**		pencil		
ĕ pet	ō go	ŭ	cut		atom		
ē be	ô paw, for	û	fur		circus		

▲ **scarecrow**

scarf *noun* A piece of cloth that is worn around the neck or head.
scarf (skärf) ◊ *noun, plural* **scarfs** *or* **scarves**

scarlet *noun* A bright red color.
◊ *adjective* Bright red.
scar·let (**skär′**lĭt) ◊ *noun, plural* **scarlets** ◊ *adjective*

scarves *noun* A plural of **scarf.**
scarves (skärvz) ◊ *noun*

scary *adjective* Frightening; terrifying.
scar·y (**skâr′**ē) ◊ *adjective* **scarier, scariest**

scatter *verb* **1.** To separate and go or cause to go in many directions: *The wind scatters seeds.* **2.** To throw here and there: *The child scattered the toys all over the floor.*
scat·ter (**skăt′** ər) ◊ *verb* **scattered, scattering**

scavenger *noun* **1.** An animal that feeds on dead animals or plants. **2.** A person who searches through trash for useful things.
scav·en·ger (**skăv′**ĭn jər) ◊ *noun, plural* **scavengers**

scene *noun* **1.** A place as seen by a viewer; view. **2.** The place where an action or event occurs: *The towing truck arrived at the scene of the wreck.* **3.** The place in which the action of a story or play occurs. **4.** A short section of a play or movie.
scene (sēn) ◊ *noun, plural* **scenes**
‖*These sound alike:* **scene, seen**

scenery *noun* **1.** The landscape. **2.** The structures or curtains on a theater stage.
scen·er·y (**sē′** nə rē) ◊ *noun, plural* **sceneries**

scenic *adjective* Of attractive natural scenery: *We drove along a scenic route in the mountains.*
sce·nic (sē′nĭk) ◊ *adjective*

scent *noun* **1.** A distinctive smell. —See Synonyms at **smell. 2.** A perfume. **3.** The trail of a hunted animal or fugitive. **4.** The sense of smell.
◊ *verb* To sense by or as if by smelling.
scent (sĕnt) ◊ *noun, plural* **scents** ◊ *verb* **scented, scenting**
‖*These sound alike:* **scent, cent, sent**

scepter *noun* A staff held by a monarch.
scep·ter (sĕp′tər) ◊ *noun, plural* **scepters**

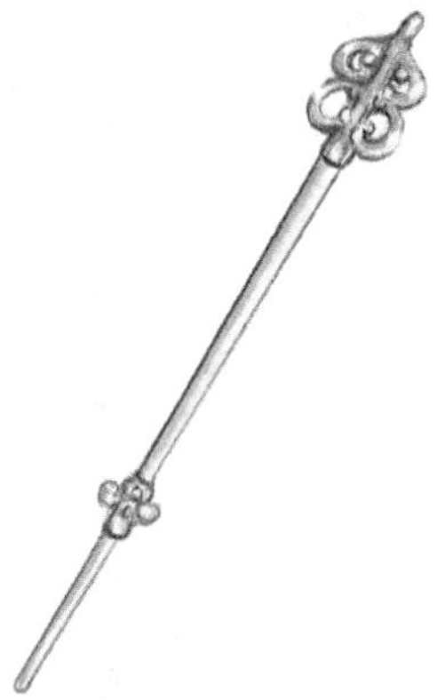
▲ **scepter**

schedule *noun* **1.** A program of events, appointments, or classes. **2.** A list of the times for departures and arrivals.
◊ *verb* To plan or appoint for a certain time.
sched·ule (skĕj′o͞ol *or* skĕj′əl) ◊ *noun, plural* **schedules** ◊ *verb* **scheduled, scheduling**

scheme *noun* **1.** A plan or plot for doing something. **2.** A chart, diagram, or outline. **3.** An orderly arrangement or combination.
◊ *verb* To make up a plan or scheme for.
scheme (skēm) ◊ *noun, plural* **schemes** ◊ *verb* **schemed, scheming**

scholar *noun* **1.** A person who has a great deal of knowledge. **2.** A student.
schol·ar (skŏl′ər) ◊ *noun, plural* **scholars**

scholarly *adjective* Of or right for a scholar or scholarship.
schol·ar·ly (skŏl′ər lē) ◊ *adjective*

scholarship *noun* **1.** A grant of money given to help a student continue with his or her education. **2.** A scholar's methods.
schol·ar·ship (skŏl′ər shĭp′) ◊ *noun, plural* **scholarships**

school¹ *noun* A large group of fish or other water animals, such as whales or porpoises, swimming together.
school¹ (sko͞ol) ◊ *noun, plural* **schools**

LANGUAGE DETECTIVE

school¹

A group of water animals such as fish or whales swimming together is called a *school.* Other words like *school* refer to groups of various kinds of living things. Some of these words refer to only one kind of living thing. For example, a *gam* is a group of whales. A *gaggle* is a group of geese. A *pride* is a group of lions and a *watch* is a group of nightingales. Other words can be used in more general ways. A *herd* is a group of animals of one kind, such as cattle, that are kept together by people. A *herd* is also a group of wild animals, such as deer. A *flock* can be a group of animals, such as sheep, that are kept together by people. A *flock* can also be a group of birds, such as geese. If the birds are in the air, you can call them a *flight.* If you see a group of bees in the air flying to make a new colony, you see a *swarm.* Good language detectives are on the lookout for *flights, gaggles, gams, herds, prides, schools, swarms,* and *watches.*

school² *noun* **1.** A place for teaching and learning. **2.** The students and teachers of a school. **3.** Study given in school; instruction; schooling.
school² (sko͞ol) ◊ *noun, plural* **schools**

HISTORY **• school¹, school²**

School¹ comes from an old Dutch word that meant "troop" and also "a group of whales." **School²** goes back to a Greek word that meant "spare time" and especially "spare time spent in learning."

schoolbook *noun* A textbook.
school·book (sko͞ol′bo͝ok′) ◊ *noun, plural* **schoolbooks**

schoolboy *noun* A boy attending school.
school·boy (sko͞ol′boi′) ◊ *noun, plural* **schoolboys**

schoolchild *noun* A child attending school.
school·child (sko͞ol′chīld′) ◊ *noun, plural* **schoolchildren**

S

schoolgirl *noun* A girl attending school.
school·girl (**sko͞ol'** gûrl') ◊ *noun, plural* **schoolgirls**

schoolhouse *noun* A school building.
school·house (**sko͞ol'** hous') ◊ *noun, plural* **schoolhouses**

schooling *noun* Instruction given at school.
school·ing (**sko͞o'** lĭng) ◊ *noun*

schoolroom *noun* A classroom in school.
school·room (**sko͞ol'** ro͞om' *or* **sko͞ol'** ro͝om') ◊ *noun, plural* **schoolrooms**

schoolteacher *noun* A person who teaches school.
school·teach·er (**sko͞ol'** tē'chər) ◊ *noun, plural* **schoolteachers**

schoolwork *noun* A student's work.
school·work (**sko͞ol'** wûrk') ◊ *noun*

schoolyard *noun* A yard next to a school.
school·yard (**sko͞ol'** yärd') ◊ *noun, plural* **schoolyards**

schooner *noun* A ship with two or more masts and sails that are set lengthwise.
schoo·ner (**sko͞o'** nər) ◊ *noun, plural* **schooners**

▲ **schooner**

ă	pat	ĭ	pit	oi	**oil**	th	ba**th**
ā	pay	ī	ride	o͝o	**book**	*th*	ba**th**e
â	care	î	fierce	o͞o	**boot**	ə	ago, item
ä	father	ŏ	pot	ou	**out**		pencil
ĕ	pet	ō	go	ŭ	cut		atom
ē	be	ô	paw, for	û	fur		circus

schwa *noun* The vowel sound found in many unstressed syllables shown in pronunciations by the symbol (ə). For example, the pronunciations of *a* in *alone* and *e* in *linen* are shown by a schwa.
schwa (shwä) ◊ *noun, plural* **schwas**

science *noun* **1.** The study and explanation of things that happen in nature and the universe. **2.** An area of knowledge in which observation, experiments, and study are used.
sci·ence (**sī'** əns) ◊ *noun, plural* **sciences**

scientific *adjective* Of, relating to, or used in science.
sci·en·tif·ic (sī'ən **tĭf'** ĭk) ◊ *adjective*

scientist *noun* Someone, such as a chemist, who is an expert in a science.
sci·en·tist (**sī'** ən tĭst) ◊ *noun, plural* **scientists**

scissors *noun* (*used with a singular or plural verb*) A cutting tool that has two pivoting blades that close against each other.
scis·sors (**sĭz'** ərz) ◊ *noun*

scold *verb* To speak angrily to for a fault: *The teacher scolded me for being late.*
scold (skōld) ◊ *verb* **scolded, scolding**

scoop *noun* **1.** A utensil that is like a small shovel, used to take up or dish out foods. **2.** The amount a scoop holds: *Add another scoop of flour to the dough.*
◊ *verb* **1.** To lift out or up with or as if with a scoop. **2.** To hollow out by digging.
scoop (sko͞op) ◊ *noun, plural* **scoops** ◊ *verb* **scooped, scooping**

scooter *noun* A child's vehicle that is made of a board with wheels, is steered by a handlebar, and is pushed with one foot.
scoot·er (**sko͞o'** tər) ◊ *noun, plural* **scooters**

scope *noun* **1.** The range of a person's ideas, thoughts, actions, or abilities. **2.** Extent or opportunity to function.
scope (skōp) ◊ *noun*

scorch *verb* To burn on the surface.
◊ *noun* A slight burn.
scorch (skôrch) ◊ *verb* **scorched, scorching** ◊ *noun, plural* **scorches**

score *noun* **1.** The number of points made by each participant in a game, contest, or test. **2.** A record of points made: *You keep the score this time.* **3.** A set or group containing 20 things. **4.** The written or printed form of a piece of music.

◊ *verb* **1.** To gain a point or points in a game, contest, or test: *We scored 24 points.* **2.** To achieve, gain, or win: *We scored a great success in the play.* **3.** To record the points in a game or contest.
score (skôr) ◊ *noun, plural* **scores** ◊ *verb* **scored, scoring**

scorn *verb* To think of as bad, worthless, or low; despise: *Don't scorn younger kids.*
◊ *noun* A feeling that someone or something is bad, worthless, or low; contempt.
scorn (skôrn) ◊ *verb* **scorned, scorning** ◊ *noun*

scornful *adjective* Full of scorn; disdainful.
scorn·ful (**skôrn′** fəl) ◊ *adjective*

scorpion *noun* An animal that is related to the spider and that has a tail giving a poisonous sting.
scor·pi·on (**skôr′** pē ən) ◊ *noun, plural* **scorpions**

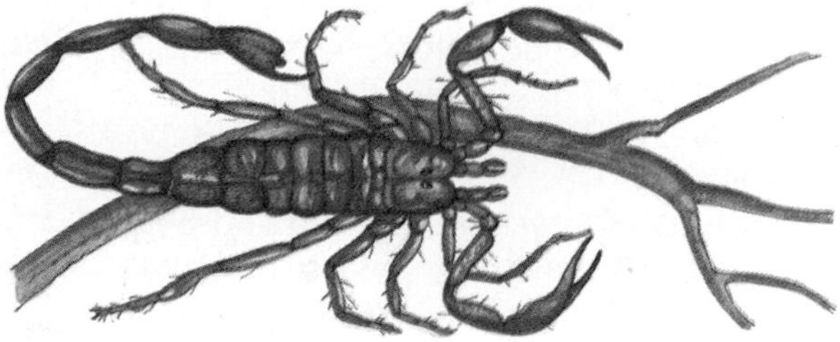

▲ **scorpion**

Scot *noun* A person who was born in or lives in Scotland.
Scot (skŏt) ◊ *noun, plural* **Scots**

Scotch *adjective* Scottish.
Scotch (skŏtch) ◊ *adjective*

Scottish *noun* (*used with a plural verb*) The people of Scotland.
◊ *adjective* Of or relating to Scotland, the Scots, or their dialect.
Scot·tish (**skŏt′** ĭsh) ◊ *noun* ◊ *adjective*

scoundrel *noun* A very wicked person.
scoun·drel (**skoun′** drəl) ◊ *noun, plural* **scoundrels**

scour *verb* To clean or polish by scrubbing: *I scoured the kitchen sink.*
scour (skour) ◊ *verb* **scoured, scouring**

scout *noun* Someone who goes out from a group to gather information.
◊ *verb* **1.** To observe or explore carefully for information. **2.** To search.
scout (skout) ◊ *noun, plural* **scouts** ◊ *verb* **scouted, scouting**

scowl *verb* To lower the eyebrows in anger or disapproval; frown.
◊ *noun* An angry frown.
scowl (skoul) ◊ *verb* **scowled, scowling** ◊ *noun, plural* **scowls**

scramble *verb* **1.** To move quickly, especially by climbing or crawling. **2.** To struggle or contend eagerly in competition with others. **3.** To mix together in a confused mass. **4.** To cook eggs by mixing together the yolks and whites and frying the mixture.
◊ *noun* **1.** A difficult climb. **2.** A disorderly struggle: *There was a scramble for the ball.*
scram·ble (**skrăm′** bəl) ◊ *verb* **scrambled, scrambling** ◊ *noun, plural* **scrambles**

scrap *noun* **1.** A fragment or particle: *I can't find a scrap of paper.* **2. scraps** Leftover bits of food or other material.
◊ *verb* To throw out or abandon as useless.
scrap (skrăp) ◊ *noun, plural* **scraps** ◊ *verb* **scrapped, scrapping**

scrapbook *noun* A book with blank pages for mounting pictures or clippings.
scrap·book (**skrăp′** bo͝ok′) ◊ *noun, plural* **scrapbooks**

scrape *verb* **1.** To rub in order to clean, smooth, or shape: *Scrape the carrots carefully.* **2.** To remove material by rubbing. **3.** To injure or damage the surface of by rubbing.
◊ *noun* **1.** Something, as an injury, that is caused by scraping. **2.** An act of scraping.
scrape (skrāp) ◊ *verb* **scraped, scraping** ◊ *noun, plural* **scrapes**

scratch *verb* **1.** To make a thin, shallow cut or mark with or as if with a sharp tool. **2.** To rub to relieve itching. **3.** To dig, scrape, damage, or wound with nails, claws, or something sharp or rough: *I fell on the cement and scratched my knee.* **4.** To strike out by drawing marks through.
◊ *noun* **1.** A thin, shallow mark or injury made by scratching. **2.** A scraping sound.
scratch (skrăch) ◊ *verb* **scratched, scratching** ◊ *noun, plural* **scratches**

S

scrawl *verb* To write quickly or in a messy way.
◊ *noun* Handwriting that is hard to read.
scrawl (skrôl) ◊ *verb* **scrawled, scrawling** ◊ *noun, plural* **scrawls**

scream *verb* To make a long, loud, piercing cry or sound.
◊ *noun* A long, loud, piercing cry or sound.
scream (skrēm) ◊ *verb* **screamed, screaming** ◊ *noun, plural* **screams**

screech *noun* A high, harsh cry or sound.
◊ *verb* To make a high, harsh cry or sound.
screech (skrēch) ◊ *noun, plural* **screeches** ◊ *verb* **screeched, screeching**

screen *noun* **1.** A light, movable frame used to divide, hide, or protect. **2.** Something that hides something else from view. **3.** A frame covered with wire mesh, used in a window or door to keep out insects. **4.** A flat surface on which slides or movies are projected or on which an electronic image appears.
◊ *verb* **1.** To hide, shelter, or protect. **2.** To separate with or as if with a screen.
screen (skrēn) ◊ *noun, plural* **screens** ◊ *verb* **screened, screening**

screw *noun* **1.** A metal pin with a spiral ridge around its length that is used to fasten things. **2.** A propeller for a ship or boat.
◊ *verb* **1.** To fasten, tighten, or attach with or as if with a screw. **2.** To twist into place: *I screwed a bulb into the lamp.*
screw (skro͞o) ◊ *noun, plural* **screws** ◊ *verb* **screwed, screwing**

screwdriver *noun* A tool that is used to turn screws.
screw·driv·er (**skro͞o′** drī′vər) ◊ *noun, plural* **screwdrivers**

scribble *verb* To write or draw carelessly.
◊ *noun* Careless writing or drawing.
scrib·ble (**skrĭb′** əl) ◊ *verb* **scribbled, scribbling** ◊ *noun, plural* **scribbles**

scribe *noun* A person who copies writing.
scribe (skrīb) ◊ *noun, plural* **scribes**

ă	pat	ĭ	pit	oi	**oi**l	th	ba**th**
ā	pay	ī	ride	o͝o	b**oo**k	*th*	ba**th**e
â	care	î	fierce	o͞o	b**oo**t	ə	ago, item
ä	father	ŏ	pot	ou	**ou**t		pencil
ĕ	pet	ō	go	ŭ	cut		atom
ē	be	ô	paw, for	û	f**ur**		circus

scrimmage *noun* In football, the action that occurs from the time the ball is snapped until it is out of play.
scrim·mage (**skrĭm′**ĭj) ◊ *noun, plural* **scrimmages**

script *noun* **1.** Letters or symbols written by hand. **2.** The written text of a play or movie or of a radio or television show.
script (skrĭpt) ◊ *noun, plural* **scripts**

Scripture *noun* **1.** The Bible. **2. scripture** Any sacred writing or book.
Scrip·ture (**skrĭp′** chər) ◊ *noun, plural* **Scriptures**

scroll *noun* A roll of parchment or paper on which something is written.
scroll (skrōl) ◊ *noun, plural* **scrolls**

scrub *verb* To clean by rubbing hard.
◊ *noun* An act of scrubbing.
scrub (skrŭb) ◊ *verb* **scrubbed, scrubbing** ◊ *noun, plural* **scrubs**

scruff *noun* The skin on the back of the neck.
scruff (skrŭf) ◊ *noun, plural* **scruffs**

scruple *noun* **1.** A principle that keeps someone from doing wrong. **2.** A guilty feeling caused by wrongdoing.
scru·ple (**skro͞o′** pəl) ◊ *noun, plural* **scruples**

scrupulous *adjective* Careful and honest.
scru·pu·lous (**skro͞o′** pyə ləs) ◊ *adjective*

scuba *noun* One or more tanks of compressed air, worn on the back by divers for breathing underwater.
scu·ba (**sko͞o′** bə) ◊ *noun*

LANGUAGE DETECTIVE

scuba

The word **scuba** is a word made up of the first letters of the word group *(s)elf-(c)ontained (u)nderwater (b)reathing (a)pparatus.* A word like **scuba** is an *acronym,* which is a word that is made up of the first letters or parts of a word group. Another *acronym* in this dictionary is **radar,** which is made up of the beginning letters or parts of the word group *(ra)dio (d)etecting (a)nd (r)anging.*

scuff *verb* **1.** To scrape or drag the feet in walking. **2.** To scrape and roughen the surface of: *Don't scuff up your new shoes.*

◊ *noun* The act or result of scuffing.
scuff (skŭf) ◊ *verb* **scuffed, scuffing** ◊ *noun, plural* **scuffs**

scuffle *verb* To struggle in a disorderly way.
◊ *noun* A disorderly struggle.
scuf·fle (**skŭf′** əl) ◊ *verb* **scuffled, scuffling** ◊ *noun, plural* **scuffles**

scull *noun* **1.** An oar used for rowing a boat. **2.** A small, light racing boat.
scull (skŭl) ◊ *noun, plural* **sculls**
‖*These sound alike:* **scull, skull**

sculptor *noun* An artist who makes sculptures.
sculp·tor (**skŭlp′** tər) ◊ *noun, plural* **sculptors**

sculpture *noun* **1.** The art of making figures or designs that have depth, as in wood, stone, or metal. **2.** A work of sculpture.
◊ *verb* To make sculptures.
sculp·ture (**skŭlp′** chər) ◊ *noun, plural* **sculptures** ◊ *verb* **sculptured, sculpturing**

▲ **sculpture**

scum *noun* **1.** A filmy material that rises to the top of a boiling liquid. **2.** An often slimy coating that forms on stagnant water.
scum (skŭm) ◊ *noun*

scurry *verb* To move lightly and quickly.
scur·ry (**skûr′** ē) ◊ *verb* **scurried, scurrying**

scurvy *noun* A disease that results from a lack of vitamin C, marked by bleeding gums.
scur·vy (**skûr′** vē) ◊ *noun*

scuttle *verb* To move with quick little steps: *Just then a crab scuttled away.*
scut·tle (**skŭt′** l) ◊ *verb* **scuttled, scuttling**

scythe *noun* A tool with a long, curved blade for mowing grass or reaping grain.
scythe (sīth) ◊ *noun, plural* **scythes**

SD The abbreviation for *South Dakota* used with a Zip Code.

S.Dak. An abbreviation for *South Dakota.*

SE *or* **S.E.** Abbreviations for *Southeast.*

sea *noun* **1.** The body of salt water that covers most of the earth; ocean. **2.** A body of salt water within an ocean and partly enclosed by land, as the Mediterranean Sea. **3.** An ocean wave.
sea (sē) ◊ *noun, plural* **seas**
‖*These sound alike:* **sea, see**

sea anemone *noun* A sea animal with a flexible, tube-shaped body and a mouth opening that is surrounded by many flowerlike tentacles.
sea a·nem·o·ne (ə **nĕm′** ə nē) ◊ *noun, plural* **sea anemones**

seacoast *noun* Land along the sea.
sea·coast (**sē′** kōst′) ◊ *noun, plural* **seacoasts**

seafaring *adjective* **1.** Earning one's living at sea. **2.** Traveling on the sea.
sea·far·ing (**sē′** fâr′ĭng) ◊ *adjective*

seafood *noun* Fish or shellfish eaten as food.
sea·food (**sē′** fōōd′) ◊ *noun*

seagoing *adjective* **1.** Made for use on the open sea. **2.** Seafaring.
sea·go·ing (**sē′** gō′ĭng) ◊ *adjective*

sea gull *noun* A gull that lives on coasts.
sea gull ◊ *noun, plural* **sea gulls**

sea horse *noun* A small ocean fish with a head that looks like a horse's head.
sea horse ◊ *noun, plural* **sea horses**

▲ **sea horse**

seal[1] *noun* **1.** An instrument, such as an engraved ring, for stamping wax or paper with a special mark. **2.** A design used as an official mark of authority. **3.** A small disk of wax, lead, or paper stamped with a design. It is used to show that a paper is genuine or to fasten an envelope. **4.** A small paper sticker used to fasten or decorate an envelope or package. **5.** A very tight closing, as on a jar.

S

◊ *verb* **1.** To stamp or mark with a seal. **2.** To close or fasten with or as if with a seal.
seal¹ (sēl) ◊ *noun, plural* **seals** ◊ *verb* **sealed, sealing**

seal² *noun* A sea mammal that lives in cold regions and has soft, thick fur and flippers.
seal² (sēl) ◊ *noun, plural* **seals**

***HISTORY* • seal¹, seal²**

Seal¹ comes from an Old French word that came in turn from a Latin word meaning "a little sign." **Seal²** comes from the old English name for this sea mammal.

▲ **seal²**

sea level *noun* The level of the surface of the ocean, used as a standard in measuring land elevation or sea depths.

sea lion *noun* A very large seal found mostly in the Pacific Ocean.
sea lion ◊ *noun, plural* **sea lions**

seam *noun* **1.** A line, fold, or groove formed by joining two pieces of material together at their edges, as by sewing. **2.** A layer: *They mined a new seam of coal.*
seam (sēm) ◊ *noun, plural* **seams**
‖*These sound alike:* **seam, seem**

ă pat	ĭ pit	oi **oil**	th **bath**
ā pay	ī ride	ŏŏ **book**	*th* **bathe**
â care	î fierce	ōō **boot**	ə ago, item
ä father	ŏ pot	ou **out**	pencil
ĕ pet	ō go	ŭ cut	atom
ē be	ô paw, for	û fur	circus

seaman *noun* **1.** A sailor or mariner. **2.** A Navy or Coast Guard enlisted person ranking below a petty officer.
sea·man (sē′mən) ◊ *noun, plural* **seamen**

seamstress *noun* A woman who makes her living by sewing.
seam·stress (**sēm′**strĭs) ◊ *noun, plural* **seamstresses**

seaplane *noun* An airplane that can take off from and land on water.
sea·plane (sē′plān′) ◊ *noun, plural* **seaplanes**

▲ **seaplane**

search *verb* **1.** To look thoroughly and carefully: *We searched for fossils in the rocks.* **2.** To look over or go through carefully to find something.
◊ *noun* An act or example of searching.
search (sûrch) ◊ *verb* **searched, searching** ◊ *noun, plural* **searches**

searchlight *noun* A powerful lamp for producing a beam of bright light.
search·light (**sûrch′**līt′) ◊ *noun, plural* **searchlights**

seashell *noun* The shell of a shellfish.
sea·shell (sē′shĕl′) ◊ *noun, plural* **seashells**

seashore *noun* Land at the edge of a sea.
sea·shore (sē′shôr′) ◊ *noun, plural* **seashores**

seasick *adjective* Dizzy and sick to one's stomach from the motion of a ship.
sea·sick (sē′sĭk′) ◊ *adjective*

season *noun* **1.** One of the four equal natural divisions of the year. The seasons are spring, summer, autumn, and winter. **2.** A period of the year marked by a certain activity or event: *Winter in New England is the skiing season.*
◊ *verb* To flavor by adding seasoning.
sea·son (sē′zən) ◊ *noun, plural* **seasons**
◊ *verb* **seasoned, seasoning**

seasonal *adjective* Of or coming with a certain season: *Baseball, gardening, and snow removal are seasonal activities.*
sea·son·al (sē′zə nəl) ◊ *adjective*

seasoning *noun* An ingredient that adds to the flavor of food.
sea·son·ing (sē′zə nĭng) ◊ *noun, plural* **seasonings**

seat *noun* **1.** Something, as a chair or bench, that may be sat in or on. **2.** A place in which someone may sit. **3.** The part of something on which a person rests in sitting.
◊ *verb* **1.** To place on a seat. **2.** To have seats for: *The hall seats 5,000 people.*
seat (sēt) ◊ *noun, plural* **seats** ◊ *verb* **seated, seating**

seat belt *noun* A safety strap or harness that is designed to hold a person securely in a seat, as in a car or airplane.
seat belt ◊ *noun, plural* **seat belts**

seating *noun* **1.** The act of providing with seats. **2.** The arrangement of seats, as in an auditorium.
seat·ing (sē′tĭng) ◊ *noun, plural* **seatings**

seaweed *noun* One of many kinds of algae, such as a kelp, that live in the sea.
sea·weed (sē′wēd′) ◊ *noun, plural* **seaweeds**

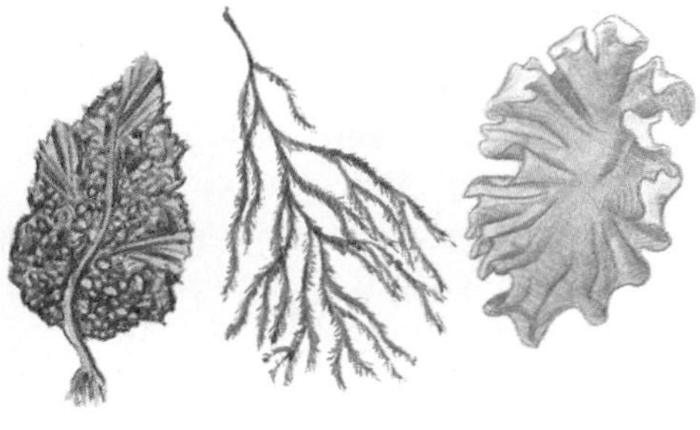

▲ **seaweed**

sec. The abbreviation for *seconds* (time division).

secede *verb* To withdraw from membership in a union or organization, as of states.
se·cede (sĭ sēd′) ◊ *verb* **seceded, seceding**

second[1] *noun* **1.** A unit of time equal to 1/60 of a minute. **2.** A very short period of time.
sec·ond[1] (sĕk′ənd) ◊ *noun, plural* **seconds**

second[2] *noun* **1.** The number in a series that matches the number two. **2.** A person or thing that is next after the first. **3.** Merchandise that has something wrong with it.
◊ *adjective* **1.** Coming after the first. **2.** Ranking below the first.
◊ *adverb* In the second place.
◊ *verb* To support: *I seconded the motion during the meeting.*
sec·ond[2] (sĕk′ənd) ◊ *noun, plural* **seconds**
◊ *adjective* ◊ *adverb* ◊ *verb* **seconded, seconding**

***HISTORY* • second[1], second[2]**

In Latin, an hour was divided into "first parts" and "second parts." The "first parts" we call **minutes**, from a Latin word meaning "something small." The "second parts" we call **seconds[1]**, from a Latin word meaning "following, coming next or second." **Second[2]** comes from a different form of the same Latin word that gave us **second[1]**.

secondary *adjective* **1.** Second in rank or importance. **2.** Not original; secondhand: *Secondary information, such as gossip, is often untrue.*
sec·on·dar·y (sĕk′ən dĕr′ē) ◊ *adjective*

secondary school *noun* A school for students between elementary school and college.
secondary school ◊ *noun, plural* **secondary schools**

secondary stress *noun* **1.** The weaker amount of stress or force used in pronouncing a word. The secondary stress is on the third syllable of *secretary* (**sĕk′**rĭ tĕr′ē). **2.** The mark (′) used to show which syllable or syllables receive a weaker stress.

second-class *adjective* Being in the rank or class that is next below the first or best.
sec·ond-class (sĕk′ənd **klăs′**) ◊ *adjective*

S

secondhand *adjective* **1.** Used before by another; not new. **2.** Selling goods that have been used before. **3.** Coming from another.
sec·ond·hand (**sĕk′**ənd **hănd′**) ◊ *adjective*

secondly *adverb* In the second place.
sec·ond·ly (**sĕk′**ənd lē) ◊ *adverb*

second-string *adjective* Of or being a substitute, as on a football team.
sec·ond-string (sĕk′ənd **strĭng′**) ◊ *adjective*

secrecy *noun* **1.** The condition of being secret. **2.** The practice of keeping secrets.
se·cre·cy (**sē′**krĭ sē) ◊ *noun*

secret *adjective* **1.** Hidden from general knowledge or view. **2.** Working in secrecy.
◊ *noun* Something that is kept hidden or is known only to a few.
◊ *idiom* **in secret** Not openly; in secrecy.
se·cret (**sē′**krĭt) ◊ *adjective* ◊ *noun, plural* **secrets**

secretary *noun* **1.** A person who is employed to handle records and letters for another person. **2.** An officer of an organization who keeps records of meetings. **3.** The head of a government department.
sec·re·tar·y (**sĕk′**rĭ tĕr′ē) ◊ *noun, plural* **secretaries**

secrete *verb* To produce a secretion.
se·crete (sĭ **krēt′**) ◊ *verb* **secreted, secreting**

secretion *noun* **1.** The act or process of secreting a substance. **2.** A substance, such as saliva, that is produced by a bodily organ.
se·cre·tion (sĭ **krē′**shən) ◊ *noun, plural* **secretions**

sect *noun* A group of people within a larger group who share interests or beliefs.
sect (sĕkt) ◊ *noun, plural* **sects**

section *noun* **1.** A part taken from a whole: *Divide the orange into sections.* **2.** A division of a book or chapter. **3.** A picture of the inside of a solid object, as if it were cut through. **4.** A part of an area or a group. —See Synonyms at **part.**
◊ *verb* To separate into parts.
sec·tion (**sĕk′**shən) ◊ *noun, plural* **sections** ◊ *verb* **sectioned, sectioning**

secure *adjective* **1.** Safe against danger or risk of loss. **2.** Not frightened or worried. **3.** Firm or strong: *The door has a secure lock.* **4.** Assured; certain: *The future of our school band is secure.*
◊ *verb* **1.** To make safe. **2.** To fasten tightly. **3.** To get; acquire: *The workers tried to secure higher wages.*
se·cure (sĭ **kyo͝or′**) ◊ *adjective* **securer, securest** ◊ *verb* **secured, securing**

security *noun* **1.** The state of being safe and secure; safety. **2.** Something that is given to guarantee the fulfillment of an agreement.
se·cu·ri·ty (sĭ **kyo͝or′**ĭ tē) ◊ *noun, plural* **securities**

sedan *noun* An automobile with two or four doors and front and rear seats.
se·dan (sĭ **dăn′**) ◊ *noun, plural* **sedans**

sediment *noun* **1.** Matter that falls to the bottom of a liquid. **2.** Sand and stones deposited by water, wind, or a glacier.
sed·i·ment (**sĕd′**ə mənt) ◊ *noun, plural* **sediments**

sedimentary *adjective* Of, like, or formed from sediment.
sed·i·men·ta·ry (sĕd′ə **mĕn′**tə rē) ◊ *adjective*

see *verb* **1.** To take in with the eyes. **2.** To understand: *I see what you mean.* **3.** To know through actual experience: *We had seen hard times.* **4.** To find out: *See if the bike can be fixed.* **5.** To visit or meet with: *The doctor will see you now.* **6.** To view: *Let's see the museums today.* **7.** To go with; accompany: *I'll see you home.* **8.** To make sure; take care: *Always see that the door is locked.*
◊ *idioms* **see through 1.** To understand the true character or nature of. **2.** To help in difficult times: *The nurse saw me through my illness.* **see to** To attend to.
see (sē) ◊ *verb* **saw, seen, seeing**
‖*These sound alike:* **see, sea**

seed *noun* **1.** A usually tiny and enclosed part of a flowering plant. A seed can grow into a plant like the one that produced it. **2.** A source; beginning.
◊ *verb* **1.** To plant seeds in; sow. **2.** To produce seeds. **3.** To remove the seeds from.
seed (sēd) ◊ *noun, plural* **seeds** *or* **seed** ◊ *verb* **seeded, seeding**

ă	pat	ĭ	pit	oi	**oil**	th	**bath**
ā	pay	ī	ride	o͝o	**book**	*th*	**bathe**
â	care	î	fierce	o͞o	**boot**	ə	**ago, item**
ä	father	ŏ	pot	ou	**out**		pencil
ĕ	pet	ō	go	ŭ	cut		atom
ē	be	ô	paw, for	û	fur		circus

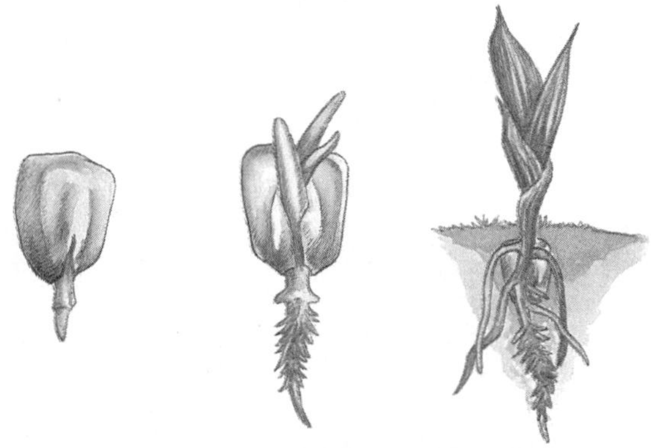

▲ **seed/seedling**
A seed evolves into a seedling.

seedcase *noun* A pod that contains seeds.
seed·case (sēd′kās′) ◊ *noun, plural* **seedcases**

seedling *noun* A newly sprouted plant.
seed·ling (sēd′lĭng) ◊ *noun, plural* **seedlings**

seek *verb* **1.** To try to find or get: *We seek a new place to live.* **2.** To attempt; try: *They sought to make the world a better place.*
seek (sēk) ◊ *verb* **sought, seeking**

seem *verb* **1.** To give the impression of being; appear to be: *You seem worried.* **2.** To appear to oneself: *I seem to recall you now.*
seem (sēm) ◊ *verb* **seemed, seeming**
‖*These sound alike:* **seem, seam**

seemingly *adverb* With an appearance that may or may not be real: *They are, seemingly, good friends.*
seem·ing·ly (sē′mĭng lē) ◊ *adverb*

seen *verb* Past participle of **see.**
seen (sēn) ◊ *verb*
‖*These sound alike:* **seen, scene**

seep *verb* To pass slowly through small openings; ooze: *Cold air seeped in.*
seep (sēp) ◊ *verb* **seeped, seeping**

seersucker *noun* A lightweight fabric of cotton or rayon that has a crinkled surface. Seersucker usually has a striped pattern.
seer·suck·er (sîr′sŭk′ər) ◊ *noun*

seesaw *noun* A long plank balanced so that with a person riding on either end, one end goes up as the other goes down.
◊ *verb* To ride on a seesaw.
see·saw (sē′sô′) ◊ *noun, plural* **seesaws**
◊ *verb* **seesawed, seesawing**

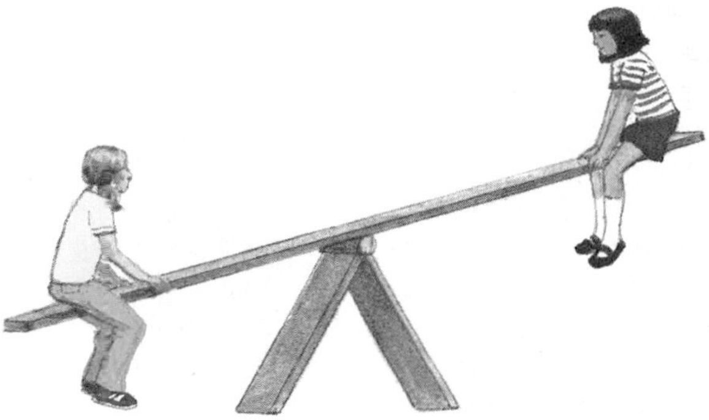

▲ **seesaw**

segment *noun* A part into which something is or can be divided.
seg·ment (sĕg′mənt) ◊ *noun, plural* **segments**

segregate *verb* To separate and set apart from others or from a main body or group.
seg·re·gate (sĕg′rĭ gāt′) ◊ *verb* **segregated, segregating**

segregation *noun* The act of segregating or the condition of being segregated.
seg·re·ga·tion (sĕg′rĭ gā′shən) ◊ *noun*

seismograph *noun* An instrument that detects and records earthquakes.
seis·mo·graph (sīz′mə grăf′) ◊ *noun, plural* **seismographs**

▲ **seismograph**

seize *verb* **1.** To take hold of suddenly: *I seized the rail as I fell.* **2.** To take possession

S

of with force: *Pirates seized the ship.*
seize (sēz) ◊ *verb* **seized, seizing**

seldom *adverb* Not often; rarely.
sel·dom (**sĕl′** dəm) ◊ *adverb*

select *verb* To choose from among several. ◊ *adjective* **1.** Carefully chosen to include the best. **2.** Of high quality.
se·lect (sĭ **lĕkt′**) ◊ *verb* **selected, selecting** ◊ *adjective*

selection *noun* **1.** The act or process of selecting. **2.** Someone or something that is chosen. —See Synonyms at **choice.**
se·lec·tion (sĭ **lĕk′** shən) ◊ *noun, plural* **selections**

self *noun* **1.** A person considered apart from any other person. **2.** A person's usual personality: *You aren't your happy self these days.*
self (sĕlf) ◊ *noun, plural* **selves**

self– The prefix *self–* means "oneself" or "itself." If one has *self-respect,* one has proper respect for oneself.

***VOCABULARY BUILDER* • self–**

Many words that are formed with **self–** are not entries in this dictionary. But you can figure out what these words mean by looking up the meanings of the root words in the dictionary. A hyphen is always used between *self–* and the root word. For example:
self-love = love of oneself
self-pity = pity for oneself

self-addressed *adjective* Addressed to be sent back to the sender.
self-ad·dressed (sĕlf′ə **drĕst′**) ◊ *adjective*

self-confidence *noun* Confidence in oneself and one's abilities.
self-con·fi·dence (**sĕlf′ kŏn′** fĭ dəns) ◊ *noun*

self-conscious *adjective* Too conscious of one's own appearance or behavior.
self-con·scious (**sĕlf′ kŏn′** shəs) ◊ *adjective*

ă	pat	ĭ	pit	oi	oil	th	bath
ā	pay	ī	ride	o͝o	book	*th*	bathe
â	care	î	fierce	o͞o	boot	ə	ago, item
ä	father	ŏ	pot	ou	out		pencil
ĕ	pet	ō	go	ŭ	cut		atom
ē	be	ô	paw, for	û	fur		circus

self-control *noun* Control over one's own emotions and behavior.
self-con·trol (sĕlf′kən **trōl′**) ◊ *noun*

self-government *noun* **1.** Political independence. **2.** Government by the people.
self-gov·ern·ment (**sĕlf′ gŭv′** ərn mənt) ◊ *noun*

selfish *adjective* Concerned mainly with oneself without thinking of others.
self·ish (**sĕl′** fĭsh) ◊ *adjective*

self-reliance *noun* Confidence in one's own abilities or resources.
self-re·li·ance (sĕlf′rĭ **lī′** əns) ◊ *noun*

self-respect *noun* Proper regard for oneself.
self-re·spect (sĕlf′rĭ **spĕkt′**) ◊ *noun*

self-righteous *adjective* Too sure of the rightness of one's behavior or beliefs.
self-right·eous (**sĕlf′ rī′** chəs) ◊ *adjective*

sell *verb* **1.** To exchange or deliver something for money or its equivalent: *I sold my bike for $50.00.* **2.** To offer for sale: *This store sells comics.* **3.** To be on sale. **4.** To be popular with buyers: *Is that item selling?*
sell (sĕl) ◊ *verb* **sold, selling**
‖*These sound alike:* **sell, cell**

selves *noun* Plural of **self.**
selves (sĕlvz) ◊ *noun*

semaphore *noun* A system for signaling in which two flags that are held one in each hand are used.
sem·a·phore (**sĕm′** ə fôr′) ◊ *noun, plural* **semaphores**

▲ **semaphore**

semester *noun* One of two terms that make up a school year.
se·mes·ter (sə **mĕs′**tər) ◊ *noun, plural* **semesters**

semicircle *noun* Half of a circle.
sem·i·cir·cle (**sĕm′**ĭ sûr′kəl) ◊ *noun, plural* **semicircles**

semicolon *noun* A punctuation mark (;) that shows a greater degree of separation between parts of a sentence than a comma does.
sem·i·co·lon (**sĕm′**ĭ kō′lən) ◊ *noun, plural* **semicolons**

semiconductor *noun* A material, such as silicon, that is used in making integrated circuits for computers.
sem·i·con·duc·tor (sĕm′ē kən **dŭk′**tər) ◊ *noun, plural* **semiconductors**

semifinal *noun* A game or match that comes before the final one, as in a tournament.
sem·i·fi·nal (sĕm′ē **fī′**nəl) ◊ *noun, plural* **semifinals**

seminary *noun* A school or college for training priests, ministers, or rabbis.
sem·i·nar·y (**sĕm′**ə nĕr′ē) ◊ *noun, plural* **seminaries**

semisolid *adjective* Partly solid and partly liquid.
◊ *noun* A substance that is partly solid and partly liquid.
sem·i·sol·id (sĕm′ē **sŏl′**ĭd) ◊ *adjective* ◊ *noun, plural* **semisolids**

Semitic *noun* A group of related languages that includes Arabic and Hebrew.
◊ *adjective* Of or relating to Semitic.
Se·mit·ic (sə **mĭt′**ĭk) ◊ *noun* ◊ *adjective*

senate *noun* Often **Senate 1.** The upper house of the United States Congress. Its members are elected every six years. **2.** The upper branch of the legislature in most states of the United States. **3.** In the Canadian government, the upper house of Parliament.
sen·ate (**sĕn′**ĭt) ◊ *noun, plural* **senates**

senator *noun* A member of a senate.
sen·a·tor (**sĕn′**ə tər) ◊ *noun, plural* **senators**

send *verb* **1.** To cause to go: *They sent me home.* **2.** To cause to move by force: *I sent the ball flying.* **3.** To transmit by mail. **4.** To cause to occur: *The sun sends out powerful rays.* **5.** To express for another to convey: *We send our love to your parents.*
send (sĕnd) ◊ *verb* **sent, sending**

SYNONYMS
send, address, dispatch, transmit
I am *sending* a birthday present to you. I *addressed* my letter to you incorrectly. Extra trains were *dispatched* to pick up the large crowd. The astronauts *transmitted* reports from the moon.
Antonym: *receive*

senior *adjective* **1.** Older: *My grandparents are the senior members of the family.* **2.** Indicating the older of two persons with the same name. **3.** Having a higher rank or longer service: *I am the senior member of the club.* **4.** Of the last year of high school or college: *The senior class graduates soon.*
◊ *noun* **1.** A person who is older or of higher rank than another. **2.** A student in the last year of high school or college.
sen·ior (**sēn′**yər) ◊ *adjective* ◊ *noun, plural* **seniors**

sensation *noun* **1.** Something that is felt, seen, tasted, smelled, or heard as a result of stimulation of a sense organ or as a result of a bodily condition: *A campfire gives us the sensation of heat.* **2.** The ability to perceive or feel. **3.** Lively public interest and excitement: *News of the discovery caused a sensation.* **4.** A cause of lively interest or excitement: *The new band was a sensation.*
sen·sa·tion (sĕn **sā′**shən) ◊ *noun, plural* **sensations**

sensational *adjective* Causing excitement.
sen·sa·tion·al (sĕn **sā′**shə nəl) ◊ *adjective*

sense *noun* **1.** A specialized bodily function, such as sight, hearing, or touch, that occurs as a reaction to stimulation of a sense organ. **2.** The taking in of something through or as if through the senses: *Their praise gave me a sense of my own worth.* **3.** An understanding or appreciation: *It's important to have a good sense of humor.* **4.** Good judgment: *Have the sense to put on a raincoat.* **5.** Sound reason: *We saw no sense in hurrying.* **6.** The meaning, or one of the meanings, of a word or phrase. —See Synonyms at **meaning. 7.** The meaning communicated by a story.
◊ *verb* To be aware of; feel.
sense (sĕns) ◊ *noun, plural* **senses** ◊ *verb* **sensed, sensing**

senseless *adjective* **1.** Without the power to feel; unconscious. **2.** Without meaning; pointless. **3.** Lacking judgment; foolish.
sense·less (sĕns′lĭs) ◊ *adjective*

sense organ *noun* A bodily organ or structure, such as the eye or ear, that reacts to a stimulus.
sense organ ◊ *noun, plural* **sense organs**

sensible *adjective* Showing good judgment; reasonable: *Be sensible and take your umbrella.*
sen·si·ble (sĕn′sə bəl) ◊ *adjective*

sensitive *adjective* **1.** Capable of receiving sense impressions: *Bats are sensitive to faint sounds.* **2.** Affected by something: *Photographic film is sensitive to light.* **3.** Easily affected, influenced, or hurt: *Don't be so sensitive to criticism.*
sen·si·tive (sĕn′sĭ tĭv) ◊ *adjective*

sensory *adjective* Of or relating to the senses or sensation.
sen·so·ry (sĕn′sə rē) ◊ *adjective*

sent *verb* Past tense and past participle of **send.**
sent (sĕnt) ◊ *verb*
‖*These sound alike:* **sent, cent, scent**

sentence *noun* **1.** A group of words, or sometimes a single word, that tells or expresses a complete thought. These are sentences: *It's almost midnight. Is it raining? Stop!* **2.** The punishment given by a court of law to a person who has been found guilty of wrongdoing; penalty.
◊ *verb* To set a punishment for.
sen·tence (sĕn′təns) ◊ *noun, plural* **sentences** ◊ *verb* **sentenced, sentencing**

sentiment *noun* **1.** A thought based on emotion or feeling: *The march music stirred up their patriotic sentiment.* **2.** Tender or sensitive feeling. **3.** A general opinion or view.
sen·ti·ment (sĕn′tə mənt) ◊ *noun, plural* **sentiments**

sentimental *adjective* **1.** Having to do with the feelings; emotional: *I have sentimental ties to my old school.* **2.** Easily influenced or affected by feelings.
sen·ti·ment·al (sĕn′tə **mĕn′**tl) ◊ *adjective*

sentry *noun* A guard who is posted at a spot to keep watch.
sen·try (sĕn′trē) ◊ *noun, plural* **sentries**

sepal *noun* One of the parts forming the outer covering of a flower. Sepals are usually green but sometimes they are brightly colored.
se·pal (sē′pəl) ◊ *noun, plural* **sepals**

▲ **sepal**

separate *verb* **1.** To divide into parts or sections: *We separated the apples into four piles.* **2.** To put or keep apart; be placed between: *A river separates the two states.* **3.** To go different ways: *We said good-by and separated.* **4.** To break a friendship or other union. **5.** To remove or be removed.
◊ *adjective* **1.** Set apart from the rest: *Libraries have a separate section for children's books.* **2.** Individual or independent: *They gave the children separate presents.*
sep·a·rate ◊ *verb* (sĕp′ə rāt′) **separated, separating** ◊ *adjective* (sĕp′ər ĭt *or* sĕp′rĭt)

SYNONYMS

separate, divide, part

I *separated* my good crayons from my old ones. *Divide* the circle into five sections. Nothing can *part* those two friends. **Antonyms:** *combine, join*

separation *noun* **1.** The act of separating or the condition of being separated. **2.** A space that separates; gap.
sep·a·ra·tion (sĕp′ə **rā′**shən) ◊ *noun, plural* **separations**

Sept. The abbreviation for *September.*

September *noun* The ninth month of the year. September has 30 days.
Sep·tem·ber (sĕp **tĕm′**bər) ◊ *noun*

ă	pat	ĭ	pit	oi	**oil**	th	**bath**
ā	pay	ī	ride	o͝o	book	*th*	**bathe**
â	care	î	fierce	o͞o	boot	ə	ago, item
ä	father	ŏ	pot	ou	**out**		pencil
ĕ	pet	ō	go	ŭ	cut		atom
ē	be	ô	paw, for	û	fur		circus

sequence *noun* **1.** The following of one thing after another in a regular or fixed way: *Show the pictures in the proper sequence.* **2.** A number of things or events that follow each other; series.
se·quence (sē′kwəns) ◊ *noun, plural* **sequences**

sequoia *noun* A very large evergreen tree that can grow as high as 300 feet.
se·quoi·a (sĭ **kwoi′** ə) ◊ *noun, plural* **sequoias**

▲ **sequoia**

serenade *noun* Music sung or played to honor someone.
◊ *verb* To sing or play a serenade.
ser·e·nade (sĕr′ə **nād′**) ◊ *noun, plural* **serenades** ◊ *verb* **serenaded, serenading**

serene *adjective* Peaceful and calm: *There was a serene look on the face of the child.*
se·rene (sə **rēn′**) ◊ *adjective*

sergeant *noun* **1.** An Army or Marine Corps officer ranking above a corporal. **2.** An Air Force officer ranking above an airman.
ser·geant (sär′jənt) ◊ *noun, plural* **sergeants**

serial *noun* A story divided into parts. The parts of a serial are presented one at a time in a magazine, on radio, or on television.
se·ri·al (sîr′ē əl) ◊ *noun, plural* **serials**
‖*These sound alike:* **serial, cereal**

serial number *noun* One of a series of numbers used to identify a person or thing.
serial number ◊ *noun, plural* **serial numbers**

series *noun* A number of similar things or events in a row or following one another: *A series of footprints led to the house.*
se·ries (sîr′ēz) ◊ *noun, plural* **series**

serious *adjective* **1.** Thoughtful or grave; solemn: *The chess players all had serious expressions.* **2.** Not joking or fooling: *Are you serious about moving away?* **3.** Not trivial; important: *Getting married is a serious matter.* **4.** Able or likely to cause harm; dangerous: *Smoking is a serious health risk.*
se·ri·ous (sîr′ē əs) ◊ *adjective*

SYNONYMS

serious, earnest, grave²

I am *serious* when I tell you not to go.
My friend made an *earnest* plea for help.
They talked about the approaching storm in *grave* voices.

sermon *noun* **1.** A speech given for religious or moral teaching as part of a religious service. **2.** A long, serious talk.
ser·mon (sûr′mən) ◊ *noun, plural* **sermons**

serpent *noun* A snake.
ser·pent (sûr′pənt) ◊ *noun, plural* **serpents**

serum *noun* **1.** The clear, yellowish liquid part of the blood. **2.** A liquid used to prevent or cure a disease. Serum is taken from the blood of an animal that has the disease.
se·rum (sîr′əm) ◊ *noun, plural* **serums**

servant *noun* **1.** A person who works for wages in someone else's household. **2.** A person who is hired to perform services for others: *Police officers are public servants.*
serv·ant (sûr′vənt) ◊ *noun, plural* **servants**

serve *verb* **1.** To do work for; be a servant to: *The butler served the family for years.* **2.** To

S

work to help; promote the interests of; aid. **3.** To spend time on: *They served 10 years in the navy.* **4.** To fill a certain job: *Our neighbor served as the school janitor.* **5.** To wait on customers in a store or restaurant. **6.** To put food on a table. **7.** To be enough for: *This can of corn serves four.* **8.** To be of use; act: *An old box served as a bed for the cat.* **9.** To be used by: *This harbor serves many ships.* **10.** To put a ball into play by hitting it in a game such as tennis.
◊ *noun* The right to put a ball into play by hitting it in a game such as tennis.
serve (sûrv) ◊ *verb* **served, serving** ◊ *noun, plural* **serves**

service *noun* **1.** The act or work of helping others; aid: *They spent their lives in service to the poor.* **2.** Work or employment for someone else. **3.** Benefit or use: *My typewriter has given me good service.* **4. services** Help given by a person with special training: *When I broke my arm I needed the services of a doctor.* **5.** The act or manner of satisfying customers' requests: *The service at that restaurant is very slow.* **6.** A set of dishes or other objects used for serving and eating food. **7.** A branch of the government: *I want a job in the civil service.* **8.** The armed forces or a branch of the armed forces. **9.** A system that supplies public needs: *Our bus service is good.* **10.** A religious ceremony or gathering. **11.** Repair or maintenance, as of a car.
◊ *verb* To repair or keep fit for use: *A mechanic serviced the washing machine.*
serv·ice (sûr′ vĭs) ◊ *noun, plural* **services** ◊ *verb* **serviced, servicing**

service station *noun* A gas station.
service station ◊ *noun, plural* **service stations**

serving *noun* A portion of food; helping.
serv·ing (sûr′ vĭng) ◊ *noun, plural* **servings**

session *noun* **1.** A single meeting or gathering together of a group. **2.** A meeting or series of meetings of a court or legislature. **3.** The time during which meetings take place: *The summer session of classes begins in June.*
ses·sion (sĕsh′ ən) ◊ *noun, plural* **sessions**

set¹ *verb* **1.** To put; place: *I set the package on the table.* **2.** To become hard or firm; harden. **3.** To put in a certain condition: *The prisoners were set free by the new ruler.* **4.** To place in a position or condition for proper use; arrange: *We set a trap for the mouse.* **5.** To adjust a device or machine to a certain position: *I set my alarm for seven o'clock.* **6.** To determine a goal or a wish: *My heart is set on being a forest ranger.* **7.** To decide on; fix: *They set a date for the party.* **8.** To establish; create: *Let's set a good example for the younger students.* **9.** To start; begin: *Let's set to work.* **10.** To disappear beneath the horizon; go down: *The sun sets in the west.*
◊ *adjective* **1.** Not changing; fixed. **2.** Ready; prepared: *We're set to go.*
◊ *idioms* **set aside** To keep for a special purpose. **set in** To begin to happen or appear: *Cold weather set in early this year.* **set off** **1.** To cause to happen: *The story set off wild laughter.* **2.** To cause to explode: *Who set off the fireworks?* **3.** To show as being different: *Quotation marks set off words that are spoken.* **set out** To start a journey or other task. **set up** **1.** To build, put up, or arrange. **2.** To establish or start: *Our city set up a free medical center for needy patients.*
set¹ (sĕt) ◊ *verb* **set, setting** ◊ *adjective*

set² *noun* **1.** A group of things of the same kind that belong or are used together: *We have a new set of china.* **2.** A radio or television and the parts that make it up. **3.** The scenery, furniture, and other objects on the stage for a play or movie. **4.** A group of games that make up one part of a match in tennis.
set² (sĕt) ◊ *noun, plural* **sets**

***HISTORY* • set¹, set²**

Set¹ is related to **sit.** It comes from an old English word that meant "to cause to sit, to put." **Set²** comes from an old French word that came from a Latin word meaning "a group of followers."

setter *noun* A large dog with long, smooth hair. Setters are often trained to show a hunter where an animal is.
set·ter (sĕt′ ər) ◊ *noun, plural* **setters**

ă	pat	ĭ	pit	oi	**oi**l	th	ba**th**
ā	pay	ī	ride	ŏŏ	b**oo**k	*th*	ba**th**e
â	care	î	fierce	ōō	b**oo**t	ə	ago, item
ä	father	ŏ	pot	ou	**ou**t		pencil
ĕ	pet	ō	go	ŭ	cut		atom
ē	be	ô	paw, for	û	fur		circus

▲ **setter**

settle *verb* **1.** To arrange or decide by agreement: *Let's settle the date of the field trip.* **2.** To come to rest or cause to come to rest in place: *The butterfly settled on a flower.* **3.** To make a home or place to live in: *Pioneers settled the West.* **4.** To go down or to the bottom; sink: *Mud settles fast in calm rivers.* **5.** To make or become calm: *After the excitement I tried to settle myself so I could study.*
set·tle (sĕt′l) ◊ *verb* **settled, settling**

settlement *noun* **1.** The act of settling. **2.** A small community; village. **3.** A colony.
set·tle·ment (sĕt′l mənt) ◊ *noun, plural* **settlements**

seven *noun* The number, written 7, that is equal to the sum of 6 + 1.
◊ *adjective* Being one more than six.
sev·en (sĕv′ən) ◊ *noun, plural* **sevens** ◊ *adjective*

seventeen *noun* The number, written 17, that is equal to the sum of 16 + 1.
◊ *adjective* Being one more than sixteen.
sev·en·teen (sĕv′ən **tēn′**) ◊ *noun, plural* **seventeens** ◊ *adjective*

seventeenth *noun* **1.** The number in a series that matches the number seventeen. **2.** One of seventeen equal parts, written 1/17.
◊ *adjective* Coming after the sixteenth.
sev·en·teenth (sĕv′ən **tēnth′**) ◊ *noun, plural* **seventeenths** ◊ *adjective*

seventh *noun* **1.** The number in a series that matches the number seven. **2.** One of seven equal parts, written 1/7.
◊ *adjective* Coming after the sixth.
sev·enth (sĕv′ənth) ◊ *noun, plural* **sevenths** ◊ *adjective*

seventieth *noun* **1.** The number in a series that matches the number seventy. **2.** One of seventy equal parts, written 1/70.
◊ *adjective* Coming after the sixty-ninth.
sev·en·ti·eth (sĕv′ən tē ĭth) ◊ *noun, plural* **seventieths** ◊ *adjective*

seventy *noun* The number, written 70, that is equal to the product of 10 × 7.
◊ *adjective* Being equal to ten times seven.
sev·en·ty (sĕv′ən tē) ◊ *noun, plural* **seventies** ◊ *adjective*

several *adjective* More than two but not many: *We live several miles away.* —See Synonyms at **many.**
◊ *noun* More than two people or things.
sev·er·al (sĕv′ər əl) ◊ *adjective* ◊ *noun*

severe *adjective* **1.** Very strict and harsh; stern. **2.** Causing great pain or difficulty. **3.** Very serious; extreme.
se·vere (sə **vîr′**) ◊ *adjective* **severer, severest**

sew *verb* To make, repair, or fasten a thing with stitches made by a needle and thread.
sew (sō) ◊ *verb* **sewed, sewn** *or* **sewed, sewing**
‖*These sound alike:* **sew, so, sow[1]**

sewage *noun* Waste material that is carried away from buildings in drains or sewers.
sew·age (sōō′ĭj) ◊ *noun*

sewer *noun* A pipe or drain, usually underground, built to carry away waste material.
sew·er (sōō′ər) ◊ *noun, plural* **sewers**

sewn *verb* A past participle of **sew.**
sewn (sōn) ◊ *verb*

sex *noun* **1.** One of the two groups, male and female, into which many living things are divided. **2.** The condition of being male or female: *We hire people according to ability, not by age or sex.*
sex (sĕks) ◊ *noun, plural* **sexes**

shabby *adjective* Being worn-out and old.
shab·by (**shăb′**ē) ◊ *adjective* **shabbier, shabbiest**

shack *noun* A small, crudely built cabin.
shack (shăk) ◊ *noun, plural* **shacks**

shad *noun* An ocean fish that swims up rivers and is caught for food.
shad (shăd) ◊ *noun, plural* **shad**

shade *noun* **1.** An area that is partly dark because light has been blocked off from it. **2.** A device that blocks off part of the light: *Pull*

S

down the window shade. **3.** One of the degrees of lightness or darkness of a color: *The garden has many shades of green.* **4.** A very small amount or degree.
◊ *verb* **1.** To keep light from: *Trees shaded the street.* **2.** To have or give different degrees of lightness and darkness.
shade (shād) ◊ *noun, plural* **shades** ◊ *verb* **shaded, shading**

shadow *noun* **1.** A shaded area made when light is blocked. **2.** Partial darkness.
shad·ow (shăd′ō) ◊ *noun, plural* **shadows**

▲ **shadow**

shady *adjective* Full of or giving shade.
shad·y (shā′dē) ◊ *adjective* **shadier, shadiest**

shaft *noun* **1.** A spear or arrow or the long slender stem of a spear or arrow. **2.** A rod that forms a handle. Devices such as hammers and golf clubs have shafts. **3.** A long bar or rod used in a machine. **4.** A ray or beam of light. **5.** A long, narrow, vertical passage or opening, as one that goes into a mine.
shaft (shăft) ◊ *noun, plural* **shafts**

shaggy *adjective* Having long, rough hair, wool, or fibers: *We have a shaggy dog.*
shag·gy (shăg′ē) ◊ *adjective* **shaggier, shaggiest**

shake *verb* **1.** To move back and forth or up and down with short, quick movements: *The nurse shook the thermometer. The branches shook in the wind.* **2.** To remove or scatter by making short, quick movements: *I shook the snow from my hat.* **3.** To clasp hands. **4.** To tremble: *I was shaking with cold.* **5.** To be a shock to; upset: *News of the accident had shaken us.* **6.** To make less firm or loyal: *Nothing could shake me from my belief.*
◊ *noun* An act of shaking.
shake (shāk) ◊ *verb* **shook, shaken, shaking** ◊ *noun, plural* **shakes**

ă pat	ĭ pit	oi **oil**	th **bath**
ā pay	ī ride	o͝o **book**	*th* **bathe**
â care	î fierce	o͞o **boot**	ə ago, item
ä father	ŏ pot	ou **out**	pencil
ĕ pet	ō go	ŭ cut	atom
ē be	ô paw, for	û fur	circus

SYNONYMS

shake, quake, shiver

Look at them *shake* with laughter. His legs *quaked* from stage fright. She *shivered* in the wind and rain.

shaken *verb* Past participle of **shake.**
shak·en (shā′kən) ◊ *verb*

shaky *adjective* **1.** Trembling or shaking: *The child answered in a shaky voice.* **2.** Likely to break down; not firm or sound: *That old table is shaky.*
shak·y (shā′kē) ◊ *adjective* **shakier, shakiest**

shale *noun* A kind of rock with thin layers that split easily.
shale (shāl) ◊ *noun*

shall *auxiliary verb* Used before a verb in the infinitive to show: **1.** Something that will take place or exist in the future: *We shall arrive tomorrow.* **2.** Something, such as an order, requirement, or obligation: *You shall obey us.* **3.** The will to do something or make something happen: *I shall not cry.*
shall (shăl) ◊ *auxiliary verb, past tense* **should**

shallow *adjective* Measuring little from bottom to top or from back to front; not deep.
shal·low (shăl′ō) ◊ *adjective* **shallower, shallowest**

shame *noun* **1.** A painful feeling that one has done something wrong or foolish. **2.** A loss of respect or honor; disgrace. **3.** Something that causes regret: *It would be a shame to miss the circus this year.*
◊ *verb* **1.** To fill with shame. **2.** To force by causing shame. **3.** To bring disgrace on.
shame (shām) ◊ *noun, plural* **shames** ◊ *verb* **shamed, shaming**

shameful *adjective* That brings, causes, or deserves shame; disgraceful.
shame·ful (**shām′** fəl) ◊ *adjective*

shampoo *noun* **1.** A liquid soap used to wash the hair or to clean rugs or furniture coverings. **2.** The act of using shampoo.
◊ *verb* To wash or clean with shampoo.
sham·poo (shăm **po͞o′**) ◊ *noun, plural* **shampoos** ◊ *verb* **shampooed, shampooing**

shape *noun* **1.** The outer form of an object; outline: *We drew circles, triangles, and other shapes.* **2.** A form in which something appears; appearance: *The jar has the shape of a bear.* **3.** Proper physical condition or mechanical order: *Athletes must stay in shape.*
◊ *verb* To give a certain shape or form to.
shape (shāp) ◊ *noun, plural* **shapes** ◊ *verb* **shaped, shaping**

-shaped The word *-shaped* combines with other words and means "having the shape or form of." An *egg-shaped* stone has the shape of an egg.

***VOCABULARY BUILDER* • -shaped**

Many words that can be formed with **-shaped** are not entries in this dictionary. But you can figure out what these words mean by looking up the meanings of the root words in the dictionary. A hyphen is always used between *-shaped* and the word with which it combines.
For example:
cone-shaped = having the form of a cone
heart-shaped = having the shape of a heart

share *verb* **1.** To have, use, or do together with another or others: *They shared the job of cleaning up. Let's share this last orange.* **2.** To take part: *We all shared in planning the show.*
◊ *noun* **1.** A part; portion. **2.** One of the many equal parts into which the ownership of a business is divided.
share (shâr) ◊ *verb* **shared, sharing** ◊ *noun, plural* **shares**

shark *noun* A large, fierce ocean fish that has a big mouth and sharp teeth.
shark (shärk) ◊ *noun, plural* **sharks**

▲ **shark**
A hammerhead shark

sharp *adjective* **1.** Having a thin edge that cuts or a fine point that pierces. **2.** Not rounded or blunt; pointed. **3.** Abrupt or sudden; not gradual: *The road made a sharp turn to the left.* **4.** Clear; distinct. **5.** Harsh; severe: *A sharp wind was blowing.* **6.** Acting strongly on the senses: *This cheese has a sharp flavor.* **7.** Alert in noticing or thinking; keen: *Someone with sharp eyes would see the tiny bird.*
◊ *adverb* **1.** Exactly; precisely: *It's three o'clock sharp.* **2.** Alertly; keenly: *Look sharp!*
sharp (shärp) ◊ *adjective* **sharper, sharpest** ◊ *adverb*

sharpen *verb* To make or become sharp.
sharp·en (**shär′** pən) ◊ *verb* **sharpened, sharpening**

shatter *verb* **1.** To break suddenly into many pieces; smash. **2.** To destroy; ruin.
shat·ter (**shăt′** ər) ◊ *verb* **shattered, shattering**

shave *verb* **1.** To remove hair from with a razor. **2.** To cut or remove thin slices from.
◊ *noun* The act of shaving.
shave (shāv) ◊ *verb* **shaved, shaved** *or* **shaven, shaving** ◊ *noun, plural* **shaves**

shaven *verb* A past participle of **shave.**
shav·en (**shā′** vən) ◊ *verb*

shaving *noun* A thin strip or slice of material, such as wood or metal.
shav·ing (**shā′** vĭng) ◊ *noun, plural* **shavings**

S

shawl *noun* A large piece of cloth worn around the shoulders, neck, or head.
shawl (shôl) ◊ *noun, plural* **shawls**

she *pronoun* The female one mentioned earlier: *My mother told me that she would return soon.*
she (shē) ◊ *pronoun*

sheaf *noun* A bundle of things of the same kind: *The folder held a sheaf of papers.*
sheaf (shēf) ◊ *noun, plural* **sheaves**

shear *verb* To remove wool or hair with a sharp tool such as scissors or clippers.
shear (shîr) ◊ *verb* **sheared, sheared** *or* **shorn, shearing**
‖*These sound alike:* **shear, sheer**

shears *noun* (*used with a plural verb*) A cutting tool like a scissors but usually larger.
shears (shîrz) ◊ *noun*

sheath *noun* A case or covering that fits tightly over the blade of a knife or sword.
sheath (shēth) ◊ *noun, plural* **sheaths**

sheaves *noun* Plural of **sheaf.**
sheaves (shēvz) ◊ *noun*

shed¹ *verb* **1.** To let fall or flow; pour out: *I shed tears easily.* **2.** To lose naturally; drop: *Most trees shed their leaves.* **3.** To send out; give off: *The moon shed a pale light.*
shed¹ (shĕd) ◊ *verb* **shed, shedding**

shed² *noun* A small, simple building for storage or shelter.
shed² (shĕd) ◊ *noun, plural* **sheds**

***HISTORY* • shed¹, shed²**

Shed¹ comes from an old English word that meant "to separate, cast off." **Shed²** first appeared in written English about 500 years ago. It is probably related to **shade.**

she'd Contraction of "she had" or "she would."
she'd (shēd) ◊ *contraction*

ă	pat	ĭ	pit	oi	**oil**	th	**bath**
ā	pay	ī	ride	o͝o	**book**	*th*	**bathe**
â	care	î	fierce	o͞o	**boot**	ə	ago, item
ä	father	ŏ	pot	ou	**out**		pencil
ĕ	pet	ō	go	ŭ	cut		atom
ē	be	ô	paw, for	û	fur		circus

sheep *noun* An animal related to the goat, with hoofs and a thick coat of wool. Sheep are raised for their wool, skin, or meat.
sheep (shēp) ◊ *noun, plural* **sheep**

▲ **sheep**

sheep dog *noun* A dog that is trained to guard and herd sheep.
sheep dog ◊ *noun, plural* **sheep dogs**

sheer *adjective* **1.** Thin enough to see through. **2.** Total; utter: *I fainted from sheer exhaustion.* **3.** Very steep.
sheer (shîr) ◊ *adjective* **sheerer, sheerest**
‖*These sound alike:* **sheer, shear**

sheet *noun* **1.** A large piece of thin cloth. Sheets are used as bed coverings, usually with one under and one over the person sleeping. **2.** A broad, thin piece of a material such as paper, metal, glass, or ice.
sheet (shēt) ◊ *noun, plural* **sheets**

sheet lightning *noun* Lightning that appears as a broad sheet of light across a part of the sky. Sheet lightning is caused by the reflection of a distant flash of lightning by clouds.

sheik *noun* The leader of an Arab family, village, or tribe.
sheik (shēk) ◊ *noun, plural* **sheiks**

shekel *noun* A unit of money used in Israel.
shek·el (shĕk′əl) ◊ *noun, plural* **shekels**

shelf *noun* **1.** A flat piece of a material such as wood, metal, or glass, attached to a wall or fastened into a frame. Shelves are used to hold or store things. **2.** Something, such as a flat ledge of rock, like a shelf.
shelf (shĕlf) ◊ *noun, plural* **shelves**

shell *noun* **1.** The hard outer covering of such

water animals as clams, crabs, oysters, and snails. **2.** The hard outer covering of certain other animals or plants. Turtles, eggs, and nuts all have shells. **3.** An outer covering or a frame. **4.** A piece of ammunition for a gun, especially a case that holds a bullet and its explosive.
◊ *verb* **1.** To remove the outer covering from. **2.** To attack with ammunition; bombard.
shell (shĕl) ◊ *noun, plural* **shells** ◊ *verb* **shelled, shelling**

she'll Contraction of "she will" or "she shall."
she'll (shēl) ◊ *contraction*

shellac *noun* A hard varnish that can be used to protect wooden floors and furniture.
◊ *verb* To apply shellac to.
shel·lac (shə **lăk'**) ◊ *noun, plural* **shellacs** ◊ *verb* **shellacked, shellacking**

shellfish *noun* A water animal that has a hard outer covering. Crabs, clams, and oysters are shellfish.
shell·fish (**shĕl'** fĭsh') ◊ *noun, plural* **shellfish** *or* **shellfishes**

shelter *noun* **1.** Something that protects or covers. **2.** The state of being protected: *If it rains, take shelter.* **3.** A place for homeless people or animals to stay.
◊ *verb* To provide protection or cover for.
shel·ter (**shĕl'** tər) ◊ *noun, plural* **shelters** ◊ *verb* **sheltered, sheltering**

shelves *noun* Plural of **shelf.**
shelves (shĕlvz) ◊ *noun*

shepherd *noun* A person who takes care of a flock of sheep.
shep·herd (**shĕp'** ərd) ◊ *noun, plural* **shepherds**

sherbet *noun* A frozen dessert similar to ice cream and flavored with fruit.
sher·bet (**shûr'** bĭt) ◊ *noun, plural* **sherbets**

sheriff *noun* A county official who is in charge of enforcing the law.
sher·iff (**shĕr'** ĭf) ◊ *noun, plural* **sheriffs**

she's Contraction of "she is" or "she has."
she's (shēz) ◊ *contraction*

shield *noun* **1.** A piece of hard material, such as metal or wood, that is carried on the arm to protect the body during battle. **2.** A badge shaped like a warrior's shield. **3.** Something used as a defense or protection: *We planted a hedge as a shield against the wind.*
◊ *verb* To protect or cover: *I shielded my head from the sun with a parasol.*
shield (shēld) ◊ *noun, plural* **shields** ◊ *verb* **shielded, shielding**

shift *verb* **1.** To move from one place or position to another; transfer: *I shifted the package to my other arm.* **2.** To change: *Let's shift seats.* **3.** To provide for one's own needs: *The older students had to shift for themselves.*
◊ *noun* **1.** A change in place, position, or direction; movement or transfer. **2.** A group of workers who work at one place during the same hours. **3.** The period of time during which a group of workers works.
shift (shĭft) ◊ *verb* **shifted, shifting** ◊ *noun, plural* **shifts**

shilling *noun* A former British coin that was worth 1/20 of a pound.
shil·ling (**shĭl'** ĭng) ◊ *noun, plural* **shillings**

shimmer *verb* To shine with a flickering light; glimmer.
shim·mer (**shĭm'** ər) ◊ *verb* **shimmered, shimmering**

shin *noun* The front part of the leg between the knee and the ankle.
◊ *verb* To climb by holding on and pulling with the hands and legs.
shin (shĭn) ◊ *noun, plural* **shins** ◊ *verb* **shinned, shinning**

shine *verb* **1.** To give off light or reflect light; glow. **2.** To make bright or glossy; polish.
◊ *noun* **1.** Light that is given off or reflected; brightness. **2.** An act of polishing. **3.** Sunny weather: *We'll go, rain or shine.*
shine (shīn) ◊ *verb* **shone, shining** ◊ *noun, plural* **shines**

shingle *noun* A thin piece of a material, such as wood, that is laid in overlapping rows to cover the roof or outside walls of a building.
◊ *verb* To put shingles on a roof or wall.
shin·gle (**shĭng'** gəl) ◊ *noun, plural* **shingles** ◊ *verb* **shingled, shingling**

shiny *adjective* Reflecting light; bright.
shin·y (**shī'** nē) ◊ *adjective* **shinier, shiniest**

ship *noun* **1.** A large vessel that can travel in deep water. A ship can be powered by a motor or sails. **2.** An airplane, airship, or spacecraft.
◊ *verb* **1.** To transport: *We ship our fresh vegetables to market by truck.* **2.** To put on board a ship. **3.** To take a job on a ship.
ship (shĭp) ◊ *noun, plural* **ships** ◊ *verb* **shipped, shipping**

S

-ship The suffix *-ship* forms nouns and means "condition" or "quality." *Friendship* is the condition of being friends. The suffix *-ship* also means "art," "skill," or "craft." *Penmanship* is the art or skill of writing with a pen. The suffix *-ship* also means "office," "position," or "rank." *Dictatorship* means the position of dictator.

***VOCABULARY BUILDER* • -ship**

Many words that are formed with **-ship** are not entries in this dictionary. But you can figure out what these words mean by looking up the meanings of the root words and the suffix. For example:
governorship = the office of governor
leadership = the quality of a leader
marksmanship = the art or skill of a marksman

shipboard *noun* The side of a ship.
◊ *idiom* **on shipboard** On board a ship.
ship·board (**shĭp′**bôrd′) ◊ *noun*

shipment *noun* **1.** The act of shipping goods. **2.** An amount of goods shipped.
ship·ment (**shĭp′**mənt) ◊ *noun, plural* **shipments**

shipping *noun* **1.** The act or business of transporting goods. **2.** The ships belonging to a port, industry, or country.
ship·ping (**shĭp′**ĭng) ◊ *noun*

shipshape *adjective* Neat and tidy.
ship·shape (**shĭp′**shāp′) ◊ *adjective*

shipwreck *noun* **1.** A wrecked ship. **2.** The destruction of a ship, as by a collision or because of a storm.
ship·wreck (**shĭp′**rĕk′) ◊ *noun, plural* **shipwrecks**

shipyard *noun* A place where ships are built, repaired, and equipped.
ship·yard (**shĭp′**yärd′) ◊ *noun, plural* **shipyards**

ă	pat	ĭ	pit	oi	**oil**	th	**bath**
ā	pay	ī	ride	ŏŏ	**book**	*th*	**bathe**
â	care	î	fierce	ōō	**boot**	ə	**ago, item**
ä	father	ŏ	pot	ou	**out**		pencil
ĕ	pet	ō	go	ŭ	cut		atom
ē	be	ô	paw, for	û	fur		circus

▲ **shipyard**

shirk *verb* To avoid doing something one ought to do: *Quit shirking and help us get this job done.*
shirk (shûrk) ◊ *verb* **shirked, shirking**

shirt *noun* A garment for the upper part of the body. A shirt usually has a collar, sleeves, and an opening in the front.
shirt (shûrt) ◊ *noun, plural* **shirts**

shiver *verb* To undergo shaking that cannot be controlled; tremble. —See Synonyms at **shake.**
◊ *noun* The act or sensation of shivering.
shiv·er (**shĭv′**ər) ◊ *verb* **shivered, shivering** ◊ *noun, plural* **shivers**

shoal *noun* A shallow place in water.
shoal (shōl) ◊ *noun, plural* **shoals**

shock[1] *noun* **1.** A heavy, violent collision, impact, or disturbance. **2.** Something that happens suddenly and that upsets the mind or emotions. **3.** A mental or emotional upset caused by such an event. **4.** A strong reaction of the body to severe injury or loss of blood. A person in shock is weak, pale, and cold. **5.** The feeling caused by the passage of an electric current through the body.
◊ *verb* **1.** To surprise or upset greatly. **2.** To subject to an electric shock.
shock[1] (shŏk) ◊ *noun, plural* **shocks** ◊ *verb* **shocked, shocking**

shock[2] *noun* **1.** A pile of grain stacked upright in a field to dry. **2.** A bushy mass.
shock[2] (shŏk) ◊ *noun, plural* **shocks**

HISTORY • shock[1], shock[2]

Shock[1] comes from an old French word that meant "to strike." **Shock[2]** may come from an old Dutch word that meant "a pile of grain sheaves."

shod *verb* Past tense and past participle of **shoe.**
shod (shŏd) ◊ *verb*

shoddy *adjective* Of very poor quality.
shod·dy (**shŏd′**ē) ◊ *adjective* **shoddier, shoddiest**

shoe *noun* **1.** An outer covering for the foot. A typical shoe has a stiff sole and heel and a flexible upper part. **2.** A horseshoe.
◊ *verb* To furnish or fit with shoes.
shoe (sho͞o) ◊ *noun, plural* **shoes** ◊ *verb* **shod, shoeing**

shoehorn *noun* A curved device that is used at the heel to help slip on a tight shoe.
shoe·horn (**sho͞o′**hôrn′) ◊ *noun, plural* **shoehorns**

shoelace *noun* A string used for lacing and fastening a shoe.
shoe·lace (**sho͞o′**lās′) ◊ *noun, plural* **shoelaces**

shone *verb* Past tense and past participle of **shine.**
shone (shōn) ◊ *verb*
‖*These sound alike:* **shone, shown**

shook *verb* Past tense of **shake.**
shook (sho͝ok) ◊ *verb*

shoot *verb* **1.** To hit, wound, or kill with a bullet, an arrow, or another projectile fired from a weapon. **2.** To fire a weapon. **3.** To set off; explode. **4.** To send or be sent forth with great force or speed: *They shot a rocket into outer space.* **5.** To aim; strive: *I'm shooting for first prize.* **6.** To move or pass quickly: *The cars shot past us.* **7.** To begin to grow or sprout. **8.** To record on film; photograph.
◊ *noun* A plant or plant part that has just begun to grow or sprout.
shoot (sho͞ot) ◊ *verb* **shot, shooting** ◊ *noun, plural* **shoots**

shooting star *noun* A meteor.
shooting star ◊ *noun, plural* **shooting stars**

shop *noun* **1.** A place where goods or services are sold to the public; store. **2.** A place where things are made or repaired. **3.** A classroom for learning how to use tools.
◊ *verb* To visit stores to look or buy.
shop (shŏp) ◊ *noun, plural* **shops** ◊ *verb* **shopped, shopping**

shoplift *verb* To steal displayed merchandise from a store.
shop·lift (**shŏp′**lĭft′) ◊ *verb* **shoplifted, shoplifting**

shopping center *noun* A group of shops that form a central market; mall.
shopping center ◊ *noun, plural* **shopping centers**

shore *noun* **1.** The land along the edge of a body of water. **2.** Land.
shore (shôr) ◊ *noun, plural* **shores**

shorn *verb* A past participle of **shear.**
shorn (shôrn) ◊ *verb*

short *adjective* **1.** Not long: *Short hair is now in style.* **2.** Not tall. **3.** Covering a small distance or taking a small amount of time: *We took a short walk.* **4.** Not being or having enough; insufficient: *Ten is two short of a dozen.* **5.** Brief in an unfriendly way; curt. **6.** Not stressed: *The line of verse had five long syllables and five short syllables.* **7.** Of or having one of the vowel sounds (ă), (ĕ), (ĭ), (ŏ), (ŭ), or (o͝o): *The "a" in "pan" is a short vowel, but the "a" in "pane" is a long vowel.*
◊ *adverb* Suddenly: *The car stopped short.*
◊ *noun* **1.** A short movie. **2.** A short circuit. **3. shorts** Pants that reach only to the knees or above the knees.
short (shôrt) ◊ *adjective* **shorter, shortest** ◊ *adverb* ◊ *noun, plural* **shorts**

shortage *noun* An amount of something that is not enough; lack.
short·age (**shôr′**tĭj) ◊ *noun, plural* **shortages**

short circuit *noun* A path of electricity that leaves the intended electric circuit and allows too much current to flow. A short circuit can cause a fire or blow a fuse.
short circuit ◊ *noun, plural* **short circuits**

shortcoming *noun* A fault or weakness.
short·com·ing (**shôrt′**kŭm′ĭng) ◊ *noun, plural* **shortcomings**

shortcut *noun* A route or method that is quicker or more direct than the usual one.
short·cut (**shôrt′**kŭt′) ◊ *noun, plural* **shortcuts**

shorten *verb* To make or become shorter.
short·en (shôr′tn) ◊ *verb* **shortened, shortening**

shortening *noun* Butter, lard, or other fat used in baking.
short·en·ing (shôr′tn ĭng) ◊ *noun*

short-lived *adjective* Living or lasting only a short time.
short-lived (shôrt′līvd′ *or* shôrt′lĭvd′) ◊ *adjective*

shortly *adverb* In a short time; soon.
short·ly (shôrt′ly) ◊ *adverb*

shortness *noun* The quality or condition of being short; brevity.
short·ness (shôrt′nĭs) ◊ *noun*

shortsighted *adjective* **1.** Unable to see distant objects clearly; nearsighted. **2.** Not planning carefully for the future.
short·sight·ed (shôrt′sī′tĭd) ◊ *adjective*

shortstop *noun* **1.** The position between second and third bases in baseball. **2.** The player who plays this position.
short·stop (shôrt′stŏp′) ◊ *noun, plural* **shortstops**

▲ **shortstop**

ă	pat	ĭ	pit	oi	**oil**	th	**bath**
ā	pay	ī	ride	o͝o	**book**	*th*	**bathe**
â	care	î	fierce	o͞o	**boot**	ə	**ago, item**
ä	father	ŏ	pot	ou	**out**		pencil
ĕ	pet	ō	go	ŭ	cut		atom
ē	be	ô	paw, for	û	fur		circus

shot¹ *noun* **1.** The firing of a weapon, such as a gun. **2.** A bullet, a metal ball, or a pellet fired from a gun. **3.** The launching of a space vehicle. **4.** A throw, drive, or stroke toward a goal or target. **5.** The distance over which something is or can be shot. **6.** A person who shoots: *You're the best shot on our hockey team.* **7.** A chance; try. **8.** A photograph. **9.** A dose of medicine given by injection.
shot¹ (shŏt) ◊ *noun, plural* **shots** *or* **shot** (for sense 2)

shot² *verb* Past tense and past participle of **shoot.**
shot² (shŏt) ◊ *verb*

shotgun *noun* A gun with a long barrel that fires cartridges filled with pellets.
shot·gun (shŏt′gŭn′) ◊ *noun, plural* **shotguns**

should *auxiliary verb* Past tense of **shall** used to show: **1.** Obligation; duty: *You should send them a note.* **2.** What is expected or likely: *We should arrive at noon.* **3.** Something, such as an action, that would lead to something else: *If they should call, tell them I'll be back soon.*
should (sho͝od) ◊ *auxiliary verb*

shoulder *noun* **1.** The part of the human body between the neck and the upper arm. **2.** A similar part on an animal. **3.** The part of a garment that covers the shoulder. **4.** A sloping side or edge, as of a road.
shoul·der (shōl′dər) ◊ *noun, plural* **shoulders**

shoulder blade *noun* A large, flat bone that forms the rear of the shoulder.
shoulder blade ◊ *noun, plural* **shoulder blades**

shouldn't Contraction of "should not."
should·n't (sho͝od′nt) ◊ *contraction*

shout *verb* To cry out or say loudly; yell.
◊ *noun* A loud cry or yell.
shout (shout) ◊ *verb* **shouted, shouting** ◊ *noun, plural* **shouts**

shove *verb* To push hard or roughly: *We shoved the heavy chest into the hall.* —See Synonyms at **push.**
◊ *noun* A hard or rough push.
shove (shŭv) ◊ *verb* **shoved, shoving** ◊ *noun, plural* **shoves**

shovel *noun* A tool with a long handle and a flattened scoop.

◊ *verb* **1.** To pick up or move with a shovel. **2.** To clear or make with a shovel: *We shoveled a path through the snow to the garage.* **3.** To put or move in a careless way or in a large mass.
shov·el (shŭv′əl) ◊ *noun, plural* **shovels** ◊ *verb* **shoveled, shoveling**

show *verb* **1.** To cause or allow to be seen: *I showed them the necklace. The dog showed its teeth.* **2.** To present for the public to see; display. **3.** To point out; demonstrate: *Show me how to knit.* **4.** To be in sight. **5.** To reveal or become revealed. **6.** To conduct; guide. **7.** To give; grant: *Show us a little consideration.* **8.** To prove; indicate.
◊ *noun* **1.** A public display. **2.** An appearance, especially a false one: *They made a big show of being sorry.* **3.** A performance that is supposed to entertain an audience.
◊ *idiom* **show off** To display or behave so as to get praise or admiration from others.
show (shō) ◊ *verb* **showed, shown** *or* **showed, showing** ◊ *noun, plural* **shows**

SYNONYMS

show, display, exhibit

I'll *show* you my microscope. The new toys were *displayed* in the store window. The science museum *exhibited* a newly discovered dinosaur skeleton.
Antonyms: *conceal, hide*

showcase *noun* A case for displaying objects, as in a store or museum.
show·case (shō′kās′) ◊ *noun, plural* **showcases**

shower *noun* **1.** A brief fall of rain. **2.** A large number of things falling or appearing together. **3.** A bath in which water is sprayed on the body. **4.** A device for spraying water.
◊ *verb* **1.** To pour down in a shower. **2.** To sprinkle or spray: *We showered the parade with confetti.* **3.** To bathe by taking a shower. **4.** To give or provide in large amounts.
show·er (shou′ər) ◊ *noun, plural* **showers** ◊ *verb* **showered, showering**

shown *verb* A past participle of **show.**
shown (shōn) ◊ *verb*
These sound alike: **shown, shone**

showoff *noun* A person who tries to get attention by displaying his or her abilities.
show·off (shō′ôf′) ◊ *noun, plural* **showoffs**

showy *adjective* Attracting attention because of bright color or size; conspicuous: *The rose has showy flowers.*
show·y (shō′ē) ◊ *adjective* **showier, showiest**

shrank *verb* A past tense of **shrink.**
shrank (shrăngk) ◊ *verb*

shred *noun* A narrow strip cut or torn off.
◊ *verb* To cut or tear into small strips.
shred (shrĕd) ◊ *noun, plural* **shreds** ◊ *verb* **shredded** *or* **shred, shredding**

shrew *noun* A small animal with a narrow, pointed snout. Shrews feed on insects.
shrew (shrōō) ◊ *noun, plural* **shrews**

▲ **shrew**

shrewd *adjective* Clever and practical: *A shrewd shopper compares prices at different stores before buying.*
shrewd (shrōōd) ◊ *adjective* **shrewder, shrewdest**

shriek *noun* A loud, shrill sound.
◊ *verb* To make a loud, shrill sound.
shriek (shrēk) ◊ *noun, plural* **shrieks** ◊ *verb* **shrieked, shrieking**

shrill *adjective* Having a high, sharp sound.
shrill (shrĭl) ◊ *adjective* **shriller, shrillest**

shrimp *noun* A small shellfish that is related to the lobster and is used as food.
shrimp (shrĭmp) ◊ *noun, plural* **shrimp** *or* **shrimps**

shrine *noun* **1.** A container or a place where sacred religious objects are kept. **2.** A place considered especially important because of its history or its associations.
shrine (shrīn) ◊ *noun, plural* **shrines**

S

shrink *verb* **1.** To make or become smaller: *If you wash the wool sweater in hot water, it will shrink.* **2.** To draw back; retreat.
shrink (shrĭngk) ◊ *verb* **shrank** *or* **shrunk, shrunk** *or* **shrunken, shrinking**

shrivel *verb* To shrink and wrinkle; wither.
shriv·el (**shrĭv′** əl) ◊ *verb* **shriveled, shriveling**

shroud *noun* **1.** A cloth used to wrap a dead body for burial. **2.** Something that covers.
◊ *verb* To wrap in or as if in a shroud.
shroud (shroud) ◊ *noun, plural* **shrouds**
◊ *verb* **shrouded, shrouding**

shrub *noun* A woody plant that is smaller than a tree. A shrub usually has many separate stems.
shrub (shrŭb) ◊ *noun, plural* **shrubs**

shrubbery *noun* A group of shrubs.
shrub·ber·y (**shrŭb′** ə rē) ◊ *noun*

shrug *verb* To raise the shoulders to show doubt, impatience, or a lack of interest.
◊ *noun* The gesture of shrugging.
shrug (shrŭg) ◊ *verb* **shrugged, shrugging**
◊ *noun, plural* **shrugs**

shrunk *verb* A past tense and a past participle of **shrink.**
shrunk (shrŭngk) ◊ *verb*

shrunken *verb* A past participle of **shrink.**
shrunk·en (**shrŭng′** kən) ◊ *verb*

shuck *noun* An outer covering, such as a corn husk, pea pod, or oyster shell.
◊ *verb* To remove the husk or shell from.
shuck (shŭk) ◊ *noun, plural* **shucks** ◊ *verb* **shucked, shucking**

shudder *verb* To tremble or shiver suddenly, especially from fear or cold: *We all shuddered as we went into the dark cave.*
◊ *noun* A shiver, especially from fear or cold.
shud·der (**shŭd′** ər) ◊ *verb* **shuddered, shuddering** ◊ *noun, plural* **shudders**

shuffle *verb* **1.** To walk slowly, while dragging the feet. **2.** To mix so as to change the order: *Shuffle the baseball cards and look at them again.*
◊ *noun* An act of shuffling.
shuf·fle (**shŭf′** əl) ◊ *verb* **shuffled, shuffling**
◊ *noun, plural* **shuffles**

shun *verb* To avoid on purpose.
shun (shŭn) ◊ *verb* **shunned, shunning**

shut *verb* **1.** To move into a closed position: *Shut the door.* **2.** To prevent entrance into; block or close. **3.** To confine.
◊ *idioms* **shut down** To stop running or work: *The old factory was shut down.* **shut up** To make or become quiet.
shut (shŭt) ◊ *verb* **shut, shutting**

shutout *noun* A game in which one side does not score.
shut·out (**shŭt′** out′) ◊ *noun, plural* **shutouts**

shutter *noun* **1.** A cover for a window or door, usually opening and closing on hinges. **2.** A movable cover over a camera lens that opens for an instant to let in light.
shut·ter (**shŭt′** ər) ◊ *noun, plural* **shutters**

shuttle *noun* **1.** A device used in weaving to carry the threads back and forth between the threads that are stretched out. **2.** A device on a sewing machine that carries the lower thread through loops in the upper thread. **3.** A train or other vehicle that makes short trips between two places.
◊ *verb* To move back and forth quickly.
shut·tle (**shŭt′** l) ◊ *noun, plural* **shuttles**
◊ *verb* **shuttled, shuttling**

shuttlecock *noun* A piece of cork with feathers in it, hit back and forth in badminton.
shut·tle·cock (**shŭt′** əl kŏk′) ◊ *noun, plural* **shuttlecocks**

shy *adjective* **1.** Feeling uneasy around people or with strangers; bashful: *The shy new student sat alone.* **2.** Easily frightened; timid: *Most birds are shy.* **3.** Less than a certain amount; short: *I am three inches shy of five feet.*
◊ *verb* To move suddenly, as if startled.
shy (shī) ◊ *adjective* **shier** *or* **shyer, shiest** *or* **shyest** ◊ *verb* **shied, shying**

ă	pat	ĭ	pit	oi	**oil**	th	ba**th**
ā	pay	ī	ride	o͝o	book	*th*	ba*th*e
â	care	î	fierce	o͞o	boot	ə	ago, item
ä	father	ŏ	pot	ou	**out**		pencil
ĕ	pet	ō	go	ŭ	cut		atom
ē	be	ô	paw, for	û	fur		circus

SYNONYMS

shy, bashful, modest

I like people but I am *shy.* He was too *bashful* to sing before the guests. Though she plays the piano well she is *modest* about it. **Antonym:** *bold*

sick *adjective* **1.** Suffering from an illness. **2.** Feeling nausea: *Riding on the plane made me sick.* **3.** Very unhappy; upset: *We're just sick about having to move.*
sick (sĭk) ◊ *adjective* **sicker, sickest**

sicken *verb* To make or become sick.
sick·en (sĭk′ən) ◊ *verb* **sickened, sickening**

sickening *adjective* **1.** Causing an illness. **2.** Causing disgust.
sick·en·ing (sĭk′ə nĭng) ◊ *adjective*

sickle *noun* A tool for cutting grain or grass. It has a curved blade on a short handle.
sick·le (sĭk′əl) ◊ *noun, plural* **sickles**

▲ **sickle**

sickly *adjective* **1.** Of, caused by, or suggesting sickness. **2.** Tending to become sick; frail: *One puppy was sickly and kept apart.*
sick·ly (sĭk′lē) ◊ *adjective* **sicklier, sickliest**

sickness *noun* **1.** The condition of being sick; illness. **2.** A disease. **3.** Nausea.
sick·ness (sĭk′nĭs) ◊ *noun, plural* **sicknesses**

side *noun* **1.** A line or surface that forms a boundary: *A triangle has three sides.* **2.** One of the surfaces of an object that connects the top and the bottom. **3.** One of the two surfaces of a flat object, such as a piece of paper. **4.** One of the two halves that an object can be divided into. **5.** Either the right or the left half of the trunk of a human or animal body. **6.** The space next to someone or something: *I stood at my parents' side.* **7.** An area identified by its direction from a center: *We live on the north side of town.* **8.** One of two or more opposing individuals, groups, teams, or positions: *Our side won the game. I support your side of the argument.* **9.** A quality or aspect: *The situation has its funny side.* **10.** A line of ancestors: *He is an uncle on my mother's side.*
◊ *verb* To take a position in a disagreement: *I sided with her in the argument.*
◊ *adjective* On or to a side: *We left the theater by a side door.*
◊ *idiom* **side by side** Next to each other.
side (sīd) ◊ *noun, plural* **sides** ◊ *verb* **sided, siding** ◊ *adjective*

sideburns *plural noun* Hair that is allowed to grow down the sides of a man's face.
side·burns (sīd′bûrnz′) ◊ *plural noun*

▲ **sideburns**

sideline *noun* **1.** A boundary line along the side of a playing field or court. **2.** An activity in addition to a regular job or occupation.
side·line (sīd′līn′) ◊ *noun, plural* **sidelines**

sidelong *adjective* To the side: *I gave them a sidelong glance as I hurried by.*
side·long (sīd′lông′) ◊ *adjective*

sidestep *verb* **1.** To step out of the way of. **2.** To avoid; evade.
side·step (sīd′stĕp′) ◊ *verb* **sidestepped, sidestepping**

sidetrack *verb* To turn aside from a main issue or course.
side·track (sīd′trăk′) ◊ *verb* **sidetracked, sidetracking**

sidewalk *noun* A walk that goes along the side of a road.
side·walk (sīd′wôk′) ◊ *noun, plural* **sidewalks**

sideways *adjective & adverb* **1.** To or from one side: *Take a sideways step.* **2.** With one side forward: *Crabs can move sideways.*
side·ways (sīd′wāz′) ◊ *adjective & adverb*

sidle *verb* **1.** To move sideways. **2.** To move casually or in order to avoid being noticed.
si·dle (sīd′l) ◊ *verb* **sidled, sidling**

siege *noun* The surrounding of a town, city, or fortress for a long time by an army that is trying to make it surrender.
siege (sēj) ◊ *noun, plural* **sieges**

sierra *noun* A rugged range of mountains.
si·er·ra (sē ĕr′ə) ◊ *noun, plural* **sierras**

sieve *noun* A utensil with tiny holes in the bottom that let water and small pieces of material pass through, but not large pieces.
sieve (sĭv) ◊ *noun, plural* **sieves**

S

sift *verb* To remove lumps or large chunks from by shaking or pushing through a sieve.
sift (sĭft) ◊ *verb* **sifted, sifting**

sigh *verb* To let out a long, deep breath because of fatigue, sorrow, or relief.
◊ *noun* The act or sound of sighing.
sigh (sī) ◊ *verb* **sighed, sighing** ◊ *noun, plural* **sighs**

sight *noun* **1.** The ability to see; vision. **2.** The act of seeing; view: *The sight of land relieved the sailors.* **3.** The range that can be seen. **4.** Something seen or worth seeing. **5.** Something that looks very strange, funny, or messy: *You were a sight, all covered with mud.* **6.** A device that is used to help in aiming an instrument, such as a telescope.
◊ *verb* To observe with the eyes; see: *The lookout sighted land.*
sight (sīt) ◊ *noun, plural* **sights** ◊ *verb* **sighted, sighting**
‖*These sound alike:* **sight, cite, site**

sightless *adjective* Unable to see; blind.
sight·less (**sīt′** lĭs) ◊ *adjective*

sightseeing *noun* The act of touring interesting places.
sight·see·ing (**sīt′**sē′ĭng) ◊ *noun*

sign *noun* **1.** Something that indicates a fact, quality, or condition: *Dark clouds are a sign of rain.* **2.** An action or gesture that gives information. **3.** Something, such as a poster, that conveys information. **4.** A mark or symbol that stands for a word, phrase, or process: *The sign for multiplication is* ×. **5.** Evidence that is left by someone or something.
◊ *verb* To write one's name on, as a form.
sign (sīn) ◊ *noun, plural* **signs** ◊ *verb* **signed, signing**

SYNONYMS

sign, indication, symptom

I saw no *sign* of boredom in the audience. Is there any *indication* that she likes him? Fever is a *symptom* of illness.

ă	pat	ĭ	pit	oi	oil	th	bath
ā	pay	ī	ride	o͝o	book	*th*	bathe
â	care	î	fierce	o͞o	boot	ə	ago, item
ä	father	ŏ	pot	ou	out		pencil
ĕ	pet	ō	go	ŭ	cut		atom
ē	be	ô	paw, for	û	fur		circus

signal *noun* A sign, gesture, or device that gives a command, a warning, or other information. —See Synonyms at **warning.**
◊ *verb* **1.** To make a signal to. **2.** To make known with or as if with signals: *A period signals the end of a sentence.*
sig·nal (**sĭg′**nəl) ◊ *noun, plural* **signals** ◊ *verb* **signaled, signaling**

signature *noun* A person's name written in that person's own handwriting.
sig·na·ture (**sĭg′** nə chər) ◊ *noun, plural* **signatures**

signboard *noun* A board with a sign on it.
sign·board (**sīn′** bôrd′) ◊ *noun, plural* **signboards**

significance *noun* **1.** The condition or quality of being significant; importance. **2.** The sense of something. —See Synonyms at **meaning.**
sig·nif·i·cance (sĭg **nĭf′** ĭ kəns) ◊ *noun*

significant *adjective* Having importance; notable: *The year 1776 is significant in American history.*
sig·nif·i·cant (sĭg **nĭf′** ĭ kənt) ◊ *adjective*

signify *verb* To serve as a sign of: *What does this monument signify?*
sig·ni·fy (**sĭg′** nə fī′) ◊ *verb* **signified, signifying**

sign language *noun* A system of communication using hand gestures instead of speech.

signpost *noun* A post with a sign attached to it, usually giving information or directions for travelers.
sign·post (**sīn′** pōst′) ◊ *noun, plural* **signposts**

silence *noun* **1.** Absence of sound; stillness. **2.** A keeping still; absence of talk.
◊ *verb* To make silent: *A look from our teacher silenced us.*
si·lence (**sī′** ləns) ◊ *noun, plural* **silences** ◊ *verb* **silenced, silencing**

silent *adjective* **1.** Making or having no sound; quiet. **2.** Saying little or nothing. **3.** Not spoken or expressed out loud: *We sat in silent thought.* **4.** Not pronounced or sounded: *The "k" in "knife" is silent.*
si·lent (**sī′** lənt) ◊ *adjective*

silhouette *noun* **1.** A drawing consisting of an outline filled in with a solid color. **2.** A dark form against a light background.
◊ *verb* To show as a dark outline against a

light background: *The tall buildings far away were silhouetted against the blue sky.*
sil·hou·ette (sĭl'o͞o ĕt') ◊ *noun, plural* **silhouettes** ◊ *verb* **silhouetted, silhouetting**

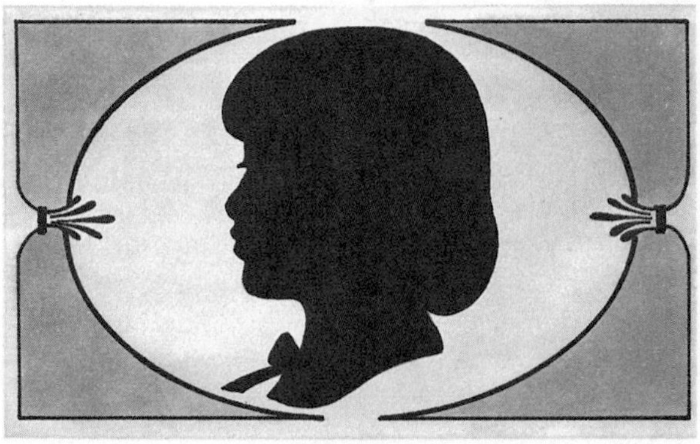

▲ **silhouette**

silicon *noun* A substance that is used in making glass, concrete, bricks, and microchips. Silicon is one of the chemical elements.
sil·i·con (sĭl'ĭ kən) ◊ *noun*

silk *noun* **1.** The fine, glossy fiber that a silkworm produces to form its cocoon. **2.** Thread or cloth that is made from the fiber produced by silkworms.
silk (sĭlk) ◊ *noun, plural* **silks**

silken *adjective* **1.** Made of silk. **2.** Silky.
silk·en (sĭl'kən) ◊ *adjective*

silkworm *noun* A caterpillar that spins a cocoon of fine, glossy fiber. People gather this fiber to make silk.
silk·worm (sĭlk'wûrm') ◊ *noun, plural* **silkworms**

silky *adjective* Soft and smooth, like silk.
silk·y (sĭl'kē) ◊ *adjective* **silkier, silkiest**

sill *noun* A piece of wood or stone across the bottom of a window frame or doorway.
sill (sĭl) ◊ *noun, plural* **sills**

silly *adjective* **1.** Not showing good sense or reason; stupid: *Forgetting that test was a silly mistake.* **2.** Not serious; ridiculous: *That story about robot animals is silly.* —See Synonyms at **foolish.**
sil·ly (sĭl'ē) ◊ *adjective* **sillier, silliest**

silo *noun* **1.** A tall, round building in which food for farm animals is stored. **2.** An underground shelter for a missile.
si·lo (sī'lō) ◊ *noun, plural* **silos**

▲ **silo**
A grain silo

silt *noun* Fine particles of earth, found at the bottom of lakes and rivers; sediment.
◊ *verb* To fill with silt: *The pond on our neighbor's farm silted up.*
silt (sĭlt) ◊ *noun* ◊ *verb* **silted, silting**

silver *noun* **1.** A soft shiny white metal that is one of the chemical elements. Silver is used to make coins, jewelry, and table utensils. **2.** Coins made of silver. **3.** Table utensils made of silver; silverware.
◊ *adjective* Being the color of silver.
sil·ver (sĭl'vər) ◊ *noun* ◊ *adjective*

silversmith *noun* A person who makes and repairs articles of silver.
sil·ver·smith (sĭl'vər smĭth') ◊ *noun, plural* **silversmiths**

silverware *noun* Utensils made of or coated with silver or another shiny metal.
sil·ver·ware (sĭl'vər wâr') ◊ *noun*

S

silvery *adjective* Shining like silver.
sil•ver•y (sĭl′ və rē) ◊ *adjective*

similar *adjective* Alike but not exactly the same: *Those two cars are similar in design.*
sim•i•lar (sĭm′ ə lər) ◊ *adjective*

similarity *noun* **1.** The condition or quality of being similar. —See Synonyms at **likeness. 2.** A way in which two or more things are similar: *Bees and wasps both sting, and they have other similarities too.*
sim•i•lar•i•ty (sĭm′ə **lăr′** ĭ tē) ◊ *noun, plural* **similarities**

simmer *verb* To cook below or just at the boiling point: *The soup simmered on the stove.*
sim•mer (sĭm′ ər) ◊ *verb* **simmered, simmering**

simple *adjective* **1.** Not complicated: *The directions are simple.* —See Synonyms at **easy. 2.** Without additions: *Please answer with a simple "yes" or "no."* **3.** Not fancy; plain.
sim•ple (sĭm′ pəl) ◊ *adjective* **simpler, simplest**

simplicity *noun* The condition or quality of being simple.
sim•plic•i•ty (sĭm **plĭs′** ĭ tē) ◊ *noun*

simplify *verb* To make or become simpler.
sim•pli•fy (sĭm′ plə fī′) ◊ *verb* **simplified, simplifying**

simply *adverb* **1.** In a simple way; plainly. **2.** Merely; just: *I was simply standing there.*
sim•ply (sĭm′ plē) ◊ *adverb*

simultaneous *adjective* Happening or existing at the same time.
si•mul•ta•ne•ous (sī′məl **tā′** nē əs) ◊ *adjective*

sin *noun* An act that breaks a religious or moral law; wrongdoing.
◊ *verb* To break a religious or moral law.
sin (sĭn) ◊ *noun, plural* **sins** ◊ *verb* **sinned, sinning**

since *adverb* **1.** From then until now: *They left town and haven't been here since.* **2.** Before now; ago: *I've long since forgotten.*
◊ *conjunction* **1.** During the time after: *They haven't been home since they graduated.* **2.** As a result of the fact that; because: *Since you're not interested, I won't tell you.*
◊ *preposition* During the period after.
since (sĭns) ◊ *adverb* ◊ *conjunction* ◊ *preposition*

sincere *adjective* Not lying or pretending; honest; genuine: *Our feelings are sincere.*
sin•cere (sĭn **sîr′**) ◊ *adjective* **sincerer, sincerest**

sincerity *noun* The quality or condition of being sincere.
sin•cer•i•ty (sĭn **sĕr′** ĭ tē) ◊ *noun*

sinew *noun* A strong cord of tissue inside the body that joins a muscle to a bone.
sin•ew (sĭn′ yo͞o) ◊ *noun, plural* **sinews**

sing *verb* **1.** To produce a series of words or vocal sounds in musical tones: *We sang as we worked.* **2.** To perform a song. **3.** To make sounds that seem musical: *Birds sing.*
sing (sĭng) ◊ *verb* **sang, sung, singing**

singe *verb* To burn slightly; scorch.
singe (sĭnj) ◊ *verb* **singed, singeing**

single *adjective* **1.** Not with another or others: *There is a single biscuit left on the plate.* **2.** Intended to be used by one person or family. **3.** Not married.
◊ *noun* A hit in baseball that allows the batter to reach first base.
◊ *verb* **1.** To choose from others; pick out: *We singled out the best oranges in the basket.* **2.** To hit a single in baseball.
sin•gle (sĭng′ gəl) ◊ *adjective* ◊ *noun, plural* **singles** ◊ *verb* **singled, singling**

single-handed *adjective* Working or done without help from others.
sin•gle-hand•ed (sĭng′gəl **hăn′** dĭd) ◊ *adjective*

singular *adjective* Of or being a form of a word that is used when speaking of only one person or thing. For example, *pencil* and *mouse* are singular nouns.
◊ *noun* The form of a word that is used when only one person or thing is meant.
sin•gu•lar (sĭng′ gyə lər) ◊ *adjective* ◊ *noun, plural* **singulars**

sinister *adjective* Suggesting evil or ill will.
sin•is•ter (sĭn′ ĭ stər) ◊ *adjective*

sink *verb* **1.** To go down or cause to go down or under the surface: *Heavy storms can sink ships.* **2.** To force or drive into the ground:

ă	pat	ĭ	pit	oi	**oi**l	th	ba**th**
ā	pay	ī	ride	o͝o	b**oo**k	*th*	ba**th**e
â	care	î	fierce	o͞o	b**oo**t	ə	ago, item
ä	father	ŏ	pot	ou	**ou**t		pencil
ĕ	pet	ō	go	ŭ	cut		atom
ē	be	ô	paw, for	û	fur		circus

We sank some posts for a new fence. **3.** To pass into a condition that seems lower or deeper; fall: *I sank into a deep sleep.* **4.** To become lower in amount. **5.** To go deeply; penetrate: *The rain sank into the dry soil.*
◊ *noun* A basin with a drain and faucets for turning on and off a water supply.
sink (sĭngk) ◊ *verb* **sank** *or* **sunk, sunk, sinking** ◊ *noun, plural* **sinks**

sip *verb* To drink a little at a time.
◊ *noun* **1.** An act of sipping. **2.** A small drink.
sip (sĭp) ◊ *verb* **sipped, sipping** ◊ *noun, plural* **sips**

siphon *noun* A U-shaped pipe or tube filled with liquid that is forced by air pressure to flow up and out of a container and into a lower container.
◊ *verb* To draw off through a siphon.
si·phon (sī′fən) ◊ *noun, plural* **siphons** ◊ *verb* **siphoned, siphoning**

▲ **siphon**

sir *noun* **1.** A polite form of address used in place of a man's name. **2. Sir** A title used before the given name, as of a knight.
sir (sûr) ◊ *noun, plural* **sirs**

Sire *noun* A form of address used at one time when speaking to a great man, such as a king.
Sire (sīr) ◊ *noun, plural* **Sires**

siren *noun* A device that makes a loud whistling or wailing sound as a signal or warning.
si·ren (sī′rən) ◊ *noun, plural* **sirens**

sirup *noun* Another spelling for **syrup.**
sir·up (sĭr′əp *or* sûr′əp) ◊ *noun, plural* **sirups**

sister *noun* **1.** A girl or woman having the same mother and father as another person. **2.** A woman who has an interest or cause in common with another. **3. Sister** A nun.
sis·ter (sĭs′tər) ◊ *noun, plural* **sisters**

sisterhood *noun* The relationship of being a sister or sisters.
sis·ter·hood (sĭs′tər hŏŏd′) ◊ *noun*

sister-in-law *noun* **1.** The sister of one's husband or wife. **2.** The wife of one's brother.
sis·ter-in-law (sĭs′tər ĭn lô′) ◊ *noun, plural* **sisters-in-law**

sit *verb* **1.** To rest on the lower part of the body where the hips and legs join. **2.** To cause to be seated. **3.** To be located. **4.** To pose for an artist or photographer. **5.** To have a position in a body of officials, such as judges. **6.** To be in session: *The court will sit next week.* **7.** To baby-sit.
sit (sĭt) ◊ *verb* **sat, sitting**

site *noun* A position or location.
site (sīt) ◊ *noun, plural* **sites**
‖*These sound alike:* **site, cite, sight**

sitting *noun* A session, as of a court.
sit·ting (sĭt′ĭng) ◊ *noun, plural* **sittings**

situate *verb* To place in a spot; locate.
sit·u·ate (sĭch′ōō āt′) ◊ *verb* **situated, situating**

situation *noun* **1.** The place where something is; location. **2.** A person's position or status. **3.** A set of circumstances.
sit·u·a·tion (sĭch′ōō ā′shən) ◊ *noun, plural* **situations**

sit-up *noun* A kind of exercise in which a person lies flat on the floor, then rises to a sitting position without using the hands or bending the legs.
sit-up (sĭt′ŭp′) ◊ *noun, plural* **sit-ups**

six *noun* The number, written 6, that is equal to the sum of 5 + 1.
◊ *adjective* Being one more than five.
six (sĭks) ◊ *noun, plural* **sixes** ◊ *adjective*

sixteen *noun* The number, written 16, that is equal to the sum of 15 + 1.
◊ *adjective* Being one more than fifteen.
six·teen (sĭk **stēn′**) ◊ *noun, plural* **sixteens** ◊ *adjective*

sixteenth *noun* **1.** The number in a series that matches the number sixteen. **2.** One of sixteen equal parts, written 1/16.
◊ *adjective* Coming after the fifteenth.
six·teenth (sĭk **stēnth′**) ◊ *noun, plural* **sixteenths** ◊ *adjective*

S

sixth *noun* **1.** The number in a series that matches the number six. **2.** One of six equal parts, written 1/6.
◊ *adjective* Coming after the fifth.
sixth (sĭksth) ◊ *noun, plural* **sixths**
◊ *adjective*

sixtieth *noun* **1.** The number in a series that matches the number sixty. **2.** One of sixty equal parts, written 1/60.
◊ *adjective* Coming after the fifty-ninth.
six·ti·eth (**sĭk′**stē ĭth) ◊ *noun, plural* **sixtieths**
◊ *adjective*

sixty *noun* The number, written 60, that is equal to the product of 10 × 6.
◊ *adjective* Being equal to ten times six.
six·ty (**sĭk′**stē) ◊ *noun, plural* **sixties**
◊ *adjective*

sizable *adjective* Fairly large.
siz·a·ble (**sī′**zə bəl) ◊ *adjective*

size *noun* **1.** The physical dimensions, proportions, or extent of something. **2.** One of a series of standard dimensions: *What is the size of that shoe?*
size (sīz) ◊ *noun, plural* **sizes**

sizzle *verb* To make the hissing sound of frying fat.
siz·zle (**sĭz′**əl) ◊ *verb* **sizzled, sizzling**

skate *noun* **1.** A boot, shoe, or metal frame having a metal blade used for gliding on ice. **2.** A roller skate.
◊ *verb* To move along on skates.
skate (skāt) ◊ *noun, plural* **skates** ◊ *verb* **skated, skating**

skateboard *noun* A short board with small wheels, on which the user stands, pushes off, and glides.
skate·board (**skāt′**bôrd′) ◊ *noun, plural* **skateboards**

skeleton *noun* The framework of bones that supports and protects the body of a human being or an animal with a backbone.
skel·e·ton (**skĕl′**ĭ tən) ◊ *noun, plural* **skeletons**

ă	pat	ĭ	pit	oi	**oi**l	th	ba**th**
ā	pay	ī	ride	o͝o	b**oo**k	*th*	ba**th**e
â	care	î	fierce	o͞o	b**oo**t	ə	ago, item
ä	father	ŏ	pot	ou	**ou**t		pencil
ĕ	pet	ō	go	ŭ	cut		atom
ē	be	ô	paw, for	û	fur		circus

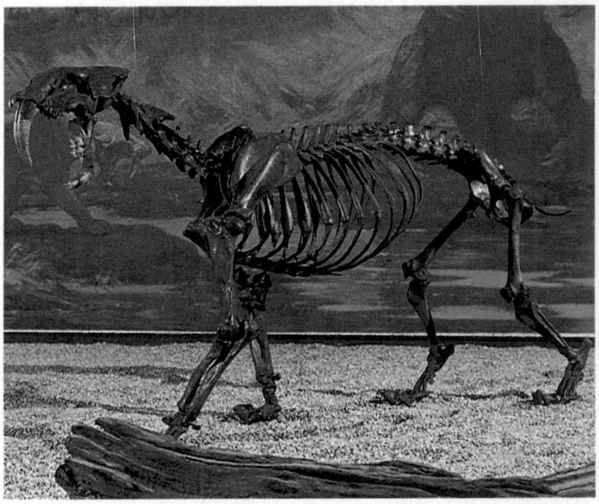

▲ **skeleton**
A dinosaur skeleton

skeptical *adjective* Doubting; questioning: *I'm skeptical about our chances of winning the game.*
skep·ti·cal (**skĕp′**tĭ kəl) ◊ *adjective*

sketch *noun* **1.** A rough drawing or outline. **2.** A short written composition.
◊ *verb* To make a sketch or sketches.
sketch (skĕch) ◊ *noun, plural* **sketches**
◊ *verb* **sketched, sketching**

sketchy *adjective* **1.** Roughly drawn or outlined. **2.** Not complete or thorough: *They could give us only sketchy information.*
sketch·y (**skĕch′**ē) ◊ *adjective* **sketchier, sketchiest**

ski *noun* One of a pair of long, narrow runners, curved slightly upward at the tip, that are attached to boots and are used for gliding on snow.
◊ *verb* To move along on skis.
ski (skē) ◊ *noun, plural* **skis** ◊ *verb* **skied, skiing**

skid *verb* To slide out of control or sideways over a slippery surface.
◊ *noun* The act of skidding.
skid (skĭd) ◊ *verb* **skidded, skidding** ◊ *noun, plural* **skids**

skiff *noun* A light rowboat.
skiff (skĭf) ◊ *noun, plural* **skiffs**

skill *noun* The ability to do something well. —See Synonyms at **ability.**
skill (skĭl) ◊ *noun, plural* **skills**

skilled *adjective* Having or using skill.
skilled (skĭld) ◊ *adjective*

skillet *noun* A frying pan.
skil·let (skĭl′ĭt) ◊ *noun, plural* **skillets**

skillful *adjective* Having, done with, or showing skill; expert.
skill·ful (skĭl′fəl) ◊ *adjective*

skim *verb* **1.** To remove from the surface of a liquid. **2.** To move lightly and quickly over: *The bird skimmed the water.* **3.** To read quickly, skipping over parts.
skim (skĭm) ◊ *verb* **skimmed, skimming**

skim milk *noun* Milk from which the cream has been removed.

skin *noun* **1.** The outer protective covering of a human or animal body. **2.** A hide or pelt removed from the body of an animal. **3.** The outer layer, as of a fruit.
◊ *verb* **1.** To remove the skin from: *Skin the grapes before you eat them.* **2.** To injure by scraping: *I fell and skinned my knee.*
skin (skĭn) ◊ *noun, plural* **skins** ◊ *verb* **skinned, skinning**

skin diving *noun* Underwater swimming with a face mask, flippers, and a breathing device.

▲ **skin diving**

skinny *adjective* Very thin. —See Synonyms at **thin.**
skin·ny (skĭn′ē) ◊ *adjective* **skinnier, skinniest**

skip *verb* **1.** To move forward by stepping and hopping lightly. **2.** To jump lightly over: *I like to skip rope.* **3.** To pass over; omit: *You skipped my name.* **4.** To be promoted to the grade beyond the next higher one.
◊ *noun* **1.** A light hopping step. **2.** The act of leaving out; omission.
skip (skĭp) ◊ *verb* **skipped, skipping** ◊ *noun, plural* **skips**

skipper *noun* The captain of a ship.
skip·per (skĭp′ər) ◊ *noun, plural* **skippers**

skirmish *noun* A minor fight between small bodies of troops.
◊ *verb* To take part in a skirmish.
skir·mish (skûr′mĭsh) ◊ *noun, plural* **skirmishes** ◊ *verb* **skirmished, skirmishing**

skirt *noun* **1.** A woman's or girl's garment or part of a garment that hangs from the waist down. **2.** A border or edging.
◊ *verb* **1.** To lie along or form the border of: *The road skirted the woods.* **2.** To pass around rather than across or through.
skirt (skûrt) ◊ *noun, plural* **skirts** ◊ *verb* **skirted, skirting**

skit *noun* A very short, often funny play.
skit (skĭt) ◊ *noun, plural* **skits**

skull *noun* The bony framework of the head that encloses and protects the brain.
skull (skŭl) ◊ *noun, plural* **skulls**
‖*These sound alike:* **skull, scull**

skunk *noun* An animal that has black and white fur and a bushy tail. A skunk can spray a bad-smelling liquid when it is attacked.
skunk (skŭngk) ◊ *noun, plural* **skunks**

▲ **skunk**

sky *noun* The part of the upper air that seems to arch over the earth; heavens.
sky (skī) ◊ *noun, plural* **skies**

S

sky diving *noun* The act or sport of jumping from an airplane and falling a great distance before opening a parachute.

skylark *noun* A brownish European bird that sings while flying high in the air.
sky·lark (**skī′**lärk′) ◊ *noun, plural* **skylarks**

skylight *noun* A window in a roof or ceiling.
sky·light (**skī′**līt′) ◊ *noun, plural* **skylights**

skyline *noun* **1.** The line along which the earth and sky appear to meet; horizon. **2.** The outline of something, such as a group of city buildings, seen against the sky.
sky·line (**skī′**līn′) ◊ *noun, plural* **skylines**

skyrocket *noun* A firework that explodes high in the air in a shower of sparks.
sky·rock·et (**skī′**rŏk′ĭt) ◊ *noun, plural* **skyrockets**

skyscraper *noun* A very tall building.
sky·scrap·er (**skī′**skrā′pər) ◊ *noun, plural* **skyscrapers**

slab *noun* A broad, flat, thick piece, as of bread, stone, or cheese.
slab (slăb) ◊ *noun, plural* **slabs**

slack *adjective* **1.** Not firm or tight; loose: *The rope broke and went slack.* **2.** Not lively or busy; slow: *Business was slack in the spring.*
◊ *verb* To make or become slack; slacken.
◊ *noun* A loose or slack part.
slack (slăk) ◊ *adjective* **slacker, slackest** ◊ *verb* **slacked, slacking** ◊ *noun*

slacken *verb* **1.** To make or become slower. **2.** To make less tight; loosen.
slack·en (**slăk′**ən) ◊ *verb* **slackened, slackening**

slacks *plural noun* Long, casual pants.
slacks (slăks) ◊ *plural noun*

slain *verb* Past participle of **slay**.
slain (slān) ◊ *verb*

slam *verb* **1.** To shut forcefully and noisily. **2.** To put forcefully: *Don't slam down the telephone.* **3.** To strike forcefully; crash.
◊ *noun* A forceful, loud blow or crash.
slam (slăm) ◊ *verb* **slammed, slamming** ◊ *noun, plural* **slams**

ă pat	ĭ pit	oi	**oil**	th	ba**th**		
ā pay	ī ride	o͝o	**book**	*th*	ba**the**		
â care	î fierce	o͞o	**boot**	ə	ago, item		
ä father	ŏ pot	ou	**out**		pencil		
ĕ pet	ō go	ŭ	**cut**		atom		
ē be	ô paw, for	û	**fur**		circus		

slander *noun* A false, usually spoken statement that harms a person's reputation.
slan·der (**slăn′**dər) ◊ *noun, plural* **slanders**

slang *noun* Special words and meanings that are used in place of standard language, as in joking with friends.
slang (slăng) ◊ *noun*

slant *verb* To have or take a direction that is not horizontal or vertical; slope: *These italic letters slant to the right.*
◊ *noun* A sloping line, surface, or direction.
slant (slănt) ◊ *verb* **slanted, slanting** ◊ *noun, plural* **slants**

slap *verb* **1.** To strike sharply with or as if with the palm of the hand. **2.** To knock against something with a sharp noise.
◊ *noun* A sharp blow with the open hand.
slap (slăp) ◊ *verb* **slapped, slapping** ◊ *noun, plural* **slaps**

slash *verb* **1.** To cut or strike with sweeping strokes. **2.** To reduce greatly: *The clothing store has slashed its prices.*
◊ *noun* **1.** A forceful, sweeping stroke, as with a knife. **2.** A long cut; gash. **3.** A big reduction, as in prices.
slash (slăsh) ◊ *verb* **slashed, slashing** ◊ *noun, plural* **slashes**

slat *noun* A narrow strip of metal or wood.
slat (slăt) ◊ *noun, plural* **slats**

slate *noun* **1.** A fine-grained rock that splits into thin layers with smooth surfaces. **2.** A piece of slate cut for use as a roofing material or blackboard. **3.** A dark bluish gray.
slate (slāt) ◊ *noun, plural* **slates**

slaughter *noun* **1.** The killing of animals for food. **2.** The killing of large numbers of people especially during a war; massacre.
◊ *verb* **1.** To butcher for food. **2.** To kill in large numbers; massacre.
slaugh·ter (**slô′**tər) ◊ *noun, plural* **slaughters** ◊ *verb* **slaughtered, slaughtering**

slave *noun* **1.** A person owned by someone else. **2.** A person who is ruled by a habit or influence: *Don't be a slave to TV.* **3.** A person who works very hard.
◊ *verb* To work very hard.
slave (slāv) ◊ *noun, plural* **slaves** ◊ *verb* **slaved, slaving**

slavery *noun* **1.** The condition of being a slave. **2.** The practice of owning slaves. **3.** Hard work.
slav·er·y (**slā′**və rē) ◊ *noun*

slay *verb* To kill violently.
slay (slā) ◊ *verb* **slew, slain, slaying**
‖*These sound alike:* **slay, sleigh**

sled *noun* A vehicle on runners for coasting over snow and ice.
◊ *verb* To ride on a sled.
sled (slĕd) ◊ *noun, plural* **sleds** ◊ *verb* **sledded, sledding**

sledgehammer *noun* A long, heavy hammer usually used with both hands.
sledge·ham·mer (**slĕj′**hăm′ər) ◊ *noun, plural* **sledgehammers**

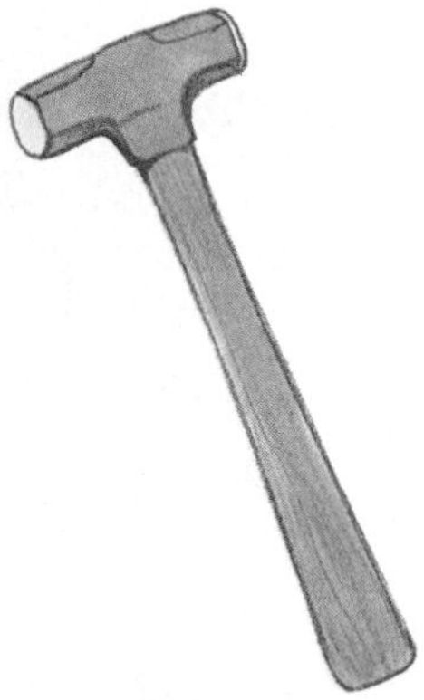
▲ **sledgehammer**

sleek *adjective* Very smooth and glossy.
sleek (slēk) ◊ *adjective* **sleeker, sleekest**

sleep *noun* **1.** A natural condition of rest that occurs regularly. **2.** A condition like sleep, such as hibernation.
◊ *verb* To be or fall asleep: *I slept for more than ten hours.*
sleep (slēp) ◊ *noun* ◊ *verb* **slept, sleeping**

sleeping bag *noun* A large, warmly lined bag in which a person may sleep outdoors.
sleeping bag ◊ *noun, plural* **sleeping bags**

sleepy *adjective* **1.** Ready for or needing sleep. **2.** Quiet; inactive: *The train sounded loud as it passed through the sleepy town.*
sleep·y (**slē′**pē) ◊ *adjective* **sleepier, sleepiest**

sleet *noun* Rain that is partly frozen.
◊ *verb* To fall as sleet.
sleet (slēt) ◊ *noun* ◊ *verb* **sleeted, sleeting**

sleeve *noun* **1.** The part of a garment that covers all or part of the arm. **2.** A case, covering, or shell that fits around something.
sleeve (slēv) ◊ *noun, plural* **sleeves**

sleigh *noun* A vehicle on runners that is usually pulled by a horse over ice or snow.
sleigh (slā) ◊ *noun, plural* **sleighs**
‖*These sound alike:* **sleigh, slay**

▲ **sleigh**

slender *adjective* Having little width. —See Synonyms at **thin.**
slen·der (**slĕn′**dər) ◊ *adjective* **slenderer, slenderest**

slept *verb* Past tense and past participle of **sleep.**
slept (slĕpt) ◊ *verb*

slew *verb* Past tense of **slay.**
slew (slo͞o) ◊ *verb*

slice *noun* A thin, flat piece cut from something, such as a loaf of bread.
◊ *verb* **1.** To cut into slices. **2.** To cut with or as if with a sharp knife: *The ship sliced through the icy water.*
slice (slīs) ◊ *noun, plural* **slices** ◊ *verb* **sliced, slicing**

slick *adjective* Having a smooth or slippery surface.
◊ *verb* To make smooth and glossy.
slick (slĭk) ◊ *adjective* **slicker, slickest** ◊ *verb* **slicked, slicking**

slid *verb* Past tense and past participle of **slide.**
slid (slĭd) ◊ *verb*

slide *verb* **1.** To move or cause to move smoothly over a surface. **2.** To move easily or quietly: *I slid into my seat just in time.* **3.** To move out of place; slip.
◊ *noun* **1.** A sliding movement. **2.** A smooth surface down which people or things can slide. **3.** A transparent photograph for projection on a screen. **4.** A small glass plate on which objects are placed for examination by microscope. **5.** An avalanche.
slide (slīd) ◊ *verb* **slid, sliding** ◊ *noun, plural* **slides**

S

slight *adjective* **1.** Small in amount or degree. **2.** Small in size; slender.
◊ *verb* **1.** To value too little: *Don't slight your English homework.* **2.** To insult or behave coldly toward.
◊ *noun* An act of slighting.
slight (slīt) ◊ *adjective* **slighter, slightest** ◊ *verb* **slighted, slighting** ◊ *noun, plural* **slights**

slim *adjective* **1.** Thin; slender. **2.** Small in degree, amount, or extent: *We had only a slim chance of winning.*
slim (slĭm) ◊ *adjective* **slimmer, slimmest**

slime *noun* Thick, soft, slippery mud or a mudlike substance.
slime (slīm) ◊ *noun*

slimy *adjective* **1.** Like slime in appearance or texture. **2.** Covered with slime.
slim·y (**slī′**mē) ◊ *adjective* **slimier, slimiest**

sling *noun* **1.** A looped belt, rope, or chain in which loads are placed for lifting or carrying. **2.** A band of cloth looped around the neck to support an injured arm or hand. **3.** A looped strap used for throwing stones.
◊ *verb* **1.** To hang so as to swing freely. **2.** To hurl or fling.
sling (slĭng) ◊ *noun, plural* **slings** ◊ *verb* **slung, slinging**

slingshot *noun* A Y-shaped stick with an elastic strap attached for shooting small stones.
sling·shot (**slĭng′**shŏt′) ◊ *noun, plural* **slingshots**

slink *verb* To move in a secret, sneaking way, as from guilt.
slink (slĭngk) ◊ *verb* **slunk, slinking**

slip¹ *verb* **1.** To move or pass smoothly and easily. **2.** To move quietly so as not to attract attention: *I slipped into the classroom.* **3.** To put on or take off quickly and easily: *Slip off your shoes.* **4.** To lose one's balance or footing on a slippery surface. **5.** To move into or away from a proper place or position: *The ladder started to slip.* **6.** To escape from: *Your name slips my mind.* **7.** To fall from a standard: *The quality of your work is slipping.* **8.** To make a mistake.
◊ *noun* **1.** An act of slipping. **2.** A decline. **3.** A small mistake. **4.** An undergarment made like a dress with shoulder straps. **5.** A pillowcase.
slip¹ (slĭp) ◊ *verb* **slipped, slipping** ◊ *noun, plural* **slips**

slip² *noun* **1.** A piece of paper on which something is recorded: *Save your sales slip in case you want to return that shirt.* **2.** A plant part cut for planting or grafting.
slip² (slĭp) ◊ *noun, plural* **slips**

***HISTORY* • slip¹, slip²**

Slip¹ may have come from an old Dutch word that meant "to move quietly." **Slip²** may have come from a different old Dutch word that meant "a cut or slit."

slipper *noun* A light, low-cut shoe that is easily slipped on and off.
slip·per (**slĭp′**ər) ◊ *noun, plural* **slippers**

slippery *adjective* Tending to slip or cause slipping.
slip·per·y (**slĭp′**ə rē) ◊ *adjective* **slipperier, slipperiest**

slit *noun* A long, narrow cut or opening.
◊ *verb* To make a long, narrow cut in.
slit (slĭt) ◊ *noun, plural* **slits** ◊ *verb* **slit, slitting**

slither *verb* To move along by gliding: *The snake slithered across the road.*
slith·er (**slĭ*th*′**ər) ◊ *verb* **slithered, slithering**

sliver *noun* A sharp-ended, thin piece, as of wood or glass; splinter.
sliv·er (**slĭv′**ər) ◊ *noun, plural* **slivers**

slogan *noun* A word or phrase used by a business, team, or other group to advertise its aims or beliefs; motto.
slo·gan (**slō′**gən) ◊ *noun, plural* **slogans**

slop *verb* To spill, flow, or spread messily.
slop (slŏp) ◊ *verb* **slopped, slopping**

slope *verb* To slant upward or downward.
◊ *noun* **1.** A slanting line, surface, or direction. **2.** A sloping stretch of ground.
slope (slōp) ◊ *verb* **sloped, sloping** ◊ *noun, plural* **slopes**

ă	pat	ĭ	pit	oi	**oi**l	th	ba**th**
ā	pay	ī	ride	ŏŏ	b**oo**k	*th*	ba***th***e
â	care	î	fierce	ōō	b**oo**t	ə	ago, item
ä	father	ŏ	pot	ou	**ou**t		pencil
ĕ	pet	ō	go	ŭ	cut		atom
ē	be	ô	paw, for	û	fur		circus

sloppy *adjective* **1.** Wet or muddy: *Our boots splashed through the sloppy ground.* **2.** Messy in appearance. **3.** Carelessly done.
slop·py (slŏp′ē) ◊ *adjective* **sloppier, sloppiest**

slot *noun* A narrow groove or opening.
slot (slŏt) ◊ *noun, plural* **slots**

sloth *noun* **1.** The state of being lazy. **2.** A slow-moving tropical American animal that hangs upside down from tree branches.
sloth (slôth) ◊ *noun, plural* **sloths**

▲ **sloth**

slouch *verb* To sit, stand, or walk with a bent or drooping posture.
◊ *noun* A bent or drooping posture.
slouch (slouch) ◊ *verb* **slouched, slouching** ◊ *noun*

slovenly *adjective* Messy or careless.
slov·en·ly (slŭv′ən lē) ◊ *adjective* **slovenlier, slovenliest**

slow *adjective* **1.** Moving or going at a low speed. **2.** Taking more time than usual. **3.** Being behind the correct time: *My watch is ten minutes slow.* **4.** Not active or lively. **5.** Not quick to learn or understand.
◊ *adverb* In a slow way.
◊ *verb* To make or become slow or slower.
slow (slō) ◊ *adjective, adverb* **slower, slowest** ◊ *verb* **slowed, slowing**

slug¹ *noun* A small, soft-bodied land animal, like a snail but usually having no shell.
slug¹ (slŭg) ◊ *noun, plural* **slugs**

slug² *noun* **1.** A bullet. **2.** A small metal disk that is often used in place of a coin.
slug² (slŭg) ◊ *noun, plural* **slugs**

slug³ *verb* To strike hard with the fist.
◊ *noun* A hard blow, as with the fist.
slug³ (slŭg) ◊ *verb* **slugged, slugging** ◊ *noun, plural* **slugs**

***HISTORY* • slug¹, slug², slug³**

Of these words, **slug¹** is the oldest, and comes from an old Scandinavian word meaning "someone who is slow." **Slug²** was then named after **slug¹** because of their similarity in shape. **Slug³** may then have been named after **slug²**, with the idea of "a punch as hard as a bullet."

sluggish *adjective* Moving or acting in a slow way.
slug·gish (slŭg′ĭsh) ◊ *adjective*

slum *noun* A very poor, dirty, overcrowded area of a city.
slum (slŭm) ◊ *noun, plural* **slums**

slumber *verb* To sleep.
◊ *noun* Sleep.
slum·ber (slŭm′bər) ◊ *verb* **slumbered, slumbering** ◊ *noun, plural* **slumbers**

slump *verb* **1.** To sink down suddenly: *I slumped into the chair.* **2.** To drop off suddenly, as in activity.
◊ *noun* A sudden, heavy drop.
slump (slŭmp) ◊ *verb* **slumped, slumping** ◊ *noun, plural* **slumps**

slung *verb* Past tense and past participle of **sling.**
slung (slŭng) ◊ *verb*

slunk *verb* Past tense and past participle of **slink.**
slunk (slŭngk) ◊ *verb*

slur *verb* To say in an unclear way.
slur (slûr) ◊ *verb* **slurred, slurring**

slush *noun* Partly melted snow or ice.
slush (slŭsh) ◊ *noun*

sly *adjective* **1.** Clever, cunning, and tricky. **2.** Secret in a tricky way. **3.** Playfully mischievous.
sly (slī) ◊ *adjective* **slier, sliest**

smack *verb* **1.** To make a sharp sound by closing and opening the lips quickly. **2.** To slap or bump loudly.
◊ *noun* **1.** The sharp sound made by smacking the lips. **2.** A sharp blow.
◊ *adverb* Directly: *I fell smack in the mud.*
smack (smăk) ◊ *verb* **smacked, smacking** ◊ *noun, plural* **smacks** ◊ *adverb*

S

small *adjective* **1.** Little in size, amount, or extent. —See Synonyms at **little.** **2.** Few in number. **3.** Not important: *It's just a small problem.* **4.** Engaged in an activity on a limited scale: *We like to support the many small businesses in our town.*
◊ *noun* A small or narrow part: *I have a pain in the small of my back.*
small (smôl) ◊ *adjective* **smaller, smallest** ◊ *noun*

small intestine *noun* The long, narrow part of the digestive system that is between the stomach and large intestine. Digested food is taken into the bloodstream from the small intestine.

smallpox *noun* A serious, very contagious disease marked by chills, fever, and pimples on the skin.
small·pox (smôl′pŏks′) ◊ *noun*

smart *adjective* **1.** Having a quick mind; bright. **2.** Brisk and lively: *We walked at a smart pace.* **3.** Fashionable; stylish.
◊ *verb* **1.** To cause or feel a stinging pain. **2.** To feel hurt, as from a scolding.
◊ *noun* A sharp stinging pain.
smart (smärt) ◊ *adjective* **smarter, smartest** ◊ *verb* **smarted, smarting** ◊ *noun, plural* **smarts**

smash *verb* **1.** To break or be broken into pieces. **2.** To throw, move, or strike violently. **3.** To destroy or defeat completely.
◊ *noun* The act or sound of smashing.
smash (smăsh) ◊ *verb* **smashed, smashing** ◊ *noun, plural* **smashes**

smear *verb* **1.** To cover or stain with a sticky or greasy substance. **2.** To become spread or blurred: *This ink smears easily.*
◊ *noun* A stain or smudge.
smear (smîr) ◊ *verb* **smeared, smearing** ◊ *noun, plural* **smears**

smell *verb* **1.** To detect the odor of by using sense organs in the nose: *I smell smoke.* **2.** To give off an odor.
◊ *noun* **1.** The sense by which odors are detected; the ability to smell. **2.** Odor; scent. **3.** The act of smelling.
smell (smĕl) ◊ *verb* **smelled** *or* **smelt, smelling** ◊ *noun, plural* **smells**

ă	pat	ĭ	pit	oi	**oil**	th	ba**th**
ā	pay	ī	ride	o͝o	book	*th*	bathe
â	care	î	fierce	o͞o	boot	ə	ago, item
ä	father	ŏ	pot	ou	**out**		pencil
ĕ	pet	ō	go	ŭ	cut		atom
ē	be	ô	paw, for	û	fur		circus

SYNONYMS

smell, fragrance, scent

The dog noticed many interesting *smells* in the old house. The *fragrance* of roses filled the room. I love the *scent* of freshly cut grass.

smelly *adjective* Having an unpleasant odor.
smell·y (smĕl′ē) ◊ *adjective* **smellier, smelliest**

smelt[1] *verb* To melt ore in order to extract the metal.
smelt[1] (smĕlt) ◊ *verb* **smelted, smelting**

smelt[2] *verb* A past tense and a past participle of **smell.**
smelt[2] (smĕlt) ◊ *verb*

smile *noun* A pleased or happy expression on the face. A person forms a smile by curving the corners of the mouth upward.
◊ *verb* **1.** To have or form a smile. **2.** To express by a smile: *They smiled their approval.*
smile (smīl) ◊ *noun, plural* **smiles** ◊ *verb* **smiled, smiling**

smock *noun* A garment like a long, loose shirt, worn over clothes to protect them.
smock (smŏk) ◊ *noun, plural* **smocks**

▲ smock

smog *noun* Fog mixed with smoke.
smog (smôg) ◊ *noun*

smoke *noun* **1.** The mixture of gases and particles of carbon that rises from burning material. **2.** A cloud of smoke.
◊ *verb* **1.** To give off smoke. **2.** To draw in and blow out smoke from burning tobacco. **3.** To preserve by exposing to smoke.
smoke (smōk) ◊ *noun* ◊ *verb* **smoked, smoking**

smokestack *noun* A very tall chimney.
smoke·stack (**smōk′**stăk′) ◊ *noun, plural* **smokestacks**

smoky *adjective* Filled with or giving off much smoke.
smok·y (**smō′**kē) ◊ *adjective* **smokier, smokiest**

smolder *verb* To burn slowly with smoke and no flame.
smol·der (**smōl′**dər) ◊ *verb* **smoldered, smoldering**

smooth *adjective* **1.** Having a surface that is not rough or uneven. **2.** Advancing evenly without sudden stops and starts.
◊ *verb* To make smooth.
smooth (smo͞o*th*) ◊ *adjective* **smoother, smoothest** ◊ *verb* **smoothed, smoothing**

smother *verb* **1.** To suffocate or cause to suffocate from lack of air. **2.** To put out a fire by removing the oxygen supply.
smoth·er (**smŭ*th*′**ər) ◊ *verb* **smothered, smothering**

smudge *verb* To smear or blur.
◊ *noun* A blotch or smear.
smudge (smŭj) ◊ *verb* **smudged, smudging** ◊ *noun, plural* **smudges**

smug *adjective* Too pleased or satisfied with oneself.
smug (smŭg) ◊ *adjective* **smugger, smuggest**

smuggle *verb* **1.** To take or carry secretly. **2.** To bring in or take out of a country secretly and illegally.
smug·gle (**smŭg′**əl) ◊ *verb* **smuggled, smuggling**

snack *noun* A light meal.
snack (snăk) ◊ *noun, plural* **snacks**

snag *noun* **1.** A tree branch that sticks out above water. **2.** A sharp or jagged part that sticks out. **3.** A difficulty that has not been anticipated.
◊ *verb* To catch or damage on a snag.
snag (snăg) ◊ *noun, plural* **snags** ◊ *verb* **snagged, snagging**

snail *noun* A slow-moving, soft-bodied land or water animal having a coiled, spiral shell.
snail (snāl) ◊ *noun, plural* **snails**

snake *noun* A reptile that has a long, narrow body and no legs. The bite of some snakes is poisonous.
◊ *verb* To move or wind like a snake.
snake (snāk) ◊ *noun, plural* **snakes** ◊ *verb* **snaked, snaking**

snap *verb* **1.** To make or cause to make a sharp cracking sound. **2.** To break or cause to break suddenly with a sharp sound. **3.** To bite, seize, or grasp with a snatching motion. **4.** To speak or utter sharply. **5.** To move swiftly and with precision. **6.** To turn on or off with a snapping sound: *Snap on the light.* **7.** To open or close with a click: *The lid snapped shut.* **8.** To take a photograph.
◊ *noun* **1.** A sharp cracking sound. **2.** A sudden breaking. **3.** A fastener that closes and opens with a snapping sound. **4.** A thin, crisp cookie. **5.** A snapshot. **6.** An easy task.
◊ *adjective* Made or done suddenly: *I made a snap decision.*
snap (snăp) ◊ *verb* **snapped, snapping** ◊ *noun, plural* **snaps** ◊ *adjective*

snapdragon *noun* A plant with flowers that open and close when their sides are pressed.
snap·drag·on (**snăp′**drăg′ən) ◊ *noun, plural* **snapdragons**

snapping turtle *noun* An American freshwater turtle with powerful hooked jaws.
snapping turtle ◊ *noun, plural* **snapping turtles**

▲ **snapping turtle**

S

snapshot *noun* A photograph taken usually with a small camera.
snap·shot (snăp′shŏt′) ◊ *noun, plural* **snapshots**

snare *noun* A device, such as a noose, that is used for capturing birds and small animals. ◊ *verb* To trap in or as if in a snare.
snare (snâr) ◊ *noun, plural* **snares** ◊ *verb* **snared, snaring**

snare drum *noun* A small drum that has cords stretched across the bottom to make a sharp, rattling tone.
snare drum ◊ *noun, plural* **snare drums**

snarl[1] *noun* An angry or threatening growl. ◊ *verb* **1.** To growl, especially with the teeth showing. **2.** To speak in an angry way.
snarl[1] (snärl) ◊ *noun, plural* **snarls** ◊ *verb* **snarled, snarling**

snarl[2] *noun* **1.** A tangled mass, as of hair or yarn. **2.** A confused or tangled situation. ◊ *verb* To tangle or become tangled.
snarl[2] (snärl) ◊ *noun, plural* **snarls** ◊ *verb* **snarled, snarling**

***HISTORY* • snarl[1], snarl[2]**

Snarl[1] comes from an old German word that was probably made up to imitate the sound it describes. **Snarl**[2] probably developed from the word **snare.**

snatch *verb* To grasp quickly; grab. ◊ *noun* **1.** An act of snatching. **2.** A short period of time. **3.** A small amount or part.
snatch (snăch) ◊ *verb* **snatched, snatching** ◊ *noun, plural* **snatches**

sneak *verb* **1.** To move or act in a sly or secret way. **2.** To bring, take, or put secretly. ◊ *noun* A person who sneaks.
sneak (snēk) ◊ *verb* **sneaked, sneaking** ◊ *noun, plural* **sneaks**

sneaker *noun* A canvas sport shoe with a soft rubber sole.
sneak·er (snē′kər) ◊ *noun, plural* **sneakers**

ă	pat	ĭ	pit	oi	**oi**l	th	ba**th**
ā	pay	ī	ride	o͝o	book	*th*	ba**th**e
â	care	î	fierce	o͞o	boot	ə	ago, item
ä	father	ŏ	pot	ou	**ou**t		pencil
ĕ	pet	ō	go	ŭ	cut		atom
ē	be	ô	paw, for	û	fur		circus

sneaky *adjective* Like a sneak; sly.
sneak·y (snē′kē) ◊ *adjective* **sneakier, sneakiest**

sneer *noun* A remark or look of contempt. ◊ *verb* **1.** To show contempt or scorn with a sneer. **2.** To utter with a sneer.
sneer (snîr) ◊ *noun, plural* **sneers** ◊ *verb* **sneered, sneering**

sneeze *verb* To force air through the nose and mouth in a sudden, violent action. ◊ *noun* The act of sneezing.
sneeze (snēz) ◊ *verb* **sneezed, sneezing** ◊ *noun, plural* **sneezes**

snicker *noun* A mean or sly little laugh. ◊ *verb* To laugh in this way.
snick·er (snĭk′ər) ◊ *noun, plural* **snickers** ◊ *verb* **snickered, snickering**

sniff *verb* **1.** To inhale in short breaths that can be heard, as in crying. **2.** To smell or try to smell by sniffing. ◊ *noun* **1.** The act or sound of sniffing. **2.** An odor or scent perceived by sniffing.
sniff (snĭf) ◊ *verb* **sniffed, sniffing** ◊ *noun, plural* **sniffs**

sniffle *verb* To sniff again and again, as when suffering from a head cold. ◊ *noun* The act or sound of sniffling.
snif·fle (snĭf′əl) ◊ *verb* **sniffled, sniffling** ◊ *noun, plural* **sniffles**

snip *verb* To cut with short, quick strokes. ◊ *noun* **1.** A small piece snipped off. **2.** A stroke made with shears or scissors.
snip (snĭp) ◊ *verb* **snipped, snipping** ◊ *noun, plural* **snips**

snipe *noun* A marsh bird with a long bill. ◊ *verb* To shoot at others, as enemies, from a hiding place.
snipe (snīp) ◊ *noun, plural* **snipe** *or* **snipes** ◊ *verb* **sniped, sniping**

sniper *noun* A person who shoots at others from a hiding place.
snip·er (snī′pər) ◊ *noun, plural* **snipers**

snob *noun* A person who feels superior to others and ignores or looks down on them.
snob (snŏb) ◊ *noun, plural* **snobs**

snoop *verb* To look or search in a nosy way. ◊ *noun* A nosy person.
snoop (sno͞op) ◊ *verb* **snooped, snooping** ◊ *noun, plural* **snoops**

snooze *verb* To take a light nap. ◊ *noun* A light nap.

snooze (snōōz) ◊ *verb* **snoozed, snoozing** ◊ *noun, plural* **snoozes**

snore *verb* To breathe with a hoarse, harsh noise while sleeping.
◊ *noun* An act or sound of snoring.
snore (snôr) ◊ *verb* **snored, snoring** ◊ *noun, plural* **snores**

snorkel *noun* A curved breathing tube used when swimming just under the surface of the water.
snor·kel (snôr′kəl) ◊ *noun, plural* **snorkels**

snort *verb* To force air noisily through the nose.
◊ *noun* An act or sound of snorting.
snort (snôrt) ◊ *verb* **snorted, snorting** ◊ *noun, plural* **snorts**

snout *noun* The long front part of the head of an animal that projects outward.
snout (snout) ◊ *noun, plural* **snouts**

snow *noun* **1.** Soft white crystals of ice that form from water vapor in the upper air and fall to earth. **2.** A fall of flakes of snow.
◊ *verb* To fall as snow.
snow (snō) ◊ *noun, plural* **snows** ◊ *verb* **snowed, snowing**

snowball *noun* A ball of pressed snow.
snow·ball (snō′bôl′) ◊ *noun, plural* **snowballs**

snowdrift *noun* A mass of snow piled up by the wind.
snow·drift (snō′drĭft′) ◊ *noun, plural* **snowdrifts**

snowfall *noun* **1.** A fall of snow. **2.** The amount of snow that falls.
snow·fall (snō′fôl′) ◊ *noun, plural* **snowfalls**

snowflake *noun* A single crystal of snow.
snow·flake (snō′flāk′) ◊ *noun, plural* **snowflakes**

snowman *noun* A figure in the form of a person made from snow.
snow·man (snō′măn′) ◊ *noun, plural* **snowmen**

snowmobile *noun* A vehicle like a sled with a motor, used for traveling over snow.
snow·mo·bile (snō′mō bēl′) ◊ *noun, plural* **snowmobiles**

snowplow *noun* A device or vehicle for removing snow, as from roads.
snow·plow (snō′plou′) ◊ *noun, plural* **snowplows**

snowshoe *noun* A rounded wooden frame with leather strips stretched across it, attached to the shoe to keep the foot from sinking into snow.
snow·shoe (snō′shōō′) ◊ *noun, plural* **snowshoes**

snowstorm *noun* A storm with heavy snow.
snow·storm (snō′stôrm′) ◊ *noun, plural* **snowstorms**

snowy *adjective* **1.** Full of or covered with snow. **2.** White like snow.
snow·y (snō′ē) ◊ *adjective* **snowier, snowiest**

snub *verb* To treat with scorn or coldness.
◊ *noun* An act or example of snubbing.
snub (snŭb) ◊ *verb* **snubbed, snubbing** ◊ *noun, plural* **snubs**

snuff *verb* To put out a candle; extinguish.
snuff (snŭf) ◊ *verb* **snuffed, snuffing**

snug *adjective* **1.** Giving comfort and protection; cozy. **2.** Fitting closely.
snug (snŭg) ◊ *adjective* **snugger, snuggest**

snuggle *verb* To lie or hold close; nestle.
snug·gle (snŭg′əl) ◊ *verb* **snuggled, snuggling**

so *adverb* **1.** In that manner; thus: *Why do you think so?* **2.** To that extent: *I'm so happy that I could cry.* **3.** To a great extent; extremely: *You are so friendly.* **4.** As a result; consequently: *I never went before and so I don't know the way.* **5.** Likewise; also: *They like the book and so do I.* **6.** In truth; indeed: *You did so lie.*
◊ *conjunction* With the result that: *You didn't eat, so you lost weight.*
◊ *pronoun* **1.** About that: *I need a yard or so of fabric.* **2.** The same: *We became friends and remained so the rest of our lives.*
so (sō) ◊ *adverb* ◊ *conjunction* ◊ *pronoun*
‖ *These sound alike:* **so, sew, sow**[1]

soak *verb* **1.** To make or become completely wet: *The rain soaked us.* **2.** To take in; absorb: *Sponges soak up moisture.*
◊ *noun* The act or process of soaking.
soak (sōk) ◊ *verb* **soaked, soaking** ◊ *noun*

soap *noun* A substance that is usually made from fat and lye and is used for washing.
◊ *verb* To treat, rub, or cover with soap.
soap (sōp) ◊ *noun, plural* **soaps** ◊ *verb* **soaped, soaping**

soapy *adjective* Like, covered with, or containing soap.
soap·y (sō′pē) ◊ *adjective* **soapier, soapiest**

S

soar *verb* **1.** To rise, fly, or glide high in the air. **2.** To rise suddenly and rapidly: *Prices began to soar.*
soar (sôr) ◊ *verb* **soared, soaring**
‖ *These sound alike:* **soar, sore**

sob *verb* To cry or utter with gasps and catching of the breath.
◊ *noun* The act or sound of sobbing.
sob (sŏb) ◊ *verb* **sobbed, sobbing** ◊ *noun, plural* **sobs**

sober *adjective* **1.** Serious or grave; solemn. **2.** Not drunk.
◊ *verb* To make or become sober.
so·ber (sō′bər) ◊ *adjective* **soberer, soberest** ◊ *verb* **sobered, sobering**

so-called *adjective* Called this, especially incorrectly: *The so-called guide was no help.*
so-called (sō′**kôld′**) ◊ *adjective*

soccer *noun* A game that is played on a field by two teams, each of which tries to kick a round ball into the goal of the opposing team.
soc·cer (sŏk′ər) ◊ *noun*

▲ **soccer**

sociable *adjective* **1.** Liking to be with company; friendly. **2.** Marked by friendly companionship: *We ate a sociable meal together.*
so·cia·ble (sō′shə bəl) ◊ *adjective*

social *adjective* **1.** Living together in communities or groups: *Bees and ants are social insects.* **2.** Of or relating to human beings as members of a community. **3.** Of, relating to, or based on one's position in society. **4.** Liking friendly companionship; sociable.
◊ *noun* An informal social gathering.
so·cial (sō′shəl) ◊ *adjective* ◊ *noun, plural* **socials**

socialism *noun* A system in which things such as factories and businesses are owned and controlled by the public or the government.
so·cial·ism (sō′shə lĭz′əm) ◊ *noun*

socialist *noun* A person who believes in or practices socialism.
so·cial·ist (sō′shə lĭst) ◊ *noun, plural* **socialists**

social studies *plural noun* A course of study including geography, history, and government.

society *noun* **1.** Human beings living and acting together; people in general: *Laws are made to protect society.* **2.** A group of people sharing an aim or interest; association. **3.** Company; companionship.
so·ci·e·ty (sə **sī′**ĭ tē) ◊ *noun, plural* **societies**

sock[1] *noun* A short, knitted or woven covering for the foot that reaches above the ankle and ends below the knee.
sock[1] (sŏk) ◊ *noun, plural* **socks**

sock[2] *verb* To hit; punch.
◊ *noun* A punch.
sock[2] (sŏk) ◊ *verb* **socked, socking** ◊ *noun, plural* **socks**

HISTORY **• sock[1], sock[2]**

Sock[1] was borrowed long ago from a Latin word for a type of light shoe. The word **sock[2]** may have been made up to imitate the sound of a hard punch.

socket *noun* A hollow piece or part for receiving or holding something: *I put a new light bulb in the socket.*
sock·et (sŏk′ĭt) ◊ *noun, plural* **sockets**

sockeye salmon *noun* A small salmon that is found along the northern Pacific coast. Its

ă	pat	ĭ	pit	oi	**oi**l	th	ba**th**
ā	pay	ī	ride	o͝o	b**oo**k	*th*	ba**th**e
â	care	î	fierce	o͞o	b**oo**t	ə	ago, item
ä	father	ŏ	pot	ou	**ou**t		pencil
ĕ	pet	ō	go	ŭ	c**u**t		atom
ē	be	ô	paw, for	û	f**u**r		circus

red flesh is much used as food.
sock·eye salmon (sŏk′ī′) ◊ *noun, plural* **sockeye salmon**

sod *noun* **1.** The layer of grass and soil that forms the surface of the ground. **2.** A piece of sod held together by matted roots.
sod (sŏd) ◊ *noun*

soda *noun* **1.** A soft drink containing carbonated water. **2.** A drink made with carbonated water, flavoring, and ice cream. **3.** Carbonated water.
so·da (sō′də) ◊ *noun, plural* **sodas**

soda fountain *noun* A counter where soft drinks, sandwiches, and ice cream are served.
soda fountain ◊ *noun, plural* **soda fountains**

soda water *noun* Water that contains carbon dioxide in the form of tiny bubbles.

sodium *noun* A soft, light, silver-white metallic chemical element. Sodium is one of the components of common salt.
so·di·um (sō′dē əm) ◊ *noun*

sofa *noun* A long upholstered seat with a back and arms.
so·fa (sō′fə) ◊ *noun, plural* **sofas**

soft *adjective* **1.** Not hard or firm: *The pillow is soft.* **2.** No longer strong: *Your leg muscles are soft.* **3.** Smooth, fine, or pleasing in feel or look: *The kitten had soft gray fur.* **4.** Not loud or harsh; quiet: *We listened to soft music on the radio.* **5.** Gentle or kind: *You have a soft heart.*
soft (sôft) ◊ *adjective* **softer, softest**

softball *noun* **1.** A game that is similar to baseball but is played with a larger, slightly softer ball. **2.** The ball used in softball.
soft·ball (sôft′bôl′) ◊ *noun, plural* **softballs**

soft drink *noun* A carbonated beverage that contains no alcohol.
soft drink ◊ *noun, plural* **soft drinks**

soften *verb* To make or become soft or softer.
soft·en (sô′fən) ◊ *verb* **softened, softening**

software *noun* Written or printed data, such as programs, that are used in operating computers.
soft·ware (sôft′wâr′) ◊ *noun*

softwood *noun* The wood of a cone-bearing tree, such as a pine.
soft·wood (sôft′wo͝od′) ◊ *noun*

soggy *adjective* Soaked with moisture.
sog·gy (sô′gē) ◊ *adjective* **soggier, soggiest**

soil¹ *noun* **1.** The loose top layer of the earth's surface in which plant life can grow. **2.** Land; country: *The settlers landed on foreign soil.*
soil¹ (soil) ◊ *noun, plural* **soils**

soil² *verb* To make or become dirty.
soil² (soil) ◊ *verb* **soiled, soiling**

***HISTORY* • soil¹, soil²**

Soil¹ comes from an old French word that meant "a patch of ground." The French word came from a Latin word meaning "a seat." **Soil²** also comes from an old French word that goes back to a Latin word. The French word meant "to make something dirty" and the Latin word meant "little pig."

sol *noun* The fifth tone of the musical scale.
sol (sōl) ◊ *noun*
‖*These sound alike:* **sol, sole, soul**

solar *adjective* **1.** Of or relating to the sun. **2.** Using, made by, or operating by energy from the sun: *Our new house has a solar heating system.*
so·lar (sō′lər) ◊ *adjective*

solar system *noun* The sun together with the nine planets and the other heavenly bodies that orbit it.

sold *verb* Past tense and past participle of **sell.**
sold (sōld) ◊ *verb*

solder *noun* An alloy, especially of tin and lead, that can be melted and used to join or mend metal parts or surfaces.
◊ *verb* To join or mend with solder.
sol·der (sŏd′ər) ◊ *noun* ◊ *verb* **soldered, soldering**

soldier *noun* A member of an army.
sol·dier (sōl′jər) ◊ *noun, plural* **soldiers**

sole¹ *noun* **1.** The bottom surface of the foot. **2.** The bottom of a shoe, boot, or slipper.
sole¹ (sōl) ◊ *noun, plural* **soles**
‖*These sound alike:* **sole, sol, soul**

sole² *adjective* **1.** Being the only one; single. **2.** Belonging only to one person or group and not to others: *My grandparents left me some money for my sole use.*
sole² (sōl) ◊ *adjective*
‖*These sound alike:* **sole, sol, soul**

S

sole³ *noun* An edible flatfish that is related to the flounder.
sole³ (sōl) ◊ *noun, plural* **sole** *or* **soles**
‖*These sound alike:* **sole, sol, soul**

***HISTORY* • sole¹, sole², sole³**

Sole¹ was borrowed long ago from a Latin word meaning "sandal." **Sole²** comes from a French word that came in turn from a Latin word meaning "alone." **Sole³** comes from the French name for this fish. The French name came from the same Latin word that gave us **sole¹**, because this flatfish is shaped a little like a sandal.

solemn *adjective* **1.** Very serious; grave: *A funeral is a solemn occasion.* **2.** Marked by serious thought and an understanding of possible consequences: *I gave a solemn promise not to tell a lie.*
sol·emn (sŏl′əm) ◊ *adjective*

solid *adjective* **1.** Having a definite shape and weight; not a liquid or a gas. **2.** Not hollow: *The chef carved a swan out of a solid block of ice.* **3.** Being of the same material, color, or kind throughout: *The plate was made of solid silver.* **4.** Without an interruption or break; continuous: *They talked for a solid hour.* **5.** Strong and firm: *The house has a solid foundation.* **6.** Respectable and dependable: *Solid citizens pay their taxes.*
◊*noun* **1.** A substance that has a definite shape and weight. **2.** A geometric figure, such as a cube, that has three dimensions.
sol·id (sŏl′ĭd) ◊ *adjective* ◊ *noun, plural* **solids**

solitary *adjective* **1.** Being or living alone: *I saw a solitary runner at the side of the road.* —See Synonyms at **alone. 2.** Happening, done, or passed alone: *I spent a solitary evening at home.*
sol·i·tar·y (sŏl′ĭ tĕr′ē) ◊ *adjective*

ă	pat	ĭ	pit	oi	**oil**	th	ba**th**
ā	pay	ī	ride	ŏŏ	book	*th*	ba**the**
â	care	î	fierce	ōō	boot	ə	ago, item
ä	father	ŏ	pot	ou	**out**		pencil
ĕ	pet	ō	go	ŭ	cut		atom
ē	be	ô	paw, for	û	fur		circus

solo *noun* A musical composition or a passage for a single voice or instrument with or without accompaniment.
◊*adjective* Done or performed without accompaniment, a partner, or a companion: *I made my first solo flight.*
◊*adverb* Alone: *Lacking a pianist, I had to sing solo.*
so·lo (sō′lō) ◊ *noun, plural* **solos** ◊ *adjective* ◊ *adverb*

soloist *noun* A person who performs a solo.
so·lo·ist (sō′lō ĭst) ◊ *noun, plural* **soloists**

soluble *adjective* Capable of being dissolved: *Soap flakes are soluble in water.*
sol·u·ble (sŏl′yə bəl) ◊ *adjective*

solution *noun* **1.** A mixture formed by dissolving a substance in a liquid: *I rinsed my mouth with a solution of salt in water.* **2.** The act, method, or process of solving a problem: *Use your books to help in the solution of difficult questions.* **3.** The answer to a problem: *Help me, but don't tell me the solution.*
so·lu·tion (sə lōō′shən) ◊ *noun, plural* **solutions**

solve *verb* To find an answer or solution to.
solve (sŏlv) ◊ *verb* **solved, solving**

somber *adjective* **1.** Dark and dull; gloomy: *The somber sky was the first sign of the approaching storm.* **2.** Melancholy; dismal: *The bad news put us into a somber mood.*
som·ber (sŏm′bər) ◊ *adjective*

sombrero *noun* A tall straw or felt hat with a broad brim that is worn especially in Mexico and the southwestern United States.
som·bre·ro (sŏm **brâr′**ō) ◊ *noun, plural* **sombreros**

▲ **sombrero**

some *adjective* Being a number or quantity that is not specified or that is not known: *We bought some apples.*
◊*pronoun* A number or quantity that is indefinite or that is not specified: *Some of the roses died.*
some (sŭm) ◊ *adjective* ◊ *pronoun*
‖*These sound alike:* **some, sum**

somebody *pronoun* A person who is not specified or who is unknown; someone: *Somebody came to see you.*
◊ *noun* An important person: *If you want to be somebody, you must work hard for it.*
some·bod·y (sŭm′bŏd′ē) ◊ *pronoun* ◊ *noun, plural* **somebodies**

someday *adverb* At a future time.
some·day (sŭm′dā′) ◊ *adverb*

somehow *adverb* In some way or another: *Early scientists knew that food and weight were somehow related.*
some·how (sŭm′hou′) ◊ *adverb*

someone *pronoun* Some person; somebody: *Someone called but didn't leave a message.*
some·one (sŭm′wŭn′) ◊ *pronoun*

somersault *noun* The act of rolling the body in a complete circle, heels over head.
◊ *verb* To perform a somersault.
som·er·sault (sŭm′ər sôlt′) ◊ *noun, plural* **somersaults** ◊ *verb* **somersaulted, somersaulting**

something *pronoun* A thing that is not definitely known or that is not specified: *I bought something for my parents. Something is wrong with the stove.*
some·thing (sŭm′thĭng) ◊ *pronoun*

sometime *adverb* **1.** At an indefinite time in the future: *Come and see us sometime.* **2.** At a time that is unknown or that is not stated: *All of that happened sometime last summer.*
some·time (sŭm′tīm′) ◊ *adverb*

sometimes *adverb* Now and then; at times: *I see them sometimes but not often.*
some·times (sŭm′tīmz′) ◊ *adverb*

somewhat *adverb* To some extent; rather: *My jacket is somewhat like yours.*
◊ *pronoun* Some extent or degree: *What you said comes as somewhat of a shock.*
some·what (sŭm′hwət) ◊ *adverb* ◊ *pronoun*

somewhere *adverb* **1.** At, in, or to a place that is not specified or is not known: *I found this turtle somewhere near the road.* **2.** At a time that is not specified: *Let's leave somewhere around noon.*
some·where (sŭm′hwâr′) ◊ *adverb*

son *noun* A male offspring or child.
son (sŭn) ◊ *noun, plural* **sons**
‖*These sound alike:* **son, sun**

sonar *noun* A system or device like radar that uses reflected sound waves for detecting and locating underwater objects.
so·nar (sō′när′) ◊ *noun*

sonata *noun* A musical composition in three or four sections, as for the piano.
so·na·ta (sə nä′tə) ◊ *noun, plural* **sonatas**

song *noun* **1.** A usually short musical piece that is meant to be sung. **2.** A musical sound that is produced by a bird.
song (sông) ◊ *noun, plural* **songs**

songbird *noun* A bird with a musical song.
song·bird (sông′bûrd′) ◊ *noun, plural* **songbirds**

son-in-law *noun* The husband of one's daughter.
son-in-law (sŭn′ĭn lô′) ◊ *noun, plural* **sons-in-law**

soon *adverb* **1.** Within a short time; before long: *We'll soon know if we passed the test.* **2.** Before the expected or usual time; early: *We arrived at the party too soon.* **3.** In a prompt manner; quickly: *We have to finish this job as soon as possible.*
soon (so͞on) ◊ *adverb* **sooner, soonest**

soot *noun* A fine, black powder produced when something, such as wood or coal, burns.
soot (so͝ot) ◊ *noun*

soothe *verb* **1.** To make calm or quiet: *The sound of the music soothed the restless baby.* **2.** To make less painful or intense; relieve: *I drank warm milk to soothe my sore throat.*
soothe (so͞oth) ◊ *verb* **soothed, soothing**

sop *verb* **1.** To dip or soak in a liquid: *Sop the bread in the beaten eggs.* **2.** To absorb or soak: *I used a mop to sop up the spilled water.*
sop (sŏp) ◊ *verb* **sopped, sopping**

sophomore *noun* A student in the second year at a high school or college.
soph·o·more (sŏf′ə môr′) ◊ *noun, plural* **sophomores**

soprano *noun* **1.** A singing voice of the highest range. **2.** A singer with this voice.
so·pran·o (sə prăn′ō) ◊ *noun, plural* **sopranos**

sore *adjective* **1.** Causing pain or distress; painful. **2.** Suffering pain; hurting: *I am sore from running.*
◊ *noun* A painful place, such as an open wound, on the body.
sore (sôr) ◊ *adjective* **sorer, sorest** ◊ *noun, plural* **sores**
‖*These sound alike:* **sore, soar**

S

sorrow *noun* **1.** Grief or sadness caused by loss or injury. **2.** A cause of sorrow.
◊ *verb* To feel or show sorrow; grieve.
sor·row (sŏr′ō) ◊ *noun, plural* **sorrows**
◊ *verb* **sorrowed, sorrowing**

sorry *adjective* **1.** Feeling sorrow, sympathy, pity, or regret: *I'm sorry I'm late.* **2.** Of poor quality; inferior: *This is a sorry collection of useless junk.*
sor·ry (sŏr′ē) ◊ *adjective* **sorrier, sorriest**

sort *noun* A group of persons or things sharing some characteristics; kind: *We bought all sorts of fruits.*
◊ *verb* To arrange according to class, kind, or size; classify: *We sorted the mail.*
sort (sôrt) ◊ *noun, plural* **sorts** ◊ *verb* **sorted, sorting**

SOS *noun* A call for rescue or help.
S·O·S (ĕs′ō **ĕs′**) ◊ *noun, plural* **SOSes** *or* **SOS's**

sought *verb* Past tense and past participle of **seek.**
sought (sôt) ◊ *verb*

soul *noun* **1.** The spiritual part of a person that is believed to include the capabilities to think, feel, and act. **2.** A person's emotional and moral nature: *I threw my whole soul into that job.* **3.** A human being: *There wasn't a soul at home.*
soul (sōl) ◊ *noun, plural* **souls**
‖*These sound alike:* **soul, sol, sole**

sound¹ *noun* **1.** A kind of vibration that travels through a substance, such as air, and can be heard. **2.** Something that is heard: *The sound of the trumpet was very loud.* **3.** The distance within which something can be heard: *They sat within sound of the waterfall.* **4.** One of the noises that make up human speech: *Pronounce the sound of "s" in "snow."*
◊ *verb* **1.** To make or cause to make a sound: *They sounded the gong.* **2.** To pronounce or be pronounced: *The words "break" and "brake" sound alike.* **3.** To seem to be: *The news sounds good.* **4.** To summon, announce, or signal by a sound: *We used the siren to sound a warning.*
sound¹ (sound) ◊ *noun, plural* **sounds** ◊ *verb* **sounded, sounding**

sound² *adjective* **1.** Free from defect, decay, damage, or disease: *Eat good food to have sound bones and teeth.* —See Synonyms at **healthy. 2.** Solid and firm: *We built our house on a sound foundation.* **3.** Sensible and correct: *You gave me some sound advice.* **4.** Deep and not interrupted: *I fell into a sound sleep.*
sound² (sound) ◊ *adjective* **sounder, soundest**

sound³ *noun* **1.** A long body of water that is wider than a channel or strait and that connects two larger bodies of water. **2.** An arm or inlet of the ocean.
sound³ (sound) ◊ *noun, plural* **sounds**

sound⁴ *verb* To measure the depth of water, especially by means of a weighted line.
sound⁴ (sound) ◊ *verb* **sounded, sounding**

HISTORY **• sound¹, sound², sound³, sound⁴**

Sound¹ comes from an old French word that came in turn from a Latin word for "something heard." **Sound²** comes from an old English word that meant "uninjured, healthy." **Sound³** comes from an old English word that meant "an act of swimming" and "a body of water narrow enough to swim across." **Sound⁴** comes from an old French word for a line used to measure the depth of water.

soundproof *adjective* Capable of keeping sound from passing through or entering.
sound·proof (**sound′**p**rōōf′**) ◊ *adjective*

soundtrack *noun* A narrow strip at the edge of a motion-picture film that carries a recording of the sound.
sound·track (**sound′**trăk′) ◊ *noun, plural* **soundtracks**

soup *noun* A liquid food prepared from meat, fish, or vegetable broth, often with various solid ingredients added.
soup (sōōp) ◊ *noun, plural* **soups**

ă	pat	ĭ	pit	oi	oil	th	bath
ā	pay	ī	ride	ŏŏ	book	*th*	bathe
â	care	î	fierce	ōō	boot	ə	ago, item
ä	father	ŏ	pot	ou	out		pencil
ĕ	pet	ō	go	ŭ	cut		atom
ē	be	ô	paw, for	û	fur		circus

sour *adjective* **1.** Having a sharp, tart, or acid taste: *Lemons are sour.* **2.** Made acid through spoiling: *The milk is sour.*
◊ *verb* To make or become sour.
sour (sour) ◊ *adjective* **sourer, sourest** ◊ *verb* **soured, souring**

source *noun* **1.** The person, place, or point from which something comes: *What is the source of the trouble?* **2.** The point of origin of a stream of water.
source (sôrs) ◊ *noun, plural* **sources**

sourness *noun* The quality of being sour.
sour·ness (**sour'**nĭs) ◊ *noun*

south *noun* **1.** The direction to the left of a person who faces the sunset. **2.** Often **South** A region in this direction. **3. South** The southeastern section of the United States. **4. South** The states that supported the Confederacy during the Civil War.
◊ *adjective* **1.** Of, in, or toward the south: *We camped on the south side of the lake.* **2.** Coming from the south: *A warm south wind blew all day.*
◊ *adverb* Toward the south: *We drove south to the camping site.*
south (south) ◊ *noun* ◊ *adjective* ◊ *adverb*

South American *noun* A person who was born in or lives in South America.
◊ *adjective* Of or relating to South America or South Americans.
South American ◊ *noun, plural* **South Americans** ◊ *adjective*

southeast *noun* **1.** The direction that is halfway between south and east. **2.** A region in this direction.
◊ *adjective* **1.** Of, in, or toward the southeast. **2.** Coming from the southeast.
◊ *adverb* Toward the southeast: *The border runs southeast along the mountains.*
south·east (south **ēst'**) ◊ *noun* ◊ *adjective* ◊ *adverb*

southerly *adjective & adverb* **1.** In or toward the south. **2.** From the south.
south·er·ly (**sŭth'**ər lē) ◊ *adjective & adverb*

southern *adjective* **1.** Often **Southern** Of, in, or toward the south. **2.** Coming from the south: *A warm southern wind is blowing today.*
south·ern (**sŭth'**ərn) ◊ *adjective*

South Pole *noun* The most southern point of the earth.

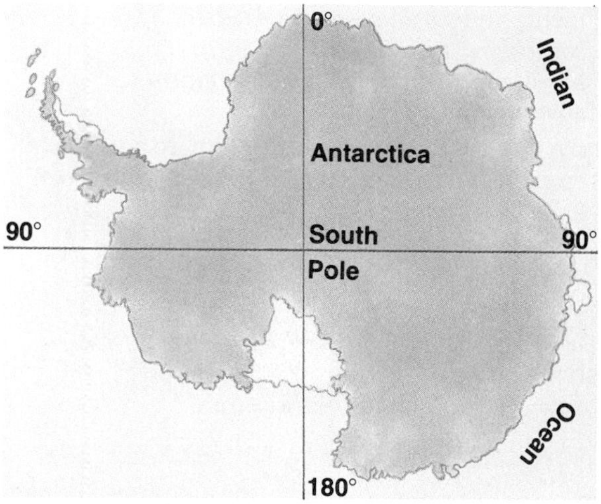

▲ **South Pole**

southward *adverb* To or toward the south: *The river flows southward.*
◊ *adjective* Moving to or toward the south: *We began our southward journey at dawn.*
south·ward (**south'**wərd) ◊ *adverb* ◊ *adjective*

southwards *adverb* Southward.
south·wards (**south'**wərdz) ◊ *adverb*

southwest *noun* **1.** The direction that is halfway between south and west. **2.** A region in this direction.
◊ *adjective* **1.** Of, in, or toward the southwest: *I was born in the southwest part of the state.* **2.** Coming from the southwest: *We're expecting a southwest wind tomorrow.*
◊ *adverb* Toward the southwest: *We sailed southwest to the island for a picnic.*
south·west (south **wĕst'**) ◊ *noun* ◊ *adjective* ◊ *adverb*

southwester *noun* A waterproof hat with a broad brim that is longer in the back to protect the neck.
south·west·er (south **wĕs'**tər *or* sou **wĕs'**tər) ◊ *noun, plural* **southwesters**

souvenir *noun* Something kept as a reminder of something, as a place or occasion.
sou·ve·nir (sōō'və **nîr'**) ◊ *noun, plural* **souvenirs**

sovereign *noun* The chief of state in a monarchy; king or queen.
◊ *adjective* **1.** Having supreme rank, authority, or power: *A monarch is a sovereign ruler.*

S

2. Not ruled or controlled by another government; independent: *The United States is a sovereign state.*
sov·er·eign (sŏv′rĭn) ◊ *noun, plural* **sovereigns** ◊ *adjective*

sow¹ *verb* **1.** To scatter or plant to produce a crop: *The farmer sowed wheat and corn.* **2.** To scatter or plant seed in or on: *We sowed our fields in the spring.*
sow¹ (sō) ◊ *verb* **sowed, sown** *or* **sowed, sowing**
‖*These sound alike:* **sow¹, sew, so**

sow² *noun* A fully grown female pig.
sow² (sou) ◊ *noun, plural* **sows**

***HISTORY* • sow¹, sow²**

Sow¹ comes from an old English word that meant "to plant seed." **Sow²** comes from a different old English word that meant "a female pig."

sown *verb* A past participle of **sow¹**.
sown (sōn) ◊ *verb*

soybean *noun* A bean plant of Asia that is widely grown for its edible, very nutritious seeds. Soybean seeds are a source of oil and flour.
soy·bean (soi′bēn′) ◊ *noun, plural* **soybeans**

space *noun* **1.** The expanse without limits in which the solar system, stars, and galaxies exist. **2.** The distance or open area between or within objects or between points: *Leave a space between the two words.* **3.** An area provided for a certain purpose: *We finally found a parking space.* **4.** An extent of time: *Two trains arrived within a space of three minutes.* ◊ *verb* To place, arrange, or organize with space between: *We spaced the tulips carefully when we planted the garden.*
space (spās) ◊ *noun, plural* **spaces** ◊ *verb* **spaced, spacing**

spacecraft *noun* A vehicle designed for travel beyond the earth's atmosphere.
space·craft (spās′krăft′) ◊ *noun, plural* **spacecraft**

spaceship *noun* A spacecraft.
space·ship (spās′shĭp′) ◊ *noun, plural* **spaceships**

space shuttle *noun* A space vehicle designed to carry astronauts back and forth between the earth and an orbiting space station.
space shuttle ◊ *noun, plural* **space shuttles**

▲ **space shuttle**

space station *noun* A large satellite that can hold a crew. A space station is placed in a permanent orbit around the earth.
space station ◊ *noun, plural* **space stations**

space suit *noun* A protective suit that allows the person wearing it to move about freely in outer space.
space suit ◊ *noun, plural* **space suits**

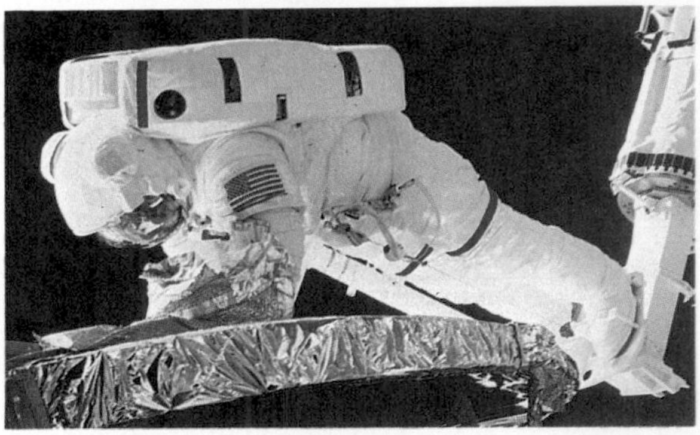

▲ **space suit**

ă	pat	ĭ	pit	oi	**oi**l	th	ba**th**
ā	pay	ī	ride	o͝o	b**oo**k	*th*	ba**the**
â	care	î	fierce	o͞o	b**oo**t	ə	ago, item
ä	father	ŏ	pot	ou	**ou**t		pencil
ĕ	pet	ō	go	ŭ	c**u**t		atom
ē	be	ô	paw, for	û	f**u**r		circus

spade *noun* A digging tool with a long handle and a flat blade that is pressed into the ground with the foot.
spade (spād) ◊ *noun, plural* **spades**

spaghetti *noun* A food made of a mixture of flour and water that is shaped into long strings and is cooked by boiling.
spa·ghet·ti (spə gĕt′ē) ◊ *noun*

span *noun* **1.** The distance between two supports, as of a bridge. **2.** The distance from the tip of the thumb to the tip of the little finger when the hand is spread out. **3.** A period of time: *We traveled for a span of four hours.*
◊ *verb* To stretch across: *The bridge spans the big river.*
span (spăn) ◊ *noun, plural* **spans** ◊ *verb* **spanned, spanning**

spangle *noun* A small disk of shiny metal or plastic used for decoration.
span·gle (spăng′gəl) ◊ *noun, plural* **spangles**

Spaniard *noun* A person who was born in or lives in Spain.
Span·iard (spăn′yərd) ◊ *noun, plural* **Spaniards**

spaniel *noun* A dog of small or medium size with drooping ears, short legs, and a silky, wavy coat.
span·iel (spăn′yəl) ◊ *noun, plural* **spaniels**

Spanish *noun* **1.** (*used with a plural verb*) The people of Spain. **2.** The language of Spain, Mexico, and most of Central America and South America.
◊ *adjective* Of or relating to Spain, the Spanish, or their language.
Span·ish (spăn′ĭsh) ◊ *noun* ◊ *adjective*

Spanish moss *noun* A plant of the southeastern United States and tropical America that grows on trees and hangs down in long, grayish threadlike masses.

spank *verb* To slap with the open hand or with a flat object.
spank (spăngk) ◊ *verb* **spanked, spanking**

spare *verb* **1.** To show mercy or consideration to: *I tried to spare your feelings by not telling you about the problem.* **2.** To free from the need to have to do something: *Order the supplies by phone and spare yourself a trip to the store.* **3.** To give up, especially if not needed: *Can you spare a dime? Can you spare a few minutes to talk?* **4.** To have left over: *We got there at noon with time to spare.*
◊ *adjective* **1.** Ready when needed: *There's a spare tire in the trunk.* **2.** Beyond what is needed; extra: *Do you have any spare cash?* **3.** Thin or lean: *The farmer is tall and spare.*
◊ *noun* Something, such as a tire, that can be used when it is needed.
spare (spâr) ◊ *verb* **spared, sparing** ◊ *adjective* **sparer, sparest** ◊ *noun, plural* **spares**

sparing *adjective* Thrifty or frugal.
spar·ing (spâr′ĭng) ◊ *adjective*

sparingly *adverb* In a thrifty way or manner.
spar·ing·ly (spâr′ĭng lē) ◊ *adverb*

spark *noun* **1.** A small bit of burning material. **2.** A quick flash of light, especially of electricity. **3.** A small amount; trace: *They didn't show a spark of interest in the story.*
◊ *verb* To give or cause to give off sparks.
spark (spärk) ◊ *noun, plural* **sparks** ◊ *verb* **sparked, sparking**

sparkle *verb* To give off sparks of light; glitter: *Diamonds sparkle.*
◊ *noun* **1.** A spark of light. **2.** A sparkling quality; glitter.
spar·kle (spär′kəl) ◊ *verb* **sparkled, sparkling** ◊ *noun, plural* **sparkles**

sparrow *noun* A small brownish or grayish bird that is often found in cities.
spar·row (spăr′ō) ◊ *noun, plural* **sparrows**

sparse *adjective* Occurring only here and there; thin: *Vegetation in the area is sparse.*
sparse (spärs) ◊ *adjective* **sparser, sparsest**

spasm *noun* A sudden involuntary contraction of a muscle or group of muscles.
spasm (spăz′əm) ◊ *noun, plural* **spasms**

spat¹ *noun* A short, unimportant quarrel.
spat¹ (spăt) ◊ *noun, plural* **spats**

spat² *verb* A past tense and a past participle of **spit²**.
spat² (spăt) ◊ *verb*

spatter *verb* To scatter or splash in drops: *Be careful not to spatter paint on your shirt.*
spat·ter (spăt′ər) ◊ *verb* **spattered, spattering**

spatula *noun* A tool with a flexible blade that is used especially for mixing or spreading soft substances.
spat·u·la (spăch′ə lə) ◊ *noun, plural* **spatulas**

spawn *verb* To lay eggs and reproduce, as fish and some other water animals do.

S

◊ *noun* The eggs of a water animal such as a fish, an oyster, or a frog.
spawn (spôn) ◊ *verb* **spawned, spawning**
◊ *noun*

▲ **spawn**

speak *verb* **1.** To utter words; talk: *Speak to me.* **2.** To express in words: *Is the witness speaking the truth?* **3.** To make a speech: *Who spoke at the school assembly today?* **4.** To use or be able to use orally: *My friend speaks Spanish.*
speak (spēk) ◊ *verb* **spoke, spoken, speaking**

> ***SYNONYMS***
>
> ***speak, chatter, talk***
>
> Would you like to *speak* to the audience? We *chattered* away about nothing. During dinner we *talk* about what each of us has done during the day.

speaker *noun* **1.** A person who speaks. **2.** A person who presides over a meeting. **3.** A loudspeaker.
speak·er (spē′kər) ◊ *noun, plural* **speakers**

spear *noun* **1.** A weapon that has a long shaft and a sharply pointed head. **2.** A slender stalk or stem, as of asparagus.
◊ *verb* To pierce or stab with or as if with a spear: *I speared the last piece of fish on the serving platter with my fork.*
spear (spîr) ◊ *noun, plural* **spears** ◊ *verb* **speared, spearing**

spearmint *noun* A mint plant whose leaves are used for flavoring.
spear·mint (**spîr′**mĭnt′) ◊ *noun*

special *adjective* **1.** Different from what is common or usual; exceptional: *Birthdays are special occasions.* **2.** Distinct from all others; unique: *We ordered a car in a special color.* **3.** Intended for a particular occasion or purpose: *If you want to become a doctor, you will need special training.*
spe·cial (**spĕsh′**əl) ◊ *adjective*

specialist *noun* A person, such as a doctor, who is involved in a particular activity or branch of study.
spe·cial·ist (**spĕsh′**ə lĭst) ◊ *noun, plural* **specialists**

specialize *verb* To be involved in a particular activity or branch of study: *Our doctor specializes in children's diseases.*
spe·cial·ize (**spĕsh′**ə līz′) ◊ *verb* **specialized, specializing**

specialty *noun* **1.** A special study, profession, or skill. **2.** A special attraction or feature: *The restaurant's specialty is seafood.*
spe·cial·ty (**spĕsh′**əl tē) ◊ *noun, plural* **specialties**

species *noun* A group of animals or plants that are similar and considered to be of the same kind.
spe·cies (**spē′**shēz′) ◊ *noun, plural* **species**

specific *adjective* Clearly stated; definite: *Please ask specific questions.*
spe·ci·fic (spĭ **sĭf′**ĭk) ◊ *adjective*

specify *verb* To state in a clear and precise way: *When you order the books, you must specify how many you want.*
spec·i·fy (**spĕs′**ə fī′) ◊ *verb* **specified, specifying**

specimen *noun* One of a group of things that can be taken to represent the group: *I collected many specimens of butterflies.*
spec·i·men (**spĕs′**ə mən) ◊ *noun, plural* **specimens**

speck *noun* **1.** A small spot or mark: *What are those brown specks on the paper?* **2.** A small bit; particle: *There are specks of dust on the table.*
speck (spĕk) ◊ *noun, plural* **specks**

ă	pat	ĭ	pit	oi	**oil**	th	**bath**
ā	pay	ī	ride	ŏŏ	**book**	*th*	**bathe**
â	care	î	fierce	ōō	**boot**	ə	ago, item
ä	father	ŏ	pot	ou	**out**		pencil
ĕ	pet	ō	**go**	ŭ	**cut**		atom
ē	be	ô	paw, for	û	**fur**		circus

spectacle *noun* **1.** An unusual or impressive public show, as of fireworks. **2. spectacles** A pair of eyeglasses.
spec·ta·cle (**spĕk′** tə kəl) ◊ *noun, plural* **spectacles**

spectacular *adjective* Being unusual or impressive; sensational: *From the helicopter we had a spectacular view of the falls.*
spec·tac·u·lar (spĕk **tăk′** yə lər) ◊ *adjective*

spectator *noun* A person who watches an event but does not take part in it.
spec·ta·tor (**spĕk′** tā′tər) ◊ *noun, plural* **spectators**

spectrum *noun* The bands of color that are seen when light, especially light from the sun, is broken up, as by a prism. You can see the colors of the spectrum in a rainbow.
spec·trum (**spĕk′**-trəm) ◊ *noun, plural* **spectrums**

▲ **spectrum**

speculate *verb* To think deeply; ponder; reflect.
spec·u·late (**spĕk′** yə-lāt′) ◊ *verb* **speculated, speculating**

sped *verb* A past tense and a past participle of **speed.**
sped (spĕd) ◊ *verb*

speech *noun* **1.** The act of speaking. **2.** The ability to speak: *Speech is a gift to be treasured.* **3.** Something that is spoken: *Their speech was full of slang.* **4.** The way in which a person speaks: *Your slurred speech shows that you are sleepy.* **5.** A public talk or address: *The president's speech was broadcast.*
speech (spēch) ◊ *noun, plural* **speeches**

speechless *adjective* Not able to speak for a short time because of shock, fear, or joy.
speech·less (**spēch′** lĭs) ◊ *adjective*

speed *noun* **1.** The condition of moving or acting rapidly; quickness: *You work with amazing speed.* **2.** Rate of motion or action: *We drove at the legal speed of 55 miles an hour.*
◊ *verb* **1.** To move or cause to move rapidly. **2.** To drive faster than is lawful or safe.
speed (spēd) ◊ *noun, plural* **speeds** ◊ *verb* **sped** *or* **speeded, speeding**

SYNONYMS

speed, accelerate, hurry

I *sped* along on my bicycle. The car *accelerated* down the hill. As I was *hurrying* to town I missed my turn.

speedometer *noun* A device that measures and indicates speed, as of an automobile.
speed·om·e·ter (spĭ **dŏm′** ĭ tər) ◊ *noun, plural* **speedometers**

speedy *adjective* Moving quickly; swift.
speed·y (**spē′** dē) ◊ *adjective* **speedier, speediest**

spell¹ *verb* **1.** To name or write the letters of in order: *The teacher asked me to spell "southern."* **2.** To be the letters of: *What does "d-o-g" spell?* **3.** To be a sign of; mean: *Those black clouds spell trouble.*
spell¹ (spĕl) ◊ *verb* **spelled** *or* **spelt, spelling**

spell² *noun* **1.** A word or group of words thought to have magic power. **2.** An irresistible influence: *We fell under the spell of the tropical island.*
spell² (spĕl) ◊ *noun, plural* **spells**

spell³ *noun* **1.** A short, indefinite period of time: *I've decided to stay at home for a spell.* **2.** A period of activity: *We each had a spell at the controls of the boat.*
◊ *verb* To take the place of for a time: *I'll spell you now at mowing the lawn.*
spell³ (spĕl) ◊ *noun, plural* **spells** ◊ *verb* **spelled, spelling**

***HISTORY* • spell¹, spell², spell³**

Spell¹ and **spell²** both go back to a Germanic word that meant "to recite." This word was borrowed long ago into French, where it came to mean "to read out letter by letter." The old French word was then borrowed into English as **spell¹**. The Germanic word had also passed into English, where it first meant "a story" and later developed the special magical sense of **spell²**. **Spell³** came from a different old English word that meant "to substitute for."

S

speller *noun* **1.** A person who spells words. **2.** A book used in teaching spelling.
spell·er (spĕl′ər) ◊ *noun, plural* **spellers**

spelling *noun* **1.** The forming of words with letters in the proper order. **2.** The way in which a word is spelled.
spell·ing (spĕl′ĭng) ◊ *noun, plural* **spellings**

spelt *verb* A past tense and a past participle of **spell[1]**.
spelt (spĕlt) ◊ *verb*

spend *verb* **1.** To pay out: *I spent $5.00 for the book.* **2.** To pay out money: *Earn your allowance before you decide to spend.* **3.** To pass: *They will spend their vacation at the beach.*
spend (spĕnd) ◊ *verb* **spent, spending**

spent *verb* Past tense and past participle of **spend.**
spent (spĕnt) ◊ *verb*

sperm *noun* A male cell of reproduction.
sperm (spûrm) ◊ *noun, plural* **sperm**

sperm whale *noun* A large whale that is the source of a valuable oil.
sperm whale ◊ *noun, plural* **sperm whales**

▲ **sperm whale**

ă	pat	ĭ	pit	oi	oil	th	bath
ā	pay	ī	ride	o͝o	book	*th*	bathe
â	care	î	fierce	o͞o	boot	ə	ago, item
ä	father	ŏ	pot	ou	out		pencil
ĕ	pet	ō	go	ŭ	cut		atom
ē	be	ô	paw, for	û	fur		circus

sphere *noun* **1.** An object shaped so that all points on its surface are the same distance from a center point. **2.** An object shaped like a sphere. **3.** A field or area of interest, activity, or knowledge: *Music is not my sphere.*
sphere (sfîr) ◊ *noun, plural* **spheres**

sphinx *noun* An ancient Egyptian figure with the body of a lion and the head of a man, ram, or hawk.
sphinx (sfĭngks) ◊ *noun, plural* **sphinxes**

▲ **sphinx**

spice *noun* **1.** A plant substance, such as nutmeg or clover, that has a pleasant or strong smell and is used to flavor food. **2.** Something that adds excitement or interest: *Variety is often called the spice of life.*
◊ *verb* To flavor with or as if with spice.
spice (spīs) ◊ *noun, plural* **spices** ◊ *verb* **spiced, spicing**

spicy *adjective* Seasoned with or containing spice.
spic·y (spī′sē) ◊ *adjective* **spicier, spiciest**

spider *noun* An animal with eight legs and a body divided into two parts that spins webs to catch insects.
spi·der (spī′dər) ◊ *noun, plural* **spiders**

spigot *noun* A faucet.
spig·ot (spĭg′ət) ◊ *noun, plural* **spigots**

spike[1] *noun* **1.** A long, heavy nail. **2.** A pointed metal piece attached to the sole of a shoe. An athlete wears spikes to get and keep a firm footing.
spike[1] (spīk) ◊ *noun, plural* **spikes**

spike² *noun* **1.** An ear of grain, as wheat. **2.** A long cluster of flowers that do not have stalks.
spike² (spīk) ◊ *noun, plural* **spikes**

> ***HISTORY* • spike¹, spike²**
>
> **Spike¹** first appears in written English about 650 years ago. Before that, the word perhaps came from Scandinavia or northern Germany. **Spike²** comes from a Latin word for an ear of grain.

spill *verb* **1.** To cause or allow to run or flow out of a container, especially by accident: *The child spilled the milk.* **2.** To run or fall out: *Water spilled over the top of the dam.* **3.** To cause to fall, as from a horse.
◊ *noun* **1.** Something spilled: *Oil spills cause great destruction.* **2.** A fall, as from a horse.
spill (spĭl) ◊ *verb* **spilled** *or* **spilt, spilling** ◊ *noun, plural* **spills**

spilt *verb* A past tense and a past participle of **spill.**
spilt (spĭlt) ◊ *verb*

spin *verb* **1.** To draw out and twist fibers into thread. **2.** To form a thread, web, or cocoon from a liquid given off by the body, as spiders do. **3.** To tell; relate: *The old sailor is good at spinning tales.* **4.** To turn about an axis at high speed; rotate: *The car's wheels were spinning on the icy pavement.* **5.** To seem to be whirling, as from dizziness: *The roller coaster made my head spin.*
◊ *noun* **1.** A rapid rotating motion: *Give the top a spin.* **2.** A short drive in or on a vehicle: *I'm going to take a spin on my bicycle.*
spin (spĭn) ◊ *verb* **spun, spinning** ◊ *noun, plural* **spins**

spinach *noun* A plant grown for its dark green leaves. Spinach is eaten as a vegetable.
spin·ach (spĭn′ĭch) ◊ *noun*

spinal *adjective* Of, relating to, or near the spine or backbone.
spi·nal (spī′nəl) ◊ *adjective*

spinal column *noun* The backbone.
spinal column ◊ *noun, plural* **spinal columns**

spinal cord *noun* A thick cord of nerve tissue that begins at the brain and goes down through the center of the backbone.
spinal cord ◊ *noun, plural* **spinal cords**

spindle *noun* **1.** A rod or pin on a spinning machine that holds and winds thread. **2.** A rod or pin like a spindle that turns, or on which something turns.
spin·dle (spĭn′dl) ◊ *noun, plural* **spindles**

spine *noun* **1.** The backbone. **2.** A part of a plant or animal that sticks out with a sharp point. The quills on a porcupine and thorns on a rose are spines.
spine (spīn) ◊ *noun, plural* **spines**

spinning wheel *noun* A device consisting of a large wheel and a spindle that is used to spin thread or yarn.
spinning wheel ◊ *noun, plural* **spinning wheels**

spinster *noun* An unmarried woman.
spin·ster (spĭn′stər) ◊ *noun, plural* **spinsters**

spiny *adjective* Full of or covered with spines.
spin·y (spī′nē) ◊ *adjective* **spinier, spiniest**

spiral *noun* **1.** A curve that gradually widens as it coils around. **2.** Something, such as the thread of a screw, that resembles a spiral.
◊ *verb* To move or cause to move in the form of a spiral: *Smoke spiraled from the chimney.*
◊ *adjective* Of, relating to, or being a spiral: *The tower had a spiral staircase.*
spi·ral (spī′rəl) ◊ *noun, plural* **spirals** ◊ *verb* **spiraled, spiraling** ◊ *adjective*

spire *noun* A structure, such as a steeple, that becomes narrow at the top.
spire (spīr) ◊ *noun, plural* **spires**

spirit *noun* **1.** The part of a human being that is believed to have control over thinking and feeling; soul. **2.** A ghost. **3. spirits** A person's mood or state of mind: *Even though I lost the tennis championship, I'm in good spirits.* **4.** Enthusiasm, courage, or pep: *Our team showed a lot of spirit.* **5.** Real meaning, sense, or intent: *We must obey the spirit and the letter of the law.*
◊ *verb* To carry off mysteriously or secretly.
spir·it (spĭr′ĭt) ◊ *noun, plural* **spirits** ◊ *verb* **spirited, spiriting**

spirited *adjective* Full of vigor or courage.
spir·it·ed (spĭr′ĭ tĭd) ◊ *adjective*

spiritual *adjective* **1.** Of or relating to the spirit. **2.** Of or relating to religion.
◊ *noun* A religious folk song that originated among southern blacks in the United States.
spir·i·tu·al (spĭr′ĭ cho͞o əl) ◊ *adjective* ◊ *noun, plural* **spirituals**

S

spit¹ *noun* **1.** A slender, pointed rod on which meat is roasted. **2.** A narrow point of land that extends into a body of water.
spit¹ (spĭt) ◊ *noun, plural* **spits**

spit² *verb* To expel saliva from the mouth.
◊ *noun* Saliva.
spit² (spĭt) ◊ *verb* **spat** *or* **spit, spitting** ◊ *noun*

> ***HISTORY* • spit¹, spit²**
>
> **Spit¹** comes from an old English word that meant "a pointed stick used for roasting." The meaning "a narrow strip of land" developed more recently. **Spit²** comes from a different old English word that was probably made up to imitate the sound of someone spitting.

spite *noun* A mean desire to hurt another person.
◊ *verb* To show ill will to another person.
◊ *idiom* **in spite of** With no thought or concern; regardless: *I'm going in spite of the risk.*
spite (spīt) ◊ *noun* ◊ *verb* **spited, spiting**

splash *verb* **1.** To scatter a liquid, such as water, all around: *The children splashed in the pool.* **2.** To make wet or dirty by splashing: *I knocked over the can and splashed paint on the rug.* **3.** To fall, move, or hit with the sound of splashing: *Rain splashed on the roof.*
◊ *noun* **1.** The act or sound of splashing. **2.** A mark or spot made by or as if by splashed liquid.
splash (splăsh) ◊ *verb* **splashed, splashing** ◊ *noun, plural* **splashes**

splashdown *noun* The landing of a spacecraft or missile in the ocean or the moment of its impact.
splash·down (**splăsh′**doun′) ◊ *noun, plural* **splashdowns**

splendid *adjective* **1.** Very beautiful or impressive; brilliant: *The ballet performance was splendid.* **2.** Very good; excellent: *Your record in school is splendid.*
splen·did (**splĕn′**dĭd) ◊ *adjective*

splendor *noun* Magnificent or beautiful appearance: *We were impressed by the splendor of the costumes.*
splen·dor (**splĕn′**dər) ◊ *noun, plural* **splendors**

splint *noun* A device that is used to hold a broken bone in place.
splint (splĭnt) ◊ *noun, plural* **splints**

splinter *noun* A sharp, thin piece, as of wood, that is broken off from a larger piece.
◊ *verb* To break into splinters.
splin·ter (**splĭn′**tər) ◊ *noun, plural* **splinters** ◊ *verb* **splintered, splintering**

split *verb* **1.** To divide or become divided into parts, especially lengthwise: *We split logs for the campfire.* **2.** To break, burst, or rip apart with force: *Pressure caused the container to split.* **3.** To divide and share: *We split the bill for the dinner.*
◊ *noun* **1.** The act or result of splitting. **2.** A division within a group: *There's a split in the team about who should be captain.*
split (splĭt) ◊ *verb* **split, splitting** ◊ *noun, plural* **splits**

spoil *verb* **1.** To damage and make less valuable or useful; injure: *A storm spoiled our picnic.* **2.** To become unfit for use, as by decaying: *The milk spoiled.* **3.** To injure the character or disposition of by too much praise or indulgence: *Don't spoil your younger brothers and sisters.* —See Synonyms at **pamper.**
◊ *plural noun* **spoils** Property that is taken away by force; plunder.
spoil (spoil) ◊ *verb* **spoiled** *or* **spoilt, spoiling** ◊ *plural noun*

spoilt *verb* A past tense and a past participle of **spoil.**
spoilt (spoilt) ◊ *verb*

spoke¹ *noun* A rod or brace that connects the rim of a wheel to its hub.
spoke¹ (spōk) ◊ *noun, plural* **spokes**

spoke² *verb* Past tense of **speak.**
spoke² (spōk) ◊ *verb*

spoken *adjective* Expressed or communicated by speaking; oral: *There is spoken dialogue in some operas.*
◊ *verb* Past participle of **speak.**
spo·ken (**spō′**kən) ◊ *adjective* ◊ *verb*

ă	pat	ĭ	pit	oi	**oil**	th	**bath**
ā	pay	ī	ride	ŏŏ	book	*th*	**bathe**
â	care	î	fierce	ōō	boot	ə	ago, item
ä	father	ŏ	pot	ou	**out**		pencil
ĕ	pet	ō	go	ŭ	cut		atom
ē	be	ô	paw, for	û	fur		circus

sponge *noun* **1.** A water animal that has a soft skeleton with many small holes that absorb water. **2.** The soft skeleton of a sponge that is used for bathing, wiping, or cleaning. **3.** A commercial product made of an absorbent material such as rubber or plastic that is used for bathing, wiping, and cleaning.
◊ *verb* To bathe, wipe, or clean with a sponge.
sponge (spŭnj) ◊ *noun, plural* **sponges** ◊ *verb* **sponged, sponging**

▲ **sponge**
An artificial and a natural sponge

sponsor *noun* **1.** A person who is responsible for or supports another person or thing: *The governor is a well-known sponsor of the arts.* **2.** A person or organization that pays the costs of a radio or television program in order to advertise a product or service. **3.** A godmother or godfather.
◊ *verb* To act as a sponsor for.
spon·sor (**spŏn′** sər) ◊ *noun, plural* **sponsors** ◊ *verb* **sponsored, sponsoring**

spontaneous *adjective* Happening, done, or produced naturally or without outside cause.
spon·ta·ne·ous (spŏn **tā′** nē əs) ◊ *adjective*

spool *noun* A small cylinder, as of wood, on which thread and wire are wound.
spool (spo͞ol) ◊ *noun, plural* **spools**

spoon *noun* A utensil with a shallow bowl at the end of its handle. Spoons are used in measuring, serving, or eating food.
◊ *verb* To scoop up with or as if with a spoon.
spoon (spo͞on) ◊ *noun, plural* **spoons** ◊ *verb* **spooned, spooning**

▲ **spool**

spore *noun* A single plant or animal cell that is able to grow into a new plant or animal.
spore (spôr) ◊ *noun, plural* **spores**

sport *noun* **1.** Recreation, competition, and games that involve physical activity. Baseball, hockey, and tennis are sports. **2.** A person judged by the way he or she reacts to winning or losing: *Try to be a good sport.*
sport (spôrt) ◊ *noun, plural* **sports**

sportsmanship *noun* The qualities and conduct of a participant in a sport.
sports·man·ship (**spôrts′** mən shĭp′) ◊ *noun*

spot *noun* **1.** A small mark or stain: *Red spots on the body can be a symptom of measles.* **2.** An area that is different, as in color, from the area around it: *My dog has brown fur with white spots.* **3.** A place or location.
◊ *verb* **1.** To mark or cause to be marked with spots. **2.** To find or locate: *It was hard to spot you in the crowd.*
spot (spŏt) ◊ *noun, plural* **spots** ◊ *verb* **spotted, spotting**

spotless *adjective* Completely clean. —See Synonyms at **clean.**
spot·less (**spŏt′** lĭs) ◊ *adjective*

spotlight *noun* A strong lamp that lights up a small area, as on a stage.
spot·light (**spŏt′** līt′) ◊ *noun, plural* **spotlights**

spouse *noun* A husband or wife.
spouse (spous) ◊ *noun, plural* **spouses**

spout *verb* To shoot or flow out hard or in spurts: *The volcano spouted lava.*
◊ *noun* A tube, pipe, or opening through which liquid spouts.
spout (spout) ◊ *verb* **spouted, spouting** ◊ *noun, plural* **spouts**

sprain *noun* An injury to a joint or muscle in which it is stretched, twisted, or torn.
◊ *verb* To cause a sprain in.
sprain (sprān) ◊ *noun, plural* **sprains** ◊ *verb* **sprained, spraining**

sprang *verb* A past tense of **spring.**
sprang (sprăng) ◊ *verb*

sprawl *verb* To sit or lie with the arms and legs spread out.
◊ *noun* The posture or act of sprawling.
sprawl (sprôl) ◊ *verb* **sprawled, sprawling** ◊ *noun, plural* **sprawls**

spray *noun* **1.** Liquid that moves through the air as mist: *The ocean spray felt good on a hot*

S

day. **2.** A jet of vapor that is forced out under pressure from a container. **3.** A device that forces out a spray of vapor or liquid.
◊ *verb* To apply in the form of spray.
spray (sprā) ◊ *noun, plural* **sprays** ◊ *verb* **sprayed, spraying**

spread *verb* **1.** To open out wide or wider: *I spread the tablecloth on the ground.* **2.** To push or move apart; stretch: *Spread your fingers as much as you can when holding the basketball.* **3.** To distribute a layer of over a surface: *I spread paint on the wall.* **4.** To make or become widely known: *The news spread rapidly.*
◊ *noun* **1.** The act or process of spreading. **2.** The extent to which something can be spread: *The wings of the bird have a 12-inch spread.* **3.** A cloth cover for a bed.
spread (sprĕd) ◊ *verb* **spread, spreading** ◊ *noun, plural* **spreads**

SYNONYMS

spread, expand, extend

I *spread* my arms as far apart as I could. The balloon *expanded* as I blew it up. We *extended* the ladder as far as possible. **Antonyms:** *contract, shrink*

spring *verb* **1.** To move upward or forward in one quick motion; leap: *I sprang from my chair.* **2.** To grow or appear suddenly: *The new houses seemed to spring up overnight.* **3.** To cause to happen unexpectedly: *Don't spring any surprises on us.*
◊ *noun* **1.** An elastic device that returns to its original shape after being pushed, pulled, twisted, or bent. **2.** The act of springing. **3.** A natural fountain or flow of water. **4.** The season of the year between winter and summer when plants begin to grow. **5.** The quality of being elastic.
spring (sprĭng) ◊ *verb* **sprang** *or* **sprung, sprung, springing** ◊ *noun, plural* **springs**

ă	pat	ĭ	pit	oi	**oil**	th	**bath**
ā	pay	ī	ride	o͝o	**book**	*th*	**bathe**
â	care	î	fierce	o͞o	**boot**	ə	**ago, item**
ä	father	ŏ	pot	ou	**out**		pencil
ĕ	pet	ō	go	ŭ	**cut**		atom
ē	be	ô	paw, for	û	**fur**		circus

springboard *noun* A flexible board used in diving or gymnastics to help a person jump high in the air.
spring·board (**sprĭng′**bôrd′) ◊ *noun, plural* **springboards**

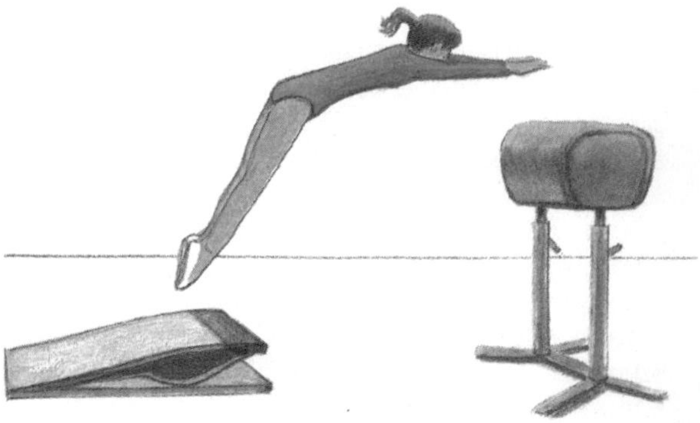

▲ **springboard**

springtime *noun* The season of spring.
spring·time (**sprĭng′**tīm′) ◊ *noun*

sprinkle *verb* **1.** To scatter in drops or particles: *Sprinkle salt on the icy steps.* **2.** To scatter drops on: *We sprinkled the lawn.* **3.** To rain slightly.
◊ *noun* **1.** An act of sprinkling. **2.** A light rain.
sprin·kle (**sprĭng′**kəl) ◊ *verb* **sprinkled, sprinkling** ◊ *noun, plural* **sprinkles**

sprinkler *noun* A device for sprinkling water on a lawn or plants.
sprin·kler (**sprĭng′**klər) ◊ *noun, plural* **sprinklers**

sprint *noun* A short race run at top speed.
◊ *verb* To run at top speed for a short distance: *I sprinted around the track.*
sprint (sprĭnt) ◊ *noun, plural* **sprints** ◊ *verb* **sprinted, sprinting**

sprout *verb* To produce or appear as new growth: *The corn sprouted after the rain.*
◊ *noun* A young plant growth, as a bud.
sprout (sprout) ◊ *verb* **sprouted, sprouting** ◊ *noun, plural* **sprouts**

spruce *noun* An evergreen tree with short needles and soft wood.
spruce (spro͞os) ◊ *noun, plural* **spruces**

▲ **spruce**

sprung *verb* A past tense and the past participle of **spring.**
sprung (sprŭng) ◊ *verb*

spry *adjective* Active; lively.
spry (sprī) ◊ *adjective* **sprier, spriest**

spun *verb* Past tense and past participle of **spin.**
spun (spŭn) ◊ *verb*

spunk *noun* Spirit; courage.
spunk (spŭngk) ◊ *noun*

spur *noun* **1.** A device with sharp points that is worn on a rider's boot. The rider uses spurs to urge on the horse. **2.** Something that makes a person do something; incentive.
◊ *verb* To urge on with or as if with spurs.
spur (spûr) ◊ *noun, plural* **spurs** ◊ *verb* **spurred, spurring**

spurn *verb* To refuse scornfully.
spurn (spûrn) ◊ *verb* **spurned, spurning**

spurt *noun* **1.** A sudden gush of liquid; jet. **2.** A short burst of energy or activity.
◊ *verb* To gush or squirt: *Oil spurted into the air.*
spurt (spûrt) ◊ *noun, plural* **spurts** ◊ *verb* **spurted, spurting**

sputter *verb* **1.** To spit out particles of saliva or food in short bursts. **2.** To make a coughing noise: *The engine sputtered and died.*
◊ *noun* The act or sound of sputtering.
sput·ter (**spŭt**′ər) ◊ *verb* **sputtered, sputtering** ◊ *noun, plural* **sputters**

spy *noun* A secret agent whose job is to obtain information about an enemy.
◊ *verb* **1.** To watch secretly and for hostile reasons: *Soldiers were spying on the enemy camp.* **2.** To catch sight of; see: *I spied a blue jay on a branch.*
spy (spī) ◊ *noun, plural* **spies** ◊ *verb* **spied, spying**

spyglass *noun* A small telescope.
spy·glass (**spī**′glăs′) ◊ *noun, plural* **spyglasses**

sq. The abbreviation for *square* used in measurements.

squab *noun* A young pigeon.
squab (skwŏb) ◊ *noun, plural* **squabs**

squabble *verb* To have a minor quarrel.
◊ *noun* A minor quarrel.
squab·ble (**skwŏb**′əl) ◊ *verb* **squabbled, squabbling** ◊ *noun, plural* **squabbles**

squad *noun* **1.** A small group of soldiers. **2.** A small organized group, as of football players.
squad (skwŏd) ◊ *noun, plural* **squads**

squadron *noun* **1.** A unit of cavalry troops. **2.** A naval unit, as a group of destroyers. **3.** A formation of at least eight airplanes.
squad·ron (**skwŏd**′rən) ◊ *noun, plural* **squadrons**

squall *noun* A brief, sudden, violent windstorm, often with rain or snow.
squall (skwôl) ◊ *noun, plural* **squalls**

squander *verb* To spend lavishly or wastefully.
squan·der (**skwŏn**′dər) ◊ *verb* **squandered, squandering**

square *noun* **1.** A rectangle having four equal sides. **2.** Something shaped like a square. **3.** An instrument shaped like an L or a T that is used for drawing or testing right angles. **4.** An open area at the intersection of two or more streets. **5.** A rectangular area enclosed by streets; block.
◊ *adjective* **1.** Having the shape of a square. **2.** Forming a right angle: *This box has square corners.* **3.** Being a unit that measures the surface of something: *A square foot is a foot long and a foot wide.* **4.** Adequate; satisfying: *You need three square meals a day to stay healthy.*
◊ *verb* To cut or form into a square.
square (skwâr) ◊ *noun, plural* **squares** ◊ *adjective* **squarer, squarest** ◊ *verb* **squared, squaring**

S

square dance *noun* A dance in which sets of four couples form squares.
square dance ◊ *noun, plural* **square dances**

▲ **square dance**

squash¹ *noun* A fleshy fruit that is related to the pumpkins and the gourds and is eaten as a vegetable.
squash¹ (skwŏsh) ◊ *noun, plural* **squashes** *or* **squash**

▲ **squash¹**

ă	pat	ĭ	pit	oi	oil	th	bath
ā	pay	ī	ride	o͝o	book	*th*	bathe
â	care	î	fierce	o͞o	boot	ə	ago, item
ä	father	ŏ	pot	ou	out		pencil
ĕ	pet	ō	go	ŭ	cut		atom
ē	be	ô	paw, for	û	fur		circus

squash² *verb* To press or be pressed into a flat mass or pulp; crush.
◊ *noun* A game played in a walled court. The players hit a hard rubber ball with a racket.
squash² (skwŏsh) ◊ *verb* **squashed, squashing** ◊ *noun*

***HISTORY* • squash¹, squash²**

Squash¹ comes from the name for this plant in the language of the Native Americans who lived in Massachusetts. Many of the plants in America were new to the European settlers, and so they often borrowed the Native American names. **Squash²** came from an old French word that came in turn from a Latin word meaning "to shatter."

squat *verb* **1.** To sit on one's heels. **2.** To settle on unoccupied or public land without having a legal right to do so.
◊ *adjective* Short and thickset.
squat (skwŏt) ◊ *verb* **squatted** *or* **squat, squatting** ◊ *adjective* **squatter, squattest**

squawk *noun* A loud, harsh screech.
◊ *verb* To make this sound.
squawk (skwôk) ◊ *noun, plural* **squawks** ◊ *verb* **squawked, squawking**

squeak *noun* A high, thin cry or sound.
◊ *verb* To make a squeak.
squeak (skwēk) ◊ *noun, plural* **squeaks** ◊ *verb* **squeaked, squeaking**

squeaky *adjective* Tending to squeak.
squeak·y (**skwē′** kē) ◊ *adjective* **squeakier, squeakiest**

squeal *noun* A high, loud cry or sound.
◊ *verb* To make a squeal.
squeal (skwēl) ◊ *noun, plural* **squeals** ◊ *verb* **squealed, squealing**

squeeze *verb* **1.** To press together with force; compress: *The baby squeezed the rubber toy.* **2.** To extract by squeezing: *Squeeze the juice from the orange.* **3.** To force by pressure: *We squeezed through the door.*
◊ *noun* An act or example of squeezing.
squeeze (skwēz) ◊ *verb* **squeezed, squeezing** ◊ *noun, plural* **squeezes**

squid *noun* A sea animal that is related to the octopus and has a long body and ten arms.
squid (skwĭd) ◊ *noun, plural* **squids** *or* **squid**

squint *verb* To look with the eyes partly open: *We squinted at the fine print.*
◊ *noun* An act of squinting.
squint (skwĭnt) ◊ *verb* **squinted, squinting** ◊ *noun, plural* **squints**

squire *noun* **1.** A young man of noble birth who served a knight. **2.** An English country gentleman.
squire (skwīr) ◊ *noun, plural* **squires**

squirm *verb* **1.** To twist about; wriggle. **2.** To feel or show signs of embarrassment.
squirm (skwûrm) ◊ *verb* **squirmed, squirming**

squirrel *noun* Any of several animals with gray, reddish-brown, or black fur and a bushy tail. Squirrels climb trees.
squir·rel (**skwûr′**əl) ◊ *noun, plural* **squirrels**

▲ **squirrel**

squirt *verb* To send out or be sent out in a thin, fast stream.
◊ *noun* A thin, fast stream of liquid or air.
squirt (skwûrt) ◊ *verb* **squirted, squirting** ◊ *noun, plural* **squirts**

Sr. The abbreviation for *Senior.*

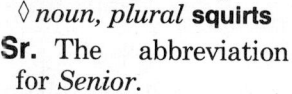

S.S. *or* **SS** Abbreviations for *Steamship.*

St. The abbreviation for *Saint.*

stab *verb* To pierce or wound with a pointed instrument.
◊ *noun* **1.** A thrust or wound made with a pointed weapon. **2.** An attempt; try: *Let's make a stab at our homework.*
stab (stăb) ◊ *verb* **stabbed, stabbing** ◊ *noun, plural* **stabs**

stability *noun* The condition of being stable.
sta·bil·i·ty (stə **bĭl′**ĭ tē) ◊ *noun*

stable[1] *adjective* **1.** Not likely to change suddenly: *We want a stable economy.* **2.** Likely to continue or survive: *We have a stable government.*
sta·ble[1] (**stā′**bəl) ◊ *adjective* **stabler, stablest**

stable[2] *noun* A building for sheltering domestic animals, as horses.
◊ *verb* To put or keep in a stable.
sta·ble[2] (**stā′**bəl) ◊ *noun, plural* **stables** ◊ *verb* **stabled, stabling**

***HISTORY* • stable[1], stable[2]**

Stable[1] and **stable[2]** come from different old French words. Both of these old French words were related to the Latin word meaning "to stand." Something that is **stable[1]** stands firm, and a **stable[2]** is a place where animals stand.

stack *noun* **1.** A large pile, as of straw, that is shaped like a cone. **2.** A pile arranged in layers: *A stack of books lay on my desk.* **3.** A vertical exhaust pipe, as a chimney.
◊ *verb* To arrange in a stack; pile.
stack (stăk) ◊ *noun, plural* **stacks** ◊ *verb* **stacked, stacking**

stadium *noun* A large structure in which athletic events are held.
sta·di·um (**stā′**dē əm) ◊ *noun, plural* **stadiums**

staff *noun* **1.** A long stick carried to help in walking. **2.** A pole on which a flag flies. **3.** A group of assistants who serve a person in a position of authority. **4.** The set of five lines and the spaces between them on which musical notes are written.
staff (stăf) ◊ *noun, plural* **staffs** *or* **staves** (senses 1, 4)

stag *noun* A fully grown male deer.
stag (stăg) ◊ *noun, plural* **stags**

stage *noun* **1.** The raised platform in a theater on which entertainers perform. **2.** Theatrical work. **3.** A stagecoach. **4.** A level, degree, or period of time during a process.
◊ *verb* To produce or direct on or as if on a stage: *We staged a class play.*
stage (stāj) ◊ *noun, plural* **stages** ◊ *verb* **staged, staging**

stagecoach *noun* A coach with four wheels that is drawn by horses. Stagecoaches were once used to carry mail, baggage, and passengers.
stage·coach (**stāj′**kōch′) ◊ *noun, plural* **stagecoaches**

stagger *verb* **1.** To move or cause to move unsteadily. **2.** To overwhelm, as with amazement: *We were staggered by the unexpected news.*
◊ *noun* A staggering walk.
stag·ger (**stăg′**ər) ◊ *verb* **staggered, staggering** ◊ *noun, plural* **staggers**

S

stagnant *adjective* **1.** Not moving or flowing. **2.** Foul or polluted as a result of not moving: *Mosquitoes breed in stagnant water.* **3.** Not changing or growing; inactive.
stag·nant (stăg′nənt) ◊ *adjective*

stagnate *verb* **1.** To be or become stagnant. **2.** To lie inactive; fail to grow or change.
stag·nate (stăg′nāt′) ◊ *verb* **stagnated, stagnating**

stain *verb* **1.** To discolor or become discolored with a substance that soaks in: *I stained my fingers with ink.* **2.** To color with dye.
◊ *noun* **1.** A discolored mark or spot. **2.** A liquid applied to material in order to stain it.
stain (stān) ◊ *verb* **stained, staining** ◊ *noun, plural* **stains**

stair *noun* **1. stairs** A series or flight of steps; staircase. **2.** One of a flight of steps.
stair (stâr) ◊ *noun, plural* **stairs**
‖*These sound alike:* **stair, stare**

staircase *noun* A flight of steps and the structure that supports it.
stair·case (stâr′kās′) ◊ *noun, plural* **staircases**

stairway *noun* A flight of stairs.
stair·way (stâr′wā′) ◊ *noun, plural* **stairways**

stake *noun* **1.** A pointed stick or post driven into the ground as a marker, barrier, or support. **2.** A share or interest in a project.
◊ *verb* To mark the location or boundaries of with or as if with stakes.
stake (stāk) ◊ *noun, plural* **stakes** ◊ *verb* **staked, staking**
‖*These sound alike:* **stake, steak**

stalactite *noun* A deposit like a cylinder or cone that projects down from the roof of a cave and is formed by dripping mineral water.
sta·lac·tite (stə lăk′tīt′) ◊ *noun, plural* **stalactites**

stalagmite *noun* A deposit like a cylinder or cone that projects up from the floor of a cave and is formed by dripping mineral water.
sta·lag·mite (stə lăg′mīt′) ◊ *noun, plural* **stalagmites**

ă	pat	ĭ	pit	oi	oil	th	bath
ā	pay	ī	ride	o͝o	book	*th*	bathe
â	care	î	fierce	o͞o	boot	ə	ago, item
ä	father	ŏ	pot	ou	out		pencil
ĕ	pet	ō	go	ŭ	cut		atom
ē	be	ô	paw, for	û	fur		circus

▲ **stalagmite**
Stalagmites and stalactites

stale *adjective* **1.** Not fresh: *The bread is stale.* **2.** Having lost its freshness or interest: *Old news is stale news.*
stale (stāl) ◊ *adjective* **staler, stalest**

stalk¹ *noun* **1.** The stem of a plant. **2.** A part that is attached to or supports a leaf or flower.
stalk¹ (stôk) ◊ *noun, plural* **stalks**

stalk² *verb* **1.** To walk in a stiff, haughty way. **2.** To move in a stealthy way as if tracking prey: *The tiger stalked through the jungle.*
stalk² (stôk) ◊ *verb* **stalked, stalking**

***HISTORY* • stalk¹, stalk²**

Stalk¹ first appeared in written English about 700 years ago. It may have come from an older English word for the sides of a ladder. **Stalk²** comes from an old English word that meant "to walk cautiously."

stall *noun* **1.** An enclosure for a single animal in a barn or stable. **2.** An enclosure for selling or displaying merchandise; booth. **3.** A sudden loss of power in an engine.
◊ *verb* **1.** To put in a stall. **2.** To slow or be slowed down: *The bill is stalled in Congress.* **3.** To try to put off action by using delays.
stall (stôl) ◊ *noun, plural* **stalls** ◊ *verb* **stalled, stalling**

stallion *noun* A mature male horse.
stal·lion (stăl′yən) ◊ *noun, plural* **stallions**

stalwart *adjective* Physically strong.
stal·wart (stôl′wərt) ◊ *adjective*

stamen *noun* An organ of a flower that consists of a slender stalk with a pollen-bearing part at its tip. Petals surround the stamen.
sta·men (stā′mən) ◊ *noun, plural* **stamens**

stammer *verb* To speak with pauses and repeated sounds; stutter.
◊ *noun* An act or example of stammering.
stam·mer (stăm′ər) ◊ *verb* **stammered, stammering** ◊ *noun, plural* **stammers**

stamp *verb* **1.** To put the foot down heavily and loudly: *The horse stamped on the ground.* **2.** To press with a device that leaves a mark, design, or message: *The immigration officer stamped our papers.* **3.** To put a postage stamp on. **4.** To show to be of a certain character: *Their behavior stamps them as brave people.*
◊ *noun* **1.** A device for stamping. **2.** A mark made by a stamp. **3.** A piece of paper that has a design or message on its face and gum on its back. **4.** A postage stamp.
◊ *idiom* **stamp out** To put a stop to: *We stamped out the fire. Doctors are trying to stamp out cancer.*
stamp (stămp) ◊ *verb* **stamped, stamping** ◊ *noun, plural* **stamps**

stampede *noun* **1.** A sudden rush of startled animals, such as cattle. **2.** A general rush or movement by many people.
◊ *verb* To take or cause to take part in a stampede.
stam·pede (stăm pēd′) ◊ *noun, plural* **stampedes** ◊ *verb* **stampeded, stampeding**

▲ **stampede**

stand *verb* **1.** To take or stay in an upright position on one's feet: *I stood next to the door.* **2.** To rest in an upright position on a base or support: *The rocket stood on the launching pad.* **3.** To be located: *An old tower stands on the hill.* **4.** To be in a certain order or rank: *I stand second in my class.* **5.** To remain still or undisturbed: *Let the mixture stand overnight.* **6.** To remain in effect: *The rule still stands.* **7.** To tolerate or endure: *My parents can't stand loud music.* **8.** To resist or withstand: *I can't stand this headache.*
◊ *noun* **1.** An act of standing. **2.** A place where a person stands. **3.** A place reserved for the stopping or parking of certain vehicles, as taxis. **4.** A small place where goods for sale are displayed. **5.** A small device for holding something, as umbrellas or music. **6.** A raised structure where people can sit or stand and be clearly seen. **7.** A position that one is prepared to defend or support: *We took a strong stand against crime.*
◊ *idioms* **stand for 1.** To be a shortened or symbolic form for; represent: *"X" stands for an unknown quantity.* **2.** To put up with; accept: *The school won't stand for tardiness.* **stand in for** To take the place of; substitute for. **stand out 1.** To attract attention. **2.** To be outstanding; excel.
stand (stănd) ◊ *verb* **stood, standing** ◊ *noun, plural* **stands**

standard *noun* **1.** Something that is accepted as a basis for measuring or as a rule or model: *Many Americans enjoy a high standard of living.* **2.** A flag, such as one used as the emblem of a military unit.
◊ *adjective* **1.** Serving as or measuring up to a standard: *The ounce is a standard unit of weight.* —See Synonyms at **normal.** **2.** Widely accepted as reliable or excellent: *This is a standard atlas.* **3.** Widely used and considered acceptable: *Most radio and TV announcers speak standard English.*
stan·dard (stăn′dərd) ◊ *noun, plural* **standards** ◊ *adjective*

standing *noun* **1.** The length of time during which something has continued, existed, or been in use: *We are friends of long standing.* **2.** The position that a person has, as in society; status.
stand·ing (stăn′dĭng) ◊ *noun, plural* **standings**

S

standpoint *noun* A way of looking at something; viewpoint.
stand·point (stănd′point′) ◊ *noun, plural* **standpoints**

standstill *noun* A stop: *The work has come to a standstill.*
stand·still (stănd′stĭl′) ◊ *noun, plural* **standstills**

stank *verb* A past tense of **stink.**
stank (stăngk) ◊ *verb*

stanza *noun* A group of lines that makes up a division of a poem.
stan·za (stăn′zə) ◊ *noun, plural* **stanzas**

staple[1] *noun* **1.** A main product that is grown or produced in a region: *Rice is a staple of Asia.* **2.** A main feature, element, or part: *Fish and vegetables are staples of our diet. Reference books are the staples of a library.*
sta·ple[1] (stā′pəl) ◊ *noun, plural* **staples**

staple[2] *noun* **1.** A U-shaped metal loop with pointed ends that is driven into a surface to hold something, as a hook or bolt, in place. **2.** A thin U-shaped piece of wire used to hold materials, such as paper, together.
sta·ple[2] (stā′pəl) ◊ *noun, plural* **staples**

***HISTORY* • staple[1], staple[2]**

Staple[1] now means "a main product" but once meant "a marketplace." **Staple[1]** comes from an old French word that meant "market." **Staple[2]** comes from an old English word that meant "pillar, post." **Staple[2]** came to mean "a U-shaped metal loop that holds something on a surface, such as that of a post or wall."

star *noun* **1.** A heavenly body that appears as a very bright point in the sky at night. **2.** A design or object that has points radiating from a center and looks like or represents a star. **3.** A performer who plays a leading role in a play, opera, or movie. **4.** An outstanding performer, as in sports.
◊ *verb* **1.** To decorate with stars. **2.** To play or present in the leading role: *I understand you are starring in the school play.*
star (stär) ◊ *noun, plural* **stars** ◊ *verb* **starred, starring**

ă	pat	ĭ	pit	oi	oil	th	bath
ā	pay	ī	ride	o͝o	book	*th*	bathe
â	care	î	fierce	o͞o	boot	ə	ago, item
ä	father	ŏ	pot	ou	out		pencil
ĕ	pet	ō	go	ŭ	cut		atom
ē	be	ô	paw, for	û	fur		circus

starboard *noun* The right-hand side of a ship or aircraft.
◊ *adjective & adverb* On, to, or toward the starboard.
star·board (stär′bôrd′) ◊ *noun* ◊ *adjective & adverb*

starch *noun* **1.** A carbohydrate that occurs widely in nature, chiefly in parts of plants, especially wheat, corn, rice, and potatoes. **2.** A product that is prepared from starch and used to stiffen fabrics.
◊ *verb* To stiffen with starch.
starch (stärch) ◊ *noun, plural* **starches** ◊ *verb* **starched, starching**

stare *verb* To look with a steady, often wide-eyed gaze.
◊ *noun* A staring gaze.
stare (stâr) ◊ *verb* **stared, staring** ◊ *noun, plural* **stares**
‖*These sound alike:* **stare, stair**

starfish *noun* A sea animal with five or more arms and a body that is shaped like a star.
star·fish (stär′fĭsh′) ◊ *noun, plural* **starfish** *or* **starfishes**

▲ **starfish**

starlight *noun* Light coming from stars.
star·light (stär′līt′) ◊ *noun*

starling *noun* A common bird with dark, glossy feathers.
star·ling (stär′lĭng) ◊ *noun, plural* **starlings**

starry *adjective* Shining like or full of stars.
star·ry (stär′ē) ◊ *adjective* **starrier, starriest**

Stars and Stripes *noun* The flag of the United States.

start *verb* **1.** To begin to move, go, or act: *We started at dawn.* —See Synonyms at **begin.** **2.** To come into operation or being: *School*

starts in September. **3.** To set going: *Start the engine.* **4.** To bring about: *Let's not start an argument.* **5.** To set up; found: *We want to start a soccer club.* **6.** To move suddenly: *I started in surprise when the door slammed.*
◊ *noun* **1.** A beginning: *We got a late start.* **2.** A place or time at which something, such as a race, begins. **3.** A sudden or involuntary movement: *I awoke with a start.*
start (stärt) ◊ *verb* **started, starting** ◊ *noun, plural* **starts**

startle *verb* **1.** To cause to make a sudden movement, as of surprise: *A thud on the roof startled us.* **2.** To fill with sudden alarm.
star·tle (stär′tl) ◊ *verb* **startled, startling**

starve *verb* **1.** To suffer or die from lack of food. **2.** To suffer or cause to suffer from a lack of something necessary: *The plants are starving for water.*
starve (stärv) ◊ *verb* **starved, starving**

state *noun* **1.** A condition or form of existence: *The radio is in a state of disrepair. Ice is water in the solid state.* **2.** A mental or emotional condition: *Try to get in a calmer state.* **3.** A body of people living under a single independent government; nation. **4.** Often **State** One of the political and geographic subdivisions of a country such as the United States: *There are 50 states in the Union. Have you traveled in the State of Maine?*
◊ *verb* To express in words: *Please state your problem.* —See Synonyms at **say.**
state (stāt) ◊ *noun, plural* **states** ◊ *verb* **stated, stating**

stately *adjective* **1.** Marked by great dignity. **2.** Impressive, especially in size; majestic: *The White House is a stately mansion.*
state·ly (stāt′lē) ◊ *adjective* **statelier, stateliest**

statement *noun* Something expressed in words; declaration.
state·ment (stāt′mənt) ◊ *noun, plural* **statements**

statesman *noun* A wise and experienced government or political leader.
states·man (stāts′mən) ◊ *noun, plural* **statesmen**

static *noun* Random noise in a radio receiver or visible specks on a television screen caused by atmospheric disturbances.
stat·ic (stăt′ĭk) ◊ *noun*

station *noun* **1.** The place or location where a person stands or is directed to stand. **2.** A place where a special service is provided or certain activities are directed: *Let's tour the fire station.* **3.** A stopping place along a route for taking on and letting off passengers: *I'll buy my ticket at the bus station.* **4.** A place with equipment to send out radio or television signals.
◊ *verb* To assign to a position; post: *We were stationed in California.*
sta·tion (stā′shən) ◊ *noun, plural* **stations** ◊ *verb* **stationed, stationing**

stationary *adjective* **1.** Not changing: *The price remained stationary.* **2.** Not capable of being moved: *The towers of a suspension bridge are stationary.*
sta·tion·ar·y (stā′shə nĕr′ē) ◊ *adjective*
‖*These sound alike:* **stationary, stationery**

stationery *noun* Materials, such as paper, notebooks, pens, and envelopes, that are used in writing.
sta·tion·er·y (stā′shə nĕr′ē) ◊ *noun*
‖*These sound alike:* **stationery, stationary**

station wagon *noun* An automobile with rows of rear seats that can be folded down to provide extra baggage space.
station wagon ◊ *noun, plural* **station wagons**

statue *noun* An image, as of a person or animal, made by an artist out of a solid substance, such as stone or metal.
stat·ue (stăch′o͞o) ◊ *noun, plural* **statues**

▲ **statue**

S

stature *noun* **1.** The natural height of a person or animal when upright. **2.** Reputation gained by achievement: *They are athletes of world stature.*
stat·ure (stăch′ər) ◊ *noun*

status *noun* A person's professional or social standing.
sta·tus (stā′təs *or* stăt′əs) ◊ *noun*

statute *noun* A law.
stat·ute (stăch′o͞ot) ◊ *noun, plural* **statutes**

stave *noun* **1.** A strip of wood that forms part of the side of a barrel or tub. **2.** A heavy stick or pole; staff.
stave (stāv) ◊ *noun, plural* **staves**

staves *noun* A plural of **staff** (senses 1, 4).
staves (stāvz) ◊ *noun*

stay *verb* **1.** To remain in one place or condition: *Stay right here. Try to stay awake.* **2.** To live for a time: *Stay overnight at my house.* **3.** To satisfy for a time: *I ate a snack to stay my hunger.* **4.** To put off for a time; postpone.
◊ *noun* **1.** A period of time in which a person lives or visits somewhere. **2.** A postponement.
stay (stā) ◊ *verb* **stayed, staying** ◊ *noun, plural* **stays**

stead *noun* The place or position of another: *A friend attended the meeting in my stead.*
stead (stĕd) ◊ *noun*

steadfast *adjective* Not changing; firm.
stead·fast (stĕd′făst′) ◊ *adjective*

steadily *adverb* In a steady way.
stead·i·ly (stĕd′l ē) ◊ *adverb*

steady *adjective* **1.** Not likely to shift, wobble, or slip; firm: *Keep a steady grip on the wheel.* **2.** Not changing: *A steady rain is falling.* **3.** Not easily excited: *You have steady nerves.* **4.** Reliable; dependable: *We appreciate steady workers.* **5.** Regular: *You are a steady customer.*
◊ *verb* To make or become steady.
stead·y (stĕd′ē) ◊ *adjective* **steadier, steadiest** ◊ *verb* **steadied, steadying**

ă	pat	ĭ	pit	oi	**oil**	th	bath
ā	pay	ī	ride	o͝o	book	*th*	bathe
â	care	î	fierce	o͞o	boot	ə	ago, item
ä	father	ŏ	pot	ou	**out**		pencil
ĕ	pet	ō	go	ŭ	cut		atom
ē	be	ô	paw, for	û	fur		circus

steak *noun* A slice of meat, as beef or fish, that is usually broiled or fried.
steak (stāk) ◊ *noun, plural* **steaks**
‖*These sound alike:* **steak, stake**

steal *verb* **1.** To take without right or permission: *They stole my bicycle.* **2.** To get or enjoy secretly: *Let's steal a glimpse of the party.* **3.** To move very quietly: *A big cat stole through the garden.*
◊ *noun* **1.** The act of stealing. **2.** Something gotten at a very low price; bargain.
steal (stēl) ◊ *verb* **stole, stolen, stealing** ◊ *noun, plural* **steals**
‖*These sound alike:* **steal, steel**

steam *noun* **1.** Water in a gaseous state, especially when hot. **2.** The mist that forms when hot water vapor cools and condenses into tiny drops. **3.** Power that is produced by water vapor under pressure.
◊ *verb* **1.** To produce or give off steam. **2.** To turn into or escape as steam. **3.** To become covered with mist or steam: *The kitchen windows steam up when we wash dishes.* **4.** To move by or as if by the power of steam: *The ship steamed into the harbor.* **5.** To treat with or expose to steam, as in cooking: *Let's steam the rice.*
steam (stēm) ◊ *noun* ◊ *verb* **steamed, steaming**

steamboat *noun* A steamship.
steam·boat (stēm′bōt′) ◊ *noun, plural* **steamboats**

steam engine *noun* An engine that is powered by steam.
steam engine ◊ *noun, plural* **steam engines**

steamroller *noun* A vehicle powered by an engine and equipped with a heavy roller for smoothing road surfaces.
steam·roll·er (stēm′rō′lər) ◊ *noun, plural* **steamrollers**

steamship *noun* A ship that is driven by a steam engine.
steam·ship (stēm′shĭp′) ◊ *noun, plural* **steamships**

steed *noun* A high-spirited horse for riding.
steed (stēd) ◊ *noun, plural* **steeds**

steel *noun* **1.** A hard, strong alloy of iron and carbon. **2.** Something, such as a sword, that is made of steel.
steel (stēl) ◊ *noun*
‖*These sound alike:* **steel, steal**

steep[1] *adjective* **1.** Rising or falling sharply: *We climbed a steep hill.* **2.** Very high: *I think $20,000 is a steep price to pay for a car.*
steep[1] (stēp) ◊ *adjective* **steeper, steepest**

steep[2] *verb* To soak or be soaked in a liquid: *Let the tea steep for a few minutes.*
steep[2] (stēp) ◊ *verb* **steeped, steeping**

> ***HISTORY* • steep[1], steep[2]**
>
> **Steep[1]** comes from an old English word that meant "high" and also "deep." **Steep[2]** can only be traced back 600 years or so, but it may be related to an older word that meant "pail."

steeple *noun* A tall tower that rises from the roof of a building, especially one on a church or courthouse.
stee·ple (stē′pəl) ◊ *noun, plural* **steeples**

▲ **steeple**

steer[1] *verb* **1.** To direct the course of: *The pilot steered the ship to the dock.* —See Synonyms at **guide. 2.** To be guided: *This car steers easily.*
steer[1] (stîr) ◊ *verb* **steered, steering**

steer[2] *noun* A young male of domestic cattle that is raised for beef.
steer[2] (stîr) ◊ *noun, plural* **steers**

> ***HISTORY* • steer[1], steer[2]**
>
> **Steer[1]** comes from an old English word that meant "to guide." **Steer[2]** comes from a different old English word for a young ox or cow.

stem[1] *noun* **1.** The main supporting part of a plant that usually grows above the ground. **2.** A slender plant part that supports another part, such as a leaf or flower; stalk. **3.** A part that looks like a stem: *The stem of the glass is slender.*
stem[1] (stĕm) ◊ *noun, plural* **stems**

stem[2] *verb* To stop the advance of: *The big dam stemmed the flood waters.*
stem[2] (stĕm) ◊ *verb* **stemmed, stemming**

> ***HISTORY* • stem[1], stem[2]**
>
> **Stem[1]** comes from an old English word that meant "a tree trunk" and also "the prow of a ship." **Stem[2]** comes from an old Scandinavian word that meant "to delay."

stencil *noun* A sheet of material, as paper or plastic, out of which letters or a design have been cut. When ink or paint is applied to the sheet, the patterns will appear on the surface beneath.
sten·cil (stĕn′səl) ◊ *noun, plural* **stencils**

step *noun* **1.** A single movement made by lifting one foot and putting it down in another spot. **2.** The distance covered by a step. **3.** The sound of a step. **4.** A footprint: *We saw steps in the sand.* **5.** A way of walking: *You move with a light step.* **6.** A fixed rhythm or pace, as in marching: *Keep in step with the band.* **7. steps** Stairs. **8.** An action or a measure taken to achieve a goal: *We are taking steps to clean up the school grounds.*

9. A degree, as of progress: *You've taken a step forward in learning French.*
◊ *verb* **1.** To move by taking steps: *Step forward when I call your name.* **2.** To press the foot down or against: *Step on the pedal.*
step (stĕp) ◊ *noun, plural* **steps** ◊ *verb* **stepped, stepping**

stepfather *noun* The husband of one's mother by a later marriage.
step·fa·ther (**stĕp′**fä′*th*ər) ◊ *noun, plural* **stepfathers**

stepladder *noun* A portable ladder with flat steps instead of rungs.
step·lad·der (**stĕp′**lăd′ər) ◊ *noun, plural* **stepladders**

stepmother *noun* The wife of one's father by a later marriage.
step·moth·er (**stĕp′**mŭ*th*′ər) ◊ *noun, plural* **stepmothers**

stereo *noun* A record player that uses more than one speaker. The speakers are placed in different parts of a room to produce more natural sound.
ste·re·o (**stĕr′**ē ō′ *or* **stîr′**ē ō′) ◊ *noun, plural* **stereos**

sterilize *verb* To rid of germs.
ster·il·ize (**stĕr′**ə līz′) ◊ *verb* **sterilized, sterilizing**

stern[1] *adjective* **1.** Grave and severe: *We received a stern lecture on table manners.* **2.** Not yielding; strict: *The stern discipline at school surprised us.*
stern[1] (stûrn) ◊ *adjective* **sterner, sternest**

stern[2] *noun* The rear part of a ship or boat.
stern[2] (stûrn) ◊ *noun, plural* **sterns**

***HISTORY* • stern[1], stern[2]**

Stern[1] comes from an old English word that meant "strict, cruel." **Stern[2]** is related to **steer[1]**, which means "to direct the course of." The **stern[2]** is where a boat is directed or steered with a rudder.

ă	pat	ĭ	pit	oi	oil	th	bath
ā	pay	ī	ride	ŏŏ	book	*th*	bathe
â	care	î	fierce	ōō	boot	ə	ago, item
ä	father	ŏ	pot	ou	out		pencil
ĕ	pet	ō	go	ŭ	cut		atom
ē	be	ô	paw, for	û	fur		circus

stethoscope *noun* A medical instrument that is used to listen to sounds made in the body, as in the lungs.
steth·o·scope (**stĕth′**ə skōp′) ◊ *noun, plural* **stethoscopes**

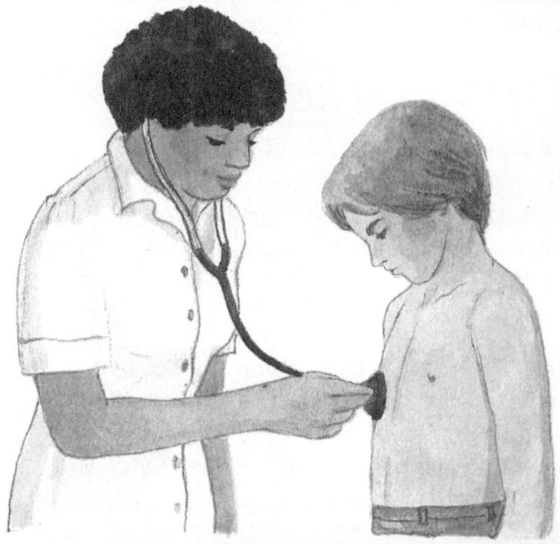

▲ **stethoscope**

stew *verb* To cook by boiling slowly.
◊ *noun* Food, such as meat and vegetables, cooked by stewing.
stew (stōō *or* styōō) ◊ *verb* **stewed, stewing** ◊ *noun, plural* **stews**

steward *noun* **1.** A person who manages another's property or household. **2.** A person who waits on passengers, as on an airplane.
stew·ard (**stōō′**ərd *or* **styōō′**ərd) ◊ *noun, plural* **stewards**

stewardess *noun* A woman who waits on passengers, as on an airplane.
stew·ard·ess (**stōō′**ər dĭs *or* **styōō′**ər dĭs) ◊ *noun, plural* **stewardesses**

stick *noun* **1.** A long, slender piece of wood, as a branch cut from a tree. **2.** Something shaped like a stick. **3.** A cane for walking.
◊ *verb* **1.** To pierce or prick with a pointed object: *I stuck my finger with a needle.* **2.** To fasten or attach by pushing in a pointed object: *Stick the pictures on the board with a pin.* **3.** To fasten or attach with an adhesive, as glue: *I stuck a stamp on the envelope.* **4.** To be and remain attached; adhere: *Jam sticks to the fingers.* **5.** To be fixed and unable to move: *The window stuck.* **6.** To put in a certain place or position: *Stick the box in the*

closet. **7.** To extend, stick out, or protrude: *I stuck my head out the door.*
stick (stĭk) ◊ *noun, plural* **sticks** ◊ *verb* **stuck, sticking**

sticky *adjective* **1.** Tending to stick; adhesive: *Honey is sticky.* **2.** Hot and humid; muggy: *It's a sticky summer day.*
stick·y (stĭk′ē) ◊ *adjective* **stickier, stickiest**

stiff *adjective* **1.** Not easily bent: *The collar is stiff.* **2.** Not moving or moved easily: *I have stiff muscles.* **3.** Not flowing easily; thick: *The batter was too stiff to beat easily.* **4.** Not natural or easy in manner; formal: *We had a stiff conversation.* **5.** Strong, steady, and forceful: *A stiff wind blew my hat off.*
stiff (stĭf) ◊ *adjective* **stiffer, stiffest**

stiffen *verb* To make or become stiff.
stiff·en (stĭf′ən) ◊ *verb* **stiffened, stiffening**

stifle *verb* **1.** To smother. **2.** To hold back; stop: *I stifled a yawn.*
sti·fle (stī′fəl) ◊ *verb* **stifled, stifling**

still *adjective* **1.** Without noise; silent: *The audience was still during the concert.* **2.** Without motion: *The air was still before the storm.*
◊ *noun* A condition of quiet; silence.
◊ *adverb* **1.** Without moving: *Sit still!* **2.** Now as before: *The trees are still green.* **3.** All the same; nevertheless: *You're not very tall, but you're still the best player on our team.*
still (stĭl) ◊ *adjective* **stiller, stillest** ◊ *noun* ◊ *adverb*

stilt *noun* One of a pair of long, slender poles each with a foot support for raising a person above the ground in walking.
stilt (stĭlt) ◊ *noun, plural* **stilts**

stimulate *verb* To make active or more active: *The book stimulates my imagination.*
stim·u·late (stĭm′yə lāt′) ◊ *verb* **stimulated, stimulating**

stimuli *noun* Plural of **stimulus.**
stim·u·li (stĭm′yə lī′) ◊ *noun*

stimulus *noun* Something that stimulates: *Praise is a stimulus for better work.*
stim·u·lus (stĭm′yə ləs) ◊ *noun, plural* **stimuli**

sting *verb* **1.** To prick or wound with a small, sharp point: *A bee stung me on the foot.* **2.** To feel or cause to feel a sharp, burning pain: *My ears stung with the cold.*
◊ *noun* **1.** The act of stinging. **2.** A stinger. **3.** A pain or wound that is caused by or as if by stinging.
sting (stĭng) ◊ *verb* **stung, stinging** ◊ *noun, plural* **stings**

stinger *noun* A sharp-pointed organ that an insect or animal uses to sting and often poison another animal or a human being.
sting·er (stĭng′ər) ◊ *noun, plural* **stingers**

stingray *noun* An ocean fish with a flat body and a long tail that looks like a whip. A stingray has a poisonous spine that can cause a painful wound.
sting·ray (stĭng′rā′) ◊ *noun, plural* **stingrays**

▲ **stingray**

stingy *adjective* Not generous.
stin·gy (stĭn′jē) ◊ *adjective* **stingier, stingiest**

stink *verb* To give off or cause to give off a strong, bad smell.
◊ *noun* A strong, bad smell.
stink (stĭngk) ◊ *verb* **stank** *or* **stunk, stunk, stinking** ◊ *noun, plural* **stinks**

stir *verb* **1.** To mix by using repeated circular motions: *I stirred the vegetables into the soup.* **2.** To move or cause to move slightly.
◊ *noun* **1.** An act of stirring. **2.** An excited reaction: *Their arrival caused quite a stir.*
◊ *idiom* **stir up** To start: *Please don't stir up trouble.*
stir (stûr) ◊ *verb* **stirred, stirring** ◊ *noun, plural* **stirs**

stirrup *noun* A ring or loop hanging by a strap from a saddle to support a rider's foot.
stir·rup (stûr′əp) ◊ *noun, plural* **stirrups**

stitch *noun* **1.** One complete movement of a threaded needle into and out of fabric in sewing or embroidering. **2.** A loop of yarn around

S

an instrument such as a knitting needle. **3.** A sudden sharp pain in the side. —See Synonyms at **pain.**
◊ *verb* To fasten or decorate with stitches.
stitch (stĭch) ◊ *noun, plural* **stitches** ◊ *verb* **stitched, stitching**

stock *noun* **1.** A supply for future use: *The farmer had a stock of grain for winter.* **2.** Animals, such as cows, sheep, or pigs, that are raised on a farm or ranch; livestock. **3.** The group of ancestors from which others descend: *Our family comes from Polish stock.* **4.** Shares in the ownership of a business. **5.** The part of something, as a firearm or fishing rod, that is used as the handle. **6.** The broth in which meat, fish, or vegetables have been cooked. **7. stocks** A wooden framework with holes for the ankles or for the ankles and wrists that was once used to punish criminals in a public place.
◊ *verb* To provide with, keep, or lay in a supply of: *We stocked the cupboard with food.*
◊ *adjective* **1.** Kept regularly on hand for sale. **2.** In common use; usual: *You gave a stock response to the question.*
stock (stŏk) ◊ *noun, plural* **stocks** ◊ *verb* **stocked, stocking** ◊ *adjective*

stockade *noun* **1.** A barrier of large, strong posts set upright in the ground. **2.** The area surrounded by a stockade.
stock·ade (stŏ **kād′**) ◊ *noun, plural* **stockades**

stocking *noun* A close-fitting, usually knitted covering for the foot and leg.
stock·ing (**stŏk′**ĭng) ◊ *noun, plural* **stockings**

stocky *adjective* Solid and sturdy in build.
stock·y (**stŏk′**ē) ◊ *adjective* **stockier, stockiest**

stockyard *noun* A yard in which livestock are kept until being slaughtered or shipped.
stock·yard (**stŏk′**yärd′) ◊ *noun, plural* **stockyards**

stole *verb* Past tense of **steal.**
stole (stōl) ◊ *verb*

ă	pat	ĭ	pit	oi	**oil**	th	**bath**
ā	pay	ī	ride	o͝o	**book**	*th*	**bathe**
â	care	î	fierce	o͞o	**boot**	ə	ago, item
ä	father	ŏ	pot	ou	**out**		pencil
ĕ	pet	ō	go	ŭ	**cut**		atom
ē	be	ô	paw, for	û	**fur**		circus

stolen *verb* Past participle of **steal.**
sto·len (**stō′**lən) ◊ *verb*

stomach *noun* **1.** The large muscular pouch into which food passes when it leaves the mouth and esophagus and in which the process of digestion begins. **2.** The belly or the abdomen.
stom·ach (**stŭm′**ək) ◊ *noun, plural* **stomachs**

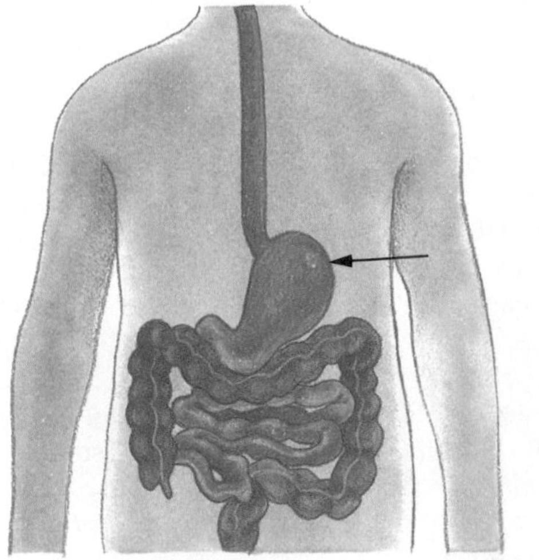

▲ **stomach**

stone *noun* **1.** A naturally hardened mass of earthy or mineral material; rock. **2.** A jewel or gem. **3.** A seed, as of a peach, with a hard covering.
stone (stōn) ◊ *noun, plural* **stones**

stood *verb* Past tense and past participle of **stand.**
stood (sto͝od) ◊ *verb*

stool *noun* **1.** A seat without arms or a back. **2.** A low support to rest the feet on while sitting; footstool.
stool (sto͞ol) ◊ *noun, plural* **stools**

stoop¹ *verb* **1.** To bend forward and down: *I stooped to pick up the flower.* **2.** To lower oneself; condescend: *Don't stoop to stealing.*
◊ *noun* **1.** The act of stooping. **2.** A forward bending of the head and shoulders, especially when it is a habit: *Do you always walk with a stoop?*
stoop¹ (sto͞op) ◊ *verb* **stooped, stooping** ◊ *noun, plural* **stoops**

stoop² *noun* A small staircase or porch leading to the entrance of a house or building.
stoop² (sto͞op) ◊ *noun, plural* **stoops**

HISTORY • stoop[1], stoop[2]

Stoop[1] comes from an old English word that meant "to bend down." **Stoop[2]** comes from an old Dutch word that meant "a front porch."

stop *verb* **1.** To cease or cause to cease moving, acting, or operating: *The police officer stopped the traffic.* **2.** To bring or come to an end: *The rain finally stopped.* **3.** To keep back; restrain: *They tried to stop us from eating too much.* **4.** To close an opening by obstructing it: *Grease stopped up the drain in the kitchen sink.*
◊ *noun* **1.** The act of stopping or the condition of being stopped. **2.** A brief or temporary stay at a place: *We made a stop at the seashore.* **3.** A place where something stops: *We waited at the bus stop.* **4.** A device that blocks or plugs something up; stopper.
stop (stŏp) ◊ *verb* **stopped, stopping** ◊ *noun, plural* **stops**

SYNONYMS

stop, halt, quit

Keep going and don't *stop. Halt!* Who goes there? Let's *quit* before we get tired. **Antonyms:** *go, start*

stoplight *noun* **1.** A set of lights used to control traffic on a road. **2.** A red light on the rear of a motor vehicle that turns on when the driver puts on the brakes.
stop·light (stŏp′lĭt′) ◊ *noun, plural* **stoplights**

stopper *noun* A device, such as a cork, put into an opening to close it.
stop·per (stŏp′ər) ◊ *noun, plural* **stoppers**

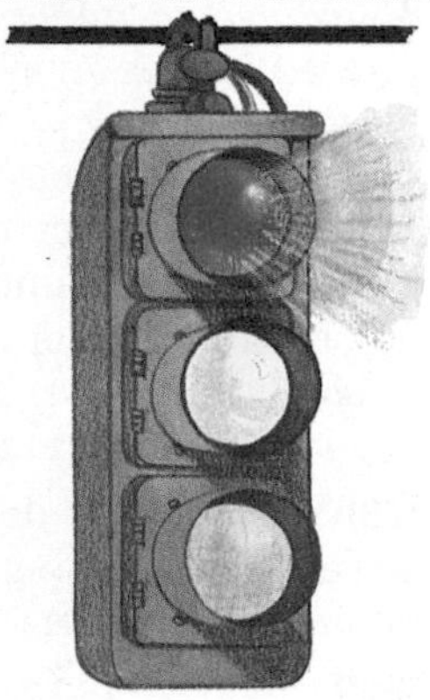

▲ **stoplight**

stopwatch *noun* A watch that can be started and stopped instantly for measuring time exactly.
stop·watch (stŏp′wŏch′) ◊ *noun, plural* **stopwatches**

storage *noun* **1.** The act of storing or the condition of being stored. **2.** A space or place for storing things. **3.** The part of a computer that keeps information for future use.
stor·age (stôr′ĭj) ◊ *noun, plural* **storages**

store *noun* **1.** A place where goods are sold; shop. **2.** A supply kept for future use; stock: *Do you have a store of wood for cold weather?*
◊ *verb* To put away for future use: *Squirrels store acorns for winter.*
◊ *idiom* **in store** Coming; waiting: *There's a surprise in store for you.*
store (stôr) ◊ *noun, plural* **stores** ◊ *verb* **stored, storing**

storehouse *noun* A place in which things are stored; warehouse.
store·house (stôr′hous′) ◊ *noun, plural* **storehouses**

storekeeper *noun* A person who owns or manages a shop or store.
store·keep·er (stôr′kē′pər) ◊ *noun, plural* **storekeepers**

stork *noun* A large wading bird with long legs and a long, straight bill.
stork (stôrk) ◊ *noun, plural* **storks**

▲ **stork**

storm *noun* **1.** A strong wind with rain, hail, sleet, or snow. **2.** A sudden strong outburst: *There was a storm of criticism.* **3.** A sudden violent attack.
◊ *verb* **1.** To blow with a strong wind and rain, hail, sleet, or snow. **2.** To rush with violence. **3.** To attack violently.
storm (stôrm) ◊ *noun, plural* **storms** ◊ *verb* **stormed, storming**

S

stormy *adjective* **1.** Of, relating to, or affected by storms: *We had stormy weather.* **2.** Showing very strong feelings.
storm·y (stôr′mē) ◊ *adjective* **stormier, stormiest**

story[1] *noun* **1.** A report about an event: *There was a newspaper story about the election.* **2.** A tale made up to entertain people: *I just read an adventure story.* **3.** A lie.
sto·ry[1] (stôr′ē) ◊ *noun, plural* **stories**

story[2] *noun* A horizontal level or division of a building.
sto·ry[2] (stôr′ē) ◊ *noun, plural* **stories**

HISTORY • story[1], story[2]

Both **story[1]** and **story[2]** go back to a Latin word meaning "story, history." The Latin word passed into French and then into English as **story[1]**. The French word then acquired another meaning, "a level of a building," perhaps because levels of church buildings contained colored-glass windows that told stories. In any case, this new meaning was borrowed into English as **story[2]**.

stout *adjective* **1.** Large and heavy in build. **2.** Not giving in easily: *Our suggestion met stout resistance.* **3.** Strong and sturdy: *Our house was made with stout timbers.*
stout (stout) ◊ *adjective* **stouter, stoutest**

stove *noun* An appliance that provides heat, as for cooking, and uses electricity or fuel, as gas, as a source of its power.
stove (stōv) ◊ *noun, plural* **stoves**

stovepipe *noun* A metal pipe that carries smoke or fumes from a stove to a chimney.
stove·pipe (stōv′pīp′) ◊ *noun, plural* **stovepipes**

stow *verb* To put away; store or pack: *We stowed our camping gear in the garage.*
stow (stō) ◊ *verb* **stowed, stowing**

ă	pat	ĭ	pit	oi	**oi**l	th	ba**th**
ā	pay	ī	ride	ŏŏ	b**oo**k	*th*	ba**the**
â	care	î	fierce	ōō	b**oo**t	ə	**a**go, it**e**m
ä	father	ŏ	pot	ou	**ou**t		penc**i**l
ĕ	pet	ō	go	ŭ	c**u**t		at**o**m
ē	be	ô	paw, for	û	f**u**r		circ**u**s

stowaway *noun* A person who hides aboard a vehicle, such as a ship, to travel without paying for a ticket.
stow·a·way (stō′ə wā′) ◊ *noun, plural* **stowaways**

straggle *verb* **1.** To wander in a random way; stray: *The line of people straggled away from the bus stop.* **2.** To spread out in a scattered way: *Vines straggled along the garden path.*
strag·gle (străg′əl) ◊ *verb* **straggled, straggling**

straight *adjective* **1.** Not curving, curling, or bending: *I have straight hair.* **2.** In the proper order or arrangement: *Try to keep your arithmetic straight.* **3.** Direct, honest, or correct: *Is that a straight answer?* **4.** Showing no emotion, especially not amusement: *It was hard for me to keep a straight face.*
◊ *adverb* **1.** In a straight line; directly: *The car came straight at us.* **2.** Without detour or delay: *Go straight to the store.* **3.** Without bending or curving: *Stand up straight.*
straight (strāt) ◊ *adjective, adverb* **straighter, straightest**
‖*These sound alike:* **straight, strait**

straighten *verb* To make or become straight: *Let's straighten up the room.*
straight·en (strāt′n) ◊ *verb* **straightened, straightening**

straightforward *adjective* Honest and frank.
straight·for·ward (strāt **fôr′** wərd) ◊ *adjective*

strain *verb* **1.** To pull or draw tight: *The dogs strained at their leashes.* **2.** To try very hard: *I strained to understand.* **3.** To injure or be injured by too much stretching or effort: *I'll strain my back if I carry that heavy box.* **4.** To press or pour through a strainer.
◊ *noun* **1.** The act of straining or the condition of being strained. **2.** An injury from too much stretching or effort.
strain (strān) ◊ *verb* **strained, straining**
◊ *noun, plural* **strains**

strainer *noun* A device, such as a filter or sieve, for separating liquids from solids.
strain·er (strā′nər) ◊ *noun, plural* **strainers**

strait *noun* A narrow passage that connects two bodies of water.
strait (strāt) ◊ *noun, plural* **straits**
‖*These sound alike:* **strait, straight**

strand[1] *verb* To leave in a difficult or helpless position: *They were stranded on the mountain*

when their car broke down.
strand¹ (strănd) ◊ *verb* **stranded, stranding**

strand² *noun* **1.** One of the threads, strings, or wires twisted together to make a rope, cord, or cable. **2.** A fiber, hair, or thread. **3.** Something, such as a string of beads, that is twisted or braided like a rope: *I bought a strand of pearls.*
strand² (strănd) ◊ *noun, plural* **strands**

***HISTORY* • strand¹, strand²**

Strand¹ goes back to an old English word that meant "seashore." About 400 years ago this word was made into a verb meaning "to force aground on a shore." **Strand¹** then came to have the meaning "to leave in a difficult position." **Strand²** first appears in written English about 500 years ago. Its origin before that is not known for certain.

strange *adjective* **1.** Not known before; unfamiliar: *We moved to a strange city.* **2.** Not ordinary; unusual.
strange (strānj) ◊ *adjective* **stranger, strangest**

stranger *noun* A person one has not known or met before.
strang·er (**strān′**jər) ◊ *noun, plural* **strangers**

strangle *verb* To be or feel to be unable to breathe; choke.
stran·gle (**străng′**gəl) ◊ *verb* **strangled, strangling**

strap *noun* A long, narrow strip of flexible material, such as leather, that is used to hold things together or keep things in place.
◊ *verb* To fasten or hold firmly with a strap.
strap (străp) ◊ *noun, plural* **straps** ◊ *verb* **strapped, strapping**

strategic *adjective* **1.** Of or relating to strategy. **2.** Very important in strategy.
stra·te·gic (strə **tē′**jĭk) ◊ *adjective*

strategy *noun* **1.** The planning and directing of a series of actions that will be useful in gaining a goal: *Military officers study strategy.* **2.** A clever system or plan: *Our strategy is to give a surprise party for them.*
strat·e·gy (**străt′**ə jē) ◊ *noun, plural* **strategies**

straw *noun* **1.** Stalks of grain, as wheat or oats, whose seeds have been removed. **2.** A thin tube made of paper or plastic through which a person can drink a liquid.
straw (strô) ◊ *noun, plural* **straws**

strawberry *noun* A small red fruit that has many tiny seeds on its surface.
straw·ber·ry (**strô′**bĕr′ē) ◊ *noun, plural* **strawberries**

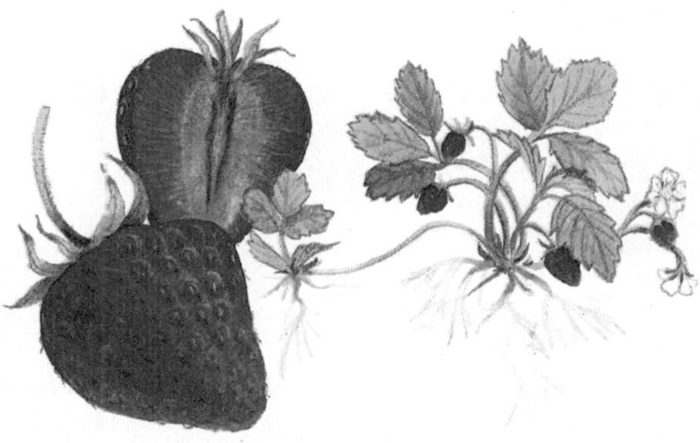

▲ **strawberry**

stray *verb* To wander or roam, especially away from a group or a proper place: *The horses strayed from the corral.*
◊ *noun* A person or animal that has strayed.
◊ *adjective* **1.** Straying or having strayed: *We fed the stray cat.* **2.** Scattered here and there: *A few stray pins lay on the floor.*
stray (strā) ◊ *verb* **strayed, straying** ◊ *noun, plural* **strays** ◊ *adjective*

streak *noun* **1.** A mark or line that differs in color or nature from its background. **2.** A character trait. **3.** A brief series: *Our team is on a winning streak.*
◊ *verb* **1.** To mark or become marked with streaks. **2.** To move at high speed; rush: *The jet streaked through the sky.*
streak (strēk) ◊ *noun, plural* **streaks** ◊ *verb* **streaked, streaking**

stream *noun* **1.** A body of water, as a brook, that flows in a bed or channel. **2.** A steady flow: *A stream of cars left the city.*
◊ *verb* **1.** To flow or move in or as if in a stream: *The crowd streamed into the store.* **2.** To float outward; wave: *Flags streamed in the breeze.*
stream (strēm) ◊ *noun, plural* **streams** ◊ *verb* **streamed, streaming**

S

streamer *noun* A long, narrow flag or strip of material often used for decoration.
stream·er (strē′mər) ◊ *noun, plural* **streamers**

streamline *verb* **1.** To design or build in a way that makes movement through air or water easier. **2.** To make simpler or more efficient: *The new manager streamlined methods for serving school lunches.*
stream·line (strēm′līn′) ◊ *verb* **streamlined, streamlining**

street *noun* **1.** A public road in a city or town. **2.** The people who live on a street: *The whole street attended our party.*
street (strēt) ◊ *noun, plural* **streets**

streetcar *noun* A vehicle that runs on rails and that carries people along regular routes on city streets.
street·car (strēt′kär′) ◊ *noun, plural* **streetcars**

▲ **streetcar**

strength *noun* **1.** The quality of being strong; power: *Elephants have enormous strength.* **2.** Power to resist strain or stress: *Test the strength of the ladder before you climb it.*
strength (strĕngkth) ◊ *noun, plural* **strengths**

strengthen *verb* To make or become strong.
strength·en (strĕngk′thən) ◊ *verb* **strengthened, strengthening**

ă	pat	ĭ	pit	oi	oil	th	bath
ā	pay	ī	ride	o͝o	book	*th*	bathe
â	care	î	fierce	o͞o	boot	ə	ago, item
ä	father	ŏ	pot	ou	out		pencil
ĕ	pet	ō	go	ŭ	cut		atom
ē	be	ô	paw, for	û	fur		circus

strenuous *adjective* **1.** Needing or showing great effort or energy: *Playing tennis is strenuous exercise.* **2.** Very active; energetic: *There was strenuous opposition to our idea.*
stren·u·ous (strĕn′yo͞o əs) ◊ *adjective*

stress *noun* **1.** Special importance; emphasis: *Don't put so much stress on making money.* **2.** Greater loudness in pronouncing a word or syllable; accent: *In the word "maple" the stress is on the first syllable.* **3.** Physical or mental pressure; strain: *The job of a firefighter involves stress.*
◊ *verb* **1.** To give special importance or emphasis to: *I stressed the need for being on time.* **2.** To pronounce a word or syllable with greater loudness; accent.
stress (strĕs) ◊ *noun, plural* **stresses** ◊ *verb* **stressed, stressing**

stretch *verb* **1.** To draw out to a greater length or width: *I stretched the rubber band.* **2.** To become or be capable of being stretched: *My sweater has stretched out of shape.* **3.** To extend or cause to extend: *The road stretches for miles. Stretch the canvas over the frame.* **4.** To put forth; hold out: *I stretched out my hand to take the letter.* **5.** To lie at full length: *Why don't you stretch out on the sofa?* **6.** To flex the muscles: *It feels good to stretch after a long drive.*
◊ *noun* **1.** An act of stretching the body or a part of the body. **2.** A continuous expanse of space or time: *We drove down a long empty stretch of highway.* **3.** The amount that something can be stretched.
stretch (strĕch) ◊ *verb* **stretched, stretching** ◊ *noun, plural* **stretches**

stretcher *noun* A portable bed or cot on which a sick or injured person can be carried.
stretch·er (strĕch′ər) ◊ *noun, plural* **stretchers**

stricken *adjective* Undergoing trouble, sickness, or sorrow: *We sent food to the stricken victims of the earthquake.*
strick·en (strĭk′ən) ◊ *adjective*

strict *adjective* **1.** Demanding or following strong discipline: *Our parents are strict about table manners.* **2.** Absolute; complete: *They told me the story in strict secrecy.* **3.** Not changing; enforced all the time: *Our school has strict playground safety rules.*
strict (strĭkt) ◊ *adjective* **stricter, strictest**

stridden *verb* Past participle of **stride.**
strid·den (strĭd′n) ◊ *verb*

stride *verb* To walk with long steps. —See Synonyms at **walk.**
◊ *noun* **1.** A long step. **2.** A step forward; advance: *We have made great strides in the field of medicine.*
stride (strīd) ◊ *verb* **strode, stridden, striding** ◊ *noun, plural* **strides**

strike *verb* **1.** To hit with or as if with the hand: *I struck the ball with the bat.* **2.** To collide with or crash into: *The car struck a pole.* **3.** To set on fire by scratching: *Strike a match.* **4.** To indicate by a sound: *The clock struck five.* **5.** To have an effect on; impress: *That struck me as a good idea.* **6.** To come upon; discover: *The miner struck gold.* **7.** To stop working in order to get better working conditions.
◊ *noun* **1.** An act or example of striking; hit. **2.** A valuable discovery, as of a precious mineral. **3.** The stopping of work by employees in order to get better working conditions. **4.** A baseball pitch that counts against the batter.
◊ *idioms* **strike out** To put or be put out in baseball by three strikes. **strike up 1.** To start to play vigorously: *Strike up the band.* **2.** To begin: *We struck up an acquaintance on the cruise.*
strike (strīk) ◊ *verb* **struck, striking** ◊ *noun, plural* **strikes**

strikeout *noun* The act of striking out or being struck out in baseball.
strike·out (strīk′out′) ◊ *noun, plural* **strikeouts**

string *noun* **1.** A cord, as of twisted fibers, for fastening or tying. **2.** Something that is like a string: *We put a string of colored lights on the tree. I put on a string of pearls.* **3.** A series of things or events: *A string of accidents happened at that corner.* **4.** A stretched cord of a musical instrument that produces a tone when it is made to vibrate. **5. strings** Musical instruments that have strings and are played with a bow.
◊ *verb* **1.** To provide with strings: *I had my tennis racket strung.* **2.** To put on a string; thread: *Children love to string beads.* **3.** To stretch from one place to another: *We strung the line from pole to pole.*
string (strĭng) ◊ *noun, plural* **strings** ◊ *verb* **strung, stringing**

string bean *noun* A long, narrow green or yellow pod that is eaten as a vegetable.
string bean ◊ *noun, plural* **string beans**

▲ **string bean**

strip¹ *verb* **1.** To take off the clothing; undress. **2.** To remove the covering from: *I stripped the peel from the banana.*
strip¹ (strĭp) ◊ *verb* **stripped, stripping**

strip² *noun* A long, narrow piece of material or land: *A paper strip marks my place in the book. We swam at a beautiful, uncrowded strip of beach.*
strip² (strĭp) ◊ *noun, plural* **strips**

***HISTORY* • strip¹, strip²**

Strip¹ comes from an old English word that meant "to plunder." **Strip²** may be a different form of the word **stripe.**

stripe *noun* **1.** A long, narrow band of color or material that is different from its background. **2.** A strip of cloth worn on the sleeve of a uniform to show years of service or rank.
◊ *verb* To mark with stripes.
stripe (strīp) ◊ *noun, plural* **stripes** ◊ *verb* **striped, striping**

strive *verb* To try hard: *We should always strive to be good sports.*
strive (strīv) ◊ *verb* **strove, striven** *or* **strived, striving**

striven *verb* A past participle of **strive.**
striv·en (strĭv′ən) ◊ *verb*

strode *verb* Past tense of **stride.**
strode (strōd) ◊ *verb*

stroke *noun* **1.** An act of striking; blow. **2.** A single complete movement that is repeated often: *Swim with even strokes.* **3.** A mark made by or as if by a pen or brush: *I paint with broad strokes.* **4.** Something unexpected with a powerful effect: *They had an amazing stroke of good luck.* **5.** A sudden illness caused by the breaking or blocking of a blood vessel in the brain.

S

◊ *verb* To move the hand over gently: *Mother stroked my head when I was sick.*
stroke (strōk) ◊ *noun, plural* **strokes** ◊ *verb* **stroked, stroking**

stroll *verb* To walk around in a slow, relaxed way. —See Synonyms at **walk.**
◊ *noun* A slow, relaxed walk.
stroll (strōl) ◊ *verb* **strolled, strolling** ◊ *noun, plural* **strolls**

strong *adjective* **1.** Having much power, energy, or strength: *A strong horse pulled the heavy cart. Strong winds can blow down trees.* **2.** Not easily broken; sturdy: *Strong walls last for many years.* **3.** Firmly established: *The patriots' belief in their cause is strong.*
strong (strông) ◊ *adjective* **stronger, strongest**

stronghold *noun* A fortress or refuge.
strong·hold (**strông′**hōld′) ◊ *noun, plural* **strongholds**

strove *verb* Past tense of **strive.**
strove (strōv) ◊ *verb*

struck *verb* Past tense and past participle of **strike.**
struck (strŭk) ◊ *verb*

structure *noun* **1.** Something, as a building or bridge, that has been built. **2.** Something that is made up of a number of parts arranged together: *Our government is a complex structure.* **3.** The way in which parts go together or are arranged to make a whole: *Our class studied the structure of the flower.*
struc·ture (**strŭk′**chər) ◊ *noun, plural* **structures**

struggle *verb* **1.** To make a great effort: *The team struggled to win.* **2.** To advance with effort: *I struggled through the tall weeds.*
◊ *noun* **1.** A great effort. **2.** A battle; fight.
strug·gle (**strŭg′**əl) ◊ *verb* **struggled, struggling** ◊ *noun, plural* **struggles**

strum *verb* To play on a stringed instrument by stroking the strings lightly with the fingers: *Please strum a tune on your guitar.*
strum (strŭm) ◊ *verb* **strummed, strumming**

ă	pat	ĭ	pit	oi	**oi**l	th	ba**th**
ā	pay	ī	ride	o͝o	book	*th*	ba*th*e
â	care	î	fierce	o͞o	boot	ə	ago, item
ä	father	ŏ	pot	ou	**ou**t		pencil
ĕ	pet	ō	go	ŭ	cut		atom
ē	be	ô	paw, for	û	fur		circus

strung *verb* Past tense and past participle of **string.**
strung (strŭng) ◊ *verb*

stub *noun* **1.** A short end that is left over after something has been used up or broken off: *It is hard to write with the stub of a pencil.* **2.** A small part of a bank check that is kept as a record. **3.** The part of a ticket that is returned to the user as proof that the ticket has been paid for.
◊ *verb* To bump one's toe or foot against something.
stub (stŭb) ◊ *noun, plural* **stubs** ◊ *verb* **stubbed, stubbing**

stubble *noun* **1.** Short, stiff stalks, as of grain, that are left on a field after a crop has been cut. **2.** A short, rough growth, especially of a beard.
stub·ble (**stŭb′**əl) ◊ *noun*

stubborn *adjective* **1.** Not willing to change a purpose or opinion in spite of urging or requests from others: *The stubborn child refused to wear boots.* —See Synonyms at **obstinate.** **2.** Hard to handle or deal with: *I have a stubborn cold.*
stub·born (**stŭb′**ərn) ◊ *adjective*

stuck *verb* Past tense and past participle of **stick.**
stuck (stŭk) ◊ *verb*

student *noun* A person who studies, as in a school.
stu·dent (**sto͞od′**nt *or* **styo͞od′**nt) ◊ *noun, plural* **students**

studio *noun* **1.** The place where an artist works. **2.** A place where an art is studied or taught. **3.** A place where movies, television and radio shows, or records are made. **4.** A place from which television or radio shows are broadcast.
stu·di·o (**sto͞o′**dē ō′ *or* **styo͞o′**dē ō′) ◊ *noun, plural* **studios**

study *noun* **1.** The act or process of learning; an effort to learn: *Much study went into the new program.* **2.** A branch of knowledge: *The study of law requires patience.* **3.** A close and careful examination: *We made a study of the map before we left.* **4.** A room used especially for studying, reading, or writing.
◊ *verb* **1.** To try to learn: *We study Spanish.* **2.** To examine closely and carefully: *Study the questions before you try to answer them.*

stud·y (stŭd′ē) ◊ *noun, plural* **studies** ◊ *verb* **studied, studying**

stuff *noun* **1.** Belongings, goods, or equipment needed or used by people: *Leave your football stuff at school.* **2.** Useless material; junk: *Get rid of that stuff in the garage.*
◊ *verb* **1.** To pack tightly; cram: *I stuffed my school bag with books.* **2.** To stop up; block: *My nose is stuffed.* **3.** To fill oneself with too much food: *We stuffed ourselves on apples.* **4.** To fill with a stuffing.
stuff (stŭf) ◊ *noun* ◊ *verb* **stuffed, stuffing**

stuffing *noun* **1.** Soft material used to stuff articles, as pillows, made of or covered with cloth. **2.** A mixture, as of seasoned bread crumbs, that is put inside meat, poultry, fish, or vegetables.
stuff·ing (stŭf′ĭng) ◊ *noun, plural* **stuffings**

stuffy *adjective* **1.** Lacking fresh air. **2.** Having blocked breathing passages.
stuff·y (stŭf′ē) ◊ *adjective* **stuffier, stuffiest**

stumble *verb* **1.** To trip and almost fall. **2.** To walk in a clumsy way. **3.** To speak or act in a clumsy way: *Sometimes I stumble over words.* **4.** To find unexpectedly: *They stumbled on a valuable coin in the shop.*
stum·ble (stŭm′bəl) ◊ *verb* **stumbled, stumbling**

stump *noun* **1.** The part of a tree trunk left in the ground after it has fallen or been cut down. **2.** A short or broken piece or part: *My pencil was worn down to a stump.*
◊ *verb* To puzzle or baffle completely: *The hard question stumped the best student.*
stump (stŭmp) ◊ *noun, plural* **stumps** ◊ *verb* **stumped, stumping**

▲ **stump**

stun *verb* **1.** To daze or make senseless by or as if by a blow. **2.** To shock or confuse.
stun (stŭn) ◊ *verb* **stunned, stunning**

stung *verb* Past tense and past participle of **sting.**
stung (stŭng) ◊ *verb*

stunk *verb* A past tense and the past participle of **stink.**
stunk (stŭngk) ◊ *verb*

stunning *adjective* **1.** Shocking or astonishing: *Our team won a stunning victory.* **2.** Strikingly attractive or handsome.
stun·ning (stŭn′ĭng) ◊ *adjective*

stunt¹ *verb* To stop or interfere with the growth or development of: *Air pollution may stunt many kinds of plants.*
stunt¹ (stŭnt) ◊ *verb* **stunted, stunting**

stunt² *noun* **1.** An act that shows unusual skill or daring. **2.** An unusual act done especially to attract attention.
stunt² (stŭnt) ◊ *noun, plural* **stunts**

HISTORY **• stunt¹, stunt²**

Stunt¹ probably comes from an old Scandinavian word that meant "short." **Stunt²** first appears in written English about 100 years ago as a slang word used in American colleges. Its origin before that is not known for certain.

stupid *adjective* **1.** Slow to understand; dull. **2.** Not sensible; foolish: *It would be stupid to wear shorts in a snowstorm.*
stu·pid (stōō′pĭd *or* **styōō′**pĭd) ◊ *adjective* **stupider, stupidest**

stupidly *adverb* In a foolish manner or way.
stu·pid·ly (stōō′pĭd lē *or* **styōō′**pĭd lē) ◊ *adverb*

sturdy *adjective* Strongly made or built.
stur·dy (stûr′dē) ◊ *adjective* **sturdier, sturdiest**

sturgeon *noun* A large food fish with bony plates on its body.
stur·geon (stûr′jən) ◊ *noun, plural* **sturgeon** *or* **sturgeons**

stutter *verb* To speak or say with many pauses and repetitions of sounds.
◊ *noun* The act or habit of stuttering.
stut·ter (stŭt′ər) ◊ *verb* **stuttered, stuttering** ◊ *noun, plural* **stutters**

S

sty *noun* A pen where pigs are kept.
sty (stī) ◊ *noun, plural* **sties**

▲ **sty**

style *noun* **1.** A way of doing or making something: *We built our house in a modern style.* **2.** A way of writing or speaking: *The style of the book is informal.* **3.** A way of dressing or acting. **4.** A way of dressing or acting that is fashionable: *My clothes are out of style.*
◊ *verb* To make and design in a special way.
style (stīl) ◊ *noun, plural* **styles** ◊ *verb* **styled, styling**

stylish *adjective* Going along with the current style; fashionable.
styl·ish (**stī′**lĭsh) ◊ *adjective*

subdivide *verb* To divide into smaller parts.
sub·di·vide (sŭb′dĭ **vīd′**) ◊ *verb* **subdivided, subdividing**

subdivision *noun* **1.** The act of subdividing. **2.** A subdivided part, as of a neighborhood.
sub·di·vi·sion (sŭb′dĭ **vĭzh′**ən) ◊ *noun, plural* **subdivisions**

subdue *verb* **1.** To defeat in battle; conquer. **2.** To bring under control: *I managed to subdue my fear and speak up.*
sub·due (səb **do͞o′** *or* səb **dyo͞o′**) ◊ *verb* **subdued, subduing**

subject *noun* **1.** One that is thought about, discussed, or represented: *I'm tired of sports; let's change the subject.* **2.** A course or field of study: *Math is my favorite subject.* **3.** One that is studied: *Scientists often use mice as subjects when they do research.* **4.** The word or group of words in a sentence that performs or receives the action of the verb. **5.** A person under the authority, rule, or control of another: *All British citizens are subjects of the monarch.*
◊ *adjective* **1.** Under the authority, rule, or control of another. **2.** Likely to have or get: *I am subject to colds.* **3.** Being dependent on: *Going on the trip to Washington is subject to my parents' approval.*
◊ *verb* **1.** To bring under rule or control. **2.** To cause to undergo: *The doctors subjected the patient to tests.*
sub·ject ◊ *noun* (**sŭb′**jĭkt), *plural* **subjects** ◊ *adjective* (**sŭb′**jĭkt) ◊ *verb* (səb **jĕkt′**) **subjected, subjecting**

submarine *noun* **1.** A ship that can operate both underwater and on the surface. **2.** A sandwich on a large, long roll.
sub·ma·rine (**sŭb′**mə rēn′ *or* sŭb′mə **rēn′**) ◊ *noun, plural* **submarines**

LANGUAGE DETECTIVE

submarine

There are many names for a large, long sandwich. Nine of these names are given here. Which ones are used where you live? Some people call this kind of sandwich a *submarine* or *sub* because the bread is shaped like a submarine. *Torpedo* is another word that refers to the shape of the sandwich. Around New York City, the sandwich is often called a *hero*, probably because it takes a brave person to eat the whole thing! The name *Italian sandwich* comes from the long loaf of Italian bread used to make it. People around New Orleans call it a *poor boy*, probably because such a big sandwich can make a whole meal that is very inexpensive. Around Philadelphia it is called a *hoagie*. In still other places it is a *grinder* or a *Coney Island sandwich*.

ă	pat	ĭ	pit	oi	oil	th	bath
ā	pay	ī	ride	o͝o	book	*th*	bathe
â	care	î	fierce	o͞o	boot	ə	ago, item
ä	father	ŏ	pot	ou	out		pencil
ĕ	pet	ō	go	ŭ	cut		atom
ē	be	ô	paw, for	û	fur		circus

▲ **submarine**

submerge *verb* **1.** To place or plunge into a liquid, especially water: *The submarine quickly submerged.* **2.** To cover with water: *Huge waves submerged the pier.*
sub·merge (səb **mûrj′**) ◊ *verb* **submerged, submerging**

submission *noun* **1.** The act of submitting. **2.** The condition of being submissive.
sub·mis·sion (səb **mĭsh′**ən) ◊ *noun, plural* **submissions**

submissive *adjective* Tending to give in to other people's wishes.
sub·mis·sive (səb **mĭs′**ĭv) ◊ *adjective*

submit *verb* **1.** To yield to the commands or authority of another; give in: *I submitted to my parents' wishes and returned the monkey to the pet shop.* —See Synonyms at **yield. 2.** To put forward for someone else's consideration, judgment, or approval: *I submitted my outline to the teacher.*
sub·mit (səb **mĭt′**) ◊ *verb* **submitted, submitting**

subordinate *adjective* Belonging to a lower rank; inferior.
◊ *noun* A person who is subordinate to another.
sub·or·di·nate (sə **bôr′**dn ĭt) ◊ *adjective* ◊ *noun, plural* **subordinates**

subscribe *verb* To pay for and receive a publication regularly.
sub·scribe (səb **skrīb′**) ◊ *verb* **subscribed, subscribing**

subscription *noun* The purchase of a certain number of future issues of a publication.
sub·scrip·tion (səb **skrĭp′**shən) ◊ *noun, plural* **subscriptions**

subsequent *adjective* Following in time or order: *Last spring we had heavy rains and subsequent floods.*
sub·se·quent (**sŭb′**sĭ kwənt) ◊ *adjective*

subside *verb* **1.** To sink to a lower or more normal level: *The flood waters finally subsided.* **2.** To become less intense or active: *The cheers for the winner finally subsided.*
sub·side (səb **sīd′**) ◊ *verb* **subsided, subsiding**

subsoil *noun* The layer of earth that lies below the topsoil.
sub·soil (**sŭb′**soil′) ◊ *noun*

substance *noun* **1.** Something that has weight and takes up space; matter. **2.** The material that a thing is made of. **3.** The content of what is said or written rather than its form or style; meaning. **4.** Truth or reality: *Is there any substance to these charges?*
sub·stance (**sŭb′**stəns) ◊ *noun, plural* **substances**

substantial *adjective* **1.** Of, relating to, or having substance. **2.** Not imaginary; real. **3.** Solidly built; strong: *The tower was a substantial structure.* **4.** Large in amount; ample.
sub·stan·tial (səb **stăn′**shəl) ◊ *adjective*

substitute *noun* Someone or something that takes the place of another; replacement: *While our teacher was sick, a substitute taught the class.*
◊ *verb* **1.** To put or use in place of another: *The cook substituted peaches for pears in the recipe.* **2.** To take the place of another.
sub·sti·tute (**sŭb′**stĭ to͞ot′ *or* **sŭb′**stĭ tyo͞ot′) ◊ *noun, plural* **substitutes** ◊ *verb* **substituted, substituting**

subtle *adjective* Having a faint, delicate quality that is hard to detect or appreciate: *Things looked almost the same, but subtle changes in the environment had taken place.*
sub·tle (**sŭt′**l) ◊ *adjective* **subtler, subtlest**

subtract *verb* To take away one number or part from another number or a whole; deduct: *If you subtract 4 from 7, you get 3.*
sub·tract (səb **trăkt′**) ◊ *verb* **subtracted, subtracting**

S

subtraction *noun* The act or process of subtracting.
sub·trac·tion (səb **trăk′**shən) ◊ *noun, plural* **subtractions**

subtrahend *noun* A number that is to be subtracted from another number.
sub·tra·hend (**sŭb′**trə hĕnd′) ◊ *noun, plural* **subtrahends**

suburb *noun* A town or district that is close to a city.
sub·urb (**sŭb′**ûrb′) ◊ *noun, plural* **suburbs**

suburban *adjective* Of, relating to, or located in a suburb.
sub·ur·ban (sə **bûr′**bən) ◊ *adjective*

suburbanite *noun* A person who lives in a suburb.
sub·ur·ban·ite (sə **bûr′**bə nīt′) ◊ *noun, plural* **surburbanites**

subway *noun* An underground railroad in a city, especially one that is powered by electricity.
sub·way (**sŭb′**wā′) ◊ *noun, plural* **subways**

▲ **subway**

succeed *verb* **1.** To come next after, as in position; follow: *B succeeds A in our alphabet.* **2.** To carry out something desired or attempted: *We succeeded in our repairs.*
suc·ceed (sək **sēd′**) ◊ *verb* **succeeded, succeeding**

ă	pat	ĭ	pit	oi	**oi**l	th	ba**th**
ā	pay	ī	ride	o͝o	b**oo**k	*th*	ba**th**e
â	care	î	fierce	o͞o	b**oo**t	ə	ago, item
ä	father	ŏ	pot	ou	**ou**t		pencil
ĕ	pet	ō	go	ŭ	c**u**t		atom
ē	be	ô	paw, for	û	f**u**r		circus

success *noun* **1.** The achievement of something: *My second attempt to jump over the bar ended in success.* **2.** The gaining of fame or wealth: *My cousin won success as a skater.* **3.** Someone or something that is successful: *The picnic was a great success.*
suc·cess (sək **sĕs′**) ◊ *noun, plural* **successes**

successful *adjective* **1.** Ending or resulting in success: *My fourth attempt to ride the bicycle was successful.* **2.** Having gained success: *My parents are successful lawyers.*
suc·cess·ful (sək **sĕs′**fəl) ◊ *adjective*

succession *noun* **1.** The process or act of following in order: *Historians study the succession of events.* **2.** A number of persons or things that follow in order: *We heard a succession of loud pops.* **3.** The order, right, or act of succeeding to a title, throne, or estate.
suc·ces·sion (sək **sĕsh′**ən) ◊ *noun, plural* **successions**

successive *adjective* Following in order.
suc·ces·sive (sək **sĕs′**ĭv) ◊ *adjective*

successor *noun* A person who succeeds another: *The vice president was the president's successor.*
suc·ces·sor (sək **sĕs′**ər) ◊ *noun, plural* **successors**

succumb *verb* To give in to something overpowering or overwhelming.
suc·cumb (sə **kŭm′**) ◊ *verb* **succumbed, succumbing**

such *adjective* **1.** Of this or that kind: *We never dreamed you could do such work.* **2.** Of the same kind; similar: *I think up two or three such jokes a week.* **3.** So much or so great: *You read with such speed!*
◊*pronoun* A person, thing, or group of that kind: *I heard some music, if it can be called such.*
such (sŭch) ◊ *adjective* ◊ *pronoun*

suck *verb* **1.** To draw liquid into the mouth by inhaling or pulling in the cheeks. **2.** To draw from in this way. **3.** To take into the mouth and pull on or lick: *The baby was sucking its thumb.*
suck (sŭk) ◊ *verb* **sucked, sucking**

sucker *noun* **1.** A part of an animal's body by which it can cling to surfaces. **2.** A freshwater fish with thick lips that suck in food. **3.** A shoot growing from the base of a plant.
suck·er (**sŭk′**ər) ◊ *noun, plural* **suckers**

suction *noun* The process of drawing something into a space, such as into a straw, by removing part of the air in that space: *We drink through straws by means of suction.*
suc·tion (sŭk′shən) ◊ *noun*

sudden *adjective* **1.** Happening or arriving without warning: *We were caught in a sudden snowstorm.* **2.** Rapid; quick: *With a sudden dive the hawk attacked the mouse.*
◊ *idiom* **all of a sudden** Very quickly and unexpectedly.
sud·den (sŭd′n) ◊ *adjective*

suds *plural noun* Soapy water.
suds (sŭdz) ◊ *plural noun*

sue *verb* To bring a lawsuit against.
sue (so͞o) ◊ *verb* **sued, suing**

suede *noun* Leather that is rubbed to give it a soft, velvety surface.
suede (swād) ◊ *noun*

suet *noun* The hard fat around the kidneys of cattle and sheep. Suet is used for feeding birds and in cooking.
su·et (so͞o′ĭt) ◊ *noun*

suffer *verb* **1.** To feel pain or distress: *The drought victims are suffering from malnutrition.* **2.** To undergo something unpleasant: *The chess team suffered defeat.* **3.** To be at a disadvantage: *The student suffered from poor preparation.*
suf·fer (sŭf′ər) ◊ *verb* **suffered, suffering**

sufficient *adjective* As much as is needed or wanted; enough.
suf·fi·cient (sə fĭsh′ənt) ◊ *adjective*

suffix *noun* A word part that is added to the end of a base word or root word. A suffix changes the meaning. The word *kindness* is made up of the base word *kind* and the suffix *-ness*.
suf·fix (sŭf′ĭks′) ◊ *noun, plural* **suffixes**

***VOCABULARY BUILDER* • suffix**

When you add a suffix to a word, you must sometimes change the spelling of the word. When you add the suffix *-ed* to *fade* to make *faded,* you drop the *e.* When you add the suffix *-ed* to *dry* to make *dried,* you change the *y* to an *i.* When you add the suffix *-ed* to *drop* to make *dropped,* you add an extra *p.*

suffocate *verb* **1.** To die from a lack of oxygen. **2.** To be hot and uncomfortable because of a lack of air.
suf·fo·cate (sŭf′ə kāt′) ◊ *verb* **suffocated, suffocating**

suffrage *noun* The right to vote.
suf·frage (sŭf′rĭj) ◊ *noun*

sugar *noun* **1.** A sweet substance gotten mainly from sugar beets or sugar cane. Sugar is used to sweeten food. **2.** Any of a number of carbohydrates that have a sweet taste.
sug·ar (sho͝og′ər) ◊ *noun, plural* **sugars**

sugar beet *noun* A beet with whitish roots from which sugar is gotten.
sugar beet ◊ *noun, plural* **sugar beets**

sugar cane *noun* A tall grass with thick, juicy stems from which sugar is gotten.

▲ **sugar cane**

sugar-free *adjective* Containing no sugar.
sug·ar-free (sho͝og′ər frē′) ◊ *adjective*

suggest *verb* **1.** To offer for consideration or action: *I suggest going to a movie tonight.* **2.** To bring or call to mind: *That cloud suggests a boat to me.* **3.** To show indirectly; hint: *A dancer may suggest feelings through movement.*
sug·gest (səg jĕst′) ◊ *verb* **suggested, suggesting**

suggestion *noun* **1.** The act of suggesting. **2.** Something that is suggested. **3.** A hint or a trace.
sug·ges·tion (səg jĕs′chən) ◊ *noun, plural* **suggestions**

S

suicide *noun* The act of intentionally killing oneself.
su·i·cide (sōō′ĭ sīd′) ◊ *noun, plural* **suicides**

suit *noun* **1.** A set of things to be used together: *We put on our gym suits for physical education class.* **2.** A case that is brought before a court of law; lawsuit.
◊ *verb* **1.** To meet the requirements of; satisfy: *The new house suited us.* **2.** To be appropriate or acceptable for; fit: *The song suited the occasion.* **3.** To please; satisfy: *Rest all day if it suits you.*
suit (sōōt) ◊ *noun, plural* **suits** ◊ *verb* **suited, suiting**

suitable *adjective* Right for a purpose or occasion; appropriate.
suit·a·ble (sōō′tə bəl) ◊ *adjective*

suitcase *noun* A rectangular or square piece of luggage.
suit·case (sōōt′kās′) ◊ *noun, plural* **suitcases**

suite *noun* **1.** A series of connected rooms used together. **2.** A set of matched or similar things: *The orchestra played a suite of dances.*
suite (swēt) ◊ *noun, plural* **suites**
‖*These sound alike:* **suite, sweet**

suitor *noun* A man who courts a woman.
suit·or (sōō′tər) ◊ *noun, plural* **suitors**

sulfur *noun* A pale-yellow chemical element used to make gunpowder and chemicals.
sul·fur (sŭl′fər) ◊ *noun*

sulk *verb* To be sullenly quiet or angry.
sulk (sŭlk) ◊ *verb* **sulked, sulking**

sulky *adjective* Tending to sulk; moody.
sulk·y (sŭl′kē) ◊ *adjective* **sulkier, sulkiest**

sullen *adjective* Showing bad humor or resentment.
sul·len (sŭl′ən) ◊ *adjective*

sum *noun* **1.** The result of the operation of addition: *The sum of 2 + 2 is 4.* **2.** The whole amount: *The sum of my knowledge is very small.* **3.** An amount of money: *The check was for the sum of $10,000.* **4.** An arithmetic problem.
◊ *verb* To find the sum of; add.
sum (sŭm) ◊ *noun, plural* **sums** ◊ *verb* **summed, summing**
‖*These sound alike:* **sum, some**

sumac *noun* A shrub or rather small tree having leaves with many leaflets and pointed clusters of small, usually red berries.
su·mac (sōō′măk′ *or* **shōō′** măk′) ◊ *noun, plural* **sumacs**

▲ **sumac**

summarize *verb* To state in a summary: *Summarize the plot of the story.*
sum·ma·rize (sŭm′ə rīz′) ◊ *verb* **summarized, summarizing**

summary *noun* A short statement of the main points of something longer.
sum·ma·ry (sŭm′ə rē) ◊ *noun, plural* **summaries**
‖*These sound alike:* **summary, summery**

summer *noun* The hottest season of the year, between spring and autumn.
sum·mer (sŭm′ər) ◊ *noun, plural* **summers**

summertime *noun* The season of summer.
sum·mer·time (sŭm′ər tīm′) ◊ *noun*

summery *adjective* Of, like, or suitable for summer: *It was a clear, summery afternoon.*
sum·mer·y (sŭm′ə rē) ◊ *adjective*
‖*These sound alike:* **summery, summary**

summit *noun* The highest point or part; top.
sum·mit (sŭm′ĭt) ◊ *noun, plural* **summits**

summon *verb* **1.** To ask to come or appear; call or send for. **2.** To find in oneself and use: *Summon your courage and go onto the stage.*
sum·mon (sŭm′ən) ◊ *verb* **summoned, summoning**

ă	pat	ĭ	pit	oi	**oi**l	th	ba**th**
ā	pay	ī	ride	ŏŏ	book	*th*	bathe
â	care	î	fierce	ōō	boot	ə	ago, item
ä	father	ŏ	pot	ou	**ou**t		pencil
ĕ	pet	ō	go	ŭ	cut		atom
ē	be	ô	paw, for	û	fur		circus

summons *noun* **1.** An official paper ordering someone to appear in court. **2.** A call or order to appear or do something.
sum·mons (sŭm′ənz) ◊ *noun, plural* **summonses**

sumptuous *adjective* Very rich, expensive, luxurious, or splendid.
sump·tu·ous (sŭmp′cho͞o əs) ◊ *adjective*

sun *noun* **1.** The star around which the earth and the other planets revolve. The sun gives light and heat to the earth and sustains all life. **2.** A star, especially one around which planets revolve. **3.** The light of the sun; sunshine.
◊ *verb* To bathe in or expose to the sun's rays.
sun (sŭn) ◊ *noun, plural* **suns** ◊ *verb* **sunned, sunning**
‖ *These sound alike:* **sun, son**

Sun. The abbreviation for *Sunday.*

sunbathe *verb* To expose the body to the light of the sun.
sun·bathe (sŭn′bāth′) ◊ *verb* **sunbathed, sunbathing**

sunbeam *noun* A ray of sunshine.
sun·beam (sŭn′bēm′) ◊ *noun, plural* **sunbeams**

sunbelt *or* **Sunbelt** *noun* The region that includes southern and southwestern states of the United States.
sun·belt *or* **Sun·belt** (sŭn′bĕlt′) ◊ *noun*

sunburn *noun* A red soreness of the skin caused by exposure to too much sunlight.
◊ *verb* To affect or be affected by sunburn.
sun·burn (sŭn′bûrn′) ◊ *noun, plural* **sunburns** ◊ *verb* **sunburned** *or* **sunburnt, sunburning**

sunburnt *verb* A past tense and a past participle of **sunburn.**
sun·burnt (sŭn′bûrnt′) ◊ *verb*

sundae *noun* Ice cream with toppings such as syrup, fruit, or nuts.
sun·dae (sŭn′dē) ◊ *noun, plural* **sundaes**

Sunday *noun* The first day of the week.
Sun·day (sŭn′dē) ◊ *noun, plural* **Sundays**

***HISTORY* • Sunday**

Three days of the week were named after planets or heavenly bodies. **Sunday** was named after the sun.

sunder *verb* To break apart.
sun·der (sŭn′dər) ◊ *verb* **sundered, sundering**

sundial *noun* An instrument that shows the time of day by the position of the shadow made by a pointer on a marked disk.
sun·di·al (sŭn′dī′əl) ◊ *noun, plural* **sundials**

▲ **sundial**

sundown *noun* Sunset.
sun·down (sŭn′doun′) ◊ *noun, plural* **sundowns**

sunflower *noun* A tall plant that has large flowers with yellow petals and dark centers. Sunflowers bear edible seeds that are rich in oil.
sun·flow·er (sŭn′flou′ər) ◊ *noun, plural* **sunflowers**

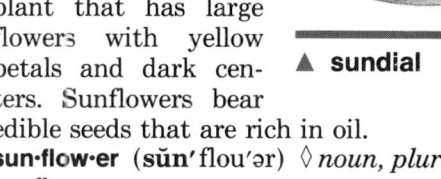

sung *verb* Past participle of **sing.**
sung (sŭng) ◊ *verb*

sunglasses *plural noun* Eyeglasses that are worn to protect the eyes from the sun's glare.
sun·glass·es (sŭn′glăs′ĭz) ◊ *plural noun*

sunk *verb* A past tense and the past participle of **sink.**
sunk (sŭngk) ◊ *verb*

sunken *adjective* **1.** Beneath the surface of a body of water; submerged: *The divers searched for sunken ships.* **2.** Below a surrounding level: *The beautiful garden had a sunken lake.*
sunk·en (sŭng′kən) ◊ *adjective*

sunlight *noun* The light of the sun.
sun·light (sŭn′līt′) ◊ *noun*

sunlit *adjective* Lighted by the sun.
sun·lit (sŭn′lĭt′) ◊ *adjective*

sunny *adjective* **1.** Full of sunshine: *Let's hope for a sunny day.* **2.** Cheerful.
sun·ny (sŭn′ē) ◊ *adjective* **sunnier, sunniest**

sunrise *noun* **1.** The daily appearance of the sun above the eastern horizon in the morning. **2.** The time when the sun rises.
sun·rise (sŭn′rīz′) ◊ *noun, plural* **sunrises**

sunset *noun* **1.** The daily disappearance of the sun below the western horizon at evening.

S

2. The time when the sun sets.
sun·set (**sŭn′**sĕt′) ◊ *noun, plural* **sunsets**

▲ **sunset**

sunshine *noun* Sunlight.
sun·shine (**sŭn′**shīn′) ◊ *noun*

sunstroke *noun* A condition marked by fever, dizziness, and collapse. Sunstroke is caused by too much heat from the sun.
sun·stroke (**sŭn′**strōk′) ◊ *noun, plural* **sunstrokes**

sunup *noun* Sunrise.
sun·up (**sŭn′**ŭp′) ◊ *noun, plural* **sunups**

super *adjective* Excellent; fabulous: *Going camping is a super idea.*
su·per (**so͞o′**pər) ◊ *adjective*

superb *adjective* Being the very best; excellent: *Your grades are superb.*
su·perb (so͝o **pûrb′**) ◊ *adjective*

superhuman *adjective* Being or seeming to be beyond ordinary or normal ability: *It would take superhuman strength to move that boulder.*
su·per·hu·man (so͞o′pər **hyo͞o′**mən) ◊ *adjective*

superintendent *noun* **1.** A person who supervises or is in charge of something. **2.** The janitor of a building.
su·per·in·ten·dent (so͞o′pər ĭn **tĕn′**dənt) ◊ *noun, plural* **superintendents**

ă	pat	ĭ	pit	oi	**oil**	th	bath
ā	pay	ī	ride	o͝o	book	*th*	bathe
â	care	î	fierce	o͞o	boot	ə	ago, item
ä	father	ŏ	pot	ou	**out**		pencil
ĕ	pet	ō	go	ŭ	cut		atom
ē	be	ô	paw, for	û	fur		circus

superior *adjective* **1.** Of higher position or rank than another. **2.** Of a higher quality: *Steel is superior to wood in strength.* **3.** Of greater ability or achievement. **4.** Considering oneself better than others; conceited: *Don't take a superior attitude toward the younger students.*
◊ *noun* A person who is higher than others, especially in rank or position.
su·pe·ri·or (so͝o **pîr′**ē ər) ◊ *adjective* ◊ *noun, plural* **superiors**

superiority *noun* The quality, condition, or fact of being superior.
su·pe·ri·or·i·ty (so͝o pîr′ē **ôr′**ĭ tē) ◊ *noun*

superlative *adjective* Being the very best: *The singer gave a superlative performance.*
◊ *noun* The form of an adjective or adverb that indicates the greatest degree of the quality described by the adjective or adverb: *"Best" is the superlative of "good."*
su·per·la·tive (so͝o **pûr′**lə tĭv) ◊ *adjective* ◊ *noun, plural* **superlatives**

supermarket *noun* A large self-service store selling food and household goods.
su·per·mar·ket (**so͞o′**pər mär′kĭt) ◊ *noun, plural* **supermarkets**

superscript *noun* A number or letter written next to and a little above another character.
su·per·script (**so͞o′**pər skrĭpt′) ◊ *noun, plural* **superscripts**

supersonic *adjective* Of, relating to, or moving at a speed greater than that of sound.
su·per·son·ic (so͞o′pər **sŏn′**ĭk) ◊ *adjective*

superstition *noun* A belief that some action that has nothing to do with a future event influences the outcome of the event.
su·per·sti·tion (so͞o′pər **stĭsh′**ən) ◊ *noun, plural* **superstitions**

superstitious *adjective* Believing in or resulting from a superstition.
su·per·sti·tious (so͞o′pər **stĭsh′**əs) ◊ *adjective*

supervise *verb* To watch over and inspect the action, work, or performance of.
su·per·vise (**so͞o′**pər vīz′) ◊ *verb* **supervised, supervising**

supervisor *noun* A person who supervises.
su·per·vi·sor (**so͞o′**pər vī′zər) ◊ *noun, plural* **supervisors**

supper *noun* The evening meal or the last meal of the day.
sup·per (**sŭp′**ər) ◊ *noun, plural* **suppers**

supplant *verb* To take the place of.
sup·plant (sə **plănt′**) ◊ *verb* **supplanted, supplanting**

supple *adjective* Bending easily; limber: *You need supple joints to bend backward and touch the floor.*
sup·ple (sŭp′əl) ◊ *adjective* **suppler, supplest**

supplement *noun* Something that is added to complete something or make up for what was missing: *The doctor told me to take vitamin pills as a supplement to my diet.*
◊ *verb* To provide a supplement to: *The teacher supplemented our reading with films.*
sup·ple·ment ◊ *noun* (**sŭp′**lə mənt), *plural* **supplements** ◊ *verb* (**sŭp′**lə mĕnt′) **supplemented, supplementing**

supply *verb* **1.** To make available for use; provide: *Large forests supply trees for lumber.* **2.** To fill; satisfy: *The new bus route supplies a real need for better transportation.*
◊ *noun* **1.** The act of supplying: *Trucks are important for the supply of fresh farm foods to consumers.* **2.** An amount available for use; stock: *Our supply of food is low.* **3. supplies** Necessary materials kept and used or given out when needed: *After three months, the explorers' supplies ran out.*
sup·ply (sə **plī′**) ◊ *verb* **supplied, supplying** ◊ *noun, plural* **supplies**

support *verb* **1.** To keep from falling; hold in position: *Two steel towers support the bridge.* **2.** To supply with things needed for life: *My parents support two children.* **3.** To show to be true; back up: *The evidence supports your theory.* **4.** To stand behind the cause of; take sides with: *Which candidate do you support?* **5.** To keep from dying out; sustain: *The desert climate supports little plant life.*
◊ *noun* **1.** The act of supporting or the condition of being supported. **2.** Someone or something that supports.
sup·port (sə **pôrt′**) ◊ *verb* **supported, supporting** ◊ *noun, plural* **supports**

suppose *verb* **1.** To be inclined to think; assume: *I suppose you're right.* **2.** To assume to be true for the sake of argument or illustration: *Suppose the earth were square instead of being round.* **3.** To expect; intend: *The spacecraft landed just as it was supposed to.*
sup·pose (sə **pōz′**) ◊ *verb* **supposed, supposing**

SYNONYMS

suppose, believe

Though I'm not sure, I *suppose* that he is telling the truth. We really *believe* that she will do what she promised.

suppress *verb* **1.** To hold back; check: *I suppressed a giggle.* **2.** To put an end to, as by force; crush: *Troops suppressed the rebellion.*
sup·press (sə **prĕs′**) ◊ *verb* **suppressed, suppressing**

supreme *adjective* **1.** Greatest in rank, power, or authority: *The monarch is the supreme ruler in that country.* **2.** Highest in degree: *This is a supreme example of bravery.*
su·preme (so͞o **prēm′**) ◊ *adjective*

Supreme Court *noun* The highest federal court of the United States, consisting of nine justices. The Supreme Court hears its cases in Washington, D.C.

▲ **Supreme Court**

sure *adjective* **1.** Feeling no doubt; certain: *I checked the spelling in the dictionary, so I'm sure it's right.* **2.** Bound to happen: *Our failure to score meant sure defeat for the team.* **3.** Steady; firm: *My grip on the railing is sure.*
sure (sho͝or) ◊ *adjective* **surer, surest**

surf *noun* **1.** The waves of the sea as they break on a shore or reef. **2.** The white foam of breaking waves.
surf (sûrf) ◊ *noun*

S

surface *noun* **1.** The outermost layer: *The surface of the moon is pitted with craters.* **2.** One of the sides of a solid object: *A cube has six surfaces.* **3.** Outward appearance: *On the surface my new neighbor seemed friendly.* ◊ *verb* **1.** To form or cover the surface of: *We surfaced the driveway with asphalt.* **2.** To rise to the surface of a liquid: *Seals surface to breathe when they are swimming.*
sur·face (sûr′fəs) ◊ *noun, plural* **surfaces** ◊ *verb* **surfaced, surfacing**

surfboard *noun* A long, flat board with rounded ends that is used for riding waves.
surf·board (**sûrf′**bôrd′) ◊ *noun, plural* **surfboards**

surge *verb* To move with gathering force, as rolling waves do: *The crowd surged forward.* ◊ *noun* **1.** A large, powerful wave. **2.** A sudden increase: *We felt a surge of excitement.*
surge (sûrj) ◊ *verb* **surged, surging** ◊ *noun, plural* **surges**

surgeon *noun* A doctor who specializes in surgery.
sur·geon (**sûr′**jən) ◊ *noun, plural* **surgeons**

surgery *noun* A branch of medicine in which injury and disease are treated by cutting into and removing or repairing parts of the body.
sur·ger·y (**sûr′**jə rē) ◊ *noun*

surmise *verb* To come to a conclusion without much evidence; suppose: *Some astronomers surmise that there is life elsewhere in the universe.*
sur·mise (sər **mīz′**) ◊ *verb* **surmised, surmising**

surmount *verb* **1.** To climb to the top of. **2.** To triumph over: *I surmounted my fear and looked down from the tower.* **3.** To be at the top: *A cross surmounts the steeple.*
sur·mount (sər **mount′**) ◊ *verb* **surmounted, surmounting**

surname *noun* A family name; last name.
sur·name (**sûr′**nām′) ◊ *noun, plural* **surnames**

ă	pat	ĭ	pit	oi	**oil**	th	**bath**
ā	pay	ī	ride	ŏŏ	**book**	*th*	**bathe**
â	care	î	fierce	ōō	**boot**	ə	**ago, item**
ä	father	ŏ	pot	ou	**out**		**pencil**
ĕ	pet	ō	**go**	ŭ	**cut**		**atom**
ē	be	ô	**paw, for**	û	**fur**		**circus**

surpass *verb* **1.** To be better, greater, or stronger than; exceed. **2.** To go beyond the limit or powers of: *The beauty of the valley surpasses description.*
sur·pass (sər **păs′**) ◊ *verb* **surpassed, surpassing**

surplus *noun* An amount or quantity greater than what is needed: *We eat most of the vegetables we grow and sell the surplus.*
sur·plus (**sûr′**plŭs′) ◊ *noun, plural* **surpluses**

surprise *verb* **1.** To come upon suddenly and without warning: *I arrived early and surprised my family.* **2.** To cause to feel astonishment: *The price of the cassette surprised me.* ◊ *noun* **1.** The act of coming upon someone or something suddenly and without warning: *The rain caught us by surprise.* **2.** Something that surprises: *The news was a surprise to me.* **3.** A feeling of astonishment.
sur·prise (sər **prīz′**) ◊ *verb* **surprised, surprising** ◊ *noun, plural* **surprises**

surrender *verb* **1.** To give up to another in response to a demand or under force: *The people surrendered the city to the invading army.* **2.** To give oneself up, as to an enemy. ◊ *noun* The act of surrendering.
sur·ren·der (sə **rĕn′**dər) ◊ *verb* **surrendered, surrendering** ◊ *noun, plural* **surrenders**

surrey *noun* A horse-drawn carriage with four wheels, two seats, and usually a fringed canopy over the seats.
sur·rey (**sûr′**ē) ◊ *noun, plural* **surreys**

▲ **surrey**

surround *verb* To be on all sides of; encircle: *Hills surround the town.*
sur·round (sə **round'**) ◊ *verb* **surrounded, surrounding**

surroundings *plural noun* The things, conditions, and circumstances that surround a person; environment.
sur·round·ings (sə **roun'**dĭngz) ◊ *plural noun*

survey *verb* **1.** To look over the parts or features of: *We surveyed the neighborhood from the roof.* **2.** To examine in order to make estimates; investigate: *The farmer surveyed the damage done by the storm.* **3.** To find out the measurements, position, boundaries, or elevation of an area of land by measuring angles and distances.
◊ *noun* **1.** A view of a broad area, field, or subject. **2.** A big investigation, as a sampling of opinions: *A survey of the voters showed that people want honest government.* **3.** The act of surveying land.
sur·vey ◊ *verb* (sər **vā'** *or* **sûr'**vā') **surveyed, surveying** ◊ *noun* (**sûr'**vā'), *plural* **surveys**

surveyor *noun* A person whose work is surveying land.
sur·vey·or (sər **vā'**ər) ◊ *noun, plural* **surveyors**

survival *noun* **1.** The act or fact of surviving. **2.** Someone or something that has survived.
sur·viv·al (sər **vī'**vəl) ◊ *noun, plural* **survivals**

survive *verb* **1.** To stay alive or in existence. **2.** To manage to live through: *Insects survive the winter by burrowing underground.* **3.** To live longer than.
sur·vive (sər **vīv'**) ◊ *verb* **survived, surviving**

survivor *noun* Someone or something that has survived.
sur·vi·vor (sər **vī'**vər) ◊ *noun, plural* **survivors**

suspect *verb* **1.** To think that someone is or may be guilty without proof. **2.** To have doubts about; distrust: *We suspected their honesty.* **3.** To believe without being sure; suppose: *I suspect they'll come.*
◊ *noun* A person suspected, as of a crime.
sus·pect ◊ *verb* (sə **spĕkt'**) **suspected, suspecting** ◊ *noun* (**sŭs'**pĕkt'), *plural* **suspects**

suspend *verb* **1.** To attach from above in order to permit free movement; hang: *We suspended the fan from the ceiling.* **2.** To stop for a time; interrupt: *We suspended our work to have lunch.* **3.** To do away with for a time: *The state suspended the restaurant's license.* **4.** To bar from a position or privilege for a time: *The principal has the authority to suspend a student.*
sus·pend (sə **spĕnd'**) ◊ *verb* **suspended, suspending**

suspenders *plural noun* A pair of supporting straps worn over the shoulders and fastened to trousers or a skirt.
sus·pend·ers (sə **spĕn'**dərz) ◊ *plural noun*

suspense *noun* Anxious uncertainty about what will happen.
sus·pense (sə **spĕns'**) ◊ *noun*

suspension *noun* **1.** The act of suspending or the condition of being suspended. **2.** The time during which someone or something is suspended.
sus·pen·sion (sə **spĕn'**shən) ◊ *noun, plural* **suspensions**

suspension bridge *noun* A bridge that is hung from cables that are stretched between supporting towers.
suspension bridge ◊ *noun, plural* **suspension bridges**

▲ **suspension bridge**

suspicion *noun* **1.** A feeling or belief that something is wrong or bad but with little evidence to support it. **2.** The condition of being suspected.
sus·pi·cion (sə **spĭsh'**ən) ◊ *noun, plural* **suspicions**

S

suspicious *adjective* **1.** Causing suspicion. **2.** Tending to suspect; distrustful. **3.** Expressing distrust.
sus·pi·cious (sə **spĭsh′** əs) ◊ *adjective*

sustain *verb* **1.** To support from below; hold or prop up: *The beams weren't strong enough to sustain the weight of the roof.* **2.** To keep up: *Choose a project that will sustain your interest.* **3.** To supply with what is needed: *Food sustains life.* **4.** To support the spirits of: *Our belief that we would be rescued sustained us.*
sus·tain (sə **stān′**) ◊ *verb* **sustained, sustaining**

S.W. *or* **SW** Abbreviations for *southwest.*

swagger *verb* To walk with a bold, proud, or defiant manner.
swag·ger (**swăg′** ər) ◊ *verb* **swaggered, swaggering**

swallow[1] *verb* **1.** To allow to pass into the stomach through the mouth and throat. **2.** To cause to disappear as if by swallowing: *The forest swallowed the hikers.* **3.** To keep from expressing; suppress: *I swallowed my nervousness.*
◊ *noun* **1.** An act of swallowing. **2.** An amount that can be swallowed at one time.
swal·low[1] (**swŏl′** ō) ◊ *verb* **swallowed, swallowing** ◊ *noun, plural* **swallows**

swallow[2] *noun* A bird with narrow, pointed wings and a forked or notched tail.
swal·low[2] (**swŏl′** ō) ◊ *noun, plural* **swallows**

> ***HISTORY* • swallow[1], swallow[2]**
>
> **Swallow[1]** comes from an old English word with much the same meaning that it has today. **Swallow[2]** comes from the old English name for this bird.

swam *verb* Past tense of **swim.**
swam (swăm) ◊ *verb*

swamp *noun* An area of spongy, muddy land that is often filled with water.
◊ *verb* **1.** To fill with or sink in water: *The stormy seas swamped our boat.* **2.** To burden or overwhelm: *My homework swamped me.*
swamp (swŏmp) ◊ *noun, plural* **swamps** ◊ *verb* **swamped, swamping**

swampy *adjective* Of or like a swamp.
swamp·y (**swŏm′** pē) ◊ *adjective* **swampier, swampiest**

swan *noun* A large, usually white water bird with webbed feet and a long, slender neck.
swan (swŏn) ◊ *noun, plural* **swans**

swap *verb* To trade or exchange.
◊ *noun* A trade or exchange.
swap (swŏp) ◊ *verb* **swapped, swapping** ◊ *noun, plural* **swaps**

swarm *noun* **1.** A large number of people, insects, or things, especially in motion. **2.** A large group of bees moving together from a hive to start a new colony.
◊ *verb* **1.** To form or move in or as if in a swarm. **2.** To be filled; teem: *The lake is swarming with fish.*
swarm (swôrm) ◊ *noun, plural* **swarms** ◊ *verb* **swarmed, swarming**

swat *verb* To hit sharply with a quick blow.
swat (swŏt) ◊ *verb* **swatted, swatting**

sway *verb* **1.** To swing or cause to swing back and forth or from side to side: *The willow trees were swaying in the wind.* **2.** To cause to change the thinking of; influence: *The candidate's promises swayed the voters.*
◊ *noun* **1.** The action or an example of swinging or being swung from side to side. **2.** A ruling influence or power: *The country was under the sway of a dictator.*
sway (swā) ◊ *verb* **swayed, swaying** ◊ *noun, plural* **sways**

swear *verb* **1.** To say or promise under oath; vow: *I solemnly swear to tell the truth.* **2.** To put under an obligation by means of an oath: *They swore us to secrecy.* **3.** To use bad language; curse.
swear (swâr) ◊ *verb* **swore, sworn, swearing**

sweat *verb* **1.** To give off salty liquid through pores in the skin; perspire. **2.** To form water in small drops on a surface, as on a pipe.
◊ *noun* **1.** The salty liquid given off in sweating; perspiration. **2.** A condition of sweating.
sweat (swĕt) ◊ *verb* **sweated** *or* **sweat, sweating** ◊ *noun*

ă pat	ĭ pit	oi **oil**	th ba**th**
ā pay	ī ride	o͝o **book**	*th* ba**th**e
â care	î fierce	o͞o **boot**	ə **a**go, it**e**m
ä father	ŏ **pot**	ou **out**	penc**i**l
ĕ pet	ō **go**	ŭ cut	at**o**m
ē be	ô paw, for	û fur	circ**u**s

sweater *noun* A knitted outer garment worn on the upper part of the body.
sweat·er (swĕt′ər) ◊ *noun, plural* **sweaters**

Swede *noun* A person who was born in or lives in Sweden.
Swede (swēd) ◊ *noun, plural* **Swedes**

Swedish *noun* The language of the Swedes.
◊ *adjective* Of or relating to Sweden, the Swedes, or their language.
Swed·ish (swē′dĭsh) ◊ *noun* ◊ *adjective*

sweep *verb* **1.** To clean with a broom or brush: *The janitor swept the hallway.* **2.** To clear away with a broom or brush: *My job was to sweep up litter.* **3.** To move or carry forcefully: *Flood waters swept away many bridges.* **4.** To move or flow with steady force: *A cold wind swept through the north.* **5.** To range throughout: *A flu epidemic is sweeping the city.* **6.** To touch or brush lightly: *Willow branches swept the river's surface.* **7.** To move or pass over a wide extent: *The searchlight swept the deserted beach.*
◊ *noun* **1.** An act or example of sweeping. **2.** A sweeping motion or course. **3.** The range or area covered by sweeping: *The object was outside the sweep of the radar equipment.* **4.** An extent of space: *There was a sweep of glistening snow on the hillside.*
sweep (swēp) ◊ *verb* **swept, sweeping**
◊ *noun, plural* **sweeps**

sweet *adjective* **1.** Having a pleasing taste like that of sugar. **2.** Not salted: *Sweet butter is delicious.* **3.** Not spoiled: *This milk is still sweet.* **4.** Having a pleasant smell. **5.** Pleasing to the eye, ear, feelings, or mind. **6.** Easy to love; gentle and kind: *You have a sweet disposition.*
◊ *noun* Something that tastes sweet.
sweet (swēt) ◊ *adjective* **sweeter, sweetest**
◊ *noun, plural* **sweets**
‖ *These sound alike:* **sweet, suite**

sweeten *verb* To make or become sweet or sweeter.
sweet·en (swēt′n) ◊ *verb* **sweetened, sweetening**

sweetener *noun* A substance that is added to food or drink to sweeten it.
sweet·en·er (swēt′n ər) ◊ *noun, plural* **sweeteners**

sweetheart *noun* **1.** A person whom one loves. **2.** A lovable person.
sweet·heart (swēt′härt′) ◊ *noun, plural* **sweethearts**

sweetmeat *noun* A piece of candy or other sweet delicacy.
sweet·meat (swēt′mēt′) ◊ *noun, plural* **sweetmeats**

sweet pea *noun* A climbing plant with fragrant, variously colored flowers.
sweet pea ◊ *noun, plural* **sweet peas**

▲ **sweet pea**

sweet potato *noun* The thick, sweet yellowish or reddish root of a tropical vine that is cooked and eaten as a vegetable.
sweet potato ◊ *noun, plural* **sweet potatoes**

swell *verb* **1.** To increase in size or volume as a result of pressure from the inside; expand: *The injured ankle swelled.* **2.** To cause to bulge: *A brisk wind swelled the sails.*
◊ *noun* **1.** The act or process of becoming larger. **2.** A long rolling wave in open water.
◊ *adjective* Fine; excellent.
swell (swĕl) ◊ *verb* **swelled, swelled** *or* **swollen, swelling** ◊ *noun, plural* **swells**
◊ *adjective* **sweller, swellest**

swelling *noun* A part that is swollen.
swell·ing (swĕl′ĭng) ◊ *noun, plural* **swellings**

swept *verb* Past tense and past participle of **sweep.**
swept (swĕpt) ◊ *verb*

swerve *verb* To turn aside suddenly from a straight course: *I swerved my bicycle to avoid hitting the dog.*
swerve (swûrv) ◊ *verb* **swerved, swerving**

swift *adjective* **1.** Moving or able to move very fast. **2.** Happening or done quickly: *I gave a swift answer.*
◊ *noun* A gray or blackish bird with long, narrow wings that often nests in chimneys.
swift (swĭft) ◊ *adjective* **swifter, swiftest**
◊ *noun, plural* **swifts**

swim *verb* **1.** To move through water by moving the arms, legs, or fins. **2.** To go across by swimming: *The horses swam the river.*

S

3. To float on or be covered with liquid.
◊ *noun* The act or a period of swimming.
swim (swĭm) ◊ *verb* **swam, swum, swimming** ◊ *noun, plural* **swims**

swindle *verb* To cheat of money or property.
◊ *noun* A dishonest act or scheme.
swin·dle (**swĭn′**dl) ◊ *verb* **swindled, swindling** ◊ *noun, plural* **swindles**

swine *noun* A pig or hog.
swine (swīn) ◊ *noun, plural* **swine**

swing *verb* **1.** To move or cause to move back and forth: *I swung my keys on a chain.* **2.** To turn or cause to turn on a hinge or pivot: *The door swung shut.* **3.** To move or cause to move in a sweeping curve: *I swung the bat.*
◊ *noun* **1.** An act of swinging. **2.** A swinging movement or rhythm. **3.** The distance traveled by something that swings. **4.** A suspended seat on which a person can ride back and forth for amusement.
swing (swĭng) ◊ *verb* **swung, swinging** ◊ *noun, plural* **swings**

▲ **swing**

swirl *verb* To move with a rotating motion; whirl or spin: *The wind swirled the snow.*
◊ *noun* **1.** The motion of whirling or spinning. **2.** Something that swirls, as a whirlpool.
swirl (swûrl) ◊ *verb* **swirled, swirling** ◊ *noun, plural* **swirls**

ă	pat	ĭ	pit	oi	**oi**l	th	ba**th**
ā	pay	ī	ride	o͝o	b**oo**k	*th*	ba**th**e
â	care	î	fierce	o͞o	b**oo**t	ə	**a**go, it**e**m
ä	father	ŏ	pot	ou	**ou**t		penc**i**l
ĕ	pet	ō	go	ŭ	c**u**t		at**o**m
ē	be	ô	paw, for	û	f**u**r		circ**u**s

swish *verb* To move with a soft hissing or rustling sound.
◊ *noun* **1.** A hissing or rustling sound. **2.** A swishing movement.
swish (swĭsh) ◊ *verb* **swished, swishing** ◊ *noun, plural* **swishes**

Swiss *noun* A person who was born in or lives in Switzerland.
◊ *adjective* Of or relating to Switzerland or the Swiss.
Swiss (swĭs) ◊ *noun, plural* **Swiss** ◊ *adjective*

switch *noun* **1.** A slender flexible rod or stick. **2.** A whipping or a blow given with a switch. **3.** A stroke or lash: *A horse drives off flies with a switch of its tail.* **4.** A device for opening or closing an electric circuit. **5.** A device for shifting a train or streetcar from one track to another. **6.** A change or shift from one thing to another: *There was a sudden switch in our plans.*
◊ *verb* **1.** To strike or whip with or as if with a switch. **2.** To move quickly from side to side: *The cat switched its tail.* **3.** To change or shift: *They switched the conversation to the weather.* **4.** To control by operating a switch: *Please switch on the television.*
switch (swĭch) ◊ *noun, plural* **switches** ◊ *verb* **switched, switching**

switchboard *noun* One or more panels that contain switches for controlling electric or telephone circuits.
switch·board (**swĭch′**bôrd′) ◊ *noun, plural* **switchboards**

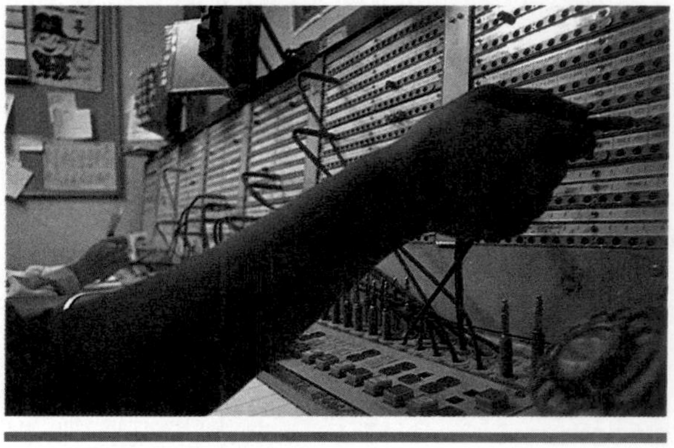

▲ **switchboard**

swivel *noun* A device that joins two parts in a way that allows either part to turn freely.
◊ *verb* To turn on or as if on a swivel.
swiv·el (**swĭv′**əl) ◊ *noun, plural* **swivels**
◊ *verb* **swiveled, swiveling**

swollen *verb* A past participle of **swell.**
swol·len (**swō′**lən) ◊ *verb*

swoon *verb* To faint.
◊ *noun* A faint.
swoon (swo͞on) ◊ *verb* **swooned, swooning**
◊ *noun, plural* **swoons**

swoop *verb* To move or attack with a sudden sweeping motion: *The owl swooped down and caught the mouse.*
◊ *noun* The act or an example of swooping.
swoop (swo͞op) ◊ *verb* **swooped, swooping**
◊ *noun, plural* **swoops**

sword *noun* A weapon having a long, pointed blade set in a handle or hilt.
sword (sôrd) ◊ *noun, plural* **swords**

swordfish *noun* A very large ocean food fish having a swordlike bone sticking out from the upper jaw.
sword·fish (**sôrd′**fĭsh′) ◊ *noun, plural* **swordfish** *or* **swordfishes**

▲ **swordfish**

swordtail *noun* A small tropical freshwater fish that has a long, narrow point extending from the tail fin. Swordtails are often kept in home aquariums.
sword·tail (**sôrd′**tāl′) ◊ *noun, plural* **swordtail** *or* **swordtails**

swore *verb* Past tense of **swear.**
swore (swôr) ◊ *verb*

sworn *verb* Past participle of **swear.**
sworn (swôrn) ◊ *verb*

swum *verb* Past participle of **swim.**
swum (swŭm) ◊ *verb*

swung *verb* Past tense and past participle of **swing.**
swung (swŭng) ◊ *verb*

sycamore *noun* A North American tree that has ball-shaped seed clusters and bark that often flakes off in large pieces.
syc·a·more (**sĭk′**ə môr) ◊ *noun, plural* **sycamores**

syllabicate *verb* To divide into syllables.
syl·lab·i·cate (sĭ **lăb′**ə kāt′) ◊ *verb* **syllabicated, syllabicating**

syllabication *noun* The act of syllabicating or the condition of being syllabicated.
syl·lab·i·ca·tion (sĭ lăb′ĭ **kā′**shən) ◊ *noun*

syllabify *verb* To syllabicate.
syl·lab·i·fy (sĭ **lăb′**ə fī′) ◊ *verb* **syllabified, syllabifying**

syllable *noun* **1.** A word or part of a word that is pronounced as a single sound. The word *ditch* has one syllable and *native* has two. **2.** A letter or group of letters used to represent a syllable. A word is divided into syllables in this dictionary with centered dots as in **syl·la·ble.** In writing or printing, a hyphen is used to divide words according to syllables at the end of a line.
syl·la·ble (**sĭl′**ə bəl) ◊ *noun, plural* **syllables**

symbiosis *noun* The relationship of two or more different organisms that live in close association. Symbiosis is often to the advantage of each of the organisms.
sym·bi·o·sis (sĭm′bī **ō′**sĭs) ◊ *noun*

symbol *noun* **1.** Something that stands for or represents something else: *The dove is a symbol of peace.* **2.** A printed or written sign used instead of a word to represent a quantity, direction, relationship, or something to be done.
sym·bol (**sĭm′**bəl) ◊ *noun, plural* **symbols**
‖*These sound alike:* **symbol, cymbal**

symbolic *adjective* Of or being a symbol.
sym·bol·ic (sĭm **bŏl′**ĭk) ◊ *adjective*

symbolize *verb* To serve as a symbol of: *The poet used rain to symbolize sorrow.*
sym·bol·ize (**sĭm′**bə līz′) ◊ *verb* **symbolized, symbolizing**

symmetric *or* **symmetrical** *adjective* Having or showing symmetry.
sym·met·ric (sĭ **mĕt′**rĭk) *or* **sym·met·ri·cal** (sĭ **mĕt′**rĭ kəl) ◊ *adjective*

S

symmetry *noun* **1.** An exact matching of parts on opposite sides of a dividing line or around a central point. **2.** A balanced arrangement of parts.
sym·me·try (sĭm′ĭ trē) ◊ *noun, plural* **symmetries**

▲ **symmetry**

sympathetic *adjective* **1.** Feeling or showing sympathy: *Some sympathetic friends visited me in the hospital.* **2.** Favorable; agreeable: *We were sympathetic to their plan.*
sym·pa·thet·ic (sĭm′pə **thĕt′**ĭk) ◊ *adjective*

sympathize *verb* **1.** To feel or show sympathy: *We sympathized with our classmate whose dog had died.* **2.** To be in favor of another's feelings or ideas: *Our parents sympathize with our ambitions.*
sym·pa·thize (**sĭm′**pə thīz′) ◊ *verb* **sympathized, sympathizing**

sympathy *noun* **1.** A feeling or expression of pity or sorrow for the distress of another. **2.** Favor; agreement: *We are in sympathy with their beliefs.*
sym·pa·thy (**sĭm′**pə thē) ◊ *noun, plural* **sympathies**

ă	pat	ĭ	pit	oi	**oil**	th	**bath**
ā	pay	ī	ride	ŏŏ	**book**	*th*	**bathe**
â	care	î	fierce	ōō	**boot**	ə	**ago, item**
ä	father	ŏ	pot	ou	**out**		pencil
ĕ	pet	ō	go	ŭ	**cut**		atom
ē	be	ô	paw, for	û	**fur**		circus

symphony *noun* **1.** A usually long piece of music for a large orchestra. **2.** A large orchestra with string, wind, and percussion sections.
sym·pho·ny (**sĭm′**fə nē) ◊ *noun, plural* **symphonies**

symptom *noun* **1.** A change in the body that is usually a sign of illness or disease. —See Synonyms at **sign. 2.** A sign or indication: *Yawning can be a symptom of boredom.*
symp·tom (**sĭmp′**təm) ◊ *noun, plural* **symptoms**

synagogue *noun* A Jewish place of worship.
syn·a·gogue (**sĭn′**ə gŏg′) ◊ *noun, plural* **synagogues**

synonym *noun* A word with the same or nearly the same meaning as another word: *The word "wide" is a synonym for "broad."*
syn·o·nym (**sĭn′**ə nĭm) ◊ *noun, plural* **synonyms**

synonymous *adjective* Being the same or almost the same in meaning.
syn·on·y·mous (sĭ **nŏn′**ə məs) ◊ *adjective*

synonymy *noun* **1.** The condition or quality of being synonymous. **2.** A list, book, or system of synonyms.
syn·on·o·my (sĭ **nŏn′**ə mē) ◊ *noun, plural* **synonomies**

synthetic *adjective* Made by people rather than found in nature.
◊ *noun* A synthetic material.
syn·thet·ic (sĭn **thĕt′**ĭk) ◊ *adjective* ◊ *noun, plural* **synthetics**

syrup *noun* **1.** A thick, sweet liquid, as that made by boiling sugar and water. **2.** The sap of a tree or plant that is boiled down.
syr·up (**sûr′**əp *or* **sĭr′**əp) ◊ *noun, plural* **syrups**

system *noun* **1.** A set of parts moving or working together as a unit: *Radiators and a furnace are parts of the heating system of a house.* **2.** A group of bodily organs or parts, such as the digestive system, that work together. **3.** An organized plan or method, as of government. **4.** An orderly way of doing something: *I have a system for washing dishes fast.*
sys·tem (**sĭs′**təm) ◊ *noun, plural* **systems**

systematic *adjective* Showing or acting according to a system: *You are a systematic worker.*
sys·tem·at·ic (sĭs′tə **măt′**ĭk) ◊ *adjective*

Turtle

Tt

T is the twentieth letter of the English alphabet. Did you know that it has a long history?

Over 3,500 years ago, people in the Middle East were using symbols that became the letters of our alphabet. This ancient Middle Eastern symbol is a form of the letter that became our letter *T*.

The ancient Greeks borrowed their alphabet from people in the Middle East. Here is a form of the Greek letter that became our letter *T*.

The ancient Romans borrowed their alphabet from a people who had taken their own letter symbols from the Greeks. Here is a form of the Roman letter *T* that was used for carving letters into stone. These letters became the model for our printed capital letters.

As people wrote quickly, especially with pens, the capital letters began to take the shapes of small letters. Here is a small-letter *t* that was used in the Middle Ages.

Tt *Tt*	Tt	Tt	Tt
Handwriting	Sans Serif Type	Serif Type	Computer Printing

t *or* **T** *noun* The twentieth letter of the English alphabet.
t *or* **T** (tē) ◊ *noun, plural* **t's** *or* **T's**

tab *noun* A small flap that is attached to something for pulling, opening, or labeling it.
tab (tăb) ◊ *noun, plural* **tabs**

table *noun* **1.** A piece of furniture that has legs and a flat top. **2.** The food that is served at a meal or the people who are gathered to eat it. **3.** A list of facts or information: *The table of contents lists the chapters in the book.*
ta·ble (tā′bəl) ◊ *noun, plural* **tables**

tablecloth *noun* A cloth to cover a table.
ta·ble·cloth (tā′bəl klôth′) ◊ *noun, plural* **tablecloths**

tablespoon *noun* **1.** A large spoon used for serving food. **2.** A unit used in cooking, equal to three teaspoons or ½ fluid ounce.
ta·ble·spoon (tā′bəl spo͞on′) ◊ *noun, plural* **tablespoons**

tablet *noun* **1.** A thin slab or sheet, as of stone or clay, used for writing or drawing. **2.** A pad of writing paper glued together along one edge. **3.** A small, flat piece of medicine.
tab·let (tăb′lĭt) ◊ *noun, plural* **tablets**

table tennis *noun* A game played on a table with wooden paddles and a small plastic ball that is hit back and forth over a low net.

tack *noun* **1.** A small nail with a sharp point and a flat head. **2.** A change in the direction of a sailing ship. **3.** A course of action: *We're not succeeding, so let's try a new tack.*
◊ *verb* **1.** To fasten with tacks. **2.** To add as an extra item: *The desk clerk tacked $10.00 onto our bill.* **3.** To sail in a zigzag course.
tack (tăk) ◊ *noun, plural* **tacks** ◊ *verb* **tacked, tacking**

tackle *noun* **1.** A set of equipment for a certain use, as in fishing; gear. **2.** A system of ropes and pulleys for lifting or moving. **3.** An act of tackling, especially in football.
◊ *verb* **1.** To begin to deal with: *Let's tackle the hardest job first.* **2.** To grab hold of and throw a person to the ground.
tack·le (tăk′əl) ◊ *noun, plural* **tackles** ◊ *verb* **tackled, tackling**

tact *noun* The ability to say or do the right thing so as not to hurt a person's feelings.
tact (tăkt) ◊ *noun*

tactic *noun* **1. tactics** (*used with a singular or plural verb*) The science of using military or naval forces to the best advantage. **2.** A method for achieving a goal.
tac·tic (**tăk′**tĭk) ◊ *noun, plural* **tactics**

tadpole *noun* A newly hatched frog or toad that lives in water and has a tail and gills.
tad·pole (**tăd′**pōl′) ◊ *noun, plural* **tadpoles**

▲ **tadpole**

taffy *noun* A chewy candy made from molasses or brown sugar boiled very thick.
taf·fy (**tăf′**ē) ◊ *noun, plural* **taffies**

tag[1] *noun* A small strip or tab attached to something else: *The price tag on the jacket says $20.00.*
◊ *verb* **1.** To label with or as if with a tag. **2.** To follow closely and constantly: *Our dog tags along wherever we go.*
tag[1] (tăg) ◊ *noun, plural* **tags** ◊ *verb* **tagged, tagging**

tag[2] *noun* A game in which a player who is called "it" chases the other players in order to touch one of them, who then becomes "it."
◊ *verb* To touch another person, as in putting out a runner in baseball.
tag[2] (tăg) ◊ *noun* ◊ *verb* **tagged, tagging**

ă	pat	ĭ	pit	oi	**oil**	th	ba**th**
ā	pay	ī	ride	o͝o	**book**	*th*	ba**the**
â	care	î	fierce	o͞o	**boot**	ə	ago, item
ä	father	ŏ	pot	ou	**out**		pencil
ĕ	pet	ō	**go**	ŭ	cut		atom
ē	be	ô	paw, for	û	fur		circus

***HISTORY* • tag[1], tag[2]**

Tag[1] first appeared in written English about 600 years ago, when it meant "a dangling piece of cloth." The origin of **tag**[2] is not known for certain.

tail *noun* **1.** A slender part that sticks out from the rear of an animal's body. **2.** The rear, last, or bottom part of something. **3.** Something that looks, hangs, or trails like an animal's tail. **4. tails** (*used with a singular or plural verb*) The side opposite the head of a coin.
◊ *verb* To follow closely in order to watch.
tail (tāl) ◊ *noun, plural* **tails** ◊ *verb* **tailed, tailing**
‖*These sound alike:* **tail, tale**

tailor *noun* A person who makes, repairs, or alters clothing.
◊ *verb* To make, repair, or alter clothing.
tai·lor (**tā′**lər) ◊ *noun, plural* **tailors** ◊ *verb* **tailored, tailoring**

take *verb* **1.** To grasp with the hands; hold: *We took the brushes and started to paint.* **2.** To capture, seize, or win. **3.** To get possession or use of. **4.** To carry along with one: *Take the book back to the library.* **5.** To accept into one's body: *Take a deep breath.* **6.** To accept as one's own: *They took all the credit.* **7.** To get by winning: *Our team took the trophy.* **8.** To come upon: *We were taken by surprise.* **9.** To charm; captivate. **10.** To perform the action of: *I took a bath.* **11.** To require or need: *What size do you take?* **12.** To use: *We'll take a bus.* **13.** To occupy: *Please take a seat.* **14.** To pick out; select. **15.** To make; do: *I took notes during the lecture.* **16.** To accept or endure: *The teacher won't take any nonsense.* **17.** To undergo: *The team took a beating.* **18.** To react to; receive: *How did they take the bad news?* **19.** To accept or believe as true; assume: *I take it you don't agree.* **20.** To subtract: *Take four from seven.* **21.** To obtain by a certain method: *The doctor took the patient's temperature.* **22.** To become affected: *I took sick at school.*
◊ *idioms* **take after** To look like; resemble. **take back** To withdraw, as something said or written. **take in** To understand: *They took in*

the situation right away. **take off 1.** To remove, as clothing. **2.** To rise up in flight, as an airplane. **take out 1.** To remove. **2.** To have a date with. **take up 1.** To shorten: *Can you take up this hem?* **2.** To start or start again: *Let's take up where we left off.*
take (tāk) ◊ *verb* **took, taken, taking**

taken *verb* Past participle of **take.**
tak·en (tā′kən) ◊ *verb*

takeoff *noun* An act of rising up in flight.
take·off (tāk′ôf′) ◊ *noun, plural* **takeoffs**

tale *noun* A story, usually an imaginary or made-up one.
tale (tāl) ◊ *noun, plural* **tales**
‖*These sound alike:* **tale, tail**

talent *noun* **1.** A natural ability to do something well: *If you give up music, you'll waste your talent.* —See Synonyms at **ability. 2.** A person with talent.
tal·ent (tăl′ənt) ◊ *noun, plural* **talents**

talented *adjective* Having talent; gifted.
tal·ent·ed (tăl′ən tĭd) ◊ *adjective*

talk *verb* **1.** To say words. —See Synonyms at **speak. 2.** To communicate by a means other than speech: *They talked with sign language.* **3.** To have a conversation; converse. **4.** To speak of; discuss: *Let's not talk politics.* **5.** To influence by speech: *They tried to talk me into hiking 12 miles on a hot day.*
◊ *noun* **1.** The act of talking; conversation. **2.** An informal speech.
talk (tôk) ◊ *verb* **talked, talking** ◊ *noun, plural* **talks**

talkative *adjective* Tending to talk a lot.
talk·a·tive (tô′kə tĭv) ◊ *adjective*

talking-to *noun* A scolding.
talk·ing-to (tô′kĭng to͞o′) ◊ *noun, plural* **talking-tos**

tall *adjective* **1.** Having greater than ordinary height. **2.** Having a stated height: *Our plant grew to be three feet tall.* **3.** Made up and often exaggerated: *Don't tell tall stories.*
tall (tôl) ◊ *adjective* **taller, tallest**

tallow *noun* A solid substance made from melted and mixed animal fats. Tallow is used to make candles and soap.
tal·low (tăl′ō) ◊ *noun*

talon *noun* The claw of a bird, such as an eagle or falcon, that hunts and catches other animals.
tal·on (tăl′ən) ◊ *noun, plural* **talons**

tambourine *noun* A small drum with jingling metal disks around the rim.
tam·bou·rine (tăm′bə-rēn′) ◊ *noun, plural* **tambourines**

▲ **tambourine**

tame *adjective* **1.** Accustomed to living with or trained to live with human beings: *We had a tame deer in our yard.* **2.** Not fierce, dangerous, or timid: *The raccoons were so tame that they let us pet them.*
◊ *verb* To make or become tame: *The children caught and tamed a rabbit.*
tame (tām) ◊ *adjective* **tamer, tamest** ◊ *verb* **tamed, taming**

tamper *verb* To handle carelessly; meddle: *Please don't tamper with the clock radio.*
tam·per (tăm′pər) ◊ *verb* **tampered, tampering**

tan *verb* **1.** To convert animal hide into leather by soaking it in certain chemicals. **2.** To make or become brown from the sun.
◊ *noun* **1.** A light yellowish brown color. **2.** The brown color of the skin that results from exposing it to the sun.
◊ *adjective* Of the color tan.
tan (tăn) ◊ *verb* **tanned, tanning** ◊ *noun, plural* **tans** ◊ *adjective* **tanner, tannest**

tang *noun* A sharp, strong flavor or taste.
tang (tăng) ◊ *noun, plural* **tangs**

tangerine *noun* A fruit that is like an orange but is smaller and peels more easily.
tan·ger·ine (tăn′jə rēn′) ◊ *noun, plural* **tangerines**

tangle *verb* To mix or become mixed together in a confused or twisted mass or state; snarl.
◊ *noun* **1.** A confused, snarled mass. **2.** A confused state or condition.
tan·gle (tăng′gəl) ◊ *verb* **tangled, tangling** ◊ *noun, plural* **tangles**

tank *noun* **1.** A large container for holding or storing liquids: *Trucks have gas tanks.* **2.** An armored combat vehicle that has guns and moves on continuous metal belts.
tank (tăngk) ◊ *noun, plural* **tanks**

tanker *noun* A ship, truck, or airplane that is equipped with tanks for carrying liquids.
tank·er (**tăng'** kər) ◊ *noun, plural* **tankers**

tantrum *noun* An outburst of bad temper.
tan·trum (**tăn'** trəm) ◊ *noun, plural* **tantrums**

tap[1] *verb* **1.** To strike gently with a light blow: *I tapped my friend on the shoulder.* **2.** To imitate or produce with light blows.
◊ *noun* A light blow or its sound.
tap[1] (tăp) ◊ *verb* **tapped, tapping** ◊ *noun, plural* **taps**

tap[2] *noun* A valve and spout for controlling the flow of a fluid at the end of a pipe; faucet.
◊ *verb* **1.** To pierce so as to draw off a liquid: *The farmer tapped the maple trees for their sap.* **2.** To make a connection into a telephone wire in order to listen secretly.
tap[2] (tăp) ◊ *noun, plural* **taps** ◊ *verb* **tapped, tapping**

> ***HISTORY* • tap[1], tap[2]**
>
> **Tap**[1] comes from an old French word that was probably made up to imitate the sound it describes. **Tap**[2] comes from an old English word for a kind of spout.

tape *noun* **1.** A long, narrow strip of material, such as cloth or paper, used especially for sealing or fastening. **2.** A long, narrow band of specially treated plastic on which sounds or images can be recorded.
◊ *verb* **1.** To fasten, wrap, or bind with tape. **2.** To record on tape: *I taped the TV show.*
tape (tāp) ◊ *noun, plural* **tapes** ◊ *verb* **taped, taping**

tape measure *noun* A tape that is marked off in units and is used for measuring length.
tape measure ◊ *noun, plural* **tape measures**

taper *noun* **1.** A gradual decrease in thickness or width in a long object. **2.** A thin candle.
◊ *verb* **1.** To make or become gradually thinner. **2.** To become slowly smaller or less.
ta·per (**tā'** pər) ◊ *noun, plural* **tapers** ◊ *verb* **tapered, tapering**
‖*These sound alike:* **taper, tapir**

tape recorder *noun* A device that records sound or electrical signals on specially treated tape and can usually play back the recording.
tape recorder ◊ *noun, plural* **tape recorders**

tapestry *noun* A rich, heavy cloth with designs and scenes woven into it. A tapestry is hung on a wall or is used to cover furniture.
tap·es·try (**tăp'** ĭ strē) ◊ *noun, plural* **tapestries**

tapeworm *noun* A long, flat, ribbonlike worm that lives as a parasite in the intestines of human beings and other animals.
tape·worm (**tāp'** wûrm') ◊ *noun, plural* **tapeworms**

tapioca *noun* A starch that is gotten from the root of a tropical plant and is used in puddings.
tap·i·o·ca (tăp'ē **ō'** kə) ◊ *noun*

tapir *noun* A tropical animal of America and Asia that has a heavy body, short legs, and a long, fleshy snout.
ta·pir (**tā'** pər) ◊ *noun, plural* **tapirs**
‖*These sound alike:* **tapir, taper**

taps *noun* (*used with a singular or plural verb*) A bugle call played at night as a signal to put out lights or at military funerals.
taps (tăps) ◊ *noun, plural* **taps**

tar *noun* A thick, oily, dark mixture made from wood, coal, or peat.
◊ *verb* To coat or cover with tar.
tar (tär) ◊ *noun* ◊ *verb* **tarred, tarring**

tarantula *noun* A large, hairy spider. Its bite is painful but not seriously poisonous.
ta·ran·tu·la (tə **răn'** chə lə) ◊ *noun, plural* **tarantulas**

▲ **tarantula**

tardy *adjective* Arriving, coming, or happening after the expected time.
tar·dy (**tär'** dē) ◊ *adjective* **tardier, tardiest**

target *noun* **1.** Something, such as a mark, circle, or an object, that is aimed or shot

ă	pat	ĭ	pit	oi	**oil**	th	**bath**
ā	pay	ī	ride	o͝o	**book**	*th*	**bathe**
â	care	î	fierce	o͞o	**boot**	ə	**ago, item**
ä	father	ŏ	pot	ou	**out**		**pencil**
ĕ	pet	ō	go	ŭ	**cut**		**atom**
ē	be	ô	paw, for	û	**fur**		**circus**

at. **2.** Someone or something that is criticized or laughed at. **3.** A goal or aim.
tar·get (tär′ gĭt) ◊ *noun, plural* **targets**

tariff *noun* A tax or duty that a government places on imported or exported goods.
tar·iff (tăr′ ĭf) ◊ *noun, plural* **tariffs**

tarnish *verb* To lose or cause to lose luster or color, as from being exposed to air or dirt.
◊ *noun* A coating formed on a surface, as of silver, when it is exposed to air or dirt.
tar·nish (tär′ nĭsh) ◊ *verb* **tarnished, tarnishing** ◊ *noun*

tarp *noun* A tarpaulin.
tarp (tärp) ◊ *noun, plural* **tarps**

tarpaulin *noun* A covering of waterproof canvas used to protect something outdoors.
tar·pau·lin (tär **pô′** lĭn) ◊ *noun, plural* **tarpaulins**

tart[1] *adjective* Having a sharp, sour, or acid taste: *I ate a tart green apple.*
tart[1] (tärt) ◊ *adjective* **tarter, tartest**

tart[2] *noun* A small, fruit-filled pie or pastry.
tart[2] (tärt) ◊ *noun, plural* **tarts**

***HISTORY* • tart[1], tart[2]**

Tart[1] comes from an old English word that meant "sharp to the taste." **Tart[2]** comes from the old French name for this kind of pastry.

tartan *noun* **1.** A fabric woven with stripes of different colors and widths that cross. Tartan was first made in Scotland. **2.** The design or pattern of a tartan.
tar·tan (tär′ tn) ◊ *noun, plural* **tartans**

tartar *noun* A hard yellowish substance that forms on the teeth and that consists of food particles, saliva, and calcium.
tar·tar (tär′ tər) ◊ *noun*

task *noun* A piece of work to be done.
task (tăsk) ◊ *noun, plural* **tasks**

SYNONYMS

task, assignment, chore, job

My *task* is to fill out all these forms. The teacher gave her the *assignment.* His *chore* is to do the dishes every day. I have a baby-sitting *job* today.

tassel *noun* **1.** A bunch of loose threads or cords bound at one end and hanging free at the other. Tassels are used as ornaments, as on curtains. **2.** Something that is like a tassel.
tas·sel (tăs′ əl) ◊ *noun, plural* **tassels**

taste *noun* **1.** The sense that picks up the difference between the sweet, sour, salty, or bitter flavors of things placed in the mouth. **2.** A sensation produced by a substance taken into the mouth; flavor: *The toothpaste has a pleasant taste.* **3.** A small amount; sample. **4.** A personal preference or liking: *It's a pretty color but not to my taste.* **5.** The ability to know, choose, and appreciate what is good or beautiful: *My cousin has good taste in clothes.*
◊ *verb* **1.** To tell the flavor of by taking into the mouth. **2.** To have a flavor: *Cider tastes sweet.* **3.** To take a small amount of: *You hardly tasted your supper.*
taste (tāst) ◊ *noun, plural* **tastes** ◊ *verb* **tasted, tasting**

tasteless *adjective* **1.** Having little or no flavor: *Oxygen is a tasteless gas.* **2.** Showing or having poor taste: *That remark you made was untactful and even tasteless.*
taste·less (tāst′ lĭs) ◊ *adjective*

tasty *adjective* Pleasing in taste.
tast·y (tā′ stē) ◊ *adjective* **tastier, tastiest**

tatter *noun* **1.** A torn and hanging piece, as of cloth; shred. **2. tatters** Ragged clothing.
tat·ter (tăt′ ər) ◊ *noun, plural* **tatters**

tattle *verb* To tell someone else's secrets.
tat·tle (tăt′ l) ◊ *verb* **tattled, tattling**

tattletale *noun* A person who tattles.
tat·tle·tale (tăt′ l tāl′) ◊ *noun, plural* **tattletales**

taught *verb* Past tense and past participle of **teach.**
taught (tôt) ◊ *verb*
‖*These sound alike:* **taught, taut**

taunt *verb* To say mean or insulting things to; mock.
◊ *noun* A mean or insulting remark.
taunt (tônt) ◊ *verb* **taunted, taunting** ◊ *noun, plural* **taunts**

taut *adjective* Pulled or drawn tight: *Tie a knot so that the rope will be taut.*
taut (tôt) ◊ *adjective* **tauter, tautest**
‖*These sound alike:* **taut, taught**

tavern *noun* An inn.
tav·ern (tăv′ ərn) ◊ *noun, plural* **taverns**

T

tax *noun* **1.** Money that people or businesses must pay in order to support a government. **2.** A heavy demand; strain or burden.
◊ *verb* **1.** To place a tax on: *The state taxes our income.* **2.** To require a tax from: *The city taxes property owners.* **3.** To make a heavy demand on: *The delay in traffic taxed my patience.*
tax (tăks) ◊ *noun, plural* **taxes** ◊ *verb* **taxed, taxing**

taxation *noun* The act of imposing taxes.
tax·a·tion (tăk **sā′** shən) ◊ *noun*

taxi *noun* A taxicab.
◊ *verb* **1.** To ride in a taxicab. **2.** To move slowly along the ground before taking off or after landing, as an aircraft does.
tax·i (**tăk′** sē) ◊ *noun, plural* **taxis** ◊ *verb* **taxied, taxiing**

taxicab *noun* An automobile that carries passengers wherever they want to go for a fare.
tax·i·cab (**tăk′** sē kăb′) ◊ *noun, plural* **taxicabs**

▲ **taxicab**

tbsp. The abbreviation for *tablespoon.*

tea *noun* **1.** A drink prepared by soaking or brewing the dried leaves of an Asian shrub in boiling water. **2.** This shrub or its dried leaves. **3.** A drink or medicine made from plant parts, as leaves or flowers. **4.** A light meal or a social gathering in the late afternoon at which tea is served.
tea (tē) ◊ *noun, plural* **teas**
‖ *These sound alike:* **tea, tee, ti**

teach *verb* **1.** To give instruction. **2.** To give knowledge of or lessons in: *The teachers taught us to read.* **3.** To show by example or experience: *The accident taught us to be more careful.*
teach (tēch) ◊ *verb* **taught, teaching**

teacher *noun* A person who teaches.
teach·er (**tē′** chər) ◊ *noun, plural* **teachers**

teacher's aide *noun* An assistant to a schoolteacher, especially in the classroom.
teacher's aide ◊ *noun, plural* **teacher's aides**

teakettle *noun* A kettle with a handle and a spout that is used for boiling water.
tea·ket·tle (**tē′** kĕt′l) ◊ *noun, plural* **teakettles**

teal *noun* A small wild duck.
teal (tēl) ◊ *noun, plural* **teal** *or* **teals**

team *noun* **1.** Two or more animals that are harnessed together to a vehicle or a piece of farm equipment: *A team of oxen pulled the plow.* **2.** A group of players on the same side in a game. **3.** A group of people who work together.
◊ *verb* To form a team: *The third and fourth grades teamed up to decorate the gym for the party.*
team (tēm) ◊ *noun, plural* **teams** ◊ *verb* **teamed, teaming**
‖ *These sound alike:* **team, teem**

teammate *noun* A fellow member of a team.
team·mate (**tēm′** māt′) ◊ *noun, plural* **teammates**

teamster *noun* A person who drives a team of animals or a truck.
team·ster (**tēm′** stər) ◊ *noun, plural* **teamsters**

teapot *noun* A covered pot with a handle and spout for making and serving tea.
tea·pot (**tē′** pŏt′) ◊ *noun, plural* **teapots**

tear[1] *verb* **1.** To pull or be pulled into pieces by force; split: *Tear the paper in half. Silk tears easily.* **2.** To make an opening in by pulling; rip: *I tore my best shirt on the fence.* **3.** To pull or remove forcefully. **4.** To move very fast; rush.
◊ *noun* An opening made by tearing; rip.
tear[1] (târ) ◊ *verb* **tore, torn, tearing** ◊ *noun, plural* **tears**

ă	pat	ĭ	pit	oi	**oi**l	th	ba**th**
ā	pay	ī	ride	ŏŏ	b**oo**k	*th*	ba**the**
â	care	î	fierce	ōō	b**oo**t	ə	ago, item
ä	father	ŏ	pot	ou	**ou**t		pencil
ĕ	pet	ō	go	ŭ	cut		atom
ē	be	ô	paw, for	û	fur		circus

tear² *noun* A teardrop.
tear² (tîr) ◊ *noun, plural* **tears**
‖*These sound alike:* **tear², tier**

> ***HISTORY* • tear¹, tear²**
>
> **Tear¹** comes from an old English word that meant "to pull apart." **Tear²** comes from a different old English word that meant "teardrop."

teardrop *noun* A drop of the clear, salty liquid that is produced by a gland of the eye.
tear·drop (**tîr′** drŏp′) ◊ *noun, plural* **teardrops**

tease *verb* To make fun of playfully; try to annoy for amusement.
◊ *noun* A person who teases.
tease (tēz) ◊ *verb* **teased, teasing** ◊ *noun, plural* **teases**

teaspoon *noun* **1.** A small spoon used for stirring liquids, as tea or coffee. **2.** A unit used in cooking, equal to ⅓ tablespoon.
tea·spoon (**tē′** spo͞on′) ◊ *noun, plural* **teaspoons**

technical *adjective* **1.** Of or relating to technique: *Painters must learn technical ability.* **2.** Of or relating to a subject or field; specialized: *The high-school science book is written in technical language.* **3.** Of or relating to applied science or the industrial or mechanical arts: *Our friend attends a technical school.*
tech·ni·cal (**tĕk′** nĭ kəl) ◊ *adjective*

technician *noun* A person who is skilled in a technical field or process: *A dental technician cleaned the patient's teeth.*
tech·ni·cian (tĕk **nĭsh′** ən) ◊ *noun, plural* **technicians**

technique *noun* A procedure or method by which a task, especially a difficult or complicated one, is carried out.
tech·nique (tĕk **nēk′**) ◊ *noun, plural* **techniques**

technology *noun* **1.** The use of scientific knowledge in industry and especially in a technical field such as engineering. **2.** The methods and materials used in technology.
tech·nol·o·gy (tĕk **nŏl′** ə jē) ◊ *noun, plural* **technologies**

teddy bear *noun* A stuffed toy bear.
ted·dy bear (**tĕd′** ē bâr′) ◊ *noun, plural* **teddy bears**

tedious *adjective* Long and tiring; boring: *Mowing the lawn can be a tedious job.*
te·di·ous (**tē′** dē əs) ◊ *adjective*

tee *noun* A small peg of wood or plastic on which a golf ball is put before being hit.
tee (tē) ◊ *noun, plural* **tees**
‖*These sound alike:* **tee, tea, ti**

▲ **tee**

teem *verb* To be full; abound: *The jungle teems with insects.*
teem (tēm) ◊ *verb* **teemed, teeming**
‖*These sound alike:* **teem, team**

teen-ager *or* **teenager** *noun* A person between the ages of 13 and 19.
teen-ag·er *or* **teen·ag·er** (**tēn′** ā′jər) ◊ *noun, plural* **teen-agers** *or* **teenagers**

teens *plural noun* The years of a person's life between the ages of 13 and 19.
teens (tēnz) ◊ *plural noun*

teeter *verb* **1.** To walk or move in an unsteady way. **2.** To seesaw.
tee·ter (**tē′** tər) ◊ *verb* **teetered, teetering**

teeter-totter *noun* A seesaw.
tee·ter-tot·ter (**tē′** tər tŏt′ər) ◊ *noun, plural* **teeter-totters**

teeth *noun* Plural of **tooth.**
teeth (tēth) ◊ *noun*

teethe *verb* To develop teeth.
teethe (tē*th*) ◊ *verb* **teethed, teething**

telegram *noun* A message sent by telegraph.
tel·e·gram (**tĕl′** ĭ grăm′) ◊ *noun, plural* **telegrams**

telegraph *noun* **1.** A system or device for sending messages by wire or radio to a receiving station. **2.** A telegram.
◊ *verb* To send by telegraph.
tel·e·graph (**tĕl′** ĭ grăf′) ◊ *noun, plural* **telegraphs** ◊ *verb* **telegraphed, telegraphing**

telephone *noun* An instrument that reproduces and receives sound, especially speech. The sound is carried over wires by electricity.
◊ *verb* To call or talk with by telephone.
tel·e·phone (**tĕl′** ə fōn′) ◊ *noun, plural* **telephones** ◊ *verb* **telephoned, telephoning**

telescope *noun* A device that uses an arrangement of lenses or mirrors in a long tube to make distant objects appear closer.
tel•e•scope (tĕl′ĭ skōp′) ◊ *noun, plural* **telescopes**

▲ **telescope**

televise *verb* To broadcast by television.
tel•e•vise (tĕl′ə vīz′) ◊ *verb* **televised, televising**

television *noun* **1.** A system for sending and receiving visual images of objects and actions with the sounds that go with them. **2.** A device that receives and reproduces the images and sounds transmitted by a television broadcast system.
tel•e•vi•sion (tĕl′ə vĭzh′ən) ◊ *noun, plural* **televisions**

tell *verb* **1.** To express in words: *I'm not going to tell a lie.* —See Synonyms at **say. 2.** To give an account of; describe: *Tell us what happened.* **3.** To make known; reveal. **4.** To discover by observing; identify: *Can't you tell whose voice this is?* **5.** To command; order: *The teacher told us to sit down.*
tell (tĕl) ◊ *verb* **told, telling**

teller *noun* A bank employee who takes in and pays out money.
tell•er (tĕl′ər) ◊ *noun, plural* **tellers**

temper *noun* **1.** A person's usual state of mind or emotions; disposition. **2.** Calmness of mind or emotions: *Don't lose your temper.* **3.** A tendency to become angry.
◊ *verb* **1.** To soften or moderate: *Temper justice with mercy.* **2.** To harden or strengthen a material by special treatment.
tem•per (tĕm′pər) ◊ *noun, plural* **tempers**
◊ *verb* **tempered, tempering**

ă	pat	ĭ	pit	oi	oil	th	bath
ā	pay	ī	ride	ŏŏ	book	*th*	bathe
â	care	î	fierce	ōō	boot	ə	ago, item
ä	father	ŏ	pot	ou	out		pencil
ĕ	pet	ō	go	ŭ	cut		atom
ē	be	ô	paw, for	û	fur		circus

temperate *adjective* **1.** Avoiding extremes; moderate. **2.** Neither very hot nor very cold.
tem•per•ate (tĕm′pər ĭt) ◊ *adjective*

temperature *noun* **1.** Relative hotness or coldness as measured on a standard scale. **2.** Body temperature above what is normal, usually the result of a disease; fever.
tem•per•a•ture (tĕm′pər ə chər) ◊ *noun, plural* **temperatures**

tempest *noun* **1.** A violent wind, often with rain, snow, or hail. **2.** An uproar.
tem•pest (tĕm′pĭst) ◊ *noun, plural* **tempests**

temple[1] *noun* A house of worship, especially a synagogue.
tem•ple[1] (tĕm′pəl) ◊ *noun, plural* **temples**

temple[2] *noun* Either of the flat regions at the sides of the head next to the forehead.
tem•ple[2] (tĕm′pəl) ◊ *noun, plural* **temples**

***HISTORY* • temple[1], temple[2]**

Temple[1] comes from a Latin word for a sacred space or building. **Temple**[2] comes through French from the Latin word for the side of the head.

tempo *noun* The rate of speed at which a piece of music is played.
tem•po (tĕm′pō) ◊ *noun, plural* **tempos**

temporary *adjective* Lasting, used, or working only for a time; not permanent.
tem•po•rar•y (tĕm′pə rĕr′ē) ◊ *adjective*

tempt *verb* **1.** To persuade or try to persuade to do something foolish or wrong: *Thirst tempted me to drink the salty water.* **2.** To appeal strongly to; attract: *Your offer tempts me.* **3.** To risk provoking: *Don't tempt fate.*
tempt (tĕmpt) ◊ *verb* **tempted, tempting**

temptation *noun* **1.** The act of tempting or the state of being tempted: *Don't give in to temptation.* **2.** Something that tempts.
temp•ta•tion (tĕmp tā′shən) ◊ *noun, plural* **temptations**

ten *noun* The number, written 10, equal to the sum of 9 + 1.
◊ *adjective* Being one more than nine.
ten (tĕn) ◊ *noun, plural* **tens** ◊ *adjective*

tenant *noun* **1.** A person who pays rent to use or live on property that is owned by another person. **2.** An occupant; inhabitant.
ten·ant (tĕn′ənt) ◊ *noun, plural* **tenants**

tend¹ *verb* **1.** To be likely; incline: *I tend to be lazy.* **2.** To move or extend in a certain direction: *The river tends toward the south.*
tend¹ (tĕnd) ◊ *verb* **tended, tending**

tend² *verb* To look after; take care of: *Will you tend my cats while I'm on vacation?*
tend² (tĕnd) ◊ *verb* **tended, tending**

***HISTORY* • tend¹, tend²**

These two words are related. **Tend¹** comes through French from a Latin word meaning "to stretch out." **Tend²** was shortened from **attend**, which came through French from a Latin word meaning "to stretch toward."

tendency *noun* An inclination to think, act, or behave in a certain way.
ten·den·cy (tĕn′dən sē) ◊ *noun, plural* **tendencies**

tender *adjective* **1.** Easily broken or damaged; fragile. **2.** Young and not yet mature. **3.** Not tough: *We enjoyed a tender steak.* **4.** Painful; sore: *Her bruised knee is still tender.* **5.** Gentle and loving: *His grandmother gave him a tender hug.*
ten·der (tĕn′dər) ◊ *adjective* **tenderer, tenderest**

tendon *noun* A band or cord of tough tissue that connects a muscle and a bone.
ten·don (tĕn′dən) ◊ *noun, plural* **tendons**

tendril *noun* **1.** A slender, coiling plant part like a stem. A climbing plant clings to a support by use of its tendrils. **2.** A curl or curled end.
ten·dril (tĕn′drəl) ◊ *noun, plural* **tendrils**

tenement *noun* A cheap apartment house that is badly maintained.
ten·e·ment (tĕn′ə mənt) ◊ *noun, plural* **tenements**

Tenn. An abbreviation for *Tennessee.*

tennis *noun* A game played by two or four players with rackets and a light ball on a court divided in two by a net.
ten·nis (tĕn′ĭs) ◊ *noun*

tenor *noun* **1.** A singing voice that is higher than a baritone. **2.** A person having such a voice.
ten·or (tĕn′ər) ◊ *noun, plural* **tenors**

tense¹ *adjective* **1.** Stretched or pulled tight; taut. **2.** Anxious or nervous.
◊ *verb* To make or become tense.
tense¹ (tĕns) ◊ *adjective* **tenser, tensest**
◊ *verb* **tensed, tensing**

tense² *noun* Any of the forms of a verb that indicate the time of an action. For example, *I eat* is in the present tense, *I ate* is in the past tense, and *I will eat* is in the future tense.
tense² (tĕns) ◊ *noun, plural* **tenses**

***HISTORY* • tense¹, tense²**

Tense¹ is related to **tend¹**, and comes from a Latin word that meant "stretched out." **Tense²** came through French from a Latin word meaning "time."

tension *noun* **1.** The act of stretching or the condition of being stretched. **2.** Stress that affects nerves, emotions, or relationships with other people; strain: *Meeting the deadline caused tension in the office.*
ten·sion (tĕn′shən) ◊ *noun, plural* **tensions**

tent *noun* A portable shelter, as of canvas, usually supported by poles.
tent (tĕnt) ◊ *noun, plural* **tents**

tentacle *noun* One of the narrow, flexible parts that certain animals use for grasping and moving.
ten·ta·cle (tĕn′tə kəl) ◊ *noun, plural* **tentacles**

▲ **tentacle**

tenth *noun* **1.** The number in a series that matches the number ten. **2.** One of ten equal parts, written 1/10.
◊ *adjective* Coming after the ninth.
tenth (tĕnth) ◊ *noun, plural* **tenths** ◊ *adjective*

T

tepee *noun* A cone-shaped tent of skins or bark used by some Native Americans.
te·pee (tē′pē′) ◊ *noun, plural* **tepees**

tepid *adjective* Somewhat warm; lukewarm.
tep·id (tĕp′ĭd) ◊ *adjective*

term *noun* **1.** A period of time, especially one with definite limits: *She began a term of six years as senator.* **2.** A word that has a certain meaning, usually in a special vocabulary: *"Shutout" is a sports term, and "tack" is a term used by sailors.* **3.** A condition that is one of the parts of an agreement or legal paper. **4. terms** Relations: *The twins aren't on speaking terms today.*
◊ *verb* To call by a term; name.
term (tûrm) ◊ *noun, plural* **terms** ◊ *verb* **termed, terming**

terminal *noun* **1.** An end part; limit. **2.** A point in an electric device or circuit where an electrical connection can be made. **3.** A station at the end of a transportation line. **4.** A video terminal.
ter·mi·nal (**tûr′**mə nəl) ◊ *noun, plural* **terminals**

termite *noun* An insect that lives in large colonies and that feeds on and destroys wood.
ter·mite (**tûr′**mīt′) ◊ *noun, plural* **termites**

terrace *noun* **1.** A porch or balcony. **2.** An open area next to a house; patio. **3.** A raised, flat bank of earth with sloping sides.
ter·race (**tĕr′**əs) ◊ *noun, plural* **terraces**

terrarium *noun* A glass bowl or box for keeping small plants and sometimes animals.
ter·rar·i·um (tə **râr′**ē əm) ◊ *noun, plural* **terrariums**

terrestrial *adjective* **1.** Of or on the earth. **2.** Living or growing on land.
ter·res·tri·al (tə **rĕs′**trē əl) ◊ *adjective*

terrible *adjective* **1.** Causing great fear; dreadful. **2.** Very great or extreme; severe: *The terrible heat kept most people indoors.* **3.** Very bad: *That was a terrible movie.*
ter·ri·ble (**tĕr′**ə bəl) ◊ *adjective*

ă	pat	ĭ	pit	oi	oil	th	bath
ā	pay	ī	ride	o͝o	book	*th*	bathe
â	care	î	fierce	o͞o	boot	ə	ago, item
ä	father	ŏ	pot	ou	out		pencil
ĕ	pet	ō	go	ŭ	cut		atom
ē	be	ô	paw, for	û	fur		circus

terrier *noun* A small, active dog that was once used for hunting small animals in their burrows.
ter·ri·er (**tĕr′**ē ər) ◊ *noun, plural* **terriers**

▲ **terrier**

terrific *adjective* **1.** Causing great fear: *A terrific storm is coming.* **2.** Excellent: *You're a terrific singer.* **3.** Very great; extreme: *The heat is terrific.*
ter·ri·fic (tə **rĭf′**ĭk) ◊ *adjective*

terrify *verb* To fill with terror: *Heights terrify some people.* —See Synonyms at **frighten.**
ter·ri·fy (**tĕr′**ə fī′) ◊ *verb* **terrified, terrifying**

territory *noun* **1.** An area of land; region. **2.** The land and waters under the control of a state, nation, or government. **3.** A part of the United States not admitted as a state.
ter·ri·to·ry (**tĕr′**ĭ tôr′ē) ◊ *noun, plural* **territories**

terror *noun* **1.** Very great fear. **2.** A cause of very great fear.
ter·ror (**tĕr′**ər) ◊ *noun, plural* **terrors**

terrorize *verb* **1.** To fill with terror. **2.** To control by fear; intimidate.
ter·ror·ize (**tĕr′**ə rīz′) ◊ *verb* **terrorized, terrorizing**

test *noun* **1.** A way of studying something to find out its nature, value, or characteristics: *A simple test will show if this is real gold.* **2.** A series of questions, problems, or tasks designed to measure knowledge or ability.
◊ *verb* To study or examine by a test.
test (tĕst) ◊ *noun, plural* **tests** ◊ *verb* **tested, testing**

testament *noun* **1.** A legal paper that tells what a person wants done with his or her property after death; will. **2. Testament** Ei-

ther of the two main divisions of the Bible, the Old Testament and the New Testament.
tes·ta·ment (tĕs′ tə mənt) ◊ *noun, plural* **testaments**

testify *verb* To make an official statement under oath: *Two witnesses testified in court.*
tes·ti·fy (tĕs′ tə fī′) ◊ *verb* **testified, testifying**

testimony *noun* **1.** A statement or series of official statements made under oath. **2.** Evidence that supports a fact; proof.
tes·ti·mo·ny (tĕs′ tə mō′nē) ◊ *noun, plural* **testimonies**

test tube *noun* A tube of glass that is usually open at one end and rounded at the other. Test tubes are used in the laboratory for experiments.
test tube ◊ *noun, plural* **test tubes**

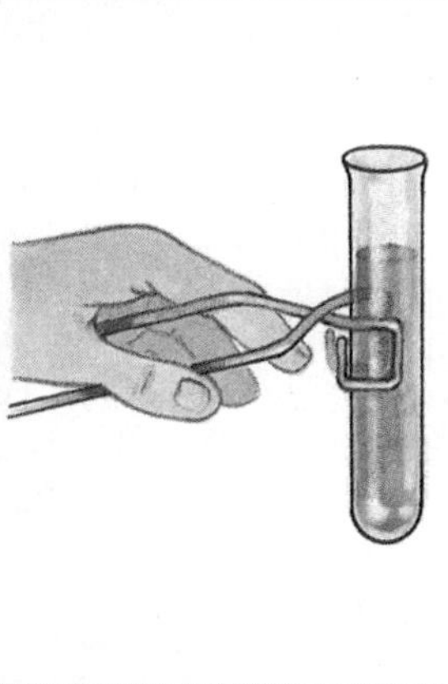
▲ **test tube**

tetanus *noun* A very serious disease caused by infected wounds. The main symptoms of this disease are stiffness in the muscles and spasms.
tet·a·nus (tĕt′n əs) ◊ *noun*

tether *noun* A rope or chain for fastening an animal and keeping it in a limited area.
◊ *verb* To fasten with a tether.
teth·er (tĕ*th*′ ər) ◊ *noun, plural* **tethers** ◊ *verb* **tethered, tethering**

Teuton *noun* A member of an ancient Germanic people who lived in northern Europe until about 100 B.C.
Teu·ton (to͞ot′n *or* tyo͞ot′n) ◊ *noun, plural* **Teutons**

text *noun* **1.** The actual words in a piece of writing or in a speech. **2.** The main body of writing in a book or on a page: *This children's book has many pictures and little text.* **3.** Subject matter; theme: *The text of the talk was democracy.* **4.** A textbook.
text (tĕkst) ◊ *noun, plural* **texts**

textbook *noun* A book used for studying a subject.
text·book (tĕkst′ bo͝ok′) ◊ *noun, plural* **textbooks**

textile *noun* Woven or knitted fabric; cloth.
tex·tile (tĕk′ stəl *or* tĕk′ stīl′) ◊ *noun, plural* **textiles**

texture *noun* The look or feel of a surface: *Velvet has a soft, smooth texture.*
tex·ture (tĕks′ chər) ◊ *noun, plural* **textures**

than *conjunction* In comparison with: *Mountains are bigger than hills.*
than (*th*ăn) ◊ *conjunction*

thank *verb* To say that one is grateful: *I thanked them for their help.*
thank (thăngk) ◊ *verb* **thanked, thanking**

thankful *adjective* Showing or feeling gratitude; grateful.
thank·ful (thăngk′ fəl) ◊ *adjective*

thankless *adjective* **1.** Not feeling or showing gratitude. **2.** Not likely to be appreciated.
thank·less (thăngk′ lĭs) ◊ *adjective*

thanks *plural noun* An expression of gratitude: *We sent our thanks for the gifts.*
◊ *interjection* A word that is used to express gratitude.
◊ *idiom* **thanks to** On account of; because of: *Thanks to your help I will be ready in time.*
thanks (thăngks) ◊ *plural noun* ◊ *interjection*

thanksgiving *noun* An act or expression of giving thanks.
thanks·giv·ing (thăngks gĭv′ ĭng) ◊ *noun, plural* **thanksgivings**

Thanksgiving Day *noun* A holiday for giving thanks, especially to God. Thanksgiving Day is the fourth Thursday of November in the United States. It is the second Monday of October in Canada.

that *adjective* **1.** Being the one farther away or at a distance: *That desk is yours and this one is mine.* **2.** Being the one indicated or just mentioned: *Did you see that lightning?*
◊ *pronoun* **1.** Who, whom, or which: *There are still some chores that have to be done.* **2.** In, on, or for which: *We called the day that we arrived.* **3.** The one farther away or at a distance: *This is a pigeon, and that is a sparrow.* **4.** The one indicated or just mentioned: *A woodchuck? What kind of animal is that?*
◊ *adverb* To that extent: *Is it that important?*
◊ *conjunction* Used to introduce a clause in a sentence: *I think that they are coming to visit.*
that (*th*ăt) ◊ *adjective, plural* **those** ◊ *pronoun, plural* **those** ◊ *adverb* ◊ *conjunction*

T

thatch *noun* Plant material, such as straw or reeds, that is used to make or cover a roof. ◊ *verb* To cover with thatch.
thatch (thăch) ◊ *noun* ◊ *verb* **thatched, thatching**

▲ **thatch**

thaw *verb* To change from a solid to a liquid by gradual warming. —See Synonyms at **melt.** ◊ *noun* The process of thawing.
thaw (thô) ◊ *verb* **thawed, thawing** ◊ *noun, plural* **thaws**

the[1] *definite article* Used before a noun or noun phrase that stands for a certain person or thing: *The student in the front row has red hair. The dog has a black tail.*
the[1] (*th*ē or *th*ə) ◊ *definite article*

the[2] *adverb* To that extent; by that much: *We should leave, and the sooner the better.*
the[2] (*th*ē or *th*ə) ◊ *adverb*

***HISTORY* • the**[1]**, the**[2]

The[1] and **the**[2] come from different forms of the same old English word.

theater *noun* **1.** A building where plays or movies are presented. **2.** The work of writing, producing, or acting in plays.
the·a·ter (thē′ə tər) ◊ *noun, plural* **theaters**

ă	pat	ĭ	pit	oi	oil	th	bath
ā	pay	ī	ride	o͝o	book	*th*	bathe
â	care	î	fierce	o͞o	boot	ə	ago, item
ä	father	ŏ	pot	ou	out		pencil
ĕ	pet	ō	go	ŭ	cut		atom
ē	be	ô	paw, for	û	fur		circus

theft *noun* The act or an instance of stealing.
theft (thĕft) ◊ *noun, plural* **thefts**

their *pronoun* Relating or belonging to them: *They put their boots in the closet.*
their (*th*âr) ◊ *pronoun*
‖*These sound alike:* **their, there, they're**

theirs *pronoun* The one or ones that belong to them: *Our car was in the repair shop so we borrowed theirs.*
theirs (*th*ârz) ◊ *pronoun*
‖*These sound alike:* **theirs, there's**

them *pronoun* The objective case of **they:** *Did you see them? The letter was from them.*
them (*th*ĕm) ◊ *pronoun*

theme *noun* **1.** The subject of a talk or a piece of writing. **2.** A short written composition. **3.** A melody in a piece of music.
theme (thēm) ◊ *noun, plural* **themes**

themselves *pronoun* Their own selves: *They blamed themselves. They themselves knew it.*
them·selves (*th*ĕm **sĕlvz′**) ◊ *pronoun*

then *adverb* **1.** At that time: *We were younger then.* **2.** After that; next: *One more game, and then we'll go home.* **3.** In that case: *If you want to go, then go.* **4.** As a result: *If 2 + 2 equals 4, then 4 – 2 equals 2.*
◊ *noun* That time: *From then on, I obeyed.*
then (*th*ĕn) ◊ *adverb* ◊ *noun*

thence *adverb* From there: *We drove to Chicago and thence westward to California.*
thence (*th*ĕns) ◊ *adverb*

thenceforth *adverb* From then on.
thence·forth (*th*ĕns **fôrth′**) ◊ *adverb*

theology *noun* **1.** The study of religion. **2.** A group of teachings about religion.
the·ol·o·gy (thē **ŏl′** ə jē) ◊ *noun, plural* **theologies**

theory *noun* **1.** A statement or group of statements designed to explain certain facts or observations without actual proof: *According to one scientific theory, there may be more than one solar system.* **2.** A set of rules for the practice of an art or science. **3.** An opinion or belief based on limited knowledge: *My theory is that we'll have a cold winter this year.*
the·o·ry (**thē′** ə rē) ◊ *noun, plural* **theories**

therapy *noun* Treatment that is supposed to heal or cure illnesses or disabilities: *The doctor prescribed walking as therapy for my weak knee.*
ther·a·py (**thĕr′** ə pē) ◊ *noun, plural* **therapies**

there *adverb* **1.** At or in that place: *Set the package there on the table.* **2.** To or toward that place: *I bicycled there and back.*
◊*pronoun* Used to introduce a sentence in which the verb comes before the subject: *There are several different kinds of pepper.*
◊*noun* That place or point: *I'll never know how we got out of there.*
◊*interjection* A word that is used to show satisfaction or sympathy: *There, I've done it!*
there (*th*âr) ◊*adverb* ◊*pronoun* ◊*noun* ◊*interjection*
‖*These sound alike:* **there, their, they're**

thereabouts *adverb* **1.** Near that number, time, or age: *It was ten o'clock or thereabouts.* **2.** In that neighborhood.
there·a·bouts (*th*âr'ə **bouts'**) ◊*adverb*

thereafter *adverb* After that; from then on.
there·af·ter (*th*âr **ăf'** tər) ◊*adverb*

thereby *adverb* By that means: *We took a shortcut, thereby saving an hour.*
there·by (*th*âr **bī'**) ◊*adverb*

therefore *adverb* For that reason: *I overslept and was therefore late getting to school.*
there·fore (***th*âr'** fôr') ◊*adverb*

there's Contraction of "there is."
there's (*th*ârz) ◊*contraction*
‖*These sound alike:* **there's, theirs**

thermal *adjective* Of, using, producing, or caused by heat.
ther·mal (**thûr'** məl) ◊*adjective*

thermometer *noun* An instrument that measures temperature, usually by the height of a liquid that expands or contracts inside a slender glass tube.
ther·mom·e·ter (thər **mŏm'** ĭ tər) ◊*noun, plural* **thermometers**

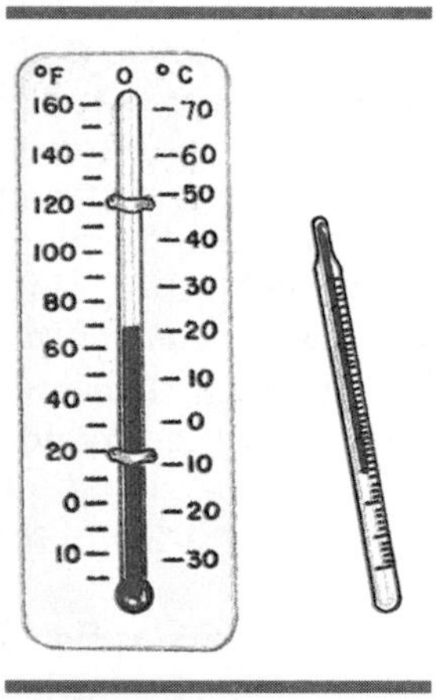

▲ **thermometer**

thermostat *noun* A device that automatically controls temperature in heating and cooling systems. Thermostats are used to regulate furnaces and refrigerators.
ther·mo·stat (**thûr'** mə stăt') ◊*noun, plural* **thermostats**

thesaurus *noun* A book or list of synonyms and antonyms. They are listed alphabetically.
the·sau·rus (thĭ **sôr'** əs) ◊*noun, plural* **thesauruses**

these *adjective & pronoun* Plural of **this:** *These houses are very old. Are these your gloves?*
these (*th*ēz) ◊*adjective & pronoun*

they *pronoun* **1.** The persons, animals, or things last mentioned; those ones: *Elephants are large, but they move quickly.* **2.** People in general: *They say it will snow today.*
they (*th*ā) ◊*pronoun*

they'd Contraction of "they had" or "they would."
they'd (*th*ād) ◊*contraction*

they'll Contraction of "they will."
they'll (*th*āl) ◊*contraction*

they're Contraction of "they are."
they're (*th*âr) ◊*contraction*
‖*These sound alike:* **they're, their, there**

they've Contraction of "they have."
they've (*th*āv) ◊*contraction*

thick *adjective* **1.** Having much space between opposite surfaces or sides; not thin: *A thick board will not break easily.* **2.** Measuring a certain amount between opposite sides: *These walls are two feet thick.* **3.** Not flowing easily: *The soup is thick.* **4.** Made of or having a large number of things close together.
◊*adverb* So as to be thick; thickly.
◊*noun* The most active or intense part: *We had to leave during the thick of the game.*
thick (thĭk) ◊*adjective, adverb* **thicker, thickest** ◊*noun*

thicken *verb* To make or become thicker.
thick·en (**thĭk'** ən) ◊*verb* **thickened, thickening**

thicket *noun* A group of shrubs or small trees that grow very close together.
thick·et (**thĭk'**ĭt) ◊*noun, plural* **thickets**

thief *noun* A person who steals.
thief (thēf) ◊*noun, plural* **thieves**

thieve *verb* To steal things.
thieve (thēv) ◊*verb* **thieved, thieving**

thieves *noun* Plural of **thief.**
thieves (thēvz) ◊*noun*

thigh *noun* The upper part of the leg, between the hip and the knee.
thigh (thī) ◊*noun, plural* **thighs**

thimble *noun* A small metal or plastic cap that is worn to protect the finger that pushes the needle when sewing.
thim·ble (thĭm′bəl) ◊ *noun, plural* **thimbles**

thin *adjective* **1.** Having little space between opposite surfaces or sides; not thick: *The sun shone through the thin curtains.* **2.** Small in diameter; fine. **3.** Having little fat on the body; slender. **4.** Having parts or units that are widely separated. **5.** Not dense. **6.** Not strong or firm, especially in tone: *The child spoke in a high, thin voice.*
◊ *adverb* So as to be thin; thinly: *Slice the bread thin.*
◊ *verb* To make or become thin or thinner.
thin (thĭn) ◊ *adjective, adverb* **thinner, thinnest** ◊ *verb* **thinned, thinning**

> **SYNONYMS**
>
> ***thin, skinny, slender***
>
> I am tall and *thin.* If you exercise your muscles more, you won't be so *skinny.* The ballet dancer was graceful and *slender.* **Antonyms:** *fat, plump, stout*

thing *noun* **1.** An object, creature, or matter that is not named: *What's that thing on the table?* **2.** A creature; person: *The baby is such a sweet little thing.* **3.** An act or deed. **4. things** Personal belongings: *Have you packed your things?* **5. things** The general state of affairs; conditions: *Things are getting better now.*
thing (thĭng) ◊ *noun, plural* **things**

think *verb* **1.** To use one's mind to form ideas and make decisions: *Think a moment before you decide what to do.* **2.** To have as a thought; imagine: *Can you think of a costume to wear?* **3.** To examine carefully in the mind; consider: *We need time to think the problem out.* **4.** To believe; suppose: *I think the storm is over.*
think (thĭngk) ◊ *verb* **thought, thinking**

ă	pat	ĭ	pit	oi	**oi**l	th	ba**th**
ā	pay	ī	ride	o͝o	b**oo**k	*th*	ba**th**e
â	care	î	fierce	o͞o	b**oo**t	ə	**a**go, it**e**m
ä	father	ŏ	pot	ou	**ou**t		penc**i**l
ĕ	pet	ō	go	ŭ	c**u**t		at**o**m
ē	be	ô	paw, for	û	f**u**r		circ**u**s

> **SYNONYMS**
>
> ***think, consider, plan, ponder***
>
> I would like to *think* it over. *Consider* all the choices. They *planned* every step of the project. We *pondered* the problem for several days.

third *noun* **1.** The number in a series that matches the number three. **2.** One of three equal parts, written 1/3.
◊ *adjective* Coming after the second.
third (thûrd) ◊ *noun, plural* **thirds** ◊ *adjective*

thirst *noun* **1.** A dry feeling in the mouth related to the need to drink. **2.** A desire to drink liquids.
◊ *verb* To feel thirsty.
thirst (thûrst) ◊ *noun, plural* **thirsts** ◊ *verb* **thirsted, thirsting**

thirsty *adjective* **1.** Feeling thirst. **2.** Needing rain or watering: *The house plants are thirsty.*
thirst·y (thûr′stē) ◊ *adjective* **thirstier, thirstiest**

thirteen *noun* The number, written 13, that is equal to the sum of 12 + 1.
◊ *adjective* Being one more than twelve.
thir·teen (thûr′tēn′) ◊ *noun, plural* **thirteens** ◊ *adjective*

thirteenth *noun* **1.** The number in a series that matches the number thirteen. **2.** One of thirteen equal parts, written 1/13.
◊ *adjective* Coming after the twelfth.
thir·teenth (thûr′tēnth′) ◊ *noun, plural* **thirteenths** ◊ *adjective*

thirtieth *noun* **1.** The number in a series that matches the number thirty. **2.** One of thirty equal parts, written 1/30.
◊ *adjective* Coming after the twenty-ninth.
thir·ti·eth (thûr′tē ĭth) ◊ *noun, plural* **thirtieths** ◊ *adjective*

thirty *noun* The number, written 30, that is equal to the product of 10 × 3.
◊ *adjective* Being equal to ten times three.
thir·ty (thûr′tē) ◊ *noun, plural* **thirties** ◊ *adjective*

this *adjective* **1.** Being the one present, nearby, or just mentioned: *I think you'll enjoy this book.* **2.** Being the one that is nearer than another: *This car is smaller than that one.*
◊ *pronoun* **1.** The one present, nearby, or just mentioned: *This is my house.* **2.** The one that

is nearer than another: *These are oak trees, and those are pines.* **3.** What is about to be said: *This will really make you laugh.*
◊ *adverb* To this extent; so: *I never knew them to stay out this late.*
this (*th*ĭs) ◊ *adjective, plural* **these** ◊ *pronoun, plural* **these** ◊ *adverb*

thistle *noun* A plant with prickles, purplish flowers, and seeds with tufts of silky fluff.
this·tle (**thĭs′** əl) ◊ *noun, plural* **thistles**

thong *noun* **1.** A strip of leather used to fasten something, such as a sandal. **2.** A sandal that is fastened by one strip of plastic or leather that goes between the toes.
thong (thông) ◊ *noun, plural* **thongs**

thorax *noun* **1.** The part of the human body that is between the neck and the abdomen, enclosed partly by the ribs; chest. **2.** The middle of the three-part body of an insect.
tho·rax (**thôr′** ăks′) ◊ *noun, plural* **thoraxes**

thorn *noun* **1.** A sharp point growing from the stem of a plant. **2.** A shrub or tree that has sharp points growing on its stems.
thorn (thôrn) ◊ *noun, plural* **thorns**

▲ **thorn**

thorny *adjective* **1.** Full of thorns. **2.** Causing trouble; difficult.
thorn·y (**thôr′** nē) ◊ *adjective* **thornier, thorniest**

thorough *adjective* **1.** Complete in every way: *I gave my room a thorough cleaning.* **2.** Not overlooking anything; very careful.
thor·ough (**thûr′** ō) ◊ *adjective*

thoroughfare *noun* A main road; highway.
thor·ough·fare (**thûr′** ō fâr′) ◊ *noun, plural* **thoroughfares**

those *adjective & pronoun* Plural of **that:** *Those socks don't match. Are those your keys?*
those (*th*ōz) ◊ *adjective & pronoun*

though *adverb* However; nevertheless: *The shirt is pretty; it doesn't fit, though.*
◊ *conjunction* Although; while: *Your report, though well planned, was badly written.*
though (*th*ō) ◊ *adverb* ◊ *conjunction*

thought *noun* **1.** The act or process of thinking. **2.** A result of thinking; an idea or group of ideas.
◊ *verb* Past tense and past participle of **think.**
thought (thôt) ◊ *noun, plural* **thoughts** ◊ *verb*

thoughtful *adjective* **1.** Thinking quietly. **2.** Well thought out: *Give a thoughtful answer to the question on the test.* **3.** Being aware of other people's needs and feelings; considerate.
thought·ful (**thôt′** fəl) ◊ *adjective*

thoughtless *adjective* **1.** Not thinking; careless: *It was thoughtless of me to forget to lock the door.* **2.** Not showing consideration of other people's needs and feelings.
thought·less (**thôt′** lĭs) ◊ *adjective*

thousand *noun* The number, written 1,000, that is equal to the product of 10 × 100.
◊ *adjective* Being ten times one hundred.
thou·sand (**thou′** zənd) ◊ *noun, plural* **thousands** ◊ *adjective*

thousandth *noun* **1.** The number in a series that matches the number 1,000. **2.** One of a thousand equal parts, written 1/1000.
◊ *adjective* Coming after the 999th.
thou·sandth (**thou′** zəndth) ◊ *noun, plural* **thousandths** ◊ *adjective*

thrash *verb* **1.** To give a beating or whipping to. **2.** To defeat utterly. **3.** To move wildly or violently: *The big fish thrashed on the line.*
thrash (thrăsh) ◊ *verb* **thrashed, thrashing**

thread *noun* **1.** A fine, thin cord made of two or more strands of fiber twisted together. Thread is used in weaving cloth and in sewing. **2.** A long, very thin stream or flow. **3.** A series of connected ideas or events: *I must have skipped a page, because I lost the thread of the story.* **4.** The ridge or groove that winds in a spiral around a screw.
◊ *verb* **1.** To pass one end of a thread through the eye of a needle or through the various hooks and holes on a sewing machine. **2.** To connect by running a thread through; string.

T

3. To proceed cautiously: *The hikers threaded their way through the thick forest.*
thread (thrĕd) ◊ *noun, plural* **threads** ◊ *verb* **threaded, threading**

threadbare *adjective* **1.** Worn so much that the nap is gone and the threads show through. **2.** Wearing old, shabby clothes.
thread·bare (**thrĕd′**bâr′) ◊ *adjective*

threat *noun* **1.** An expression indicating that punishment or harm will follow. **2.** A warning of danger: *The night air held a threat of frost.* **3.** Something regarded as a danger: *A speeding driver is a threat to everyone else on the road.*
threat (thrĕt) ◊ *noun, plural* **threats**

threaten *verb* **1.** To express threats against. **2.** To be a threat to; endanger: *Landslides threatened the village.* **3.** To give signs of; warn of: *Dark skies threaten rain.*
threat·en (**thrĕt′**n) ◊ *verb* **threatened, threatening**

three *noun* The number, written 3, that is equal to the sum of 2 + 1.
◊ *adjective* Being one more than two.
three (thrē) ◊ *noun, plural* **threes** ◊ *adjective*

thresh *verb* To separate the grain or seeds from by striking or beating.
thresh (thrĕsh) ◊ *verb* **threshed, threshing**

thresher *noun* A machine used for threshing.
thresh·er (**thrĕsh′**ər) ◊ *noun, plural* **threshers**

threshold *noun* **1.** The piece of wood or stone put beneath a door. **2.** An entrance. **3.** The point where something begins: *Scientists are on the threshold of new discoveries.*
thresh·old (**thrĕsh′**ōld′) ◊ *noun, plural* **thresholds**

threw *verb* Past tense of **throw.**
threw (thro͞o) ◊ *verb*
‖*These sound alike:* **threw, through**

thrift *noun* Careful and wise management of one's money and other resources.
thrift (thrĭft) ◊ *noun*

ă	pat	ĭ	pit	oi	oil	th	bath
ā	pay	ī	ride	o͝o	book	*th*	bathe
â	care	î	fierce	o͞o	boot	ə	ago, item
ä	father	ŏ	pot	ou	out		pencil
ĕ	pet	ō	go	ŭ	cut		atom
ē	be	ô	paw, for	û	fur		circus

thrifty *adjective* Practicing thrift; careful not to waste money or resources.
thrift·y (**thrĭf′**tē) ◊ *adjective* **thriftier, thriftiest**

thrill *verb* To feel or cause to feel a sudden sensation of joy, fear, or excitement: *The acrobat thrilled the spectators.*
◊ *noun* A sudden, exciting sensation.
thrill (thrĭl) ◊ *verb* **thrilled, thrilling** ◊ *noun, plural* **thrills**

thrive *verb* **1.** To be or stay in a healthy condition: *Some plants thrive in damp, sandy soil.* **2.** To be successful; flourish: *The little town thrived.*
thrive (thrīv) ◊ *verb* **thrived** *or* **throve, thrived** *or* **thriven, thriving**

thriven *verb* A past participle of **thrive.**
thriv·en (**thrĭv′**ən) ◊ *verb*

throat *noun* **1.** The part of the digestive tract that forms a passage between the mouth and the esophagus. **2.** The front part of the neck. **3.** A narrow passage or part, as of a violin.
throat (thrōt) ◊ *noun, plural* **throats**

throb *verb* To beat rapidly or loudly; pound: *My heart was throbbing after the race.*
◊ *noun* A strong, heavy beat or vibration.
throb (thrŏb) ◊ *verb* **throbbed, throbbing** ◊ *noun, plural* **throbs**

throne *noun* **1.** The special chair that a monarch sits on. **2.** A monarch's rank or position.
throne (thrōn) ◊ *noun, plural* **thrones**
‖*These sound alike:* **throne, thrown**

throng *noun* A very large group; crowd.
◊ *verb* **1.** To crowd into; fill: *People thronged the beaches.* **2.** To move in a crowd: *The audience thronged toward the exits.*
throng (thrông) ◊ *noun, plural* **throngs** ◊ *verb* **thronged, thronging**

throttle *noun* **1.** A valve in an engine that controls the flow of fuel or steam. **2.** A pedal or lever that opens and closes such a valve.
◊ *verb* To control an engine with a throttle.
throt·tle (**thrŏt′**l) ◊ *noun, plural* **throttles** ◊ *verb* **throttled, throttling**

through *preposition* **1.** In one side and out the other side of: *We walked through the park.* **2.** In the midst of; among or between: *A garden path winds through the flowers.* **3.** By means of: *I met them through a friend.* **4.** As a result of: *We lost the book through our carelessness.* **5.** Here and there in; around: *We traveled through Africa.* **6.** From the be-

ginning to the end of: *I'll be staying at camp through July.* **7.** At or to the end of: *We are through school at two thirty.*
◊ *adverb* **1.** From one side or end to the other. **2.** In every part; completely: *We were soaked through.* **3.** From beginning to end: *I watched the movie through again.* **4.** To the end: *Let's see the game through.* **5.** All the way: *This road runs through to the coast.*
◊ *adjective* **1.** Passing or permitting passage from one end or side to another: *This is a through street.* **2.** Going all the way without stopping: *I took a through bus to Saint Louis.* **3.** Finished; done: *Since I'm through, may I leave?*
through (thro͞o) ◊ *preposition* ◊ *adverb* ◊ *adjective*
‖ *These sound alike:* **through, threw**

throughout *preposition* In, to, or through every part of: *We hiked throughout the area until we got tired.*
◊ *adverb* In or through every part; everywhere: *The book was interesting throughout.*
through·out (thro͞o **out′**) ◊ *preposition* ◊ *adverb*

throve *verb* A past tense of **thrive.**
throve (thrōv) ◊ *verb*

throw *verb* **1.** To send through the air with a fast motion of the arm; fling: *We threw the ball back and forth.* **2.** To bring or be brought to the ground with force: *The horse threw me.* **3.** To put on or off in a hurry or in a careless way: *I threw on a coat and went out.*
◊ *noun* **1.** An act of throwing. **2.** A scarf, shawl, or light cover.
◊ *idioms* **throw away 1.** To get rid of; discard. **2.** To fail to use: *Don't throw away the opportunity to get a good education.* **throw out** To get rid of; discard. **throw up** To vomit.
throw (thrō) ◊ *verb* **threw, thrown, throwing** ◊ *noun, plural* **throws**

SYNONYMS

throw, hurl, toss

Throw the ball over here. She *hurled* the javelin as far as it would go. I *tossed* my socks on the floor.

thrown *verb* Past participle of **throw.**
thrown (thrōn) ◊ *verb*
‖ *These sound alike:* **thrown, throne**

thrush *noun* Any of several songbirds that usually have a brownish back and a spotted breast. A robin is a kind of thrush.
thrush (thrŭsh) ◊ *noun, plural* **thrushes**

▲ **thrush**

thrust *verb* To push with force: *We thrust the curtains aside and peered out.* —See Synonyms at **push.**
◊ *noun* **1.** A forceful push; shove. **2.** A lunge, as with a sword.
thrust (thrŭst) ◊ *verb* **thrust, thrusting** ◊ *noun, plural* **thrusts**

thruway *noun* A highway for high-speed traffic, usually having four or more lanes.
thru·way (**thro͞o′** wā′) ◊ *noun, plural* **thruways**

thud *noun* A dull sound: *The big dictionary fell to the floor with a thud.*
◊ *verb* To strike heavily with a dull sound.
thud (thŭd) ◊ *noun, plural* **thuds** ◊ *verb* **thudded, thudding**

thumb *noun* **1.** The short, thick first finger of the human hand. **2.** The part of a glove or mitten that fits over the thumb.
◊ *verb* To turn pages rapidly with or as if with the thumb: *I thumbed through the magazine.*
thumb (thŭm) ◊ *noun, plural* **thumbs** ◊ *verb* **thumbed, thumbing**

thumbtack *noun* A tack that has a broad flat head.
thumb·tack (**thŭm′** tăk′) ◊ *noun, plural* **thumbtacks**

thump *noun* **1.** A blow with a blunt object. **2.** A dull sound made by such a blow.
◊ *verb* **1.** To strike with a blunt object. **2.** To beat, hit, or fall so as to make a thump.

T

thump (thŭmp) ◊ *noun, plural* **thumps** ◊ *verb* **thumped, thumping**

thunder *noun* **1.** The deep, rumbling noise that goes with or comes after a flash of lightning. **2.** A deep, rumbling noise: *We could hear the thunder of the waves.*
◊ *verb* **1.** To produce thunder: *It thundered and rained all night.* **2.** To make sounds like thunder: *The waves thundered.* **3.** To roar; shout.
thun·der (thŭn′dər) ◊ *noun* ◊ *verb* **thundered, thundering**

thunderbolt *noun* A flash of lightning along with thunder.
thun·der·bolt (thŭn′dər bōlt′) ◊ *noun, plural* **thunderbolts**

thundercloud *noun* A large, dark cloud that produces lightning and thunder.
thun·der·cloud (thŭn′dər kloud′) ◊ *noun, plural* **thunderclouds**

thunderstorm *noun* A heavy storm with lightning and thunder.
thun·der·storm (thŭn′dər stôrm′) ◊ *noun, plural* **thunderstorms**

thunderstruck *adjective* Very amazed; astonished.
thun·der·struck (thŭn′dər strŭk′) ◊ *adjective*

Thurs. The abbreviation for *Thursday.*

Thursday *noun* The fifth day of the week.
Thurs·day (thûrz′dē) ◊ *noun, plural* **Thursdays**

> ***HISTORY* • Thursday**
>
> Four of the seven days of the week were named after the gods that the English believed in before they became Christians. **Thursday** was named after *Thor,* the god of thunder.

thus *adverb* **1.** In this way: *Please print your name; written thus, it is easier to read.* **2.** To this extent; so: *We dug thus far and found no treasure.* **3.** As a result; consequently: *Balsa wood is softer and thus it is easier to carve.*
thus (*th*ŭs) ◊ *adverb*

ă	pat	ĭ	pit	oi	**oil**	th	ba**th**
ā	pay	ī	ride	ŏŏ	**book**	*th*	ba**th**e
â	care	î	fierce	ōō	**boot**	ə	ago, item
ä	father	ŏ	pot	ou	**out**		pencil
ĕ	pet	ō	go	ŭ	**cut**		atom
ē	be	ô	paw, for	û	**fur**		circus

thwart *verb* To keep from being successful; frustrate.
thwart (thwôrt) ◊ *verb* **thwarted, thwarting**

thyme *noun* A low-growing plant with spicy-smelling leaves used to flavor food.
thyme (tīm) ◊ *noun*
‖*These sound alike:* **thyme, time**

thyroid gland *noun* A gland in the neck. The thyroid gland makes and gives off a hormone that controls body growth and metabolism.
thy·roid gland (thī′roid′) ◊ *noun*

ti *noun* The seventh note of the musical scale.
ti (tē) ◊ *noun*
‖*These sound alike:* **ti, tea, tee**

tick¹ *noun* **1.** A sharp clicking sound made by a device, especially a clock or wristwatch. **2.** A light mark that is used to check off an item on a list.
◊ *verb* **1.** To make a tick or a series of ticks: *The clock was ticking.* **2.** To make a light mark next to; check off: *I ticked off each name on the list.*
tick¹ (tĭk) ◊ *noun, plural* **ticks** ◊ *verb* **ticked, ticking**

tick² *noun* A small, eight-legged animal that is related to the spiders. Ticks suck blood from the skin of animals and human beings.
tick² (tĭk) ◊ *noun, plural* **ticks**

> ***HISTORY* • tick¹, tick²**
>
> **Tick¹** first appeared in writing about 550 years ago and meant "a tap, pat." **Tick²** may come from the old English name for this insect.

ticket *noun* **1.** A paper slip or card that gives a person the right to a service, such as a bus ride or entrance to a theater. **2.** A price tag or label attached to something being sold. **3.** A legal summons given to a person accused of breaking a traffic law.
◊ *verb* **1.** To attach a tag to; label. **2.** To give a legal summons to: *The driver was ticketed for parking in front of a fire hydrant.*
tick·et (tĭk′ĭt) ◊ *noun, plural* **tickets** ◊ *verb* **ticketed, ticketing**

tickle *verb* **1.** To touch the body lightly, caus-

ing a tingling sensation and sometimes jerky movements and laughter. **2.** To feel a prickling sensation. **3.** To delight or amuse; please. ◊ *noun* The act or sensation of tickling.
tick·le (tĭk′əl) ◊ *verb* **tickled, tickling** ◊ *noun, plural* **tickles**

tidal *adjective* Of or affected by tides.
tid·al (tīd′l) ◊ *adjective*

tidal wave *noun* A huge, often destructive ocean wave caused by an underwater earthquake or volcanic eruption.
tidal wave ◊ *noun, plural* **tidal waves**

tidbit *noun* A choice piece of food or news.
tid·bit (tĭd′bĭt′) ◊ *noun, plural* **tidbits**

tide *noun* **1.** The regular rising and falling of the surface level of the oceans, caused by the attraction of the moon and the sun. High tide and low tide occur twice each day along the shores of large bodies of water. **2.** A movement that pulls things along with it.
tide (tīd) ◊ *noun, plural* **tides**

tidings *plural noun* News; information: *Have you heard the glad tidings?*
tid·ings (tī′dĭngz) ◊ *plural noun*

tidy *adjective* **1.** Orderly and neat: *My job was to keep the store tidy.* **2.** Quite large; considerable: *That computer cost a tidy sum.*
◊ *verb* To put in order; make neat: *Tidy your room before going to the movies.*
ti·dy (tī′dē) ◊ *adjective* **tidier, tidiest** ◊ *verb* **tidied, tidying**

tie *verb* **1.** To fasten or secure with a cord or rope: *Wrap the package and tie it with string.* **2.** To fasten by drawing together and knotting strings or laces: *Please tie your shoes.* **3.** To form a knot in: *Can you tie a necktie?* **4.** To be equal to in points in a contest: *We tied the opponents' record last year.*
◊ *noun* **1.** A cord, string, or ribbon used for fastening. **2.** Something that holds or keeps people together; bond: *Our classmates have close ties of friendship.* **3.** A necktie. **4.** An equal score or number. **5.** A contest, such as an election, that ends with an equal score for both sides. **6.** One of the timbers that are laid across and underneath railroad tracks.
tie (tī) ◊ *verb* **tied, tying** ◊ *noun, plural* **ties**

tier *noun* One of a series of rows or layers placed one above another.
tier (tîr) ◊ *noun, plural* **tiers**
‖*These sound alike:* **tier, tear²**

tiger *noun* A large animal of Asia that belongs to the cat family. A tiger has light brown fur with black stripes.
ti·ger (tī′gər) ◊ *noun, plural* **tigers**

▲ **tiger**

tight *adjective* **1.** Not letting water or air pass through: *We were warm that night in our tight little cabin.* **2.** Held or closed firmly in place; not coming undone easily: *I tied a tight knot.* **3.** Fitting close or too close to the skin: *This coat is too tight.* **4.** Stretched out fully; taut. **5.** Leaving no room or time to spare: *My schedule is tight today.* **6.** Not generous; stingy. **7.** Difficult to deal with or get out of: *Losing my wallet put me in a tight spot.* **8.** Even or nearly even in score or outcome; close.
◊ *adverb* **1.** Firmly; securely: *Shut the door tight.* **2.** Soundly: *Sleep tight.*
tight (tīt) ◊ *adjective, adverb* **tighter, tightest**

tighten *verb* To make or become tight.
tight·en (tīt′n) ◊ *verb* **tightened, tightening**

tightrope *noun* A rope or wire stretched high above the ground. Acrobats and circus performers walk and balance on a tightrope.
tight·rope (tīt′rōp′) ◊ *noun, plural* **tightropes**

tights *plural noun* A tight-fitting, stretchable garment covering the body from the waist or neck down. Acrobats and gymnasts wear tights.
tights (tīts) ◊ *plural noun*

tigress *noun* A female tiger.
ti·gress (tī′grĭs) ◊ *noun, plural* **tigresses**

T

tile *noun* A thin slab of baked clay or plastic, laid in rows to cover floors, walls, or roofs. ◊ *verb* To cover with tiles: *We tiled the walls.*
tile (tīl) ◊ *noun, plural* **tiles** ◊ *verb* **tiled, tiling**

till[1] *verb* To prepare land for growing crops by plowing and fertilizing.
till[1] (tĭl) ◊ *verb* **tilled, tilling**

till[2] *preposition* Until: *I slept till noon.* ◊ *conjunction* **1.** Until: *Wait till it warms up.* **2.** Before or unless: *I can't pay you till you sign this slip.*
till[2] (tĭl) ◊ *preposition* ◊ *conjunction*

till[3] *noun* A drawer or box for keeping money, especially in a store.
till[3] (tĭl) ◊ *noun, plural* **tills**

***HISTORY* • till[1], till[2], till[3]**

Till[1] comes from an old English word that first meant "to work" and also "to work with a plow." **Till**[2] was borrowed from a Scandinavian preposition. It later combined with a different Scandinavian preposition to form **until.** The origin of **till**[3] is not known.

tiller *noun* A lever that is used to turn a boat's rudder.
til·ler (tĭl′ər) ◊ *noun, plural* **tillers**

tilt *verb* To slope or slant, as by raising one end; tip: *I tilted the barrel to empty it.* ◊ *noun* **1.** An act of tilting. **2.** A slope. ◊ *idiom* **at full tilt** At full speed.
tilt (tĭlt) ◊ *verb* **tilted, tilting** ◊ *noun, plural* **tilts**

timber *noun* **1.** Trees or land covered with trees. **2.** Wood for building; lumber. **3.** A long, heavy piece of wood for building; beam.
tim·ber (tĭm′bər) ◊ *noun, plural* **timbers**

timberline *noun* The height or limit that trees do not grow beyond, as on a mountain.
tim·ber·line (tĭm′bər līn′) ◊ *noun, plural* **timberlines**

ă	pat	ĭ	pit	oi	oil	th	bath
ā	pay	ī	ride	o͝o	book	*th*	bathe
â	care	î	fierce	o͞o	boot	ə	ago, item
ä	father	ŏ	pot	ou	out		pencil
ĕ	pet	ō	go	ŭ	cut		atom
ē	be	ô	paw, for	û	fur		circus

time *noun* **1.** The past, the present, and the future. Time is a quantity that can be measured by counting the number of occurrences of a regular event like the sunrise or the turns of a clock's hands. **2.** A period with a beginning and an end, during which something exists or continues: *The time the test took was 50 minutes.* **3.** A certain point in the past, present, or future, as shown on a clock or calendar: *The time right now is 3:30 in the afternoon.* **4.** A period in history; era. **5.** A period when something happens or is supposed to happen: *It was almost time to go to school.* **6.** One of a number of repeated actions: *I knocked three times.* **7.** A person's experiences and feelings during a certain period: *I had a good time at the beach.* **8.** A rate of speed; tempo: *We did the dishes in double time.* **9.** The beat in music: *The audience kept time to the song by clapping.* ◊ *verb* **1.** To set the time for: *The alarm clock is timed to go off at six o'clock.* **2.** To regulate or adjust so that each of a series of events happens at the correct time: *I timed my swing just right and hit a home run.* **3.** To record or measure the time or speed of: *I'll time you for the 100-yard dash.* ◊ *idioms* **at times** Sometimes; occasionally. **for the time being** For now; temporarily. **from time to time** Once in a while; occasionally. **in time 1.** Not too late; early enough. **2.** In the end; eventually: *In time you'll understand what I mean.* **on time** According to a schedule; promptly.
time (tīm) ◊ *noun, plural* **times** ◊ *verb* **timed, timing**
‖*These sound alike:* **time, thyme**

timeless *adjective* Not affected by time: *The beauty of nature is timeless.*
time·less (tīm′lĭs) ◊ *adjective*

timely *adjective* Coming at just the right time.
time·ly (tīm′lē) ◊ *adjective* **timelier, timeliest**

timepiece *noun* An instrument, such as a watch or clock, that tells time.
time·piece (tīm′pēs′) ◊ *noun, plural* **timepieces**

times *preposition* Multiplied by: *Eight times three equals twenty-four.*
times (tīmz) ◊ *preposition*

timetable *noun* A schedule of arrival and departure times, as of trains or buses.

time·ta·ble (tīm′tā′bəl) ◊ *noun, plural* **timetables**

S.P. AFTERNOON EXPRESS			
TRAIN NO.	TRACK NO.	DEPART	ARRIVE
20	6	2:10 PM	4:45 PM
67	7	3:30 PM	6:05 PM
3	5	4:00 PM	6:35 PM
98	6	5:00 PM	7:35 PM
14	7	5:30 PM	8:00 PM
6	4	6:00 PM	8:35 PM
WILLOW TO GRANT			

▲ **timetable**

timid *adjective* Easily frightened; shy.
tim·id (tĭm′ĭd) ◊ *adjective*

tin *noun* **1.** A soft, shiny metal that hardly rusts at all and is used to coat other metals. Tin is a chemical element. **2.** Sheets of iron or steel coated with tin. **3.** A container made of or coated with tin.
tin (tĭn) ◊ *noun, plural* **tins**

tinder *noun* A material that catches fire easily and that is used to kindle fires.
tin·der (tĭn′dər) ◊ *noun*

tinfoil *noun* A thin, flexible sheet of aluminum or a tin alloy, used for wrapping foods.
tin·foil (tĭn′foil′) ◊ *noun*

tinge *verb* **1.** To color slightly; tint: *The sunset tinged the sky with red.* **2.** To give a slight trace or touch to; affect slightly: *My admiration for them was tinged with a little envy.*
◊ *noun* A faint trace.
tinge (tĭnj) ◊ *verb* **tinged, tingeing** *or* **tinging** ◊ *noun, plural* **tinges**

tingle *verb* To have a prickling sensation.
◊ *noun* A prickling or stinging sensation.
tin·gle (tĭng′gəl) ◊ *verb* **tingled, tingling** ◊ *noun, plural* **tingles**

tinker *verb* To make minor repairs or adjustments without skilled or certain knowledge.
◊ *noun* A person who once traveled about, mending pots and pans and other utensils.
tin·ker (tĭng′kər) ◊ *verb* **tinkered, tinkering** ◊ *noun, plural* **tinkers**

tinkle *verb* To make or cause to make light, ringing sounds.
◊ *noun* A light ringing sound.
tin·kle (tĭng′kəl) ◊ *verb* **tinkled, tinkling** ◊ *noun, plural* **tinkles**

tinsel *noun* Thin sheets, strips, or threads of a glittering material used as decoration.
tin·sel (tĭn′səl) ◊ *noun*

tint *noun* **1.** A shade of a color, especially a pale or delicate shade. **2.** A slight coloring.
◊ *verb* To give a tint to; color slightly.
tint (tĭnt) ◊ *noun, plural* **tints** ◊ *verb* **tinted, tinting**

tiny *adjective* Extremely small. —See Synonyms at **little.**
ti·ny (tī′nē) ◊ *adjective* **tinier, tiniest**

tip[1] *noun* **1.** The end or farthest point of something. **2.** A piece meant to be fitted on the end of something else: *The crutches have rubber tips so they won't slip.*
◊ *verb* To put a tip on.
tip[1] (tĭp) ◊ *noun, plural* **tips** ◊ *verb* **tipped, tipping**

tip[2] *verb* **1.** To knock over; upset: *The cat tipped over the vase.* **2.** To slant; tilt: *I tipped the pail to drain off some water.* **3.** To touch or raise one's hat as a greeting.
tip[2] (tĭp) ◊ *verb* **tipped, tipping**

tip[3] *noun* **1.** A small extra sum of money given to someone who has provided a service: *He paid the bill and then left a tip for the waiter.* **2.** A piece of useful information; helpful hint.
◊ *verb* To give a small, extra sum of money to: *She tipped the taxi driver.*
◊ *idiom* **tip off** To give secret information to.
tip[3] (tĭp) ◊ *noun, plural* **tips** ◊ *verb* **tipped, tipping**

***HISTORY* • tip[1], tip[2], tip[3]**

Tip[1] comes from an old Scandinavian word that is related to **top[1]**. **Tip[2]** and **tip[3]** are probably both related to **tip[1]**, but their origins are not known for certain.

tiptoe *verb* To walk softly, as if on the tips of one's toes.
tip·toe (tĭp′tō′) ◊ *verb* **tiptoed, tiptoeing**

tire[1] *verb* **1.** To make or become weak from work or effort; weary: *The long walk tired me.* **2.** To make or become bored; lose interest: *I took up juggling, but soon tired of it.*
tire[1] (tīr) ◊ *verb* **tired, tiring**

T

tire² *noun* A covering for a wheel, usually made of rubber and filled with air.
tire² (tīr) ◊ *noun, plural* **tires**

> ***HISTORY* • tire¹, tire²**
>
> **Tire¹** comes from an old English word that meant "to fail, become weary." **Tire²** first appeared in writing about 500 years ago and refers to metal strips put on the rim of a wheel. It was probably shortened from *attire,* meaning "clothing."

tired *adjective* **1.** Weakened from work or effort; needing rest. **2.** Impatient; bored.
tired (tīrd) ◊ *adjective*

tireless *adjective* Capable of working a long time without getting tired.
tire•less (tīr′lĭs) ◊ *adjective*

tiresome *adjective* Causing a person to be tired, bored, or annoyed.
tire•some (tīr′səm) ◊ *adjective*

'tis Contraction of "it is."
'tis (tĭz) ◊ *contraction*

tissue *noun* **1.** A mass of similar cells that make up a particular part or organ of a plant or animal. **2.** Often **tissue paper** Light, thin paper used for wrapping. **3.** A piece of soft, absorbent paper used as a handkerchief.
tis•sue (tĭsh′o͞o) ◊ *noun, plural* **tissues**

title *noun* **1.** An identifying name given to a book, painting, song, or other work. **2.** A word or name given to a person to show his or her rank, office, or occupation. Some titles are *Mr., Ms., Dr., Senator,* and *Judge.* **3.** Legal ownership. —See Synonyms at **right. 4.** An official document, such as a deed to land, that shows legal ownership. **5.** A championship, especially in a sport.
◊ *verb* To give a title to.
ti•tle (tīt′l) ◊ *noun, plural* **titles** ◊ *verb* **titled, titling**

ă	pat	ĭ	pit	oi	**oi**l	th	ba**th**
ā	pay	ī	ride	o͝o	b**oo**k	*th*	ba**the**
â	care	î	fierce	o͞o	b**oo**t	ə	**a**go, it**e**m
ä	father	ŏ	**p**ot	ou	**ou**t		penc**i**l
ĕ	pet	ō	**g**o	ŭ	c**u**t		at**o**m
ē	be	ô	paw, for	û	f**u**r		circ**u**s

titleholder *noun* A person who holds a title, especially for a championship in a sport.
ti•tle•hold•er (tīt′l hōl′dər) ◊ *noun, plural* **titleholders**

TN The abbreviation for *Tennessee* used with a Zip Code.

to *preposition* **1.** In a direction toward: *I whistled as I walked to school.* **2.** Reaching as far as: *This apple is rotten to the core.* **3.** In contact with; against: *Apply the lotion to the burn.* **4.** Through; until: *I slept from three to five.* **5.** For the attention, benefit, or possession of: *Tell it to me.* **6.** For the purpose of; for: *We went to lunch.* **7.** Concerning or regarding: *What do you say to that?* **8.** In agreement with: *That music is not to my liking.* **9.** As compared with: *The score was four to three.* **10.** Before: *The time is now ten to five.* **11.** Used with verbs: *I'd like to go.*
to (to͞o) ◊ *preposition*
‖*These sound alike:* **to, too, two**

toad *noun* An animal that is similar to a frog, but has rougher, drier skin. Toads live mostly on land when they are fully grown.
toad (tōd) ◊ *noun, plural* **toads**

▲ **toad**

toadstool *noun* A mushroom that is not good to eat, especially one of the poisonous kinds.
toad•stool (tōd′sto͞ol′) ◊ *noun, plural* **toadstools**

toast¹ *verb* **1.** To heat and brown by placing close to heat: *I like to have my bread toasted.* **2.** To warm thoroughly: *We toasted our bare feet by the fire.*
◊ *noun* Sliced bread heated and browned.
toast¹ (tōst) ◊ *verb* **toasted, toasting** ◊ *noun*

toast² *noun* **1.** The act of drinking in honor of or to the health of a person or thing. **2.** A person who receives much attention or praise: *The singer became the toast of London.*
◊ *verb* To drink in honor of or to the health of: *The guests toasted the bride and groom.*
toast² (tōst) ◊ *noun, plural* **toasts** ◊ *verb* **toasted, toasting**

HISTORY • toast[1], toast[2]

Toast[1] comes from an old French word that came in turn from a Latin word meaning "to parch." **Toast[2]** probably refers to an old custom of flavoring drinks with bits of spiced **toast[1]**. To **toast[2]** a guest of honor was to suggest that his or her presence added interest or excitement to the occasion.

toaster *noun* An electrical appliance that is used to toast bread.
toast·er (tō′stər) ◊ *noun, plural* **toasters**

tobacco *noun* **1.** A plant grown for its large leaves, which are dried, cut up, and used for smoking or chewing. **2.** The dried and shredded leaves of this plant. **3.** Cigarettes, cigars, and other products made from tobacco.
to·bac·co (tə băk′ō) ◊ *noun, plural* **tobaccos** *or* **tobaccoes**

toboggan *noun* A long, narrow sled without runners. A toboggan curves upward at the front.
◊ *verb* To ride on a toboggan.
to·bog·gan (tə bŏg′ən) ◊ *noun, plural* **toboggans** ◊ *verb* **tobogganed, tobogganing**

▲ **toboggan**

today *adverb* **1.** During or on the present day. **2.** During or at the present time.
◊ *noun* The present day, time, or age: *Are the athletes of today better than those of the past?*
to·day (tə dā′) ◊ *adverb* ◊ *noun*

toddle *verb* To walk with short, unsteady steps, as a very small child does.
tod·dle (tŏd′l) ◊ *verb* **toddled, toddling**

toe *noun* **1.** One of the parts that stick out from the foot. Human beings have five toes on each foot. **2.** The part of a sock, stocking, shoe, or boot that fits over the toes.
toe (tō) ◊ *noun, plural* **toes**
‖*These sound alike:* **toe, tow**

toenail *noun* The nail on a toe.
toe·nail (tō′nāl′) ◊ *noun, plural* **toenails**

together *adverb* **1.** In or into a single group or place; with each other: *Many people were crowded together. We went to school together.* **2.** In relationship to one another: *How are they getting along together?* **3.** At the same time: *The firecrackers all went off together.* **4.** In agreement or cooperation: *We stand together on this issue.*
to·geth·er (tə gĕ*th*′ər) ◊ *adverb*

toil *verb* **1.** To work hard and for a long time. **2.** To move or go with a lot of effort.
◊ *noun* Hard, tiring work; labor.
toil (toil) ◊ *verb* **toiled, toiling** ◊ *noun*

toilet *noun* A bowl with a seat on it and a connected water supply with a flushing device. A toilet is used for getting rid of body wastes.
toi·let (toi′lĭt) ◊ *noun, plural* **toilets**

token *noun* **1.** Something that stands for something else; sign: *A white flag is a token of surrender.* **2.** A reminder; souvenir. **3.** A piece of stamped metal used as a substitute for money, as on buses and subways.
to·ken (tō′kən) ◊ *noun, plural* **tokens**

told *verb* Past tense and past participle of **tell.**
told (tōld) ◊ *verb*

tolerable *adjective* Capable of being tolerated; bearable.
tol·er·a·ble (tŏl′ər ə bəl) ◊ *adjective*

tolerance *noun* The willingness to let other people hold opinions or follow practices that are different from one's own.
tol·er·ance (tŏl′ər əns) ◊ *noun*

tolerant *adjective* Showing or having tolerance.
tol·er·ant (tŏl′ər ənt) ◊ *adjective*

tolerate *verb* **1.** To allow without trying to stop; permit: *Our coach would not tolerate rough play.* **2.** To put up with; endure: *How*

T

can you tolerate that terrible noise?
tol·er·ate (tŏl′ ə rāt′) ◊ *verb* **tolerated, tolerating**

toll¹ *noun* **1.** A fee or tax paid for a privilege: *We had to pay a toll to cross the bridge.* **2.** A charge for a service, as a long-distance telephone call.
toll¹ (tōl) ◊ *noun, plural* **tolls**

toll² *verb* To sound a bell slowly and regularly.
◊ *noun* The sound of a bell tolling.
toll² (tōl) ◊ *verb* **tolled, tolling** ◊ *noun, plural* **tolls**

***HISTORY* • toll¹, toll²**

Toll¹ was borrowed long ago from a Latin word that came in turn from a Greek word meaning "tax." **Toll²** may have come from an old English word that meant "to pull," in this case to pull a bell rope.

tomahawk *noun* A light ax that can be used as a tool or weapon.
tom·a·hawk (tŏm′ ə hôk′) ◊ *noun, plural* **tomahawks**

tomato *noun* The fleshy fruit of a widely grown plant. Tomatoes are usually reddish when ripe and are eaten raw or cooked.
to·ma·to (tə mā′ tō *or* tə mä′ tō) ◊ *noun, plural* **tomatoes**

LANGUAGE DETECTIVE

tomato

All over the United States most people pronounce *tomato* as (tə **mā′** tō). If you live in New England or eastern Virginia, you have probably heard people say (tə-**mä′** tō). A popular song was even written about the different ways of pronouncing *tomato*.

ă	pat	ĭ	pit	oi	oil	th	bath
ā	pay	ī	ride	o͝o	book	*th*	bathe
â	care	î	fierce	o͞o	boot	ə	ago, item
ä	father	ŏ	pot	ou	out		pencil
ĕ	pet	ō	go	ŭ	cut		atom
ē	be	ô	paw, for	û	fur		circus

▲ **tomato**

tomb *noun* A grave, chamber, or structure for holding a dead body.
tomb (to͞om) ◊ *noun, plural* **tombs**

tomboy *noun* An adventurous, athletic girl.
tom·boy (tŏm′ boi′) ◊ *noun, plural* **tomboys**

tombstone *noun* A stone marking a grave.
tomb·stone (to͞om′ stōn′) ◊ *noun, plural* **tombstones**

tomorrow *noun* **1.** The day after today. **2.** The near future.
◊ *adverb* On or for the day after today: *I will return your book tomorrow.*
to·mor·row (tə **môr′** ō) ◊ *noun* ◊ *adverb*

tom-tom *noun* A small drum that is beaten with the hands.
tom-tom (tŏm′ tŏm′) ◊ *noun, plural* **tom-toms**

ton *noun* A unit of weight and mass equal to either 2,000 pounds or 2,240 pounds.
ton (tŭn) ◊ *noun, plural* **tons**

tone *noun* **1.** A sound that has a certain pitch, length, loudness, or quality: *The deepest tones of the organ echoed through the auditorium.* **2.** The characteristic quality of an instrument or voice. **3.** A color or a shade of a color. **4.** A way of speaking or writing that conveys a feeling: *Our teacher's tone was gentle.* **5.** A general quality or feeling: *The tone of the poem was playful.* **6.** A healthy, firm condition of the muscles.
◊ *verb* To give a healthy firmness to: *These exercises will tone up your muscles.*
◊ *idiom* **tone down** To make quieter or softer; soften.
tone (tōn) ◊ *noun, plural* **tones** ◊ *verb* **toned, toning**

tongs *plural noun* A tool for holding and lifting things, made up of two movable arms joined at one end.
tongs (tôngz) ◊ *plural noun*

tongue *noun* **1.** A fleshy part of the body attached to the bottom of the mouth. The tongue is used in chewing, tasting, and swallowing. Human beings also use it in speaking. **2.** The tongue of an animal, such as a cow, used as food. **3.** A flap of material under the laces or buckles of a shoe. **4.** A spoken language. **5.** The power of speech: *I held my tongue.* **6.** A way of speaking: *You have a sharp tongue sometimes.*
tongue (tŭng) ◊ *noun, plural* **tongues**

tongue-tied *adjective* Being unable to speak clearly, as from surprise or embarrassment.
tongue-tied (**tŭng′**tīd′) ◊ *adjective*

tonic *noun* Something, as a medicine or an influence, that gives a person new strength or energy.
ton·ic (**tŏn′**ĭk) ◊ *noun, plural* **tonics**

tonight *adverb* On or during this night or the night of this day: *I'll see you at ten tonight.*
◊ *noun* This night or the night of this day.
to·night (tə **nīt′**) ◊ *adverb* ◊ *noun*

tonnage *noun* **1.** The amount of cargo that a ship can hold. **2.** The total shipping of a country or port, measured in tons.
ton·nage (**tŭn′**ĭj) ◊ *noun, plural* **tonnages**

tonsil *noun* Either of two small masses of tissue on the sides of the throat in the back of the mouth.
ton·sil (**tŏn′**səl) ◊ *noun, plural* **tonsils**

tonsillitis *noun* Inflammation, soreness, or swelling of the tonsils.
ton·sil·li·tis (tŏn′sə **lī′**tĭs) ◊ *noun*

too *adverb* **1.** As well; also. **2.** More than enough: *Don't hold your pen too tightly.* **3.** Very; extremely: *I'm only too happy to help.*
too (to͞o) ◊ *adverb*
‖*These sound alike:* **too, to, two**

took *verb* Past tense of **take.**
took (to͝ok) ◊ *verb*

tool *noun* A device, such as a hammer or an axe, that is specially made or shaped to help a person do work.
◊ *verb* To shape or decorate with tools.
tool (to͞ol) ◊ *noun, plural* **tools** ◊ *verb* **tooled, tooling**

toot *verb* To sound a horn or whistle in short blasts.
◊ *noun* A short blast on a horn or whistle.
toot (to͞ot) ◊ *verb* **tooted, tooting** ◊ *noun, plural* **toots**

tooth *noun* **1.** One of a set of hard, bony parts in the mouth that are used to chew and bite. **2.** A part that is one of a row and that sticks out, as on a comb, saw, or gear.
tooth (to͞oth) ◊ *noun, plural* **teeth**

toothache *noun* An aching pain in a tooth.
tooth·ache (**to͞oth′**āk′) ◊ *noun, plural* **toothaches**

toothbrush *noun* A small brush that is used to clean the teeth.
tooth·brush (**to͞oth′**brŭsh′) ◊ *noun, plural* **toothbrushes**

toothpaste *noun* A paste used to clean the teeth.
tooth·paste (**to͞oth′**pāst′) ◊ *noun, plural* **toothpastes**

toothpick *noun* A small, thin stick of wood that is used to remove food from between the teeth.
tooth·pick (**to͞oth′**pĭk′) ◊ *noun, plural* **toothpicks**

top¹ *noun* **1.** The highest or upper part, point, or surface: *I stood on the top of the hill.* **2.** The highest rank or position. **3.** The highest degree or pitch: *I yelled at the top of my voice.* **4.** An upper covering; lid.
◊ *adjective* **1.** At or being the top; highest. **2.** Most important or prominent; leading.
◊ *verb* **1.** To give a top to; form the top of: *A bell tower topped the old church.* **2.** To do better than; surpass.
top¹ (tŏp) ◊ *noun, plural* **tops** ◊ *adjective* ◊ *verb* **topped, topping**

top² *noun* A cone-shaped toy that can be made to spin on its pointed end.
top² (tŏp) ◊ *noun, plural* **tops**

***HISTORY* • top¹, top²**

Top¹ comes from an old English word meaning "the highest point." The origin of **top²** is not known for certain.

topaz *noun* A mineral, usually yellow, that is used as a gem.
to·paz (**tō′**păz′) ◊ *noun, plural* **topazes**

T

topcoat *noun* An overcoat that is light in weight.
top·coat (tŏp′kōt′) ◊ *noun, plural* **topcoats**

topic *noun* A subject treated in a speech, conversation, or piece of writing.
top·ic (tŏp′ĭk) ◊ *noun, plural* **topics**

topmost *adjective* Being the very highest.
top·most (tŏp′mōst′) ◊ *adjective*

topple *verb* **1.** To fall because of being too heavy on top. —See Synonyms at **tumble.** **2.** To cause to topple.
top·ple (tŏp′əl) ◊ *verb* **toppled, toppling**

topsoil *noun* The layer of soil at the surface of the ground.
top·soil (tŏp′soil′) ◊ *noun*

topsy-turvy *adverb* **1.** Upside-down. **2.** In great disorder or confusion: *The high winds blew everything topsy-turvy.*
top·sy-tur·vy (tŏp′sē tûr′vē) ◊ *adverb*

torch *noun* **1.** A flaming light, such as a stick burning at one end, that can be carried around. **2.** A device that shoots out a hot flame, as for welding or cutting metals.
torch (tôrch) ◊ *noun, plural* **torches**

▲ **torch**

ă	pat	ĭ	pit	oi	**oi**l	th	ba**th**
ā	pay	ī	ride	ŏŏ	b**oo**k	*th*	ba**the**
â	care	î	fierce	ōō	b**oo**t	ə	ago, item
ä	father	ŏ	pot	ou	**ou**t		pencil
ĕ	pet	ō	go	ŭ	cut		atom
ē	be	ô	paw, for	û	fur		circus

tore *verb* Past tense of **tear**[1].
tore (tôr) ◊ *verb*

torment *noun* **1.** Great physical or mental pain. **2.** A source of great pain or trouble.
◊ *verb* **1.** To cause to undergo great pain. **2.** To tease; annoy.
tor·ment ◊ *noun* (tôr′mĕnt′), *plural* **torments**
◊ *verb* (tôr **mĕnt′**) **tormented, tormenting**

torn *verb* Past participle of **tear**[1].
torn (tôrn) ◊ *verb*

tornado *noun* A violent, whirling wind. A tornado is accompanied by a funnel-shaped cloud that comes down from a thundercloud. A tornado can be very destructive along its narrow path.
tor·na·do (tôr **nā′**dō) ◊ *noun, plural* **tornadoes** *or* **tornados**

torpedo *noun* A shell shaped like a cigar that moves underwater by its own power and explodes when it hits or is near its target.
◊ *verb* To attack or destroy with a torpedo.
tor·pe·do (tôr **pē′**dō) ◊ *noun, plural* **torpedoes** ◊ *verb* **torpedoed, torpedoing**

torrent *noun* A fast-moving stream of liquid; violent flow or downpour.
tor·rent (**tôr′**ənt) ◊ *noun, plural* **torrents**

torrid *adjective* Very hot; scorching.
tor·rid (**tôr′**ĭd) ◊ *adjective*

tortilla *noun* A round, flat bread made from cornmeal and water and baked on a grill.
tor·til·la (tôr **tē′**yə) ◊ *noun, plural* **tortillas**

tortoise *noun* A turtle, especially one that lives only on land.
tor·toise (**tôr′**təs) ◊ *noun, plural* **tortoises**

torture *noun* **1.** The causing of severe pain as a punishment or as a way of forcing someone to do something against his or her will. **2.** Great physical or mental pain; torment.
◊ *verb* To subject to great pain.
tor·ture (**tôr′**chər) ◊ *noun, plural* **tortures**
◊ *verb* **tortured, torturing**

toss *verb* **1.** To throw with a quick, easy motion: *We tossed the ball to the baby.* —See Synonyms at **throw.** **2.** To rock or swing to and fro: *Heavy seas tossed the ship.* **3.** To flip a coin to decide something.
◊ *noun* An act of tossing.
toss (tôs) ◊ *verb* **tossed, tossing** ◊ *noun, plural* **tosses**

tot *noun* A small child.
tot (tŏt) ◊ *noun, plural* **tots**

total *noun* **1.** A number gotten by adding; sum. **2.** An entire amount; all of a quantity.
◊ *adjective* **1.** Being the whole of something: *What is the total population of the state?* **2.** Absolute; complete: *Our play was a total success.*
◊ *verb* **1.** To find the sum of: *I totaled my expenses with a calculator.* **2.** To equal a total of; amount to: *Your bill totals $25.00.*
to·tal (tōt′l) ◊ *noun, plural* **totals** ◊ *adjective* ◊ *verb* **totaled, totaling**

totem *noun* **1.** An animal, plant, or natural object that, among Native Americans and certain other peoples, stands for a clan or family and the ancestors of the clan or family. **2.** An image or representation of a totem.
to·tem (tō′təm) ◊ *noun, plural* **totems**

totter *verb* **1.** To sway as if about to fall. **2.** To walk unsteadily.
tot·ter (tŏt′ər) ◊ *verb* **tottered, tottering**

toucan *noun* A tropical American bird with brightly colored feathers and a very large bill.
tou·can (to͞o′kăn′) ◊ *noun, plural* **toucans**

▲ **toucan**

touch *verb* **1.** To come or bring into contact with: *The two canoes almost touched each other in passing.* **2.** To feel with a part of the body, especially with the hand: *I will touch wildflowers but not pick them.* **3.** To meet, border on, or get as far as: *New Hampshire just touches the ocean.* **4.** To tap, press, or strike lightly. **5.** To affect; concern: *The issue of clean air and water touches us all.* **6.** To affect emotionally; move: *The sad movie touched us all.*
◊ *noun* **1.** An act or way of touching: *I woke the sleeping puppy with a touch of my hand.* **2.** The sense by which one becomes aware of things in contact with one's skin; feeling. **3.** Contact; communication: *I'll be in touch with you by telephone.* **4.** A little bit; trace: *I think the soup needs a touch of pepper.* **5.** A mild case or attack: *I have a touch of the flu.* **6.** A detail that improves or completes something: *This room needs a few touches to make it look beautiful.*
◊ *idiom* **touch up** To improve in small ways.
touch (tŭch) ◊ *verb* **touched, touching** ◊ *noun, plural* **touches**

touchdown *noun* **1.** A score of six points in football, usually made by running with the ball, or catching a teammate's pass, across the opposing team's goal line. **2.** The landing of an aircraft or spacecraft.
touch·down (tŭch′doun′) ◊ *noun, plural* **touchdowns**

touching *adjective* Causing a tender emotion such as sympathy; moving.
touch·ing (tŭch′ĭng) ◊ *adjective*

touchy *adjective* **1.** Easily insulted or made angry; irritable. **2.** Requiring special care or tact; delicate: *Tardiness is a touchy subject with our teacher.*
touch·y (tŭch′ē) ◊ *adjective* **touchier, touchiest**

tough *adjective* **1.** Strong and not likely to break or tear with use or wear. **2.** Hard to chew. **3.** Able to stand hardships; rugged: *The sailor had a tough, wiry build.* **4.** Difficult to do; demanding: *Painting ceilings is a tough job.* **5.** Unwilling to give in; stubborn. **6.** Disorderly; lawless; rough.
◊ *noun* A rough, disorderly person; hoodlum.
tough (tŭf) ◊ *adjective* **tougher, toughest** ◊ *noun, plural* **toughs**

toughen *verb* To make or become tough.
tough·en (tŭf′ən) ◊ *verb* **toughened, toughening**

tour *noun* **1.** A trip during which many interesting places are visited. —See Synonyms at **trip. 2.** A brief trip through a place in order to see it: *The owner took us on a tour of the factory.* **3.** A series of engagements in different places: *The band went on a concert tour.*
◊ *verb* **1.** To go on a tour: *We toured through Spain.* **2.** To make a tour of.
tour (to͝or) ◊ *noun, plural* **tours** ◊ *verb* **toured, touring**

T

tourist *noun* A person who travels to various places for pleasure.
tour·ist (tŏŏr′ĭst) ◊ *noun, plural* **tourists**

tournament *noun* **1.** A contest in which a number of competitors take part. **2.** A medieval contest between jousting knights.
tour·na·ment (**tûr′**nə mənt) ◊ *noun, plural* **tournaments**

tourney *noun* A tournament.
tour·ney (**tûr′**nē) ◊ *noun, plural* **tourneys**

tourniquet *noun* A device, such as a tightly twisted band, that is used to stop bleeding.
tour·ni·quet (**tûr′**nĭ kĭt) ◊ *noun, plural* **tourniquets**

tow *verb* To draw or pull along behind with a chain, rope, or cable: *The wrecker towed our car to the garage.* —See Synonyms at **pull.**
◊ *noun* **1.** An act of towing. **2.** The condition of being towed: *The tug had a barge in tow.*
tow (tō) ◊ *verb* **towed, towing** ◊ *noun, plural* **tows**
‖*These sound alike:* **tow, toe**

toward *preposition* **1.** In the direction of: *We walked toward the school.* **2.** In a position facing: *He sat with his chair turned toward the window.* **3.** Somewhat before in time; near: *It started to rain toward dawn.* **4.** With regard to: *The coach likes my attitude toward sports.* **5.** In partial payment of: *She gave $20.00 toward the bill for the gift.*
to·ward (tôrd *or* tə **wôrd′**) ◊ *preposition*

towards *preposition* Toward.
to·wards (tôrdz *or* tə **wôrdz′**) ◊ *preposition*

towel *noun* A piece of cloth or paper used for wiping or drying something that is wet.
◊ *verb* To wipe or rub dry with a towel.
◊ *idiom* **throw in the towel** To admit defeat.
tow·el (**tou′**əl) ◊ *noun, plural* **towels** ◊ *verb* **toweled, toweling**

tower *noun* A very tall building or a tall structure that is part of a larger building.
◊ *verb* To rise or reach very high.
tow·er (**tou′**ər) ◊ *noun, plural* **towers** ◊ *verb* **towered, towering**

ă	pat	ĭ	pit	oi	**oil**	th	ba**th**
ā	pay	ī	ride	ŏŏ	**book**	*th*	ba**th**e
â	care	î	fierce	ōō	**boot**	ə	**ago, item**
ä	father	ŏ	pot	ou	**out**		pencil
ĕ	pet	ō	go	ŭ	cut		atom
ē	be	ô	paw, for	û	fur		circus

▲ **tower**

towering *adjective* Very tall.
tow·er·ing (**tou′**ər ĭng) ◊ *adjective*

towhead *noun* A person who has white-blond hair.
tow·head (**tō′**hĕd′) ◊ *noun, plural* **towheads**

town *noun* **1.** A populated area that is larger than a village but smaller than a city. **2.** A city. **3.** The people who live in a town.
town (toun) ◊ *noun, plural* **towns**

township *noun* A unit of local government that is part of a county.
town·ship (**toun′**shĭp′) ◊ *noun, plural* **townships**

towpath *noun* A path beside a river or canal used by people or animals towing boats.
tow·path (**tō′**păth′) ◊ *noun, plural* **towpaths**

toxic *adjective* Of, relating to, or caused by a poison.
tox·ic (**tŏk′**sĭk) ◊ *adjective*

toy *noun* Something for children to play with.
◊ *verb* To amuse oneself; play: *As I talked on the phone I was toying with a pencil.*
toy (toi) ◊ *noun, plural* **toys** ◊ *verb* **toyed, toying**

trace *noun* **1.** A visible mark or sign of the former presence or existence of something: *As we walked through the woods we found no trace of deer.* **2.** A very small amount.
◊ *verb* **1.** To follow the track, course, or trail of: *The post office tried to trace the lost letter.* **2.** To follow the stages in the history or development of: *Historians traced the beginnings*

of the war. **3.** To copy by following lines seen through a sheet of transparent paper.
trace (trās) ◊ *noun, plural* **traces** ◊ *verb* **traced, tracing**

trachea *noun* The windpipe.
tra·che·a (trā′kē ə) ◊ *noun*

track *noun* **1.** A mark, such as a footprint, that is left behind by something that has moved by: *We saw rabbit tracks in the snow.* **2.** A path or course made for racing or running. **3.** A course of action: *You're on the wrong track.* **4.** A rail or set of rails for vehicles such as trains to run on. **5.** A sport that includes running, jumping, and throwing.
◊ *verb* **1.** To follow the footprints or trail of. **2.** To follow the course of something such as an airplane: *Radar is used to track weather balloons.* **3.** To carry on the feet and leave as marks: *Don't track mud on the rug.*
track (trăk) ◊ *noun, plural* **tracks** ◊ *verb* **tracked, tracking**

tract *noun* **1.** An area of land: *There's a tract of woods behind our cabin.* **2.** A system of body organs and tissues that performs a special function: *The digestive tract includes the stomach.*
tract (trăkt) ◊ *noun, plural* **tracts**

traction *noun* The resistance to uncontrolled movement that keeps a moving body from slipping on a surface.
trac·tion (**trăk′**shən) ◊ *noun*

tractor *noun* **1.** A vehicle that is driven by an engine and is equipped with large tires that have deep treads. A tractor is used especially for pulling farm machinery. **2.** A truck that has a cab and no body and is used for pulling trailers.
trac·tor (**trăk′**tər) ◊ *noun, plural* **tractors**

trade *noun* **1.** The business of buying and selling goods; commerce. **2.** An exchange of one thing for another: *Let's make a trade—my sled for your bicycle.* **3.** A kind of work; craft: *My neighbor is learning the tailor's trade.* **4.** The people who work in a business or industry.
◊ *verb* **1.** To take part in buying, selling, or bartering. **2.** To give in exchange or make an exchange; swap: *My friend and I traded seats.*
trade (trād) ◊ *noun, plural* **trades** ◊ *verb* **traded, trading**

trademark *noun* A device, as a name or symbol, that identifies a product. A trademark can legally be used only by the owner.
trade·mark (**trād′**märk′) ◊ *noun, plural* **trademarks**

trading post *noun* A store in a frontier area where local products, such as furs or hides, are exchanged for food and supplies.
trading post ◊ *noun, plural* **trading posts**

tradition *noun* **1.** The passing down of ideas, customs, and beliefs from one generation to the next. **2.** An idea, custom, or belief that is passed down by tradition.
tra·di·tion (trə **dĭsh′**ən) ◊ *noun, plural* **traditions**

traditional *adjective* Of, passed down by, or in agreement with tradition: *It's traditional to have turkey for Thanksgiving dinner.*
tra·di·tion·al (trə **dĭsh′**ə nəl) ◊ *adjective*

traffic *noun* **1.** The movement of vehicles and people along roads and streets, of ships on the seas, or of aircraft in the sky. **2.** The number of vehicles, ships, or aircraft in movement: *Traffic is heavy during rush hour.* **3.** The exchange of goods in commerce; trade.
◊ *verb* To carry on trade.
traf·fic (**trăf′**ĭk) ◊ *noun* ◊ *verb* **trafficked, trafficking**

tragedy *noun* **1.** A serious play that ends with great misfortune, disaster, or ruin. **2.** A terrible event; disaster.
trag·e·dy (**trăj′**ĭ dē) ◊ *noun, plural* **tragedies**

tragic *adjective* **1.** Of or relating to dramatic tragedy. **2.** Very unfortunate; disastrous.
trag·ic (**trăj′**ĭk) ◊ *adjective*

trail *verb* **1.** To drag, allow to drag, or be dragged along behind: *The child trailed a toy cart. The long coat trailed over the floor.* **2.** To follow the traces or scent of; track. **3.** To lag behind: *The home team trailed by 12 points.* **4.** To grow along or over a surface.
◊ *noun* **1.** A mark, trace, or path left by a moving body: *The wagon left a trail of dust.* **2.** The scent of a person or animal. **3.** A path or track, especially through woods.
trail (trāl) ◊ *verb* **trailed, trailing** ◊ *noun, plural* **trails**

trailer *noun* **1.** A vehicle that is pulled by a tractor or truck. **2.** A vehicle that can be pulled, as by an automobile or truck, and that is used as a home or office.
trail·er (**trā′**lər) ◊ *noun, plural* **trailers**

T

train *noun* **1.** A string of connected railroad cars drawn by a locomotive or driven by electricity. **2.** A long moving line of persons, animals, or vehicles: *A train of camels crossed the desert.* **3.** A part of a long dress that trails behind the wearer.
◊ *verb* **1.** To instruct in a way of behaving or performing: *My parents have trained me to be polite.* **2.** To instruct in an art, trade, or profession. **3.** To make or become fit for an athletic performance: *Coaches are training the players for the team.* **4.** To cause to grow in or take on a desired course or shape: *We trained ivy to grow up the wall.*
train (trān) ◊ *noun, plural* **trains** ◊ *verb* **trained, training**

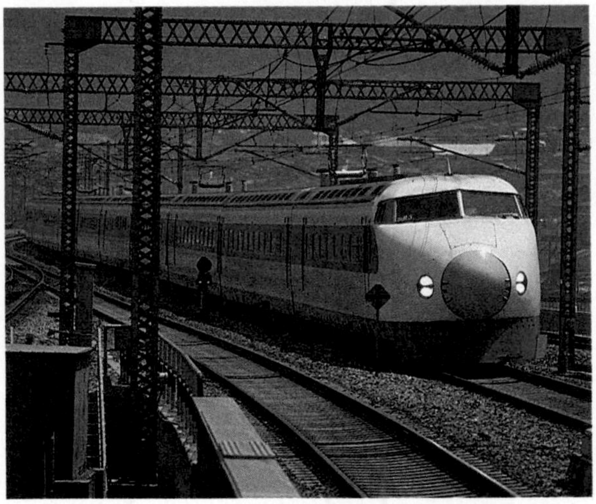

▲ **train**

training *noun* **1.** The act, process, or routine of training or being trained. **2.** Good physical condition, as for a sport.
train·ing (**trā′**nĭng) ◊ *noun*

trait *noun* A quality that helps to set off one person or thing from another; characteristic: *Honesty is one of your best traits.*
trait (trāt) ◊ *noun, plural* **traits**

ă	pat	ĭ	pit	oi	**oil**	th	ba**th**
ā	pay	ī	ride	o͝o	book	*th*	ba**th**e
â	care	î	fierce	o͞o	boot	ə	ago, item
ä	father	ŏ	pot	ou	**out**		pencil
ĕ	pet	ō	go	ŭ	cut		atom
ē	be	ô	paw, for	û	fur		circus

traitor *noun* A person who betrays a cause, a trust, or his or her country.
trai·tor (**trā′**tər) ◊ *noun, plural* **traitors**

tramp *verb* **1.** To walk with a heavy step: *They tramped up the stairs.* **2.** To go through on foot: *We tramped the woods in search of wild raspberries.* **3.** To step on heavily: *I tramped down the snow to make a path.*
◊ *noun* **1.** The sound of heavy walking or marching. **2.** A walking trip; hike. **3.** A person who wanders around and usually has no regular job or place to stay.
tramp (trămp) ◊ *verb* **tramped, tramping** ◊ *noun, plural* **tramps**

trample *verb* To tread heavily on; crush.
tram·ple (**trăm′**pəl) ◊ *verb* **trampled, trampling**

trampoline *noun* A sheet of canvas fastened with springs inside a metal frame. A trampoline is used by gymnasts for springing and tumbling.
tram·po·line (**trăm′**pə lēn′) ◊ *noun, plural* **trampolines**

trance *noun* **1.** A mental condition somewhat like sleep that can be caused by being hypnotized. **2.** A dazed or dreamy condition, as of a person lost in thought.
trance (trăns) ◊ *noun, plural* **trances**

tranquil *adjective* Peaceful and quiet. —See Synonyms at **calm.**
tran·quil (**trăng′**kwĭl) ◊ *adjective*

trans– The prefix *trans–* means "across" or "beyond." A *transcontinental* trip will take you across a continent.

***VOCABULARY BUILDER* • trans–**

Many words that are formed with **trans–** are not entries in this dictionary. But you can figure out what these words mean by looking up the meanings of the root words and the prefix. For example:
transmarine = going across the sea
transpolar = traveling across a polar region

transcontinental *adjective* Crossing a continent: *We took a transcontinental flight from New York to Los Angeles.*
trans·con·ti·nen·tal (trăns′kŏn tə **nĕn′**tl *or* trănz′kŏn tə **nĕn′**tl) ◊ *adjective*

transfer *verb* **1.** To cause to move from one place to another: *Bees transfer pollen among flowers.* **2.** To move from one vehicle to another: *I got off the subway and transferred to a bus.* **3.** To move from one job, school, or location to another. **4.** To move a design from one surface to another: *Trace the design and then transfer it to the leather.*
◊ *noun* **1.** An act of transferring or example of being transferred. **2.** Someone or something that transfers or is transferred. **3.** A ticket that permits a passenger to change from one bus or train to another.
trans·fer ◊ *verb* (trăns **fûr′** *or* **trăns′**fər) **transferred, transferring** ◊ *noun* (**trăns′**fər), *plural* **transfers**

transform *verb* **1.** To change very much in form or appearance: *The cold weather transformed the green leaves into gold ones.* **2.** To change the nature, function, or condition of; convert: *A steam engine transforms heat into energy.* —See Synonyms at **change.**
trans·form (trăns **fôrm′**) ◊ *verb* **transformed, transforming**

transformation *noun* The act of transforming or the condition of being transformed.
trans·for·ma·tion (trans′fər **mā′**shən) ◊ *noun, plural* **transformations**

transformer *noun* A device that is used to transfer electric energy from one circuit to another.
trans·form·er (trăns **fôr′**mər) ◊ *noun, plural* **transformers**

transfusion *noun* A putting of blood or plasma into a person's or an animal's bloodstream.
trans·fu·sion (trăns **fyo͞o′**zhən) ◊ *noun, plural* **transfusions**

transistor *noun* A small electronic device used to control the flow of electricity, especially in radios, television sets, and computers.
tran·sis·tor (trăn **zĭs′**tər) ◊ *noun, plural* **transistors**

transit *noun* **1.** The act of passing over, across, or through; passage. **2.** The act of carrying things from one place to another: *The letters were lost in transit.* **3.** The transportation of people or goods, especially on public vehicles.
tran·sit (**trăn′**sĭt) ◊ *noun*

transition *noun* A change from one form, state, subject, or place to another: *It is a big transition from elementary school to junior high.*
tran·si·tion (trăn **zĭsh′**ən) ◊ *noun, plural* **transitions**

translate *verb* To put into or express in another language: *Together they translated the book from Russian into English.*
trans·late (trăns **lāt′**) ◊ *verb* **translated, translating**

translation *noun* **1.** The act or process of translating. **2.** Something that has been translated.
trans·la·tion (trăns **lā′**shən) ◊ *noun, plural* **translations**

translucent *adjective* Letting some but not all light through: *The frosted glass in the window was translucent.* —See Synonyms at **clear.**
trans·lu·cent (trăns **lo͞o′**sənt) ◊ *adjective*

transmission *noun* **1.** The act or process of transmitting. **2.** Something transmitted, as by radio or television. **3.** A series of gears by which power is carried from the engine to the wheels of a motor vehicle.
trans·mis·sion (trăns **mĭsh′**ən) ◊ *noun, plural* **transmissions**

transmit *verb* **1.** To send from one person, place, or thing to another: *If you sneeze you may transmit your cold to other people in the room.* —See Synonyms at **send. 2.** To send out an electric or electronic signal by wire or radio. **3.** To cause or allow to travel through a material or substance: *Glass transmits light.*
trans·mit (trăns **mĭt′**) ◊ *verb* **transmitted, transmitting**

transmitter *noun* A device that sends out electrical, radio, or television signals.
trans·mit·ter (trăns **mĭt′**ər) ◊ *noun, plural* **transmitters**

transom *noun* A small, often hinged window above a door or above another window.
tran·som (**trăn′**səm) ◊ *noun, plural* **transoms**

transparent *adjective* **1.** Allowing light to pass through so that objects on the other side can be seen clearly: *Lenses for eyeglasses are transparent.* —See Synonyms at **clear. 2.** Easily detected; obvious: *That was a transparent excuse.*
trans·par·ent (trăns **pâr′**ənt *or* trăns**păr′**ənt) ◊ *adjective*

T

transplant *verb* **1.** To remove a living plant and plant it again in another place. **2.** To transfer tissue or an organ from one body or body part to another. **3.** To transfer to and establish in a new place: *The family was transplanted from New York to Chicago.*
◊ *noun* **1.** Something transplanted, especially tissue or an organ transplanted by surgery. **2.** The act or operation of transplanting: *The doctor performed a heart transplant.*
trans·plant ◊ *verb* (trăns **plănt′**) **transplanted, transplanting** ◊ *noun* (**trăns′**plănt′), *plural* **transplants**

transport *verb* **1.** To carry from one place to another. —See Synonyms at **carry.** **2.** To fill with strong emotion.
◊ *noun* **1.** The act of carrying from one place to another. **2.** A ship for carrying troops or military equipment. **3.** A vehicle, as an aircraft, ship, or train, for carrying passengers or freight.
trans·port ◊ *verb* (trăns **pôrt′**) **transported, transporting** ◊ *noun* (**trăns′**pôrt′), *plural* **transports**

transportation *noun* **1.** The act or process of transporting. **2.** A means of transporting: *Planes are fast transportation.* **3.** The business of transporting passengers or goods.
trans·por·ta·tion (trăns′pər **tā′**shən) ◊ *noun*

trap *noun* **1.** A device for catching animals. **2.** Something that is used to trick and catch a person who is not on guard: *The detective set a trap for the suspect.* **3.** A device for collecting waste materials from the liquid that flows through a drain.
◊ *verb* **1.** To catch in or as if in a trap. —See Synonyms at **catch.** **2.** To set traps for animals, especially as a business.
trap (trăp) ◊ *noun, plural* **traps** ◊ *verb* **trapped, trapping**

trap door *noun* A hinged or sliding door in a floor, ceiling, or roof.
trap door ◊ *noun, plural* **trap doors**

trapeze *noun* A short horizontal bar hung from two parallel ropes used for acrobatics.
tra·peze (tră **pēz′**) ◊ *noun, plural* **trapezes**

▲ **trapeze**

trapper *noun* A person who traps animals for their fur.
trap·per (**trăp′**ər) ◊ *noun, plural* **trappers**

trash *noun* Material or objects to be thrown away; refuse.
trash (trăsh) ◊ *noun*

travel *verb* **1.** To go from one place to another; journey: *The whole family traveled around the world.* **2.** To journey over or through: *We traveled a road along the river.* **3.** To be transmitted; pass: *A rumor travels from person to person.*
◊ *noun* **1.** The act or process of traveling. **2. travels** A series of journeys.
trav·el (**trăv′**əl) ◊ *verb* **traveled, traveling** ◊ *noun, plural* **travels**

traveler *noun* A person who travels.
trav·el·er (**trăv′**ə lər) ◊ *noun, plural* **travelers**

trawl *noun* A large, cone-shaped net that is towed along the sea bottom to catch fish.
◊ *verb* To fish or catch with a trawl.
trawl (trôl) ◊ *noun, plural* **trawls** ◊ *verb* **trawled, trawling**

trawler *noun* A boat used for trawling.
trawl·er (**trô′**lər) ◊ *noun, plural* **trawlers**

tray *noun* A flat, shallow container with a raised edge or rim for carrying, holding, or showing articles.
tray (trā) ◊ *noun, plural* **trays**

ă	pat	ĭ	pit	oi	**oil**	th	ba**th**
ā	pay	ī	ride	ŏŏ	book	*th*	ba**th**e
â	care	î	fierce	ōō	boot	ə	ago, item
ä	father	ŏ	pot	ou	**out**		pencil
ĕ	pet	ō	go	ŭ	cut		atom
ē	be	ô	paw, for	û	fur		circus

treacherous *adjective* **1.** Betraying trust; disloyal: *The treacherous spies betrayed their country.* **2.** Not to be trusted; dangerous: *The surf at this beach is treacherous.*
treach·er·ous (**trĕch′**ər əs) ◊ *adjective*

treachery *noun* **1.** An act of betraying trust. **2.** Treacherous behavior.
treach·er·y (**trĕch′**ə rē) ◊ *noun, plural* **treacheries**

tread *verb* **1.** To walk on, over, or along. **2.** To set the foot down in walking; step: *Tread softly or you'll wake the baby.* **3.** To press beneath the foot; trample. **4.** To make a path or trail by walking.
◊ *noun* **1.** The act, way, or sound of treading. **2.** The horizontal part of a step in a staircase. **3.** The part of a wheel or shoe sole that touches the ground. **4.** The grooves on a tire that enable it to grip the road.
tread (trĕd) ◊ *verb* **trod, trodden** *or* **trod, treading** ◊ *noun, plural* **treads**

treadle *noun* A pedal or lever that is pushed up and down or back and forth with the foot to drive a wheel, as in a sewing machine.
tread·le (**trĕd′**l) ◊ *noun, plural* **treadles**

treadmill *noun* A device that is operated by walking on the moving steps of a wheel or on an endless moving belt.
tread·mill (**trĕd′**mĭl′) ◊ *noun, plural* **treadmills**

▲ **treadmill**

treason *noun* The crime of betraying or plotting against one's country, especially by helping an enemy during a war.
trea·son (**trē′**zən) ◊ *noun*

treasure *noun* **1.** Wealth, such as jewels or money, that has been collected or hidden. **2.** A very precious or valuable person or thing.
◊ *verb* To value very highly; cherish.
treas·ure (**trĕzh′**ər) ◊ *noun, plural* **treasures** ◊ *verb* **treasured, treasuring**

treasurer *noun* A person who has charge of the funds of a government or an organization.
treas·ur·er (**trĕzh′**ər ər) ◊ *noun, plural* **treasurers**

treasury *noun* **1.** A place where funds are kept and managed. **2.** A place where treasure is kept. **3. Treasury** A government department that is in charge of public funds.
treas·ur·y (**trĕzh′**ə rē) ◊ *noun, plural* **treasuries**

treat *verb* **1.** To act or behave toward: *The teacher treats us fairly.* **2.** To deal with, handle, or cover: *The science book treats the growth of plants and animals in detail.* **3.** To regard or consider: *Don't treat friendly advice as an insult.* **4.** To give medical attention to; try to relieve or cure: *We treated the rash with an ointment.* **5.** To cause to undergo a physical or chemical process: *The cloth was treated with dye.* **6.** To provide food or entertainment for at one's own expense: *I treated my friend to a movie.*
◊ *noun* **1.** Something, such as food or entertainment, that is paid for or given by one person to another. **2.** Something that gives special enjoyment.
treat (trēt) ◊ *verb* **treated, treating** ◊ *noun, plural* **treats**

treatment *noun* **1.** An act or way of treating. **2.** The use of something to relieve or cure a disease.
treat·ment (**trēt′**mənt) ◊ *noun, plural* **treatments**

treaty *noun* An official agreement between two or more countries, national governments, or rulers.
trea·ty (**trē′**tē) ◊ *noun, plural* **treaties**

treble *adjective* **1.** Triple. **2.** Of, having, or performing the highest musical part, or range.
◊ *noun* The highest musical part, voice, instrument, or range.
◊ *verb* To triple.
treb·le (**trĕb′**əl) ◊ *adjective* ◊ *noun, plural* **trebles** ◊ *verb* **trebled, trebling**

tree *noun* **1.** A usually tall woody plant with one main stem. **2.** Something like a tree, such as a pole for hanging up clothes.

T

◊ *verb* To chase and force to climb a tree: *The dogs treed the cat.*
tree (trē) ◊ *noun, plural* **trees** ◊ *verb* **treed, treeing**

tree farm *noun* An area of land where trees are planted and grown for commercial use.
tree farm ◊ *noun, plural* **tree farms**

trek *verb* To make a slow, hard journey.
◊ *noun* A slow, hard journey.
trek (trĕk) ◊ *verb* **trekked, trekking** ◊ *noun, plural* **treks**

trellis *noun* A frame of crossed slats used to support or train climbing plants.
trel·lis (**trĕl'**ĭs) ◊ *noun, plural* **trellises**

▲ **trellis**

tremble *verb* **1.** To shake from or as if from fear or cold; shiver. **2.** To be afraid or worried.
◊ *noun* An act of trembling.
trem·ble (**trĕm'**bəl) ◊ *verb* **trembled, trembling** ◊ *noun, plural* **trembles**

tremendous *adjective* Very great, large, or intense: *A meteor falls with tremendous speed.*
tre·men·dous (trĭ **mĕn'**dəs) ◊ *adjective*

tremor *noun* **1.** A shaking or vibrating movement, especially of the earth. **2.** A rapid shaking or trembling of the body.
trem·or (**trĕm'**ər) ◊ *noun, plural* **tremors**

trench *noun* A long, narrow ditch, especially one used to protect soldiers in battle.
trench (trĕnch) ◊ *noun, plural* **trenches**

trend *noun* A general tendency or course: *The trend of gasoline prices is still upward.*
trend (trĕnd) ◊ *noun, plural* **trends**

trespass *verb* **1.** To do something that is wrong; sin. **2.** To go onto the property of another without the owner's permission.
◊ *noun* **1.** An act of trespassing. **2.** A sin.
tres·pass (**trĕs'**pəs) ◊ *verb* **trespassed, trespassing** ◊ *noun, plural* **trespasses**

tress *noun* A braid or lock of hair.
tress (trĕs) ◊ *noun, plural* **tresses**

trestle *noun* **1.** A framework that supports a bridge or railroad tracks. **2.** A horizontal beam or bar held up by two pairs of legs and used as a support, as for the top of a table.
tres·tle (**trĕs'**əl) ◊ *noun, plural* **trestles**

trial *noun* **1.** The studying and deciding of a case in a court of law. **2.** The act or process of testing and trying. **3.** An effort to do something; attempt. **4.** Something that tests a person's patience or endurance.
tri·al (**trī'**əl) ◊ *noun, plural* **trials**

triangle *noun* **1.** A figure with three sides and three angles. **2.** Something that is shaped like a triangle. **3.** A musical instrument made of a bar of metal bent into the form of a triangle. A triangle is played by being struck with a small steel rod.
tri·an·gle (**trī'**ăng'gəl) ◊ *noun, plural* **triangles**

triangular *adjective* Of, relating to, or shaped like a triangle.
tri·an·gu·lar (trī **ăng'**gyə lər) ◊ *adjective*

tribal *adjective* Of or characteristic of a tribe.
trib·al (**trī'**bəl) ◊ *adjective*

tribe *noun* **1.** A group of people who share a common ancestry, language, and culture. **2.** A group of people of the same kind.
tribe (trīb) ◊ *noun, plural* **tribes**

tributary *noun* A river or stream that flows into a larger river or stream.
trib·u·tar·y (**trĭb'**yə tĕr'ē) ◊ *noun, plural* **tributaries**

tribute *noun* **1.** Something given to show thanks or respect. **2.** Money paid by a weaker ruler or nation to a stronger one.
trib·ute (**trĭb'**yo͞ot') ◊ *noun, plural* **tributes**

trice *noun* A short period of time; instant.
trice (trīs) ◊ *noun*

trick *noun* **1.** An act that requires a special skill; stunt: *The entertainer did several juggling tricks.* **2.** A clever device, method, or technique. **3.** Something, such as a scheme, that is used to cheat or deceive. **4.** A mischievous action; prank. **5.** A mean, stupid, or

ă	pat	ĭ	pit	oi	oil	th	bath
ā	pay	ī	ride	o͝o	book	*th*	bathe
â	care	î	fierce	o͞o	boot	ə	ago, item
ä	father	ŏ	pot	ou	out		pencil
ĕ	pet	ō	go	ŭ	cut		atom
ē	be	ô	paw, for	û	fur		circus

childish act: *That was a rotten trick!*
◊ *verb* To persuade, deceive, fool, or cheat by using tricks.
trick (trĭk) ◊ *noun, plural* **tricks** ◊ *verb* **tricked, tricking**

trickery *noun* The use of tricks to deceive.
trick·er·y (trĭk′ə rē) ◊ *noun, plural* **trickeries**

trickle *verb* **1.** To flow or fall in drops or in a thin stream. **2.** To pass, come, or go as if by trickling: *The audience trickled into the theater in twos and threes.*
◊ *noun* A small flow or thin stream.
trick·le (trĭk′əl) ◊ *verb* **trickled, trickling** ◊ *noun, plural* **trickles**

tricky *adjective* **1.** Likely to use tricks. **2.** Requiring caution or skill: *Riding a skateboard is tricky and dangerous.*
trick·y (trĭk′ē) ◊ *adjective* **trickier, trickiest**

tricycle *noun* A vehicle with three wheels, usually propelled by pedals.
tri·cy·cle (trī′sĭk′əl) ◊ *noun, plural* **tricycles**

tried *adjective* Tested and found trustworthy.
◊ *verb* Past tense and past participle of **try.**
tried (trīd) ◊ *adjective* ◊ *verb*

trifle *noun* **1.** Something unimportant or worthless. **2.** A small amount of money.
◊ *verb* **1.** To behave without being serious or respectful: *Don't trifle with the principal of the school.* **2.** To play carelessly; toy: *I trifled with a pencil while waiting for the start of the examination.*
tri·fle (trī′fəl) ◊ *noun, plural* **trifles** ◊ *verb* **trifled, trifling**

trifling *adjective* Having little importance or value: *Don't let trifling matters disturb you.*
tri·fling (trī′flĭng) ◊ *adjective*

trigger *noun* The small lever on a gun that is used to fire it.
trig·ger (trĭg′ər) ◊ *noun, plural* **triggers**

trill *noun* A vibrating sound like the one that is made by some birds.
trill (trĭl) ◊ *noun, plural* **trills**

trillion *noun* One thousand billions.
◊ *adjective* Being equal to one thousand billions.
tril·lion (trĭl′yən) ◊ *noun, plural* **trillions** ◊ *adjective*

trim *verb* **1.** To make neat or even, especially by cutting: *Trim the crust from the bread.* **2.** To put decorations on; ornament: *The monarch's robe was trimmed with ermine.* **3.** To adjust sails and yards on a boat to catch the wind properly.
◊ *noun* **1.** Something, such as braid on clothing, that is used for trimming or decorating. **2.** An act of clipping or cutting: *Your hair needs a trim.* **3.** Proper order or condition.
◊ *adjective* **1.** In good order; neat. **2.** Well proportioned, with simple or slim lines.
trim (trĭm) ◊ *verb* **trimmed, trimming** ◊ *noun, plural* **trims** ◊ *adjective* **trimmer, trimmest**

trimming *noun* **1.** Something that is used to decorate, trim, or ornament. **2.** Something that goes with and completes something else: *We eat turkey with all the trimmings at Thanksgiving.* **3.** A small piece that is trimmed off a larger piece.
trim·ming (trĭm′ĭng) ◊ *noun, plural* **trimmings**

trinket *noun* A small ornament.
trin·ket (trĭng′kĭt) ◊ *noun, plural* **trinkets**

trio *noun* **1.** A group of three. **2.** A musical composition for three performers.
tri·o (trē′ō) ◊ *noun, plural* **trios**

trip *noun* **1.** A passage from one place to another; journey. **2.** A stumble or mistake.
◊ *verb* **1.** To strike the foot against something and stumble. **2.** To cause to stumble. **3.** To make or cause to make a mistake. **4.** To move lightly with quick steps; skip.
trip (trĭp) ◊ *noun, plural* **trips** ◊ *verb* **tripped, tripping**

SYNONYMS

trip, expedition, journey, tour

I am taking a *trip* to visit my relatives. The explorers left on their *expedition.* The travelers' *journey* took several months. Our guide made our *tour* of Europe very interesting.

triple *adjective* **1.** Of or having three parts. **2.** Being three times as great or as many.
◊ *verb* To make or become three times as great or as many.
trip·le (trĭp′əl) ◊ *adjective* ◊ *verb* **tripled, tripling**

triplet *noun* **1.** A group or set of three. **2.** One of three children born at one birth.
trip·let (trĭp′lĭt) ◊ *noun, plural* **triplets**

T

tripod *noun* A stand with three legs, used especially to support a camera.
tri·pod (**trī′**pŏd′) ◊ *noun, plural* **tripods**

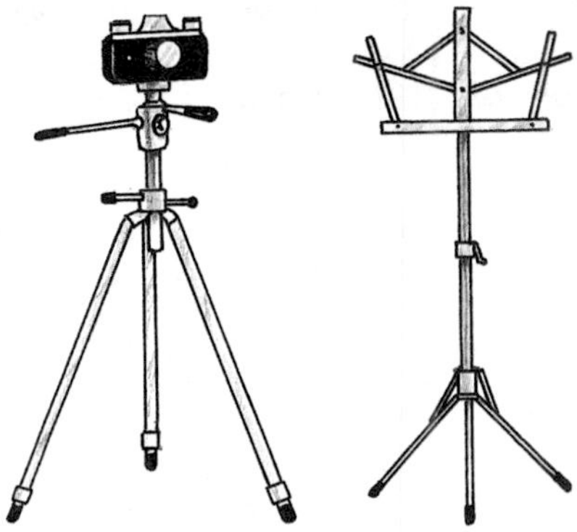

▲ **tripod**

triumph *verb* To be victorious; win.
◊ *noun* **1.** The fact of being victorious. **2.** Joy from victory or success: *When the team won, we gave yells of triumph.*
tri·umph (**trī′**əmf) ◊ *verb* **triumphed, triumphing** ◊ *noun, plural* **triumphs**

triumphal *adjective* Of, relating to, or celebrating a triumph.
tri·um·phal (trī **ŭm′**fəl) ◊ *adjective*

triumphant *adjective* **1.** Victorious or successful. **2.** Rejoicing over victory or success.
tri·um·phant (trī **ŭm′**fənt) ◊ *adjective*

trivial *adjective* That is not important; trifling: *Don't worry about trivial matters.*
triv·i·al (**trĭv′**ē əl) ◊ *adjective*

trod *verb* Past tense and a past participle of **tread.**
trod (trŏd) ◊ *verb*

trodden *verb* A past participle of **tread.**
trod·den (**trŏd′**n) ◊ *verb*

troll *noun* An imaginary dwarf or a giant that was supposed to live in places such as caves.
troll (trōl) ◊ *noun, plural* **trolls**

trolley *noun* **1.** An electrically operated car that runs on a track; streetcar. **2.** A device, such as a wheel at the end of a metal pole, that is used to carry electricity from an overhead wire to run the motor of a streetcar.
trol·ley (**trŏl′**ē) ◊ *noun, plural* **trolleys**

trombone *noun* A large brass instrument that has a low tone. A player changes tones on a trombone by sliding a U-shaped tube over two other fixed tubes.
trom·bone (trŏm **bōn′**) ◊ *noun, plural* **trombones**

▲ **trombone**

troop *noun* **1.** A group of persons, animals, or things. **2.** A group of soldiers mounted on horses or riding in motor vehicles. **3. troops** Military forces.
◊ *verb* To move or go in or as if in a troop: *The students trooped into the auditorium.*
troop (tro͞op) ◊ *noun, plural* **troops** ◊ *verb* **trooped, trooping**
‖*These sound alike:* **troop, troupe**

trooper *noun* **1.** A cavalry soldier. **2.** A state police officer.
troop·er (**tro͞o′**pər) ◊ *noun, plural* **troopers**

trophy *noun* A prize given or received as a symbol of victory or achievement.
tro·phy (**trō′**fē) ◊ *noun, plural* **trophies**

tropical *adjective* Of or typical of the tropics: *The mango is a tropical fruit.*
trop·i·cal (**trŏp′**ĭ kəl) ◊ *adjective*

tropics *plural noun* The warm regions of the earth that are near the equator.
trop·ics (**trŏp′**ĭks) ◊ *plural noun*

trot *noun* **1.** A four-footed animal's slow running gait in which the left front foot and the right hind foot move forward together, as do the right front foot and the left hind foot. **2.** A person's slow running gait.

ă	pat	ĭ	pit	oi	**oi**l	th	ba**th**
ā	pay	ī	ride	o͝o	bo**o**k	*th*	ba**th**e
â	care	î	fierce	o͞o	bo**o**t	ə	ago, item
ä	father	ŏ	pot	ou	**ou**t		pencil
ĕ	pet	ō	go	ŭ	cut		atom
ē	be	ô	paw, for	û	fur		circus

◊ *verb* **1.** To move or cause to move at a trot: *The horses trotted down the road.* **2.** To run slowly; jog.
trot (trŏt) ◊ *noun, plural* **trots** ◊ *verb* **trotted, trotting**

trouble *noun* **1.** A difficult, dangerous, or upsetting situation: *The damaged ship was in trouble.* **2.** A cause of difficulty, annoyance, or distress: *Our dog isn't any trouble in the house.* **3.** Extra work or effort. **4.** Failure to work properly: *The airplane had engine trouble.* **5.** A physical ailment: *The patient has stomach trouble.*
◊ *verb* **1.** To upset or become upset; worry. **2.** To cause bother to: *May I trouble you for the time?*
trou·ble (**trŭb′** əl) ◊ *noun, plural* **troubles** ◊ *verb* **troubled, troubling**

trough *noun* **1.** A long, narrow container for holding water or food for animals. **2.** A long, narrow hollow, as between ocean waves.
trough (trôf) ◊ *noun, plural* **troughs**

trounce *verb* **1.** To beat severely; thrash. **2.** To defeat soundly.
trounce (trouns) ◊ *verb* **trounced, trouncing**

troupe *noun* A company or group, especially of touring actors, singers, or dancers.
troupe (tro͞op) ◊ *noun, plural* **troupes**
‖ *These sound alike:* **troupe, troop**

trousers *plural noun* An outer garment that reaches from the waist to the ankles and is divided into sections that fit the legs.
trou·sers (**trou′** zərz) ◊ *plural noun*

trout *noun* A freshwater fish that often has a spotted body and is related to the salmon.
trout (trout) ◊ *noun, plural* **trout**

trowel *noun* **1.** A tool with a flat blade for spreading plaster and cement. **2.** A gardening tool with a blade shaped like a scoop.
trow·el (**trou′** əl) ◊ *noun, plural* **trowels**

truant *noun* **1.** A student who is absent from school without permission. **2.** A person who avoids doing his or her work or duty.
tru·ant (**tro͞o′** ənt) ◊ *noun, plural* **truants**

truce *noun* A temporary stop in fighting.
truce (tro͞os) ◊ *noun, plural* **truces**

truck *noun* A motor vehicle that is designed to carry large or heavy loads.
◊ *verb* To carry by truck.
truck (trŭk) ◊ *noun, plural* **trucks** ◊ *verb* **trucked, trucking**

trudge *verb* To walk slowly and with effort; plod: *I trudged through the deep snow.*
trudge (trŭj) ◊ *verb* **trudged, trudging**

true *adjective* **1.** Being in agreement with fact or reality; accurate. **2.** Faithful and loyal: *You are a true friend.* **3.** Being so by a legal or honest claim: *The prince is the true heir to the throne.* **4.** Properly so called; genuine: *The spider isn't a true bug.* —See Synonyms at **real.**
◊ *adverb* Truly or accurately.
true (tro͞o) ◊ *adjective, adverb* **truer, truest**

truly *adverb* **1.** In a true manner: *Please speak truly and frankly.* **2.** In fact; indeed: *The view from the roof is truly beautiful.*
tru·ly (**tro͞o′** lē) ◊ *adverb*

trumpet *noun* **1.** A brass wind instrument, usually a coiled tube with a mouthpiece at one end and a flaring bell at the other. **2.** A loud sound like that of a trumpet. **3.** Something that is shaped like a trumpet.
◊ *verb* **1.** To play a trumpet. **2.** To make a loud sound like that of a trumpet: *The elephants in the zoo were trumpeting loudly.*
trum·pet (**trŭm′** pĭt) ◊ *noun, plural* **trumpets** ◊ *verb* **trumpeted, trumpeting**

trunk *noun* **1.** The often tall, thick, woody main stem of a tree. **2.** The main part of the body of a human being apart from the arms, legs, and head. **3.** A sturdy box in which clothes or belongings can be packed for travel or storage. **4.** The covered compartment of an automobile, used for storage. **5.** The long, flexible snout of an elephant, used for grasping and feeding. **6. trunks** Men's shorts worn especially for athletics.
trunk (trŭngk) ◊ *noun, plural* **trunks**

trust *verb* **1.** To have or put confidence in; depend on: *Trust your parents' judgment on these matters.* —See Synonyms at **rely.** **2.** To hope or assume: *I trust you're feeling well.*
◊ *noun* **1.** Firm belief in the honesty, character, or strength of someone or something; confidence: *Don't betray your friend's trust.* **2.** A very serious and important responsibility or duty; charge: *Holding a high public office is a public trust.*
trust (trŭst) ◊ *verb* **trusted, trusting** ◊ *noun*

trustee *noun* A person or firm legally responsible for another person's property.
trus·tee (trŭs **tē′**) ◊ *noun, plural* **trustees**

T

trustful *adjective* Full of trust.
trust·ful (**trŭst′** fəl) ◊ *adjective*

trustworthy *adjective* Worthy of trust; dependable: *My friend is an extremely trustworthy person.*
trust·wor·thy (**trŭst′** wûr′*th*ē) ◊ *adjective*

trusty *adjective* Dependable: *I took my trusty binoculars and went out early to watch the birds.*
trust·y (**trŭs′** tē) ◊ *adjective* **trustier, trustiest**

truth *noun* **1.** The quality or condition of being true or accurate: *There was truth in what she said.* **2.** Something that is true: *I told him the truth.* **3.** A true statement.
truth (trōōth) ◊ *noun, plural* **truths**

truthful *adjective* **1.** Telling the truth; honest: *You should be truthful at all times.* **2.** Being true: *That is not a truthful statement.*
truth·ful (**trōōth′** fəl) ◊ *adjective*

try *verb* **1.** To test, as to evaluate quality, strength, or effect: *I decided to try a new route to school.* **2.** To decide the guilt or innocence of or to study in a court of law: *The suspect was tried for theft. A judge tries legal cases.* **3.** To cause to undergo strain or hardship: *The commercials on TV try my patience.* **4.** To make an effort; attempt: *Try to sleep now.*
◊ *noun* An attempt; effort.
◊ *idiom* **try on** To put on so as to test fit or appearance: *We tried on new running shoes.*
try (trī) ◊ *verb* **tried, trying** ◊ *noun, plural* **tries**

trying *adjective* Causing strain or hardship.
try·ing (**trī′** ĭng) ◊ *adjective*

tryout *noun* A test to learn a person's qualifications, as to perform a role in a play.
try·out (**trī′** out′) ◊ *noun, plural* **tryouts**

T-shirt *noun* A close-fitting shirt or undershirt with short sleeves and no collar.
T-shirt (**tē′** shûrt′) ◊ *noun, plural* **T-shirts**

tsp. The abbreviation for *teaspoon.*

tub *noun* **1.** A low, round vessel, as one used for packing or storing. **2.** A bathtub.
tub (tŭb) ◊ *noun, plural* **tubs**

ă	pat	ĭ	pit	oi	**oil**	th	**bath**
ā	pay	ī	ride	ŏŏ	**book**	*th*	**bathe**
â	care	î	fierce	ōō	**boot**	ə	ago, item
ä	father	ŏ	pot	ou	**out**		pencil
ĕ	pet	ō	go	ŭ	**cut**		atom
ē	be	ô	paw, for	û	**fur**		circus

tuba *noun* A large brass wind instrument with a full, rich tone and a low range.
tu·ba (**tōō′** bə *or* **tyōō′** bə) ◊ *noun, plural* **tubas**

tube *noun* **1.** A hollow cylinder, as of glass or rubber, that is used to carry liquids. **2.** A tubelike part, as of the body. **3.** A flexible container from which substances such as toothpaste can be squeezed out. **4.** Something, as a subway tunnel, that is shaped like a tube.
tube (tōōb *or* tyōōb) ◊ *noun, plural* **tubes**

tuber *noun* A thickened, usually underground stem, as that of a potato, that bears buds from which new plants grow.
tu·ber (**tōō′** bər *or* **tyōō′** bər) ◊ *noun, plural* **tubers**

tuberculosis *noun* A contagious disease that is caused by bacteria and that destroys body tissues, especially in the lungs.
tu·ber·cu·lo·sis (tōō bûr′kyə **lō′** sĭs *or* tyōō-bûr′kyə **lō′** sĭs) ◊ *noun*

tuck *noun* A pleat or fold that is stitched into the fabric of a garment to adjust the fit or to decorate it.
◊ *verb* **1.** To make tucks in. **2.** To turn or push under the end or edges of: *Tuck in your shirt.* **3.** To cover snugly by tucking in sheets and blankets: *We tucked the baby in.*
tuck (tŭk) ◊ *noun, plural* **tucks** ◊ *verb* **tucked, tucking**

Tues. The abbreviation for *Tuesday.*

Tuesday *noun* The third day of the week.
Tues·day (**tōōz′** dē *or* **tyōōz′** dē) ◊ *noun, plural* **Tuesdays**

***HISTORY* • Tuesday**

Four of the seven days of the week were named after the gods that the English believed in before they became Christians. **Tuesday** was named after *Tiu,* the god of the sky.

tuft *noun* A bunch of strands, as of hair, that grow or are held close together at the base.
tuft (tŭft) ◊ *noun, plural* **tufts**

tug *verb* **1.** To pull at strongly or move by pulling strongly. **2.** To tow with a tugboat.

◊ *noun* **1.** A hard pull. **2.** A tugboat.
tug (tŭg) ◊ *verb* **tugged, tugging** ◊ *noun, plural* **tugs**

tugboat *noun* A small, very powerful boat that tows larger vessels.
tug·boat (tŭg′bōt′) ◊ *noun, plural* **tugboats**

▲ **tugboat**

tuition *noun* A fee paid for instruction.
tu·i·tion (to͞o ĭsh′ən *or* tyo͞o ĭsh′ən) ◊ *noun, plural* **tuitions**

tulip *noun* A garden plant that grows from a bulb and has colorful cup-shaped flowers. Tulips are planted in the fall and bloom in the spring and early summer.
tu·lip (to͞o′lĭp *or* tyo͞o′lĭp) ◊ *noun, plural* **tulips**

tumble *verb* **1.** To perform feats such as somersaults and leaps. **2.** To roll or toss about. **3.** To spill out in confusion, haste, or disorder: *The kids tumbled out of the bus.* **4.** To fall suddenly.
◊ *noun* An act of tumbling; fall.
tum·ble (tŭm′bəl) ◊ *verb* **tumbled, tumbling** ◊ *noun, plural* **tumbles**

SYNONYMS

tumble, collapse, fall, topple

The kittens *tumbled* around on the floor. The building *collapsed* during the fire. Don't *fall* over the edge of the cliff. We put on one too many blocks and our tower *toppled*.

tumbler *noun* **1.** A person who tumbles. **2.** A drinking glass with no handle or stem.
tum·bler (tŭm′blər) ◊ *noun, plural* **tumblers**

tumbleweed *noun* A plant that breaks off from its roots when it is dried up and is rolled about by the wind.
tum·ble·weed (tŭm′bəl wēd′) ◊ *noun*

▲ **tumbleweed**

tumor *noun* An abnormal mass of tissue within the body.
tu·mor (to͞o′mər *or* tyo͞o′mər) ◊ *noun, plural* **tumors**

tumult *noun* **1.** Noise and commotion; uproar. **2.** Agitation of the mind or emotions.
tu·mult (to͞o′məlt *or* tyo͞o′məlt) ◊ *noun, plural* **tumults**

tuna *noun* An often large ocean fish caught in great numbers for food. Some tuna can be as long as 14 feet and can weigh 1,600 pounds.
tu·na (to͞o′nə *or* tyo͞o′nə) ◊ *noun, plural* **tuna** *or* **tunas**

tundra *noun* An area of the arctic regions that has no trees and very few other plants.
tun·dra (tŭn′drə) ◊ *noun, plural* **tundras**

tune *noun* **1.** A melody, especially one that is simple and easy to remember. **2.** Correct musical pitch: *The old piano was out of tune.*
◊ *verb* **1.** To adjust so as to be in the correct musical pitch: *I tuned my cello.* **2.** To adjust so as to get good radio or TV reception: *Tune to the next channel.*
tune (to͞on *or* tyo͞on) ◊ *noun, plural* **tunes** ◊ *verb* **tuned, tuning**

tunic *noun* **1.** A loose garment usually reaching the knees. Ancient Greeks and Romans wore tunics. **2.** A jacket or blouse usually reaching the hips.

T

tu·nic (to͞o′nĭk *or* **tyo͞o′**nĭk) ◊ *noun, plural* **tunics**

tuning fork *noun* A metal device that sounds a tone when it is struck. A tuning fork is used in tuning musical instruments to the correct pitch.
tuning fork ◊ *noun, plural* **tuning forks**

▲ **tuning fork**

tunnel *noun* An underground or underwater passage.
◊ *verb* To make or dig a tunnel.
tun·nel (**tŭn′**əl) ◊ *noun, plural* **tunnels** ◊ *verb* **tunneled, tunneling**

turban *noun* **1.** A long cloth wound around the head, worn especially by Moslems. **2.** A woman's hat like a turban.
tur·ban (**tûr′**bən) ◊ *noun, plural* **turbans**

turbine *noun* A device in which mechanical power is produced by making flowing water, air, or steam turn the blades or vanes of a rotating wheel.
tur·bine (**tûr′**bĭn *or* **tûr′**bīn′) ◊ *noun, plural* **turbines**

turbulent *adjective* Marked by or causing agitation or disturbance: *The water underneath the waterfall was turbulent.*
tur·bu·lent (**tûr′**byə lənt) ◊ *adjective*

tureen *noun* A deep dish, often with a cover, for serving foods such as soup and stew.
tu·reen (to͞o **rēn′** *or* tyo͞o **rēn′**) ◊ *noun, plural* **tureens**

turf *noun* The top layer of grassy land, including matted plant roots and soil.
turf (tûrf) ◊ *noun*

turkey *noun* A large North American bird that is raised for food.
tur·key (**tûr′**kē) ◊ *noun, plural* **turkeys**

ă	pat	ĭ	pit	oi	**oil**	th	**bath**
ā	pay	ī	ride	o͝o	**book**	*th*	**bathe**
â	care	î	fierce	o͞o	**boot**	ə	ago, item
ä	father	ŏ	pot	ou	**out**		pencil
ĕ	pet	ō	go	ŭ	cut		atom
ē	be	ô	paw, for	û	fur		circus

▲ **turkey**

turmoil *noun* Great confusion; uproar.
tur·moil (**tûr′**moil′) ◊ *noun*

turn *verb* **1.** To move or cause to move around a center; rotate: *I heard the key turn in the lock.* **2.** To perform by rotating: *The children turned somersaults.* **3.** To change or cause to change direction or course: *I turned and waved.* **4.** To take a course around or about: *The car turned the corner.* **5.** To direct: *I turned my attention to the speaker.* **6.** To transform; change: *Some caterpillars turn into moths.* **7.** To change or cause to change color: *The leaves turn in the fall.* **8.** To injure by twisting: *I turned my ankle.* **9.** To make sick; upset: *Greasy foods turn my stomach.* **10.** To change or cause to change one's feelings or opinions: *My friends turned against me. Don't try to turn one friend against another.* **11.** To change so as to be; become: *You suddenly turned pale.*
◊ *noun* **1.** The act of turning or the condition of being turned around a center; rotation. **2.** A change in direction, motion, or position: *Make a sharp right turn here.* **3.** A place where something turns. **4.** A time or point of change: *The house was built at the turn of the century.* **5.** A change, as in a course of events: *Things took a turn for the worse.* **6.** A chance or time to do something: *It's my turn to drive the boat.* **7.** Natural inclination or aptitude: *You have a scientific turn of mind.* **8.** An action that affects another: *Try to do a good turn every day.* **9.** A short ride or walk: *We took a turn around the park after lunch.* **10.** A single twist, as of wire around a spool.
◊ *idioms* **turn down 1.** To reduce the volume,

degree, speed, or flow of: *Turn down the radio.* **2.** To refuse to accept; reject: *Did you turn down their offer to help?* **turn off** To stop the operation, activity, or flow of: *We turned the radio off.* **turn on** To start the operation, activity, or flow of: *Turn the radio on.* **turn out** To turn off: *Turn out the lights when you go to bed.* **turn up 1.** To find or be found: *The missing wallet turned up in a wastebasket.* **2.** To make an appearance: *A big crowd turned up for the sale.*
turn (tûrn) ◊ *verb* **turned, turning** ◊ *noun, plural* **turns**

turnip *noun* The large, rounded, yellowish or white edible root of a garden plant.
tur·nip (**tûr′**nĭp) ◊ *noun, plural* **turnips**

turnout *noun* The number of people present at a gathering; attendance.
turn·out (**tûrn′**out′) ◊ *noun, plural* **turnouts**

turnpike *noun* A wide highway that drivers have to pay a toll for in order to use.
turn·pike (**tûrn′**pīk′) ◊ *noun, plural* **turnpikes**

turnstile *noun* A vertical post with horizontal bars that revolve around it to let one person at a time into or out of a public area.
turn·stile (**tûrn′**stīl′) ◊ *noun, plural* **turnstiles**

turntable *noun* **1.** A rotating circular platform on which a phonograph record is placed for playing. **2.** A circular platform with a railway track that rotates to turn locomotives.
turn·ta·ble (**tûrn′**tā′bəl) ◊ *noun, plural* **turntables**

turpentine *noun* An oil that is gotten from the wood or resin of certain pine trees. It is used as a paint thinner and as a solvent.
tur·pen·tine (**tûr′**pən tīn′) ◊ *noun*

turquoise *noun* A bluish-green mineral that is a valuable gem.
tur·quoise (**tûr′**koiz′ *or* **tûr′**kwoiz′) ◊ *noun, plural* **turquoises**

turret *noun* **1.** A small tower on a building. **2.** A structure, as on a tank or warship, on which usually rotating guns are mounted.
tur·ret (**tûr′**ĭt) ◊ *noun, plural* **turrets**

turtle *noun* Any of a group of reptiles that live on water or land and have a body covered by a hard, rounded shell. The turtle can pull its head, legs, and tail into the shell for protection.
tur·tle (**tûr′**tl) ◊ *noun, plural* **turtles**

▲ **turtle**

turtleneck *noun* **1.** A high, turned-down collar that fits closely around the neck. **2.** A sweater having a high, turned-down collar.
tur·tle·neck (**tûr′**tl nĕk′) ◊ *noun, plural* **turtlenecks**

tusk *noun* A long, pointed tooth, usually one of a pair, that projects outside the closed mouth. Elephants have tusks.
tusk (tŭsk) ◊ *noun, plural* **tusks**

▲ **tusk**

tutor *noun* A person who gives individual instruction to a student; private teacher. ◊ *verb* To act as a tutor to.
tu·tor (**to͞o′**tər *or* **tyo͞o′**tər) ◊ *noun, plural* **tutors** ◊ *verb* **tutored, tutoring**

T.V. *or* **TV** Abbreviations for *television.*

twang *noun* **1.** A sharp, ringing sound. **2.** A nasal tone of voice or way of speaking.

T

◊ *verb* **1.** To make or cause to make a twang. **2.** To talk with a nasal twang.
twang (twăng) ◊ *noun, plural* **twangs** ◊ *verb* **twanged, twanging**

tweed *noun* A coarse woolen fabric.
tweed (twēd) ◊ *noun, plural* **tweeds**

tweet *noun* A high chirping sound.
◊ *verb* To make this sound, as birds do.
tweet (twēt) ◊ *noun, plural* **tweets** ◊ *verb* **tweeted, tweeting**

twelfth *noun* **1.** The number in a series that matches the number twelve. **2.** One of twelve equal parts, written 1/12.
◊ *adjective* Coming after the eleventh.
twelfth (twĕlfth) ◊ *noun, plural* **twelfths** ◊ *adjective*

twelve *noun* The number, written 12, that is equal to the sum of 11 + 1.
◊ *adjective* Being one more than eleven.
twelve (twĕlv) ◊ *noun, plural* **twelves** ◊ *adjective*

twentieth *noun* **1.** The number in a series that matches the number twenty. **2.** One of twenty equal parts, written 1/20.
◊ *adjective* Coming after the nineteenth.
twen·ti·eth (**twĕn′** tē ĭth) ◊ *noun, plural* **twentieths** ◊ *adjective*

twenty *noun* The number, written 20, that is equal to the product of 2 × 10.
◊ *adjective* Being one more than nineteen.
twen·ty (**twĕn′** tē) ◊ *noun, plural* **twenties** ◊ *adjective*

twice *adverb* **1.** Two times: *He saw the movie twice.* **2.** In doubled degree or amount: *She works twice as hard as we do.*
twice (twīs) ◊ *adverb*

twiddle *verb* To turn around and around; twirl: *They just sat there, twiddling their thumbs.*
twid·dle (**twĭd′** l) ◊ *verb* **twiddled, twiddling**

twig *noun* A small branch or shoot of a tree or shrub.
twig (twĭg) ◊ *noun, plural* **twigs**

ă	pat	ĭ	pit	oi	**oil**	th	**bath**
ā	pay	ī	ride	ŏŏ	**book**	*th*	**bathe**
â	care	î	fierce	ōō	**boot**	ə	**ago, item**
ä	father	ŏ	pot	ou	**out**		pencil
ĕ	pet	ō	go	ŭ	**cut**		atom
ē	be	ô	paw, for	û	**fur**		circus

twilight *noun* The light or time at dawn or sunset when the sun is below the horizon but there is a little light in the sky.
twi·light (**twī′** līt′) ◊ *noun, plural* **twilights**

twin *noun* **1.** One of two offspring born at the same time to one mother. **2.** One of two things that are exactly alike.
◊ *adjective* **1.** Being one or both of two offspring born at the same time to one mother: *My twin brothers dress alike.* **2.** Being one or both of two identical things.
twin (twĭn) ◊ *noun, plural* **twins** ◊ *adjective*

twine *noun* A strong cord or string consisting of two or more strands, as of hemp, that have been twisted together.
◊ *verb* **1.** To twist together. **2.** To grow in a coil: *Ivy twined around the fence.*
twine (twīn) ◊ *noun* ◊ *verb* **twined, twining**

twinge *noun* A sudden, sharp pain.
◊ *verb* To feel a sudden, sharp pain.
twinge (twĭnj) ◊ *noun, plural* **twinges** ◊ *verb* **twinged, twinging**

twinkle *verb* **1.** To shine or cause to shine with slight, quick flashes of light; sparkle: *Stars twinkled in the sky.* **2.** To be bright, as with happiness: *Your eyes are twinkling.*
◊ *noun* **1.** A slight, quick flash of light. **2.** A sparkle, as of happiness, in the eyes.
twin·kle (**twĭng′** kəl) ◊ *verb* **twinkled, twinkling** ◊ *noun, plural* **twinkles**

twinkling *noun* A very short period of time.
twin·kling (**twĭng′** klĭng) ◊ *noun, plural* **twinklings**

twirl *verb* To rotate quickly; spin.
◊ *noun* An act of twirling.
twirl (twûrl) ◊ *verb* **twirled, twirling** ◊ *noun, plural* **twirls**

twist *verb* **1.** To wind together to form a single strand. **2.** To coil around; twine: *We twisted string around the package.* **3.** To move in a winding course; meander: *A river twisted across the valley.* **4.** To injure by turning: *She twisted her ankle.* **5.** To change in meaning; distort.
◊ *noun* **1.** Something that is twisted. **2.** The act of twisting or the condition of being twisted. **3.** A sudden departure from what is expected: *The story ended with an exciting twist on the last page.*
twist (twĭst) ◊ *verb* **twisted, twisting** ◊ *noun, plural* **twists**

twister *noun* A tornado.
twist·er (twĭs′tər) ◊ *noun, plural* **twisters**

twitch *verb* To move with a quick jerk.
◊ *noun* An act of twitching.
twitch (twĭch) ◊ *verb* **twitched, twitching** ◊ *noun, plural* **twitches**

twitter *verb* To make high chirping sounds.
◊ *noun* A series of high chirping sounds.
twit·ter (twĭt′ər) ◊ *verb* **twittered, twittering** ◊ *noun, plural* **twitters**

two *noun* The number, written 2, that is equal to the sum of $1+1$.
◊ *adjective* Being one more than one.
two (to͞o) ◊ *noun, plural* **twos** ◊ *adjective*
‖*These sound alike:* **two, to, too**

twofold *adjective* Being twice as much or as many; double.
two·fold (to͞o′fōld′) ◊ *adjective*

twosome *noun* Two people together; pair.
two·some (to͞o′səm) ◊ *noun, plural* **twosomes**

TX The abbreviation for *Texas* used with a Zip Code.

tycoon *noun* A wealthy and powerful businessman.
ty·coon (tī ko͞on′) ◊ *noun, plural* **tycoons**

type *noun* **1.** A group, kind, or class sharing common traits or characteristics: *What type of sailboat is that?* **2.** Small blocks, usually of metal, with raised letters that leave a printed impression when they are inked and pressed onto paper.
◊ *verb* To write with a typewriter.
type (tīp) ◊ *noun, plural* **types** ◊ *verb* **typed, typing**

typewriter *noun* A machine that prints letters and characters by means of keys that are pressed by hand.
type·writ·er (tīp′rī′tər) ◊ *noun, plural* **typewriters**

▲ **typewriter**

typhoid fever *noun* A very serious contagious disease that is marked by high fever and is caused by germs in dirty food or water.
ty·phoid fever (tī′foid′) ◊ *noun*

typhoon *noun* A severe tropical hurricane occurring in the western Pacific Ocean.
ty·phoon (tī fo͞on′) ◊ *noun, plural* **typhoons**

typical *adjective* Showing the special traits or characteristics of a group, kind, or class: *A typical summer day in Arizona is hot and dry.* —See Synonyms at **normal.**
typ·i·cal (tĭp′ĭ kəl) ◊ *adjective*

typist *noun* A person who operates a typewriter.
typ·ist (tī′pĭst) ◊ *noun, plural* **typists**

tyrannical *adjective* Of, relating to, or like a tyrant.
ty·ran·ni·cal (tĭ răn′ĭ kəl) ◊ *adjective*

tyranny *noun* **1.** A government in which one ruler has all the power. **2.** Total power, especially when it is used unjustly or cruelly.
tyr·an·ny (tîr′ə nē) ◊ *noun, plural* **tyrannies**

tyrant *noun* A person, especially a ruler, who uses power unjustly or cruelly.
ty·rant (tī′rənt) ◊ *noun, plural* **tyrants**

T

Unicorn

Uu

U is the twenty-first letter of the English alphabet. Did you know that it has a long history?

Over 3,500 years ago, people in the Middle East were using symbols that became the letters of our alphabet. This ancient Middle Eastern symbol is a form of the letter that became our letter *U*.

The ancient Greeks borrowed their alphabet from people in the Middle East. Here is a form of the Greek letter that became our letter *U*.

The ancient Romans borrowed their alphabet from a people who had taken their own letter symbols from the Greeks. The letter *U* is a later development of the Roman letter *V*. Here is a form of the Roman letter *V* that was used for carving letters into stone. These letters became the model for our printed capital letters.

As people wrote quickly, especially with pens, the capital letters began to take the shapes of small letters. Here is a small-letter *u* that was developed about 1,200 years ago.

Uu *Uu*	Uu	Uu	Uu
Handwriting	Sans Serif Type	Serif Type	Computer Printing

u *or* **U** *noun* The twenty-first letter of the English alphabet.
u *or* **U** (yo͞o) ◊ *noun, plural* **u's** *or* **U's**

ugh *interjection* An expression that is used to show disgust or horror.
ugh (ŭg) ◊ *interjection*

ugly *adjective* **1.** Not pleasing to look at: *I think the new coat is ugly.* **2.** Showing a tendency to be nasty, mean, or rude. **3.** Not agreeable; unpleasant: *We stayed home because the weather was ugly.*
ug·ly (ŭg′lē) ◊ *adjective* **uglier, ugliest**

ukulele *noun* A small guitar that has four strings.
u·ku·le·le (yo͞o′kə **lā′**lē) ◊ *noun, plural* **ukuleles**

ă	pat	ĭ	pit	oi	**oil**	th	ba**th**
ā	pay	ī	ride	o͝o	**book**	*th*	ba**the**
â	care	î	fierce	o͞o	**boot**	ə	ago, item
ä	father	ŏ	pot	ou	**out**		pencil
ĕ	pet	ō	go	ŭ	cut		atom
ē	be	ô	paw, for	û	fur		circus

HISTORY • ukulele

Ukulele comes from two words that mean "jumping" and "flea" in the language of the original inhabitants of Hawaii. These words were probably used to name the instrument because the fingers moving on its strings made people think of a jumping flea.

ultimate *adjective* **1.** Being the last one, as in a series; final: *The ultimate result of not studying was failing the test.* **2.** Most basic; fundamental: *In a democracy the ultimate power belongs to the people.*
◊ *noun* The final or greatest stage or degree.
ul·ti·mate (ŭl′tə mĭt) ◊ *adjective* ◊ *noun*

umbrella *noun* A device that is composed of a cloth covering stretched over a folding frame mounted on a handle. An umbrella is used for protection from rain or sun.
um·brel·la (ŭm **brĕl′**ə) ◊ *noun, plural* **umbrellas**

umpire *noun* A person who rules on plays in sports, such as baseball.
um·pire (ŭm′pîr′) ◊ *noun, plural* **umpires**

un– The prefix *un–* means "not." If you are *unhappy*, you are not happy. The prefix *un–* also means "opposite of" or "contrary to." If a law in *unconstitutional*, it is contrary to the constitution of a government. The prefix *un–* also means "to do the opposite of." When you *untie* a knot, you do the opposite of tying it.

> ***VOCABULARY BUILDER* • un–**
>
> Many words that are formed with **un–** are not entries in this dictionary. But you can figure out what these words mean by looking up the meanings of the root words and the prefix. For example:
> **unbuckle** = do the opposite of buckle
> **undependable** = not dependable
> **ungraceful** = opposite of graceful

UN *or* **U.N.** Abbreviation for *United Nations.*

unable *adjective* Not able: *I was unable to catch the school bus.*
un·a·ble (ŭn ā′bəl) ◊ *adjective*

unaccustomed *adjective* Not used to or accustomed to: *I am unaccustomed to cold weather.*
un·ac·cus·tomed (ŭn′ə kŭs′təmd) ◊ *adjective*

unanimous *adjective* **1.** Sharing the same opinion: *The children were unanimous in their wish to take the trip.* **2.** Based on or showing complete agreement: *My friend was elected class president by a unanimous vote.*
u·nan·i·mous (yo͞o năn′ə məs) ◊ *adjective*

unaware *adjective* Not aware: *They were unaware of my presence.*
un·a·ware (ŭn′ə wâr′) ◊ *adjective*

unawares *adverb* By surprise; unexpectedly: *The storm caught me unawares.*
un·a·wares (ŭn′ə wârz′) ◊ *adverb*

unbearable *adjective* Not capable of being endured: *The heat seemed unbearable.*
un·bear·a·ble (ŭn bâr′ə bəl) ◊ *adjective*

unbecoming *adjective* Not attractive or proper: *Pink is an unbecoming color for me.*
un·be·com·ing (ŭn′bĭ kŭm′ĭng) ◊ *adjective*

unbelievable *adjective* Not to be believed; incredible: *That excuse for your tardiness is unbelievable; I cannot accept it.*
un·be·liev·a·ble (ŭn′bĭ lē′və bəl) ◊ *adjective*

unbreakable *adjective* Difficult or impossible to break.
un·break·a·ble (ŭn brā′kə bəl) ◊ *adjective*

unbroken *adjective* **1.** Not broken; whole. **2.** Not interrupted: *We worked along in unbroken silence.* **3.** Not tamed: *The rancher had an unbroken pony for sale.*
un·bro·ken (ŭn brō′kən) ◊ *adjective*

uncalled-for *adjective* Not wanted, necessary, or needed; improper: *That was an uncalled-for remark.*
un·called-for (ŭn kôld′fôr′) ◊ *adjective*

uncanny *adjective* Mysterious and strange: *An uncanny light seemed to be coming from the castle.*
un·can·ny (ŭn kăn′ē) ◊ *adjective* **uncannier, uncanniest**

uncertain *adjective* **1.** Not certain; doubtful: *I'm still uncertain of the answer.* **2.** Subject to change; not dependable: *We didn't have the picnic because the weather was uncertain.*
un·cer·tain (ŭn sûr′tn) ◊ *adjective*

uncertainty *noun* **1.** The condition of being uncertain; doubt. **2.** Something uncertain.
un·cer·tain·ty (ŭn sûr′tn tē) ◊ *noun, plural* **uncertainties**

uncle *noun* **1.** The brother of one's mother or father. **2.** The husband of one's aunt.
un·cle (ŭng′kəl) ◊ *noun, plural* **uncles**

uncomfortable *adjective* **1.** Feeling a lack of comfort; uneasy: *You make me uncomfortable when you stare at me.* **2.** Causing a lack of comfort: *I sat down in an uncomfortable wooden chair.*
un·com·fort·a·ble (ŭn kŭm′fər tə bəl) ◊ *adjective*

uncommon *adjective* Rare or unusual.
un·com·mon (ŭn kŏm′ən) ◊ *adjective* **uncommoner, uncommonest**

unconcerned *adjective* **1.** Not concerned or interested; indifferent. **2.** Not anxious or worried.
un·con·cerned (ŭn′kən sûrnd′) ◊ *adjective*

unconscious *adjective* **1.** Being without consciousness for a time: *I was knocked unconscious when the baseball hit me on the head.* **2.** Not aware: *We were totally unconscious of the time and so we were late.*
un·con·scious (ŭn kŏn′shəs) ◊ *adjective*

U

unconstitutional *adjective* Not in agreement with a country's constitution, especially the Constitution of the United States.
un·con·sti·tu·tion·al (ŭn′kŏn stĭ **to͞o′**shə nəl *or* ŭn′kŏn stĭ **tyo͞o′**shə nəl) ◊ *adjective*

uncouple *verb* To disconnect or unfasten: *They uncoupled the railroad cars.*
un·cou·ple (ŭn **kŭp′**əl) ◊ *verb* **uncoupled, uncoupling**

uncover *verb* **1.** To remove the cover from. **2.** To make known; reveal or expose: *The detectives uncovered the evidence.*
un·cov·er (ŭn **kŭv′**ər) ◊ *verb* **uncovered, uncovering**

undecided *adjective* **1.** Not yet settled: *Our plans are still undecided.* **2.** Not having arrived at a decision: *I'm undecided about what to do next.*
un·de·cid·ed (ŭn′dĭ **sī′**dĭd) ◊ *adjective*

undeniable *adjective* Not capable of being denied; obviously true: *It's an undeniable fact that the accident happened on this spot.*
un·de·ni·a·ble (ŭn′dĭ **nī′**ə bəl) ◊ *adjective*

under *preposition* **1.** Lower than; below: *A boat passed under the bridge.* **2.** Beneath and covered or concealed by: *I hid the kitten under my coat.* **3.** Beneath the surface of: *The plumber laid a pipe under the ground.* **4.** Less, smaller, or lower than: *Children under five years of age are admitted free.* **5.** Subject to the control, guidance, or authority of: *We studied under a famous musician.* **6.** Within the group, category, or classification of: *The book is listed under fiction.*
◊ *adverb* In or into a place below or beneath something: *The strong current pulled the boat under.*
un·der (**ŭn′**dər) ◊ *preposition* ◊ *adverb*

under– The prefix *under–* means "beneath" or "below." *Underwater* means below or underneath the surface of the water. The prefix *under–* also means "less than what is required, normal, or proper." If an animal is *underweight,* it weighs less than it should.

ă	pat	ĭ	pit	oi	oil	th	bath
ā	pay	ī	ride	o͝o	book	*th*	bathe
â	care	î	fierce	o͞o	boot	ə	ago, item
ä	father	ŏ	pot	ou	out		pencil
ĕ	pet	ō	go	ŭ	cut		atom
ē	be	ô	paw, for	û	fur		circus

VOCABULARY BUILDER • under–

Many words that are formed with **under–** are not entries in this dictionary. But you can figure out what these words mean by looking up the meanings of the root words and the prefix. For example:
undernourish = to nourish less than is required for good health
underskirt = a skirt worn beneath another skirt

underbrush *noun* Small trees and shrubs that grow close together under taller trees.
un·der·brush (**ŭn′**dər brŭsh′) ◊ *noun*

underclothes *plural noun* Underwear.
un·der·clothes (**ŭn′**dər klōz′) ◊ *plural noun*

underdog *noun* A person or group that is not expected to win a contest or struggle: *The underdog won a surprising victory in the election for president.*
un·der·dog (**ŭn′**dər dôg′) ◊ *noun, plural* **underdogs**

underfoot *adverb* **1.** Under the feet: *The ground was dry underfoot.* **2.** In the way: *Don't get underfoot in the kitchen.*
un·der·foot (ŭn′dər **fo͝ot′**) ◊ *adverb*

undergarment *noun* A garment that is worn under an outer garment.
un·der·gar·ment (**ŭn′**dər gär′mənt) ◊ *noun, plural* **undergarments**

undergo *verb* To have as an experience: *Many insects undergo three changes during their lives.*
un·der·go (ŭn′dər **gō′**) ◊ *verb* **underwent, undergone, undergoing**

undergone *verb* Past participle of **undergo.**
un·der·gone (ŭn′dər **gôn′**) ◊ *verb*

underground *adjective* **1.** Located below the surface of the ground: *An underground passage connects the two buildings.* **2.** Acting, happening, or done in secret.
◊ *adverb* **1.** Below the surface of the ground: *Miners were digging coal underground.* **2.** In secret: *The spy worked underground to avoid being caught.*
un·der·ground (**ŭn′**dər ground′) ◊ *adjective* ◊ *adverb*

undergrowth *noun* Underbrush.
un·der·growth (**ŭn′**dər grōth′) ◊ *noun*

underhand *adjective & adverb* With the hand below shoulder level: *I made an underhand throw. Throw the ball underhand.*
un·der·hand (**ŭn′** dər hănd′) ◊ *adjective & adverb*

underhanded *adjective* Done in a sly or secret way.
un·der·hand·ed (ŭn′ dər **hăn′** dĭd) ◊ *adjective*

underline *verb* To draw a line under: *Underline the title of the book.*
un·der·line (**ŭn′** dər līn′) ◊ *verb* **underlined, underlining**

underneath *preposition* Beneath; under: *We put newspapers underneath the leaking pail.* ◊ *adverb* In a place beneath; below: *I moved the stone and found a worm underneath.*
un·der·neath (ŭn′dər **nēth′**) ◊ *preposition* ◊ *adverb*

underpass *noun* A passage that runs under a road or railroad.
un·der·pass (**ŭn′** dər păs′) ◊ *noun, plural* **underpasses**

▲ **underpass**

underprivileged *adjective* Lacking the advantages or opportunities enjoyed by others, especially because of poverty.
un·der·priv·i·leged (ŭn′dər **prĭv′** ə lĭjd) ◊ *adjective*

undersea *adjective* Located, living, done, or used under the surface of the sea: *The divers studied undersea plants.*
◊ *adverb* Beneath the surface of the sea.
un·der·sea (ŭn′dər **sē′**) ◊ *adjective* ◊ *adverb*

underseas *adverb* Undersea.
un·der·seas (ŭn′dər **sēz′**) ◊ *adverb*

undershirt *noun* An undergarment that is worn under another shirt next to the skin.
un·der·shirt (**ŭn′** dər shûrt′) ◊ *noun, plural* **undershirts**

underside *noun* The side or surface that is underneath: *Ants crawled on the underside of the rock.*
un·der·side (**ŭn′** dər sīd′) ◊ *noun, plural* **undersides**

understand *verb* **1.** To get the meaning of: *Do you understand my question?* **2.** To be very familiar with; know well: *I wish I understood Spanish.* **3.** To be tolerant, kind, or sympathetic toward: *A good teacher understands children.* **4.** To learn in an indirect way; gather: *I understand they left for their trip on Thanksgiving.*
un·der·stand (ŭn′dər **stănd′**) ◊ *verb* **understood, understanding**

understanding *noun* **1.** Comprehension of the meaning of something: *If you do these problems, you will have a better understanding of arithmetic.* **2.** Agreement in thought or feeling: *The two countries are working toward a better understanding of each other.* **3.** A mutual agreement: *The owners and workers reached an understanding about wages.*
◊ *adjective* Showing or having kind, tolerant, or sympathetic feelings.
un·der·stand·ing (ŭn′dər **stăn′** dĭng) ◊ *noun, plural* **understandings** ◊ *adjective*

understood *verb* The past participle of **understand.**
un·der·stood (ŭn′dər **stŏŏd′**) ◊ *verb*

undertake *verb* **1.** To take upon oneself to do: *The librarian undertook the job of packing the books.* **2.** To attempt; try: *The carpenter undertook to finish the work by the end of the week.*
un·der·take (ŭn′dər **tāk′**) ◊ *verb* **undertook, undertaken, undertaking**

undertaken *verb* The past participle of **undertake.**
un·der·tak·en (ŭn′dər **tā′** kən) ◊ *verb*

undertaker *noun* A person who prepares the dead for burial and makes funeral arrangements.
un·der·tak·er (**ŭn′** dər tā′kər) ◊ *noun, plural* **undertakers**

U

undertone *noun* A low tone: *The students talked in undertones before class.*
un·der·tone (ŭn′dər tōn′) ◊ *noun, plural* **undertones**

undertook *verb* The past tense of **undertake.**
un·der·took (ŭn′dər to͝ok′) ◊ *verb*

underwater *adjective* Located, living, done, or used under the surface of the water: *The company drilled for underwater oil.*
◊ *adverb* Under the surface of the water: *Do you know how to swim underwater?*
un·der·wa·ter (ŭn′dər wô′tər) ◊ *adjective* ◊ *adverb*

underwear *noun* Clothing that is worn next to the skin and under outer clothes.
un·der·wear (ŭn′dər wâr′) ◊ *noun*

underweight *adjective* Weighing less than is normal, usual, or required.
un·der·weight (ŭn′dər wāt′) ◊ *adjective*

underwent *verb* Past tense of **undergo.**
un·der·went (ŭn′dər wĕnt′) ◊ *verb*

undid *verb* Past tense of **undo.**
un·did (ŭn dĭd′) ◊ *verb*

undo *verb* **1.** To do away with or reverse the result or effect of: *They wished they could undo the mistakes of the past.* **2.** To unfasten and open: *I tried to undo the knot in my shoelace but I finally had to cut it.* **3.** To open by removing the wrappings from: *We undid our Christmas gifts.*
un·do (ŭn do͞o′) ◊ *verb* **undid, undone, undoing**

undone *verb* Past participle of **undo.**
un·done (ŭn dŭn′) ◊ *verb*

undress *verb* To remove the clothing of or take one's clothes off.
un·dress (ŭn drĕs′) ◊ *verb* **undressed, undressing**

undying *adjective* Having no end: *You have our undying gratitude.*
un·dy·ing (ŭn dī′ĭng) ◊ *adjective*

unearth *verb* **1.** To dig up out of the ground: *The scientists have unearthed some ancient pottery.* **2.** To discover; find: *The detective unearthed all the evidence.*
un·earth (ŭn ûrth′) ◊ *verb* **unearthed, unearthing**

ă	pat	ĭ	pit	oi	**oi**l	th	ba**th**
ā	pay	ī	ride	o͝o	b**oo**k	*th*	ba**th**e
â	care	î	fierce	o͞o	b**oo**t	ə	**a**go, it**e**m
ä	father	ŏ	pot	ou	**ou**t		penc**i**l
ĕ	pet	ō	go	ŭ	cut		at**o**m
ē	be	ô	paw, for	û	fur		circ**u**s

uneasy *adjective* **1.** Worried or nervous: *We felt uneasy before the test.* **2.** Awkward or uncomfortable: *I was uneasy speaking to a large crowd.*
un·eas·y (ŭn ē′zē) ◊ *adjective* **uneasier, uneasiest**

unequal *adjective* **1.** Not the same, as in quantity or size: *We cut the bread into unequal pieces.* **2.** Not properly matched or balanced: *We lost the game in an unequal contest.*
un·e·qual (ŭn ē′kwəl) ◊ *adjective*

uneven *adjective* **1.** Not level, smooth, or straight: *The surface of coral is uneven.* **2.** Varying, as in quality: *Your homework is uneven.* **3.** Not balanced; unequal. **4.** Not capable of being divided by two; odd: *Seven and nine are uneven numbers.*
un·e·ven (ŭn ē′vən) ◊ *adjective* **unevener, unevenest**

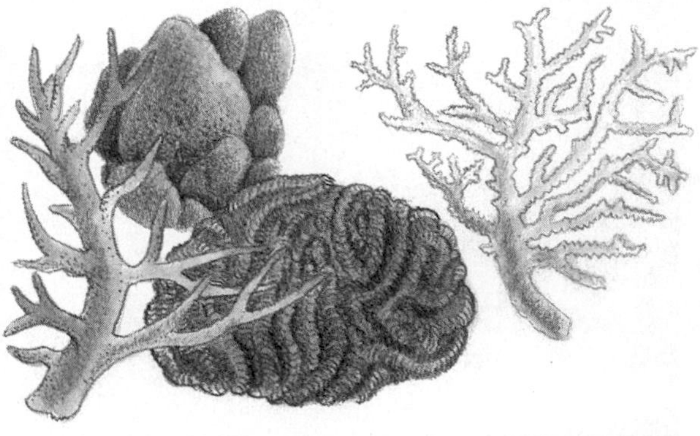

▲ **uneven**
Coral has uneven edges.

unexpected *adjective* Taking place without warning: *You paid me an unexpected visit.*
un·ex·pect·ed (ŭn′ĭk spĕk′tĭd) ◊ *adjective*

unfair *adjective* Not fair: *We think the punishment is unfair.*
un·fair (ŭn fâr′) ◊ *adjective* **unfairer, unfairest**

unfamiliar *adjective* **1.** Not known; strange: *We saw an unfamiliar face at the door.* **2.** Not acquainted: *I am unfamiliar with the streets in this neighborhood.*
un·fa·mil·iar (ŭn′fə mĭl′yər) ◊ *adjective*

unfeeling *adjective* **1.** Not kind or sympathetic. **2.** Not capable of feeling.
un·feel·ing (ŭn **fē′**lĭng) ◊ *adjective*

unfit *adjective* Not suitable: *The water from the river is unfit to drink.*
un·fit (ŭn **fĭt′**) ◊ *adjective*

unfold *verb* **1.** To open the folds of and spread out: *I unfolded the letter and read it.* **2.** To spread out to view; become visible: *A beautiful view unfolded before us.*
un·fold (ŭn **fōld′**) ◊ *verb* **unfolded, unfolding**

unforgettable *adjective* Not likely to be forgotten.
un·for·get·ta·ble (ŭn′fər **gĕt′**ə bəl) ◊ *adjective*

unfortunate *adjective* Not fortunate.
un·for·tu·nate (ŭn **fôr′**chə nĭt) ◊ *adjective*

unfriendly *adjective* Not friendly; hostile.
un·friend·ly (ŭn **frĕnd′**lē) ◊ *adjective* **unfriendlier, unfriendliest**

unfurl *verb* To spread or open out: *They unfurled the flag and let it flutter in the wind.*
un·furl (ŭn **fûrl′**) ◊ *verb* **unfurled, unfurling**

unhappy *adjective* Not happy; sad.
un·hap·py (ŭn **hăp′**ē) ◊ *adjective* **unhappier, unhappiest**

unhealthy *adjective* **1.** In poor health; sick: *If you don't eat proper foods, you'll be unhealthy.* **2.** Resulting from poor health: *Extreme paleness may be an unhealthy sign.* **3.** Harmful to one's health: *Living conditions in the city's slums are unhealthy.*
un·health·y (ŭn **hĕl′**thē) ◊ *adjective* **unhealthier, unhealthiest**

unheard-of *adjective* Never known before.
un·heard-of (ŭn **hûrd′**ŭv′) ◊ *adjective*

unicorn *noun* An imaginary animal similar to a horse but with a single long horn in the middle of the forehead.
u·ni·corn (**yōō′**nĭ kôrn′) ◊ *noun, plural* **unicorns**

uniform *noun* Clothing that identifies those who wear it as members of a certain group, such as a police force.
◊ *adjective* **1.** Being always the same; not changing: *We drove at a uniform rate of speed.* **2.** Having the same appearance, form, or measurements as others: *There are rows and rows of uniform brick houses in our neighborhood.*
u·ni·form (**yōō′**nə fôrm′) ◊ *noun, plural* **uniforms** ◊ *adjective*

▲ **uniform**

unify *verb* To make or form into a unit; unite: *Patriotism unified all the people in the community.*
u·ni·fy (**yōō′**nə fī′) ◊ *verb* **unified, unifying**

union *noun* **1.** The act of uniting two or more people or things into a larger group or whole. **2.** An organization of workers formed to protect and promote their interests, as by getting higher wages and better working conditions. **3. Union** The United States of America, especially during the Civil War.
un·ion (**yōōn′**yən) ◊ *noun, plural* **unions**

unique *adjective* **1.** Being the only one of its kind: *Rhode Island is unique because it is the smallest state in the United States.* **2.** Very unusual; remarkable: *We were offered a unique opportunity to spend the summer with a family in Europe.*
u·nique (yōō **nēk′**) ◊ *adjective*

unit *noun* **1.** A thing, group, or person that is part of a larger group or whole: *We think of the family as the basic unit of society.* **2.** An exact quantity used as a standard of measurement: *The meter is a unit of distance.* **3.** A piece of equipment or part of a larger machine or device that does a certain job: *The freezer unit of our refrigerator is broken.* **4.** The first whole number that is represented by the numeral 1.
u·nit (**yōō′**nĭt) ◊ *noun, plural* **units**

unite *verb* **1.** To bring together in order to form a whole: *Leaders of the Revolution had*

a plan to unite the Colonies under one government. —See Synonyms at **join. 2.** To join together for a single purpose: *People everywhere should unite to fight poverty.*
u·nite (yo͞o **nīt′**) ◊ *verb* **united, uniting**

United Nations *noun* An international organization that includes members from most of the countries in the world. It was formed in 1945 to promote world peace, understanding, and economic and social development.

▲ **United Nations**

unity *noun* **1.** The quality or condition of being united: *In unity there is strength.* **2.** Agreement, as in purpose: *The president was working to achieve national unity.*
u·ni·ty (**yo͞o′**nĭ tē) ◊ *noun*

universal *adjective* **1.** Affecting the whole world: *Sickness and poverty are universal problems.* **2.** Of, for, or shared by all or everyone: *Is there a universal desire for peace?*
u·ni·ver·sal (yo͞o′nə **vûr′**səl) ◊ *adjective*

universe *noun* Everything that exists, including the earth, the planets, and the stars.
u·ni·verse (**yo͞o′**nə vûrs′) ◊ *noun, plural* **universes**

ă	pat	ĭ	pit	oi	**oil**	th	ba**th**
ā	pay	ī	ride	o͝o	**book**	*th*	ba**the**
â	care	î	fierce	o͞o	**boot**	ə	ago, item
ä	father	ŏ	pot	ou	**out**		pencil
ĕ	pet	ō	**go**	ŭ	**cut**		atom
ē	be	ô	paw, for	û	**fur**		circus

university *noun* A school of higher learning that offers degrees in professions such as medicine and law in addition to regular college instruction.
u·ni·ver·si·ty (yo͞o′nə **vûr′**sĭ tē) ◊ *noun, plural* **universities**

un·kempt *adjective* **1.** Not combed. **2.** Not neat or tidy; messy.
un·kempt (ŭn **kĕmpt′**) ◊ *adjective*

unkind *adjective* Harsh or cruel.
un·kind (ŭn **kīnd′**) ◊ *adjective* **unkinder, unkindest**

unknown *adjective* Not known or familiar; strange: *We bought a drawing by an unknown artist.*
un·known (ŭn **nōn′**) ◊ *adjective*

unless *conjunction* Except on the condition that: *You can't go out unless you finish your homework first.*
un·less (ŭn **lĕs′**) ◊ *conjunction*

unlike *adjective* Not like; different: *Those puppies couldn't have been more unlike.* ◊ *preposition* **1.** Different from: *I had heard a sound unlike any other.* **2.** Not typical of: *It's unlike you not to say hello.*
un·like (ŭn **līk′**) ◊ *adjective* ◊ *preposition*

unlikely *adjective* **1.** Not likely: *That's an unlikely story.* **2.** Likely to fail: *You're unlikely to win.*
un·like·ly (ŭn **līk′**lē) ◊ *adjective* **unlikelier, unlikeliest**

unlimited *adjective* Having no limits: *The possibilities of success seem unlimited.*
un·lim·it·ed (ŭn **lĭm′**ĭ tĭd) ◊ *adjective*

unload *verb* **1.** To remove a load from: *We unloaded the truck.* **2.** To remove from a container or vehicle: *The crew unloaded crates from the ship.* **3.** To remove the ammunition from a firearm.
un·load (ŭn **lōd′**) ◊ *verb* **unloaded, unloading**

unlock *verb* To undo the lock of.
un·lock (ŭn **lŏk′**) ◊ *verb* **unlocked, unlocking**

unloose *verb* To let loose; release.
un·loose (ŭn **lo͞os′**) ◊ *verb* **unloosed, unloosing**

unlucky *adjective* Having or bringing bad luck.
un·luck·y (ŭn **lŭk′**ē) ◊ *adjective* **unluckier, unluckiest**

unmanned *adjective* **1.** Lacking or without a

crew. **2.** Designed to operate without a crew: *Unmanned spacecraft orbit the earth.*
un·manned (ŭn **mănd′**) ◊ *adjective*

unmindful *adjective* Careless or forgetful.
un·mind·ful (ŭn **mīnd′**fəl) ◊ *adjective*

unmistakable *adjective* Not able to be mistaken or misunderstood; obvious.
un·mis·tak·a·ble (ŭn′mĭ **stā′**kə bəl) ◊ *adjective*

unnatural *adjective* Different from what usually happens in nature: *It is unnatural for birds to fly north in the winter.*
un·nat·u·ral (ŭn **năch′**ər əl) ◊ *adjective*

unoccupied *adjective* **1.** Vacant or empty: *I took the first unoccupied seat on the bus.* **2.** Not busy or active; not in use: *Since I don't have a summer job, I've been unoccupied during vacation.*
un·oc·cu·pied (ŭn **ŏk′**yə pīd′) ◊ *adjective*

unofficial *adjective* Not official: *Do you believe the unofficial reports about the election?*
un·of·fi·cial (ŭn′ə **fĭsh′**əl) ◊ *adjective*

unopened *adjective* Not opened; closed.
un·o·pened (ŭn **ō′**pənd) ◊ *adjective*

unpack *verb* **1.** To remove the contents of a container or vehicle, such as a suitcase or car: *I unpacked the old trunk.* **2.** To remove from a container or package: *We unpacked our new home computer.*
un·pack (ŭn **păk′**) ◊ *verb* **unpacked, unpacking**

unpopular *adjective* Not generally liked or approved of.
un·pop·u·lar (ŭn **pŏp′**yə lər) ◊ *adjective*

unprepared *adjective* **1.** Not prepared; not ready: *I am unprepared to take the test.* **2.** Done without preparation: *That was an unprepared speech.*
un·pre·pared (ŭn′prĭ **pârd′**) ◊ *adjective*

unquestionable *adjective* Not open to question, doubt, or argument; certain: *We have unquestionable rights under the Constitution.*
un·ques·tion·a·ble (ŭn **kwĕs′**chə nə bəl) ◊ *adjective*

unravel *verb* **1.** To separate or straighten out, as tangled threads or a confused situation: *I unraveled the yarn. The detectives unraveled the mystery.* **2.** To undo a woven or knitted fabric; pull apart.
un·rav·el (ŭn **răv′**əl) ◊ *verb* **unraveled, unraveling**

▲ **unravel**

unreasonable *adjective* **1.** Not having or showing good sense: *My fear of heights is unreasonable.* **2.** Too great; excessive: *They are asking an unreasonable price for that old car.*
un·rea·son·a·ble (ŭn **rē′**zə nə bəl) ◊ *adjective*

unreliable *adjective* Not to be depended on or trusted.
un·re·li·a·ble (ŭn′rĭ **lī′**ə bəl) ◊ *adjective*

unrest *noun* A lack of ease or calm; disturbance.
un·rest (ŭn **rĕst′**) ◊ *noun*

unruly *adjective* Hard to discipline or control: *The cowboy broke the unruly horse.*
un·ru·ly (ŭn **rōō′**lē) ◊ *adjective* **unrulier, unruliest**

unsatisfactory *adjective* Not satisfactory.
un·sat·is·fac·to·ry (ŭn′săt ĭs **făk′**tə rē) ◊ *adjective*

unscramble *verb* To straighten out: *I had to unscramble a big pile of papers.*
un·scram·ble (ŭn **skrăm′**bəl) ◊ *verb* **unscrambled, unscrambling**

unsettled *adjective* **1.** Not peaceful or orderly; disturbed: *Conditions in the coastal towns were unsettled after the hurricane.* **2.** Not decided or resolved: *The strike that closed the factory is still unsettled.* **3.** Not populated: *A large part of the southwestern United States is unsettled desert.*
un·set·tled (ŭn **sĕt′**ld) ◊ *adjective*

unshaken *adjective* Being very firm and certain: *Americans' faith in democracy remains unshaken.*
un·shak·en (ŭn **shā′**kən) ◊ *adjective*

unsightly *adjective* Not pleasant to look at; ugly: *That vacant lot is unsightly.*

U

un·sight·ly (ŭn **sīt′** lē) ◊ *adjective* **unsightlier, unsightliest**

unskilled *adjective* **1.** Lacking skill or special training. **2.** Not needing or requiring special skill or training: *With no education, you will get only unskilled work.*
un·skilled (ŭn **skĭld′**) ◊ *adjective*

unsound *adjective* **1.** Not strong or solid; weak: *That old bridge looks unsound to me.* **2.** Not based on logic or clear thinking: *Don't listen to unsound advice.*
un·sound (ŭn **sound′**) ◊ *adjective*

unstable *adjective* **1.** Not steady or solid: *The table is unstable because one leg is a little shorter than the others.* **2.** Likely to change: *The price of gasoline is unstable.*
un·sta·ble (ŭn **stā′** bəl) ◊ *adjective* **unstabler, unstablest**

unsteady *adjective* Not steady; shaky.
un·stead·y (ŭn **stĕd′** ē) ◊ *adjective* **unsteadier, unsteadiest**

unthinkable *adjective* Impossible to imagine or consider; out of the question.
un·think·a·ble (ŭn **thĭng′** kə bəl) ◊ *adjective*

untie *verb* To loosen or undo.
un·tie (ŭn **tī′**) ◊ *verb* **untied, untying**

▲ **untie**

until *preposition* **1.** Up to the time of: *They studied until dinner.* **2.** Before: *You can't have the bike until Monday.*
◊ *conjunction* **1.** Up to the time that: *They studied until it was time for dinner.* **2.** Before: *You can't go out until you finish your homework.* **3.** To the point or extent that: *They played soccer until they were tired.*
un·til (ŭn **tĭl′**) ◊ *preposition* ◊ *conjunction*

untold *adjective* **1.** Not told or revealed: *Those secrets are still untold.* **2.** Too many to be counted or too much to be measured: *There is untold wealth in that newly discovered gold mine.*
un·told (ŭn **tōld′**) ◊ *adjective*

untruthful *adjective* **1.** Not being true; false. **2.** Likely to lie or deceive others. —See Synonyms at **dishonest.**
un·truth·ful (ŭn **tro͞oth′** fəl) ◊ *adjective*

unused *adjective* **1.** Not in use or never having been used. **2.** Not accustomed: *I am unused to chopping wood.*
un·used (ŭn **yo͞ozd′**) ◊ *adjective*

unusual *adjective* Not usual, common, or ordinary: *It's unusual for me not to eat; I must be sick.*
un·u·su·al (ŭn **yo͞o′** zho͞o əl) ◊ *adjective*

up *adverb* **1.** From a lower to a higher position: *I threw the ball up.* **2.** In, at, or to a higher position: *Don't look up.* **3.** In an upright position; on one's feet: *Please help me up.* **4.** Out of bed: *I get up every morning at seven o'clock.* **5.** Above the horizon: *The sun came up.* **6.** Entirely; thoroughly: *The dog ate up its dinner.* **7.** Into notice, view, or consideration: *May I bring up another problem?* **8.** To a higher volume, pitch, or intensity: *Turn the radio up.*
◊ *adjective* **1.** Moving or directed upward: *The up escalator in the store was broken.* **2.** In a high position; not down: *The shades are up.* **3.** Out of bed: *Are you up yet?* **4.** Being above the horizon: *The sun is up.*
◊ *preposition* **1.** From a lower to a higher position or place in or on: *We walked up the hill.* **2.** At or to a farther point in or on: *I took my dog for a walk up the street.* **3.** Toward the source of: *We took a boat ride up the Hudson River.*
◊ *idiom* **up to 1.** Busy with: *What are you up to?* **2.** Depending on the action or will of someone: *The decision is up to you.* **3.** Having enough power, ability, or training for: *I don't*

ă	pat	ĭ	pit	oi	**oi**l	th	ba**th**
ā	pay	ī	ride	o͝o	b**oo**k	*th*	ba**th**e
â	care	î	fierce	o͞o	b**oo**t	ə	ago, item
ä	father	ŏ	pot	ou	**ou**t		pencil
ĕ	pet	ō	go	ŭ	cut		atom
ē	be	ô	paw, for	û	fur		circus

think this old tractor is up to that job.
up (ŭp) ◊ *adverb* ◊ *adjective* ◊ *preposition*

upbringing *noun* The care and training received during childhood.
up·bring·ing (**ŭp′**brĭng′ĭng) ◊ *noun*

upheld *verb* Past tense and past participle of **uphold.**
up·held (ŭp **hĕld′**) ◊ *verb*

uphill *adjective* Going up a hill or slope.
◊ *adverb* Up a hill or slope: *We hiked three miles uphill.*
up·hill (**ŭp′**hĭl′) ◊ *adjective* ◊ *adverb*

uphold *verb* To agree with; give support to: *The coach upheld the referee's decision.*
up·hold (ŭp **hōld′**) ◊ *verb* **upheld, upholding**

upholster *verb* To fit furniture with stuffing, springs, and a fabric covering.
up·hol·ster (ŭp **hōl′**stər) ◊ *verb* **upholstered, upholstering**

upkeep *noun* The act of putting or keeping something in proper condition or repair: *The estate had three gardeners to see to the upkeep of the yards.*
up·keep (**ŭp′**kēp′) ◊ *noun*

upon *preposition* On: *We stopped and sat down upon a flat rock.*
up·on (ə **pŏn′**) ◊ *preposition*

upper *adjective* Higher in place, position, or rank: *A fire spread through the upper floors of the deserted building.*
up·per (**ŭp′**ər) ◊ *adjective*

upper hand *noun* A position of control or advantage: *Our team lost the upper hand when our star quarterback was injured.*

uppermost *adjective* Highest in place, position, or rank: *The children's education is the teacher's uppermost concern.*
◊ *adverb* In the first or highest place, position, or rank; first: *Keep this explanation uppermost in your mind.*
up·per·most (**ŭp′**ər mōst′) ◊ *adjective* ◊ *adverb*

upright *adjective* **1.** Vertical: *We attached some boards to four upright posts.* **2.** Good or honest; moral: *Upright people do not lie, steal, or cheat.*
◊ *adverb* Straight up: *I taught my dog to sit upright and beg for a biscuit.*
up·right (**ŭp′**rīt′) ◊ *adjective* ◊ *adverb*

uproar *noun* Noisy excitement and confusion: *The fans were in an uproar when we won the game at the last minute.*
up·roar (**ŭp′**rôr′) ◊ *noun, plural* **uproars**

uproot *verb* **1.** To remove a plant and its roots from the ground: *The hurricane uprooted several trees in the coastal town.* **2.** To force to leave: *Many people were uprooted from their homes by the flood.*
up·root (ŭp **ro͞ot′** *or* ŭp **ro͝ot′**) ◊ *verb* **uprooted, uprooting**

▲ **uproot**

upset *verb* **1.** To knock over or tip over; overturn: *The cat upset a vase of flowers.* **2.** To disturb the order or arrangement of; interfere with: *Bad weather upset our plans to go for a sail.* **3.** To make sad or worried: *The bad news upset me.* **4.** To disturb the stomach; cause sickness or nausea: *Onions upset my stomach.* **5.** To defeat unexpectedly in a game or contest: *Everyone was surprised when our*

U

team upset the state champions.
◊ *noun* An unexpected defeat or victory in a game or contest: *If I win the race, it will be a real upset.*
◊ *adjective* **1.** Knocked over or overturned: *Look at the upset sailboat.* **2.** Sad or worried: *We are still upset by the bad news.* **3.** Sick: *I have an upset stomach.*
up·set ◊ *verb* (ŭp **sĕt′**) **upset, upsetting** ◊ *noun* (**ŭp′**set′), *plural* **upsets** ◊ *adjective* (ŭp **sĕt′**)

upside down *adverb* **1.** With the top and bottom parts reversed in position: *Turn the bucket upside down.* **2.** In or into disorder or confusion: *I turned my room upside down looking for my wallet.*
up·side down (**ŭp′**sīd) ◊ *adverb*

upside-down *adjective* Having the top part at the bottom: *Can you read upside-down letters?*
◊ *adverb* Another spelling of **upside down.**
up·side-down (**ŭp′**sīd **doun′**) ◊ *adjective* ◊ *adverb*

upstairs *adverb* **1.** Up the stairs: *I ran upstairs to get my books.* **2.** On or to an upper floor: *We do our homework upstairs.*
◊ *adjective* On an upper floor: *Turn off the light in the upstairs hallway.*
◊ *noun* The upper floor of a building: *The whole upstairs is dirty and needs cleaning.*
up·stairs (**ŭp′**stârz′) ◊ *adverb* ◊ *adjective* ◊ *noun*

upstream *adverb* In the direction toward the source of a stream; against the current: *It is hard to paddle a canoe upstream by yourself.*
◊ *adjective* At or toward the source of a stream: *Upstream fishing was good today.*
up·stream (**ŭp′**strēm′) ◊ *adverb* ◊ *adjective*

up-to-date *adjective* Showing or using the latest improvements, facts, or style: *We bought a new, up-to-date home computer.*
up-to-date (**ŭp′**tə **dāt′**) ◊ *adjective*

upward *adverb* Toward a higher place, level, or condition: *The plane flew upward and out of sight.*
◊ *adjective* Moving toward a higher place, level, or condition: *We could feel the upward flow of the river's current.*
up·ward (**ŭp′**wərd) ◊ *adverb* ◊ *adjective*

upwards *adverb* Upward.
up·wards (**ŭp′**wərdz) ◊ *adverb*

uranium *noun* A heavy, silvery-white metal that is radioactive and is used as a source of nuclear energy. Uranium is a chemical element.
u·ra·ni·um (yo͝o **rā′**nē əm) ◊ *noun*

Uranus *noun* The seventh planet of the solar system in order of increasing distance from the sun. Its diameter is about 29,000 miles, its average distance from the sun is about 1,790 million miles, and it takes about 84 years to orbit the sun.
U·ra·nus (yo͝o **rā′**nəs *or* **yo͝or′**ə nəs) ◊ *noun*

urban *adjective* Of, relating to, or located in a city: *Traffic is a serious urban problem.*
ur·ban (**ûr′**bən) ◊ *adjective*

urge *verb* **1.** To push, force, or drive onward: *We urged the team on with loud cheers.* **2.** To try to convince; plead with: *My parents urged me to study harder.* **3.** To recommend or argue for strongly: *The citizens urged the mayor to approve the plans for a new hospital.*
◊ *noun* A strong desire; impulse: *I had a sudden urge to go swimming.*
urge (ûrj) ◊ *verb* **urged, urging** ◊ *noun, plural* **urges**

urgent *adjective* Needing immediate attention: *You have received an urgent message.*
ur·gent (**ûr′**jənt) ◊ *adjective*

urine *noun* A clear or yellow-colored fluid produced by the kidneys and discharged as waste from the body.
u·rine (**yo͝or′**ĭn) ◊ *noun*

urn *noun* **1.** A large vase set on a base and often used for decoration. **2.** A large metal container with a faucet, used for making and serving coffee or tea.
urn (ûrn) ◊ *noun, plural* **urns**
‖ *These sound alike:* **urn, earn**

us *pronoun* The objective case of **we:** *The movie impressed us greatly. They told us the latest news. The neighbors left their cat with us when they went on their vacation.*
us (ŭs) ◊ *pronoun*

ă	pat	ĭ	pit	oi	**oil**	th	**bath**
ā	pay	ī	ride	o͝o	**book**	*th*	**bathe**
â	care	î	fierce	o͞o	**boot**	ə	ago, item
ä	father	ŏ	pot	ou	**out**		pencil
ĕ	pet	ō	go	ŭ	cut		atom
ē	be	ô	paw, for	û	fur		circus

U.S. The abbreviation for *United States.*

U.S.A. The abbreviation for *United States of America.*

usage *noun* **1.** A way of using something; treatment: *Rough usage will ruin your radio.* **2.** The usual way people use words: *The teacher said that I had a problem with the usage of some verbs.*
us·age (**yo͞o′**sĭj) ◊ *noun, plural* **usages**

use *verb* **1.** To bring or put into service for a purpose: *Use the soap when you wash.* **2.** To spend or consume by using: *We don't always use our time wisely.* **3.** Used to show a former fact, condition, or practice: *I used to ride my bicycle everywhere when I was younger.*
◊ *noun* **1.** The act of using or the condition of being used: *The telephone is in use right now.* **2.** The way of using something; usage: *No one has ever shown me the correct use of a saw.* **3.** The right or privilege to use something: *We have the use of the auditorium tonight to practice our play.* **4.** The power or ability to use something: *When I broke my kneecap, I lost the use of my leg for six weeks.* **5.** The need to use something: *Do you have any use for this old newspaper?*
use ◊ *verb* (yo͞oz) **used, using** ◊ *noun* (yo͞os), *plural* **uses**

used *adjective* **1.** Not new; secondhand: *We bought a used car.* **2.** Familiar; accustomed: *I have never become used to riding my bike on icy streets.*
used (yo͞ozd) ◊ *adjective*

useful *adjective* Being of use or service; helpful: *Our map of Chicago was useful when we visited there.*
use·ful (**yo͞os′**fəl) ◊ *adjective*

> ***SYNONYMS***
>
> ***useful, handy, helpful***
>
> A hammer is a *useful* tool. This sewing machine is *handy* even for those who have difficulty with machines. Thank you for being so *helpful* with my homework.

usher *noun* A person who shows people to their seats, as in a theater or church.
◊ *verb* To act as an usher; escort.
ush·er (**ŭsh′**ər) ◊ *noun, plural* **ushers** ◊ *verb* **ushered, ushering**

▲ **usher**

U.S.S.R. The abbreviation for *Union of Soviet Socialist Republics.*

usual *adjective* Happening at regular intervals or all the time; customary.
u·su·al (**yo͞o′**zho͞o əl) ◊ *adjective*

UT The abbreviation for *Utah* used with a Zip Code.

utensil *noun* An instrument or container, such as one used in a kitchen.
u·ten·sil (yo͞o **tĕn′**səl) ◊ *noun, plural* **utensils**

utility *noun* A company that provides a public service. Telephone, gas, and electric companies are utilities.
u·til·i·ty (yo͞o **tĭl′**ĭ tē) ◊ *noun, plural* **utilities**

utter¹ *verb* **1.** To speak; say: *We didn't utter a word during the test.* **2.** To express out loud: *I uttered a sigh of relief when the test was over.*
ut·ter¹ (**ŭt′**ər) ◊ *verb* **uttered, uttering**

utter² *adjective* Complete or total: *There was utter silence during the test.*
ut·ter² (**ŭt′**ər) ◊ *adjective*

> ***HISTORY* • utter¹, utter²**
>
> **Utter¹** and **utter²** are both related to the word **out. Utter¹** comes from an old Dutch word that meant "to speak out." **Utter²** goes back to an old English word that meant "further out" and "extremely."

U

Vulture

Vv

V is the twenty-second letter of the English alphabet. Did you know that it has a long history?

The ancient Greeks borrowed their alphabet from people in the Middle East. Here is a form of the Greek letter that became our letter *V*.

Over 3,500 years ago, people in the Middle East were using symbols that became the letters of our alphabet. This ancient Middle Eastern symbol is a form of the letter that became our letter *V*.

V

The ancient Romans borrowed their alphabet from a people who had taken their own letter symbols from the Greeks. Here is a form of the Roman letter *V* that was used for carving letters into stone. These letters became the model for our printed capital letters.

As people wrote quickly, especially with pens, the capital letters began to take the shapes of small letters. Here is a small-letter *v* that was used in the Middle Ages.

Vv Vv	Vv	Vv	Vv
Handwriting	Sans Serif Type	Serif Type	Computer Printing

v *or* **V** *noun* **1.** The twenty-second letter of the English alphabet. **2.** The Roman numeral for the number 5.
v *or* **V** (vē) ◊ *noun, plural* **v's** *or* **V's**

VA The abbreviation for *Virginia* used with a Zip Code.

Va. An abbreviation for *Virginia.*

vacancy *noun* **1.** The condition of being vacant. **2.** An unoccupied job, position, or place.
va·can·cy (**vā′**kən sē) ◊ *noun, plural* **vacancies**

vacant *adjective* **1.** Not occupied or rented. —See Synonyms at **empty. 2.** Having no expression on the face; blank.
va·cant (**vā′**kənt) ◊ *adjective*

ă	pat	ĭ	pit	oi	oil	th	bath
ā	pay	ī	ride	o͝o	book	*th*	bathe
â	care	î	fierce	o͞o	boot	ə	ago, item
ä	father	ŏ	pot	ou	out		pencil
ĕ	pet	ō	go	ŭ	cut		atom
ē	be	ô	paw, for	û	fur		circus

vacate *verb* To go away from and no longer occupy: *We vacated our apartment when we bought a house.*
va·cate (**vā′**kāt′) ◊ *verb* **vacated, vacating**

vacation *noun* A time of rest from work, school, or other regular activities.
◊ *verb* To take or spend a vacation.
va·ca·tion (vā **kā′**shən) ◊ *noun, plural* **vacations** ◊ *verb* **vacationed, vacationing**

vaccinate *verb* To inoculate with a vaccine in order to protect against disease.
vac·ci·nate (**văk′**sə nāt′) ◊ *verb* **vaccinated, vaccinating**

vaccination *noun* The act of vaccinating.
vac·ci·na·tion (văk′sə **nā′**shən) ◊ *noun, plural* **vaccinations**

vaccine *noun* A preparation of weak or dead germs that are injected into a person or animal as a protection against the disease caused by those germs.
vac·cine (văk **sēn′**) ◊ *noun, plural* **vaccines**

vacuum *noun* **1.** A space that does not have any air in it. **2.** A vacuum cleaner.

◊ *verb* To clean with a vacuum cleaner.
vac·u·um (**văk′** yo͞o əm *or* **văk′** yo͞om)
◊ *noun, plural* **vacuums** ◊ *verb* **vacuumed, vacuuming**

vacuum cleaner *noun* An electrical appliance that picks up dust and dirt, as from floors and furniture.
vacuum cleaner ◊ *noun, plural* **vacuum cleaners**

vague *adjective* Not clear or distinct: *The witness could give only a vague description of the accident.*
vague (vāg) ◊ *adjective* **vaguer, vaguest**

> ***SYNONYMS***
> ***vague, hazy***
> I felt a *vague* discomfort in the crowded room. My memories of that time are *hazy* now. **Antonyms:** *clear, distinct*

vain *adjective* **1.** Having no success: *Firefighters made a vain attempt to save the burning building.* **2.** Thinking too much of one's own appearance, qualities, or achievements.
vain (vān) ◊ *adjective* **vainer, vainest**
‖*These sound alike:* **vain, vane, vein**

valentine *noun* **1.** A small gift or greeting card sent on Valentine's Day to a friend, relative, or loved one. **2.** A person to whom such a card or gift is sent.
val·en·tine (**văl′** ən tīn′) ◊ *noun, plural* **valentines**

▲ **valentine**

Valentine's Day *noun* February 14, a day when people send valentines to their friends, relatives, and sweethearts.

valiant *adjective* Acting with or showing courage: *Valiant efforts saved the very sick child.*
val·iant (**văl′** yənt) ◊ *adjective*

valid *adjective* **1.** Having facts, evidence, and good judgment as support; sound. **2.** Acceptable according to the law or rules: *My library card is valid until September.*
val·id (**văl′** ĭd) ◊ *adjective*

valise *noun* A small suitcase.
va·lise (və **lēs′**) ◊ *noun, plural* **valises**

valley *noun* **1.** A long, narrow area of low land between mountains or hills, often with a river running along the bottom. **2.** A large region of land drained by a river system.
val·ley (**văl′** ē) ◊ *noun, plural* **valleys**

valuable *adjective* **1.** Worth a lot of money: *This is a valuable necklace.* **2.** Of great importance, use, or service: *I have always appreciated your valuable advice.*
◊ *noun* Often **valuables** A valuable personal possession, as jewelry: *We have a safe to put our valuables in.*
val·u·a·ble (**văl′** yo͞o ə bəl) ◊ *adjective* ◊ *noun, plural* **valuables**

> ***SYNONYMS***
> ***valuable, precious, priceless***
> I learned a *valuable* lesson by losing the game Good friends are more *precious* than gold. Love is a *priceless* gift.
> **Antonym:** *worthless*

value *noun* **1.** What something is worth in exchange for something else: *These shoes will give you good value for your money.* **2.** The quality that makes something worth having; importance: *You should recognize the value of a good education.* **3.** Estimated or determined worth: *The jeweler put a value of $9,000 on the diamond ring.*
◊ *verb* **1.** To believe to be of great worth or importance: *I value your opinions.* **2.** To estimate or determine how much something is worth.
val·ue (**văl′** yo͞o) ◊ *noun, plural* **values** ◊ *verb* **valued, valuing**

V

valve *noun* **1.** A device that blocks or uncovers an opening so as to control the flow of a liquid, gas, or loose material through a pipe or channel: *Turn the valve to start the sprinkler.* **2.** One of the two parts of a sea animal's shell. The shells of clams and oysters have valves.
valve (vălv) ◊ *noun, plural* **valves**

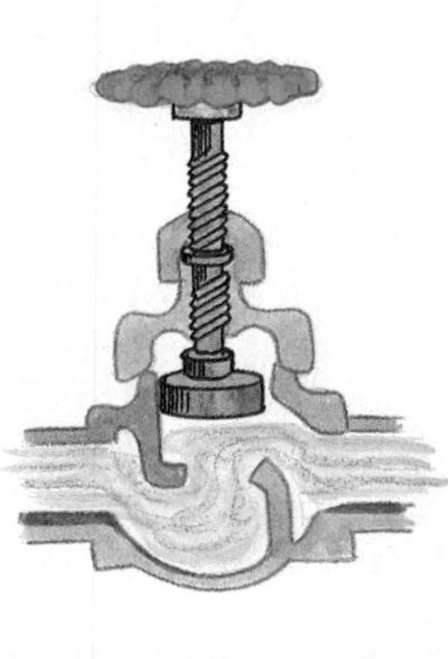
▲ **valve**

van *noun* A covered vehicle that is used for moving goods, animals, or people.
van (văn) ◊ *noun, plural* **vans**

vandalism *noun* The deliberate damaging or destroying of property.
van·dal·ism (**văn′** dl ĭz′əm) ◊ *noun*

vane *noun* A thin, flat piece of wood or metal, often having the shape of an arrow or a rooster, that turns on a vertical pivot to show the direction of the wind. Vanes are often placed on top of buildings.
vane (vān) ◊ *noun, plural* **vanes**
‖*These sound alike:* **vane, vain, vein**

▲ **vane**

ă	pat	ĭ	pit	oi	**oi**l	th	ba**th**
ā	pay	ī	ride	ŏŏ	b**oo**k	*th*	ba**th**e
â	care	î	fierce	ōō	b**oo**t	ə	**a**go, it**e**m
ä	father	ŏ	pot	ou	**ou**t		penc**i**l
ĕ	pet	ō	go	ŭ	cut		at**o**m
ē	be	ô	paw, for	û	fur		circ**u**s

vanilla *noun* A flavoring made from the seed pods of a tropical plant. Vanilla is used in various foods.
va·nil·la (və **nĭl′**ə) ◊ *noun*

vanish *verb* **1.** To disappear or become invisible: *My smile vanished when I heard the bad news.* **2.** To stop existing: *Dinosaurs vanished millions of years ago.*
van·ish (**văn′**ĭsh) ◊ *verb* **vanished, vanishing**

vanity *noun* Too much pride in one's looks, appearance, or ability; conceit.
van·i·ty (**văn′**ĭ tē) ◊ *noun*

vapor *noun* **1.** Fine particles of matter in the air. Mist, steam, smoke, and smog are forms of vapor. **2.** A gas formed from something that is solid or liquid at normal temperatures. Clouds are made of water vapor.
va·por (**vā′** pər) ◊ *noun, plural* **vapors**

variable *adjective* Likely to change or be changed: *Chicago often has variable weather.* ◊ *noun* Something that is not always the same: *The weather is one variable that will determine if we go on our hike.*
var·i·a·ble (**vâr′** ē ə bəl) ◊ *adjective* ◊ *noun, plural* **variables**

variation *noun* **1.** A change from the normal or usual: *The days were boring, with very little variation.* **2.** Something that is similar to something else, but with slight changes: *The play is a variation on an old fairy tale.*
var·i·a·tion (vâr′ē **ā′** shən) ◊ *noun, plural* **variations**

varied *adjective* Of many kinds and forms; full of variety.
var·ied (**vâr′** ēd) ◊ *adjective*

variety *noun* **1.** Difference or change: *We enjoy variety in our meals.* **2.** A number of different kinds within the same group or category: *Our library has a wide variety of books to read.* **3.** A kind or type: *Hospitals deal with diseases of every variety.*
va·ri·e·ty (və **rī′**ĭ tē) ◊ *noun, plural* **varieties**

various *adjective* **1.** Of different kinds: *We were unable to go for various reasons.* **2.** Several: *I spoke to various members of the class about trying out for the play.*
var·i·ous (**vâr′** ē əs) ◊ *adjective*

varnish *noun* A liquid similar to paint that dries to leave a thin, hard, clear surface: *We put a coat of shiny varnish on the chair.* ◊ *verb* To put varnish on.

var·nish (vär′nĭsh) ◊ *noun, plural* **varnishes** ◊ *verb* **varnished, varnishing**

vary *verb* **1.** To be or become different: *The temperature varies from day to day.* **2.** To make different; give variety to: *I try to vary my activities on weekends.*
var·y (vâr′ē) ◊ *verb* **varied, varying**

vase *noun* An open container used to hold flowers or as an ornament.
vase (vās) ◊ *noun, plural* **vases**

▲ **vase**

vassal *noun* A person who was granted protection, land, or the use of land by a lord in return for loyal support and military service to the lord.
vas·sal (văs′əl) ◊ *noun, plural* **vassals**

vast *adjective* Very great in area, size, or amount: *The ship sailed the vast ocean.*
vast (văst) ◊ *adjective* **vaster, vastest**

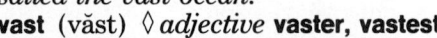

vat *noun* A large tank or container used for storing liquids.
vat (văt) ◊ *noun, plural* **vats**

vault¹ *noun* **1.** A storeroom with arched walls and ceiling, especially one that is underground. **2.** A place for keeping valuables safe.
vault¹ (vôlt) ◊ *noun, plural* **vaults**

vault² *verb* To jump or leap over, especially with the help of one's hands or a pole: *I vaulted over the fence.*
◊ *noun* A high jump or leap made with the help of one's hands or a pole.
vault² (vôlt) ◊ *verb* **vaulted, vaulting** ◊ *noun, plural* **vaults**

***HISTORY* • vault¹, vault²**

Vault¹ and **vault²** both go back to a Latin word meaning "to turn." A form of the word passed into French, took on a new meaning of "something bent or arched," and was then borrowed into English as **vault¹**. Another form of the word meant "to turn a horse, to leap," and was borrowed into English as **vault²**.

VCR The abbreviation for *videocassette recorder.*

veal *noun* The meat of a calf.
veal (vēl) ◊ *noun*

vegetable *noun* A plant whose roots, leaves, stems, flowers, or other parts are used as food.
veg·e·ta·ble (vĕj′ĭ tə bəl) ◊ *noun, plural* **vegetables**

vegetarian *noun* A person who eats foods from plants and does not eat meat.
◊ *adjective* Eating, serving, or containing no meat.
veg·e·tar·i·an (vĕj′ĭ târ′ē ən) ◊ *noun, plural* **vegetarians** ◊ *adjective*

vegetation *noun* Plant life: *Forests and jungles have thick vegetation.*
veg·e·ta·tion (vĕj′ĭ tā′shən) ◊ *noun*

vehicle *noun* Something used for carrying people or goods from one place to another, especially one that moves on wheels or runners. Cars, trucks, trains, and airplanes are vehicles.
ve·hi·cle (vē′ĭ kəl) ◊ *noun, plural* **vehicles**

veil *noun* **1.** A piece of fine, thin fabric worn by women over the head or face: *The bride wore a lace veil.* **2.** Something that covers or conceals like a veil: *A veil of secrecy surrounds their activities.*
◊ *verb* To cover or hide with or as if with a veil.
veil (vāl) ◊ *noun, plural* **veils** ◊ *verb* **veiled, veiling**

▲ **veil**

V

vein *noun* **1.** One of the blood vessels through which blood returns to the heart from all parts of the body. **2.** One of the narrow tubes that form the framework of a leaf or an insect's wing. **3.** A long, narrow deposit of a mineral in rock: *They hit a vein of silver in the mine.* **4.** A streak of different color in marble or wood.
vein (vān) ◊ *noun, plural* **veins**
‖*These sound alike:* **vein, vain, vane**

▲ **vein**

velocity *noun* The speed at which something moves in a given direction: *The velocity of light is about 186,000 miles per second.*
ve·loc·i·ty (və **lŏs′**ĭ tē) ◊ *noun, plural* **velocities**

velvet *noun* A soft fabric with a short, thick pile. Velvet is made of silk, cotton, rayon, or other materials.
vel·vet (**vĕl′**vĭt) ◊ *noun, plural* **velvets**

vending machine *noun* A machine that delivers small items, such as candy and stamps, when coins are dropped into a slot.
vend·ing machine (**vĕn′**dĭng) ◊ *noun, plural* **vending machines**

vendor *noun* A person who sells something, such as newspapers.
ven·dor (**vĕn′**dər) ◊ *noun, plural* **vendors**

Venetian blind *noun* A window blind made of many horizontal slats. The slats can be raised and lowered or slanted to change the amount of light admitted.
Ve·ne·tian blind (və **nē′**shən) ◊ *noun, plural* **Venetian blinds**

venison *noun* The meat of a deer, used as food.
ven·i·son (**vĕn′**ĭ sən) ◊ *noun*

venom *noun* A poison produced by some snakes, spiders, scorpions, and other animals. Venom is usually passed into a victim through a bite or sting.
ven·om (**vĕn′**əm) ◊ *noun, plural* **venoms**

venomous *adjective* Containing or producing poison; poisonous.
ven·om·ous (**vĕn′**ə məs) ◊ *adjective*

vent *noun* An opening through which a liquid or gas can escape.
vent (vĕnt) ◊ *noun, plural* **vents**

ventilation *noun* The circulation of fresh air: *Windows on two sides of a room provide good ventilation.*
ven·ti·la·tion (vĕn′tl **ā′**shən) ◊ *noun*

ventilator *noun* Something, as an exhaust fan, that provides ventilation.
ven·ti·la·tor (**vĕn′**tl ā′tər) ◊ *noun, plural* **ventilators**

ventricle *noun* Either of the two chambers of the heart that contract to pump blood into the arteries.
ven·tri·cle (**vĕn′**trĭ kəl) ◊ *noun, plural* **ventricles**

ventriloquist *noun* A person who can produce vocal sounds that seem to come from somewhere else.
ven·tril·o·quist (vĕn **trĭl′**ə kwĭst) ◊ *noun, plural* **ventriloquists**

venture *noun* A task or activity that is risky or dangerous: *Our first venture to the moon was a great success.*
ven·ture (**vĕn′**chər) ◊ *noun, plural* **ventures**

Venus *noun* The second planet of the solar system in order of increasing distance from the sun. Venus is brighter than any other heavenly body except the sun and the moon.
Ve·nus (**vē′**nəs) ◊ *noun*

veranda *noun* A long porch, usually with a roof, that runs along one or more sides of a building.
ve·ran·da (və **răn′**də) ◊ *noun, plural* **verandas**

ă	pat	ĭ	pit	oi	**oil**	th	**bath**
ā	pay	ī	ride	o͝o	**book**	*th*	**bathe**
â	care	î	fierce	o͞o	**boot**	ə	**ago, item**
ä	father	ŏ	pot	ou	**out**		pencil
ĕ	pet	ō	go	ŭ	**cut**		atom
ē	be	ô	paw, for	û	**fur**		circus

▲ **veranda**

verb *noun* Any of a class of words that express action or state of being. The words *do, run,* and *be* are verbs.
verb (vûrb) ◊ *noun, plural* **verbs**

verbal *adjective* **1.** Of or having to do with words: *The students were tested on their verbal aptitude.* **2.** Expressed in words: *They made a verbal agreement.*
ver·bal (vûr′ bəl) ◊ *adjective*

verdict *noun* The decision reached by a jury at the end of a trial.
ver·dict (vûr′ dĭkt) ◊ *noun, plural* **verdicts**

verify *verb* **1.** To prove the truth of: *Modern astronomers have verified many of the findings of the ancient Greeks.* **2.** To test or check the accuracy of: *Verify your addition before handing in your paper.*
ver·i·fy (vĕr′ ə fī′) ◊ *verb* **verified, verifying**

versatile *adjective* **1.** Able to do many things well: *You are a versatile athlete because you run, play soccer, and swim well.* **2.** Having many uses: *The potato is a versatile vegetable.*
ver·sa·tile (vûr′ sə təl) ◊ *adjective*

verse *noun* **1.** Words put together in a rhythmic pattern and often in rhyme: *That play is written in verse.* **2.** One section or stanza of a poem or song.
verse (vûrs) ◊ *noun, plural* **verses**

version *noun* A description or account from a particular point of view: *Each driver gave a different version of the accident.*
ver·sion (vûr′ zhən) ◊ *noun, plural* **versions**

vertebra *noun* One of the small bones that form the backbone.
ver·te·bra (vûr′ tə brə) ◊ *noun, plural* **vertebras**

vertebrate *noun* Any of a large group of animals that have backbones. Fish, amphibians, reptiles, birds, and mammals are vertebrates.
ver·te·brate (vûr′ tə brĭt *or* vûr′ tə brāt′) ◊ *noun, plural* **vertebrates**

vertical *adjective* Straight up and down; perpendicular to a level surface: *A flagpole is set in a vertical position.*
ver·ti·cal (vûr′ tĭ kəl) ◊ *adjective*

SYNONYMS

vertical, perpendicular

The smoke coiled up in a *vertical* direction. The wall was *perpendicular* to the street. **Antonym:** *horizontal*

very *adverb* **1.** To a high degree; extremely: *I am a very happy person today.* **2.** Truly; absolutely: *This is the very best watch money can buy.* **3.** Precisely; exactly: *I said the very same thing.*
◊ *adjective* **1.** Complete; absolute: *I am at the very end of the lesson.* **2.** Exactly the same; identical: *That is the very question I was about to ask.* **3.** Precise; exact: *A large tree stands in the very center of town.*
ver·y (vĕr′ ē) ◊ *adverb* ◊ *adjective*

vessel *noun* **1.** A ship or large boat. **2.** A hollow container or holder, such as a bowl, pitcher, or jar. **3.** A narrow tube that a body fluid flows or circulates through. Arteries and veins are blood vessels.
ves·sel (vĕs′ əl) ◊ *noun, plural* **vessels**

vest *noun* A short, sleeveless article of clothing that is worn over a shirt.
vest (vĕst) ◊ *noun, plural* **vests**

veteran *noun* **1.** A person who has had long experience in a profession or activity: *The coach is a veteran of many football games.* **2.** A person who has served in the armed forces, especially during a war.
vet·er·an (vĕt′ ər ən) ◊ *noun, plural* **veterans**

veterinarian *noun* A doctor who is trained to treat animals.
vet·er·i·nar·i·an (vĕt′ər ə nâr′ ē ən) ◊ *noun, plural* **veterinarians**

V

veto *noun* **1.** The right or power of a president, governor, or mayor to reject a bill that has been passed by a legislature and to keep it from becoming a law. **2.** A prohibiting of something by a person in charge.
◊ *verb* **1.** To prevent from becoming law by using the power of veto: *The President vetoed the tax bill passed by Congress.* **2.** To refuse to consent to; forbid: *My parents vetoed my plan to go to the movies on a school night.*
ve·to (vē′tō) ◊ *noun, plural* **vetoes** ◊ *verb* **vetoed, vetoing**

via *preposition* By way of: *We are flying from New York to Seattle via Chicago.*
vi·a (vī′ə *or* vē′ə) ◊ *preposition*

viaduct *noun* A bridge used to carry a road or railroad over a valley, river, or highway.
vi·a·duct (vī′ə dŭkt′) ◊ *noun, plural* **viaducts**

vibrate *verb* To move or cause to move back and forth rapidly: *Plucking a guitar string causes it to vibrate and produce a sound.*
vi·brate (vī′brāt′) ◊ *verb* **vibrated, vibrating**

vibration *noun* Rapid movement back and forth.
vi·bra·tion (vī brā′shən) ◊ *noun, plural* **vibrations**

vice admiral *noun* A Navy or Coast Guard officer ranking above a rear admiral.
vice admiral (vīs) ◊ *noun, plural* **vice admirals**

vice president *noun* An officer ranking just below a president.
vice president ◊ *noun, plural* **vice presidents**

vice versa *adverb* The other way around: *We help our neighbors and vice versa.*
vi·ce ver·sa (vī′sə vûr′sə *or* vīs′ vûr′sə) ◊ *adverb*

vicinity *noun* A nearby or surrounding area.
vi·cin·i·ty (vĭ sĭn′ĭ tē) ◊ *noun, plural* **vicinities**

vicious *adjective* **1.** Cruel and mean. **2.** Evil; wicked. **3.** Savage and dangerous.
vi·cious (vĭsh′əs) ◊ *adjective*

ă	pat	ĭ	pit	oi	oil	th	bath
ā	pay	ī	ride	o͝o	book	*th*	bathe
â	care	î	fierce	o͞o	boot	ə	ago, item
ä	father	ŏ	pot	ou	out		pencil
ĕ	pet	ō	go	ŭ	cut		atom
ē	be	ô	paw, for	û	fur		circus

victim *noun* **1.** A person or animal that is harmed, killed, or made to suffer. **2.** A person who is treated badly, as by being tricked or cheated: *I was the victim of a bad joke.*
vic·tim (vĭk′tĭm) ◊ *noun, plural* **victims**

victorious *adjective* **1.** Having won a victory: *They held a parade for the victorious team.* **2.** Of or causing victory: *Nothing could stop the army's victorious advance.*
vic·to·ri·ous (vĭk tôr′ē əs) ◊ *adjective*

victory *noun* The defeat of an opponent or enemy; success.
vic·to·ry (vĭk′tə rē) ◊ *noun, plural* **victories**

video *adjective* Of or used in the visual part of a television broadcast or a display of computer data.
◊ *noun* The picture part of television.
vid·e·o (vĭd′ē ō′) ◊ *adjective* ◊ *noun*

videocassette *noun* A videotape recording or film that is contained in a cassette.
vid·e·o·cas·sette (vĭd′ē ō kə sĕt′) ◊ *noun, plural* **videocassettes**

videocassette recorder *noun* A device that records television programs onto videocassettes and then plays them back on the screen.
videocassette recorder ◊ *noun, plural* **videocassette recorders**

video display screen *noun* The screen of a computer on which information is shown.
video display screen ◊ *noun, plural* **video display screens**

▲ **video display screen**

video game *noun* An electronic or computerized game played by moving images around on a television or computer screen.
video game ◊ *noun, plural* **video games**

videotape *noun* A special type of magnetic recording tape that is used to record television programs.
vid·e·o·tape (vĭd′ē ō tāp′) ◊ *noun, plural* **videotapes**

videotape recorder *noun* A device that records television programs onto videotape and then plays them back on the screen.
videotape recorder ◊ *noun, plural* **videotape recorders**

video terminal *noun* A computer keyboard and screen used to put information into the computer, take information out of the computer, and display information on the screen.
video terminal ◊ *noun, plural* **video terminals**

Vietnamese *noun* **1.** A person who was born in or lives in Vietnam. **2.** The language of Vietnam.
◊ *adjective* Of or relating to Vietnam, the Vietnamese, or their language.
Vi·et·na·mese (vē ĕt′nə **mēz′**) ◊ *noun, plural* **Vietnamese** ◊ *adjective*

view *noun* **1.** The act of seeing something; sight: *Their first view of the city was from an airplane.* **2.** Something that can be seen: *The view from my window is lovely.* **3.** Range or field of sight: *The airplane disappeared from view.* **4.** A way of showing or seeing something: *This picture shows a side view of the house.* **5.** A way of thinking; opinion: *The candidates gave us their views on education.*
◊ *verb* **1.** To look at: *We viewed the stars through a telescope.* **2.** To think about; consider: *You shouldn't view your homework as a chore.*
view (vyōō) ◊ *noun, plural* **views** ◊ *verb* **viewed, viewing**

viewpoint *noun* A way of thinking about something; point of view.
view·point (**vyōō′**point′) ◊ *noun, plural* **viewpoints**

vigor *noun* **1.** Physical energy or strength: *You seem to be full of health and vigor.* **2.** Great force or energy: *Defend your beliefs with vigor.*
vig·or (**vĭg′**ər) ◊ *noun*

vigorous *adjective* **1.** Full of energy; lively: *The nest held three vigorous young birds.* **2.** Done with energy or spirit: *They took a vigorous hike through the woods.*
vig·or·ous (**vĭg′**ər əs) ◊ *adjective*

Viking *noun* One of a daring group of Scandinavian sailors who raided the coasts of northern and western Europe from the eighth to the tenth century. The Vikings made early voyages to the New World.
Vi·king (**vī′**kĭng) ◊ *noun, plural* **Vikings**

village *noun* **1.** A group of houses that make up a community smaller than a town. **2.** The people who live in a village.
vil·lage (**vĭl′**ĭj) ◊ *noun, plural* **villages**

villain *noun* A wicked person.
vil·lain (**vĭl′**ən) ◊ *noun, plural* **villains**

vine *noun* A plant with a long, thin stem that climbs on, creeps along, or twines around something for support. Grapes, pumpkins, and cucumbers grow on vines.
vine (vīn) ◊ *noun, plural* **vines**

vinegar *noun* A sour liquid that is made by fermenting wine, cider, or other liquids. Vinegar is used in flavoring and preserving food and in salad dressing.
vin·e·gar (**vĭn′**ĭ gər) ◊ *noun, plural* **vinegars**

vineyard *noun* A piece of land on which grapevines are grown.
vine·yard (**vĭn′**yərd) ◊ *noun, plural* **vineyards**

▲ **vineyard**

vinyl *noun* Any of several plastics that are tough, flexible, and shiny. Vinyls are used for boots, raincoats, and floor coverings.
vi·nyl (**vī′**nəl) ◊ *noun, plural* **vinyls**

viola *noun* A stringed musical instrument of the violin family. A viola is slightly larger

than a violin and has a deeper, mellower tone.
vi·o·la (vē ō′lə) ◊ *noun, plural* **violas**

violate *verb* To fail to keep or obey; break: *Don't violate the law.*
vi·o·late (vī′ə lāt′) ◊ *verb* **violated, violating**

violence *noun* **1.** The use of physical force to cause damage or injury. **2.** Great force or strength: *The violence of the tornado destroyed many homes.*
vi·o·lence (vī′ə ləns) ◊ *noun*

violent *adjective* **1.** Showing or caused by great physical force: *The boat sank in a violent storm at sea.* —See Synonyms at **intense.** **2.** Showing or caused by very strong feelings.
vi·o·lent (vī′ə lənt) ◊ *adjective*

violet *noun* **1.** A low-growing plant having small flowers that are usually bluish purple but can be yellow or white. **2.** A bluish purple color.
◊ *adjective* Bluish purple.
vi·o·let (vī′ə lĭt) ◊ *noun, plural* **violets**
◊ *adjective*

violin *noun* A musical instrument that has four strings and is played with a bow.
vi·o·lin (vī′ə lĭn′) ◊ *noun, plural* **violins**

violinist *noun* A person who plays the violin.
vi·o·lin·ist (vī′ə lĭn′ĭst) ◊ *noun, plural* **violinists**

virgin *adjective* In the original or natural state: *No trees have ever been cut in this virgin forest.*
vir·gin (vûr′jĭn) ◊ *adjective*

virtual *adjective* Being so for all practical purposes: *Uncontrolled hunting led to the virtual extinction of the buffalo.*
vir·tu·al (vûr′cho͞o əl) ◊ *adjective*

virtue *noun* **1.** Moral goodness. **2.** An example of moral goodness: *Patience is a virtue.*
vir·tue (vûr′cho͞o) ◊ *noun, plural* **virtues**

virtuous *adjective* Having or showing virtue.
vir·tu·ous (vûr′cho͞o əs) ◊ *adjective*

virus *noun* A form of matter that exists only in living cells and is too small to be seen with an ordinary microscope. Viruses cause many diseases, such as polio, measles, and mumps.
vi·rus (vī′rəs) ◊ *noun, plural* **viruses**

vise *noun* A device having a pair of jaws that are opened and closed by means of a screw or lever. A vise is used to hold firmly an object that is being worked on.
vise (vīs) ◊ *noun, plural* **vises**

visibility *noun* **1.** The quality or condition of being visible. **2.** The distance to which it is possible to see under given weather conditions: *Visibility in the fog was only 15 feet.*
vis·i·bil·i·ty (vĭz′ə bĭl′ĭ tē) ◊ *noun*

visible *adjective* **1.** Capable of being seen: *The planet Pluto is visible only through a telescope.* **2.** Easily noticed: *The students showed visible signs of boredom.*
vis·i·ble (vĭz′ə bəl) ◊ *adjective*

vision *noun* **1.** The ability to see; the sense of sight: *My vision is poor.* **2.** The ability to look ahead in the imagination; foresight: *Thomas Jefferson had great vision as a leader.* **3.** A mental picture produced by the imagination: *I had visions of being rich and famous.*
vi·sion (vĭzh′ən) ◊ *noun, plural* **visions**

visit *verb* **1.** To go or come to see: *Visit your doctor once a year.* **2.** To stay with as a guest: *I am visiting an old friend in California.*
◊ *noun* A short stay or call: *I paid a visit to my former teacher.*
vis·it (vĭz′ĭt) ◊ *verb* **visited, visiting** ◊ *noun, plural* **visits**

visitor *noun* A person who visits.
vis·i·tor (vĭz′ĭ tər) ◊ *noun, plural* **visitors**

visor *noun* **1.** A part that sticks out on the front of a cap to protect the eyes. **2.** A movable shade above the windshield of a car to protect against glare. **3.** The movable front piece on a helmet that protects the face.
vi·sor (vī′zər) ◊ *noun, plural* **visors**

visual *adjective* **1.** Of or having to do with vision: *Eyeglasses can correct many visual defects.* **2.** Based on or designed for the sense of sight: *The teacher used films, charts, and other visual aids.*
vis·u·al (vĭzh′o͞o əl) ◊ *adjective*

vital *adjective* **1.** Of or having to do with life: *The heartbeat is one of the vital signs that indicate whether an animal or human being is alive.* **2.** Necessary to life: *The heart and lungs are vital organs.* **3.** Very important; es-

ă	pat	ĭ	pit	oi	**oi**l	th	ba**th**
ā	pay	ī	ride	o͝o	book	*th*	ba**th**e
â	care	î	fierce	o͞o	boot	ə	ago, item
ä	father	ŏ	pot	ou	**ou**t		pencil
ĕ	pet	ō	go	ŭ	cut		atom
ē	be	ô	paw, for	û	fur		circus

sential: *A good education is vital to a successful career.*
vi·tal (vīt′l) ◊ *adjective*

vitamin *noun* Any of a group of substances that occur in small amounts in animal and plant tissue and are necessary to the health and normal functioning of the body.
vi·ta·min (vī′tə mĭn) ◊ *noun, plural* **vitamins**

vivid *adjective* **1.** Bright and strong; brilliant: *The coat was a vivid blue.* **2.** Active; lively: *You have a vivid imagination.* **3.** Sharp and clear: *We still have vivid memories of our trip to Washington, D.C.*
viv·id (vĭv′ĭd) ◊ *adjective*

vocabulary *noun* **1.** All the words of a language: *The English vocabulary comes from many sources.* **2.** The stock of words used by a particular person, group, or profession: *Your cousin has a large vocabulary for a young child.* **3.** A list of words and phrases, usually in alphabetical order, with their meanings.
vo·cab·u·lar·y (vō **kăb**′yə lĕr′ē) ◊ *noun, plural* **vocabularies**

vocal *adjective* **1.** Of, relating to, or produced by the voice: *A baby makes vocal sounds before it can speak.* **2.** Meant to be sung: *My teacher can perform both instrumental and vocal music.*
vo·cal (vō′kəl) ◊ *adjective*

vocal cords *plural noun* A pair of bands or folds of tissue in the larynx. Sound is produced when these bands are pulled together and air from the lungs causes them to vibrate.

voice *noun* **1.** Sound produced by using the mouth and vocal cords in speaking, singing, or shouting: *I recognized your voice on the telephone.* **2.** The ability to produce such sound: *I caught a bad cold and lost my voice.* **3.** The right to express a choice or opinion: *The students had no voice in making the rules.*
voice (vois) ◊ *noun, plural* **voices**

volcanic *adjective* Of or having to do with a volcano.
vol·can·ic (vŏl **kăn**′ĭk) ◊ *adjective*

volcano *noun* **1.** An opening in the earth's crust through which lava, dust, ash, and hot gases are ejected. **2.** A mountain that is formed by the material ejected during a volcanic eruption.
vol·ca·no (vŏl **kā**′nō) ◊ *noun, plural* **volcanoes** *or* **volcanos**

▲ **volcano**

volleyball *noun* **1.** A game played by two teams who hit a ball back and forth over a high net. **2.** The ball used in this game.
vol·ley·ball (vŏl′ē bôl′) ◊ *noun, plural* **volleyballs**

volt *noun* A unit for measuring the force of an electric current.
volt (vōlt) ◊ *noun, plural* **volts**

voltage *noun* The amount of force of an electric current measured in volts.
volt·age (vōl′tĭj) ◊ *noun*

volume *noun* **1.** A book: *The library owns thousands of volumes.* **2.** One book of a set: *We are missing two volumes of this encyclopedia.* **3.** Amount of space occupied: *A tall, narrow box may have the same volume as a short, wide one.* **4.** Degree of loudness of sound: *Don't play your radio at full volume.*
vol·ume (vŏl′yəm *or* vŏl′yo͞om) ◊ *noun, plural* **volumes**

voluntary *adjective* **1.** Made, done, given, or acting of one's own free will: *I made a voluntary decision to give up the movies tonight.* **2.** Controlled by the will: *We move our arms and legs with voluntary muscles.*
vol·un·tar·y (vŏl′ən tĕr′ē) ◊ *adjective*

volunteer *noun* **1.** Someone who does a job or gives services freely and usually without pay: *We need volunteers to give blood.* **2.** A person who enlists in the armed forces.
◊ *adjective* Of, relating to, or made up of volunteers.

V

◊ *verb* To give or offer, usually without being asked: *I volunteered to lead the younger children on an overnight hike.*
vol·un·teer (vŏl′ən **tîr′**) ◊ *noun, plural* **volunteers** ◊ *adjective* ◊ *verb* **volunteered, volunteering**

vomit *verb* To expel part or all of the contents of the stomach through the mouth.
vom·it (**vŏm′**ĭt) ◊ *verb* **vomited, vomiting**

vote *noun* **1.** A formal expression of choice, made in or as if in an election. **2.** The number of votes cast in an election or to settle an issue: *The vote was 70 to 51 in favor of our proposal.* **3.** The right to express a choice in or as if in an election: *Only members of the team have a vote.*
◊ *verb* **1.** To cast a vote: *Our parents voted in the last election.* **2.** To make available: *The committee voted funds for flood control.*
vote (vōt) ◊ *noun, plural* **votes** ◊ *verb* **voted, voting**

vow *noun* A solemn promise: *Doctors make a vow to help the sick.*
◊ *verb* To make a solemn promise.
vow (vou) ◊ *noun, plural* **vows** ◊ *verb* **vowed, vowing**

vowel *noun* One of the letters *a, e, i, o, u,* and sometimes *y.*
vow·el (**vou′**əl) ◊ *noun, plural* **vowels**

voyage *noun* A long journey to a distant place, made on a ship, aircraft, or spacecraft.
voy·age (**voi′**ĭj) ◊ *noun, plural* **voyages**

VT The abbreviation for *Vermont* used with a Zip Code.

Vt. An abbreviation for *Vermont.*

vulture *noun* Any of several large birds that usually have dark feathers and a bare head and neck. Vultures feed on dead animals.
vul·ture (**vŭl′**chər) ◊ *noun, plural* **vultures**

ă	pat	ĭ	pit	oi	oil	th	bath
ā	pay	ī	ride	ŏŏ	book	*th*	bathe
â	care	î	fierce	ōō	boot	ə	ago, item
ä	father	ŏ	pot	ou	out		pencil
ĕ	pet	ō	go	ŭ	cut		atom
ē	be	ô	paw, for	û	fur		circus

▲ vulture

Walrus

Ww

W is the twenty-third letter of the English alphabet. Did you know that it has a long history?

Over 3,500 years ago, people in the Middle East were using symbols that became the letters of our alphabet. This ancient Middle Eastern symbol is a form of the letter that became our letter *W*.

The ancient Greeks borrowed their alphabet from people in the Middle East. Here is a form of the Greek letter that became our letter *W*.

The ancient Romans borrowed their alphabet from a people who had taken their own letter symbols from the Greeks. The letter *W* is a development of the Roman letter *V*. *W* is made up of two *V*'s written together. Here is a form of the Roman letter *V* that was used for carving letters into stone. These letters became the model for our printed capital letters.

As people wrote quickly, especially with pens, the capital letters began to take the shapes of small letters. Here is a small-letter *w* that was used in the Middle Ages.

Ww *Ww*	Ww	Ww	Ww
Handwriting	Sans Serif Type	Serif Type	Computer Printing

w *or* **W** *noun* The twenty-third letter of the English alphabet.
w *or* **W** (**dŭb′**əl yo͞o′) ◊ *noun, plural* **w's** *or* **W's**

W. *or* **W** Abbreviation for *west.*

WA The abbreviation for *Washington* used with a Zip Code.

wad *noun* **1.** A soft mass of material, such as cotton, used for padding or packing. **2.** A tight roll of papers or paper money.
◊ *verb* To form into a wad.
wad (wŏd) ◊ *noun, plural* **wads** ◊ *verb* **wadded, wadding**

waddle *verb* To take short steps and sway from side to side as a duck does.
◊ *noun* The act of waddling.
wad·dle (**wŏd′**l) ◊ *verb* **waddled, waddling** ◊ *noun, plural* **waddles**

wade *verb* **1.** To walk through something, such as water or mud, that keeps the feet from moving freely: *On our hike we had to wade across a stream.* **2.** To make one's way with difficulty: *I had to wade through several books in order to write my report.*
wade (wād) ◊ *verb* **waded, wading**

wafer *noun* A thin flat cookie, cracker, or candy.
wa·fer (**wā′**fər) ◊ *noun, plural* **wafers**

waffle *noun* A light, crisp cake made of batter. A waffle is cooked in an appliance that presses a pattern into it.
waf·fle (**wŏf′**əl) ◊ *noun, plural* **waffles**

wag *verb* To move, swing, or wave back and forth or up and down: *The friendly dog wagged its tail.*
◊ *noun* A wagging movement.
wag (wăg) ◊ *verb* **wagged, wagging** ◊ *noun, plural* **wags**

wage *noun* Payment for work or services.
◊ *verb* To take part in or carry on: *We are waging a campaign against poverty.*
wage (wāj) ◊ *noun, plural* **wages** ◊ *verb* **waged, waging**

wagon *noun* A four-wheeled vehicle for carrying loads or passengers.
wag·on (**wăg′**ən) ◊ *noun, plural* **wagons**

waif *noun* A lost or stray person or animal.
waif (wāf) ◊ *noun, plural* **waifs**

wail *verb* To utter a long cry of grief, sadness, or pain.
◊ *noun* A long cry or similar sound: *I heard the wail of a locomotive whistle.*
wail (wāl) ◊ *verb* **wailed, wailing** ◊ *noun, plural* **wails**

waist *noun* **1.** The part of the human body between the ribs and the hips. **2.** The part of a garment that fits around the waist.
waist (wāst) ◊ *noun, plural* **waists**
‖*These sound alike:* **waist, waste**

wait *verb* **1.** To do nothing or stay in a place until something expected happens: *Wait for me here.* **2.** To be temporarily put off or not done: *This job can wait.*
◊ *noun* Time spent in waiting.
◊ *idiom* **wait on** To serve or attend as a waiter, salesperson, or servant.
wait (wāt) ◊ *verb* **waited, waiting** ◊ *noun, plural* **waits**
‖*These sound alike:* **wait, weight**

waiter *noun* A man who serves food and drink to people, as in a restaurant.
wait·er (wā′tər) ◊ *noun, plural* **waiters**

waiting room *noun* A room, as in a doctor's office, for people who are waiting.
waiting room ◊ *noun, plural* **waiting rooms**

waitress *noun* A woman who serves food and drink to people, as in a restaurant.
wait·ress (wā′trĭs) ◊ *noun, plural* **waitresses**

waive *verb* **1.** To give up something by one's own choice: *The family waived their claim to the land.* **2.** To set aside or postpone: *We waived the formalities and got right down to the purpose of the meeting.*
waive (wāv) ◊ *verb* **waived, waiving**
‖*These sound alike:* **waive, wave**

wake¹ *verb* **1.** To stop or cause to stop sleeping; awaken: *I woke before daybreak.* **2.** To become or cause to become active; rouse: *Every time we visit the natural history museum my interest in science wakes again.*
◊ *noun* A watch kept over the body of a dead person before the burial.
wake¹ (wāk) ◊ *verb* **woke** *or* **waked, waked, waking** ◊ *noun, plural* **wakes**

wake² *noun* **1.** The track or path of waves, ripples, or foam left in the water by a moving boat or ship. **2.** The track or course left behind something that has passed: *The hurricane left destruction in its wake.*
wake² (wāk) ◊ *noun, plural* **wakes**

***HISTORY* • wake¹, wake²**

Wake¹ comes from an old English word that meant "to remain awake." **Wake²** probably comes from an old Dutch word that meant "a channel in ice."

waken *verb* To wake.
wak·en (wā′kən) ◊ *verb* **wakened, wakening**

walk *verb* **1.** To move or cause to move on foot at an easy, steady pace. **2.** To go over, across, or through by walking: *We walked the whole length of the town.* **3.** To help to walk; escort on foot: *My parents used to walk me to school.* **4.** To go or advance to first base in baseball after four balls have been pitched.
◊ *noun* **1.** An act of walking: *We took a walk on the beach.* **2.** A distance covered or to be covered in walking: *The walk to school is less than a mile.* **3.** A place, such as a path, that is set apart or designed for walking. **4.** A way of walking; gait: *You have a fast walk.* **5.** The advance of a baseball batter to first base after four balls have been pitched.
walk (wôk) ◊ *verb* **walked, walking** ◊ *noun, plural* **walks**

SYNONYMS

walk, march, stride, stroll

I *walked* to the store. The band *marched* in the parade. The sheriff *strides* toward the outlaws. We *strolled* slowly around the park.

walkie-talkie *noun* A portable radio transmitter and receiver operated by a battery.
walk·ie-talk·ie (wô′kē tô′kē) ◊ *noun, plural* **walkie-talkies**

ă	pat	ĭ	pit	oi	oil	th	bath
ā	pay	ī	ride	o͝o	book	*th*	bathe
â	care	î	fierce	o͞o	boot	ə	ago, item
ä	father	ŏ	pot	ou	out		pencil
ĕ	pet	ō	go	ŭ	cut		atom
ē	be	ô	paw, for	û	fur		circus

▲ walkie-talkie

wall *noun* A solid structure that forms an upright side of a building or room or that divides two areas.
◊ *verb* To surround, divide, or protect with or as if with a wall.
wall (wôl) ◊ *noun, plural* **walls** ◊ *verb* **walled, walling**

wallet *noun* A small, flat folding case for holding money, cards, and photographs.
wal·let (wŏl′ĭt) ◊ *noun, plural* **wallets**

wallop *verb* To hit with a hard blow.
◊ *noun* **1.** A hard blow. **2.** The power to hit with hard blows.
wal·lop (wŏl′əp) ◊ *verb* **walloped, walloping** ◊ *noun, plural* **wallops**

wallow *verb* To roll about in or as if in mud.
wal·low (wŏl′ō) ◊ *verb* **wallowed, wallowing**

wallpaper *noun* Heavy paper printed in colors and patterns. Wallpaper is used to cover and decorate walls.
◊ *verb* To cover with wallpaper.
wall·pa·per (wôl′pā′pər) ◊ *noun, plural* **wallpapers** ◊ *verb* **wallpapered, wallpapering**

walnut *noun* An edible nut that grows on a tall tree and has a hard, rough shell.
wal·nut (wôl′nŭt′) ◊ *noun, plural* **walnuts**

walrus *noun* A large sea animal that is related to the seals and sea lions. Walruses have tough, wrinkled skin and large tusks and live in the Arctic.
wal·rus (wôl′rəs) ◊ *noun, plural* **walrus** *or* **walruses**

▲ walrus

waltz *noun* **1.** A smooth, gliding dance to music with three beats to the measure. **2.** Music to accompany the waltz.
◊ *verb* To dance a waltz.
waltz (wôlts) ◊ *noun, plural* **waltzes** ◊ *verb* **waltzed, waltzing**

wampum *noun* Small beads that are made from pieces of polished shells. Wampum was once used by Native Americans as money.
wam·pum (wŏm′pəm) ◊ *noun*

wan *adjective* Pale, as from illness.
wan (wŏn) ◊ *adjective* **wanner, wannest**

wand *noun* A slender rod or stick, especially one used by a magician.
wand (wŏnd) ◊ *noun, plural* **wands**

wander *verb* **1.** To move from place to place without a special purpose or destination; roam: *We wandered around town.* **2.** To stray from a particular place, group, or subject: *My attention wandered.* **3.** To follow a winding or irregular course.
wan·der (wŏn′dər) ◊ *verb* **wandered, wandering**

wane *verb* **1.** To grow gradually less light. **2.** To become smaller, as in size or importance: *My interest in the problem waned.*
wane (wān) ◊ *verb* **waned, waning**

want *verb* **1.** To wish or desire: *They wanted to play outdoors.* **2.** To have a need for; require: *The grass wants cutting.*
◊ *noun* **1.** The condition of needing something; lack: *They lost the election for want of support.* **2.** A need, desire, or requirement: *I have few wants.*
want (wŏnt) ◊ *verb* **wanted, wanting** ◊ *noun, plural* **wants**

W

war *noun* **1.** Fighting or combat between nations, states, or groups of people. **2.** A struggle; fight: *The government is carrying on a war against poverty.*
◊ *verb* To make or take part in war; fight.
war (wôr) ◊ *noun, plural* **wars** ◊ *verb* **warred, warring**

warbler *noun* A small songbird, often having brightly colored feathers.
war·bler (**wôr′**blər) ◊ *noun, plural* **warblers**

ward *noun* **1.** A section of a hospital. **2.** A division of a city or town, especially an election district. **3.** A person put under the care or protection of a guardian or a court.
ward (wôrd) ◊ *noun, plural* **wards**

warden *noun* **1.** An official who makes sure that certain laws, as those relating to hunting and fishing, are obeyed. **2.** An official in charge of running a prison.
war·den (**wôrd′**n) ◊ *noun, plural* **wardens**

wardrobe *noun* **1.** A person's clothes. **2.** A closet or tall piece of furniture in which clothes are kept.
ward·robe (**wôr′**drōb′) ◊ *noun, plural* **wardrobes**

warehouse *noun* A large building where merchandise is stored.
ware·house (**wâr′**hous′) ◊ *noun, plural* **warehouses**

wares *plural noun* Goods for sale: *At the fair all the merchants displayed their wares.*
wares (wârz) ◊ *plural noun*

warfare *noun* Armed combat; war.
war·fare (**wôr′**fâr′) ◊ *noun*

warlike *adjective* **1.** Quick to make war; hostile. **2.** Threatening war: *Violating a treaty is a warlike action.*
war·like (**wôr′**līk′) ◊ *adjective*

warm *adjective* **1.** Somewhat hot: *I took a bath in warm water.* **2.** Giving off or retaining heat: *We walked in the warm sun. I'm wearing a warm sweater.* **3.** Having a feeling of bodily warmth: *I was warm after jogging.* **4.** Enthusiastic, friendly, or affectionate: *We gave the foreign students a warm welcome.*
◊ *verb* To make or become warm or warmer.
◊ *idiom* **warm up** To make or become ready to do something, as by exercising beforehand.
warm (wôrm) ◊ *adjective* **warmer, warmest** ◊ *verb* **warmed, warming**

ă	pat	ĭ	pit	oi	**oil**	th	**bath**
ā	pay	ī	ride	o͝o	**book**	*th*	**bathe**
â	care	î	fierce	o͞o	**boot**	ə	**ago, item**
ä	father	ŏ	**pot**	ou	**out**		pencil
ĕ	pet	ō	**go**	ŭ	**cut**		atom
ē	be	ô	**paw, for**	û	**fur**		circus

warm-blooded *adjective* Having blood that stays at about the same temperature no matter how much the temperature of the surrounding air or water changes.
warm-blood·ed (**wôrm′blŭd′**ĭd) ◊ *adjective*

warmth *noun* **1.** Moderate heat. **2.** Warm or friendly feelings: *We spoke about our old friends with warmth.*
warmth (wôrmth) ◊ *noun*

warn *verb* **1.** To make aware of danger; alert: *The news report warned us that the roads were icy.* **2.** To advise or caution: *We warned them not to run beside the swimming pool.*
warn (wôrn) ◊ *verb* **warned, warning**
‖*These sound alike:* **warn, worn**

warning *noun* Something that serves to warn: *The red light is a warning to stop.*
warn·ing (**wôr′**nĭng) ◊ *noun, plural* **warnings**

> ***SYNONYMS***
>
> ***warning, alarm, signal***
>
> The signs were posted as a *warning* that swimming there was dangerous. The smoke *alarm* woke up the family. The *signal* told the pilot where to land.

warp *verb* To bend, curve, or twist out of shape: *The door has warped and we can't close it.*
warp (wôrp) ◊ *verb* **warped, warping**

warrant *noun* An official paper that gives the police authority, as for making a search or an arrest.
◊ *verb* **1.** To call for; justify or deserve: *Your excellent work warrants a grade of A.* **2.** To guarantee: *My new watch is warranted for a year.*
war·rant (**wôr′**ənt) ◊ *noun, plural* **warrants** ◊ *verb* **warranted, warranting**

warrant officer *noun* A military officer ranking between an enlisted person and a commissioned officer.
warrant officer ◊ *noun, plural* **warrant officers**

warrior *noun* A person who is involved or experienced in war or fighting.
war·ri·or (wôr′ ē ər) ◊ *noun, plural* **warriors**

warship *noun* A ship that is built and equipped with weapons for battle.
war·ship (wôr′ shĭp′) ◊ *noun, plural* **warships**

wart *noun* A small hard lump that grows on the skin and is caused by a virus.
wart (wôrt) ◊ *noun, plural* **warts**

wary *adjective* On one's guard against danger; cautious: *Be wary of the icy steps.*
war·y (wâr′ ē) ◊ *adjective* **warier, wariest**

was *verb* First and third person singular past tense of **be.**
was (wŏz *or* wŭz) ◊ *verb*

wash *verb* **1.** To clean using water and often soap: *Whose turn is it to wash the dishes?* **2.** To remove by or as if by washing: *I washed the spot from my shirt.* **3.** To make oneself clean with soap and water: *Please be sure to wash before supper.* **4.** To carry or be carried away by moving water: *Rain washed the soil down the hill.*
◊ *noun* **1.** The act or process of washing. **2.** A quantity, as of clothes or linens, washed or to be washed. **3.** The flow or sound of moving water: *We could hear the wash of the waves against the shore.*
wash (wŏsh *or* wôsh) ◊ *verb* **washed, washing** ◊ *noun, plural* **washes**

Wash. An abbreviation for *Washington.*

washer *noun* **1.** A washing machine. **2.** A flat ring, as of rubber, put between a nut and a bolt to reduce friction and give a tighter fit.
wash·er (wŏsh′ ər *or* wô′ shər) ◊ *noun, plural* **washers**

washing *noun* A batch of articles washed or to be washed.
wash·ing (wŏsh′ ĭng *or* wô′ shĭng) ◊ *noun, plural* **washings**

washing machine *noun* A machine used for washing clothes and household articles.
washing machine ◊ *noun, plural* **washing machines**

wasn't Contraction of "was not."
was·n't (wŏz′ ənt *or* wŭz′ ənt) ◊ *contraction*

wasp *noun* A flying insect with a narrow middle section. A wasp can give a painful sting.
wasp (wŏsp *or* wôsp) ◊ *noun, plural* **wasps**

▲ **wasp**

waste *verb* **1.** To spend or use foolishly or needlessly: *Don't waste the whole day watching television.* **2.** To grow or cause to grow weaker or thinner: *If you miss your meals, you'll just waste away.*
◊ *noun* **1.** The act of wasting or the condition of being wasted. **2.** Worthless or useless material, such as garbage. **3.** Material that is left over after food has been digested. **4.** A barren or wild area or region: *Few animals can exist in the frozen wastes of the Arctic.*
◊ *adjective* **1.** Worthless or useless: *Throw out that waste paper.* **2.** Barren or wild.
waste (wāst) ◊ *verb* **wasted, wasting** ◊ *noun, plural* **wastes** ◊ *adjective*
‖*These sound alike:* **waste, waist**

wastebasket *noun* An open container that is used to hold things to be thrown away.
waste·bas·ket (wāst′ băs′kĭt) ◊ *noun, plural* **wastebaskets**

wasteful *adjective* Spending or using more than is needed.
waste·ful (wāst′ fəl) ◊ *adjective*

wasteland *noun* A lonely, usually barren place, such as a desert, where few plants or animals can live.
waste·land (wāst′ lănd′) ◊ *noun, plural* **wastelands**

watch *verb* **1.** To look or look at with care or attention: *People stopped to watch the parade.* **2.** To be alert and looking: *Watch for the street sign.* **3.** To keep guard or keep guard over: *We're watching our neighbors' house while they're away.*
◊ *noun* **1.** A small device for telling time that can be worn on the wrist or carried in a pocket. **2.** The act of guarding or watching.

W

3. A person or group of persons that guards or protects. **4.** The period of time when a person keeps a lookout.
watch (wŏch) ◊ *verb* **watched, watching** ◊ *noun, plural* **watches**

SYNONYMS
watch, gaze, look
I *watched* while the ship went by. I could *gaze* for hours at the ocean. *Look* over here.

watchdog *noun* A dog that is trained to protect people or property.
watch·dog (**wŏch′** dôg′) ◊ *noun, plural* **watchdogs**

watchful *adjective* Carefully watching; alert.
watch·ful (**wŏch′** fəl) ◊ *adjective*

watchman *noun* A person whose job is to watch and guard property, especially at night.
watch·man (**wŏch′** mən) ◊ *noun, plural* **watchmen**

water *noun* The liquid that falls from the sky as rain and forms rivers, oceans, and lakes. ◊ *verb* **1.** To sprinkle, wet, or supply with water: *I have to water the lawn.* **2.** To mix with or as if with water. **3.** To produce tears: *My eyes water when I chop onions.*
wa·ter (**wô′** tər) ◊ *noun* ◊ *verb* **watered, watering**

water color *noun* **1.** A paint in which the coloring material is mixed with water instead of oil. **2.** A picture done with these paints.
water color ◊ *noun, plural* **water colors**

watercress *noun* A plant that grows in running water. Its leaves are used in salads and as a garnish.
wa·ter·cress (**wô′** tər krĕs′) ◊ *noun*

waterfall *noun* A natural stream of water that falls from a high place.
wa·ter·fall (**wô′** tər fôl′) ◊ *noun, plural* **waterfalls**

ă	pat	ĭ	pit	oi	**oi**l	th	ba**th**
ā	pay	ī	ride	o͝o	book	*th*	ba**the**
â	care	î	fierce	o͞o	boot	ə	ago, item
ä	father	ŏ	pot	ou	**ou**t		pencil
ĕ	pet	ō	go	ŭ	cut		atom
ē	be	ô	paw, for	û	fur		circus

waterfront *noun* Land or a part of a town or city at the edge of a body of water.
wa·ter·front (**wô′** tər frŭnt′) ◊ *noun, plural* **waterfronts**

water lily *noun* A water plant with broad, floating leaves and colorful flowers.
water lily ◊ *noun, plural* **water lilies**

watermelon *noun* A very large melon with a hard, thick, green rind and sweet, watery pink or reddish flesh.
wa·ter·mel·on (**wô′** tər mĕl′ən) ◊ *noun, plural* **watermelons**

water moccasin *noun* A poisonous snake of swampy regions of the southern United States.
water moccasin ◊ *noun, plural* **water moccasins**

water polo *noun* A water sport played by two teams of swimmers who try to push, throw, or carry the ball toward the opponents' goal.

waterpower *noun* The energy produced by falling or running water that is used to run machines and to generate electricity.
wa·ter·pow·er (**wô′** tər pou′ər) ◊ *noun*

waterproof *adjective* Capable of keeping water from coming through: *Raincoats are made of waterproof material.*
◊ *verb* To make waterproof.
wa·ter·proof (**wô′** tər pro͞of′) ◊ *adjective* ◊ *verb* **waterproofed, waterproofing**

watershed *noun* **1.** A ridge of mountains or high land that separates two different systems of rivers. **2.** The region draining into a river or lake.
wa·ter·shed (**wô′** tər shĕd′) ◊ *noun, plural* **watersheds**

water-ski *noun* One of a pair of short, broad skis worn for gliding over water while the person skiing holds a rope attached to a motorboat.
◊ *verb* To glide over water on water-skis.
wa·ter-ski (**wô′** tər skē′) ◊ *noun, plural* **water-skis** ◊ *verb* **water-skied, water-skiing**

waterway *noun* A body of water, as a river or canal, on which ships and boats can travel.
wa·ter·way (**wô′** tər wā′) ◊ *noun, plural* **waterways**

water wheel *noun* A wheel that is turned by the power of flowing water.
water wheel ◊ *noun, plural* **water wheels**

▲ water wheel

watery *adjective* **1.** Filled with or containing water: *My eyes were watery from the cold wind.* **2.** Having too much water; thin: *The soup was watery.*
wa·ter·y (wô′ tə rē) ◊ *adjective* **waterier, wateriest**

watt *noun* A unit of electrical power.
watt (wŏt) ◊ *noun, plural* **watts**

wave *verb* **1.** To move back and forth or up and down; flap or flutter: *The flags waved in the breeze.* **2.** To move a hand or something held in the hand back and forth as a signal or greeting. **3.** To fall or arrange in curls or curves.
◊ *noun* **1.** A ridge or swell moving along the surface of a body of water: *The waves tossed our boat up and down.* **2.** A motion back and forth or up or down that passes energy from point to point; vibration. Light, sound, and heat travel in waves. **3.** An act of waving: *I greeted them with a wave of my hand.* **4.** A curve or arrangement of curves: *You have a soft wave in your hair.* **5.** A widespread condition of very hot or cold weather: *We are experiencing a terrible heat wave.*
wave (wāv) ◊ *verb* **waved, waving** ◊ *noun, plural* **waves**
‖*These sound alike:* **wave, waive**

waver *verb* **1.** To sway back and forth. **2.** To be uncertain; falter: *I never wavered in my choice.* **3.** To be unsteady: *My voice wavered.*
wa·ver (wā′ vər) ◊ *verb* **wavered, wavering**

wax¹ *noun* **1.** A substance that is produced by bees and is used to make honeycombs. Wax is hard but becomes soft when heated. **2.** A substance like wax. **3.** A substance containing wax that is used for polishing.
◊ *verb* To cover, coat, or polish with wax.
wax¹ (wăks) ◊ *noun, plural* **waxes** ◊ *verb* **waxed, waxing**

wax² *verb* **1.** To grow gradually more light. **2.** To increase, as in size, strength, or intensity.
wax² (wăks) ◊ *verb* **waxed, waxing**

> ***HISTORY* • wax¹, wax²**
>
> **Wax¹** comes from an old English word that first meant "beeswax." **Wax²** comes from a different old English word that meant "to grow."

way *noun* **1.** A manner or fashion: *I answered in a polite way.* **2.** A method, means, or technique: *Do you know a better way of solving the problem?* **3.** An aspect or feature: *They are improving the city in many ways.* **4.** A road or route from one place to another: *We found a way through the woods.* **5.** Room enough to pass or go: *Make way for the fire truck.* **6.** Progress or travel along a route or course: *Lead the way home.* **7.** Distance: *Is it a long way to school?* **8.** A specific direction: *Which way did the taxi go?* **9.** What one wants; wish or will: *If I had my way, we'd go to the movies tonight.*
◊ *adverb* Far: *The sweetest apples are way at the top of the tree.*
way (wā) ◊ *noun, plural* **ways** ◊ *adverb*
‖*These sound alike:* **way, weigh**

wayside *noun* The side or edge of a road.
way·side (wā′ sīd′) ◊ *noun, plural* **waysides**

we *pronoun* The people who are the speakers or the writers: *We went to the circus.*
we (wē) ◊ *pronoun*
‖*These sound alike:* **we, wee**

weak *adjective* **1.** Lacking strength, power, or energy; feeble: *My left arm is weaker than my right arm.* **2.** Likely to break or fail under pressure or stress: *A chain breaks at the weakest link.*
weak (wēk) ◊ *adjective* **weaker, weakest**
‖*These sound alike:* **weak, week**

W

weaken *verb* To make or become weak or weaker.
weak·en (wē′kən) ◊ *verb* **weakened, weakening**

weakling *noun* A weak person or animal.
weak·ling (wēk′lĭng) ◊ *noun, plural* **weaklings**

weakly *adverb* In a weak way.
weak·ly (wēk′lē) ◊ *adverb*
‖*These sound alike:* **weakly, weekly**

weakness *noun* **1.** The condition or feeling of being weak. **2.** An imperfection; flaw: *My biggest weakness is putting off the chores.* **3.** A special liking: *I have a weakness for good food.*
weak·ness (wēk′nĭs) ◊ *noun, plural* **weaknesses**

wealth *noun* **1.** A great amount of money or valuable possessions. **2.** A large amount of something: *The library contains a wealth of information.*
wealth (wĕlth) ◊ *noun*

wealthy *adjective* Having wealth; rich.
wealth·y (wĕl′thē) ◊ *adjective* **wealthier, wealthiest**

weapon *noun* Something, such as a gun or claw, that is used in defense or attack.
weap·on (wĕp′ən) ◊ *noun, plural* **weapons**

wear *verb* **1.** To have on the body. **2.** To show: *They were all wearing smiles.* **3.** To damage, make less, or use up by long use, rubbing, or scraping: *Waves wore away the cliff.* **4.** To make or become as a result of rubbing: *I wore a hole in my sock.* **5.** To withstand long use: *My jacket wore well.*
◊ *noun* **1.** The act of wearing or the condition of being worn. **2.** Clothing: *This store sells outdoor wear.* **3.** Damage that comes from long use: *The rug shows signs of wear.*
◊ *idiom* **wear out 1.** To use or be used so as to become useless: *I wore out my best jacket.* **2.** To cause to be exhausted; tire: *The long trip wore them out.*
wear (wâr) ◊ *verb* **wore, worn, wearing** ◊ *noun*

weary *adjective* **1.** Needing rest; tired: *The weary children went straight to bed.* **2.** Causing or showing tiredness: *I gave a weary sigh.*
◊ *verb* To make or become weary; tire.
wea·ry (wîr′ē) ◊ *adjective* **wearier, weariest** ◊ *verb* **wearied, wearying**

weasel *noun* An animal with soft fur and a long, narrow body. Weasels feed on small animals and birds.
wea·sel (wē′zəl) ◊ *noun, plural* **weasels**

▲ **weasel**

weather *noun* The condition or activity of the atmosphere with respect to whether it is hot or cold, sunny or cloudy, windy or calm, or wet or dry.
◊ *verb* **1.** To change because of being exposed to the weather: *The old barn weathered to a soft gray.* **2.** To pass through safely; survive: *We weathered the big storm at sea.*
weath·er (wĕ*th*′ər) ◊ *noun* ◊ *verb* **weathered, weathering**

weather vane *noun* A moving vane that shows which way the wind is blowing.
weather vane ◊ *noun, plural* **weather vanes**

weave *verb* **1.** To make something, such as cloth or a basket, by passing something, such as threads or twigs, over and under one another. **2.** To move in and out, back and forth, or from side to side: *I weaved through the line of cars.* **3.** To spin, as a spider's web.
◊ *noun* A pattern or method of weaving.
weave (wēv) ◊ *verb* **wove** *or* **weaved** (for sense 2), **woven, weaving** ◊ *noun, plural* **weaves**
‖*These sound alike:* **weave, we've**

ă pat	ĭ pit	oi oil	th bath
ā pay	ī ride	ŏŏ book	*th* bathe
â care	î fierce	ōō boot	ə ago, item
ä father	ŏ pot	ou out	pencil
ĕ pet	ō go	ŭ cut	atom
ē be	ô paw, for	û fur	circus

web *noun* **1.** A network of fine, silky threads that are spun by a spider; cobweb. **2.** Something formed by or as if by weaving: *From the airplane window I could see a web of city streets.* **3.** A fold of tissue that connects the toes of certain animals, such as frogs.
web (wĕb) ◊ *noun, plural* **webs**

webbed *adjective* Connected or formed with a web: *A goose has webbed feet.*
webbed (wĕbd) ◊ *adjective*

web-footed *adjective* Having feet with toes joined by a web: *Ducks are web-footed.*
web-foot·ed (**wĕb′ fo͝ot′** ĭd) ◊ *adjective*

wed *verb* **1.** To take as a husband or wife; marry. **2.** To unite in marriage.
wed (wĕd) ◊ *verb* **wedded, wed** *or* **wedded, wedding**

Wed. The abbreviation for *Wednesday.*

we'd Contraction of "we had," "we should," or "we would."
we'd (wēd) ◊ *contraction*
‖*These sound alike:* **we'd, weed**

wedding *noun* A marriage ceremony.
wed·ding (**wĕd′** ĭng) ◊ *noun, plural* **weddings**

wedge *noun* **1.** A block of material, such as wood, that is wide at one end and tapers to a point at the other. A wedge is used for splitting, tightening, or holding things in place. **2.** Something shaped like a wedge: *I cut the melon into wedges.*
◊ *verb* **1.** To split, force apart, or fix in place with a wedge: *I wedged the door open.* **2.** To crowd or squeeze into a limited space: *We were all wedged into one tiny room.*
wedge (wĕj) ◊ *noun, plural* **wedges** ◊ *verb* **wedged, wedging**

wedlock *noun* The state of being married.
wed·lock (**wĕd′** lŏk′) ◊ *noun*

Wednesday *noun* The fourth day of the week.
Wednes·day (**wĕnz′** dē) ◊ *noun, plural* **Wednesdays**

HISTORY • Wednesday

Four of the seven days of the week were named after the gods the English believed in before they became Christians. *Wednesday* was named after *Woden,* the king of the gods.

wee *adjective* Very little; tiny.
wee (wē) ◊ *adjective* **weer, weest**
‖*These sound alike:* **wee, we**

weed *noun* A plant that grows easily where it is not wanted and is considered to be troublesome, useless, or harmful.
◊ *verb* To rid of weeds: *If you weed the garden, the plants will grow better.*
weed (wēd) ◊ *noun, plural* **weeds** ◊ *verb* **weeded, weeding**
‖*These sound alike:* **weed, we'd**

weedy *adjective* Full of weeds.
weed·y (**wē′** dē) ◊ *adjective* **weedier, weediest**

week *noun* **1.** A period of seven days: *We'll be there in a week.* **2.** The period from Sunday through the next Saturday. **3.** The part of a week during which one works or goes to school.
week (wēk) ◊ *noun, plural* **weeks**
‖*These sound alike:* **week, weak**

weekday *noun* Any day of the week except Saturday and Sunday.
week·day (**wēk′** dā′) ◊ *noun, plural* **weekdays**

weekend *noun* The period of time from Friday evening through Sunday evening.
week·end (**wēk′** ĕnd′) ◊ *noun, plural* **weekends**

weekly *adverb* Once a week or every week: *Our relatives visit us weekly.*
◊ *adjective* **1.** Done, happening, or coming weekly: *Our club has weekly meetings.* **2.** Made or figured by the week: *My weekly allowance is very good.*
◊ *noun* A weekly newspaper or magazine.
week·ly (**wēk′** lē) ◊ *adverb* ◊ *adjective* ◊ *noun, plural* **weeklies**
‖*These sound alike:* **weekly, weakly**

weep *verb* To shed tears; cry.
weep (wēp) ◊ *verb* **wept, weeping**

weevil *noun* A beetle with a long snout. Weevils do damage to plants and crops.
wee·vil (**wē′** vəl) ◊ *noun, plural* **weevils**

weigh *verb* **1.** To find out the weight of. **2.** To have a particular weight: *The car weighs 2,800 pounds.* **3.** To consider carefully; think about: *We weighed our choices of movies before we decided which one to see.*
◊ *idiom* **weigh down** To cause to bend: *Snow weighed down the branches of the trees.*
weigh (wā) ◊ *verb* **weighed, weighing**
‖*These sound alike:* **weigh, way**

W

weight *noun* **1.** The measure of how heavy something is: *The weight of the box is 100 pounds.* **2.** The force of gravity pulling on an object. **3.** A unit, such as a pound, for measuring weight. **4.** An object with a known weight: *I lift ten-pound weights to strengthen my muscles.* **5.** Something heavy used to press or hold down objects, such as papers.
weight (wāt) ◊ *noun, plural* **weights**
‖*These sound alike:* **weight, wait**

weightless *adjective* **1.** Having little or no weight. **2.** Experiencing little or no pull of gravity, as an astronaut does when traveling inside a space vehicle orbiting the earth.
weight·less (**wāt′**lĭs) ◊ *adjective*

weighty *adjective* **1.** Having great weight; heavy. **2.** Of great importance.
weight·y (**wā′**tē) ◊ *adjective* **weightier, weightiest**

weird *adjective* **1.** Mysterious and often frightening; eerie: *A weird light came from the woods.* **2.** Strange, odd, or unusual: *Purple trousers, an orange shirt, and a pointed hat make a weird outfit.*
weird (wîrd) ◊ *adjective* **weirder, weirdest**

welcome *verb* **1.** To greet with pleasure, hospitality, or special ceremony: *We stood to welcome our guests.* **2.** To accept or receive gladly: *I welcome your suggestions.*
◊ *noun* The act of welcoming.
◊ *adjective* **1.** Greeted, received, or accepted with pleasure: *You are always a welcome visitor.* —See Synonyms at **pleasant. 2.** Freely permitted to have, do, or use: *You're welcome to have the apple.* **3.** Used in the phrase "You're welcome" to respond to "Thank you."
wel·come (**wĕl′**kəm) ◊ *verb* **welcomed, welcoming** ◊ *noun, plural* **welcomes** ◊ *adjective*

weld *verb* **1.** To join metal or plastic parts by heating and then pressing the materials together. **2.** To bring together; unite: *A season of playing baseball together welded us into a fine team.*
◊ *noun* A joint formed by welding materials.
weld (wĕld) ◊ *verb* **welded, welding** ◊ *noun, plural* **welds**

welfare *noun* **1.** Health, happiness, or prosperity; well-being. **2.** Help, such as money, that is given to those who are in need.
wel·fare (**wĕl′**fâr′) ◊ *noun*

well[1] *noun* **1.** A deep hole that is dug or drilled into the ground to get to a natural deposit, such as water, oil, or gas. **2.** Something like a well, as an opening for stairs that goes between the floors of a building.
◊ *verb* To rise and flow forth: *Tears of joy welled up in my eyes.*
well[1] (wĕl) ◊ *noun, plural* **wells** ◊ *verb* **welled, welling**

well[2] *adverb* **1.** In a way that is good, proper, skillful, satisfactory, or successful: *My dog behaves well. You play the piano well. I slept well. We got along well with them.* **2.** Thoroughly: *Blend the ingredients well.* **3.** To a great degree or extent; much: *It was well after sunset when we arrived.* **4.** In a favorable way: *People speak well of you.* **5.** In a close way; familiarly: *I know them well.*
◊ *adjective* **1.** In good health; not sick: *I'm well, thank you.* —See Synonyms at **healthy. 2.** All right; satisfactory: *All is well.*
◊ *interjection* **1.** Used to show relief, doubt, or surprise: *Well! I never expected to see you so soon.* **2.** Used to begin a remark or to fill time when one is thinking of what to say: *I guess you're right, but, well, I'm not sure.*
well[2] (wĕl) ◊ *adverb* **better, best** ◊ *adjective* ◊ *interjection*

HISTORY • well[1], well[2]

Well[1] comes from an old English word that meant "a spring of water." **Well[2]** is related to **wealth** and originally meant "in a good manner, prosperously."

we'll Contraction of "we will" or "we shall."
we'll (wēl) ◊ *contraction*

well-being *noun* Health, happiness, or prosperity; welfare.
well-be·ing (**wĕl′bē′**ĭng) ◊ *noun*

well-bred *adjective* Having or showing good training in manners; polite.
well-bred (**wĕl′brĕd′**) ◊ *adjective*

ă	pat	ĭ	pit	oi	**oil**	th	ba**th**
ā	pay	ī	ride	o͝o	book	*th*	ba*th*e
â	care	î	fierce	o͞o	boot	ə	ago, item
ä	father	ŏ	pot	ou	**out**		pencil
ĕ	pet	ō	go	ŭ	cut		atom
ē	be	ô	paw, for	û	fur		circus

well-known *adjective* Known to many people: *They are a well-known singing group and will give a concert next month.*
well-known (wĕl′nōn′) ◊ *adjective*

well-to-do *adjective* Having enough money to live in comfort; prosperous.
well-to-do (wĕl′tə **dōō′**) ◊ *adjective*

went *verb* Past tense of **go.**
went (wĕnt) ◊ *verb*

wept *verb* Past tense and past participle of **weep.**
wept (wĕpt) ◊ *verb*

were *verb* **1.** Second person singular past tense of **be. 2.** First, second, and third person plural past tense of **be.**
were (wûr) ◊ *verb*

we're Contraction of "we are."
we're (wîr) ◊ *contraction*

weren't Contraction of "were not."
weren't (wûrnt) ◊ *contraction*

west *noun* **1.** The direction in which the sun is seen setting in the evening. **2.** Often **West** A region in the west. **3. West** The western part of the United States, especially the part west of the Mississippi River. **4. West** The part of the earth west of Asia, especially Europe and North and South America.
◊ *adjective* **1.** Of, in, or toward the west: *We camped on the west side of the large lake.* **2.** Coming from the west: *A west wind blew all day.*
◊ *adverb* Toward the west: *We drove west.*
west (wĕst) ◊ *noun* ◊ *adjective* ◊ *adverb*

westerly *adjective & adverb* **1.** In or toward the west. **2.** From the west: *Our sailboat was blown off course by westerly winds.*
west·er·ly (**wĕs′** tər lē) ◊ *adjective & adverb*

western *adjective* **1.** Often **Western** Of, in, or toward the west. **2.** Coming from the west.
◊ *noun* Often **Western** A book, movie, or television program about frontier life in the western United States.
west·ern (**wĕs′** tərn) ◊ *adjective* ◊ *noun, plural* **westerns**

westward *adverb* To or toward the west.
◊ *adjective* Moving to or toward the west: *We began our westward journey at dawn.*
west·ward (**wĕst′** wərd) ◊ *adverb* ◊ *adjective*

westwards *adverb* Westward.
west·wards (**wĕst′** wərdz) ◊ *adverb*

wet *adjective* **1.** Being covered, moistened, or soaked with a liquid, especially water. **2.** Rainy: *We've had a week of wet weather.* **3.** Not yet dry or hardened: *Don't touch the wet paint.*
◊ *verb* To make wet.
wet (wĕt) ◊ *adjective* **wetter, wettest** ◊ *verb* **wet** *or* **wetted, wetting**

we've Contraction of "we have."
we've (wēv) ◊ *contraction*
‖*These sound alike:* **we've, weave**

whale *noun* An often very large sea animal that looks like a fish but is a mammal that breathes air.
whale (hwāl) ◊ *noun, plural* **whales**

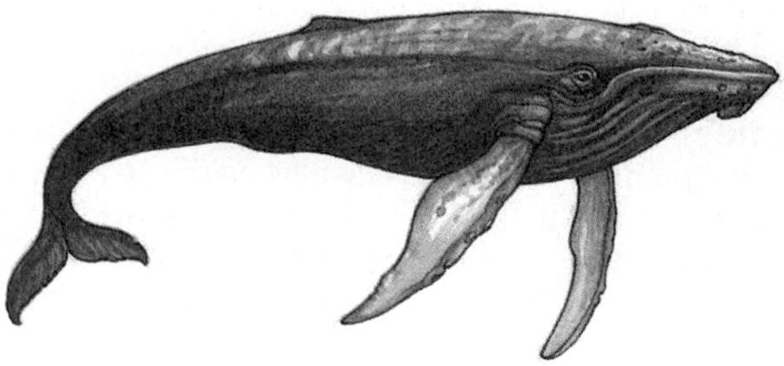

▲ **whale**

whaler *noun* **1.** A person who hunts whales. **2.** A ship used in hunting whales.
whal·er (**hwā′** lər) ◊ *noun, plural* **whalers**

wharf *noun* A landing place built along a shore where ships can load or unload.
wharf (hwôrf) ◊ *noun, plural* **wharves** *or* **wharfs**

wharves *noun* A plural of **wharf.**
wharves (hwôrvz) ◊ *noun*

what *pronoun* **1.** Used to ask questions about things or persons: *What are we having for supper? What do you think I am?* **2.** That which; the thing that: *I saw what you did.* **3.** Whatever: *Say what you want.*
◊ *adjective* **1.** Used to ask questions about things or persons: *What train do I take?* **2.** Of any kind; whatever: *Ask what questions you*

W

like. **3.** How surprising or remarkable: *What an exciting movie!*
◊ *adverb* In which way; how: *What does it matter, after all?*
◊ *interjection* An expression used to show surprise: *What! More snow?*
what (hwŏt) ◊ *pronoun* ◊ *adjective* ◊ *adverb* ◊ *interjection*

whatever *pronoun* **1.** Anything that: *Please do whatever you can to help.* **2.** No matter what: *Whatever you do, come early.* **3.** Which thing or things; what: *Whatever made her say that?*
◊ *adjective* **1.** Of any number or kind that; any or all: *Buy whatever clothing you need.* **2.** Of any kind at all: *He ate nothing whatever at dinner.*
what·ev·er (hwŏt **ĕv′** ər) ◊ *pronoun* ◊ *adjective*

wheat *noun* A cereal grass that bears grain. The grain is often ground to make flour.
wheat (hwēt) ◊ *noun*

wheel *noun* **1.** A round device that can turn on a point in its center. A wheel can be used to move a vehicle or to drive a machine. **2.** Something that is shaped like a wheel, that is used like a wheel, or that has a wheel as its main part: *The driver uses a steering wheel to turn the car.*
◊ *verb* **1.** To move or roll on wheels: *Please wheel the cart to the library.* **2.** To turn and change direction: *The horse wheeled and ran away.*
wheel (hwēl) ◊ *noun, plural* **wheels** ◊ *verb* **wheeled, wheeling**

wheelbarrow *noun* A cart for carrying small loads that has one or two wheels in front and two handles at the back for pushing.
wheel·bar·row (**hwēl′** băr′ō) ◊ *noun, plural* **wheelbarrows**

wheelchair *noun* A chair on wheels in which a sick or disabled person can move about.
wheel·chair (**hwēl′** châr′) ◊ *noun, plural* **wheelchairs**

ă	pat	ĭ	pit	oi	oil	th	bath
ā	pay	ī	ride	o͝o	book	*th*	bathe
â	care	î	fierce	o͞o	boot	ə	ago, item
ä	father	ŏ	pot	ou	out		pencil
ĕ	pet	ō	go	ŭ	cut		atom
ē	be	ô	paw, for	û	fur		circus

wheeze *verb* To breathe with difficulty, making a hoarse whistling or hissing sound.
wheeze (hwēz) ◊ *verb* **wheezed, wheezing**

whelk *noun* A large sea snail with a pointed spiral shell.
whelk (hwĕlk) ◊ *noun, plural* **whelks**

when *adverb* **1.** At what time: *When did you leave?* **2.** At which time: *I know when to leave for school.*
◊ *conjunction* **1.** At or during the time that: *Start when I give the signal.* **2.** As soon as: *I'll call you when I get there.* **3.** At any time that; whenever: *I'm not afraid when I'm alone.* **4.** Although: *I played when I should have been studying.* **5.** Considering that; if: *How can you win the competition when you won't practice?*
when (hwĕn) ◊ *adverb* ◊ *conjunction*

whenever *adverb* At whatever time: *Come whenever possible.*
◊ *conjunction* At whatever time that: *We can start whenever you're ready.*
when·ev·er (hwĕn **ĕv′** ər) ◊ *adverb* ◊ *conjunction*

where *adverb* At, in, or to what place: *Where is the telephone?*
◊ *conjunction* **1.** At, in, or to what or which place: *I am going to my room, where I can study.* **2.** At, in, or to a place at, in, or to which: *The bike is where I left it.* **3.** Wherever: *I'll go where you go.*
◊ *pronoun* What or which place: *Where did they come from?*
where (hwâr) ◊ *adverb* ◊ *conjunction* ◊ *pronoun*

whereabouts *adverb* At or near what place: *Whereabouts did I leave my notebook?*
◊ *noun* (*used with a singular or plural verb*) The place where someone or something is: *My friend's whereabouts is* (or *are*) *unknown.*
where·a·bouts (**hwâr′** ə bouts′) ◊ *adverb* ◊ *noun*

wherever *conjunction* At, in, or to whatever place or situation that: *I'll miss you wherever you go.*
wher·ev·er (hwâr **ĕv′** ər) ◊ *conjunction*

whether *conjunction* **1.** Used to show a choice between things: *Whether we win or lose, we will be glad we tried.* **2.** If: *Ask whether the museum is open.*
wheth·er (**hwĕ*th*′** ər) ◊ *conjunction*

whew *interjection* An expression used to show tiredness, relief, or surprise.
whew (hwyo͞o) ◊ *interjection*

whey *noun* The watery part of milk that separates from the curds, as in making cheese.
whey (hwā) ◊ *noun*

which *pronoun* **1.** What one or ones: *Which is your house?* **2.** The one or ones that; any that: *Take those which are yours.* **3.** The one or ones mentioned: *They bought the car, which was expensive.*
◊ *adjective* Being what one or ones: *Which coat is yours?*
which (hwĭch) ◊ *pronoun* ◊ *adjective*

whichever *pronoun* Whatever one or ones; no matter which: *Buy whichever you like best.*
◊ *adjective* Being any one or ones that: *Buy whichever toy you like best.*
which·ev·er (hwĭch ĕv′ər) ◊ *pronoun* ◊ *adjective*

whiff *noun* **1.** A slight puff, as of air or smoke. **2.** A trace of a smell: *A whiff of the freshly baked bread made us hungry.*
whiff (hwĭf) ◊ *noun, plural* **whiffs**

while *noun* **1.** A period of time: *Please stay for a while.* **2.** Time or effort used: *It's not worth my while to plant bulbs in poor soil.*
◊ *conjunction* **1.** During the time that: *Our vacation was great while it lasted.* **2.** At the same time that; although: *She is tall, while her brother is short.*
◊ *verb* To pass or spend in a pleasant or relaxed way: *We whiled away the morning sitting on the porch.*
while (hwīl) ◊ *noun* ◊ *conjunction* ◊ *verb* **whiled, whiling**

whim *noun* A sudden wish, desire, or idea: *We had a whim to go sailing today.*
whim (hwĭm) ◊ *noun, plural* **whims**

whimper *verb* To cry with weak, broken, whining sounds.
◊ *noun* A whimpering sound.
whim·per (**hwĭm′**pər) ◊ *verb* **whimpered, whimpering** ◊ *noun, plural* **whimpers**

whine *verb* **1.** To make a high, shrill sound or cry: *The electric saw whined as it cut the wood.* **2.** To complain in a childish, annoying way: *Don't whine about your homework.*
◊ *noun* A whining sound or cry.
whine (hwīn) ◊ *verb* **whined, whining** ◊ *noun, plural* **whines**

whinny *noun* A horse's gentle neigh.
◊ *verb* To make a whinny.
whin·ny (**hwĭn′**ē) ◊ *noun, plural* **whinnies** ◊ *verb* **whinnied, whinnying**

whip *noun* A rod or stick with a handle, often with a lash at the end. A whip is used especially for driving or controlling animals such as cattle or horses.
◊ *verb* **1.** To strike, beat, or lash with or as if with a whip. **2.** To move, pull, or put suddenly and quickly: *I whipped out my pen and began to write.* **3.** To beat something, such as cream, into a foam. **4.** To defeat, as in a fight; beat: *You can't whip our team this year.*
whip (hwĭp) ◊ *noun, plural* **whips** ◊ *verb* **whipped, whipping**

whippoorwill *noun* A plump, brownish bird of North America that is active at night. The whippoorwill has a call that sounds like its name.
whip·poor·will (**hwĭp′**ər wĭl′) ◊ *noun, plural* **whippoorwills**

▲ **whippoorwill**

whir *verb* To move quickly with a buzzing or humming sound.
◊ *noun* A buzzing or humming sound.
whir (hwûr) ◊ *verb* **whirred, whirring** ◊ *noun, plural* **whirs**

whirl *verb* **1.** To spin or cause to spin quickly: *Snow whirled in the air.* **2.** To feel dizzy.
◊ *noun* **1.** A whirling movement. **2.** A dizzy or confused condition: *My thoughts have been in a happy whirl since I won first prize.*
whirl (hwûrl) ◊ *verb* **whirled, whirling** ◊ *noun, plural* **whirls**

whirlpool *noun* A current of water that rotates very rapidly.
whirl·pool (**hwûrl′**po͞ol′) ◊ *noun, plural* **whirlpools**

whirlwind *noun* A current of air that rotates rapidly and often violently.
whirl·wind (**hwûrl′**wĭnd′) ◊ *noun, plural* **whirlwinds**

whisk *verb* **1.** To brush or sweep with quick, light movements: *I whisked the crumbs off the*

W

table. **2.** To move or carry very quickly: *The parents whisked the naughty child out the door.*
whisk (hwĭsk) ◊ *verb* **whisked, whisking**

whisker *noun* **1. whiskers** A man's mustache and beard. **2.** One of the hairs growing on a man's face. **3.** A stiff, long hair growing near the mouths of certain animals, such as cats, rats, and rabbits.
whisk·er (**hwĭs′** kər) ◊ *noun, plural* **whiskers**

whiskey *noun* A strong alcoholic drink made from a grain such as corn or rye.
whis·key (**hwĭs′** kē) ◊ *noun, plural* **whiskeys**

whisper *verb* **1.** To speak, tell, or say in a very low, soft voice. **2.** To make a soft hissing or rustling sound: *The breeze whispered through the pines.*
◊ *noun* **1.** A whispering sound. **2.** Something whispered.
whis·per (**hwĭs′** pər) ◊ *verb* **whispered, whispering** ◊ *noun, plural* **whispers**

whistle *verb* **1.** To make a clear, high sound by forcing air out between the teeth or lips. **2.** To blow on a device that makes this sound. **3.** To make or move with a sound like whistling: *The wind whistled through the trees.* **4.** To make, signal, or call by whistling: *The child whistled a tune.*
◊ *noun* **1.** A device that makes a high, clear sound when air is blown through it. **2.** A sound made by or as if by whistling.
whis·tle (**hwĭs′** əl) ◊ *verb* **whistled, whistling** ◊ *noun, plural* **whistles**

white *noun* **1.** A color that is the opposite of black; the color of snow. **2.** The part of something, such as an egg, that is light in color. **3.** A person with light skin.
◊ *adjective* **1.** Of the color white: *The fence is white.* **2.** Light in color. **3.** Having little color; pale: *The sick child's face was very white.* **4.** Having light skin. **5.** Pale gray or silvery: *White hair is attractive.*
white (hwīt) ◊ *noun, plural* **whites** ◊ *adjective* **whiter, whitest**

ă	pat	ĭ	pit	oi	**oil**	th	ba**th**
ā	pay	ī	ride	ŏŏ	book	*th*	ba*th*e
â	care	î	fierce	ōō	**boot**	ə	ago, item
ä	father	ŏ	pot	ou	**out**		pencil
ĕ	pet	ō	go	ŭ	cut		atom
ē	be	ô	paw, for	û	fur		circus

white blood cell *noun* A colorless cell in the blood that helps fight infection by destroying disease germs.
white blood cell ◊ *noun, plural* **white blood cells**

white cap *noun* An ocean wave with a foaming white crest.
white cap ◊ *noun, plural* **white caps**

White House *noun* **1.** The official home of the President of the United States, in Washington, D.C. **2.** The office or power of the President of the United States.

whiten *verb* To make or become white.
whit·en (**hwīt′**n) ◊ *verb* **whitened, whitening**

whitewash *noun* A mixture of lime and water used to whiten surfaces such as walls.
white·wash (**hwīt′** wŏsh′) ◊ *noun*

whitish *adjective* Somewhat white.
whit·ish (**hwī′** tĭsh) ◊ *adjective*

whittle *verb* **1.** To cut small bits or shavings from wood with a knife. **2.** To make or shape in this way: *We whittled a wooden toy.*
whit·tle (**hwĭt′**l) ◊ *verb* **whittled, whittling**

whiz *or* **whizz** *verb* To move quickly with a buzzing or hissing sound: *The express train whizzed past the station.*
whiz *or* **whizz** (hwĭz) ◊ *verb* **whizzed, whizzing**

who *pronoun* **1.** What or which person or persons: *Who called?* **2.** The person or group that: *The friend who was here has left.*
who (hōō) ◊ *pronoun*

who'd Contraction of "who would."
who'd (hōōd) ◊ *contraction*

whoever *pronoun* Anyone that: *Whoever comes to our school should be welcomed.*
who·ev·er (hōō **ĕv′** ər) ◊ *pronoun*

whole *adjective* **1.** Having no part missing; complete: *The whole class laughed.* **2.** Not divided; in one piece: *Our playing field covers a whole acre.* **3.** Entire; full: *The baby cried the whole time.*
◊ *noun* **1.** Something complete: *Two halves make a whole.* **2.** An entire group or system: *The class as a whole voted to visit the city.*
whole (hōl) ◊ *adjective* ◊ *noun, plural* **wholes**
‖ *These sound alike:* **whole, hole**

whole number *noun* A number such as 1, 2, 15, or 126 as opposed to a fraction or decimal.
whole number ◊ *noun, plural* **whole numbers**

wholesale *noun* The sale of goods in large quantities, usually to retail stores.
whole·sale (hōl′sāl′) ◊ *noun*

wholesome *adjective* Good for the health; healthful: *You should always try to eat wholesome food.*
whole·some (hōl′səm) ◊ *adjective*

who'll Contraction of "who will" or "who shall."
who'll (ho͞ol) ◊ *contraction*

wholly *adverb* To the complete extent; entirely: *I did the job wholly by myself.*
whol·ly (hō′lē) ◊ *adverb*
‖*These sound alike:* **wholly, holy**

whom *pronoun* The objective case of **who.**
whom (ho͞om) ◊ *pronoun*

whomever *pronoun* The objective case of **whoever.**
whom·ev·er (ho͞om ĕv′ər) ◊ *pronoun*

whoop *noun* A loud cry or shout.
◊ *verb* To cry out or shout loudly.
whoop (ho͞op *or* hwo͞op *or* wo͞op) ◊ *noun, plural* **whoops** ◊ *verb* **whooped, whooping**

whooping crane *noun* A large crane with white feathers and a loud cry.
whooping crane ◊ *noun, plural* **whooping cranes**

▲ **whooping crane**

who's Contraction of "who is" or "who has."
who's (ho͞oz) ◊ *contraction*
‖*These sound alike:* **who's, whose**

whose *pronoun* Of, relating to, or belonging to whom or which: *Whose car is this? Let's fix the bike whose tire is flat.*
whose (ho͞oz) ◊ *pronoun*
‖*These sound alike:* **whose, who's**

why *adverb* For what reason: *Why did you have to leave?*
◊ *conjunction* The reason for which: *I don't know why they bought that car.*
◊ *interjection* An expression used to show feelings such as surprise, pleasure, or doubt: *Why, I'd be glad to help you.*
why (hwī) ◊ *adverb* ◊ *conjunction* ◊ *interjection*

WI The abbreviation for *Wisconsin* used with a Zip Code.

wick *noun* A cord or strand of soft fibers, as in a candle or oil lamp, that draws up fuel, such as melted wax or oil, to be burned.
wick (wĭk) ◊ *noun, plural* **wicks**

wicked *adjective* Bad, evil, or mean.
wick·ed (wĭk′ĭd) ◊ *adjective* **wickeder, wickedest**

wicker *noun* A flexible twig or thin branch, as of a willow tree. Wicker is woven together to make baskets and furniture.
wick·er (wĭk′ər) ◊ *noun, plural* **wicker**

wicket *noun* A wire arch through which a croquet player tries to hit the ball.
wick·et (wĭk′ĭt) ◊ *noun, plural* **wickets**

wide *adjective* **1.** Taking up a large amount of space from side to side; broad: *We live on a wide street.* **2.** Measuring a particular amount from side to side: *The ribbon is two inches wide.* **3.** Having a large range or scope: *This store has a wide selection of clothes.* **4.** Fully open: *I saw that the child's eyes were wide with surprise.*
◊ *adverb* To the full extent: *The door was wide open.*
wide (wīd) ◊ *adjective, adverb* **wider, widest**

widen *verb* To make or become wide or wider: *The city is widening this street.*
wid·en (wīd′n) ◊ *verb* **widened, widening**

widespread *adjective* **1.** Existing, happening, believed, or used in many places by many people: *There is widespread interest in saving energy.* **2.** Fully open: *The eagle glides with widespread wings.*
wide·spread (wīd′sprĕd′) ◊ *adjective*

widow *noun* A woman whose husband has died.
wid·ow (wĭd′ō) ◊ *noun, plural* **widows**

widower *noun* A man whose wife has died.
wid·ow·er (wĭd′ō ər) ◊ *noun, plural* **widowers**

W

width *noun* The measure of something from side to side: *The width of the room is 20 feet.*
width (wĭdth) ◊ *noun, plural* **widths**

wife *noun* A woman who is married.
wife (wīf) ◊ *noun, plural* **wives**

wig *noun* A covering for the head that is made of real or artificial hair.
wig (wĭg) ◊ *noun, plural* **wigs**

wiggle *verb* To move or cause to move from side to side with short, quick motions.
wig·gle (wĭg′əl) ◊ *verb* **wiggled, wiggling**

wigwam *noun* A Native American dwelling with a frame made of poles covered with a material such as bark or hides.
wig·wam (wĭg′wŏm′) ◊ *noun, plural* **wigwams**

wild *adjective* **1.** Not grown, cared for, or controlled by people: *We picked wild berries. The polar bear is a wild animal.* **2.** Having or showing no discipline or control: *The wild herd of cattle stampeded.*
◊ *adverb* Not under human control: *Flowers grow wild by the lake.*
◊ *noun* An area in a natural state; wilderness.
wild (wīld) ◊ *adjective, adverb* **wilder, wildest** ◊ *noun, plural* **wilds**

wildcat *noun* A small or medium-sized wild animal, such as the lynx, that is related to the domestic cat.
wild·cat (wīld′kăt′) ◊ *noun, plural* **wildcats**

wilderness *noun* A region in a wild, natural state in which there are few or no people.
wil·der·ness (wĭl′dər nĭs) ◊ *noun, plural* **wildernesses**

wildlife *noun* Wild animals living in their natural surroundings.
wild·life (wīld′līf′) ◊ *noun*

will[1] *noun* **1.** The power to choose or decide what to do. **2.** Strong purpose; determination: *The coach told the team that they must have the will to win.* **3.** An official paper that tells what a person wants done with his or her property after death.
◊ *verb* **1.** To use the will to choose or decide: *I willed myself to stay awake.* **2.** To give by a will: *Our parents willed their house to us.*
will[1] (wĭl) ◊ *noun, plural* **wills** ◊ *verb* **willed, willing**

will[2] *auxiliary verb* Used to show or express: **1.** Something that is going to take place or exist in the future: *They will arrive in the morning.* **2.** An order, requirement, or obligation: *You will report to the principal's office.* **3.** A wish or an intention; willingness: *I will help you.* **4.** Ability or capacity: *This bottle will hold a quart.* **5.** A usual or frequent action: *They will spend hours shooting baskets.*
will[2] (wĭl) ◊ *auxiliary verb, past tense* **would**

HISTORY **• will[1], will[2]**

Will[1] comes from an old English word that meant "desire." **Will[2]** comes from a related old English verb that meant "to desire."

willful *adjective* Wanting one's own way: *The willful child would not obey.*
will·ful (wĭl′fəl) ◊ *adjective*

willing *adjective* Acting or ready to act gladly: *You're a willing helper.*
will·ing (wĭl′ĭng) ◊ *adjective*

willow *noun* A tree with slender twigs that bend easily and narrow, pointed leaves.
wil·low (wĭl′ō) ◊ *noun, plural* **willows**

▲ **willow**

ă	pat	ĭ	pit	oi	**oil**	th	**bath**
ā	pay	ī	ride	o͝o	**book**	*th*	**bathe**
â	care	î	fierce	o͞o	**boot**	ə	**ago, item**
ä	father	ŏ	pot	ou	**out**		pencil
ĕ	pet	ō	go	ŭ	cut		atom
ē	be	ô	paw, for	û	fur		circus

wilt *verb* To lose freshness; droop.
wilt (wĭlt) ◊ *verb* **wilted, wilting**

win *verb* **1.** To gain victory in a game, contest, or battle: *Which team won?* **2.** To receive as a prize or reward: *We won a trip to New Orleans.* **3.** To get by hard work; earn. —See Synonyms at **get.**
◊ *noun* A victory.
win (wĭn) ◊ *verb* **won, winning** ◊ *noun, plural* **wins**

winch *noun* A machine for pulling or lifting heavy objects.
winch (wĭnch) ◊ *noun, plural* **winches**

wind¹ *noun* **1.** Air that is in motion. **2.** The ability to breathe; breath: *The fall from the horse knocked the wind out of me.* **3. winds** Musical instruments that are played by blowing air through them; wind instruments.
wind¹ (wĭnd) ◊ *noun, plural* **winds**

wind² *verb* **1.** To wrap or be wrapped around something: *The vines wind around the posts.* **2.** To tighten the spring of: *I forgot to wind my watch.* **3.** To move along with twists and turns: *The river winds through our valley.*
◊ *idiom* **wind up** To bring to an end.
wind² (wīnd) ◊ *verb* **wound, winding**

***HISTORY* • wind¹, wind²**

Wind¹ is from an old English word that meant "air in motion." **Wind²** is from an old English word that meant "to move with force or speed" and also "to twist."

windbreak *noun* Something, as a hedge, that decreases the force of the wind.
wind·break (wĭnd′brāk′) ◊ *noun, plural* **windbreaks**

wind instrument *noun* A musical instrument that is played by blowing air through it. Clarinets, trumpets, and flutes are wind instruments.
wind instrument ◊ *noun, plural* **wind instruments**

windmill *noun* A mill or other machine that uses the power of the wind to turn a wheel or a set of vanes at the top of a tower. Windmills can be used for pumping water or producing electricity.
wind·mill (wĭnd′mĭl′) ◊ *noun, plural* **windmills**

▲ **windmill**

window *noun* **1.** An opening in a wall that lets in light and air. **2.** A window with its frame and a pane or panes of glass.
win·dow (wĭn′dō) ◊ *noun, plural* **windows**

windowpane *noun* A pane of glass in a window.
win·dow·pane (wĭn′dō pān′) ◊ *noun, plural* **windowpanes**

windpipe *noun* A tube that goes from the throat to the lungs and is used in breathing.
wind·pipe (wĭnd′pīp′) ◊ *noun*

windshield *noun* A sheet of glass or plastic at the front of a motor vehicle to protect against the wind.
wind·shield (wĭnd′shēld′) ◊ *noun, plural* **windshields**

windstorm *noun* A storm with high winds but little or no rain.
wind·storm (wĭnd′stôrm′) ◊ *noun, plural* **windstorms**

W

windy *adjective* Having much wind.
wind·y (wĭn′dē) ◊ *adjective* **windier, windiest**

wine *noun* An alcoholic drink made from the juice of fruits such as grapes.
wine (wīn) ◊ *noun, plural* **wines**

wing *noun* **1.** One of a pair of movable parts that allow a bird, bat, or insect to fly. **2.** Something like a wing in use or shape: *The wings of the airplane are silver.* **3.** A part of a building that sticks out from the main structure: *The west wing of the hospital is new.* **4. wings** An area on either side of a theater stage.
wing (wĭng) ◊ *noun, plural* **wings**

wink *verb* To close and then open one eye quickly, often as a signal.
◊ *noun* The act of winking.
wink (wĭngk) ◊ *verb* **winked, winking** ◊ *noun, plural* **winks**

winner *noun* A person or group that wins.
win·ner (wĭn′ər) ◊ *noun, plural* **winners**

winter *noun* The season of the year between fall and spring, lasting from late December to late March in the Northern Hemisphere.
win·ter (wĭn′tər) ◊ *noun, plural* **winters**

wintergreen *noun* A small evergreen plant with red berries. The oil gotten from wintergreen is used in medicine and flavoring.
win·ter·green (wĭn′tər grēn′) ◊ *noun*

wintry *adjective* Of, relating to, or like winter; cold.
win·try (wĭn′trē) ◊ *adjective* **wintrier, wintriest**

wipe *verb* **1.** To clean or dry by rubbing: *Wipe the dishes with a towel.* **2.** To remove by rubbing: *Wipe the dust off the table.*
◊ *noun* The act of wiping.
wipe (wīp) ◊ *verb* **wiped, wiping** ◊ *noun, plural* **wipes**

wire *noun* **1.** A usually flexible thin metal strand or rod. **2.** Wires joined or twisted together to form a cable, as for carrying electricity. **3.** A telegram.
◊ *verb* **1.** To join or fasten with wire. **2.** To install electrical wires in. **3.** To send a telegram.
wire (wīr) ◊ *noun, plural* **wires** ◊ *verb* **wired, wiring**

wiry *adjective* **1.** Made of or like wire: *The dog has wiry hair.* **2.** Thin but tough or strong: *The athlete has a wiry build.*
wir·y (wīr′ē) ◊ *adjective* **wirier, wiriest**

Wis. *or* **Wisc.** Abbreviations for *Wisconsin.*

wisdom *noun* Intelligence and good judgment in knowing what to do and being able to tell the difference between good and bad and right and wrong.
wis·dom (wĭz′dəm) ◊ *noun*

wise *adjective* Having or showing intelligence and good judgment: *A wise student studies for tests. Studying for tests is a wise decision.*
wise (wīz) ◊ *adjective* **wiser, wisest**

-wise The suffix *-wise* forms adverbs and means "in a certain way, direction, or position." If one person does something one way and you do it a different or other way, you do it *otherwise.* If you make a cut *lengthwise* in a piece of paper, you cut in the direction of the length.

VOCABULARY BUILDER • -wise

Many words that are formed with **-wise** are not entries in this dictionary. But you can figure out what these words mean by looking up the meanings of the root words and the suffix. For example:
crabwise = in the way a crab moves
slantwise = in a slanting position or direction

wish *noun* **1.** A strong desire for something: *My only wish is to be a teacher.* **2.** An expression of a desire or hope: *We send you our best wishes for a happy birthday.*
◊ *verb* **1.** To long for; want: *I wish you were here.* **2.** To have or express a wish for: *We wish you a safe trip.*
wish (wĭsh) ◊ *noun, plural* **wishes** ◊ *verb* **wished, wishing**

wishbone *noun* A bone shaped like the letter Y in the front of the breastbone of most birds.
wish·bone (wĭsh′bōn′) ◊ *noun, plural* **wishbones**

ă	pat	ĭ	pit	oi	**oil**	th	ba**th**
ā	pay	ī	ride	o͝o	book	*th*	ba**the**
â	care	î	fierce	o͞o	boot	ə	ago, item
ä	father	ŏ	pot	ou	**out**		pencil
ĕ	pet	ō	go	ŭ	cut		atom
ē	be	ô	paw, for	û	fur		circus

LANGUAGE DETECTIVE

wishbone

If you live in the northern United States, you probably use the word *wishbone.* If you live in the southern United States, you might call it a *pully-bone* or a *pull-bone.* And still another word for it is *lucky-bone. Lucky-bone* is used by some people in northern New England and eastern Virginia. All these words refer to the custom of making a wish and then pulling the two ends of the bone until it breaks. The person who gets the larger piece is supposed to get the wish that he or she made.

wishful *adjective* Having or showing a wish or desire, often for something that is not likely to happen.
wish·ful (**wĭsh′**fəl) ◊ *adjective*

wisp *noun* **1.** A small bunch or strand: *Wisps of hair were in my eyes.* **2.** A thin streak: *A wisp of smoke came out of the chimney.*
wisp (wĭsp) ◊ *noun, plural* **wisps**

wisteria *noun* A climbing vine with woody stems and large bunches of purple or white flowers that droop from the vine.
wis·ter·i·a (wĭ **stîr′**ē ə) ◊ *noun*

wit *noun* **1.** The ability to describe things, people, or situations in a clever, funny, or unusual way. **2.** Often **wits** The ability to think and reason clearly: *Keep your wits about you and swim to shore.*
wit (wĭt) ◊ *noun, plural* **wits**

witch *noun* A person thought to have magical and especially evil powers.
witch (wĭch) ◊ *noun, plural* **witches**

with *preposition* **1.** In the company of: *Come with me.* **2.** In possession of; having: *Look at that clown with the red nose.* **3.** In a way showing: *They drove with care.* **4.** In the opinion or judgment of: *I'll go if it's all right with you.* **5.** In support of: *We're right with you on your plan.* **6.** By means of; using: *We started the fire with a match.* **7.** Because of: *I was jumping with joy.* **8.** In regard to: *I am pleased with my new teacher.* **9.** In the same direction as: *Trees bend with the wind.* **10.** Against: *Don't argue with me.* **11.** From: *I hate to part with my dog even for a day.*
with (wĭ*th* or wĭth) ◊ *preposition*

withdraw *verb* **1.** To take back or away; remove: *I withdrew money from the bank.* **2.** To move back or away: *The army withdrew from the city.*
with·draw (wĭ*th* **drô′** *or* wĭth **drô′**) ◊ *verb* **withdrew, withdrawn, withdrawing**

withdrawn *verb* Past participle of **withdraw.**
with·drawn (wĭ*th* **drôn′** *or* wĭth **drôn′**) ◊ *verb*

withdrew *verb* Past tense of **withdraw.**
with·drew (wĭ*th* **dro͞o′** *or* wĭth **dro͞o′**) ◊ *verb*

wither *verb* To dry or cause to dry up: *The flowers withered without water.*
with·er (**wĭ*th*′**ər) ◊ *verb* **withered, withering**

withheld *verb* Past tense and past participle of **withhold.**
with·held (wĭth **hĕld′** *or* wĭ*th* **hĕld′**) ◊ *verb*

withhold *verb* **1.** To keep in check; restrain: *Please withhold your laughter in class.* **2.** To refuse to give, allow, or grant: *The teacher withheld approval of the project.* —See Synonyms at **keep.**
with·hold (wĭth **hōld′** *or* wĭ*th* **hōld′**) ◊ *verb* **withheld, withholding**

within *preposition* **1.** Inside of: *The heart is an organ within the body.* **2.** Not going beyond the limits of: *It is within the teacher's power to give you permission to leave early.*
with·in (wĭ*th* **ĭn′** *or* wĭth **ĭn′**) ◊ *preposition*

without *preposition* **1.** Not having; lacking: *We built the campfire without help.* **2.** Not showing or accompanied by: *It's unusual to have smoke without a fire.*
with·out (wĭ*th* **out′** *or* wĭth **out′**) ◊ *preposition*

withstand *verb* To resist the effect or action of: *This building is strong enough to withstand earthquakes.*
with·stand (wĭth **stănd′** *or* wĭ*th* **stănd′**) ◊ *verb* **withstood, withstanding**

withstood *verb* Past tense and past participle of **withstand.**
with·stood (wĭth **sto͝od′** *or* wĭ*th* **sto͝od′**) ◊ *verb*

witness *noun* **1.** Someone who has seen or heard something: *I was a witness to the argument.* **2.** A person who is called to testify before a court of law and promises to tell the truth. **3.** A person who signs an official paper

in order to show that he or she saw the writer of the paper also sign it.
◊ *verb* **1.** To be a witness of; see: *We both witnessed the storm.* **2.** To sign as a witness.
wit·ness (wĭt′nĭs) ◊ *noun, plural* **witnesses** ◊ *verb* **witnessed, witnessing**

witty *adjective* Having or showing humor: *The witty remark made everyone laugh.*
wit·ty (wĭt′ē) ◊ *adjective* **wittier, wittiest**

wives *noun* Plural of **wife.**
wives (wīvz) ◊ *noun*

wizard *noun* **1.** A man thought to have magical powers; magician. **2.** A person who has a very great skill or talent.
wiz·ard (wĭz′ərd) ◊ *noun, plural* **wizards**

wk. The abbreviation for *week.*

wobble *verb* To move unsteadily from side to side: *This old table wobbles.*
wob·ble (wŏb′əl) ◊ *verb* **wobbled, wobbling**

woke *verb* A past tense of **wake[1].**
woke (wōk) ◊ *verb*

wolf *noun* A wild animal that is related to the dog and lives mostly in northern regions. Wolves often attack livestock but rarely bother people.
◊ *verb* To eat quickly and greedily.
wolf (wo͝olf) ◊ *noun, plural* **wolves** ◊ *verb* **wolfed, wolfing**

▲ **wolf**

ă	pat	ĭ	pit	oi	**oil**	th	ba**th**
ā	pay	ī	ride	o͝o	book	*th*	ba**the**
â	care	î	fierce	o͞o	boot	ə	ago, item
ä	father	ŏ	pot	ou	**out**		pencil
ĕ	pet	ō	go	ŭ	cut		atom
ē	be	ô	paw, for	û	fur		circus

wolfhound *noun* Any of several kinds of large dogs originally trained to hunt wolves.
wolf·hound (wo͝olf′hound′) ◊ *noun, plural* **wolfhounds**

wolverine *noun* An animal related to the weasel that lives in northern regions and has thick, dark fur and a bushy tail. Wolverines feed on the flesh of other animals.
wol·ver·ine (wo͝ol′və **rēn′**) ◊ *noun, plural* **wolverines**

wolves *noun* Plural of **wolf.**
wolves (wo͝olvz) ◊ *noun*

woman *noun* **1.** A fully grown female human being. **2.** Women as a group.
wom·an (wo͝om′ən) ◊ *noun, plural* **women**

womanhood *noun* **1.** The condition or time of being a woman. **2.** Women as a group. **3.** The qualities or characteristics of a woman.
wom·an·hood (wo͝om′ən ho͝od′) ◊ *noun*

womankind *noun* Women as a group.
wom·an·kind (wo͝om′ən kīnd′) ◊ *noun*

wombat *noun* An Australian animal that looks like a small bear.
wom·bat (wŏm′băt′) ◊ *noun, plural* **wombats**

women *noun* Plural of **woman.**
wom·en (wĭm′ĭn) ◊ *noun*

won *verb* Past tense and past participle of **win.**
won (wŭn) ◊ *verb*
‖*These sound alike:* **won, one**

wonder *noun* **1.** Something very unusual or remarkable; marvel: *The Grand Canyon in Arizona is one of the natural wonders of the world.* **2.** The feeling of great amazement or admiration caused by something unusual or remarkable: *We watched in wonder as the astronauts walked on the moon.*
◊ *verb* To be curious about; want to know: *I wonder what went wrong. I wonder if they'll attend our party.*
won·der (wŭn′dər) ◊ *noun, plural* **wonders** ◊ *verb* **wondered, wondering**

wonderful *adjective* **1.** Causing wonder; marvelous: *We are studying the wonderful plants and animals of our land.* **2.** Very good; excellent: *I read a wonderful book about life on the frontier.*
won·der·ful (wŭn′dər fəl) ◊ *adjective*

won't Contraction of "will not."
won't (wōnt) ◊ *contraction*

wood *noun* **1.** The hard material beneath the bark of trees and shrubs that makes up the trunk and branches. Wood is used as fuel and for building. **2.** Often **woods** A thick growth of trees; forest.
wood (wo͝od) ◊ *noun, plural* **woods**
‖*These sound alike:* **wood, would**

woodchuck *noun* A North American mammal that has brownish fur, short legs, and a bushy tail. The woodchuck digs holes and spends the winter underground.
wood·chuck (**wo͝od′**chŭk′) ◊ *noun, plural* **woodchucks**

wooded *adjective* Having trees or woods.
wood·ed (**wo͝od′**ĭd) ◊ *adjective*

wooden *adjective* Made of wood.
wood·en (**wo͝od′**n) ◊ *adjective*

woodland *noun* Land covered with trees.
wood·land (**wo͝od′**lənd) ◊ *noun, plural* **woodlands**

woodpecker *noun* A bird that has a hard, pointed bill. The woodpecker drills tiny holes into the bark of trees to get insects.
wood·peck·er (**wo͝od′**pĕk′ər) ◊ *noun, plural* **woodpeckers**

▲ **woodpecker**

woodwork *noun* The wooden parts found inside a house. Window frames and doors are woodwork.
wood·work (**wo͝od′**wûrk′) ◊ *noun*

woodworking *noun* The art or skill of making things from wood.
wood·work·ing (**wo͝od′**wûr′kĭng) ◊ *noun*

woody *adjective* Of, like, or containing wood: *Some plants have woody stems.*
wood·y (**wo͝od′**ē) ◊ *adjective* **woodier, woodiest**

wool *noun* **1.** The soft, thick, curly or wavy hair of animals such as sheep. **2.** Yarn, cloth, or clothing made of wool.
wool (wo͝ol) ◊ *noun, plural* **wools**

woolen *adjective* Made of wool.
wool·en (**wo͝ol′**ən) ◊ *adjective*

woolly *adjective* Made of or covered with wool or a material like wool.
wool·ly (**wo͝ol′**ē) ◊ *adjective* **woollier, woolliest**

word *noun* **1.** A sound or group of sounds that has meaning as a unit of spoken language. **2.** The written or printed letters that stand for a spoken word. **3.** A remark or comment: *The teacher gave us a word of advice before we took the test.* **4.** A short conversation: *May I have a word with you?* **5. words** Remarks made in a quarrel: *We had words over who was to blame.* **6.** A promise: *I give you my word that I will not tell your secret.* **7.** News: *We received word of your safe arrival in the city.*
◊ *verb* To express in words: *Word your answers clearly on the paper.*
word (wûrd) ◊ *noun, plural* **words** ◊ *verb* **worded, wording**

wording *noun* The way in which something is expressed; choice of words.
word·ing (**wûr′**dĭng) ◊ *noun, plural* **wordings**

wordy *adjective* Using or having too many words.
word·y (**wûr′**dē) ◊ *adjective* **wordier, wordiest**

wore *verb* Past tense of **wear.**
wore (wôr) ◊ *verb*

work *noun* **1.** The physical or mental effort that is required to do something; labor: *Cleaning the house is hard work.* **2.** An activity by which a person earns money; job: *Our neighbor is looking for work as a teacher.* **3.** A task or a number of tasks: *There is enough work here to last all day.* **4.** The way in which someone does a job: *Your work is improving.* **5.** Something that has been done or made: *I stopped sewing and put my work in the basket.* **6. works** The moving parts of a device such as a machine: *The works of the watch are rusted.*
◊ *verb* **1.** To put or cause to put out effort to do or make something: *We work hard to get good grades. The teacher works the sixth*

W

graders hard. **2.** To have a job: *My parents work in a hospital.* **3.** To operate or cause to operate properly: *The radio is not working. We are learning how to work the computer.* **4.** To bring about; accomplish: *The new medicine works well.* **5.** To form or shape by applying pressure; mold: *We worked the clay into a ball.*
◊ *idiom* **work out 1.** To develop or bring about by effort: *We are working out a plan.* **2.** To be successful: *The scheme didn't work out very well.* **3.** To do athletic exercises: *I work out at the gym every day.*
work (wûrk) ◊ *noun, plural* **works** ◊ *verb* **worked, working**

workable *adjective* Capable of being worked, used, or put into effect.
work·a·ble (**wûr′** kə bəl) ◊ *adjective*

workbench *noun* A sturdy table where manual work is done, as by a carpenter.
work·bench (**wûrk′** bĕnch′) ◊ *noun, plural* **workbenches**

▲ **workbench**

workbook *noun* A book for students that has pages of exercises and problems.
work·book (**wûrk′** bo͝ok′) ◊ *noun, plural* **workbooks**

ă	pat	ĭ	pit	oi	oil	th	bath
ā	pay	ī	ride	o͝o	book	*th*	bathe
â	care	î	fierce	o͞o	boot	ə	ago, item
ä	father	ŏ	pot	ou	out		pencil
ĕ	pet	ō	go	ŭ	cut		atom
ē	be	ô	paw, for	û	fur		circus

worker *noun* **1.** A person who works. **2.** A female insect, such as an ant, bee, or termite, that does the work of the colony or hive and does not have offspring.
work·er (**wûr′** kər) ◊ *noun, plural* **workers**

workman *noun* A person who does manual work.
work·man (**wûrk′** mən) ◊ *noun, plural* **workmen**

workmanship *noun* The skill with which something is made: *The table shows fine workmanship on the part of the carpenter.*
work·man·ship (**wûrk′** mən shĭp′) ◊ *noun*

world *noun* **1.** The earth: *The world is round.* **2.** A particular part of the earth: *The United States is in the western world.* **3.** All of the people who live on earth: *Pollution is a threat to the world.* **4.** A field of activity: *Our neighbor is well known in the business world.* **5.** A large amount: *The vacation did me a world of good.*
world (wûrld) ◊ *noun, plural* **worlds**

worldwide *adjective* Extending or spread throughout the world: *There is worldwide interest in space exploration.*
world·wide (**wûrld′ wīd′**) ◊ *adjective*

worm *noun* Any of several kinds of animals that have soft bodies and no backbone. Worms have no legs and move by crawling.
◊ *verb* To move by or as if by crawling: *We wormed our way through the crowd.*
worm (wûrm) ◊ *noun, plural* **worms** ◊ *verb* **wormed, worming**

worn *verb* Past participle of **wear**.
worn (wôrn) ◊ *verb*
‖ *These sound alike:* **worn, warn**

worn-out *adjective* **1.** No longer usable or in good condition: *I threw away the worn-out sweater.* **2.** Very tired; exhausted: *The worn-out climbers made camp for the night.*
worn-out (**wôrn′ out′**) ◊ *adjective*

worry *verb* **1.** To feel or cause to feel uneasy: *Your bad cough worries me.* **2.** To tug at and shake with the teeth repeatedly: *The kitten was worrying a ball of yarn.*
◊ *noun* **1.** An uneasy feeling. **2.** Something that causes worry.
wor·ry (**wûr′** ē) ◊ *verb* **worried, worrying** ◊ *noun, plural* **worries**

worse *adjective* **1.** Comparative of **bad. 2.** Comparative of **ill.**
worse (wûrs) ◊ *adjective*

worship *noun* **1.** Great respect and devotion for a sacred being, especially God. **2.** Religious ceremonies and prayers.
◊ *verb* **1.** To honor and love. **2.** To take part in a religious service.
wor·ship (wûr′shĭp) ◊ *noun* ◊ *verb* **worshiped, worshiping** *or* **worshipped, worshipping**

worst *adjective* **1.** Superlative of **bad. 2.** Superlative of **ill.**
worst (wûrst) ◊ *adjective*

worth *noun* **1.** The quality that makes someone or something expensive, valuable, useful, or important: *Your education will prove its worth.* **2.** The amount that a certain sum of money will buy: *We bought five dollars' worth of gasoline.*
◊ *adjective* **1.** Equal in value to: *Her stamp collection is worth $1,000.00.* **2.** Having wealth that amounts to: *His father is worth over a million dollars.* **3.** Deserving of; good enough for: *The book is not worth reading.*
worth (wûrth) ◊ *noun* ◊ *adjective*

worthless *adjective* Without worth; useless.
worth·less (wûrth′lĭs) ◊ *adjective*

worthwhile *adjective* Worth the time, effort, or cost involved.
worth·while (wûrth′hwīl′) ◊ *adjective*

worthy *adjective* **1.** Having merit or value: *We contribute to worthy causes.* **2.** Deserving or meriting: *Teachers are worthy of respect.*
wor·thy (wûr′thē) ◊ *adjective* **worthier, worthiest**

would *auxiliary verb* Past tense of **will²** used to show or express: **1.** Something that is likely: *They would be here if they had left on time.* **2.** Something that is planned or intended: *They said that they would help.* **3.** A usual or frequent action: *They would walk for hours every day.* **4.** A request: *Would you be able to come?*
would (wo͝od) ◊ *auxiliary verb*
‖*These sound alike:* **would, wood**

wouldn't Contraction of "would not."
would·n't (wo͝od′nt) ◊ *contraction*

wound¹ *noun* An injury in which body tissue is cut or broken.
◊ *verb* **1.** To hurt by cutting or breaking body tissue. **2.** To hurt the feelings of: *Their thoughtless remarks wounded me.*
wound¹ (wo͞ond) ◊ *noun, plural* **wounds**
◊ *verb* **wounded, wounding**

wound² *verb* Past tense and past participle of **wind².**
wound² (wound) ◊ *verb*

wove *verb* A past tense of **weave.**
wove (wōv) ◊ *verb*

woven *verb* Past participle of **weave.**
wo·ven (wō′vən) ◊ *verb*

wrap *verb* **1.** To wind or fold as a covering: *I wrapped a shawl around my shoulders.* **2.** To cover by winding or folding: *Wrap the baby in a blanket.* **3.** To wind or clasp: *I wrapped my arms around the dog's neck.* **4.** To put a covering on: *Wrap the package for mailing.*
◊ *noun* An outer garment, such as a coat, that is worn for warmth.
wrap (răp) ◊ *verb* **wrapped, wrapping** ◊ *noun, plural* **wraps**
‖*These sound alike:* **wrap, rap**

wrapper *noun* A piece of material, such as paper, in which something is wrapped.
wrap·per (răp′ər) ◊ *noun, plural* **wrappers**

wrapping *noun* Material used to wrap.
wrap·ping (răp′ĭng) ◊ *noun, plural* **wrappings**

wrath *noun* Very great anger; rage.
wrath (răth) ◊ *noun*

wreath *noun* A circle of leaves, flowers, or branches that are twisted or tied together.
wreath (rēth) ◊ *noun, plural* **wreaths**

wreathe *verb* To decorate with or as if with a wreath.
wreathe (rēth) ◊ *verb* **wreathed, wreathing**

wreck *verb* **1.** To damage badly or destroy, as by breaking up: *The collision wrecked both cars. The crew wrecked the building in five days.* —See Synonyms at **ruin. 2.** To bring to ruin; cause the end of: *The rain wrecked our plans for a picnic.*
◊ *noun* **1.** Destruction: *We saw a bad car wreck.* **2.** Something that has been badly damaged or destroyed: *They hope to raise the wreck of the big ship from the ocean floor.*
wreck (rĕk) ◊ *verb* **wrecked, wrecking**
◊ *noun, plural* **wrecks**

wreckage *noun* The remains of something that has been wrecked.
wreck·age (rĕk′ĭj) ◊ *noun*

W

wrecker *noun* A motor vehicle that removes wreckage.
wreck·er (rĕk′ər) ◊ *noun, plural* **wreckers**

wren *noun* A small brownish songbird that holds its tail pointed upward.
wren (rĕn) ◊ *noun, plural* **wrens**

▲ **wren**

wrench *noun* **1.** A sudden hard, sharp pull: *I had to give the window a wrench to open it.* **2.** An injury caused by twisting or straining. **3.** A tool that has jaws for gripping nuts, bolts, or pieces of pipe so that they can be turned.
◊ *verb* **1.** To twist or pull with sudden force: *I wrenched the door open.* **2.** To injure by twisting or straining: *I fell and wrenched my ankle.*
wrench (rĕnch) ◊ *noun, plural* **wrenches**
◊ *verb* **wrenched, wrenching**

wrestle *verb* **1.** To struggle with and try to force or throw an opponent to the ground. **2.** To struggle to solve or overcome: *I wrestled with the arithmetic problems for an hour.*
wres·tle (rĕs′əl) ◊ *verb* **wrestled, wrestling**

wrestler *noun* A person who wrestles, especially as a sport.
wres·tler (rĕs′lər) ◊ *noun, plural* **wrestlers**

wrestling *noun* A sport in which two opponents try to force or throw each other to the ground.
wres·tling (rĕs′lĭng) ◊ *noun*

wretched *adjective* **1.** Very unhappy or unfortunate; miserable: *The wretched cat sought shelter from the cold.* **2.** Deserving contempt; hateful: *They are wretched cowards.*
wretch·ed (rĕch′ĭd) ◊ *adjective*

ă	pat	ĭ	pit	oi	oil	th	bath
ā	pay	ī	ride	o͝o	book	*th*	bathe
â	care	î	fierce	o͞o	boot	ə	ago, item
ä	father	ŏ	pot	ou	out		pencil
ĕ	pet	ō	go	ŭ	cut		atom
ē	be	ô	paw, for	û	fur		circus

wriggle *verb* To twist and turn from side to side: *The fish wriggled out of my grasp.*
wrig·gle (rĭg′əl) ◊ *verb* **wriggled, wriggling**

wring *verb* **1.** To twist or squeeze so as to force out liquid: *Wring out the wet clothes.* **2.** To force out by or as if by twisting or squeezing: *Wring the water from the towel.*
wring (rĭng) ◊ *verb* **wrung, wringing**
‖*These sound alike:* **wring, ring**

wringer *noun* A device for squeezing water from clothes after washing.
wring·er (rĭng′ər) ◊ *noun, plural* **wringers**

wrinkle *noun* A small fold or crease.
◊ *verb* To form or cause to form wrinkles.
wrin·kle (rĭng′kəl) ◊ *noun, plural* **wrinkles**
◊ *verb* **wrinkled, wrinkling**

wrist *noun* The joint between the hand and the arm.
wrist (rĭst) ◊ *noun, plural* **wrists**

wristwatch *noun* A watch worn on a band around the wrist.
wrist·watch (rĭst′wŏch′) ◊ *noun, plural* **wristwatches**

write *verb* **1.** To form letters or words on a surface with a pen or pencil. **2.** To form the letters or words of: *I wrote my name.* **3.** To communicate by writing: *I wrote the good news to my friend.* **4.** To send a letter to: *I wrote my friend just the other day.* **5.** To set down stories, articles, or books to be read: *The author writes for a living.*
write (rīt) ◊ *verb* **wrote, written, writing**
‖*These sound alike:* **write, right**

writer *noun* A person who writes, especially for a living.
writ·er (rī′tər) ◊ *noun, plural* **writers**

writhe *verb* To twist or squirm, as in pain.
writhe (rī*th*) ◊ *verb* **writhed, writhing**

writing *noun* **1.** Written form: *Put your request in writing.* **2.** Handwriting: *Your writing is easy to read.* **3.** A written work, as a book.
writ·ing (rī′tĭng) ◊ *noun, plural* **writings**

written *verb* Past participle of **write.**
writ·ten (rĭt′n) ◊ *verb*

wrong *adjective* **1.** Not correct or true: *You gave the wrong answer.* —See Synonyms at **false. 2.** Not right or moral; bad: *It is wrong to steal.* **3.** Not intended or wanted: *I dialed the wrong telephone number.* **4.** Not proper or suitable: *You picked the wrong time to call.*

5. Not operating properly: *Something is wrong with the television set.*
◊ *adverb* In a wrong way: *You spelled my name wrong.*
◊ *noun* **1.** Something that is wrong: *There's a big difference between right and wrong.* **2.** The condition of being mistaken or of being at fault.
◊ *verb* To do a wrong to: *Even if they have wronged you, try to forgive them.*
wrong (rông) ◊ *adjective* ◊ *adverb* ◊ *noun, plural* **wrongs** ◊ *verb* **wronged, wronging**

wrongdoer *noun* A person who does wrong.
wrong·do·er (**rông′** do͞o′ər) ◊ *noun, plural* **wrongdoers**

wrongdoing *noun* A mean or illegal act.
wrong·do·ing (**rông′** do͞o′ĭng) ◊ *noun, plural* **wrongdoings**

wrote *verb* Past tense of **write.**
wrote (rōt) ◊ *verb*

wrung *verb* Past tense and past participle of **wring.**
wrung (rŭng) ◊ *verb*
‖*These sound alike:* **wrung, rung**

wt. The abbreviation for *weight.*

WV The abbreviation for *West Virginia* used with a Zip Code.

W.Va. An abbreviation for *West Virginia.*

WY The abbreviation for *Wyoming* used with a Zip Code.

Wyo. An abbreviation for *Wyoming.*

W

Xiphias

Xx

X is the twenty-fourth letter of the English alphabet. Did you know that it has a long history?

X — About 3,000 years ago, the ancient Greeks borrowed their alphabet from people in the Middle East. The ancient Greeks, however, added the symbol *X* to their alphabet. Here is a form of the Greek letter that became our letter *X*.

X — The ancient Romans borrowed their alphabet from a people who had taken their own letter symbols from the Greeks. Here is a form of the Roman letter *X* that was used for carving letters into stone. These letters became the model for our printed capital letters.

x — As people wrote quickly, especially with pens, the capital letters began to take the shapes of small letters. Here is a small-letter *x* that was developed about 1,200 years ago.

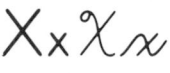

Xx Xx	Xx	Xx	Xx
Handwriting	Sans Serif Type	Serif Type	Computer Printing

x *or* **X** *noun* **1.** The twenty-fourth letter of the English alphabet. **2.** The Roman numeral for the number 10. **3.** An unknown quantity.
x *or* **X** (ĕks) ◊ *noun, plural* **x's** *or* **X's**

Xerox *noun* A trademark for a machine or process that makes photographic copies of written or printed material.
Xe·rox (zîr′ŏks′) ◊ *noun*

xiphias *noun* A swordfish.
xiph·i·as (zĭf′ē əs) ◊ *noun, plural* **xiphias**

Xmas *noun* Christmas.
X·mas (**krĭs′**məs *or* **ĕks′**məs) ◊ *noun, plural* **Xmases**

x-ray *or* **X-ray** *noun* **1.** A powerful light ray that can pass through substances that ordinary rays of light cannot go through. X-rays are used to take pictures of parts of the body that cannot be seen from the outside, such as organs and bones. **2.** A photograph obtained by the use of x-rays.
◊ *verb* To photograph with x-rays.
x-ray *or* **X-ray** (**ĕks′**rā′) ◊ *noun, plural* **x-rays** *or* **X-rays** ◊ *verb* **x-rayed, x-raying** *or* **X-rayed, X-raying**

ă	pat	ĭ	pit	oi	**oil**	th	ba**th**
ā	pay	ī	ride	o͝o	book	*th*	ba**th**e
â	care	î	fierce	o͞o	boot	ə	ago, item
ä	father	ŏ	pot	ou	**out**		pencil
ĕ	pet	ō	go	ŭ	cut		atom
ē	be	ô	paw, for	û	fur		circus

***HISTORY* • x-ray**

Scientists and mathematicians often use the letter *x* as a symbol for something that is unknown. This symbol *x* is used in the word **x-ray** because the scientist who discovered these rays did not completely understand them.

xylophone *noun* A musical instrument that is made up of two rows of wooden bars of varying lengths. A xylophone is played by striking the bars with small wooden hammers.
xy·lo·phone (zī′lə fōn′) ◊ *noun, plural* **xylophones**

Yak

Yy

Y is the twenty-fifth letter of the English alphabet. Did you know that it has a long history?

Over 3,500 years ago, people in the Middle East were using symbols that became the letters of our alphabet. This ancient Middle Eastern symbol is a form of the letter that became our letter *Y*.

The ancient Greeks borrowed their alphabet from people in the Middle East. Here is a form of the Greek letter that became our letter *Y*.

The ancient Romans borrowed their alphabet from a people who had taken their own letter symbols from the Greeks. The Romans later took the symbol *Y* directly from the Greeks. Here is a form of the Roman letter *Y* that was used for carving letters into stone. These letters became the model for our printed capital letters.

As people wrote quickly, especially with pens, the capital letters began to take the shapes of small letters. Here is a small-letter *y* that was used in the Middle Ages.

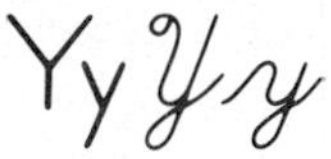

Handwriting

Yy

Sans Serif Type

Yy

Serif Type

Computer Printing

y *or* **Y** *noun* The twenty-fifth letter of the English alphabet.
y *or* **Y** (wī) ◊ *noun, plural* **y's** *or* **Y's**

-y The suffix *-y* forms adjectives and means "having the qualities of" or "full of." When you say a wind is *icy*, you mean that it has the qualities of ice. When you say a sidewalk is *icy*, you mean that it is full of ice. The suffix *-y* also means "inclined to" or "tending to." When you say you feel *sleepy*, you are inclined to go to sleep.

VOCABULARY BUILDER • -y

Many words that are formed with **-y** are not entered in this dictionary. But you can figure out what these words mean by looking up the meanings of the root words and the suffix. For example:
bouncy = inclined to bounce
clingy = tending to cling
leafy = full of leaves
waxy = having the qualities of wax

yacht *noun* A small, graceful ship used for pleasure trips or racing.
yacht (yät) ◊ *noun, plural* **yachts**

yak *noun* A long-haired ox of the mountains of central Asia. Yaks are raised for their milk and meat and are used as work animals.
yak (yăk) ◊ *noun, plural* **yaks**

yam *noun* **1.** The starchy root of a climbing vine that grows in the tropics. The yam is eaten as a vegetable or ground into flour. **2.** A sweet potato having reddish flesh.
yam (yăm) ◊ *noun, plural* **yams**

yank *verb* To pull with a sudden, sharp movement: *We yanked the heavy door open.* ◊ *noun* A sudden, sharp pull.
yank (yăngk) ◊ *verb* **yanked, yanking** ◊ *noun, plural* **yanks**

yard¹ *noun* **1.** A unit of length equal to 3 feet or 36 inches. **2.** A long pole attached crosswise to a mast on a boat to support a sail.
yard¹ (yärd) ◊ *noun, plural* **yards**

yard² *noun* **1.** A piece of ground near a building: *I mowed the grass in the yard.* **2.** An

area, often fenced, used for a purpose or business: *We bought some wood at the lumber yard.* **3.** An area where railroad cars are switched from track to track, made up into trains, stored, or repaired.
yard² (yärd) ◊ *noun, plural* **yards**

> ***HISTORY* • yard¹, yard²**
>
> **Yard¹** comes from an old English word for a measuring rod. **Yard²** comes from a different old English word that meant "an enclosed space."

yardstick *noun* A measuring stick that is one yard long.
yard·stick (yärd′stĭk′) ◊ *noun, plural* **yardsticks**

yarn *noun* **1.** Natural or manmade fibers, as wool or nylon, twisted or spun into long strands for use in weaving or knitting. **2.** A long, exciting story.
yarn (yärn) ◊ *noun, plural* **yarns**

yawn *verb* **1.** To open the mouth wide with a deep inward breath, as when sleepy or bored. **2.** To open wide: *The entrance to the tunnel yawned before us.*
◊ *noun* A deep inward breath with the mouth wide open.
yawn (yôn) ◊ *verb* **yawned, yawning** ◊ *noun, plural* **yawns**

yd. The abbreviation for *yard* or *yards* (unit of measurement).

yea *adverb* Yes.
◊ *noun* A vote or voter in favor of something.
yea (yā) ◊ *adverb* ◊ *noun, plural* **yeas**

year *noun* **1.** The period of time in which the earth makes one complete trip around the sun. **2.** A period of 365 days, or 366 days in a leap year, divided into 52 weeks or 12 months, beginning January 1 and ending December 31. **3.** A period of 12 months: *We plan to return a year from now.* **4.** A period of time, usually less than 12 months, devoted to a special activity: *The school year usually begins in September and ends in June.*
year (yîr) ◊ *noun, plural* **years**

yearly *adjective* **1.** Taking place once a year; annual: *I make a yearly trip to the mountains.* **2.** For or during a single year: *Rainfall this year exceeded the yearly average.*
◊ *adverb* Once a year or every year; annually: *Oak trees shed their leaves yearly.*
year·ly (yîr′lē) ◊ *adjective* ◊ *adverb*

yearn *verb* To have a deep longing: *I yearn to see my old friends again.*
yearn (yûrn) ◊ *verb* **yearned, yearning**

yeast *noun* A substance that is used to make bread dough rise. Yeast consists of tiny one-celled plants that grow quickly.
yeast (yēst) ◊ *noun, plural* **yeasts**

yell *verb* To shout or cry out loudly.
◊ *noun* A loud shout or cry.
yell (yĕl) ◊ *verb* **yelled, yelling** ◊ *noun, plural* **yells**

yellow *noun* **1.** The color of ripe lemons or of dandelions. **2.** Something having this color, as the yolk of an egg.
◊ *adjective* Of the color yellow.
◊ *verb* To turn yellow: *The pages of the old book have yellowed with time.*
yel·low (yĕl′ō) ◊ *noun, plural* **yellows** ◊ *adjective* **yellower, yellowest** ◊ *verb* **yellowed, yellowing**

yellowish *adjective* Somewhat yellow.
yel·low·ish (yĕl′ō ĭsh) ◊ *adjective*

yellow jacket *noun* A small wasp that has bands of black and yellow around its body.
yellow jacket ◊ *noun, plural* **yellow jackets**

▲ **yellow jacket**

ă	pat	ĭ	pit	oi	**oi**l	th	ba**th**
ā	pay	ī	ride	ŏŏ	b**oo**k	*th*	ba**the**
â	care	î	fierce	ōō	b**oo**t	ə	ago, item
ä	father	ŏ	pot	ou	**ou**t		pencil
ĕ	pet	ō	go	ŭ	cut		atom
ē	be	ô	paw, for	û	fur		circus

yen *noun* A unit of money used in Japan.
yen (yěn) ◊ *noun, plural* **yen**

yeoman *noun* **1.** A farmer in England, especially in former times, who owned the small piece of land on which he worked. **2.** A petty officer in the Navy or Coast Guard who performs clerical duties.
yeo·man (yō′mən) ◊ *noun, plural* **yeomen**

yes *adverb* It is true; I agree: *Yes, that is the correct spelling.*
◊ *noun* **1.** An answer that shows acceptance or approval: *We said yes to the offer.* **2.** A vote or voter in favor of something.
yes (yěs) ◊ *adverb* ◊ *noun, plural* **yeses**

yesterday *noun* **1.** The day before today: *Yesterday was windy.* **2.** The recent past: *The science fiction of yesterday is reality today.*
◊ *adverb* On the day before today.
yes·ter·day (yěs′tər dē) ◊ *noun* ◊ *adverb*

yesteryear *noun* **1.** Last year. **2.** Years gone by; the past.
yes·ter·year (yěs′tər yîr′) ◊ *noun, plural* **yesteryears**

yet *adverb* **1.** At this time; now: *You can't go yet.* **2.** Up to now; so far: *They have not returned yet.* **3.** Up to that time; still: *We had not yet told them.* **4.** Besides; in addition: *We had yet another reason not to go.* **5.** Nevertheless: *We are young yet wise.* **6.** At some future time; eventually: *I will do it yet.*
◊ *conjunction* But; nevertheless; however: *We said we would be late, yet we arrived on time.*
yet (yět) ◊ *adverb* ◊ *conjunction*

yew *noun* An evergreen tree or shrub with poisonous dark-green needles and red berries. The tough wood of the yew is used for making archery bows.
yew (yo͞o) ◊ *noun, plural* **yews**
‖*These sound alike:* **yew, ewe, you**

yield *verb* **1.** To give forth; produce: *Soybeans yield many useful products.* **2.** To give up; surrender: *The army yielded the fort to the enemy.* **3.** To give in; submit: *We yielded to their arguments.* **4.** To give way to physical pressure or force: *The soft dough yields when pressed with a finger.*
◊ *noun* An amount produced: *We hope to increase our yield of tomatoes this year.*
yield (yēld) ◊ *verb* **yielded, yielding** ◊ *noun, plural* **yields**

SYNONYMS

yield, relent, submit

I *yielded* in the argument because I saw that she was right. He *relented* when he realized he had been too strict with them. The army could not win and so it *submitted* to the other side.
Antonym: *withstand*

yodel *verb* To sing so that the voice alternates between its normal range and a much higher range.
◊ *noun* A sound that is yodeled.
yo·del (yōd′l) ◊ *verb* **yodeled, yodeling** ◊ *noun, plural* **yodels**

yogurt *noun* A thick, creamy food made by adding certain bacteria to milk. Yogurt is slightly sour and often sweetened or flavored.
yo·gurt (yō′gərt) ◊ *noun, plural* **yogurts**

yoke *noun* **1.** A wooden frame with two U-shaped pieces that fit around the necks of a pair of oxen or other work animals. **2.** A frame or pole placed across a person's shoulders to hold equal loads at each end. **3.** A part of a garment that fits closely around the neck and shoulders.
◊ *verb* To join with a yoke: *The farmer yoked the oxen to the plow.*
yoke (yōk) ◊ *noun, plural* **yokes** ◊ *verb* **yoked, yoking**
‖*These sound alike:* **yoke, yolk**

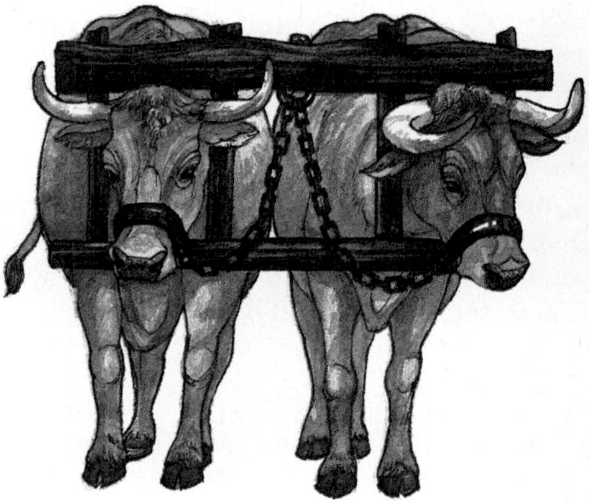

▲ **yoke**

Y

yolk *noun* The yellow part of an egg. The yolk contains protein and fat to nourish the young animal before it is hatched.
yolk (yōk) ◊*noun, plural* **yolks**
‖*These sound alike:* **yolk, yoke**

Yom Kippur *noun* The holiest Jewish holiday, celebrated on the tenth day following Rosh Hashanah in September or October.
Yom Kip·pur (yŏm **kĭp′**ər) ◊*noun*

yonder *adjective* At a distance but able to be seen or pointed out: *A dragon is supposed to dwell in yonder cave.*
◊*adverb* In, to, or at that place; over there: *The town lies yonder in the valley.*
yon·der (**yŏn′**dər) ◊*adjective* ◊*adverb*

you *pronoun* **1.** The one or ones spoken or written to: *When will you return? We'll pick you up at eight o'clock. This package is addressed to you.* **2.** Anyone at all: *Whenever you cross the street you should look in both directions.*
you (yo͞o) ◊*pronoun*
‖*These sound alike:* **you, ewe, yew**

you-all *pronoun* You two or more; all of you.
you-all (yo͞o **ôl′** *or* **yo͞o′**ôl′ *or* yôl) ◊*pronoun*

LANGUAGE DETECTIVE

you-all
The word *you-all* is not used much in the northern United States. However, in the southern United States it is used by many people when they speak. *You-all* is not used very much in writing.

you'd Contraction of "you had" or "you would."
you'd (yo͞od) ◊*contraction*

you'll Contraction of "you will" or "you shall."
you'll (yo͞ol) ◊*contraction*
‖*These sound alike:* **you'll, Yule**

ă	pat	ĭ	pit	oi	oil	th	bath
ā	pay	ī	ride	o͝o	book	*th*	bathe
â	care	î	fierce	o͞o	boot	ə	ago, item
ä	father	ŏ	pot	ou	out		pencil
ĕ	pet	ō	go	ŭ	cut		atom
ē	be	ô	paw, for	û	fur		circus

young *adjective* **1.** Being in an early stage of life or growth; not fully developed: *A lamb is a young sheep. We were a young country full of pioneer spirit.* **2.** Not far advanced; newly begun: *The evening is young.* **3.** Having the qualities of youth; fresh and vigorous: *Our parents are young at heart.*
◊*noun (used with a singular or plural verb)* Offspring in an early stage of development: *The young of a frog is called a tadpole. The young of many birds are covered with down when they hatch.*
young (yŭng) ◊*adjective* **younger, youngest** ◊*noun, plural* **young**

SYNONYMS

young, immature
I am too *young* to drive. It was *immature* of me not to make my bed.
Antonyms: *mature, old*

youngster *noun* A young person or child.
young·ster (**yŭng′**stər) ◊*noun, plural* **youngsters**

your *adjective* Relating or belonging to you: *Where did you put your books?*
your (yo͝or) ◊*adjective*
‖*These sound alike:* **your, you're**

you're Contraction of "you are."
you're (yo͝or) ◊*contraction*
‖*These sound alike:* **you're, your**

yours *pronoun* The one or ones that belong to you: *They need extra books, so why don't you lend them yours?*
yours (yo͝orz) ◊*pronoun*

yourself *pronoun* Your own self: *Don't cut yourself with the scissors.*
your·self (yo͝or **sĕlf′**) ◊*pronoun, plural* **yourselves**

yourselves *pronoun* Plural of **yourself.**
your·selves (yo͝or **sĕlvz′**) ◊*pronoun*

youth *noun* **1.** The state or quality of being young: *Enjoy your youth while you have it.* **2.** The time of life between being a child and being an adult: *They had worked hard since their youth.* **3.** A young person, especially a boy or young man. **4.** Young people in general: *The youth of today are eager to learn.*
youth (yo͞oth) ◊*noun, plural* **youths**

youthful *adjective* **1.** Being in one's youth;

young: *The youthful athlete won the medal.* **2.** Of or typical of youth: *You all have youthful energy.* **3.** Having the look of youth.
youth·ful (yo͞oth′fəl) ◊ *adjective*

you've Contraction of "you have."
you've (yo͞ov) ◊ *contraction*

yowl *noun* A loud howling or wailing cry. ◊ *verb* To make this sound.
yowl (youl) ◊ *noun, plural* **yowls** ◊ *verb* **yowled, yowling**

yo-yo *noun* A toy that looks like a flat spool wound in the center with string. The string is looped around a finger and used to spin the yo-yo up and down.
yo-yo (yō′yō′) ◊ *noun, plural* **yo-yos**

yr. The abbreviation for *year* and *your.*

yucca *noun* A plant that grows in dry regions of North and Central America. It has pointed leaves and a cluster of whitish flowers.
yuc·ca (yŭk′ə) ◊ *noun, plural* **yuccas**

▲ **yucca**

Yule *or* **yule** *noun* Christmas or the Christmas season.
Yule *or* **yule** (yo͞ol) ◊ *noun, plural* **Yules** *or* **yules**
‖*These sound alike:* **Yule, you'll**

Y

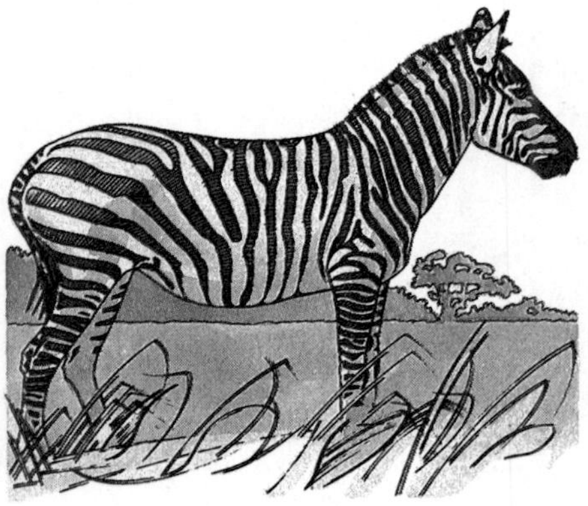

Zebra

Zz

Z is the twenty-sixth letter of the English alphabet. Did you know that it has a long history?

Over 3,500 years ago, people in the Middle East were using symbols that became the letters of our alphabet. This ancient Middle Eastern symbol is a form of the letter that became our letter *Z*.

The ancient Greeks borrowed their alphabet from people in the Middle East. Here is a form of the Greek letter that became our letter *Z*.

The ancient Romans borrowed their alphabet from a people who had taken their own letter symbols from the Greeks. The Romans later took the symbol *Z* directly from the Greeks. Here is a form of the Roman letter *Z* that was used for carving letters into stone. These letters became the model for our printed capital letters.

As people wrote quickly, especially with pens, the capital letters began to take the shapes of small letters. Here is a small-letter *z* that was used in the Middle Ages.

Zz	Zz	Zz	Zz
Handwriting	Sans Serif Type	Serif Type	Computer Printing

z *or* **Z** *noun* The twenty-sixth letter of the English alphabet.
z *or* **Z** (zē) ◊ *noun, plural* **z's** *or* **Z's**

zebra *noun* A wild animal of Africa that is related to the horse. Zebras have a light-colored coat marked with black stripes.
ze·bra (zē′brə) ◊ *noun, plural* **zebras**

zenith *noun* **1.** The point in the sky that is directly overhead. **2.** The highest point: *Being elected class president was the zenith of my years in high school.*
ze·nith (zē′nĭth) ◊ *noun, plural* **zeniths**

zero *noun* **1.** The numerical figure 0. **2.** The temperature indicated by the numeral 0 on a temperature scale. **3.** A point, as in a scale or system of measurement, shown by the numeral 0.
ze·ro (zîr′ō) ◊ *noun, plural* **zeros** *or* **zeroes**

zest *noun* Added flavor or interest: *Spices give zest to simple foods.*
zest (zĕst) ◊ *noun*

zigzag *noun* **1.** A line or course that runs first one way and then another in a series of short, sharp turns. **2.** One of a series of short, sharp turns from one direction to another.
◊ *adjective* Having or moving in a zigzag: *A zigzag path led through the snow.*
◊ *adverb* In a zigzag: *The ship moved zigzag across the ocean.*
◊ *verb* To move in or follow the form of a zigzag: *The trail zigzagged up the mountain.*
zig·zag (zĭg′zăg′) ◊ *noun, plural* **zigzags** ◊ *adjective* ◊ *adverb* ◊ *verb* **zigzagged, zigzagging**

zinc *noun* A shiny bluish-white metal, used as a coating for iron and in electric batteries. Zinc is one of the chemical elements.
zinc (zĭngk) ◊ *noun*

ă	pat	ĭ	pit	oi	**oil**	th	**bath**
ā	pay	ī	ride	ŏŏ	**book**	*th*	**bathe**
â	care	î	fierce	ōō	**boot**	ə	**ago, item**
ä	father	ŏ	**pot**	ou	**out**		pencil
ĕ	pet	ō	**go**	ŭ	**cut**		atom
ē	be	ô	paw, for	û	**fur**		circus

zinnia *noun* A garden plant with bright flowers of various colors.
zin·ni·a (zĭn′ē ə) ◊ *noun, plural* **zinnias**

zip *verb* To fasten or close with a zipper: *Zip up your jacket.*
zip (zĭp) ◊ *verb* **zipped, zipping**

Zip Code *noun* A trademark for a system designed to speed mail sorting and delivery. A series of numbers is assigned to each delivery area in the United States. The Zip Code appears on an envelope after the abbreviation for the state.
Zip Code ◊ *noun, plural* **Zip Codes**

zipper *noun* A fastener that consists of two rows of metal or plastic teeth on separate edges that are joined by a sliding tab.
zip·per (zĭp′ər) ◊ *noun, plural* **zippers**

zither *noun* A musical instrument made of a flat box with 30 to 40 strings stretched across it. A zither is played by plucking the strings with the fingers or a pick.
zith·er (zĭth′ər) ◊ *noun, plural* **zithers**

▲ **zither**

zodiac *noun* An imaginary belt in the heavens that contains the paths of the sun, moon, and most of the planets. It is divided into 12 equal parts, each of which is named for a constellation.
zo·di·ac (zō′dē ăk′) ◊ *noun*

zone *noun* **1.** An area or region set off from others by a special characteristic or use: *You must drive slowly in a school zone.* **2.** Any of the five regions into which the surface of the earth is divided according to climate and latitude. There are two frigid zones, two temperate zones, and one torrid zone, which includes the equator.
◊ *verb* To divide or mark off into zones: *This part of town is zoned for business only.*
zone (zōn) ◊ *noun, plural* **zones** ◊ *verb* **zoned, zoning**

zoo *noun* A public place, such as a park or large enclosed area, where living animals are kept and exhibited.
zoo (zo͞o) ◊ *noun, plural* **zoos**

zoogeography *noun* The scientific study of the distribution of animals.
zo·o·ge·og·ra·phy (zō′ə jē ŏg′rə fē) ◊ *noun*

zoology *noun* The scientific study of animals.
zo·ol·o·gy (zō ŏl′ə jē) ◊ *noun*

zoom *verb* **1.** To move rapidly with a loud buzzing or humming sound: *The jet zoomed across the sky.* **2.** To climb suddenly and sharply: *The eagle zoomed into the sky.*
zoom (zo͞om) ◊ *verb* **zoomed, zooming**

zucchini *noun* A long, narrow squash with a green skin.
zuc·chi·ni (zo͞o kē′nē) ◊ *noun, plural* **zucchini** *or* **zucchinis**

Children's American Heritage Reference Library

Table of Contents

Children's Thesaurus

This is a thesaurus. A **thesaurus** contains synonyms. Synonyms are words with the same or nearly the same meaning. Your thesaurus gives you the meanings that the synonyms share. It also gives you sample sentences that show you how to use the synonyms. Your thesaurus includes many antonyms, too. Antonyms are words with opposite or nearly opposite meanings from the synonyms. In your thesaurus the entry words are red and arranged in alphabetical order. You will find a group of synonyms following each entry word. Here is a sample entry:

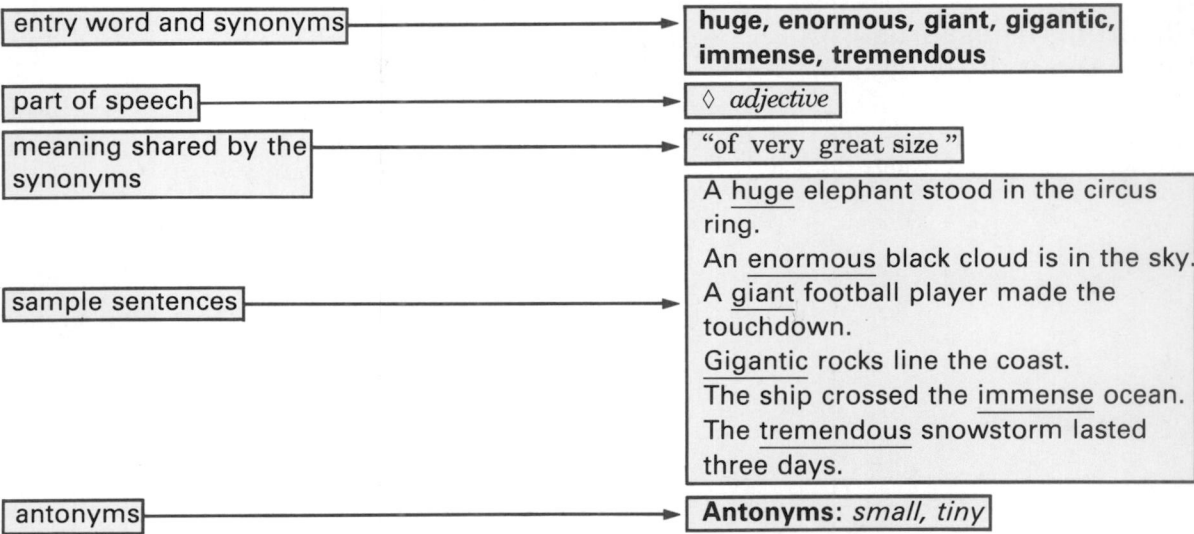

entry word and synonyms →	**huge, enormous, giant, gigantic, immense, tremendous**
part of speech →	◊ *adjective*
meaning shared by the synonyms →	"of very great size"
sample sentences →	A huge elephant stood in the circus ring. An enormous black cloud is in the sky. A giant football player made the touchdown. Gigantic rocks line the coast. The ship crossed the immense ocean. The tremendous snowstorm lasted three days.
antonyms →	**Antonyms:** *small, tiny*

A thesaurus can help you make your writing more interesting. Suppose you wrote this sentence: "Our school has a huge stadium." You might want to use a different word from *huge*. Look up *huge* in your thesaurus. You will find five other words to choose from: *enormous, giant, gigantic, immense,* and *tremendous.* You can see from the sample sentences that any one of these five words might be used in place of *huge* in your sentence. Try using your thesaurus in this way the next time you write. Use the **index** on pages 837–838 to find the right word.

ask, examine, question ◊ *verb* These synonyms can all share the meaning "to try to get information from someone."

I asked them whether they could hear me.

The lawyer examined the witness carefully about the accident.

The coach questioned us about our plans for extra soccer practice.

Antonyms: *answer, reply*

bad, inferior, poor ◊ *adjective* These synonyms can all share the meaning "not coming up to the proper standard."

The light over here is bad for reading.

My jacket shrank in the wash because it was made of inferior material.

If you don't study, you will make a poor grade on the test.

Antonyms: *good, superior*

begin, commence, embark, start ◊ *verb* These synonyms can all share the meaning "to get going or take the first step."

Soon I will begin to do my homework.

The speaker commenced his talk with a joke.

The ship embarked on a long cruise.

She'd better start on her way right now.

Antonyms: *close, conclude, end, finish, stop*

big, great, large ◊ *adjective* These synonyms can all share the meaning "above average in size or amount."

I had a big helping of fresh fruit.

A great bowl of fresh flowers stood on the table.

Our neighbors have a large boat.

Antonyms: *little, small*

brave, courageous, fearless, valiant ◊ *adjective* These synonyms can all share the meaning "having or showing the ability to face danger or difficulty."

You were brave when you dove off the board for the first time.

The courageous leader stood up for what was right.

The fearless cowboy tamed the wild horse.

A valiant volunteer rescued the animals from the forest fire.

Antonym: *cowardly*

change, convert, transform ◊ *verb* These synonyms can all share the meaning "to make or become different."

As a joke I changed the spelling of my name.

We converted part of our front yard into a garden.

Freezing temperatures transformed the water into ice.

chief, main, principal ◊ *adjective* These synonyms can all share the meaning "first in rank or importance."

The President is the chief executive of the United States.

The main street of the town was full of cars.

The principal thing to remember about fire is that it burns.

choice, alternative, preference, selection ◊ *noun* These synonyms can all share the meaning "the act or opportunity of choosing."

We had a wide choice of food to bring to the picnic.

The alternatives are to take this train or the next one.

What is your preference—apples or oranges?

We had a hard time making our selection of new spring clothes.

copy, imitate, mimic ◊ *verb* These synonyms can all share the meaning "to follow someone or something taken as a model."

I tried to copy the picture that I liked.

I can imitate the way my friend laughs.

We can teach certain birds to mimic human speech.

dark, dim, murky ◊ *adjective* These synonyms can all share the meaning "lacking in light or clearness."

It was a dark night and we could see nothing.

I saw my friend standing in a dim corner of the big room.

The waters of the lake were murky after the storm.

Antonyms: *clear, light*

do, accomplish, execute, fulfill, perform ◊ *verb* These synonyms can all share the meaning "to carry out successfully or completely."

We like to watch the clowns do tricks.

I hope I can accomplish all of my goals in school.

The acrobats executed some exciting tumbling routines.

You have fulfilled your duties well.

The doctor performs difficult operations every day.

education, knowledge, learning ◊ *noun* These synonyms can all share the meaning "known facts, ideas, and skills that one has been taught."

A person's education includes knowing how to read and write well.

Doing science projects increases our knowledge of the world around us.

The teachers in our school are men and women of learning.

Antonym: *ignorance*

expensive, costly, high ◊ *adjective* These synonyms can all share the meaning "high in cost or value."

I didn't want to buy an expensive watch.

The prince and princess wore costly jewels.

The price of the boat is high.

Antonyms: *cheap, inexpensive*

faithful, loyal, true ◊ *adjective* These synonyms can all share the meaning "firm and unchanging in attachment to someone or something."

The manager retired after 25 years of faithful service to the company.

Loyal friends helped our family build a new barn.

A true friend can always be depended on for help when it is needed.

Antonyms: *disloyal, false, unfaithful*

good, desirable, pleasing ◊ *adjective* These synonyms can all share the meaning "having positive or attractive qualities."

Our teacher said that our behavior was good on the field trip.

Honesty and hard work are desirable qualities in a person.

You have very pleasing manners.

Antonyms: *bad, undesirable*

grow, increase, swell ◊ *verb* These synonyms can all share the meaning "to become bigger or greater."

I hope to grow two or three inches in height this year.

Our knowledge increases as we mature.

My twisted ankle began to swell.

Antonym: *decrease*

happy, cheerful, glad, joyful ◊ *adjective* These synonyms can all share the meaning "having or showing good spirits."

Happy children played games at the birthday party.

We were cheerful because we made good grades on our tests.

You have a glad smile on your face today.

The two old friends were joyful at seeing each other again.

Antonyms: *depressed, gloomy, glum, sad, sorrowful, unhappy*

healthy, fit, sound, well ◊ *adjective* These synonyms can all share the meaning "in good physical condition."

I've been healthy so far this year and haven't had a cold yet.

My parents stay fit by walking every day.

Drink milk to build sound bones and teeth.

Are you feeling well?

Antonyms: *sick, unhealthy, unwell*

hide, bury, conceal ◊ *verb* These synonyms can all share the meaning "to keep from the sight or knowledge of others."

Let's hide the birthday presents until the party.

We searched for treasure that had been buried on the island.

Natural camouflage helps to conceal some animals from their enemies.

honest, candid, direct, frank ◊ *adjective* These synonyms can all share the meaning "speaking or spoken freely, accurately, and sincerely."

When the teacher asks you a question, please give an honest answer.

The candidate for mayor gave a candid reply to the reporter's hard question.

Our parents gave us direct suggestions about improving our table manners.

The coach's frank criticism of our swimming style has made us a better team.

Antonyms: *dishonest, indirect*

huge, enormous, giant, gigantic, immense, tremendous ◊ *adjective* These synonyms can all share the meaning "of very great size."

A huge elephant stood in the circus ring.

An enormous black cloud is in the sky.

A giant football player made the touchdown.

Gigantic rocks line the coast.

The ship crossed the immense ocean.

The tremendous snowstorm lasted three days.

Antonyms: *small, tiny*

important, major, significant, weighty ◊ *adjective* These synonyms can all share the meaning "having much influence or being worth noticing."

The President of the United States of America is an important person.

We read a major news story for current events.

Scientists have made significant discoveries in recent years.

The governor has to make weighty decisions every day.

Antonyms: *insignificant, minor, unimportant*

join, connect, unite ◊ *verb* These synonyms can all share the meaning "to bring or come together."

We joined hands and ran around the room.

This road connects two major highways.

Our town is uniting in favor of building a new park with tennis courts.

Antonyms: *part, separate*

late, overdue, tardy ◊ *adjective* These synonyms can all share the meaning "not happening or appearing at the usual, expected, or proper time."

I'm sorry to be late, but the traffic was very heavy.

My book is overdue two days because I forgot to return it to the library.

We have never been tardy to school.

Antonym: *early*

like, enjoy, love ◊ *verb* These synonyms can all share the meaning "to be attracted to or take pleasure in."

I like swimming.

We enjoy visiting the city every weekend.

They loved every minute of the play.

Antonyms: *dislike, hate*

make, build, construct, form, manufacture ◊ *verb* These synonyms can all share the meaning "to create by putting together materials."

We made a fort out of the snow.

We built a dock on the river.

Let's construct a model airplane.

I formed a pot out of modeling clay.

This factory manufactures cars.

necessary, essential, required ◊ *adjective* These synonyms can all share the meaning "much needed."

A pen, a pencil, and paper are necessary items on every student's desk.

Water is essential to living things.

Five is the required number of players for a basketball team.

Antonym: *unnecessary*

new, fresh, original ◊ *adjective* These synonyms can all share the meaning "not known or used before."

Inventors develop and build new things.

Let's try a fresh approach to this mathematics problem.

Your design for the costumes is original.

Antonym: *old*

nice, agreeable, pleasant ◊ *adjective* These synonyms can all share the meaning "pleasing in nature."

You have nice manners.

My friend has an agreeable personality.

They have such pleasant smiles.

Antonym: *unpleasant*

opponent, competitor, rival ◊ *noun* These synonyms can all share the meaning "a person who is in a contest or a struggle with another person."

My best friend will be my opponent in the chess match.

There will be 20 competitors in the race.

Let's read just for fun and not be rivals to see who can read the most books.

possible, practical, workable ◊ *adjective* These synonyms can all share the meaning "likely to be done or capable of being done."

It is not possible to fly to the moon in a hang glider.

Give me a practical suggestion for solving the problem.

Let's try to figure out a workable schedule for finishing our science projects.

Antonyms: *impossible, impractical, unworkable.*

pull, drag, haul, tow ◊ *verb* These synonyms can all share the meaning "to cause to move toward."

I pulled the rope toward me as hard as I could.

We dragged the huge sacks of grain over the ground.

The horses hauled the heavy logs to the mill.

The truck towed our car to the garage.

Antonyms: *push, shove*

rise, climb, leap ◊ *verb* These synonyms can all share the meaning "to move upward."

I like to watch the sun rise over the ocean.

The powerful engines made the rocket climb rapidly.

The dog leaped into the air to catch the ball.

Antonyms: *drop, fall*

rough, jagged, uneven ◊ *adjective* These synonyms can all share the meaning "not smooth or even."

The bark on the old tree felt rough when I touched it.

The lid of the can has a jagged edge.

The coast of Maine is rocky and uneven.

Antonyms: *even, smooth*

run, dash, race ◊ *verb* These synonyms can all share the meaning "to move on foot at a very fast pace."

I run a mile every morning for exercise.

We dashed home from school.

The children raced down the street after the ball.

Antonyms: *stroll, walk*

save, deliver, rescue ◊ *verb* These synonyms can all share the meaning "to free from danger or risk."

Knowing how to give artificial respiration can save a life.

Lifeguards delivered the swimmers from the stormy sea.

I rescued my cat from the tall tree.

see, notice, observe, view ◊ *verb* These synonyms can all share the meaning "to become

aware of, by using the eyes or the mind."
We can see wheat fields from our house.
I noticed a train coming from far away.
We can observe the sailboats on the lake from our front porch.
We viewed the valley from a tall tower on top of the mountain.

short, brief, concise ◊ *adjective* These synonyms can all share the meaning "lasting or intended to last for only a limited time."
We gave a short play at assembly last week.
The principal's speech on the first day of school was brief.
The President will give a concise, five-minute statement to the reporters.
Antonyms: *lengthy, long*

slide, glide, skid ◊ *verb* These synonyms can all share the meaning "to move smoothly over or as if over a surface."
Watch me slide down the hill on my sled.
The fish glided quietly through the water.
The truck skidded on the slippery road.

strange, peculiar, unusual ◊ *adjective* These synonyms can all share the meaning "not ordinary or normal."
My friend wore a strange costume to the party.
Some jungle birds make very peculiar sounds.
The store is painted an unusual shade of yellow.
Antonyms: *familiar, ordinary, usual*

talk, chatter, speak ◊ *verb* These synonyms can all share the meaning "to use speech to express oneself or to communicate a message."
During dinner we talk about current events.
We chattered happily on the bus to school.
Please speak to the class about your science project.

tall, high, lofty ◊ *adjective* These synonyms can all share the meaning "having more height than is usual or normal."
The Empire State Building is a tall structure.
This room has a high ceiling.
We looked up at the lofty mountains.
Antonyms: *low, short*

teach, instruct, train, tutor ◊ *verb* These synonyms can all share the meaning "to share knowledge or information with."
Please teach your baby brother how to tie his shoes.
Our teacher instructs us in language arts, social studies, science, and math.
Her coach is training her in gymnastics.
I will tutor you in arithmetic after school.
Antonym: *learn*

thin, lean, skinny, slender ◊ *adjective* These synonyms can all share the meaning "having little fat or flesh on the body."
The captain of our basketball team is tall and thin.
The beef is lean.
The stray dog is skinny because it doesn't eat much.
A slender, graceful dancer performed the solo.
Antonyms: *fat, plump, stout*

think, believe, consider ◊ *verb* These synonyms can all share the meaning "to have a belief or an opinion."
I think that swimming is fun.
Our teacher believes that field trips to historic places help us to understand history better.
We consider fruit and vegetables to be good for our health.

time, period, season ◊ *noun* These synonyms can all share the meaning "a span with a beginning and an end, during which something exists or goes on."
Harvest time comes at the end of the summer.
January is a slow period for business.
November and December are months in the holiday season.

unclear, cloudy, faint ◊ *adjective* These synonyms can all share the meaning "not clearly seen or able to be seen."
We had an unclear view of the ship in the fog.
When the skies are cloudy, you can't see the stars well.
I could see a faint glow from the candle.
Antonym: *clear*

undo, loosen, unfasten, untie ◊ *verb* These synonyms can all share the meaning "to free from ties or fasteners."
Let's undo the pretty bow and open the present.
We loosened the ropes on the boat and moved away from the dock.
Can you unfasten the pin?
Help the little child untie those shoes.
Antonyms: *fasten, tie*

unhappy, depressed, gloomy, glum, sad, sorrowful ◊ *adjective* These synonyms can all share the meaning "having or showing low spirits."
I was unhappy because I missed the birthday party.

We were depressed when we heard the bad news.

You have a gloomy expression on your face today.

We were glum because we made poor grades on our tests.

When my best friend moved away, I was very sad.

Our neighbors were sorrowful over losing their dog.

Antonyms: *bright, cheerful, happy*

upset, frantic, nervous ◊ *adjective* These synonyms can all share the meaning "feeling troubled or disturbed."

I was upset when I missed the ball game.

Our kitten became frantic during the thunder storm.

We were nervous before we walked onto the stage.

Antonym: *calm*

use, apply, utilize ◊ *verb* These synonyms can all share the meaning "to put into action or use."

Students use pens, pencils, and paper when they write.

We will apply our knowledge of math when we measure the boards for our tree house.

I utilized my skills in Spanish when we visited Puerto Rico last year.

vision, eyesight, sight ◊ *noun* These synonyms can all share the meaning "the ability to see."

The school nurse checked my vision.

A pilot must have excellent eyesight.

My sight has improved now that I have glasses.

want, crave, desire, wish ◊ *verb* These synonyms can all share the meaning "to have a strong need for."

I want new skis this winter.

I crave fresh strawberries every summer.

Don't you desire to have a large group of friends?

The children wished for a swimming pool in their neighborhood.

way, method, system ◊ *noun* These synonyms can all share the meaning "a plan or procedure for doing a job."

Please show me the right way to read this map.

What is your method of writing an outline?

Our family has a system for distributing the chores fairly.

work, job, occupation ◊ *noun* These synonyms can all share the meaning "what a person does to earn a living."

My cousin's work is farming.

I have a job mowing lawns after school.

Exploring space is an exciting occupation.

Index to the Children's Thesaurus

This alphabetical **index** shows you where to look for synonyms in your thesaurus. For example, the index entry

enormous *adjective* Look at **huge.**

tells you that if you want to find synonyms for the word *enormous,* you must look at the entry for *huge* to find the synonyms. When you turn to *huge,* what synonyms do you find? You find these synonyms: *huge, enormous, giant, gigantic, immense,* and *tremendous.*

desire *verb* Look at **want.**
dim *adjective* Look at **dark.**
direct *adjective* Look at **honest.**
drag *verb* Look at **pull.**
embark *verb* Look at **begin.**
enjoy *verb* Look at **like.**
enormous *adjective* Look at **huge.**
essential *adjective* Look at **necessary.**
examine *verb* Look at **ask.**
execute *verb* Look at **do.**
eyesight *noun* Look at **vision.**
faint *adjective* Look at **unclear.**
fearless *adjective* Look at **brave.**
fit *adjective* Look at **healthy.**
form *verb* Look at **make.**
frank *adjective* Look at **honest.**
frantic *adjective* Look at **upset.**
fresh *adjective* Look at **new.**
fulfill *verb* Look at **do.**
giant *adjective* Look at **huge.**
gigantic *adjective* Look at **huge.**
glad *adjective* Look at **happy.**
glide *verb* Look at **slide.**
gloomy *adjective* Look at **unhappy.**
glum *adjective* Look at **unhappy.**
great *adjective* Look at **big.**
haul *verb* Look at **pull.**
high *adjective* **1.** Look at **tall.**
2. Look at **expensive.**
imitate *verb* Look at **copy.**
immense *adjective* Look at **huge.**
increase *verb* Look at **grow.**
inferior *adjective* Look at **bad.**
instruct *verb* Look at **teach.**
jagged *adjective* Look at **rough.**
job *noun* Look at **work.**
joyful *adjective* Look at **happy.**
knowledge *noun* Look at **education.**
large *adjective* Look at **big.**
lean *adjective* Look at **thin.**
leap *verb* Look at **rise.**
learning *noun* Look at **education.**
lofty *adjective* Look at **tall.**
loosen *verb* Look at **undo.**
love *verb* Look at **like.**
loyal *adjective* Look at **faithful.**
main *adjective* Look at **chief.**
major *adjective* Look at **important.**
manufacture *verb* Look at **make.**
method *noun* Look at **way.**
mimic *verb* Look at **copy.**
murky *adjective* Look at **dark.**
nervous *adjective* Look at **upset.**
notice *verb* Look at **see.**
observe *verb* Look at **see.**
occupation *noun* Look at **work.**
original *adjective* Look at **new.**
overdue *adjective* Look at **late.**
peculiar *adjective* Look at **strange.**
perform *verb* Look at **do.**
period *noun* Look at **time.**
pleasant *adjective* Look at **nice.**
pleasing *adjective* Look at **good.**
poor *adjective* Look at **bad.**
practical *adjective* Look at **possible.**
preference *noun* Look at **choice.**
principal *adjective* Look at **chief.**
question *verb* Look at **ask.**
race *verb* Look at **run.**
required *adjective* Look at **necessary.**
rescue *verb* Look at **save.**
rival *noun* Look at **opponent.**
sad *adjective* Look at **unhappy.**
season *noun* Look at **time.**
selection *noun* Look at **choice.**
sight *noun* Look at **vision.**
significant *adjective* Look at **important.**
skid *verb* Look at **slide.**
skinny *adjective* Look at **thin.**
slender *adjective* Look at **thin.**
sorrowful *adjective* Look at **unhappy.**
sound *adjective* Look at **healthy.**
speak *verb* Look at **talk.**
start *verb* Look at **begin.**
swell *verb* Look at **grow.**
system *noun* Look at **way.**
tardy *adjective* Look at **late.**
tow *verb* Look at **pull.**
train *verb* Look at **teach.**
transform *verb* Look at **change.**
tremendous *adjective* Look at **huge.**
true *adjective* Look at **faithful.**
tutor *verb* Look at **teach.**
uneven *adjective* Look at **rough.**
unfasten *verb* Look at **undo.**
unite *verb* Look at **join.**
untie *verb* Look at **undo.**
unusual *adjective* Look at **strange.**
utilize *verb* Look at **use.**
valiant *adjective* Look at **brave.**
view *verb* Look at **see.**
weighty *adjective* Look at **important.**
well *adjective* Look at **healthy.**
wish *verb* Look at **want.**
workable *adjective* Look at **possible.**

Facts about the States

Key ❶ Location ❷ Origin of Name ❸ Date of Admission ❹ Capital ❺ Nicknames ❻ Official Data ❼ Interesting Facts

Alabama

❶ Southeast, between Mississippi and Georgia
❷ *Alabama* comes from a tribal name that meant "people who clear away thickets."
❸ 1819
❹ Montgomery
❺ Heart of Dixie, Cotton State, Yellowhammer State
❻ *bird:* yellowhammer; *flower:* camellia; *song:* "Alabama"; *tree:* southern pine
❼ Alabama's capital, Montgomery, was also the first capital of the Confederacy (1861).

Alaska

❶ Northwest North America, west and north of British Columbia, Canada
❷ *Alaska* comes from an Eskimo word that meant "the mainland."
❸ 1959
❹ Juneau
❺ The Last Frontier, The Land of the Midnight Sun
❻ *bird:* willow ptarmigan; *fish:* king salmon; *flower:* forget-me-not; *song:* "Alaska's Flag"
❼ Alaska was purchased from Russia in 1867 for two cents an acre.

Arizona

❶ Southwest, between California and New Mexico
❷ *Arizona* comes from a Native American name that means "place of the little spring."
❸ 1912
❹ Phoenix
❺ Grand Canyon State
❻ *bird:* cactus wren; *flower:* saguaro cactus blossom; *song:* "Arizona"; *tree:* paloverde
❼ The Grand Canyon in northern Arizona is 217 miles long, 4 to 18 miles wide, and 1 mile deep.

Arkansas

❶ South-central, between Missouri and Louisiana
❷ *Arkansas* is from a Native American word meaning "people who live down the river."
❸ 1836
❹ Little Rock
❺ Land of Opportunity
❻ *bird:* mockingbird; *flower:* apple blossom; *song:* "Arkansas"; *tree:* pine
❼ Arkansas has many natural hot springs where the water temperature averages 147 degrees Fahrenheit.

California

❶ Southwest, on the Pacific Ocean
❷ The name *California* was first used in an old Spanish poem.
❸ 1850
❹ Sacramento
❺ Golden State
❻ *animal:* grizzly bear; *bird:* valley quail; *colors:* blue and gold; *fish:* golden trout; *flower:* golden poppy; *song:* "I Love You, California"; *tree:* redwood
❼ Gold was discovered in California on January 24, 1848, in a stream near Sacramento.

Colorado

❶ West-central, between Utah and Kansas
❷ *Colorado* comes from a Spanish word meaning "having a reddish color."
❸ 1876
❹ Denver
❺ Centennial State, Silver State
❻ *animal:* bighorn sheep; *bird:* lark bunting; *colors:* blue and white; *flower:* columbine; *tree:* blue spruce
❼ Denver is called the Mile-High City because it is 5,280 feet above sea level.

Connecticut

❶ Northeast, between New York and Rhode Island
❷ *Connecticut* is from a Native American word meaning "by the long river."
❸ 1788
❹ Hartford
❺ Nutmeg State
❻ *bird:* robin; *flower:* mountain laurel; *song:* "Yankee Doodle Dandy"; *tree:* white oak
❼ In 1639 settlers here adopted the first constitution in the New World that was based on the consent of the people.

Delaware

❶ East-central, between Maryland and the Atlantic Ocean
❷ *Delaware* comes from the name of Lord De La Warr, the first governor of Virginia.
❸ 1787
❹ Dover
❺ First State, Diamond State
❻ *bird:* blue hen chicken; *flower:* peach blossom; *song:* "Our Delaware"; *tree:* American holly
❼ Delaware was the first state to ratify the federal Constitution.

Florida

❶ Southeast, between the Gulf of Mexico and the Atlantic Ocean
❷ *Florida* comes from a Spanish word meaning "flowery."
❸ 1845
❹ Tallahassee
❺ Sunshine State
❻ *bird:* mockingbird; *flower:* orange blossom; *song:* "Swanee River"; *tree:* Sabal palmetto palm
❼ In 1565 the Spanish founded the first permanent settlement in Florida at St. Augustine on the northeast coast.

Georgia

❶ Southeast, between Alabama and South Carolina
❷ Georgia was named after King George II of England.
❸ 1788
❹ Atlanta
❺ Empire State of the South, Peach State, Goober State
❻ *bird:* brown thrasher; *flower:* Cherokee rose; *song:* "Georgia On My Mind"; *tree:* live oak
❼ Georgia produces more peanuts, also called "goobers," than any other state.

Key ❶ Location ❷ Origin of Name ❸ Date of Admission ❹ Capital ❺ Nicknames ❻ Official Data ❼ Interesting Facts

Hawaii

❶ Central Pacific Ocean
❷ *Hawaii* probably comes from the name that the original inhabitants gave to their homeland.
❸ 1959
❹ Honolulu
❺ Aloha State
❻ *bird:* nene (goose); *flower:* hibiscus; *song:* "Hawaii Ponoi"; *tree:* kukui (candlenut)
❼ Two of Hawaii's volcanos, Kilauea and Mauna Loa, are still active.

Idaho

❶ Northwest, between Washington and Montana
❷ *Idaho* may have come from the name of a Native American tribe.
❸ 1890
❹ Boise
❺ Gem State, Gem of the Mountains, Panhandle State
❻ *bird:* mountain bluebird; *flower:* syringa; *song:* "Here We Have Idaho"; *tree:* white pine
❼ Idaho is famous for the large potatoes grown there.

Illinois

❶ North-central, south of Wisconsin
❷ *Illinois* comes from the name of a Native American tribe that meant "perfect men."
❸ 1818
❹ Springfield
❺ Prairie State, The Inland Empire
❻ *bird:* cardinal; *flower:* violet; *slogan:* Land of Lincoln; *song:* "Illinois"; *tree:* white oak
❼ The Cahokia Mounds are a group of about 85 earthworks built by Native Americans between 1300 and 1700.

Indiana

❶ North-central, between Illinois and Ohio
❷ *Indiana* comes from "Indian" plus a Latin ending and means "land of the Indians."
❸ 1816
❹ Indianapolis
❺ Hoosier State
❻ *bird:* cardinal; *flower:* peony; *song:* "On the Banks of the Wabash"; *tree:* tulip poplar
❼ Indiana has many Native American mounds, built more than a thousand years ago.

Iowa

❶ North-central, between Minnesota and Missouri
❷ *Iowa* comes from a Native American word that probably meant "sleepy ones."
❸ 1846
❹ Des Moines
❺ Hawkeye State
❻ *bird:* eastern goldfinch; *colors:* red, white, and blue; *flower:* wild rose; *song:* "Song of Iowa"; *tree:* oak
❼ Iowa is in the heart of the Corn Belt. Most of the state's land area is used for farming.

Kansas

❶ Central, between Nebraska and Oklahoma
❷ *Kansas* comes from a tribal name that may have meant "people of the south wind."
❸ 1861
❹ Topeka
❺ Sunflower State, Jayhawk State
❻ *animal:* buffalo; *bird:* western meadowlark; *flower:* sunflower; *song:* "Home on the Range"; *tree:* cottonwood
❼ Kansas is in the exact center of the continental United States.

Kentucky

❶ East-central, north of Tennessee
❷ *Kentucky* comes from a Native American name that meant "meadowland."
❸ 1792
❹ Frankfort
❺ Bluegrass State
❻ *bird:* Kentucky cardinal; *flower:* goldenrod; *song:* "My Old Kentucky Home"; *tree:* Kentucky coffee tree
❼ Kentucky's nickname comes from the bluish-green grass that grows in the northern hills. Many horse farms are in this area.

Louisiana

❶ South-central, between Texas and Mississippi
❷ Louisiana was named by French explorers after King Louis XIV of France.
❸ 1812
❹ Baton Rouge
❺ Pelican State, Creole State, Sugar State
❻ *bird:* pelican; *flower:* magnolia; *song:* "Give Me Louisiana"; *tree:* bald cypress
❼ The Mississippi River ends its long journey to the Gulf of Mexico near New Orleans, Louisiana.

Maine

❶ Northeast, between the Atlantic Ocean and New Hampshire
❷ *Maine* comes from an older English word meaning "mainland."
❸ 1820
❹ Augusta
❺ Pine Tree State
❻ *bird:* chickadee; *flower:* white pine cone and tassel; *song:* "State of Maine Song"; *tree:* white pine
❼ Maine lies south of the 49th parallel, which is the border between much of the United States and Canada.

Maryland

❶ East-central, between Virginia and Delaware
❷ Maryland was named in honor of Queen Henrietta Maria of England.
❸ 1788
❹ Annapolis
❺ Old Line State, Free State
❻ *bird:* Baltimore oriole; *dog:* Chesapeake Bay retriever; *fish:* rockfish; *flower:* black-eyed Susan; *song:* "Maryland, My Maryland"; *tree:* white oak
❼ Maryland donated the land for Washington, D.C., in 1790.

Key ❶ Location ❷ Origin of Name ❸ Date of Admission ❹ Capital ❺ Nicknames ❻ Official Data ❼ Interesting Facts

Massachusetts

❶ Northeast, on the Atlantic Ocean
❷ *Massachusetts* comes from a Native American word that meant "big hill."
❸ 1788
❹ Boston
❺ Bay State, Old Colony State
❻ *bird:* chickadee; *flower:* mayflower; *song:* "All Hail to Massachusetts"; *tree:* American elm
❼ In 1621 the Pilgrims celebrated the first Thanksgiving Day here with members of a Native American tribe.

Michigan

❶ North-central, on two peninsulas in the Great Lakes
❷ *Michigan* is from a Native American name meaning "big lake."
❸ 1837
❹ Lansing
❺ Wolverine State
❻ *animal:* wolverine; *bird:* robin; *fish:* trout; *flower:* apple blossom; *song:* "Michigan, My Michigan"; *tree:* white pine
❼ Detroit, Michigan, is known as the Automobile Capital of the World.

Minnesota

❶ North-central, south of Canada
❷ *Minnesota* is from a Native American name that meant "white water," or water that is very rough and frothy.
❸ 1858
❹ St. Paul
❺ North Star State, Gopher State, Land of 10,000 Lakes
❻ *bird:* common loon; *flower:* lady's-slipper; *song:* "Hail, Minnesota"; *tree:* red pine
❼ Minnesota has between 12,000 and 15,000 lakes.

Mississippi

❶ Southeast, between Louisiana and Alabama
❷ *Mississippi* is from a Native American name meaning "great river."
❸ 1817
❹ Jackson
❺ Magnolia State
❻ *bird:* mockingbird; *flower:* magnolia; *song:* "Go, Mississippi"; *tree:* magnolia
❼ Hernando de Soto explored this area in 1540 and discovered the Mississippi River in 1541.

Missouri

❶ Central, between Kansas and Illinois
❷ *Missouri* comes from a tribal name that may have meant "big canoes."
❸ 1821
❹ Jefferson City
❺ Show Me State
❻ *bird:* bluebird; *colors:* red, white, and blue; *flower:* hawthorn; *song:* "Missouri Waltz"; *tree:* dogwood
❼ Missouri was the starting point for many westward-bound pioneers in the nineteenth century.

Montana

❶ Northwest, between Idaho and North Dakota
❷ *Montana* takes its name from a Latin word that meant "mountainous."
❸ 1889
❹ Helena
❺ Treasure State
❻ *bird:* western meadowlark; *flower:* bitterroot; *song:* "Montana"; *tree:* ponderosa pine
❼ Glacier National Park is a popular tourist attraction in Montana. It includes more than 50 glaciers and 200 lakes.

Nebraska

❶ Central, between South Dakota and Kansas
❷ *Nebraska* is from a Native American word that meant "flat water."
❸ 1867
❹ Lincoln
❺ Cornhusker State, Beef State
❻ *bird:* western meadowlark; *flower:* goldenrod; *fossil:* mammoth; *rock:* prairie agate; *song:* "Beautiful Nebraska"; *tree:* cottonwood
❼ Nebraska has huge wheat, rye, and corn fields.

Nevada

❶ Western, between California and Utah
❷ *Nevada* was shortened from the Spanish words *sierra nevada,* meaning "snow-covered mountains."
❸ 1864
❹ Carson City
❺ Sagebrush State, Silver State
❻ *bird:* mountain bluebird; *flower:* sagebrush; *song:* "Home Means Nevada"; *tree:* single-leaf piñon
❼ Hoover Dam is one of the largest dams in the world.

New Hampshire

❶ Northeast, between Vermont and Maine
❷ New Hampshire was named after Hampshire, a county in England.
❸ 1788
❹ Concord
❺ Granite State
❻ *bird:* purple finch; *flower:* purple lilac; *songs:* "Old New Hampshire," "New Hampshire, My New Hampshire"; *tree:* white birch
❼ New Hampshire is a popular state with skiers and winter vacationers.

New Jersey

❶ East-central, on the Atlantic Ocean
❷ New Jersey was named after Jersey, an island in the English Channel.
❸ 1787
❹ Trenton
❺ Garden State
❻ *bird:* eastern goldfinch; *colors:* buff and blue; *flower:* purple violet; *tree:* red oak
❼ Many Revolutionary War battles were fought in New Jersey, including the Battles of Trenton (1776) and Princeton (1777).

Key ❶ Location ❷ Origin of Name ❸ Date of Admission ❹ Capital ❺ Nicknames ❻ Official Data ❼ Interesting Facts

New Mexico

❶ Southwest, between Arizona and Texas
❷ New Mexico was named after Mexico by an early Spanish explorer.
❸ 1912
❹ Santa Fe
❺ Land of Enchantment, Sunshine State
❻ *animal:* black bear; *bird:* roadrunner; *flower:* yucca; *song:* "O Fair New Mexico"; *tree:* piñon
❼ Carlsbad Caverns are the largest caverns in the world.

New York

❶ Northeast, between Pennsylvania and the Canadian border
❷ New York was named after the Duke of York, who took charge of the colony in 1664.
❸ 1788
❹ Albany
❺ Empire State
❻ *bird:* bluebird; *flower:* rose; *tree:* sugar maple
❼ New York City is the largest city in the United States. The Dutch originally settled the city in 1626, calling it New Netherlands.

North Carolina

❶ Southeast, on the Atlantic Ocean
❷ North Carolina was named for King Charles I of England.
❸ 1789
❹ Raleigh
❺ Tar Heel State
❻ *bird:* cardinal; *colors:* red and blue; *flower:* dogwood; *shell:* Scotch bonnet; *song:* "The Old North State"; *tree:* pine
❼ The first English colony in America was founded here in 1585 on Roanoke Island.

North Dakota

❶ North-central, between South Dakota and the Canadian border
❷ North Dakota was named after the Dakota tribe. *Dakota* meant "allies."
❸ 1889
❹ Bismarck
❺ Sioux State, Flickertail State
❻ *bird:* western meadowlark; *flower:* wild prairie rose; *song:* "North Dakota Hymn"; *tree:* American elm
❼ Until 1889 North Dakota was part of the state of South Dakota.

Ohio

❶ North, on Lake Erie between Pennsylvania and Indiana
❷ *Ohio* comes from a Native American name meaning "beautiful river."
❸ 1803
❹ Columbus
❺ Buckeye State
❻ *bird:* cardinal; *flower:* scarlet carnation; *gem:* flint; *song:* "Beautiful Ohio"; *tree:* buckeye
❼ Nine Presidents were born or lived in Ohio.

Oklahoma

❶ South-central, between Kansas and Texas
❷ *Oklahoma* is from a Native American phrase that meant "red people."
❸ 1907
❹ Oklahoma City
❺ Sooner State
❻ *bird:* scissortail flycatcher; *colors:* green and white; *flower:* mistletoe; *song:* "Oklahoma"; *tree:* redbud
❼ On April 22, 1889, more than 50,000 settlers entered Oklahoma when the area was opened for homesteads.

Oregon

❶ Northwest, on the Pacific Ocean
❷ *Oregon* was formerly the name for the Columbia River.
❸ 1859
❹ Salem
❺ Beaver State
❻ *animal:* beaver; *bird:* western meadowlark; *fish:* Chinook salmon; *flower:* Oregon grape; *song:* "Oregon, My Oregon"; *tree:* Douglas fir
❼ Large numbers of settlers began arriving along the overland Oregon Trail in 1843.

Pennsylvania

❶ East, between New York and Maryland
❷ Pennsylvania was named after its founder, William Penn.
❸ 1787
❹ Harrisburg
❺ Keystone State
❻ *bird:* ruffed grouse; *colors:* blue and gold; *dog:* Great Dane; *flower:* mountain laurel; *insect:* firefly; *tree:* hemlock
❼ Philadelphia was the leading city of the new nation from 1776 to 1800.

Rhode Island

❶ Northeast, on the Atlantic Ocean
❷ Rhode Island was probably named after the Greek island of Rhodes, off the southwestern coast of Turkey.
❸ 1790
❹ Providence
❺ Ocean State
❻ *bird:* Rhode Island Red; *colors:* blue, white, and gold; *flower:* violet; *song:* "Rhode Island"; *tree:* red maple
❼ Rhode Island is the smallest state in the United States.

South Carolina

❶ Southeast, on the Atlantic Ocean
❷ South Carolina was named for King Charles I of England. The word *Carolina* is Latin for "pertaining to Charles."
❸ 1788
❹ Columbia
❺ Palmetto State
❻ *bird:* Carolina wren; *flower:* Carolina yellow jessamine; *song:* "Carolina"; *tree:* palmetto
❼ In 1860 South Carolina was the first state to secede from the Union.

Key ❶ Location ❷ Origin of Name ❸ Date of Admission ❹ Capital ❺ Nicknames ❻ Official Data ❼ Interesting Facts

South Dakota

❶ North-central, north of Nebraska
❷ South Dakota was named after the Dakota tribe.
❸ 1889
❹ Pierre
❺ Sunshine State, Coyote State
❻ *animal:* coyote; *bird:* ring-necked pheasant; *fish:* walleye; *flower:* pasqueflower; *song:* "Hail! South Dakota"; *tree:* spruce
❼ Mount Rushmore has huge sculptures of Washington, Jefferson, Lincoln, and Theodore Roosevelt.

Tennessee

❶ Southeast, south of Kentucky
❷ *Tennessee* is from a Native American name that was first used for a town in the area.
❸ 1796
❹ Nashville
❺ Volunteer State
❻ *animal:* raccoon; *bird:* mockingbird; *flower:* iris; *horse:* Tennessee walking horse; *song:* "Tennessee Waltz"; *wild flower:* passion flower
❼ Nashville is an important center for country music.

Texas

❶ South-central, north of Mexico
❷ *Texas* comes from a Native American greeting that was also used as a tribal name.
❸ 1845
❹ Austin
❺ Lone Star State
❻ *bird:* mockingbird; *flower:* bluebonnet; *song:* "Texas, Our Texas"; *tree:* pecan
❼ Texas was originally controlled by Mexico. American settlers organized an independent republic in 1836 and applied for statehood nine years later.

Utah

❶ West, between Nevada and Colorado
❷ *Utah* comes from a Native American tribal name.
❸ 1896
❹ Salt Lake City
❺ Beehive State
❻ *bird:* seagull; *emblem:* beehive; *flower:* sego lily; *song:* "Utah, We Love Thee"; *tree:* blue spruce
❼ Great Salt Lake is the largest natural lake west of the Mississippi River. It is so salty that no fish can live in it.

Vermont

❶ Northeast, between New York and New Hampshire
❷ *Vermont* comes from two French words that mean "green" and "mountains."
❸ 1791
❹ Montpelier
❺ Green Mountain State
❻ *animal:* Morgan horse; *bird:* hermit thrush; *flower:* red clover; *song:* "Hail, Vermont!"; *tree:* sugar maple
❼ Vermont was the first state to join the Union after the original 13.

Virginia

❶ East-central, between Maryland and North Carolina
❷ Virginia was named for Queen Elizabeth I of England, who was sometimes called "the Virgin Queen."
❸ 1788
❹ Richmond
❺ The Old Dominion, Mother of Presidents
❻ *bird:* cardinal; *flower:* dogwood; *song:* "Carry Me Back to Old Virginia"; *tree:* flowering dogwood
❼ The English first settled at Jamestown in 1607.

Washington

❶ Northwest, on the Pacific Ocean
❷ Washington was named after President George Washington.
❸ 1889
❹ Olympia
❺ Evergreen State
❻ *bird:* willow goldfinch; *colors:* green and gold; *fish:* steelhead trout; *flower:* rhododendron; *song:* "Washington, My Home"; *tree:* western hemlock
❼ Washington is the only state named after a President.

West Virginia

❶ East-central, between Ohio and Virginia
❷ West Virginia was named for "the Virgin Queen," a popular name for Queen Elizabeth I of England.
❸ 1863
❹ Charleston
❺ Mountain State
❻ *animal:* black bear; *bird:* cardinal; *flower:* rhododendron; *song:* "West Virginia, Home Sweet Home"; *tree:* sugar maple
❼ West Virginia was part of Virginia until 1861.

Wisconsin

❶ North-central, between Minnesota and Michigan
❷ *Wisconsin* is from a Native American name that was first used for the Wisconsin River.
❸ 1848
❹ Madison
❺ Badger State
❻ *animals:* badger, white-tailed deer, dairy cow; *bird:* robin; *fish:* muskellunge; *flower:* wood violet; *song:* "On, Wisconsin"; *tree:* sugar maple
❼ Wisconsin is famous for its dairy products.

Wyoming

❶ West, between Montana and Colorado
❷ *Wyoming* is from a Native American name meaning "at the big flats."
❸ 1890
❹ Cheyenne
❺ Equality State
❻ *bird:* meadowlark; *flower:* Indian paintbrush; *gem:* jade; *insignia:* bucking horse; *song:* "Wyoming"; *tree:* cottonwood
❼ Wyoming was the first territory or state to allow women the right to vote (1869).

The World

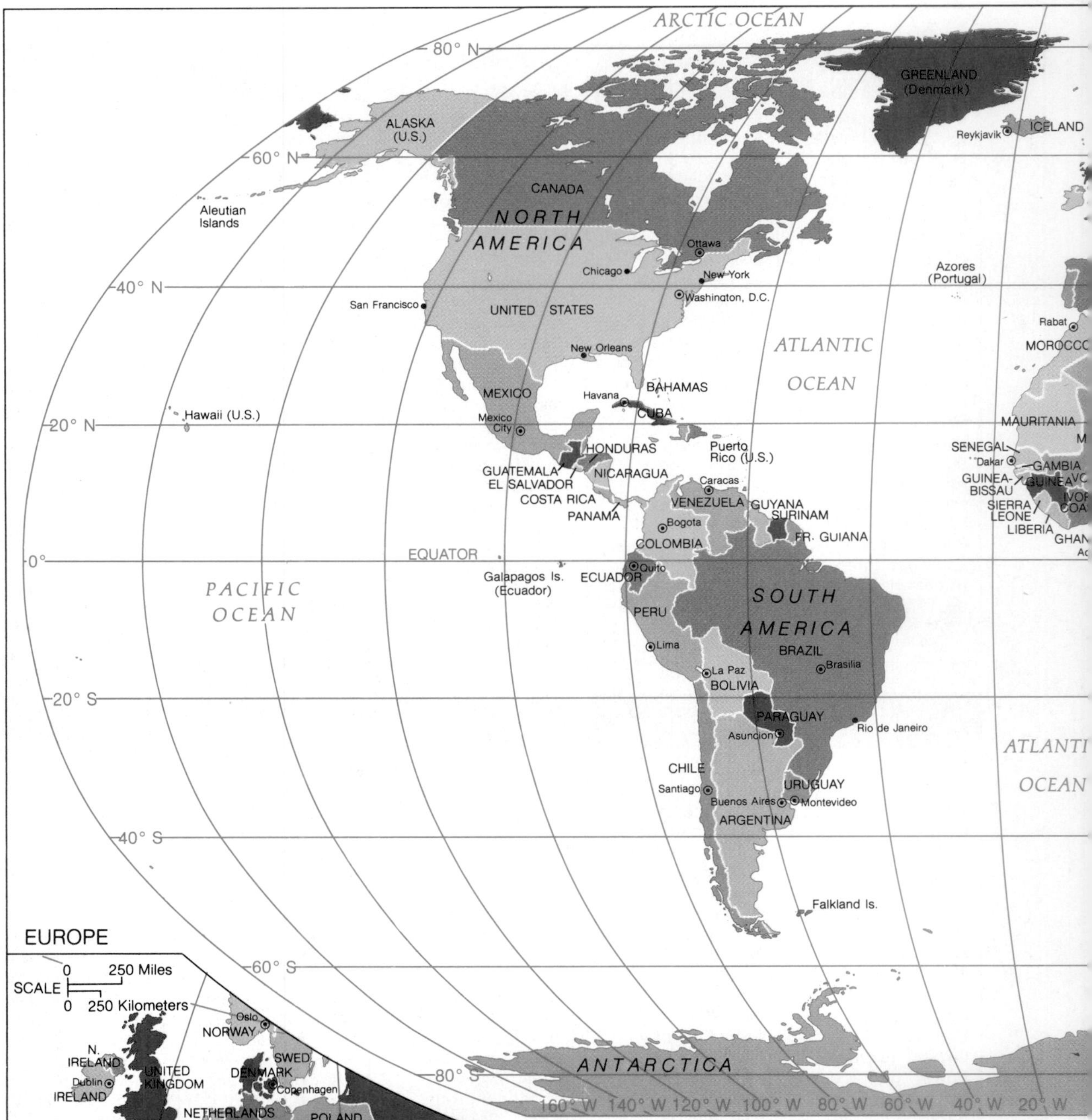

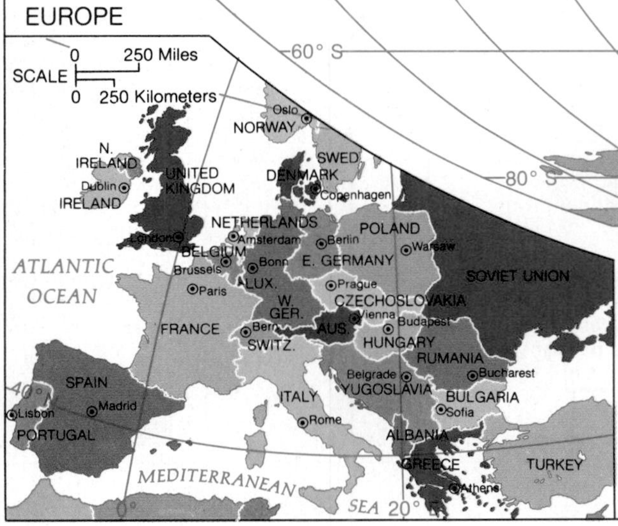

ABBREVIATIONS

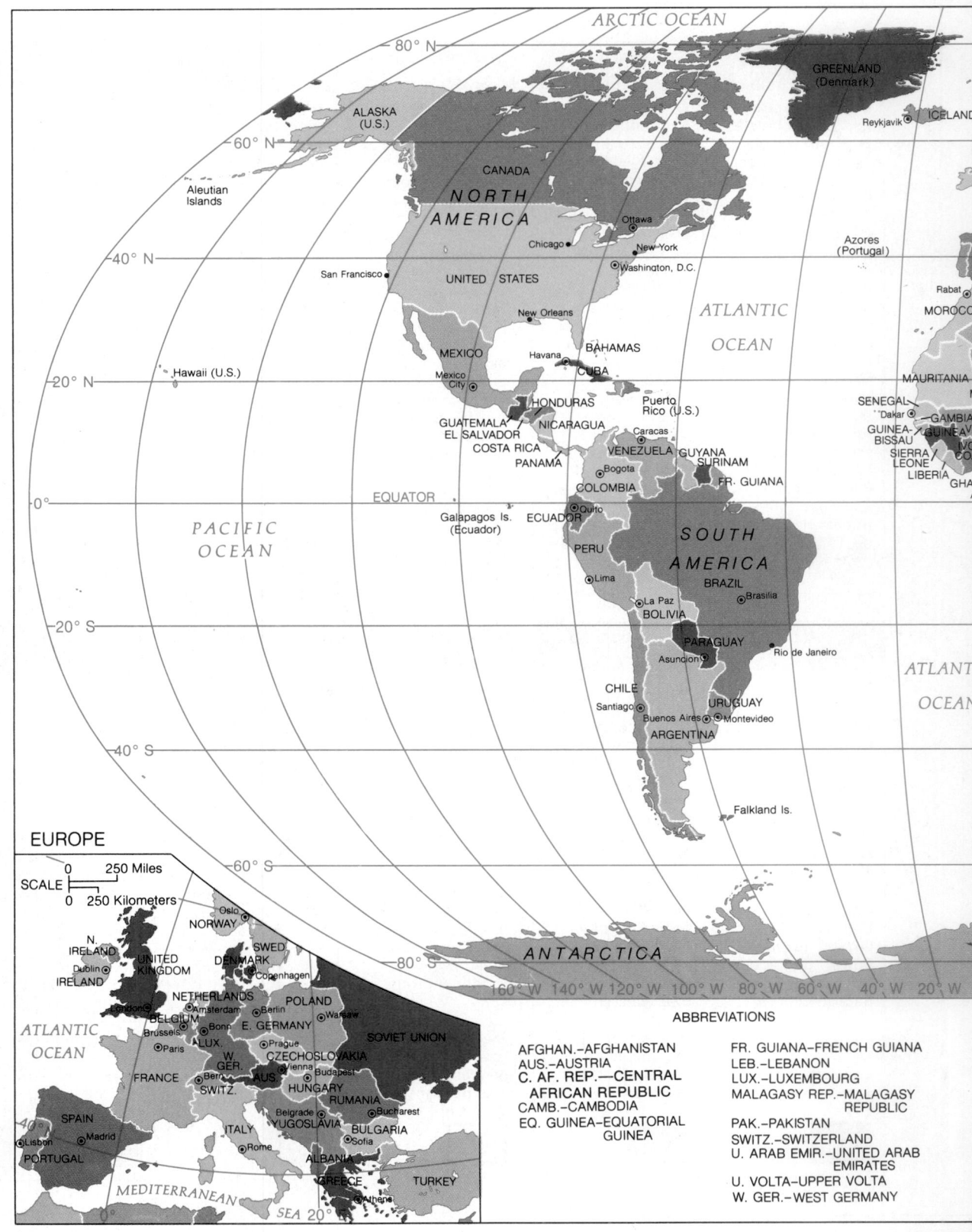

AFGHAN.–AFGHANISTAN
AUS.–AUSTRIA
C. AF. REP.—CENTRAL AFRICAN REPUBLIC
CAMB.–CAMBODIA
EQ. GUINEA–EQUATORIAL GUINEA
FR. GUIANA–FRENCH GUIANA
LEB.–LEBANON
LUX.–LUXEMBOURG
MALAGASY REP.–MALAGASY REPUBLIC
PAK.–PAKISTAN
SWITZ.–SWITZERLAND
U. ARAB EMIR.–UNITED ARAB EMIRATES
U. VOLTA–UPPER VOLTA
W. GER.–WEST GERMANY

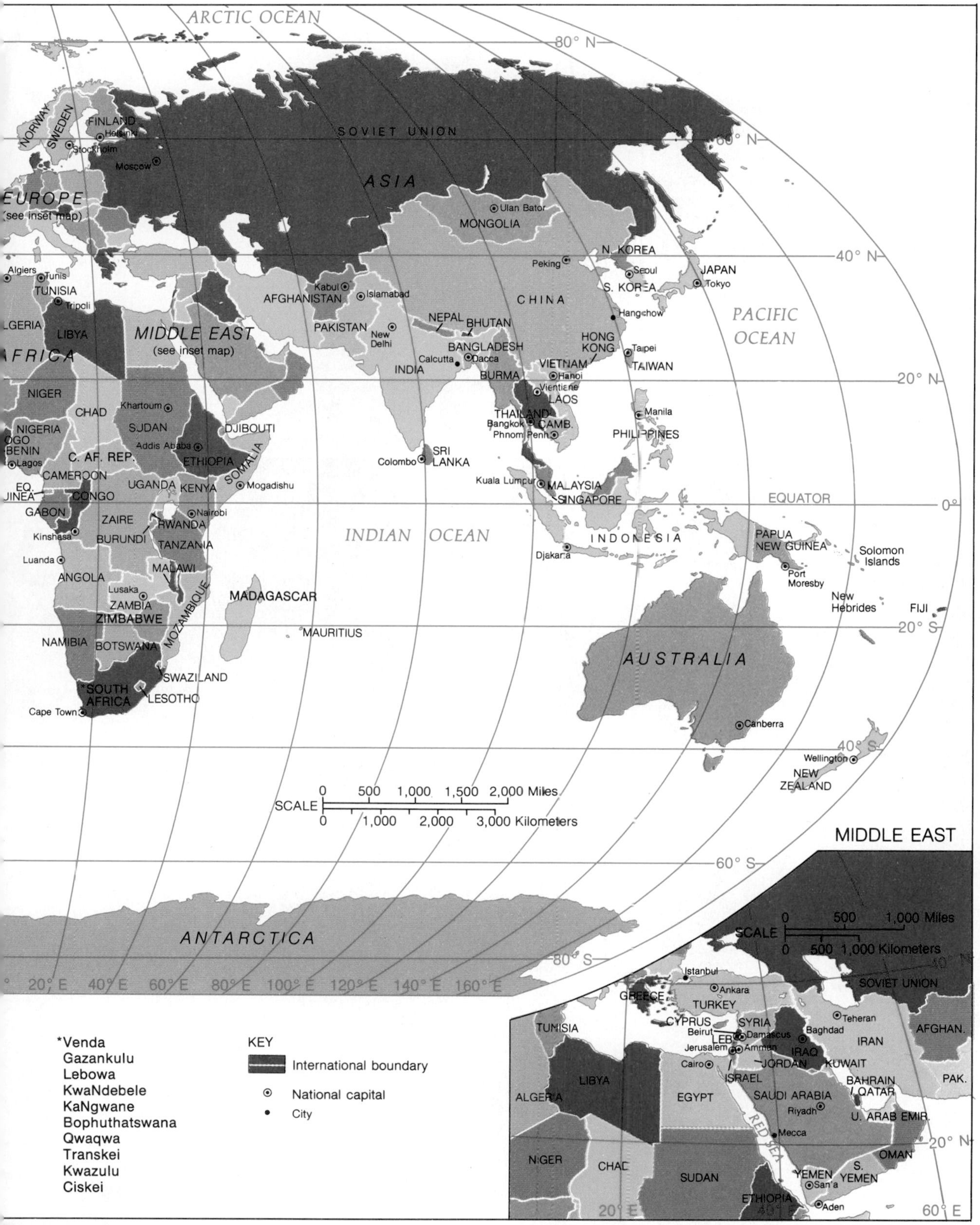
ARCTIC OCEAN
80° N
60° N
40° N
20° N
0°
20° S
40° S
60° S
80° S
NORWAY
SWEDEN
FINLAND
Helsinki
Stockholm
Moscow
SOVIET UNION
ASIA
EUROPE
(see inset map)
Ulan Bator
MONGOLIA
N. KOREA
Peking
Seoul
S. KOREA
JAPAN
Tokyo
Algiers
Tunis
TUNISIA
Tripoli
Kabul
Islamabad
AFGHANISTAN
CHINA
PACIFIC OCEAN
Hangchow
NEPAL
BHUTAN
PAKISTAN
New Delhi
LGERIA
LIBYA
MIDDLE EAST
(see inset map)
FRICA
BANGLADESH
Calcutta
Dacca
INDIA
HONG KONG
Taipei
TAIWAN
VIETNAM
Hanoi
BURMA
Vientiane
LAOS
NIGER
CHAD
Khartoum
SUDAN
DJIBOUTI
THAILAND
Bangkok
CAMB.
Phnom Penh
Manila
PHILIPPINES
NIGERIA
OGO
BENIN
Lagos
Addis Ababa
ETHIOPIA
C. AF. REP.
SOMALIA
Colombo
SRI LANKA
CAMEROON
UGANDA
KENYA
Mogadishu
Kuala Lumpur
MALAYSIA
SINGAPORE
EQ. GUINEA
CONGO
GABON
EQUATOR
Nairobi
ZAIRE
RWANDA
Kinshasa
BURUNDI
INDIAN OCEAN
INDONESIA
PAPUA NEW GUINEA
Solomon Islands
TANZANIA
Luanda
Djakarta
Port Moresby
MALAWI
ANGOLA
Lusaka
ZAMBIA
MOZAMBIQUE
MADAGASCAR
New Hebrides
FIJI
ZIMBABWE
MAURITIUS
NAMIBIA
BOTSWANA
AUSTRALIA
SWAZILAND
*SOUTH AFRICA
LESOTHO
Cape Town
Canberra
Wellington
NEW ZEALAND
0 500 1,000 1,500 2,000 Miles
SCALE
0 1,000 2,000 3,000 Kilometers
ANTARCTICA
20° E 40° E 60° E 80° E 100° E 120° E 140° E 160° E
MIDDLE EAST
0 500 1,000 Miles
SCALE
0 500 1,000 Kilometers
Istanbul
Ankara
GREECE
TURKEY
SOVIET UNION
CYPRUS
SYRIA
Teheran
TUNISIA
Beirut
LEB.
Damascus
Baghdad
AFGHAN.
Jerusalem
Amman
IRAQ
IRAN
Cairo
JORDAN
KUWAIT
LIBYA
ISRAEL
BAHRAIN
QATAR
PAK.
ALGERIA
EGYPT
SAUDI ARABIA
Riyadh
U. ARAB EMIR.
RED SEA
Mecca
20° N
NIGER
CHAD
SUDAN
YEMEN
S. YEMEN
OMAN
San'a
ETHIOPIA
Aden
20° E
40° E
60° E
*Venda
Gazankulu
Lebowa
KwaNdebele
KaNgwane
Bophuthatswana
Qwaqwa
Transkei
Kwazulu
Ciskei
KEY
International boundary
National capital
City

The United States of America

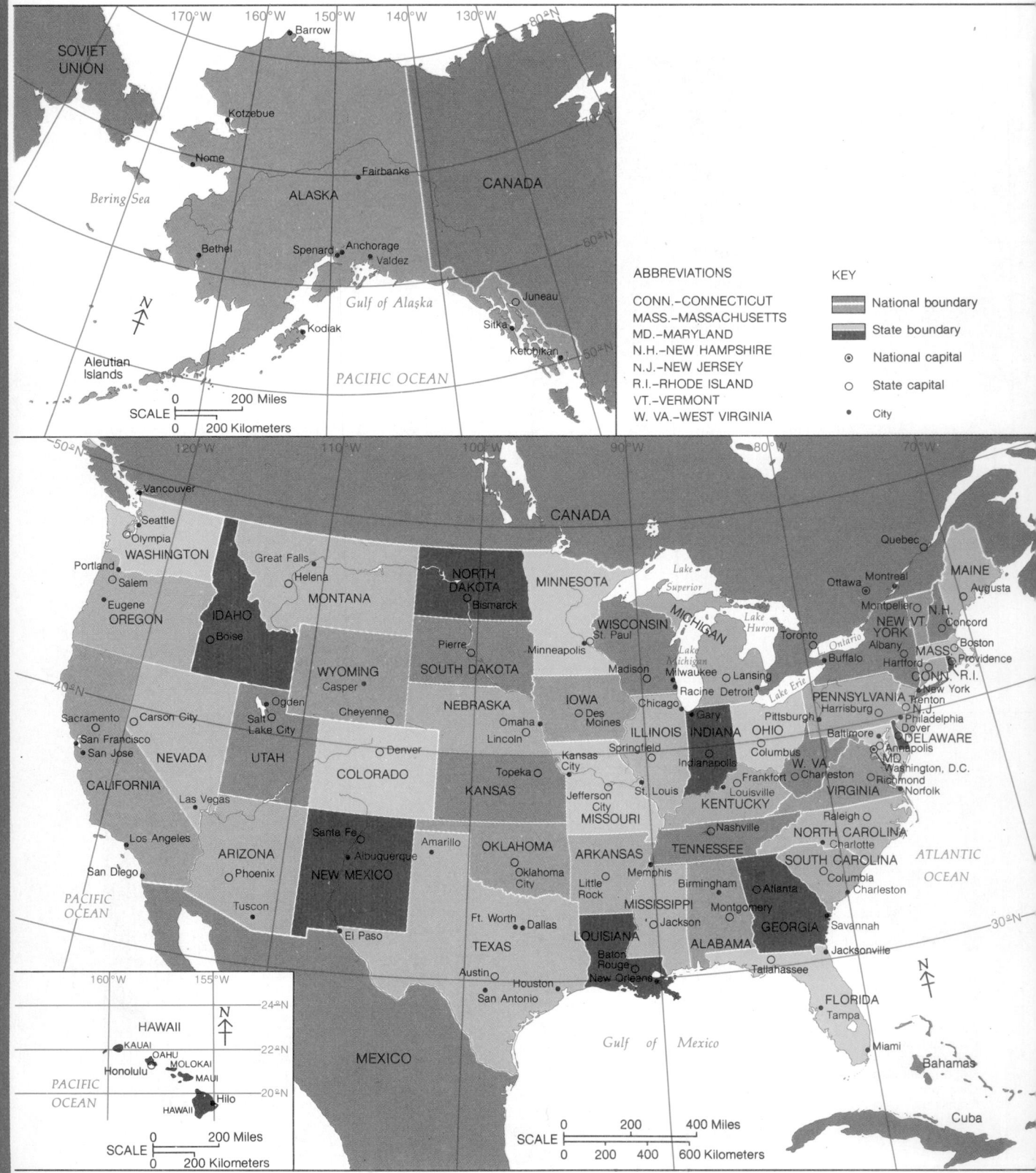

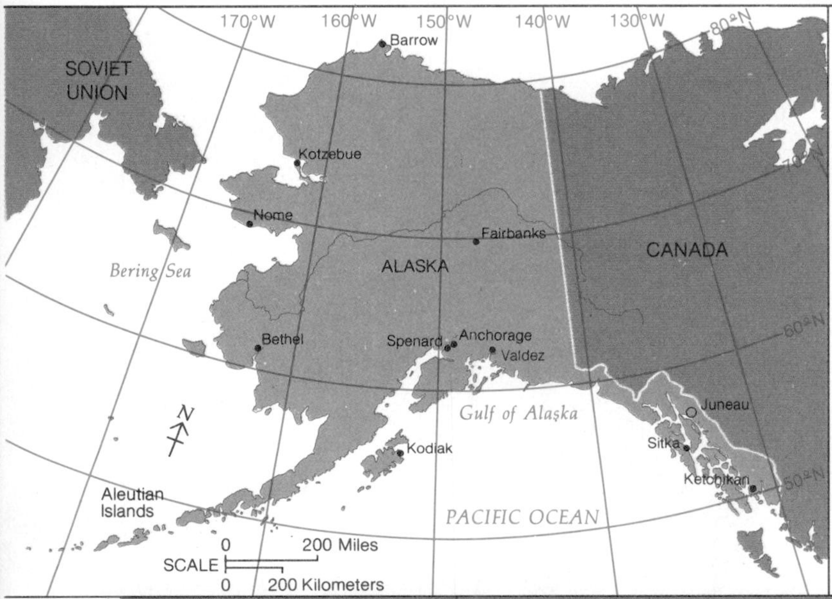

ABBREVIATIONS

CONN.–CONNECTICUT
MASS.–MASSACHUSETTS
MD.–MARYLAND
N.H.–NEW HAMPSHIRE
N.J.–NEW JERSEY
R.I.–RHODE ISLAND
VT.–VERMONT
W. VA.–WEST VIRGINIA

KEY

- National boundary
- State boundary
- ⊙ National capital
- ○ State capital
- • City

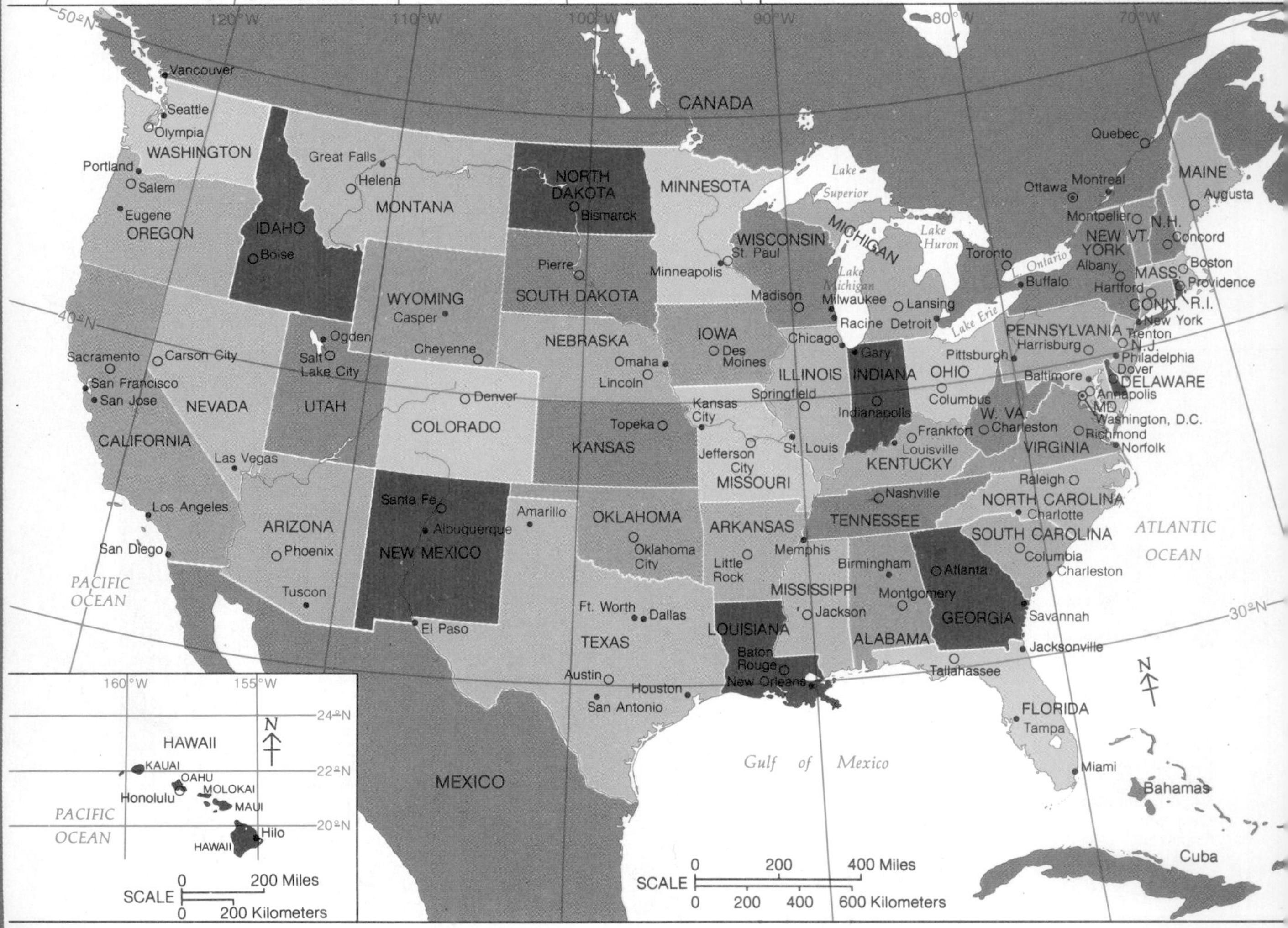

Picture Credits

Illustrations

Floyd Cooper boomerang
Lorraine Epstein acorn, hemlock, hickory, holly, huckleberry, Indian paintbrush, indigo, iris, lichen, lily of the valley, linden, loganberry, okra
Al Fiorentino binoculars
Frank Fretz amoeba, constellation, continent, mantis, metamorphosis, mollusk
Christa Kieffer abreast, acute angle, adder, adhesive, angle, anvil, apprentice, balance, baton, beard, bellhop, bleachers, booth, breastbone, calico, carriage, cello, chandelier, chopsticks, clarinet, cone, corsage, cradle, curtsy, cymbal, dewlap, dimple, doublet, double bass, duck[2], dumbbell, dwarf, earmuffs, eggplant, embroidery, English horn, excavate, eyeglasses, eyepiece, feeler, fiddle, flax, flute, flying fish, forceps, freckle, French horn, globe, goggles, graft, grasshopper, grindstone, grouse, Halloween, hammock, handlebar, harp, hurdle, infant, jasmine, juggler, jute, kelp, kettledrum, kilt, knapsack, lantern, leggings, mackinaw, marionette, medal, mitt, muffler, neckerchief, nook, nursery, oboe, overshoe, piccolo, prospector, puppet, queen, quiver[2], ramp, ranger, receiver, recorder, rowboat, sari, saxophone, seesaw, semaphore, shadow, sideburns, skin diving, smock, sombrero, springboard, stethoscope, swing, tambourine, telescope, toboggan, treadmill, trombone, tuning, uniform, unravel, untie, usher, veil, walkie-talkie, workbench, zither
Sharron O'Neil African violet, agate, almond, anthill, arbor, architecture, azalea, balloon, banjo, bicuspid, bouquet, broccoli, brooch, castanet, cauliflower, churn, cleat, colonnade, comet, compass, convertible, cornet, cricket, crossbones, cube, currant, dart, detour, diameter, diaphragm, dike, disk, dispenser, driftwood, eaves, elbow, emblem, encyclopedia, engraving, ensign, exhibit, extinguisher, eye, fang, feather, file[2], fingerprint, fixture, forefoot, fossil, fringe, frond, frying pan, funnel, gear, geometric, gladiolus, gnome, gourd, hare, heart, heather, herb, hieroglyphic, hive, hoe, honeycomb, hourglass, ice skate, igloo, imprint, inkwell, inscription, insignia, instrument, jack-o'-lantern, jib, jonquil, junction, keyboard, kidney, knothole, ladybug, larkspur, laurel, ledge, lighthouse, locomotive, lotus, mainspring, mallet, mango, marigold, melon, menu, moat, morning glory, mushroom, narcissus, nasturtium, needle, needlepoint, network, nightingale, North Pole, notion, nucleus, obtuse angle, octagon, onion, opal, partridge, passenger pigeon, patchwork, pavilion, peninsula, pentagon, pestle, pimiento, piston, polygon, potato, prism, program, prow, pussy willow, quill, racket, rectangle, reel[1], respiratory system, rhubarb, right angle, rook, rung, saddle, scarecrow, scepter, schooner, sickle, silhouette, siphon, sledgehammer, South Pole, spectrum, spool, spruce, stomach, stoplight, strawberry, stringbean, sumac, sundial, sweet pea, symmetry, tentacle, test tube, thatch, thermometer, thorn, timetable, tower, trellis, tripod, uneven, valentine, valve, vane, vase, vein, whippoorwill, woodpecker, wren, yucca
Jim Pearson adrift, aqueduct, arrowhead, bagpipe, barge, beacon, boxcar, buggy, buoy, canoe, carburetor, catapult, chariot, checkerboard, clipper, coach, compact, convoy, crow's-nest, cupola, daredevil, deck, den, depot, derrick, dinosaur, dirigible, discus, dome, dory, earphone, electric guitar, engine, equipment, exercise, fisher, flipper, food chain, foothill, forge[1], fort, fuselage, galleon, goalie, gyroscope, helmet, home, hydroplane, isthmus, jigsaw, junk[2], mail[2], maul, megaphone, milestone, minaret, nest, nutmeg, organ, outboard motor, outrigger, palmetto, pear, persimmon, phlox, plum, poison ivy, prickly pear, pulley, raspberry, reaper, rescue, robot, rocker, rose, seaweed, seed/seedling, sepal, shortstop, sperm whale, sponge, squash, starfish, stingray, stump, sugarcane, surrey, swordfish, tadpole, tarantula, tee, thrush, tomato, turkey
Pat Traub adult, alligator, ant, apricot, armadillo, avocado, bat[2], beech, cactus, cedar, centipede, chestnut, claw, cocoon, collie, comb, conch, copperhead, cottontail, crayfish, crest, crustacean, Dalmatian, eel, exotic, gander, gerbil, gopher, Great Dane, gull, hawk[1], hedgehog, hippopotamus, hoof, horned toad, husky[3], inchworm, leopard, lizard, llama, lobster, longhorn, lynx, magnolia, mammoth, meadowlark, mink, mistletoe, mockingbird, moose, mountain goat, mule, muzzle, newt, opossum, orangutan, otter, owl, ox, parrot, peacock, pelican, pheasant, piggyback, platypus, plover, poodle, porcupine, prairie dog, pug, raven, reindeer, reptile, retriever, rhinoceros, salmon, scallop, scorpion, sea horse, seal, setter, shark, sheep, shrew, skunk, sloth, snapping turtle, squirrel, stork, terrier, tiger, toad, turtle, tusk, walrus, weasel, whale, whooping crane, wolf, yoke
Lou Vaccaro all illustrations pages B7–B16.

Photographs

abbey Peter Bennett, Stockphotos; **access code** Eric Fordham, courtesy of Data General Corp.; **acrobat** Harold Lambert, Frederic Lewis; **airport** Sharon L. Fox, The Picture Cube; **albatross** Sheri Blaney, The Picture Cube; **algae** Runk/Schoenberger, Grant Heilman; **alpaca** George H. Harrison, Grant Heilman; **ambulance** Barry L. Runk, Grant Heilman; **amphibian** Frank J. Staub, The Picture Cube; **amphitheater** Dick Schiffmann, Index Stock; **anaconda** Bucky Reeves, Photo Researchers; **anteater** François Gohier, Photo Researchers; **antique** Milton Feinberg, The Picture Cube; **aphid** J.G. Miller, The Picture Cube; **aspen** Grant Heilman; **aster** Gil Fahey, The Picture Cube; **astronaut** Photo Researchers; **auk** George H. Harrison, Grant Heilman.

bacteria Runk/Schoenberger, Grant Heilman; **bald eagle** Leonard Lee Rue III, Photo Researchers; **bareback** Elisabeth Weiland, Photo Researchers; **barnacle** Runk/Schoenberger, Grant Heilman; **baseball** Mike Mazzaschi, Stock, Boston; **bazaar** Brent Jones; **beaver** Tom McHugh, Photo Researchers; **blacksmith** Dan McCoy, Rainbow; **blastoff** Hank Morgan, Photo Researchers; **blowtorch** Lou Jones; **bluejay** Bruce Ando, Index Stock; **bobcat** Harold Lambert, Frederic Lewis; **Braille** Paul Keel, Photo Researchers; **bramble** David Witbeck, The Picture Cube; **bridle** Courtesy of Edgar Berube; **Brussels sprout** Barry L. Runk, Grant Heilman; **buck** Grant Heilman; **bulldog** Russ Kinne, Photo Researchers; **bullfrog** George H. Harrison, Grant Heilman; **burro** Bernie Suess, Index Stock; **butterfly** Grant Heilman.

camel Martin Rogers, Stock, Boston; **canal** L. Stimmel, The Picture Cube; **canyon** Frank J. Staub, The Picture Cube; **capsule** George Thompson, Stockphotos; **cardinal** David C. Bitters, The Picture Cube; **cascade** Frank J. Staube, The Picture Cube; **channel** Richard Pasley, Stock, Boston; **cheetah** R.S. Virdee, Grant Heilman; **chickadee** Jose Anzel, Woodfin Camp; **chimpanzee** Toni Angermayer, Photo Researchers; **chipmunk** V. Gates, Frederic Lewis; **circus** Cynthia W. Sterling, The Picture Cube; **citrus** Barry L. Runk, Grant Heilman; **clam** A.L. Lowry, Photo Researchers; **cliff** John Serrao, Photo Researchers; **clown** Jim Roderick, Index Stock; **cockatoo** Andy Gardner, Stockphotos; **coliseum** Roderick Beebe, Photo Researchers; **commencement** Jan Halaska, Photo Researchers; **component** V. Gates, Frederic Lewis; **computer** Ellis Herwig, The Picture Cube; **condor** Jeffrey T. Apoian, Photo Researchers; **confetti** Joe Bilbao, Photo Researchers; **congress** Art Stein, Photo Researchers; **contact lens** Steve Dapkiewicz, The Picture Cube; **control tower** Joseph Nettis, Photo Researchers; **court** Sherge McNee, Stockphotos; **courtyard** Paulo Koch, Photo Researchers; **creek** M. Goodner, Stockphotos; **crocodile** M.P. Kahl, Photo Researchers.

dandelion A.K. Moon, Stock, Boston; **daybreak** M.E. Warren, Photo Researchers; **deer** Index Stock; **delta** NASA, Grant Heilman; **demonstration** Roger Clark, Jr., Photo Researchers; **dentist** Brent Jones; **destroyer** Ellis Herwig, Stock, Boston; **director** Southern Living, Photo Researchers; **disaster** Tom McHugh, Photo Researchers; **disc jockey** Bruce Ando, Index Stock; **diver** John Deitz, Photo Researchers; **dock** J.S. Larson, Photo Researchers; **dogwood** Russ Kinne Photo Researchers; **dolphin** Tom & Michelle Grimm,

International Stock; **dragonfly** Tony Ruta, Index Stock; **drawbridge** Donald Dietz, Stock, Boston; **dugout** Max Hunn, Frederic Lewis; **dune** Michael P. Gadomski, Photo Researchers.

eclipse George F. Thompson, Stockphotos; **elephant** George H. Harrison, Grant Heilman; **elevator** Barbara Alper, Stock, Boston; **elk** Peter Hoyland, Stockphotos; **emu** A.B. Joyce, Photo Researchers; **erosion** Russ Kinne, Photo Researchers; **etching** Steve Hansen, Stock, Boston; **eucalyptus** A.B. Joyce, Photo Researchers; **evergreen** Frank J. Staub, The Picture Cube; **expressway** M.E. Warren, Photo Researchers.

factory Frank Grant, International Stock; **fairground** Jane Latta, Kay Reese; **falcon** George Galicz, Photo Researchers; **farm, fawn** Harold Lambert, Frederic Lewis; **Ferris wheel** Brent Jones; **fig** Richard Parker, Photo Researchers; **finch** John S. Dunning, Photo Researchers; **fireworks** Carl Purcell, Photo Researchers; **fjord** T.W. Bennett, Taurus Photos; **flamingo** M.P. Kahl, Photo Researchers; **float** Lawrence Schiller, Photo Researchers; **flood** Harold Lambert, Frederic Lewis; **foliage** Peter Kaplan, Photo Researchers; **forget-me-not** S.J. Krasemann, Photo Researchers; **fox** Steven Krasemann, DRK Photo; **furrow** Harold Lambert, Frederic Lewis.

gangway Barry M. Winiker, Kay Reese; **garden** Alexander Lowry, Photo Researchers; **gauge** Barry L. Runk, Grant Heilman; **gazelle** Kenneth W. Fink, Photo Researchers; **geyser** Georg Gerster, Photo Researchers; **Gila monster** J.H. Robinson, Photo Researchers; **glacier** Tom Bean, DRK Photo; **gondola** Angelina Lax, Photo Researchers; **gorilla** Ray Hunold, Photo Researchers; **granary** B. Llewellyn, The Picture Cube; **grape** Stockphotos; **greenhouse** Barry L. Runk, Grant Heilman; **grizzly bear** Tom McHugh, Photo Researchers; **guard** Mel Wright, Art Resource.

hang glider Philip Rudy, Stockphotos; **hatchery** Alec Duncan, Taurus Photos; **headdress** Susan van Etten, The Picture Cube; **helicopter** George F. Thompson, Stockphotos; **high-rise** Allen Green, Photo Researchers; **horizon** Ross Horowitz, Stockphotos; **hot-air balloon** Jeffrey Blackman, Index Stock; **hummingbird** Werner Roberg, Stockphotos.

iguana J.H. Robinson, Photo Researchers; **impala** Robert Caputo, Photo Researchers; **inaugurate** UPI/Bettman Newsphotos; **incubator** Lou Jones; **ingot** M.E. Warren, Photo Researchers; **intersection** Stacy Pick, Stock, Boston; **irrigation** Donald Dietz, Stock, Boston.

jack rabbit Steven Krasemann, Photo Researchers; **jaw** Tom McHugh, Photo Researchers; **jellyfish** Stan Wayman, Photo Researchers; **jungle** N.H. Cheatham, DRK Photo.

kingfisher Index Stock; **kite** L.L.T. Rhodes, Taurus Photos; **koala** Tom McHugh, Photo Researchers.

lacrosse A.J. Wright, Taurus Photos; **leap** Phaneuf/Gurdziel, The Picture Cube; **levee** Eric Kroll, Taurus Photos; **liftoff** NASA; **lion** M.P. Kahl, Photo Researchers; **litter** Walter Chandoha; **loon** Townsend P. Dickinson, Photo Researchers; **lowland** Albert Rose, Frederic Lewis; **lunar module** NASA.

make-up Richard Hutchings, Photo Researchers; **martin** Leonard Lee Rue III, Photo Researchers; **masquerade** Mark Mittleman, Taurus Photos; **memorial** W.G. Williams, Stockphotos; **merry-go-round** Nigel Stone, Stockphotos; **microchip** Dean, Frederic Lewis; **microscope** R.D. Ullman, Taurus Photos; **milkweed** Townsend P. Dickinson, Photo Researchers; **mill wheel** Lynn McLaren, The Picture Cube; **minicomputer** Courtesy of NCR Corporation; **mongoose** H. Uible, Photo Researchers; **monorail** Jeff Albertson, The Picture Cube; **monument** John E. Fogle, The Picture Cube; **mosaic** Claire Taplin, Taurus Photos; **mother-of-pearl** Runk/Schoenberger, Grant Heilman; **mural** Porterfield/Chickering, Photo Researchers; **musk ox** Leonard Lee Rue III, Photo Researchers.

nose cone NASA.

observatory Robin Scagell, Photo Researchers; **octopus** B. Griffiths, Photo Researchers; **Olympic games** Tom McHugh, Photo Researchers; **orchestra** Katrina Thomas, Photo Researchers; **ostrich** R. Webb, Stockphotos.

paddle wheel Grant Heilman; **palace** W. Finch, Stock, Boston; **palomino** E. Simpson, After Image, Inc.; **panda** George Holton, Photo Researchers; **parachute** Howard Ross, Stockphotos; **periscope** U.S. Navy; **Pilgrim** courtesy of Plimoth Plantation; **pinto** Karen Buchanan, The Picture Cube; **planet** NASA; **poinsettia** W.M. Thompson, Stockphotos; **polar bear** Stephen J. Krasemann, Photo Researchers; **porpoise** Bill Curtsinger, Photo Researchers; **precipice** Index Stock; **pronghorn** Leonard L. Rue III, Photo Researchers; **propeller** Brent Jones; **pueblo** Alan Pitcairn, Grant Heilman; **pumpkin** Guy Gillette, Photo Researchers; **pyramid** Index Stock.

quarry Larry Lefever, Grant Heilman.

radar Joseph Nettis, Photo Researchers; **rainbow** Frank J. Staub, The Picture Cube; **rapids** Tim Davis, Photo Researchers; **relay race** David S. Strickler, The Picture Cube; **rigging** Dani Carpenter, The Picture Cube; **rink** Owen Franken, Stock, Boston; **robot** Peter Menzel, After Image; **roller coaster** Touchstone/Bensky, Stockphotos; **roundup** Grant Heilman.

sandbar Jeff Dunn, The Picture Cube; **satellite** Globe/Stockphotos; **sculpture** Owen Franken, Stock, Boston; **seaplane** Tom Walker, Stock, Boston; **seismograph** William Felger, Grant Heilman; **sequoia** Jeff Foott, DRK Photo; **shipyard** David Witbeck, The Picture Cube; **silo** Isaac Geib, Grant Heilman; **skeleton** Tom McHugh, Photo Researchers/Natural History Museum of Los Angeles County; **sleigh** Guy Gillette, Photo Researchers; **soccer** Robert Martin, Stockphotos; **space suit** NASA: **spawn** S. Rannels, Grant Heilman; **sphinx** Index Stock; **square dance** Jon L. Barkam, The Picture Cube; **stalagmite** Runk/Schoenberger, Grant Heilman; **stampede** Index Stock; **statue** Vance Henry, Taurus Photos; **steeple** David Herman, Frederic Lewis; **streetcar** Gregg Mancuso, Stockphotos; **sty** Grant Heilman; **submarine** Arnold Meisner, Stockphotos; **subway** Richard Wood, The Picture Cube; **Supreme Court** Gary Krueger, Stockphotos; **suspension bridge** Sarah Putnam, The Picture Cube; **switchboard** Larry Lefever, Grant Heilman.

taxicab George E. Jones III, Photo Researchers; **torch** Agency Vandystadt, Photo Researchers; **toucan** John S. Dunning, Photo Researchers; **train** M.P. Kahl, Photo Researchers; **trapeze** Michael P. Manheim, After Image; **tugboat** Lawrence Migdale, Photo Researchers; **tumbleweed** Tom McHugh, Photo Researchers; **typewriter** James Simon, The Picture Cube.

underpass Karen Buchanan Feeney, The Picture Cube; **uproot** W.G. Williams, Stockphotos; **United Nations** Courtesy of United Nations.

veranda Barbara Alper, Stock, Boston; **video display screen** Courtesy of the Computer Museum; **vineyard** Grant Heilman; **volcano** Peter Menzel, Stock, Boston; **vulture** Anthony Mercieca, Photo Researchers.

wasp Russ Kinne, Photo Researchers; **water wheel** David C. Bitters, The Picture Cube; **willow** Townsend P. Dickinson, Photo Researchers; **windmill** Vance Henry, Taurus Photos.

yellow jacket James H. Robinson, Photo Researchers.

HIJKLMNOPQR-DOW-998765432